25 -

MODERN EQUITY

AUSTRALIA AND NEW ZEALAND
The Law Book Company Ltd.
Sydney : Melbourne : Perth

CANADA AND U.S.A.
The Carswell Company Ltd.
Agincourt, Ontario

INDIA
N. M. Tripathi Private Ltd.
Bombay
and
Eastern Law House Private Ltd.
Calcutta and Delhi
M.P.P. House
Bangalore

ISRAEL
Steimatzky's Agency Ltd.
Jerusalem : Tel Aviv : Haifa

PAKISTAN
Pakistan Law House,
Karachi

HANBURY AND MAUDSLEY

MODERN EQUITY

BY

Harold Greville Hanbury, Q.C., D.C.L.

AND

Ronald Harling Maudsley,
LL.D, B.C.L., M.A., Hon. LL.D. (U.S.D.), S.J.D.

THIRTEENTH EDITION

BY

JILL E. MARTIN, ll.m. (Lond.)
Reader in Laws, King's College, London

London
Stevens & Sons
1989

First Edition	1935	Second Impression	1971
Second Edition	1937	Third Impression	1973
Third Edition	1943	Fourth Impression	1974
Fourth Edition	1946	Fifth Impression	1975
Fifth Edition	1949	Tenth Edition	1976
Sixth Edition	1952	Second Impression	1979
Seventh Edition	1957	Eleventh Edition	1981
Eighth Edition	1962	Twelfth Edition	1985
Ninth Edition	1969	Thirteenth Edition	1989

Published by
Stevens & Sons Limited of
South Quay Plaza, 183 Marsh Wall, London E14 9FT
Computerset by CCI Technical Services Ltd., Hitchin, Herts.
Printed in Great Britain by
Richard Clay (The Chaucer Press) Ltd., Bungay, Suffolk

British Library Cataloguing in Publication Data
Hanbury, Harold Greville.
 Modern Equity.—13th ed/by Jill E. Martin.
 1. England. Law. Equity.
 I. Title   II. Maudsley, R. H.
 (Ronald Harling)   III. Martin, Jill E.
 344.206′04

 ISBN 0-420-48130-3
 ISBN 0-420-48140-0   Pbk

PREFACE

There have been many interesting and important developments in the law of Equity and Trusts in the four years since the twelfth edition. One of my objectives has been to include them without increasing the overall length of the book. In this I have been assisted by a change in the type-face, so that it even appears that the thirteenth edition is shorter than its predecessor. Some material has been deleted to make way for the new; in particular, the treatment of express trusts for sale (formerly in Chapter 11), which may be found in the land law books. Space has also been saved by avoiding certain areas of duplication in the treatment of certainty of objects and gifts to unincorporated associations which occurred in previous editions.

The old Chapter 11 on Trusts for Sale and the Doctrine of Conversion has been replaced by a new chapter entitled Trusts of the Family Home. This utilises some of the material previously found in the chapters on Resulting and Constructive Trusts, together with a substantial amount of new case-law, in particular the decision of the Court of Appeal in *Grant* v. *Edwards* on the acquisition of interests in the home. The material on Conversion has gone to join the other equitable doctrines in Chapter 26.

There has been substantial rewriting of the section of the Constructive Trusts chapter dealing with the degree of knowledge required for the imposition of constructive trusteeship on a recipient of trust property, to accommodate *Re Montagu's S.T.* Much of Chapter 9 (Taxation) has been rewritten in the light of the replacement of capital transfer tax with inheritance tax by the Finance Act 1986. The section on Voidable Trusts in Chapter 13 has been completely recast to deal with the Insolvency Act 1986, which was still in Bill form at the publication of the previous edition. The treatment of "reservation of title clauses" in Chapter 22 has been somewhat expanded. There has also been substantial rewriting of the Undue Influence section of Chapter 25. In addition to the decision of the House of Lords in *National Westminster Bank* v. *Morgan*, which came just too late for the twelfth edition, there have been many new cases, especially on the principle that a lender who has made the borrower his agent in securing the cooperation of a third party is prejudiced by any undue influence exercised by the borrower over the third party.

Statutory developments not already mentioned include the Charities Act 1985, modifying the *cy-près* doctrine. Chapter 15 deals also with the recent Woodfield Report on the administration of charities.

Of the many relevant cases decided since the twelfth edition, apart from those referred to above, mention might be made of *Ashburn Anstalt* v. *Arnold* on the enforceability of contractual licences against third parties by means of a constructive trust; *Re Basham* and *Coombes* v. *Smith* on proprietary estoppel; and *Space Investments Ltd.* v. *Canadian Imperial Bank of Commerce Trust Co. (Bahamas) Ltd.* and *Re Att.-Gen.'s Reference (No. 1 of 1985)*, offering different views on tracing. There have been, as always, countless cases on injunctions, of which perhaps the most significant was *Att.-Gen.* v. *Guardian Newspapers Ltd. (No. 2)* (the *Spycatcher* case), dealing with breach of confidence and the effect of injunctions on third parties. No less interesting is the recent emergence of the "world-wide" *Mareva* injunction. Indeed, the Court of Appeal decision in *Derby and Co. Ltd.* v. *Weldon (No. 3 and No. 4)* was reported only at the page proof stage and could not be fully dealt with. The principles here, it seems, are still to be worked out.

Also incorporated is the recent periodical literature and the various recommendations of the Law Commission in recent Reports and Working Papers, wherever relevant. It is disappointing to note, however, that only very few of the recommendations of the Law Reform Committee on the Powers and Duties of Trustees (23rd Report, 1982) have yet been implemented.

I would like to thank those of my colleagues at King's College who have given me advice and assistance, especially Jeffrey Price, who has once again revised the sections on income tax and capital gains tax in Chapter 9. I would also like to mention the continued support of Professor Harold Hanbury, and to offer him congratulations on his recent ninetieth birthday. Thanks are also due to the editorial staff of Sweet & Maxwell for their help.

My intention has been to state the law as at January 1, 1989.

King's College London   Jill Martin
January 1, 1989

CONTENTS

PART III

TRUSTEES

PART IV

EQUITABLE REMEDIES

PART V

MISCELLANEOUS EQUITABLE DOCTRINES AND EQUITIES

TABLE OF CASES

Bold page numbers indicate where a case is fully discussed in the text

ix

TABLE OF STATUTES

The bold type indicates the page on which the section is set out more fully

TABLE OF ABBREVIATIONS

Books

Annual Report	*Annual Report by the Charity Commissioners.*
A.S.C.L.	*Annual Survey of Commonwealth Law.*
Cheshire	Cheshire and Burn, *The Modern Law of Real Property.* (14th ed., 1988).
Farrand	Farrand, *Contract and Conveyance* (4th ed., 1983).
Farwell	*Farwell on Powers* (3rd ed., 1916).
Goff and Jones	Goff and Jones, *The Law of Restitution* (3rd ed., 1986).
Harris	Harris, *Variation of Trusts.*
Hayton and Marshall	Hayton and Marshall, Cases and Commentary on the Law of Trusts (8th ed., 1986).
Holdsworth *H.E.L.*	Holdsworth, *History of English Law.*
Lewin	*Lewin on Trusts* (16th ed., 1964).
Maitland	*Maitland's Equity* (2nd ed., 1936).
M. & W.	Megarry and Wade, *The Law of Real Property* (5th ed., 1984).
Morris and Leach	Morris and Leach, *The Rule Against Perpetuities* (2nd ed., 1962).
Parker and Mellows	Parker and Mellows, *The Modern Law of Trusts* (5th ed., 1983).
Pettit	Pettit, *Equity and the Law of Trusts* (5th ed., 1983).
Preston and Newsom	Preston and Newsom, *Limitation of Actions* (3rd ed., 1953).
Scott	Scott, *Trusts* (3rd ed., 1967).
Snell	Snell, *Principles of Equity* (28th ed., 1982).
Spry	Spry, *Equitable Remedies* (3rd ed., 1984).
Tudor	*Tudor on Charities* (7th ed., 1984).

Journals

All E.R. Rev.	All England Law Reports Annual Review.
B.T.R.	British Tax Review.
C.L.J.	Cambridge Law Journal.

C.B.R.	Canadian Bar Review.
Col. L.R.	Columbia Law Review.
Conv.	Conveyancer and Property Lawyer.
Conv. (N.S.)	Conveyancer and Property Lawyer (New Series).
Crim. L.R.	Criminal Law Review.
C.L.P.	Current Legal Problems.
E.G.	Estates Gazette.
Fam. Law	Family Law
H.L.R.	Harvard Law Review.
I.C.L.Q.	International and Comparative Law Quarterly.
J.B.L.	Journal of Business Law.
J.L.H.	Journal of Legal History.
L.Q.R.	Law Quarterly Review.
L.S.	Legal Studies.
L.S.Gaz.	Law Society's Gazette.
M.L.R.	Modern Law Review.
N.L.J.	New Law Journal.
S.J.	Solicitor's Journal.

Acts of Parliament

A.E.A.	Administration of Estates Act.
C.G.T.A.	Capital Gains Tax Act.
F.A.	Finance Act.
I.C.T.A.	Income and Corporation Taxes Act.
I.H.T.A.	Inheritance Tax Act.
L.C.A.	Land Charges Act.
L.P.A.	Law of Property Act.
L.P.(A.).A.	Law of Property (Amendment) Act.
S.L.A.	Settled Land Act.
T.A.	Trustee Act.
T.I.A.	Trustee Investments Act.
V.T.A.	Variation of Trusts Act.

General

B.S.	Building Society.
Comm.	Commissioners.
I.R.C.	Inland Revenue Commissioners.
R.S.C.	Rules of the Supreme Court.
S.	Section.
S.E.	Settled Estates.
S.T.	Settlement Trusts.
W.T.	Will Trusts.

PART I

INTRODUCTION

CHAPTER 1

HISTORY AND PRINCIPLES

1. GENERAL

EQUITY is a word with many meanings. In a wide sense, it means that which is fair and just, moral and ethical; but its legal meaning is much narrower. Equity is the branch of the law which, before the Judicature Act of 1873 came into force, was applied and administered by the Court of Chancery.[1] It is not synonymous with justice in a broad sense. A plaintiff asserting some equitable right or remedy must show that his claim has "an ancestry founded in history and in the practice and precedents of the court administering equity jurisdiction. It is not sufficient that because we may think that the 'justice' of the present case requires it, we should invent such a jurisdiction for the first time."[2]

Developed systems of law have often been assisted by the introduction of a discretionary power to do justice in particular cases where the strict rules of law cause hardship.[3] Rules formulated to deal with

---

[1] This is "but a poor thing to call a definition"; Maitland, p. 1.

[2] *Re Diplock* [1948] Ch. 465 at pp. 481, 482, *post*, p. 625. See also Jessel M.R. in *Re National Funds Assurance Co.* (1878) 10 Ch.D. 118 at p. 128: "This court is not, as I have often said, a Court of Conscience, but a Court of Law."

[3] The Praetor performed such a function in Roman Law: Buckland and McNair, *Roman Law and Common Law* (2nd ed.), pp. 1–6.

3

particular situations may subsequently work unfairly as society develops. Equity is the body of rules which evolved to mitigate the severity
of the rules of the common law. Its origin was the exercise by the
Chancellor of the residual discretionary power of the King to do justice
among his subjects in circumstances in which, for one reason or
another, justice could not be obtained in a common law court.

Principles of justice and conscience are the basis of equity jurisdiction, but it must not be thought that the contrast between law and
equity is one between a system of strict rules and one of broad discretion. Equity has no monopoly of the pursuit of justice. As Harman
L.J. has said, equitable principles are "rather too often bandied about
in common law courts as though the Chancellor still had only the
length of his own foot to measure when coming to a conclusion. Since
the time of Lord Eldon, the system of equity for good or evil has been a
very precise one, and equitable jurisdiction is exercised only on well-
known principles."[4] In similar vein Lord Radcliffe, speaking of common lawyers, said that equity lawyers were "both surprised and dis-
comfited by the plenitude of jurisdiction and the imprecision of rules
that are attributed to 'equity' by their more enthusiastic colleagues."[5]
Just as the common law has escaped from its early formalism, so over
the years equity has established strict rules for the application of its
principles. Indeed, at one stage the rules became so fixed that a "*rigor
aequitatis*"[6] developed; equity itself displayed the very defect which it
was designed to remedy. We will see that today some aspects of equity
are strict and technical, while others leave considerable discretion to
the court.

The field of equity is delineated by a series of historical events, and
not by a pre-conceived theory; an outline of these events will be given
in the next section. We will then see that, until the Judicature Act 1873,
the Court of Chancery had almost exclusive equity jurisdiction[7]; rules
of equity were not enforced in the common law courts. If a defendant
to a common law action had an equitable defence to it, he had to go to
Chancery to obtain an injunction to stay the proceedings in the common law court and then start a new action in Chancery to establish his
equitable rights. This complicated system led to a number of difficulties, as we shall see. The Judicature Acts of 1873 and 1875 created the
Supreme Court of Judicature, all of whose branches exercise common
law and equity jurisdiction. The division between law and equity is less
marked, therefore, than it was prior to those Acts, but it is still

---

[4] *Campbell Discount Co. Ltd.* v. *Bridge* [1961] 1 Q.B. 445 at p. 459.
[5] *Bridge* v. *Campbell Discount Co. Ltd.* [1962] A.C. 600 at p. 626.
[6] Allen's *Law in the Making* (7th ed.), p. 417.
[7] For the equity jurisdiction of the Court of Exchequer, see Radcliffe and Cross,
English Legal System (6th ed.), p. 171. The Common Law Procedure Act 1854 had
given common law courts a limited power to issue injunctions.

necessary for various reasons to know whether a rule has its origins in law or in equity.[8]

2. Historical Outline

The long history of the Court of Chancery is a fascinating story, the details of which must be sought elsewhere[9]; it is not possible here to do more than mention, in broad outline, those aspects of the history which are essential to the understanding of modern equity.

A. The Medieval Chancellor

In the medieval period the Chancellor was the most important personage in the country next to the King himself: Maitland described him as "the king's prime minister,"[10] "the king's secretary of state for all departments."[11] One very important function of the Chancery was to issue the royal writs which began an action at law.[12] By varying existing writs or inventing new ones, the Chancellor could have some influence on the development of the law; a limited influence, however, for the decision to issue a writ did not create a new form of action. The litigant could not proceed without it; but the common law court could still decide that the writ disclosed no claim recognised by the law.

B. Petitions to the Chancellor[13]

An injured plaintiff could only sue at common law if his complaint came within the scope of an existing writ. And in the thirteenth century the available writs covered very narrow ground. Even if the claim came within the scope of an existing writ, it may have been that for some reason, such as the power and influence of the defendant, the plaintiff could not get justice before a common law court. The King in his Council still retained wide discretionary power to do justice among his subjects, and the plaintiff could petition to the King and Council praying for a remedy.

Petitions were addressed to the Chancellor in situations in which a

---

[8] *Post*, pp. 17 *et seq.*.
[9] Spence, *The Equitable Jurisdiction of the Court of Chancery* (1846–1849); Kerly, *An Historical Sketch of the Equitable Jurisdiction of the Court of Chancery* (1890); Potter, *Historical Introduction to English Law and its Institutions* (4th ed.); Maitland Lectures I-IV; Holdsworth; *H.E.L.* i, Chap. 5; iv, pp. 407–480; v, pp. 215–338; vi, pp. 518–551, 640–671; ix, pp. 335–408; xii, pp. 178–330; xiii, pp. 574–668; xvi, pp. 5–135; Plucknett, *Concise History of the Common Law* (5th ed.), Part V; Simpson, *An Introduction to the History of the Land Law* (2nd ed.), Chap. 8; Milsom, *Historical Foundations of the Common Law* (2nd ed.), Chaps. 4, 9; Yale, *Lord Nottingham's Two Treatises*; Yale, *Introduction to the Selden Society*, Vols. 73 and 79; Jones, *The Elizabethan Court of Chancery*; (1965) 81 L.Q.R. 562; (1966) 82 L.Q.R. 215 (J.L. Barton); Keeton and Sheridan's *Equity* (3rd ed.), Chap. 2.
[10] Maitland, p. 3.
[11] Maitland, p. 2.
[12] See Maitland, *Forms of Action at Common Law*.
[13] Holdsworth, *H.E.L.* i, pp. 402 *et seq.*; Milsom, at pp. 82 *et seq.*

petitioner complained that his case was beyond the ordinary mechanism, and he sought another way. Milsom points out that, in its origins,
this would not be regarded as an application of a separate and superior
body of rules to those applied by the common law courts. "Not only
was there no equity as a nascent body of rules different from those of
the common law. There was no common law, no body of substantive
rules from which equity could be different."[14] If the mechanism
appeared to work unfairly, as where juries were misled, corrupted or
intimidated, the petitioner would seek another way. The Chancery
"was the head office of the organisation, and it was here that application was made when the ordinary mechanisms appeared to be incapable of working. The approach to the chancellor has no more
mysterious origin than that."[15]

Later the petition was used to obtain relief in cases where the
common law was inflexible and incapable of providing a remedy. The
common law developed into a comprehensive system, but an injured
plaintiff could only sue at common law if his complaint came within the
scope of an existing writ. By the sixteenth century local jurisdictions,
where many matters not covered by common law writs had been dealt
with, played a much smaller part. The common law was taking on the
aspect of a substantive as well as a comprehensive system, and the
application to Chancery was ceasing to look like a request for the same
justice, withheld below by some mechanical fault. There seemed to be
two parallel systems, and the relationship between them had to be
explained in theory and worked out in practice.

C. The Chancellor's Discretion

Maitland points out that in the thirteenth and fourteenth centuries
the Chancellor probably did not regard himself as administering a new
body of law.[16] He was trying to give relief in hard cases, and the
medieval Chancellor was peculiarly well fitted for this work. He was
usually an ecclesiastic, generally a bishop, and learned in the civil and
canon law.[17] The Chancellor would give or withhold relief, not according to any precedent, but according to the effect produced upon his
own individual sense of right and wrong by the merits of the particular
case before him. No wonder that Seldon could say that "Equity is a
roguish thing. For law we have a measure . . . equity is according to the
conscience of him that is Chancellor, and as that is longer or narrower,
so is equity. 'Tis all one as if they should make the standard for the
measure a Chancellor's foot."[18]

[14] Milsom, at p. 84.
[15] *Ibid.*
[16] Maitland, p. 5.
[17] There were some lay Chancellors at this period; see Trevelyan, *England in the Age of
Wycliffe* (1899).
[18] *Table Talk of John Selden* (ed. Pollock, 1927), p. 43; quoted Holdsworth, *H.E.L.* i,
pp. 467–468.

D. Attendance of the Defendant

In exercising this jurisdiction, the Chancellor was faced with the problem of ensuring the attendance of the defendant without the issue of a royal writ. "The Chancellor, having considered the petition or bill as it is called, orders the (defendant) to come before him and answer the complaint. The writ whereby he does this is called a *subpoena*— because it orders the man to appear upon pain of forfeiting a sum of money—*e.g. subpoena centum librarum.*"[19] The examination will be made under oath; it need not be restricted to specific questions raised in the complaint; and issues of fact as well as issues of law will be decided by the Chancellor.

E. Enforcement

A further question is that of enforcement. If the petition is successful, the Chancellor's conclusion will usually be different from that which the common law court would have reached; otherwise the matter would have been litigated at common law. If the Chancellor finds that Blackacre is owned by A, but that, in conscience, it should be beneficially owned by B, he may order A to convey the land to B, or to hold the legal estate for the exclusive benefit of B. The Chancellor does not and cannot in these circumstances hold that B is the owner. A's right at law is undoubted, and the Chancellor cannot change the law. What the Chancellor does is to issue an order to A either to convey the land to B, or to refrain from action interfering with B's right, as the case may be. The Chancellor's jurisdiction is against the person; *in personam*,[20] and directed to the conscience of the individual in question. And the Chancellor has the power to back up his orders with the threat of imprisonment for those in contempt. Although there is, theoretically, no interference with common law property rights, there is in substance an interference with common law jurisdiction. This was the subject of dispute later on.[21]

F. The Use[22]

"If we were asked what is the greatest and most distinctive achievement performed by Englishmen in the field of jurisprudence I cannot think that we should have any better answer to give than this, namely the development from century to century of the trust idea."[23] Such was

---

[19] Maitland, p. 5.

[20] *Post*, p. 18.

[21] *Post*, p. 11.

[22] Holdsworth, *H.E.L.* iv, pp. 407–480; Ames, *Lectures on Legal History*, pp. 233–247; Plucknett, *Concise History of the Common Law*, p. 575; Simpson, *Introduction to the History of Land Law* (2nd ed.), Chap. 8; Milsom, Chap. 9; (1965) 81 L.Q.R. 562; (1966) 82 L.Q.R. 215 (J.L. Barton).

[23] *Selected Essays*, p. 129.

the view of Maitland. Let us now examine the origins of that development.

In medieval times, the Chancellor's jurisdiction was vague and undefined; as wide as the subject-matter of the petitions which invoked it. The basis of intervention was that it was necessary on grounds of conscience. His authority was unquestioned in cases of fraud and breach of confidence. The boundaries do not concern us here. As stated above, the most significant and far-reaching sphere of his jurisdiction was the enforcement of the use of land.

If land is given to A on A's undertaking to hold the land to the use and benefit of B, it is unconscionable for A to keep it for his own benefit. B however has no legal claim or title to the land. The conveyance to A gives him whatever legal estate was conveyed, and, at common law, A can exercise all the rights which that estate gives to him.

Land might be given to A to the use of B for various reasons. If B were going on a crusade, then there must be someone to perform and receive the feudal services. If B were a community of Franciscan friars which, because of the rule of poverty, is incapable of holding property, it is necessary for someone to hold the land for its benefit.[24] Perhaps, however, B is trying to escape from his creditors; or fears that a conviction for felony will result in the loss of his lands.[25] For various reasons it may be advisable or necessary to put the legal title to B's land in A. If B conveys to A subject to an undertaking to hold to the use of B, B would have no protection at common law beyond that given in the fourteenth century to covenants under seal; and if a third party conveyed the land to A to hold to the use of B, no relationship recognised by the common law existed between A and B.

The Chancellor interfered to compel A to hold the land for the exclusive use and benefit of B. The Chancellor cannot say that B is the owner; A is. But all the beneficial interest in the land can be given to B by compelling A to keep the legal title only, and to give all the benefit of the land to B. This is what happens when the use is enforced. And, although the jurisdiction against A is a jurisdiction *in personam*, the Chancellor will enforce B's rights, not only against A, but against other persons who take the land from A.[26] It is not long before we are saying that A is the owner at law, B the owner in equity. In the terminology of the time, A is the feoffee to uses, B the *cestui que use*. The use is the forerunner, as we will see, of the trust.

Gradually the Chancellors established the circumstances in which uses would be enforced. They had to decide also what equitable estates they would recognise; for example, if land were conveyed to A to the

---

[24] Maitland, p. 25; Holdsworth, *H.E.L.* iv, p. 415; Milsom, pp. 203 *et seq.*

[25] *Davies* v. *Otty (No. 2)* (1865) 35 Beav. 208.

[26] Except a bona fide purchaser of a legal estate for value without notice, *post*, p. 33; Maitland, pp. 113–115.

use of B for life and then to the use of C, should this be enforced? Broadly, the answer is that, in accordance with the maxim that equity follows the law, the estates and interests which could be created in equity corresponded with those which existed at law.

G. The Advantages of the Use

The employment of the use made it possible to avoid some of the feudal incidents. Under feudal law, the lord was entitled to a payment when an heir succeeded to feudal land, and to other valuable rights arising when the land was held by a minor heir, and the right of escheat where there was no heir.[27] These burdens could be avoided if the land was vested in a number of feoffees to uses. They were unlikely to die together or without heirs. Those who died could be replaced, and the feoffees would never be minors. Thus, the use, to feudal land owners, had something of the appeal of tax planning techniques at the present day. It was possible also, in spite of the rule that freehold land could not be devised, to create effective dispositions of equitable interests on death by vesting the land in feoffees and declaring the uses on which the land was to be held after the settlor's death. Further, uses made possible new methods of conveyancing,[28] and also the creation of new types of interests in land which were not possible at common law.[29] For a time also, until prevented by statute, land held to uses could be enjoyed by religious houses in defiance of the Statutes of Mortmain,[30] or be placed beyond the reach of creditors.

H. The Statute of Uses 1535

Henry VIII found that his purse was being emptied by the avoidance of feudal incidents which the system of uses made possible. To small tenants who had no tenants of their own, the system of uses was entirely beneficial. To large landowners, it was beneficial in so far as they were tenants, and harmful in so far as they were lords. To the King, it was entirely harmful, because he was lord of all and tenant of none. The first part of Henry VIII's reign had been expensive, and he was determined to restore the revenues of the Crown by attacking uses. The Statute of Uses of 1535 was intended to reduce greatly the

---

[27] Cheshire and Burn, pp. 12 *et seq.*

[28] *i.e.* the bargain and sale. An agreement for consideration to sell land to a purchaser raised a use in the purchaser's favour.

[29] *e.g.* springing and shifting interests; M. & W., pp. 1169, 1179; Cheshire and Burn, p. 67.

[30] Which forbade the conveyance of land to religious houses without permission of the Crown. Milsom, p. 204.

scope of the use. After a grandiloquent preamble[31] it provided, according to Maitland's summary of the first clause[32]: "where any person or persons shall be seised of any lands or other hereditaments to the use, confidence, or trust of any other person or persons, in every such case such person and persons that shall have any such use, confidence or trust in fee simple, fee tail, for term of life or for years or otherwise shall stand and be seised deemed and adjudged in lawful seisin estate and possession of and in the same lands and hereditaments in such like estates as they had or shall have in the use." In other words, the feoffees to uses were to disappear. The *cestui que use* was to have the legal estate.

The Statute did not however suppress all uses.[33] It only applied where the feoffee was *seised* to the use of another. If the feoffee held only a term of years, he would not be seised, and the Statute would not apply. Again it did not apply to situations where the feoffees had active duties to perform. The feoffees were then necessary participants, and the Chancellor held that a duty to sell the land, or to collect the rents and profits of the land and pay them to X, was a sufficiently active duty to exclude the Statute.[34]

I. A Use upon a Use. The Trust

It was possible, after the Statute, to create equitable interests in land by imposing a use upon a term of years, or by requiring the legal owners of freehold land to collect the rents and profits and to pay them over to the beneficiaries. Such uses were not executed; nor were they invalid.[35] Passive uses of freehold land were however a different matter. Such a use was executed by the Statute. What would happen if a second use were imposed? If land were limited to A to the use of B to the use of C, is it possible to argue that the first use will be executed, and that B will hold the legal estate to the use of C? Such a solution was reached by about 1700[36]; the second use is called a trust. A shorter form, which became settled practice, was to omit A, and to make the disposition "unto and to the use of B in trust for C."

The story of this development is confused and uncertain.[37] Most accounts start with the proposition that through the sixteenth century,

---

[31] Discussed in *H.E.L.* iv, pp. 460–461, and described as: "far from being a sober statement of historical fact. Rather it is an official statement of the numerous good reasons which had induced the government to pass so wise a statute—the sixteenth century equivalent of a leading article in a government newspaper upon a government measure."

[32] Maitland, p. 35.

[33] Holdsworth, *H.E.L.* iv, pp. 467–473.

[34] Maitland, pp. 38–41; M. & W., p. 1167.

[35] Simpson, *Introduction to the History of Land Law* (2nd ed.), p. 195.

[36] Simpson, *loc. cit.*, p. 203.

[37] Milsom, p. 208 suggests that the origin is in a situation in which a settlor wishes to settle upon himself with remainders over; (1977) 93 L.Q.R. 33 (J.H. Baker).

the second use was repugnant to the first, and void.[38] It was then said that the turning-point came with *Sambach* v. *Dalston* in 1634[39]; but this is now discredited,[40] and the present view is that the change came at the end of the sixteenth century.[41] Barton[42] however says that it was earlier and that "the trust of freehold was an accepted institution at any rate in the latter part of the sixteenth century"[43]; and this is supported by the recent discovery of two unpublished manuscripts.[44] However that may be, it is clear that after the Restoration in 1660, a number of factors combined to facilitate the recognition of passive trusts of freeholds. The abolition of military tenures[45] and the consequent freedom to devise all freehold land,[46] the reduction in the value of money which followed the development of the New World, and the changes in the constitutional and financial structure of the country in the seventeenth century, all helped to make the collection of feudal dues a minor factor in the royal revenues. The Civil War determined once and for all that the Government was to be financed by Parliamentary vote. There was now no reason of policy why passive trusts of freeholds should not be enforced as were active trusts and trusts of leaseholds. The enforcement of the second use as a trust was so similar to that of the enforcement of the use against a feoffee to uses centuries before that Lord Hardwicke was able to say, in 1738, in a remark of greater dramatic power than legal or mathematical accuracy: " ... by this means a statute made upon great consideration, introduced in a solemn and pompous manner, by this strict construction, has had no other effect than to add at most, three words to a conveyance."[47]

J. The Struggle over Injunctions

The story of the use and of the trust has taken us away from the chronological sequence. For it was at the close of the sixteenth century that the quarrel over the power of the Chancery to issue injunctions

---

[38] Maitland, p. 42; Ames, *Lectures on Legal History*, pp. 243–247; Holdsworth, *H.E.L.* iv, pp. 471–473; Plucknett, *Concise History of the Common Law*, pp. 600–601; Simpson, *loc. cit.*, pp. 201 *et seq.*; *Jane Tyrell's Case* (1557) Dyer 155a.

[39] (1634) Tothill 188.

[40] (1958) 74 L.Q.R. 550 (J. E. Strathdene); (1957) 15 C.L.J. 72 (D. E. C. Yale).

[41] Simpson, *loc. cit.*, pp. 202–203.

[42] (1966) 82 L.Q.R. 215 (J. L. Barton).

[43] *Ibid.* at p. 221.

[44] (1977) 93 L.Q.R. 33 (J. H. Baker).

[45] Tenures Abolition Act 1660.

[46] Previously only two-thirds of land held by knight service could be devised.

[47] *Hopkins* v. *Hopkins* (1739) 1 Atk. 581 at p. 591; see Holdsworth, *H.E.L.* iv, pp. 449 *et seq.*

came to a head. The orthodox view is that the clash was inevitable.[48] The use of the injunction had the effect of rendering the common law inoperative; no wonder that the Chancellor was charged that he left "the common law of the realm, and you presume much upon your own mind, and think that your conceit is far better than the common law."[49] That the clash did not come earlier was due partly to the statesmanlike qualities of men like More; and no doubt also to the reluctance to challenge the powers of royal officers in Tudor times. Chief Justice Coke was not willing to see the common law treated in this way, and in a number of cases decided that imprisonment for disobedience to injunctions issued by Chancery was unlawful.[50] In one case it was said that "if any court of equity doth inter-meddle with any matters properly triable at the common law, or which concern freehold, they are to be prohibited."[51] Coke further argued that the jurisdiction of the Chancellor was contrary to the Statute of Praemunire of 1353[52] and also to a statute of 1402.[53] Lord Chancellor Ellesmere, equally determined, claimed that he was in no sense interfering with the common law; he was merely acting *in personam*, directing the individual that, on equitable grounds, he must not proceed to sue at law or enforce a judgment already obtained at law.

James I stepped in and referred the matter to Bacon,[54] then Attorney-General, and others learned in the law. Acting on their recommendations, and no doubt in accordance with his own political views and interests, he decided in favour of the Chancery.[55] The victory did not remain long unchallenged. The success of the Parliament and of the common lawyers in the political struggles of the seventeenth century provided further impetus for the attack on the Chancery. As late as 1690, following the Revolution, a Bill was introduced in the House of Commons to restrain the interference by Chancery in any

---

[48] See, however, Jones, *The Elizabethan Court of Chancery*, pp. 22 *et seq.* He points out that common law judges often sat in Chancery, and that the legal structure of England was a single institution, and not just a set of disjointed parts. Disputes between the parts could arise for various reasons—competition over jurisdiction, fees, privileges—and these disputes "could be exacerbated by personal infelicities. ... The seventeenth-century dispute between Egerton [Lord Ellesmere] and Coke, which must not be exaggerated, has its origins in the inability of sensitive men to escape from a wooden deference to their own accustomed procedures, methods and modes of argument. This was one of the most senseless quarrels ever to be staged between two such outstanding intelligences, and even James I, part fumbling and part devious, had the wit to perceive this." See Milsom, p. 91.

[49] Reply of a serjeant to the Doctor and Student, *Harg. Law. Tracts* 323 at p. 328, quoted Holdsworth, *H.E.L.* i, p. 460.

[50] *Heath* v. *Rydley* (1614) Cro.Jac. 335; *Bromage* v. *Genning* (1617) 1 Rolle 368; *Throckmorton* v. *Finch* (1598) Third Institute 124 at p. 125; Holdsworth, *H.E.L.* i, p. 461.

[51] *i.e.* liable to be subject to the writ of Prohibition; *Heath* v. *Rydley* (1614) Cro.Jac. 335.

[52] 27 Edward III, St. 1, c. 1.

[53] 4 Henry IV, c. 23.

[54] For Bacon's remarkable career, see Holdsworth, *H.E.L.* v, pp. 238–254.

[55] *Reports of Cases in Chancery*, App. 1, p. 49; 21 E.R. 588.

suit for which the proper remedy was at common law.[56] The Bill was not passed, and from that time the Chancellor's jurisdiction was not seriously challenged. Thereafter, law and equity worked together, as parts of a consistent whole; and this enabled Maitland to say that Equity had come, not to destroy the law, but to fulfil it.[57]

K. The Transformation of Equity into the Modern System[58]

From the beginning of the Chancellorship of Lord Nottingham in 1673 and to the end of that of Lord Eldon in 1827, equity was transformed from a jurisdiction based upon the personal interference of the Chancellor into a system of established rules and principles. We have seen that the early Chancellors were ecclesiastics. Lawyers and others were sometimes appointed during the Tudor and Stuart periods. But the retirement of Lord Shaftesbury[59] in 1672 was the last occasion on which a non-lawyer held the Great Seal. This factor influenced the development of the system into one based on rules and precedents rather than on individual conscience. The first reported Chancery cases are dated 1557[60] and these cases are treated as authorities and followed.[61]

Lord Nottingham did much to weld together, consolidate and stiffen the whole system. To him we owe the doctrine that there can be no "clog on the equity of redemption,"[62] a classification of trusts,[63] and the modern rule against perpetuities.[64] Throughout the eighteenth century, equity, in a period of legislative stagnation, became the great force that moulded the progress of the law right up to the beginning of the nineteenth century. In this period the modern law of trusts develops and is shaped to meet entirely new conditions of social life; equity took in hand the administration of the estates of deceased persons, on which depend the doctrines of election,[65] satisfaction,[66] ademption,[67] marshalling of assets,[68] and performance,[69] and in many cases it is

---

[56] Holdsworth, *H.E.L.* i, pp. 463–465.

[57] *Equity*, p. 19.

[58] Pollock, *Essays in Legal History*, p. 286.

[59] A member of the Cabal of Charles II; he had been educated as a lawyer, but never practised; Holdsworth, *H.E.L.* i, p. 411; vi, pp. 525–526.

[60] "Choyce Cases in Chancery"; Holdsworth, *H.E.L.* v, pp. 274–278; Jones, *The Elizabethan Court of Chancery*, p. 3.

[61] In the preface to Nelson's reports, at pp. 2–3, the author said that "Equity became artificial Reason, and hath ever since such a mixture of law in it, that it would be much easier now for a Lawyer to preach, than for a Prelate to be a Judge of that Court"; Holdsworth, *H.E.L.* vi, p. 669.

[62] *Howard* v. *Harris* (1681) 1 Vern. 33.

[63] *Cook* v. *Fountain* (1676) 3 Swan. 585. See Holdsworth, *H.E.L.* vi, pp. 545–548, 643.

[64] *Duke of Norfolk's Case* (1683) 2 Swan. 454. For a collection of Lord Nottingham's Cases, see Yale, *Introduction to the Selden Society*, Vols. 73 and 78.

[65] *Post*, pp. 810 *et seq.*

[66] *Post*, pp. 821 *et seq.*

[67] *Post*, pp. 821 *et seq.*

[68] Snell, p. 332.

[69] *Post*, pp. 826 *et seq.*

possible to point to the Chancellor who first applied them.[70] In this period there were many great Chancellors, Talbot (1733–37), Hardwicke (1737–60), Camden (1766–71), Thurlow (1778–93), culminating in Lord Eldon (1801–06, 1807–27), one of the greatest equity lawyers. His decisions were thorough, painstaking, learned and clear. As Holdsworth said: "He had a thorough grasp of existing rules and principles; but he looked as anxiously into all the facts and circumstances of each case ... as if there were no such rules and as if, therefore, he was under the necessity of determining each case as one of first impression."[71] The judgments were masterly. But it is hardly surprising that the business of the court was scandalously in arrears. The pattern and principles of equity were now established. "Nothing would inflict on me greater pain in quitting this place," he said, "than the recollection that I had done anything to justify the reproach that the equity of this court varies like the Chancellor's foot."[72]

L. The Nineteenth Century and the Judicature Acts 1873 and 1875

The nineteenth century was a period of great development of the equitable jurisdiction, based upon the principles established by the end of Lord Eldon's tenure. The enormous industrial, international and imperial expansion of Britain in this period necessitated developments in equity to deal with a host of new problems. The accumulation of business fortunes required rules for the administration of companies and partnerships; and the change in emphasis from landed wealth to stocks and shares necessitated the development of new concepts of property settlements.

Clearly the old organisation of the Chancery Court, overloaded in Lord Eldon's time, could not hope to deal with the mass of business. "Remember this," said Maitland to his students at the turn of the twentieth century, "that until 1813 there were only two judges in the Court of Chancery. There was the Lord Chancellor, and there was the Master of the Rolls, and it was but by degrees that the latter had become an independent judge; for a long time he appears merely as the Chancellor's assistant.[73] In 1813 a Vice-Chancellor was appointed. In 1841 two more Vice-Chancellors. In 1851 two Lords Justices of Appeal in Chancery. When the Court was abolished in 1875, it had seven judges. Cases in the first instance were taken before the Master of the Rolls, or one of the three Vice-Chancellors, and there was an Appeal Court constituted by the Chancellor and the two Lords Justices; but the Chancellor could sit as a judge of first instance if he pleased and

---

[70] *Re Hallet's Estate* (1880) 13 Ch.D. 696 at p. 710.

[71] Holdsworth, *H.E.L.* i, p. 468; Dickens, *Bleak House*, Chap. 1.

[72] Holdsworth, *H.E.L.* i, pp. 468–469; *Gee* v. *Pritchard* (1818) 2 Swan. 402 at p. 414.

[73] For a modern and detailed account of the position of the Master of the Rolls as an administrative officer, see Jones, *The Elizabethan Court of Chancery*, pp. 51–58.

sometimes did so."[74] At least however, the judges and Chancery officials could deal with their work without the fear of opposition from the common law. The two courts had now become, "not rivals but partners in the work of administering justice."[75] The time had come for the fusion of these jurisdictions into a single Supreme Court.

Some limited steps were taken towards this fusion in the middle of the nineteenth century. The Common Law Procedure Act 1854 gave to the common law courts a certain power to give equitable remedies, and the Chancery Amendment Act 1858, commonly known as Lord Cairns' Act, gave to the Court of Chancery power to award damages in addition to, or in substitution for, an injunction or a decree of specific performance.[76] The major change however came with the Judicature Acts 1873 and 1875. These Acts abolished the old separate Courts of Queen's Bench, Exchequer, Common Pleas, Chancery, Probate, the Divorce Court, and the Court of Admiralty; it created the Supreme Court of Judicature with a High Court divided into Divisions known as the Queen's Bench Division, Chancery Division, and the Probate, Divorce and Admiralty Division. The latter was re-named the Family Division in 1970.[77] Its Admiralty jurisdiction was assigned to the Queen's Bench Division, and Probate business, other than non-contentious and common form probate business, to the Chancery Division. Each Division exercises both legal and equitable jurisdiction.[78] Thus any issue can be adjudicated in any Division; and any point of law or equity can be raised and determined in any Division; but, for the sake of administrative convenience, cases are allocated to the Divisions according to their general subject-matter.[79] Thus the court "is now not a Court of Law or a Court of Equity, it is a Court of complete jurisdiction."[80]

It was foreseen that a court which applied the rules both of common law and of equity would face a conflict where the common law rules would produce one result, and equity another. The Supreme Court of Judicature Act 1873 therefore made provision, in the first 10 subsections of section 25, for the solution of many problems in which those

---

[74] Maitland, p. 14. There are now 13 judges, headed by the Vice-Chancellor, allocated to the Chancery Division.

[75] Holdsworth, *H.E.L.* v, p. 668.

[76] *Post*, pp. 684, 738.

[77] Administration of Justice Act 1970, s.1.

[78] Judicature Act 1873, s.24; Judicature Act 1925, ss.36–44; Supreme Court Act 1981, s.49.

[79] See Supreme Court Act 1981, Sched. 1, *post*, p. 41

[80] *Pugh* v. *Heath* (1882) 7 App.Cas. 235 at p. 237 (*per* Lord Cairns). Thus the three-fold division of the content of equity into the exclusive, concurrent and auxiliary jurisdictions lost importance after the Judicature Acts; Snell, pp. 13–14.

rules would conflict.[81] Subsection 11 contained a general residual clause. It provided that:

"Generally, in all matters not hereinbefore particularly mentioned in which there is any conflict or variance between the rules of equity and the rules of common law with reference to the same matter, the rules of equity shall prevail."

The effect of the Judicature Act is best shown by the leading case of *Walsh* v. *Lonsdale.*[82]

The landlord (defendant) entered into an agreement in writing to grant to the tenant (plaintiff) a lease of a mill for seven years. The agreement provided that the rent was payable in advance if demanded. No grant by deed of the lease—as required for the grant of a lease exceeding three years *at law*—was ever made.

The tenant entered and paid rent quarterly, not in advance. He became in arrears and the landlord demanded a year's rent in advance. It was not paid, and the landlord distrained. The tenant brought this action for illegal distress.[83]

The action failed. The distress would have been illegal at law, because no seven-year lease had been granted, and the yearly legal tenancy which arose because of the entering into possession and payment of rent did not include the provision for payment of rent in advance.[84] In equity, however, the agreement for the lease was as good as a lease. The tenant was held liable to pay a year's rent in advance and the distress was held to be lawful.

It will be seen that the effect of the Act is procedural only.[85] The rights of the parties, whether dependent on the rules of law or of equity, were under the Act determined at a single trial. But the same result would ultimately have been reached if the case had arisen before 1875; the procedure only would have differed. The claim, being one for damages for illegal distress, would have been brought at common

[81] Now Supreme Court Act 1981, s.49. Examples are found in s.25(1) of the Act of 1873, dealing with the order of priority of payment of debts of a person dying insolvent; and the refusal of common law but not of equity to recognise the assignment of debts and choses in action (s.25(6)). These matters are now dealt with by A.E.A. 1925, s.34(1) and L.P.A. 1925, s.136 respectively. See *Job* v. *Job* (1877) 6 Ch.D. 562; *Lowe* v. *Dixon* (1885) 16 Q.B.D. 455; *Berry* v. *Berry* [1929] 2 K.B. 316; *Mitas* v. *Hyams* [1951] 2 T.L.R. 1215.

[82] (1882) 21 Ch.D. 9; *Warmington* v. *Miller* [1973] Q.B. 877; *Tottenham Hotspur Football and Athletic Co. Ltd.* v. *Princegrove Publishers Ltd.* [1974] 1 W.L.R. 113; (1974) 90 L.Q.R. 149 (M.J. Albery); (1987) 7 O.J.L.S. 60 (S. Gardner).

[83] A landlord may distrain (*i.e.* issue a distress) upon a tenant who is in arrear, and in doing so may take and sell sufficient goods of the tenant (with exceptions) as are necessary to pay the arrears; M. & W., p. 709; Cheshire and Burn, p. 404.

[84] Because a yearly tenancy which arises in these circumstances includes only such terms of any agreement as are consistent with a yearly tenancy. An agreement to pay a year's rent in advance is not consistent with a yearly tenancy; M. & W., p. 641; Cheshire and Burn, p. 361.

[85] See (1966) 4 Alberta L.R. 134 (J. E. Coté).

law. To the tenant's argument that he held only on a lease from year to year, of which the covenant to pay rent a year in advance was not a term, the landlord would have had no reply in a court of law. This claim to specific performance by the tenant of his agreement to take a lease was one that could only have been made in equity. The landlord would have had to obtain an injunction to stop the tenant's action at law, and then to obtain specific performance of the agreement; and then to have returned to the common law court with the lease duly sealed by the tenant in conformity with the decree of Chancery. With the lease sealed, the landlord would have had a good defence in the common law court. The effect of the Judicature Acts was to enable the court to treat as done that which ought to be done, and to allow the landlord to use his equitable defence (based on his right to specific performance) to the common law claim. *Walsh* v. *Lonsdale*[86] was a case involving a landlord and a tenant, and was concerned with an agreement for a lease. The principle that equity treats as done that which ought to be done is not new. The significance of the case is the recognition of that principle in a case involving a legal claim. The principle is not limited to cases dealing with agreements for leases, but is applicable to all cases where there is a contract of which equity will decree specific perform-ance, by a legal estate owner to convey or create a legal estate.[87] This is an Estate Contract, typical examples of which are contracts to sell, to grant a lease or a mortgage.[88] And the principle has been applied "once removed"; as where A agreed to sell Blackacre to B who had agreed to grant a lease to C. C was treated as the lessee in equity of the land.[89] C would not become a lessee at law until the legal lease had been properly granted.

Whether developments in the century following the Judicature Acts have had the effect of fusing, not only the jurisdictions but law and equity themselves[90] is a disputed question which can best be considered after looking into the nature of equitable rights.

3. The Nature of Equitable Rights

There has for many years been a learned and unsettled controversy on the question of the nature of equitable rights; and particularly of the nature of the interest of a beneficiary under a trust. In its simplest

---

[86] (1882) 21 Ch.D. 9.

[87] L.C.A. 1972, s.2(4).

[88] A similar situation arises where there is a contract to grant an easement (*McManus* v. *Cook* (1887) 35 Ch.D. 681); or a profit à prendre (*Mason* v. *Clark* [1955] A.C. 778). Such an interest would appear to be registrable as a land charge Class D. (iii), but see Lord Denning's comments in *Ives (E.R.) Investments Ltd.* v. *High* [1967] 2 Q.B. 379, at pp. 395–396.

[89] *Industrial Properties (Barton Hill) Ltd.* v. *Associated Electrical Industries Ltd.* [1977] Q.B. 580; (1977) 40 M.L.R. 718 (P. Jackson).

[90] (1961) 24 M.L.R. 116 (V. T. H. Delaney).

form, one view emphasises the fact that a beneficiary's remedy, historically and practically, is in the form of an action against the trustee; a right *in personam*. On the other hand, equitable interests under trusts are in the form of equitable proprietary interests, corresponding to legal estates, and the beneficiary can properly be regarded as the owner of the beneficial interest; and ownership is a right *in rem*. The controversy attracted many of the great scholars of the English-speaking world; with Langdell, Ames, Maitland and Holland on one side, and Austin, Salmond, Pomeroy and Scott on the other.[91] Hanbury, in early editions of this work, took a middle course; arguing that the beneficiary's interest was less than ownership because of its liability to destruction before a bona fide purchaser of a legal estate for value without notice[92]; but more proprietary than ownership at common law because of the availability, to equitable owners alone, of the tracing remedy.[93]

Much of this controversy was carried out in the context of discussing whether the beneficiary's right was a right *in personam* or a right *in rem*. This was because Austin, following the classifications of Roman law, laid down that rights must be of one type or the other.[94] But, for the discussion to become meaningful, it is necessary to know what these Latinisms mean. They mean different things in different contexts. Thus a right *in rem* is sometimes used to signify a right against a specific item of property. It is used also, and with hardly a word of criticism, to distinguish the tracing remedy from a personal action for damages.[95] It can also be used to distinguish a right to property from a chose in action.[96] It seems that its proper meaning in the present context is "a right enforceable against the world with respect to a particular thing."[97] It seems to be assumed throughout that a legal owner does have rights *in rem*. Rights, that is, against all the world with respect to property. The civilians would have said that he had a right *in rem* because he had a right in the thing itself. Which may be true of legal ownership of chattels. But it is difficult to see how that could be so in the case of intangibles such as investments, or a bank account. And also with land, for the feudal theory established that the feudal tenant did not own the land. He owned an estate in the land. How, then, does a beneficiary under a trust measure up to this test; that of asking whether he has rights against all the world with respect to property?

The basis of equitable jurisdiction, historically and presently, is that,

---

[91] (1967) 45 C.B.R. at p. 221 (D. W. M. Waters); (1917) 17 Col.L.R. 269 (A. W. Scott); (1917) 17 Col.L.R. 467 (H. F. Stone); (1962) 40 C.B.R. at p. 270 (E. J. Mockler).
[92] *Post*, p. 33.
[93] *Post*, p. 624.
[94] See generally [1982] Conv. 118, 177 (A. R. Everton), discussing the emergence of a third, intermediate category, described as a "right of quasi-property."
[95] *Re Diplock* [1948] Ch. 465; [1951] A.C. 251, *post*, p. 625.
[96] *Scott on Trusts*, § 130.
[97] (1962) 40 C.B.R. at p. 279.

in accordance with the maxim, equity acts *in personam*, equitable rights grew up where the Chancellor was willing to intervene. The use has its origin in the insistence of the Chancellor that the feoffees to uses should administer the property in a particular way—to the use and benefit of the *cestui que use*. Similarly with the trust. "Equity did not say that the *cestui que trust* was the owner of the land, it said that the trustee was the owner of the land, but added that he was bound to hold the land for the benefit of the *cestui que trust*."[98] We will see later[99] that this situation inevitably raised the question of the effect of the sale of the land by the trustee. The answer was that the beneficiary's interest was effective against everyone, with the exception of a bona fide purchaser for valuable consideration without notice, actual or constructive, of the equitable interest. He took the legal estate free from the equitable interest.

Indeed equity could not have done differently. Its remedies of specific performance and injunction were decrees *in personam*. They ordered the defendant to do something or to refrain from doing something; and behind them was the threat that a recalcitrant defendant would be put in prison for contempt if he refused.

There is no space here to run through every aspect of equity jurisdiction to establish this point. The reader is invited to bear it in mind whenever any question of equitable rights or interests arises during the course of this book. It will be seen on every occasion that equity is acting *in personam*. One practical application of this proposition is the fact that a court of equity will exercise jurisdiction to decree specific performance of a contract for the sale of land abroad[1]; or to administer assets abroad if the executors are in England[2]; or to restrain a mother, who was a British subject and ordinarily resident in England and who had been served while in the United States under R.S.C., Order XI, r. 1,[3] from keeping abroad her children who had been made wards of court.[4]

But this does not prevent us from treating a beneficiary under a trust as having equitable ownership. A beneficiary's interest behind a trust has long been treated as having the basic characteristics of a proprietary interest in that it can be bought, sold, mortgaged, and devised or bequeathed. Even though, historically, the protection of *cestui que use* was based on the Chancellor's willingness to proceed *in personam* against the trustee, that protection has ended up by creating rights in

---

[98] Maitland, p. 17.

[99] *Post*, p. 33.

[1] *Penn* v. *Lord Baltimore* (1750) 1 Ves.Sen. 444; *Richard West and Partners (Inverness) Ltd.* v. *Dick* [1969] Ch. 424; *post*, p. 652; *Hamlin* v. *Hamlin* [1986] Fam. 11 (jurisdiction to restrain disposal of foreign land under Matrimonial Causes Act 1973, s.37(2), where defendant amenable to jurisdiction).

[2] *Ewing* v. *Orr-Ewing (No. 1)* (1883) 9 App.Cas. 34.

[3] It permits the service of a writ in certain cases upon a person who is out of the jurisdiction.

[4] *Re Liddell's Settlement* [1936] Ch. 365.

the nature of ownership.[5] To argue that a beneficiary's rights are proprietary is not to say that legal rights are the same as equitable, or that equitable ownership is the same as legal. Rather, it is to accept the basic peculiarity of ownership under the English law of trusts. The trustee is the owner at law; and the beneficiary is the owner in equity.

In relation to some claims affecting the trust property, the trustee is able to sue and not the beneficiary. Thus, the trustee sues for rent,[6] or for possession; and, with personalty, the trustee, not the beneficiary, sues for conversion of the trust property.[7] The beneficiary's right is to compel the trustee to take action; though he may, in some cases, take action himself, joining the trustee as defendant.[8] This right may sometimes be inadequate; as where the trustee has sold the property to a bona fide purchaser of the legal estate for value without notice, who will defeat the equitable ownership of the beneficiary.[9] Does this require us to say that his rights are personal against the trustee, and are not properly regarded as proprietary? This was the deciding test for the supporters of the theory that equitable rights must be regarded as being *in personam*. But it shows the inadequacy of the test which is being applied as a means of distinguishing equitable ownership from legal ownership; which is accepted as being a right *in rem*. For legal rights of ownership are not good against all the world. There are many ways in which the legal owner of a chattel or chose in action may be involuntarily deprived of legal ownership.[10] The situation of the bona fide purchaser is not determinative of the question whether the beneficiary's interest is proprietary; or whether his rights are *in rem* or *in personam*. It demonstrates again that legal and equitable ownership may have different effects.

At which stage, the reader may well ask whether there is any significance to the discussion. "It is a moot question whether the whole discussion raised by the arbitrary classifications borrowed from Roman law and distorted to fit in with new facts is not a merely academical tourney with no real bearing upon the protection of the law, and, being faulty in hypothesis and unsatisfactory in result, would be better abandoned altogether."[11] To a large extent, that is true. But related questions of great significance have arisen in the tax field, in

---

[5] *Per* Lord Atkin [1914] A.C. 398 at p. 444; (1954) 70 L.Q.R. 326 at p. 331 (Lord Evershed M.R.).

[6] *Schalit* v. *Nadler Ltd.* [1933] 2 K.B. 79; the beneficiary's right is not to the rent, but to an account.

[7] The beneficiary can sue if he has a right to immediate possession; *Healey* v. *Healey* [1915] 1 K.B. 938.

[8] See *Les Affréteurs Réunis Société Anonyme* v. *Leopold Walford (London) Ltd.* [1919] A.C. 801.

[9] The beneficiary in such circumstances will have a personal right against the trustee for compensation: *post*, p. 597.

[10] Sale of Goods Act 1979, ss.21–26; Factors Act 1889, ss.2, 8, 9; Consumer Credit Act 1974, Sched. 4, para. 22. A legal owner of stolen goods may not assert his title against a bona fide purchaser who buys them in market overt.

[11] Turner, *Equity of Redemption* (1931 ed.), p. 152.

which it has been material to determine whether a beneficiary was the owner of certain property, or had merely a personal right against a trustee. The point has arisen in a wide variety of circumstances in different tax legislations in different parts of the Commonwealth. There is no space to examine them all. The answers given are as confusing as the circumstances are various,[12] some courts dealing with the matter on a pragmatic basis, relating to the policy of the particular taxing statute, and some basing themselves on the old theoretical analysis. Two leading cases, one from the House of Lords, and one from the Privy Council, will be sufficient to demonstrate the practical difficulties of the problems in this field.

In *Baker* v. *Archer-Shee*,[13] Lady Archer-Shee, an American citizen resident in England, was the income beneficiary of a New York trust established by a New York settlor. The New York trustee received the dividends, paid out money due for local taxes, expenses and their fees, and retained the balance in the account in New York. The question was whether Lady Archer-Shee was liable to income tax in England upon this income. She would be liable if taxable on an "arising" basis, but not if she were taxable on a "remittance" basis; that is only on such part of the money as was remitted to her in England. That, in turn, depended on whether she was regarded as the owner of the dividends as they arose; or whether the trustees were the owners, and her right was to require them to pay to her the balance after expenditures.[14] The House of Lords, by a majority of 3–2, held that she was liable on an "arising" basis. She was the owner of the dividends.[15]

Baker v. *Archer-Shee*[16] was of course concerned with an established trust. Would the same view be taken of the interest of a legatee under the unadministered estate of a deceased person?[17] Here it is clearly more difficult to say that the beneficiary is the owner of the estate or of any part thereof. For parts of the estate will be used to pay debts and taxes, and it may turn out that the estate is insolvent. Until administration is complete, it is impossible to say what it consists of. It is much easier to think of the legatee's right as being one to require the due administration of the estate by the executor or administrator. And so it is usually stated.

---

[12] See (1967) 45 C.B.R. 219 (D. W. M. Waters).

[13] [1927] A.C. 844.

[14] See also *Syme* v. *Commissioner of Taxes* [1914] A.C. 1013; *Nelson* v. *Adamson* [1941] 2 K.B. 12.

[15] New York law was applicable to the trust. In the absence of expert evidence, it was assumed that New York law was the same as English law. Subsequently, in *Archer-Shee* v. *Garland* ([1931] A.C. 212), expert evidence was given to show that New York law regarded the income beneficiary as having only a personal right to sue the trustee; and the taxpayer was held to be liable only on a remittance basis.

[16] [1927] A.C. 844.

[17] *Cooper* v. *Cooper* (1874) 7 H.L. 53; *Sudeley* v. *Att.-Gen.* [1897] A.C. 11; *Barnado's Homes* v. *Special Commissioners of Income Tax* [1921] 2 A.C. 1; *Re Gibbs* [1951] Ch. 933; *Re Cunliffe-Owen* [1953] Ch. 544.

In *Commissioner of Stamp Duties (Queensland)* v. *Livingston*,[18] a husband died domiciled in New South Wales, and his widow became entitled to a one-third share of his estate. The estate contained land in Queensland. The widow died intestate, also domiciled in New South Wales, prior to the completion of the administration of her husband's estate. The question was whether the Queensland authorities could levy succession duty in respect of the Queensland land upon the widow's death. The Privy Council held that they could not; because the widow was not the owner of the land. She had a right, which was situated in New South Wales, to require the true administration of the estate. She owned no property in Queensland.

These cases are introduced to show the current position on two aspects of this matter. They do not help to resolve all the conflicting cases; nor do they determine the answer to the *in rem-in personam* dispute. The dispute on the theoretical question will continue indefinitely; though there is less interest in the matter at the present day. From a more practical point of view, the best that can be said is that when a question arises in which the beneficiary requires to assert his right through the medium of the trustee, the old theory that equity acts *in personam* is wholly acceptable.[19] But, in other cases, usually tax cases, the theoretical view is overtaken by a pragmatic approach; and the result determined by the language of the statute and a number of policy questions relating to the purposes of the particular statute. This is an area where practical questions arise; and one where Austin's theoretical analysis is the least helpful. Perhaps the better view is that the beneficiary's interest is *sui generis*.[20]

4. THE RELATIONSHIP BETWEEN LAW AND EQUITY: FUSION

The Judicature Act clearly "fused" the administration of law and equity by the creation of the High Court of Judicature exercising both law and equity and gave supremacy to equity in cases of conflict. A disputed question is whether that Act, or the development of law and equity in the century which has followed, should be regarded as having effected the fusion of law and equity themselves.

The orthodox view is that the jurisdictions have been fused but not the system. The changes made by the Judicature Act gave rise to no new cause of action, remedy, or defence, which was not available before. In a famous "fluvial" metaphor, Ashburner said "the two streams of jurisdiction, though they run in the same channel; run side

---

[18] [1965] A.C. 694; *post,* p. 59.
[19] "Where the problem concerns the working of the trust machinery" (1967) 45 C.B.R. at p. 280 (D. W. M. Waters).
[20] Pettit, p. 69.

by side, and do not mingle their waters."[21] Thus, legal rights remain legal rights, and equitable rights remain equitable rights, though administered in the same court. Other bills which were introduced prior to the Judicature Act would indeed have fused the systems; but they failed, and the Judicature Act was a more cautious measure.[22]

There are, however, statements by great judges to the effect that the systems are fused. Sir George Jessel said, as early as 1881; "there are not two estates as there were formerly, one estate in common law by reason of the payment rent from year to year, and an estate in equity under the agreement. There is only one court, and equity rules prevail in it."[23] More recently, Lord Diplock[24] discussed Ashburner's metaphor, and declared:

> "By 1977, this metaphor has in my view become most mischievous and deceptive. The innate conservatism of English lawyers may have made them slow to recognise that by the Supreme Court of Judicature Act 1873, the two systems of substantive and adjectival law formerly administered by courts of law and Courts of Chancery (as well as those administered by Courts of Admiralty, Probate and Matrimonial Causes), were fused."

Others, less extreme, have expressed views to the effect that we ought to be addressing our minds to the *combined effect* of the systems of law and equity, and that to keep the systems always distinct is pedantic, and an impediment to the natural development of the law.[25]

It is important, in this discussion, to be clear as to what is meant by the claim that law and equity are fused. If it means that there is now no distinction or difference between legal rights and remedies and equitable rights and remedies, it cannot be supported.[26] It is still clear that legal ownership is different from equitable ownership; all the provisions of the legislation of 1925, dealing with unregistered land, are

---

[21] *Principles of Equity* (2nd ed.), p. 18. See also (1954) 70 L.Q.R. 326 (Lord Evershed M.R.); (1966) 24 M.L.R. 116 (V. T. H. Delaney); (1977) 93 L.Q.R. 529 (P. V. Baker); (1977) 6 A.A.L.R. 119 (T. G. Watkin).

[22] (1977) 93 L.Q.R. 529 at p. 530 (P. V. Baker); (1870) 14 S.J. 548.

[23] *Walsh* v. *Lonsdale* (1882) 21 Ch.D. 14. He had previously expressed the orthodox view of the effect of the Act, in *Salt* v. *Cooper* (1880) 16 Ch.D. 544 at p. 549.

[24] *United Scientific Holdings Ltd.* v. *Burnley Borough Council* [1978] A.C. 904 at p. 925. All the members of the House indicated their general acceptance of the principle of fusion. Lord Diplock is described as "the most forceful exponent of the fusion fallacy," in Heydon, Gummow and Austin, *Cases and Materials on Equity and Trusts* (2nd ed.), p. 23. See also *Chief Constable of Kent* v. *V.* [1983] Q.B. 34 at p. 41.

[25] See (1948) J.S.P.T.L. 180 (Lord Evershed); (1952) C.L.P. 1 (Lord Denning); *The Court of Appeal in England*, p. 13 (Lord Evershed); (1961) 24 M.L.R. 116 (V. T. H. Delaney); Lord Denning, *Landmarks in the Law*, p. 86 ("the fusion is complete"); Keeton and Sheridan's *Equity* (3rd ed.), pp. 28–30.

[26] (1977) 93 L.Q.R. 529 at p. 532 (P. V. Baker).

based on that assumption.[27] Again, the law of trusts assumes a distinction between legal and equitable rights. Further, it is still basically
true to say that an equitable claim will provide an equitable remedy
and that a common law claim will provide only a common law
remedy.[28] This is seen in the context of remedies for fraudulent and
innocent misrepresentation,[29] and with remedies for contracts induced
by undue influence. And equitable doctrines, such as the doctrine of
part performance, attract only the equitable remedy of specific performance.[30] And the equitable tracing remedy is available only to a
plaintiff who can show a breach of a fiduciary relation.[31] The illustrations could be multiplied.

Nor is it true, at the other extreme, to say that rights exercisable in
the High Court today are the same as those existing in 1875; nor that
the application of equitable doctrines in the courts has not had the
effect of refining and developing the common law rules.[32] Both legal
and equitable rules have developed in the last century; and the development of legal rules has sometimes been influenced by established
equitable doctrine, with the effect that a situation which would at one
time have been treated differently at law and in equity is now treated in
the same manner. If that is what is meant by fusion, there is evidence of
it, as shown below. It is a healthy and welcome development; and there
are other situations which might be candidates for future inclusion.

In *Boyer* v. *Warbey*,[33] the question arose whether covenants in a
lease that touched and concerned the land bound assignees, not only
where the lease had been sealed, but also where the lease was a valid
written lease (not exceeding three years). The Court of Appeal held
that, whatever the position before 1875, this was not an area where
distinctions based on formalities were now acceptable, and that the
covenant should bind. It was further suggested that the same result
would follow if there was merely a contract for a lease which was
enforceable in equity. Whether it was law or equity that regarded the
lease as effective, the rule as to the running of covenants should be the
same. In a limited sense this is "fusion" in that the reasons why a
particular lease is effective are ignored in favour of a uniform conse-
quential rule.

In *Australian Blue Metal Ltd.* v. *Hughes*,[34] a question arose concern-

---

[27] The distinction between legal and equitable ownership is of little significance in
registered land. But that is due to the classification of interests for the purposes of the
system, and is unconnected with any question of fusion.
[28] See also *Allied Arab Bank Ltd.* v. *Hajjar* [1988] 2 W.L.R. 942 (writ *ne exeat regno* still
requires an equitable claim).
[29] Subject to change by statute; Misrepresentation Act 1967; *post*, p. 787.
[30] Subject also to intervention by statute: Lord Cairns' Act 1858, *post*, p. 684.
[31] *Post*, p. 624.
[32] (1977) 93 L.Q.R. 536 (P.V. Baker).
[33] [1953] 1 Q.B. 234, especially at pp. 245–247, *per* Denning and Romer L.JJ. *post*,
p. 688.
[34] [1963] A.C. 74, especially at pp. 101–102, *per* Lord Devlin.

ing the form of notice that might be required for a party to a certain type of obligation to resile from it. Common law approached the question by implying a need for reasonable notice, equity by allowing a reasonable period of grace. In the view of the Privy Council, such a theoretical distinction should not lead to different results. The only test was that of what was reasonable and fair between the parties, and nothing here depended on whether the origin of the protection was legal or equitable. In consequence, the rule can be fully stated without reference to its origins. In *United Scientific Holdings Ltd.* v. *Burnley Borough Council*[35] the question was whether a landlord who failed to keep strictly to the timetable laid down by a rent review clause was deprived of his right to obtain the increased rent. The House of Lords held that the Law of Property Act 1925, s.41[36] applied; and that time was not of the essence under the rules of equity. Similarly, it has been held that set-off, whether legal or equitable, can be raised as a defence whether the relief sought by the plaintiff is legal or equitable.[37]

Much of the modern development of the law of estoppel, especially in the form of promissory estoppel and proprietary estoppel, has been achieved without enquiring whether the doctrines are doctrines of equity, or of law or of both. The doctrine of promissory estoppel works negatively; to give protection to the party who relied on the promise, but not to give him a new cause of action.[38] But proprietary estoppel operates positively[39] and is capable of creating new rights. The distinction between an estoppel which operates negatively and one which operates positively was once thought to demonstrate a distinction between "equitable estoppel" and "common law estoppel."[40] But this is now discredited, and only a proprietary estoppel creates new rights. Such rights are recognised in equity only, and, in unregistered land, are enforceable against all but a bona fide purchaser of a legal estate for value without notice.[41] Proprietary estoppel must be regarded as a development in equity. Other estoppels can be regarded as being based on common law or equity.

One indication of fusion is a situation where the legal remedy may be given for breach of an equitable right. The converse, an equitable remedy for breach of a legal right, has been accepted in various situations, such as an injunction to restrain a nuisance, or other tort, or to restrain a breach of contract. And, prior to the Judicature Act, Lord Cairns' Act authorised, in certain circumstances, courts of common

---

[35] [1978] A.C. 904.

[36] "Stipulations in a contract, as to time or otherwise, which according to rules of equity are not deemed to be or to have become of the essence of the contract, are also construed and have effect at law in accordance with the same rules."

[37] *B.I.C.C. plc* v. *Burndy Corp.* [1985] Ch. 232; (1985) 101 L.Q.R. 145.

[38] *Combe* v. *Combe* [1951] 2 K.B. 215, *post*, p. 849.

[39] *Post*, p. 850.

[40] *Williams* v. *Pinckney* (1897) 67 L.J.Ch. 34, *per* Vaughan-Williams L.J.; (1952) 15 M.L.R. 325 (L. A. Sheridan); Spencer-Bower, p. 10.

[41] *Post*, p. 858.

law to grant specific performance or an injunction instead of damages, and courts of equity to award damages. And, as will be seen, this Act, although overtaken by the Judicature Act, still has scope for operation.[42]

Generally, however, the breach of an equitable right will provide an equitable remedy only. Thus, a breach of a restrictive covenant by a non-contracting party is remedied by an injunction, not damages; innocent misrepresentation, apart from statute, by rescission and not damages; and breach of fiduciary duty by various equitable remedies.[43] The stage has not yet been reached at which it is immaterial whether a breach is of a legal or equitable duty. This situation was approached in *Seager* v. *Copydex Ltd.*,[44] where the defendants had used a technical idea communicated to them in confidence by the plaintiff in marketing a carpet grip. Equity's familiar remedies to protect a plaintiff injured in this manner are an injunction and an account. But the circumstances of this case suggested that the most just solution was an assessment of damages. Can an action for common law damages lie, however, for a breach of confidence, which is protected only in equity? The Court of Appeal held that the appropriate remedy must be granted; fictions of implied contracts or notional injunctions were not now necessary[45]; damages were thus ordered to be assessed.

But this does not mean that law and equity are fused. Sufficient examples have been given to show that this is not so. What can be said is that a century of fused jurisdiction has seen the two systems working more closely together; each changing and developing and improving from contact with the other; and each willing to accept new ideas and developments, regardless of their origin. They are coming closer together. But they are not yet fused.

---

[42] *Post*, p. 684.

[43] Which may include the payment of money.

[44] [1967] 1 W.L.R. 923. Heydon, Gummow and Austin, *Cases and Materials on Equity and Trusts* (2nd ed.), pp. 11 *et seq.*, treat this case as an example of "fusion fallacies," *i.e.* cases where the results are explicable by the application of neither law nor equity, and could only result from a legislative change in substantive principles which is not found in the Judicature Act. Similarly *Cuckmere Brick Co. Ltd.* v. *Mutual Finance Ltd.* [1971] Ch. 949 (notions of common law damages and duty of care imported into mortgagee's power of sale).

[45] *i.e.* to enable damages to be granted in lieu under Lord Cairns' Act, *post*, p. 684. See *Seager* v. *Copydex Ltd., supra*, at pp. 931–932. *cf. Nicrotherm Electrical Co. Ltd.* v. *Percy* [1957] R.P.C. 272. See also *Fraser* v. *Thames Television Ltd.* [1984] Q.B. 44, where damages were awarded for breach of confidence without any argument on this point; *Stephens* v. *Avery* [1988] 2 W.L.R. 1280. In employment cases, of course, use of confidential information may be a breach of contract sounding in damages. Lord Goff has recently said that damages are available for breach of confidence, despite the equitable nature of the wrong, "through a beneficent interpretation of the Chancery Amendment Act 1858 (Lord Cairns' Act) . . ."; *Att.-Gen.* v. *Guardian Newspapers Ltd. (No. 2)* [1988] 3 W.L.R. 776, at p. 810.

5. THE MAXIMS OF EQUITY

The maxims of equity embody the general principles which evolved in the Court of Chancery. They are not rules which must be rigorously applied in every case, but are more in the nature of general guidelines illustrating the way in which equitable jurisdiction is exercised. A few examples of their operation must suffice,[46] but they should be borne in mind when considering the various rules and doctrines of equity.

i. Equity will not suffer a wrong to be without a remedy. The principle behind this maxim is that equity will intervene to protect a right which, perhaps because of some technical defect, is not enforceable at law. It is not sufficient that the defendant may be guilty of some moral wrong: the plaintiff's right must be suitable for enforcement by the court. The classic example is the enforcement of trusts. The beneficiary had no remedy at common law if the trustee claimed the property for himself, as the trustee was the legal owner, but he could enforce his rights in equity. The maxim is also reflected in the area of equitable remedies, which may be granted where the defendant's wrong is one not recognised by the common law. Thus equity may grant specific performance of a contract relating to land which is supported by an act of part performance, even though it is not evidenced in writing and is therefore unenforceable at law.[47] In the field of injunctions, the plaintiff may obtain a *quia timet* injunction to restrain a threatened wrong although he has no cause of action at law until the wrong is committed[48]; similarly, he may be granted an interlocutory injunction to preserve his rights until the trial in situations where the common law remedy of damages would be quite inadequate and in any event not available until the case is proved at trial.[49]

ii. Equity follows the law. Clearly equity may not depart from statute law, nor does it refuse to follow common-law rules save in exceptional circumstances.[50] Thus equitable interests in land correspond with the legal estates and interests.[51] For example, the rights and duties of the parties under an equitable lease are the same as if the lease were legal.

iii. He who seeks equity must do equity. A plaintiff who seeks equitable relief must be prepared to act fairly towards the defendant. The operation of this principle can be seen where equity, in allowing rescission of a contract for mistake, puts the plaintiff on terms which

[46] For a more detailed survey, see Snell, Chap. 3.
[47] *Post*, p. 658.
[48] *Post*, p. 732.
[49] *Post*, p. 697.
[50] For the conflicts between the rules of law and equity, see *ante*, p. 15.
[51] Equity, however, recognised certain future interests which were not recognised at law. See Megarry and Wade, *The Law of Real Property* (5th ed.), p. 1179.

appear to the court to be just and equitable.[52] A plaintiff seeking an injunction will not succeed if he is unable or unwilling to carry out his own future obligations.[53] This maxim is also the foundation of the doctrine of election.[54]

iv. He who comes to equity must come with clean hands. This principle is closely related to the last one, save that the latter looks to the plaintiff's future conduct, while the "clean hands" principle looks to his previous conduct. Thus equity will not grant relief against forfeiture for breach of covenant where the breach in question was flagrant.[55] Similarly, a licensee may be debarred from invoking the doctrine of estoppel if he has been guilty of grave misconduct.[56] Examples abound in the field of equitable remedies[57]: a tenant cannot get specific performance of a contract for a lease if he is already in breach of his obligations[58]; nor could a purchaser if he had taken advantage of the illiteracy of the vendor who was not separately advised[59]; so also in the case of injunctions,[60] but equitable relief will only be debarred on this ground if the plaintiff's blameworthy conduct has some connection with the relief sought. The court is not concerned with the plaintiff's general conduct. Thus in *Argyll (Duchess)* v. *Argyll (Duke)*,[61] the fact that the wife's adultery had led to the divorce proceedings was no ground for refusing her an injunction to restrain her husband from publishing confidential material; her adultery did not license her husband to "broadcast unchecked the most intimate confidences of earlier and happier days."[62] If both parties have "unclean hands," the court should consider only those of the applicant, and need not balance the misconduct of one against that of the other.[63]

v. Where the equities are equal the law prevails.

vi. Where the equities are equal the first in time prevails. These two related maxims, dealing with the priorities of competing interests, may

---

[52] See the terms imposed in *Solle* v. *Butcher* [1950] 1 K.B. 671 and *Grist* v. *Bailey* [1967] Ch. 532, *post*, p. 780.

[53] See *Chappell* v. *Times Newspapers Ltd.* [1975] 1 W.L.R. 482, *post*, p. 738, where employees failed to get an injunction to restrain their dismissal where they refused to undertake not to become involved in strikes.

[54] *Post*, p. 810.

[55] See *Shiloh Spinners Ltd.* v. *Harding* [1973] A.C. 691.

[56] See *Williams* v. *Staite* [1979] Ch. 291; *J. Willis & Son* v. *Willis* [1986] 1 E.G.L.R. 62. See also, on the acquisition of equitable interests, *Winkworth* v. *Edward Baron Development Co. Ltd.* [1986] 1 W.L.R. 1512.

[57] *Post*, Part IV.

[58] *Coatsworth* v. *Johnson* (1886) 54 L.T. 520.

[59] *Mountford* v. *Scott* [1975] Ch. 258.

[60] See *Hubbard* v. *Vosper* [1972] 2 Q.B. 84, *post*.

[61] [1967] Ch. 302.

[62] *Ibid.* at p. 333.

[63] *Sang Lee Investment Co. Ltd.* v. *Wing Kwai Investment Co. Ltd.*, *The Times*, April 14, 1983.

be dealt with together. They provide the foundation for the doctrine of notice.[64] Thus a prior equitable interest in land can only be defeated by a bona fide purchaser of a legal estate without notice. If the purchaser is bona fide and without notice, then the equities are equal and his legal estate prevails. If he took with notice the position is otherwise, as the equities are not equal. If he does not acquire a legal estate then the first in time, *i.e.* the prior equitable interest, prevails, as equitable interests rank in order of creation. The two maxims are also the foundation of the law on priority of mortgages of land, but have lost some of their importance since the introduction in 1925 of the system of registration of certain interests in land.[65]

vii. Equity imputes an intention to fulfil an obligation. Where a person is obliged to do some act, and does some other act which could be regarded as a performance of it, then it will be so regarded in equity. This is the basis of the doctrines of performance and satisfaction.[66] For example, if a debtor leaves a legacy to his creditor (of an amount at least as great as the debt), this is presumed to be a repayment of the debt so that, unless the presumption is rebutted, the creditor cannot take the legacy and sue to recover the debt.

viii. Equity regards as done that which ought to be done. Where there is a specifically enforceable obligation equity regards the parties as already in the position which they would be in after performance of the obligation. A contract relating to land is specifically enforceable if there is writing or part performance.[67] Therefore in equity a specifically enforceable contract for a lease creates an equitable lease. This is the doctrine of *Walsh* v. *Lonsdale*.[68] Similarly, a specifically enforceable contract for the sale of land transfers the equitable interest to the purchaser, the vendor holding the legal title on constructive trust until completion.[69] The maxim is also the basis of the doctrine of conversion, whereby an interest under a trust for sale of land is regarded as an interest in the proceeds of sale,[70] and the rule in *Howe* v. *Dartmouth*,[71] concerning the duty to convert unauthorised investments.

ix. Equity is equality. Where two or more persons are entitled to an interest in the same property, then the principle of equity is equal division, if there is no good reason for any other basis for division. Equity, therefore, dislikes the joint tenancy where, by the doctrine of

---

[64] *Post*, p. 33.
[65] *Post*, p. 37.
[66] *Post*, p. 821.
[67] L.P.A. 1925, s.40.
[68] (1882) 21 Ch.D. 9, *ante*, p. 16. See also *Industrial Properties (Barton Hill) Ltd.* v. *Associated Electrical Industries Ltd.* [1972] Q.B. 580.
[69] *Post*, p. 304. See *Lake* v. *Bayliss* [1974] 1 W.L.R. 1073.
[70] *Post*, p. 806.
[71] (1802) 7 Ves. 137, *post*, p. 510.

survivorship, the last survivor takes all. This may be contrasted with the tenancy in common, where the interest of each party devolves upon his personal representative on his death. In the absence of an express declaration to the effect that the equitable interest is held jointly, equity presumes a tenancy in common in three cases where at law the parties are joint tenants: first, where the purchase money has been provided in unequal shares, equity presumes a tenancy in common in shares proportionate to the contributions; secondly, where parties lend money on mortgage, whether equally or unequally, the mortgagees are presumed as between themselves to be entitled as tenants in common[72]; and thirdly, where partners acquire property, they are presumed to be tenants in common.[73] Even where the equitable interest is held jointly, equity leans in favour of severance, meaning that equity is ready to regard an act or dealing as an act of severance, whereby the equitable interest is converted to a tenancy in common, thus excluding the possibility of survivorship.[74]

Another area where the maxim can be seen in operation is entitlement to matrimonial property. Where the parties have both made substantial contributions to the acquisition of property, whether directly or indirectly, then, if no other basis for division clearly appears, equity prefers to treat the parties as equally entitled rather than to examine their precise contributions.[75]

x. Equity looks to the intent rather than the form. This principle does not mean that formalities may be ignored in equity, but rather that equity looks at the substance rather than the form. Thus equity will regard a transaction as a mortgage even though it is not so described, if in substance it appears that the property was transferred by way of security. Similarly a trust may be created although the word "trust" has not been used.[76] A covenant will be regarded as a restrictive covenant if negative in substance even if it is worded in a positive form.[77] Although a party to a contract under seal can enforce the contract at law even though no consideration has been given, equity regards such a party as a volunteer and will not decree specific performance in his favour.[78]

---

[72] Although as against the mortgagor they remain joint tenants, so that the survivor can give a good receipt on repayment. L.P.A. 1925, s.111.

[73] *cf. Barton* v. *Morris* [1985] 1 W.L.R. 1257 (express declaration of beneficial joint tenancy). See also *Malayan Credit Ltd.* v. *Jack Chia-MPH Ltd.* [1986] A.C. 549 (presumption of tenancy in common where legal joint tenants held premises for their several individual business purposes).

[74] See *Burgess* v. *Rawnsley* [1975] Ch. 429.

[75] *Post*, p. 259.

[76] *Post*, p. 93.

[77] *Tulk* v. *Moxhay* (1848) 18 L.J.Ch. 83 (covenant "to keep uncovered by buildings" held negative).

[78] *Cannon* v. *Hartley* [1949] Ch. 213, *post*, p. 122.

xi. Delay defeats equities. Equity aids the vigilant and not the indolent. This is the foundation of the doctrine of laches, whereby a party who has slept upon his rights cannot obtain equitable relief. This doctrine is superseded where the Limitation Act 1980 deals with the matter.[79] For example, actions against trustees for breach of trust must, by section 21, be brought within six years, and delay short of this will not bar relief. Where, however, the plaintiff has a legal right, for example, upon a contract, delay may prevent the grant of an equitable remedy such as specific performance even though the legal right is not statute-barred.[80] Interlocutory injunctions must always be sought promptly, but it seems that delay may not prevent the grant of a final injunction where the cause of action is not statute-barred.[81]

The doctrine of laches continues to apply to those equitable claims which are outside the Limitation Act 1980, for example a claim to set aside a purchase of trust property by a trustee.[82] Similarly, claims to rescission and rectification may be barred by delay.[83]

xii. Equity acts *in personam.* Equity has jurisdiction over the defendant personally. The personal nature of the jurisdiction is illustrated by the fact that failure to comply with an order, such as specific performance or an injunction, is a contempt of court punishable by imprisonment. Provided that the defendant is within the jurisdiction (or can be served outside it), it is no objection that the property which is the subject-matter of the dispute is outside it.[84] Thus in the leading case of *Penn* v. *Lord Baltimore*,[85] specific performance was ordered of an agreement relating to land boundaries in Pennsylvania and Maryland, the defendant being in this country.

6. EQUITABLE REMEDIES

At common law, the normal form of relief is an award of damages, to which a plaintiff who has proved his case is entitled as of right. One of the greatest contributions of equity has been to supplement the limited range of legal remedies by introducing a wide range of equitable remedies,[86] which can be awarded both to enforce rights which are

---

[79] Either expressly or by analogy; *post*, p. 618.
[80] *Post*, p. 677. See Limitation Act 1980, s.36(1).
[81] *Fullwood* v. *Fullwood* (1878) 9 Ch.D. 176; *H.P. Bulmer Ltd. & Showerings Ltd.* v. *J. Bollinger S.A.* [1977] 2 C.M.L.R. 625, *post*, p. 734.
[82] *Post*, p. 618.
[83] *Post*, pp. 794, 801.
[84] See *Chellaram* v. *Chellaram* [1985] Ch. 409 (appointment and removal of foreign trustees of foreign settlement); *post*, p. 479.
[85] (1750) 1 Ves.Sen. 444, *post*, p. 652; *Hamlin* v. *Hamlin* [1986] Fam. 11. See also Civil Jurisdiction and Judgments Act 1982, s.30(1).
[86] See generally Meagher, Gummow and Lehane, *Equity—Doctrines and Remedies*; Heydon, Gummow and Austin, *Cases and Materials on Equity and Trusts*; Spry, *Equitable Remedies*, Chap. 1.

exclusively equitable and those which are legal. Their common features are that they are discretionary, their availability depends upon the inadequacy of common law remedies (which, in the case of exclusive equitable rights, will not be available at all) and they are governed by the doctrine that equity acts *in personam*.

The most significant of these remedies are specific performance, whereby the court orders a party to a contract to perform his contractual obligations, and an injunction, whereby the court orders a person to do, or, more commonly, to refrain from doing, some particular act. These, plus the remedies of rescission and rectification of contracts, will be examined in Part IV. Other equitable remedies include delivery up and cancellation of documents,[87] account[88] and receivers.[89]

Mention might also be made of certain procedural remedies, equitable in origin, which have now been incorporated into the general rules of litigation. Examples include discovery of documents[90] and suits for the perpetuation of testimony.[91] Similarly the writ *ne exeat regno*, which has recently enjoyed something of a revival.[92] The remedy of the declaration had some connection with equity in origin,[93] but the jurisdiction to grant it is now governed wholly by statute.[94] Finally, although not remedies in the traditional sense, the constructive trust and the doctrine of tracing are sometimes so described. These will be examined elsewhere.[95]

The differing character of equitable remedies must be appreciated. First, it is obvious that factors such as fraud, misrepresentation and mistake are relevant to the exercise of discretionary jurisdiction to issue injunctions and decrees of specific performance. Here, the question is ordinarily one of the manner in which an already existing legal or equitable right is enforced.[96] The right itself is not affected. Thus if equity refuses to decree specific performance of a contract due to a defendant's mistake, the plaintiff's right to sue for damages still subsists[97]: it is merely that a supplementary method of enforcement is

---

[87] Snell, pp. 608 *et seq.*
[88] Snell, pp. 620 *et seq.*
[89] Snell, pp. 663 *et seq.*
[90] R.S.C. Ord. 24; Snell, p. 566.
[91] R.S.C. Ord. 39, r. 15; Snell, p. 566; Pettit, p. 576.
[92] Snell, p. 567; Keeton and Sheridan's *Equity* (3rd ed.), pp. 546–547; *Felton* v. *Callis* [1969] 1 Q.B. 200; *Lipkin Gorman* v. *Cass, The Times*, May 29, 1985; *Al Nahkel for Contracting and Trading Ltd.* v. *Lowe* [1986] 2 W.L.R. 317; *Allied Arab Bank Ltd.* v. *Hajjar* [1988] Q.B. 787; *Thaha* v. *Thaha* (1987) 17 Fam.Law 234; *cf. Bayer A.G.* v. *Winter* [1986] 1 W.L.R. 497; (1986) 45 C.L.J. 189 (C. Harpum); (1987) 104 L.Q.R. 246 and (1987) 137 N.L.J. 584 (L. Anderson); (1987) 84 L.S.G. 2345 (G. Mitchell); (1988) 47 C.L.J. 364 (N. Andrews); *post*, p. 771.
[93] See de Smith, *Judicial Review of Administrative Action*, (4th ed.), pp. 517–518.
[94] *Tito* v. *Waddell (No. 2)* [1977] Ch. 106 at p. 259 (Megarry V.-C.). See also *Chapman* v. *Michaelson* [1909] 1 Ch. 238; Snell, pp. 567–568.
[95] *Post*, pp. 285, 621.
[96] *Post*, pp. 674, 734.
[97] *Wood* v. *Scarth* (1855) 2 K. & J. 33 (in equity); (1858) 1 F. & F. 293 (at law); *Webster* v. *Cecil* (1861) 30 Beav. 62; *Johnson* v. *Agnew* [1980] A.C. 367, *post*, p. 675.

denied to a plaintiff. But secondly, other equitable remedies are larger in their effect; if equity rescinds a deed or a contract, a right to sue on that contract or deed ceases to be available at law. Equity will exercise this jurisdiction on grounds on which law takes no similar action, for instance, in cases of constructive fraud or wholly innocent misrepresentations, so that the equitable remedy affects the substance of a plaintiff's rights, and not merely the manner of their enforcement. This is also true when the equitable remedy of rectification is called into operation, a remedy by which a term of an obligation, contained in a document, is varied so as to make it accord with the parties' real intentions. Thirdly, it should be noted that an equitable remedy may fulfil a task intermediate between the situations so far considered, the task of enabling a plaintiff to take full advantage of a right at common law. A plaintiff may, for instance, have a right at common law to rescind a contract for fraud, but may be at common law unable to exercise that right[98] because a precise *restitutio in integrum* is not possible. Equity has a wider discretion to bring about a rescission in such a case by devising a fair, if not a precise, return of the parties to something approaching their original positions.[99]

As we shall see, it is in the field of remedies that equity displays perhaps the greatest inventiveness and capacity for development, providing relief in new situations as they arise.[1]

7. THE BONA FIDE PURCHASER OF THE LEGAL ESTATE FOR VALUE WITHOUT NOTICE

As we have seen, the use was enforceable against the feoffee to uses because the feoffee's conscience was bound by the undertaking which he had given to hold the property to the use and benefit of the *cestui que use*. Similarly with a trustee and beneficiary. So long as the same person remained trustee, this theory works quite simply. But if the legal estate passes from him to another person, how is the conscience of the transferee affected? The question is then one of determining, as a matter of policy, whether this new holder of the legal estate is to be bound by the trust.[2] Any way in which the equitable ownership of a beneficiary is destroyed is of course a serious weakening of the position of the beneficiary; and equity strives always to protect him.[3]

Thus, a trust is binding on a person to whom the trustee gave the

---

[98] And would be confined to an action for damages.
[99] *Spence* v. *Crawford* [1939] 3 All E.R. 271; a decision showing that equity may be more willing to do so in cases of actual fraud than in others.
[1] See particularly the *Anton Piller* and *Mareva* injunctions, *post*, pp. 766, 770.
[2] Maitland, pp. 111 *et seq*. The principles here discussed are those which developed before the days of registration of title. Different principles apply to registered land.
[3] *Ibid.* at p. 220.

property[4]; or a mere occupier[5] or adverse possessor,[6] and also on a purchaser who bought it if he knew or could by reasonable inquiries have found out about the existence of the trust.[7] In short, the trust is binding on everyone coming to the land except the bona fide purchaser of a legal estate for value without notice actual, constructive or imputed. "Such a purchaser's plea of purchase for valuable consider-ation without notice is an absolute, unqualified, unanswerable defence, and an unanswerable plea to the jurisdiction of this Court. Such a purchaser . . . may be interrogated and tested to any extent as to the valuable consideration which he has given in order to show the *bona fides* or *mala fides* of his purchase, and also the presence or absence of notice; but when once he has gone through that ordeal, and has satisfied the terms of the plea of purchase for valuable consider-ation without notice, then, according to my judgment, this Court has no jurisdiction whatever to do anything more than let him depart in possession of that legal estate, that legal right, that legal advantage which he has obtained, whatever it may be. In such a case, a purchaser is entitled to hold that which, without breach of duty, he has had conveyed to him."[8]

The doctrine is of general application throughout the law, except in relation to the statutory system of registration of title to land, which makes no distinction between legal and equitable rights so far as the enforcement of rights is concerned.[9] With unregistered land, the means of giving and obtaining notice was, as will be seen, revo-lutionised by the Land Charges Act 1925, now replaced by the Land Charges Act 1972.

A. Purchaser for Value

The purchaser must have given consideration in money, or money's worth,[10] or the consideration of marriage.[11] Otherwise he is a donee, and bound by the trust regardless of notice. A purchaser includes a mortgagee[12] or lessee.

---

[4] *Re Diplock* [1948] Ch. 465, at pp. 544–545.
[5] *Mander* v. *Falcke* [1891] 2 Ch. 554.
[6] *Re Nisbet and Pott's Contract* [1906] 1 Ch. 386; affirming [1905] 1 Ch. 391.
[7] *Pilcher* v. *Rawlins* (1872) L.R. 7 Ch.App. 250.
[8] *Per* James L.J. in *Pilcher* v. *Rawlins, supra,* at pp. 268–269.
[9] *Parkash* v. *Irani Finance Ltd.* [1970] Ch. 101, *per* Plowman J. at p. 109. But even here traces are visible; *Barclays Bank Ltd.* v. *Taylor* [1974] Ch. 137. Overriding interests (L.R.A. 1925, s.70(1)) are binding on a purchaser of registered land, regardless of notice, and whether legal or equitable; *Hodgson* v. *Marks* [1971] Ch. 892; *Williams & Glyn's Bank Ltd.* v. *Boland* [1981] A.C. 487.
[10] *Thorndike* v. *Hunt* (1859) 3 De G. & J. 563; *Midland Bank Trust Co. Ltd.* v. *Green* [1981] A.C. 513.
[11] *i.e.* a future marriage. An ante-nuptial settlement is deemed to be made for value in respect of the spouses and the issue of the marriage, *post*, p. 120.
[12] *Kingsnorth Finance Co.* v. *Tizard* [1986] 1 W.L.R. 783; see L.P.A. 1925, s.205(xxi); L.C.A. 1972, s.13.

B. Legal Estate

This doctrine is based on the maxim that when the equities are equal the law prevails. In the case of a purchase of a legal estate for value without notice, the equities are equal between the purchaser and the beneficiaries; the purchaser's legal estate is allowed to prevail.

The position is different where the purchaser is a purchaser of an *equitable* interest only. The competition then is between two equitable interests; and the rule here is that the first in time prevails.[13]

There is, however, as we shall see, a situation in which the precedence given to a purchaser for value applies to the case of a purchaser of an equitable interest. This is so where the competition is between the purchaser of an equitable interest for value without notice and a person claiming to be entitled to a mere equity.

Mere equities "such as rights to rectification or to set aside a conveyance"[14] are thus distinguished from equitable interests. The matter is discussed in more detail below.[15] The extent to which mere equities are binding on third parties is uncertain. But it seems that a bona fide purchaser of an equitable interest in the land for value without notice will take free of them,[16] and, *a fortiori*, a purchaser of a legal estate.[17]

C. Notice

i. Meaning of Notice. Apart from legislation[18] a purchaser is taken to have notice of an equitable interest unless he can show that "he took all reasonable care and made inquiries, and that, having taken that care and made inquiry, he received no notice of the trust which affected the property."[19] He must show that he had no notice actual, constructive or imputed.

Actual notice is the simple case where the purchaser subjectively knew of the equitable interest.

Constructive notice exists where knowledge of the equitable interest would have come to him if he had made all such inquiries as a prudent purchaser would have made.

Imputed notice covers actual or constructive notice to his agent who was acting as such in the transaction in question.[20]

---

[13] *Phillips* v. *Phillips* (1862) 4 De G.F. & J. 208 at p. 218; *Re Morgan* (1881) 18 Ch.D. 93; *McCarthy and Stone Ltd.* v. *Hodge & Co.* [1971] 1 W.L.R. 1547; (1972) 30 C.L.J. 34; L.C.A. 1972, s.4(5), (6).

[14] *Shiloh Spinners Ltd.* v. *Harding* [1973] A.C. at p. 721, *per* Lord Wilberforce.

[15] *Post*; pp. 865 *et seq.*

[16] *National Provincial Bank Ltd.* v. *Ainsworth* [1965] A.C. 1175 at p. 1238, *per* Lord Upjohn; *Phillips* v. *Phillips, supra.*

[17] *Smith* v. *Jones* [1954] 1 W.L.R. 1089.

[18] Especially L.C.A. 1972, *post*, p. 37.

[19] *Per* Fry J. in *Re Morgan* (1881) 18 Ch.D. 93 at p. 102.

[20] L.P.A. 1925, s.199.

ii. Duty to Make Inquiries. As we have seen, a purchaser will be held
to have constructive notice of such equitable interests as would have
come to his notice if he had made such inquiries as a reasonable and
prudent purchaser would make. The inquiries which should be made
will depend on the type of property in question. A purchaser,
however, should always inspect the premises. The rule before 1926,
and still sometimes applicable, is that a purchaser has notice of the
interest of a person in occupation of the property.[21]

(a) *Purchase of Freeholds*. Unless the title is registered, a vendor
satisfies a purchaser of his ownership of the land and of his entitlement
to sell by producing his title deeds which trace the history of the
ownership of the land. The title should start with a good root of title[22]
at least 15 years old.[23] A prudent purchaser should examine that
document and every one subsequent to it; he will normally be held to
have constructive notice of every equitable interest which appears on
the title[24]; but not of those disclosed by earlier deeds with which he is
not concerned. If he agrees to accept a title which begins later than the
statutory period of 15 years, he does so at his own risk, and will be
bound by equitable interests disclosed by documents which are within
the statutory period but prior to the agreed date.[25] It is said that he is
normally deemed to have constructive notice of interests disclosed by
the deeds. There is an exception where there are in fact deeds which
disclose an equitable interest, but the vendor is able to produce an
apparently perfect title after suppressing some of them. Thus in *Pilcher
v. Rawlins*[26]:

Rawlins was the fee simple owner of land. He conveyed it by way
of mortgage to the trustees of Pilcher's settlement as security for a
loan. Later the surviving trustee of the settlement improperly recon-
veyed the land to Rawlins although the loan was not fully repaid.
The legal estate was later conveyed by Rawlins to other mortgagees,
Rawlins making title without disclosing the conveyance to the trustees of the Pilcher settlement and the re-conveyance to him. He thus
appeared to be an unencumbered owner in fee simple.

---

[21] *Barnhart* v. *Greenshields* (1853) 9 Moo.P.C. 18; *Hunt* v. *Luck* [1902] 1 Ch. 428;
Kingsnorth Finance Co. Ltd. v. *Tizard* [1986] 1 W.L.R. 783; *cf. Bristol and West
Building Society* v. *Henning* [1985] 1 W.L.R. 778. As to the effect on this rule of the
provisions of the 1925 legislation relating to the registration of land charges, see *post*,
p. 37; *Hollington Bros.* v. *Rhodes* [1951] 2 All E.R. 578n.; *Smith* v. *Jones* [1954] 1
W.L.R. 1089; *Midland Bank Trust Co. Ltd.* v. *Green* [1981] A.C. 513.
[22] *i.e.* "a document which describes the land sufficiently to identify it, which shows a
disposition of the whole legal and equitable interest contracted to be sold, and which
contains nothing to throw any doubt on the title"; M. & W., p. 608; Cheshire and
Burn, p. 715.
[23] L.P.A. 1969, s.23, reducing the period from 30 years laid down in L.P.A. 1925, s.44.
[24] *Carter* v. *Carter* (1857) 3 K. & J. 617. But see *Pilcher* v. *Rawlins, infra*.
[25] *Re Nisbet and Pott's Contract* [1906] 1 Ch. 386; affirming [1905] 1 Ch. 391.
[26] (1872) L.R. 7 Ch.App. 259.

The beneficiaries under the settlement claimed that the mortgagees took subject to their equitable interests. The mortgagees claimed to be purchasers of the legal estate for value without notice. There was no way in which they could have discovered that the land had been conveyed to the trustees of the settlement and had become subject to the trusts, because Rawlins' title appeared to be perfect when he disclosed only the deeds by which the land was first conveyed to him. As we have seen, the court decided that the test for constructive notice was whether the mortgagees had made all reasonable inquiries, and concluded that they had; they therefore took free of the trusts.

(b) *Leases*. A person intending to enter into a lease is not entitled to examine the title of the lessor (the freeholder).[27] In spite of this, it was held before 1926 that a lessee was bound by constructive notice of equitable interests which he would have discovered if he had examined it.[28] That rule was reversed in 1926.[29] The lessee is however bound by land charges which are registered under the Land Charges Act.[30]

(c) *Personalty*. The doctrine of constructive notice applies differently with personalty. There is no duty on the purchaser to examine the seller's title; and usually there are no documents of title.[31] A purchaser of chattels need not search the register of bills of sale and will not be bound by entries on it.[32] The holder of a negotiable instrument may be a "holder in due course" without taking steps to inquire into the title of the transferor.[33] And a purchaser of shares is not required to inquire about beneficial ownership, nor may notice of any trust affecting the shares be entered on the company's register of shareholders. However, where some equitable interest or charge is disclosed to a purchaser of personalty or presents itself to his notice, he will be bound by it if it is not satisfied out of the purchase money.[34]

iii. Registration of Charges under the Land Charges Act 1972. The Land Charges Act 1925 introduced a system of registration of various charges and obligations created after 1925 upon unregistered land.[35] These are now contained in Land Charges Act 1972, s.2, except for

---

[27] L.P.A. 1925, s.44(3).
[28] *Patman* v. *Harland* (1881) 17 Ch.D. 353.
[29] L.P.A. 1925, s.44(3); *Shears* v. *Wells* [1936] 1 All E.R. 832.
[30] *White* v. *Bijou Mansions* [1937] Ch. 610 at p. 619; (1940) 56 L.Q.R. 361 (D.W. Logan); (1956) 14 C.L.J. 230–234 (H. W. R. Wade).
[31] See Factors Act 1889, s.1(4). The registration book of a car is not a document of title: *Joblin* v. *Watkins and Roseveare (Motors) Ltd.* [1949] 1 All E.R. 47.
[32] *Joseph* v. *Lyons* (1884) 15 Q.B.D. 280.
[33] *London Joint Stock Bank* v. *Simmons* [1892] A.C. 201, 221; *Ellis* v. *Hinds* [1947] K.B. 475 at p. 483.
[34] *Nelson* v. *Larholt* [1948] 1 K.B. 339.
[35] L.C.A. 1972 does not apply to registered land; but all the interests contained in it can be protected by notice or caution under L.R.A. 1925.

those relating to local land charges, which are dealt with in the Local
Land Charges Act 1975. Most of the registrable charges are equitable,
but some are legal, such as a legal mortgage where the mortgagee does
not take possession of the title deeds,[36] and one is a statutory creation.[37] Registration pursuant to the Land Charges Act is deemed to be
actual notice to all persons so long as the registration remains in
force.[38] And land charges classes B, C, D and F are void against a
purchaser for value[39] of any interest in the land unless registered.[40]

It will be seen that this enactment has vitally affected the old
doctrines of notice. Where a charge is registrable, the old rules as to
notice no longer apply. A purchaser is deemed to have notice of a
charge if it is registered. If the charge is not registered, it has been held
that he takes free even if he actually knows about it,[41] or if the interest
in question is that of a person who is in actual occupation of the land,[42]
and the House of Lords has recently held that the court cannot enquire
into the good faith of the purchaser, nor into the adequacy of the
consideration paid by him.[43]

D. Over-Reaching

More important for our present purposes than the list of charges and
obligations made registrable by the Land Charges Act 1972 are equitable beneficial interests generally: that is to say, the equitable interests
enjoyed by beneficial owners of land under a trust for sale or strict
settlement. Under the Law of Property Act 1925, s.1(1), the only legal
estates which can exist in land after 1925 are the fee simple absolute in
possession and the term of years absolute. Thus, in every case in which
the beneficial ownership of land is split into successive interests (other
than leases), the interests are equitable.

The 1925 legislation also provides that all successive beneficial
interests in land must be held either behind a trust for sale or under a
settlement.[44] In the case of a trust for sale, the legal estate is vested in
the trustees for sale, and is held by them on trust to sell and the
beneficial interests are imposed upon the proceeds of sale and upon

---

[36] L.C.A. 1972, s.2(4) Class C(i).
[37] Class F. See Matrimonial Homes Act 1983.
[38] L.P.A. 1925, s.198(1).
[39] This includes marriage consideration.
[40] L.C.A. 1972, s.4. In the case of land charges class D, and an estate contract entered
into after January 1, 1926, the charge only becomes void in favour of a purchaser of a
legal estate for money or money's worth.
[41] *Hollington Brothers* v. *Rhodes* [1951] 2 All E.R. 578n.
[42] *Smith* v. *Jones* [1954] 1 W.L.R. 1089.
[43] *Midland Bank Trust Co. Ltd.* v. *Green* [1981] A.C. 513; (1981) 97 L.Q.R. 518 (B.
Green); (1981) 40 C.L.J. 213 (C. Harpum); [1981] Conv. 361 (H. Johnson); (son,
holding unregistered option to purchase valuable land granted by father, not protected when father sold to mother for £500).
[44] S.L.A. 1925, s.1.

the rents and profits until sale.[45] Where therefore the trustees for sale sell the land in performance of their duty to sell, the land which the purchaser takes is unaffected by any trusts; the trusts are, and always have been, imposed upon the purchase money. The Law of Property Act, s.2(1)(ii), provides that the purchaser takes free from the beneficial interests.

This process of transfer of the beneficial interests from the land to the purchase money is called "overreaching." Provided the money is paid to at least two trustees, the purchaser takes free of the beneficial interests even if he knew of them. There is no room for the application of the doctrine that occupation by the beneficiaries gives constructive notice to the purchaser.[46] Nor, in unregistered land, is there any machinery for the registration of such interests.

Where, however, the purchase money is paid to a sole trustee (for example, a husband who is sole legal owner of a house in which his wife has a share in equity), the doctrine of overreaching cannot apply. In such a case the doctrine of notice remains applicable in unregistered land, so that occupation by the wife is likely to give constructive notice to a purchaser or mortgagee.[47]

A strict settlement within the Settled Land Act 1925 is, broadly speaking, another method of achieving the same result.[48] Here the legal fee simple is vested in the tenant for life who holds it on trust for himself for life and then on trust for the other beneficiaries under the settlement. Every settlement of successive interests is a strict settlement unless the land is subject to a trust for sale.[49] The Settled Land Act 1925 provides that if the purchaser observes the provisions of the Act (including the payment of the purchase money to at least two trustees and not to the tenant for life), the beneficial interests under the settlement shall be taken from the land and transferred to the purchase money.[50] Thus the purchaser takes the land free from the beneficial interests; which is what he wants. The beneficiaries have interests in the purchase money which are equivalent to those which they previously had in the land. And there is no problem of a bona fide purchaser destroying the interests of the beneficiaries.

The old rules of notice therefore apply today only in the cases of equitable interests and charges relating to unregistered land which are neither registrable nor overreachable, such as a restrictive covenant

[45] L.P.A. 1925, s.2; *post*, p. 261. See the definition of "statutory trust" in L.P.A. 1925, s.35. The trustees have a power to postpone sale indefinitely; *ibid.*, s.25.

[46] *City of London Building Society* v. *Flegg* [1988] A.C. 54; *cf.* Law Com. Working Paper No. 106 (1988), *Trusts of Land, Overreaching.*

[47] *Kingsnorth Finance Co. Ltd.* v. *Tizard* [1986] 1 W.L.R. 783; *cf. Bristol and West Building Society* v. *Henning* [1985] 1 W.L.R. 778 (equitable owner who acquiesced in mortgage by legal owner deemed to intend to cede priority to mortgagee).

[48] See Law Commission Working Paper No. 94 (1985), *Trusts of Land, post*, p. 278.

[49] S.L.A. 1925, s.1(7).

[50] S.L.A. 1925, ss.18, 72, 75.

entered into before 1926 and a few other examples.[51] The cases seem "to show that there may well be rights, of an equitable character outside the provisions as to registration and which are incapable of being overreached."[52]

It is important to appreciate, however, that the doctrine of notice still has much scope for operation, as mentioned above, in the context of beneficial interests under a trust for sale where the doctrine of overreaching cannot apply because there is only one trustee.[53] Although such interests cannot be registered, a wife's statutory right to occupy the matrimonial home is registrable.[54] This, however, has no effect on the enforceability of any equitable interest she may have.

E. Purchase with Notice from Purchaser without Notice

A purchaser of a legal estate for value without notice, taking a good title, free, as we have seen, from the equitable interests may pass his good title to a purchaser who *has* notice. Otherwise, if the equitable claims become publicly known, the property would become unsaleable. The limits of this rule were expressed in *Wilkes* v. *Spooner*[55] where—

> X, the lessee of two High Street shops, Nos. 137 and 170, assigned the lease of No. 170 to the plaintiff, and covenanted, in effect, not to compete with the plaintiff's business as a general butcher. This restriction upon the user of No. 137 premises was such as to be binding in equity on the land under the doctrine of *Tulk* v. *Moxhay*.[56]
>
> X surrendered the lease of No. 137 for value to the landlord, who, not knowing of the restrictive covenant, accepted the surrender; and then granted a new lease to X's son, who did know of it.
>
> The Court of Appeal held that the covenant was not binding. The landlord was a purchaser for value without notice. The covenant was destroyed, and did not revive on the passing of the land to the son. They approved a quotation from Ashburner.[57] "A purchaser for valuable consideration without notice can give a good title to a purchaser from him with notice. The only exception is that a trustee who has sold property in breach of trust, or a person who has

---

[51] *Post,* p. 867; *E.R. Ives Investment Ltd.* v. *High* [1967] 2 Q.B. 379 (equitable easement); *Poster* v. *Slough Estates Ltd.* [1968] 1 W.L.R. 1518 (right to enter to remove fixtures); *Shiloh Spinners Ltd.* v. *Harding* [1973] A.C. 691 (equitable right of entry); *Hodgson* v. *Marks* [1971] Ch. 892 (bare trust). It has been proposed that a bare trust should be overreachable; Law Com. Working Papers 94 (1985), pp. 73 and 106 (1988), p. 42.

[52] *Per* Lord Wilberforce in *Shiloh Spinners* v. *Harding* [1973] A.C. 691 at p. 721.

[53] *Ante,* p. 39.

[54] Matrimonial Homes Act 1983; Land Charges Act 1972, s.2(7) (Class F).

[55] [1911] 2 K.B. 473.

[56] (1848) 2 Ph. 774.

[57] Ashburner, *Principles of Equity* (2nd ed.), p. 55.

acquired property by fraud cannot protect himself by purchasing it from a bona fide purchaser for value without notice."[58]

8. THE SUBJECT-MATTER OF EQUITY

In this Introduction, it has only been possible to mention certain heads of equitable jurisdiction as they became relevant, and it may be helpful to the understanding of equity to list the subjects which should properly be included within it. No list can be exhaustive. Certain matters however are assigned to the Chancery Division by the Supreme Court Act 1981.[59] They are:

The sale, exchange or partition of land, or the raising of charges on land;

The redemption or foreclosure of mortgages[60];

The execution of trusts;

The administration of the estates of deceased persons;

Bankruptcy;

The dissolution of partnerships or the taking of partnership or other accounts;

The rectification, setting aside or cancellation of deeds or other instruments in writing;

Probate business, other than non-contentious or common form business;

Patents, trade marks, registered designs or copyright;

The appointment of a guardian of a minor's estate[61];

All causes and matters involving the exercise of the High Court's jurisdiction under the enactments relating to companies.

---

[58] *Bovey* v. *Smith* (1682) 1 Vern. 60; *Lowther* v. *Carlton* (1741) 2 Atk. 242; *Sweet* v. *Southcote* (1786) 2 Bro.C.C. 66; *Re Stapleford Colliery Co., Barrow's Case* (1880) 14 Ch.D. 432.

[59] s.61 and Sched. 1. For the transfer of business to the Mayor's and City of London County Court, see *Practice Direction (Chancery: Transfer of Business)* [1988] 1 W.L.R. 741.

[60] See also R.S.C. Ord. 88, r. 2.

[61] This work was transferred from the Chancery Division to the Family Division by the Administration of Justice Act 1970. Now see Supreme Court Act 1981, Sched. 1, para. 3.

All divisions of the High Court, however, exercise co-ordinate jurisdiction. Where a matter arises which has not been assigned to one division, it should go to whichever division is the more appropriate and convenient; in many cases the plaintiff's counsel will be able to choose. If the action is brought in the wrong Division, it may be retained or transferred at the discretion of the judge.[62]

9. THE TRUST IN MODERN LAW

Trusts are primarily about money and the preservation of wealth. The idea of the trust developed as a means for providing for the family. This has decreased in importance as society has changed. In its place has emerged a modern and significant role for the trust concept in the constitution of pension funds,[63] charities and various endowments. Thus the trust continues to be a form of property-holding of ever-increasing importance because of its adaptability and convenience in effecting complicated forms of settlement. Indeed, "as the principles of equity permeate the complications of modern life, the nature and variety of trusts ever grow."[64] If a settlor wishes to give property to his wife for life and after her death to various other members of the family, it would be possible to arrange a system of law by which it could be done without using a trust. Indeed, the early common law did so, in an elementary form. And Roman law did so[65]; as do those countries which have followed modernised systems of Roman law.[66]

In England, full use has been made of the convenience of the system whereby the legal estate is in the trustees and the equitable or beneficial ownership is kept separate. We have seen that this is insisted upon for the creation of successive or concurrent interests in land under the 1925 legislation.[67] The legal title can be kept clear of beneficial interests; the land can be sold free of them to a purchaser, who can over-reach them. Thus a most elaborate system of beneficial interests can be created without complicating the title to the land.

The same advantages exist with personalty. Most modern settle-

---

[62] Supreme Court Act 1981, ss.61(6), 65.
[63] See *Cowan* v. *Scargill* [1985] Ch. 270; *Mason* v. *Farbrother* [1983] 2 All E.R. 1078; *In Re Courage Group's Pension Scheme* [1987] 1 W.L.R. 495. See generally Moffat and Chesterman, *Trusts Law Text and Materials*, Chap. 14.
[64] *Re a Solicitor* [1952] Ch. 328 at p. 332 (*per* Roxburgh J.).
[65] Buckland and McNair: *Roman Law and Common Law* (2nd ed.), pp. 173 *et seq.*
[66] See (1980) *Journal of Legal History*, p. 6 (B. Beinart); (1974) 48 Tulane L.Rev. 917 (J. H. Merryman).
[67] *Ante*, p. 39. Similarly a trust is necessary where there is incapacity to hold a legal estate in land, as in the case of a minor.

ments deal wholly or partly with personalty in the form of investments. No system of legal future interests in personalty ever developed; for settlements of personalty did not arise until the system of trusts was well advanced. In this sphere also, it is most convenient to separate legal and equitable ownership; by doing so, the trustees can buy and sell shares without the purchaser being concerned with the beneficial interests.[68] The beneficial interests attach to whatever is held by the trustees for the time being.

Those are the simple cases. Settlors may wish to create other forms of settlement.[69] With a gift for charitable purposes, for example, there is no beneficial owner; such a gift is effected by a special form of trust.[70] A settlor may wish to protect a beneficiary from his own extravagance by making it impossible for creditors to proceed against his limited interest; this is done by protective trust.[71] The settlor may wish to allow his trustees to determine from time to time how the capital and income shall be distributed among the beneficiaries; this is done by a discretionary trust.[72] He may wish to provide for someone, such as his mistess, by will without identifying her in that document; this is done by a secret trust.[73] Each sort of trust will be considered in its proper place. It will in each case be seen that the desired result could have been effected without the existence of a trust; but that the trust is a very satisfactory and convenient way of effecting it; and that this has become the only way in which it can now be effected in English law. In some cases, however, the trust has not afforded a solution, for example, in the case of gifts for abstract non-charitable purposes.[74] Theoretical difficulties have also been encountered with the property of unincorporated associations.[75] Finally, it should never be forgotten that there is one factor which dominates all others in the context of the creation of trusts in modern law: taxation. Although the law of equity and trusts can be understood without it, it will be appreciated that the popular forms of trust in recent years have been those which reduce to a minimum the liability to tax. The Chancery lawyer's job is to be able to advise on these matters and to create the most appropriate trusts to meet the wishes of the settlor.

[68] No notice of any trust can be entered on the register of shareholders (Companies Act 1985, s.360). The interests of a beneficiary can be protected by serving a notice on the company (known as a stop notice) requiring the company, on receiving a request to transfer the shares, to report this fact to the person giving the notice. Such person, if he wishes to take steps to prevent the transfer, must do so within fourteen days; R.S.C., Ord. 50, rr. 11–14.

[69] It should not be forgotten that the trust may also be created unintentionally. See Resulting and Constructive Trusts, *post*, Chaps. 10, 12.

[70] *Post*, p. 369. Also a gift for a non-human object, such as the maintenance of an animal or a tombstone; *post*, pp. 349 *et seq.*

[71] *Post*, p. 181.

[72] *Post*, p. 191.

[73] *Post*, p. 140.

[74] *Post*, p. 342.

[75] *Post*, p. 354.

10. The Creativity of Equity

One question which has arisen is whether the category of equitable interests is closed, or whether new ones might be created.[76] One clear example is the restrictive covenant, which, since Lord Eldon's day, has evolved from a contractual right to an equitable interest enforceable against the covenantor's successors in title. It seems that we may be witnessing the emergence of another equitable interest in the shape of the contractual licence, although the matter awaits clarification in the House of Lords.[77] One view is that the modern machinery for law reform should be relied upon in preference to judicial creativity.[78]

Bagnall J., in a case concerning matrimonial property, warned against unwarranted extensions of equitable jurisdiction in the following words:

"In any individual case the application of these propositions may produce a result which appears unfair. So be it; in my view that is not an injustice. I am convinced that in determining rights, particularly property rights, the only justice that can be obtained by mortals, who are fallible and are not omniscient, is justice according to law; the justice which flows from the application of sure and settled principles to proved or admitted facts. So in the field of equity, the length of the Chancellor's foot has been measured or is capable of measurement. This does not mean that equity is past childbearing; simply that its progeny must be legitimate—by precedent out of principle. It is well that this should be so; otherwise no lawyer could safely advise on his client's title and every quarrel would lead to a law suit."[79]

Throughout this book it will be seen that the principles of equity have constantly developed and found new fields of application.[80] The reader, when examining these developments, might consider whether the words of Bagnall J. have been heeded. A few examples must suffice here.

Many new develements have been seen in the field of injunctions, notably the evolution of the so-called *Anton Piller* and *Mareva* injunctions, designed respectively to prevent removal or destruction of evidence and to prevent the assets of the defendant from being

---

[76] Eveleigh L.J. in *Pennine Raceway Ltd.* v. *Kirklees Metropolitan Council* [1983] Q.B. 382 at p. 392, said, "There has been a considerable development in the law in relation to equitable interests and I do not think that it is right to regard the category as closed." But at p. 397, Stephenson L.J. preferred to express no view.

[77] *Post*, p. 841. See *Ashburn Anstalt* v. *Arnold* [1988] 2 W.L.R. 706.

[78] See, for example, the "deserted wife's equity" and the Matrimonial Homes Act 1983, *post*, p. 269.

[79] *Cowcher* v. *Cowcher* [1972] 1 W.L.R. 425 at p. 430.

[80] In some fields, however, the role of equity has declined. The entitlement to the funds on dissolution of an unincorporated association, for example, is today treated as more a matter of contract than of trusts. See *post*, p. 231.

dissipated.[81] Equity's excursions into the criminal law, however, have been restricted.[82]

The constructive trust has also proved to be a fertile field, assisting in the enforcement of contractual licences against third parties[83]; enabling the remedy of tracing to be exercised in new situations[84]; and allowing unprotected minor interests to be enforced against purchasers of registered land.[85] Constructive and resulting trusts have operated to give security to unsecured creditors[86]; and to determine the ownership of matrimonial and "quasi-matrimonial" property.[87] Here we have seen the "new model constructive trust," a term first used by Lord Denning M.R. in the case concerning the claim of a mistress to a share in the home, where he said, "Equity is not past the age of childbearing. One of her latest progeny is a constructive trust of a new model. Lord Diplock brought it into the world[88] and we have nourished it."[89]

Other areas where equity's creativity has shown itself in recent years include proprietary estoppel,[90] the rescission of contracts on the ground of mistake,[91] and the restriction of the rights of a mortgagee.[92] This brief survey indicates the dynamism of equity. The developments discussed above, and others, will be examined in the relevant parts of this book.

---

[81] *Post*, pp. 766, 770.
[82] *R.C.A. Corp.* v. *Pollard* [1983] Ch. 135, not following *Ex p. Island Records Ltd.* [1978] Ch. 122; *post*, p. 702.
[83] *Ashburn Anstalt* v. *Arnold, supra; post*, p. 313.
[84] *e.g.* by finding a fiduciary relationship to have arisen by reason of a mistaken payment: *Chase Manhattan N.A.* v. *Israel-British Bank (London) Ltd.* [1981] Ch. 105, *post*, p. 628. Other developments in tracing have proved more problematical. See the decisions on "retention of title" clauses after *Aluminium Industrie Vaassen B.V.* v. *Romalpa Aluminium Ltd.* [1976] 1 W.L.R. 676, *post*, p. 633.
[85] *Peffer* v. *Rigg* [1977] 1 W.L.R. 285; *Lyus* v. *Prowsa Ltd.* [1982] 1 W.L.R. 1044, *post*, p. 314.
[86] *Barclays Bank Ltd.* v. *Quistclose Investments Ltd.* [1970] A.C. 567, *post*, p. 51; *Carreras Rothmans Ltd* v. *Freeman Mathews Treasure Ltd.* [1985] Ch. 207; *In Re E.V.T.R. Ltd.*, [1987] B.C.L.C. 647. See also *Hussey* v. *Palmer* [1972] 1 W.L.R. 1286; *Re Kayford* [1975] 1 W.L.R. 279.
[87] *Post*, pp. 250, 310.
[88] In *Gissing* v. *Gissing* [1971] A.C. 886.
[89] *Eves* v. *Eves* [1975] 1 W.L.R. 1338 at p. 1341; *cf. Allen* v. *Snyder* [1977] 2 N.S.W.L.R. 685 at p. 701: "the legitimacy of the new model is at least suspect; at best it is a mutant from which further breeding should be discouraged." It seems that the "new model" is in decline; *post*, p. 316.
[90] *Post*, p. 850.
[91] *Solle* v. *Butcher* [1950] 1 K.B. 671; *post*, p. 780.
[92] *Quennell* v. *Maltby* [1979] 1 W.L.R. 318 (right to possession must be exercised bona fide and to protect security).

Chapter 2

NATURE AND CLASSIFICATION OF TRUSTS

1. DISTINCTIONS

MANY attempts have been made to define a trust, but none of them has been wholly successful.[1] It is not thought that a dissection and criticism of earlier definitions are very rewarding; rather it is better to describe than to define a trust, and then to distinguish it from related but distinguishable concepts.

A trust is a relationship recognised by equity which arises where property is vested in (a person or) persons called the trustees, which those trustees are obliged to hold for the benefit of other persons called *cestuis que trust*[2] or beneficiaries. The interests of the beneficiaries will usually be laid down in the instrument creating the trust, but may be implied or imposed by law.[3] The beneficiary's interest is proprietary[4] in

---

[1] Co.Litt. 272b; Underhill, *Law of Trusts and Trustees* (14th ed.), p. 3; used by Cohen J. in *Re Marshall's W.T.* [1945] Ch. 217 at p. 219 and by Romer L.J. in *Green* v. *Russell* [1959] 2 Q.B. 226 at p. 241; Snell, p. 90; *Halsbury's Laws of England* (4th ed.), Vol. 48, p. 272; *Restatement of Trusts* (U.S.A.) § 2; Scott, *Law of Trusts*, § 2; (1955) 71 L.Q.R. 39 (A. W. Scott).

[2] This is the correct plural; (1910) 26 L.Q.R. 196 (C. Sweet).

[3] *Post*, pp. 69, 70.

[4] *Ante*, p. 17. Discretionary trusts and trusts for persons for particular purposes need separate consideration: *post*, Chaps. 8 and 14.

the sense that it can be bought and sold, given away or disposed of by will; but it will cease to exist if the legal estate in the property comes into the hands of a bona fide purchaser for value without notice of the beneficial interest.[5] The subject-matter of the trust must be some form of property. Commonly, it is legal ownership of land or of invested funds; but it may be of any sort of property—land, money, chattels, equitable interests,[6] choses in action,[7] etc. There may also be trusts for charitable purposes; such trusts are enforced at the suit of the Attorney-General.[8] But there is much doubt and uncertainty as to the status and validity of trusts for non-charitable purposes—as a trust for the building of a monument[9] or for the maintenance of the testator's horses, dogs, and cats.[10]

A trust must be distinguished from certain other legal phenomena which resemble the trust, but which must be kept separate from it. The point of such distinguishing is threefold: first, to compare the different legal consequences of a trust and the related concept; secondly, to identify the circumstances in which the one concept must exist to the exclusion of the other; and thirdly, to identify the circumstances in which a trust may co-exist with the related concept, as may be the case, for example, with certain contracts and debts.

A. Bailment

Blackstone defined bailment as "a delivery of goods in trust upon a contract expressed or implied, that the trust shall be faithfully executed on the part of the bailee."[11] This is a fruitful source of confusion. Bailment is a relationship recognised by the common law, and arises where a chattel owned by A is, with A's permission, in the possession of B.[12] It may exist in different forms, the details of which are not relevant here.[13] The rights of the parties may or may not be governed by a contract. In a sense, the bailor, A, is relying on B; he expects, and is entitled to, a certain standard of care by B in his stewardship of A's chattel. But this is very different from a trust. For there is no transfer of ownership from A to B; B's duties are dependent on the rules of common law and not upon equity; and these duties are entirely different from, and minimal in character as compared with, those which

---

[5] *Pilcher* v. *Rawlins* (1872) L.R. 7 Ch.App. 259; *ante*, p. 36.
[6] For example, where a beneficiary under a settlement makes a settlement of his beneficial interest.
[7] For example, a trust of a promise, or of a debt, or of a bank balance.
[8] See *post*, Chap. 15.
[9] *Mussett* v. *Bingle* [1876] W.N. 170; *Re Endacott* [1960] Ch. 232; *post*, p. 349.
[10] *Pettingall* v. *Pettingall* (1842) 11 L.J.Ch. 176; *Re Dean* (1889) 41 Ch.D. 552; *post*, p. 350.
[11] Bl.Com. II, p. 451; Maitland, p. 45.
[12] Crossley Vaines, *Personal Property* (5th ed.), Chap. 6; *Aluminium Industrie Vaassen B.V.* v. *Romalpa Aluminium Ltd.* [1976] 1 W.L.R. 676, *post*, p. 634.
[13] *Ibid.* and see *Coggs* v. *Barnard* (1703) 2 Ld.Ray. 909.

would exist if B held the property as trustee for A. Again the bailor, A, could lose his legal ownership only through one of the ways in which legal owners may be deprived.[14] But if the property was held by B on trust for A, A's equitable title could be defeated by the transfer of the legal title in the property to a bona fide purchaser for value without notice of the trust.[15]

B. Agency

In many ways the relationship of principal and agent resembles that of beneficiary and trustee.[16] Agents, like trustees, must act personally in the business of the agency,[17] and are accountable to their principals, as are trustees to beneficiaries, for any profits made out of the property or business entrusted to them.[18] The relationship of beneficiary and trustee is a fiduciary relationship, while that of principal and agent may or may not be.[19] But the vital difference is that a trust is *proprietary*. The beneficiary is equitable and beneficial owner of the property. Where money is due on an account between principal and agent, it is recoverable on the basis of a personal claim.

A right to claim £100 against a defendant may be just as good as beneficial ownership of £100 in the hands of the defendant as trustee; so long as the defendant can pay. But if the defendant is insolvent, the distinction becomes clear. The personal claim is one against the general assets of the defendant; and will abate with the claims of other creditors if the defendant cannot pay in full. However, if the claim is a proprietary one, the property held by the defendant as trustee is not available for the trustee's debts. It may be claimed by the beneficiary as his own if it is identifiable; and, for the purposes of identification, a "tracing remedy"[20] is available where the assets have been mixed with the trustee's own funds. "Equity," as Maitland said, "has been always striving to prevent the *cestui que trust* from falling to the level of an unsecured creditor."[21] On the other hand, property for which the agent is liable to account to his principal is subject only to a personal claim; the principal is not owner at law or in equity of the money due, and the tracing remedy is not available.[22] Further, there is usually a contractual relationship between a principal and agent, but not between a trustee and beneficiary. And many of the rules governing principal and agent

---

[14] *e.g.* through estoppel, or the operation of the Factors Act 1899, ss.2, 8, 9; Sale of Goods Act 1979, ss.21–26; or the Consumer Credit Act 1974, Sched. 4, para. 22.
[15] *Ante*, pp. 33 *et seq.*
[16] See Hanbury, *Principles of Agency* (2nd ed.), pp. 3–10; Bowstead, *Agency* (15th ed.), pp. 16–17.
[17] *Post*, p. 532.
[18] *Post*, p. 565.
[19] *Post*, p. 566.
[20] *Re Hallett's Estate* (1880) 13 Ch.D. 696, *post*, p. 624.
[21] Maitland, p. 220.
[22] *Lister* v. *Stubbs* (1890) 45 Ch.D. 1, *post*, p. 627.

are based on the common law; the trust relationship is exclusively equitable.

C. Contract

Trust and contract are quite different concepts. A contract is a common law personal obligation resulting from agreement between the parties. A trust is an equitable proprietary relation which can arise independently of agreement. However, there are various situations in which the distinction may be difficult to draw, or where the facts may give rise to both.[23]

(i) **Settlements and Covenants to Settle.** Property which is vested in the trustees of a settlement is held upon the trusts of the settlement, and the beneficiaries are the owners in equity of their interests under the settlement. But if the property has not yet been conveyed to the trustees, and is merely subject to a covenant to settle, then the beneficiaries will only be able to enforce the covenant if they have given consideration. Equity will not assist a volunteer.[24]

(ii) **Third Party Rights under a Contract.** There has been much discussion of the question whether the problem of the inability of a third party beneficiary to sue upon a contract can be overcome by finding that one of the parties to the contract contracted as trustee for him. But this is not really a question of distinguishing a trust from a contract. The question is whether there is a trust of the benefit of the contract. The answer to that question depends, in accordance with the rule relating to the creation of express trusts, on whether there is a manifestation of an intention to create a trust of the benefit of the contract; this question is discussed elsewhere.[25]

(iii) **Unincorporated Associations.** An unincorporated association is not a legal entity. Where there is a gift to an unincorporated association, there is often doubt whether the property is held by the donees on trust for the members of the association, or for the purposes of the association, or subject to the members' contractual rights.[26] On the dissolution of such an association the ownership of its funds has sometimes been determined by applying trust principles, but today the matter is more commonly treated as one of contract.[27]

---

[23] As, for example, in the case of a constructive trust arising out of a specifically enforceable contract for sale, *post*, p. 304; or possibly in the case of a contractual licence, discussed below. Consideration does not negative a trust; *Carreras Rothmans Ltd.* v. *Freeman Mathews Treasure Ltd.* [1985] Ch. 207.

[24] *Post*, Chap. 4.

[25] *Post*, p. 125. For a recent illustration, see *Swain* v. *The Law Society* [1983] 1 A.C. 598, *post*, p. 567.

[26] *Post*, p. 354.

[27] *Post*, p. 231.

(iv) Contractual Licences. A contractual licence, normally involving the occupation of land, is created by agreement of the parties, applying the normal principles of the law of contract. There is some authority,[28] however, especially in the context of enforceability against third parties, that a contractual licence may give rise to a constructive trust, thus giving the licensee an equitable interest in the land in addition to his contractual rights. The development of this theory is discussed elsewhere.[29]

D. Debt

A debt may or may not be contractual. Whether the obligation is contractual or not, the duty of the debtor is to pay money to the creditor; that of a trustee is to hold the trust property on trust for the beneficiary. The debtor's obligation, like that of the agent, is personal. The trust is proprietary. We have seen that the distinction becomes crucial if the obligor is insolvent[30]; and what has been said in relation to the insolvency of an agent as opposed to a trustee is relevant here also.[31] Further, a trustee must, where practicable, apply trust funds in income-bearing investments, and account to the beneficiaries for the income. With a debtor, or a stakeholder, this is a matter of agreement, express or implied.[32]

On the other hand, it may be to a person's own advantage to be a trustee rather than a person subject to a personal obligation. If money is borrowed and then stolen from the borrower, it must still be repaid; but a trustee is not liable for loss which is not due to his own lack of care.[33] Similarly, where a testator attaches obligations to a legacy, they must be complied with in full if they are personal obligations,[34] but only to the extent of the property available if the obligations are subject to a trust or charge.[35] A debt may, of course, be the subject-matter of a

---

[28] *Binions* v. *Evans* [1972] Ch. 359; *D.H.N. Food Distributors Ltd.* v. *London Borough of Tower Hamlets* [1976] 1 W.L.R. 852; *Ashburn Anstalt* v. *Arnold* [1988] 2 W.L.R. 706.

[29] *Post*, p. 844.

[30] See generally *Space Investments Ltd.* v. *Canadian Imperial Bank of Commerce Trust Co. (Bahamas) Ltd.* [1986] 1 W.L.R. 1072; (1987) 103 L.Q.R. 433 (R. M. Goode); *post*, p. 630; *Ross* v. *Lord Advocate* [1986] 1 W.L.R. 1077; (1987) 50 M.L.R. 231 (M. Percival).

[31] *Ante*, p. 48.

[32] *Potters* v. *Loppert* [1973] Ch. 399 (estate agent held entitled to retain interest earned by deposit held as stakeholder. There was difficulty in seeing how the receipt of a deposit by a stakeholder "could impose upon the latter simultaneously an obligation to hold the specific deposit and its investment as trust property and a liability to repay a fixed sum equal to the amount of the deposit.") See now Estate Agents Act 1979, s.13.

[33] *Morley* v. *Morley* (1678) 2 Ch.Cas. 2.

[34] *Rees* v. *Engelback* (1871) L.R. 12 Eq. 225; *Re McMahon* [1901] 1 I.R. 489; *Duffy* v. *Duffy* [1920] 1 I.R. 122; *Re Lester* [1942] Ch. 324.

[35] *Re Cowley* (1885) 53 L.T. 494.

trust,[36] but the question here considered is whether the making of a loan can create a trust in favour of the lender, either initially or at some later stage. Sometimes a form of words is construed as creating both forms of obligation.[37] There is no reason why, in certain circumstances, a debt and a trust cannot co-exist; a loan to be held by the borrower on trust is repayable in debt if the purpose for which the money was lent is carried out, and may be held in trust for the lender if performance is impossible. In *Barclays Bank Ltd.* v. *Quistclose Investments Ltd.*[38]:

> Rolls Razor Ltd., very much indebted to Barclays Bank, was in need of £209,719 8s. 6d. to pay dividends which had been declared on its shares. This sum was borrowed from Quistclose under an arrangement whereby the loan was to be used only for that purpose. The money was paid into a separate account at Barclays Bank, the Bank having notice of the nature of the arrangement.
>
> Before the dividend was paid, Rolls Razor went into liquidation. The question was whether the money in the account was owned beneficially by Rolls Razor in which case Barclays Bank claimed to set it off against the overdraft,[39] or whether Rolls Razor had received the money as trustees and still held it as such on trust for Quistclose.
>
> The House of Lords unanimously decided that the money had been received upon trust to apply it for the payment of dividends; that purpose having failed, the money was held on trust for Quistclose. The fact that the transaction was a loan, recoverable by an action at law, did not exclude the implication of a trust. The legal and equitable rights and remedies could co-exist. The Bank, having notice of the trust, could not retain the money against Quistclose.

The principle is that "equity fastens on the conscience of the person who receives from another property transferred for a specific purpose only and not therefore for the recipient's own purposes, so that such person will not be permitted to treat the property as his own or to use it

---

[36] For an unusual example, see *Barclays Bank plc* v. *Willowbrook International Ltd.* [1987] 1 F.T.L.R. 386, C.A., holding that where A charges to B a debt owed to A by C, any money paid by C to A is held by A on constructive trust for B.

[37] *Welby* v. *Rockcliffe* (1830) 1 Russ. & M. 571; *Wright* v. *Wilkin* (1862) 2 B. & S. 232 at p. 260.

[38] [1970] A.C. 567; (1980) 43 M.L.R. 489 (W. Goodhart and G. Jones); *Selangor United Rubber Estates* v. *Cradock (No. 3)* [1968] 1 W.L.R. 1555. For other circumstances where an unsecured creditor can acquire a proprietary interest, see *Swiss Bank Corporation* v. *Lloyds Bank Ltd.* [1982] A.C. 584, and some of the "tracing" cases, *post*, pp. 633–638.

[39] See Insolvency Act 1986, s.323.

for other than the stated purpose."[40] The principle applies also where only part of the money lent is used for the specific purpose: the part not so applied is held on trust for the lender.[41]

The court in *Re Kayford Ltd. (In Liquidation)*[42] went one step further, holding that circumstances apparently giving rise to a debt in fact created a trust which did not co-exist with the debt but excluded it. In that case, customers of a mail-order company paid in advance when ordering goods. The company, being in financial difficulties, decided to protect its customers in the event of its insolvency by opening a separate bank account, called "Customers' Trust Deposit Account," into which the purchase money was paid. In liquidation proceedings it was held that the money was held on trust for the customers and did not form part of the assets of the company. The customer could create a trust by using appropriate words or, as here, the company could do it by taking suitable steps on or before receiving the money, thus transforming the obligations from debt to trust. The customers never became creditors, so no question of a fraudulent preference[43] of creditors could arise.[44]

In the context of informal family transactions, it may be difficult to determine whether a payment was intended to create a debt or not. Thus in *Hussey* v. *Palmer*,[45] where the plaintiff paid £607 for an extension to her son-in-law's house, Cairns L.J. held that it was a loan,

---

[40] *Carreras Rothmans Ltd.* v. *Freeman Mathews Treasure Ltd.* [1985] Ch. 207 at p. 222. See generally (1985) 101 L.Q.R. 269 (P. J. Millett), examining who can enforce such a trust and where the beneficial interest lies. Presumably if the payer intends a specific purpose only, as in *Quistclose*, a trust exists without any intention to create a trust on the part of the recipient. But where the payer did not intend the money to be used for a specific purpose only, there is no trust unless the recipient has evinced an intention to create a trust.

[41] *In Re EVTR Ltd.* [1987] B.C.L.C. 647 (loan for buying equipment, part of which never delivered and money refunded to debtor by vendor).

[42] [1975] 1 W.L.R. 279. See the Report of the Review Committee on Insolvency Law and Practice (1982, Cmnd. 8558), paras. 1048–1056. *Re Kayford Ltd.* was distinguished in *Re Multi Guarantee Co. Ltd.* [1987] B.C.L.C. 257, where a separate account was designated but no trust of the money was established because the company contemplated having further resort to the money. The decision is criticised at (1988) 85 L.S.G. No. 36, p. 14 (I.M. Hardcastle).

[43] The preference rules are now found in Insolvency Act 1986, s.239.

[44] *Cf.* (1980) 43 M.L.R. 489 at pp. 494 *et seq.* (W. Goodhart and G. Jones). The point that the customers never became creditors seems unconvincing. For this to be so, the trust must already have existed when the company received the money. In *Re Chelsea Cloisters* (1981) 41 P. & C.R. 98, tenants' deposits against damage were paid into a separate bank account, any balance to be credited to them at the end of the lease. On the liquidation of the managing company, the Court of Appeal held that a trust had been created, but doubted (on the authority of *Potters* v. *Loppert* [1973] Ch. 399, *supra*, n. 32, concerning purchaser's deposit with estate agent), whether it had arisen at the outset. (See now Landlord and Tenant Act 1987, s.42). See also Heydon, Gummow and Austin, *Cases and Materials on Equity and Trusts* (2nd ed.), p. 357, suggesting that *Re Kayford Ltd.* and the *Quistclose* case "provide startling opportunities for well-advised lenders to obtain protection against the prospect of the borrower's insolvency."

[45] [1972] 1 W.L.R. 1286.

Lord Denning M.R. held that it was not, and Phillimore L.J. thought that it "might be" a loan. The decision of the majority was that the payment gave rise to a resulting (or constructive) trust on the basis that it would be inequitable for the son-in-law to deny that she had an interest in the house.[46] If the payment was neither a gift nor a loan, this conclusion is not surprising, but Phillimore L.J. held that a resulting trust could arise even if it was a loan.[47] There is much force in the dissenting judgment of Cairns L.J., holding that a resulting trust of money paid by way of a loan could not arise. The question arose again in *Re Sharpe*,[48] where an aunt lent money to her nephew towards the purchase of a house on the understanding that she could live with him for the rest of her life. On the nephew's bankruptcy, the aunt claimed an interest in the house. Although her claim succeeded on other grounds,[49] the argument that the loan gave rise to a resulting trust was rejected, *Hussey* v. *Palmer* being distinguished as a case on "very special" facts.

E. Conditions and Charges

It is sometimes difficult to determine whether a gift of property is subject to a trust or whether it is conditional upon, or charged with, the duty of making certain payments. Thus a bequest to X "but he is to pay £50 to Y" could give rise to several possible constructions, each of them having different consequences.[50]

The bequest could be construed as a gift to X upon trust to pay Y £50.[51] In that situation, Y would immediately become entitled in equity to the £50, provided that the property bequeathed was of sufficient value; a trustee is not required to produce money of his own to make up deficiencies in the trust property.[52] Similarly with a loan for a specified purpose which, for some reason, cannot be carried out.[53] If there is a surplus, a trustee is not, on principle, entitled to obtain any benefit from the trust and the surplus will usually be held upon a resulting trust.[54] But a possible construction is that, even if there was a

---

[46] See *post*, p. 228.

[47] This would not be within the principle of *Barclays Bank Ltd.* v. *Quistclose Investments Ltd., supra*, as the money *was* applied to the purpose for which it was paid. A further distinction is that the trust in *Quistclose* was of the money lent, whereas the trust in *Hussey* v. *Palmer* was apparently of a proportionate share of the house.

[48] [1980] 1 W.L.R. 219. See also *Spence* v. *Brown* (1988) 18 Fam.Law 291.

[49] *Post*, p. 845.

[50] (1952) 11 C.L.J. 240 (T. C. Thomas).

[51] *Re Frame* [1939] Ch. 700 (devise to housekeeper "on condition that she adopt my daughter Alma and also gives to my daughters Jessie and May the sum of £5 each, and a like sum to my son Alexander."); *cf. Re Brace* [1954] 1 W.L.R. 955, *infra*.

[52] *Re Cowley* (1885) 53 L.T. 494.

[53] *Toovey* v. *Milne* (1819) 2 B. & A. 683; *Edwards* v. *Glyn* (1859) 2 E. & E. 29; *Re Rogers* (1891) 8 Morr. 243; *Barclays Bank Ltd.* v. *Quistclose Investment Ltd, supra*.

[54] *King* v. *Denison* (1813) 1 V. & B. 260, *per* Lord Eldon at p. 272; *cf. Croome* v. *Croome* (1888) 59 L.T. 582; *Re West* [1900] 1 Ch. 84; *Re Rees' W.T.* [1950] Ch. 204; *post*, p. 156.

trust of the £50, X was intended to take the surplus beneficially, the trust being applicable only to the £50.[55]

The bequest might also be construed as a gift to X conditional upon his performing the obligation. In that situation, Y obtains no interest in the £50; X has the choice of keeping the property and paying £50 or of declining both.[56] The condition must of course not be so vague as to be unintelligible.[57]

It could also be construed so as to impose a charge on the property. Here again, X will only be obliged to make the payment if he receives the property. His obligation will be limited to the value of the property,[58] and he will be entitled to retain any surplus,[59] Y will have an equitable right by virtue of the charge[60]; but this right is a different one from that of a beneficiary under a trust.[61]

Again, it could be construed as imposing merely a personal obligation on X if he accepts the gift. The position then is similar to one in which X is a debtor for the sum in question and this is discussed above.[62]

F. Interest under a Will or Intestacy

The relationship between a personal representative and a legatee or devisee bears many similarities to that of trustee, and beneficiary. The origins of the relationship, however, are quite distinct, the former originating in the Ecclesiastical Court and the latter in Chancery and their basic function is different. The trustee's duty is to manage the trust so long as it continues. The personal representative's duty is to liquidate the estate and distribute the assets; either to individual beneficiaries, or, if a trust is established by the will, to the trustees of the trust. Commonly, the executors and the trustees are the same persons, and, as we shall see,[63] in the case of personalty the transfer to themselves is notional; in the case of land an assent is required. Although the two relationships often coalesce or overlap, there are important distinctions between them. They can be regarded from two aspects:

(i) Whether a Personal Representative is a Trustee. The definition of

---

[55] *Re Foord* [1922] 2 Ch. 519 ("To my sister, Margaret Juliet, absolutely on trust to pay my wife per annum" £300); distinguished in *Re Osoba* [1979] 1 W.L.R. 247.

[56] *Att.-Gen.* v. *The Cordwainers Co.* (1833) 3 Myl. & K. 534.

[57] *Re Brace* [1954] 1 W.L.R. 955; "on condition that she will always provide a home for my daughter Doris at . . . ."

[58] *Re Cowley* (1885) 53 L.T. 494.

[59] *Re Oliver* (1890) 62 L.T. 533.

[60] *Parker* v. *Judkin* [1931] 1 Ch. 475.

[61] See, however, *Barclays Bank plc* v. *Willowbrook International Ltd.* [1987] 1 F.T.L.R. 386, C.A., holding that where a debt due to a company was charged by the company to the bank, the company held the money paid to it by the debtor on constructive trust for the bank.

[62] *Ante*, p. 50.

[63] *Post*, p. 55.

trustee in the Trustee Act 1925 includes a personal representative[64] where the context so admits; and the Trustee Act 1925, except where otherwise expressly provided, applies to executorships and administratorships,[65] and a personal representative is sometimes treated in Administration of Estates Act 1925 as a trustee.[66] A personal representative is under fiduciary duties which are very similar to those of a trustee. There are, however, a number of ways in which a personal representative has been held not to be a trustee:

(a) *Different Periods of Limitation Apply.* Generally, an action for the recovery of trust property or for a breach of trust must be brought against a trustee within six years.[67] An action against a personal representative in respect of a claim to personal estate must be brought within 12 years,[68] and an action for the recovery of arrears of interest on legacies within six years.[69]

(b) *Power of Disposition of Personalty.* The power of personal representatives to dispose of pure personalty is *several*; that of trustees is *joint*.[70] This means that one of several executors can pass title to a chattel; but in a sale by trustees, all must combine. It thus becomes important to ascertain when a personal representative becomes a trustee. Where, of course, a will appoints certain persons as executors and other persons as trustees, the executors, on the completion of the administration, must assent to the vesting of the property subject to the trust in the trustees. In the case of personalty the assent may be oral, or even implied[71]; in the case of a legal estate in land however an assent must be in writing, and it becomes an essential document of title.[72]

When however, the executors are appointed trustees also, or where no provision is made for the appointment of trustees in a will which provides for property to be held in trust after the completion of

---

[64] s.68(17); A.E.A. 1925, s.33; *contra*, I.C.T.A. 1988, s.686(6).

[65] s.69.

[66] A.E.A. 1925, ss.33, 46, 49; Intestates' Estates Act 1952.

[67] Limitation Act 1980, s.21(3); there is an exception for fraud, and in respect of property retained by a trustee; *ibid.* s.21(1) and (2).

[68] Limitation Act 1980, s.22; *Ministry of Health* v. *Simpson* [1951] A.C. 251; affirming *sub nom. Re Diplock* [1948] Ch. 465.

[69] Limitation Act 1980, s.22.

[70] *Jacomb* v. *Harwood* (1751) 2 Ves.Sen. 265; *Attenborough* v. *Solomon* [1913] A.C. 76; *Collier* v. *Hollinshead* (1984) 272 E.G. 941. The Law Reform Committee on Powers and Duties of Trustees (23rd Report, Cmnd. 8733 (1982)) recommended that the power should be joint in the case of personal representatives also.

[71] *Attenborough* v. *Solomon* [1913] A.C. 76.

[72] "An assent to the vesting of a legal estate shall be in writing, signed by the personal representative, and shall name the person in whose favour it is given and shall operate to vest in that person the legal estate to which it relates; and an assent not in writing or not in favour of a named person shall not be effectual to pass a legal estate." A.E.A. 1925, s.36(4); *post*, p. 58. This does not apply to the vesting of an equitable interest in land; *Re Edwards's W.T.* [1982] Ch. 30.

administration, the question arises of the way in which, and of the time at which, the executors become trustees. The principle is that the transition from executors to trustees occurs automatically after completion of the administration, but as far as powers of disposition of property are concerned, there must also have been a sufficient assent by the executors in their own favour as trustees.

In *Attenborough* v. *Solomon*,[73] the House of Lords held that a pledge of silver plate by one of two executors, which was made 13 years after the completion of the administration of the estate, passed no title to the pledgee. The executors had long since become trustees; an assent in their own favour could be inferred from their conduct; and trustees must act jointly.

A similar view was taken in the cases allowing a personal representative to act as a trustee in the exercise of the statutory power of appointing new trustees.[74]

There is no distinction with regard to the power of disposition of realty,[75] the power being joint in both cases.[76] It seems however that one of two or more personal representatives, acting with the authority of the other, may enter into a contract to sell; though the contract can only be implemented and the sale carried out with the concurrence of the others or by order of the court.[77] Where there is only a single personal representative, he may give a receipt for capital money arising on the sale,[78] while at least two trustees or a trust corporation are required in the case of a conveyance by a tenant for life or trustees for sale.[79] It is necessary for all personal representatives who are registered shareholders of a company to execute any transfer of the shares, and they may do this even if they have not been registered as members of the company.[80]

(c) *Tenure of Office.* Formerly a personal representative held his office for life,[81] unless the grant was for a limited period. An executor could, of course, decline to accept office, but once he had taken steps in the administration of the estate (and once an administrator had been

---

[73] [1913] A.C. 76.
[74] *Re Ponder* [1921] 2 Ch. 59; *Re Pitt* (1928) 44 T.L.R. 371; *Re Cockburn* [1957] Ch. 438. See also [1984] Conv. 423 (C. Stebbings).
[75] Including leaseholds after 1925; A.E.A. 1925, s.3(1).
[76] *Ibid.* s.2(2).
[77] *Fountain Forestry Ltd.* v. *Edwards* [1975] Ch. 1; where, however, specific performance was refused because the contracting administrator purported to contract with the concurrence of his co-administratrix, when she had not in fact agreed; *Sneesky* v. *Thorne* (1855) 7 De G.M. & G. 399. See also *Collier* v. *Hollinshead* (1984) 272 E.G. 941.
[78] L.P.A. 1925, s.27(2), as amended by L.P.(A.)A. 1926.
[79] T.A. 1925, s.14; *post*, p. 529.
[80] Companies Act 1985, s.183(3).
[81] *Re Timmis* [1908] 1 Ch. 176 at p. 183, *per* Kekewich J.; *Attenborough* v. *Solomon*, *supra*; *Harvell* v. *Foster* [1954] 2 Q.B. 367.

appointed) he could not retire. Now, however, the court may discharge an executor or administrator and appoint a substitute.[82] A
trustee, on the other hand, may retire without a court order.[83] Subject
to the above, a personal representative's duties terminate with the
completion of the administration of the estate, but his liabilities are
limited only by effluxion of time. Thus, solicitors, who were sureties of
an administrator and who handed over the residue of the estate to the
administrator (who then absconded) were held liable on their bond.[84]

(d) *Duty to Estate: Duty to Beneficiaries.* Executors and trustees are
both subject to fiduciary duties. A trustee's duty is to the beneficiaries,
and he must "hold the balance evenly between the beneficiaries to
whom the property belongs."[85] With an unadministered estate, no
legatee, devisee or next of kin, has, as will be seen,[86] beneficial ownership of the assets. The executor's duty is to the estate as a whole.[87] In
Re Hayes' Will Trusts,[88] a testator appointed four persons, including
his son, executors and trustees of his will, and gave power to "my
trustees ... to sell ... to any person ... including my son despite his
being a trustee and in his case at the value placed upon the same for
purposes of estate duty." He gave his residuary estate to his widow for
life and after her death to such of his children as should be living at his
death. Two of the questions which arose are relevant to the present
distinction. First, the fact that the power was given to the "trustees"
did not prevent them from exercising the power in their capacity as
executors. If it had been given to them in the capacity of trustees only,
it would not have been exercisable by them, but by the tenant for life.[89]
Secondly, in agreeing the estate duty valuation of the farm, the executors were not obliged to consider the implications of the fact that a
low valuation benefited the son, a high one benefited the other beneficiaries. They negotiated in the usual way with the District Valuer and
agreed as low a valuation for tax purposes as they could obtain. This
was the usual correct procedure, and they were right to sell to the son
at that price.

(e) *Vesting of a Legal Estate.* A further question arises, however,
with a legal estate in land. Where trustees under an existing trust make
an appointment of a new trustee under a statutory power given to them
by Trustee Act 1925, s.36,[90] the legal estate in the trust property vests

---

[82] Administration of Justice Act 1985, s.50.
[83] T.A. 1925, ss.36, 39; *post*, p. 477.
[84] *Harvell* v. *Foster, supra.*
[85] *Re Hayes' W.T.* [1971] 1 W.L.R. 758 at p. 764; *post*, p. 508.
[86] *Post*, p. 59.
[87] *Re Charteris* [1917] 2 Ch. 379, where a postponement of sale of some assets acted to
the disadvantage of the life tenant, although it was in the interest of the estate.
[88] [1971] 1 W.L.R. 758; (1971) 36 Conv.(N.S.) 136 (J. F. Mummery).
[89] *Ibid.* at p. 762; Settled Land Act 1925, s.108.
[90] *Post*, p. 469.

in the new trustee under section 40.[91] Personal representatives cannot appoint successors to their offices. If the last executor dies, the office passes to his executor if he appoints one. If he does not, then a new grant of administration *de bonis non* must be obtained. Personal representatives, however, may, after they have become trustees following the completion of the administration of the estate,[92] appoint additional or successor trustees.

But in *Re King's Will Trusts*,[93] Pennycuick J. held that Trustee Act 1925, s.40 did not apply to an appointment of a new trustee by the surviving executor and trustee of a will, who had not previously assented in writing to the vesting of the legal estate in himself in his capacity as trustee. We have seen that an assent in writing is necessary for the vesting of a legal estate in land, and that it constitutes an essential document of title.[94] The executor could have assented to the vesting of the legal estate in himself and the new trustee after the appointment; or he could have assented, before the appointment, to the vesting in himself as trustee; in which case s.40 would have applied.

This decision has been criticised,[95] and it may upset a number of titles which have relied on the practice established by earlier cases.[96] A purchaser is well advised to insist upon an assent in writing whenever the legal estate in land has been in the hands of personal representatives. While the terms of the Administration of Estates Act 1925, s.36(4),[97] do not seem to make a written assent essential in a case where the legal estate owner is merely changing the capacity in which he holds, such a requirement is consistent with the principle of the 1925 legislation that every dealing with a legal estate in land should be supported by a document of title. An assent to the vesting of an

---

[91] Some forms of property are excepted.
[92] *Supra*, n. 74. See also Parry and Clark, *The Law of Succession* (9th ed.), pp. 381–385.
[93] [1964] Ch. 542; Mellows, *The Law of Succession* (4th ed.), pp. 281–282.
[94] *Ante*, p. 55.
[95] (1964) 28 Conv.(N.S.) 298 (J. F. Garner); (1964) 80 L.Q.R. 328 (R. R. A. Walker); (1976) 29 C.L.P. 60 (E. C. Ryder); see also Farrand, *Contract and Conveyance* (4th ed.), p. 10. The requirement of an assent is however supported by Key and Elphinstone, *Conveyancing Precedents* (15th ed.), Vol. 1, p. 238 (§ 14) and p. 248 (note p); Prideaux, *Conveyancing Forms and Precedents* (25th ed.), Vol. 3, p. 909; Wolstenholme and Cherry, *Conveyancing Statutes* (12th ed.), Vol. 2, p. 1470, but the support is qualified in 13th ed., Vol. 5, p. 61; (ed. J. T. Farrand). See Law Commission Working Paper No. 105 (1987), *Transfer of Land, Title on Death*, tentatively suggesting that an assent should be deemed to have been made under certain conditions; paras. 4.23, 4.24.
[96] *Re Ponder* [1921] 2 Ch. 59; *Re Cockburn* [1957] Ch. 438 (not apparently cited in *Re King's Will Trusts* [1964] Ch. 542); (1964) 28 Conv.(N.S.) 302; see also *Re Stirrup's Contract* [1961] 1 W.L.R. 449; [1984] Conv. 423 (C. Stebbings).
[97] *Ante*, p. 55.

equitable interest in land need not, however, be in writing, and may be inferred from conduct.[98]

(ii) The Nature of the Interest of a Legatee or Devisee.

A legatee or devisee does not, on the testator's death, become equitable owner of any part of the estate. The executor takes full title to the testator's property, not merely a bare legal estate.[99] He is, by virtue of his office, subjected to various fiduciary duties, which can be enforced against him by persons interested; and these duties are inconsistent with his holding the property on trust for the legatee or devisee.[1]

The fiduciary duties of the personal representatives are "to preserve the assets, to deal properly with them, and to apply them in a due course of administration for the benefit of those interested according to that course, creditors, the death duty authorities, legatees of various sorts, and the residuary beneficiaries. They might just as well have been termed 'duties in respect of the assets' as trusts. What equity did *not*[2] do was to recognise or create for residuary legatees a beneficial interest in the assets in the executor's hand during the course of administration."[3] It may be, as with an insolvent estate, that nothing is left which can be applied for the benefit of those entitled under the will. Even if the estate is solvent, the devisee or legatee is not the owner in equity of any asset in the estate.[4] He has a chose in action, a right to compel the administration of the estate. Thus, in the *Livingston* case,[5] the question was whether succession duty was payable under a Queensland statute which applied to property situated in Queensland. A widow died domiciled in New South Wales, and was

---

[98] *Re Edwards's W.T.* [1982] Ch. 30. But see [1982] Conv. 4 (P. W. Smith) for the view that only an executor, and not an administrator, can make such an implied assent.

[99] *Commissioner of Stamp Duties (Queensland)* v. *Livingston* [1965] A.C. 694 at pp. 707, 708, 712; *ante*, p. 22. But, for the purposes of inheritance tax, a person who would become entitled to a residuary estate (or part thereof) on the completion of the administration is treated as having become entitled at the death of the deceased. Inheritance Tax Act 1984, s.91.

[1] *Sudeley (Lord)* v. *Att.-Gen.* [1897] A.C. 11; *Barnado's (Dr.) Homes* v. *Income Tax Special Commissioners* [1920] 1 K.B. 468 at p. 479; [1921] 2 A.C. 1; *Corbett* v. *Commissioners of Inland Revenue* [1938] 1 K.B. 567 at pp. 575–577; *Passant* v. *Jackson (Inspector of Taxes)* [1986] S.T.C. 164; see also, for differing views, *Cooper* v. *Cooper* (1874) L.R. 7 H.L. 53; *McCaughey* v. *Commissioner of Stamp Duties* (1945) 46 S.R., N.S.W. 192; *Smith* v. *Layh* (1953) 90 C.L.R. 102; *Skinner* v. *Att.-Gen.* [1940] A.C. 350. See *ante*, p. 21; and for a full discussion of the Commonwealth cases, see (1967) 45 C.B.R. 219 (D. W. M. Waters).

[2] Italics supplied.

[3] *Per* Lord Radcliffe [1965] A.C. 694 at p. 707; *Re Hayes' Will Trusts* [1971] 1 W.L.R 758, *ante*, p. 57; (1967) 45 C.B.R. 219 (D. W. M. Waters).

[4] There is some doubt as to the position concerning a specific gift. Although the property may be used to discharge debts, earlier authorities support the view that the property belonged to the legatee in equity as from the testator's death. See *Re Neeld* [1962] Ch. 643 at p. 688; Snell, p. 338. But some statements in the *Livingston* case may cast doubt on the correctness of this proposition. See *infra*, n. 10.

[5] [1965] A.C. 694; *ante*, p. 22.

residuary legatee under her husband's will. The estate, which was not administered at the date of the widow's death, contained land in Queensland. The Privy Council held that succession duty was not payable on that property. The widow was not the owner of it. She was the owner of a chose in action, and that was situated in New South Wales, the state of her domicile. In *Eastbourne Mutual Building Society* v. *Hastings Corporation*,[6] a husband occupied a house on his wife's intestacy, and he was unable to claim compensation for the value of the house on compulsory purchase, because the estate was not administered, and he had no interest in the house. Similarly, in *Lall* v. *Lall*,[7] a widow wished to defend an action for possession of the matrimonial home, which had been owned by her deceased husband. No grant of administration of his estate had yet been made. The widow could have required the house to be appropriated towards her share of her husband's intestate estate under Intestates' Estates Act 1952, s.5, Sched. 2. But this gave her no *locus standi* to defend the action. And in *Re K. (deceased)*[8] residuary beneficiaries under an unadministered estate had not acquired an "interest in property" within section 2(7) of the Forfeiture Act 1982 so as to preclude the court from giving relief under the Act from the forfeiture rule in favour of an applicant who had killed the testator. On the other hand, in *Re Leigh's Will Trust*,[9] a bequest by a widow of "all the shares which I hold and any other interest or assets which I may have" in a particular company was held to be wide enough to include a claim to her husband's unadministered estate which contained such share; and her claim passed under her will.

A devisee or legatee may be said to become the equitable owner of specific property once property has been allocated by the executor for the purpose.[10] In the case of a residuary gift or a claim on intestacy, the allocation cannot occur until the residuary accounts are prepared.[11] That is the time at which the executors are turning into trustees. The interest of the person entitled then becomes that of a beneficiary under a trust.

---

[6] [1965] 1 W.L.R. 861.

[7] [1965] 1 W.L.R. 1249; (1965) 23 C.L.J. 44 (S. J. Bailey).

[8] [1986] Ch. 180; *post*, p. 309. It was left open in the High Court, [1985] Ch. 85, whether s.2(7) would apply if administration of the estate had been completed. This was not dealt with on appeal.

[9] [1970] Ch. 277; (1970) 86 L.Q.R. 20 (P.V.B.).

[10] *Phillipo* v. *Munnings* (1837) 2 Myl. & Cr. 309; "Nevertheless, there are passages in the judgment (of the *Livingston* case [1965] A.C. 694 at pp. 707, 708) which seem to imply that it is not confined to gifts of residue and intestacies but extends also to virtually every type of testamentary gift." (1965) C.L.J. 44 at p. 45 (S.J. Bailey).

[11] *Re Claremont* [1923] 2 K.B. 718.

G. Powers[12]

(i) Trusts Imperative; Powers Discretionary. The distinction between trusts and powers is fundamental. Trusts are imperative; powers
are discretionary. Trustees must perform the duties connected with
their trusts. A donee of a power may exercise it, or not, at his choice. If
the donee of a power created by will predeceases the testator then the
power lapses, but it is otherwise in the case of a trust, which does not
fail for lack of a trustee.[13]

Trustees are under a duty to hold the trust property for the benefit of
the beneficiaries in accordance with the terms of the trust. The beneficiaries under a trust are the owners in equity of the trust property.
Objects of a power own nothing, unless and until the donee of the
power makes an appointment in their favour.[14] Thus, if a testator by his
will leaves property to his widow for life and after her death to his
children in equal shares, the widow and the children obtain vested
interests in the property. Compare this with a gift to the widow for life
and after her death as she shall appoint among the children, and, in
default of appointment, to charity. Then the children obtain nothing
unless and until an appointment is made in their favour.

Whether a trust or a power has been created is dependent upon the
construction of the language of the instrument. A properly drafted
instrument will leave no room for doubt.

We have seen that the beneficiaries under a trust are the owners in
equity of the trust property. Objects of a power, on the other hand,
own nothing. They merely have a hope that the power will be exercised
in their favour. Until the power is exercised, equitable ownership in
such a case is in those who will take in default of an appointment, their
interest being subject to defeasance on its exercise.

This distinction is however complicated by the fact that a trust may
give to the trustees considerable discretion. A trustee may be given a
discretion to select beneficiaries from a specified class, or to determine
the proportions in which specified beneficiaries are to take. This is the
basis of a discretionary trust. Under such a trust no member of a class
of the discretionary beneficiaries has an interest in a specific part of the
trust property until the discretion of the trustees has been exercised in

[12] *Farwell on Powers* (3rd ed.); Halsbury's *Laws of England* (4th ed.), Vol. 36, p. 529;
(1957) 35 C.B.R. 1060 (O. R. Marshall); (1953) 69 L.Q.R. 334 (D. M. Gordon);
(1949) 13 Conv.(n.s.) 20 (J. G. Fleming); (1954) 18 Conv.(n.s.) 565 (F. R. Crane);
(1971) C.L.J. 68 (J. A. Hopkins); (1971) 87 L.Q.R. 31 (J. W. Harris). For current
views on the changing nature of trusts and powers, see [1970] A.S.C.L. 187 (J. D.
Davies); (1974) 37 M.L.R. 643 (Y. Grbich). *Post*, Chap. 6.
[13] *Brown* v. *Higgs* (1803) 8 Ves. 561.
[14] *Vestey* v. *I.R.C.* [1980] A.C. 1148.

his favour.[15] The beneficiaries as a whole, however, are the owners of the trust property. If all are adult and under no disability, they may combine together to terminate the trust and demand a distribution of the property.[16] And the trustees throughout are under a trustee's obligation to perform the trust; that is to say, in the context of a discretionary trust, to exercise their discretion; and so to make a selection after proper consideration. "If the trustees fail to exercise their discretion, the court can compel them to exercise the trust."[17] Thus a beneficiary under a discretionary trust cannot demand payment. He has, however, the right to demand that the trustees exercise their discretion in accordance with the trust. What happens if the trustees refuse to do so is one of the matters discussed in *McPhail* v. *Doulton*.[18] The court could replace obstructive trustees with willing ones; and, if no suitable trustees would act, the court ultimately would need to make a selection. The point is that a discretionary trust is a trust. The trustees are under an obligation. Their duty is to make a selection. This is very different from a mere power to appoint; for in that case there is no duty to make a selection.

It must not be thought, however, that the donee of a mere power of appointment has no duties. While not obliged to exercise the power, he must consider periodically whether to exercise it, consider the range of objects, and the appropriateness of individual appointments. If he does decide to exercise the power, he must do so in a responsible manner according to its purpose and, of course, refrain from making any appointment which is not within the terms of the power.[19] This is the case where the power is given to a trustee as such; the duties described above are necessary to the performance of his fiduciary role. Where, however, the donee of the power is not a fiduciary, he is not subjected to these fiduciary duties, although he must, of course, keep within the terms of the power and "refrain from acting capriciously."[20]

But it is difficult in borderline cases to draw a dividing line between

---

[15] This fact provided, for many years up to 1969, a great opportunity for estate duty saving on the deaths of beneficiaries. Under the estate duty law, duty was payable when property passed on a death. Since no beneficiary under a discretionary trust owned any property under the trust, none passed on his death. *Gartside* v. *I.R.C.* [1968] A.C. 553. This is also the case with inheritance tax, but the creation of the discretionary trust is taxable; *post*, Chap. 9.

[16] *Re Smith* [1928] Ch. 915; *Re Nelson* (1918) [1928] Ch. 926; *Vestey* v. *I.R.C. (Nos. 1 and 2)* [1980] A.C. 1148.

[17] *Per* Lord Guest in *McPhail* v. *Doulton* [1971] A.C. 424 at p. 444; *Re Locker's S.T.* [1977] 1 W.L.R. 1323.

[18] [1971] A.C. 424; *post*, p. 98.

[19] *Re Hay's S.T.* [1982] 1 W.L.R. 202; [1982] Conv. 432 (A. Grubb). The power cannot be exercised by merely obeying the settlor's instructions without independent consideration, or even appreciation that the discretion is that of the donee and not the settlor. An appointment made in such circumstances is void; *Turner* v. *Turner* [1984] Ch. 100, *post*, p. 168.

[20] *Re Hay's S.T.*, *supra*, at p. 209.

discretionary trusts and powers.[21] The decision turns on the proper construction of the language of the instrument.[22]

The matter is made more difficult by reason of the fact that a discretionary trust may be "exhaustive" or "non-exhaustive." An exhaustive discretionary trust is one where the trustees' duty to exercise their discretion can only be satisfied by making a distribution. A non-exhaustive discretionary trust, on the other hand, is one where the settlor has given the trustees power to decide not to distribute all of the income, for example, by giving them power to accumulate it for a certain period.[23] It must be admitted that the identification of the precise duty in the case of a non-exhaustive discretionary trust is a difficult task. The distinction from a power of appointment is a fine one, and the matter will be further discussed in Chapter 8. For present purposes the position may be summarised as follows: whereas the donee of a fiduciary power of appointment need only consider exercising the power, the trustee of a discretionary trust must actually exercise it, although in the case of a non-exhaustive discretionary trust this duty may be satisfied by deciding to accumulate rather than to distribute.

(ii) Terminology.[24] Nor is the matter helped by the terminology. The problem is to determine whether a limitation is a trust or a power; and commonly arises where a limitation which is phrased as a power is construed as a trust. It has been referred to as a "power in the nature of a trust," or "a power coupled with a duty," or even as a "trust power." Terminology of this type adds to confusion. The situation is that if the limitation, on its proper construction, is held to impose a duty, then the limitation creates a trust—though one in which the trustees have a power of selection. And the usual rules applicable to discretionary trusts (*e.g.* as to formality, certainty, liability of trustees, etc.) then apply.[25]

(iii) Significance of the Distinction. The question may be material in a number of circumstances.

(a) *Whether the Class Takes if the Discretion is not Exercised.* If there is a gift in favour of such members of a class as X shall select, and X fails to make a selection, will the gift take effect in favour of the class, or will it fail? If the power is construed as a mere power, the non-exercise of

---

[21] *Re Leek* [1969] 1 Ch. 563; *Re Gulbenkian's Settlements* [1970] A.C. 508 at p. 525, *per* Lord Upjohn. *McPhail* v. *Doulton, supra,* at p. 448; *Vestey* v. *I.R.C., supra.* See also, in the context of charity, *Re Cohen* [1973] 1 W.L.R. 415.

[22] *Re Scarisbrick's W.T.* [1951] Ch. 622 at p. 635, *per* Lord Evershed M.R.

[23] This led some commentators to take the view that there is no longer any analytical distinction between trusts and powers. See [1970] A.S.C.L. 187 (J. D. Davies); (1974) 37 M.L.R. 643 (Y. Grbich); (1976) 54 C.B.R. 229 (M. C. Cullity).

[24] (1976) 54 C.B.R. 229 at p. 230 (M. C. Cullity).

[25] *Post,* Chap. 3.

the power will cause it to fail; and the property will then pass on default of appointment, or go on resulting trust for the grantor. But if the gift is construed as a gift to the class subject to X's power of selection, the trust in favour of the class will take effect.[26]

In *Burrough* v. *Philcox*[27] a testator provided that the survivor of his children should have power, by will, "to dispose of all my real and personal estates amongst my nephews and nieces, or their children, either all to one of them or to as many of them as my surviving child shall think proper." No appointments were made and the members of the class were held to take equally as a trust had been created. On the other hand in *Re Weekes' Settlement*,[28] a testatrix gave to her husband a power "to dispose of all such property by will amongst our children," and there was held to be no trust. In neither case was there a gift over in default.

The question is whether, on the proper construction of the limitation, it is possible to show an intention to benefit the objects of the power in the event of no appointment being made.[29] It has been said that the courts are more inclined to such a construction when the objects of the power are small in number, such as children under a marriage settlement.[30] But in *McPhail* v. *Doulton*,[31] a deed was held to create a trust which provided that the trustees "shall apply the net income in making at their absolute discretion" grants to employees, past and present, and their dependants. The principle to be applied in these cases was laid down by Lord Cottenham in *Burrough* v. *Philcox*,[32] "When there appears a general intention in favour of a class, and a particular intention in favour of individuals of a class to be selected by another person, and the particular intention fails, from that selection not being made, the Court will carry into effect the general intention in favour of the class." The presence of a gift over in default of appointment destroys any such implication; the gift over shows that the settlor is providing for a situation where the donee does not appoint to the class; and this is inconsistent with a trust in favour of the class.[33] But

---

[26] *Brown* v. *Higgs* (1799) 4 Ves. 708; *Burrough* v. *Philcox, supra*; *Wilson* v. *Duguid* (1883) 24 Ch.D. 244; *Re Llewellyn's Settlement* [1921] 2 Ch. 281; *Re Arnold's Trusts* [1947] Ch. 131. See also (1967) 31 Conv.(N.S.) 117 (A. J. Hawkins); (1971) 29 C.L.J. 68 (J. A. Hopkins); (1976) 54 C.B.R. 229 (M. C. Cullity).

[27] (1840) 5 Myl. & Cr. 72. Such a trust, it is submitted, should be regarded as a fixed trust subject to defeasance by exercise of the power of selection, and thus unaffected by *McPhail* v. *Doulton, infra*. See *post*, p. 107.

[28] [1897] 1 Ch. 289; *Re Combe* [1925] Ch. 210; *Re Perowne* [1951] Ch. 785.

[29] *Harding* v. *Glyn* (1739) 1 Atk. 469; *Brown* v. *Higgs* (1799) 4 Ves.Jr. 708, 5 Ves.Jr. 495, 8 Ves.Jr. 561, 18 Ves.Jr. 192; *Re Llewellyn's Settlement* [1921] 2 Ch. 281; *Re Arnold* [1947] Ch. 131.

[30] *Re Perowne* [1951] Ch. 785 at p. 790.

[31] [1971] A.C. 424.

[32] (1840) 5 Myl. & Cr. 72 at p. 92.

[33] This is so even if the gift is void; *Re Sprague* (1880) 43 L.T. 236. But it would not be so because of a residuary gift, or a gift over in default of there being any objects of the power; *Re Brierly* (1894) 43 W.R. 36; *Re Leek* [1969] 1 Ch. 563.

there is no hard and fast rule that a trust is intended if there is no gift over.[34]

Where the court finds that there is a trust, the question arises of the share which each of the beneficiaries will take. This will depend upon many factors. In the nineteenth century cases, where the question usually arose in the context of division among a family group, the rule of equal division was applied, on the principle that equality was equity.[35] Such a solution would be particularly inappropriate in the context of modern trusts in favour of employees of companies and their dependants. In *McPhail* v. *Doulton*,[36] the House of Lords, as we have seen, was more courageous, and accepted the obligation, where necessary, of itself making a decision on division.

(b) *The Test of Certainty*. With both trusts and powers, it is necessary for the beneficiaries, or the objects, to be defined with sufficient certainty to enable the trustees or the donees to exercise their functions, and for the court to supervise them. Before the decision of the House of Lords in *McPhail* v. *Doulton*,[37] it was necessary to draw a distinction between the requirement of certainty in the case of trusts (fixed and discretionary) and that required for mere powers. *McPhail* v. *Doulton* however decided that the test was the same for discretionary trusts and mere powers. The test came from *Re Gulbenkian's Settlements*,[38] a case on a power, and is whether "it can be said with certainty that any given individual is or is not a member of the class."[39] This test will be discussed in detail in Chapter 3. But it may be said here that the assimilation of the test of certainty for discretionary trusts and mere powers has greatly reduced the practical significance of the distinction between them. Prior to *McPhail* v. *Doulton*,[40] most of the litigation on the distinction between discretionary trusts and mere powers arose in the determination of the question whether a limitation was required to comply only with the above test; or whether it was void for failure to comply with a stricter test which had earlier been applicable to all trusts.[41] That test was whether the description of the beneficiaries enabled the trustee to draw up a full list of the beneficiaries. That test still remains applicable to "fixed" as opposed to discretionary

---

[34] *Re Weekes* [1879] 1 Ch. 289; *Re Combe* [1925] Ch. 210; *Re Perowne* [1951] Ch. 785; *McPhail* v. *Doulton* [1971] A.C. 424.

[35] This will still be the result if such was the settlor's intention; *post*, p. 107.

[36] [1971] A.C. 424. Equal division would not be possible in any event if the total membership of the class was not known. As will be seen, the certainty test propounded in *McPhail* v. *Doulton* does not require all the objects to be ascertained.

[37] *Supra*.

[38] [1970] A.C. 508.

[39] *Per* Lord Wilberforce in *McPhail* v. *Doulton*, *ante*, at p. 456; *Re Baden's Deed Trusts (No. 2)* [1973] Ch. 9, *post*, p. 99.

[40] [1971] A.C. 424.

[41] *I.R.C.* v. *Broadway Cottages Trust Ltd.* [1955] Ch. 20.

trusts; that is to say trusts which purport to give a specific share to each beneficiary. Unless the court could make a complete list of all the beneficiaries, it would be impossible to make a division, or to supervise the trustees if they failed to distribute.

(c) *Terminating the Trust.* Where all the beneficiaries of a discretionary trust are adult and under no disability they may determine the trust and require the trust property to be shared out.[42] On the other hand, objects of a power can never claim any proprietary interest in the property until the power has been exercised in their favour.

2. CLASSIFICATION OF TRUSTS

Trusts have been variously classified and subdivided. The names given to different types of trusts are not terms of art; but they are commonly (even in statutes)[43] assumed to be so. The categories are not exclusive; some trusts could appear in more than one category.

The basic division is between private trusts, and public or charitable trusts. Charitable trusts, which are dealt with in Chapter 15, are trusts for certain selected purposes; which purposes are so beneficial to the community that the Attorney-General undertakes responsibility for their enforcement; and they are accorded special privileges by the law both in terms of non-liability to tax, and in terms of perpetual duration. Private trusts, on the other hand, are trusts for persons, the beneficiaries; and the beneficiaries are the people who can enforce the trust. It may also be noted here that there are a few anomalous cases in which trusts for non-charitable purposes, usually for the building of monuments or the upkeep of particular animals, have been upheld. Such trusts are usually called non-charitable purpose trusts, or trusts of imperfect obligation. The latter name indicates one of their main anomalies; who will enforce such a trust? These trusts are dealt with in Chapter 14.

Private trusts are divided into express, constructive and resulting trusts; and express trusts may be divided into executed and executory, and into completely constituted and incompletely constituted trusts.

Sometimes implied trusts are included as a further category of private trusts.[44] This classification, it is submitted, serves little purpose, and the examples commonly given might preferably be regarded as express, resulting or constructive trusts, as the case may be. Trusts have often been established although express words to that effect have not been used,[45] yet such trusts are "express" because the settlors

[42] *Re Smith* [1928] 1 Ch. 915. For the position regarding a non-exhaustive discretionary trust, see *post*, p. 200.
[43] L.P.A. 1925, s.53(2); *post*.
[44] Such a classification at times appears in statutes, for example, L.P.A. 1925 s.53(2).
[45] See *Paul* v. *Constance* [1977] 1 W.L.R. 527, and the cases discussed under the heading 'Certainty of Intention,' *post*, p. 93.

intended to create them. Trusts based on the presumed intention of the settlor as, for example, in the case of a voluntary conveyance, are sometimes described as implied trusts, but will here be treated as resulting trusts. Mutual wills are also sometimes described as implied trusts,[46] but will here be treated as constructive trusts. The term may be used as meaning any private trust which is not express, but the matter is purely one of terminology.

A. Express Trusts

An express trust is one intentionally declared by the creator of the trust, who is known as the settlor, or, if the trust is created by will, the testator. A trust is created by a manifestation of an intention to create a trust; though certain formalities, as will be seen, are required in the case of *inter vivos* trusts of land and of all testamentary trusts.

Two subdivisions of express trusts should be mentioned.

(i) Executed and Executory. An executed trust is one in which the testator or settlor has marked out in appropriate technical expressions what interests are to be taken by all the beneficiaries; where he has, as the saying goes, "been his own conveyancer."[47] On the other hand, in an executory trust, the execution of some further instrument is required, in order to define the beneficial interests with precision. The property is immediately subject to a valid trust, but it remains executory until the further instrument is duly executed.

The practical significance of the distinction is that while the language of executed trusts is governed by strict rules of construction, executory trusts are construed more liberally. Where, in the case of an executed trust, the settlor has made use of technical expressions, as to the interpretation of which the law has laid down rules, equity will follow the law and give effect to such interpretation.[48] In the case of an executory trust, however, equity will attach less importance to the use or omission of technical words, but will seek to discover the settlor's true intention, and order the preparation of a final deed which gives effect to such intention. It is necessary, however, for the court to be able to ascertain, from the language of the instrument, the trusts which are intended to be imposed on the property.[49]

Executory trusts appeared most commonly in marriage articles, which often provided that certain property belonging to one of the parties should be settled upon them and their issue, and in wills. They are rarely met at the present day; due no doubt to the fact that many

---

[46] Snell, p. 190.
[47] *Per* Lord St. Leonards in *Egerton* v. *Lord Brownlow* (1853) 4 H.L.Cas. 1 at p. 210. In *Re Flavel's W.T.* [1969] 1 W.L.R. 444, Stamp J. refused to apply this principle to the setting up of a trust for employees of a company.
[48] *Re Bostock's Settlement* [1921] 2 Ch. 469; see also L.P.A. 1925, s.60(1); *cf. Re Arden* [1935] Ch. 326.
[49] *Re Flavel's Will Trusts* [1966] 1 W.L.R. 445 at p. 447 ("for formation of a superannuation and bonus fund for the employees").

modern trusts have tax-saving implications, and it is necessary, for such purposes, to be precise and specific in drafting the trust.

In earlier days the courts, in construing executory trusts in marriage articles, were assisted by a presumption that the settlor's intention was to provide for the issue of the marriage. Accordingly, the interests given to the husband and wife would be construed as being life interests, unless there was clear indication to the contrary. For, if the husband or wife received an entail or an absolute interest, the property could be alienated and the issue deprived.[50] The most significant example of the operation of this presumption in the case of marriage articles was that a gift of land before 1926 on trust for the husband and wife for life with remainder on trust to the heirs of their bodies would not attract the application or the rule in *Shelley's Case*.[51] In the case of executory trusts arising under wills, the court would seek to ascertain the testator's intention without the aid of the presumption.[52] It was still not bound by technical rules; and in *Sweetapple* v. *Bindon*,[53] the testator provided that lands should be settled "to the only use of M and her children," and if M died without issue, "the land to be divided between her brothers and sisters then living." It was held that M took an estate tail.

(ii) Completely and Incompletely Constituted Trusts. There cannot be a trust unless the trust is completely constituted. This heading is therefore irrational; it is dealing, not with two different types of trust, but with a rule for distinguishing what is a trust from something that is void. Nevertheless, it is convenient to make the point here, and to deal in more detail with the matter below.[54]

A trust is only valid if the title to the property is in the trustee and if the trusts have been validly declared. A declaration that A holds on trust for B is ineffective if the property is not vested in A. The trust becomes constituted and valid when the property is vested in A. The vesting in A raises questions of the proper method of effecting such vesting, dependent on the nature of the property—land, chattel, money, shares in a company, copyrights, patents, debts or other choses in action—and the appropriate method must of course be used.[55] And in the case of a trust of land there must be written evidence of the declaration of trust.[56] The settlor may of course declare himself trustee, and there is then an automatic constitution, because title was

---

[50] *Sackville-West* v. *Viscount Holmesdale* (1870) L.R. 4 H.L. 543 (a case of an executory trust under a will).
[51] *Jervoise* v. *Duke of Northumberland* (1820) 1 Jac. & W. 559; *Papillon* v. *Voice* (1728) 2 P.Wms. 471.
[52] *Sackville-West* v. *Viscount Holmesdale, supra*, at p. 554, *per* Lord Hatherley; *Miles* v. *Harford* (1879) 12 Ch.D. 691.
[53] (1705) 2 Vern. 536. See also *Re Bannister* (1921) 90 L.J.Ch. 415.
[54] *Post*, Chap. 4.
[55] *Post*, pp. 114 *et seq*.
[56] L.P.A. 1925, s.53; *post*, p. 80.

in the settlor throughout.[57] Testamentary trusts are always completely constituted; for the personal representatives, if not the trustees themselves, are under a duty to transfer the trust property to the nominated trustees.

It was said that no trust was created unless the trust was completely constituted. This is true; but there are situations where intended beneficiaries under an incompletely constituted trust may compel the necessary transfer of the property to the trustees. In general, they can do so if they have given consideration,[58] but not if they are volunteers, for there is yet no trust and "equity will not assist a volunteer."[59]

B. Resulting Trusts[60]

A resulting trust exists where property has been conveyed to another, but the beneficial interest returns, or "results" to the transferor. This may happen in various situations; the simplest one is where the property is conveyed to trustees upon certain trusts which fail or which do not exhaust the whole beneficial interest. The part undisposed of results to the settlor. For example, if there is a gift on trust for A for life and then on trust for X if X attains the age of 21, but X dies under 21 in A's lifetime, the property will result on A's death to the settlor. Or if property is given to trustees upon trust to pay £1,000 a year to A, and on A's death to B absolutely, and the income during A's lifetime is £5,000 a year, there will be a resulting trust of the surplus £4,000.

Such a resulting trust may be described as "automatic,"[61] meaning that it arises by operation of law, without depending on the intention of the settlor. Indeed it may be what he most wished to avoid, because, for example, it imposes a tax liability upon him.[62] Resulting trusts of this kind are akin to constructive trusts in so far as they arise independently of intention. Indeed, some of the more recent cases treat the two kinds of trust as almost synonymous.[63]

Another type of resulting trust is the "presumed" resulting trust, where intention is not irrelevant. A resulting trust may be presumed in favour of the transferor where property is conveyed to a volunteer. The presumption is rebuttable by evidence of an intention to make a gift or, where the volunteer is the transferor's wife or child, by the presumption of advancement.[64]

---

[57] *Post*, p. 117.
[58] This includes, as we shall see, "marriage consideration."
[59] *Post*, p. 110.
[60] *Post*, p. 226.
[61] *Per* Megarry J. in *Re Vandervell's Trust (No. 2)* [1974] Ch. 269 at p. 291.
[62] *Vandervell* v. *I.R.C.* [1967] 2 A.C. 291.
[63] *Per* Lord Denning M.R. in *Hussey* v. *Palmer* [1972] 1 W.L.R. 1286 at p. 1289; *Cooke* v. *Head* [1972] 1 W.L.R. 518; *Eves* v. *Eves* [1975] 1 W.L.R. 1338; *Burns* v. *Burns* [1984] Ch. 317; *Passee* v. *Passee* [1988] 1 F.L.R. 263 at p. 269.
[64] *Post*, p. 240.

C. Constructive Trusts[65]

While express trusts arise from the act of the parties, constructive trusts arise by operation of law. Equity just says that in certain circumstances the legal owner of property must hold it on trust for others. The absence of the need for formalities in such circumstances is obvious. There is, however, much dispute and uncertainty as to the occasions on which constructive trusts arise, and also as to their nature.

The term has indeed been used in different senses. It can cover the duty of a trustee who has obtained benefits by fraud; the obligation incumbent on a transferee from an express trustee, unless he proves he was a bona fide purchaser for value without notice, to hold the transferred property on the trusts previously applicable[66]; the obligation incumbent on a trustee who has made a profit, however innocently, through his office, to hold such profit for the benefit of his beneficiaries[67]; the position of a stranger to the trust who meddles with the trust property in such a way that equity will regard him as a *trustee de son tort*[68]; the relationship of vendor and purchaser between the signing of the contract and the execution of the conveyance[69]; and other relationships, such as licensees, and claimants to a matrimonial home, where the introduction of a constructive trust was considered to be necessary to enable the court to reach a just solution.[70] Modern developments in this field follow long established practice in the United States, where the concept of a constructive trust has been said to be "one of the instrumentalities which a court of equity may employ to prevent the unjust enrichment of one person at the expense of another."[71] But the American doctrine regards a constructive trust, not as a substantive trust, but as a "remedial institution,"[72] an equitable remedy of a proprietary nature, available to prevent unjust enrichment whenever the personal remedy is inadequate.[73] Statements in modern English cases, as will be seen, go beyond that; they have suggested the recognition of a constructive trust "of a new model,"[74] which will be imposed "whenever justice and good conscience required it . . . " as an equitable

---

[65] *Post*, p. 280. Waters, *The Constructive Trust*; Oakley, *Constructive Trusts* (2nd ed.).
[66] See Maitland, p. 82.
[67] *Keech* v. *Sandford* (1726) Sel.Cas.t. King 61; *Boardman* v. *Phipps* [1967] 2 A.C. 46; *Industrial Develoment Consultants Ltd.* v. *Cooley* [1972] 1 W.L.R. 443.
[68] *Barnes* v. *Addy* (1874) L.R. 9 Ch.App. 244; *Re Barney* [1892] 2 Ch. 265; *Selangor United Rubber Estates* v. *Cradock (No. 3)* [1968] 1 W.L.R. 1555; *Carl Zeiss Stiftung* v. *Herbert Smith and Co. (No. 2)* [1969] 2 Ch. 276; *post*, p. 288.
[69] *Post*, p. 304.
[70] *Hussey* v. *Palmer* [1972] 1 W.L.R. 1286; *Binions* v. *Evans* [1972] Ch. 359 (licensees); (1972) 36 Conv.(N.S.) 266 (J. Martin); *Eves* v. *Eves* [1975] 1 W.L.R. 1338 (mistress); *Re Densham* [1975] 1 W.L.R. 1519 (wife). See *post*, p. 309.
[71] Scott and Scott, *Cases on Trusts* (5th ed.), p. 869; Scott, *Trusts*, Chap. 13; (1955) 71 L.Q.R. 39 (A. W. Scott).
[72] (1920) 33 H.L.R. 420 at p. 421 (R. Pound).
[73] (1959) 75 L.Q.R. 234 (R. H. Maudsley); Waters, *The Constructive Trust*; Goff and Jones, p. 62; (1963) 21 C.L.J. 119 (L. J. Sealy); (1977) 28 N.I.L.Q. 123 (R. H. Maudsley); (1978) 56 C.B.R. 346 (R. L. Campbell); *post*, Chap. 12.
[74] *Eves* v. *Eves* [1975] 1 W.L.R. 1338, *per* Lord Denning M.R.

remedy "by which the court can enable an aggrieved party to obtain restitution."[75] The implications of this development will be discussed in Chapter 12.

D. Bare Trusts

A distinction is sometimes made between bare or simple trusts, on the one hand, and "special" trusts on the other. The distinction has been complicated by the different explanations which have been given of it and which have appeared in different contexts; they will not be examined here.[76] According to current practice, there is said to be a bare trust when the trustee holds trust property in trust for a single beneficiary absolutely. In such a situation the beneficiary may call for a conveyance of the legal estate at any time, and the trustee must comply.[77] In the meantime the trustee will deal with the trust property in accordance with the instructions of the beneficiary. But that situation would not arise if the trustee had specific duties to perform in addition to those included in the trustee's fiduciary obligations.[78] It will be seen that a bare trust is similar to the type of use which was executed by the Statute of Uses in the case of a use of freehold land. In a jurisdiction which retained the Statute of Uses[79] or has a similar policy[80] such a trust would be "executed" and the legal title would vest in the beneficiary.

A bare trust arises in various situations; where for example, shares are held by a nominee for the beneficial owner,[81] or where the legal title to shares was vested by an employer stockbroker in one of the employees of the firm for the stockbroker's convenience.[82] It will also arise where a beneficiary becomes absolutely entitled as against the trustees; as where a life tenant dies and the remainderman becomes absolutely entitled; or where a minor beneficiary becomes absolutely entitled upon attaining majority. It can often arise, also, outside the context of express trusts; as where a resulting trust arises in favour of the settlor where property is conveyed to a trustee without any declaration of the beneficial interests,[83] or where a transfer is made by fraud, or without intending a beneficial interest to pass.[84] Such a situation will be of significance where the subject-matter of the trust is land. For

---

[75] *Hussey* v. *Palmer* [1972] 1 W.L.R. 1286 at p. 1289, *per* Lord Denning M.R.

[76] See Pettit, p. 59.

[77] As, indeed, could a multiplicity of beneficiaries, all adult and under no disability; *Saunders* v. *Vautier* (1841) 4 Beav. 115; *post*, p. 579.

[78] *Re Dowcra* (1885) 29 Ch.D. 693; *Re Cunningham and Fray* [1891] 2 Ch. 567; *Schalit* v. *Joseph Nadler Ltd.* [1933] 2 K.B. 79.

[79] Repealed in England in 1925; L.P.A. 1925, Sched. 7.

[80] As in New York: Estates Powers and Trusts Law: Part 7.

[81] *Re Vandervell's Trusts* [1971] A.C. 912. This does not include a custodian trustee: *I.R.C.* v. *Schwartz Ltd.* [1951] Ch. 521; *post*, p. 465.

[82] *Hardoon* v. *Belilios* [1901] A.C. 118. The employers were held liable to pay a call on the shares, which was made against the employee: *post*, p. 556.

[83] *Re Vandervell's Trusts* (*supra*).

[84] *Hodgson* v. *Marks* [1971] Ch. 892.

there is in such a case no strict settlement or trust for sale, and difficult questions can arise if the trustee sells the property to a purchaser who claims to have no notice of the trust.[85] If the sale is of personal property such as stocks and shares the beneficiary has no remedy, in the absence of fraud, against the purchaser. His remedy is against the trustee alone.

It is said that all other trusts are "special" trusts. The description however, is not generally used except as a mode of contrast with a bare or simple trust.

E. Trusts in the Higher Sense and Trusts in the Lower Sense

The word "trust" is used in various contexts which have no relationship to the legal meaning of the term. A lender may make a loan to a borrower only because he "trusts" him. But that, in ordinary circumstances, will create no more than a loan. Similarly, with ministers and other public officials, the Crown may entrust them with property perhaps providing that they shall hold it "in trust" for the benefit of some person or body of persons. While such a situation is capable of creating a trust in the legal or "lower" sense, " 'trust' is not a term of art in public law and when used in relation to matters which lie within the field of public law, the words 'in trust' may do no more than indicate the existence of a duty owed to the Crown by the officer of state as servant of the Crown, to deal with the property for the benefit of the subject for whom it is expressed to be held in trust, such duty being enforced administratively or by disciplinary sanctions and not otherwise; *Kinlock* v. *Secretary of State for India*.[86],[87] Similarly, where it is alleged that the Crown is trustee for members of the public. In *Tito* v. *Waddell*[88] phosphate had been mined on Ocean Island by a British company from 1900 until 1920, when the mining rights were acquired by the governments of the United Kingdom, Australia and New Zealand. Thereafter the mining undertaking was carried on by the British Phosphate Commissioners. The Ocean Islanders (the Banabans) claimed, *inter alia*, that the Crown stood in a fiduciary position to them in respect of two transactions, and that, consequently, the Crown was liable to them for various breaches of trust. The claim failed. Although the relevant documents and Mining Ordinances used the word "trust,"

---

[85] *Ante*, p. 33; *Hodgson* v. *Marks, supra*. It has been suggested that bare trusts should be made subject to the doctrine of overreaching; Law Commission Working Paper No. 94, *Trusts of Land* (1985), p. 73; Working Paper No. 106, *Trusts of Land; Overreaching* (1988), pp. 16–17.

[86] (1882) 7 App.Cas. 619.

[87] *Per* Lord Diplock in *Town Investments Ltd.* v. *Department of the Environment* [1978] A.C. 359 at p. 382. But the Crown can be a trustee in the "lower sense"; *Civilian War Claimants Association Ltd.* v. *R.* [1932] A.C. 14.

[88] (*No.* 2) [1977] Ch. 106.

their wording was, as a matter of construction, consonant with the creation of a governmental obligation, for the breach of which the court was powerless to give relief. This governmental obligation, or "trust in the higher sense," was not a true trust in the conventional sense. It created no fiduciary obligation, and was not justiciable in the courts.

PART II

TRUSTS AND POWERS

CHAPTER 3

REQUIREMENTS OF A TRUST

1. CAPACITY TO CREATE A TRUST

CAPACITY to create a trust is, generally speaking, co-extensive with the ability to hold and dispose of a legal or equitable interest in property. But there are two special situations which require to be mentioned.

A. Minors

A settlement made by a minor is voidable; he may repudiate it during minority, or within a reasonable time of attaining his majority,[1] which is the age of 18.[2]

A minor may not, since 1925, hold a legal estate in land.[3] If a minor becomes entitled to a fee simple absolute in possession, the land

---

[1] *Edwards* v. *Carter* [1893] A.C. 360.
[2] Family Law Reform Act 1969, s.1.
[3] L.P.A. 1925, s.1(6).

77

becomes settled land[4] and the trustees of the settlement have the powers of the tenant for life.[5]

B. Mentally Incapacitated Persons

Mental abnormality may affect the ability of a person to make a will, or a gift, or to create a trust. In the case of a gratuitous transfer *inter vivos*, it seems that the test varies according to the size of the transfer and its relationship to the sum of the assets owned by the donor. In *Re Beaney*[6] a mother who was suffering from senile dementia made a gift of her house, the only substantial asset of her estate, to one daughter, Valerie, who had stayed at home to look after her mother for many years; but this had the effect of virtually disinheriting the other two (married) children. Martin Nourse Q.C.[7] summarised the matter as follows[8]:

> "In the circumstances, it seems to me that the law is this. The degree or extent of understanding required in respect of any instrument is relative to the particular transaction which it is to effect. In the case of a will the degree required is always high. In the case of a contract, a deed made for consideration or a gift *inter vivos*, whether by deed or otherwise, the degree required varies with the circumstances of the transaction. Thus, at one extreme, if the subject-matter and value of a gift are trivial in relation to the donor's other assets a low degree of understanding will suffice. But, at the other, if its effect is to dispose of the donor's only assets of value and thus for practical purposes to pre-empt the devolution of his estate under his will or on his intestacy, then the degree of understanding required is as high as that required for a will, and the donor must understand the claims of all potential donees and the extent of the property to be disposed of."

And he held that Mrs. Beaney's gift to Valerie was void, because she was not capable of understanding the conflicting claims of her other children. These problems can be avoided if steps are taken to place the affairs of the person suffering from mental abnormality under the control of the Court of Protection.

Under the Mental Health Act 1983 the Court of Protection has wide powers of dealing with the property and affairs of a person whom the judge is satisfied is incapable, by reason of mental disorder, of manag-

---

[4] S.L.A. 1925, s.1(1)(ii)(*d*).

[5] *Ibid.* s.26.

[6] [1978] 1 W.L.R. 770; [1978] Conv. 387 (F.R. Crane). See also *Simpson* v. *Simpson* (1989) 19 Fam.Law 20 (life-time gift which upset the balance of the will held void for want of mental capacity. Transferee of bank deposits held them on resulting trust).

[7] At p. 774, sitting as Deputy Judge of the High Court.

[8] *Ball* v. *Manion* (1829) 3 Bli.(N.s.) 1; *Birkin* v. *Wang* (1890) 63 L.T. 80; *Manches* v. *Trimborn* (1946) 115 L.J.K.B. 305; *Gibbons* v. *Wright* (1954) 91 C.L.R. 423.

ing and administering his property and affairs.[9] The judge may make an order providing for the maintenance or benefit of the patient or of members of his family, or for making[10] provision for other persons or purposes for whom or for which the patient might be expected to provide if he were not mentally disordered, or otherwise for administering the patient's affairs.[11] There is also power to vary such settlement if any material fact was not disclosed when the settlement was made or if there has been any substantial change in circumstances.[12]

The guiding principle for the court is the consideration of what the patient would be likely to do if he were not subject to the disability. Thus, in *Re T.B.*,[13] the court approved the creation of a revocable trust in favour of the patient's illegitimate child; the property would otherwise have passed on intestacy to collateral relatives. If the matter had arisen after 1969, the court might have dealt with the problem by authorising the making of a will for the patient. Since that date,[14] the court has had power to make a will for an adult mental patient, if the judge has reason to believe that the patient lacks testamentary capacity. The judge must make such a will as the actual, and not a hypothetical patient, acting reasonably, would have been likely to make if restored to full mental capacity, memory and foresight, taking into account the beliefs, affections and antipathies he had (provided they were not "beyond reason") before losing testamentary capacity.[15]

Applications to the court for the approval of schemes affecting the patient's property have commonly been brought in circumstances in which it was desirable in the interests of the family to reduce the tax liability of a rich patient. The applicant must show that the scheme is for the benefit of the patient.[16] It is not essential that provision should be made for revocation if the patient recovers.[17] It is sufficient that it is the sort of settlement which the patient would be likely to make in favour of other members of the family if he had been subject to no mental abnormality.[18] Similarly, if a patient has a life interest under an existing settlement, an application may be made under the Variation of Trusts Act 1958 to vary the settlement for fiscal purposes.[19]

---

[9] M.H.A. 1983, s.95; for the general jurisdiction to do what is beneficial, see *Re Ryan* [1911] W.N. 56.

[10] A judge may order a settlement for this purpose; M.H.A. 1983, s.96(1)(*d*).

[11] M.H.A. 1983, s.95(1). *Re C.M.G.* [1970] Ch. 574. For the jurisdiction of the Court of Chancery, see *Re K.'s S.T.* [1969] 2 Ch. 1.

[12] M.H.A. 1983, s.96(3).

[13] [1967] Ch. 247.

[14] A.J.A. 1969, adding the provisions now found in M.H.A. 1983, ss.96(1)(*e*) and 97; (1970) 34 Conv.(N.S.) 150 (D. E. Hart and M. E. Reed); *Practice Direction* [1970] 1 W.L.R. 259; *Practice Note* [1983] 1 W.L.R. 1077. See *Re Davey* [1981] 1 W.L.R. 164.

[15] *Re D.(J.)* [1982] Ch. 237.

[16] See *Re Ryan, supra.*

[17] *Re Greene* [1928] Ch. 528; *Re C.W.M.* [1951] 2 K.B. 714.

[18] See *Re C.W.M. (supra)*; *Re C.* [1960] 1 W.L.R. 92; *Re C.E.F.D.* [1963] 1 W.L.R. 329.

[19] *Re Sanderson's S.T.* [1961] 1 W.L.R. 36: *Practice Direction* [1960] 1 W.L.R. 17; *Re C.L.* [1969] 1 Ch. 587.

2. FORMALITIES

A. Inter Vivos

(i) Creation. The basic rule is that a settlor may create a trust by manifesting an intention to create it.[20] No formalities are required for the creation of an *inter vivos* trust of personalty.[21] Evidence in writing is required for the creation of a trust of land, and all testamentary trusts must be in writing, signed by the testator and attested by two witnesses as required by the Wills Act 1837, s.9, as amended.[22]

It is necessary, however, to observe literally every word of the basic rule. The intention must be to *create a trust*; a general intention to benefit someone will not suffice.[23] The words or acts of the settlor must be sufficient to establish an intention that either another person (or persons), or the settlor himself, shall be trustee of property for the beneficiary. In practice *inter vivos* trusts are created in writing and usually by deed. Such trusts usually have as one of their objects the saving of tax, and this can only be achieved where there is clear documentary proof of the date and terms of the trust.

With regard to trusts of land, the Law of Property Act 1925, s.53(1) (*b*), provides:

"A declaration of trust respecting any land or any interest therein must be manifested and proved by some writing signed by some person who is able to declare such trust or by his will."[24]

It will be seen that the writing is required as evidence of intention; the declaration need not itself be in writing. And it seems that, as in the case of failure to comply with the Law of Property Act 1925, s.40,[25] a failure to comply with the requirements of s.53(1)(*b*) renders the trust unenforceable, and not void.[26] The signature must be that of the settlor himself and not that of his agent.

These requirements apply to express trusts only, and not to resulting, implied or constructive trusts,[27] although, as will be seen from the case-law discussed below, dispositions of interests arising under resulting or constructive trusts are subject to the formality requirements.

---

[20] Maitland, p. 56; Scott, *Law of Trusts*, Vol. 1, § 23.

[21] *M'Fadden* v. *Jenkyns* (1842) 1 Ph. 153; *Paul* v. *Constance* [1977] 1 W.L.R. 521; *Re Kayford* [1975] 1 W.L.R. 279.

[22] *Post*, p. 91.

[23] *Jones* v. *Lock* (1865) L.R. 1 Ch.App. 25; *post*, p. 118; *Paul* v. *Constance* [1977] 1 W.L.R. 521.

[24] Replacing Statute of Frauds 1677, s.7.

[25] Relating to contracts for the sale of land or other disposition of land or any interest in land s.40 is to be repealed; see *post*, p. 658, n.44.

[26] Pettit, p. 73; Hayton and Marshall (8th ed.), p. 56. See (1984) 43 C.L.J. 306 (T. G. Youdan).

[27] L.P.A. 1925, s.53(2); *Davies* v. *Otty (No. 2)* (1865) 35 Beav. 208; *Rochefoucauld* v. *Boustead* [1897] 1 Ch. 196; *Bannister* v. *Bannister* [1948] 2 All E.R. 133; *Hodgson* v. *Marks* [1971] Ch. 892; *Binions* v. *Evans* [1972] Ch. 359.

Where an oral declaration of a trust of land is alleged, it has been held that the claimant cannot assert a constructive trust and thereby avoid section 53(1)(*b*) unless he has acted to his detriment in reliance on the declaration.[28]

(ii) Disposition.[29] A disposition of an equitable interest, on the other hand, is required to be in writing; otherwise, the disposition is void. Section 53(1)(*c*) provides[30]:

> "A disposition of an equitable interest or trust subsisting at the time of the disposition must be in writing signed by the person disposing of the same, or by his agent thereunto lawfully authorised in writing or by will."

"The subsection . . . " said Lord Wilberforce,[31] "is certainly not easy to apply to the various transactions in equitable interests which now occur." Such transactions include attempts to avoid stamp duty on share transfers, and the practice of putting shareholdings in nominees. Recent litigation has established some fine, and not always logical, distinctions.

Of course, it might be said that the equitable interest is disposed of whenever an absolute owner declares himself trustee of the property. Such a view would, however, make section 53(1)(*b*) meaningless. The word "subsisting" in section 53(1)(*c*) indicates that the subsection only applies where the equitable interest has already been separated from the legal estate.

(a) *Assignment of Equitable Interest.* The simple case is where a beneficiary under a trust assigns his interest to another. This is a disposition of an equitable interest, and is void unless in writing. This is so, whether the beneficial interest is a limited interest, such as a life interest, or an absolute interest which is held on a bare trust by a nominee. The subsection applies to equitable interests in both land and personalty. It will be seen that the disposition must actually be in writing, and not merely evidenced in writing,[32] but a number of connected documents can provide the necessary writing.[33]

---

[28] *Midland Bank Ltd.* v. *Dobson* [1986] 1 F.L.R. 171; *cf. Re Densham* [1975] 1 W.L.R. 1519. See also [1987] Conv. 246 (J. D. Feltham), discussing the enforceability of informal declarations by third party beneficiaries.

[29] (1966) 24 C.L.J. 19 (G. H. Jones): (1967) 31 Conv.(N.S.) 175 (S. M. Spencer): [1979] Conv. 17 (G. Battersby); [1975] Ottawa L.R. 483 (G. Battersby) discussing the English cases in a Canadian context; (1978) 94 L.Q.R. 170 (D. Sugarman and F. Webb).

[30] Re-enacting Statute of Frauds 1677, s.9, with some alterations, the most significant one being that s.9 applied to "all grants and assignments of any trust or confidence" while s.53(1)(*c*) applies to a "disposition of an equitable interest."

[31] In *Vandervell* v. *I.R.C.* [1967] 2 A.C. 291 at p. 329.

[32] *cf.* L.P.A. 1925, ss.40, 53(1)(*b*).

[33] *Re Danish Bacon Co. Staff Pension Fund Trusts* [1971] 1 W.L.R. 248 at p. 255.

(b) *Direction to Trustees to Hold on Trust for Another.* Where a beneficiary is absolutely entitled and directs the trustee to hold upon other trusts, there is a disposition of the beneficiary's interest. This is the basis of *Grey* v. *I.R.C.*,[34] which was concerned with an attempt by an intending settlor to save stamp duty on shares being put into the settlement. At that time *ad valorem* stamp duty (*i.e.* varying with the value of the interest transferred) was payable on deeds of gift, although this is no longer the position.[35] Where stamp duty is payable, it is payable upon instruments whereby property is transferred, and not upon transactions.[36]

In *Grey* v. *I.R.C.*,[37] the settlor made six settlements of nominal sums in favour of his grandchildren. Later, he transferred shares of substantial value to the trustees, as his nominees, on trust for himself. That transfer attracted only nominal stamp duty. Then he orally instructed the trustees to hold that property upon the trusts of the six settlements. Finally, the trustees executed documents confirming that they held the shares upon the trusts of the settlements. The settlor, though not expressed to be a party, executed the documents.

There was no doubt that the trusts were validly declared. The question was whether they were declared by the settlor's oral declaration, in which case the subsequent documents were truly confirmatory, and passed no beneficial interest; or whether, as the Revenue argued, the document effected a disposition of an existing equitable interest within section 53(1)(c). If the Revenue was correct, the documents created the trust, and were subject to *ad valorem* duty.

In argument, Pennycuick Q.C. posed the question thus[38]:
"If X holds property in trust for A as absolute owner and A then directs X to hold the property on the settlement trusts for the benefit of B, C, and D, and X accepts the trust, is that direction a 'disposition' of a subsisting equitable interest within the meaning of section 53?" The House of Lords answered affirmatively. While the trustees held the shares as nominees for the settlor, the settlor owned the entire beneficial interest. When the trustees held them upon the trusts of the settlements, the beneficial interest passed from the settlor to the beneficiaries under the settlements. That, according to the natural

---

[34] [1960] A.C. 1; (1960) C.L.J. 31 (J. W. A. Thornely); see also [1958] Ch. 375, and [1958] Ch. 690; [1979] Conv. 17 (G. Battersby); (1984) 47 M.L.R. 385 (B. Green).
[35] F.A. 1985, s.82, abolishing the duty in the case of *inter vivos* gifts on or after March 26, 1985.
[36] *I.R.C.* v. *Angus* (1889) 23 Q.B.D. 579; *Oughtred* v. *I.R.C.* [1960] A.C. 206 at p. 227, *per* Lord Radcliffe.
[37] See note 34, *supra*.
[38] [1960] A.C. 1 at p. 4.

meaning of the word, was a disposition. It was different from a declaration of a trust of the beneficial interest. *Ad valorem* stamp duty was payable on the documents.

It would be interesting to speculate whether the settlor's objectives would have been achieved if he had either (i) orally declared himself trustee of the shares for the beneficiaries while still the legal owner; following the declaration with a confirmatory document; and retiring, when he wished, in favour of other trustees; or (ii) as in the previous example except that he had conveyed the legal title to the nominees before the oral declaration of trust, the declaration imposing some active duties upon himself, in order to create a sub-trust rather than an assignment[39]; or (iii) surrendered his equitable interest to the trustees. It has been suggested that a surrender of a beneficial interest is not a disposition within section 53(1)(c).[40] This is doubtful, but if this were so it would have provided a convenient way of avoiding stamp duty, for an owner could have conveyed the property to the intended donee on trust for himself and then orally surrendered this interest. None of these situations is fully covered by decided cases.

(c) *Conveyance of Legal Estate by Nominee.* But the subsection does not apply where the nominee conveys the legal estate to a stranger with the consent or at the direction of a beneficiary absolutely entitled. In that situation, "prima facie a transfer of the legal estate carries with it the absolute beneficial interest in the property transferred."[41]

In *Vandervell* v. *I.R.C.*,[42] Mr. Vandervell wished to give sufficient money to the Royal College of Surgeons to found a Chair of Pharmacology. He decided to do so by arranging for the transfer to the College of all the "A" shares in Vandervell Products Ltd., subject to an option exercisable by Vandervell Trustees Ltd., a company which acted as trustee for various Vandervell family trusts, to repurchase the shares for £5,000. The shares were held by the National Provincial Bank Ltd. as nominees for Vandervell.

The Bank transferred the shares to the College subject to the option. Dividends amounting to £250,000 were declared on the shares and paid to the College, and the income in the hands of the College, being a charity, was not subject to liability to income tax. But the Revenue claimed surtax from Vandervell on the ground that he had not completely divested himself of the beneficial interest in the property.[43] The Revenue succeeded on the ground that there

---

[39] See section (e), *post*, p. 87.
[40] [1960] B.T.R. 20 (J. G. Monroe); *cf.* Meagher, Gummow and Lehane, p. 214; Pettit, p. 78. A surrender is not the same as a disclaimer.
[41] *Per* Diplock L.J. [1966] Ch. 261 at p. 287.
[42] [1967] 2 A.C. 291; (1966) 24 C.L.J. 19 (G. H. Jones); (1967) 31 Conv.(n.s.) 175 (S. M. Spencer); (1967) 30 M.L.R. 461 (N. Strauss); (1975) 38 M.L.R. 557 (J. W. Harris).
[43] I.T.A. 1952, s.415; now I.C.T.A. 1988, ss.684, 685.

had been no declaration of the trusts on which the option was held by Vandervell Trustees Ltd., and that, in the absence of such a declaration of trust, they held it on a resulting trust for Vandervell. This aspect of the case is considered in Chapter 10 below.

A second argument of the Revenue was to the effect that, since the Bank had held the shares on trust for Vandervell, the transfer by the Bank to the College transferred only the bare legal estate; and the equitable interest could not leave Vandervell except by a disposition in writing signed by him. If A holds property on trust for B, and A transfers the legal title to X, who is not a bona fide purchaser of the legal estate for value without notice, the ordinary rule would suggest that X took subject to B's beneficial interest; that the beneficial interest, in short, did not pass on the transfer of the legal title by A.[44] Certainly this would be the case if the transfer was in breach of trust, or was only the appointment of a new trustee.[45] On the other hand, there could be no argument in favour of the application of the section in the case of a transfer by a person who was the sole owner, at law and in equity[46]; and the House of Lords held that the section was similarly not applicable in the case of a transfer by a trustee on the directions of a beneficial owner of the whole interest. Lord Upjohn, after referring to the *Grey*[47] and *Oughtred*[48] cases, explained the object of the section as being to prevent hidden oral transactions relating to equitable interests. "But when the beneficial owner owns the whole beneficial estate and is in a position to give directions to his bare trustee with regard to the legal as well as the equitable estate there can be no possible ground for invoking the section where the beneficial owner wants to deal with the legal estate as well as the equitable estate.[49]

Presumably, however, the subsection would apply if the beneficial owner were to direct that the legal title should be transferred to X, who should hold on trust for Y. In such a case the equitable interest, although passing at the same time as the legal title, would remain separated from it.[50]

(d) *Declaration of Trust with Consent of Beneficial Owner.* That decision did not exhaust the subtleties of the section in its application to Mr. Vandervell's affairs. Faced with the surtax claim by the Reve-

---

[44] *I.R.C.* v. *Hood-Barrs (No. 2)* (1963) 41 T.C. 339 at p. 362, *per* Wilberforce J.
[45] (1967) 31 Conv.(N.S.) 175 at p. 177 (S. M. Spencer).
[46] Such a transfer would include the equitable interest unless there is evidence that such was not intended, or where the presumption of resulting trust applies; *post*, p. 227.
[47] [1960] A.C. 1.
[48] [1960] A.C. 206; *post*, p. 87.
[49] [1967] 2 A.C. 291 at p. 311.
[50] But compare the position in *Re Vandervell's Trusts (No. 2)*, *infra*, where the subsection did not apply to a transaction whereby the legal title passed to the trustees and the equitable interest to the children's settlement, having previously been united in the Royal College of Surgeons. On the latter point it is distinguishable from the example in the text, and is in fact the converse of *Vandervell* v. *I.R.C.*

nue in 1961 in respect of the dividends paid to the Royal College of Surgeons, he instructed Vandervell Trustees Ltd. to exercise the option. They did so, in the same year, using £5,000 from the Vandervell children's settlement for the purpose, manifesting an intention with Vandervell's consent that the shares which they thereby acquired should be held on the trusts of the children's settlement, and so informing the Revenue. In 1965, Vandervell executed a deed formally assigning to Vandervell Trustees Ltd. any right or interest he might still have in the option or the shares.

The Revenue assessed Vandervell to surtax in respect of the years 1961–65. Up to 1961, there was a resulting trust in his favour of the option. He had not, until 1965, they argued, disposed of that beneficial interest in writing, and therefore he must still have it; though now in the shares into which the option had been converted.

The executors of Vandervell's estate stepped in before the Revenue's claim was litigated, and claimed from Vandervell Trustees Ltd. the dividends paid during 1961–65.[51] They applied to join the Revenue as second defendants. But Vandervell Trustees Ltd. objected, and the objection was upheld.[52] The executors' claim to the dividends succeeded before Megarry J.; on the ground that the resulting trust which applied to the option applied also to the shares, and there had been no valid declaration of trust in favour of the children's settlement. This was reversed by the Court of Appeal, which took the view that the trustee company held the dividends on the trusts of the children's settlement. Four reasons were given: first, that the trustees used funds of the children's settlement to exercise the option; secondly, that the trustees and Vandervell showed an intention that the shares should be held on the trusts of that settlement; thirdly, that there had been a perfect gift of the dividends to the children's settlement; and fourthly, that the resulting trust attached to the option and not to the shares, and the trust of the option came to an end with the exercise of the option. Neither the extinction of the trust of the option nor the creation of the new trust of the shares, nor the two, viewed as a whole, amounted to a disposition by Vandervell of an interest within section 53(1)(*c*).

The subsection did not apply where a trustee, with the consent of the beneficiary, declared new trusts of what could be regarded as new property.

The decision of the Court of Appeal leaves many problems in its wake. Essential to the decision was the finding of a valid declaration of trust in favour of the children's settlement, but the three things relied on as constituting the declaration are unconvincing.[53] Surely an element of intention is necessary in the declaration of a trust, yet none of the parties had such an intention, but merely acted on the assumption

---

[51] *Re Vandervell's Trusts (No. 2)* [1974] Ch. 269; (1975) 38 M.L.R. 557 (J. W. Harris).
[52] *Vandervell Trustees Ltd.* v. *White* [1971] A.C. 912.
[53] *Post*, p. 119.

that the children's settlement was entitled. It is difficult to accept the proposition that the use of the money from the settlement resulted in the acquisition of the beneficial ownership of the shares. Is not the owner of an option entitled to the fruits of it? The fact that it was exercised with X's money gives rights to X, but not equitable ownership.[54] Equally doubtful is the point that there was a "perfect gift" of the dividends to the children's settlement. A valid gift requires a donative intention and capacity to give. Here the dividends were paid to the children's settlement not with a donative intention but on the assumption that the children were already entitled to them.

Other criticisms can be directed at the proposition that Vandervell had no interest in the shares but only in the option, so that when the option terminated (upon its exercise) there was no question of any interest in the shares passing from him to the children's settlement. Underlying the entire decision is the supposition that, if the children's claim failed, there would be a resulting trust of the shares to Vandervell. How could this be if he had no interest in them? Indeed, the House of Lords, in *Vandervell* v. *I.R.C.*,[55] had held that he had. He was liable to surtax on the dividends because his beneficial ownership of the option meant that he retained some interest in the *shares*.[56] Certainly this was not the entire beneficial interest, but it cannot be said that he had no interest in the shares.

Difficulty arose from the point that the acts relied on as constituting the declaration of trust were acts of the trustees, hence the emphasis on the fact of Vandervell's "approval" of these acts. Why should his approval be necessary if he had no interest in the shares? Even assuming a valid declaration of trust, it would have to occur no later than the exercise of the option in order to avoid a resulting trust to Vandervell, whereby any subsequent declaration would be a disposition of his interest.[57] Yet two of the three acts relied on as constituting the declaration occurred after the exercise of the option. Finally, how did the equitable interest in the shares pass from the college to the children's settlement without satisfying the subsection?[58] As the college was at that time also the legal owner, perhaps section 53(1)(*c*) did not apply.[59]

---

[54] *Ibid.*
[55] [1967] 2 A.C. 291.
[56] See I.C.T.A. 1988, ss.684, 685.
[57] As in *Grey* v. *I.R.C.* [1960] A.C. 1, *supra.*
[58] See (1975) 38 M.L.R. 557 (J. W. Harris).
[59] On the basis that there was no "subsisting" separate equitable interest. Compare the reasoning of *Vandervell* v. *I.R.C.*, *supra.* It might also be argued that the exercise of the option gave rise to a contract, which gave rise to a constructive trust, as in the *Oughtred* argument. Thus the equitable interest passed from the college, by virtue of s.53(2), without the need for a written disposition. But this would not solve the problem of where it went to. Presumably it would go to the beneficial owner of the option unless he had disposed of his interest elsewhere, which was the very issue.

(e) *Declaration by Equitable Owner of Himself as Trustee.* A further aspect of the matter which has not yet been worked out is the situation in which a beneficiary, absolutely entitled, declares himself trustee of his equitable interest for another. On the one hand, it can be argued that this is, on its face, a declaration of trust, and not a disposition. It is a sub-trust, the subject-matter not being identical to that of the original trust.[60] On the other hand, it was said in *Grainge* v. *Wilberforce*[61] that "where A was trustee for B, who was trustee for C, A holds in trust for C, and must convey as C directed." Thus, B "disappears from the picture,"[62] and C becomes the beneficiary. This looks like a disposition. But this will presumably only occur if B has, under the trust, no active duties to perform; and the applicability of the subsection may depend on that.[63]

(f) *Specifically Enforceable Oral Contracts for Sale.* *Oughtred* v. *I.R.C.*,[64] like *Grey*, concerned an attempt to avoid stamp duty on a share transfer.

Mrs. Oughtred was the owner of 72,700 shares in a company and was also tenant for life under a settlement which contained 100,000 preference shares and 100,000 ordinary shares. Her son, Peter, was entitled in remainder. In order to reduce the estate duty which would be payable on Mrs. Oughtred's death, an oral agreement was made in 1956 under which Peter would surrender his remainder interest in the settled shares in consideration for the transfer to him of his mother's 72,700 shares.

A deed was executed by Mrs. Oughtred and Peter which recited that the settled shares were then held in trust for Mrs. Oughtred absolutely. The trustees then executed formal transfers of the shares to Mrs. Oughtred; and she transferred the 72,700 shares to Peter. The question was whether *ad valorem* stamp duty was payable on the documents. The document selected for the purpose of the claim was the transfer of the shares from the trustees to Mrs. Oughtred.

The question depended on whether or not Mrs. Oughtred was owner in equity of the shares before the formal transfer. Provided a contract is specifically enforceable, a constructive trust is said to arise as soon as the contract is entered into, whereby the equitable interest passes to the purchaser by virtue of his right to specific performance.[65]

---

[60] Compare the reasoning of *Re Vandervell's Trusts (No. 2)*, *supra*.

[61] (1889) 5 T.L.R. 436 at p. 437; *post*, p. 113; see also *D.H.N. Food Distributors Ltd.* v. *Tower Hamlets L.B.C.* [1976] 1 W.L.R. 852; (1977) 93 L.Q.R. 171 (D. Sugarman and F. Webb).

[62] *Per* Upjohn J. in *Grey* v. *I.R.C.* [1958] Ch. 375 at p. 382.

[63] *Re Lashmar* [1891] 1 Ch. 258 at p. 268; see (1958) 74 L.Q.R. 180 (P.V.B.); (1984) 37 M.L.R. 385 at p. 396 (B. Green), suggesting that all sub-trusts are within the subsection.

[64] [1960] A.C. 206.

[65] *Post*, p. 304.

Contracts for the sale of land are normally specifically enforceable, provided section 40 of the Law of Property Act 1925 (requiring written evidence or part performance)[66] is complied with. Contracts for the sale of personalty are specifically enforceable only if the remedy of damages would be inadequate. Thus contracts to sell shares in a public company are not normally specifically enforceable, but the position is otherwise in the case of shares in a private company, which are not available for purchase on the market. Mrs. Oughtred was accordingly able to claim that the equitable interest had passed to her by virtue of her right to specific performance of the contract; or, putting the same point another way, that Peter, after the agreement, held the shares as constructive trustee for her. The later document would then be only a formal transfer of the bare legal estate.

The House of Lords, however, by three to two, held to the contrary. For the majority, Lord Jenkins, with whose speech Lord Keith expressed entire agreement, accepted that Mrs. Oughtred's interest, after the agreement, was similar to that of a purchaser of land between contract and conveyance. The purchaser's interest "is no doubt a proprietary interest of a sort, which arises, so to speak, in anticipation of the execution of the transfer for which the purchaser is entitled to call. But its existence has never (so far as I know) been held to prevent a subsequent transfer, in performance of the contract, of the property contracted to be sold from constituting for stamp duty purposes a transfer on sale of the property in question."[67] So here, the transfer of the legal estate is nevertheless an instrument attracting duty.

Lord Radcliffe, in a dissenting speech, took the view that Mrs. Oughtred became equitable owner of the reversionary interest in the settled shares by virtue of the specifically enforceable agreement to exchange. She became the absolute owner in equity. "There was . . . no equity to the shares that could be asserted against her, and it was open to her, if she so wished, to let the matter rest without calling for a written assignment,[68] from her son. . . . It follows that, in my view, this transfer cannot be treated as a conveyance of the son's equitable reversion at all."[69] This argument is compelling, and it points out a number of questions relating to the nature of the interest which Mrs. Oughtred held before the legal transfer from the trustees; the majority speeches leave these questions unanswered. It has always been held that stamp duty is payable on a conveyance of land, even though the beneficial interest in the property passed on the signing of the contract; similarly with a purchase of shares. This factor may have influenced

---

[66] s.40 is to be repealed and replaced by a requirement that the contract be *in* writing; Law of Property (Miscellaneous Provisions) Bill; *post*, p. 658.

[67] [1960] A.C. 206, at p. 240.

[68] For an example of a contract for the sale of land which was left uncompleted in order to save stamp duty, see *Industrial Properties (Barton Hill) Ltd.* v. *Associated Electrical Industries Ltd.* [1977] Q.B. 580.

[69] [1960] A.C. 206 at p. 228.

the court's approach to the application of section 53. *Oughtred* may thus be viewed as a policy decision.

Later decisions in varying contexts have tended to support the view that an equitable interest can pass under a contract without formality, although the point is rarely fully argued. In *Re Holt's Settlement*,[70] concerning the Variation of Trusts Act 1958, Megarry J., relying on the minority judgments in *Oughtred*, accepted the proposition that where there is a specifically enforceable agreement, the beneficial interest passes to the purchaser under a constructive trust without writing. Similarly in *D.H.N. Food Distributors Ltd.* v. *Tower Hamlets London Borough Council*,[71] concerning compulsory purchase, the Court of Appeal assumed that an equitable interest in land could pass without writing where the transaction was not a gift. In *Chinn* v. *Collins*,[72] concerning a capital gains tax avoidance scheme, Lord Wilberforce said that

> "The legal title to the shares was at all times vested in a nominee . . . and dealings related to the equitable interest in these required no formality. As soon as there was an agreement for their sale accompanied or followed by payment of the price, the equitable title passed at once to the purchaser . . . and all that was needed to perfect his title was notice to the trustees or the nominee . . . "

It seems then, that a specifically enforceable contract can shift the equitable interest without formality, but that where the title is perfected by an instrument, the constructive trust argument will not succeed in the stamp duty context.[73]

In view of these uncertainties, the precise scope of section 53(2), providing that the section does not "affect the creation or operation of resulting, implied or constructive trusts," remains to be determined. As far as constructive trusts are concerned, it is probable that this provision was intended to embrace the kind of constructive trust which is imposed to prevent fraud,[74] and did not envisage the anomalous constructive trust arising on a specifically enforceable contract for sale. The latter is in any event only a qualified trust.[75] In favour of the *Oughtred* decision it might also be said that in the case of a contract there is a transfer of the equitable interest from the vendor to the purchaser, whereas in the case of resulting trusts and constructive

---

[70] [1969] 1 Ch. 100, at p. 116.
[71] [1976] 1 W.L.R. 852, at pp. 865, 867.
[72] [1981] A.C. 533, at p. 548.
[73] See also *Henty and Constable (Brewers) Ltd.* v. *I.R.C.* [1961] 1 W.L.R. 1504, at p. 1510.
[74] As in *Bannister* v. *Bannister* [1948] 2 All E.R. 133; *Hodgson* v. *Marks* [1971] Ch. 892. See also *Midland Bank Ltd.* v. *Dobson* [1986] 1 F.L.R. 171, *post*, p. 311.
[75] *Post*, p. 304. See Hayton and Marshall, p. 67; Heydon, Gummow and Austin, *Cases and Materials on Equity and Trusts* (2nd ed.), pp. 136–137.

trusts imposed to prevent fraud, contemplated by section 53(2), there is no *passing* of the equitable interest, which remains throughout in the true beneficial owner.

(g) *Disposition to Fiduciary*. The subsection is concerned with the disposition of an equitable interest, and not with the creation of further trusts upon the interest disposed of. "There is nothing in section 53 which requires that, where the assignee is to hold in a fiduciary capacity, the writing shall comprise the particulars of the trust."[76] Thus, if X holds a fund on resulting trust for Y, and Y, in writing, instructs X to hold it upon trusts already declared, the written disposition by Y satisfies the statute and it is no objection that the terms of the trust were orally declared.[77]

(h) *Variation of Trusts Act 1958*. We shall see in Chapter 21 that the Variation of Trusts Act 1958 gave power to the court to approve, on behalf of categories of persons unable to make the decision for themselves, variations of the existing beneficial interests under trusts where it is for the benefit of the beneficiaries to do so. The Act was mainly used, before the introduction of capital transfer tax (now inheritance tax), for the purpose of avoiding liability to estate duty; by amending old-fashioned trusts which would attract estate duty on the death of beneficiaries, in favour of modern tax-saving trusts instead. Many variations had been approved by the courts in the first 11 years of the operation of the Act, when suddenly, in *Re Holt's Settlement*,[78] Megarry J. asked whether it was not necessary for the disposition of each existing beneficial interest to be in writing under section 53. Megarry J. was able to satisfy himself that writing was not necessary, and the threat of invalidity to most of the variations previously approved was removed. The details of the matter are best postponed until the Act is explained.[79]

(i) *Right of Nomination under Staff Pension Fund*. The rules of the pension fund of the *Danish Bacon Co. Ltd.* provided, *inter alia*, that employees could nominate a person to receive moneys due in the case of the death of an employee before qualifying for a pension. Such a nomination could be regarded as a disposition, *inter vivos*, of an equitable interest under the pension fund trust; or as a testamentary disposition in that it took effect only in the event of the employee's death. In *Re Danish Bacon Co. Staff Pension Fund Trusts*,[80] Megarry J. held that it was not a testamentary disposition. He very much

---

[76] [1967] 1 W.L.R. 1269 at p. 1275.
[77] *Re Tyler* [1967] 1 W.L.R. 1269; *Ottaway* v. *Norman* [1972] Ch. 698; *post*, p. 150.
[78] [1969] 1 Ch. 590.
[79] *Post*, p. 586.
[80] [1971] 1 W.L.R. 248. For the special position of trusts for the benefit of employees in relation to inheritance tax, see Inheritance Tax Act 1984, ss.28, 86, *post*, p. 222.

doubted "whether the nomination falls within section 53(1)(*c*)"[81]; but held that, even if it did, the necessary writing was supplied by two connecting documents.

(j) *Disclaimer.* In *Re Paradise Motor Co. Ltd.*,[82] a stepfather made a gift of shares to his stepson. The transfer, though technically defective, was sufficient to make the stepson equitable owner of the shares.[83] The stepson knew nothing of the transfer. When he became aware of the circumstances,[84] he stated in unmistakable language that he wished to make no claim to the shares. But when the company was in liquidation, he changed his mind and claimed his share of the proceeds. One question was whether there could be a disclaimer of an equitable interest without compliance with section 53. That section was held to be irrelevant, because "a disclaimer operates by way of avoidance and not by way of disposition."[85] The disclaimer was effective and the claim failed.

However, the position seems otherwise as far as tax matters are concerned,[86] where it has been found necessary to make express provision that a disclaimer shall not be treated as a disposition for inheritance tax purposes.[87]

B. By Will

Additional formalities are required for the creation of a testamentary trust. Wills Act 1837, s.9, as amended by Administration of Justice Act 1982, s.17, provides:

"No will shall be valid unless:

(a) it is in writing, and signed by the testator, or by some other person in his presence and by his direction; and

(b) it appears that the testator intended by his signature to give effect to the will; and

(c) the signature is made or acknowledged by the testator in the presence of two or more witnesses present at the same time; and

(d) each witness either—

(i) attests and signs the will; or

---

[81] *Ibid.* at p. 256.
[82] [1968] 1 W.L.R. 1125.
[83] *Post*, p. 115.
[84] As is required for a disclaimer: *Lady Naas* v. *Westminster Bank Ltd.* [1940] A.C. 366.
[85] *Re Paradise Motor Co. Ltd., supra*, at p. 1143; *Dewar* v. *Dewar* [1975] 1 W.L.R. 1532. But see L.P.A. 1925, s.205(1)(ii).
[86] *Re Stratton's Disclaimer* [1958] Ch. 42 (estate duty).
[87] Inheritance Tax Act 1984, s.17.

(ii) acknowledges his signature,

in the presence of the testator (but not necessarily in the presence of any other witness),

but no form of attestation shall be necessary."

No attempt will be made here to deal with the details of this enactment. Such treatment is more appropriate to a treatise on wills. The question of the validity of trusts taking effect on a testator's death which fail to comply with these provisions—the so-called "secret trusts"—will be discussed in Chapter 5.[88]

3. CERTAINTY

A private express trust cannot be created unless the three certainties[89] are present; certainty of intention; certainty of subject matter; and certainty of beneficiaries. Each of these heads will be considered below. Different considerations apply to each; yet they are interrelated. "Uncertainty in the subject of the gift has a reflex action upon the previous words, and shows doubt upon the intention of the testator, and seems to show that he could not possibly have intended his words of confidence, hope, or whatever they may be—his appeal to the conscience of the first taker—to be imperative words."[90]

Similar, but distinct, questions about certainty may arise by reason of the application of a condition to the gift; whether a condition precedent to taking,[91] or a condition of defeasance.[92] Further, the requirement of certainty of beneficiaries operates differently, as will be seen, with discretionary as opposed to fixed trusts.[93] And the requirement of certainty operates differently with trusts for the purposes as opposed to trusts for people. There is some doubt, as will be seen, whether a trust for a non-charitable purpose is valid; many such trusts have failed; but where such a trust has been upheld, the court has insisted that the purpose be described with sufficient certainty.[94] With charitable trusts, there is no need to specify in any way which charity is to be benefited; but the language of the gift must clearly establish that the gift is applicable for charitable purposes only.[95]

---

[88] *Post*, p. 140.

[89] See Lord Langdale in *Knight* v. *Knight* (1840) 3 Beav. 148 at p. 173. Extrinsic evidence is not generally admissible to aid the construction of a trust deed; *Rabin* v. *Gerson Berger Association Ltd.* [1986] 1 W.L.R. 526.

[90] *Mussourie Bank* v. *Raynor* (1882) 7 App.Cas. 321 at p. 331, *per* Sir Arthur Hobhouse.

[91] *Re Allen* [1953] Ch. 810; *Re Barlow's W.T.* [1979] 1 W.L.R. 278.

[92] *Clayton* v. *Ramsden* [1943] A.C. 320; *Blathwayt* v. *Lord Cawley* [1976] A.C. 397.

[93] *Post*, p. 97, *ante*, p. 65.

[94] *Re Astor's S.T.* [1952] Ch. 534; *post*, p. 346.

[95] *Post*, p. 378.

A. Certainty of Intention

We have already said that a trustee is under an imperative obligation, but that the obligation may be inferred from the nature and
manner of the gift, considered as a whole.[96] Technical words are not
required. The question in each case is whether, on the proper construction of the words used, the settlor or testator has manifested an
intention to create a trust.[97] A trust may be created without using the
word "trust," and, conversely, the use of the word "trust" does not
conclusively indicate the existence of a trust.[98] An expression of hope
or desire, or suggestion or request, is not sufficient. The words in each
case must be examined to see whether the intention was to impose the
obligation of a trust upon the donee. It is not surprising that, on such
questions of construction, the courts have not always been consistent.

The Court of Chancery at one time leaned in favour of construing
expressions of desire on the part of a testator as intended to create a
binding trust.[99] The reason why the court would so readily find a trust
appears to be that, according to the rule established by the Ecclesiastical Courts,[1] an executor who had administered an estate was entitled
to keep for himself any surplus which was undisposed of by the will. In
1830, however, the Executors Act provided that undisposed-of residue
should be held on trust for the next-of-kin; and from about the middle
of the nineteenth century, a stricter construction was placed upon
expressions of this type, usually called "precatory words." Where,
however, an express trust is construed from precatory words, it is, of
course, just as much a trust as any other.[2]

The older cases are therefore unhelpful as guides to construction.
Lambe v. *Eames*[3] is usually regarded as the case which marks the
"turning of the tide"; but the process was gradual and there is much
overlapping between the decisions.[4]

> In *Lambe* v. *Eames*[5] the testator gave his estate to his widow "to
> be at her disposal in any way she may think best, for the benefit of
> herself and her family." By her will she gave part of the estate
> outside the family; it was held that she had been absolutely entitled
> to the property and that the gift was valid.

[96] *Ante*, p. 61. In the context of charity, see *Re Cohen* [1973] 1 W.L.R. 415.
[97] *Ante*, p. 80.
[98] *Tito* v. *Waddell (No. 2)* [1977] Ch. 106 (a case concerning the Crown), *ante*, p. 72.
[99] This tendency appears not to be in accordance with the views of Lord Nottingham, see
    Cook v. *Fountain* (1676) 3 Swan. 585.
[1] Which exercised jurisdiction over the estates of deceased persons until 1858.
[2] In *Re Williams* [1897] 2 Ch. 12 at p. 27 Rigby L.J. protested against the use of the term
    "precatory trust," calling it a "misleading nickname."
[3] (1871) L.R. 6 Ch. 597 at p. 599. James L.J. observed that to turn a widow into a
    trustee might be a "very cruel kindness indeed." This case was approved by the Court
    of Appeal in *Re Adams and the Kensington Vestry* (1884) 27 Ch.D. 394.
[4] See *Curnick* v. *Tucker* (1874) L.R. 17 Eq. 320; *Le Marchant* v. *Le Marchant* (1874)
    L.R. 18 Eq. 414, for cases adopting the older approach; *cf. Re Diggles* (1888) 39 Ch.D.
    253.
[5] (1871) L.R. 6 Ch. 597.

The matter is best summarised in the words of Lopes L.J. in *Re Hamilton*[6]: " ... it seems to me perfectly clear that the current of decisions with regard to precatory trusts is now changed, and that the result of the change is this, that the court will not allow a precatory trust to be raised unless on the consideration of all the words employed it comes to the conclusion that it was the intention of the testator to create a trust."

In *Re Adams and the Kensington Vestry*[7] a testator gave his real and personal estate "unto and to the absolute use of my dear wife, Harriet . . . in full confidence that she will do what is right as to the disposal thereof between my children, either in her lifetime or by will after her decease."

The Court of Appeal held that she took absolutely. It was argued that " . . . the testator would be very much astonished if he found he had given his wife power to leave the property away." To which Cotton L.J responded[8]: "He would be much surprised if the wife to whom he had left his property absolutely should so act as not to provide for the children. . . . That is a very different thing."

But a trust will be found from precatory words if on a proper construction of the language of the will such was the intention of the testator.

In *Comiskey* v. *Bowring-Hanbury*,[9] a testator gave to his wife "the whole of my real and personal estate . . . in full confidence that she will make such use of it as I should have made myself and that at her death she will devise it to such one or more of my nieces as she may think fit and in default of any disposition by her thereof by her will . . . I hereby direct that all my estate and property acquired by her under this my will shall at her death be equally divided among the surviving said nieces." A majority of the House of Lords held that there was an intention in the testator to make a gift to his wife, with an executory gift over of the whole property at her death to such of her nieces as should survive her, shared according to the wife's will, and otherwise equally.[10]

Where a form of words has once been held to create a trust, the testator's intention may be held to be such as to reach the same result,

---

[6] [1895] 2 Ch. 370 at p. 374.
[7] (1884) 27 Ch.D. 394; *Mussourie Bank* v. *Raynor* (1882) 7 App.Cas. 321 ("feeling confident that she will act justly to our children in distributing the same"); *Re Diggles* (1888) 39 Ch.D. 253 ("it is my desire that she allows . . . an annuity of £25); *Re Johnson* [1939] 2 All E.R. 458 ("I request that my mother will on her death leave the property or what remains of it . . . to my four sisters"). See also *Swain* v. *The Law Society* [1983] 1 A.C. 598 (words "on behalf of" did not create a trust).
[8] At p. 409.
[9] [1905] A.C. 84.
[10] Lord Lindley construed the limitation as showing an intention to give an absolute gift to the wife.

at any rate where the words have been used as a precedent, even though the words used, when subjected to the stricter modern construction, might be expected to produce a different result.[11] And if the gift is contained in a will and the precatory expression in a codicil, the inference in favour of a trust is much stronger than where the gift and the precatory words are contained in the same instrument.[12]

Where the words used are held not to create a trust, the donee of the property takes beneficially. By the rule in *Lassence* v. *Tierney*,[13] a gift to which certain words are attached, which fail to create a trust, takes effect as an absolute gift. This must be distinguished from the situation where there is certainty of intention to create a trust, but uncertainty as to the objects or the shares they are to take. In such cases, as we shall see, there is a resulting trust.

The question of certainty of intention may also arise in other situations, for example, where there is no document to construe. The question then is whether the acts or words of the parties indicate an intention to create a trust; as where a man tells his mistress that she can share his bank account[14]; or where a mail order company puts money sent by customers into a separate bank account.[15] This aspect of the problem will be further discussed in Chapter 4, where the requirements of the declaration of trust are examined.[16]

B. Certainty of Subject-Matter

The subject-matter may take many forms. It may be an interest in land, whether in possession or in remainder or in reversion; it may be chattels or money; it may be a chose in action, such as a promise[17] or a debt. Whatever form it takes, it must be specified with reasonable certainty. Testamentary gifts have failed where they concerned "the bulk of my estate,"[18] or "such parts of my . . . estate as she shall not have sold,"[19] or "anything that is left,"[20] or "the remaining part of what

---

[11] *Re Steele's W.T.* [1948] Ch. 603; following *Shelley* v. *Shelley* (1868) L.R. 6 Eq. 540; (1968) 32 Conv.(N.S.) 361 (P. St. J. Langan).

[12] *Re Burley* [1910] 1 Ch. 215.

[13] (1849) 1 Mac. & Cr. 551; *Hancock* v. *Watson* [1902] A.C. 14; *Watson* v. *Holland* [1985] 1 All E.R. 290; *cf. Re Pugh's W.T.* [1967] 1 W.L.R. 1261.

[14] *Paul* v. *Constance* [1977] 1 W.L.R. 527. See also *Re Vandervell's Trusts (No. 2)* [1974] Ch. 269; *Swain* v. *The Law Society* [1983] 1 A.C. 598, All E.R. Rev. 1982, at p. 315 (P. J. Clarke); *Universe Tankships Inc. of Monrovia* v. *International Transport Workers' Federation* [1983] 1 A.C. 366.

[15] *Re Kayford Ltd. (in Liquidation)* [1975] 1 W.L.R. 279, *ante*, p. 52; *cf. Re Multi Guarantee Co. Ltd.* [1987] B.C.L.C. 257, ante, p. 52; *Carreras Rothmans Ltd.* v. *Freeman Mathews Treasure Ltd.* [1985] Ch. 207; *cf. Re Chelsea Cloisters Ltd.* (1981) 41 P. & C.R. 98.

[16] *Post*, p. 117.

[17] *Fletcher* v. *Fletcher* (1844) 4 Hare 67; *post*, p. 126.

[18] *Palmer* v. *Simmonds* (1854) 2 Drew. 221.

[19] *Re Jones* [1898] 1 Ch. 438.

[20] *In the Estate of Last* [1958] P. 137.

is left"[21] or "all my other houses"[22]—*i.e.* those remaining after a choice had been made by another beneficiary who died before choosing. But these cases should be contrasted with one where the subject-matter of the gift is to be determined in the discretion of a trustee. In *Re Golay's Will Trusts*,[23] a gift directing the executors to allow a beneficiary to "enjoy one of my flats during her lifetime and to receive a reasonable income from my other properties" was upheld. The executors could select the flat. The words "reasonable income" were not intended to allow the trustees to make a subjective decision: but they provided a sufficient objective determinant to enable the court, if necessary, to quantify the amount.

The problem, however, is that no objective determination of words such as "reasonable" can be made unless the context is known. In *Re Golay's Will Trusts*,[24] it seems to have been assumed that the yardstick by which to measure it was the beneficiary's previous standard of living. The word "reasonable" in isolation has little meaning. If a testator were to give "a reasonable legacy" to X, then no doubt the gift would fail, unless it was clear that the amount was to be fixed by the executors.

Where the subject-matter of the trust is uncertain, then no trust is created. There is nothing to form the subject-matter of a resulting trust. If the purported trust has been attached to an absolute gift, then the absolute gift takes effect.

It may be, however, that the property itself is certain, but the beneficial shares are not. Unless the trustees have a discretion to determine the amounts, then the trust will fail, and the property will be held on a resulting trust for the settlor. This was the case in *Boyce* v. *Boyce*,[25] where the determination was to be made by a beneficiary who died before choosing. Sometimes the problem will be solved by the principle that equity is equality,[26] or by the court determining what is the proper division according to the circumstances.[27]

Before leaving the question of certainty of subject-matter, it might be said that uncertainty as to the precise scope of property subjected to a secret trust,[28] or a trust arising under mutual wills,[29] has not proved fatal to its validity.

---

[21] *Sprange* v. *Barnard* (1789) 2 Bro.C.C. 585.
[22] *Boyce* v. *Boyce* (1849) 16 Sim. 476.
[23] [1965] 1 W.L.R. 969.
[24] *Supra.*
[25] (1849) 6 Sim. 476.
[26] *Burrough* v. *Philcox* (1840) 5 Myl. & Cr. 72; (1967) 31 Conv.(N.S.) 117 (A. J. Hawkins).
[27] *McPhail* v. *Doulton* [1971] A.C. 424 (concerning the selection of beneficiaries); *post,* p. 100.
[28] *Ottaway* v. *Norman* [1972] Ch. 698, *post,* p. 150.
[29] *Re Cleaver* [1981] 1 W.L.R. 939, *post,* p. 302.

C. Certainty of Objects: The Beneficiaries[30]

"It is clear law that a trust (other than a charitable trust)[31] must be for ascertainable beneficiaries."[32] In the case of future interests, the beneficiaries must be ascertainable within the period of perpetuity.[33] The test to be applied to determine certainty of objects depends upon the nature of the trust. With a "fixed" trust, it is, and always has been, that a trust is void unless it is possible to ascertain each and every beneficiary. With a discretionary trust, the House of Lords decided in *McPhail* v. *Doulton*[34] that the test was: can it be said with certainty that any individual is or is not a member of the class?[35] That is the same test as was established for certainty of objects of a mere power in *Re Gulbenkian's Settlements*.[36] This assimilation of the tests for powers and discretionary trusts destroys what used to be one of the most important reasons for distinguishing between trusts and powers.[37]

(i) Fixed Trusts. A fixed trust is one in which the share or interest of the beneficiaries is specified in the instrument. The beneficiary is the owner of the equitable interest allocated to him. This situation is contrasted with a discretionary trust; where the trustees hold the trust property on trust for such member or members of a class of beneficiaries as they shall in their absolute discretion determine. In that situation, no beneficiary owns any part of the trust fund unless and until the trustees have exercised their discretion in his favour.[38]

Commonly, but not necessarily, there is a fixed trust where there are successive interests in favour of individual beneficiaries; such as a trust for A for life and after A's death for B absolutely. Where there is a gift for a class then, as we have seen,[39] it is necessary in the case of a fixed trust to lay down what share each beneficiary is to take; a discretionary trust will provide for the trustees to exercise a discretion in the selection of a beneficiary. The requirement of certainty in discretionary trusts is considered in (ii) below. The point here is that if trust property is to be divided among a class of beneficiaries in equal (or in any other fixed) shares, the trust cannot, in the nature of things, be administered unless the number and identify of beneficiaries are known. Some of the

---

[30] (1971) 24 C.L.P. 133 (H. Cohen); (1971) 87 L.Q.R. 31 (J. W. Harris); (1971) 29 C.L.J. 68 (J. A. Hopkins); (1973) 5 N.Z.U.L.R. 348; (1974) 37 M.L.R. 643 (Y. F. R. Grbich); (1973) 7 V.U.W.L.R. 258 (L. McKay); (1975) 4 Anglo-American L.R. 442 (S. Fradley); (1982) 98 L.Q.R. 551 (C. T. Emery); Law Com. No. 58 para. 63.
[31] *Post*, p. 369.
[32] *Per* Lord Denning in *Re Vandervell's Trusts (No. 2)* [1974] Ch. 269 at p. 319; *Re Wood* [1949] Ch. 498.
[33] *Re Flavel's W.T.* [1969] 1 W.L.R. 444 at pp. 446–447.
[34] [1971] A.C. 424.
[35] *Per* Lord Wilberforce [1971] A.C. 424 at pp. 454, 456.
[36] [1970] A.C. 508; *post*, p. 99.
[37] *Re Gestetner Settlement* [1953] Ch. 672.
[38] *Post*, p. 199.
[39] *Supra*.

language in *McPhail* v. *Doulton*[40] might suggest the new rule applied to all trusts. But the decision is upon a discretionary trust, and the cases which it examines are cases of discretionary trusts.[41] Although the rule of certainty should be the minimum necessary to make the trust workable, a stricter rule is needed for fixed trusts. How could the trustee or the court administer a trust which provides for the income or capital to be held on trust for "my employees, ex-employees and their relatives and dependants in equal shares?"[42]

To summarise the position, what is required of a fixed trust is that the description of beneficiaries should involve neither conceptual nor evidential uncertainty.[43] But the court will strive to uphold the trust and a common-sense approach will be taken. Furthermore, provided the identity of the beneficiaries is known, it is no objection that their whereabouts or continued existence is not discoverable, as their shares can be paid into court.[44] The requirement is that a list will be able to be drawn, which is on balance of probabilities complete, as to the maximum number of shares, at the time for distribution.

(ii) Discretionary Trusts; Trust Powers.[45] The rule of certainty should be no stricter than is necessary to permit trustees to perform their duties. We have seen that,[46] where the trust property is to be divided into specific shares, it is necessary for the trustees to know exactly how many beneficiaries there are. Until 1971, the same rule applied to discretionary trusts.[47] If the trustees should fail or refuse to carry out their duty to select the beneficiaries and distribute, the court must be able to do so; and, it was argued, the court would necessarily distribute equally on the basis that equality is equity and, for that purpose, the beneficiaries must be identifiable.[48] The fallacy of this argument was shown in *McPhail* v. *Doulton*.[49]

Bertram Baden executed a deed in which he declared that he wished to establish a fund to provide benefits for the staff of *Matthew Hall & Co. Ltd.* and their relatives and dependants.

---

[40] [1971] A.C. 424.
[41] *Re Ogden* [1933] Ch. 678; *I.R.C.* v. *Broadway Cottages Trust* [1955] Ch. 678. For a contrary view, see Parker and Mellows, *The Modern Law of Trusts* (5th ed.), p. 79.
[42] *McPhail* v. *Doulton, supra.* See [1984] Conv. 22 (P. Matthews), suggesting that complete ascertainment is not necessary in the case of fixed trusts. This is doubted at [1984] Conv. 304 (J. Martin) and 307 (D. Hayton).
[43] *Post*, p. 101.
[44] (1982) 98 L.Q.R. 551 (C. T. Emery); *cf.* [1984] Conv. 22 (P. Matthews).
[45] For a possible distinction between these two terms, see *post*, p. 107.
[46] *Ante*, p. 97.
[47] *I.R.C.* v. *Broadway Cottages Trust* [1955] Ch. 678.
[48] [1971] A.C. 424 at p. 442, *per* Lord Hodson.
[49] *Supra*, (1970) 34 Conv.(N.S.) 287 (F. R. Crane). One result of the decision is to confirm that a trust may be valid although it is impossible to state who is entitled to the equitable interest. See [1982] Conv. 118 (A. R. Everton).

Clause 9(*a*) provided as follows: "The trustees shall apply the net income of the fund in making at their absolute discretion grants to or for the benefit of any of the officers and employees or ex-officers or ex-employees of the company or to any relatives or dependants of any such persons in such amounts at such times and on such conditions (if any) as they think fit."

The trustees were not obliged to exhaust the income of any year. Capital could be realised for the purpose of making grants if the income was insufficient. And clause 10 provided that no person had any interest in the fund otherwise than pursuant to the exercise of the trustees' discretion.

We have seen that the deed created a discretionary trust not a mere power.[50] It was not possible to make a list of all the members of the class of beneficiaries. The House of Lords, however, held that the test for certainty in discretionary trusts was that applied to powers in *Re Gulbenkian's Settlements*[51]: "Can it be said with certainty that any given individual is or is not a member of the class?"[52] The case was referred to the Chancery Division for the determination of the question whether the test was satisfied. The Court of Appeal held that it was.[53]

In reaching a decision on the question of the test to be applied, it was necessary to deal with two main arguments in favour of the stricter test. First, that a trustee's duty to distribute could only be performed if he was able to consider every possible claimant; and secondly, that the court could only execute the trust, on failure of the trustees to do so, by equal division of the fund. If these arguments could be answered, there was much to be said for assimilating the test with that for powers; for, although the distinction between trust and power is, in some contexts, basic to a lawyer, it is often difficult to ascertain which exists in any particular case; and "a layman and, I suspect, also a logician would find it hard to understand what difference there is."[54] Thus a relaxation of the test was needed to save many trusts from failure.

A trustee's duty to distribute requires a consideration of the claims of possible recipients. "If [a trustee] has to distribute the whole of a fund's income, he must necessarily make a wider and more systematic survey if his duty is expressed in terms of a power to make grants"[55]; and later, "a wider and more comprehensive range of inquiry is called for in the case of a trust power than in the case of a power."[56] But the difference is only one of degree; there is no need for a trustee of a

[50] *Ante*, p. 98.
[51] [1970] A.C. 508.
[52] *Per* Lord Wilberforce [1971] A.C. 424 at pp. 454, 456.
[53] [1973] Ch. 9; *post*, p. 101.
[54] *Per* Lord Wilberforce [1971] A.C. 424 at p. 448.
[55] *Ibid.* at pp. 449, 457; (1971) 87 L.Q.R. 31 at pp. 61–62.
[56] [1973] Ch. 9 at p. 27.

discretionary trust to "require the preparation of a complete list of names."[57] The difference does not justify a stricter rule for certainty in discretionary trusts.

The main question is whether the court can execute the trust upon the failure of the trustees to do so. This is a theoretical rather than a practical problem. In the cases which have reached the court there have been no examples of trustees refusing to execute a discretionary trust; if a trustee did so, he could be removed and replaced.[58] Secondly, "it does not follow that execution is impossible unless there can be equal division."[59] There are a number of cases, prior to 1801,[60] in which the court exercised a discretion in relation to distribution, deciding in accordance with guidance given by the circumstances of the case.[61] In many of these situations equal division would have been inappropriate. As indeed it would be in modern forms of discretionary trusts for the benefit of employees and their dependants. It would have been paradoxical if the trust in *McPhail* v. *Doulton*[62] had failed because of the court's inability to divide equally; for equal division would have been a nonsensical solution. Thus, the court, if called upon to execute a discretionary trust, will do so in the manner best calculated to give effect to the testator's intentions. "It may do so by appointing new trustees, or by authorising or directing representative persons of the classes of beneficiaries to prepare a scheme of distribution, or even, should the proper basis for this distribution appear, by itself directing the trustees so to distribute."[63] Or, in cases where the trustees have failed to exercise their discretion within a reasonable time, the court may direct them to do so, provided there is no evidence of bias or obstinacy.[64] There is no need therefore to require a stricter rule for discretionary trusts than that accepted in *Gulbenkian*[65] as applicable to powers.

It is thought that this less stringent test will also apply to purpose trusts upheld on the principle of *Re Denley's Trust Deed*[66] as being for the benefit of ascertainable individuals.

---

[57] [1971] A.C. 424 at p. 449.

[58] *Post*, p. 469.

[59] *Ibid.* at p. 451.

[60] *Kemp* v. *Kemp* (1801) 5 Ves.Jr. 849.

[61] *Mosely* v. *Mosely* (1673) Fin. 53; *Clarke* v. *Turner* (1694) Free Ch. 198; *Warburton* v. *Warburton* (1702) 4 Bro.P.C. 1; *Richardson* v. *Chapman* (1760) 7 Bro.P.C. 318.

[62] [1971] A.C. 424.

[63] *Ibid.* at p. 457, *per* Lord Wilberforce; Scott, *Trusts*, § 122.

[64] *Re Locker's Settlement* [1977] 1 W.L.R. 1323; (1978) 94 L.Q.R. 177. The distribution must be in favour of those who were objects at the time the discretion should have been exercised. It is otherwise in the case of a mere power, where the default gift will operate if the power is not exercised within the proper time limits.

[65] [1970] A.C. 508.

[66] [1969] 1 Ch. 373, *post*, p. 344. See *R.* v. *District Auditor, ex p. West Yorkshire Metropolitan County Council* (1986) 26 R.V.R. 24, holding that "administrative unworkability" (*infra*) was fatal to a *Re Denley* type of purpose trust.

(iii) Conceptual Uncertainty[67] and Evidential Difficulties. In *Re Baden's Deed Trusts (No. 2)*, Brightman J.,[68] and then the Court of Appeal,[69] had to apply the test laid down by the House of Lords, and consider in particular whether the words "dependants" and "relatives" were too uncertain. In applying the test "it is essential to bear in mind the difference between conceptual uncertainty and evidential difficulties."[70] The test is concerned with the former; "the court is never defeated by evidential uncertainty."[71] The illustration given of a conceptual question is that of the contrasting cases "someone under a moral obligation," which is conceptually uncertain and "first cousins," which is conceptually certain.[72] It would be possible in the latter case, but not in the former, to say with certainty "that any given individual is or is not a member of the class."[73] It is no objection that it may be difficult to establish whether or not any given person satisfies the description, so long as the description is conceptually clear.[74] In each case the precise words must of course be examined to see whether the test is satisfied. Once the class is determined as being conceptually certain the question of inclusion is an issue of fact. "Relatives" and "dependants" were both sufficiently certain.

Provided the class is certain in the above sense, it does not matter that the whereabouts or continued existence of an object is not known.[75]

(iv) Problems with the Test. The test is not without its difficulties, theoretical and practical.

(a) *What is Conceptually Certain?* Different minds may take different views on the question of whether a particular description is conceptually certain or not. Indeed, the illustrations referred to in the previous paragraph, which were selected to make the point, are not wholly persuasive. The problem is that few descriptions of the kind likely to be encountered in trusts and powers are so clear as to admit of no borderline cases. Most fall between those which are indisputably certain, for example "Nobel prize winners," and those which are

---

[67] Sometimes called linguistic or semantic uncertainty.

[68] [1972] Ch. 607.

[69] [1973] Ch. 9; (1973) 36 Conv.(N.S.) 351 (D. J. Hayton); *Re Bethel* [1971] 17 D.L.R. (3d) 652; [1971] A.S.C.L., p. 377.

[70] *Per* Sachs L.J. [1973] Ch. 9 at p. 19; see also, *per* Lord Wilberforce [1971] A.C. 424 at p. 457.

[71] *Ibid.* at p. 20; in *Re Tuck's S.T.* [1978] Ch. 49 at p. 59, Lord Denning M.R. in the context of a condition precedent, confessed that he found "the dichotomy most unfortunate."

[72] *Ibid.*

[73] *Ante*, p. 99.

[74] This is discussed further below. Such evidential difficulties would, however, invalidate a fixed trust; *ante*, p. 97.

[75] *Re Gulbenkian's Settlement Trusts* [1970] A.C. 508; (1982) 98 L.Q.R. 551 (C. T. Emery). This point is more significant in the case of fixed trusts.

conceptually unclear, for example "friends." To insist on complete certainty would be to defeat most gifts. Dispositions ought if possible to be upheld, and "should not be held void on a peradventure."[76] Words such as "relatives" may cause difficulties,[77] but trustees can be expected to act sensibly and not to select a remote kinsman.[78] The best solution, it is submitted, is to regard such words as conceptually certain, leaving it to the claimant to establish his case, as discussed below. Words such as "friends," on the other hand, must fall on the wrong side of the line. Although "old friends" was upheld in *Re Gibbard*,[79] this was the result of applying a test which has not survived later decisions,[80] namely that it was sufficient that there was some person who could be shown to be within the class. Browne-Wilkinson J., in *Re Barlow's Will Trusts*,[81] attempted to clarify who a "friend" was. But that was in the context of a gift subject to a condition precedent, which, as we shall see,[82] is governed by a less strict test.

  Conceptual uncertainty may, however, be cured by a provision that the opinion of a third party is to settle the matter.[83] A gift to persons "having a moral claim" on the donor would be conceptually uncertain, but a gift to "such persons as the company may consider to have a moral claim" on the donor would satisfy the test.[84] Similarly, any uncertainty in the requirement of being of the Jewish faith and married to an "approved wife" could be cured by a provision that disputes were to be decided by a chief rabbi.[85]

  (b) *Proof of Inclusion and Exclusion; Proving Negatives.* Read strictly, the test means that it must be possible to show either that any person is within the class or that he is not within it. But, how could you show that a person is, for example, not your relative? Sachs L.J.[86] said

---

[76] *Re Hay's Settlement Trusts* [1982] 1 W.L.R. 202 at p. 212.

[77] *Infra.*

[78] *Re Baden's Deed Trusts (No. 2)* [1973] Ch. 9.

[79] [1967] 1 W.L.R. 42, *cf. Re Lloyd's Trust Instruments*, June 24, 1970 (unreported; but referred to in *Brown* v. *Gould* [1972] Ch. 53 at pp. 56–57).

[80] See *Gulbenkian's Settlement Trusts (No. 1)* [1970] A.C. 508.

[81] [1979] 1 W.L.R. 278. It was said that a trust or power in favour of "friends" would probably fail.

[82] *Post*, p. 108.

[83] Except on a matter of law. See further *Re Coxen* [1948] Ch. 747 at 761, *post*, p. 481.

[84] *Re Leek* [1969] 1 Ch. 563; *cf. Re Jones* [1953] Ch. 125; *Re Wright's W.T.* (1981) 78 L.S.G. 841 (gift to trustees "for such people and institutions as they think have helped me or my late husband" regarded as uncertain). See also *Re Coates* [1955] Ch. 495 (for any friends the testator's wife might feel he had forgotten). In the case of a discretionary trust, difficulties might arise if the court is called upon to execute it.

[85] *Re Tuck's Settlement Trusts* [1978] Ch. 49. For a contrary view, see Hayton and Marshall (8th ed.), pp. 149–150. See also *Re Tepper's Will Trusts* [1987] Ch. 358, holding that the meaning of "Jewish faith" could be elucidated by extrinsic evidence of the faith as practised by the testator; All E.R. Rev. 1987, p. 159 (P. J. Clarke) and 260 (C. H. Sherrin). *Cf.* A.J.A. 1982, s.21.

[86] [1973] Ch. 9; and see (1973) 32 C.L.J. 36 (J. A. Hopkins).

that the claimant needs to show that he is within the class; if he cannot do that, he is not within it. His Lordship was here referring to evidential uncertainty. Clearly conceptual uncertainty cannot be cured by casting the onus of proof on to the claimant, because the matter would not be susceptible of proof.[87] Megaw L.J. said that the test was satisfied[88] "If, as regards at least a substantial number of objects, it can be said with certainty that they fall within the trust; even though, as regards a substantial number of other persons ... the answer would have to be, not 'they are outside the trust,' but 'it is not proven whether they are in or out.' " His Lordship suggested that to require proof that every person was or was not within the class would return to the old rule requiring the making of a list. This seems doubtful. To be in a position to accept or reject the claim of any given person does not require ascertainment of the whole class. The "substantial number" test might be thought to be a return to the *Gibbard*[89] test which was rejected in *Gulbenkian*.[90] This is not so, as the *Gibbard*[91] test allowed a degree of conceptual uncertainty, while the statement of Megaw L.J. quoted above concerns evidential uncertainty. It is submitted that the majority view is to be preferred to the somewhat stricter test laid down by Stamp L.J., which seems to require that the trustees be in a position to say affirmatively whether any given person is within or outside the class. His Lordship considered that the validity or invalidity of a discretionary trust depended on[92] "whether you can say of any individual—and the accent must be on that word 'any' for it is not simply the individual whose claim you are considering who is spoken of—[that he] 'is or is not a member of the class,' for only thus can you make a survey of the range of objects or possible beneficiaries." If Stamp L.J. had not been able to construe "relatives" as meaning "next-of-kin" or "nearest blood relations" he would have held the trust void for uncertainty.[93]

(c) *Width of the Class; Administrative Unworkability.* Lord Wilberforce in *McPhail* v. *Doulton*[94] indicated that there might be a difference in one situation between the test to be applied to discretionary trusts and that for mere powers. A description of beneficiaries which might comply with the certainty test laid down might be "so hopelessly

---

[87] *Cf. Re Barlow's Will Trusts* [1979] 1 W.L.R. 278, *post*, p. 108.
[88] [1973] Ch. 9 at p. 24.
[89] [1967] 1 W.L.R. 42.
[90] [1970] A.C. 508.
[91] *Supra.*
[92] [1973] Ch. 9 at p. 28.
[93] The view of the majority was that it meant "descendants from a common ancestor." It has long been established that "relatives" should be confined to next of kin only if this is necessary to save the gift, *e.g.* where the "list test" applies. See *Re Shield's W.T.* [1974] 2 W.L.R. 885; *Re Barlow's W.T.* [1979] 1 W.L.R. 278; *Re Poulton's W.T.* [1987] 1 W.L.R. 795.
[94] [1971] A.C. 424; criticised on this point in (1974) 38 Conv.(n.s.) 269 (L. McKay); (1974) 37 M.L.R. 643 (Y. F. R. Grbich).

wide as not to form 'anything like a class,' so that the trust is administratively unworkable,"[95] and he hesitatingly gave as an example a
class consisting of "all the residents of Greater London." This was said
in the context of a discretionary trust. The question has arisen whether
this concept applies also to mere powers. Buckley L.J. assumed *obiter*
that it did in *Blausten* v. *I.R.C.*[96] This was doubted in *Re Manisty's
Settlement*,[97] where Templeman J. held that a mere power could not be
invalid on the ground of width of numbers, preferring the view that its
validity should depend on whether or not it was capricious. This point
is discussed below. *Manisty* was preferred to *Blausten* by Megarry
V.-C. in *Re Hay's Settlement Trusts*.[98] A mere power, whether or not
vested in a fiduciary, was not invalid on the ground of the size of the
class. Mere numbers could not prevent the trustee from considering
whether to exercise the power nor from performing his other duties,[99]
nor prevent the court from controlling him. But it was suggested that a
discretionary trust in favour of the same wide class[1] as the mere power
would have been void as administratively unworkable, as the duties of
a discretionary trustee were more stringent, and the objects of a
discretionary trust had rights of enforcement which objects of a mere
power lacked. A similar view was taken in *R.* v. *District Auditor, ex p.
West Yorkshire Metropolitan County Council*,[2] where a local
authority, purporting to act under statutory powers,[3] resolved to set up
a trust "for the benefit of any or all or some of the inhabitants of the
County of West Yorkshire."[4] There were 2,500,000 potential beneficiaries. The court was prepared to assume that "inhabitant" was sufficiently certain, but held the trust void for administrative unworkability
as the class was far too large, applying Lord Wilberforce's dictum in
McPhail v. *Doulton*.[5] *Re Manisty's Settlement*[6] was distinguished as
concerning a power, where the function of the court was more restricted. The weight of authority, therefore, supports the view that
"administrative unworkability" can invalidate discretionary trusts but
not mere powers.[7]

---

[95] *Ibid.* at p. 427.
[96] [1972] Ch. 256. The power was upheld because the trustees' power to include any
other person as an object was subject to the settlor's consent. The settlor had,
therefore, put "metes and bounds" on the otherwise unrestricted class.
[97] [1974] Ch. 17.
[98] [1982] 1 W.L.R. 202.
[99] *i.e.* to make no unauthorised appointment; to consider the range of objects; to
consider the appropriateness of any individual appointment.
[1] Any person except the settlor, settlor's spouse or trustees.
[2] (1986) 26 R.V.R. 24 (Q.B.D.); (1986) 45 C.L.J. 391 (C. Harpum).
[3] Local Government Act 1972, s.137(1).
[4] The details of the trust, which was not charitable, are given in Chap. 14, *post*, p. 345.
[5] *Supra.*
[6] *Supra.*
[7] *Cf.* [1982] Conv. 432 at p. 434 (A. Grubb) and (1982) 98 L.Q.R. 551 (C. T. Emery),
taking the view that it applies also to powers, and Riddall, *The Law of Trusts* (3rd ed.),
p. 24, taking the view that it applies also to fixed trusts.

(d) *Capriciousness.* There is no general principle of English law that a capricious disposition is invalid. Wigram V.-C. in *Bird* v. *Luckie*[8] said, "No man is bound to make a will in such a manner as to deserve approbation from the prudent, the wise, or the good. A testator is permitted to be capricious and improvident, and moreover is at liberty to conceal the circumstances and the motives by which he has been actuated in his dispositions."

But while a capricious legacy may be valid, the position may be otherwise in a discretionary trust or power. Unlike a straightforward gift in a will, discretionary trusts and powers involve fiduciary obligations, the performance of which may be rendered impossible if their terms are capricious. In upholding a power of great width in *Re Manisty's Settlement*[9] Templeman J. held that the terms of the power need not provide guidance to the trustees; an absolute discretion did not preclude a sensible consideration of whether and how to exercise the power. The example of a class comprising "residents of Greater London" would be capricious and void, not on the basis of numbers, but on the ground that the terms of the power negatived any sensible intention on the settlor's part and any sensible consideration by the trustees. The objects must either be unlimited, in which case the trustees can perform their obligations sensibly, or limited to a "sensible" class. The disposition would be void if membership of the class of objects was accidental and irrelevant to any purpose or to any method of limiting or selecting beneficiaries.[10]

Is "capriciousness" the same notion as "administrative unworkability?"[11] The latter, as we have seen, has been held inapplicable to mere powers, while the former has been held applicable to both mere powers and discretionary trusts.[12] In *R.* v. *District Auditor, ex p. West Yorkshire Metropolitan County Council*[13] a trust for the benefit of 2,500,000 inhabitants of West Yorkshire was held void for administrative unworkability (as being too large a class) even though it was not capricious because the local authority (the settlor) had every reason to wish to benefit the inhabitants in the ways specified. Thus it appears that the two concepts are distinct, although the same example may give rise to invalidity on both grounds. Capriciousness has no necessary connection with width of numbers, which is the characteristic of administrative unworkability.

It might also be mentioned that the capricious exercise of a fiduciary

---

[8] (1850) 8 Hare 301. See also *Re James's Will Trusts* [1962] Ch. 226.

[9] [1974] Ch. 17.

[10] *Ibid.* at p. 26. See [1982] Conv. 432 at p. 435 (A. Grubb) explaining that the "appointment criteria," necessary to avoid invalidity on the ground of capriciousness, need not be apparent from the power itself.

[11] See (1982) 98 L.Q.R. 551 (C. T. Emery) for the view that they are the same.

[12] See *Re Manisty's Settlement, supra*; *Re Hay's Settlement Trusts* [1982] 1 W.L.R. 202.

[13] (1986) 26 R.V.R. 24, (1986) 45 C.L.J. 391 (C. Harpum); *ante,* p. 104.

power or trust, as where objects are chosen by height or complexion, will be invalid even though the power or trust is valid.[14]

(e) *Duty to Survey the Field.* Clearly the trustees of a discretionary trust are not obliged to consider every object, as the trust may be valid although the identity of all the objects is not known. But, as we have seen, Lord Wilberforce in *McPhail* v. *Doulton*,[15] considered that the trustees ought to make such a survey of the range of objects as would enable them to carry out their fiduciary duty, and that a wider or more comprehensive range of enquiry was called for in the case of discretionary trusts than in the case of powers. In the case of a wide-ranging discretionary trust, where the number of objects may run to hundreds of thousands, the trustees' duty is to assess in a businesslike way "the size of the problem."[16] Megarry V.-C. in *Re Hay's Settlement Trusts*,[17] said:

> "The trustee must not simply proceed to exercise the power in favour of such of the objects as happen to be at hand or claim his attention. He must first consider what persons or classes of persons are objects of the power . . . there is no need to compile a complete list of the objects, or even to make an accurate assessment of the number of them: what is needed is an appreciation of the width of the field, and thus whether a selection is to be made merely from a dozen or, instead, from thousands or millions. . . . Only when the trustee has applied his mind to the 'size of the problem' should he then consider in individual cases whether, in relation to other possible claimants, a particular grant is appropriate. In doing this, no doubt he should not prefer the undeserving to the deserving; but he is not required to make an exact calculation whether, as between deserving claimants, A is more deserving than B."

This was the duty which had emerged from cases concerning discretionary trusts, but "plainly the requirements for a mere power cannot be more stringent than those for a discretionary trust."[18] The duties of a trustee of a discretionary trust are more stringent than those of the donee of a fiduciary mere power because of the obligation to distribute. The precise scope of the less onerous duty to survey in the case of a mere power awaits clarification.[19]

---

[14] *Re Manisty's Settlement, supra; Re Hay's Settlement Trusts, supra.*

[15] [1971] A.C. 424; criticised in (1974) 37 M.L.R. 643 (Y. F. R. Grbich).

[16] *Re Baden's Deed Trusts (No. 2)* [1973] Ch. 9 at p. 20 (*per* Sachs, L.J.).

[17] [1982] 1 W.L.R. 202 at pp. 209–210.

[18] *Ibid.* This may be contrasted with the view of Harman J. in *Re Gestetner* [1953] Ch. 672 at p. 688: " . . . there is no obligation on the trustees to do more than consider from time to time the merits of such persons of the specified class as are known to them. . . ." See also Templeman J. in *Re Manisty's Settlement* [1974] Ch. 14 at p. 25.

[19] See [1982] Conv. 432 at p. 437 (A. Grubb), suggesting that the duty is merely to consider those who press claims and present themselves for inspection; there is no need to "go forth and search out worthy candidates."

(f) *Many Certain Categories; One Uncertain.* Further difficulties could arise with a definition of a class of beneficiaries which contained a long series of categories which complied with the *McPhail* v. *Doulton* test, but to which there was added one category which did not. What, for example, would the court say to a trust in the same language as that in *McPhail* v. *Doulton* but to which there was added "any other person to whom I may be under a moral obligation and any of my old friends?" ... which is, let it be assumed, conceptually uncertain. The same problem could arise in a case of power.[20]

In this situation, the class as the whole does not satisfy the test. It would however be unfortunate to declare the whole trust void because of the final addition. After all, the trust is eminently workable as it is. Such a trust, however, may be held void unless it is possible to excise the offending phrase by the operation of a species of severance; a suggestion which is made on more than one occasion.[21] It would of course be valid if a return was made to the *Gibbard* test.[22]

(v) **Effect of Certainty Tests on Rights of Objects.** When, prior to *McPhail* v. *Doulton*,[23] complete ascertainment of objects was required in the case of a discretionary trust, it was thought that each object had a right to be considered, and to share in the fund if the trustees failed in their duty to exercise their discretion. Clearly this is no longer accurate, now that the trust may be valid without the necessity of ascertaining the full membership of the class. The question of equal division in default of exercise has already been dealt with.[24] Any right to be considered must be confined to the situation where the claim is brought to the attention of the trustees. The right of the object is simply to require that the trustees perform their obligation to allocate the fund after surveying the range of objects, as described above.[25] If the unknown or unascertainable object is not considered by the trustees, at any rate he is no worse off than he would have been prior to *McPhail* v. *Doulton*,[26] when the possibility of his existence would have caused the discretionary trust to fail.

(vi) **Trust-Powers in the Old Sense; Trusts with a Power of Selection.** If, as a matter of construction, it can be inferred that the settlor's intention was that the entire class should take if the trustee failed to make a selection, then no doubt equal division is still appropriate, in which case the "complete ascertainment" test must still be satisfied.

---

[20] *Post*, Chap. 6.
[21] *Per* Sachs L.J. in *Re Leek* [1969] 1 Ch. 563 at p. 586; and in the case of a power, by Winn L.J. in *Re Gulbenkian's Settlements* [1968] Ch. 126 at p. 138 (C.A.). *Cf.* decisions on trusts which are not exclusively charitable; *post*, p. 424.
[22] [1967] 1 W.L.R. 42.
[23] [1971] A.C. 424.
[24] *Ante*, p. 99.
[25] See generally *Re Hay's Settlement Trusts*, *supra*; *Turner* v. *Turner* [1984] Ch. 100.
[26] *Supra*.

This is more likely to be the case in a family trust, where the objects are not large in number, as in *Burrough* v. *Philcox*.[27] It may be that the minority and the majority in *McPhail* v. *Doulton*[28] were talking at cross-purposes, the former having in mind the more old-fashioned trust-power as described above, while the latter analysed the modern discretionary trust in favour of a large class, where the settlor could not have contemplated equal division.[29]

(vii) Gifts Subject to a Condition Precedent. A less strict test than that laid down in *McPhail* v. *Doulton*[30] applies where there is a gift subject to a condition precedent as opposed to a discretionary trust or power. A degree of conceptual uncertainty does not invalidate such a gift.[31] The test, as laid down in *Re Allen*,[32] is that the gift is valid if it is possible to say that one or more persons qualify, even though there may be difficulty as to others.

This test fell to be considered by Browne-Wilkinson J. in *Re Barlow's Will Trust*,[33] where the testatrix left a valuable collection of paintings, directing her executor to sell those not specifically bequeathed, subject to a proviso that "any friends of mine who may wish to do so" be allowed to purchase any of them at a price below the market value. This disposition was held sufficiently certain. Total ascertainment of the testatrix's friends was not required. A "friend" was a person who had a relationship of long standing with the testatrix, which was a social as opposed to a business or professional relationship, and who had met her frequently when circumstances permitted.[34] The effect of the gift was to confer on her friends a series of options to purchase. There was no legal necessity to inform them of their rights, although this would be desirable. The claimant must prove "by any reasonable test" that he qualified.[35] In case of doubt, the executors could apply to the court for directions. The justification for this less strict test was that in the case of individual gifts, unlike trusts and

---

[27] (1840) 5 Myl. & Cr. 72; *ante*, p. 64.

[28] *Supra*.

[29] See (1974) 37 M.L.R. 643 (Y. F. R. Grbich); (1982) 98 L.Q.R. 551 (C. T. Emery). For the proper meaning of "trust power", see [1984] Conv. 227 (R. Bartlett and C. Stebbings).

[30] [1971] A.C. 424.

[31] A stricter test applies to a condition subsequent. The distinction, though criticised by Lord Denning M.R. in *Re Tuck's Settlement Trusts* [1978] Ch. 49, was acknowledged by the House of Lords in *Blathwayt* v. *Lord Cawley* [1976] A.C. 397 at p. 425; *post*, p. 320. See also *Re Tepper's Will Trusts* [1987] Ch. 358.

[32] [1953] Ch. 810. It is suggested in (1982) 98 L.Q.R. 551 (C. T. Emery) that this should also apply to non-fiduciary mere powers.

[33] [1979] 1 W.L.R. 278; criticised [1980] Conv. 263 (L. McKay), (1982) 98 L.Q.R. 551 (C. T. Emery). See also Hayton and Marshall (8th ed.), pp. 147–149.

[34] [1979] 1 W.L.R. 278 at p. 282.

[35] *Cf. Re Baden's Deed Trusts (No. 2)* [1973] Ch. 9, where the onus of proof on the claimant concerns evidential, and not conceptual, uncertainty.

powers, uncertainty as to some beneficiaries did not affect the quantum of the gift in respect of those who clearly qualified. To uphold the gift in the case of the latter gave effect, at least in part, to the donor's intention.[36]

Although the "condition precedent" test is now settled, this decision illustrates the difficulties inherent in it. The trustees could be in real difficulty in giving effect to such a disposition. The solution that trustees could apply to court in cases of doubt is unsatisfactory. How can the court be in any better position than the trustees to pronounce on the question whether X is a "friend" of Y?

[36] This has not been regarded as sufficient to justify a less strict test in the case of trusts and powers.

CHAPTER 4

CONSTITUTION OF TRUSTS
EQUITY WILL NOT ASSIST A VOLUNTEER

1. THE GENERAL PROBLEM

A. Requirements of Conveyance and Declaration

We have seen that the interest of the beneficiary under a trust is a proprietary interest.[1] The legal title is in the trustee; the equitable and benficial title is in the beneficiary. The trust may be of any form of property—land, chattels, money, choses in action—and for any interest known to the law, whether legal or equitable, in possession, remainder[2] or reversion. A manifestation of an intention to create a trust is, as we have seen, one of the requirements for the creation of an express trust.[3] But it is not sufficient in itself. To declare that A is to hold Blackacre on trust for B does not create a trust unless Blackacre is conveyed to A. Similarly, a conveyance to A does not create a trust of

---

[1] *Ante*, p. 17; *post*, p. 199.
[2] *Re Ralli's W.T.* [1964] Ch. 288.
[3] *Ante*, p. 93.

110

Blackacre for B unless the trust is properly declared. In short, it is necessary both to declare the trust *and* to convey the property to the trustee.

This is self-evident. But many difficulties have been caused by failure to observe these basic propositions. And, even where they are observed, complications can arise. And a number of questions are left open. Is it necessary that the conveyance and the declaration be contemporaneous? If X conveys Blackacre to A to hold upon trust for B, a trust is created in favour of B; or if X conveys to A upon trust and later declares the trusts.[4] If X conveys Blackacre to A, can he then tell A to hold on trust for B? No; because after the conveyance A became the absolute owner. May the declaration precede the conveyance? May X create a trust for B by declaring that A is to hold on trust for B; and later convey Blackacre to A? This question raises a number of difficulties as we will see; they will be discussed in this chapter and also in Chapter 5.

B. Methods of Benefiting an Intended Donee

There are various ways in which an owner of property can benefit another person. If X is the owner at law and in equity, he can make B the beneficial owner in any one of three ways:

(i) Outright Transfer. He can transfer legal and equitable ownership to B. In the case of land, this transaction is called a conveyance. With a chattel, it is called a sale or gift; with a chose in action, it is called an assignment; with shares it is usually called a transfer. Whatever type of transaction, X, by following the correct procedure appropriate to the type of property, can transfer his absolute interest, legal and equitable, to B. The converse is almost too obvious to state: if X does not follow the correct procedure, he will not transfer the legal or beneficial interest to B. This self-evident proposition is stated here because arguments have unsuccessfully been raised to the effect that an attempted but unsuccessful transfer to B might be construed as a declaration of trust for B. It is not.[5]

(ii) Transfer to Trustee. X may transfer the legal title in the property to A to hold on trust for B. Provided that the legal title is correctly transferred to A, according to the type of property concerned, A will become legal owner; and provided that an intention to create a trust in favour of B is sufficiently manifested, B will become equitable and beneficial owner. A holds on trust for B.

(iii) Declaration of Self as Trustee. X may declare that he holds the

---

[4] *Re Tyler* [1967] 1 W.L.R. 1269; *post*, p. 156. *Grey* v. *I.R.C.* [1960] A.C. 1; *ante*, p. 82.
[5] *Post*, pp. 113 *et seq.*

property on trust for B. In this situation all that is necessary is a declaration of trust in favour of B. There is no problem of the legal estate being vested in the trustee. It was, and remains, in X, who is the trustee, holding on trust for B. These three situations should be borne in mind in the discussion which follows.

C. Contracts to Convey or to Create a Trust

Situations (ii) and (iii) concern the creation of trusts in the strict sense. B in each case will obtain an equitable proprietary interest. In such a situation, it is immaterial whether B gave consideration or not. A gift confers title just as effectively as a sale.

If, however, the transaction in question had been *in*effective to transfer the legal title from X to B in situation (i), what is B's position? If B gave no consideration there is nothing more that he can do; the gift fails, just as it would fail if a Christmas present were promised and not given. Equity will not assist a volunteer. But if B gave consideration, the position is different. B would be in a contractual relation with X, and could either sue X for damages for breach, or, in appropriate circumstances, obtain specific performance of the contract.[6] If, in situation (ii), B gave consideration for the promise by X to convey to A on trust for B, or—more realistically, for this question usually arises in connection with marriage settlements—if B is treated as being within the marriage consideration,[7] B can compel his trustee A to take proceedings against X, either to obtain the property or damages for breach, and to hold the property or the damages on the trusts declared. Thus, B, being treated as one who gave consideration and not as a volunteer, is entitled to enforce the promise; and, in accordance with the principle that equity considers as done that which ought to be done, may be treated as entitled in equity to the property which was the subject of the promise.[8]

D. Absolute Beneficial Owner under a Trust

Reference should also be made here to the question of the way in which an absolute owner in equity (the legal title being in trustees) may create interests in favour of other persons out of his equitable interest.

In a well-known statement in *Timpson's Executors* v. *Yerbury*,[9] Romer L.J. said: "Now the equitable interest in property in the hands of a trustee can be disposed of by the person entitled to it in favour of a third party in any one of four . . . ways. The person entitled to it (1) can assign it to a the third party directly; (2) can direct the trustees to hold the property in trust for the third party (see *per* Sargant J. in *Re Chrimes*[10]); (3) can contract for valuable consideration to assign the

---

[6] *Post*, pp. 651 *et seq.*
[7] *Post*, pp. 120 *et seq.*
[8] See *Pullan* v. *Koe* [1913] 1 Ch. 9; *post*, p. 121.
[9] [1936] 1 K.B. 645 at p. 664; *Grey* v. *I.R.C.* [1958] Ch. 690 at p. 709 (C.A.).
[10] [1917] 1 Ch. 30.

equitable interest to him; or (4) can declare himself to be a trustee for him of such interest." Category (2), as Lord Evershed pointed out in *Grey* v. *I.R.C.*[11] "appears ... to have been regarded as distinct from both an assignment, on the one hand, and a declaration of trust of the interest in the beneficial owner's hands, on the other."

We know however that such a direction is a "disposition" within Law of Property Act 1925, s.53, according to the wide construction put upon that word by the House of Lords,[12] and required therefore to be in writing. The writing need not include the names of the new beneficiaries.[13] And if the beneficial owner does not direct the trustees to hold the property on particular trusts, but authorises them to transfer the legal estate to donees, then the beneficial interest passes to the donees without express mention.[14]

It should also be noted that category (4) creates what is usually called a sub-trust; a situation in which A holds property on trust for B, and B declares himself to be trustee of his interest for C. Unless B has specific duties to perform, he is a bare trustee and drops out, the original trustee A holding on trust for C.[15]

2. TRANSFER OF THE PROPERTY TO TRUSTEES UPON TRUST

A. Legal Interests

The classic statement of the law relating to the requirement of a transfer of the property to trustees is that of Turner L.J. in *Milroy* v. *Lord*[16]:

> "I take the law of this Court to be well settled, that, in order to render a voluntary settlement valid and effectual, the settlor must have done everything which, according to the nature of the property comprised in the settlement, was necessary to be done in order to transfer the property and render the settlement binding upon him. He may, of course, do this by actually transferring the property to the persons for whom he intends to provide, and the provision will then be effectual, and it will be equally effectual if he transfers the property to a trustee for the purposes of the settlement, or declares that he himself holds it in trust for those purposes; and if the property be personal, the trust may, as I apprehend, be declared either in writing or by parol; but, in order to render the settlement binding, one or other of these modes must, as I understand the law

[11] [1958] Ch. 690 at p. 709 (C.A.).
[12] *Grey* v. *I.R.C.* [1960] A.C. 1; *ante*, p. 82.
[13] *Re Tyler* [1967] 1 W.L.R. 1269.
[14] *Vandervell* v. *I.R.C.* [1967] 2 A.C. 291; *ante*, p. 83.
[15] *Grainge* v. *Wilberforce* (1889) 5 T.L.R. 436, *per* Chitty J. at p. 437; *Grey* v. *I.R.C.* [1958] Ch. 375 at p. 382, *per* Upjohn J.; queried (1966) 25 C.L.J. 22; *ante*, p. 87.
[16] (1862) 4 De G.F. & J. 264 at pp. 274–275. For the position where the trustee disclaims, see *Mallott* v. *Wilson* [1903] 2 Ch. 494; [1981] Conv. 141 (P. Matthews).

of this court, be resorted to, for there is no equity in this court to perfect an imperfect gift. The cases, I think, go further to this extent, that if the settlement is intended to be effectuated by one of the modes to which I have referred, the Court will not give effect to it by applying another of those modes. If it is intended to take effect by transfer, the court will not hold the intended transfer to operate as a declaration of trust, for then every imperfect instrument would be made effectual by being converted into a perfect trust."

The transfer to the trustees must accord with the rules applicable to the property concerned. Legal estates in land must be transferred by deed,[17] shares by the appropriate form of transfer,[18] equitable interests[19] and copyright[20] by writing, chattels by deed of gift or by an intention to give coupled with a delivery of possession,[21] a bill of exchange by endorsement.[22]

In *Milroy* v. *Lord*,[23] a settlor executed a voluntary deed purporting to transfer shares in the Bank of Louisiana to Samuel Lord to be held on trust for the plaintiff. The shares, however, could only be transferred by the appropriate transfer form followed by registration of the name of the transferee in the books of the Bank. Lord held a power of attorney to act on behalf of the settlor, and it would have enabled him to take all necessary further steps to obtain registration. But this was not done. The Court of Appeal in Chancery held that there was no trust, although the intention clearly was to benefit the intended beneficiary.

On the other hand, once the property has been vested in the trustees, and the trusts declared, the trust is constituted, and the settlor is unable to reclaim the property, even though the beneficiaries may be volunteers.[24] And the trust may be constituted where the property is vested in the trustees, even though it reached them in a capacity distinct from their office as trustees of the trust in question.

---

[17] L.P.A. 1925, s.52(1). Registration is necessary if the title is registered under L.R.A. 1925. See *Mascall* v. *Mascall, post*, p. 117.

[18] See Companies Act 1985, ss.182, 183; Stock Transfer Act 1963, s.1.

[19] L.P.A. 1925, s.53(1).

[20] Copyright Designs and Patents Act 1988, s.90(3).

[21] *Ryall* v. *Rolls* (1750) 1 Ves.Sen. 348; *Irons* v. *Smallpiece* (1819) 2 B. & A. 551; *Cochrane* v. *Moore* (1890) 25 Q.B.D. 57; *Lock* v. *Heath* (1892) 8 T.L.R. 295; *Kilpin* v. *Raltey* [1892] 1 Q.B. 582; *Re Cole* [1964] Ch. 175; *Thomas* v. *Times Book Co. Ltd.* [1966] 1 W.L.R. 911; (1953) 12 C.L.J. 355 (J. W. A. Thornely); (1964) 27 M.L.R. 357 (A. C. Diamond).

[22] Bills of Exchange Act 1882, s.31; *Whistler* v. *Forster* (1863) 14 C.B.(N.S.) 248; see, however, Cheques Act 1957, ss.1, 2.

[23] (1862) 4 De G.F. & J. 264.

[24] *Paul* v. *Paul* (1882) 20 Ch.D. 742; *Jefferys* v. *Jefferys* (1841) Cr. & Ph. 138; *Re Ellenborough* [1903] 1 Ch. 697 (the assets received under her sister's will); *Re Bowden* [1936] Ch. 71; similarly for voluntary covenants to settle: *Re Adlard* [1954] Ch. 29.

In *Re Ralli's Will Trusts*,[25] a testator left his residuary estate on trust for his widow for life and then for his two daughters Irene and Helen. Helen's marriage settlement included a covenant to settle after-acquired property in favour of (in the events which happened) volunteers. Helen died and then the widow died. The plaintiff was the sole surviving trustee both of the testator's will and also of Helen's marriage settlement. Buckley J. had to decide on what trusts the residue was held. He concluded, as one ground for his decision, that the vesting of the property in the plaintiff was sufficient to constitute the trusts of the marriage settlement even though the property came to him in his other capacity as trustee of the will. "The circumstances that the plaintiff holds the fund because he was appointed a trustee of the will is irrelevant. He is at law the owner of the fund, and the means by which he became so have no effect upon the quality of his legal ownership."[26]

B. Equitable Interests

The same general principle applies where the settlor's interest is equitable. A correct transfer of the equitable interest to a trustee upon properly declared trusts is necessary to create a trust of that equitable interest. A disposition of an equitable interest must, as has been seen, be in writing.[27]

In *Kekewich* v. *Manning*,[28] shares were held on trust for A for life and then for B. B assigned his equitable interest in remainder to trustees to hold on certain trusts, and this was held to create a trust of the equitable interest in remainder.

C. Act of Third Party Required to Perfect Title

Difficulties can arise where the act of a third party is necessary to perfect the transfer of legal title. The problem commonly involves shares, the legal title to which is transferable by the execution of the form of transfer required by the company's articles, followed by registration in the share register of the company.[29] If the transaction is for consideration, the purchaser becomes equitable owner of the shares from the date of the execution of the document of transfer, and is entitled to dividends declared after that date.[30]

The transfer of shares in a private company is restricted, and the Articles usually provide that the directors shall have power at their discretion to refuse to register the transfer. A difficult situation arises where a settlor makes a voluntary settlement of shares in such a

---

[25] [1964] Ch. 288; *cf. Brooks' S.T.* [1939] 1 Ch. 993, where the contrary conclusion is reached.
[26] *Ibid.* at p. 301.
[27] L.P.A., s.53(1)(*c*); *ante*, p. 81.
[28] (1851) 1 De G.M. & G. 176; *Gilbert* v. *Overton* (1864) 22 H. & M. 110.
[29] See Companies Act 1985, ss.182, 183. Stock Transfer Act 1963, s.1.
[30] *Black* v. *Homersham* (1878) 4 Ex.D. 24; *Re Wimbush* [1940] Ch. 92.

company, executing a transfer which purports to transfer the shares to
trustees to be held on the trusts of the settlement. The expectation is
that the registration of the transfer will follow and the trust become
constituted. The directors however may refuse to register the transfer.
In that case, under the strict rule of *Milroy* v. *Lord*,[31] the trust will be
incompletely constituted and a nullity. The validity of the trust would
be dependent upon the uncontrollable discretion of the directors.
And, even if they do register it, the date on which this happens may be
crucial in determining whether the transfer is liable to inheritance tax
at the full death rate applicable to gifts made within three years of
death or at the lower rates for gifts made three to seven years before
death.[32]

In *Re Rose*,[33] a settlor by voluntary deed transferred shares in a
private company to trustees to be held on certain trusts. The directors, who had power to refuse to register transfers, registered this
transfer some two months later. The deceased died at a time at
which the shares would be treated as part of his estate for estate
duty[34] purposes if the date of the transfer were the date of registration; but would not be so treated if the date was the date of the deed.
The Court of Appeal held that the relevant date was that of the
deed; for the settlor had at that time done everything possible to
divest himself of the property. All that was needed in addition was
the formal act of registration by the third party.

Evershed M.R. went so far as to say that after the execution of the
transfer, the settlor held the shares as trustee for the beneficiaries.[35]
He did not however give any convincing answer to the Crown's argument that, consistently with Turner L.J.'s judgment in *Milroy* v.
Lord,[36] the transfer was either a valid transfer at law; or a declaration

---

[31] (1862) 4 De. G.F. & J. 264. There, however, the correct transfer form was not used.
[32] I.H.T.A. 1984, s.7; *post*, p. 213.
[33] [1952] Ch. 499; *Re Fry* [1946] Ch. 312; *Re Rose* [1949] Ch. 78; *Re Paradise Motor Co.
Ltd.* [1968] 1 W.L.R. 1125; *Vandervell* v. *I.R.C.* [1967] 2 A.C. 291 at p. 330.
[34] *Inter vivos* gifts were not liable to estate duty unless they were made within a specified
number of years before the death. Estate duty was replaced by Capital Transfer Tax,
in turn replaced by Inheritance Tax in Finance Act 1986. This tax is chargeable on
death and, on a sliding scale, on gifts made within seven years of death. It is also
chargeable on certain lifetime gifts made outside the seven-year period, but at half the
death rate.
[35] "If a man executes a document transferring all his equitable interest, say, in shares,
that document, operating, and intended to operate, as a transfer, will give rise to and
take effect as a trust; for the assignor will then be a trustee of the legal estate in the
shares for the person in whose favour he has made an assignment of his beneficial
interest." [1952] Ch. 499 at p. 510. See Oakley, *Constructive Trusts* (2nd ed.), p. 178,
suggesting that a constructive trust arises in these circumstances.
[36] (1862) 4 De G.F. & J. 264; *ante*, p. 113.

of trust; or it was ineffective. The settlor clearly did not intend to declare himself a trustee,[37] and would have been surprised to have been told that, if the directors had refused to register, he was unable to withdraw from the transfer because he was a trustee; or that he was required to exercise the voting powers conferred by the shares in the interests of the beneficiaries.[38] *Re Rose* thus creates a number of theoretical difficulties.[39] It is submitted, however, that it is an eminently sensible decision in a context in which the liability to tax may be affected by the date on which the transfer is treated as being effective. The transfer of shares, for this reason, may be treated as a special situation.[40] *Re Rose* can be contrasted with *Re Fry*,[41] where the donor was domiciled abroad, and had not, at the critical time, done everything that was needed of him, as he had not obtained Treasury consent to the transfer.

The *Re Rose* principle was applied to a transfer of registered land in *Mascall* v. *Mascall*,[42] where a father executed a transfer of a house to his son, a volunteer, and handed over the land certificate. After the transfer had been sent to the Inland Revenue for stamping, and returned, the father (having fallen out with the son), sought a declaration that the transfer was ineffective. The son had not yet sent the documents to the Land Registry in order to become registered proprietor and had, therefore, not acquired legal title.[43] It was held that the gift was complete. The father had done all that he could, as the application to the Land Registry could be made by the son, from whom the father had no right to recover the transfer and land certificate.

3. Declaration of Self as Trustee

There is no difficulty in the way of a settlor who wishes to declare himself trustee of some or all of his property. All that is needed is a manifestation of an intention to declare a trust; and, if the property is land, evidence in writing of such intent. The settlor "need not use the words, 'I declare myself a trustee,' but he must do something which is equivalent to it, and use expressions which have that meaning; for, however anxious the Court may be to carry out a man's intention, it is not at liberty to construe words otherwise than according to their proper meaning."[44] It is necessary to show, not only an intention to

---

[37] *Jones* v. *Lock* (1865) L.R. 1 Ch.App. 25.

[38] *Butt* v. *Kelsen* [1952] Ch. 197; *cf. Re George Whichelow Ltd.* [1954] 1 W.L.R. 5.

[39] (1976) 40 Conv.(n.s.) 139 (L. McKay), criticising the reasoning.

[40] *Re Rose* was described in *Rowlandson* v. *National Westminster Bank Ltd.* [1978] 1 W.L.R. 798 at p. 802 as a "gloss" on the principle of perfect gifts.

[41] [1946] Ch. 312 (he had, however, applied for consent); *Re Transatlantic Life Assurance Co. Ltd.* [1980] 1 W.L.R. 79; Keeton & Sheridan's *Equity* (3rd ed.), p. 246.

[42] (1985) 49 P. & C.R. 119. See also Meagher, Gummow and Lehane, *Equitable Doctrines and Remedies*, pp. 163–164.

[43] L.R.A. 1925, s.19.

[44] *Richards* v. *Delbridge* (1874) L.R. 18 Eq. 11 at p. 14, *per* Jessel M.R.

benefit someone; but an intention to be trustee for that person. "Men often mean to give things to their kinsfolk, they do not often mean to constitute themselves trustees. An imperfect gift is no declaration of trust."[45]

The issues which arise in this section are quite different from those discussed in section 2. There, the question was whether the property was vested in the trustee. Here, there is no such problem; if there is a trust the settlor is trustee. The question here is whether a trust has properly been declared. The problems in this section usually arise in cases where the settlor's intention was to make a gift to a donee but the gift failed, and the question is whether the intent to benefit the donee can be construed as a declaration of trust in his favour.

The rule is that equity will not construe a void gift as a declaration of trust. What is needed is a manifestation of an intention to declare a trust.

In *Jones* v. *Lock*,[46] a father, being chided for failing to bring a present from Birmingham for his nine-month-old son, produced a £900 cheque payable to himself, saying: "Look you here, I give this to baby; it is for himself." He gave it to the child, who was about to tear it up, and the father took it away and put it in an iron safe. The father died and the cheque was found among his effects.

The question was whether the child was entitled to the cheque or whether it formed part of the father's estate. It would belong to the father unless he gave it to the child, or declared himself trustee of it. Clearly, he had not given it to the child, because a gift of a non-bearer cheque requires endorsement.[47] Had he declared himself trustee? No. He intended to give it to the child. But there was no evidence of the fact that he intended to declare himself trustee of it, and to burden himself with a trustee's duties in respect of it, including that of investing it in trustee securities and being personally liable for failure to do so. There was no such intention here; nor was there an effective gift. The child took nothing.[48]

Similarly, in *Richards* v. *Delbridge*,[49] a grandfather, who was entitled to leasehold premises on which he carried on business, endorsed on the lease a memorandum as follows: "This deed and all thereto belonging I give to [R who was a minor] from this time forth, with all the stock-in-trade." He delivered the document to R's mother, and then died, making no mention of the property in his will. Jessel M.R. held that no interest passed; not at law, because the

[45] Maitland, p. 72.

[46] (1865) L.R. 1 Ch.App. 25.

[47] Under the Cheques Act 1957, s.2, indorsements in blank of cheques payable to order are no longer necessary so far as the rights of a collecting bank are concerned.

[48] *cf. Re Rose* [1952] Ch. 499; *ante,* p. 116.

[49] (1874) L.R. 18 Eq. 11; *cf. Middleton* v. *Pollock* (1876) 2 Ch.D. 104, where there was evidence in a memorandum of the declaration of trust.

endorsement was ineffective to assign a lease; and not in equity, for the words were inappropriate for the declaration of a trust.

These cases may be contrasted with the situation where the legal owner has not attempted to transfer the property to the third party, but has shown that he considers himself to hold the property as trustee for the third party. Whether or not, in any case, the evidence is sufficient will depend on the facts of the case; it has been held that the intent can be implied from conduct where the evidence is clear.[50]

So in *Paul* v. *Constance*[51] the conduct of the parties was sufficient to manifest an intention to declare a trust. In that case Mr. Constance was separated from his wife, and lived with the plaintiff. He received, as damages for an injury suffered at work, a cheque for £950 and he and the plaintiff decided to put it into a deposit account at Lloyds Bank. The account was opened in the name of Mr. Constance only; because he and the plaintiff felt an embarrassment in opening a joint account in different names. Mr. Constance indicated on many occasions that the money was as much the plaintiff's as his. On his death, the widow claimed the assets in the account as part of her husband's estate. The question was whether the assets were owned beneficially by Mr. Constance, or whether, on the particular facts, he had manifested an intention to hold the property as trustee for the plaintiff, or as trustee for the two of them in equal shares. The Court of Appeal found, affirming the county court judge, that the evidence was sufficient to manifest an intention in Mr. Constance to declare himself a trustee; although it was not easy to pinpoint a specific moment of declaration.[52] The plaintiff was thus able to recover half of the proceeds of the account.

A lenient view of the requirements of a declaration of trust was taken by the Court of Appeal in *Re Vandervell's Trusts (No. 2)*.[53] An option to purchase certain shares was held by trustees on a resulting trust for Vandervell. The trustees exercised the option, using money from Vandervell's children's settlement. It was held that the shares were henceforth held on trust for the children's settlement. There was no declaration of trust by Vandervell, but such a declaration could be inferred from certain acts of the trustees: first, the use of the money from the children's settlement; secondly, the subsequent payment of the dividends to that settlement; and thirdly, the trustees' notification

---

[50] *Gee* v. *Liddell* (1866) 35 Beav. 621; *New, Prance and Garrard's Trustee* v. *Hunting* [1897] 2 Q.B. 19. See also *Re Kayford Ltd.* [1975] 1 W.L.R. 279; *Re Chelsea Cloisters Ltd.* (1981) 41 P. & C.R. 98; *ante*, p. 52.

[51] [1977] 1 W.L.R. 54; convincingly criticised in Heydon, Gummow and Austin, *Cases and Materials on Equity and Trusts* (2nd ed.), pp. 118–119: "The law of express trusts normally requires an intention to benefit the *cestui que trust* specifically by way of trust—a mere intention to benefit him in some way is insufficient."

[52] This could cause problems. See Heydon, Gummow and Austin, *op. cit.*, at p. 119.

[53] [1974] Ch. 269; *ante*, p. 85; *post*, p. 239.

to the Revenue that they now held the shares on trust for that settlement. Although trustees cannot normally declare a trust, these acts were "acquiesced in" by Vandervell. The inadequacy of these three acts as establishing a declaration of trust lies in the fact that the second and third merely indicate what the trustees thought the position to be, while the first ignores Vandervell's beneficial ownership of the option. This is further examined elsewhere.[54]

It will be noted that it is not necessary that the beneficiary should be aware of the declaration of trust.[55] The beneficiary becomes equitable owner just as he would become legal owner if the property had been transferred by conveyance *inter vivos*.

4. COVENANTS TO SETTLE

If a settlor has neither conveyed the property to trustees nor declared himself a trustee, no trust is created. If he has covenanted by deed to settle the property, the crucial question is whether or not the intended beneficiary can compel him to carry out the covenant and settle it. A beneficiary who has given consideration can do so by obtaining specific performance of the covenant; one who has not given consideration cannot do so. Equity will not assist a volunteer.

For this purpose, "consideration" has a wider meaning than that which it bears at common law. The term includes everything which would be included by the common law[56]; but equity also treats as having given consideration, in the case of a covenant in a marriage settlement, the husband and wife and issue of the marriage.[57] They are said to be "within the marriage consideration."[58] It appears that the "issue" of the marriage refers not only to children but also to more remote issue.[59] It seems, however, that illegitimate children,[60] children by a former marriage, and children to whom one of the parties stands *in loco parentis*, cannot be included unless their interests are so closely intertwined with those of the natural issue of the marriage that the

---

[54] *Ante*, p. 85; *post*, p. 239.
[55] *Middleton* v. *Pollock* (1876) 2 Ch.D. 104; *Standing* v. *Bowring* (1885) 31 Ch.D. 282.
[56] Cheshire, Fifoot and Furmston, *The Law of Contract* (11th ed.), Chap. 4; Treitel, *The Law of Contract* (7th ed.), Chap. 3.
[57] *Harvey* v. *Ashley* (1748) 3 Atk. 607 at p. 610; *Hill* v. *Gomme* (1839) 5 Myl. & Cr. 250 at p. 254; *De Mestre* v. *West* [1891] A.C. 264; *Att.-Gen.* v. *Jacobs-Smith* [1895] 2 Q.B. 341.
[58] This is so whether the settlement is made on the marriage, or made before but in consideration of the marriage, or a post-nuptial settlement in pursuance of an ante-nuptial agreement.
[59] *MacDonald* v. *Scott* [1893] A.C. 642.
[60] This principle seems unaffected by the Family Law Reform Act 1987, which in general equates the rights of children of married and unmarried parents.

latter may be said to take only on terms which admit the former to a participation with them.[61]

In *Pullan* v. *Koe*,[62] a marriage settlement of 1859 settled property on trusts in favour of husband and wife and prospective children, and also contained a covenant by the wife to settle on the same trusts any property she later acquired of the value of £100 and upwards. In 1879 the wife received £285, part of which was used for her own purposes and part invested in bearer bonds, which remained at the bank in the husband's name until his death in 1909. The question was whether the trustees could then take steps to obtain the bonds from his executors and hold them on the trusts of the settlement.

Swinfen-Eady J. held that it was the duty of the trustees to enforce the covenant on behalf of those who were within the marriage consideration. Indeed, the wife and children could have taken action themselves if the trustees had refused to do so. Here, however, the common law action on the covenant was barred by the lapse of time; but the court held that the £285 was impressed with the trust at the moment the wife received it, and that the trust could be enforced against the bonds.

Such a covenant would not however be enforceable in favour of next-of-kin, for they are volunteers.[63] Thus, if a marriage settlement contained a similar covenant to settle after-acquired property, and there were no children of the marriage, there is no way in which the husband and wife could be prevented from ignoring the covenant and keeping after-acquired property for themselves. The next-of-kin, or other persons who take in default of children, will not be able to enforce the covenant. It was however suggested in one case that the wife could not keep both her interest under the settlement and also the after-acquired property, but should be put to her election.[64] It is doubtful whether the doctrine of election would be applied so generally.

Where the covenant is enforced by persons within the marriage consideration, the court may order the covenantor to settle the property in accordance with the covenant; or, as in *Pullan* v. *Koe*,[65] declare that the property is subject to the trusts of the settlement. However where one of the intended beneficiaries is a party[66] to the

---

[61] See *Att.-Gen.* v. *Jacobs-Smith* [1895] 2 Q.B. 341; *Rennell* v. *I.R.C.* [1962] Ch. 329 at p. 341, *per* Lord Evershed M.R., affd. [1964] A.C. 173; *Re Cook's S.T.* [1965] Ch. 902 at p. 914.

[62] [1913] 1 Ch. 9. See (1979) 32 C.L.P. 1 at pp. 4–5 (C. E. F. Rickett).

[63] *Re D'Angibau* (1880) 15 Ch.D. 228; *Re Plumptre's Marriage Settlement* [1901] 1 Ch. 609; *Re Cook's S.T.* [1965] Ch. 902. Nor will it be enforceable on this principle if, although for consideration, the covenant is not specifically enforceable, as in the case of a covenant to pay money; *Stone* v. *Stone* (1869) 5 Ch.App. 74; Pettit, p. 89.

[64] *Re Vardon's Trusts* (1885) 31 Ch.D. 275; *post*, p. 819.

[65] [1913] 1 Ch. 9, *supra*.

[66] For the meaning of which, see *Beswick* v. *Beswick* [1968] A.C. 58 at p. 102.

covenant, even though a volunteer, there is no reason why an action on the covenant for damages should not be brought, although the equitable remedy of specific performance would not lie.

In *Cannon* v. *Hartley*,[67] a settlement upon a separation, to which the spouses and a daughter were parties, provided that the father should pay to the daughter any sum exceeding £1,000 which he might inherit from his parents. Having inherited, he failed to make the payment. The daughter was a volunteer; she could not take advantage of the rule about marriage consideration because the settlement was not one made in consideration of marriage. She could however sue upon her father's covenant under seal, and recover damages for breach of covenant at common law.

5. ACTION FOR DAMAGES BY THE TRUSTEES. TRUSTS OF CHOSES IN ACTION

There is no special difficulty in enforcing a trust of a chose in action.[68] Where a contractual right is held by A on trust for B, A may sue and obtain damages or a decree of specific performance on behalf of B[69]; or B may obtain such relief on his own account if A refuses to act, joining A as a co-defendant in the action.[70]

It may well be asked why this doctrine is not applied to assist a volunteer in the case of a covenant to settle existing or after-acquired property.[71] If a husband or wife covenants with a trustee A to settle after-acquired property in favour of the children of the marriage, and in default in favour of the next-of-kin, we have seen that the next-of-kin, being volunteers, are unable to sue on the covenant.[72] Could not the trustees sue, recover damages, and hold them in trust for the next-of-kin?[73] Or could not the next-of-kin argue that there is already a completely constituted trust of the benefit of the covenant, a trust of a

---

[67] [1949] Ch. 213. See generally (1988) 8 L.S. 172 (M.R.T. Macnair), suggesting that there is some historical support for allowing specific performance of covenants in favour of volunteers.

[68] *Post*, p. 125. For recent examples, see *Barclays Bank plc* v. *Willowbrook International Ltd.* [1987] 1 F.T.L.R. 386; *Harrison* v. *Tew, The Times*, November 30, 1988.

[69] *Lloyd's* v. *Harper* (1880) 16 Ch.D. 290. See, however, *Jackson* v. *Horizon Holidays Ltd.* [1975] 1 W.L.R. 1468; disapproved in *Woodar Investment Developments Ltd.* v. *Wimpey Construction (U.K.) Ltd.* [1980] 1 W.L.R. 277.

[70] *Les Affréteurs Réunis Société Anonyme* v. *Leopold Walford Ltd.* [1919] A.C. 801.

[71] *i.e.* a covenant to settle property which might come subsequently to one of the beneficiaries under a settlement. It was common in a marriage settlement for each of the spouses to covenant to add to the trusts of the settlement any property which they subsequently might acquire.

[72] *Ante*, p. 121; *Re D'Angibau* (1880) 15 Ch.D. 228; *Re Plumptre's Marriage Settlement* [1910] 1 Ch. 609; *Re Cook's S.T.* [1965] Ch. 902.

[73] (1960) 76 L.Q.R. 100 (D. W. Elliott).

chose in action for which they are the beneficiaries, and thus entitled to enforce?[74]

Modern developments have given volunteers no comfort in this respect. In *Re Pryce*,[75] Eve J. held that the trustees should not be compelled to pursue whatever remedy they may have at law on the covenant, and in *Re Kay's Settlement*,[76] Simonds J. decided that they should be instructed not to do so; and in *Re Cook's Settlement Trusts*,[77] Buckley J. distinguished *Fletcher* v. *Fletcher*,[78] *Williamson* v. *Codring-ton*[79] and *Re Cavendish-Browne's Settlement Trusts*,[80] and refused to allow volunteers to enforce a covenant even though another person had given consideration. These however are all decisions of courts of first instance, and the matter should be analysed more closely.

A. Suit by the Trustees

There are certain difficulties which lie in the way of the proposition that the trustees, as parties to the covenant under seal, can sue to recover damages with a view to holding the money received on trust for the (volunteer) beneficiaries.

(i) **Decision to Enforce.** If the trustees were able to recover damages, but could not be compelled by the beneficiaries to sue, the trustees would be left with the decision whether or not to enforce the trust. It is true that many discretions may be left to trustees.[81] But, as we have seen, a trust necessarily involves a duty on the trustees to administer the trust in some way. To give the trustee, as a party to the covenant, the right to decide whether or not anything shall be done for any of the beneficiaries is not consistent with his office of trustee.[82] It is submitted that it is better to limit the trustees' intervention to cases where the beneficiaries can compel them to take action.

(ii) **Nominal or Substantial Damages.** The next question is whether the trustee would recover substantial damages in an action at law on the covenant. If he can recover only nominal damages, the action will be of no help to the beneficiary.[83]

---

[74] (1962) 78 L.Q.R. 228 (J. A. Hornby); *Perspectives of Law* (ed. R. Pound), p. 239; (1969) 85 L.Q.R. 213 (W. A. Lee); (1975) 91 L.Q.R. 236 (J. L. Barton); (1976) 92 L.Q.R. 427 (R. P. Meagher and J. R. F. Lehane); (1979) 32 C.L.P. 1 and (1981) 34 C.L.P. 189 (C. E. F. Rickett).

[75] [1917] 1 Ch. 234.

[76] [1939] Ch. 329.

[77] [1965] Ch. 902; (1965) 24 C.L.J. 46 (G. H. Jones); (1966) 29 M.L.R. 397 (D. Matheson); (1966) 8 Malaya L.R. 153 (M. Scott); [1967] A.S.C.L. 387 *et seq.* (J. D. Davies); (1969) 85 L.Q.R. 213 (W. A. Lee).

[78] (1844) 4 Hare 67.

[79] (1750) 1 Ves.Sen. 511.

[80] [1916] W.N. 341.

[81] Chap. 19 and pp. 473–474.

[82] *Post*, p. 457; *cf.* the problems in relation to purpose trusts, *post*, p. 346; and in relation to discretionary trusts, *post*, p. 198, (1969) 85 L.Q.R. 213 at p. 255 (W. A. Lee).

[83] See (1950) 3 C.L.P. 30 at p. 43 (O. R. Marshall).

The general rule is that the plaintiff may recover in an action for breach of contract damages sufficient to compensate him for his loss. Just as third parties cannot normally sue upon a contract, damages suffered by third parties are not recoverable by the plaintiff: unless, as explained below, the plaintiff contracted as trustee for the third parties. An attempt by the Court of Appeal in *Jackson* v. *Horizon Holidays Ltd.*[84] to permit the plaintiff to recover damages in respect of the loss suffered by third parties has been firmly disapproved by the House of Lords.[85]

The real question, however, is this: what does the common law regard as the plaintiff's own loss? In the context of a voluntary covenant to settle, it has been said that "for breach of a covenant to pay a certain sum the measure of damages (if that is the appropriate expression) is the certain sum; and for breach of a covenant to transfer property worth a certain sum, it is the value of the property."[86] There is no doubt that this is the usual rule, as shown by the cases where the volunteer beneficiary is a party to the covenant.[87] Applying this rule, substantial damages should be recoverable at law by B where A covenants to pay a certain sum (or to transfer Blackacre) to B to be held on trust for C. It is no answer at common law to say that B suffers no loss by the breach of such a covenant. At law the position is no different from that of a trustee of a completely constituted trust, who may recover substantial damages for the breach of any contract he may make as trustee even though he personally suffers no loss. There is, however, little direct authority in the context of an incompletely constituted trust. Of the cases usually quoted on this question, *Re Cavendish-Browne's Settlement Trusts*[88] is most clearly in point.

> The covenantor was absolutely entitled under two wills to a share of unconverted real estate in Canada, which he entered into a voluntary covenant to settle. The trustees sued for damages and were awarded a sum equivalent to the value of the property which would have come into their hands if the covenant had been per-

[84] [1975] 1 W.L.R. 1468.

[85] *Woodar Investment Developments Ltd.* v. *Wimpey Construction (U.K.) Ltd.* [1980] 1 W.L.R. 277. See also (1976) 39 M.L.R. 202 (D. Yates); *Forster* v. *Silvermere Golf and Equestrian Centre Ltd.* (1981) 42 P. & C.R. 255. See also *Beswick* v. *Beswick* [1968] A.C. 58; *post*, p. 128.

[86] (1960) 76 L.Q.R. 100 at p. 112 (D. W. Elliott); (1975) 91 L..R. 236 at p. 238 (J. L. Barton); [1988] Conv. 19 at p. 21 (D. Goddard). See also [1982] Conv. 280 at p. 281 (M. W. Friend), agreeing that substantial damages are available on the basis of debt in the case of a voluntary covenant to pay money, but suggesting that this is less clear in the case of specific property other than money.

[87] *Cannon* v. *Hartley* [1949] Ch. 213; *Synge* v. *Synge* [1894] 1 Q.B. 466.

[88] [1916] W.N. 341; (1916) 61 S.J. 27; *Re Parkin* [1892] 3 Ch. 510; *Ward* v. *Audland* (1847) 16 M. & W. 863. *cf. Perspectives of Law* (ed. R. Pound), p. 243; (1969) 85 L.Q.R. 213 at p. 219. The decision was prior to the cases holding that a trustee cannot sue; *ante*, p. 123. See, however, (1979) 32 C.L.P. 1 (C. E. F. Rickett), suggesting that the decision was based on the "trust of the promise" theory (discussed below).

formed, and this money was to be held on the trusts of the settlement.

This, then, supports the view that a covenantee may recover substantial damages at law for breach of a covenant to pay money or to transfer specific property, although he has suffered no loss personally. But even if this be correct, it may not follow that the same view would prevail in the context of cases like *Re Pryce*[89] and *Re Kay's Settlement*.[90] The covenant in those cases was not to pay a sum of money or to transfer specific property, but to transfer after-acquired property to the covenantee.[91]

Even though substantial damages may be available at law in an action by the trustee-covenantee, this would not be the end of the difficulties, for it may be argued that any such damages would be held on a resulting trust for the covenantor (settlor) and not for the volunteer beneficiaries.[92] This is because, in the absence of any completely constituted trust of either the property or the benefit of the covenant (discussed below), the volunteers would have no claim. The trustee-covenantee, it need hardly be added, could not keep the money himself.

B. Trust of the Benefit of the Covenant

If there is a completely constituted trust of the benefit of the covenant, there is no difficulty, as has been seen,[93] in enforcing it, either by the trustees on behalf of the beneficiaries, or by the beneficiaries themselves. It was said, however, in *Re Cook's Settlement Trusts*,[94] that a covenant to settle future property cannot be the subject-matter of a trust, because it does not "create a debt enforceable at law . . . that is to say, a property right."[95] It is submitted tht this restriction is not supportable.[96] Of course, future property itself, or unascertained property, or a mere *spes*, cannot be the subject-matter of a trust.[97] But a

---

[89] [1917] 1 Ch. 234.

[90] [1939] Ch. 329. In this case and in *Re Pryce, supra*, it was assumed that the trustees, if they sued at law, would recover substantial damages. See also *Coulls* v. *Bagot's Trustee* (1967) 40 A.L.J.R. 471; *Cannon* v. *Hartley* [1949] Ch. 213.

[91] See, however, [1988] Conv. 19 at p. 21 (D. Goddard), suggesting that *Re Cavendish-Browne's S.T.* did involve after-acquired property. The testators from whom the property in question derived had died, but their estates were unadministered at the date of the covenant.

[92] See Underhill and Hayton, *Law of Trusts and Trustees* (14th ed.), pp. 130–132. *cf. Re Cavendish-Browne's S.T., supra*.

[93] *Ante*, p. 122.

[94] [1965] Ch. 902; [1967] A.S.C.L. 387 *et seq.* (J. D. Davies); (1969) 86 L.Q.R. 213 (W. A. Lee). *Cf. Davenport* v. *Bishopp* (1843) 2 Y. & C.C.C. 451.

[95] [1965] Ch. 902 at p. 913; (1976) 92 L.Q.R. 427 (R. P. Meagher and J. R. F. Lehane).

[96] (1965) 24 C.L.J. 46 at p. 49 (G. H. Jones); *cf.* (1969) 85 L.Q.R. 213 at p. 223 (W. A. Lee). See also (1979) 32 C.L.P. 1 and (1981) 34 C.L.P. 189 (C. E. F. Rickett); (1982) 98 L.Q.R. 17 (J. D. Feltham); [1982] Conv. 280 (M. W. Friend); [1982] Conv. 352 (S. Smith).

[97] *Post*, p. 131; *Williams* v. *C.I.R.* [1965] N.Z.L.R. 395.

covenant to pay a sum to be ascertained in the future is just as good a chose in action as a covenant to pay a specified sum, and it creates legal property of value. The trust *res* is the benefit of the covenant, the chose in action; not the property which will be obtained by its performance.[98] There is no difficulty in a trust of a bank account, which is itself a chose in action, its value varying with the state of the account from day to day. And the obligation in *Lloyd's* v. *Harper*[99] was an obligation to pay an undetermined sum. The decision in *Re Cook's Settlement Trusts*[1] is not inconsistent with this view; for there was in that case no manifestation of an intention to create a trust of the benefit of the covenant; though Meagher and Lehane assume the contrary.[2]

On the assumption that there is no difficulty in the concept of a trust of the benefit of a covenant, there is nevertheless considerable difficulty in any particular case in deciding whether or not there is a manifestation of an intention to create one.[3] The cases show a great divergence.

The critical case is *Fletcher* v. *Fletcher*,[4] a decision which presents certain difficulties.

> Ellis Fletcher entered into a voluntary covenant with trustees to pay to them £60,000 to be held on trust, in the events which happened, for his natural son Jacob. The trustees did not wish to accept the trust or to receive the money unless they were required by the court to do so. Vice-Chancellor Wigram held that Jacob was able to claim the money, saying that equity would either allow Jacob to use the name of the trustee to sue at law, or to recover in his own name in a court of equity.

Wigram V.-C. was of course fully aware of the rule forbidding aid being given to a volunteer, and this argument was pressed upon him:

> "According to the authorities, I cannot, I admit, do anything to perfect the liability of the author of the trust, if it is not already perfect. This covenant, however, is already perfect. The covenantor is liable at law, and the Court is not called upon to do any act to perfect it. One question made in argument has been whether there can be a trust of a covenant the benefit of which shall belong to a third party; but I cannot think that there is any difficulty in that. . . .

---

[98] *Williamson* v. *Codrington* (1750) 1 Ves.Sen. 511; *Fletcher* v. *Fletcher* (1844) 4 Hare 67; *Lloyd's* v. *Harper* (1880) 16 Ch.D. 290; *Re Cavendish-Browne's S.T.* [1916] W.N. 341; (1975) 91 L.Q.R. 236 at p. 238 (J. L. Barton); (1976) 92 L.Q.R. at p. 428; *The Restatement of Trusts* (2nd ed.), § 17(e).

[99] (1880) 16 Ch.D. 290.

[1] [1965] Ch. 902.

[2] (1976) 92 L.Q.R. 427 at p. 428; criticised in [1982] Conv. 280 (M. W. Friend).

[3] *Re Engelbach's Estate* [1924] 2 Ch. 348; *Vandepitte* v. *Preferred Accident Insurance Corp. of New York* [1933] A.C. 70; *Re Schebsman* [1944] Ch. 83; *Green* v. *Russell* [1959] 2 Q.B. 266; *Scruttons Ltd.* v. *Midland Silicones Ltd.* [1962] A.C. 446; *Beswick* v. *Beswick* [1968] A.C. 58; *Swain* v. *Law Society* [1983] 1 A.C. 598.

[4] (1844) 4 Hare 67.

The proposition, therefore, that in no case can there be a trust of a covenant is too large, and the real question is whether the relation of trustee and *cestui que trust* is established in the present case."[5]

There was, then, a trust of the benefit of the covenant, and the plaintiff, as beneficiary of the trust, could enforce it. The trustees were, analytically, in the same position as Lloyd's were in *Lloyd's* v. *Harper*.[6] It was there decided that Lloyd's had contracted with Harper as trustee for the persons insured, and that, therefore, Lloyd's could sue, on behalf of the person insured, and recover the damages which they, the beneficiaries, had suffered. The crucial question in these cases is whether or not there has been a manifestation of an intention to declare a trust of a chose in action, and this is a matter in which the courts have not, over the years, maintained a consistent approach. There are some difficulties in holding that there was a trust of the chose in action on the facts of *Fletcher* v. *Fletcher*.[7] In the first place, positive evidence of intention is lacking. Ellis Fletcher, the covenantor, covenanted that he would pay the £60,000 to trustees "to be held on the following trusts." There is clearly a trust which will affect the money once it is received by the trustee, but no manifestation of an intention by either party to create a trust of a chose in action. It cannot be assumed from the fact that the property itself is to be subjected to a trust that a trust of the benefit of the covenant was also intended.[8]

Another question is whether the relevant intention is that of the covenantor (settlor) or the covenantee (trustee). Certainly there was no intention to create a trust of the chose in action on the part of the trustees, if that is the requirement, in *Fletcher* v. *Fletcher*[9]: they did not know about the arrangement, and wished to decline the trust upon hearing of it. A trust of tangible property is declared by the owner of the property, whether he declares himself trustee or transfers it to another on trust. As a general rule, a trust of a debt is declared by the creditor. It is submitted, however, that a distinction must be drawn between covenants supported by valuable consideration and those which are not. Where there is consideration, the relevant intention to create a trust of the chose in action is that of the covenantee.[10] This will

---

[5] *Ibid.* at p. 74. The position will be otherwise if the covenant is statute-barred. *cf. Pullan* v. *Koe* [1913] 1 Ch. 9; *ante*, p. 121, where the beneficiaries' interest, owing to the presence of consideration, was not merely in the covenant but in the property itself.

[6] (1880) 16 Ch.D. 290.

[7] (1844) 4 Hare 67.

[8] *cf.* (1982) 98 L.Q.R. 17 (J. D. Feltham), suggesting that such an assumption should be made, in order to avoid the absurdity that voluntary covenants to settle are otherwise unenforceable.

[9] (1844) 4 Hare 67.

[10] See the insurance cases: *Vandepitte* v. *Preferred Accident Insurance Corp. of New York* [1933] A.C. 70; *Swain* v. *The Law Society* [1983] 1 A.C. 598. The question in these cases is whether the policy-holder intended to hold the company's obligation on trust. See (1982) 98 L.Q.R. 17 (J. D. Feltham).

usually be proved by showing that the latter covenanted as trustee for the persons nominated by the covenantor. Where, on the other hand, the covenant is voluntary, as in *Fletcher* v. *Fletcher*,[11] the better view is that "the promisor is the creator of the trust, and if he manifests an intention that the promisee's rights under the promise shall be held in trust, the promisee immediately becomes trustee of his rights under the promise."[12]

C. Specific Performance at the Suit of the Contracting Party

Beswick v. *Beswick*[13] suggests the possibility of a new approach to this problem. If the administratrix of old Mr. Beswick could in that case obtain specific performance against young Mr. Beswick and compel him to perform his promise to make payments to the widow Beswick (a volunteer), can it not be argued that the trustees in a marriage settlement situation should be able to obtain specific performance of the promise to settle after-acquired property in favour of volunteers? At least in *Beswick* v. *Beswick* the House of Lords saw no objection to a solution which permitted the widow to obtain by this indirect method what she could not obtain directly[14]; Simonds J. in *Re Kay's Settlement*[15] had taken the opposite view.

It is submitted however that the principle of *Beswick* v. *Beswick*[16] does not apply to the case of voluntary covenants. In that case, old Mr. Beswick (A) gave consideration for the promise of young Mr. Beswick (B). He had a right of action for damages against B *in respect of his own loss*. When the loss was shown to be nil, and the damages therefore nominal, specific performance became available instead. That remedy is available where the legal remedy of damages is inadequate.[17] Where valuable consideration has been given, the remedy of nominal damages is inadequate, although there is no loss to the contracting party, because the result is the unjust enrichment of the defendant. In the case of a voluntary covenant to pay to trustees the situation (assuming that damages would be nominal[18]) is different. There is no unjust enrichment; nominal damages are therefore adequate. Specific performance in any event is not available to a volunteer, and most trustees

---

[11] *Supra.*
[12] *The Restatement of Trusts* (2nd ed.), para. 26. See also (1979) 32 C.L.P. 1 at p. 13 (C. E. F. Rickett); Heydon, Gummow and Austin, *Cases and Materials on Equity and Trusts* (2nd ed.), p. 469. Difficulties could arise in cases such as *Re Cook's S.T.* [1965] Ch. 902, where the covenant is made with persons of whom some, but not all, have given consideration.
[13] [1968] A.C. 58; *post*, pp. 689 *et seq.*; [1967] A.S.C.L. 387 *et seq.* (J. D. Davies); (1988) 8 L.S. 14 (N. H. Andrews).
[14] *Per* Lord Pearce [1968] A.C. 58 at p. 89.
[15] [1939] Ch. 329 at p. 342.
[16] [1968] A.C. 58. See also *Snelling* v. *John G. Snelling Ltd.* [1973] Q.B. 87.
[17] *Post*, p. 652.
[18] Which may not be correct; *ante*, p. 123.

are volunteers.[19] Furthermore, the availability of specific performance in *Beswick* v. *Beswick*[20] was not hampered by the principle that trustees are not allowed to sue,[21] because the plaintiff there was not a trustee.[22]

We have seen that it made no difference in *Re Cook's Settlement Trusts*[23] that one of the parties had given consideration.

> In *Re Cook's Settlement Trusts*, F, on a resettlement of the family capital, covenanted with H, his father, and the trustees, that he would pay to the trustees any money received from any sale during H's lifetime of some valuable pictures owned absolutely by F. The beneficiaries under the settlement were volunteers, and Buckley J. held that the trustees were unable to demand the payment to them of the proceeds of sale of a picture.

The decision preceded *Beswick* v. *Beswick*,[24] in which it was apparently not cited. A similarity between the two cases appears on close analysis. H entered into a contract for consideration with F, one of the terms of which was that F would confer a benefit on X. If H had sued F, could he succeed, as in *Beswick* v. *Beswick*, by saying that the damages awardable for the breach were inadequate, and that specific performance of the covenant to pay should be decreed in favour of X? The covenant was not in terms to pay to the volunteers, but to the trustees, who would hold the money in trust for them; but this seems immaterial. It is H who, on this reasoning, could sue and not the trustees; but the action should not be dependent upon H's physical survival, for his estate, on the reasoning of *Beswick*, should be able to do so.[25]

It was however suggested in *Coulls* v. *Bagot's Trustee*,[26] where the contract was not in the form of a covenant, that where the promise is made both to H (who gave the consideration) *and* to X (the volunteer), *both of whom* are parties[27] to the contract or covenant, X can sue by joining H (irrespective of H's wishes) although X has provided no consideration. Enforcement would then be on the basis of contract.

It has been said that "The dicta in *Coulls* and the decision in *Beswick* may be the most important developments in specific performance this

---

[19] Nominal consideration is not sufficient in equity. See (1966) 8 Malaya L.R. 153 at p. 158 (M. Scott).

[20] [1968] A.C. 58.

[21] *Ante*, p. 123.

[22] She was a personal representative, but the position was exactly the same as if Mr. Beswick senior had been in a position to bring the action himself. There was no trust.

[23] [1965] Ch. 902; *ante*, p. 123.

[24] [1968] A.C. 58.

[25] *cf.* (1979) 32 C.L.P. 1 at p. 14 (C. E. F. Rickett).

[26] (1967) 40 A.L.J.R. 471 at p. 477, *per* Barwick C.J.; [1967] A.S.C.L. at p. 395 (J. D. Davies); (1978) 37 C.L.J. 301 (B. Coote). Compare the facts of *Cannon* v. *Hartley* [1949] 1 Ch. 213, *ante*, p. 122, where another party to the covenant had given consideration.

[27] But see (1978) 37 C.L.J. 301 (B. Coote), doubting whether the wife, although a signatory, was properly to be regarded as a party to the contract.

century."[28] But, as in *Beswick*, there was no trust involved in *Coulls*, and hence no need to surmount the obstacle that trustees cannot sue.[29] Both were cases where valuable consideration had been furnished to the promisor. It is doubtful whether they will enable trustees to enforce voluntary covenants to settle. But in the case of a covenant by a third party in a marriage settlement to settle after-acquired property, that person, or his estate after his death, having provided consideration, and being a party to the transaction, may, on the authority of *Beswick* v. *Beswick*[30] be able to obtain specific performance for the benefit of the volunteers.

That line of reasoning is wholly separate from the question of the enforcement of a covenant in the *Fletcher* v. *Fletcher* type of situation.[31] There, no consideration was given. The covenant was voluntary. It would be enforceable by, or on behalf of the beneficiaries if, and only if, there was found to be a trust of the chose in action. That brings us back to the most basic question of all in relation to the creation of trusts: whether the settlor has manifested an intention to create a trust.

The question whether such an intention can be found has been the subject of much litigation since the privity rule was established by *Tweddle* v. *Atkinson*,[32] and it is well known, both that the courts have been inconsistent in their decisions, and that, since *Walford's* case,[33] they have been more reluctant to find such an intention. It was very different in Jacob Fletcher's day which predated *Milroy* v. *Lord*,[34] *Jones* v. *Lock*[35] and *Tweddle* v. *Atkinson*.[36] There is little doubt that a modern court would fail to find the necessary manifestation of intention on the facts of *Fletcher* v. *Fletcher*. On the other hand, if the existence of an intention to create a trust of a chose in action were to be found now on evidence as flimsy as it was in that case, there would be a different answer to many of the cases on covenants to settle after-acquired property—and also of the cases on the privity rule.

---

[28] Heydon, Gummow and Austin, *Cases and Materials on Equity and Trusts* (2nd ed.), p. 806.
[29] *Ante*, p. 123.
[30] [1968] A.C. 58.
[31] (1844) 4 Hare 67.
[32] (1861) 3 B. & S. 393.
[33] *Les Affréteurs Réunis Société Anonyme* v. *Leopold Walford (London) Ltd.* [1919] A.C. 801. See *Swain* v. *The Law Society* [1983] 1 A.C. 598 (the Law Society did not contract as trustee by using words "on behalf of all solicitors" in insurance contract. But solicitors, although not parties, could enforce the contract directly as a result of Solicitors Act 1974, s.37, providing a statutory exception to the privity rule). Outside the contract area, however, an intention to create a trust has been upheld without strong evidence; see *Paul* v. *Constance* [1977] 1 W.L.R. 54, *ante*, p. 119.
[34] (1862) 4 De G.F. & J. 264.
[35] (1865) L.R. 1 Ch.App. 25.
[36] *Supra*.

D. Summary

The proper solution to this question, it is submitted, is dependent upon the question of policy, whether the covenantor should or should not be made to implement his undertaking on behalf of the volunteers. If it is thought that he should, the means are at hand, whether by finding a trust of the chose in action, or by allowing specific performance of the covenant or, indeed, by abrogating the rule that third parties cannot sue on a contract.[37] But if it is thought that he should not, cases like *Re Kay's Settlement*[38] must stand; they are at least consistent with the established rules requiring strict construction of expressions of intention to create trusts, and of the older principles relating to the availability of specific performance.

6. TRUSTS OF FUTURE PROPERTY

A contract for consideration to convey future property to trustees upon trust is valid[39] and, in most cases, specifically enforceable.[40] A voluntary covenant to convey future property to trustees is actionable at law by a beneficiary who is a party to the covenant.[41] If the beneficiary is not a party he is unable to sue, being in no better a position than the volunteer in the case of a covenant relating to present property. Indeed, he may be worse off if it is correct to say that the argument that there is a trust of the benefit of the covenant is not available in the case of future property.[42] A purported assignment of an expectancy[43] cannot be a conveyance because there is nothing to convey. Nor can there be a valid declaration of trust of property not yet existing.[44] If consideration is given for a purported conveyance, it will be construed as a contract to assign and enforceable as such.[45] But if it is made gratuitously it is a nullity.[46]

In *Re Ellenborough*,[47] the sister of Lord Ellenborough purported to convey by voluntary settlement the property which she would receive under her brother's will. On his death she declined to

---

[37] See criticisms of this rule by the House of Lords in *Woodar Investment Developments Ltd.* v. *Wimpey Construction (U.K.) Ltd.* [1980] 1 W.L.R. 277; *Swain* v. *The Law Society* [1983] 1 A.C. 598.

[38] [1939] Ch. 329; (1975) 91 L.Q.R. 236 (J. L. Barton).

[39] *Re Lind* [1915] 2 Ch. 345; *Re Gillott's Settlements* [1934] Ch. 97; *Re Haynes' W.T.* [1949] Ch. 5.

[40] *Pullan* v. *Koe* [1913] 1 Ch. 9.

[41] *Cannon* v. *Hartley* [1949] Ch. 213; *ante*, p. 122.

[42] *Ante*, p. 125.

[43] *Williams* v. *C.I.R.* [1965] N.Z.L.R. 345; ("the first £500 of the net income which shall accrue to the assignor ... from the Trust."). An assignment of the assignor's life interest under the trust would, of course, have been valid.

[44] cf. *Re Ralli's W.T.* [1964] Ch. 288; *ante*, p. 115. See also *Simpson* v. *Simpson* (1989) 19 Fam.Law 20.

[45] *Re Burton's Settlement* [1955] Ch. 82.

[46] *Meek* v. *Kettlewell* (1842) 1 Hare 464; *Re Ellenborough* [1903] 1 Ch. 697; *Re Brooks' S.T.* [1939] Ch. 993; *Williams* v. *C.I.R.* [1965] N.Z.L.R. 345.

[47] [1903] 1 Ch. 697; cf. *Re Bowden* [1936] Ch. 71; *Re Adlard* [1954] Ch. 29.

transfer the property to the trustees, and Buckley J. held that the trustees could not compel her to do so.

A further question is whether such a gratuitous covenant, assign-ment or declaration in respect of future property can subsequently be treated as an effective declaration of trust if the property does later vest in the trustee. The situation can arise if the property, on falling in, is transferred to trustees without a further declaration of the trusts, or where the property vests in the settlor after he has declared the trusts on which he is to hold it.

We have seen that a covenant in a marriage settlement to settle after-acquired property is not enforceable at the suit of the next-of-kin because they are volunteers[48]; and it is clear that a deed purporting to grant future property upon trust is ineffective.[49] But if, in either of these cases, the property found its way into the hands of the trustees, it would presumably be held upon the trusts declared in the relevant documents.[50] If the settlor, in either case, conveyed the property to the trustees, that action could be construed as a further declaration of the trusts; but if the property reached the trustees by another route, being conveyed perhaps by the executors of the testator from whom the property came,[51] or coming into the hands of the trustee in a different capacity,[52] the possibility of finding that there was a further declaration of trust is less strong. There appear to be three possible solutions to such a case: that the trustees take beneficially, that they hold on trust for the settlor, or that they hold on the trusts declared in the previous document. The first is obviously unsatisfactory. The second involves the proposition that the settlor could claim back in equity property which he had covenanted or purported to settle.[53] The third avoids the necessity of making the ultimate destination of the property depend upon the route by which it reached the trustees; it is consistent with the expressed intention of the parties and appears to be the most satis-factory solution.[54]

Where the property comes to the settlor himself, it is possible for the court to hold that a previous declaration of trust,[55] followed by the vesting of the property in himself as a trustee, constitutes the trust. The question is whether he will be treated as making the declaration at the

---

[48] *Re D'Angibau* (1880) 15 Ch.D. 228; *Re Plumptre's Settlement* [1910] 1 Ch. 609.
[49] *Re Ellenborough* [1903] 1 Ch. 697; *Re Brooks' S.T.* [1939] Ch. 993.
[50] *Re Ellenborough, supra*. Miss Emily Towry Law had already handed over to the trustees the property which she received under her sister's will; and no attempt was made to recover it; *Re Adlard* [1954] Ch. 29; *Re Ralli's W.T.* [1964] Ch. 228.
[51] *Re Adlard* [1954] Ch. 29.
[52] *Re Ralli's W.T.* [1964] Ch. 288.
[53] Dicta in *Re Ralli's W.T.* [1964] Ch. 288, indicate that this could be regarded as unconscionable.
[54] So held in *Re Ralli's W.T., supra*, discussed *ante*, p. 115.
[55] As opposed to a mere covenant to settle or purported assignment; *Re Ellenborough, supra*.

moment he receives the property.[56] It is clear that a previous declaration is not of itself sufficient[57]; subsequent confirmation of a previous declaration is sufficient.[58] In less obvious cases it is no doubt a question of construction to determine whether or not the settlor is to be taken to have made a subsequent declaration or to have affirmed a previous one. If he made the declaration every day, the last declaration being made the moment before he received the property, this would no doubt be sufficient. But in the absence of authority, it is unsafe to predict to what extent an argument on these lines might be acceptable. What is clear in these cases is that the beneficiaries must show that the trust was properly declared and properly constituted. In connection with the declaration, there are again very difficult points of construction, the solution of which will largely depend on the view the court takes on the policy question whether or not trusts ought to be created in this way. There appears to be nothing intrinsically wrong in holding that the declaration of a trust may precede its constitution.

7. EXCEPTIONS TO THE RULE THAT EQUITY WILL NOT ASSIST A VOLUNTEER

A. The Rule in Strong v. Bird[59]

Where an incomplete gift is made during the donor's lifetime, and the donor appointed the donee as executor,[60] or, in the case of the intestacy, the donee is appointed administrator,[61] the vesting of the property in the donee in his capacity as executor or administrator may be treated as the completion of the gift, overriding the claims of the beneficiaries under the will or intestacy. Similarly with the release of a debt owed to the donor.

> In *Strong* v. *Bird*,[62] B borrowed £1,100 from A, his stepmother, who lived in his house, paying £212 10s. a quarter for board, and it was agreed that the debt should be paid off by a deduction of £100 from each quarter's payment. Deductions of this amount were made for two quarters; but on the third quarter-day, A paid the full amount. She continued to do so to the time of her death, some four years later. B was appointed her sole executor, and proved the will.

---

[56] *Restatement of Trusts*, para. 26, comments *k* and *l*; para. 86, comment *c*.

[57] *Matter of Gurlitz*, 105 Misc. 30, 172 N.Y. Supp. 523 (1918); *Brennan* v. *Morphett* (1908) 6 C.L.R 22; *Permanent Trustee Co.* v. *Scales* (1930) 30 S.R. (N.S.W.) 391 at p. 393; *Williams* v. *C.I.R.* [1965] N.Z.L.R. 345.

[58] *Re Northcliffe* [1925] Ch. 651.

[59] See [1982] Conv. 14 (G. Kodilinye).

[60] (1874) L.R. 18 Eq. 315. It is sufficient if he is appointed one of the executors; *Re Stewart* [1908] 2 Ch. 251.

[61] *Re James* [1935] Ch. 449; *Re Gonin* [1979] Ch. 16 (where, however, doubts were expressed by Walton J.); (1977) 93 L.Q.R. 485. In *Strong* v. *Bird* itself, the rule was said only to apply to an executor.

[62] (1874) L.R. 18 Eq. 315; *Re James* [1935] Ch. 449 (a gift of realty).

Later A's next-of-kin claimed for the balance of the debt. It was held that the appointment of B as executor released the debt.

It is necessary to show that the donor intended to make an immediate *inter vivos* gift,[63] and also that he had a continuing intention to give until the date of his death. Thus, an intention to make a testamentary gift is not sufficient.[64] The intention must relate to a specific item of property. It is not sufficient that there was a vague desire to provide something for the donee. In *Re Gonin*[65] a mother wished to leave her house to her daughter, who had given up a career to look after her parents, but thought for some reason that she could not do so because the daughter was illegitimate. Instead, she wrote a cheque for £33,000 in the daughter's favour, which was found after her death. (The cheque could not be cashed, as the death terminated the bank's mandate to pay it.) The daughter became administratrix, but failed in her claim to the house. There was no evidence of a continuing intention that the daughter should have an immediate gift of the house. The drawing of the cheque, as a substitute, pointed the other way. And a donee executor will fail if the testator, subsequently to the act on which the executor relies as establishing the intention to give a chattel, acted inconsistently with that intention by giving or lending the chattel to someone else,[66] or if the testator, having once had an intention to give, forgot the gift, and treated the property as his own.[67]

B. Donatio Mortis Causa

(i) The Principle. A *donatio mortis causa* is a gift made *inter vivos* which is conditional upon, and which takes effect upon, death. It must be distinguished on the one hand from a normal *inter vivos* gift, under which title passes immediately to the transferee; and, on the other hand, from a testamentary gift which takes effect under the provisions of a properly executed will.[68] It may therefore be regarded as an exception either to the rules governing *inter vivos* gifts, or to the rules governing gifts which take effect upon death. In the present context, we are concerned with the former aspect. But the assistance of equity will not be required by the donee in all cases. Where the subject-matter is a chattel which has been delivered to the donee, the donee's title is complete on the donor's death, no further act being necessary. In the case of a chose in action, on the other hand, the donee's title is not

---

[63] *cf. Re Ralli's W.T.* [1964] Ch. 288, *ante*, p. 115 (covenant to settle in the future). See also *Simpson* v. *Simpson* (1989) 19 Fam.Law 20 (future gift).

[64] *Re Stewart* [1908] 2 Ch. 251; *Re Innes* [1910] Ch. 188.

[65] [1979] Ch. 16; (1977) 93 L.Q.R. 488.

[66] *Re Freeland* [1952] Ch. 110.

[67] *Re Wale* [1956] 1 W.L.R. 1346.

[68] For the distinction between a *donatio mortis causa* and a legacy, see Snell's *Principles of Equity* (28th ed.), pp. 382–383. As to availability to meet deceased donor's debts, see [1978] Conv. 130 (S. Warnock-Smith).

complete on the donor's death as the legal title vests in the donor's personal representatives. The donee can seek the assistance of equity to compel the personal representatives to do whatever is necessary to perfect the donee's title.[69] It is in this latter situation that the doctrine of *donatio mortis causa* can be seen as an exception to the rule that equity will not assist a volunteer to perfect an imperfect gift.

The three essentials for a valid *donatio mortis causa* were laid down by Lord Russell C.J. in *Cain* v. *Moon*.[70]

(a) The gift must have been in contemplation, though not necessarily in the expectation, of death[71];

(b) the subject-matter of the gift must have been delivered to the donee[72];

(c) the gift must have been made under such circumstances as to show that the property is to revert to the donor if he should recover.[73]

(ii) Contemplation of Death. The donor must have been contemplating death more particularly than by merely reflecting that we must all die some day. Commonly, *donationes mortis causa* are made in reference to a particular illness, but the principle applies equally to other causes such as the embarkation on a hazardous journey,[74] or possibly even to the contemplation of active service in war.[75] If death occurs, the *donatio* may still be valid even though it comes from a cause different from that contemplated.

In *Wilkes* v. *Allington*[76] the donor was suffering from an incurable disease, and made a gift in the knowledge that he had not long to live; as things turned out, he had an even shorter time than he imagined, for he died two months later of pneumonia. It was held that the gift remained valid.

(iii) Delivery of Subject-matter. A *donatio mortis causa* will not be valid without a delivery of the property to the donee[77] with the intention of parting with the "dominion" over it. It will not suffice if the property is handed over merely for safe custody.[78]

(a) *Chattels.* The donor must hand over either the chattel itself or the

[69] *Duffield* v. *Elwes* (1827) 1 Bli.(N.S.) 497; *Re Lillingston* [1952] 2 All E.R. 184.

[70] [1896] 2 Q.B. 283; *Re Craven's Estate* [1937] Ch. 423 at p. 426; *Delgoffe* v. *Fader* [1939] Ch. 922.

[71] *Wilkes* v. *Allington* [1931] 2 Ch. 104.

[72] *Cain* v. *Moon* [1896] 2 Q.B. 283.

[73] *Re Lillingston* [1952] 2 All E.R. 184.

[74] cf. *Thompson* v. *Mechan* [1958] O.R. 357: the ordinary risks of air travel do not suffice.

[75] *Agnew* v. *Belfast Banking Co.* [1896] 2 I.R. 204 at p. 221.

[76] [1931] 2 Ch. 104. A valid *donatio mortis causa* cannot be made in contemplation of suicide; *Re Dudman* [1925] 1 Ch. 553. This is probably not affected by the Suicide Act 1961, whereby suicide is no longer a crime.

[77] *Ward* v. *Turner* (1752) 2 Ves.Sen. 431.

[78] *Hawkins* v. *Blewitt* (1798) 2 Esp. 663.

means of getting control over it such as, for example, a key to the box or place where the subject-matter is located.[79]

(b) *Choses in Action.* The position is more difficult if the title to the chose in action does not pass by mere delivery of any document. The donor must hand over such documents as constitute "the essential indicia or evidence of title, possession or production of which entitles the possessor to the money or property purported to be given."[80] Thus the delivery of a bank deposit pass-book,[81] a Post Office Savings Bank-book,[82] national savings certificates[83] or a cheque or promissory note payable to the donor[84] have been held to create a *donatio mortis causa* of the chose in action represented by the document in question, so that, on the death of the donor, the donee can compel the personal representatives to perfect his legal title.

(iv) **The Intention of the Donor.** The donor's intention must be to make a gift which is conditional upon death, and revocable upon recovery by the donor. Thus, there is no *donatio mortis causa* if the intention is to make an immediate unconditional gift, even though the gift may fail,[85] nor where the intention is to make a future gift.[86] The conditional nature of the gift need not be expressed, but may be implied from the circumstances.[87]

(v) **Revocation.** In addition to automatic revocation upon the donor's recovery,[88] the donor may revoke expressly, or by recovering dominion over the subject-matter,[89] but he cannot revoke by will, the reason being that the donee's title is complete before the will takes effect.[90] Where the gift is revoked the donee holds the subject-matter as trustee for the donor.[91] It might be added that the gift fails if the donee predeceases the donor.[92]

---

[79] *Re Wasserberg* [1915] 1 Ch. 195; *Re Lillingston* [1952] 2 All E.R. 184; *Re Cole* [1964] Ch. 175; *Re Mustapha* (1891) 8 T.L.R. 160; it will not suffice if the donor retains a duplicate key; *Re Craven's Estate* [1937] Ch. 423, at p. 427.

[80] *Birch* v. *Treasury Solicitor* [1951] Ch. 298 at p. 311. *cf. Re Weston* [1902] 1 Ch. 680; *Delgoffe* v. *Fader* [1939] Ch. 922.

[81] *Birch* v. *Treasury Solicitor* [1951] Ch. 298.

[82] *Re Weston* [1902] 1 Ch. 608. It is otherwise if withdrawals may be made without producing the book; *Delgoffe* v. *Fader* [1939] Ch. 922.

[83] *Darlow* v. *Sparks* [1938] 2 All E.R. 235.

[84] Even though unendorsed and therefore not transferable by delivery. See *Re Mead* (1880) 15 Ch.D. 651.

[85] *Edwards* v. *Jones* (1836) 1 My. & Cr. 226.

[86] *Solicitor to the Treasury* v. *Lewis* [1900] 2 Ch. 812.

[87] *Re Lillingston* [1952] 2 All E.R. 184.

[88] *Staniland* v. *Willott* (1852) 3 Mac. & G. 664.

[89] *Bunn* v. *Markham* (1816) 7 Taunt. 224.

[90] *Jones* v. *Selby* (1710) Prec.Ch. 300 at p. 303.

[91] *Re Wasserberg* [1915] 1 Ch. 195.

[92] *Tate* v. *Hilbert* (1793) 2 Ves. 111 at p. 120.

(vi) Exceptions. It seems that not every kind of property is capable of being the subject-matter of a *donatio mortis causa*:

(a) *Donor's Own Cheque or Promissory Note.* It has been held that a *donatio mortis causa* cannot be made of the donor's own cheque[93] or promissory note.[94] The former is merely a revocable mandate to the bank,[95] while a gift of the latter is merely a gratuitous promise, thus they are not the "property" of the donor at all. It may be otherwise if the cheque is actually paid in the donor's lifetime, or before the bank has been informed of his death, or if it has been negotiated for value.[96]

(b) *Land.* Although there is no English authority directly on the point, Lord Eldon has doubted whether it is possible to make a *donatio mortis causa* of land.[97] The reason may lie in the supposed difficulty of parting with the "dominion" over land. The possibility has recently been rejected in Australia after a full review of the authorities.[98]

(c) *Stocks and Shares.* There is some authority that such property cannot form the subject-matter of a *donatio mortis causa*. It was held in *Ward* v. *Turner*[99] that South Sea annuities could not be the subject-matter of such a gift. The decision may have been based on the inadequacy of the transfer on the facts,[1] but it has been applied in cases concerning railway stock[2] and building society shares.[3] On the other hand, it has been held that shares in a public company can be the subject-matter of a *donatio mortis causa*.[4] This exception is, therefore, a doubtful one.

C. Modifications by the 1925 Legislation

Two statutory exceptions arise and, for the sake of completeness, must be mentioned, although their real significance is in respect of the machinery of the 1925 legislation relating to the settlement of land, rather than to the present topic.

(i) Settled Land Act 1925, s.27. A conveyance (whether it is for value or not) which purports to convey a legal estate to a minor[5] operates as

---

[93] *Re Beaumont* [1902] 1 Ch. 886.
[94] *Re Leaper* [1916] 1 Ch. 579.
[95] Only a holder for value can sue.
[96] *Tate* v. *Hilbert* (1793) 2 Ves. 111.
[97] *Duffield* v. *Elwes* (1827) 1 Bli.(n.s.) 497. This case upheld a *donatio mortis causa* of a mortgage of land.
[98] *Bayliss* v. *Public Trustee* (1988) 12 N.S.W.L.R. 540, examining English, Australian, Canadian and American decisions.
[99] (1752) 2 Ves.Sen. 431.
[1] See Pettit, *loc. cit.*, p. 104.
[2] *Moore* v. *Moore* (1874) L.R. 18 Eq. 474.
[3] *Re Weston* [1902] 1 Ch. 680.
[4] *Staniland* v. *Willott* (1852) 3 Mac. & G. 664.
[5] Who is incapable of holding a legal estate; L.P.A. 1925, s.1(6).

an agreement for valuable consideration to execute a settlement in favour of the minor, and in the meantime to hold the land in trust for him.[6]

(ii) Settled Land Act 1925, s.9. In various situations in which a settlement is inadequately created for lack of the correct instruments,[7] the most significant of which, by section 9(1)(iii), is that of an instrument *inter vivos* intended to create a settlement which does not comply with the requirements of the Settled Land Act 1925, the trustees may, and on the request of the tenant for life or statutory owner shall, execute a principal vesting deed for the purpose of perfecting the settlement.[8] This is so whether or not the beneficiary is a volunteer.

It may be doubted, however, whether this is a true exception. A trust may be valid under the general law, yet not create a settlement for the purpose of the Settled Land Act 1925; in which case the provisions of that Act, for example the overreaching machinery, will not apply to it. Section 9(1)(iii) requires an instrument, therefore there will be writing, as required by section 53(1)(*b*)[9] of the Law of Property Act, and thus a valid trust of land under the general law. But not every instrument creating a trust of land will satisfy the requirements of section 4(3) of the Settled Land Act 1925 for a trust instrument under that Act. Section 9 will operate in such a case, converting the trust which is already valid under the general law into a settlement for the purpose of the Settled Land Act 1925.

D. Proprietary Estoppel

It has long been settled that estoppel works as a shield and not as a sword.[10] In other words, where one person has been led to act upon the statement of another, he can prevent that other person from acting inconsistently with his statement.

There is another doctrine of long standing,[11] which received its modern formulation in the dissenting speech of Lord Kingsdown in *Ramsden* v. *Dyson*,[12] and a more precise formulation by Fry J. in *Willmott* v. *Barber*,[13] and which can have the effect of creating a proprietary interest in a volunteer although there was no valid gift or trust in his favour. The doctrine is based on acquiescence and is often

---

[6] S.L.A. 1925, s.27(1).
[7] S.L.A. 1925, s.9(1).
[8] S.L.A. 1925, s.9(2).
[9] *Ante*, p. 80.
[10] *Combe* v. *Combe* [1951] 2 K.B. 215; (1952) 15 M.L.R. 1 (Denning L.J.); *cf.* (1965) 81 L.Q.R. 84 at p. 223 (D. C. Jackson).
[11] *Huning* v. *Ferrers* (1711) Gilb.Eq. 85; *East India Co.* v. *Vincent* (1740) 2 Atk. 83; *Att.-Gen.* v. *Balliol College, Oxford* (1744) 9 Mod. 407 at p. 411; *Stiles* v. *Cowper* (1748) 3 Atk. 692 at p. 693; Snell, p. 558.
[12] (1866) L.R. 1 H.L. 129 at p. 170.
[13] (1880) 15 Ch.D. 96 at p. 105. See now *Taylors Fashions Ltd.* v. *Liverpool Victoria Trustees Co. Ltd.* [1982] Q.B. 133, where a broader approach is formulated.

confused with estoppel,[14] due in part, no doubt, to the fact that it has in modern times acquired the name of Proprietary Estoppel.

Most of the modern applications of this doctrine have been in the context of licences to occupy land, and the matter will be fully discussed in Chapter 27. It will there be seen that, in applying the doctrine, the court exercises a wide discretion in reaching a solution which is appropriate to the facts of a particular case. Solutions will be seen to vary from finding, in some cases, that a volunteer has acquired a proprietary interest[15]; in others that negative protection is appropriate,[16] with many variations in between.[17]

---

[14] See *Crabb* v. *Arun D.C.* [1976] Ch. 179 at pp. 187, 193. Spencer Bower and Turner, *The Law Relating to Estoppel by Representation* (3rd ed., 1977), paras. 289–292, 308.

[15] *Dillwyn* v. *Llewelyn* (1862) 4 De G.F. & J. 517; *Plimmer* v. *Wellington Corporation* (1884) 9 App.Cas. 699; *Chalmers* v. *Pardoe* [1963] 1 W.L.R. 677; *E.R. Ives Investment Ltd.* v. *High* [1967] 2 Q.B. 379; *Crabb* v. *Arun D.C.* [1976] Ch. 179; *Pascoe* v. *Turner* [1979] 1 W.L.R. 431.

[16] *Hopgood* v. *Brown* [1955] 1 W.L.R. 213; *Inwards* v. *Baker* [1965] 2 Q.B. 29; *Jones* v. *Jones* [1977] 1 W.L.R. 438.

[17] *Dodsworth* v. *Dodsworth* (1973) 228 E.G. 1115; *Griffiths* v. *Williams* (1977) 248 E.G. 947.

CHAPTER 5

TESTAMENTARY GIFTS NOT COMPLYING
WITH THE WILLS ACT 1837. SECRET TRUSTS[1]

1. GENERAL

WE have seen that certain formalities are necessary for the creation of *inter vivos* trusts of land and for testamentary dispositions. A trust of land must be evidenced in writing[2]; and all testamentary dispositions must be in writing and signed by the testator, in the presence of two or more attesting witnesses present at the same time.[3] We now have to consider the effect of intended dispositions of these types which fail to comply with the necessary formalities.

The problem over the enforcement of secret trusts is the fact that the terms of the trusts are not expressed in a form which complies with the formal requirements of the Wills Act; though, in cases in which the testator's intention is clear and there is no possibility of doubt or fraud, there is a real compulsion to enforce the secret trust. The question is whether the enforcement of the secret trust is a defiance of the Wills Act; or whether there is recognised legal doctrine which allows secret trusts to be enforced in spite of the provisions of the Wills Act. What should be done, for example, where an intended trustee fraudulently shelters behind the provisions of the statutes? Where, for example, a transferee procures the conveyance of land to him by means of an oral

[1] (1947) 12 Conv.(N.S.) 28 (J.G. Fleming); (1951) 67 L.Q.R. 314 (L.A. Sheridan); (1963) 27 Conv.(N.S.) 92 (J. A. Andrews); (1972) 36 Conv.(N.S.) 113 (R. Burgess).
[2] L.P.A. 1925, s.53(1)(*b*); *ante*, p. 80.
[3] Wills Act 1837, s.9, as amended by Administration of Justice Act 1982; *ante*, p. 91; there are exceptions for wills made by members of the forces in actual military service or mariners or seamen in similar circumstances.

promise to hold on trust for a third party? Or a legatee or devisee persuades the testator to make a will in his favour in reliance on a similar oral promise? Or an intestate successor similarly persuades the intending testator not to make a will at all?

Equity, where possible, will not permit a statute to be a cloak for fraud.[4] However, a statute is a statute, and all courts must obey it. The question therefore is whether or not equity can, by acting *in personam* against the fraudulent party, prevent the fraud without disregarding the statute. If A conveys land to B on an oral trust for C, and B fraudulently claims the land for himself, how can equity interfere? Clearly, by operating *in personam* against B to deprive him of the benefit. Should the beneficial interest then be enjoyed by C, or held on a resulting trust for A? A resulting trust for A is all that is necessary to prevent B's unjust enrichment by his fraud; to give the beneficial interest to C looks perilously like a disregard of the statute. It is a question of balancing the policy of the formality requirement against the injustice which may be caused by relying on the formality rule. The rule appears to be that B will be compelled to hold on trust for C.[5]

In *Rochefoucauld* v. *Boustead*,[6] the plaintiff was the mortgagor of the Delmar Estates in Ceylon. They were sold by the mortgagee to the defendant, who had orally agreed to hold the estates on trust for the plaintiff subject to the repayment to the defendant of the purchase price, and expenses. The defendant sold the land at a price higher than that which he had paid, but did not account to the plaintiff. The defendant became bankrupt.

The plaintiff obtained an order for an account. The Court of Appeal refused to allow the Statute of Frauds to prevent the proof of fraud; and " . . . it is a fraud on the part of a person to whom land is conveyed as a trustee, and who knows it was so conveyed, to deny the trust and claim the land himself. Consequently, notwithstanding the statute, it is competent for a person claiming land conveyed to another to prove by parol evidence that it was so conveyed upon trust for the claimant, and that the grantee, knowing the facts, is denying the trust and relying upon the form of conveyance and the statute, in order to keep the land himself."[7]

The case of a conveyance by A to B on an oral trust for A is a simpler

---

[4] *Davies* v. *Otty* (1865) 35 Beav. 208; *McCormick* v. *Grogan* (1869) L.R. 4 H.L. 82; *Rochefoucauld* v. *Boustead* [1897] 1 Ch. 196; *Bannister* v. *Bannister* [1948] 2 All E.R. 133; *Re Nicholls* [1974] 1 W.L.R. 296 at p. 301. A related jurisdiction is that which gave rise to the doctrine of part performance.

[5] *Taylor* v. *Salmon* (1838) 4 Myl. & Cr. 134; (1915) 28 H.L.R. 237, at p. 366 (G. P. Costigan).

[6] [1897] 1 Ch. 196. See (1984) 43 C.L.J. 306 (T. G. Youdan); (1986) 36 N.I.L.Q. 358 (M. P. Thompson); [1987] Conv. 246 (J. D. Feltham) (taking the view that the "instrument of fraud" principle does not enable C to benefit); *cf* [1988] Conv. 267 (T. G. Youdan) (taking the view that B holds on trust for C).

[7] *Per* Lindley L.J. at p. 206.

one, for, by preventing B taking the beneficial interest, the effect will be to require him to hold on trust for A.[8] The problem appears more commonly with wills than with conveyances *inter vivos*. In the case of wills, it is more complicated; for the alternative solution of a resulting trust for the settlor is less satisfactory; in the *inter vivos* case a living settlor can think again; with a will he is dead, and a resulting trust for the residuary estate is often what the testator most wished to avoid.

There may be many reasons why a testator wishes to be secret about his testamentary dispositions. In many of the older cases, the reason was that he wished to make a gift to support an illegitimate child and its mother. To include the gift in the will would give unwanted publicity; either among members of the family when its provisions are disclosed, or to any person who makes official application to examine the will. At the present day, the usual reason is that the testator cannot make up his mind upon all the details of the disposition of his estate.[9] By using a secret trust, he is able to escape from the policy of the Wills Act, and to retain for himself a power to make future gifts which do not comply with the formalities required by the Act. There seems to be no good reason why he should be able to do so. It is also common to make a settlement *inter vivos* and then, by will, to add further property to the settlement. The details of the disposition do not in that case appear in the will; but this is not a proper case of a secret trust, but of incorporating the other document into the will by reference.

To create a secret trust the testator will usually arrange to leave a legacy to a trusted friend (often his solicitor) who undertakes to hold it upon certain trusts; or he may give it to him "to be held upon such trusts as I have declared to him." The question in the former case is whether the friend could keep the legacy for himself; if not, and clearly in the latter case he cannot, who can claim it: the intended beneficiaries, or the estate?

Different considerations apply to these two situations, as will be seen. The former case is known as a fully secret trust; the latter a half- or semi-secret trust.

2. OTHER METHODS OF INFORMAL DISPOSITION ON DEATH

Before attempting to answer these questions in the context of secret trusts, it is necessary to mention other ways in which a testator may establish a trust which is to take effect on his death without spelling out the terms of the trust in his will.

---

[8] *Davies* v. *Otty* (1865) 35 Beav. 208; *Bannister* v. *Bannister* [1948] 2 All E.R. 133.
[9] This has been described as an abuse of the doctrine, as secrecy is irrelevant; [1981] Conv. 335 (T. G. Watkin). See *Re Snowden* [1979] Ch. 528.

A. Incorporation by Reference[10]

" . . . if a testator, in a testamentary paper duly executed, refers to an existing unattested testamentary paper, the instrument so referred to becomes part of his will; in other words it is incorporated into it; but it is clear that, in order that the informal document should be incorporated in the validly executed document, the latter must refer to the former as a written instrument then existing—that is at the time of execution—in such terms that it may be ascertained."[11] It is not sufficient that the document was in existence; it must be *referred to as an existing document*. If therefore it is a future document at the date of the will, but in existence at the date of a codicil, it is not saved by the rule that a later codicil republishes the will.[12] Where the doctrine of incorporation applies, the incorporated document is admitted to probate, and the advantage of secrecy is lost. We will see that this doctrine appears to be in the minds of some judges when they are dealing with cases of secret trusts, and that the rules applicable to this doctrine have sometimes been applied to secret trust cases.[13]

B. Facts of Independent Legal Significance

It is possible, in some circumstances, for a testator to make a valid testamentary disposition even though the identification of the beneficiaries or of the property must be determined by extrinsic evidence. Thus a gift to my valet, or to the chauffeur of X, or to the testator's partners,[14] or of the contents of a bank account, or of the furniture in a particular room is identifiable only by inquiry. The details of the disposition do not appear in the will; and the disposition will vary with changes which take place in the class of beneficiaries or in the location of the property.

However there are limits. A testator may not make a disposition in favour of the persons whose names appear in an unattested paper, or of such property as shall be indicated to them. The distinction is difficult to draw precisely. Jarman says[15]: "the question is, therefore: is the supplementary act testamentary? If it is, the devise is void; if it is not, then, although it is the sole act of the testator, the devise is good." The American authorities lay down that such a disposition is valid if it can be ascertained from facts which have significance apart from their

---

[10] *Allen* v. *Maddock* (1858) 11 Moo.P.C.C. 427; *In bonis Smart* [1902] P. 238; *Re Jones* [1942] Ch. 328; *Re Edwards' W.T.* [1948] Ch. 440; *Re Schintz's W.T.* [1951] Ch. 870; *Re Tyler* [1967] 1 W.L.R. 1269.

[11] *Per* Gorell-Barnes J. in *In bonis Smart* [1902] P. 238 at p. 240.

[12] *Ibid.* at p. 241. Unless the will is so worded that, speaking from the date of the codicil, it refers to the document as then existing: *In the Goods of Truro* (1886) 1 P. & D. 201.

[13] For differing views as to whether this doctrine is the basis of half secret trusts, see [1979] Conv. 360 (P. Matthews); [1980] Conv. 341 (D. R. Hodge); [1981] Conv. 335 (T. G. Watkin).

[14] *Stubbs* v. *Sargon* (1838) 3 Myl. & Cr. 507.

[15] *Jarman on Wills* (8th ed.), p. 153.

effect upon the disposition in the will.[16] If the facts (as with the unattested paper) have no independent legal significance, the disposition will be void.

C. Gift to Trustees of an Existing Settlement

It is common practice to make a bequest to trustees of an existing settlement to be held by them upon the trusts of that settlement. There is no difficulty in doing so if the existing settlement is incorporated by reference in the will. In such a situation a variation by the court of the terms of the settlement, after the will has taken effect on the testator's death, or on the divorce of a beneficiary, or presumably under the Variation of Trusts Act 1958, does not affect the trusts of the bequest.[17]

However, the doctrine of incorporation by reference is incapable of dealing with a situation in which an *inter vivos* settlement is amended after the date of the will. In *Re Jones*,[18] a testamentary gift which attempted to include future alterations of the settlement was held void even though no alterations were made. The testator was there attempting to reserve for himself a power to dispose of his property by future unattested document.[19] Is this so whenever there is a testamentary addition to a settlement which includes a power of revocation or amendment? A strict application of the rules of incorporation by reference would suggest that it is; but the courts have been willing, where possible, to find a construction which will allow the testamentary gift to be upheld.[20]

In *Re Schintz's Will Trusts*,[21] a settlor made a settlement in which he expressly reserved a power to amend or to revoke. His will provided that the residuary estate should be held on the trusts of the settlement and those which might be created by future deeds executed under the power of amendment or revocation "or as near thereto as the situation will admit." No new trusts were declared. Wynn-Parry J. upheld the gift, finding, as a matter of construction, that the words referring to the future deeds were "otiose and . . . really no more than descriptive of the terms of the settlement."[22] *Re Jones*[23] was distinguished on that ground.

The matter is one of importance, as there is need for some doctrine more acceptable than the fine points of construction which have emerged from the cases. Admittedly, it is not common for a settlor to reserve a power of revocation and amendment, for tax reasons. But it

---

[16] Scott, *Law of Trusts*, § 54(2).

[17] *Re Gooch* [1929] 1 Ch. 740.

[18] [1942] Ch. 328; *Re Edwards' W.T.* [1948] Ch. 440; *Re Schintz's W.T.* [1951] Ch. 870.

[19] The gift was to the trustees of the settlement "or any substitution therefor or modification thereof or addition thereto which I may hereafter execute."

[20] *Re Edwards' W.T., supra; Re Schintz's W.T., supra.*

[21] [1951] Ch. 870.

[22] *Ibid.* at p. 877.

[23] [1942] Ch. 328.

is common to include in settlements a provision for the trustees to have power to amend the trusts, or to appoint upon new trusts, or to terminate the settlement; and it is necessary to know the effect of these factors upon a testamentary addition to the settlement.

If the settlement has not been changed at the date of the testator's death, the question is whether the testamentary addition is valid or not. Where the settlement has been altered, there are three possible solutions; first, that the testamentary addition is void; secondly, that it takes effect upon the settlement in its original form; thirdly, that it takes effect upon the settlement as amended. The testator's intention would in most cases be the third choice. He will know of the amendment of the trust which will have been made before his death, and which may have been made for tax or for family reasons. But clearly the doctrine of incorporation by reference is incapable of incorporating an amendment made after the date of the will. We have seen that the courts can sometimes escape the necessity of holding the gift void. But the second solution is not satisfactory on any argument.

The difficulty could be overcome by applying to this situation a doctrine such as that discussed under B. If the *inter vivos* settlement has independent legal significance, the testator would be able, in this situation as in others, to make a disposition the details of which need not be spelled out in the will; and the technicalities of the doctrine of incorporation by reference would no longer be troublesome. This rule would not conflict with *Re Jones*,[24] for it appears that no property had been transferred to the trustees of the *inter vivos* settlement, which therefore had no independent legal significance.

On this reasoning, the third solution could be selected, and the testamentary gift held upon the trusts of the settlement as amended. This may well seem to be a considerable departure from the present English law. So it seemed in Canada[25] and the United States where it was thought best to deal with the problem by statute. The Uniform Testamentary Additions to Trusts Act 1960, now adopted in a large majority of the States, provides, subject to a contrary expression of intention by the testator, that the testamentary disposition shall become part of the settlement and that it shall be disposed of in accordance with any amendments made to the trusts existing at the date of the testator's death.

In the absence of a statute in England, the courts can only do their best with the doctrine available to them. In some situations, as we have seen, a testator is able to make some testamentary dispositions without

---

[24] *Supra.*
[25] Report of the Ontario Law Commission on Testamentary Additions to Trusts (1967).

spelling out all the details, and *Re Playfair*[26] suggests that some such doctrine is in operation, though unrecognised.[27]

In *Re Playfair*, the testator bequeathed £20,000 to trustees to be held on the trusts of an irrevocable marriage settlement and which was expressed to be an addition to the trust funds. The testator's son, who had a vested interest under the marriage settlement, predeceased the testator. The question was whether his estate was able to benefit from the bequest. It would do so if the bequest formed an addition to the funds of the marriage settlement, under which he held a vested interest at the time of his death; but it would lapse if it were a testamentary gift on the trusts declared in the marriage settlement[28]—as it would be if the settlement were incorporated by reference into the will. It was held that the bequest was an addition to the funds of the marriage settlement and that the son's estate was entitled.[29]

3. Trusts Uncommunicated During the Testator's Lifetime Cannot be Enforced

We have seen that testamentary dispositions are void unless they comply with the formalities required by the Wills Act.[30] A gift is "testamentary" if it is one which takes effect only upon the death of the testator; until the testator dies, there is no gift; a will may be changed, destroyed, or revoked by the testator at any time before his death. Thus a gift "to X when I die" is a testamentary gift and is void unless it observes the proper formalities; and in any case may be revoked at any time before death. But a gift to myself for life and after my death to X is a gift *inter vivos* restricting the donor's present interest to a life interest and giving X a present interest in remainder. The formalities for validity are those applicable to *inter vivos* gifts.[31] If the gift is expressly made revocable, some difficult borderline cases can arise.[32]

Once a gift is effectively made, it is impossible for the donor to take it back, or to impress trusts upon it. It follows that, after the gift in the case of *inter vivos* transactions, and after death in the case of a gift by

---

[26] [1951] Ch. 4.

[27] See also *Berchtoldt* v. *Hertford* (1844) 7 Beav. 172; *Ford* v. *Buxton* (1844) 1 Coll. N.C. 403; *Re Palmer* (1858) 3 H. & N. 26; *Re Finch and Chew's Contract* [1903] 2 Ch. 486; *Re Beaumont* [1913] 1 Ch. 325; *Re Powell* [1918] 1 Ch. 407. The difficulty is that the facts of a case such as *Re Playfair, supra,* are hardly distinguishable from those where the doctrine of incorporation by reference was held applicable.

[28] See *Jarman on Wills* (8th ed.), Chap. XIV.

[29] A possible explanation may be that the testator can exclude the operation of the doctrine of lapse, and may be taken to have done so where he makes a gift by will on the trusts of a marriage settlement in which a vested interest is held by a beneficiary who, to the testator's knowledge, is now dead.

[30] 1837, s.9; *ante*, p. 91; for *donationes mortis causa*, see *ante*, p. 134.

[31] *Ante*, pp. 80 *et seq.*

[32] *Re Danish Bacon Co. Ltd. Staff Pension Fund Trust* [1971] 1 W.L.R. 248.

will, there is no way in which the donor or testator can impose trusts upon the property. If a testator by his will leaves property to X absolutely, this absolute ownership vests in X by virtue of the gift, and it is not possible to reduce X to the status of a trustee. A note in the testator's hand, found among his papers, but not executed as a will and not incorporated with it,[33] is not effective to impose a trust upon the property.[34]

4. FULLY SECRET TRUSTS

A. Informal Disclosure of the Existence and the Terms of the Trust

Where, however, a testator makes a gift by will to a legatee in reliance upon the legatee's express or implied[35] undertaking to hold the property upon certain trusts, or to dispose of it in a certain way by his will,[36] it would not be satisfactory to permit the legatee to take advantage of the requirement of testamentary formality and to keep the property for himself.[37] The doctrine applies also where the deceased failed to revoke an existing gift,[38] or revoked a codicil so as to revive a previous testamentary gift,[39] or where an intestate, in reliance on the undertaking of those entitled on intestacy, failed to make a will,[40] or where a legatee used force[41] or undue influence.[42] "It is altogether immaterial whether the promise is made before or after the execution of the will, that being a revocable instrument."[43]

If the legatee or intestate successor is not allowed to take the property beneficially, the next question is whether the oral trust should be enforced, or whether the legatee or intestate successor should be required to hold as trustee, without trusts being declared, and therefore holding on resulting trust for the estate. The rule in these cases is that the secret trust is enforced in favour of the beneficiary.[44]

This result is justifiable if it is correct to say, as explained below,[45]

---

[33] *Re Louis* (1916) 32 T.L.R. 313 ("to have a drink or smoke with Louis every day").

[34] *Wallgrave* v. *Tebbs* (1855) 2 K. & J. 313; *McCormick* v. *Grogan* (1869) L.R. 4 H.L. 82; *Re Boyes* (1884) 26 Ch.D. 531; *Re Hawkesley's Settlement* [1934] Ch. 384.

[35] "Acquiescence either by words of consent or by silence": *per* Wood V.-C. in *Moss* v. *Cooper* (1861) 1 J. & H. 352 at p. 366. The communication may be by the testator or by his agent.

[36] *Re Gardner* [1920] 2 Ch. 523; *Re Young* [1951] Ch. 344; *Ottaway* v. *Norman* [1972] Ch. 698.

[37] *Drakeford* v. *Wilks* (1747) 3 Atk. 539; *Stickland* v. *Aldridge* (1804) 9 Ves.Jr. 516; *Wallgrave* v. *Tebbs* (1855) 2 K. & J. 313 at p. 320. For the position where the trustee revokes his acceptance during the testator's lifetime, see Hayton and Marshall, *Cases and Commentary on the Law of Trusts* (8th ed.), p. 103.

[38] *Chamberlaine* v. *Chamberlaine* (1678) Free. Ch. 34; *Moss* v. *Cooper, supra.*

[39] *Tharp* v. *Tharp* [1916] 1 Ch. 142; [1916] 2 Ch. 205.

[40] *Stickland* v. *Aldridge, supra*, at p. 519; (1948) 12 Conv.(N.S.) 28 (J. G. Fleming).

[41] *Dixon* v. *Olmius* (1787) 1 Cox. Eq. 414.

[42] *Bulkley* v. *Wilford* (1834) 2 Cl. & F. 102.

[43] *Per* Wood V.-C. in *Moss* v. *Cooper* (1861) 1 J. & H. 352 at p. 367.

[44] See Scott, *Law of Trusts*, § 55(1); *Thynn* v. *Thynn* (1684) 1 Vern. 296.

[45] *Post*, p. 157.

that a secret trust is enforced because the testator validly declared an *inter vivos* trust during his lifetime, and the trust became constituted by the vesting of the property on his death in the trustee. That, as will be seen below, is the modern theoretical explanation of the enforcement of secret trusts. That is not, however, the reason which has been relied on historically to enforce fully secret trusts. Without that theory, the courts were in real difficulty in that the Wills Act laid down the requirements for the creation of a testamentary trust, and those requirements were not met. If, therefore, the trusts were enforced, was not the Wills Act being disregarded? Or, as they said, did the courts not "give the go-by" to it?[46] The courts searched for a justification in not observing the terms of the Wills Act. And the justification was found in the doctrine of fraud; and the fact that it would be a fraud in the legatee to take beneficially in the circumstances. The fraud theory was laid down in the clearest terms by Lord Hatherley L.C. and Lord Westbury in *McCormick* v. *Grogan*,[47] although the House of Lords held in that case that the testator had not intended to impose an obligation on Grogan, the sole executor, and that, therefore, no trust existed on the facts of the case. To base the court's intervention on the ground of fraud could well be a sufficient justification for not applying the Wills Act; but the next step was not so obvious; it would be wrong for the legatee to keep the property, but it was difficult to see how the prevention of fraud would justify the projection forward of the beneficial interest to the beneficiary. As we will see, this matter became all the more clear when the courts were dealing with the question of half-secret trusts; that is to say the case in which the testator requires the legatee to take the property as trustee, without saying in the will who the beneficiaries are. In that situation, there was no possibility of the legatee being fraudulent, in the sense of enriching himself, because he was expressed to take as trustee. In *Blackwell* v. *Blackwell*[48] the leading case on half-secret trusts, the enforcement of the half-secret trust was justified by saying that the intention of the testator was clear, and that it was communicated to and acquiesced in by the legatee. As explained above, the modern view is to justify the enforcement of secret trusts upon the theory that the trust has been declared *inter vivos* and that it is constituted by the testamentary gift to the legatee. There are, as will be seen, some theoretical difficulties in this view also.[49]

B. Proof

Related to the question whether the doctrine of secret trusts is based upon a fraud of the legatee is the question of the standard of proof required to establish a secret trust. A high standard of proof is required

---

[46] *Re Pitt-Rivers* [1902] 1 Ch. 403 at p. 407; *Blackwell* v. *Blackwell* [1929] A.C. 318 at p. 337.
[47] (1869) L.R. 4 H.L. 82.
[48] [1929] A.C. 318.
[49] *Post*, p. 157.

to prove fraud, and there are dicta in many cases indicating that a secret trust can only be proved where there is "clear evidence,"[50] and suggesting that the standard is the same as that required to support the rectification of a written instrument.[51] In *Re Snowden*,[52] however, Megarry V.-C. disregarded the historical connection of the doctrine of secret trusts and the requirement of fraud; and laid down that the standard required to prove communication and acceptance is the ordinary civil standard of proof required to establish an ordinary trust.[53] The evidence may, of course, establish an intention to create a trust, and its acceptance by the legatee, without establishing who the beneficiaries were. The legatee would then hold on resulting trust.[54] If questions of fraud or other special factors arose, the standard required would rise. The onus is on the person contending that the trust exists.[55]

C. Disclosure to the Legatee of the Existence of the Trust but not its Terms

If the testator discloses to the legatee the fact that he is to hold the legacy on trust, but does not disclose the terms of the trust before his death, the legatee will hold on resulting trust for the estate.[56] The intended trust, not being declared before the death, cannot be enforced. The imposition of the resulting trust will prevent the unjust enrichment of the legatee.

In *Re Boyes*,[57] a legacy was given to the testator's solicitor, who had undertaken to hold the property according to directions which he would receive by letter. The letter was found only after the death. The solicitor accepted that he held as trustee, and wished to carry out the trust. Kay J. held that there was a resulting trust in favour of the next-of-kin; and explained the rule by saying: "The essence of all these decisions is that the devisee or legatee accepts a particular trust which thereupon becomes binding upon him, and which it would be a fraud in him not to carry into effect.[58]

A further point must be mentioned. This situation is similar to that of half-secret trusts in that the legatee takes as a trustee. But there is an important difference. In *Re Boyes*,[59] the gift was absolute on its face;

---

[50] See *McCormick* v. *Grogan* (1869) L.R. 4 H.L. 82 at p. 87, *per* Lord Westbury; *Ottaway* v. *Norman* [1972] Ch. 698 at p. 699.

[51] *Fowler* v. *Fowler* (1859) 4 De G. & J. 250 at p. 264; *Crane* v. *Hegaman-Harris Co. Inc.* [1939] 4 All E.R. 68 at p. 71; *Joscelyne* v. *Nissen* [1970] 2 Q.B. 86 at p. 98; *Ottaway* v. *Norman, supra.*

[52] [1979] Ch. 528; (1979) 38 C.L.J. 260 (C. E. F. Rickett).

[53] *Ibid.* at p. 537.

[54] *Re Boyes* (1884) 26 Ch.D. 531.

[55] *Jones* v. *Badley* (1868) L.R. 3 Ch.App. 362.

[56] Similarly if the terms, although disclosed, are unlawful or uncertain. See *Re Pugh's W.T.* [1967] 1 W.L.R. 1262.

[57] (1884) 26 Ch.D. 531; *Re Hawkesley's Settlement* [1934] Ch. 384.

[58] *Ibid.* at p. 536.

[59] (1884) 26 Ch.D. 531.

the trust could have been enforced if the terms had been declared before death.[60] Where the existence of a trust is disclosed on the face of the will, the communication, as we shall see, must be prior to or contemporaneously with the execution of the will.[61]

D. Methods of Communication

We have seen that the trust must be communicated before the testator's death. The communication may be made orally or in writing; and it appears that, just as "a ship which sails under sealed orders, is sailing under orders though the exact terms are not ascertained by the captain till later,"[62] a testator may, during his lifetime, give to the legatee a sealed envelope which is not to be opened until the testator's death. This is sufficient provided the legatee knows that it contains details of the trust.

E. Additions to the Secret Trust

A testator must communicate not only the trust and the terms, but also the identity of the property to be held on trust.

In *Re Colin Cooper*,[63] the testator left £5,000 to two persons as trustees, and informally communicated to them the terms of the trust. By a later codicil he purported to increase the sum to be devoted to the secret trust to £10,000, they "knowing my wishes regarding that sum." This addition was not communicated to the trustees. It was held that the first instalment could be devoted to the secret trusts; but the later instalment went on a resulting trust.[64]

F. Undertaking to Leave by Will

A secret trust may impose an obligation not only to hold on trust for a beneficiary on the testator's death; but also an obligation to make provision for an intended beneficiary after the legatee's death.

In *Re Gardner (No. 1)*,[65] a wife left her estate to her husband for life, and there was an agreement that the property should be divided among certain beneficiaries on his death. The husband died intestate, and the Court of Appeal decided that he held the property, after his life interest, on trust for the beneficiaries.

Ottaway v. *Norman*[66] took the matter a stage further. The testator agreed with his housekeeper that she should have a bungalow after his death, and she agreed to leave it to the testator's son by her will. The testator left the bungalow to her absolutely. She first made a will

---

[60] *Re Gardner* [1920] 2 Ch. 523.
[61] *Post*, p. 154.
[62] *Per* Lord Wright in *Re Keen* [1937] Ch. 236 at p. 242; *Re Boyes, supra*, at p. 536.
[63] [1939] Ch. 811.
[64] Had it been a fully secret trust, the legatees would have been beneficially entitled to the addition.
[65] [1920] 2 Ch. 523; *Re Young* [1951] Ch. 344; *post*, p. 158.
[66] [1972] Ch. 698; (1972) 36 Conv.(n.s.) 129 (D. J. Hayton).

in favour of the testator's son; but she then changed that will, and left the bungalow to the defendant. Brightman J. held that the son was entitled.

The enforcement of a secret trust in this situation creates a number of problems concerning the status of the trust during the housekeeper's lifetime, and the theoretical basis on which secret trusts are enforced. This question is discussed in section 7 below, but some of the questions arising from *Ottaway* v. *Norman*[67] are more conveniently considered in Chapter 12.

G. Tenants in Common and Joint Tenants

Where a testamentary gift is made to two or more persons as tenants in common, and secret trusts are communicated to some but not all of the tenants in common, those to whom the communication was made are bound, the others taking beneficially.[68] "To hold otherwise would enable one beneficiary to deprive the rest of their benefits by setting up a secret trust."[69]

But where a gift is made to them as joint tenants, a distinction is made between the case where the trust is communicated before the making of the will, and that where the communication is between the will and the death.[70] In the former case, all joint tenants are bound.[71] In the latter, only those who have accepted the trust are bound by it,[72] "the reason being that the gift is not tainted with any fraud in procuring the execution of the will."[73]

Farwell J. was dissatisfied with his own explanation. He confessed that he was "unable to see any difference between a gift made on the faith of an antecedent promise and a gift left unrevoked on the faith of a subsequent promise."[74] It has been suggested that gifts upon secret trusts to joint tenants and tenants in common should be decided on the principle of *Huguenin* v. *Baseley*,[75] that "'no man may profit by the fraud of another.'"[76] Thus "if A induces B to make or leave unrevoked a will leaving property to A and C,"[77] whether as joint tenants or tenants in common, C will be bound "if the testator would not have made any gift to C unless A had promised. . . . If the testator would still have left property to C even if A had not promised, C is not bound. . . . Whether A and C are joint tenants or tenants in common, and whether A's

---

[67] *Supra.*
[68] *Tee* v. *Ferri* (1856) 2 K. & J. 357.
[69] *Re Stead* [1900] 1 Ch. 237 at p. 241.
[70] See Maitland, p. 62.
[71] *Russell* v. *Jackson* (1852) 10 Hare 204; *Jones* v. *Badley* (1868) L.R. 3 Ch.App. 362; *Re Gardom* [1914] 1 Ch. 662; *Re Spence* [1949] W.N. 237; *Re Young* [1951] Ch. 344.
[72] *Burney* v. *MacDonald* (1845) 15 Sim. 6; *Moss* v. *Cooper* (1861) 1 J. & H. 352.
[73] *Per* Farwell J. in *Re Stead* [1900] 1 Ch. 237 at p. 241.
[74] *Ibid.*
[75] (1807) 14 Ves. 273.
[76] (1972) 88 L.Q.R. 225 at p. 226 (B. Perrins).
[77] *Per* Farwell J. in *Re Stead* [1900] 1 Ch. 237 at p. 241.

promise was before or after the making of the will are matters of
evidence that may help to determine whether or not there was such an
inducement, but of themselves both matters are inconclusive."[78] The
argument is persuasive; but the cases say otherwise. The wrong turning
was taken in *Rowbotham* v. *Dunnett*.[79]

The principles discussed above have emerged from cases concerning
fully secret trusts. Of course, in the case of half-secret trusts there
could be no question of the legatees taking beneficially. The issue
would be whether a valid half-secret trust could be created by communication to fewer than the whole number of trustees. It seems that the
principles applicable to fully secret trusts would be applied by analogy,
bearing in mind that half-secret trustees will invariably be joint
tenants, and that communication after the will is ineffective in the case
of half-secret trusts, as explained below. Hence communication to one
of the trustees prior to the making of the will is effective.[80]

5. HALF-SECRET TRUSTS

Where the will gives property to a legatee *upon trust*, without,
however, saying what the intended trusts are, the question of the
enforcement of a secret trust communicated to the legatee has been
treated very differently from the case where the property was given to
the legatee *absolutely* in the will. The courts have found it more
difficult to enforce a secret trust in the former case—where the legatee
takes expressly as trustee—than in the latter case. It is difficult to see
any sense, however, in a rule which allows a secret trust to be enforced
if the trust is nowhere mentioned in the will; but holds it void if the
testamentary gift discloses the fact that the legatee takes as trustee.
And, if it be right to say that secret trusts are express trusts operating
wholly outside the scope of the Wills Act, it is difficult to see why the
two situations should not be treated alike.

But there is a historical explanation. We saw that the nineteenth
century judges said that secret trusts were enforced to prevent fraud[81]
to prevent the legatee taking for himself what he had promised the
testator to hold upon trust. The element of fraud, however, was not
present in the case of the gift to a legatee as trustee. As he took in a
fiduciary capacity, he could in no circumstances take the property for
himself. There was no possibility of fraud, and no justification, so the
argument ran, for not applying the Wills Act. And it was at one time
held that the mention of the existence of a trust did prevent the

---

[78] (1972) 88 L.Q.R. 225 at p. 226 (B. Perrins).
[79] (1878) 8 Ch.D. 430.
[80] See *Re Gardom* [1914] 1 Ch. 662.
[81] *Ante*, p. 148.

operation of the doctrine of secret trusts.[82] The validity of half-secret trusts was not finally established until the House of Lords decision in *Blackwell* v. *Blackwell*[83] in 1929.

In *Blackwell* v. *Blackwell*,[84] the testator by a codicil gave a legacy of £12,000 to legatees upon trust to apply the income "for the purposes indicated by me to them." The trust had been accepted prior to the execution of the codicil. The House of Lords enforced the trust. They were assisted by *Re Fleetwood*[85] and *Re Huxtable*[86] where it was held that the secret trust doctrine applied although the gift was in terms a gift upon trust, and where therefore there was no question of fraud in the legatee. Lord Sumner concluded that "it is communication of the purpose to the legatee, coupled with acquiescence or promise on his part, that removes the matter from the provision of the Wills Act and brings it within the law of trusts, as applied in this instance to trustees, who happen also to be legatees."[87] The effect of the bequest "remains to be decided by the law as laid down by the Courts before and since the [Wills] Act, and does not depend on the Act itself."[88] Thus the trust operated outside the Act and could be enforced without proof of fraud.

In *Blackwell* v. *Blackwell*[89] the trusts were communicated before the will and were stated to have been so communicated. Will the same rule apply where the trusts are or may be declared in the future? On the one hand, there is logically no difference between declarations of trusts before and after the will; for the will is ambulatory and of no effect until the death.[90] The distinction is not made, as we have seen, with fully secret trusts.[91] And, if the trust operates independently of the Wills Act, the date of the will should be immaterial. On the other hand, it is more difficult to *assume* acquiescence where the communication is after the will; in the absence of proof of express agreement, the fact of non-revocation may be the only basis on which to presume acquiescence. And more important, "a testator cannot reserve to himself a power of making future unwitnessed dispositions by merely naming a trustee and leaving the purposes of the trust to be supplied afterwards . . . ."[92] To allow that to be done by half-secret trust would

[82] *Moss* v. *Cooper* (1861) 1 J. & H. 352 at p. 367; *Le Page* v. *Gardom* (1915) 84 L.J.Ch. 749 at p. 752; (1937) 53 L.Q.R. 501 (W. S. Holdsworth).
[83] [1929] A.C. 318.
[84] *Supra.*
[85] (1880) 15 Ch.D. 594.
[86] [1902] 2 Ch. 793.
[87] [1929] A.C. 318 at pp. 339–340; *Ottaway* v. *Norman* [1972] Ch. 698 at p. 711.
[88] *Ibid.* at p. 339.
[89] [1929] A.C. 318.
[90] (1937) 53 L.Q.R. 501 (W. S. Holdsworth); Holdsworth, *Essays in Law and History*, p. 199.
[91] *Ante*, p. 150; *Re Gardner* [1920] 2 Ch. 523.
[92] *Per* Lord Sumner in *Blackwell* v. *Blackwell* [1929] A.C. 318 at p. 339.

be to give a wider rule for secret trusts (which might be oral) than that which as we have seen is applied in the case of incorporation of documents by reference.[93] It would be surprising if the law of wills permitted this; but, if the proper explanation of the enforcement of secret trusts is that they operate outside the will and independently of the Wills Act, then the rules relating to incorporation by reference are, as has been pointed out, quite irrelevant.[94] And what Lord Sumner feared can always be achieved by a fully secret trust.

With half-secret trusts however the distinction appears to be made.

In *Re Keen*[95] the testator gave a sum of money to trustees "to be held upon trust and disposed of by them among such person, persons or charities as may be notified by me to them or either of them during my lifetime. ... " Otherwise the money was to fall into residue. Previously, one of the trustees had been given a sealed envelope containing the name of the beneficiary of the intended trust. In deciding in favour of the residuary legatees, the Court of Appeal held that the handing over of the sealed envelope was a communication of the trust, but that this, being *prior* to the date of the will,[96] was inconsistent with the terms of the will which provided for "a future definition . . . of the trust subsequent to the date of the will," while "the sealed letter relied on as notifying the trust was communicated . . . before the date of the will."[97]

The trust would, however, have failed independently of the question of inconsistency. The provision in the will contained a power to declare trusts in the future. This was void, for it "would involve a power to change a testamentary disposition by an unexecuted codicil and would violate section 9 of the Wills Act."[98]

The criticisms of this rule have been discussed. The contrary rule exists in Ireland[99] and in most of the American jurisdictions.[1] The matter is still open to the House of Lords; it may be that the true ratio of *Re Keen*[2] is the narrow point of inconsistency; but it was followed in *Re Bateman's Will Trusts*,[3] where, it seems, the rule was not challenged. The present position is unsatisfactory; there is no sense in a rule which (in the case of communication between the will and the

---

[93] *In bonis Smart* [1902] P. 238; [1979] Conv. 360 (P. Matthews).
[94] (1937) 53 L.Q.R. 501 (W. S. Holdsworth); *Moss* v. *Cooper* (1861) 1 J. & K. 352 at p. 367.
[95] [1937] Ch. 236; *Johnson* v. *Ball* (1851) 5 De G. & Sm. 85; (1972) 23 N.I.L.Q. (R. Burgess).
[96] *Re Huxtable* [1902] 2 Ch. 793.
[97] *Re Keen, supra,* at p. 248; *Re Rees' W.T.* [1950] Ch. 204.
[98] *Re Keen, supra,* at p. 247; *Johnson* v. *Ball* (1851) 5 De G. & Sm. 85; *Re Hetley* [1902] 2 Ch. 866.
[99] *Riordan* v. *Banon* (1876) 10 Ir.R.Eq. 469; *contra Balfe* v. *Halfpenny* [1904] 1 Ir.R. 486; *Re Browne* [1944] Ir.R. 90; (1951) 67 L.Q.R. 413 (L. A. Sheridan).
[1] Scott, *Law of Trusts,* § 55(8); *Restatement of Trusts,* § 55, comment (*c*), (*h*).
[2] [1937] Ch. 236.
[3] [1970] 1 W.L.R. 1463.

death) enforces a trust in a bequest "to X" but disregards the trust in a bequest "to X upon trust."

In support of the communication rules, however, it has been said that secret trusts are best explained in terms of the extrinsic evidence rule, whereby such evidence may not be admitted to contradict the terms of a will in the absence of fraud (or other vitiating factors), but may sometimes be admitted to explain an ambiguity. Thus in the case of a fully secret trust extrinsic evidence of the acceptance of a trust before or after execution of the will is admissible to contradict the apparently absolute terms of the gift in order to prevent fraud. In the case of a half-secret trust, where no fraud is possible, extrinsic evidence of a prior communication is admissible because this does not contradict the will and does not amount to upholding an "unexecuted codicil" because the testator is entitled to incorporate the arrangements by reference. The extrinsic evidence is necessary to elucidate what the will means when it refers to a trust. Where, however, the communication is after the will extrinsic evidence is not admissible to elucidate the reference to a trust because this would amount to allowing an "unexecuted codicil" and, as has been said, cannot be justified on the basis of fraud.[4]

Another view is that consistency should be achieved by requiring the communication to be before the will even in the case of a fully secret trust. If the trusteeship was accepted after the will, the legatee would hold on trust for the residuary legatee or next-of-kin. This would have the advantage of preventing reliance on the doctrine of secret trusts by testators who are merely indecisive[5] and thus not within the rationale of the doctrine.[6]

6. CAN THE SECRET TRUSTEE TAKE A BENEFIT?

The legatee may claim that the testator intended him to take some benefit from the gift, perhaps, for example, a specific sum, or possibly any surplus after performing the trust. Two separate questions arise here; first, was this the testator's intention? Secondly, how far is evidence of such an intention admissible in favour of the trustee?

To consider first the question of intention, it is necessary to construe the language of the will to determine whether the testator's intention was to make the legatee a trustee of the whole of the property given, or to make a beneficial gift to him subject to his performing certain

---

[4] [1985] Conv. 248 (B. Perrins).
[5] As in *Re Snowden* [1979] Ch. 528.
[6] [1981] Conv. 335 (T. G. Watkin). See also the discussion of how the suggested reform would operate in the case of a person who refrains from making a will in reliance upon the acceptance of a trust by the next-of-kin.

obligations.[7] In the former case, any surplus left after carrying out the trusts is held upon resulting trusts[8]; in the latter, the legatee may keep it.[9] There is thus no difficulty in a case where the will itself makes it clear that the trust does not extend to the whole of the legacy, but the will may be silent on the matter, and the only evidence extrinsic. This leads us to the second question, namely whether the trustee may be permitted to prove his claim to benefit by relying on documentary or even oral evidence.

The difficulty, whether the trust be fully or half-secret, is the danger of fraud by the secret trustee. A further problem in the case of a half-secret trust is that the evidence would contradict the terms of the will, which impose a trust on the entire legacy.[10]

In *Re Rees' W.T.*[11] the testator by will appointed a friend and his solicitor (thereinafter called his trustees) to be executors and trustees. He left the whole estate "unto my trustees absolutely they well knowing my wishes concerning the same."

The testator had told the trustees that he wished them to make certain payments and to retain any surplus for themselves. A substantial surplus remained. It was held that the trustees were not entitled to the surplus, which passed as on intestacy. The will, on its true construction, imposed a trust on the whole, and evidence was not admissible to show that the trustees were to take a benefit. It was not without significance that the trustee was the testator's solicitor. As Evershed M.R. said, "In the general public interest it seems to me desirable that, if a testator wishes his property to go to his solicitor and the solicitor prepares the will, that intention on the part of the testator should appear plainly in the will and should not be arrived at by the more oblique method of what is sometimes called a secret trust."[12]

In *Re Tyler*,[13] however, there are suggestions that evidence is admissible as to all the terms of a trust, including any in favour of the trustee himself, although such evidence will not lightly be admitted. Pennycuick J. found difficulty in the reasoning of *Re Rees*. But evidence

---

[7] *Ante*, p. 53. This construction is more likely where the legatee is a relative for whom the testator may be supposed to have been intending to provide. See *Irvine* v. *Sullivan* (1869) L.R. 8 Eq. 673 (fiancée).

[8] *Ante*, p. 53.

[9] *Ante*, p. 54; *Irvine* v. *Sullivan* (1869) L.R. 8 Eq. 673.

[10] We have seen, in the context of communication, that evidence inconsistent with the will is not admissible; *Re Keen* [1937] Ch. 236, *ante*, p. 154.

[11] [1950] Ch. 204. See also *Re Pugh's W.T.* [1967] 1 W.L.R. 1262, suggesting that it is easier to infer an intention that a sole trustee should take beneficially than that two or more trustees should do so.

[12] [1950] Ch. 204 at p. 211.

[13] [1967] 1 W.L.R. 1269 (concerning an *inter vivos* trust). See also *Ottaway* v. *Norman* [1972] Ch. 698, *ante*, p. 150, where the secret trustee took a benefit in the form of a life interest. This was clearly the testator's intention and the point was not discussed. In any event, the interest had already been enjoyed.

contained in the (now deceased) trustee's own written memorandum did not suffice.[14]

Finally, we have seen that if a secret trust fails for non-compliance with the communication rules, or for uncertainty, the secret trustee holds on trust for the residuary legatee or next-of-kin. He could not claim the legacy for himself if the trust was half-secret, or, although fully secret, if he had accepted trusteeship. A question might arise as to whether the secret trustee could take the property if he himself was the residuary legatee or next-of-kin. There is no reason in principle why he should not, as he would be claiming in a different capacity, but the court might intervene if he disclaimed the legacy in order to benefit.[15]

7. THEORETICAL BASIS OF SECRET TRUSTS

A. Inter Vivos Trust Dehors the Will

The formal requirements for a will, contained in the Wills Act 1837, are based upon a sound policy. It is important to avoid doubt, fraud and uncertainty in connection with testamentary dispositions; and it is essential to rely upon written formalities as there is no other way of ascertaining the intention of the testator. If secret trusts, which effectively create dispositions of property on death, are to be allowed, it is important to justify the failure to apply the provisions of the Wills Act. In terms of policy, it is easy to favour an exception in cases in which the intention of the testator is clear, and is opposed only by the formalities which were set up in the hope of establishing it. But further justification is needed. The Wills Act is a statute, and not merely an expression of policy. The question is whether some theory can be found to justify the enforcement of secret trusts.

We have seen that the early cases were explained on the ground of fraud[16]; the fear that the legatee would otherwise keep the property for himself. And there is substantial authority for a refusal to allow a statute to be used as an instrument of fraud. But the fraud theory will not justify the enforcement of half-secret trusts.[17] The legatee, being named as a trustee, cannot claim. Nor is it sufficient to say as did Lord Sumner in *Blackwell* v. *Blackwell*[18] that secret trusts are based upon

---

[14] Although generally such a memorandum is *admissible* under the Civil Evidence Act 1968 to prove the terms of the trust.

[15] See *Blackwell* v. *Blackwell* [1929] A.C. 318 at p. 341. Disclaimer might in any event not cause a half-secret trust to fail, by reliance on the maxim that a trust does not fail for want of a trustee; but it has been said that a fully secret trust will fail if the trustee disclaims; *Re Maddock* [1902] 2 Ch. 220 at p. 231; *cf. Blackwell* v. *Blackwell, supra*; Oakley, *Constructive Trusts* (2nd ed.), p. 122.

[16] *Ante*, p. 148; Oakley, *Constructive Trusts* (2nd ed.), pp. 117–118.

[17] But see [1980] Conv. 341 (D. R. Hodge), expressing the view that the fraud theory is the proper basis; there can be a fraud on the testator or secret beneficiary even if there is no gain to the secret trustee. See *Riordan* v. *Banon* (1876) 10 Ir.R.Eq. 469; *Re Fleetwood* (1880) 15 Ch.D. 594.

[18] [1929] A.C. 318 at p. 340; *ante*, p. 153.

the essential elements of intention, communication and acquiescence, for this assumes a new basis for the enforcement of testamentary dispositions which is wholly inconsistent with the Wills Act, and suggests that a testator could "contract out of" the Wills Act, and create testamentary dispositions by a different method. The modern view is that secret trusts can be enforced because they are not trusts created by will; but are trusts arising outside and independently of (or dehors) the will[19]; that they arise by reason of the personal obligation accepted by the legatee.[20]

In *Re Young*,[21] the testator made a bequest to his wife with a direction that on her death she should leave the property for the purposes which he had communicated to her. One of the purposes was that she would leave a legacy of £2,000 to the chauffeur. The chauffeur had witnessed the will. A witness may not normally take a legacy, and the question was whether he had thereby forfeited his interest.[22] Danckwerts J. held that he had not; the trust in his favour was not a trust contained in the will but one created separately and imposed upon the legatee.[23]

It is one thing to say that the trust operates outside the will, but it is another to say just how and when the trust takes effect. If some of the propositions discussed in Chapter 4[24] are sound, the most natural way for this to occur is to treat the communication to the trustee as the declaration of trust, and the vesting of the property in the trustee by the will as the constitution of the trust. If this is so, the declaration is *inter vivos*, and the Wills Act has no effect upon it; the only statutory formalities that are relevant are Law of Property Act 1925, s.53(1)

---

[19] *Per* Lord Westbury in *Cullen* v. *Att.-Gen. for Northern Ireland* (1866) L.R. 1 H.L. 190 at p. 198; *per* Lord Sumner in *Blackwell* v. *Blackwell* [1929] A.C. 318 at p. 340.

[20] "I think the solution is to be found by bearing in mind that what is enforced is not a trust imposed by the will, but one arising from the acceptance by the legatee of a trust communicated to him by the testator, on the faith of which acceptance the will was made or left unrevoked, as the case might be": *per* Lord Warrington of Clyffe in *Blackwell* v. *Blackwell* [1929] A.C. 318 at p. 342.

[21] [1951] Ch. 344; *Cullen* v. *Att.-Gen. for Northern Ireland* (1866) L.R. 1 H.L. 190.

[22] Wills Act 1837, s.15. *cf. Re Fleetwood* (1880) 15 Ch.D. 594; *O'Brien* v. *Condon* [1905] Ir.R. 51. If it is the secret trustee who attests there should be no difficulty if it is a half-secret trust, as he takes no beneficial interest on the face of the will. If it is fully secret, the position is less clear. For the view that it would fail, see Oakley, *Constructive Trusts* (2nd ed.), p. 120.

[23] To the contrary is *Re Maddock* [1902] 2 Ch. 220, where the property subject to a fully secret trust was treated as being subject to a specific bequest for the purpose of the payment of debts out of the estate. No doubt the legacy would be treated as part of the estate for tax purposes and for the purposes of the Inheritance (Provision for Family and Dependants) Act 1975, rather than as property disposed of prior to the death. Another question which could arise would be whether, in the case of a misapplication, the secret beneficiary would have a personal action against the recipient. Such actions apparently do not lie in the case of *inter vivos* trusts; *post*, p. 645.

[24] *Ante*, pp. 110 *et seq*.

(*b*),[25] which requires that declarations of trusts of land should be evidenced in writing; but this would not affect the rule requiring a fraudulent trustee in a fully secret trust of land to hold on a constructive trust.[26] There would be no awkward distinction between declarations prior to and subsequent to the will in half-secret trusts[27]; the sole question would be whether or not a trust was declared of the property before the death, and whether that trust became properly constituted by the vesting of the property in the trustee.

We have seen that the usual rule in the case of property coming to a person who had previously declared himself trustee of it was that the trust did not become constituted without a further manifestation of intention.[28] It was submitted that where a third person accepted an instruction to hold the property on certain trusts and the settlor subsequently transferred the property to him without further declaration, the trust would be constituted. It should make no difference whether the property passed to the trustee by conveyance *inter vivos* or by a will.[29] It will probably fail however if the trustee predeceases the testator, at any rate in the case of a fully secret trust.[30] Assuming its terms were known, it may be that a half-secret trust could be saved by the maxim "a trust does not fail for want of a trustee."[31]

Ottaway v. *Norman*[32] raises a further complication. Assuming that it is correct to say that the testator made an *inter vivos* declaration that the bungalow was to be held on trust for his son after the housekeeper's death, and that the trust was constituted by the vesting of the property in the housekeeper as trustee, the question arises, as has been seen, of the nature of the trust during the housekeeper's lifetime. Does the trust arise on the testator's death, or upon the housekeeper's? If it arises on the testator's death, is the housekeeper's interest effectively reduced to a life interest? If it arises on the housekeeper's death, what is the position during her lifetime? Brightman J. said that it was "in suspense ... but attaches to the estate of the [housekeeper] at the

---

[25] *Ante*, p. 80. *Re Baillie* (1886) 2 T.L.R. 660 at p. 661; but there was no writing in *Ottaway* v. *Norman* [1972] Ch. 698; *post*, p. 161.

[26] L.P.A. 1925, s.53(2). As to whether he should hold on trust for the secret beneficiaries, see *post*, p. 161.

[27] *Re Keen* [1937] Ch. 236; *ante*, p. 154.

[28] *Ante*, p. 133; *Brennan* v. *Morphett* (1908) 6 C.L.R. 22; *Matter of Gurlitz*, 105 Misc. 30, 172 N.Y. Supp. 523 (1918); *Re Northcliffe* [1925] Ch. 651.

[29] As with the property received by Miss Towry Law from her sister and conveyed to the trustees: *Re Ellenborough* [1903] 1 Ch. 697; *Re Adlard* [1954] Ch. 29; *Re Ralli's W.T.* [1964] Ch. 288.

[30] *Per* Cozens-Hardy L.J. in *Re Maddock* [1902] 2 Ch. 220 at p. 251; Oakley, *Constructive Trusts* (2nd ed.), p. 120.

[31] Unless the particular trustee is regarded as essential to the trust. For an example in another context, see *Re Lysaght* [1966] 1 Ch. 191. The question of disclaimer by the secret trustee has already been considered; *ante*, p. 157.

[32] [1972] Ch. 698; (1972) 36 Conv.(N.S.) 129 (D. J. Hayton); (1972) 36 Conv.(N.S.) at p. 115 (R. Burgess); [1971] A.S.C.L. 375 at p. 384 (J. J. Hackney).

moment of the latter's death."[33] A sort of "floating trust,"[34] such as was recognised by the High Court of Australia in *Birmingham* v. *Renfrew*[35] but which can hardly be said to be a recognised legal concept. The situation during the housekeeper's lifetime is similar to that existing during the lifetime of the survivor of makers of mutual wills. But the origin of the trust is of course quite different. In the former case it is based upon the declaration of the trust, followed by communication and acquiescence and the vesting of the property in the trustee; in the case of mutual wills, it is based on the contract between the parties followed by the receipt of the benefits by the survivor. Once the trust has attached, however, the problems are similar, and will be discussed in Chapter 12.

Until the property has so vested, there is no completely constituted trust; the declaration can have no effect, and cannot create property rights. It can be revoked or altered, or the property may be disposed of during the testator's lifetime; and no doubt, if the settlor (or testator) acts as if he had forgotten the declaration or assumed it to be no longer existent, it will be treated as having expired. And no rational theory, it is suggested, can be found which will justify the remarkable decision in *Re Gardner (No. 2)*.[36] We have seen that a wife left her estate to her husband for life,[37] and that after his death it was to be held on secret trust for five named beneficiaries. One of the beneficiaries predeceased the wife. The representatives of the deceased beneficiary successfully claimed the share.

A gift by will normally lapses if the donee predeceases the testator,[38] and the estate of the donee can only claim if the donee acquired some interest in the property before he died. No such interest could exist in this case; and the theory which suggests that a secret trust can be treated as a declaration of trust *inter vivos* does not suggest that any interest is obtained by any beneficiary prior to the constitution of the trust by vesting of the legal estate in the trustee.

B. Express or Constructive Trust

Closely connected with the theoretical basis of secret trusts is the question whether a secret trust is properly categorised as an express or

---

[33] *Ibid.* at p. 713.

[34] (1972) 36 Conv.(n.s.) at p. 132 (D. J. Hayton).

[35] (1937) 57 C.L.R. 666. Applied in *Re Cleaver* [1981] 1 W.L.R. 939.

[36] [1923] 2 Ch. 230. See Oakley, *Constructive Trusts* (2nd ed.), p. 121, suggesting that there is no clear rule against a non-testamentary trust for a dead person. This is doubtful, as such a beneficiary has no legal personality, unless it is clear that his estate is intended to take.

[37] *Re Gardner (No. 1)* [1920] 2 Ch. 523; *ante*, p. 150.

[38] A special exception is made in the case of children of the testator who predecease him, leaving issue: Wills Act 1837, s.33, as amended by Administration of Justice Act 1982. Such a gift takes effect in favour of the issue.

constructive trust.[39] The question is not merely academic, for, as we have seen,[40] constructive trusts of land are excepted from the requirement of written evidence. Is an oral secret trust of land valid?

An express trust is one declared by the settlor; a constructive trust is one imposed by the law.[41] Our analysis of secret trusts as being declarations dehors the will categorises them as express trusts, whether they are fully or half secret. In the case of a half secret trust the will itself expressly declares a trust. While this element is absent with a fully secret trust, such a trust may claim to be express on the basis of the testator's express declaration to the secret trustee. There is authority that a half-secret trust of land is not enforceable without written evidence.[42] In *Ottaway* v. *Norman*,[43] however, a fully secret trust of land was upheld without written evidence, but the point was not discussed.

Fully secret trusts however have, as it were, another string to their bow. They were enforced long before secret trusts were thought of as taking effect outside the will. We have seen that they have been said on high authority to be enforceable on the ground of fraud,[44] and they can claim also to be constructive trusts. It is submitted that fully secret trusts can be enforced under either head.

If it becomes established that even a fully secret trust is express, it does not follow that the secret trustee would take beneficially if the trust fails for lack of compliance with the formality requirements. The result in such a case would be that, having accepted trusteeship, he would hold on trust for the residuary beneficiary or next-of-kin.[45]

C. Conclusion

Ultimately, the enforcement of secret trusts is a matter of policy relating to testamentary dispositions. The strict rules of the Wills Act 1837 are intended to achieve a reasonable degree of certainty in respect of the validity of testamentary dispositions. The stricter the rules,[46] however, the more likely that injustice will be done if a mistake

[39] One view is that the attempt to classify as express or constructive is misguided because the secret trust 'doctrine is concerned with the procedural question of admitting evidence of a trust and not with the nature of the trust itself; [1985] Conv. 248, at p. 253 (B. Perrins).

[40] *Ante*, p. 80.

[41] *Post*, p. 280.

[42] *Re Baillie* (1886) 2 T.L.R. 660 at p. 661.

[43] [1972] Ch. 698. See also *Strickland* v. *Aldridge* (1804) 9 Ves.Jr. 516. Similarly with *inter vivos* transfers; *Rochefoucauld* v. *Boustead* [1897] 1 Ch. 196.

[44] *McCormick* v. *Grogan* (1869) L.R. 4 H.L. 82; *ante*, p. 148.

[45] See Oakley, *Constructive Trusts* (2nd ed.), p. 130; [1985] Conv. 248 (B. Perrins); (1986) 36 N.I.L.Q. 358 (M. P. Thompson). Another view is that both fully and half-secret trusts are constructive, as both are imposed to prevent fraud on the testator, which may occur without any benefit to the secret trustee; [1980] Conv. 341 (D.R. Hodge). *cf.* (1951) 67 L.Q.R. 413 (L. A. Sheridan).

[46] The formality requirements of s.9 of the Wills Act 1837 have been relaxed in some respects by the Administration of Justice Act 1982.

is made. Secret trusts have, in effect, created a wide gap in the law relating to testamentary dispositions. We have seen that the machinery is available to widen it still further.[47] The extent to which it should be so used is a matter of policy. It is possible to take the view that secret trusts should not be enforced beyond preventing the unjust enrichment of the fraudulent legatee; or, on the other hand, to hold that the testator's intention should be upheld in every case. This is really a matter for the legislature, and it is submitted that it would be more satisfactory to review the whole matter and to incorporate into the statutory scheme as much of the secret trust doctrine as it is desired to retain.

[47] *Re Keen* [1937] Ch. 236; *Re Young* [1951] Ch. 344; *ante*, p. 158.

POWERS

1. POWERS[1] AND TRUSTS

A POWER is an authorisation to do certain things which affect property to which the appointor is not solely entitled, and in which he may have no beneficial interest at all. A person may hold a power in a personal or an official capacity, a distinction relevant to the question whether he has fiduciary obligations; and the source of the power may be express grant or a statute. Thus trustees have by statute powers of investment,[2] sale,[3] and so on. They may also be given other powers by the terms of the trust instrument, such as a power of appointment which enables those holding the power to effect the disposal of the settlor's property by "appointing" it to other people. It is with "powers" in the latter sense that this chapter is concerned.

It has been seen that there are important points of distinction between powers and trusts.[4] Essentially a trust is imperative and a power discretionary. But the dividing line is not as clear as one would hope; for many trusts contain discretionary elements; and many powers are given to trustees who are governed by fiduciary duties in the exercise of their powers.

---

[1] See Farwell; and Halsbury (4th ed.), Vol. 36, p. 529; Keeton & Sheridan's *Equity* (3rd ed.), Chap. 9.

[2] T.I.A. 1961; *post*, pp. 491 *et seq.*

[3] *Post*, p. 527.

[4] *Ante*, pp. 61 *et seq.*

The practical importance of the distinction lies in the extent of the obligations imposed on a trustee as compared with the donee of a power, for example, the question how far he is obliged to consider the claims of possible recipients[5]; also the extent of the rights of objects of a trust as compared with a mere power, including the question of entitlement to the property in default of exercise and the question whether the beneficiaries, all being adult and under no disability, can terminate the trust and either divide the trust property[6] or alienate it.[7]

Whether a particular disposition creates a mere power or a discretionary trust (or "trust-power") is a question of construction. This has already been discussed.[8]

2. BARE POWERS AND FIDUCIARY POWERS

A distinction must also be made between a bare power and a power to which some fiduciary obligation is attached, such as a power given to trustees of property exercisable in relation to that property. Several manifestations of this distinction will be explained in connection with powers of appointment. Of general application however is the rule that a bare power given to an individual can only be exercised by him,[9] and a "bare power given to two or more by name cannot be executed by the survivor."[10] But a power given to trustees is prima facie given to them *ex officio*, and may be exercised by the survivor,[11] or by their successors in office,[12] and powers given to two or more trustees jointly may be exercised by the survivor or survivors of them, or by the personal representatives of the last of them, pending the appointment of new trustees.[13]

3. POWERS OF APPOINTMENT

A power of appointment is one given (by the donor of the power) to the donee of the power (the appointor) to appoint property to some

---

[5] *McPhail* v. *Doulton* [1971] A.C. 424; *esp.* at p. 456, *per* Lord Wilberforce; *ante*, p. 106.

[6] *Saunders* v. *Vautier* (1841) 4 Beav. 115; *Anson* v. *Potter* (1879) 13 Ch.D. 141; *Re Brockbank* [1948] Ch. 206; *ante*, p. 62; *post*, p. 200.

[7] *Re Smith* [1928] Ch. 915; *Re Nelson* (1918) [1928] Ch. 920 n.

[8] *Ante*, p. 64.

[9] *Re Harding* [1923] 1 Ch. 182; *Re Lysaght* [1966] Ch. 191.

[10] Farwell, p. 514; Halsbury (4th ed.), Vol. 36, § 861; *Re Beesly's W.T.* [1966] Ch. 223 (contrary intention).

[11] *Re Bacon* [1907] 1 Ch. 475; *Bersel Manufacturing Co. Ltd.* v. *Berry* [1968] 2 All E.R. 552; T.A. 1925, s.18(1).

[12] *Re Smith* [1904] 1 Ch. 139; *Re De Sommery* [1912] 2 Ch. 662.

[13] T.A. 1925, s.18, and see *ibid.* s.36(7); *Re Wills' Trust Deeds* [1964] Ch. 219, *post*, p. 179.

person (the appointee). Such powers are useful in that they make it possible for the donee of the power to take into consideration circumstances existing at the date of the appointment which the settlor or testator could not have foreseen. Thus, a husband may give his estate to his widow for her life, and after her death to their children. He may leave his widow to decide upon the shares which each child is to receive by giving to her a power to appoint among the children in such shares as she shall in her absolute discretion select, with a gift in default of appointment to the children in equal shares. Powers feature in trusts of all sorts, and modern trusts commonly give various powers of appointment to the trustees in addition to imposing the obligation to hold the property upon trust. In such situations the property is owned by the beneficiaries who are entitled in default of appointment, subject to defeasance upon the exercise of the power.[14]

A. General, Special and Intermediate (or Hybrid) Powers
A gift to A for life with remainder to whomsoever he shall appoint is a general power; A may appoint to himself and become absolute owner. A general power is in most cases equivalent to ownership.[15] If, however, in the illustration given above, the power were exercisable only by will, it would still be a general power even though A would then be unable to appoint to himself. A special power is one in which the choice of appointees is restricted by the terms of the power: for example a power to appoint in favour of one's own children, or of the employees of a company and their families and dependants.[16] The power is special even though the appointor is himself a member of the restricted group.[17] A power which does not fit neatly into these categories is one where the donee is given power to appoint to anyone except certain people or groups of people, for instance himself,[18] or all persons except the settlor and his wife,[19] or to all persons living at the death of the donee[20]; such powers are called intermediate or hybrid powers,[21] and they may be treated as general powers for some purposes, and special for others.[22] Intermediate powers are classified as

---

[14] *Re Brooks' S.T.* [1939] Ch. 993 at p. 997; Farwell, p. 310.
[15] See, for example, Inheritance Tax Act 1984, s.5(2); Inheritance (Provision for Family and Dependants) Act 1975, s.25(1).
[16] *Re Gestetner* [1953] Ch. 672; *Re Sayer* [1957] Ch. 423.
[17] *Re Penrose* [1933] Ch. 793. See, however, Perpetuities and Accumulations Act 1964, s.7.
[18] *Re Park* [1932] 1 Ch. 580; *Re Byron's Settlement* [1891] 3 Ch. 475 (except "her husband or any friend or relative of his.") *Re Abraham's W.T.* [1969] 1 Ch. 463 at p. 474; *Re Lawrence's W.T.* [1972] Ch. 418 (except his "wife's relatives").
[19] To avoid aggregation of the income of the trust with that of the settlor; I.C.T.A. 1988, ss.673, 683. Also to avoid "reservation of benefit" under the inheritance tax system.
[20] *Re Jones* [1945] Ch. 105.
[21] *Re Lawrence's W.T.* [1972] Ch. 418; *Re Manisty's Settlement* [1974] Ch. 17; *Re Hay's S.T.* [1982] 1 W.L.R. 202.
[22] "This division (*i.e.* of powers into general and special) is neither precise nor exhaustive, for there are some powers which may be general for some purposes and not for others." (Halsbury (4th ed.), Vol. 36, § 805.)

special powers for the purpose of the Wills Act 1837, s.27,[23] and for the purposes of the rule against perpetuities.[24]

A power may be exercisable by deed, or by will, or by will or deed. A power which is exercisable by will only is called a testamentary power; and may be general or special.

B. The Requirement of Certainty; Wide Powers; Capricious Powers

These matters have been dealt with in Chapter 3, where the requirements of trusts and powers are compared.[25]

C. Duties of Donee of Power; Rights of Objects

A donee of a power is not, as such, under any fiduciary duties. In the example given above of the power given to the wife to determine the shares in which the children shall receive the property from their father's estate, the widow is under no obligation to exercise the power or even to consider its exercise, although if she does exercise it, then of course she must keep within the terms of the power.[26] This is a bare, or personal, power of appointment. This must be contrasted with a fiduciary power held by a trustee *virtute officii*, which in turn must be distinguished from the obligation of a trustee of a discretionary trust.

A discretionary trust is a trust in which the property is held by the trustees on trust, not for named beneficiaries in fixed proportions, but on trust for such members of a class of beneficiaries as the trustees shall in their absolute discretion select. That situation has many points of similarity with a power of appointment held by trustees to appoint among a group of objects. The distinction however remains that a trust is obligatory, a power permissive.[27] In many aspects the distinction is theoretical only. We have seen that the test for certainty of objects has been assimilated, but clear distinctions remain in the area of the rights and duties of the parties.

Although a power is discretionary and permissive, a trustee who is the donee of a power must act in accordance with his fiduciary duty. The duties in the case of a fiduciary power arise, as it were, not from the power, but those inherent in the office of trustee. Thus, a trustee may not disregard a power, or forget about it, or release it. His fiduciary duty requires him to give consideration to the exercise of the power, and particularly to any application made to him by an object of the power requesting an exercise in his favour.[28] "Trustees of a power must consider from time to time whether and how to exercise the

---

[23] *Post*, p. 169.
[24] P.A.A. 1964, s.7, affirming *Re Churston's S.E.* [1954] Ch. 334; *Re Earl of Coventry's Indentures* [1974] Ch. 77. For the significance of the distinction in the context of perpetuity, see Maudsley, *The Modern Law of Perpetuities*, pp. 60–64, 162–166.
[25] See also Chap. 2, pp. 65 *et seq.*
[26] *Re Hay's S.T.* [1982] 1 W.L.R. 202.
[27] *Ante*, p. 61.
[28] *Re Gestetner* [1953] Ch. 672 at p. 688, *per* Harman J.; *Re Manisty's Settlement* [1974] Ch. 17 at p. 25.

power."[29] "A settlor or testator who entrusts a power to his trustees must be relying on them in their fiduciary capacity so they cannot simply push aside the power and refuse to consider whether it ought in their judgment to be exercised."[30]

The duties of the donee of a fiduciary power were recently analysed by Megarry V.-C. in *Re Hay's Settlement Trusts*.[31] He must make no unauthorised appointment; he must consider periodically whether to exercise the power; he must consider the range of objects[32]; and he must consider the appropriateness of individual appointments. These duties, which were not intended to be exhaustive,[33] were further explained as follows: the donee, if he exercises the power, must do so "in a responsible manner according to its purpose. It is not enough for him to refrain from acting capriciously; he must do more. He must 'make such survey of the range of objects or possible beneficiaries' as will enable him to carry out his fiduciary duties."[34] He must not simply exercise the power in favour of those objects who happen to be at hand or to claim his attention. He must first consider who the objects are. He need not compile a list or assess the number: " . . . what is needed is an appreciation of the width of the field, and thus whether a selection is to be made merely from a dozen or, instead, from thousands or millions. . . . Only when the trustee has applied his mind to 'the size of the problem' should he then consider in individual cases whether, in relation to other possible claimants, a particular grant is appropriate. In doing this, no doubt he should not prefer the undeserving to the deserving; but he is not required to make an exact calculation whether, as between deserving claimants, A is more deserving than B."[35]

The question arises of what the court will do if the trustees fail in their duty to consider the exercise of the power. "Normally the trustee is not bound to exercise it, and the court will not compel him to do so. That, however, does not mean that he can simply fold his hands and ignore it, for normally he must from time to time consider whether or not to exercise the power, and the court may direct him to do this."[36] A recalcitrant trustee may be removed. Where the power has been exercised, the court "will intervene if the trustees exceed their power, and possibly if they are proved to have exercised it capriciously."[37] The

---

[29] [1974] Ch. 17 at p. 22, *per* Templeman J.; *Re Gestetner (supra)*; *Re Abraham's W.T.* [1969] 1 Ch. 463 at p. 474, *per* Cross J.; *Re Gulbenkian's Settlements* [1970] A.C. 508 at p. 518, *per* Lord Reid; *McPhail* v. *Doulton* [1972] A.C. 424 at p. 456, *per* Lord Wilberforce.

[30] *Re Gulbenkian's Settlements, supra*, at p. 518.

[31] [1982] 1 W.L.R. 202.

[32] Further discussed in Chap. 3.

[33] For the duty not to delegate, and to appoint in good faith, see *post*, pp. 171, 173.

[34] [1982] 1 W.L.R. 202 at p. 209, quoting from *McPhail* v. *Doulton* [1971] A.C. 424 at p. 449.

[35] *Ibid*, at p. 210.

[36] *Ibid*, at p. 209.

[37] [1971] A.C. 424 at p. 456, *per* Lord Wilberforce.

court will also intervene if the trustees have failed in any other respect to discharge the duties described above. Thus, in *Turner* v. *Turner*,[38] the exercise of a power of appointment was invalid when the trustees, who were not professional trustees, failed to appreciate their powers and duties and left all the decision-making to the settlor (who was not a trustee). They executed documents of appointment at his behest without reading them, and without understanding that they had a discretion. The settlor "held the reins," and the trustees acted as a "rubber-stamp." This was a breach of their duty to consider the exercise of the power and the appropriateness of the appointments made. There was no effective exercise at all, and the appointments accordingly were null and void, save to the extent that one appointment concerned land and was effective to transfer the legal title, which was held on trust by the appointee for the trustees of the settlement.

Thus the court's intervention is based upon the breach by the trustee of his fiduciary duty, and not upon any property right or entitlement among the objects of the power to compel a payment to them. The right of an object is not to compel an exercise of the power, in his own favour or at all, but merely to insist that the trustees consider the exercise of the power, to restrain any invalid exercise of the power, and, of course, to retain any property duly appointed to him.[39]

D. Power to Apply for Purposes

There seems to be no reason why a power should not permit the application of money for specific purposes, as opposed to being paid to persons. The purposes must be sufficiently certain to enable a court to determine whether any particular application is within the terms of the power or not. Such a power may be useful as a means of permitting the application of money to non-charitable purposes; a trust for non-charitable purposes lacks a means of enforcement and is void. That is a problem which is not faced by a power. The matter is discussed in Chapter 14.

4. EXERCISE OF POWERS OF APPOINTMENT

A. General Rule

(i) **Inter Vivos**. No technical words are required for the exercise of a power. "All that is requisite is an intention on the part of the donee that the fund shall pass to some one who is an object of the power."[40] If the appointment relates to land, it must comply with Law of Property Act 1925, s.53(1), and be in writing, signed by the donee of the power

---

[38] [1984] Ch. 100. See also *Re Hastings-Bass* [1975] Ch. 25.
[39] *Vestey* v. *I.R.C. (No. 2)* [1979] Ch. 198 (Walton J.). Affirmed [1980] A.C. 1148.
[40] Farwell, p. 218; *Re Ackerley* [1913] 1 Ch. 510; *Re Lawrence's W.T.* [1972] Ch. 418.

or by his authorised agent; an appointment of personalty may be made orally. The terms of the power may require certain further formalities[41] for its exercise, or specific reference to the power or to the property subject thereto,[42] and such requirements must be strictly complied with. Thus, "if a power is to be executed by deed, it cannot be validly exercised by will,"[43] and "a power to be executed by will cannot be validly exercised by any instrument to take effect in the lifetime of the donee of the power."[44]

(ii) By Will. Before 1838, a general devise[45] did not apply to land over which the testator had a power of appointment, unless he owned no land except that which was the subject of the power.[46] Wills Act 1837, section 27, reversed this rule by providing, in relation to both realty and personalty, and subject to the expression of a contrary intention, that, where a testator shall have a "power to appoint in any manner he may think proper," a general devise or bequest shall operate as an execution of the power. This clearly excludes special powers, and also intermediate or hybrid powers, which in any way restrict the donee's freedom of choice.[47] But the section applies even though the will was executed before the power was created.[48]

Any power to which the section does not apply is only exercised by will if "there is an indication of intention to exercise the power," a sufficient indication being "either a reference to the power or a sufficient reference to the property subject to the power.[49] Whether or not this is so in any particular case is often a question of great difficulty.[50]

B. Excessive Execution[51]

The donee has only the power which is given to him by the instrument. Thus he may not exercise it in favour of non-objects; nor in breach of the perpetuity rule; nor impose unauthorised conditions.[52] Any such purported exercise will be void. Difficult questions can arise

---

[41] *Hawkins* v. *Kemp* (1803) 3 East 410; subject to L.P.A. 1925, s.159, *post*, p. 171.

[42] *Re Lane* [1908] 2 Ch. 581; *Re Waterhouse* (1907) 98 L.T. 30; *Re Knight* [1957] Ch. 441; *Re Priestley's W.T.* [1971] Ch. 562, 858; *Re Lawrence's W.T.* [1972] Ch. 418; (1971) 121 N.L.J. 41, 597, 808 (C. H. Sherrin).

[43] Farwell, p. 197; *Lord Darlington* v. *Pulteney* (1797) 3 Ves.Jr. 384; *Lady Cavan* v. *Doe* d. *Pulteney* (1795) 6 Bro.P.C. 175; *Re Phillips* (1884) 41 Ch.D. 417 at p. 419.

[44] Farwell, p. 198; *Reid* v. *Shergold* (1805) 10 Ves.Jr. 370; *Re Evered* [1910] 2 Ch. 147 at p. 156.

[45] *e.g.* a devise which refers generally to realty and not specifically to separate pieces; *e.g.* "all my realty."

[46] Hawkins and Ryder, *Construction of Wills*, pp. 35 *et seq.*

[47] *Re Ackerley* [1913] 1 Ch. 510; *Re Byron's Settlement* [1893] 3 Ch. 474 (where the death of excluded persons made the power general).

[48] *Boyes* v. *Cook* (1880) 14 Ch.D. 53.

[49] *Re Ackerley, supra,* at p. 513, *per* Sargant J.; *Re Priestley's W.T.* [1971] Ch. 858.

[50] *Re Ackerley, supra*; *Re Priestley's W.T.* [1971] Ch. 562, 858; *Re Lawrence's W.T.* [1972] Ch. 418; (1971) 121 N.L.J. 41, 597, 808 (C. H. Sherrin).

[51] See Farwell, Chap. 6; Halsbury (4th ed.), Vol. 36, para. 951.

[52] See *Re Hay's S.T.* [1982] 1 W.L.R. 202, *post*, p. 172.

when an appointment is partly good and partly bad, as where there is an appointment of a sum greater than that authorised; or where some of the appointees are objects and some are not. The rule is that the court will sever the good from the bad where possible: " . . . if there is a complete execution of the power with the addition of something improper, the execution is good and the excess bad, whereas if there is no complete execution, or if the boundaries between the excess and the execution are not distinguishable, the whole appointment fails. In order to be valid, the appointment must be distinct and absolute."[53] It is believed that this rule will apply where the exercise of a power makes an appointment and contains a release; if the release is invalid, the rest of the appointment may stand.[54]

C. Defective Execution

The donee of a power should exercise it in accordance with the provisions of the instrument creating it. Thus the necessary formalities should be observed, and the required consents obtained. Failure to comply will usually render the exercise void. But there is a jurisdiction in equity and under statute to validate certain cases of defective execution.

(i) In Equity. Where the donee, "in discharge of moral or natural obligations, shows an intention to execute [a] power"[55] equity will act upon the conscience of those entitled in default to compel them to make good the defect in the execution. Relief may be obtained in favour of purchasers for value, creditors, charities, and persons to whom the donee is under a natural or moral obligation to provide.[56]

The essential features of the intended execution must be proved; these are "the intention to pass the property . . . the persons to be benefited . . . the amount of the benefit and . . . good consideration."[57] There will never be relief against the non-execution of a power,[58] except perhaps in the case of fraud by the person entitled in default.[59]

The jurisdiction applies to the execution of express powers generally, but not to defective execution of statutory powers; for "it is

---

[53] Halsbury, (4th ed.) Vol. 36, para. 951; *Re Holland* [1914] 2 Ch. 595; see also Halsbury, (4th ed.) Vol. 36, paras. 952–955, for illustrations of the general rule. The rule applies also where part of the appointment is void under the doctrine of "fraud on a power," *post*, p. 173.

[54] *Post*, p. 178.

[55] Farwell, p. 378; *Chapman* v. *Gibson* (1791) 3 Bro.C.C. 229 at p. 230.

[56] White and Tudor, *Leading Cases*, Vol. II, pp. 255–259, 273–274; Halsbury, (4th ed.) Vol. 36, para. 957.

[57] Farwell, p. 379; *Garth* v. *Townsend* (1869) L.R. 7 Eq. 220; *Kennard* v. *Kennard* (1872) L.R. 8 Ch.App. 227.

[58] *Tollet* v. *Tollet* (1728) 2 P.Wms. 489 at p. 490; *Holmes* v. *Coghill* (1806) 12 Ves.Jr. 206.

[59] *Luttrell* v. *Olmius* (1787) cited at 11 Ves.Jr. 638; *Bath and Montague's Case* (1693) 3 Ch.Cas. 84 at pp. 108, 122; *Vane* v. *Fletcher* (1717) 1 P.Wms. 352 at p. 355; Farwell, pp. 383–385.

difficult to see how the court can give validity to any such act if done otherwise than in accordance with the statutory requirements; to give relief in such a case would be to legislate afresh."[60] It seems however that an agreement for a lease is enforceable against a tenant for life acting under a statutory power so as to bind the interest of the tenant to the extent to which he is able to bind it.[61]

(ii) By Statute. (a) *Appointment Inter Vivos.* Law of Property Act 1925, s.159, provides that the execution of a deed of appointment will be valid if executed in the presence of and attended by two or more witnesses,[62] even though it does not comply with additional formalities stipulated in the instrument. This provision does not however dispense with any necessary consents, nor does it apply to any acts required to be performed which have no relation to the mode of executing and attesting the document.[63] Nor does it require a power to be exercised by deed where another method of exercise complies with the terms of the power.

(b) *Appointment by Will.* Similarly, an appointment by will is valid as regards execution and attestation if the provisions of the Wills Acts relating to the formalities of wills are complied with.[64]

D. Contract to Exercise

A valid contract to exercise a general power, if capable of specific performance, operates as a valid exercise of the power in equity; but there can never be specific performance of a contract to exercise a testamentary power, and the only remedy for breach is an action for damages against the estate.[65] A contract to exercise a special testamentary power is not enforceable[66]; but a release, in appropriate circumstances,[67] can be effective, as can a contract not to exercise the power[68]; the property will then go in default of appointment.

5. DELEGATION OF POWERS

In general, a person to whom a discretion has been given, whether personally or by virtue of his being in a fiduciary relationship, may not

---

[60] Farwell, p. 394.
[61] *Dyas* v. *Cruise* (1845) 2 Jo. & La T. 460; explaining *Harnett* v. *Yielding* (1805) 2 Sch. & Lef. 549; Farwell, p. 399.
[62] "in the manner in which deeds are ordinarily executed and attested."
[63] Subs. (2).
[64] Wills Act 1837, s.10; Wills Act 1963, s.2; *Taylor* v. *Meads* (1865) 4 De G.J. & S. 597 at p. 601. See also, as to powers to grant leases, L.P.A. 1925, s.152(1).
[65] *Re Parkin* [1892] 3 Ch. 510; *post*, p. 670.
[66] *Re Bradshaw* [1902] 1 Ch. 436; *Re Cooke* [1922] 1 Ch. 292.
[67] *Post*, p. 177.
[68] *Re Evered* [1910] 2 Ch. 147.

delegate his discretion to others. *Delegatus non potest delegare.*[69] A
donee may delegate the performance of merely ministerial acts[70]; and
the donee of a general power equivalent to absolute ownership may
appoint to a class in such proportions as another shall select.[71] But
many powers involve a personal discretion and this prevents delegation.[72] There is no objection however to a testator or settlor giving an
intermediate power of appointment to a trustee.[73] Special questions
arise as to the validity of powers inserted in wills which in effect
delegate to the donees the testator's power of testamentary disposition.[74] A tenant for life may not delegate his statutory powers.[75] In the
absence of express provision in the instrument creating a special
power,[76] the donee may not appoint on discretionary trust.[77] This
question recently arose in *Re Hay's Settlement Trusts.*[78]

> Trustees had a power to appoint to "such persons or purposes" as
> they should in their discretion select, except the settlor, her hus-
> band, or the trustees. Prior to the appointment, the income was to
> be applied, at the trustees' discretion, for the settlor's nephews and
> nieces, or for charity. The trustees exercised the power of appoint-
> ment by appointing the property to themselves on a discretionary
> trust for similar purposes. Prior to the distribution, the income was
> to be applied to any person or charity. Megarry V.-C. held that the
> exercise of the power was void, so that the property vested in the
> persons entitled in default of appointment (the period during which
> the power was exercisable having expired). The appointment did
> not designate the persons appointed, as the settlement required. It
> merely provided a mechanism whereby the appointees might be
> ascertained. The power was to appoint persons, and not to nominate
> persons to make an appointment. Intermediate powers were subject
> to the rule against unauthorised delegation, and it was immaterial

---

[69] *Post*, p. 532.

[70] *Att.-Gen.* v. *Scott* (1750) 1 Ves.Sen. 413 at p. 417; *Re Hetling and Merton's Contract*
[1893] 3 Ch. 269; Farwell, pp. 503–504.

[71] Farwell, p. 505; *White* v. *Wilson* (1852) 1 Drew. 298 at p. 304; *Re Triffitt's Settlement*
[1958] Ch. 852 (explained in *Re Hay's S.T.* [1982] 1 W.L.R. 202 as showing that the
rule does not apply to bare powers).

[72] *Combe's Case* (1613) 9 Co.Rep. 75a; *De Bussche* v. *Alt* (1878) 8 Ch.D. 286; *Re Morris'*
Settlement [1951] 2 All E.R. 528; *Re Hunter's W.T.* [1963] Ch. 372; (1954) 23
Conv.(N.S.) 27, 423 (D. W. M. Waters).

[73] *Houston* v. *Burns* [1918] A.C. 337; *Att.-Gen.* v. *National Provincial Bank* [1922] A.C.
262; *Re Manisty's Settlement* [1974] Ch. 17 at p. 26; *Re Park* [1932] 1 Ch. 580; *Re*
Abraham's W.T. [1969] 1 Ch. at p. 475.

[74] (1953) 69 L.Q.R. 334 (D. M. Gordon); *post*, p. 347; *Re Triffitt's Settlement, supra*;
Tatham v. *Huxtable* (1950) 81 C.L.R. 639; (1974) 9 Melbourne U.L.R. 650 (I. J.
Hardingham); (1976) 54 C.B.R. 229 at p. 273 (M. C. Cullity).

[75] S.L.A. 1925, s.104; but trustees for sale may delegate their powers of management to
the tenant for life; L.P.A. 1925, s.29.

[76] *Per* Evershed M.R. in *Re Morris' Settlement, supra*, at pp. 530–531.

[77] *Re Morris' Settlement* [1951] 2 All E.R. 528 at pp. 532–533, *per* Jenkins L.J.

[78] [1982] 1 W.L.R. 202.

that the donees of the power were the same persons as the trustees of the discretionary trust.

If the donee appoints on protective trusts,[79] the determinable life interest will be valid, but the discretionary trusts due to take effect on forfeiture of the life interest are void and the trusts in default take effect.[80] There is no objection, however, to the inclusion in an appointment of a power of advancement.[81] Before 1926, the inclusion of such a power of advancement "had become a common form of conveyancing practice"[82]; and "legislative recognition has now been given to the old practice in the form of the statutory power of advancement conferred by section 32(1) of the Trustee Act 1925, so that the question is no longer likely to arise."[83] Generally, where it is desired that the donee should be able to make an appointment which itself includes a power of appointment or involves any other delegation of discretion, express provision should be made in the instrument creating the power.[84]

6. Fraud on a Power

An appointor, in the typical case of a special power of appointment with a gift over in default, is under no duty to exercise the power; but if he chooses to exercise the power, he must exercise it honestly.[85] Unless he is a fiduciary,[86] he need not weigh the merits of the possible beneficiaries; he may appoint all the available assets to any one beneficiary, who may indeed be himself.[87] But he must exercise it within the limits imposed by the donor or testator who created it.[88] If, of course, he expressly exceeds those limits the exercise of the power will be void unless it can be cut down by severing the invalid excess.[89] But the doctrine of fraudulent exercise of a power goes further than this, for it extends to the intent with which a power is exercised. The theory is that, in the case of a special power, the property is vested in those entitled in default of its exercise subject to its being divested by a proper exercise of the power[90]; and that an exercise of the power for

---

[79] *Post*, pp. 181 *et seq.*
[80] *Re Boulton's S.T.* [1928] Ch. 703; *Re Morris' Settlement, supra*; *Re Hunter* [1963] Ch. 372.
[81] *Re May's Settlement* [1926] Ch. 136; *Re Joicey* [1915] 2 Ch. 115; *Re Mewburn's Settlement* [1934] Ch. 112; *Re Morris' Settlement* [1951] 2 All E.R. 528; *Re Wills' W.T.* [1959] Ch. 1; *Pilkington* v. *I.R.C.* [1964] A.C. 612, *post*, p. 550.
[82] *Per* Evershed M.R. in *Re Morris' Settlement, supra*.
[83] *Per* Jenkins L.J., *loc. cit.* pp. 532–533; see also Maugham L.J. in *Re Mewburns' Settlement, supra*.
[84] For powers commonly included in discretionary trusts, see *post*, pp. 193 *et seq.*
[85] *Cloutte* v. *Storey* [1911] 1 Ch. 18.
[86] In which case, see *Re Hay's S.T.* [1982] 1 W.L.R. 202, *ante*, p. 172.
[87] *Re Penrose* [1933] Ch. 793.
[88] (1977) 3 Monash L.R. 210 (Y. Grbich), describing the doctrine of fraud on a power as an "*ultra vires* appointments" doctrine.
[89] *Churchill* v. *Churchill* (1867) L.R. 5 Eq. 44; *Re Oliphant* (1917) 86 L.J.Ch. 452.
[90] *Re Brook's S.T.* [1939] Ch. 993.

"any bye or sinister object" is not proper, is a fraud on those entitled in default, and void.[91]

A. Prior Agreement

The first type of case in which an apparently valid exercise of a power will be void for what in this context is termed fraud[92] is where the appointment is made as the result of a prior agreement or bargain with the appointee as to what he will do with the proceeds. Such an exercise of a power will be wholly void save when the appointor is the person entitled in default, or where the person entitled in default is a party to it.[93]

B. Benefit to Appointor

A second type of case is where the power is exercised so as to benefit the appointor. The benefit is usually financial in character, as where an appointment is made to an ailing child by its father, who will benefit on the child's death,[94] but it is not restricted to financial benefit.[95] For the exercise of the power to be void, there must be more than a hope of benefit. Thus an appointment to a healthy child by a father will be valid.[96] For fraud to operate, the appointment must have been made with intent to benefit the appointor. An appointment is sometimes made, however, which in fact benefits the appointor, but which is clearly intended to, and does, benefit the appointees; this is true of many an appointment that forms part of the variation of a trust, for the tax savings achieved will often be a benefit to the appointor. Thus in *Re Merton*,[97] Wynn-Parry J. decided that there was no inflexible rule that forced him to declare such an exercise of a power to be void. The intent that renders an appointment void is a matter "of fact or of inference rather than of law,"[98] and must be ascertained as a single fact after consideration of all the relevant evidence.[99] In the context of variation of trust however, modern cases have shown a reluctance to apply this benevolent view.[1]

---

[91] *Portland* v. *Topham* (1864) 11 H.L.Cas. 32 at p. 54, *per* Lord Westbury; *Vatcher* v. *Paul* (as in n.93) [1915] A.C. 372. *cf. Re Greaves* [1954] Ch. 434 at p. 446, *per* Evershed M.R.

[92] See the classification in Farwell, p. 460, and also Sheridan, *Fraud in Equity*, pp. 116 *et seq.*

[93] See generally *Vatcher* v. *Paull* [1915] A.C. 372.

[94] *Lord Hichinbroke* v. *Seymour* (1789) 1 Bro.C.C. 395; *Lady Wellesley* v. *Earl Mornington* (1855) 2 K. & J. 143.

[95] *Cochrane* v. *Cochrane* [1922] 2 Ch. 230.

[96] *Henty* v. *Wrey* (1882) 21 Ch.D. 332.

[97] [1953] 1 W.L.R. 1096 especially at p. 1100; *Re Robertson's W.T.* [1960] 1 W.L.R. 1050.

[98] *Re Holland* [1914] 2 Ch. 595 at p. 601, *per* Sargant J.

[99] *Re Crawshay* [1948] Ch. 123.

[1] *Re Wallace's Settlements* [1968] 1 W.L.R. 711; *Re Brook's Settlement* [1968] 1 W.L.R. 1661; *post*, p. 591; [1968] B.T.R. 199 (J.G.M.); (1969) 32 M.L.R. 317 (S. M. Cretney).

C. Non-objects

An appointment is sometimes drafted so that the intent appears to be to benefit objects of the power, but the real intent is to benefit non-objects. It will then be void, even though the appointee was in no sense a party, and might not even have known of the appointment or its intent. It may still be true that the "execution of the power is alien in reality . . . to the power conferred."[2] Thus, in *Re Dick*[3]:

> A widow had a power to appoint amongst her brothers and sisters and their issue, but she wished to provide for a family who were looking after her. She had inadequate free capital to do so. She appointed by will to her favourite sister, but coupling the appointment with a request "without imposing any trust or legal obligation" that the sister should provide an annuity for the family concerned. The Court of Appeal held that the absence of obligation on the appointee was not crucial; but rather that the whole intent in making the appointment was to secure a benefit to non-objects by subjecting the appointee to "strong moral suasion to benefit a non-object, which suasion the [appointee] would, in the appointor's opinion, be unable to resist."[4] This intent was enough to constitute the exercise of the power as fraudulent.

Difficulties arise from this rule as to real intent, for it is not easy to distinguish cases such as *Re Dick*[5] from cases where there was a real intent to benefit the appointee but coupled with a hope that the appointee would benefit a non-object, which cases are of course not within the doctrine of fraud on a power. But the intent in many cases is simply dual—genuinely to benefit the appointee but also to subject him to strong moral persuasion as to part of the benefit appointed. It may therefore be relevant in *Re Dick*[6] that a substantial proportion of the sum appointed would have been absorbed by the annuity and that a great deal of planning and discussion had gone into the making of the appointment coupled with the expression of the request in formal memoranda. For the danger inherent in extending the doctrine too far is that, if the appointment is void, the appointee loses all benefit unless

---

[2] *Re Nicholson's Settlement* [1939] Ch. 11 at p. 19, *per* Clauson L.J. This case decided that the doctrine as to the real intent behind an appointment did not apply to a power exercisable only in favour of one person and so exercised. But see the criticism in Sheridan, *Fraud in Equity*, p. 122, and Keeton & Sheridan's *Equity* (3rd ed.), p. 297.

[3] [1953] Ch. 343; *Re Kirwan* (1884) 25 Ch.D. 373. *cf. Re Marsden's Trusts* (1859) 4 Drew. 594.

[4] The matter was put in this way by Cohen L.J. in *Re Crawshay* [1948] Ch. 123 at p. 135, a case which contained the additional vitiating factor of a covenant by the appointee assigning to non-objects any benefits received by the exercise of the power; (1948) 64 L.Q.R. 221 (H. G. Hanbury).

[5] [1953] Ch. 343.

[6] *Supra.*

the appointor is alive to reappoint,[7] a loss to the appointee which is not justified if intent to benefit him was a substantial element in the exercise of the power.

D. Excessive Exercise; Severance

That the intent with which a power is exercised cannot be investigated too rigidly is also shown by the cases which cut down a power excessively exercised. If there is a genuine intent to benefit the appointee, something expressly superadded so as to benefit a non-object can be severed, leaving the appointment valid.[8] But severance will not occur in the absence of such a genuine intent.[9] Again if, in a will by which he exercises a power, a testator makes a gift of *his own* property conditional on the appointee resettling the *appointed* property, this is a valid condition on his own gift and the exercise of the power also is valid, provided there was a genuine intent to benefit the appointee.[10] This would be difficult to reconcile with strict emphasis on the intent with which a power was exercised as being "entire and single."[11]

E. Releases

The doctrine of fraud on a power does not apply to releases, for releases simply benefit those entitled in default. It is irrelevant that the appointor, in releasing his power, is intended to benefit thereby, as he has no duty in respect of the disappointed objects.[12] Nor does the doctrine apply to the revocation of the exercise of a power.[13] An appointment may only be revoked where such right of revocation has been reserved. Where such right exists, it seems that the appointor is under no duty to the appointees. It has even been said that, in revoking, he may stipulate for a benefit, but it would be strange if, by first exercising a power and then revoking it, an appointor could obtain a benefit rightly denied him on an appointment, and it is significant that, in the leading case,[14] the revocation was followed by a release.[15]

---

[7] There can be no severance in these cases as there is nothing to sever. But *Re Chadwick's Trusts* [1939] 1 All E.R. 850 shows that a fresh appointment is valid if free from the element that vitiated a prior one.

[8] *Re Kerr's W.T.* (1878) 4 Ch.D. 600; *Re Holland* [1914] 2 Ch. 595; followed in *Re Burton's Settlements* [1955] Ch. 82.

[9] *Re Cohen* [1911] 1 Ch. 37. Severance will not of course occur when there has been a prior agreement with the appointee.

[10] *Re Burton's Settlements* [1955] Ch. 82.

[11] In *Re Simpson* [1952] Ch. 412, Vaisey J. had held that *Re Crawshay* and *Re Dick* impelled him to take this strict view on facts analogous to those in *Re Burton's Settlements*, in which case, however, Upjohn J. rightly refused to follow the lead.

[12] *Re Somes* [1896] 1 Ch. 250. Releases may be an important element in the variation of a trust: *Re Ball's Settlement Trusts* [1968] 1 W.L.R. 899, *post*, p. 591.

[13] *Re Greaves* [1954] Ch. 434.

[14] *Ibid.*

[15] *cf.* Evershed M.R. in *Re Greaves, supra*, at p. 448.

F. Position of Third Parties

The position of a bona fide purchaser, for instance a mortgagee, of an interest appointed to his vendor in such a manner as to amount to a fraud on the power is complicated. Those entitled in default of appointment who can challenge the exercise of the power as fraudulent have an interest in the property appointed which in principle prevails over the interest of its bona fide purchasers for value,[16] it being significant, of course, that no legal title passes under the ordinary power of appointment since 1925. The Law of Property Act 1925, s.157, protects such purchasers, but only if the vendor-appointee was at least 25 years of age at the time of sale, and only to the extent to which he was presumptively entitled in default of appointment. Apart from this curious and limited protection, a fraudulent appointment is void even against a bona fide purchaser.

7. RELEASE OF POWERS

A. Why Release?

As a power is always discretionary, it may be asked why it becomes advantageous to release it as opposed merely to not exercising it. This may be for various reasons; for example, to create indefeasible interests in those entitled in default,[17] to make a gift charitable by releasing a power to appoint to anyone else,[18] to avoid the "reservation of benefit" rules under the inheritance tax system by excluding the settlor from the class of objects,[19] and especially to avoid the effect of Income and Corporation Taxes Act 1988, ss.671–675. They provide for the income of a settlement to be treated as that of the settlor in certain circumstances; where, for example, the settlor or his wife may benefit from the revocation of a revocable settlement[20]; or from the exercise of a power of appointment. Until 1958, it had been common to include the wife of the settlor as a member of the discretionary class; and it thus became important to exclude her.[21] This was usually done by exercising the trustees' power to appoint on new trusts which were identical with the old ones except that the wife was omitted. This is in effect a partial release of the earlier power, and is treated as such.[22] As we will

---

[16] *Cloutte* v. *Storey* [1911] 1 Ch. 18. See also *Turner* v. *Turner* [1984] Ch. 100, *ante*, p. 168, on the effect of appointments made in breach of the duty to consider; and *Re Hay's S.T.* [1982] 1 W.L.R. 202, *ante*, p. 172, on the effect of an appointment in breach of the duty not to delegate.

[17] *Re Mills* [1930] 1 Ch. 654.

[18] *Re Wills* [1964] Ch. 219.

[19] *Post*, p. 216.

[20] *I.R.C.* v. *Cookson* [1977] 1 W.L.R. 962.

[21] F.A. 1958, s.22, now I.C.T.A. 1988, s.674; *Blausten* v. *I.R.C.* [1972] Ch. 256; (1972) 36 Conv.(N.S.) 127 (D. J. Hayton).

[22] *Re Wills, supra*; *Muir* v. *I.R.C.* [1966] 1 W.L.R. 251 and 1269; *Blausten* v. *I.R.C.* (*supra*).

see, many of the releases which have been made in this way are of
doubtful validity.

B. How to Effect a Release

Trustees may in effect surrender their trusts and powers by paying
the money into court under the Trustee Act 1925, s.63[23]; or they may
apply to the court for an administration order; or they may ask the
court for directions as to the way in which they should act on questions
arising in the administration of the trust. Usually, however, the court
will not give general directions concerning the exercise of discretionary
powers in the future.[24]

They may also effect a release of a power, in appropriate circumstances, by executing a deed of release, or by a contract not to exercise
the power.[25] A power may also be extinguished by implication by any
dealing with the property by the donee which is inconsistent with its
further exercise[26]; or by obtaining the approval of the court to an
arrangement which is so inconsistent. There is much uncertainty concerning the validity of releases in some circumstances, and it is important that express provision should be made in the instrument creating
the power which expressly authorises the donees of the power to
release it.[27]

C. Validity of Release

It is not possible to lay down with confidence what are the circumstances in which, in the absence of express provision, a release will be
valid. The matter is not made easier by a great confusion in
terminology.

Powers used to be divided into those which are appendant,[28] in
gross,[29] or collateral. The two former could be released; but collateral
powers "that is a power to a stranger, who has no interest in the land,"
or "where it is to be exercised for the benefit of another"[30] could not.
But this rule was changed in 1881 by the predecessor to the Law of
Property Act 1925, s.155, which enacts that: "A person to whom any

---

[23] *Post*, p. 506; this is now rare; (1968) 84 L.Q.R. 67 (A. J. Hawkins).
[24] *Re Allen-Meyrick's W.T.* [1966] 1 W.L.R. 499; (1967) 31 Conv.(N.S.) 117 (A. J.
Hawkins); *post*, p. 505.
[25] L.P.A. 1925, ss.155, 160.
[26] *Foakes* v. *Jackson* [1900] 1 Ch. 807; *Re Christie-Miller's Settlement* [1961] 1 W.L.R.
462; *Re Wills* [1964] Ch. 219; *Muir* v. *I.R.C.* [1966] 1 W.L.R. 251, 1269; *Re Courtauld's Settlement* [1965] 2 All E.R. 544; *Blausten* v. *I.R.C.* [1972] Ch. 256; (1968) 84
L.Q.R. 92–93 (A. J. Hawkins).
[27] *Muir* v. *I.R.C.* [1966] 1 W.L.R. 1269; *Blausten* v. *I.R.C.* (*supra*).
[28] Exercisable by a person having an interest in the property, which interest is capable of
being affected by the exercise of the power.
[29] Exercisable by a person having an interest in the property, which interest cannot be
affected by the exercise of the power.
[30] *West* v. *Berney* (1819) 1 Russ. & My. 431 at p. 434.

power, whether coupled with an interest or not, is given may by deed release or contract not to exercise, the power."[31]

Almost immediately the question arose whether this provision applied to a situation where the donees of the power were trustees who held the power in a fiduciary capacity. Admittedly they cannot be compelled to exercise it; but can they be allowed to release it? The courts answered this question in the negative[32]; and the search at the present day is for a test to determine which are the cases to which the statute does not apply.

(i) **Trusts.** The first category is that discussed above where the situation is not really a power but a discretionary trust. Here the trustees are under a duty to appoint; if they fail to do so, the court will declare the property to be held on trust for the class of possible appointees.[33] There is no question of release here.

(ii) **Fiduciary Powers.** Where a power is conferred upon a person *virtute officii*, he may not release it. *"In the absence of words in the trust deed authorising [him] so to do."*[34] Here there may be a gift over in default, either to the class of appointees or to a different class. This is a power proper, and not a trust. But the power is one given to the trustees to be exercised in a fiduciary capacity. They cannot discard it; they are, as has been seen,[35] under a duty to consider from time to time whether and how to exercise the power.[36] This is so whether it is given to them as trustees, or whether it is given to persons by name "if on the true view of the facts, they were selected as donee of the power because they were trustees."[37] Conversely, persons selected as individuals may be described as trustees. In *Re Wills' Trust Deeds*[38] a power of appointment in respect of property which was the subject of a *settlement* was given to the trustees of the settlor's *will*; this was not given *virtute officii*. The question of the release of a fiduciary power

---

[31] This does not apply to a tenant for life of settled land; S.L.A. 1925, s.104.

[32] *Re Eyre* (1883) 49 L.T. 259; *Weller* v. *Kerr* (1866) L.R. 1 Sc. & D. 11; *Saul* v. *Pattinson* (1886) 55 L.J.Ch. 831.

[33] *Brown* v. *Higgs* (1803) 8 Ves.Jr. 561; *Burrough* v. *Philcox* (1840) 5 Myl. & Cr. 72; *Re Weekes* [1897] 1 Ch. 289; *Re Combe* [1925] Ch. 210; *Re Perowne* [1951] Ch. 785; (1967) 31 Conv.(N.S.) 117 (A. J. Hawkins). Equal division is not necessary in the case of the modern discretionary trust; *ante*, p. 100.

[34] *Muir* v. *I.R.C.* [1966] 1 W.L.R. 1269 at p. 1283, *per* Harman L.J.; the italics are original; *Blausten* v. *I.R.C.* [1972] Ch. 256.

[35] *Ante*, p. 167.

[36] *Re Gestetner Settlement* [1953] Ch. 672 at p. 688; *Re Gulbenkian's Settlements* [1970] A.C. 508 at p. 518; *McPhail* v. *Doulton* [1971] A.C. 424 at p. 456; *Re Manisty's Settlements* [1974] Ch. 17 at p. 22.; *Re Hay's S.T.* [1982] 1 W.L.R. 202; *Turner* v. *Turner* [1984] Ch. 100.

[37] Lewin, p. 387; *Lane* v. *Debenham* (1853) 11 Hare 188; *Hall* v. *May* (1857) 3 K. & J. 585; *Re Cookes' Contract* (1877) 4 Ch.D. 454.

[38] [1964] Ch. 219.

recently arose in *Re Courage Group's Pension Schemes*,[39] where fiduciary powers were vested in a committee set up to manage a pension scheme. It was held that even if existing members of the committee could release, fetter, or agree not to exercise their powers (which was not decided), they could not deprive their successors of the right to exercise their powers.

(iii) Bare Powers. Where the power is given to a person in his private capacity, the donee is prima facie able to release it.[40] In *Re Wills' Trust Deeds*[41] Buckley J. made as an exception to this rule the case where, in default of appointment, there was a trust in favour of the objects of the power[42]; but it seems that such a power can be released,[43] even if the release operates in favour of the donee, as where a father releases a power so that the shares of his sons (who are entitled in default) become absolute, and that of a deceased son passes to the donee.[44] A release, or a covenant not to exercise it, (which will be equivalent to a release)[45] may be effective if it refers only to part of the property,[46] or if it relates only to one or more of several objects.[47]

(iv) Variation of Trusts Act 1958. Section 1 of the Variation of Trusts Act 1958 makes no express reference to powers. Many powers are vested in trustees, as in the case of discretionary or protective trusts; and a variation of such powers, with the consent of the court, will no doubt be covered by the provisions of the sections relating to variation of trusts. It appears however that an arrangement under the Act which recites the release of a power,[48] or one which is inconsistent with the future exercise of the power,[49] will effectively release it.

---

[39] [1987] 1 W.L.R. 495.
[40] This is Buckley J.'s fifth category in *Re Wills' Trust Deeds* [1964] Ch. 219.
[41] [1964] Ch. 219.
[42] Buckley J.'s second category: [1964] Ch. 219.
[43] *Smith* v. *Houblon* (1859) 26 Beav. 482.
[44] *Re Radcliffe* [1892] 1 Ch. 227; an appointment in favour of the estate of the deceased son would have been a fraud on the power.
[45] *Per* Buckley L.J. in *Re Evered* [1910] 2 Ch. 147 at p. 161.
[46] *Re Evered, supra.*
[47] *Re Brown's Settlement* [1939] Ch. 944; Farwell, p. 16.
[48] *Re Christie-Miller's S.T.* [1961] 1 W.L.R. 462.
[49] *Re Courtauld's Settlement* [1965] 2 All E.R. 544; *Re Ball's S.T.* [1968] 1 W.L.R. 899.

CHAPTER 7

PROTECTIVE TRUSTS

1. The General Problem

A DEBTOR's property is in principle available for the satisfaction of his creditors and, if he becomes bankrupt, it will pass to his trustee in bankruptcy; but it is possible, by making use of a protective trust, to obtain a measure of protection against such a calamity.

In the development of protective trusts the courts have been torn between two conflicting pressures. On the one hand, no man should have the power of defeating his creditors by putting his property beyond their grasp; on the other, a settlor should be able to create a trust in any form he wishes, so long as it is not unlawful; and there is much to be said for allowing some means of protecting a person's dependants from the ill-effects of his extravagance. The technique of protective trusts involves the giving of a determinable life interest with an executory gift over upon the happening of certain eventualities. Originally, the gift over was usually in favour of other members of the family[1]; but the modern practice is to provide for a gift over to trustees to hold on discretionary trusts in favour of a class which includes the life tenant and members of his family; and this pattern is provided for by the Trustee Act 1925, s.33.[2] In most American jurisdictions, it is possible to make an equitable life interest inalienable whether voluntarily or involuntarily. This is known as a "spendthrift trust,"[3] and is justified on the ground that the settlor, in creating the trust, should be allowed to create such equitable interests as he wishes. There are statutory provisions in many States which allow creditors to reach income which is surplus to the amount needed for the maintenance and

---

[1] *e.g. Brooke* v. *Pearson* (1859) 27 Beav. 181; *Re Detmold* (1889) 40 Ch.D. 585.

[2] *Post*, p. 184.

[3] Scott, *Law of Trusts*, §§ 151–153; Griswold, *Spendthrift Trusts*; Keeton, *Modern Developments in the Law of Trusts,* Chap. 15; *Broadway National Bank* v. *Adams* 133 Mass. 170; 43 Am.Rep. 504 (1882).

education of the beneficiary. This has never been allowed in England[4];
but, as will be seen, the technique of the protective trust is at least an
equivalent protection.

2. DETERMINABLE AND CONDITIONAL INTERESTS

A distinction is made in law between an interest subject to a condition
subsequent and a determinable interest.[5] The former exists where
there is a gift of an absolute interest which is then cut down by the
application of a condition; such as a gift to X absolutely, but if he
should change his nationality, then over to Y. A determinable interest
exists where something less than an absolute interest is given in the first
place; as a gift to X until he changes (or so long as he retains) his
nationality. The distinction is subtle[6]; it depends entirely upon the
language of the gift; but it is a distinction that has importance in several
contexts. The relevance in the present context is twofold: first, that a
condition against alienation is void[7]; secondly, that a condition subsequent, being one which effects a forfeiture of an existing interest, is
strictly construed[8]; if the condition is held void, the interest becomes
absolute.[9] The determining event, however, in the case of a determinable interest is less strictly construed; and if it should be held invalid,
the whole interest fails.[10]

  Thus it is clear that a *condition* so drafted as to terminate an interest
upon alienation[11] or bankruptcy[12] is void and the prior interest is
absolute. But an interest *determinable* on alienation or bankruptcy is
valid.[13] Further, courts place an even more generous construction

---

[4] But from the early 19th century until 1935 it was possible to create a trust for the
separate use of a married woman and to impose a restraint upon the anticipation or
alienation. See Law Reform (Married Women and Tortfeasors) Act 1935 and Married
Women (Restraint upon Anticipation) Act 1949.

[5] *Post,* p. 320; *Brandon* v. *Robinson* (1811) 18 Ves.Jr. 429 at p. 433 (Lord Eldon);
Rochford v. *Hackman* (1852) 9 Hare 475; M. & W., pp. 69 *et seq.*; Cheshire and Burn,
pp. 326 *et seq.* The clue to the existence of a determinable limitation is the use of
words such as "until," "so long as," "whilst," as distinct from phraseology such as "but
if" and "when, if ever."

[6] "Little short of disgraceful to our jurisprudence," *per* Porter M.R. in *Re King's Trusts*
(1892) 29 L.R.Ir. 401 at p. 410, quoted M. & W., p. 70.

[7] Co.Litt. 223a; *Re Brown* [1954] Ch. 39.

[8] *Clavering* v. *Ellison* (1859) 7 H.L.Cas. 707; *Sifton* v. *Sifton* [1938] A.C. 656.

[9] Co.Litt. 206a, b; *Re Greenwood* [1903] 1 Ch. 749.

[10] *Re Moore* (1888) 39 Ch.D. 116. (Gift of a weekly sum to T's sister "whilst . . . living
apart from her husband" construed as a gift determinable upon returning to her
husband, and held void); *Re Tuck's S.T.* [1978] Ch. 49.

[11] *Brandon* v. *Robinson* (1811) 18 Ves.Jr. 429; *Graves* v. *Dolphin* (1826) 1 Sim. 66;
Rochford v. *Hackman* (1852) 9 Hare 475; *Re Dugdale* (1888) 38 Ch.D. 176; *Re Brown*
[1954] Ch. 39; (1943) 59 L.Q.R. 343 (Glanville Williams).

[12] *Younghusband* v. *Gisborne* (1846) 15 L.J.Ch. 355; *Re Sanderson's Trust* (1857) 3 K. &
J. 497.

[13] *Post,* p. 184; see also the earlier authorities relied on by Turner V.-C. in *Rochford* v.
Hackman, supra.

upon the validity of determining events in the case of life interests.[14]
The basis of protective trusts is therefore a determinable life interest.

3. SELF-PROTECTION

A settlor cannot make a settlement which will protect himself against
his own bankruptcy.[15]

> In *Re Burroughs-Fowler,*[16] the settlor, by ante-nuptial settlement,
> settled property upon trust to pay the income to himself for life or
> until one of certain events should occur, including his bankruptcy,
> after which event the income was to be paid to his wife. The settlor
> was adjudicated bankrupt during the wife's lifetime. It was held that
> the life interest vested indefeasibly in his trustee in bankruptcy, who
> could validly dispose of it.

A settlor may however protect himself against other forms of alienation, voluntary or involuntary. And if the limitation, as is usual,
provides for the termination of his interest upon any one of such events
or upon his bankruptcy, the gift over, as we have seen, is void in the
event of bankruptcy, but valid in all other cases.[17] If the gift over has
taken effect upon, for example, an attempt to charge the life interest,
the subsequent bankruptcy of the settlor has no effect upon it.

> In *Re Detmold,*[18] a marriage settlement of the settlor's own pro-
> perty provided for the payment of the income to the settlor for life or
> "till he shall become bankrupt or shall . . . suffer something whereby
> the same . . . would . . . by operation of law . . . become . . . payable
> to some other person . . . " and, after such determination, on trust to
> pay the income to his wife. In July 1888, an order was made appoint-
> ing a judgment creditor to be receiver of the income; and in Septem-
> ber 1888 the settlor was adjudicated bankrupt. It was held that the
> forfeiture took place upon the involuntary alienation of the income
> by process of law. The wife then became entitled to the income, and
> she did not lose the right on the subsequent bankruptcy.

[14] Jarman, p. 1486.

[15] *Wilson* v. *Greenwood* (1818) 1 Swan. 471 at p. 481, note (*a*); *Mackintosh* v. *Pogose*
[1895] 1 Ch. 505; *Re Wombwell* (1921) 125 L.T. 437; this rule is preserved by T.A.
1925, s.33(3). Nor may he settle his property on a third party to prejudice his own
creditors *post,* pp. 330 *et seq.*

[16] [1916] 2 Ch. 251.

[17] *Re Detmold* (1889) 40 Ch.D. 585; *Re Brewer's Settlement* [1896] 2 Ch. 503; *Re Johnson*
[1904] 1 K.B. 134.

[18] (1889) 40 Ch.D. 585; *Brooke* v. *Pearson* (1859) 27 Beav. 181; *Knight* v. *Browne* (1861)
30 L.J.Ch. 649; *Re Brewer's Settlement* [1896] 2 Ch. 503.

4. Protected Life Interests in Persons Other than the Settlor

Though a man cannot make a settlement of his own property upon himself until bankruptcy, and then over, yet a trust created by A to pay the income to B until B dies or becomes bankrupt alienates or charges his life interest and then over to C is good in the event of the occurrence of any of those events, including B's bankruptcy.[19] The essence of the device of protected life interests[20] is that, on the occurrence of a determining event, such as alienation or bankruptcy, the interest of the life tenant determines, and the trustees then hold the property on discretionary trusts for the benefit of the life tenant and his family.

Some early attempts to reach this result failed, owing to the absence of any clear gift over of the income.[21] Eventually, however, discretionary trusts became accepted,[22] and in recent years quite independently of protective trusts, and largely because of the fiscal advantages which they enjoyed prior to the introduction of capital transfer tax (now inheritance tax) by the Finance Act 1975,[23] they have formed the basis of a large percentage of modern family settlements.

5. Trustee Act 1925, s.33

Before 1926 it was necessary to set out expressly the terms of the trusts; and a settlor may still do so if he wishes.[24] In relation, however, to trusts coming into operation after 1925, Trustee Act 1925, s.33, "provides a shorthand arrangement whereby a settlor may establish a trust without setting forth in detail all the terms upon which the property is to be held."[25] The section applies although the statutory formula "on protective trusts" may not be used, so long as the intention is clear.[26] The section then applies subject to any modification contained in the instrument creating the trust.[27]

Section 33(1) provides:

"Where any income, including an annuity or other periodical

---

[19] *Billson* v. *Crofts* (1873) L.R. 15 Eq. 314; *Re Aylwin's Trusts* (1873) L.R. 16 Eq. 585; *Re Ashby* [1892] 1 Q.B. 872.

[20] (1957) 21 Conv.(n.s.) 110 (L. A. Sheridan).

[21] *Snowdon* v. *Dales* (1834) 6 Sim. 524; the point is discussed in *Rochford* v. *Hackman* (1852) 9 Hare 475.

[22] And may take effect where the forfeiture precedes the settlement; as where the bankruptcy began before the testator died: *Metcalfe* v. *Metcalfe* [1891] 3 Ch. 1. See also *Re Forder* [1927] 2 Ch. 291; *Re Walker* [1939] Ch. 974.

[23] *Post*, p. 212.

[24] *Re Shaw's Settlement* [1951] Ch. 833; *Re Rees (decd.)* [1954] Ch. 202; *Re Munro's S.T.* [1963] 1 W.L.R. 145.

[25] Griswold, *Spendthrift Trusts*, p. 375.

[26] *Re Wittke* [1944] Ch. 166 ("under protective trusts for the benefit of my sister"); *Re Platt* (1949) unreported; C.L.C. 10917 ("for a protective life interest").

[27] T.A. 1925, s.33(2).

income payment, is directed to be held on protective trusts for the benefit of any person (in this section called 'the principal benefici-ary') for the period of his life or for any less period, then, during that period (in this section called the 'trust period') the said income shall, without prejudice to any prior interest, be held on the following trusts, namely:—

(i) Upon trust for the principal beneficiary during the trust period or until he . . . does or attempts to do or suffers any act or thing, or until any event happens, other than an advance under any statutory or express power, whereby, if the said income were payable during the trust period to the principal beneficiary absolutely during that period, he would be deprived of the right to receive the same or any part thereof,[28] in any of which cases . . . this trust of the said income shall fail or determine;

(ii) [and during the remainder of the trust period] . . . upon trust for the application thereof for the maintenance or support, or otherwise for the benefit, of all or any one or more exclusively of the other or others of the following persons[29] (that is to say)—

    (*a*) the principal beneficiary and his or her wife or husband, if any, and his or her children or more remote issue, if any; or

    (*b*) if there is no wife or husband or issue of the principal beneficiary in existence, the principal beneficiary and the persons who would, if he were actually dead, be entitled to the trust property or the income thereof to the annuity fund, if any, or arrears of the annuity, as the case may be; as the trustees in their absolute discretion, without being liable to account for the exercise of such discretion, think fit."

6. FORFEITURE OF THE LIFE TENANT'S INTEREST

It is necessary in each case to decide whether or not the event which has occurred is sufficient to determine the interest of the life tenant, and thus to bring the discretionary trusts into operation.[30] The question usually arises under trusts governed by the Trustee Act 1925, s.33. Where the question arises in respect of an express protective trust, the question will be dependent upon the construction of the particular trust under consideration.[31] The principles applicable will however be the same.

It will be appreciated that a forfeiture is not in these cases a disaster. The forfeiture deprives the life tenant of his life interest, which would

---

[28] See *Re Smith's Will Trusts* (1981) 131 N.L.J. 292.

[29] Relationships are to be construed in accordance with s.1 of the Family Law Reform Act 1987 (*i.e.* without regard to legitimacy); F.L.R.A. 1987, Sched. 2, para. 2.

[30] *Re Brewer's Settlement* [1896] 2 Ch. 503.

[31] *Ibid.* at p. 507; *Re Dennis' S.T.* [1942] Ch. 283 at p. 286; *Re Hall* [1944] Ch. 46.

otherwise have become available to his creditors. The effect of the forfeiture is to allow the protective provisions to come into effect, and to keep the principal beneficiary's interest from his trustee in bankruptcy.

A. Determining Events

If the principal beneficiary alienates his interest, or goes bankrupt, a forfeiture obviously occurs. In other circumstances, it is often difficult to draw a clear dividing line between those which will and those which will not effect a forfeiture. The matter is best explained by illustrations. The first three are cases of express protective trusts in which the instrument provided that the life interest should be determinable upon the happening of some event whereby some or all of the income became payable to another person.

In *Re Balfour's Settlement Trusts*,[32] the trustees had, at the life tenant's request, and in breach of trust, advanced parts of the capital to him. They then asserted their right to retain the income of the fund in order to make good the breach. Subsequently, the life tenant became bankrupt. Farwell J. held that the life tenant's interest had determined because the trustees became entitled to the income.[33] The life interest was thus saved from the bankruptcy.

In *Re Baring's Settlement Trusts*,[34] a sequestration order was made against the property of a mother who failed to obey a court order to return her children to the jurisdiction. Morton J. held that the order effected a forfeiture, although the mother's loss of income was only temporary.

In *Re Dennis' Settlement Trusts*,[35] the settlor's son was entitled to a protective life interest under a family settlement. A rearrangement took place on his attaining the age of 21, and provided that for the next six years the trustees should pay to him only part of the income and should accumulate the rest for him. The rearrangement caused a forfeiture.

In *Re Gourju's Will Trusts*,[36] the protective trust was one governed by the Trustee Act 1925, s.33. The life tenant ceased to be entitled to receive the income of the trust because she lived in Nice, which became enemy occupied country during the Second World War. This caused a forfeiture. The Custodian of Enemy Property

---

[32] [1938] Ch. 928; *Re Gordon* [1978] Ch. 145; *post*, p. 819.

[33] Distinguishing *Re Brewer's Settlement* [1896] 2 Ch. 503, where bankruptcy took place before the trustees exercised their right.

[34] [1940] Ch. 737.

[35] [1942] Ch. 283.

[36] [1943] Ch. 24; *Re Wittke* [1944] Ch. 166; *Re Allen-Meyrick's Will Trusts* [1966] 1 W.L.R. 499. See also Trading with the Enemy (Custodian) (No. 2) Order, 1945 (S.R. & O. 1945 No. 887) providing that vesting in the Custodian should not take place if it would cause a forfeiture.

had no claim; nor could the trustees treat the tenant for life as still entitled, and retain income for her until the end of the war. The discretionary trusts came into effect, and the income was payable to one or more members of the class of beneficiaries.

On the other hand, residence in enemy occupied territory did not cause a forfeiture in *Re Hall*,[37] where forfeiture was to take place if the annuitant (*inter alia*) should "do or suffer any act" whereby the annuity should be payable elsewhere. The annuity could no longer be paid to the annuitant; but this was not due to anything that she had done or permitted; the Custodian of Enemy Property was entitled. Nor was there a forfeiture where a life tenant under a protective trust (terminable if the income became "payable to ... some other person") assigned his interest to the trustees of his marriage settlement (of which he was tenant for life), authorised the trustees to charge their expenses to the fund and appointed them his attorneys to receive the income.[38] Again there was no forfeiture where the life tenant was of unsound mind and a receiver was appointed.[39] Nor does the fact that a receiver's fees become payable out of the estate of such a person effect a forfeiture.[40] And an authority to pay to creditors the dividends due from a company for a period of time during which the company declared no dividend did not cause a forfeiture.[41]

B. Order of the Court under Trustee Act 1925, s.57[42]

The court may make an order under Trustee Act 1925, s.57, which may affect the operation of a trust. If an order is made authorising the trustees to raise money to pay the debts of a life tenant under a protective trust, there is no forfeiture; for the power must be treated as if it had been "inserted in the trust instrument as an over-riding power."[43] And if the order provides that the life tenant effects an insurance policy to secure a like amount of money at his death, and that the trustees shall pay the premiums out of the income if the life tenant fails to do so, there is no forfeiture so long as the life tenant makes the payments; but if the life tenant fails to pay and they become payable by the trustees from the income, there would be a forfeiture.[44]

C. Order of the Court under Matrimonial Causes Acts 1859–1973

It is not clear whether a forfeiture is effected when an order is made in the Family Division of the High Court which alters a protected life

---

[37] [1944] Ch. 46; *Re Harris* [1945] Ch. 316; *Re Pozot's S.T.* [1952] Ch. 427.
[38] *Re Tancred's Settlement* [1903] 1 Ch. 715. Similarly an assignment of income already accrued; *Re Greenwood* [1901] 1 Ch. 887.
[39] *Re Oppenheimer's W.T.* [1950] Ch. 633; *Re Marshall* [1920] 1 Ch. 284.
[40] *Re Westby's Settlement* [1950] Ch. 296, overruling *Re Custance's Settlement* [1946] Ch. 42; Mental Health Act 1983, s.106(6).
[41] *Re Longman* [1955] 1 W.L.R. 197.
[42] *Post*, p. 583.
[43] *Re Mair* [1935] Ch. 562 at p. 565, *per* Farwell J.
[44] *Re Salting* [1932] 2 Ch. 57 at p. 65.

interest under a marriage settlement.[45] In *Re Richardson's Will Trusts*,[46] the court ordered that the principal beneficiary should charge his interest with an annual payment of £50 in favour of his divorced wife. The charge was held to create a forfeiture. On the other hand, in *General Accident Fire and Life Assurance Corporation Ltd.* v. *I.R.C.*[47] an order of the Divorce Court diverting part of the income from the life tenant in favour of a former wife was held not to effect a forfeiture.

These cases are distinguishable on a narrow ground of construction of section 33.[48] But the broader ground of the decision, that this situation has no relevance to the real purpose of protective trusts, would seem to apply to the charge in *Re Richardson's Will Trusts*[49] as much as to the diversion of part of the income in the *General Accident* case.[50] It is submitted that the principle of the *General Accident* case is sound. As Donovan L.J. said[51]: " . . . the section is intended as a protection to spendthrift or improvident or weak life tenants. But it can give . . . no protection against the effect of a court order such as was made here. Furthermore, if such an order involves a forfeiture much injustice could be done." Perhaps the problem can be rationalised with the cases on section 57 by saying with Russell L.J., who made clear, however, that he did not rest his decision on this approach: "the settlement throughout was potentially subject in all its trusts to such an order as was made."[52] *Re Richardson's Will Trusts*[53] was not mentioned; but an earlier case on the Matrimonial Causes Act 1859 in favour of forfeiture, *Re Carew*,[54] was overruled. It is tempting to say that *Re Richardson's Will Trusts* is wrong; but it should be noted that in that case, as in *Re Carew*, the decision in favour of forfeiture forwarded the broad policy of section 33; for the forfeiture in those cases allowed the discretionary trusts to operate when otherwise the trustee in bankruptcy would have claimed the interest.

---

[45] Which the court has power to do under Matrimonial Causes Act 1973, s.24(1). (See also, as to overseas divorces, Matrimonial and Family Proceedings Act 1984, s.17).

[46] [1958] Ch. 504; *Edmonds* v. *Edmonds* [1965] 1 W.L.R. 58. *Re Richardson* illustrates the advantage of establishing a series of protective trusts, "one set until the beneficiary is twenty-five, another from twenty-five to thirty-five, a third from thirty-five to forty-five, and another for the rest of his life." A forfeiture of, or a charge upon, the principal beneficiary's interest in one of the trusts would not affect his interest in subsequent trusts. He would get a fresh start. (1958) 74 L.Q.R. 182 (R.E.M.).

[47] [1963] 1 W.L.R. 1207.

[48] *Ibid.* See Donovan L.J. at p. 1217 and Russell L.J. at p. 1221; (1963) 27 Conv.(N.S.) 517 (F. R. Crane).

[49] [1958] Ch. 504.

[50] [1963] 1 W.L.R. 1207.

[51] [1963] 1 W.L.R. 1207, *per* Donovan L.J. at p. 1218.

[52] *Ibid.* at p. 1222.

[53] [1958] Ch. 504.

[54] (1910) 103 L.T. 658.

7. Advancements

Section 33(1) expressly exempts, as a cause of forfeiture, an advancement under any statutory or express power. This means that if the life tenant is the donee of an express power of advancement and makes an advancement, or consents to one being made by the trustees under the provisions of section 32,[55] the fact that he no longer receives the income of the part of the capital which has been advanced does not effect a forfeiture.[56] It appears that the same rule applies in the case of an express protective trust,[57] *Re Stimpson*[58] is to the contrary, but is regarded as of doubtful authority.

8. Effect of Forfeiture

When a forfeiture has taken place, the life interest of the principal beneficiary is terminated, and the trusts in section 33(1)(ii), or those expressly contained in the instrument, as the case may be, come into play. The termination is not, however, an occasion of charge to inheritance tax.[59] Under section 33 there are discretionary trusts in favour of the principal beneficiary and other persons, depending on whether or not a spouse or issue of the principal beneficiary is in existence. The trustees may apply the income for the remainder of the trust period for any member of the discretionary class. The principal beneficiary is not entitled to any income; but the trustees may, if they wish, pay it to him. They must pay the income to one or more of the members.[60] If the trustees decide to pay some income to the principal beneficiary, they face the problem that the money may be claimed by the trustee in bankruptcy as the assignee of his "interest" under the discretionary trust[61]; or perhaps only the surplus above that needed for his "mere support."[62] And if the trustees pay money to the beneficiary after receiving notice of the assignment of his interest, they will be liable to the assignee.[63] They may, however, in their absolute discretion, apply

---

[55] *Post,* p. 549.
[56] See however *General Accident, etc.* v. *I.R.C.* [1963] 1 W.L.R. 1207 which suggests that an advancement does not effect a forfeiture and that the proviso to s.33 is *ex abundanti cautela.*
[57] *Re Hodgson* [1913] 1 Ch. 34; *Re Shaw's Settlement* [1951] Ch. 833; *Re Rees (decd.)* [1954] Ch. 202.
[58] [1931] 2 Ch. 77.
[59] Inheritance Tax Act 1984, s.88 *post,* p. 222.
[60] *Re Gourju's W.T.* [1943] Ch. 24.
[61] *Re Coleman* (1888) 39 Ch.D. 443; *Lord* v. *Bunn* (1843) 2 Y. & C.Ch. 98.
[62] *Re Ashby* [1892] 1 Q.B. 872 at p. 877.
[63] *Re Neil* (1890) 62 L.T. 649; *Re Bullock* (1891) 64 L.T. 736 at p. 738.

the money for his use and benefit.[64] Thus, "if the trustees were to pay an hotel-keeper to give him a dinner he would get nothing but the right to eat a dinner, and that is not property which could pass by assignment or bankruptcy."[65] It is safer to pay the money to third persons in satisfaction of services provided for the bankrupt.

[64] *Re Bullock (supra)*; *Re Coleman (supra)*; *Re Smith* [1928] Ch. 915 at p. 919; *Public Trustees* v. *Ferguson* [1947] N.Z.L.R. 746. Scott, *Law of Trusts*, § 155(1) comments that "The distinction thus drawn between payments to the beneficiary and applying trust funds for his benefit seems to be arbitrary and without any sound basis in public policy."

[65] *Re Coleman, supra*, at p. 451.

CHAPTER 8

DISCRETIONARY TRUSTS

1. GENERAL

IT has been seen that discretionary trusts were used as a means of dealing with the income of a protective trust after the interest of the principal beneficiary had determined. Conveyancers appreciated the advantages which discretionary trusts could offer, especially in the context of estate duty saving, and they developed into one of the principal tools of estate and tax planners. Estate duty was replaced by capital transfer tax (now inheritance tax) in the Finance Act 1975. An explanation of the current tax position will be delayed until the next chapter, so that the fiscal situation of different types of trusts may be considered together. It will then be seen that discretionary trusts suffered substantially upon the introduction of capital transfer tax, and became at a disadvantage in relation to other trusts.[1] The disadvantage has been increased now that the discretionary trust is the only form of trust to be initially chargeable to inheritance tax upon its creation *inter vivos*. Outright gifts and non-discretionary trusts are generally potentially exempt (*i.e.* chargeable only if the transferor dies within seven

---

[1] Although the rules applicable to discretionary trusts were substantially amended and rationalised by the Finance Act 1982. It should be added that the rates of inheritance tax under F.A. 1988 are not high, the maximum being 40 per cent. on death and 20 per cent. for chargeable lifetime transactions.

years).[2] The importance of discretionary trusts has been reduced, but they need to be examined because large numbers of them still exist and, as will be seen, one of the problems of trusts lawyers is to advise what should be done with them; secondly, because they retain many advantages outside the fiscal field; and thirdly, because they raise a number of interesting and important theoretical questions in the law of trusts.

2. Uses of Discretionary Trusts

There are various reasons why a settlor may prefer to establish discretionary trusts rather than fixed trusts. As previously indicated, the most important reason used to be the saving of estate duty, and this will be referred to in Chapter 9. The emphasis is now on the other advantages.

A. To Protect the Beneficiary Against Creditors

If one member of a class of beneficiaries under a discretionary trust goes bankrupt, the trustee in bankruptcy is not entitled to claim any part of the fund.[3] The trustee in bankruptcy is however entitled to goods and money paid over by the trustees to the beneficiary in the exercise of their discretion[4]; or perhaps only to the amount in excess of that needed for the maintenance of the beneficiary.[5] The trustee in bankruptcy is however excluded if the trustees make the maintenance payments to third parties, such as a hotel keeper[6] or tradesman.[7]

We have already seen that discretionary trusts are employed under protective trusts as a means whereby a protected life tenant may continue to receive some benefit from settled funds after his bankruptcy.[8] Indeed, this was their earliest use.

B. To Continue to Exercise Control over Young or Improvident Beneficiaries

Many take the view that it is unwise to put large sums of money at the disposal of beneficiaries if they are young or extravagant. This is due

---

[2] See F.A. 1986, s.101, introducing the potentially exempt transfer for lifetime gifts other than trusts, and Finance (No. 2) Act 1987, s.96, extending this to non-discretionary trusts.
[3] *Re Ashby* [1892] 1 Q.B. 872 at p. 877; *Re Bullock* (1891) 64 L.T. 736; *Holmes* v. *Penney* (1856) 3 K. & J. 90. If the bankrupt is the sole member of the discretionary class, the interest passes to the trustee in bankruptcy: *Green* v. *Spicer* (1830) 1 Russ. & M. 395. See also *Re Trafford's Settlement* [1985] Ch. 32, *post*, p. 199.
[4] *Re Coleman* (1888) 39 Ch.D. 443.
[5] *Re Ashby, supra*, at p. 877 *per* Vaughan Williams J.; *Page* v. *Way* (1840) 3 Beav. 20, *per* Lord Langdale M.R.; *ante*, p. 189.
[6] *Re Coleman, supra*, at p. 451; *ante*, p. 190.
[7] *Godden* v. *Crowhurst* (1842) 10 Sim. 642 at p. 656.
[8] *Ante*, pp. 189–190.

not only to the fear of the loss of family capital in case of insolvency; but also because a rich young beneficiary may be encouraged to develop habits of idleness and extravagance, and waste the inheritance; older beneficiaries may already have done so. While the discretionary trust is in operation, each member of the class of beneficiaries is entitled only to the money which the trustees see fit to allocate to him in the exercise of their discretion. The settlor may, whether or not he is a trustee, be able to influence the selection so as to exercise some element of control over the beneficiaries.[9]

C. To React to Changes in Circumstances

The trustees can exercise their discretion in relation to distribution of income and capital according to the circumstances existing at the time. When the trust is set up, there is no way of knowing how the beneficiaries will fare in the future; which of them will be most in need; which will be deserving, which spendthrift, which inebriate; which will marry millionaires, and which missionaries. The trustees can take all these factors into consideration in making their decisions; and will be much influenced by the wishes of the settlor if he is still alive, or if he has expressed his wishes to them. In making these decisions, they will also take tax factors into consideration; it is more economical to give income to those with smaller incomes; and capital given to rich beneficiaries may bear high rates of inheritance tax when disposed of by them. Decisions by trustees which favour one beneficiary over another may of course give rise to criticism and resentment by disappointed beneficiaries.[10] All these factors need to be taken into consideration. The wider the trustees' discretion, the more difficult it may be to make, but the better the chance of making the right decision in the end.

3. USUAL FORM OF DISCRETIONARY TRUSTS

A. Trustees' Discretion

The essential feature of a discretionary trust is that the property is conveyed to trustees to be held by them on trust to apply the income or the capital or both for the benefit of the members of a class of beneficiaries in such proportions as the trustees shall, in their absolute discretion, think fit. Most discretionary trusts are concerned with distribution of income; the distribution of capital is commonly effected under a power to appoint. It used to be common to include a wider class of beneficiaries as objects of the power of appointment, and a narrower, more specific class of beneficiaries of the discretionary

---

[9] But if he influences the trustees to such an extent that they fail to exercise their discretion independently, the appointment will be void; *Turner* v. *Turner* [1984] Ch. 100, *post*, p. 204.

[10] The trustees need not disclose the reasons for their decisions; *Re Beloved Wilkes's Charity* (1851) 3 Mac. & G. 440 *post*, p. 480.

trusts.[11] But, since *McPhail* v. *Doulton*,[12] the test of certainty of beneficiaries of a discretionary trust has been assimilated, as has been seen,[13] to that of objects of a mere power, and the wider class can now be employed for both purposes. During the period of the trust, no individual beneficiary is entitled to any share of the property, income or capital; he receives what the trustees see fit to give him and no more.

B. The Trust Period

Provision will be made for the discretionary trust to continue for the trust period; which can be any desired period which is not in excess of the perpetuity period. Discretionary trusts provide a special situation for the application of the perpetuity rule. Since no individual beneficiary has any interest under the trust, property only vests in a beneficiary upon the exercise of the trustees' discretion in his favour; and such a vesting is void unless it takes place within the perpetuity period.[14] A discretionary trust can only exist, therefore, for the duration of the perpetuity period.

A discretionary trust will therefore be designed to terminate before the end of the period. This is normally done by postulating the "trust period" at the conclusion of which the discretionary trust will terminate, and providing for a gift over on fixed trusts which will themselves vest within the perpetuity period. Until 1964, the duration of discretionary trusts was usually governed by a "royal lives" clause.[15] Since that date, a period of years not exceeding 80 years may instead be specified.[16]

The beneficiaries of the fixed trust must themselves be individually ascertainable. The old certainty rule of *I.R.C.* v. *Broadway Cottages Trust*[17] still applies to fixed trusts.

C. Power to Accumulate

In many cases the income beneficiaries will not need the trust income each year, and it may be that, because the beneficiaries' income tax rates are higher than those of the trust, the tax payable will be higher if the income is paid out than it would be if it were retained in the trust.[18] The trustees are commonly given a power to accumulate. Without such a power, they will be obliged to distribute the income[19];

---

[11] *Re Gestetner* [1953] Ch. 672.

[12] [1971] A.C. 424.

[13] *Ante,* p. 98.

[14] *Re Coleman* [1936] Ch. 521.

[15] See M. & W., p. 252, Cheshire and Burn, p. 281; Maudsley, *The Modern Law of Perpetuities,* p. 88; Morris and Leach, p. 67.

[16] P.A.A. 1964, s.1.

[17] [1955] Ch. 20.

[18] Even though the additional rate is payable on the whole of the trust income: I.C.T.A. 1988, s.686; F.A. 1988, s.24(3).

[19] *Re Gourju's W.T.* [1943] Ch. 24; *Re Locker's S.T.* [1977] 1 W.L.R. 1323; subject to T.A. 1925, s.31, *post,* p. 542.

not to any particular beneficiary, but among the beneficiaries. It was noted above[20] that such a power makes the distinction between exhaustive and non-exhaustive discretionary trusts. The trust is non-exhaustive as to the income if the income is not required to be distributed each year; and non-exhaustive as to the capital if the trustees are not obliged to distribute all the capital during the currency of the trust.

There are, however, statutory restrictions upon powers of accumulation. Until 1964, the accumulation periods were of limited scope in the case of an *inter vivos* settlement. The Perpetuities and Accumulations Act 1964, however, provided a period in gross of 21 years. The permitted periods are (by the Law of Property Act 1925, s.164)[21]:

"(*a*) the life of the grantor or settlor; or
(*b*) a term of 21 years from the death of the grantor, settlor or testator; or
(*c*) the duration of the minority or respective minorities of any person or persons living or *en ventre sa mère* at the death of the grantor, settlor or testator; or
(*d*) the duration of the minority or respective minorities only of any person or persons who under the limitations of the instrument directing the accumulations would, for the time being, if of full age be entitled to the income directed to be accumulated."

To which the 1964 Act added, in respect of instruments coming into effect after July 16, 1964:

"(*e*) a term of 21 years from the date of the making of the disposition; and
(*f*) the duration of the minority or respective minorities of any person or persons in being at that date."

The settlor may select whichever period he wishes. If he selects a period which is in excess of those permitted, the accumulation will be invalid only as to the excess. The court will select whichever period is the most appropriate to the settlor's intent.[22] At the conclusion of the period of accumulation, the income must be distributed.

D. Power to Add to, or to Exclude from, the Class of Beneficiaries

The trustees may be given a power to add new members to the class of beneficiaries, or to exclude existing members.[23] The power to exclude members became important when Finance Act 1958[24] provided that a settlor should be liable to income tax upon the income of a settlement if the settlor or the spouse of the settlor might benefit from

[20] *Ante*, p. 63.
[21] The section does not apply to a corporate settlor: *Re Dodwell & Co. Ltd.'s Trust Deed* [1979] Ch. 301; [1979] Conv. 319 (J.T.F.).
[22] Maudsley, *The Modern Law of Perpetuities*, p. 208; Morris & Leach, p. 272.
[23] *Re Manisty's Settlement* [1974] Ch. 17; *Blausten* v. *I.R.C.* [1972] 1 Ch. 256.
[24] s.22; now I.C.T.A. 1988, s.674. See *Watson* v. *Holland* [1985] 1 All E.R. 290.

the income or property of the settlement. Many settlements in existence at that date included the spouse of the settlor as a member of the class of beneficiaries, and the Act provided that the settlor should notbe so liable if, *inter alia,* the power to make the payments was not exercisable after April 9, 1959.[25] Similar situations may arise in the future. A difficulty could arise if the trustees decided to exclude a member of the class for no good reason. Arbitrary exclusion will be inconsistent with the trustees' fiduciary duties.[26] It might also be construed as an improper release of a power held in a fiduciary capacity.[27] Yet it is difficult to see how the excluded member could establish that he had suffered loss; because, as a member of a class of beneficiaries under a discretionary trust, he was not entitled to any interest under the trust, and would be deprived of nothing except his hope or expectation of favourable consideration by the trustees.

It may be useful also to give power to the trustees to add new members to the class. Care has to be taken to ensure that the trustees cannot include persons, such as the settlor or his spouse, whose inclusion would have damaging tax consequences.[28] The power to add new members to the class is usually done by defining a class of excepted persons, and giving to the trustees a power to include in the class of beneficiaries any person who was not a member of the excepted class. Such a provision was upheld in *Re Manisty's Settlement,*[29] concerning a power of appointment, and the settlor's mother, and any person who should become his widow were added to the class of beneficiaries. The validity of trusts and powers in favour of very large classes was discussed in Chapter 3.

E. Power to Appoint Upon New Trusts

It is common to give to trustees power to appoint on further trusts, including discretionary and protective trusts, and also in favour of trustees of a foreign settlement[30] and to give them full power of delegation.[31] This makes possible a resettlement on new trusts at the end of the accumulation period, or at any time at which it becomes advantageous for fiscal or other reasons, to do so. Such an appointment must keep within the perpetuity period as measured from the date of the original settlement.[32] And it may not provide for accumulation for any period beyond that which was available to the original

---

[25] *Blausten* v. *I.R.C., supra.*

[26] *Post,* pp. 201 *et seq.*

[27] *Ante,* p. 177.

[28] Inclusion of the settlor (but probably not the settlor's spouse) would, for example, attract the "reservation of benefit" rules of inheritance tax; *post,* p. 216.

[29] [1974] Ch. 17; the power was described as an "intermediate" power; *ante,* p. 165: *Re Park* [1932] 1 Ch. 580; *Re Abraham's W.T.* [1969] 1 Ch. 463. See also *Re Hay's S.T.* [1982] 1 W.L.R. 202.

[30] *Post,* p. 476.

[31] See Hallett, *Conveyancing Precedents,* p. 772.

[32] *Pilkington* v. *I.R.C.* [1964] A.C. 612.

settlor.[33] The periods of perpetuity and of accumulation will only start again if appointments are made to a beneficiary who resettles; but such a course would result in a double transfer of the capital, which may have damaging inheritance tax consequences.

F. Miscellaneous Administrative Provisions

Trustees of every trust need to be given the powers necessary to enable them to perform their duties. Obvious powers which they need are the power to sell, to invest, to apply income for the maintenance of minor beneficiaries, to make advancements, to make payments to, and accept receipts from, guardians of minors, etc. It was at one time necessary to include all such powers in the settlement. But all the basic necessary powers are given to trustees by the Trustee Act 1925 and amendments thereto, discussed in detail below.[34] The statutory powers can be added to, or restricted, by the terms of the trust instrument.[35] It is usual, in the case of a discretionary trust, to give to the trustees the widest and most extensive powers. In terms of bulk, these administrative provisions will form the greater part of the trust instrument.

4. THE SELECTION OF TRUSTEES

The selection of the right trustees is important in the case of any trust; but particularly so in the case of a discretionary trust, where the trustees are given such extensive discretionary powers. The technical aspects of the matter are postponed to Chapter 16; but it may be useful here to anticipate some of that discussion. The settlor, in confiding such broad discretion, will wish to select individuals whose judgment and co-operation he respects. He can select his most trusted friends, but they may have no expertise in investment, accounting or law or taxes.[36] He may thus favour the inclusion of some professionals; who should do the job more efficiently; but they will need to be paid for their work. In a case of executorships or trusts generally, it is becoming common to appoint a corporate trustee, usually the Executor and Trustee Company of a bank, but there may be reluctance to appoint a corporate trustee in a case of a discretionary trust, because it may be felt that the trust officer will not be in as good a position as a personal friend to exercise the broad discretions contained in a discretionary trust. It is common to select a mixture of professionals and non-professionals; and there is no legal reason why a corporation and an individual should not be trustees.

---

[33] Because the appointors cannot be given powers in excess of those available to the settlor.

[34] *Post*, Chap. 19.

[35] T.A. 1925, s.69.

[36] For an illustration of the dangers of appointing such persons without the inclusion of professionals, see *Turner* v. *Turner* [1984] Ch. 100, *post,* p. 204.

As the disposition of the property is dependent upon the discretion of the trustees, the settlor may wish to be appointed trustee in order to be able to participate in decisions on distribution. Such an appointment has, in the past, been considered unadvisable because it might be possible for him to obtain a benefit under the settlement, and, under the estate duty system, this would have had the effect of treating the trust property as being part of the settlor's estate for estate duty purposes.[37] Under the system of inheritance tax the old estate duty concept of "reservation of benefit" has been reintroduced.[38] In the context of the discretionary trust, this means that the property is treated as remaining part of the settlor's estate if he is within the class of objects.[39] If the settlor is merely a trustee it is unlikely that the "reservation of benefit" rules will apply, but it will be otherwise if he can in fact derive benefit from his trusteeship, for example by way of remuneration. In view of these uncertainties, the appointment of the settlor as trustee is best avoided.

Even if he is not a trustee, it is possible for the settlor to exert some influence upon the trustees in the way in which they exercise their discretion. However, if the settlor effectively dictates the distribution of the property in such a way that the trustees exercise no independent discretion, any appointments so made will be void.[40]

5. The Nature of the Interest of the Beneficiaries under a Discretionary Trust

The nature of the interest of beneficiaries under a discretionary trust raises some important theoretical and practical questions. The discussion will tie in with some of the points made earlier in the distinction between trusts and powers.[41] In that context, the present discussion will justify the recognition of the basic difference between trusts and powers as being one of obligation or discretion. But it will be clear, as pointed out by modern writers,[42] that the "duty" concept in the case of discretionary trusts is a very different duty from that recognised in the case of fixed trusts.

A. Exhaustive and Non-exhaustive Discretionary Trusts

If the trustees are required to distribute the whole of the income, the discretionary trust is said to be exhaustive. Where, as in the case of most modern discretionary trusts, the trustees may apply the income

---

[37] *Oakes* v. *Stamp Duty Commissioner for N.S.W.* [1954] A.C. 51.
[38] F.A. 1986, s.102 and Sched. 20.
[39] See (1986) 83 L.S.G. 3728.
[40] *Turner* v. *Turner, supra.*
[41] *Ante*, p. 61.
[42] (1976) 54 C.B.R. 229 (M. C. Cullity); [1970] A.S.C.L. 187 (J. D. Davies); (1974) 37 M.L.R. 643 (Y. Grbich).

for some purposes other than distribution among the beneficiaries, as where there is a power to accumulate income not so applied, there is said to be a non-exhaustive discretionary trust. The rights of the beneficiaries are more complex in the case of a non-exhaustive discretionary trust. For the income beneficiaries cannot argue that they are, as a group, *entitled* to the income. The income may be accumulated in whole or in part and added to the capital.

B. The Nature of the Interest of the Beneficiaries

(i) Individual Beneficiaries. In the case of a fixed trust, we saw that the beneficiary's interest is regarded as proprietary. He is the owner of an equitable interest under the trust. This is not so in the case of a beneficiary under a discretionary trust. He is dependent upon the exercise by the trustees of their power of selection in his favour.[43] This point was crucial to the success of discretionary trusts in the estate duty days; because estate duty was payable when property "passed" on a death.[44] Property passed on the death of a life tenant under a trust.[45] The question of liability to duty on the death of a beneficiary under a discretionary trust was not seriously tested until 1968. In *Gartside* v. *I.R.C.,*[46] which concerned the death of a beneficiary under a non-exhaustive discretionary trust, the Revenue argued that, as one beneficiary *might* receive all the income, he should be treated as being entitled to all the income, and estate duty charged accordingly upon the whole of the fund. But that argument, as Lord Reid pointed out, would mean that estate duty would be chargeable upon the whole of the fund on the death of each beneficiary; which "would be a monstrous result which could never have been intended."[47] He could not be said to be entitled to any quantifiable share. He therefore owned no part of the property and no property passed on his death. The position is similar under the inheritance tax system. As we will see, the death of a discretionary beneficiary is not an event upon which the trust fund is taxable. Inheritance tax is, however, payable on a payment to a beneficiary and on certain other occasions.[48]

A sole member of a class of discretionary beneficiaries cannot claim entitlement to the income so long as there is a possibility that another member could come into existence.[49]

---

[43] He can renounce his position as class member; *Re Gulbenkian's Settlement (No. 2)* [1970] Ch. 408.

[44] F.A. 1894, s.2.

[45] *Earl Cowley* v. *I.R.C.* [1899] A.C. 198.

[46] [1968] A.C. 553; *Vestey* v. *I.R.C.* [1980] A.C. 1148 at pp. 1171, 1189; *Pearson* v. *I.R.C.* [1981] A.C. 753.

[47] *Ibid.* at p. 605.   [48] *Post*, Chap. 9.

[49] *Re Trafford's Settlement* [1985] Ch. 32. See also *Browne* v. *Browne*, *The Times*, November 25, 1988 (where sole beneficiary, trust fund was "financial resources" within M.C.A. 1973, ss.23, 24).

(ii) The Class. Whether or not the class of beneficiaries is properly regarded as the owner is a different matter. We have seen that a sole beneficiary of a discretionary trust and the remaindermen expectant upon the determination of the trust on his death, may, if all are adult and under no disability, call for the capital to be paid over to them, or may validly assign to a third party who will become the beneficiary.[50]

Cases on estate duty have indicated that a class of beneficiaries may not hold a proprietary interest which "passes" for estate duty purposes. "Two or more persons," said Lord Reid, "cannot have a single right unless they hold it jointly or in common. But clearly objects of a discretionary trust do not have that: they have individual rights, they are in competition with each other and what the trustees give to one is his alone."[51] This was said in *Gartside* v. *I.R.C.*[52] which, as has been seen, was a case of a non-exhaustive discretionary trust, but in *Re Weir's Settlement*[53] and *Sainsbury* v. *I.R.C.*[54] the same analysis was applied to exhaustive discretionary trusts. Lord Reid's rejection of the "group or class" interest concept "seems equally applicable, whether the trust is exhaustive or not exhaustive."[55] The question ceased to be of significance in relation to estate duty in 1969,[56] but is relevant to determine where the beneficial interest is in a discretionary trust; and whether the class of beneficiaries, all being adult and under no disability, is able to call for a transfer of the legal title and to terminate the trust. It is submitted that the beneficial ownership should be in all those persons in whose favour the discretion may be exercised, including the beneficiaries of an accumulation provision under a non-exhaustive trust; and that, on the principle of *Re Smith,*[57] they should be able to terminate the trust in appropriate circumstances, if all adult and under no disability.

C. Power and Duties

It may be useful at this stage to recapitulate some of the points, discussed above,[58] in connection with the nature of rights, duties and discretions in the context of trusts and powers. It will be seen that the basic distinction between trusts and powers continues to be that between obligations and discretions; but it is important to be able to identify what the trustees' duty is in the case of a discretionary trust. There are various contexts in which the question of the distinction between trusts and powers arises.

---

[50] *Green* v. *Spicer* (1830) 1 Russ. & My. 395; *Re Smith* [1928] Ch. 915.
[51] *Per* Lord Reid [1968] A.C. 553 at pp. 605–606.
[52] [1968] A.C. 553.
[53] [1969] 1 Ch. 657, reversed on a different point [1971] Ch. 145.
[54] [1970] Ch. 712.
[55] [1970] Ch. 712 at p. 724, *per* Ungoed-Thomas J.
[56] F.A. 1969, s.36.
[57] [1928] Ch. 915; *supra*; *Saunders* v. *Vautier* (1841) 4 Beav. 115, affirmed Cr. & Ph. 240.
[58] *Ante*, p. 61.

(i) **Fixed Trust.** At one end of the spectrum is the case of the trustee of a fixed trust. This is clearly an obligation upon the trustee. Having once accepted the trusteeship, he has no choice of whether or not to perform the trust. He is obliged to do so; he can be required by the court to perform, and is personally liable for breach. Some of the trustees' duties will require the exercise of a discretion in their performance. Thus, a trustee is under a duty to invest[59]; but, he will of course exercise a discretion in the selection of investments.[60] The trustees' duty may be seen as a correlative of the beneficiaries' rights. His position is wholly different from that at the other end of the spectrum; that of the donee of a power held in a non-fiduciary capacity. As will be seen, the question whether to exercise such a power is wholly a matter of the donee's discretion.

(ii) **Trust with a Power of Selection.** We have seen that there are cases in which the trustees hold property upon trust for a specified group of persons, subject to a power to select the shares and proportions in which those persons shall take. Thus in *Burrough* v. *Philcox*[61] the disposition was "among my nephews and nieces, or their children, either all to one or to as many of them as my surviving child shall think proper." We saw that, in the absence of an appointment being made, the nieces and nephews took in equal shares. The nieces and nephews thus held a vested interest under the trust, subject to divestment upon an appointment being made. Their situation is exactly the same as it would have been if the testamentary provisions had given to a donee a power to appoint, and in default of appointment to my nephews and nieces in equal shares. Those entitled in default are treated as owners in equity subject to divestment on the exercise of the power.[62] The trust in their favour is a fixed trust.[63] The division into equal shares makes it necessary to identify each member, and to know how many there are. This case is the same as that of a fixed trust; but the beneficiaries' interests are subject to defeasance. The trustee's duty to the beneficiaries is clear. It is a question of construction whether the instrument creates such a trust or creates a discretionary trust, discussed below.

(iii) **Discretionary Trusts: Exhaustive and Non-exhaustive.** A discretionary trust may require the trustees to distribute all the income; or it may give to the trustees a power to accumulate for a period allowed by law. Similarly, it may require the trustees to dispose of the capital during the trust period, or it may provide for a gift over of the assets of the trust at the end of the trust period. Whether the trust is exhaustive

---

[59] *Post*, p. 486.
[60] The trust instrument may expressly require investment in a specific security.
[61] (1840) 5 My. & Cr. 72.
[62] *Re Brooks' S.T.* [1939] Ch. 993 at p. 997; *ante*, p. 64.
[63] And thus not affected by the decision in *McPhail* v. *Doulton* [1971] A.C. 424, *ante*, p. 98. See (1982) 98 L.Q.R. 551 (C. T. Emery).

or non-exhaustive, an individual beneficiary, as has been seen, is not regarded as having any proprietary interest in the trust property.[64] If the trust is exhaustive, there is authority to say the class as a whole, if adult and under no disability, can terminate the trust.[65]

This raises the question: what is the trustee's duty? Clearly, it is different from the case of a fixed trust. Where are the beneficiary's correlative rights? This situation does not fit neatly into the right-duty correlation. The beneficiary has no proprietary rights. Is it correct to describe the situation as a trust; which, by definition, involves an obligation and a duty? The answer, it is submitted, is: yes; this is a trust, and it involves an obligation on the trustee and a duty. The duty is different from that in the case of a fixed trust.

The duty here is to exercise the discretion. In the case of an exhaustive discretionary trust, a selection must be made; whereas if the discretionary trust is non-exhaustive, the discretion may be exercised by deciding to accumulate. As Harris argued[66] persuasively, "the discretionary trust in fact depends on a rule-concept of duty, with no such necessity for correlative rights." Herein is the trustee's duty in a discretionary trust; and here is the point of distinction between a discretionary trust and a mere power. Each member of the class of beneficiaries under a discretionary trust has standing to sue in order to have the trustees' duty performed. Not that such a beneficiary will necessarily benefit by the performance of the trustees' duty; as it is a duty, not to pay to that beneficiary, but to exercise their discretion as described above.

In *Re Locker's Settlement*,[67] the terms of an exhaustive discretionary trust required the trustees to pay, divide and apply the income for charitable purposes or among the class of beneficiaries as the trustees "shall in their absolute discretion determine."

Because of subsequent expressions of wishes by the settlor, the trustees failed to make distributions of income from 1965 to 1968. The question arose in 1975 what should be done with that income, and particularly whether the trustees' discretion had expired.

Goulding J. held that the discretion still continued, and that the trustees should apply their discretion in the distribution of the money among those who were members of the class of beneficiaries in the relevant years.[68] In discussing the question of the trustees' duty and the court's power to enforce the exercise of the discretion, he said,[69] "it is common ground that it was the duty of the trustees to distribute the

---

[64] *Ante,* p. 199.
[65] *Re Smith* [1928] Ch. 915; *Re Nelson* [1928] Ch. 920n.; *ante,* p. 200.
[66] (1971) 87 L.Q.R. 231.
[67] [1977] 1 W.L.R. 1323; *Re Gourju's W.T.* [1943] Ch. 241; *McPhail* v. *Doulton* [1971] A.C. 424.
[68] Further beneficiaries were added in 1972.
[69] [1977] 1 W.L.R. 1323 at p. 1325.

trust income within a reasonable time. . . . A court of equity, where the trustees have failed to discharge their duty of prompt discretionary distribution of income, is concerned to make them, as owners of the trust assets at law, dispose of them in accordance with the requirements of conscience. . . . " If the trustees refuse to perform their duty, the court can itself execute the trust—"by appointing new trustees, or by authorising or directing representative persons of the classes of beneficiaries to prepare a scheme for distribution, or even, should the proper basis for distribution appear, by itself directing the trustees so to distribute."[70] The trustees in *Locker*,[71] as is usual in these cases,[72] were ready and willing to perform, and did so.

The point is that the trustees under these circumstances are under a duty to distribute. That is an obligation which is subject to enforcement by the court in one of the ways stated. *Locker*[73] was a case of an exhaustive discretionary trust; though the individuals in the class of beneficiaries were not, as a class, entitled to the whole of the income, because the trustees could make payments to charity. The duty and obligation of the trustees, however, is the same in the case of a non-exhaustive discretionary trust as in *McPhail* v. *Doulton*[74] itself. The difference is that in a non-exhaustive trust the duty to exercise the discretion can be satisfied by deciding to accumulate.

(iv) Powers Held as Trustee. Fiduciary Powers.[75] The situation is quite different where the trustees, as one of the terms of the trust instrument, are given a power of appointment. Here there is no duty to exercise; and the court will not order the trustee to exercise the discretion. Typical is *Re Allen Meyrick's Trust*[76] where

A will gave property to trustees to hold "upon trust that they may apply the income thereof in their absolute discretion for the maintenance of my said husband and subject to the exercise of their discretion on trust for my two godchildren . . . in equal shares absolutely." Various difficulties arose. The husband was an undischarged bankrupt. Some of the money was applied in paying the rent and certain debts. The trustees could not agree on the disposal of other income, and attempted to surrender their discretion to the court.

The court refused to accept, and was willing only to hear applications for directions in particular circumstances as they arose. Nor were

[70] *Ibid.* at p. 1325, quoting Lord Wilberforce in *McPhail* v. *Doulton* [1971] A.C. 424 at p. 457.
[71] *Supra.*
[72] As pointed out by Lord Wilberforce at p. 449.
[73] *Supra.*
[74] *Supra.*
[75] See Chap. 6.
[76] [1966] 1 W.L.R. 499.

the trustees ordered to exercise their discretion. The trust here was in favour of the godchildren, subject to the overriding power. If the trustees could not reach unanimity as to the exercise of the power, the godchildren became entitled.

This is not, of course, to say that the trustees in this situation are not subject to duties in relation to the exercise of the power. They hold the power in a fiduciary capacity, and are subject to the highest fiduciary duties in the way in which they make their decision. They must do more than refrain from acting capriciously. Their duty is to consider periodically whether to exercise the power, and to consider the range of objects in such manner as will enable them to carry out their fiduciary duties. If they decide to exercise the power they must, of course, keep within its terms; they must exercise it in a responsible manner according to its purpose and consider the appropriateness of individual appointments.[77] Furthermore, they must not delegate their powers without authority.[78] They must appreciate that the discretion is theirs and not that of the settlor. If they merely obey the settlor's instructions without any independent consideration, they will be in breach of the duties described above, and any appointment made in such circumstances will be void.[79] These duties stem from the fact that the power is fiduciary; not from any duty to exercise the power. If they decide not to do so, the court will not interfere.

(v) **Powers Held in a Non-fiduciary Capacity.** As is seen in Chapter 6, no duty is imposed upon a donee who holds a power in a non-fiduciary capacity. If a grandparent leaves property on trust for his grandchildren, and gives his son a power to appoint in favour of charity, the son is under no duty to appoint or even to consider the rival claims of charity or the grandchildren. He is, of course, if he makes an appointment, required to keep within the terms of the power, and to avoid exercising the power for an improper purpose.

(vi) **The Rule of Certainty in Ascertaining Beneficiaries or Objects.** Reference should be made to Chapter 3, where this aspect of discretionary trusts is fully discussed.

(vii) **Discretionary Trusts Since 1974.** Because of the change in tax policy, discretionary trusts of this type became unpopular in tax planning circles. As will be seen, such trusts created after March 1974 suffer higher rates of tax than those existing before the capital transfer tax legislation came into operation.[80] Since the introduction of inheritance

---

[77] *Re Hay's S.T.* [1982] 1 W.L.R. 202; [1982] Conv. 432 (A. Grubb). These duties, which were laid down in *McPhail* v. *Doulton* [1971] A.C. 424, *Re Gestetner* [1953] Ch. 672, and *Re Gulbenkian's S.T.* [1970] A.C. 508, are not necessarily exhaustive.
[78] *Ibid.*
[79] *Turner* v. *Turner* [1984] Ch. 100.
[80] Relief was given on distributions before April 1983 from pre-1974 discretionary trusts; F.A. 1975, Sched. 5, para. 14; F.A. (No. 2) 1979, s.23(1)(*b*).

tax, we have seen that discretionary trusts have suffered further by reason of their exclusion from the "potentially exempt transfer" regime.[81] The lifetime creation of such trusts is, therefore, taxable even if the settlor survives a further seven years. For this reason few discretionary trusts of substantial size are likely to be created under the present tax system,[82] although more modest discretionary trusts falling within the settlor's inheritance tax "nil rate band"[83] may still be attractive.

[81] *Ante*, p. 191.
[82] Unless they are within the class of discretionary trusts which are given preferential treatment, *e.g.* accumulation and maintenance trusts, *post*, p. 220.
[83] *Post*, p. 214. The reduction of the maximum lifetime rate to 20 per cent. by F.A. 1988 will alleviate the position to some extent.

CHAPTER 9

TAXATION AND TRUSTS[1]

1. Estate and Tax Planning

THE most significant factor in the creation of trusts *inter vivos* has been the avoidance of taxation. A wealthy person may benefit his family by giving presents to them or paying their bills, and then leave his property to them by will. But tax legislation imposes higher rates on larger accumulations of property, and this wealthy person will seek ways of conferring benefits on his family and at the same time reducing his tax liability. The tax payable by 10 people on incomes of £5,000 each is less in total than that payable by one person with an income of £50,000. Similarly, tax on capital is at its highest in large concentrations. More details of the income, and especially of the capital tax system, will be given below. The point here is that a wealthy man can best preserve the family fortune by sharing out, and that this has commonly been done by creating trusts in his lifetime. This tax planning of an estate is one of the most important and sophisticated functions of trust lawyers.

Until comparatively recently the courts in determining the tax effectiveness of any scheme of tax avoidance applied the principle laid down by Lord Tomlin in *I.R.C.* v. *Duke of Westminster*[2]: "Every man is entitled if he can to order his affairs so that the tax attaching under the appropriate Acts is less than it otherwise would be."[3] But starting in *W.*

---

[1] See Thomas, *Taxation and Trusts*; Maudsley and Burn, *Trusts and Trustees*; *Cases and Materials* (3rd ed.), Part 3. Parker and Mellows, *The Modern Law of Trusts* (5th ed.), Chap. 15; *Butterworths UK Tax Guide* (6th ed.), Chapter 11 (income tax), Chapter 18 (capital gains tax) and Chapters 40 and 41 (inheritance tax). Assets held on trust have been estimated at 6 per cent. of total personal wealth; Thomas, *op. cit.*, p. 1.
[2] [1936] A.C. 1.
[3] *Ibid.* at p. 19.

T. Ramsay v. *I.R.C.*,[4] the House of Lords has begun to elaborate a new and much more restrictive principle to apply in dealing with questions of the effectiveness of complex tax avoidance schemes. Where there occurs a pre-ordained series of transactions designed to reduce tax payable by a particular taxpayer the court is free to disregard any of those transactions if they are inserted for no good commercial purposes other than the reduction of tax. The transactions will be treated as a single composite whole and taxed accordingly. The extent to which this reasoning applies to the creation and manipulation of trusts rather than commercial and corporate dealings is as yet unclear,[5] but there seems to be no good reason why the new principle should not apply with equal force to trusts-based tax avoidance schemes.

As the circumstances of each individual differ, so each situation needs individual treatment. The estate- or tax-planner, with the assistance of accountants and other specialists, will present to the client various possible solutions, indicating the tax implications of each. The client must then decide how much to give away immediately and irrevocably, and to whom; and how much to keep for himself; and, in days of inflation, many people will hesitate before making gifts, and thereby running the risk of leaving themselves short of capital in their old age. What he keeps will be disposed of by his will, and a testamentary trust may be created. Those whose fortunes are insufficient to create tax problems will not be concerned with *inter vivos* tax planning; but may, again, create testamentary trusts on their deaths.

2. THE TAX STRUCTURE

To explain how best to avoid liability to tax, it is essential to explain the tax system in detail. There is no room to do that here, and only a few highlights can be given. It is in any case dangerous, in a book of this nature, to include too much detail; for each annual Budget may be expected to make some changes in the rates; and, if there is a change of Government, the policy behind the tax system also changes. Tax policy is often dictated more by political philosophy than by the search for a system which is rational and just.

The greatest revenue raiser is, of course, income tax. The net receipts from capital taxes have been disappointingly small. A Government in need of money has therefore an interest in keeping income tax rates high; though the logic of the matter would seem to be

---

[4] [1982] A.C. 300. See also *I.R.C.* v. *Burmah Oil Co. Ltd.* (1981) 54 T.C. 200, *Furniss* v. *Dawson* [1984] A.C. 474; *Craven (Inspector of Taxes)* v. *White* [1988] 3 W.L.R. 423 (where the House of Lords refused to extend this principle).

[5] For some suggestions see [1984] B.T.R. 109 (C. N. Beattie) and, generally, [1982] B.T.R. 200 (H. H. Monroe); [1983] B.T.R. 221 (R. K. Ashton); (1982) 98 L.Q.R. 209 (P. J. Millett); [1984] Conv. 296 (G. K. Morse); (1984) 43 C.L.J. 259 (D. Hayton); All E.R.Rev. 1984 p. 276 and 1987 p. 267 (J. Tiley).

that you should pay lower taxes on the money that you work for, than on inheritances.[6] There was a substantial argument to the effect that income tax rates, reaching up to 83 per cent.,[7] resulted in the stifling of initiative and enterprise.[8] The Conservative Government in 1979[9] heeded that argument and reduced the top rate to 60 per cent., and it has since been reduced to 40 per cent.[10] What the future holds in store cannot be known. The tax system has hitherto been regarded not only as a revenue raiser, but also as a means of promoting the social, economic and political philosophy of the Government.

A. Income Tax

Tax is chargeable upon an individual's taxable income[11] at the rates laid down annually in the Finance Act. At the present time, the basic rate is 25 per cent. on a taxable income up to £19,300, and 40 per cent. thereafter.[12] The additional rate payable by individuals on investment income has been abolished.[13] There are a number of allowances and reliefs to which individuals are entitled.

We are concerned, however, with the taxation of trusts. Trustees are not individuals for income tax purposes. Trusts as such therefore enjoy no personal allowances. The income of a trust is chargeable at the basic rate, and the trustees are assessable.[14] In a wide range of circumstances the income arising under a trust may be treated as the settlor's income.[15] The trustees need take no action in respect of income from most stock exchange investments which effectively is paid net of basic rate tax. The beneficiary who is entitled to the income is responsible for the payment of any higher rate tax which may be due; and it is often convenient to arrange for the dividends to be paid direct to him. The trustees will, however, need to deduct and account for income tax which is due on any income of the trust which has been received without deduction of tax at the basic rate, such as income from land or

---

[6] A general review of the tax structure was carried out by the Meade Committee which reported in 1978: *The Structure and Reform of Direct Taxation* (The Meade Report for the Institute for Fiscal Studies 1978); [1978] B.T.R. 176 (A. R. Prest); [1979] B.T.R. 25 (B. Bracewell-Milnes); [1979] B.T.R. 168 (D. M. Bensusan-Butt). For a thorough study in Canada, see the Report of the Royal Commission on Distribution of Income and Wealth No. 1 (Cmnd. 6171) and No. 4 (Cmnd. 6626).

[7] On incomes over £21,000 in 1979.

[8] For different views, see Kay and King, *The British Tax System* (4th ed.), Chap. 1.

[9] F.A. 1979 (No. 2), s.5.

[10] F.A. 1988, s.24(1).

[11] I.C.T.A. 1988, s.835; and means income calculated in accordance with Scheds. A–F, I.C.T.A. 1988, ss.15–20. Schedule B was abolished by F.A. 1988, s.65 and Sched. 6.

[12] F.A. 1988, ss.23, 24(1).

[13] F.A. 1984, s.17(2) and Sched. 7. The additional rate payable by trustees is not affected.

[14] There is no specific statutory provision. The higher rates do not apply to trustees because they are not "individuals"; I.C.T.A. 1988, s.1(2). See generally *Butterworth's U.K. Tax Guide* (6th ed.), pp. 431–435.

[15] I.C.T.A. 1988, Part XV. See *Watson* v. *Holland* [1985] 1 All E.R. 290. These provisions are intended to prevent and penalise tax avoidance.

for profits if they carry on a trade, and also for the additional rate which becomes due in the case of the income of a trust where there is no person currently entitled to the income.[16]

With such a trust, the income may either be paid out or, if the trust contains such a power, it may be accumulated. If it is accumulated, there is no tax liability beyond income tax at the basic rate plus the additional rate (a total in 1988–89 of 35 per cent.). Where the income is paid to or for the benefit of a beneficiary, the ultimate tax liability is dependent upon the beneficiary's tax situation.[17] He is treated as having received the value of the payment grossed up to reflect basic and additional rate tax.[18] If the beneficiary's income is in excess of £19,300, he will be liable to make up the difference between the tax already paid (35 per cent.) and the tax due at his marginal rate (40 per cent.). On the other hand, if his other income does not exhaust his allowances and reliefs, he may claim a repayment of an appropriate amount on producing to the Revenue the trustees' certificate of deduction of tax. It will thus be seen that income tax may be saved if the trustees have a discretion as to the distribution of income, and use it to make payments to those on low incomes whose tax rate is lower than the trust's. Thus, £1,300 of trust income after tax at 35 per cent.,[19] if paid to a beneficiary whose taxable income, including the payment, is £25,000, will bear another £100 in tax; but if paid to a child with no income, the child would get a rebate of £700.[20] There is, of course, no choice where the beneficiaries are entitled to the income or a share thereof. Moreover none of the above consequences apply if the sum as received by the beneficiary is capital in his hands, for example where it is paid pursuant to a power of appointment restricted to capital or out of accumulated income.[21]

B. Capital Gains Tax

Capital gains tax was introduced by the Finance Act 1965, and originally imposed at a rate of 30 per cent.[22] upon the gains accruing upon the disposal of an asset.[23] The Finance Act 1988 wrought significant changes in the tax. First, the flat rate of capital gains tax was abolished.[24] Instead the tax is to be charged at income tax rates (25 and

---

[16] I.C.T.A. 1988, s.686; F.A. 1988, s.24(3). This includes income of a discretionary trust or an accumulation and maintenance trust; *post*, p. 220. The additional rate is 10 per cent. on the whole income of the trust, after deducting expenses properly chargeable to income under the general law; *Carver* v. *Duncan (Inspector of Taxes)* [1985] A.C. 1082.

[17] But where the payment is in favour of the infant and unmarried child of the settlor, the income is treated as that of the settlor: I.C.T.A. 1988, s.663; *post*, p. 547.

[18] I.C.T.A. 1988, s.687.

[19] Basic income tax at 25 per cent. plus additional rate of 10 per cent.

[20] The child is entitled to the personal allowance of £2,605; F.A. 1988, s.25.

[21] I.C.T.A. 1988, s.687(1). See also *Stevenson* v. *Wishart* [1987] S.T.C. 266.

[22] C.G.T.A. 1979, s.3.

[23] C.G.T.A. 1979, s.1.

[24] F.A. 1988, s.98.

40 per cent. respectively). Secondly, in many cases the gain accruing on a disposal of an asset is now computed as though the disposer's acquisition cost had been the market value of the asset on March 31, 1982.[25] Thus gains attributable to a period of ownership prior to the 1982 date escape tax.[26] Capital gains tax is payable upon a sale under a bargain at arm's length, and was originally payable upon a gift. However, in respect of gifts made after April 5, 1980, the gain may be "held over" in the case of a gift to an individual, if both parties agree, so as to avoid liability on the gift, and to pass the donor's acquisition cost to the donee.[27] This provision applies to gifts to individuals and to gifts in trust.[28] Capital gains tax is not payable on death, though the deceased's property is deemed to be acquired by his personal representatives on his death at a consideration equal to its then market value. This generally involves a "tax-free uplift" in the notional acquisition cost of the assets in question, since their market value at death is usually greater than the acquisition cost enjoyed by the deceased.[29] When the personal representatives pass the assets to the legatee[30] no disposal is deemed to occur and the legatee acquires the assets with an acquisition cost equal to that of the personal representatives. Finally, capital gains tax is payable where disposals are deemed to occur, as where a capital sum is derived from an asset.[31]

There are many exemptions from liability to capital gains tax, the most important being an annual exemption of gains of £5,000 for individuals and £2,500 for a trust[32]; the taxpayer's main or only residence,[33] a chattel worth less than £3,000[34] and dated gilt-edged securities.[35]

The settlor will be liable to capital gains tax on making the settlement since this is a disposal even where the settlor declares himself trustee.[36] Under the settlement, the trustees will be affected in two quite different ways. First, in relation to the disposition of assets of the trust. On a disposal, the trustees are liable to tax on gains, as individuals would be. This situation normally arises where trustees switch investments in the ordinary course of administration of the trust. There is no liability, however, on the trustees of a trust where the majority of the trustees are resident abroad, and the management of

---

[25] F.A. 1988, s.96. The date is that of the introduction of indexation allowance.
[26] This is not so in all cases; s.96(2).
[27] F.A. 1980, s.79.
[28] F.A. 1982, s.82.
[29] C.G.T.A. 1979, s.49.
[30] Defined in s.47(2) to include "any person taking under a testamentary disposition or on an intestacy or partial intestacy, whether he takes beneficially or as trustee ... "
[31] *Ibid.*, ss.20–22. See also *Zim Properties* v. *Proctor* [1985] S.T.C. 90.
[32] F.A. 1988, s.108.
[33] C.G.T.A. 1979, s.101.
[34] *Ibid.* s.128.
[35] C.G.T.A. 1979, s.67.
[36] *Ibid.*, s.53. Holdover relief is available under F.A. 1980, s.79.

the trust is carried on abroad; liability is imposed on resident beneficiaries in relation to their interests under the trust. In certain circumstances gains of a non-resident trust may be attributed to beneficiaries for the purposes of liability.

Secondly, on certain occasions on which a disposal is deemed to have been made. Disposals are deemed to be made on various occasions, but the only one in this context on which tax is chargeable is that on which a person becomes absolutely entitled against the trustee[37]; as, for example, where the beneficiary becomes absolutely entitled upon fulfilling a condition, such as majority, or where an advancement is made to a beneficiary. As originally enacted, tax was chargeable as on a deemed disposal on the death of a life tenant, but that was changed by the Finance Act 1971[38] to bring the settlement provisions in line with the death rule for free estates.

C. Inheritance Tax

Inheritance tax is a modified version of its predecessor, capital transfer tax. Estate duty was replaced by capital transfer tax by the Finance Act 1975,[39] with effect from March 26, 1974. This was part of a complete reorganisation of the structure of the taxation of capital, which was extended to lifetime gifts. A wealth tax, in the form of an annual tax on ownership of assets, was planned in 1974. It was never introduced, nor is there any present likelihood of its introduction. The application of capital transfer tax to lifetime gifts was largely removed by the Finance Act 1986, in which the tax was renamed as inheritance tax.

(i) **Estate Duty.** Before March 26, 1974, estate duty was the only tax on private capital. It was a death tax only, and payable upon property passing on a death.[40] It could therefore be avoided by disposing of property before death; save that transfers made within seven years before death were subject to the tax.[41]

The disposal would often be by the creation of an *inter vivos* trust. The settlor would wish to avoid estate duty, not only on his death, but also upon the deaths of the beneficiaries. It was held that estate duty was payable upon the whole capital of a trust upon the death of a life tenant, or of the holder of some other limited interest.[42] The members of a class of beneficiaries of a discretionary trust owned no interest, however, in the fund[43]; they had no more than a hope that the trustees'

---

[37] *Ibid.* s.54. A deemed disposal, whether or not tax is charged, has the effect of establishing the acquisition value in the hands of the recipient.

[38] F.A. 1965, s.25(4); F.A. 1971, Sched. 12, para. 1.

[39] The provisions are now consolidated by the Inheritance Tax Act 1984, hereafter referred to as I.H.T.A. 1984.

[40] F.A. 1894, ss.1, 2.

[41] F.A. 1968, s.35.

[42] *Cowley (Earl)* v. *I.R.C.* [1899] A.C. 198.

[43] Eventually so decided in *Gartside* v. *I.R.C.* [1968] A.C. 553; *ante*, p. 199.

discretion would be exercised in their favour. It was possible, therefore, to avoid liability to estate duty, until 1969, on the death of the
settlor and of any of the beneficiaries by creating a discretionary trust
at least seven years before the death of the settlor.[44] No wonder that
the tax was called a "voluntary tax." An attempt was made in 1969 to
impose liability upon the deaths of beneficiaries under a discretionary
trust. The Finance Act 1969 imposed a charge upon the death of any
beneficiary who had received payments of income in the past seven
years.[45] The charge was on a portion of the capital equivalent to the
share of the income received by the deceased during the "relevant"
period. This system had little time to work, and would not in any case
have been very effective because the trustees of a discretionary trust
could pay the income to those whom they judged least likely to die in
the near future; and so long as the income was thus disposed of, there
was no objection to making capital payments to the old and sick
beneficiaries.[46]

(ii) **Capital Transfer Tax.** In a White Paper on Capital Transfer Tax[47]
and a Green Paper on Wealth Tax,[48] the Labour Government in 1974
announced its intention of imposing both taxes. The policy was to
effect a levelling of wealth[49]; estate duty, with all its loopholes, had
conspicuously failed to do so. Capital transfer tax was a tax on capital
transfers, whether *inter vivos* or on death, and was planned to tax
family capital, whether or not settled, at least once a generation. The
Wealth Tax would go further, and impose a tax annually on capital.
The imposition of a wealth tax would take some time, and the Government appreciated that it needed to be preceded by capital transfer tax.
   Capital transfer tax in its original form was a cumulative tax applying
to all transfers of value made by an individual after March 26, 1974
until his final transfer on death. Rates were progressive, and those
chargeable on death (or on transfers within three years of death) were
double those chargeable on lifetime transfers. The tax was modified by
subsequent Conservative Governments, in particular by alleviating
the cumulation principle. Instead of cumulating all transfers (made
after March 26, 1974), only those made within the previous 10 years
had to be cumulated, the figure finally being reduced to seven years.[50]
The rates of tax being progressive, these amendments were beneficial

[44] See *Pearson* v. *I.R.C.* [1980] Ch. 1, *per* Templeman L.J. at p. 25.
[45] s.36, creating the "substituted" F.A. 1894, s.2(1)(*b*); s.37; and in some other circumstances not here relevant.
[46] See F.A. 1969, s.37(3)(*b*).
[47] Cmnd. No. 5705 of 1974.
[48] Cmnd. No. 5704 of 1974; [1976] B.T.R. 7 (A. R. Prest).
[49] "The Government is committed to use the taxation system to promote greater social
   and economic equality. This requires a redistribution of wealth as well as income."
   Preface to Green Paper.
[50] F.A. 1986, s.101.

to the transferor. Further substantial modifications were made by the Finance Act 1986, which renamed the tax as inheritance tax, to which we now turn.

(iii) Inheritance Tax. The most significant changes brought about by the 1986 Act were the introduction of the "potentially exempt transfer" and the reintroduction of the estate duty principle of "reservation of benefit." These are explained in the outline of inheritance tax which follows.

The central concept of inheritance tax is the transfer of value, which may be chargeable, exempt or potentially exempt.[51] There is a transfer of value where a person makes a disposition as a result of which the value of his estate immediately after the disposition is less than it would have been but for the transfer, and the value transferred is the amount by which the estate is the less.[52] On a death, the deceased is treated as making a transfer of value of the whole of his estate immediately before the death.[53] There are special rules relating to settled property,[54] which will be examined below, and a number of exemptions and reliefs. The most important exemptions relate to transfers of any amount between spouses, whether *inter vivos* or on death,[55] and certain foreign property,[56] considered below, and certain personal exemptions.[57] Other reliefs and exemptions relate to situations which were familiar with estate duty, and include gifts to charities, works of art, agricultural or business property, and woodlands. They cannot be examined here.

The exemptions referred to above may be described as substantive exemptions, to distinguish them from the potentially exempt transfer, introduced by the Finance Act 1986.[58] A lifetime transfer by an individual made on or after March 18, 1986 is potentially exempt. As in the days of estate duty, it becomes chargeable if the transferor does not survive for seven years. If he dies within three years, the rates are those chargeable on a death. If he dies between three and seven years from the transfer, there is a taper relief on a sliding scale.[59] In certain exceptional cases, in particular the creation of a discretionary trust, a

[51] I.H.T.A. 1984, ss.1, 2.
[52] *Ibid.* s.3. It may include an omission to claim an entitlement: s.3(3), [1978] Conv. 291 (H. Baxter).
[53] *Ibid.* s.4.
[54] *Ibid.* Pt. III.
[55] *Ibid.* s.18.
[56] *Ibid.* s.6, *post*, p. 224, not strictly an exemption; but effectively so.
[57] *Ibid.* ss.19 *et seq.* These include £3,000 per donor per year; £250 per donee per year; normal expenditure out of income; gifts in consideration of marriage of various permitted amounts up to £5,000; and payments for the maintenance of dependants. (s.11). They give considerable scope for tax saving. It is obviously important for a donor to start his giving early, especially since the introduction of the potentially exempt transfer.
[58] I.H.T.A. 1984, s.3A, introduced by F.A. 1986, s.101 and Sched. 19.
[59] *Ibid.*, s.7, as amended.

lifetime disposition is *immediately* chargeable,[60] although at half the rates applicable on death.[61] If the settlor dies within seven years, the rates are increased as described above.

In the case of a lifetime transfer which is either initially chargeable or which becomes so by reason of death within seven years, and in the case of a transfer on death, the rates of tax are affected by any chargeable transfers within the previous seven years, which must be cumulated.[62] No tax will, however, be payable if the transfer falls within the "nil rate band," which stands at £110,000 at the time of writing.[63] Thereafter the rate is 40 per cent. if the transfer was on death or within three years of death, and 20 per cent. in the case of an initially chargeable lifetime transfer. As mentioned above, there is a sliding scale applicable to a potentially exempt transfer which becomes chargeable.[64]

In the case of an initially chargeable lifetime transfer, the tax may be paid by the transferor or the transferee. If it is paid by the transferor, the value of the chargeable transfer is the amount by which his estate is reduced, therefore the amount of the transfer for tax purposes must include the tax. It will be necessary to "gross up" the sum transferred. The amount of tax payable on any sum varies, not only with the size of the sum, but also with the total of prior chargeable transfers within the previous seven years. The calculations in any particular case can be formidable, and will be worked out in each case from grossing up tables. On the other hand, if the transferee pays the tax, the actual amount of the transfer is treated as the gross gift, and added to the transferor's total gifts. The amount of tax payable will be less; but the amount received by the transferee will also be less.

The last transfer which a person makes is that of his estate on his death. The rates applicable are those which begin at the total value of any taxable lifetime gifts within the previous seven years, grossed up as necessary. There is no question of grossing up the estate at death. Any tax is deducted prior to distribution. The incidence of tax as between specific and residuary beneficiaries is another problem.[65]

It is thus necessary to keep a "score" of taxable lifetime gifts, pay tax on them as due, and apply the seven-year cumulation rule when calculating the tax liability on subsequent chargeable gifts, and ultimately on death. The tax planner's job is to enable the client to make the best use of available exemptions and reliefs, and of the potentially exempt transfer. The adviser's dilemma is that his calculations have to

---

[60] *Ibid.*, s.3A. The lifetime creation of an interest in possession trust was initially chargeable under the 1986 Act, but this rule was abrogated by F.(No. 2)A. 1987, s.96 and Sched. 7.
[61] *Ibid.*, s.2.
[62] *Ibid.*, s.7.
[63] *Ibid.*, s.7 and Sched. 1; F.A. 1988, s.136.
[64] *Ibid.*, s.7(4).
[65] I.H.T.A. 1984, ss.38, 39; *Pinson on Revenue Law* (17th ed.), pp. 526 *et seq.*

be made on a number of assumptions about future events and tax liabilities.

Before examining the special rules relating to trusts, mention must be made of the principle of reservation of benefit. Although familiar under the estate duty regime, this concept was not relevant to capital transfer tax. It was reintroduced by the Finance Act 1986 and is a fundamental feature of inheritance tax. The object of this principle is that the donor should not be permitted to take advantage of the potentially exempt transfer rule by making gifts where he effectively retains his interest.

Where an individual makes a gift on or after March 18, 1986 the property is treated as subject to a reservation in two cases. First, where possession and enjoyment of the property is not bona fide assumed by the donee prior to the seven-year period ending with the donor's death (or, if the donor died within seven years of the gift, at the date of the gift). Secondly, where the property is not enjoyed "to the entire exclusion, or virtually to the entire exclusion, of the donor and of any benefit to him by contract or otherwise" at any time during the seven years ending with his death (or, if the donor died within seven years of the gift, at any time after the gift[66]). There are certain exceptions, for example where the donor occupies the property for full consideration in money or money's worth.[67] Nor does the principle apply where the gift falls within certain of the substantive exemptions, for example the spouse exemption.[68]

The effect of a gift with reservation of benefit is that the property is treated as remaining in the estate of the donor. Hence the making of a gift with reservation normally has no immediate inheritance tax consequence, but the property will be treated as part of the donor's estate on his death (at its value at that time) and taxed accordingly.[69] If during his lifetime there is a change of circumstances so that there is no longer a reservation of benefit, for example where the donor renounces any benefit he has retained, a potentially exempt transfer is treated as made at that time, so that the donor must survive a further seven years if tax is to be avoided.[70] If he dies within seven years, the property is taxed on its value at the date of the release of benefit, not of the prior gift. In the rare case where the lifetime gift is initially chargeable, as in the case of the creation of a discretionary trust, the property subject to a reservation will be treated as part of the settlor's estate on his death and taxed again, but relief is given against this double charge.[71]

[66] F.A. 1986, s.102.
[67] *Ibid.*, Sched. 20, para. 6.
[68] *Ibid.*, s.102(5).
[69] *Ibid.*, s.102(3).
[70] *Ibid.*, s.102(4).
[71] *Ibid.*, s.104; Inheritance Tax (Double Charges Relief) Regulations 1987 (S.I. 1987/1130).

There is, as yet, no authority on the interpretation of these provisions, but the cases on estate duty and comparable Commonwealth legislation afford guidance as to what is a reservation of benefit.[72] In the context of trusts, the settlor will be treated as reserving a benefit if he is among the class of objects of a discretionary trust,[73] even though he receives nothing. Similarly if the settlor is a remunerated trustee of the settlement.[74] The settlor does not, however, reserve a benefit by reason of being an unpaid trustee,[75] nor if he has a reversionary interest in the settled property, because the subject-matter of the gift does not include the reversion.[76]

3. INHERITANCE TAX AND SETTLEMENTS[77]

Family trusts have been used for many years as ways of avoiding tax. Not surprisingly, trusts in general, and discretionary trusts in particular, were treated harshly by the new legislation. There are, for inheritance tax purposes, two broad categories of settlements; those in which there is an interest in possession and those in which there is not, these being primarily discretionary trusts. The rules relating to reservation of benefit, discussed above,[78] must be borne in mind in relation to both categories.

When the Finance Act 1986 introduced the potentially exempt transfer, the only type of trust to benefit from it was the accumulation and maintenance trust.[79] The lifetime creation of other settlements was initially chargeable irrespective of seven-year survival. This position was subsequently modified so that the lifetime creation of an interest in possession settlement is now potentially exempt.[80] The lifetime creation of a discretionary trust (other than an accumulation and maintenance trust) remains initially chargeable.

A. Settlements in Which There is an Interest in Possession

This category deals with the standard form situation of a fixed trust for successive beneficiaries, whose interests are specified in the trust instrument; as a trust for Mrs. X for her life, and after her death for her

---

[72] See *Chick* v. *Commissioner of Stamp Duties of New South Wales* [1958] A.C. 435; *Nichols* v. *I.R.C.* [1975] 1 W.L.R. 534; *Munro* v. *Commissioner of Stamp Duties of New South Wales* [1934] A.C. 61; *St. Aubyn* v. *Att.-Gen.* [1952] A.C. 11. See also (1986) 83 L.S.G. 3728.

[73] *Att.-Gen.* v. *Heywood* (1887) 19 Q.B.D. 326. It does not seem that the inclusion of his spouse would have this effect; (1986) 83 L.S.G. 3728.

[74] *Oakes* v. *Commissioner of Stamp Duties of New South Wales* [1954] A.C. 57.

[75] *Commissioner of Stamp Duties of New South Wales* v. *Perpetual Trustee Co. Ltd.* [1943] A.C. 425; (1986) 83 L.S.G. 3728.

[76] *Ibid.*

[77] I.H.T.A. 1984, Pt. III. "Settlement" is defined in s.43(2).

[78] *Ante*, p. 215.

[79] *Post*, p. 220.

[80] F.(No. 2)A. 1987, s.96 and Sched. 7.

children in equal shares. A beneficiary has an interest in possession if he is entitled to the income as it arises. He is so entitled even though the trustees have a power to revoke or to appoint elsewhere, but not if they have a power to accumulate the income, even if unexercised.[81] A person entitled to an interest in possession under such a trust is treated for the purposes of inheritance tax as being beneficially entitled to the property in which his interest subsists.[82] Mrs. X would thus be regarded, for purposes of inheritance tax, not merely as the owner of a life interest in the trust property, but as the owner of the property itself. There are special provisions to deal with cases where there is a shared entitlement to the income,[83] or where the beneficiary is entitled to a fixed amount,[84] and also for the beneficiary who is entitled to the use and enjoyment of property which does not produce income.[85]

When an interest in possession comes to an end, the person entitled to the interest is treated as having at that time made a transfer of value of his interest. His interest is regarded as coming to an end on his disposing of or surrendering his interest, or on its termination in whole or in part by an appointment being made of the property in which his interest subsisted.[86] Where the interest in possession terminates during the lifetime of the person entitled to it, the transfer is potentially exempt.[87] If the disposal is for a consideration in money or money's worth, the value of the property is treated as reduced by the amount of the consideration[88]; but in determining that amount, the value of a reversionary interest in the property (which the tenant for life may acquire on a partition) must be left out of account.[89] Additionally, depreciatory transactions between the trustees and the persons interested under the settlement (as where the value of the trust property is reduced by granting a long lease of the property at a low rent) are treated as transfers of value.[90] Where a person dies entitled to an interest in possession, he is treated as having made a transfer of value immediately before his death of the property in which the interest subsisted.[91]

---

[81] See [1976] B.T.R. 49 (R. Walker); Press Release February 12, 1976; *Pearson* v. *I.R.C.* [1981] A.C. 753; (1980) 43 M.L.R. 712 (W. T. Murphy); (1980) 39 C.L.J. 246 (J. Tiley); (1981) 97 L.Q.R. 1; *Re Trafford's Settlement* [1985] Ch. 32; *Swales* v. *I.R.C.* [1984] 3 All E.R. 16; *Miller* v. *I.R.C.* [1987] S.T.C. 108.
[82] I.H.T.A. 1984, s.49. Accordingly, reversionary interests are "excluded property" (s.48); but there are exceptions (*ibid.*).
[83] *Ibid.* s.50(1).
[84] *Ibid.* s.50(2).
[85] *Ibid.* s.50(5).
[86] *Ibid.* ss.51, 52.
[87] F.(No. 2)A. 1987, s.96.
[88] Which will be less than the value of the property in which the interest subsisted. See I.H.T.A. 1984, s.49(2), dealing with the case where more than the actuarial value is paid.
[89] *Ibid.* s.52(2).
[90] *Ibid.* s.52(3).
[91] *Ibid.* s.4.

As the coming to an end of an interest in possession is treated as a transfer of value by the person beneficially entitled to that interest, the *rate* of any tax chargeable is determined by his personal scorecard.[92] There is, however, no question of grossing up; for the value of the transfer is not the loss to the transferor, but the value of the property in which the interest subsisted.[93]

There are certain reliefs and exemptions.[94] No tax is payable where an interest in possession comes to an end and (subject to certain qualifications) it reverts to the settlor,[95] or to the spouse, widow or widower of the settlor.[96]

There is total or partial relief where the person whose interest comes to an end becomes on the same occasion entitled either to the property or to another interest in possession in the property; there is a potentially exempt transfer only to the extent that the value of the property to which he becomes entitled is less than the value of the property in which his interest subsisted.[97] If, however, the life tenant becomes absolutely entitled by purchasing the reversion, he makes a potentially exempt transfer of the amount of the purchase price.[98] The result of these rules in the case of partition is that there is a potentially exempt transfer of that part of the fund to which the remainderman becomes absolutely entitled.

Some of the general exemptions which apply to transfers of non-settled property apply also to terminations of interests in possession, for example, transfers to a spouse or to charity, the annual exemption (£3,000) and marriage consideration[99]; and also transfers for family maintenance.[1] Finally, quick succession relief reduces the rate of tax where tax is payable on the termination of an interest in possession in settled property within five years of a previous chargeable transfer.[2]

B. Settlements in Which There is No Interest in Possession

(i) **Discretionary Trusts.** In the context of inheritance tax, a discretionary trust means a settlement in which there is no interest in possession. Such trusts were hard hit by the original provisions of the

---

[92] *Ibid.* s.52(1). But the tax is payable out of the settled property, and the trustees are responsible for it, concurrently with the beneficiary; *ibid.* s.201.

[93] *Ibid.* s.52(1).

[94] Terminations under protective trusts are dealt with below. (*post*, p. 222). See also I.H.T.A. 1984, s.90 (trustees' annuities).

[95] *Ibid.* s.54(1).

[96] *Ibid.* s.54(2).

[97] *Ibid.* s.53(2).

[98] Otherwise the life tenant could reduce the value of his taxable estate, as his free estate is reduced by the payment, while the value of the trust property in his estate is unaffected. See I.H.T.A. 1984, ss.10, 55.

[99] *Ibid.* s.57. But the small gifts exemption (£250) does not apply. Valuation reliefs on business and agricultural property are also available to settlements.

[1] *Ibid.* s.11.

[2] *Ibid.* s.141.

1975 Act, but the position was somewhat rationalised and ameliorated by the modifications of the Finance Act 1982.[3] The present code applies to "relevant property,"[4] meaning settled property in which there is no interest in possession, other than certain types of settlements which are preferentially treated.[5] As explained above, the lifetime creation of a discretionary trust is initially chargeable, although at half the rate applicable on death.[6]

(a) *The "Exit" Charge.* Tax is chargeable on any part of the funds which ceases to be "relevant property."[7] This covers not only the simple case of a payment of capital to a beneficiary, including the winding-up of the trust, but also the situation where the trustees convert the trust into a settlement with an interest in possession or into an accumulation and maintenance settlement.[8] There are certain exceptions to this rule; for example, no tax is payable in respect of a payment of costs or expenses, nor where the payment is income for income tax purposes in the hands of the recipient.[9] Only a limited number of the general exemptions, such as distributions to charity, are available.[10]

(b) *The Decennial Charge.* The "exit" charge alone is not sufficient, for the capital may not be distributed until the end of the trust period, which, as has been seen, may not occur until just before the end of the perpetuity period.[11] It is provided, therefore, that tax is payable on the whole of the settled funds every 10 years, although only at 30 per cent. of the "effective rate," as described below.[12] Thus the capital is fully taxed broadly once a generation, whether the capital is distributed or retained, or the trust is converted into another form.

(c) *Rates of Tax.* Different rules apply to the "exit" charge and the decennial charge, although in both cases the rates applicable to lifetime transfers are used. Only an outline can be given here.

In the case of the decennial charge, tax is charged on the value of the "relevant property" on the day before the 10-year anniversary, at 30

---

[3] It has also been mitigated by the reduction in rates; *post,* p. 220.

[4] *Ibid.* s.58.

[5] *Ibid.* The exceptions include accumulation and maintenance trusts, discussed below, and the special trusts mentioned in section C., *infra.*

[6] *Ante,* p. 216.

[7] I.H.T.A. 1984, s.65(1)(*a*). Tax is also chargeable where the trustees make a disposition resulting in the reduction in the value of the property; s.65(1)(*b*). See *I.R.C.* v. *Macpherson* [1988] 2 W.L.R. 1261.

[8] *Post,* p. 220; *Inglewood (Lord)* v. *I.R.C.* [1983] 1 W.L.R. 366.

[9] I.H.T.A. 1984, s.65(5); *Stevenson (Inspector of Taxes)* v. *Wishart* [1987] 1 W.L.R. 1204. See also s.65(4), (6)–(8).

[10] The annual exemption (£3,000) is not available, nor does quick succession relief apply. The valuation reliefs, however, available for business and agricultural property, do apply.

[11] *Ante,* p. 194.

[12] I.H.T.A. 1984, ss.64, 66. No such charge can arise before April 1, 1983; s.61(3).

per cent. of the "effective rate" which would have been charged on a hypothetical transfer at that time, on the assumption that the hypothetical transferor's cumulative total to be taken into account includes the settlor's chargeable transfers during the seven years preceding the creation of the settlement, plus the amounts, if any, subjected to an "exit charge" in the 10 years before the 10-year anniversary in question.[13]

In the case of the "exit" charge, the rate depends on whether the charge is payable before or after the first 10-year anniversary. In both cases the amount on which tax is payable is the amount by which the value of the "relevant property" is diminished by the event in question.[14] The rate before the first 10-year anniversary is the "appropriate fraction" of the rate payable on an assumed chargeable transfer made at the time of the "exit" charge, where the amount is the value of the settled property at the date of the settlement, and the hypothetical cumulative total is the settlor's chargeable transfers during the seven years prior to the creation of the settlement. The "appropriate fraction" is $\frac{3}{10} \times \text{N}/40$, where N is the number of completed quarters (*i.e.* three-month periods) between the creation of the settlement and the chargeable event.[15] Different rules apply to settlements made before March 27, 1974.[16]

Where an "exit" charge arises after a 10-year anniversary, tax is charged at the "appropriate fraction" of the rate at which it was charged on the last 10-year anniversary. The "appropriate fraction" is $\text{N}/40$, where N is the number of completed quarters between the last ten year anniversary and the chargeable event.[17] This rule applies also to settlements made before March 27, 1974.

Although discretionary trusts are treated more harshly than other settlements, the rates outlined above are not high. Now that the maximum lifetime rate is 20 per cent.,[18] the rate of the decennial charge cannot exceed 6 per cent. (being 30 per cent. of the rate applicable to an actual transfer, as explained above). Furthermore, a discretionary trust within the nil rate band[19] retains some attraction.

(ii) Accumulation and Maintenance Settlements. An accumulation and maintenance settlement is one in which no interest in possession exists, but one or more beneficiaries will, on attaining a specified age not exceeding 25 years, become entitled to an interest in possession.[20]

---

[13] *Ibid.* s.66. For settlements created before March 27, 1974, see s.66(6).
[14] "Grossing-up" occurs, *ibid* s.65(2).
[15] *Ibid.* s.68.
[16] *Ibid.* s.68(6).
[17] *Ibid.* s.69.
[18] F.A. 1988, s.136.
[19] *Ante*, p. 214. On tax planning for discretionary trusts, see *Butterworths U.K. Tax Guide* (6th ed.), p. 1091.
[20] I.H.T.A. 1984, s.71. There are other conditions. See *Inglewood (Lord)* v. *I.R.C.* [1983] 1 W.L.R. 366.

It has long been common practice to create accumulation and maintenance settlements in favour of minor relatives, and to give to the trustees power to apply the income at their discretion for the maintenance and education of the minors, and to accumulate any income not so applied; and power to advance some or all of the capital for the advancement or benefit of the beneficiaries. The powers are now statutory,[21] subject to the expression of a contrary intention, and are discussed in more detail in Chapter 19.

Such trusts offer considerable attraction to a settlor who wishes to reduce his tax liability by setting up a trust for members of the family.[22] The income of the trust will be taxed at the basic rate plus the additional rate.[23] Where income is paid to or applied for the maintenance and education of a beneficiary, the income, if the settlement is irrevocable,[24] is taxed according to the tax status of the beneficiary. But there is one important limitation. If the beneficiary is a minor unmarried child *of the settlor*,[25] any income paid to or applied for his maintenance or education is aggregated for tax purposes with the income of the settlor.[26] There is no aggregation, however, if such income is accumulated.

The lifetime creation of an accumulation and maintenance settlement is a potentially exempt transfer.[27] The advantage of such a trust is that it is not taxed under the principles, discussed above, which apply to settlements in which there is no interest in possession.[28] Such trusts are favourably treated because of the difficulties in the way of giving capital or income to a minor absolutely. Hence the decennial charge is not payable; nor is there any charge when a payment of capital is made to a beneficiary, as on an advancement, or when his interest vests; nor on the death of a beneficiary before becoming entitled.[29] Because of these advantages, tax is payable when a discretionary trust is converted into an accumulation and maintenance settlement.[30] In any event, the advantages of such a settlement are not permanently available. The trust will cease to qualify as an accumulation and maintenance settlement after 25 years have elapsed since its commencement, unless all the beneficiaries are grandchildren of a common grandparent.[31] Tax becomes chargeable when the settlement ceases to qualify.[32]

---

[21] T.A. 1925, s.31; *post*, p. 542.

[22] See (1976) 73 L.S.Gaz. 310 (R. P. Ray).

[23] *Ante*, p. 209.

[24] I.C.T.A. 1988, ss.663–665.

[25] *cf.* grandchildren of the settlor.

[26] I.C.T.A. 1988, s.663; *ante*, p. 209, n. 17.

[27] I.H.T.A. 1984, s.3A.

[28] *Ibid.*, s.58(1)(*b*).

[29] *Ibid.* s.71(4). The beneficiary's interest in the income normally vests at the age of 18; T.A. 1925, s.31(1)(ii).

[30] *Ibid.* s.65(1)(*a*); *Inglewood (Lord)* v. *I.R.C., supra.*

[31] *Ibid.* s.71(2).

[32] *Ibid.* s.71(3)(*a*). Also where the trustees enter into a "depreciatory transaction." Tax is charged in the same manner as under s.70 (temporary charitable trusts).

C. Protective and Other Trusts

Other forms of trusts which are entitled to special treatment are protective trusts,[33] superannuation schemes,[34] trusts for the benefit of employees[35] and for disabled persons,[36] charitable trusts,[37] newspaper trusts,[38] maintenance funds for historic buildings,[39] and various special compensation funds, such as those maintained by Lloyd's and the Law Society.[40]

A protective trust does not fit neatly into the two categories into which trusts are divided for inheritance tax purposes; for there is an interest in possession during the currency of the interest of the principal beneficiary, but a discretionary trust after the forfeiture. There is a charge to inheritance tax upon the death of the principal beneficiary; but not on the forfeiture of his interest, which, for the purpose of inheritance tax, is deemed to continue during the currency of the discretionary trusts which then arise.[41]

4. FOREIGN TRUSTS[42]

Much of the burden of United Kingdom tax liability can be avoided by moving out of the jurisdiction.[43] It is not difficult to find places abroad which are less heavily taxed; and some jurisdictions, the "tax havens," have developed an economy which is largely dependent upon the settlement there of tax refugees from Britain and other heavily taxed countries. Similarly, foreign trusts have some tax advantages even for settlors and beneficiaries resident in England, and there are benefits in setting up the trust abroad or in exporting it to a foreign jurisdiction. But the advantages to be gained have been much reduced by recent tax and economic changes.

A. Income Tax

Persons resident in the United Kingdom are liable to income tax on income from foreign investments. There is therefore no tax advantage to trustees resident in the United Kingdom in the selection of foreign investments; except where the income is mandated to a beneficiary

---

[33] I.H.T.A. 1984, s.88; *ante,* Chap. 7.
[34] *Ibid.* ss.58(1)(*d*), 151.
[35] *Ibid.* s.86.
[36] *Ibid.* s.89.
[37] *Ibid.* s.58(1)(*a*). As to temporary charitable trusts, see s.70.
[38] *Ibid.* s.87.
[39] *Ibid.* s.58(1)(*c*) and Sched. 4.
[40] *Ibid.* s.58(1)(*e*).
[41] *Ibid.* s.88. See *Cholmondeley* v. *I.R.C.* [1986] S.T.C. 384.
[42] See Parker and Mellows, *The Modern Law of Trusts* (5th ed.), pp. 429 *et seq.*; (1987) 2 *Trust Law & Practice* 59 (M. Jacobs).
[43] The transfer of sterling out of the country was formerly restricted by the Exchange Control Act 1947. These controls came to an end in 1979.

resident abroad.[44] When foreign income has borne foreign tax, relief is normally available against double taxation.[45]

Where the trustees are resident abroad,[46] they are not liable to United Kingdom income tax upon income from foreign investments. But a United Kingdom resident cannot take advantage of this rule to create a trust with trustees resident in, say, Jersey, with the income being accumulated for the ultimate benefit of the settlor. For the income is treated for tax purposes as the income of the United Kingdom resident settlor if he transfers an asset abroad and the income becomes payable to a foreign resident but the settlor enjoys or has power to enjoy the income,[47] as where the settlor transfers assets abroad to a foreign company which he controls. There is an exception where it can be shown that the transaction was not carried out for the purposes of avoiding tax.[48] Further, where the foreign trust income becomes payable to an individual other than the settlor, who is ordinarily resident in the United Kingdom but who is not subject to income tax under section 739, that individual is liable to income tax on the payment to him to the extent of the untaxed trust income.[49]

B. Capital Gains Tax

Capital gains tax is payable in respect of gains made by persons who are resident or ordinarily resident in the United Kingdom.[50] In the case of settlements, the trustees are normally chargeable. In order to avoid any element of double taxation, generally no charge to capital gains tax arises upon the disposal of a beneficial interest by a beneficiary.[51] However, trustees cease to be liable for capital gains tax if they are resident and ordinarily resident abroad. For these purposes trustees are treated as a single and continuing body and thus have a single "residence." Trustees are treated as being resident abroad if a majority of the trustees are so resident and ordinarily resident, and the general administration of the trust is carried on outside the United Kingdom.[52]

Where the trustees of a settlement are resident abroad and so are not chargeable to capital gains tax, then the exemption from tax applicable to a beneficiary disposing of his beneficial interest ceases to apply.[53] Further, if the settlor was domiciled and resident or ordinarily resident in the United Kingdom at the creation of a settlement then gains

---

[44] *Williams* v. *Singer* [1921] 1 A.C. 65.
[45] By treaty under I.C.T.A. 1988, s.788, or unilaterally under s.790.
[46] Or, seemingly, where any one of a number of trustees is resident abroad; *Dawson* v. *I.R.C.* [1988] 1 W.L.R. 930.
[47] I.C.T.A. 1988, ss.739–745. See *Vestey* v. *I.R.C.* [1980] A.C. 1148.
[48] *Ibid.* s.741.
[49] I.C.T.A. 1988, s.740.
[50] C.G.T.A. 1979, s.2(1).
[51] *Ibid.* s.58.
[52] *Ibid.* s.52.
[53] F.A. 1981 s.88(1).

accruing to the non-resident trustees will be cumulated.[54] Any capital payment out of the trust to a beneficiary will be identified with those cumulated gains and will be chargeable in the beneficiary's hands, provided that the beneficiary was domiciled and resident or ordinarily resident in the United Kingdom at some time during the year.[55]

C. Inheritance Tax

(i) **Excluded Property.** Various categories of property are excluded from the calculation of value transferred, *inter vivos* or on death.[56] One category is property outside the United Kingdom (other than settled property) if the person beneficially entitled to the property is an individual domiciled outside the United Kingdom.[57] Settled property is excluded only if the property is situated outside the United Kingdom, and the settlor was domiciled[58] outside the United Kingdom at the time when the settlement was made[59]; and a reversionary interest[60] in settled property situated outside the United Kingdom is excluded if the person beneficially entitled to it is domiciled outside the United Kingdom. Thus tax is theoretically chargeable on the death of a life tenant, resident and domiciled abroad, of a trust whose trustees are resident abroad and the property situated abroad, if the settlement was created by a settlor who was domiciled in the United Kingdom.[61] Whether or not the tax could be collected is another matter.[62] It will also be noted that property situated in the United Kingdom is subject to tax regardless of the residence or domicile of the owner, or, in the case of a trust, of the settlor.[63]

(ii) **Liability of the Settlor.** Thus liability to inheritance tax cannot be avoided by the creation of a foreign trust by a settlor domiciled in the United Kingdom, or by exporting an existing settlement made by such a settlor. The problem of collecting tax due in respect of foreign trusts is partly met by making the settlor himself, while still living, one of the persons liable for tax due under a settlement whose trustees are not for the time being resident in the United Kingdom.[64] Thus, a settlor

---

[54] *Ibid.* s.80(1).
[55] *Ibid.* s.80(6). See (1984) 81 L.S.G. 97 (C. Cox).
[56] I.H.T.A. 1984, s.6.
[57] *Ibid.* s.6(1).
[58] For the meaning of domicile in this context, see *post*, p. 225.
[59] *Ibid.* s.48(3).
[60] Reversionary interests in settled property situated in England are excluded unless the interest has at any time been acquired for a consideration in money or money's worth, or is an interest expectant on the determination of a lease for a life or lives, or is one to which either the settlor or his spouse is or has been beneficially entitled; s.48(1).
[61] See *I.R.C.* v. *Stype Trustees (Jersey) Ltd.* [1985] 1 W.L.R. 1290.
[62] A country will not enforce the tax laws of another country.
[63] There are exceptions, *e.g.* Government securities in the beneficial ownership of persons neither domiciled nor ordinarily resident in the United Kingdom; I.H.T.A. 1984, s.6(2). See also ss.6(3), 157.
[64] *Ibid.* s.201(1)(*d*). For the duties of professional advisers, see I.H.T.A. 1984, s.218.

domiciled in the United Kingdom, who now creates a discretionary trust with trustees resident abroad, will not only be liable to pay tax on the creation of the settlement, but also on the subsequent occasions for charge during his lifetime; and the settlor of a trust created many years ago which had become free of estate duty liability, may become liable for inheritance tax.[65] A settlor who proposes to create a foreign settlement should acquire a foreign domicile before doing so.

(iii) Meaning of Domicile. There are a number of technical factors which influence the basic definition of domicile, and the details cannot be considered here.[66] Basically, a new domicile is obtained by physical presence in another country with the intent of making that country a permanent home. Countries included in the Scheduled Territories are the easiest choice for those emigrating for tax purposes, for those countries present no restrictions on the transfer of capital. The easiest and nearest are the Channel Islands and the Isle of Man.

For the purpose of inheritance tax, however, domicile bears a special meaning, with the result that it is harder to acquire foreign domicile for tax purposes than under the general law. Foreign domicile may be acquired, for inheritance tax purposes, only after an interval of three years starting with the acquisition under the general law of the foreign domicile.[67]

---

[65] Although settlements existing prior to December 9, 1974 are subject to inheritance tax, the extended meaning of domicile in I.H.T.A. 1984, s.267 does not apply to such settlements; s.267(3).

[66] Dicey & Morris, *The Conflict of Laws* (11th ed.), Chap. 7; Law Com. No. 168, *Private International Law: The Law of Domicile.*

[67] I.H.T.A. 1984, s.267(1)(*a*). See also s.267(1)(*b*), as to persons resident in the U.K. for 17 of the 20 years prior to the transfer in question. The special rule preventing a person with U.K. domicile from acquiring Channel Islands or Isle of Man domicile was abrogated by F.(No. 2)A. 1983, s.12.

CHAPTER 10

RESULTING TRUSTS

1. GENERAL

A RESULTING trust is a situation in which a transferee is required by equity to hold property on trust for the transferor; or for the person who provided the purchase money for the transfer. The beneficial interest results, or comes back to the transferor or to the party who makes the payment. This situation can arise in a wide variety of circumstances, and it has been seen that the resulting trusts overlap with other categories.[1]

Resulting trusts are not subject to all the rules of express trusts. Their creation is not dependent on compliance with formalities[2]; their objects do not need to be immediately identifiable[3]; a minor may be a resulting trustee.[4] But since 1964, they are subject to the rule against perpetuities.[5]

---

[1] *Ante*, pp. 66, 69.
[2] L.P.A. 1925, s.53(2).
[3] *Re Gillingham Bus Disaster Fund* [1958] Ch. 300.
[4] *Re Vinogradoff* [1936] W.N. 68.
[5] Perpetuities and Accumulations Act 1964, s.12.

226

There are five basic types of situation in which resulting trusts arise.

A. Where the Trust is Implied

If A transfers property to B in circumstances in which it is clear from the acts or statements of the parties that A intended that B should hold on trust for him, B will hold on resulting trust. This may be better classified as an express trust. But, like the distinction between express and implied contracts, the precise dividing line between the two is impossible to find. In *Barclays Bank Ltd.* v. *Quistclose Investments Ltd.*[6] as has been seen, an intention was found that the Bank should hold the funds on trust for the plaintiffs, who provided them, if they could not be used to pay the Rolls Razor dividend; but there was no formal declaration. This could be regarded as an express or resulting trust. Similarly in *Hodgson* v. *Marks*[7] there was an oral agreement that a transferor of land should remain the beneficial owner. The oral agreement was unenforceable, but the intention was effected by the imposition of a resulting trust.

B. Conveyance to Trustees

Where property is conveyed to a person in the capacity of a trustee, there will be a resulting trust for the grantor of any part of the beneficial interest which is not disposed of. This result arises by operation of law. It is sometimes called an automatic[8] resulting trust. It will be discussed in more detail in section 2.

C. Voluntary Conveyance

A conveyance to a third party will in some circumstances give rise to a resulting trust for the transferor. The trust, in the absence of a manifestation of the parties' intention, will be raised by a presumption of a resulting trust. The presumption may of course be rebutted. In the case of a conveyance to the transferor's wife or child or to a person to whom the transferor is *in loco parentis*, the presumption is reversed by the presumption of advancement. These matters are discussed in section 3.

D. Purchase Money Resulting Trust

Closely related to the previous category are conveyances to trans-ferees who provide none or only part of the purchase price. This category includes cases where the conveyance is made to A, but some or all of the purchase price is provided by B, or where the conveyance

---

[6] [1970] A.C. 567; *ante* p. 51. See also *Carreras Rothmans Ltd.* v. *Freeman Mathews Treasure Ltd.* [1985] Ch. 207 (contractual arrangement whereby money paid into a special bank account for a specific purpose created a trust); *cf. Re Multi Guarantee Co. Ltd.* [1987] B.C.L.C. 257; *In Re E.V.T.R. Ltd.* [1987] B.C.L.C. 647 (*Quistclose* principle applied to loan for specific purpose which partially failed).

[7] [1971] Ch. 892 *post*, p. 241.

[8] *Re Vandervell's Trusts (No. 2)* [1974] Ch. 269, by Megarry J.

is to persons jointly, but the purchase price is provided unequally. The complex questions of the division of property ownership between spouses, where the contribution to the matrimonial partnership may be in ways other than the payment of money, will be dealt with in outline in Chapter 11. The details of this subject must be found in books on family law.[9] The ascertainment of the share of the ownership of the matrimonial home is only the first step to dealing with the problems of separated spouses, one of whom wishes to sell, while the other needs the house as a home. These matters are also discussed in Chapter 11. No attempt is made to deal with the court's powers over property of the spouses on a divorce.[10]

E. To Reach the Just Result

In some situations, it is necessary in the interests of justice that a transferee should hold property on trust for the transferor; for example if the transfer is obtained by fraud. *Bannister* v. *Bannister*[11] and *Hodgson* v. *Marks*[12] may be regarded as coming within this category. And there are other situations where, in the absence of fraud, a trust for the transferor is necessary to reach a just result. These situations clearly overlap with constructive trusts. Lord Denning in *Hussey* v. *Palmer*[13] said "Although the plaintiff alleged that there was a resulting trust, I should have thought that the trust in this case, if there was one, was more in the nature of a constructive trust; but this is more a matter of words than anything else. The two run together." These situations are considered in Chapter 12.

2. Conveyance to Trustees

A. Where a Trust Fails

A resulting trust may arise on the failure, for a variety of reasons, of an express trust. In *Morice* v. *Bishop of Durham*,[14] the trusts were void; so also in *Re Diplock*,[15] where a large sum of money was left to be

---

[9] Bromley, *Family Law* (7th ed.); Cretney, *The Principles of Family Law* (4th ed.); Miller, *Family Property and Financial Provision* (2nd ed.).

[10] Matrimonial Causes Act 1973; Matrimonial and Family Proceedings Act 1984.

[11] [1948] 2 All E.R. 133.

[12] [1971] Ch. 892; *post*, p. 241.

[13] [1972] 1 W.L.R. 1286 at p. 1289; *Heseltine* v. *Heseltine* [1971] 1 W.L.R. 342; *Binions* v. *Evans* [1972] Ch. 359; *Cooke* v. *Head* [1972] 1 W.L.R. 518; *Eves* v. *Eves* [1975] 1 W.L.R. 1338; *Re Densham* [1975] 1 W.L.R. 1519. See also *Passee* v. *Passee* [1988] 1 F.L.R. 263 at 269, suggesting that a trust arising from a contribution to the acquisition of the home could be called implied, constructive or resulting, the latter being "not inappropriate".

[14] (1804) 8 Ves. 399; (1805) 10 Ves. 522; *post*, p. 347. See also *Simpson* v. *Simpson* (1989) 19 Fam.Law 20 (transferee of bank deposit held on resulting trust for transferor where the latter lacked mental capacity to make a gift).

[15] [1941] Ch. 253; [1944] A.C. 341; *sub nom. Chichester Diocesan Fund and Board of Finance (Incorporated)* v. *Simpson*; [1948] Ch. 465; [1951] A.C. 251, *sub. nom. Ministry of Health* v. *Simpson*; *post*, p. 625.

applied for purposes which the executors thought to be charitable, and was applied by distribution among a number of charitable institutions. The trusts were void. The next-of-kin were entitled under a resulting trust; and they were able to recover the bulk of the money from the charities. In *Essery* v. *Cowlard*,[16] an intending wife executed a pre-nuptial settlement in which she conveyed the trust property to trustees upon trust for herself, the intended husband and the issue of the marriage. The marriage never took place, but the parties cohabited and children were born. Six years later, the plaintiff successfully reclaimed the property. The trusts failed as the "contract to marry had been definitely and absolutely put an end to."

In *Re Ames' Settlement*[17] property had been settled by the husband's father upon the trusts of a marriage settlement, and the marriage took place. Eighteen years later the wife obtained a decree of nullity (which then had the effect of declaring the marriage void *ab initio*).[18] Vaisey J. decided, after the husband's death, that the property was held on a resulting trust for the executors of the settlor.

B. Incomplete Disposal of Beneficial Interest

Unskilful draftsmanship and the failure to foresee and provide for contingencies which occur in the future may leave the beneficial ownership incomplete.[19] A resulting trust will then arise, although, as will be seen, some sets of circumstances can render this result so inconvenient that other solutions are sought.

The fact that an equitable interest is not fully disposed of may not become apparent until some time has elapsed since the constitution of the trust.

> In *Re Trusts of the Abbott Fund*[20] a sum of money was collected, to be used for the maintenance of two deaf and dumb ladies. It was held by Stirling J. that the ladies had no enforceable interests in the capital sum and that on their death, the sum remaining went on resulting trust to the subscribers.

The consequent problem of distribution on resulting trust among subscribers becomes acute when the number of subscribers is great, and the gifts are mostly anonymous, as in *Re Gillingham Bus Disaster Fund*.[21]

---

[16] (1884) 26 Ch.D. 191; *Burgess* v. *Rawnsley* [1975] Ch. 429 (if conveyance taken jointly for a purpose which fails, resulting trust to each party of his share. Majority view that must be a common purpose).

[17] [1946] Ch. 217.

[18] A decree of nullity after July 31, 1971, in respect of a voidable marriage shall operate to annul the marriage only from the date of the decree absolute; Matrimonial Causes Act 1973, s.16. See also the court's powers to make property adjustments under s.24.

[19] See *Re Cochrane* [1955] Ch. 309; *Re Flower's Settlement* [1957] 1 W.L.R. 401.

[20] [1900] 2 Ch. 326, *post*, p. 231.

[21] [1958] Ch. 300, *post*, p. 343.

A number of marine cadets were injured or killed when a bus was driven into the rear of a marching column. The mayors of three towns appealed for subscriptions to a fund that would initially care for the disabled and thereafter be available for "worthy causes" in memory of those killed. More money was contributed than could be used for the first object (liability at common law for the accident having been accepted) and the second object failed as it had not been confined within the limit of legal charity.[22] Harman J. held that, despite the manifest inconvenience of such a decision, a resulting trust arose. All subscribers, large or small, intended to contribute to a specific purpose; on that purpose being attained or no longer attainable, each donor had an interest by way of resulting trust. There was no evidence on which to arrive at any other conclusion. The suggestion that the money should be treated as *bona vacantia* was regarded by Harman J. as taking the line of least resistance in a manner unauthorised by law. "The resulting trust arises where [the donors'] expectation is for some unforeseen reason cheated of fruition and is an inference of law based on after-knowledge of the event."[23]

C. Methods of Disposal of Surplus Funds

A resulting trust is not, however, the most appropriate solution in many situations; and, although something of a digression, it will be convenient here to examine other solutions. The question arises particularly in two contexts: First, those of gifts to persons for stated purposes, without specifying what is to be done when the purposes are completed; and, secondly, in the context of the dissolution of unincorporated associations.

In determining the correct solution in each of these contexts, two points will be of particular significance. First, did the transferor intend to dispose of his whole interest; or did he intend to transfer for a particular purpose only? Secondly, was the transfer made to a person in a capacity of trustee? If so, a resulting trust may be expected of the surplus.

(i) Transfer to Persons for Particular Purposes. If property is given for the care and maintenance of certain persons, what is to happen to the property when the period of maintenance comes to an end? Do the intended beneficiaries (or their estates) keep the property, or does it

---

[22] Charities Act 1960, s.14 (*post*, p. 440) provides the most convenient solution to this type of case. It is regrettable that it applies only when the gift is charitable, as many donors, especially those contributing by way of collection boxes, have no notion of the line between charity and non-charity. To impute to such donors any intent beyond an intent to give is unrealistic. The fund was finally wound up in 1965, when the remainder of the money was paid into court. For a different solution, see *Re West Sussex Constabulary's Widows, Children and Benevolent Fund Trust* [1971] Ch. 1, *post*.

[23] [1958] Ch. 300 at p. 310.

return on the resulting trust to the donor? The answer will depend on the intention of the donor, which has to be ascertained from all the surrounding circumstances. The construction of the gift in *Re Trusts of The Abbott Fund*[24] may be regarded as unusual. More commonly, the gift is regarded as absolute. The principle of construction was laid down in *Re Sanderson's Trust*[25] as follows: "If a gross sum be given, or if the whole income of the property be given, and a special purpose be assigned for that gift, the court always regards the gift as absolute, and the purpose merely as the motive of the gift, and therefore holds that the gift takes effect as to the whole sum or the whole income, as the case may be." Thus,

In *Re Andrew's Trust*,[26] a fund was subscribed for the infant children of a deceased clergyman. An accompanying letter showed that the contributions were made "for or towards their education; ... as being necessary to defray the expenses of all, and that solely in the matter of education." After their formal education was completed, the question arose of the disposal of the surplus. Kekewich J. decided that the children were entitled in equal shares.

In *Re Osoba*[27] there was a gift by will of a residuary estate, consisting, for present purposes, of a freehold house in London, to the testator's widow on trust to be used "for her maintenance and for the training of my daughter up to University grade and for the maintenance of my aged mother ... " The mother predeceased the testator; the widow died in 1970, and the daughter's education up to University grade was completed in 1975. The children under an earlier marriage claimed the residue on intestacy.

The Court of Appeal found that the testator's intention was to provide absolute gifts for the beneficiaries, the references to maintenance and to education being expressions of motive. In the absence of words of severance, the beneficiaries took as joint tenants, with the daughter becoming entitled, on her mother's death, to the whole.

(ii) Surplus Funds on Dissolution of Unincorporated Association.[28]

(a) *Trust or Contract.* As will be seen in Chapter 14, funds of such an association will sometimes be held by trustees on trust for the members and sometimes by the treasurer or committee; in either case the property rights in the assets of the society are likely to be governed by the rules of the society which operate as a contract between members

---

[24] [1900] 2 Ch. 326.

[25] *Per* Page Wood V.-C. (1857) 3 K. & J. 497 at p. 503; *Barlow* v. *Grant* (1684) 1 Vern. 255.

[26] [1905] 2 Ch. 48.

[27] [1979] 1 W.L.R. 247.

[28] See generally Warburton, *Unincorporated Associations: Law & Practice.* For the meaning of "unincorporated association" see *Conservative and Unionist Central Office* v. *Burrell* [1982] 1 W.L.R. 522, *post*, p. 354.

and the society, and between the members themselves. The question whether the property is held upon the terms of the trust created by the donor, or whether it is held according to the contractual rights of the members is relevant here also.[29] The question commonly arises on a dissolution. It will be seen in the analysis which follows that the distinction between rights governed by a trust and those governed by a contract has not always been kept clear. In the case of a failure of a trust, the most appropriate solution is by way of resulting trust. In a case of dissolution of a society where the rights of the members are governed by a contract (*i.e.* by the rules of the society) the likely solution is in accordance with the terms of the contract; and if the contract is silent; by equal division among the members. The Crown might claim the fund as *bona vacantia*. It may also have to be considered whether any third party contributors may have a claim to participate in the distribution along with the members. Whether the matter is regarded as one of trust or contract affects the question of who is entitled and the calculation of the share. All these solutions will be demonstrated here, although the analysis in the earlier cases was subject to criticism by Walton J. in *Re Bucks Constabulary Fund (No. 2).*[30]

(b) *Meaning of Dissolution.* An association may be wound up in a formal manner, but in the absence of a formal dissolution, the question arises as to the circumstances which will justify a finding that the body has ceased to exist. In *Re G.K.N. Bolts and Nuts Ltd. (Automotive Division) Birmingham Works, Sports and Social Club*,[31] the trustees of a social club had purchased a sports ground for £2,200 in 1946. In 1975, membership cards ceased to be issued and the last annual general meeting was held. No further accounts were taken, the stock of drinks was sold and the steward dismissed. A special meeting was convened on December 18, 1975 to deal with an offer to buy the land. Resolutions were passed that the land be sold, but no sale then took place. In 1978, the trustees sold the land for £253,000. One question which arose was when the club ceased to exist.[32] It was held that mere inactivity did not suffice, unless it was so prolonged or so circumstanced that the only reasonable inference was spontaneous dissolution, in which case the court must select a date. On the facts, it ceased to exist on December

---

[29] See also *Universe Tankships Inc. of Monrovia* v. *International Transport Workers' Federation* [1983] 1 A.C. 366, (1982) 45 M.L.R. 564 and (1983) 46 M.L.R. 361 (B. Green). (No trust involved in payment to welfare fund.)

[30] [1979] 1 W.L.R. 936; *post*, p. 235.

[31] [1982] 1 W.L.R. 774; [1983] Conv. 315 (R. Griffith). See also *Abbatt* v. *Treasury Solicitor* [1969] 1 W.L.R. 1575; *Re William Denby & Sons Ltd. Sick and Benevolent Fund* [1971] 1 W.L.R. 973; *Re Bucks Constabulary Widows' and Orphans' Fund Friendly Society (No. 2)* [1979] 1 W.L.R. 936.

[32] The question of entitlement to the money is dealt with *post*, p. 237.

18, 1975, on the basis of inactivity coupled with positive acts to wind it up. This would be so even if the resolution to sell the land was invalid, as by that date the club's activities had ceased and it had become incapable of carrying out its objects.

(c) *Resulting Trust for Members*. In *Re Printers' and Transferrers' Society*,[33] a society was founded to raise funds by weekly contributions to defend and support its members in maintaining reasonable remuneration for their labour, and to provide strike and lock-out benefits for members. The scale of payments varied according to the length of time a claimant had been a member of the society, and different conditions applied to printers and transferrers respectively. No provision was made by the rules for the distribution of the funds of the society on a dissolution. At the time of its dissolution the society consisted of 201 members, and its unexpended funds amounted to £1,000. The question, therefore, arose as to how the sum was to be distributed. The Attorney-General made no claim to the fund as *bona vacantia*. It was held that there was a resulting trust in favour of those who had subscribed to the fund, and that the money was divisible amongst the existing members at the time of the dissolution, in proportion to the amount contributed by each member of the funds of the society irrespective of fines, or payments made to members in accordance with the rules.

In *Re Hobourn Aero Components Air Raid Distress Fund*,[34] a fund was established during the Second World War for employees of a company who were on war service or who sustained loss in air raids. The fund was financed by voluntary subscriptions among the employees, but it was not charitable. The Crown made no claim to the fund as *bona vacantia*. After the end of the war, the fund was found to have a surplus. It was held that each contributor, past or present, had an interest in the surplus by way of resulting trust in proportion to the amount he had contributed, but subject to adjustment in relation to any benefit he had received from the fund.

This conclusion, although logically consistent with the resulting trust analysis, is less convenient than the decision in *Re Printers' and Transferrers' Society*,[35] in that it concentrates attention on all the contributors to a society, however remote in time past, and not on those who have retained a connection with it. There is much to be said for the simpler solution of the earlier case, which, however, Cohen J. in the present case thought defensible only in cases where the ascertainment of the true entitlements would be too difficult.

---

[33] [1899] 2 Ch. 184.
[34] [1946] Ch. 86 (affirmed *ibid.* at p. 194), see especially pp. 97–98; following *Re British Red Cross Balkan Fund* [1914] 2 Ch. 419, (which is criticised in Tudor, *Charities* (7th ed.), at p. 271, n. 86).
[35] [1899] 2 Ch. 184.

(d) *Contractual Basis*. In *Cunnack* v. *Edwards*,[36] a society governed
by the Friendly Societies Act 1829[37] had been established in 1810 to
raise a fund, by the subscriptions, fines and forfeitures of its members,
to provide annuities for the widows of its deceased members. By 1879
all the members had died. The last widow-annuitant died in 1892, the
society then having a surplus unexpended fund of £1,250. A claim to
the assets was made by the personal representatives of the last surviving members. It was held that there was no resulting trust in favour of
the legal personal representatives of the members of the society. Each
member had paid away his money in return for the protection given to
his widow, if he left one. "Except as to this he abandoned and gave up
the money for ever."[38] The assets went to the Crown as *bona
vacantia*.[39]

In *Re West Sussex Constabulary's Widows, Children and Benevolent
(1930) Fund Trust*,[40] a fund had been established to provide benefits to
widows and certain dependants of members who died. The income of
the fund came from members' subscriptions, the proceeds of entertainments, sweepstakes, raffles and collecting boxes and various donations
and legacies. On the amalgamation of the West Sussex Constabulary
with other police forces on January 1, 1968, the question arose of the
distribution of the fund.

Goff J. held that the surviving members had no claim because first,
the members had received all that they had contracted for, and
secondly, the money was paid on the basis of contract, and not of trust.
The funds went as *bona vacantia* to the Crown. The possibility that
living members may have a contractual claim on the basis of frustration
of the contract or failure of consideration was met by the Crown giving
an indemnity to the trustees.

Contributions from outside sources were divided into three categories. The first two, proceeds of entertainments, etc., and collecting
boxes, could not be the subject of a resulting trust[41]; they were out-
and-out payments.[42] Identifiable donations however and legacies were
in a different position. The object of the gift had failed, and the
property was held on resulting trust. On the latter point, it is difficult to
see why third party contributors, even if identifiable, should have any

---

[36] [1896] 2 Ch. 679; *Braithwaite* v. *Att.-Gen.* [1909] 1 Ch. 510; (1966) 30 Conv.(N.S.) 117
(H.A. Hickling); (1980) 43 M.L.R. 626 (B. Green). The decision was distinguished in
Re Bucks Constabulary Fund (No. 2), *infra*, as turning upon the combined effect of
the rules and the 1829 Act.

[37] For the special position of Friendly Societies, see Warburton, *Unincorporated Associations: Law & Practice*, pp. 5–6.

[38] [1896] 2 Ch. 679 at p. 683.

[39] Ing; *Bona Vacantia*.

[40] [1971] Ch. 1; (1971) 87 L.Q.R. 464 (M.J. Albery) arguing that a purpose trust in such
circumstances should be void for perpetuity.

[41] Not following *Re Gillingham Bus Disaster Fund* [1958] Ch. 300, *ante*, p. 229.

[42] *Re Welsh Hospital (Netley) Fund* [1921] 1 Ch. 655; *Re Hillier's Trusts* [1954] 1 W.L.R.
9; *Re Ulverston and District New Hospital Building Trust* [1956] Ch. 672.

claim in such circumstances. The validity of the initial gift is usually explained on the basis that it is a gift to the members of the association, subject to their contract.[43] If that is so, such contributions should be dealt with on the same basis as the rest of the funds. It is submitted that there is no room here for a resulting trust for third parties.

The more acceptable modern solution to the distribution of assets of an unincorporated society is among the members. The matter is regarded as one of contract between the members, express or implied. On this analysis, the resulting trust solution is no longer appropriate. This is so, even though the assets of the society may be vested in trustees; as is indeed required in the case of Friendly Societies.[44] The trustees then hold the assets on trust for the members according to the rules of the society. The rules may provide for the distribution upon dissolution. Otherwise, the assets will be divided among the members at the time of the dissolution.

Re Bucks Constabulary Fund (No. 2)[45] was another case of the distribution of a fund established to provide benefits for the widows and orphans of deceased police officers and the provision of payments on the death of a member or during sickness. The Bucks Constabulary amalgamated with other constabularies to form the Thames Valley Constabulary, and in 1968 the fund was wound up. Resolutions at the dissolution meeting provided for the expenditure of the funds on (i) purchasing annuities to meet the fund's commitments to members, (ii) making a grant of £40,000 to the Thames Valley fund, and (iii) the balance of the assets to a separate Bucks fund, the Bucks Constabulary Benevolent Fund. Megarry V.-C.[46] held that the payments under (ii) and (iii) were improper, because they were not payments toward the objects of the society, as required by the Friendly Societies Act 1896, s.79(4).

The question of the proper method of distribution then came before Walton J., who held that the assets should be divided equally among members alive at the date of dissolution. If the society was moribund, as where there were no members or only one member left, the property would be ownerless. Only then would the Crown be entitled.[47] Walton J. emphasised the distinction between property held under the terms of the trust, and that governed by contract. In such a case, quoting Brightman J.,[48] "The right of the

---

[43] *Post*, p. 358.
[44] Friendly Societies Act 1974 s.49(1); Baden Fuller, *The Law of Friendly Societies* (4th ed., 1926), p. 186.
[45] [1979] 1 W.L.R. 936; (1980) 39 C.L.J. 88 (C.E.F. Rickett); (1980) 43 M.L.R. 626 (B. Green).
[46] [1978] 1 W.L.R. 641.
[47] *cf.* Landlord and Tenant Act 1987, s.42(7) (surplus monies in tenants' service charge fund on termination of last lease to go to landlord).
[48] *Re William Denby and Sons Ltd. Sick and Benevolent Fund* [1971] 1 W.L.R. 973 at p. 978.

member of the fund to receive benefits is a contractual right and the member ceases to have any interest in the fund if and when he has received the totality of the benefits to which he was contractually entitled. In other words, there is no possible claim by any member founded on a resulting trust. ... If it has been dissolved or terminated, the members entitled to participate would prima facie be those persons who were members at the date of dissolution or termination."[49]

The *West Sussex*[50] decision, although distinguishable on the ground that it did not involve a Friendly Society, was criticised by Walton J. on the basis that the principle of law applicable to the members' club cases should have governed the distribution. It made no difference whether or not the association was for the benefit of the members themselves. They controlled the assets, which were theirs all along. Thus *bona vacantia* was not an appropriate solution in that case.

(e) *Methods of Distribution Among the Members*. If entitlement is on the basis of a resulting trust, the distribution will be made amongst all members, past and present, including personal representatives of deceased members, in shares proportionate to their contributions. Past members will be excluded if the calculation would prove too difficult.[51] We have seen, however, that the resulting trust analysis is not favoured today. It is also unlikely, in view of *Re Bucks Constabulary Fund (No. 2)*,[52] that the Crown will establish a claim to the assets as *bona vacantia* in many cases, or, as submitted above,[53] that outside contributors will have any claim. Assuming that the contractual basis is adopted, only those members existing at the date of dissolution will be entitled. Unless the rules provide otherwise, the distribution will be on a *per capita* basis, prima facie in equal shares, and ignoring actual contributions.

In *Re Sick and Funeral Society of St. John's Sunday School, Golcar*,[54] a society was formed in 1866 to provide sickness and death benefits for its members. Those under 13 paid ½d per week, and the others paid 1d. The benefits for those paying the whole subscription were twice those of the smaller subscribers. Upon the winding up of the society, the surplus funds were held distributable among the members as at that date on a *per capita* basis, but as the benefits and burdens differed among the two classes of members, the proper basis for distribution was full shares for full members and half shares for the children. The *per capita* basis did not favour new members at the

[49] [1979] 1 W.L.R. 936 at p. 948.
[50] *Supra.*
[51] *Re Hobourn Aero Components Air Raid Distress Fund* [1946] Ch. 86 at p. 97.
[52] [1979] 1 W.L.R. 936.
[53] *Ante*, p. 235.
[54] [1973] Ch. 51.

expense of older ones, as each got what he paid for: the newer members had had the benefits of membership for a short time and the older members for a longer time. The latter could not complain if they did not receive more in the winding up.

In Re *Bucks Constabulary Fund (No. 2)*,[55] Walton J. held that the prima facie rule of equal division applied also to Friendly Society cases, although in the past some of those cases had favoured a distribution in proportion to contributions.[56] This approach was also adopted in *Re G.K.N. Bolts & Nuts Ltd. (Automotive Division) Birmingham Works, Sports and Social Club*,[57] where those entitled to share the assets on a *per capita* basis were the full members and the ordinary members. Honorary, temporary and associate members, who neither paid subscriptions nor had voting rights, were excluded.[58]

(iii) Trust and Charge. Here also the distinction between a trust and a charge is important.[59] A distinction was drawn by Lord Eldon in *King* v. *Denison*[60] between devises *charged with payment* of debts, and devises *on trust to pay* debts. In the former case it is assumed that the testator intended a beneficial interest for the devisee, subject to the payment of debts; in the latter case it is assumed that he intended merely to use the devisee as a vehicle for payment of the debts, and not to confer any benefit upon him. In the latter case there will, therefore, be a resulting trust of any surplus for the residuary devisee, or those entitled on intestacy; but there will be no resulting trust in the former case. In construing the language of a gift, it must be remembered that equity will not allow trustees themselves to give evidence that what was intended was a conditional gift.[61]

D. No Declaration of Trust

Where property is conveyed to persons in circumstances in which they are intended to take as trustees, then, if no beneficial interests are declared, they will hold on resulting trust for the grantor; as where a

---

[55] *Supra.*
[56] *Re Printers' and Transferrers' Society* [1899] 2 Ch. 184; *Re Lead Workmens Fund Society* [1904] 2 Ch. 196.
[57] [1982] 1 W.L.R. 774. The facts have been given, *ante*, p. 232. See also *Re St. Andrew's Allotment Association* [1969] 1 W.L.R. 229.
[58] A resolution passed to authorise distribution on the basis of length of service to the company was invalid, as no proper notice of the proposed change in the rules had been given.
[59] *Ante*, p. 53.
[60] (1813) 1 Ves. & Bea. 260; *ante*, p. 53; *Smith* v. *Cooke* [1891] A.C. 297; *Re West* [1900] 1 Ch. 84; *Re Foord* [1922] 2 Ch. 519, distinguished in *Re Osoba* [1979] 1 W.L.R. 247, *ante*, p. 231.
[61] *Re Rees* [1950] Ch. 204; *Re Pugh* [1967] 1 W.L.R. 1262; *Re Tyler* [1967] 1 W.L.R. 1269; *ante*, p. 156, *cf. Smith* v. *Cooke* (*supra*).

transfer is made to a nominee.[62] We have seen this principle in operation in the case of testamentary gifts to legatees as trustees, without
the trusts upon which they are to hold being declared prior to the
testator's death.[63]

The *Vandervell* litigation serves as a fearsome warning of the crucial
importance of attention to detail in tax planning.[64] There were two
visits to the House of Lords and three to the Court of Appeal. The
problem was caused by the fact that Mr. Vandervell's advisers overlooked the possibility of the existence of a resulting trust; when all that
Mr. Vandervell was doing was trying to give away a large sum of
money to charity.

In 1958 Vandervell decided to found a Chair of Pharmacology at
the Royal College of Surgeons with a gift of £250,000. This was to be
effected by a scheme under which a block of shares in Vandervell
Products Ltd. would be transferred to the College, and the necessary dividends subsequently declared on them. Such dividends, in
the hands of the College, would be free of liability to income tax and
surtax.[65] The shares were to be transferred subject to an option to
repurchase for £5,000 in favour of Vandervell Trustees Ltd., a
private company whose only function was to act as trustee for
various trusts connected with the Vandervell family and business. It
was trustee of the Vandervell children's trust.

The transfer of the shares was made in 1958, and between then
and 1961, the necessary dividends were paid to the College. The
Revenue assessed Vandervell for surtax on the dividends on the
ground that he had not entirely disposed of all his interest in the
property,[66] because, in the absence of a declaration of trust of the
option, it was held on resulting trust for Vandervell. The Revenue
succeeded. That was *Vandervell* v. *I.R.C.*[67] Before discussing the
reasoning, it will be best to complete the story.

On receiving the Revenue's claim in 1961, Vandervell ordered
Vandervell Trustees Ltd. to exercise the option, and they did so,
taking £5,000 from the children's settlement to finance it. All the
dividends since that date were paid to Vandervell Trustees Ltd.,
who applied them to the children's settlement. They so informed the
Revenue.

The Revenue assessed Vandervell to surtax in respect of the years
1961–65 on the footing that the shares were held on trust for him

---

[62] *Hodgson* v. *Marks* [1971] Ch. 892; *Vandervell* v. *I.R.C.* [1967] 2 A.C. 291; *D.H.N.
Food Distributors Ltd.* v. *Tower Hamlets L.B.C.* [1976] 1 W.L.R. 852, *per* Goff L.J. at
p. 864, *ante*, p. 82.
[63] *Re Boyes* (1884) 26 Ch.D. 531; *ante*, p. 149; *Re Pugh's W.T.* [1967] 1 W.L.R. 1262.
[64] *Per* Lord Reid, [1967] 2 A.C. 291 at p. 305.
[65] Because the College is a charity. *Post*, p. 375.
[66] I.T.A. 1952, s.415(2). Now I.C.T.A. 1988, s.685.
[67] [1967] 2 A.C. 291; (1966) 24 C.L.J. 19 (G.H. Jones); (1967) 31 Conv.(n.s.) 175 (S.M.
Spencer); (1967) 30 M.L.R. 461 (N. Strauss).

during that period. In 1965 he at last executed a deed which transferred all or any interest which he may have in the shares in favour of
the children's settlement. In 1967, he died.

Before this claim of the Revenue was litigated, Vandervell's
estate stepped in and claimed the dividends from Vandervell Trustees Ltd. If the plaintiffs succeeded, the Revenue's claim was clearly
good; and the Revenue attempted to join the litigation in support.
The defendants successfully excluded them.[68] In *Re Vandervell's
Trusts (No. 2)* the estate succeeded before Megarry J., but failed
before the Court of Appeal.[69]

In the first case, *Vandervell* v. *I.R.C.*[70] the Revenue succeeded by a
majority of three to two. The option was held on trust for Vandervell.
He was effectively the grantor of the option, although it was in form
the grant of the Royal College. It was taken by Vandervell Trustees
Ltd. upon trust, but no effective trusts of the option were declared,
"and so the defendant company held the option on an automatic trust
for Mr. Vandervell."[71] In this situation, there was, as Lord Wilberforce
said "no need, or room to invoke a presumption. The conclusion, on
the facts found, is simply that the option was vested in the trustee
company as a trustee on trusts, not defined at the time, possibly to be
defined later. But the equitable, or beneficial interest, cannot remain
in the air: the consequence in law must be that it remains in the
settlor."[72] An indication of the parties' intention, as opposed to what
they might be supposed to have desired, would of course have changed
the whole situation. But the donor's mere "intention not to have the
beneficial interest can[not] prevail" in an automatic resulting trust.[73]

In *Re Vandervell's Trusts (No. 2)*,[74] the Court of Appeal, reversing Megarry J., found that the resulting trust of the option in favour
of Vandervell terminated with the exercise of the option; and that a
declaration of trust of the shares in favour of the children's settlements was manifested by three factors, without, however, making
clear whether any one of them would be sufficient in itself. These
were, first, that the option was paid for by money from the children's
settlement; secondly, that the dividends had all been paid to the
children's settlement; and, thirdly, that the trustees had informed
the Revenue that they now held the shares on the trusts of the
children's settlement. Further, Vandervell, having agreed to the

[68] *Re Vandervell's Trusts (No. 1)* [1971] A.C. 912.
[69] [1974] Ch. 269.
[70] [1967] 2 A.C. 291.
[71] [1974] Ch. 269 at p. 296, *per* Megarry J.
[72] [1967] 2 A.C. 291 at p. 329.
[73] [1974] Ch. 269 at p. 298, *per* Megarry J.
[74] [1974] Ch. 269; (1974) 38 Conv.(N.S.) 405 (P.J. Clarke); (1975) 38 M.L.R. 557 (J.W.
Harris); (1975) 7 D.L.R. 483 (G. Battersby).

transfer of the shares to the trustee company and to the payment of the dividends, was estopped from claiming them back; and his estate after his death could be in no better position. "Even a court of equity," said Lord Denning M.R., "would not allow him to do anything so inequitable an unjust."[75]

Three comments may be made upon this decision. It is difficult to see how any one of these factors could be sufficient to create a new trust of the shares. The last reason is clearly inadequate, the second also, for that could not do more than indicate what the trustees thought. Similarly, with the first. If A held a valuable option on trust for B, how could A, the trustee, change the beneficial interest by taking money from C, and using it to exercise the option? Secondly, and following closely on the first, even if the acts of the trustees were sufficient to manifest an intention to create a new trust, how could the option and the shares be separated? Is it right to say: "Before the option was exercised, there was a gap in the beneficial ownership. So there was a resulting trust for Mr. Vandervell. But, as soon as the option was exercised and the shares registered in the trustees' name, there was created a valid trust of the shares in favour of the children's settlement"?[76] Thirdly, following closely on the second, and repeating the points made in Chapter 4, even if a valid trust was declared, how did the beneficial interest previously held by Vandervell leave him without a disposition in writing as required by Law of Property Act 1925, s.53(1)(c)? The Revenue has not pursued its claim to surtax for the years 1961–1965, and, in the absence of further litigation, these questions will remain unanswered. Enough is enough, and no one will disagree with Megarry J.'s pungent understatement that Mr. Vandervell had been "singularly unfortunate."[77]

3. VOLUNTARY CONVEYANCE AND THE PRESUMPTIONS

A. Presumption of Resulting Trust: Conveyance to a Third Party

(i) **Land.** One of the effects of the Statute of Uses was to prevent the operation of resulting uses. Previously, a resulting use arose on a voluntary conveyance which did not declare a use; the beneficial interest reverted to the grantor. After the Statute of Uses, the use was executed, and the grantor retained the legal estate; the conveyance was thus ineffectual. When equitable interests returned under the name of trusts, the beneficial interest might again return to the grantor in cases both of realty and personality, where the grantee was not

---

[75] *Ibid.* at p. 321.
[76] *Per* Lord Denning M.R. at p. 320; Lawton L.J. made the same point: "There could not be a resulting trust of a chose in action which was no more": *ibid.* at p. 325.
[77] [1974] Ch. 269 at p. 281.

intended to take beneficially. A number of problems remain in the ascertainment of the intention to be ascribed to the grantor.

The Law of Property Act 1925, s.60(3), helps in solving these problems in relation to land.[78] While before 1926 it was necessary, in a voluntary conveyance, to insert a use in favour of the grantee in order to prevent a resulting trust arising, section 60(3) makes this no longer essential. Section 60(3) however, only prevents the implication of a resulting trust *merely* by reason that the conveyance is not expressed to be for the benefit of the grantee. If it is intended to take effect as a gift, it is still preferable to make this clear in the conveyance, as section 60(3) does not preclude the implication of a resulting trust on general equitable principles.[79] Where it is clear that no gift was intended, section 60(3) does not prevent the finding of a resulting trust.

In *Hodgson* v. *Marks*,[80] Mrs. Hodgson was an old lady who was the registered owner of a house. A lodger, Evans, lived there. Mrs. Hodgson developed an affection for Evans, and trusted him to look after all her affairs. Her nephew disapproved of Evans, and tried to persuade Mrs. Hodgson to turn him out. To protect Evans, she transferred the house to him, under an oral agreement that she would continue to be beneficial owner. Evans, as registered owner, sold it to a bona fide purchaser, Marks, and the question was whether Mrs. Hodgson was protected against Marks.

The Court of Appeal held that she remained beneficial owner in equity, and that this was an overriding interest.[81] The express oral agreement in her favour was unenforceable under the Law of Property Act 1925, s.53(1)(*b*). Evidence of her intention was however admissible, and this gave rise to "a resulting trust of the beneficial interest to the plaintiff, which would not, of course, be affected by section 53(1)."[82] Section 60(3) was not discussed.

(ii) Personalty. In relation to personalty, the initial presumption probably remains that a voluntary transfer to a third party is accompanied by the inference of a resulting trust.

In *Re Vinogradoff*,[83] the testatrix had transferred a sum of £800 War Loan, then standing in her name, into the joint names of herself and her granddaughter, then four years old. The testatrix continued to receive the dividends until her death.

---

[78] "In a voluntary conveyance a resulting trust for the grantor shall not be implied merely by reason that the property is not expressed to be conveyed for the use or benefit of the grantee."

[79] See Parker and Mellows, *The Modern Law of Trusts* (5th ed.), p. 135; *Hodgson* v. *Marks* [1971] Ch. 892 at p. 933.

[80] [1971] Ch. 892; *ante*, p. 227.

[81] Because she was in actual occupation; L.R.A. 1925, s.70(1)(*g*).

[82] *Ibid.* at p. 933.

[83] [1935] W.N. 68; *Standing* v. *Bowring* (1885) 16 Ch.D. 282 at p. 287; *Re Muller* [1953] N.Z.L.R. 879; see *Fowkes* v. *Pascoe* (1875) L.R. 10 Ch. App. 343.

Farwell J. held that, even though an infant may not be appointed a trustee, the presumption of resulting trust applied, and the granddaughter held the property on resulting trust for the estate of the testatrix.

It is questionable whether such a result coincides with the real intention of the transferor. If, however, as would be one possible construction, her intention was to keep the property as her own during her lifetime and to give it to the granddaughter upon her death, such an attempted disposition would be testamentary, and void for failure to comply with the formal requirements of the Wills Act. A valid gift could be effected if intended to be held by the transferor for her life and after her death for the donee, or if a form of joint tenancy with a right of survivorship was created.[84]

It is even more doubtful whether the presumption accords with the transferor's intention in the case of a transfer to the grantee alone. The majority of such transfers must be intended as gifts. Although it seems correct to say that the presumption of a resulting trust exists in such cases,[85] it gives way to the slightest contrary evidence. The common sense of the transaction frequently prevails, and the rules of evidence do not prevent the sense of the transaction being deduced.

B. Presumption of Advancement

The presumption of advancement is a presumption working in the opposite direction. It arises where certain relationships exist, situations where the donor or purchaser is under an obligation recognised in equity, to support or provide for the person advanced.[86] It arises if the person to whom a voluntary conveyance is made is the wife or child of the donor, or someone to whom he stands *in loco parentis*. Like the presumption of resulting trust, it is rebuttable by evidence that the donor intended to keep the beneficial interest for himself.

(i) Husband and Wife. (a) *Gift by Husband.* The presumption of advancement applies where a husband makes a gift to his wife. The strength of the presumption is diminished in modern times.[87] "It would in my view," said Lord Diplock in *Pettitt* v. *Pettitt*,[88] "be an abuse of the legal technique for ascertaining or imputing intention to apply to transactions between the post-war generation of married couples 'presumptions' which are based upon inferences of fact which an earlier generation of judges drew as the most likely intentions of earlier

---

[84] *Fowkes* v. *Pascoe* (1875) L.R. 10 Ch. App. 343; *post*, p. 247.

[85] *George* v. *Havard* (1819) 7 Price 646 at p. 651, *per* Richards C.B.

[86] See *Cavalier* v. *Cavalier* (1971) 19 F.L.R. 199 (S.C.N.S.W.) at p. 205, where Carmichael J. challenged this statement of the basis of the principle; [1974] A.S.C.L. p. 527 (J. Hackney).

[87] *Pettitt* v. *Pettitt* [1970] A.C. 777; *Gissing* v. *Gissing* [1971] A.C. 886; *Falconer* v. *Falconer* [1970] 1 W.L.R. 1333; (1971) N.L.J. 96 at p. 126 (T.K. Earnshaw).

[88] *Supra*, at p. 824. See also *Simpson* v. *Simpson* (1989) 19 Fam.Law 20.

generations of spouses belonging to the propertied classes of a different social era." *Pettitt* v. *Pettitt* was a case of a claim to a share in the ownership of a matrimonial home, as to which special considerations apply, and will be discussed in Chapter 11.

In *Re Eykyn's Trusts*[89] in 1877, Malins V.-C. said: "The law of this court is perfectly settled that where a husband transfers money or other property into the name of his wife only, then the presumption is, that it is intended as a gift or advancement to the wife absolutely at once ... " Gifts of chattels to a wife are within the presumption; and so is the matrimonial home which is conveyed to the wife although paid for by the husband. In *Tinker* v. *Tinker*,[90] the presumption was readily applied, in spite of the comments upon the presumption in *Pettitt* v. *Pettitt*; but there was ample evidence to show that the wife was intended to benefit.

The presumption also applies where the gift is made before marriage, but with a specific marriage (which in fact takes place) in mind.[91] There is no presumption of advancement where a man puts property into the name of his mistress,[92] nor is there such a presumption where a wife puts property into the name of her husband.[93] With a matrimonial home, at least, very little evidence will suffice to establish a sharing of the beneficial interest.[94]

(b) *Rebuttal*. The presumption can be rebutted by evidence which tends to show that no gift was intended. Thus, in *Anson* v. *Anson*,[95] a husband guaranteed his wife's banking account, and eventually the guarantee was called and he was obliged to pay a sum of money to the bank as a result. Pearson J. held that the husband could recover that sum from the wife, as the transaction was not in the nature of the advancement. There will be no advancement if, for example, a joint account was opened for the purposes of making it easier for the wife to

[89] (1877) 6 Ch.D. 115 at p. 118; quoted in *Pettitt* v. *Pettitt, supra*, at p. 815.
[90] [1970] P. 136.
[91] *Moate* v. *Moate* [1948] 2 All E.R. 486; *Ulrich* v. *Ulrich* [1968] 1 W.L.R. 180; (1975) 119 S.J. 108 (E. Ellis). In this connection there was a vital distinction between a wholly void ceremony of marriage and a voidable marriage which was later annulled: *Dunbar* v. *Dunbar* [1909] 2 Ch. 639. The latter occurrence did not affect the operation of the presumption, even though a nullity decree then had retrospective effect. This is no longer the case. As to engaged couples, see Law Reform (Miscellaneous Provisions) Act 1970, s.2(1). One effect of s.2(1) is that the presumption of advancement applies to resolve disputes between couples whose engagement has ended; *Mossop* v. *Mossop* [1988] 2 W.L.R. 1255; [1988] Conv. 284 (J.E.M.).
[92] *Diwell* v. *Farnes* [1959] 1 W.L.R. 624; but the other rules for ascertaining the ownership of the home apply; *post*, p. 257.
[93] *Mercier* v. *Mercier* [1903] 2 Ch. 98; *Heseltine* v. *Heseltine* [1971] 1 W.L.R. 342. The Law Commission recommends otherwise; Law Com. No. 175 (1988), *Matrimonial Property* (dealing with personalty).
[94] Per Lord Upjohn in *Pettitt* v. *Pettitt* [1970] A.C. 777 at p. 815.
[95] [1953] 1 Q.B. 636; *Re Salisbury-Jones* [1938] 3 All E.R. 459. Similarly where the husband lacked mental capacity to make a gift; *Simpson* v. *Simpson* (1989) 19 Fam.Law 20.

draw money from an account, the husband being ill.[96] A joint account though opened for the general use of both husband and wife, will frequently lead to the inference of a joint tenancy in law and equity.[97]

(c) *Rebutting Evidence Excluded on Grounds of Unlawfulness.* Where the evidence which is produced to rebut an intention to make a gift discloses an illegal purpose, the evidence is inadmissible. The principle is of general application, and not confined to transfers between husband and wife.[98] But it is convenient to consider it here because the cases all deal with this situation.

In *Re Emery's Investment Trusts*,[99] American bonds, bought by the husband, were placed in the name of the wife (an American citizen) to evade an American tax, though the intention was that the husband and wife should own them in equal proportions in equity. But technically there was a presumption of advancement, which the husband had to rebut. It was held that he could do so only with the aid of proof of the intent to evade tax, and this intent he would not be allowed to prove. The wife could thus retain the whole, despite the fact that she was a party to the scheme.

In *Tinker* v. *Tinker*,[1] the reason why the property was conveyed into the wife's name was to protect it from the creditors of the husband if a new garage business which he had purchased was not a success. The attempt to rebut the presumption of advancement failed. The husband was "on the horns of a dilemma. . . . As against his wife he wants to say that it belongs to *him*. As against his creditors, that it belongs to *her*. That simply will not do. . . . The presumption is that it was conveyed to her for her own use; and he does not rebut that presumption by saying that he only did it to defeat his creditors. I think it belongs to her."[2]

In *Heseltine* v. *Heseltine*,[3] however, a wealthy wife transferred two sums of £20,000 to her husband; the first to equalise their property for estate duty purposes, and the second to enable him to qualify as an underwriter at Lloyd's. She was able to reclaim both sums on the basis of a resulting trust when the marriage broke up. This is not easy to explain on the basis of the presumptions, for it

---

[96] *Marshal* v. *Crutwell* (1875) L.R. 20 Eq. 328; *Simpson* v. *Simpson*, *supra*. The problem of housekeeping money was dealt with by the Married Women's Property Act 1964, under which equality of ownership is presumed in the absence of other evidence; *cf. Re Figgis* [1969] Ch. 123.

[97] *Re Bishop* [1965] Ch. 450; *Re Figgis* [1969] Ch. 123; (1969) 85 L.Q.R. 530 (M.C. Cullity); *cf. Thompson* v. *Thompson* (1970) 114 S.J. 455; *Heseltine* v. *Heseltine* [1971] 1 W.L.R. 342 (money provided by wife).

[98] See the general statements to this effect in *Ayerst* v. *Jenkins* (1873) L.R. 16 Eq. 275, *per* Lord Selborne L.C.

[99] [1959] Ch. 410; *Gascoigne* v. *Gascoigne* [1918] 1 K.B. 223; *Chettiar* v. *Chettiar* [1962] A.C. 294.

[1] [1970] P. 136; *Cantor* v. *Cox* (1975) 239 E.G. 121.

[2] *Ibid.* at p. 141, *per* Lord Denning M.R.

[3] [1971] 1 W.L.R. 342; *cf. Knightly* v. *Knightly* (1981) 11 Fam.Law. 122.

would seem that she must have intended the beneficial interest to pass to her husband, in order to achieve the stated purposes, thereby rebutting the presumption of a resulting trust. Perhaps the decision is best explained as an example of a trust imposed to achieve a just result.[4]

Equity will refuse its aid to a plaintiff who has to rely on an illegality to support his claim.[5] The same is true of assignments in fraud of creditors, though a plaintiff may in this type of case not be refused equity's aid if the transaction deceived nobody and nothing had been done under it.[6]

(ii) Father and Child. There is a presumption of advancement between a father and his legitimate child. The presumption here is stronger, and "should not . . . give way to slight circumstances."[7]

In *Re Roberts*,[8] a father took out an insurance policy on the life of his son and paid the premiums on it. The father was expressed to be trustee of the policy, and it was contended after his death that the amounts paid by way of premium were recoverable by his estate. Evershed J. held that the presumption of advancement prevailed over the other evidence, and that each premium paid by the father during his lifetime was a separate advancement to the son. The use of the word "trustee" was indicative less of a contrary intent than a means of enforcement against the insurers.

(iii) Other Relationships. But the moment one passes from this type of case to gifts from a mother to a child (whether or not the father is dead), from a father to an illegitimate child,[9] from grandparents, aunts and uncles, then the presumptions fade. Whether or not the presumption is technically in favour of a resulting trust, or technically in favour of advancement, the important consideration is whether or not there is evidence that the donor or purchaser regarded himself or herself as being *in loco parentis*, and the donee as being someone for whom an obligation to provide is felt.[10] The issue is treated as one of fact in the modern cases, and it is only in the absence of any evidence that the

---

[4] *Ante*, p. 228; *post*, p. 309.
[5] See the general statements to this effect in *Ayerst* v. *Jenkins* (1873) L.R. 16 Eq. 275, *per* Lord Selbourne L.C.
[6] *Gascoigne* v. *Gascoigne* [1918] 1 K.B. 223; *Symes* v. *Hughes* (1870) L.R. 9 Eq. 475.
[7] *Per* Viscount Simonds in *Shephard* v. *Cartwright, infra; cf.* Lord Upjohn in *Pettitt* v. *Pettitt, supra*, at p. 815.
[8] [1946] Ch. 1; *B.* v. *B.* (1976) 65 D.L.R. (3ᵈ) 460 (purchase of lottery ticket in name of 12-year-old daughter). A case where the presumption was rebutted is *Re Gooch* (1890) 62 L.T. 384 (father purchased shares to qualify son as director, and son handed over dividends to his father). See also *McEvoy* v. *Belfast Banking Co.* [1935] A.C. 24.
[9] This principle seems unaffected by the Family Law Reform Act 1987, which in general removes the property law disadvantages of children of unmarried parents.
[10] See, *per* Page-Wood V.-C. in *Tucker* v. *Burrow* (1865) 2 H. & M. 515 at pp. 525–527; *Re Paradise Motor Co. Ltd.* [1968] 1 W.L.R. 1125.

technical presumptions prevail.[11] Although, therefore, in cases other than that of father and legitimate child, the presumption may technically be in favour of a resulting trust, this is not, for the vast majority of cases, a decisive factor. The point is well brought out by the cases dealing with widowed mothers and their children.[12] In this situation, equity does not recognise in the mother, as it would have done in the father, an obligation to provide, hence there is no presumption of advancement. But the strangeness of this conclusion is wholly mitigated by the ease with which, on very little evidence, the courts will find the intent to advance.[13]

(iv) **Admissibility of Donor's Statements.** In *Shephard* v. *Cartwright*,[14] C. caused shares in companies he was promoting to be allotted to himself, his wife and his three children. Between 1929, when the allotments took place, and 1934, the companies made considerable profits and in the latter year a public company was formed, the original shareholders received partly new shares and partly cash by way of payment for their old shares. C., in fact, controlled the whole family wealth, and the shares and money were divided between his wife and children for tax reasons. The wife and children at all times acquiesced in C.'s activities, and signed powers of attorney and powers to withdraw money at his wish.

By 1936, the cash had all been withdrawn by C. and spent by him. Dividends declared on the shares allotted to the children were, however, treated as the income of the children, not the income of C. To a claim by the children against C.'s estate to recover the cash drawn by him on their bank accounts, it was argued that C.'s conduct showed that he had not intended the beneficial interest to vest in the children, but that they at all times held on resulting trust for C. himself. The House of Lords rejected this contention. The onus of rebutting the presumption of advancement lay on C.'s executors, and there was nothing in C.'s conduct that was truly inconsistent with the presumption. The children had acquiesced in their father's conduct, rather than acted as trustees for him. The House of Lords also applied the rule that evidence of declarations and conduct subsequent to the original transaction is admissible only against the party making them, though those made at the time of the original transaction are admissible for or against him. Subsequent declarations, for or against, appear now to be admissible under the Civil Evidence Act 1968.[15]

[11] *Re Vinogradoff* [1935] W.N. 68.
[12] *Bennet* v. *Bennet* (1879) 10 Ch.D. 474, discussing *Sayre* v. *Hughes* (1868) L.R. 5 Eq. 376 (where there was held to be a presumption).
[13] See especially Jessel M.R. in *Bennet* v. *Bennet, supra.*
[14] [1955] A.C. 431. Mellish L.J.'s judgment in *Fowkes* v. *Pascoe* (1875) L.R. 10 Ch.App. 343, emphasising the sense of the transaction, was expressly approved.
[15] s.2.

4. PURCHASE MONEY RESULTING TRUSTS

A. Purchase in the Name of Another

(i) Presumptions in Favour of the Purchaser. Where a purchaser of realty or personalty takes a conveyance in the name of a third party, but there is nothing to indicate an intention on his part of not appropriating to himself the beneficial interest, then there is a presumption that he intended to obtain the beneficial interest for himself, and a resulting trust will be decreed in his favour. In the words of Eyre C.B.: "The trust of a legal estate ... results to the man who advances the purchase-money."[16] The strength of the presumption, as has been seen,[17] is much reduced in cases concerning husband and wife. This situation is discussed in Chapter 11.

The presumption arises when a purchase is made in the joint names of a purchaser and a third party, and where a purchase is made in the name of third party alone; and also where property purchased with the contributions of more than one person is conveyed into the name of only one of them.

The classic case is *Fowkes* v. *Pascoe*.[18]

Mrs. B. purchased stock in the names of herself and the son of her widowed daughter-in-law. The son was outside the relationships where the presumption of advancement would arise, hence he would prima facie be presumed to hold on resulting trust for Mrs. B. But the Court of Appeal in Chancery held that the strength of the presumption varied according to the circumstances and that, once there is some evidence to rebut it, the court must look at the facts from a common-sense point of view. In the present case, the only rational inference was that Mrs. B. intended the purchase as a gift, so that the presumption of resulting trust was rebutted, though the effect of the gift would not be apparent until Mrs. B.'s death, for the court also held that any income declared on the stock during Mrs. B's lifetime would belong beneficially to her. Such a gift does not infringe the Wills Act 1837, as the legal title passes by the transfer; the legal title carries with it the right of survivorship, and all that happens on the death of Mrs. B. is that her equitable right ceases to

---

[16] *Dyer* v. *Dyer* (1788) 2 Cox 92 at p. 93. The principle applies also to personalty; *Re Policy 6402* [1902] 1 Ch. 282; *Shephard* v. *Cartwright* [1955] A.C. 431; *Crane* v. *Davis, The Times*, May 13, 1981.

[17] *Ante*, p. 242.

[18] (1875) L.R. 10 Ch.App. 343; see also *Pettitt* v. *Pettitt* [1970] A.C. 777; *Hoare* v. *Hoare* (1983) 13 Fam.Law 142.

be outstanding.[19] There is thus no *testamentary* gift provided the transfer *inter vivos* is complete and not revocable.[20]

(ii) Presumption of Advancement. As in the case of voluntary conveyances, a purchase in the name of a wife or child or other person to whom the purchaser stands *in loco parentis* raises a contrary presumption, as the purchase is presumed in these cases to be an advancement. As Lord Eldon said in *Marlees* v. *Franklin*,[21] "The general rule that on a purchase by one man in the name of another, the nominee is trustee for the purchaser is subject to exception where the purchaser is under a species of natural obligation to provide for the nominee." The presumption is weak in the case of husband and wife. It is stronger with a parent and child, but may be rebutted. In *Warren* v. *Gurney*[22]:

> A father bought a house for his daughter, who was shortly to get married, to live in. The conveyance was taken in the name of the daughter, but the father retained the title deeds. On his death 15 years later, the daughter claimed to be the beneficial owner of the house. The Court of Appeal held that there was a presumption of advancement in her favour, but that it had been rebutted by the fact of the retention of the title deeds, accompanied by evidence contemporaneous with the purchase in 1929. Retention of the deeds by itself is probably insufficient evidence, however. The court also rejected as inadmissible a document prepared by the father in 1943.

B. Purchase by Several in the Name of One

The general principle is that the legal title is held on trust for the purchasers in the proportions in which they contributed to the purchase price.[23] The purchasers thus have more than a charge on the property for the amount of their contributions. They have a concurrent interest and can claim the due proportion of the proceeds on any eventual sale of the property to include a proportion of any increase in the value of the property.[24] The resulting trust may arise where the land is purchased subject to a mortgage which is paid off by instal-

---

[19] *Young* v. *Sealey* [1949] Ch. 278. The argument is not an easy one, but Romer J. preferred to take this view as no previous English case had taken this point under the Wills Act, and gifts of this sort had not previously been thought to raise difficulties. He also had the authority of the Supreme Court of Ontario in *Re Reid* (1921) 50 Ont.L.R. 595.

[20] But in the case of a joint bank account opened by a husband in the name of himself and his wife so that either can draw on it (the account being kept in credit by the husband), there is a gift to the wife of what happens to be in the account at the date of the husband's death. The difficulties of this reasoning are discussed by Megarry J. in *Re Figgis* [1969] Ch. 123, where however *Young* v. *Sealey, supra*, was followed. (1969) 85 L.Q.R. 530 (M.C. Cullity).

[21] (1818) 1 Swans. 13 at p. 17.

[22] [1944] 2 All E.R. 472; see also *Pettitt* v. *Pettitt* [1970] A.C. 777.

[23] *Wray* v. *Steele* (1814) 2 V. & B. 388.

[24] *Diwell* v. *Farnes* [1959] 1 W.L.R. 624; *cf. Hussey* v. *Palmer* [1972] 1 W.L.R. 1286. See further, *post*, p. 260.

ments.[25] No resulting trust however arose where one member of a group was tenant of a flat, and all the residents shared the payment of the rent.[26]

Cases of this kind can give rise to serious conveyancing difficulties. The true facts of the purchase may be proved by oral evidence[27] and, not being part of the title, may not be known to a purchaser; who may then find himself dealing with a case of co-ownership without having any way of discovering this.[28]

Many cases under this head are concerned with the question of the ownership of a matrimonial home. That is a sufficiently specialised topic to require a Chapter on its own.

[25] *Moate* v. *Moate* [1948] 2 All E.R. 486.
[26] *Savage* v. *Dunningham* [1974] Ch. 181; (1973) 37 Conv.(N.S.) 440 (F.R. Crane).
[27] *Heard* v. *Pilley* (1869) L.R. 4 Ch.App. 548.
[28] *Cook* v. *Cook* [1962] P. 235; *post*, p. 266.

CHAPTER 11

TRUSTS OF THE FAMILY HOME

1. INTRODUCTION

IN the last chapter we saw the part played by the doctrine of resulting trusts in the acquisition of property interests. Most of the modern cases involve disputes between married or unmarried couples over owner-ship of the home. In this chapter we will examine the special consider-ations which apply to the matrimonial or "quasi-matrimonial" home (here called, for simplicity, the family home). The first part of the chapter will deal with the establishment of a proprietary interest in the home, for example under the doctrines of resulting or constructive trusts. The second part of the chapter will examine the problems of co-ownership and the operation of the trust for sale which, by statute, is imposed upon it. To complete the picture, reference should also be made to Chapter 27, where it will be seen that those who cannot establish an interest under a trust of the family home might neverthe-less acquire rights as licensees or under the doctrine of estoppel.

2. ACQUISITION OF INTERESTS IN THE HOME[1]

A. Background to the Problem

In the case of a married couple, one problem which arises is that the older rules of property law, which became established at a time when

[1] See generally (1969) 28 C.L.J. 196 (G. H. Jones); (1970) 29 C.L.J. 210 (J. Tiley); (1972) 88 L.Q.R. 333 (J. M. Eekelaar); (1973) 36 M.L.R. 345 (D. A. Nevitt and J. Levin); (1975) 53 C.B.R. 366 (D. W. M. Waters); (1973) 23 U. of Toronto L.R. 148 (H. Lesser); (1976) 92 L.Q.R. 489 (F. Webb); (1978) 94 L.Q.R. 26 (A. A. S. Zuckerman); Murphy and Clark, *The Family Home.*

the wife was less likely to be earning her living than is the case today, do not properly recognise her contribution to the relationship. The modern view is that marriage is a partnership between equals, in which the wife has an economic contribution to make. But she does not always insist on the matrimonial home being conveyed to the spouses jointly; or on a declaration of trust of a share of the house in favour of herself. Nor is justice done to her by the presumption of a resulting trust, based on payment of the purchase money; first, because much of her work in the house is not money-producing; and secondly, because even if she has a job, her earnings may be spent on household expenses and not in contributing to the purchase price of the house. "The cock can feather the nest because he does not have to spend most of his time sitting on it."[2]

Another problem stems from the fact that today an increasing proportion of couples cohabit outside marriage. Should their relationship break down, the court has no statutory power to adjust their property interests. Married couples, on the other hand, can invoke the court's discretionary powers, exercisable on a divorce, nullity, or judicial separation, to order a distribution of the property of the spouses.[3] This statutory jurisdiction will not be discussed here, but its significance must be emphasised. The following account deals only with the general law, which applies, subject to minor exceptions, equally to married and unmarried couples.[4] A difficulty frequently encountered, as will be seen, is that the parties do not formulate their intentions at the time the property is acquired, but consider the matter only when their relationship breaks down.

The question then is how to ensure that the ownership of the home is fairly shared. The possibility of giving the court, in the case of married couples, a wide discretionary power to declare what are the appropriate shares to be held by disputing spouses in any particular case has been rejected[5]; likewise the concept of community of property.[6] But there is much to be said in favour of a system in which the matrimonial

---

[2] Per Sir Jocelyn Simon, extrajudicially quoted by Lord Hodson in *Pettitt* v. *Pettitt* [1970] A.C. 777 at p. 811.

[3] Matrimonial Causes Act 1973, s.23; Matrimonial Homes and Property Act 1981, ss.7, 8; Matrimonial and Family Proceedings Act 1984, s.3; *Wachtel* v. *Wachtel* [1973] Fam. 72; (1974) 118 S.J. 431 (S. M. Cretney). Property disputes between spouses are best settled under this jurisdiction; *Kowalczuk* v. *Kowalczuk* [1973] 1 W.L.R. 930 at pp. 933–934; *Williams* v. *Williams* [1976] Ch. 278 at p. 286; *Suttill* v. *Graham* [1977] 1 W.L.R. 819 at p. 824. The statutory jurisdiction does not apply to engaged couples by reason of Law Reform (Miscellaneous Provisions) Act 1970, s.2(1); *Mossop* v. *Mossop* [1988] 2 W.L.R. 1255; [1988] Conv. 286 (J.E.M.).

[4] *Pettitt* v. *Pettitt* [1970] A.C. 777; *Gissing* v. *Gissing* (*supra*); *Bernard* v. *Josephs* [1982] Ch. 391; *Gordon* v. *Douce* [1983] 1 W.L.R. 563; *Burns* v. *Burns* [1984] Ch. 317. See Miller: *Family Property and Financial Provision* (2nd ed.), pp. 17 *et seq*.

[5] *Gissing* v. *Gissing* [1971] A.C. 886.

[6] Law Com. No. 52, para. 59. See also Law Com. No. 90, para. 5.20.

home is shared equally.[7] Until the enactment of any such reforms, the rights of the parties are determined according to the principles of property law, making whatever use is appropriate of evidence of agreement, declarations of trust (which comply with the necessary formalities applicable to trusts of land) and of inferences and presumptions.

The first question to determine is whether each party owns some share. If so, there is co-ownership, and the house is held upon the statutory trusts, even though it may be vested only in one.[8] The next question is to determine what is the share of each party, so that the purchase money can be divided accordingly.[9] A number of other problems can arise, such as a decision on sale if one party wishes to sell and the other to retain; questions as to the right to possession and the payment of rent; and the protection of an occupying co-owner if the sole legal owner sells to a third party.

B. Conveyance to One Party Only

If the house is conveyed to one party only, to the man, let us assume, for that is the usual case, then he will prima facie be the owner of the whole beneficial interest as well.[10] If the documents of title expressly declare the beneficial interests, that, in the absence of fraud or mistake, is conclusive,[11] although those who were not parties to the deed cannot be prejudiced by such a declaration if they have contributed.[12] Failing that, the woman may claim a share of the beneficial interest in various ways. First, there may be an express contract or trust in her favour, evidenced in writing.[13] Secondly, there may be an oral contract or declaration which is not so evidenced. Such a contract is unenforceable unless supported by part performance, while an oral declaration of a trust of land is unenforceable unless it has been acted upon so as to give rise to a constructive trust.[14] This is discussed below. If there is no express agreement or declaration, direct contributions in money or money's worth give rise to a resulting trust. Failing that, the question is whether a common intention to share, which has been acted upon, may be inferred from the parties' conduct. Indirect contributions in money or money's worth which are referable to the acquisition of the property

---

[7] Third Report on Family Property (Law Com. No. 86), *post*, p. 278. These proposals are flawed by registration requirements, and at the time of writing, there is no plan to implement them; H.L. Deb., cols. 658–664 (December 15, 1982); [1983] Conv. pp. 87–88.

[8] *Post*, p. 261.

[9] *Post*, p. 259.

[10] *Gissing* v. *Gissing* [1971] A.C. 886, *per* Viscount Dilhorne at p. 900, *per* Lord Pearson at p. 901, *per* Lord Diplock at p. 910; *Burns* v. *Burns* [1984] Ch. 317.

[11] *Per* Lord Upjohn in *Pettitt* v. *Pettitt* [1970] A.C. 777 at p. 813; *Goodman* v. *Gallant* [1986] Fam. 106.

[12] See *City of London Building Society* v. *Flegg* [1988] A.C. 54.

[13] L.P.A. 1925, ss.40, 53(1)(*b*). s.40 is to be repealed; see p. 658, n.44.

[14] *Midland Bank Ltd.* v. *Dobson and Dobson* [1986] 1 F.L.R. 171; *Grant* v. *Edwards* [1986] Ch. 638.

will normally support such an inference.[15] Finally, a trust has been imposed in some cases simply in the interests of justice.[16]

(i) *Express Agreement or Declaration.* If the declaration is contained in the documents of title, then it will be conclusive, as stated above. If it is not contained in the documents of title but is nevertheless evidenced in writing, it is enforceable under section 53(1)(*b*) of the Law of Property Act 1925. These formality requirements do not apply to resulting or constructive trusts.[17] Resulting trusts are dealt with below. In the present context, the question arises as to the circumstances necessary for the imposition of a constructive trust where there is an express oral declaration or agreement. Clearly the oral declaration itself does not suffice. It was held in *Midland Bank Ltd.* v. *Dobson and Dobson*[18] that the claimant must have acted to her detriment pursuant to the declaration or agreement if a constructive trust is to arise. This was a case where the spouses were asserting an agreement to share, of which there was no contemporary evidence, in order to preserve a share of the home against the husband's creditors. It was held that no constructive trust arose in the absence of detrimental reliance. The wife was simply a volunteer, whom equity would not assist. A similar principle was suggested in *Grant* v. *Edwards*,[19] where it was said that if the parties had made their common intention clear by means of an express oral declaration, the claimant must show that she had acted upon it. The incurring of expenditure referable to the acquisition of the property would clearly suffice, but was not essential; any detrimental act relating to the joint lives of the parties would be sufficient. The scope of this concept is not yet clear, but it seems to provide an opportunity for a sympathetic treatment of a female claimant who has made no financial contribution.[20]

(ii) *Presumption of Resulting Trust; Direct Contributions.* There will be a purchase money resulting trust in favour of a person who has contributed to the purchase price. Beneficial ownership will be enjoyed in the proportion in which the purchase money has been provided.[21] If the purchase money is provided equally, the parties are beneficial joint tenants. If the contributions are unequal, they are tenants in common. Payment of, or substantial contributions to the

---

[15] *Grant* v. *Edwards, supra*; *post*, p. 256.
[16] [1971] A.C. 886 at p. 905, *per* Lord Diplock; (1971) 115 S.J. 715 (S. M. Cretney); *Cooke* v. *Head* [1972] 1 W.L.R. 518; (1973) C.L.P. 17 at p. 25 (A. J. Oakley); *Eves* v. *Eves* [1975] 1 W.L.R. 1338.
[17] L.P.A. 1925, s.53(2).
[18] [1986] 1 F.L.R. 171; *cf. Re Densham* [1975] 1 W.L.R. 1519.
[19] [1986] Ch. 638; *infra*.
[20] (1987) 50 M.L.R. 94 (B. Sufrin); [1987] Conv. 16 (J. Montgomery). See *Lloyd's Bank Ltd.* v. *Rosset* [1988] 3 W.L.R. 1301.
[21] *Re Roger's Question* [1948] 1 All E.R. 328; *Bull* v. *Bull* [1955] 1 Q.B. 234; *Cowcher* v. *Cowcher* [1972] 1 W.L.R. 425; *Grant* v. *Edwards, supra*.

mortgage instalments, will usually suffice[22]; but for a resulting trust to arise, the payments must be in money or money's worth.[23]

The presumption of advancement may similarly arise in a case where a husband has transferred or arranged for the transfer of the legal estate to his wife; but, as has been seen, statements in *Pettitt* v. *Pettitt*[24] show that the influence of the presumptions has been much reduced. But, a husband will be unable to rebut a presumption of advancement if the evidence that a gift was not intended involves the disclosure of improper activities.[25] There is no presumption of advancement where a wife has transferred to her husband[26]; nor in the case of an unmarried couple.[27]

In the case of direct contributions, it does not seem that any actual intention to share must be proved, because the effect of the doctrine of resulting trusts is that such an intention is rebuttably presumed. In the absence of any direct contribution or express agreement, however, the question is whether a common intention to share, which has been acted upon, may be inferred from the parties' conduct. In particular, the question arises as to the kind of indirect contribution which will support this inference.

(iii) *Inferred Common Intention; Indirect Contributions*. It is important to appreciate at the outset that, since *Gissing* v. *Gissing*,[28] the court does not decide how the parties might have ordered their affairs; it only finds how they did. "The court cannot devise agreements which the parties never made. The court cannot ascribe intentions which the parties in fact never had."[29]

In *Gissing* v. *Gissing*[30] The parties had married in 1935. The wife worked throughout their married life, and obtained employment for the husband when he was out of work at the company where she worked.

In 1951, the matrimonial home was purchased out of money found by the husband, and it was conveyed to him. The wife paid some £220 for furnishings and for laying a lawn, and she paid some household expenses. The husband left, and, on the divorce, the

[22] *Re Roger's Question, ante.*

[23] *Button* v. *Button* [1968] 1 All E.R. 1064; *Muetzel* v. *Muetzel* [1970] 1 W.L.R. 188; *Wachtel* v. *Wachtel* [1973] Fam. 72 at p. 92, *per* Lord Denning M.R.

[24] [1970] A.C. 777. See also *Simpson* v. *Simpson* (1989) 19 Fam.Law 20.

[25] *Ante*, p. 244.

[26] *Heseltine* v. *Heseltine* [1971] 1 W.L.R. 342 (personalty).

[27] Unless they were engaged; Law Reform (Miscellaneous Provisions) Act 1970, s.2(1); *Mossop* v. *Mossop* [1988] 2 W.L.R. 1255.

[28] [1971] A.C. 886.

[29] *Ibid.*, *per* Lord Morris of Borth-y-Gest at p. 898; *cf. Bristol and West Building Society* v. *Henning* [1985] 1 W.L.R. 778, *post*, p. 269.

[30] *Supra.*

question arose of the ownership of the house. The House of Lords held that, since the wife had made no contribution to the purchase price, she was not entitled to any beneficial interest. A claim must be based upon accepted principles of property law.

This decision seems to establish that financial contributions which are not referable to the costs of acquisition will not give rise to a share on the basis of presumed common intention. This may be contrasted with the later decision in *Falconer* v. *Falconer*,[31] where a husband who guaranteed the wife's mortgage payments, purchased some extras and gave housekeeping money to the wife was held entitled to a half share.

And in subsequent cases the Court of Appeal[32] found that ownership was shared as a result of indirect contributions in money or money's worth[33]; "It may be *indirect*," said Lord Denning,[34] "as where both go out to work, and one pays the houskeeping and the other the mortgage instalments. . . . So long as there is a substantial financial contribution towards the family expenses, it raises the inference of a trust." This broad statement is difficult to reconcile with *Pettitt* v. *Pettitt*[35] and *Gissing* v. *Gissing*[36] without further defining the substantial financial contribution. Where there is no express agreement, an indirect contribution must be referable to the acquisition of the property.[37] Such is the case where, for example, the payment of household expenses by one party enables the other to discharge the mortgage payments, or where one party contributes physical labour on the property[38] or does unpaid work in the family business which enables the other to put the money saved towards the acquisition of property.[39] Domestic duties in the home, on the other hand, do not suffice. In *Burns* v. *Burns*,[40] concerning an unmarried couple, the woman's housework, decorating and the purchase of chattels for the home over a period of 17 years gave her no share. If this was unjust, it was suggested that the remedy lay with Parliament.

---

[31] [1970] 1 W.L.R. 1333.
[32] *Davis* v. *Vale* [1971] 1 W.L.R. 1022; *Hargrave* v. *Newton* [1971] 1 W.L.R. 1611; *Hazell* v. *Hazell* [1972] 1 W.L.R. 301; (1972) 88 L.Q.R. 333 (J. M. Eekelaar). *Kowalczuk* v. *Kowalczuk* [1973] 1 W.L.R. 930; *Finch* v. *Finch* (1975) 119 S.J. 793. See also *Farquharson* v. *Farquharson* (1971) 115 S.J. 444; *Cooke* v. *Head* [1972] 1 W.L.R. 518.
[33] *Wachtel* v. *Wachtel* [1973] Fam. 72 at p. 92.
[34] *Falconer* v. *Falconer, ante*, at p. 1336; *Hargrave* v. *Newton, ante*, at p. 1613; *Hazell* v. *Hazell, ante*, at p. 304; *cf. Cowcher* v. *Cowcher* [1972] 1 W.L.R. 425..
[35] [1970] A.C. 777.
[36] [1971] A.C. 886.
[37] A strict view of this requirement was taken in *Winkworth* v. *Edward Baron Development Co. Ltd.* [1986] 1 W.L.R. 1512, where, however, the protection of creditors was a significant factor. See [1987] Conv. 217 (J. Warburton).
[38] *Cooke* v. *Head* [1972] 1 W.L.R. 518. For improvements, see *post*, p. 258.
[39] *Nixon* v. *Nixon* [1969] 1 W.L.R. 1676.
[40] [1984] Ch. 317; (1984) 47 M.L.R. 341 (N. V. Lowe and A. Smith) and 735 (J. Dewar); [1984] Conv. 381 (S. Coneys); (1984) 43 C.L.J. 277 (R. Ingleby); All E.R. Rev. 1984, p. 167 (R. Deech). See also *Richards* v. *Dove* [1974] 1 All E.R. 888; *Layton* v. *Martin* (1986) 16 Fam. Law 212 (contribution must relate to specific assets).

The whole area has recently been reviewed by the Court of Appeal in *Grant* v. *Edwards*.[41]

An unmarried couple decided to live together. A house was bought in the name of the man and his brother (who had no beneficial interest). The man told the woman that the matrimonial proceedings pending between her and her husband might be prejudiced if her name was on the title. The man raised the purchase price by a capital payment and two mortgages. The woman made substantial indirect contributions to the mortgage by applying her earnings to the joint household expenses in addition to keeping house and bringing up the children. After they separated, the woman was held entitled to a half share.

The claimant in such a case must, in the absence of an express agreement or direct contribution, establish a common intention inferred from the parties' conduct, which she has acted upon.[42] In order to support such an inference, the court must look for expenditure referable to the acquisition of the house. This expenditure will also satisfy the requirement of detrimental reliance. Where, however, the common intention is made plain by oral declarations, all that is necessary is that the claimant should have acted upon it. In this situation, the conduct need not be expenditure referable to the acquisition of the property. What type of conduct would suffice was left open, but it was suggested that any detrimental act relating to the joint lives of the parties was sufficient.[43] In the present case, as in *Eves* v. *Eves*,[44] the man's excuse was regarded as establishing an express intention that the woman should have an interest.[45] Her indirect contributions were clearly referable to the acquisition of the property, and hence it was not necessary to decide what lesser acts might have satisfied the requirement of acting upon an express common intention.

Indirect contributions are thus relevant for four purposes: (i) as evidence from which a common intention (which has not been expressed) can be inferred; (ii) as corroboration of any direct evidence of intention; (iii) as showing detrimental reliance; and (iv) to quantify the extent of the beneficial interest. In formulating these principles,

---

[41] [1986] Ch. 638; [1986] Conv. 291 (J. Warburton); (1986) 45 C.L.J. 394 (D. Hayton); (1986) 136 N.L.J. 324; (1987) 50 M.L.R. 94 (B. Sufrin); [1987] Conv. 16 (J. Montgomery) and 93 (J. Eekelaar).

[42] The onus is upon the legal owner to prove that any detrimental act was not done in reliance upon the common intention; *Greasley* v. *Cooke* [1980] 1 W.L.R. 1306. See also *Maharaj (Sheila)* v. *Chand (Jai)* [1986] A.C. 898, suggesting that it should be inferred that the detrimental act was done in reliance on the common intention rather than out of love and affection unless there is evidence to the contrary.

[43] *Cf. Coombes* v. *Smith* [1986] 1 W.L.R. 808; *post*, p. 851. See also *Cadman* v. *Bell* [1988] E.G.C.S. 139; *Lloyd's Bank Ltd.* v. *Rosset* [1988] W.L.R. 1301 (decorating and supervising builders sufficed).

[44] [1975] 1 W.L.R. 1338.

[45] This conclusion has been criticised; (1986) 136 N.L.J. 324; (1987) 50 M.L.R. 94 (B. Sufrin).

the view of the court was that the principles of proprietary estoppel afford useful guidance. Although the requirement of detrimental reliance adds little where the claimant has made a contribution which is referable to the acquisition of the property (because the contribution founds the inference of a common intention and supplies the ingredient of acting upon it), the flexible principles of estoppel may indeed be a preferable basis to a search for an artificial common intention.[46] While the scope of the concept of detrimental reliance remains uncertain, the fact that it can include contributions which are not referable to the acquisition of the property in the cases of express common intention may afford opportunities to the non-earning woman,[47] even though *Burns* v. *Burns*[48] remains authority for the proposition that domestic work will not support the inference of a common intention. In conclusion, the approach of the courts in this area has been less liberal since the decisions of Lord Denning's Court of Appeal, but *Grant* v. *Edwards*[49] partly reverses this trend. It is likely, however, that a strict approach will be maintained where the claimant seeks to establish an interest in order to defeat the creditors of the legal owner.[50]

It seems that the principles applicable to stable relationships between unmarried couples are the same as those applicable between husband and wife,[51] but the nature of the relationship is an important factor when considering what inferences should be drawn from the way the parties have conducted their affairs and in the ascertainment of their common intention.[52] The whole question is of reduced importance in the case of married couples, as mentioned above,[53] because of the wide discretionary powers given to the court to make a distribution of property upon a divorce, nullity or judicial separation under the Matrimonial Causes Act 1973.

(iv) *Constructive Trust Imposed to Achieve Justice.* We have seen

---

[46] [1987] Conv. 93 (J. Eekelaar).

[47] (1987) 50 M.L.R. 94 (B. Sufrin); [1987] Conv. 16 (J. Montgomery). Quantification of her share could be problematic.

[48] [1984] Ch. 317; *ante.*   [49] *Supra.*

[50] *Midland Bank Ltd.* v. *Dobson* [1986] 1 F.L.R. 171; *Winkworth* v. *Edward Baron Development Co. Ltd.* [1986] 1 W.L.R. 1512; *Bristol and West Building Society.* v. *Henning* [1985] 1 W.L.R. 778; *post* p. 269. *cf. Lloyd's Bank Ltd.* v. *Rosset* [1988] 3 W.L.R. 1301.

[51] *Cooke* v. *Head* [1972] 1 W.L.R. 518; *Richards* v. *Dove* [1974] 1 All E.R. 888; *Eves* v. *Eves* (*ante*); *Crisp* v. *Mullings* (1975) 239 E.G. 119; *Robinson* v. *Robinson* (1976) 241 E.G. 153; *Burns* v. *Burns* [1984] Ch. 317. There is of course no presumption of advancement; *ante*, p. 242. See generally (1980) 96 L.Q.R. 248 (A.A.S. Zuckerman); (1976) 40 Conv.(N.S.) 351 (M. Richards).

[52] *Bernard* v. *Josephs* [1982] Ch. 391; (1982) 98 L.Q.R. 517 (J. M. Thomson); [1982] Conv. 444 (J. Warburton); All E.R. Rev. 1982, 150 (R. Deech) and 169 (P. J. Clarke). (1983) 42 C.L.J. 30 (K. Gray). See also *Gordon* v. *Douce* [1983] 1 W.L.R. 563. As to engaged couples, see Law Reform (Miscellaneous Provisions) Act 1970, s.2; *Mossop* v. *Mossop* [1988] 2 W.L.R. 1255.

[53] *Ante*, p. 251.

that the guidelines laid down in *Grant* v. *Edwards*[54] employ the constructive trust as a means of acquiring an interest in the home. The trust is constructive because it is neither express, nor, in the absence of a direct contribution, resulting. It exists only if the conduct of the parties supports the inference of a common intention to share, which has been acted upon. While, of course, the court has a measure of discretion in applying these principles, they are far removed from the notion that the court may impose a constructive trust wherever the justice of the case so requires. The latter may be described as the "new model" constructive trust, which is discussed in Chapter 12.[55] Some decisions after *Gissing* v. *Gissing*,[56] and inconsistently with it, have imposed trusts on the basis that it would be inequitable to do otherwise.[57] In *Eves* v. *Eves*[58] a woman did extensive decorative work and heavy gardening, but made no financial contribution. The man had made an excuse (that she was under 21) for not putting the property into joint names. This decision was analysed in *Grant* v. *Edwards*[59] as a case where the woman's work would not have been sufficient to support the inference of a common intention. It was, however, conduct which amounted to acting on an express oral common intention, which the man's excuse was held to constitute. Lord Denning's judgment proceeded on the broad principle that it would be "most inequitable for him to deny her any share in the house. The law will impute or impose a constructive trust by which he was to hold it in trust for both of them."[60] The Court of Appeal in *Grant* v. *Edwards*, while not disagreeing with the result, regarded Lord Denning's approach as at variance with the principles of *Gissing* v. *Gissing*.[61] It seems likely, therefore, that the "new model" constructive trust, based on broad principles of justice, has been replaced by a constructive trust based on the more specific guidelines laid down in *Grant* v. *Edwards*.

(v) *Substantial Improvements.* Some of the problems of indirect contributions arose where one of the parties had made a substantial contribution in time or money to the improvement of the property subsequent to the purchase. Following the recommendations of the Law Commission,[62] Matrimonial Proceedings and Property Act 1970, s.37, which applies only to married couples,[63] provides as follows:

[54] [1986] Ch. 638; *ante*, p. 253.
[55] *Post*, p. 309. For Commonwealth views, see *post*, p. 316.
[56] [1971] A.C. 886.
[57] *Falconer* v. *Falconer* [1970] 1 W.L.R. 1333; *ante*, p. 255. See also *Baumgartner* v. *Baumgartner* (1988) 62 A.L.J. 29; [1988] Conv. 259 (D. Hayton) (remedial constructive trust to prevent unjust enrichment).
[58] [1975] 1 W.L.R. 1338.
[59] *Supra.*
[60] [1975] 1 W.L.R. 1338, at 1341.
[61] *Supra.*
[62] Report on Financial Provision in Matrimonial Proceedings (Law Com. No. 25).
[63] And to engaged couples by reason of Law Reform (Miscellaneous Provisions) Act 1970, s.2(1).

"It is hereby declared that where a husband or wife contributes in money or money's worth to the improvement of real or personal property in which or in the proceeds of sale of which either or both of them has or have a beneficial interest, the husband or wife so contributing shall, if the contribution is of a substantial nature and subject to any agreement between them to the contrary express or implied, be treated as having then acquired by virtue of his or her contribution a share or an enlarged share, as the case may be, in that beneficial interest of such an extent as may have been then agreed or, in default of such agreement, as may seem in all the circumstances just to any court before which the question of the existence or extent of the beneficial interest of the husband or wife arises (whether in proceedings between them or in any other proceedings)."[64]

Lord Denning has said that this provision was declaratory of the previous law,[65] indeed the language of the statute is declaratory. As far as unmarried couples are concerned, substantial improvements may give rise to an interest on the basis of agreement, inferred common intention or estoppel, even though section 37 does not apply.[66]

(vi) *Size of the Share.* The size of the share of each party may similarly be determined on resulting trust principles, or on the basis of an agreement inferred by the court. The time of acquisition of the property is the starting point for the ascertainment of the shares, but later events, up to and after separation, can be taken into account.[67] If the question is determined on the basis of past contributions to the purchase price, ownership will be in the proportion in which the price was paid. But the difficulty is very great where contributions have been made to mortgage payments,[68] or to improvements,[69] or where a guarantee is given.[70] The tendency to divide equally on the principle that Equality is Equity has been criticised.[71] The division should be in

---

[64] *Griffiths* v. *Griffiths* [1973] 1 W.L.R. 1454; *Re Nicholson (decd.)* [1974] 1 W.L.R. 476.

[65] *Davis* v. *Vale* [1971] 1 W.L.R. 1021; *Jansen* v. *Jansen* [1965] P. 478.

[66] *Thomas* v. *Fuller-Brown* [1988] 1 F.L.R. 237 (where the claim failed because the inference was that the expenditure was in return for rent-free accommodation); *Cadman* v. *Bell* [1988] E.G.C.S. 139 (licence for life); *Passee* v. *Passee* [1988] 1 F.L.R. 263; [1988] Conv. 361 (J. Warburton). It is otherwise if the money was advanced as a loan; *Spence* v. *Brown* (1988) 18 Fam. Law 291; *cf. Hussey* v. *Palmer* [1972] 1 W.L.R. 1286, *ante*, p. 52.

[67] *Bernard* v. *Josephs* [1982] Ch. 391; *Gordon* v. *Douce* [1983] 1 W.L.R. 563; *Burns* v. *Burns* [1984] Ch. 317.

[68] *Re Rogers' Question* [1948] 1 All E.R. 328; *Passee* v. *Passee, supra* (wrong to disregard contributions to mortgage payments on the ground that mainly interest). See also Insolvency Act 1986, s.338.

[69] *Ante*; Matrimonial Proceedings and Property Act 1970, s.37; *Griffiths* v. *Griffiths, ante*; *Re Nicholson (decd.), ante*; *Passee* v. *Passee, supra*.

[70] *Falconer* v. *Falconer* [1970] 1 W.L.R. 1333.

[71] *Gissing* v. *Gissing* [1971] A.C. 886 at p. 897, *per* Lord Reid; at p. 903, *per* Lord Pearson.

accordance with the inferred agreement. But there is little that the court can do except to make a determination on the basis of what seems to be reasonable according to all the circumstances at the time of the decision.[72] Of course, any express declaration as to the size of the shares is conclusive.[73]

(vii) *Date for Valuation of the Share.* If it is established that a person is entitled to a share of the home under a trust (express, constructive or resulting), it follows that he or she is entitled to share proportionately in any increase (or decrease) in its value, until such time as the property is sold.[74] This principle has now been firmly upheld by the Court of Appeal,[75] disapproving earlier authority favouring the date of separation as the relevant date.[76] Separation may bring the *purpose* of the trust to an end (which is relevant to the question whether a sale should be ordered),[77] but cannot terminate the trust itself.

C. Legal Estate in Both Parties.[78] Where the legal title is in both parties, the beneficial interest will prima facie also be shared.[79] They will hold as joint tenants if the purchase money was provided in equal shares,[80] and as tenants in common if it is provided unequally.[81] There may of course be a contrary provision, which will govern.[82] And the presumption of resulting trust to determine proportions will apply, and also, for what it is worth, the presumption of advancement in the case of a married couple. But where a wife is the purchaser, and has the property conveyed into the joint names, this may be sufficient indication of an intention to rebut the presumption of a resulting trust. In modern circumstances there would seem to be no explanation other than a wish to hold equally.[83]

---

[72] *Davis* v. *Vale* [1971] 1 W.L.R. 1021 at p. 1027, *per* Lord Denning M.R.; *Cooke* v. *Head (ante); Eves* v. *Eves (ante).*

[73] *Ante,* p. 252.

[74] Or the co-ownership ends in another way, *e.g.* if one buys the other out.

[75] *Turton* v. *Turton* [1987] 3 W.L.R. 622; [1987] Conv. 378 (J. Warburton); (1987) 103 L.Q.R. 500; (1988) 18 Fam. Law 72 (J. Montgomery); *Gordon* v. *Douce* [1983] 1 W.L.R. 563; *Walker* v. *Hall* [1984] 14 Fam. Law 21; *Passee* v. *Passee* [1988] 1 F.L.R. 263. See also *Cousins* v. *Dzosens* (1984) 81 L.S.Gaz 2855; *Bernard* v. *Josephs* [1982] Ch. 391.

[76] *Hall* v. *Hall* [1982] 3 F.L.R. 379. (Interest at 10 per cent. was awarded until realisation).

[77] *Post,* p. 271.

[78] (1970) 34 Conv.(N.S.) 156 (G. Miller).

[79] *Pettitt* v. *Pettitt* [1970] A.C. 777 at pp. 813–814; *Crisp* v. *Mullings* (1976) 239 E.G. 119; *Bernard* v. *Josephs* [1982] Ch. 391; *Burns* v. *Burns* [1984] Ch. 317; Law Com. Working Paper No. 94 (1985), *Trusts of Land,* para. 16.9.

[80] *Re Eyken's Trusts* (1877) 6 Ch.D. 115.

[81] M. & W., p. 427; Cheshire and Burn, p. 210..

[82] See *Goodman* v. *Gallant* [1986] Fam. 106; (1986) 45 C.L.J. 205 (S. Juss); [1986] Conv. 355 (J.E.M.). (Severance of beneficial joint tenancy must result in equal shares even though unequal contributions). For the position where the declaration contains inconsistent provisions, see *Martin* v. *Martin* (1987) 54 P. & C.R. 238.

[83] *Pettitt* v. *Pettitt* [1970] A.C. 777 at p. 815, *per* Lord Upjohn.

3. Co-Ownership and the Operation of the Trust for Sale

A. The 1925 Legislation

The two forms of co-ownership existing under the modern law are the joint tenancy and the tenancy in common. Here only a brief outline will be given, as the details may be found in the land law books.[84] The purpose of the 1925 legislation in this context was to provide that both forms of co-ownership could exist only behind a trust for sale. The plan was that the legal estate would be held by trustees for sale holding as joint tenants, the beneficial interests existing in equity behind the trust for sale. The beneficial owners could hold their interest either jointly or in common, while the legal owners could only hold jointly. To facilitate conveyancing, the legal joint tenancy could not be severed, but severance of any equitable joint tenancy could be effected by any of the means applicable before 1926[85]; and also by notice in writing to the other joint tenants.[86] The purpose of severance is to convert the joint tenancy into a tenancy in common and thereby prevent the application of the doctrine of survivorship (whereby the survivor of joint tenants takes the whole).

The relevant legislation is the Law of Property Act 1925, section 34 (tenancies in common), and section 36 (joint tenancies). Section 35 lays down the "statutory trusts," whereby the trustees hold on trust to sell and to hold the proceeds of sale, and the income until sale, on trust for the beneficiaries.[87] The intention was to impose a trust for sale on all forms of co-ownership. The drafting was defective, but the courts have followed the scheme of the legislation, even though the language of the statute had to be strained to reach this result.[88] In this the courts have been assisted by the Settled Land Act 1925, s.34(6), which provides that an undivided share can only take effect behind a trust for sale. In the leading case of *Bull* v. *Bull*[89] a mother and son provided the purchase money but the conveyance was in the son's name alone. A resulting trust arose in favour of the mother in relation to the share of the money which she provided. The Court of Appeal, relying on the Settled Land Act 1925, s.36(4), held that their equitable tenancy in common gave rise to a statutory trust for sale.

---

[84] M. & W., pp. 417 *et seq.*; Cheshire and Burn, pp. 207 *et seq.*

[85] M. & W., pp. 429 *et seq.*; Cheshire and Burn, pp. 212 *et seq.*

[86] L.P.A. 1925, s.36(2); *Re Draper's Conveyance* [1969] 1 Ch. 486; *Harris* v. *Goddard* [1983] 1 W.L.R. 1203.

[87] For termination of the trust for sale, see M. & W., pp. 439–441; Cheshire and Burn, pp. 226–227.

[88] M. & W., pp. 437–438; Cheshire and Burn, p. 221; (1963) 27 Conv.(N.S.) 51 (B. A. Rudden). But see [1982] Conv. 213 (M. Friend and J. Newton) suggesting that no trust for sale was intended in the case of a conveyance to one person only.

[89] [1955] 1 Q.B. 234; *Re Buchanan-Wollaston's Conveyance* [1939] Ch. 217; *Williams and Glyn's Bank Ltd.* v. *Boland* [1981] A.C. 487 at p. 507 (*per* Lord Wilberforce); *City of London Building Society* v. *Flegg* [1988] A.C. 54, at p. 77.

B. Single Trustee; Plural Beneficiaries

This situation creates a number of problems which were not fore-seen by the draftsman. The legislation assumed that trusts for sale would be created either expressly or by a conveyance to more than one person, so that there would be at least two trustees for sale. Cases like *Bull* v. *Bull*[90] raise problems between the co-owners and also in rela-tion to a purchaser. They can be examined under six heads. First, is the claimant entitled to a beneficial interest? This was discussed in the earlier part of this chapter. Secondly, assuming that there is co-owner-ship, is there a trust for sale? Thirdly, assuming that there is co-ownership, can the legal estate owner evict the equitable co-owner; so as, for example, to sell with vacant possession? Fourthly, can the legal estate owner demand rent from the equitable co-owner? Fifthly, if there is co-ownership and a trust for sale, can the sole trustee for sale pass a good title to a purchaser? Sixthly, what can the equitable co-owner do in order to effect or to prevent a sale? For the present purpose it will be assumed that, as in *Bull* v. *Bull*,[91] the beneficial interest is shared; and that the beneficial ownership creates a trust for sale. We start therefore with the third question.

(i) *Can the Legal Owner Evict the Equitable Co-owner?* The right of occupation of the land pending sale is not explicitly dealt with in the statutory provisions imposing the trust for sale, and the position has been described as obscure.[92] A claim between spouses to possession of the matrimonial home will be determined under the wide discretion which is given to the High Court by the Married Women's Property Act 1882, s.17, or under the Matrimonial Homes Act 1983.[93] Other situations raise more basic questions.

In *Bull* v. *Bull*,[94] the son attempted to evict his mother. The legal relationship between the two parties was dual. They were equitable tenants in common; and the son was trustee of the legal estate which he held on trust for sale in favour of himself and his mother. The question was whether a trustee of land held upon trust for sale could obtain vacant possession from a beneficiary.

The son failed, Denning L.J. treated the dispute as one between equitable tenants in common whose rights were the same as legal tenants in common before 1926. " ... until a sale takes place those equitable tenants in common have the same right to enjoy the land as legal tenants in common used to have ... and neither of them is

---

[90] *Supra.*
[91] *Supra.*
[92] *Williams & Glyn's Bank Ltd.* v. *Boland* [1981] A.C. 487 at p. 507 (*per* Lord Wilberforce).
[93] Cretney, *Principles of Family Law* (4th ed.), Chap. 9. See also the jurisdiction to grant injunctions in relation to the matrimonial home; and the Domestic Violence and Matrimonial Proceedings Act 1976; *post*, p. 761.
[94] [1955] 1 Q.B. 234.

entitled to turn the other out."[95] But the competition was not only between tenants in common; rather it was between a trustee and a beneficiary behind a trust for sale. The rule before 1926 was that beneficiaries under trusts were not entitled to possession as of right, but only at the discretion of the trustees, and subject to control by the court[96]; and the same rule was applied in *Re Bagot's Settlement*[97] to beneficiaries under a trust for sale. And *Re Landi*,[98] in the context of the Limitation Act 1874, decided that, in the case of statutory trusts for sale after 1925, the right to possession is in the trustees for sale by virtue of their legal estate. It is submitted therefore that the beneficiaries under a trust for sale are not entitled to possession as of right.[99] The trustees should give possession in appropriate cases, and especially in pursuance of their duty under Law of Property Act 1925, s.26(3).[1] The discretionary nature of the right to possession is shown in *Barclay* v. *Barclay*.[2]

Mrs. Barclay died intestate, and her property, which included the bungalow in question, passed to her husband. Mr Barclay died in 1954, and his will provided that the bungalow should be sold and the proceeds divided into five equal shares, the beneficiaries being his children and their spouses.

One son, Allan, separated from his wife and returned to live in the bungalow. Another son, Frank, was appointed executor in the will, but took no steps to administer the estate.

In 1966, a daughter-in-law, who was a beneficiary in her own right and also entitled to her deceased's husband's share, took out letters of administration of the estate of both parents. She intended to sell, and succeeded in her action to evict Allan.

Bull v. *Bull*[3] was distinguished. Lord Denning M.R. said that the prime object there was that the house should be occupied by the parties and that they were tenants in common of the house itself. On the other hand, in *Barclay* v. *Barclay*, "the prime object of the testator was that the bungalow should be sold and the proceeds divided. So the beneficiaries were not tenants in common of the bungalow, but only of the proceeds after it was sold."[4] It is difficult to see how the nature of

[95] [1955] 1 Q.B. at p. 237. This was accepted by the House of Lords in *Williams & Glyn's Bank Ltd.* v. *Boland* [1981] A.C. 487 at pp. 507 and 510, and in *City of London Building Society* v. *Flegg* [1988] A.C. 54. See also *Jones* v. *Jones* [1977] 1 W.L.R. 438, *post*, p. 264; [1978] Conv. 193 at pp. 203 *et seq.* (H. Forrest).
[96] *Re Earl of Stamford and Warrington* [1925] Ch. 165; (1955) 19 Conv.(n.s.) at p. 147 (F. R. Crane).
[97] [1894] 1 Ch. 177.
[98] [1939] Ch. 828.
[99] Nor, however, is the trustee. He must not profit from his trust; *post*, p. 556.
[1] Which requires the trustees of a statutory trust for sale to give effect, so far as consistent with the general interest of the trust, to the wishes of the beneficiaries.
[2] [1970] 2 Q.B. 677; (1971) 29 C.L.J. 44 (M. J. Prichard).
[3] [1955] 1 Q.B. 234.
[4] [1970] 2 Q.B. at p. 684.

the interests of the beneficiaries behind a trust for sale can be made to depend on the question of intent.[5] It is submitted that the cases are better distinguished as being instances of the exercise of the court's discretion which exists in cases of claims to possession by beneficiaries under trusts for sale.[6] On that basis, it would seem that the court's discretionary power was properly exercised in *Barclay* v. *Barclay*[7] in favour of granting a possession order; just as in *Bull* v. *Bull*,[8] an order for possession was rightly refused.

It should be noted that a further ground was available to the court. In *Barclay* v. *Barclay*[9] the estate had not been administered, and it could therefore be said that no beneficiary was as yet entitled to any equitable interest in the property, whether real or personal.[10] The point was not, however, relied on by the court.

(ii) *Can the Legal Owner Demand Rent from the Equitable Co-owner?*[11] A question related to the right of occupation discussed above is whether a co-owner in sole occupation can be made to pay rent to the other co-owner.

In *Jones* (*A.E.*) v. *Jones* (*F.W.*),[12] a father bought a house for £4,000, of which £1,000 was contributed by his son, who thereby acquired a one-quarter share as tenant in common in equity. On his death, the father left the house by will to his new wife, in whom the house was subsequently vested. Her claim that the son should pay three-quarters of a fair rent for his occupation was rejected by the Court of Appeal. As tenants in common, they were equally entitled to occupation, and one of them could not claim rent from the other even though that other occupied the whole of the house. It would be otherwise, however, in a case of ouster. This point subsequently arose in *Dennis* v. *McDonald*,[13] where an unmarried couple were tenants in common. As a result of the man's violence, the woman left the home.

---

[5] But see the views expressed by Lord Denning M.R. in *Williams & Glyn's Bank Ltd.* v. *Boland* [1979] Ch. 312 at p. 329, referred to with apparent approval by Lord Wilberforce in [1981] A.C. 487 at p. 507.

[6] (1970) 34 Conv.(N.S.) 344 (F. R. Crane).

[7] [1970] 2 Q.B. 677.

[8] [1955] 1 Q.B. 234.

[9] [1970] 2 Q.B. 677.

[10] *Commissioner of Stamp Duties for Queensland* v. *Livingston* [1965] A.C. 694; *ante*, p. 22; (1970) 87 L.Q.R. 443 (P.V.B.).

[11] This question can also arise where both parties are legal owners; see *Dennis* v. *McDonald, infra*.

[12] [1977] 1 W.L.R. 438; (1977) 41 Conv.(N.S.) 279 (F. R. Crane); (1978) 41 M.L.R. 208 (J. Alder). See also *Chhokar* v. *Chhokar* [1984] F.L.R. 313.

[13] [1982] Fam. 63; (1982) 98 L.Q.R. 519 (F. Webb); All E.R. Rev. 1982, p. 172 (P. J. Clarke).

The Court of Appeal held that rent[14] was payable by the man as, in effect, he had ousted the woman. In *Bernard* v. *Josephs*,[15] on the other hand, which also concerned an unmarried couple, an occupation rent was ordered although only one member of the Court of Appeal seemed to regard the case as one of ouster.

The ouster principle has not always been applied in matrimonial cases, for example in applications under section 17 of the Married Woman's Property Act 1882.[16] In *Harvey* v. *Harvey*[17] an occupation rent was ordered in a divorce case as a term of postponing the sale of the matrimonial home in an application under section 25 of the Matrimonial Causes Act 1973. This is a convenient solution, but the source of the jurisdiction needs clarification.[18]

(iii) *Can the Single Trustee for Sale Pass a Good Title to a Purchaser?*
It was assumed, as has been seen, that wherever a legal joint tenancy or tenancy in common arose after 1925, there would be a conveyance in such terms to the co-owners who, under the statute, would be trustees for sale, and could make a title to a purchaser. Where there are two trustees for sale, the interests of the beneficiaries will be overreached. Even if in occupation, they cannot rely on the doctrine of notice in unregistered land nor assert any overriding interest in registered land. This has recently been confirmed by the House of Lords in *City of London Building Society* v. *Flegg*,[19] although the response of the Law Commission is that overreaching should not occur without the consent of an occupying beneficiary of full age.[20] Where, however, the legal title is in one person only, as in *Bull* v. *Bull*,[21] and many of the husband and wife cases, the question arises whether the purchaser can obtain a good title from a single trustee for sale. The situation of a single trustee

---

[14] Assessed at half of the sum which would be payable as a fair rent, under Rent Act 1977, s.70(1),(2), if there had been a protected tenancy of the house, taking into account mortgage repayments by the man. It was held in the High Court that L.P.A. 1925, s.30 could not be used directly to order the payment of rent, unless ancillary to an order for sale; [1982] Fam. 63. See Law Com. Working Paper No. 94 (1985), *Trusts of Land*, pp. 40–41.

[15] [1982] Ch. 391; (1982) 98 L.Q.R. 517 (J.M.T.); [1982] Conv. 444 (J. Warburton); All E.R. Rev. 1982, p. 150 (R. Deech) and p. 169 (J. Clarke); (1983) 42 C.L.J. 30 (K. Gray). See also *Cousins* v. *Dzosens* (1984) 81 L.S.Gaz. 2855 (unmarried couple).

[16] See *Bedson* v. *Bedson* [1965] 2 Q.B. 666 (rent of £1 per week ordered); *Leake* v. *Bruzzi* [1974] 1 W.L.R. 1528; *Suttill* v. *Graham* [1977] 1 W.L.R. 819; (1978) Conv. (N.S.) 161 (F. R. Crane); (1978) 97 Law Notes 78 (J. A. Treleaven).

[17] [1982] Fam. 83; All E.R. Rev. 1982, pp. 148 and 158 (R. Deech). See also *Brown* v. *Brown* [1982] 3 F.L.R. 161.

[18] See [1982] Conv. 305 (J. Martin); [1984] Conv. 103 (M. P. Thompson) and 198 (R. Cocks).

[19] [1988] A.C. 54, rejecting an argument based on s.14 of the Law of Property Act 1925. See (1987) 103 L.Q.R. 520 (R. J. Smith); (1987) 46 C.L.J. 329 (C. Harpum); [1987] Conv. 451 (W. J. Swadling); All E.R. Rev. 1987, p. 149 (P. J. Clarke); [1988] Conv. 108 (M. P. Thompson) and 141 (P. Sparkes).

[20] Working Paper No. 106 (1988), *Trusts of Land, Overreaching*; (1988) 51 M.L.R. 365 (S. Gardner).

[21] [1955] 1 Q.B. 234.

holding the legal estate on trust for sale creates a number of conveyancing difficulties. A disposition by the single trustee will not bring
the overreaching provisions of the Law of Property Act 1925, s.2 into
operation, yet the purchaser will see the title vested in one person only,
and may be unaware of the fact that there is beneficial co-ownership.
The fate of the beneficial interests may differ according to whether the
title to the property was registered or not.

If the land is unregistered,[22] the question whether the purchaser or
mortgagee is bound by the equitable interests depends, first, on the
question whether the beneficiary has an interest in the land; and if he
or she does, the second question is whether the purchaser, assuming
him to be bona fide, has notice, actual or constructive, of the interest of
the beneficiary. In theory, the beneficiary's interest is not in the land,
but in the proceeds of sale; and this, under the doctrine of conversion,
is so, whether or not the land has been sold. But there are many
situations in which this theory is not followed[23]; and it is accepted that
the equitable interest of a beneficiary behind a trust for sale will be
binding on anyone coming to the land with the exception of the bona
fide purchaser for value without notice.

This leaves open the difficult question of the circumstances in which
a purchaser or mortgagee is to be held to have constructive notice of
the interest under the trust for sale. In these cases, many of which are
cases of co-ownership between husband and wife, the equitable co-
ownership arises by virtue of one party having contributed to the
purchase price, or to the mortgage payments; and there will be nothing
in the documents of title to put a purchaser on notice. Should it be said
that the purchaser or mortgagee is put upon notice if the vendor or
mortgagor has living with him a spouse, mistress, or parent, or sister,
or mother-in-law? Because spouses, mistresses, parents, sisters or
mothers-in-law commonly contribute, these days, to the purchase
price or mortgage payments of the home. It was at one time held that a
bank mortgagee dealing with the husband as sole legal owner did not
have constructive notice of the wife's equitable interest by contribution, even though the bank knew that the parties lived together in the
house.[24] This view is now discredited.[25] So many wives today have a
share in the home that a reasonable purchaser or mortgagee should
consider the possibility. If he makes insufficient inquiries, the fact of
the wife's (or other beneficiary's) occupation will give him constructive
notice of her rights. The difficulty which remains is in deciding whether
a purchaser or mortgagee has made sufficient inquiries to absolve him
of constructive notice. This arose in *Kingsnorth Finance Co.* v.

---

[22] *i.e.* not subject to the provisions of the Land Registration Acts.
[23] *Post*, p. 274.
[24] *Caunce* v. *Caunce* [1969] 1 W.L.R. 286.
[25] *Hodgson* v. *Marks* [1971] Ch. 892 at pp. 934–935; *Williams & Glyn's Bank Ltd.* v.
Boland [1981] A.C. 487; *Kingsnorth Finance Co.* v. *Tizard* [1986] 1 W.L.R. 783.

Tizard,[26] where a wife had a half share in a house which was vested in her husband alone. When the marriage broke down she slept elsewhere but came to the house every day to look after the children and kept her possessions there. The husband mortgaged the property, falsely stating that he was single. The mortgagee's surveyor inspected the house at a time when the husband had arranged for the wife to be out. He saw evidence of the children's occupation and was told that the wife had left. No further inquiries were made as to her rights. The husband later emigrated, leaving the loan of £66,000 unpaid. It was held that the mortgagee had constructive notice of the wife's interest. In order for physical presence to amount to occupation, it did not need to be exclusive, continuous or uninterrupted, nor was it negatived by regular absences.[27] The wife was accordingly in occupation for the purpose of constructive notice. When the surveyor discovered that the mortgagor was married, he was put on enquiry as to the wife's rights. The mortgagee would not have notice if a reasonable inspection had been made which did not reveal the occupier or evidence of occupation. What amounts to a reasonable inspection depends on the circumstances, but the judge considered that the pre-arranged inspection in the present case did not discharge the obligation. If this is so, there is indeed a heavy onus on the purchaser or mortgagee.[28]

Such is the problem of constructive notice in the case of unregistered land. It should be added, however, that where spouses occupy a matrimonial home, a spouse who has no legal title may protect his or her statutory rights of occupation by registration of a Class F land charge under the Matrimonial Homes Act 1983, whether or not that spouse has any equitable interest in the home; and such registration is notice to all the world. But there is at present no possibility of protecting a substantive equitable interest by registration.

One might reasonably expect that, in the case of registered land, the issue would be made clear by the legislation. Notice plays no part in the registered land system.[29] Equitable interests are binding on a purchaser only if proper steps have been taken to protect them, as by a notice, restriction or caution; or if the interest is held to be an "overriding interest"; which is binding regardless of notice or of any means of discovery. The issue came to a head in *Williams & Glyn's Bank Ltd.* v. *Boland*[30]:

> Mr. and Mrs. Boland each contributed towards the purchase of, and to the mortgage payments due upon, a matrimonial home. Title

---

[26] *Supra.*
[27] See also *Lloyd's Bank Ltd.* v. *Rosset* [1988] 3 W.L.R. 1301; (1988) 138 N.L.J. 685 (S. Bright); (1988) 104 L.Q.R. 507 (R. J. Smith); [1988] Conv. 453 (M. P. Thompson).
[28] See [1986] Conv. 283 (M. P. Thompson); (1987) 46 C.L.J. 28 (P. G. McHugh).
[29] [1981] A.C. 487 at p. 504, *per* Lord Wilberforce.
[30] [1981] A.C. 487; [1980] Conv. 361 (J. Martin); (1980) 43 M.L.R. 692 (S. Freeman); (1980) 39 C.L.J. 243 (M. J. Prichard); (1981) 97 L.Q.R. 12 (R. J. Smith).

was taken in the sole name of Mr. Boland, and he was registered under the Land Registration Act 1925 as sole proprietor.

Later, Mr. Boland mortgaged the house by way of legal mortgage to the Bank; the Bank, in accordance with the entry on the Register, treating Mr. Boland as sole beneficial owner. On default being made in the mortgage payments, the Bank started proceedings for possession.

The wife resisted this claim on the ground that she was entitled to an equitable interest in the house which the Bank could not override. She had taken no steps to protect her interest by restriction or caution.

It was accepted, first of all, that the wife had, by virtue of her financial contribution, an equitable interest in the house; that this created beneficial co-ownership; and that the husband held the legal title upon trust for sale. The question whether this interest was valid against the Bank depended on whether or not it was an overriding interest under the Land Registration Act 1925, s.70(1)(g)[31]; it could not be binding as a minor interest, because the wife had taken no steps to protect it. Nor could it be overreached by the payment to a sole trustee.

The House of Lords unanimously held[32] that the wife's interest behind the trust for sale was capable of existing as an overriding interest. It was right "subsisting in reference" to registered land; and, on the plain words of sub-paragraph (g), the wife was "in actual occupation" at the execution of the mortgage.[33] Lord Scarman emphasised the importance of construing the legislation in the light of current social policy, and of protecting the "beneficial interest which English law now recognizes that a married woman has in the matrimonial home."[34] The result however created conflict with conveyancing and banking practice. For purchasers and mortgagees had previously considered themselves secure by a search of the Land Register, and by ascertaining that the vendor was in occupation. It is now necessary to make inquiries of other persons in occupation, whether spouse, mistress, or other persons; for their interests are capable of being binding

---

[31] s.70(1) reads: "All registered land shall, unless . . . the contrary is expressed in the register, be deemed to be subject to such of the following overriding interests as may be for the time being subsisting in reference thereto . . .

　　(g) The rights of every person in actual occupation of the land or in receipt of the rents and profits thereof, save where enquiry is made of such person and the rights are not disclosed; . . ."

[32] There were other technical arguments on the construction of sections of L.P.A. 1925 which, though "formidable," did not affect the result: *ibid.* pp. 506 *et seq.*

[33] This is the relevant date for the application of s.70(1)(g), rather than the later date of registration of the legal charge; *Lloyds Bank Ltd.* v. *Rosset* [1988] 3 W.L.R. 1301; criticised at (1988) 104 L.Q.R. 507 (R. J. Smith) and [1988] Conv. 453 (M. P. Thompson).

[34] *Ibid.* at p. 510.

as overriding interests on the purchaser or mortgagee.[35] It may be, however, that the difficulties have been overstated.[36]

The principles discussed above are subject to an important proviso. A doctrine recently propounded is that an equitable co-owner in occupation can rely neither on constructive notice (in unregistered land) nor on section $70(1)(g)$ (in registered land) where he or she was aware of the mortgage transaction and did not bring the equitable interest to the attention of the mortgagee.[37] This seems to be a version of the doctrine of estoppel. The principle formulated by the Court of Appeal is that in such circumstances it is impossible to infer any common intention other than that the equitable owner authorised the legal owner to raise money by mortgage which would have priority to any beneficial interest. Apparently it is not relevant that the mortgagee failed to make the inquiries which might have revealed the interest. As has been said, this seems to be a reversal of the doctrine of notice; the onus has shifted to the occupier to declare his rights to a purchaser (mortgagee) of whom he has notice, or be deemed to concede priority.[38] The effect of this doctrine is to diminish the importance of *Williams & Glyn's Bank Ltd.* v. *Boland*[39] and *Kingsnorth Finance Co.* v. *Tizard*,[40] which will have more application to subsequent mortgages than to acquisition mortgages, of which the co-owner is more likely to have been aware.[41]

(iv) *The Deserted Wife.* It may be helpful though not strictly relevant to trusts for sale, to show the various ways in which the plight of the deserted wife who has no interest in the land has been recognised. From *Bendall* v. *McWhirter* in 1952,[42] a doctrine developed which treated a deserted wife as a licensee with a right to remain in the matrimonial home which was effective, not only against her husband, but against third parties. This development came to an end in 1965 when *National Provincial Bank Ltd.* v. *Ainsworth*[43] decided that a deserted wife had, as such, no interest in the land, and none therefore which was capable of giving her protection against third parties. The

---

[35] This point is essentially the same as that decided by the Court of Appeal in *Hodgson* v. *Marks* [1971] Ch. 892; criticised (1973) 36 M.L.R. 25 (R. H. Maudsley), but accepted by all later cases.

[36] See H.L.Deb., cols. 658–664 (December 15, 1982); [1983] Conv., pp. 87–88.

[37] *Bristol and West Building Society* v. *Henning* [1985] 1 W.L.R. 778; *Paddington Building Society* v. *Mendelsohn* (1985) 50 P. & C.R. 244; criticised [1985] Conv. 361 (P. Todd); [1986] Conv. 57, (1986) 49 M.L.R. 255 and (1986) 6 L.S. 140 (M. P. Thompson).

[38] (1985) 44 C.L.J. 354 (M. Welstead).

[39] *Supra.*

[40] [1986] 1 W.L.R. 783, *ante*, p. 266.

[41] *cf. Lloyd's Bank Ltd.* v. *Rosset* [1988] 3 W.L.R. 1301 (wife unaware of initial mortgage).

[42] [1952] 2 Q.B. 466.

[43] [1965] A.C. 1175.

Legislature intervened by passing the Matrimonial Homes Act 1967,[44] which gave a "right of occupation" to a spouse who was not entitled to occupation by virtue of any estate or interest; and the statutory "right of occupation" was registrable as a land charge class F, and, if registered, was binding on third parties in the usual way.

The Act was not without its difficulties,[45] not least in that a bride may feel no need to register a class F land charge on her wedding-day; and, by the time that the marriage has deteriorated to a stage at which the need to register becomes clear, it may be too late. One difficulty has, however, been met. As has been seen, there is doubt whether or not a beneficiary behind a trust for sale is entitled to possession.[46] A wife, therefore, who had made contributions to the matrimonial home which would entitle her to some share in the beneficial interest in the house might fall between two stools. If the beneficial interest gave her an entitlement to occupation, she would be unable to register; yet she could find that her interest was destroyed by a bona fide purchaser. The Matrimonial Proceedings and Property Act 1970, s.38 therefore amended the 1967 Act by adding a provision, now found in section 1(11) of the Act of 1983, to the effect that a spouse who has an equitable interest in the land or the proceeds of sale, without holding the legal estate, shall be treated for the purposes of the Act as not being entitled to occupy the house. She may therefore register a statutory right of occupation. If she fails to register, she may still assert her equitable interest, and this, as has been seen, will be valid against a purchaser with actual or constructive notice in the case of unregistered land, and, in the case of registered land, valid as a minor interest if protected by restriction or caution; or as an overriding interest if the spouse is in actual occupation.[47]

(v) *What can the Equitable Co-owner Do to Effect a Sale?* A number of questions arise as to the way in which the co-owners can exercise their rights. Where the legal estate is vested in all the co-owners on trust for sale in the usual way, the trustees decide whether or not to sell. They must act unanimously.[48] In the absence of a unanimous decision to exercise the power to postpone sale, their duty, in accordance with the trust, is to sell. In case of dispute, they can apply to the court under the Law of Property Act 1925, s.30 for an order directing that a proposed transaction be carried out, and the court may make such order as it thinks fit. The question may arise, not only where there is disagreement between trustees, but also where the legal estate is

---

[44] Now the Act of 1983.

[45] Discussed [1974] Ch. 30 at p. 45; (1968) 32 Conv.(N.S.) 85 (F. R. Crane).

[46] *Ante*, p. 262.

[47] *Ante*, p. 266.

[48] *Re Hilton* [1909] 2 Ch. 548; *Re Mayo* [1943] Ch. 302; *post*, p. 462. The parties may have made express provision for sale or for one to buy the other out; *Miller* v. *Lakefield Estates Ltd.*, *The Times*, May 16, 1988.

vested in one co-owner only, as where the husband holds the legal title, and the beneficial interest is held by him and his wife as tenants in common. The wife is a "person interested,"[49] and may make the application. After decree absolute, however, applications should properly be made to the Family Division under the relevant provisions of the Matrimonial Causes Act 1973.[50] A wife may also, if a question arises as to the title to, or possession of property, ask the court for an order for sale,[51] or apply under the Matrimonial Homes Act 1983 for an order relating to the spouse's right of occupation.[52] The question of sale may also arise on the death of a co-owner, if his or her share devolves on a third party.[53]

The principle upon which the court exercises its discretion under the Law of Property Act 1925, s.30, is that it will look to see whether the object or purpose of the trust for sale has been carried out.[54] In matrimonial cases, the principal question is whether the marriage still continues in law,[55] or in fact.[56] The provision of a home for the children may also be a material, but not decisive factor.[57] The court will look into all the circumstances. The difficulty is that both parties may be acting reasonably; the one wishing to retain a home, the other to realise an investment by turning it into cash.

The modern view is that the court should have regard to the needs of the family as a whole before ordering a sale. A new approach was indicated by the Court of Appeal in *Williams* v. *Williams*,[58] where it

---

[49] So also a chargee (*Stevens* v. *Hutchinson* [1953] Ch. 299); or a trustee in bankruptcy; *Re Solomon* [1967] Ch. 573; *Re Turner* [1974] 1 W.L.R. 1556; *Re McCarthy* [1975] 1 W.L.R. 807; *Re Bailey* [1977] 1 W.L.R. 278; *Re Holliday* [1981] Ch. 405; *Re Lowrie* [1981] 3 All E.R. 353. See also *First National Securities Ltd.* v. *Hegerty* [1985] Q.B. 850; *Midland Bank plc.* v. *Pike* [1988] 2 All E.R. 434 (charging order).

[50] As amended by the Matrimonial and Family Proceedings Act 1984; *Williams* v. *Williams* [1976] Ch. 278; (1977) 93 L.Q.R. 176 (M. W. Bryan). See also *Ward* v. *Ward and Greene* [1980] 1 W.L.R. 4; Matrimonial Homes and Property Act 1981, ss.7, 8.

[51] M.W.P.A. 1882, s.17; *Bedson* v. *Bedson* [1965] 2 Q.B. 666; Cretney: *Principles of Family Law*, pp. 670 *et seq.*; Murphy and Clark, *The Family Home*, pp. 61 *et seq.*

[52] s.1(2). Such an order may also be made where both spouses have legal title; *ibid.* s.9.

[53] See *Stott* v. *Ratcliffe* (1982) 79 L.S.Gaz. 643 (co-owners were unmarried couple. The man's share devolved on his widow on his death intestate. No order for sale made on widow's application).

[54] *Re Buchanan-Wollaston's Conveyance* [1939] Ch. 738; *Re Mayo* [1943] Ch. 302; *Jones* v. *Challenger* [1961] 1 Q.B. 176; *Rawlings* v. *Rawlings* [1964] P. 398; *Barclay* v. *Barclay* [1970] 2 Q.B. 677; *Re Johns' Assignment Trusts* [1970] 1 W.L.R. 955; *Jackson* v. *Jackson* [1971] 1 W.L.R. 1539; (1971) 87 L.Q.R. 153 (P.V.B.); *Burke* v. *Burke* [1974] 1 W.L.R. 1063; *Williams* v. *Williams* [1976] Ch. 278; *Martin* v. *Martin* [1978] Fam. 12; *Jones* (*A.E.*) v. *Jones* (*F.W.*) [1977] 1 W.L.R. 438; *Bernard* v. *Josephs* [1982] Ch. 391; *Walker* v. *Hall* (1984) 14 Fam. Law 21.

[55] *Jones* v. *Challenger, supra.*

[56] *Rawlings* v. *Rawlings, supra; Re Solomon, supra.*

[57] *Burke* v. *Burke, supra.*

[58] [1976] Ch. 278, where the approach taken in *Jones* v. *Challenger* and *Burke* v. *Burke* was said to be outdated. See also *Martin* v. *Martin* [1978] Fam. 12; *Re Evers' Trust* [1980] 1 W.L.R. 1327 (unmarried couple); *Eshak* v. *Nowojewski, The Times,* November 19, 1980; *Gordon* v. *Douce* [1983] 1 W.L.R. 563 (unmarried couple); (1984) 47 M.L.R. 735 (J. Dewar). See generally [1981] Conv. 404 (M. Hayes and G. Battersby).

was said that the court is bound to have regard to the provisions of the Matrimonial Causes Act 1973 relating to matrimonial property, in particular the court's power to order a transfer of the home from one spouse to the other. The primary object of the court should be to provide a home for the remaining partner and children, and steps should be taken to preserve the property as a home for them, but giving the outgoing partner such compensation, by way of a charge or being bought out,[59] as is reasonable in the circumstances. In some cases the remaining spouse has been ordered to pay an occupation rent to the other spouse.[60] Other factors to be taken into consideration include the conduct of the parties: the suitability of the house as a home for the spouse and children, if any; the financial circumstances of the parties and the amount which each has invested in the property.[61]

Where, however, the sale is requested by the trustee in bankruptcy of one spouse, different considerations arise. "Bankruptcy has, in relation to the matrimonial home, its own claim to protection."[62] The rights of the creditors are in competition with the interests of all the beneficiaries. They do not automatically defeat the interests of the family; but the reported cases indicate that it is only in special circumstances that the trustee in bankruptcy is unlikely to succeed.[63]

The law in this area has recently been amended by the Insolvency Act 1986, following an examination by the Review Committee on Insolvency Law and Practice.[64] Where the trustee in bankruptcy applies for an order for sale of a dwelling house owned by the bankrupt and his spouse, the court shall make such order as is just and reasonable, having regard to the interests of the creditors, any conduct of the spouse contributing to the bankruptcy, the needs and resources of the spouse, the needs of any children, and all the circumstances other than the needs of the bankrupt. Where, however, the application is made after a year from the vesting in the trustee in bankruptcy, the court must assume that the interests of the creditors outweigh all other

---

[59] *Bernard* v. *Josephs* [1982] Ch. 391 (unmarried couple); *M.* v. *M.*, *The Times*, August 26, 1987.

[60] *Ante*, p. 264. Or the order may be made, but suspended on terms; *Bernard* v. *Josephs*, *supra*.

[61] *Bedson* v. *Bedson* [1965] 2 Q.B. 666; *Jackson* v. *Jackson* [1971] 1 W.L.R. 1539; (1972) 36 Conv.(N.S.) 104–108 and [1978] Conv. 301 (J. G. Miller).

[62] *Re Bailey* [1977] 1 W.L.R. 278 at p. 279 (*per* Megarry V.-C.).

[63] *Re Solomon* [1967] Ch. 573; *Re Turner* [1974] 1 W.L.R. 1556; *Re McCarthy* [1975] 1 W.L.R. 807; *Re Bailey* [1977] 1 W.L.R. 278; *Re Lowrie* [1981] 3 All E.R. 353; *Re Densham* [1975] 1 W.L.R. 1519. *cf. Re Holliday (a Bankrupt)* [1981] Ch. 405 (no order until 1985, where debtor's divorced wife burdened with obligation to provide a home for the children, and debtor bankrupt on his own petition); (1981) 97 L.Q.R. 200 (C. Hand); [1982] Conv. 74 (A. Sydenham); [1983] Conv. 219 (C. Hand). For the equity of exoneration, see *In re Pittortou (a bankrupt)* [1985] 1 W.L.R. 58.

[64] 1982, Cmnd. 8558. Some jurisdictions offer greater protection by "homestead legislation." See Joint Family Homes Act 1964 (New Zealand); Gray, *Elements of Land Law*, pp. 881–883.

considerations save in exceptional circumstances.[65] This provision, therefore, gives some protection to the family by delaying the sale, but the trustee will normally succeed after a year. There are similar provisions for the protection of children under 18 living with the bankrupt, whether or not there is a spouse with rights of occupation.[66] No new rights, however, are given to cohabitees, who must rely on the general law.

Where the trustee in bankruptcy is for any reason unable to dispose of a dwelling occupied by the bankrupt or his spouse, he may apply to court for an order imposing a charge on it for the benefit of the creditors. The property then revests in the bankrupt, subject to the charge. The object here is to enable a trustee who is unable to dispose of the dwelling to obtain his release without leaving the property vested in the official receiver.[67]

Finally, similar problems may arise prior to any bankruptcy in weighing the competing claims of the wife and any creditor of the husband who seeks a charging order on his share in the home.[68]

(vi) *What can the Equitable Co-owner Do to Prevent a Sale?* A co-owner who is a joint holder of the legal estate can of course refuse to sell, and, if proceedings are taken under Law of Property Act 1925, s.30, he will oppose. Where the co-owner, as is often the situation in the husband and wife cases, is an owner in equity only, there is usually no opportunity for protection under section 30, because the sale takes place without the spouse's knowledge. She can protect herself, as has been seen, by registration of her right of occupation as a class F land charge, and this will no doubt prevent a sale.[69] Or, with registered land, she may protect her equitable interest by the entry of a restriction or caution, and, if in occupation, may assert an overriding interest against the purchaser.[70] In addition, she may, if she hears in time of her husband's intention to sell, invoke the court's jurisdiction under the Married Women's Property Act 1882, s.17, to restrain the husband from selling or in any other way giving a right to another person to evict her.[71]

She may also seek an injunction to prevent sale without the appointment of a second trustee to safeguard the proceeds of sale, and to

---

[65] Insolvency Act 1986, s.336(3)–(5). s.336(2) reverses the rule that a spouse's right of occupation under the Matrimonial Homes Act 1983 does not bind the trustee in bankruptcy. See [1986] Conv. 393 (J. G. Miller); (1987) 17 Fam. Law 316 (N. Furey).

[66] *Ibid.* s.337.

[67] *Ibid.* s.313; (1987) 137 N.L.F. 347 (E. Bailey and C. Berry).

[68] Guidelines are given in *Harman* v. *Glencross* [1986] Fam. 81 (wife seeking transfer order in divorce proceedings); [1986] Conv. 218 (J. Warburton); All E.R. Rev. 1986, p. 184 (P. J. Clarke).

[69] *Ante*, p. 270; *Wroth* v. *Tyler* [1974] Ch. 30.

[70] *Williams & Glyn's Bank Ltd.* v. *Boland* [1981] A.C. 487.

[71] *Lee* v. *Lee* [1952] 2 Q.B. 489n.

restrain the husband from disregarding section 26(3) of the Law of Property Act 1925, requiring consultation of the beneficiaries.[72]

C. The Nature of the Interest of a Beneficiary under a Trust for Sale

A strict application of the doctrine of Conversion[73] would lead to the conclusion that a beneficiary under a trust for sale does not own an interest in land. This, however, is contrary to the realities of the matter in some situations, and it will have been observed that the courts have varied in their answers to the questions.[74]

There is no doubt that an interest under a trust for sale passes as personalty on death, whether in respect of intestate succession before 1926 or under a gift of personalty after 1925.[75] One question which arose was whether beneficiaries under a statutory trust for sale owned any "land or interest in land" for the purpose of the making of a charging order under the Administration of Justice Act 1956, s.35. The section, and its predecessors, was held not to apply to interests under a trust for sale,[76] unless the debtors were the legal owners as well as equitable owners under the trust for sale, in which case the whole property, as opposed to the separate beneficial interests of the debtors, could be charged.[77] Following recommendations from the Law Commission,[78] section 35 was replaced by section 2 of the Charging Orders Act 1979, which provides that a charge may be imposed on any interest held by the debtor beneficially under any trust, thus enabling a judgment creditor to obtain a charge upon a beneficial interest under a trust for sale.[79] Such a charge, however, is not registrable against the owner of the legal estate.[80]

Difficult questions have also arisen under section 63 of the Law of Property Act 1925, the "all-estates" provision, whereby "Every conveyance is effectual to pass all the estate, right, title, interest, claim, and demand which the conveying parties respectively have in, to or on the property[81] conveyed . . . " so long as there is no contrary intention expressed in the conveyance. In *Cedar Holdings Ltd.* v. *Green*,[82] a

---

[72] *Waller* v. *Waller* [1967] 1 W.L.R. 451.

[73] *Post*, Chapter 26.

[74] (1971) 29 C.L.J. 44 (M. J. Prichard); (1984) 100 L.Q.R. 86 (S. Anderson); [1986] Conv. 415 (J. Warburton).

[75] *Re Kempthorne* [1930] 1 Ch. 268; *Re Newman* [1930] 2 Ch. 409; *Re Cook* [1948] Ch. 212.

[76] *Irani Finance Ltd.* v. *Singh* [1971] Ch. 59; (1970) 34 Conv.(N.S.) 49, 420 (F. R. Crane).

[77] *National Westminster Bank Ltd.* v. *Allen* [1971] 2 Q.B. 718; (1971) 35 Conv.(N.S.) 427 (F. R. Crane); (1971) 121 N.L.J. 724 (S. M. Cretney).

[78] Law Com. No. 46: Charging Orders on Land, pp. 15–24.

[79] *National Westminster Bank Ltd.* v. *Stockman* [1980] 1 W.L.R. 67; [1981] Conv. 91 (A. Sydenham); *First National Securities Ltd.* v. *Hegerty* [1985] Q.B. 850. For the position of the co-owner of the debtor, see *Harman* v. *Glencross* [1986] Fam. 81.

[80] Unless the conditions of s.2(1)(b) of the 1979 Act are satisfied; *Perry* v. *Phoenix Assurance plc* [1988] 1 W.L.R. 940; [1988] Conv. 286 (J.E M.) (not an interest in "land").

[81] The word "land" is not used.

[82] [1981] Ch. 129; [1979] Conv. 372 (F. R. Crane); (1980) 43 M.L.R. 225 (B. Berkovits).

husband and wife were joint legal owners. The husband executed a legal charge over the property in favour of a bank. The wife knew nothing about this, and the charge was executed by a woman impersonating her. This was ineffective as a legal charge, and the Court of Appeal held also that it could not take effect under section 63 as a charge over the husband's equitable interest in the proceeds of sale, as this was not an interest in the "property conveyed." Although not expressly overruled, this decision was disapproved, *obiter*, by the House of Lords in *Williams & Glyn's Bank Ltd.* v. *Boland.*[83] In the subsequent case of *First National Securities Ltd.* v. *Hegerty,*[84] on similar facts, Bingham J. considered, not following *Cedar Holdings* v. *Green*, that the purported legal charge was effective to create an equitable charge on the husband's beneficial interest. In *Thames Guaranty Ltd.* v. *Campbell,*[85] on the other hand, *Cedar Holdings* v. *Green* was applied in a case where one joint tenant deposited the title deeds by way of security without the consent of the other. This did not create a charge over the legal estate, nor over the debtor's beneficial interest. The deposit was completely ineffective as, without the consent of the other joint tenant, the creditor was not entitled to retain custody of the deeds until repayment. The disapproval of *Cedar Holdings* v. *Green* by the House of Lords did not affect this particular point. Although the husband, having agreed to charge the property, could have been ordered to grant a charge on whatever interest he had in the property, the doctrine of partial performance was subject to an exception in the case of hardship to a third party. Such an order would expose the wife to the risk of proceedings for sale, and so should not be made. One distinction between this case and *First National Securities Ltd.* v. *Hegerty*[86] is that the plaintiffs in *Campbell* had been "the architects of their own misfortune,"[87] having been content to continue dealing solely with the husband after acquiring knowledge of the wife's interest, whereas the plaintiffs in *Hegerty* could have done little to protect themselves. A similar situation involving a purchaser arose in *Ahmed* v. *Kendrick,*[88] where a husband forged his wife's signature on a registered transfer to a purchaser of a house of which they were joint legal owners. The wife found out and registered an inhibition before the purchaser could be registered as proprietor. It was held that the

---

[83] [1981] A.C. 487, *infra*.
[84] [1985] Q.B. 850. A charging order was made under the 1979 Act although probably an equitable charge subsisted without it, and would have sufficed to enable the creditor to initiate proceedings under L.P.A. 1925, s.30. The charging order was upheld by the Court of Appeal without analysis of the point discussed in the text.
[85] [1985] Q.B. 210; (1984) 81 L.S.Gaz. 641 (P. H. Kenny). All E.R. Rev. 1984, p. 184 (P. J. Clarke); [1985] Conv. 129 (P. F. Smith). See also *Ainscough* v. *Ainscough (Cedar Holdings Ltd. intervening)*, noted (1987) 17 Fam. Law 347; *Wollam* v. *Barclays Bank plc* (1988) 18 Fam. Law 381.
[86] *Supra*.
[87] [1985] Q.B. 210 at p. 240.
[88] (1988) 56 P. & C. R. 120. The wife agreed to be bought out by the purchaser.

husband's beneficial interest passed to the purchaser under section 63 of the Law of Property Act 1925, the legal title remaining in the husband and wife. The authority of *Cedar Holdings Ltd.* v. *Green*[89] on the point had been destroyed by the House of Lords in *Williams & Glyn's Bank Ltd.* v. *Boland*.[90]

There are many situations in which an interest under a trust for sale is treated as an interest in land. First, the co-owners together, if adult and under no disability, or a sole survivor of beneficial joint tenants, can terminate the trust for sale and demand a conveyance of the land.[91] Secondly, the trustees under a statutory trust for sale are required to give effect to the wishes of the majority of the beneficiaries according to the value of their combined interests.[92] Thirdly, a beneficiary, as has been seen, is a person "interested" who may apply to the court for an order relating to the land.[93] Fourthly, the beneficiary's interest is sufficient to protect him, within the court's discretion, from eviction by the holder of the legal estate.[94] Fifthly, unless the overreaching provisions apply,[95] the interest of a beneficiary under a trust for sale in unregistered land is binding on a purchaser with notice.[96] With registered land the interest of a beneficiary under a trust for sale is a minor interest,[97] and was held to be the proper subject of a caution by the beneficiary.[98] It has been seen that an interest under a trust for sale in registered land may be an overriding interest if the beneficiary is in occupation.[99] The nature of a beneficial interest behind a trust for sale was not discussed in detail in the speeches in the House of Lords in *Williams & Glyn's Bank Ltd.* v. *Boland*,[1] but Ormrod L.J. in the Court of Appeal described the trust for sale as a legal fiction, whose primary objective was to simplify conveyancing. "But to press this legal fiction to its logical conclusion and beyond the point which is necessary to achieve the primary object is not justifiable, particularly when it involves the sacrifice of the interests of a class or classes of person. The consequence is that the interests of persons in the position of the (equitable co-owner) ought not to be dismissed as a mere interest in

---

[89] *Supra.*
[90] *Supra.*
[91] *Saunders* v. *Vautier* (1841) 4 Beav. 115; *Re Horsnaill* [1909] 1 Ch. 631, at p. 635; (1971) 34 M.L.R. 441 (S. M. Cretney).
[92] L.P.A. 1925, s.26(3).
[93] *Ibid.* s.30: *ante*, p. 270.
[94] *Bull* v. *Bull* [1955] 1 Q.B. 234; *Cook* v. *Cook* [1962] P. 235; *Gurasz* v. *Gurasz* [1970] P. 11: *ante*, p. 262.
[95] L.P.A. 1925, ss.2(1), 27(1)(2); *City of London Building Society* v. *Flegg* [1988] A.C. 54.
[96] *Caunce* v. *Caunce* [1969] 1 W.L.R. 286; *Williams & Glyn's Bank Ltd.* v. *Boland, infra*; *Kingsnorth Finance Co. Tizard* [1986] 1 W.L.R. 783.
[97] L.R.A. 1925, s.3(xv).
[98] *Elias* v. *Mitchell* [1972] Ch. 652; (1972) 36 Conv.(N.S.) 206 (D.J. Hayton); see also L.R.A. 1925, s.78(4); *cf. Re Rayleigh Weir Stadium* [1954] 1 W.L.R. 286.
[99] *Ante*, p. 267.
[1] [1981] A.C. 487.

the proceeds of sale except where it is essential to the working of the scheme to do so."[2] Similarly, Lord Wilberforce described the view that such an interest was merely in the proceeds of sale as "just a little unreal."[3] However, by way of contrast, it seems that interests under a strict settlement may not be overriding interests; because, the Land Registration Act 1925, s.86(2) provides that such interests "take effect as minor interests and not otherwise." It may seem strange that interests under settlements and under trusts for sale should be treated differently in this respect; and the situation has been described as "anomalous and probably accidental."[4] Finally, a contract for the sale of the beneficiary's interest under a trust for sale is held to be within Law of Property Act 1925, s.40, and is unenforceable unless evidenced in writing and signed by the party to be charged.[5]

"It is thus chimerical to suppose that a single 'correct' answer can be given to the problem whether the beneficiary's interest is or is not an 'interest in land'; in some cases it is, in others it is not."[6] It is necessary therefore to consider carefully each situation as it arises. The problem would, however, disappear if the reform discussed below,[7] whereby trusts for sale would be replaced by trusts of land with a power of sale, were to be enacted. The removal of the *duty* to sell would render the doctrine of conversion inapplicable.

4. Suggested Reforms

The trust for sale is a conveyancing mechanism. It enables beneficial interests very conveniently to be overreached because, under the doctrine of conversion, they are attached to the proceeds of sale.[8] But, as has been seen, the introduction of the doctrine has created many difficulties, and is not followed to its logical conclusion in all cases. Further, an inquiring layman, wanting to retain the land, whether as a co-owning spouse or a squire of hereditary acres, may well ask why the land has to be held in trust to *sell*.[9]

It is not necessary to use the trust for sale as a machinery in order to effect overreaching. Such an effect has been achieved for over a century under the Settled Land Act legislation. Since 1925, the Settled Land Act machinery is used whenever successive interests exist in

---

[2] [1979] Ch. 312 at p. 336. See [1981] Conv. 108 (A. E. Boyle).
[3] [1981] A.C. 487 at p. 507.
[4] (1958) 22 Conv.(n.s.) 14 at p. 24 (F. R. Crane). See also Law Com. No. 158 (1987), *Third Report on Land Registration*, para. 2.69.
[5] *Cooper* v. *Critchley* [1955] Ch. 431. This is expressly provided by the Law of Property (Miscellaneous Provisions) Bill, which replaces s.40; *post*, p. 658.
[6] (1971) 34 M.L.R. 441 (S. M. Cretney).
[7] *Post*, p. 278.
[8] Although the doctrine of conversion is not necessary to overreaching.
[9] Survey of the Land Law of Northern Ireland (1971), para. 89.

land,[10] unless the land is held upon trust for sale.[11] This duality of available machinery has caused confusion and litigation, and there is much to be said for the view that a single machinery would be better.[12]

Reform along these lines has recently been considered by the Law Commission.[13] The preferred solution is that the Settled Land Act 1925 should be repealed, and the present dual system of settlements and trusts for sale should be replaced by a new form of trust with a power of sale, applying to both successive and concurrent interests. If this proposal were to be adopted, the doctrine of conversion would no longer apply.[14] In the absence of any duty to sell, the interests of the beneficiaries would be recognised as interests in land. Another consequence would be that one trustee would not be able to force a sale, because a power of sale, as opposed to a duty, would require unanimity.[15] Hence one trustee would be able to prevent a sale. The doctrine of overreaching would still apply to a sale by two trustees,[16] as under the present law. Finally, recommendations are made to broaden the scope of section 30 of the Law of Property Act 1925 in various ways.[17]

As far as the matrimonial home is concerned, the Law Commission had previously recommended that, subject to various exceptions, it should be shared equally between the spouses as beneficial joint tenants.[18] The major difficulty of this proposal was the requirement that a spouse who was not the legal owner would have to register his or her equitable interest under the Land Charges Act 1972 in unregistered land and by entry of a restriction in registered land.[19] It seems unrealistic to expect registration by an equitable owner,[20] and at present there is no plan to implement these proposals.[21]

---

[10] S.L.A. 1925, s.1.

[11] *Ibid.* s.1(7).

[12] Cheshire and Burn, pp. 203–205; (1957) 10 C.L.P. 152 (E. H. Scamell); (1961) 24 M.L.R. 123 (G. A. Grove).

[13] Working Paper No. 94 (1985), *Trusts of Land*; [1987] Conv. 29 (M. P. Thompson); (1987) 40 C.L.P. 159 (M. Grant).

[14] *Ibid.* p. 64.

[15] *Ibid.* p. 35.

[16] *Ibid.* p. 42. See also Working Paper No. 106 (1988), *Trusts of Land, Overreaching*, p. 42, proposing an exception for occupying beneficiaries.

[17] *Ibid.* pp. 39, 41, 44–94.

[18] Law Com. No. 86: Third Report on Family Property, para. 1.1. See also [1978] Conv. 194 (H. Forrest).

[19] The Third Report recommended that s.70(1)(g) of the Land Registration Act 1925 should not apply to such an interest. This view was maintained in Law Com. No. 115 (1982), but the Third Report on Land Registration (Law Com. No. 158, 1987), pp. 23–32, accepts that it should.

[20] *cf.* Third Report on Land Registration, Law Com. No. 158 (1987), para. 2.6; Law Com. Working Paper No. 106 (1988), *Trusts of Land, Overreaching*, para. 6.4. The Matrimonial Homes Act 1983 raises similar problems. See *Williams & Glyn's Bank Ltd.* v. *Boland* [1979] Ch. 312 at p. 328 (Lord Denning M.R.).

[21] H.L. Deb., cols. 658–664 (December 15, 1982); [1983] Conv. pp. 87–88. Subsequently a Government Bill, the Law of Property and Land Registration Bill 1985, under which only co-owners who were spouses could rely on s.70(1)(g), was withdrawn as unworkable.

More recently, proposals have been made for legal and beneficial co-ownership of the home and certain other assets during marriage, coupled with equal division of all financial gains and liabilities arising during marriage upon death, divorce or bankruptcy.[22]

---

[22] Institute of Fiscal Studies, *Property and Marriage: an integrated approach* (1988); (1988) 18 Fam. Law 327 (J. Masson). See also Law Com. Working Paper No. 90, *Transfer of Money between Spouses*, paras. 5.20–5.22.

CHAPTER 12

CONSTRUCTIVE TRUSTS

1. GENERAL

A CONSTRUCTIVE trust is one which arises by operation of law, and not by reason of the intention of the parties, express or implied. "English law provides no clear and all-embracing definition of a constructive trust. Its boundaries have been left perhaps deliberately vague, so as not to restrict the court by technicalities in deciding what the justice of a particular case may demand."[1] The principle is that where a person who holds property in circumstances in which in equity and good conscience it should be held or enjoyed by another, he will be compelled to hold the property on trust for that other.[2] Such a statement can be criticised as being too general to be helpful. It used to be said that equity had developed pragmatically in this field, relying on the

[1] *Carl Zeiss Stiftung* v. *Herbert Smith & Co.* [1969] 2 Ch. 276 at p. 300 (*per* Edmund Davies L.J.).
[2] See *Beatty* v. *Guggenheim Exploration Co.*, 225 N.Y. 380 at p. 386 (1919); *Soar* v. *Ashwell* [1893] 2 Q.B. 390; (1913–14) 27 Harv.L.R. 125 (A. W. Scott); (1955) 72 L.Q.R. 39 (A. W. Scott); *Restatement of Restitution*, § 160; Waters, *The Constructive Trust*; Oakley, *Constructive Trusts*. See also *Att.-Gen.* v. *Guardian Newspapers Ltd. (No.2)* [1988] 3 W.L.R. 776 (*dicta* that *Spycatcher* copyright held on constructive trust for Crown).

precedents and paying too little attention to the general principle. In recent years, the pendulum has swung the other way, and a constructive trust has been used as a means of reaching a desired result over a wide variety of cases; constructive trusts of a "new model,"[3] "wherever justice and good conscience require it."[4] It may be, however, the the "new model" has lost momentum.[5] The best approach is to examine a number of situations in which constructive trusts have long been established as the appropriate solution, and then to consider the modern developments, and attempt to find a common principle which will help in the solution of future cases. But, first, some points of general application need to be made.

A. Overlap in Classification

We saw, in discussing the classification of trusts,[6] that there is an overlap between resulting and constructive trusts. If a settlor conveys property to trustees to hold upon certain trusts which fail, we can say that the beneficial interest returns to the settlor, because that was the implied intention, or because it is a case of a resulting trust, or that it is right and just that it should do so.[7] It makes little practical difference whether a trust is described as constructive or resulting. The formality rules, for example, apply to neither type.[8] But the tendency to merge the two categories makes any definition of a constructive trust even harder to formulate.[9] "It has been suggested that nomenclature in this context is unimportant. There is, however, some risk that confusion of terminology may lead to confusion of thought."[10] On the other hand, it has been said that, "In labelling and categorising we may well be restricting and ossifying potentially and actually useful legal doctrines and ideas."[11]

The constructive trust is usually regarded as a residual category; one which is called into play where the court desires to impose a trust and no other suitable category is available.

B. Establishing the Existence or the Terms of the Trust

The imposition of a constructive trust is often a determination that previously declared trusts are enforceable against someone other than the original trustee, or extend to additional property.[12] Thus, a pur

---

[3] *Eves* v. *Eves* [1975] 1 W.L.R. 1338 at p. 1341.
[4] *Hussey* v. *Palmer* [1972] 1 W.L.R. 1286 at p. 1290, *per* Lord Denning M.R.; *ante*, p. 71.
[5] *Post*, p. 316.
[6] *Ante*, p. 69.
[7] *Ante*, p. 69.
[8] L.P.A. 1925, s.53, *ante*, p. 80.
[9] The distinction has been maintained in Canada; *Pettkus* v. *Becker* (1980) 117 D.L.R. (3d.) 257.
[10] The Child & Co. Oxford Lecture (1984) "The Informal Creation of Interests in Land," at p. 4 (Sir Christopher Slade).
[11] [1982] Conv. 424 at p. 431 (F. Bates).
[12] Bowen L.J. in *Soar* v. *Ashwell* [1893] 2 Q.B. 390 at p. 396.

chaser of unregistered land, not being a bona fide purchaser of the legal estate for value without notice from a trustee, holds the property subject to the existing trusts. And a trustee who makes an improper profit holds the profit on the trusts which had previously been declared of the property out of which the profit was made.[13]

It may be, however, that the constructive trust doctrine will determine the trusts on which a person, admittedly a trustee, will hold the property. Thus, in a case of mutual wills, the executor of the second party to die needs to know whether he holds on the trusts of that party's will, or under the agreement which was the basis of the mutual wills.[14]

Or it may be that the doctrine determines both these questions. A person who fraudulently persuades a testator to leave a legacy to him by giving an undertaking to hold it on trust for a third party will be compelled by equity to hold the legacy on trust, and on trust for the third party even though the trust was never properly declared according to the provisions of the Wills Act 1837.[15]

These are, it is submitted, all cases of constructive trusts, for they are situations in which either the existence of the trusteeship or the terms of the trust or both are determined by operation of law.

C. The Duties of a Constructive Trustee

The duties and liabilities of a constructive trustee are not necessarily the same as those of an express trustee. This matter will be considered in more detail in Chapter 17. The point here is that a decision that X holds as constructive trustee does not necessarily subject him to the usual trustees' duties in respect of investments, etc.[16] If a person purchases land with constructive but not actual notice of a trust, he will take as constructive trustee; the beneficiaries may enforce the trust against him; but if he is not informed of their claims for some years, it seems that he will not be subjected also to liability for failure to invest in trustee investments and to the usual standard of *exacta diligentia* which is required of express trustees in the performance of their duties.[17] The duties of a constructive trustee have not been made clear; they probably vary with the circumstances and will be greater for a fraudulent trustee than for the purchaser in the situation just discussed.[18]

D. Distinction Between Constructive Trusts, Accountability and Proprietary Remedies.

Circumstances giving rise to a constructive trust may give rise to other remedies also. A person can only be a trustee if there is vested in

---

[13] *Post*, p. 287.
[14] *Post*, p. 298.
[15] *Ante*, pp. 140 *et seq.*; *post*, p. 306.
[16] *Post*, pp. 486 *et seq*.
[17] *Post*, p. 457.
[18] *Restatement of Restitution*, §§ 202–204.

him certain property which he holds upon trust.[19] A constructive trust therefore can only exist where the property in question is vested in the trustees; as, for example, where a trustee of a lease obtains a benefit for himself by negotiating a renewal of the lease in his own favour; the new lease is vested in him and is held on constructive trust for the beneficiary.[20] This type of situation is the subject-matter of the present chapter.

There are two other remedies which may also exist in the same situation (and also in others). These are the equitable proprietary remedy of tracing, and a personal action in equity against a fiduciary for an account. They should be borne in mind when considering constructive trusts; but they must be distinguished from them. They are considered in more detail below.[21]

It has been seen that a trustee who obtains a benefit for himself in breach of trust may be compelled to hold on constructive trust the specific property which he wrongly obtained. If, however, that property is no longer vested in him, he can no longer be trustee of it. The best that can be done in such a situation is to allow the plaintiff to sue for its value. If the trustee in the previous example of the constructive trust of the lease had conveyed the legal estate to a bona fide purchaser for value without notice,[22] and disposed of the proceeds of sale, there could be no constructive trust because there is no property vested in the defendant which can be the subject of the trust. The defendant has done wrong, and the plaintiff may sue him. But this is only a personal action. The defendant is *accountable*; he is not a constructive trustee of any property. And if, at the time of the suit, he has insufficient assets, the plaintiff will be unable to obtain compensation in full.

There is, however, an intermediate step. It may be possible to show that the property, wrongly obtained and disposed of, is now represented by some other property in the trustee's (defendant's) hands; and, by use of the equitable proprietary remedy, to "follow" the original property into that for which it has been exchanged. Direct exchange is of course unlikely; usually the property is sold, and money received in exchange, which is perhaps paid into his bank account. This immediately raises the question how to identify the money in the defendant's assets. This is done by the technique of "tracing"[23]; in short, the money will be treated as that money in the defendant's assets if the plaintiff can show that the defendant's bank account was, since the receipt, always in credit to the amount of the sum in question. The

---

[19] *Re Barney* [1892] 2 Ch. 265 at p. 272, *per* Kekewich J.; (1977) 28 N.I.L.Q. 123 (R. H. Maudsley). *cf.* Pettit, p. 56, suggesting that a constructive trustee who parts with the property retains his status as constructive trustee; his obligation to restore the fund constitutes the trust property.

[20] *Keech* v. *Sandford* (1726) Sel.Cas.t. King 61; *post*, p. 562.

[21] *Post*, pp. 597 *et seq.*

[22] Who would therefore take free from the trust.

[23] *Post*, p. 624.

defendant is treated as spending his own money first. If the balance in his account has never been reduced below the amount of the trust money, that money is treated as having always remained in the account.

The advantages of "tracing" the money in this way are twofold. First, if the defendant should become insolvent, the plaintiff takes in priority to the general creditors, for the money "traced" is trust money, and is kept out of the defendant's insolvency.[24] Secondly, if the money has been invested successfully by the defendant, the plaintiff is allowed to claim the share of the investments which is proportionate to the share which the trust money contributed to the invested fund.[25] A distinction between constructive trusteeship and liability to the "tracing" remedy is that the latter may be available against a person who is not liable as constructive trustee. For example, where trust property is transferred to an innocent volunteer, *i.e.* a person who is not a purchaser and who thus takes subject to the trust but who has neither actual nor constructive knowledge of it, the volunteer is not liable as constructive trustee,[26] but the "tracing" remedy lies against him while he still has the property or its identifiable proceeds.[27] This example illustrates also that this proprietary remedy may lie against a person who has no personal liability to account arising from breach of fiduciary duty.[28]

There are thus three separate matters to consider: constructive trusts, proprietary remedies, and personal actions. They are all interrelated, but each is distinct. Many statements of the law and many decisions fail to make these distinctions, and fail to make clear whether the issue is one of accountability or one of trust.[29] Referring to the decisions on profits made by fiduciaries, Lord Lane C.J. has recently said, "We find it impossible to reconcile much of the language used in these decisions."[30] An attempt in this chapter will be made to limit the discussion of constructive trusts to cases which are properly concerned with trusts. Accountability and the question of liability to proprietary remedies are considered later.[31]

---

[24] *Re Hallett's Estate* (1880) 13 Ch.D. 696.

[25] *Re Tilley's W.T.* [1967] Ch. 1179.

[26] *Post*, p. 639; *Restatement of Restitution*, § 203.

[27] *Re Diplock* [1948] Ch. 465, *post*, p. 625.

[28] The personal action in *Re Diplock*, *supra*, was on a different basis; *post*, p. 644. See *Restatement of Restitution*, § 203.

[29] *Reading* v. *Att.-Gen.* [1951] A.C. 507; *Boardman* v. *Phipps* [1967] 2 A.C. 46; *Selangor United Rubber Estates Ltd.* v. *Cradock* (*No. 3*) [1968] 1 W.L.R. 1555; *Karak Rubber Co. Ltd.* v. *Burden* (*No. 2*) [1972] 1 W.L.R. 602; *cf. Lister* v. *Stubbs* (1890) 45 Ch.D. 1, *post*, p. 627; (1959) 75 L.Q.R. 234 (R. H. Maudsley).

[30] *Re Att.-Gen.'s Reference (No. 1 of 1985)* [1986] Q.B. 491 at p. 503.

[31] *Post*, p. 597.

E. Substantive Trust or Remedy: The American View

We saw that the duties of a constructive trustee bear little relation to those of an ordinary trustee. If the plaintiff merely wishes to have the property returned, the question is whether a constructive trust need be considered as anything beyond a means of demanding the return of the property to which he is entitled in equity, and which is wrongly held by another. This is the way in which constructive trusts are regarded in most jurisdictions in the United States of America and in the *Restatement.* "Where a person holding title to property is subject to an equitable duty to convey it to another on the ground that he would be unjustly enriched if he were permitted to retain it, a constructive trust arises."[32] Thus the duty is to convey to those entitled; not to hold on trust for them.

The constructive trust is regarded as a "remedial rather than substantive" institution.[33] It becomes one of the equitable proprietary remedies, and the substantive constructive trust of the kind found in *Keech* v. *Sandford*[34] disappears. The extent of liability of the defendant will depend on whether or not he was fraudulent, and a number of elaborate rules are established.[35]

The proprietary remedy of a constructive trust is available under this doctrine whenever it is needed to prevent unjust enrichment. It is the proprietary remedy in circumstances in which an action in quasi-contract is the personal remedy. "A constructive trust differs from an express trust in much the same way as a quasi-contractual obligation differs from a contractual obligation"[36]; and, like other equitable remedies, is available where the legal remedy is inadequate, or perhaps not available at all. Thus, in a case of unjust enrichment the plaintiff will sue in quasi-contract for recovery; but if the defendant still has the property, and either the plaintiff wants specific recovery, or the defendant is insolvent, or the property has increased in value while the defendant held it, the plaintiff will be able to rely on the proprietary remedy of a constructive trust.

This concept has much to recommend it. The English cases have however, traditionally regarded the constructive trust as a substantive institution[37]; that is to say, as creating a trust, with trustee and beneficiaries. As pointed out above,[38] the question of the extent to which the usual duties of a trustee will be imposed upon a constructive trustee has

---

[32] *Restatement of Restitution*, § 160; (1955) 71 L.Q.R. 71 (A. W. Scott); *ante*, p. 70; *Carl Zeiss Stiftung* v. *Herbert Smith & Co.* [1969] 2 Ch. 276 at p. 300.

[33] (1920) 33 Harv.L.R. 420 (R. Pound). See also [1988] Conv. 259 (D. Hayton).

[34] (1726) Sel.Cas.t. King 61; *post*, p. 562.

[35] *Post*, p. 619; Goff & Jones, Chap. 2; (1959) 75 L.Q.R. 234 (R. H. Maudsley); (1971) 34 M.L.R. 12 (F. O. B. Babafemi).

[36] *Restatement of Restitution*, § 160, Comment (*a*).

[37] See *Re Sharpe* [1980] 1 W.L.R. 219, where the notion of imposing a constructive trust as a remedy was described as a novel concept in English law.

[38] *Ante*, p. 282.

not been worked out. In many cases, as where the constructive trustee holds property on trust for another person absolutely, the beneficiary has a right to call for a conveyance of the property. But when the beneficiaries are persons entitled by way of succession, or where the beneficiary is a minor,[39] the duties of a constructive trustee look much more like those of an ordinary trustee.

It may be, however, that we are moving towards the remedial concept, at any rate in the banking cases.[40] It has been said that the constructive trust is "now so extensively available as a vehicle for a proprietary remedy that it more closely resembles the American remedial trust than the traditional institutional model created by English law. ... It is no exaggeration to say [when the court is dealing with receipt by a bank of money improperly paid into an account, or improperly transferred out of an account, by its customer] that a bank's potential liability as a constructive trustee has become even more formidable than its more well known exposure to common law claims in contract and tort."[41]

Another aspect of the remedy/institution question is this: is a constructive trust something which follows inevitably from a defined set of circumstances, as a resulting trust does, or is it something which the court can impose or withhold at its discretion, like an injunction? Traditionally, it is the former, but, as we shall see,[42] some of the modern developments appear to resemble the latter, although this approach seems now to be losing favour.

The question of the nature of a constructive trust is separate from the question of the circumstances in which a constructive trust will be found to exist. The two questions are unified under the American doctrine, because the principle of unjust enrichment determines the occasions on which the constructive trust arises, and also the nature of the remedy. Not so in England. We will now examine the circumstances in which a constructive trust has been held to exist. The question of availability of a proprietary "tracing" remedy is postponed to Chapter 22; where it will be seen that the remedy is available only where the plaintiff can show that he was entitled to an equitable proprietary interest in the property claimed: usually by reason of the existence of a fiduciary relationship. But recent developments show how easily such a relationship can be found in deserving cases[43]; and we are getting nearer, in the context of the tracing remedy, to the American view that it should be available wherever the personal remedy is inadequate.

[39] *Keech* v. *Sandford* (1726) Sel. Cas. t. King 61; *post*, p. 562.
[40] *Post*, pp. 289 *et seq.*
[41] (1983) 3 L.S. 283 at p. 292 (R. M. Goode); *cf. Lipkin Gorman* v. *Karpnale Ltd.*, *The Times*, November 19, 1988.
[42] *Post*, p. 309.
[43] *Chase Manhattan Bank N.A.* v. *Israel-British Bank (London) Ltd.* [1980] Ch. 105; (1980) 39 C.L.J. 272 (A. Tettenborn); *ibid.* at p. 275 (G. Jones).

2. WHEN A CONSTRUCTIVE TRUST ARISES

Constructive trusts can arise over a wide variety of situations. No claim is made that those discussed in this section cover the whole field; they are merely illustrations. It will be seen that some of the selected categories lay down specific rules; others rely on general principles, which have been stated in the widest terms.

We have seen that one quality at least that constructive trusts should have in common is the holding of the property in question by the defendant who is held to be a constructive trustee.[44] For a person to be a trustee, the trust property must be vested in him. This principle is followed in the analysis presented here; but that is not done in all judicial and other statements. That is the factor which distinguishes a constructive trust from a situation of accountability. In the latter case, a fiduciary may well be fixed "with liability as a constructive trustee."[45] The plaintiff's remedy is in those cases necessarily a personal claim against the defendant. In the case of a constructive trust, it is against the property in the defendant's hands.

A. Unauthorised Profit by a Trustee or Fiduciary

The principle is that a person in a fiduciary position may not make use of his position to gain a benefit for himself. Trustees, personal representatives,[46] tenants for life[47] and agents[48] are by their "position debarred from keeping a personal advantage derived directly or indirectly out of his fiduciary or quasi-fiduciary position."[49] In the case of bribes, however, it has long been established that no constructive trust arises, the liability being personal only.[50] With other fiduciaries, such

---

[44] *Ante*, p. 283.

[45] *Per* Brightman J. in *Karak Rubber Co. Ltd.* v. *Burden* [1972] 1 W.L.R. 602 at p. 632.

[46] *James* v. *Dean* (1808) 15 Ves.Jr. 236.

[47] *Taster* v. *Marriott* (1768) Amb. 688; *Rawe* v. *Chichester* (1773) Amb. 715; *Pickering* v. *Vowles* (1783) 1 Bro.C.C. 197; *Lloyd Jones* v. *Clark Lloyd* [1919] 1 Ch. 424. But a tenant for life is not accountable in respect of tax reliefs for improvements effected under S.L.A. 1925, s.72(1)(iv), whose cost has been repaid to him under s.75(2); *Re Pelly's W.T.* [1975] Ch. 1.

[48] *De Bussche* v. *Alt* (1878) 8 Ch.D. 286 at p. 310; *Boardman* v. *Phipps* [1967] 2 A.C. 67.

[49] *Re Biss* [1903] 2 Ch. 40 at p. 56.

[50] *Metropolitan Bank* v. *Heiron* (1880) 5 Ex.D. 319; *Lister & Co.* v. *Stubbs* (1890) 45 Ch.D. 1; *Islamic Republic of Iran Shipping Lines* v. *Denby* [1987] 1 F.T.L.R. 30; *post*, p. 627. For the principal's right to rescind any contract with the third party, see *Logicrose Ltd.* v. *Southend United Football Club Ltd.* [1988] 1 W.L.R. 1256, holding also that the principal can recover the bribe from the agent whether he affirms or repudiates the transaction between the agent and the third party.

as company directors,[51] partners,[52] mortgagors[53] and mortgagees,[54] the question is one of fact whether the benefit was obtained by reason or independently of, the fiduciary relationship.[55] The category of fiduciaries is not closed.[56]

These matters are dealt with in Chapter 20. We will there see that a trustee must not renew in his own favour any lease held on trust; nor may he purchase the reversion on any such lease; nor may he purchase the trust property. He must not make any incidental profits out of his trusteeship. In the present context, one example must suffice.

> In *Boardman* v. *Phipps*,[57] the trustees held a minority shareholding in a private company which was not being efficiently managed. Boardman acted as solicitor to the trust, and was therefore a fiduciary. He decided that the beneficiaries would be in a better position if the trustees had control of the company, but no trust money was available to buy the extra shares. Boardman and one of the beneficiaries therefore bought the necessary shares themselves and reorganised the company. All this was done in good faith and with the object of enhancing the trust holding. Both the personal and the trust holdings increased in value. A majority of the House of Lords held that Boardman was constructive trustee of the profit made on his personal shareholding. The opportunity to make the profit arose out of his fiduciary relationship with the trust, and certain confidential information had been used in the process. However, compensation was ordered from the trust in recognition of the work and skill involved.

B. Liability of Strangers to the Trust[58]

Persons, not appointed trustees, may be liable as if they were so appointed, if they intermeddle with the trust funds or with the admi-

---

[51] *Williams* v. *Barton* [1927] 2 Ch. 9; *Re Macadam* [1946] Ch. 73; *cf. Re Dover Coalfield Extension Ltd.* [1908] 1 Ch. 65; *Re Sykes* [1909] 2 Ch. 241; *Re Gee* [1948] Ch. 284; *Re Northcote's W.T.* [1949] 1 All E.R. 442; *Re Llewellin's W.T.* [1949] Ch. 225; *Regal (Hastings)* v. *Gulliver* [1967] 2 A.C. 134; *Selangor United Rubber Estates Ltd.* v. *Cradock (No. 3)* [1968] 1 W.L.R. 1555; *Guinnes plc* v. *Saunders* [1988] 1 W.L.R. 863.

[52] *Featherstonhaugh* v. *Fenwick* (1810) 17 Ves.Jr. 298; *Clegg* v. *Fishwick* (1849) 1 Mac. & G. 294; *Clegg* v. *Edmondson* (1857) 8 De G.M. & G. 787.

[53] *Leigh* v. *Burnett* (1885) 29 Ch.D. 231.

[54] *Nelson* v. *Hannam and Smith* [1943] Ch. 59. A mortgagee is not a trustee of his power of sale, but is trustee of any surplus proceeds. This trust was originally imposed by equity, but is now statutory; L.P.A. 1925, s.105.

[55] Presumably joint tenants and tenants in common should be added because of the trust for sale introduced by L.P.A. 1925, ss.34–36. Previously, there was no fiduciary relationship; *Kennedy* v. *De Trafford* [1897] A.C. 180 (tenants in common); *Re Biss* [1903] 2 Ch. 40; *Re Jarvis* [1958] 1 W.L.R. 815 (joint tenants); *Savage* v. *Dunningham* [1974] Ch. 181. See generally (1981) 97 L.Q.R. 51 (J. C. Shepherd).

[56] *English* v. *Dedham Vale Properties Ltd.* [1978] 1 W.L.R. 93. See also *Swain* v. *Law Society* [1983] A.C. 598; *Appleby* v. *Cowley, The Times*, April 14, 1982.

[57] [1967] 2 A.C. 67, *post*, p. 571.

[58] See generally (1985) 27 Malaya Law Rev. 313 (D. Hayton); (1986) 102 L.Q.R. 114 and 267 (C. Harpum).

nistration of the trust. Intermeddling can take an unlimited number of different forms; but the cases have traditionally been regarded as falling into two distinct categories: "knowing assistance" and "knowing receipt."[59] It is doubtful, however, for reasons examined below, whether this classification should be retained.[60] But whatever the heading of liability, the existence of the trust must be established. Knowledge of a "doubtful equity" does not suffice; hence a solicitor was not a constructive trustee of moneys received in payment of costs and expenses paid by a client for work done in defending an action in which the plaintiff was claiming that the client was a trustee of the whole of its assets.[61] It would be otherwise if he knew that the plaintiff's claim was well-founded.

(i) "Knowing Assistance"[62]

(a) *Terminology*. An agent or other fiduciary may be liable to make good the loss to a trust without the trust property being vested in him and without his purporting to act as trustee; as where an agent knowingly participates with a trustee in a breach of trust.

Ungoed-Thomas J. said in *Selangor United Rubber Estates* v. *Cradock (No. 3)*[63] that such a person is not a trustee *de son tort*; and it is submitted that, as no trust property is vested in him, he should not be called a constructive, or any other kind of trustee. The question at issue however is only one of personal liability; and the matter is thus merely one of terminology. It makes no practical difference whether we speak of the personal liability as a constructive trustee, or of the liability of a fiduciary to account. It may be said however that, as there is no trusteeship, the matter should not be considered in this chapter, but hereafter; that is so; but because the cases are closely allied with

---

[59] The categories are based on Lord Selborne's speech in *Barnes* v. *Addy* (1874) L.R. 9 Ch. App. 244 at pp. 251–252, which was conveniently summarised as follows by Buckley L.J. in *Belmont Finance Corporation* v. *Williams Furniture Ltd. (No. 2)* [1980] 1 All E.R. 393 at p. 405, "If a stranger to a trust (a) receives and becomes chargeable with some part of the trust fund or (b) assists the trustees of a trust with knowledge of the facts in a dishonest design on the part of the trustees to misapply some part of a trust fund, he is liable as a constructive trustee." See also Brightman J. in *Karak Rubber Co. Ltd* v. *Burden (No. 2)* [1972] 1 W.L.R. 602 at p. 633; *per* Ungoed-Thomas J. in *Selangor United Rubber Estates Ltd.* v. *Cradock (No. 3)* [1968] 1 W.L.R. 1555.

[60] See *post*, p. 296.

[61] *Carl Zeiss Stiftung* v. *Herbert Smith & Co. (No. 2)* [1969] 2 Ch. 276; (1969) 85 L.Q.R. 160 (P.V.B.); (1986) 102 L.Q.R. 267 at p. 287 (C. Harpum). See also *Williams* v. *Williams* (1881) 17 Ch.D. 437; *Competitive Insurance Co. Ltd.* v. *Davies Investments Ltd.* [1975] 1 W.L.R. 1240.

[62] See further (1986) 102 L.Q.R. 114 (C. Harpum). In *Logicrose Ltd.* v. *Southend United Football Club Ltd.* [1988] 1 W.L.R. 1256, these authorities were held applicable to the case where a third party bribes an agent, in order to determine whether he should be treated as taking the risk that the agent would conceal the matter (with the result that the principal who recovers the bribe from the agent is not obliged to return it to the third party if the contract is rescinded).

[63] [1968] 1 W.L.R. 1555 at p. 1579.

those of trusteeship *de son tort,* it will be convenient to discuss the question here.

(b) *Knowledge of the Breach.* In *Barnes* v. *Addy,*[64] Lord Selborne laid down the test of liability as that of "actually participating in any fraudulent conduct of the trustee to the injury of the *cestui que trust*" and as assisting "with knowledge in a dishonest and fraudulent design on the part of the trustees."

In that case trust funds were misapplied by a sole trustee. The defendant, a solicitor, had advised against the appointment of the sole trustee, and of the transfer of the funds to him; but he prepared the necessary documents. He was held not liable.

In *Soar* v. *Ashwell,*[65] Lord Esher M.R. put the test in similar words. " . . . a person not nominated a trustee may be bound to liability as if he were a nominated trustee, namely, where he has knowingly assisted a nominated trustee in a fraudulent and dishonest disposition of the trust property."

Thus, a fraudulent or dishonest[66] breach of trust must be proved under this head, though not, as we shall see, under the second.[67]

(c) *Actual or Constructive Knowledge.* These statements leave open the question whether it is necessary to show that the defendant subjectively knew of the dishonest design, or whether it is sufficient that he ought to have known. This is a matter of great practical importance, because fraudulent designs in the financial world are highly complex, and can involve participants who never suspect any wrongdoing. Such was the case with the District Bank in *Selangor United Rubber Estates Ltd.* v. *Cradock (No. 3).*[68]

---

[64] (1874) L.R. 9 Ch.App. 244 at pp. 251, 252; *Selangor United Rubber Estates Ltd.* v. *Cradock (No. 3), supra,* at p. 1590; *Karak Rubber Co. Ltd.* v. *Burden (No. 2)* [1972] 1 W.L.R. 602 at p. 634.

[65] [1893] 2 Q.B. 390 at pp. 394–395; *Carl Zeiss Stiftung* v. *Herbert Smith & Co., supra,* at p. 291. The allegation of dishonesty must be clearly and unequivocally pleaded; *Belmont Finance Corporation* v. *Williams Furniture Ltd. (No. 1)* [1979] Ch. 250 at p. 268; (*Lipkin Gorman* v. *Karpnale Ltd., The Times,* November 19, 1988.

[66] In this context the meaning of the words is the same, *Belmont (No. 1)* [1979] Ch. 250 at p. 267.

[67] *Belmont (No. 2)* [1980] 1 All E.R. 393, *post,* p. 293.

[68] [1968] 1 W.L.R. 1555; (1969) 85 L.Q.R. 167 (P.V.B.); followed by *Karak Rubber Co. Ltd.* v. *Burden (No. 2)* [1972] 1 W.L.R. 602; *Baden, Delvaux and Lecuit* v. *Société Generale pour Favoriser le Développement du Commerce et de l'Industrie en France S.A.* [1983] B.C.L.C. 325. In *Rowlandson* v. *National Westminster Bank Ltd.* [1978] 1 W.L.R. 798, the bank opened a "trust account" on the instructions of Mrs. Mathews, which was for the benefit of her four grandchildren. Two of her sons were the signatories. One son applied the money for his own purposes. The bank was held liable, applying *Selangor,* on the ground that it should have questioned the withdrawals. It appears, however, that some of the bank cases could have been argued on the basis of "knowing receipt" (*infra*); (1986) 102 L.Q.R. 114 at p. 151 (C. Harpum). See also *Lipkin Gorman* v. *Karpnale Ltd., supra,* preferring a contract analysis.

A complex scheme involved a number of transactions whose basic objective was to use the company's money for the purchase of its own shares. This was an improper and dishonest application of the company's assets.[69] The company, in liquidation, sought to impose equitable liability upon the defendants. The first defendant, who was the leading spirit in these operations, was bankrupt. Some of the defendants were unaware of the nature of the transactions. Others did know.

Ungoed-Thomas J. held them all liable. It was sufficient, in the case of the directors, that they acted on the directions of Cradock who of course knew all the facts; and in the case of the District Bank that they should have known that the payments were a dishonest application of the company's funds.

This rule places an undue burden on innocent defendants, and it is thought that the better rule is to require that the stranger have actual knowledge of the fraudulent or dishonest design.[70] This was the view of the Court of Appeal in *Belmont Finance Corporation* v. *Williams Furniture Ltd. (No. 1)*,[71] where Buckley L.J. said that the degree of knowledge required was actual knowledge; constructive notice was insufficient save in the sense that, "If he wilfully shuts his eyes to dishonesty, or wilfully or recklessly fails to make such inquiries as an honest and reasonable man would make, he may be found to have involved himself in the fraudulent character of the design, or in any case to be disentitled to rely on lack of actual knowledge of the design as a defence."[72] Goff L.J. also doubted whether constructive notice "in the section 199 sense" was enough.[73] It has subsequently been held that liability will also arise where the defendant had knowledge of circumstances which would have indicated the facts to an honest and reasonable man, or knowledge of circumstances which would have put an honest and reasonable man on inquiry, although such knowledge should only be imputed in exceptional circumstances in commercial

---

[69] [1968] 1 W.L.R. 1555 at pp. 1610, 1611; Companies Act 1948, s.54. See now Companies Act 1985, ss.151–158.

[70] *Carl Zeiss Stiftung* v. *Herbert Smith & Co.* [1969] 2 Ch. 276; *Competitive Insurance Co. Ltd.* v. *Davies Investments Ltd.* [1975] 1 W.L.R. 1240; *Belmont Finance Corporation Ltd.* v. *Williams Furniture Ltd. (No. 1)* [1979] Ch. 250; *Consul Development Pty. Ltd.* v. *D.P.C. Estates Ltd.* (1975) 132 C.L.R. 373; *Re Montagu's S.T.* [1987] Ch. 264 at p. 272; *Lipkin Gorman* v. *Karpnale Ltd.*, *The Times*, November 19, 1988; (1976) 92 L.Q.R. 4; (1976) 92 L.Q.R. 360 at p. 399 (R. M. Goode); (1977) 51 A.L.J. 635 (J. D. Heydon); (1985) 27 Malaya Law Rev. 313 (D. Hayton); (1986) 102 L.Q.R. 114 (C. Harpum); (1987) 1 *Trust Law & Practice* 130 (M. J. Brindle and R. J. A. Hooley). Oakley, *Constructive Trusts*, (2nd ed.) p. 102.

[71] [1979] Ch. 250. The discussion was *obiter*.

[72] *Ibid.* at p. 267.

[73] *Ibid.* at p. 275, referring to L.P.A. 1925, s.199. His Lordship preferred the statements in *Carl Zeiss* and *Competitive Insurance* to those in *Selangor* and *Karak*.

contexts.[74] It is submitted, however, that the views of the Court of Appeal in *Belmont* are to be preferred. Of course, there will be no liability if the design is not dishonest or fraudulent.[75] The claim under this head failed in the *Belmont Finance* case.[76]

(ii) "Knowing Receipt and Dealing"[77]

(a) *Personal and Proprietary Remedies.* A basic principle of property law is that any person who receives trust property, not being a purchaser for value without notice, takes subject to the trust. This is so whether he took with actual or constructive notice. So long as he retains the property he is bound to return it, and the proprietary remedy of tracing[78] is available in respect of the property or its identifiable proceeds. However, this is different from the question whether the recipient should be under a *personal* liability as constructive trustee. The distinction is important if he no longer has the property. If he is a constructive trustee, his liability remains. If he is not a constructive trustee, his liability is confined to the return of the property or its proceeds while still in his possession. It will be appreciated that not every transferee who fails to prove that he was a bona fide purchaser of the legal estate without notice is subjected to the additional liability of a constructive trustee. An "innocent volunteer,"[79] for example, who took without notice that the property was trust property transferred in breach of trust cannot take free of the trust, but will not incur the liability of a constructive trustee.

(b) *Actual or Constructive Knowledge.* While constructive knowledge clearly suffices where the question is whether the recipient took the property subject to the trust, the position is less clear where the question is whether he has incurred the personal liability of a construc-

---

[74] *Baden, Delvaux and Lecuit* v. *Société Generale pour Favoriser le Développement du Commerce et de l'Industrie en France S.A.* [1983] B.C.L.C. 325 (Peter Gibson J.), following *Selangor* and *Karak* in preference to *Carl Zeiss* and *Belmont*. See All E.R. Rev. 1983, p. 352 (P. J. Clarke); (1985) 1 Insolvency Law & Practice 108 (R. Gregory); (1986) 102 L.Q.R. 114 at p. 154 (C. Harpum).

[75] *Competitive Insurance Co. Ltd.* v. *Davies Investments Ltd.* [1975] 1 W.L.R. 1240: *Belmont Finance Corporation Ltd.* v. *Williams Furniture Ltd. (No. 1), supra.*

[76] *Post,* p. 293.

[77] Constructive trustees within this category were described in *Selangor United Rubber Estates* v. *Cradock (No. 3)* [1968] 1 W.L.R. 1555 as trustees *de son tort,* by analogy with executors *de son tort.* The distinction was once significant in the context of the defence of limitation, but is of no significance today; *ibid.,* at p. 1579.

[78] *Post,* Chapter 22.

[79] *Re Diplock* [1948] Ch. 465 at pp. 478–479; *ante,* p. 284; *post,* p. 625. The innocent volunteers in that case were not personally liable as constructive trustees because they were under no duty to investigate the validity of the gift and were entitled to assume that the executors were acting properly; *ibid.,* at pp. 477–479. They were, however, personally liable in equity as having received property to which another was entitled (*post,* p. 644). The latter heading of personal liability somewhat undermines the rule that there is no personal liability as constructive trustee unless the conscience is affected.

tive trustee. The weight of authority favours the view that constructive knowledge suffices here also. On this view it is still important to distinguish "knowing assistance" and "knowing receipt," as actual knowledge seems to be necessary in the former category. More recent cases, however, favour the view that actual knowledge is necessary to found personal liability in the "knowing receipt" category also. If this view becomes established, it will no longer be necessary to distinguish between "knowing assistance" and "knowing receipt," save that the breach of trust in the former case, but not in the latter, must have been fraudulent.[80]

The traditional view is that where a person, not nominated as a trustee "has received trust property with actual or constructive notice that it is trust property transferred in breach of trust, or because (not being a bona fide purchaser for value without notice), he acquires notice subsequent to such receipt and then deals with the property in a manner inconsistent with the trust,"[81] he is a constructive trustee.

The question can arise in a wide variety of circumstances. Commonly, in these cases, the defendant is aware of the trust; indeed, he may be trying to administer it. Some decisions, however, hold that liability can arise where he does not know, but ought to know. Thus, in *Belmont Finance Corporation* v. *Williams Furniture Ltd. (No. 2)*[82]:

> The defendant company owned all the shares in City Industrial Finance Ltd. (City) which, in turn owned all the shares in Belmont. One James was Chairman and controlling shareholder in all these companies; and Grosscurth was Chairman and controlling shareholder in Maximum Finance Ltd. (Maximum).
>
> A scheme was arranged under which Belmont would purchase all the shares in Maximum for £500,000 in cash, a sum grossly in excess of its asset value; and Grosscurth would buy from City all the shares in Belmont. Various other terms provided for Belmont to have sufficient cash for the purchase of Maximum; and for Grosscurth accordingly to be able to pay City for the Belmont shares. The transaction was held to be unlawful under Companies Act 1948, s.54, under which it was unlawful for a company to give any financial assistance towards the purchase of its own shares.[83]
>
> In the subsequent insolvency of Belmont, the receiver claimed damages for conspiracy, and claimed also to recover from City and its directors the £489,000 which City received on the sale of the Belmont shares, on the ground that that sum had been received by

---

[80] *Ante*, p. 290.
[81] *Per* Brightman J. in *Karak Rubber Co. Ltd.* v. *Burden, supra* at p. 632.
[82] [1980] 1 All E.R. 393; see also (*No. 1*) [1979] Ch. 250; (1979) 42 M.L.R. 707 and (1981) 44 M.L.R. 107 (R. Gregory); (1979) 38 C.L.J. 278 and (1980) 39 C.L.J. 276 (L. S. Sealy). It is also assumed in *Re Diplock* [1948] Ch. 465 at pp. 477–479 that constructive knowledge would suffice.
[83] See now Companies Act 1985, ss.151–158.

the directors in breach of their fiduciary duty in respect of the funds of the company. Foster J., finding that the transactions were bona fide business operations, dismissed the action. The Court of Appeal reversed, and found for the receiver under the conspiracy claim and under that as constructive trustee.

The liability of City as constructive trustee was established by showing that the payment of £500,000 to Grosscurth was a misapplication of the funds of the company,[84] and that £489,000 of this effectively returned to City. City, through its agents and directors, had knowledge of all the facts which established the improper use of the funds, and knew or ought to have known that the £489,000 which it received was money impressed with a trust. It was immaterial that, as the judge found, the directors of City did not act fraudulently. Even assuming, though the Court of Appeal appeared to accept the judge's conclusion with reluctance, that the directors of City regarded the purchase of Maximum as a sound and bona fide commercial transaction, they and City were liable. Liability arose by receipt of the trust monies; there was no need to prove fraud.

Similarly in *International Sales and Agencies Ltd.* v. *Marcus*,[85] where the defendant, a moneylender, lent £30,000 to F personally. F was a major shareholder in the plaintiff company. This debt was repaid after F's death (insolvent) by his friend M, a director and shareholder of the company, who used company money to do so. The defendant was liable to return the money. He took it as constructive trustee, having been aware that it belonged to the company and that the payment by M was a breach of M's fiduciary duty. This was a case of actual knowledge, but constructive knowledge would have sufficed:

" . . . the knowing recipient of trust property for his own purposes will become a constructive trustee of what he receives if either he was in fact aware at the time that his receipt was affected by a breach of trust, or if he deliberately shut his eyes to the real nature of the transfer to him (this could be called 'imputed notice'), or if an ordinary reasonable man in his position and with his attributes ought to have known of the relevant breach. This I equate with constructive notice. Such a position would arise where such a person would have been put on inquiry as to the probability of a breach of trust. I am satisfied that in respect of actual recipients of trust property to be used for their own purposes the law does not require proof of knowing participation in a fraudulent transaction or want of probity, in the sense of dishonesty on the part of the recipient."[86]

More recently, however, it has been held that actual knowledge is

---

[84] *Russell* v. *Wakefield Waterworks Co.* (1875) L.R. 20 Eq. 474 at p. 479, *per* Jessel M.R.
[85] [1982] 3 All E.R. 551. A defence based on European Communities Act 1972, s.9(1), failed.
[86] *Ibid.* at p. 558 (*per* Lawson J.).

required to found personal liability as constructive trustee in the receipt cases. The question arose in *Re Montagu's S.T.*[87]

Trustees transferred certain settled chattels to the beneficiary (the tenth Duke) absolutely, in breach of trust. The situation resulted from an "honest muddle" by all concerned. The Duke's solicitor had at an earlier stage been aware of the terms of the settlement. The Duke disposed of a number of the chattels during his lifetime. After his death, the eleventh Duke claimed that his predecessor had become a constructive trustee of them. Megarry V.-C. held that, while the tenth Duke's estate must return any remaining chattels or their traceable proceeds, the Duke was not liable as constructive trustee because he had no actual knowledge that the chattels were trust property transferred in breach of trust. Even if he had once understood the terms of the settlement, there was nothing to suggest that he remembered them so as to be aware at the date of receipt that the chattels were trust property. Nor was there any reason to impute the solicitor's knowledge to the Duke, by analogy with the doctrine of imputed notice.

The Vice-Chancellor emphasised that the relevant question was whether the recipient had *knowledge*, not whether he had *notice* according to the rules established under the doctrine of notice. If "constructive notice" was not enough in the "assistance" cases, there was no reason why it should be here. The doctrine of notice dealt with the question whether an equitable interest was binding on a transferee. The question in the present context was whether a person was to have imposed on him the burdens of trusteeship. "I do not see why one of the touchstones for determining the burdens on property should be the same as that for deciding whether to impose a personal obligation on a man. The cold calculus of constructive and imputed notice does not seem to me to be an appropriate instrument for deciding whether a man's conscience is sufficiently affected for it to be right to bind him by the obligations of a constructive trustee."[88] The fundamental question was whether the conscience of the recipient was bound, that is, whether there was a "want of probity." It would be difficult to reconcile all the authorities, but the position could be summarised as follows: the doctrine of tracing and the imposition of a constructive trust are governed by different rules; a constructive trust should not be imposed unless the conscience of the recipient is affected; this depends on knowledge, not "notice"; "want of probity" includes actual knowledge, shutting one's eyes to the obvious, or wilfully and recklessly

---

[87] [1987] Ch. 264 (decided 1985). The decision was followed by Alliot J. in *Lipkin Gorman* v. *Karpnale Ltd.* [1987] 1 W.L.R. 987, where a solicitor embezzled client's money and spent it on gambling, but the Court of Appeal decided on other grounds; *The Times*, November 19, 1988.

[88] [1987] Ch. 264 at p. 273.

failing to make such enquiries as a reasonable and honest man would make; it does not include knowledge of circumstances which would indicate the facts to an honest and reasonable man or would put the latter on enquiry; a person is not treated as having knowledge of a fact he has genuinely forgotten; it is doubtful whether there is a doctrine of "imputed knowledge."

This formulation, it is submitted, has much to recommend it, although it cannot yet be said to be established in law.[89] Constructive notice remains relevant to the question of priorities and tracing, but should play no part in establishing personal liability as constructive trustee.[90] For this purpose actual knowledge is required, whether the case is one of "knowing assistance" or "knowing receipt." Both categories should be unified by the principle of "want of probity."

(iii) **Agent of Trustees Holding Trust Property**[91] An agent of the trustees, such as a solicitor, banker, or stockbroker is not necessarily a constructive trustee whenever he is in possession of the trust property, knowing it to be such. Although in receipt of the property, it will not normally have been transferred to him in breach of trust, as required by the "knowing receipt" rule, but in the ordinary process of delegation.[92] Of course, if it was transferred to him in breach of trust he will be liable under the principles discussed above, provided he had the necessary degree of knowledge. Likewise he will be liable under the "knowing assistance" rule if he knowingly assists the trustees in a fraudulent breach of trust. Indeed, most of the cases on "knowing assistance" involve agents of the trustees. In the absence of such circumstances, he will only be subjected to a trustee's liability if he receives the property into his hands in connection with his assumption of the trustee's office and duties. In *Williams-Ashman* v. *Price and Williams*,[93] Bennett J. treated *Mara* v. *Browne*[94] as authority for the proposition that "an agent in possession of money which he knows to be trust money, so long as he acts honestly, is not accountable to the beneficiaries interested in the trust money unless he intermeddles in the trust by doing acts characteristic of a trustee and outside the duties of an agent." Thus, where a solicitor received trust money through his own account, and invested it in unauthorised mortgages on the instructions of the trustees, the solicitor was held to be acting in his capacity as a solicitor, and not liable as a constructive trustee.[95] And a stockbroker

---

[89] See (1986) 102 L.Q.R. 267 and (1987) 50 M.L.R. 217 (C. Harpum); (1987) 1 *Trust Law & Practice* 130 (M. J. Brindle and R. J. A. Hooley).
[90] See Oakley, *Constructive Trusts* (2nd ed.), p. 109; (1985) 27 Malaya Law Rev. 313 and (1987) 46 C.L.J. 395 (D. Hayton).
[91] See (1986) 102 L.Q.R. 114 at pp. 130 *et seq.* (C. Harpum).
[92] *Post*, p. 532.
[93] [1942] Ch. 219 at p. 228.
[94] [1896] 1 Ch. 199.
[95] *Mara* v. *Browne* [1896] 1 Ch. 199 (any negligence action would have been statute-barred); *Williams-Ashman* v. *Price and Williams* [1942] Ch. 219.

would not be liable as constructive trustee for receiving trust money and investing it on the trustee's instructions in an unauthorised investment. The remedy is against the trustees.

If the agent does not know that the property is trust property, he is not liable if he acts honestly and within the scope of his agency, even if the facts were such as to put him on enquiry.[96] It has been suggested, however, that if the agent applies the property for his own benefit, constructive knowledge of the trust would be a sufficient basis for liability.[97]

(iv) Liability of Partner of Constructive Trustee.

In *Re Bell's Indenture,*[98] trustee-beneficiaries of a marriage settlement dissipated nearly £30,000 of the trust fund with the knowledge and assistance of H, a partner in a firm of solicitors acting for the trustees. The misappropriated trust monies passed through the firm's client account. When the dissipation was discovered, the beneficiaries sought to make H's partner, who, it was conceded, had acted honestly and reasonably throughout,[99] liable as constructive trustee. H's liability was not disputed. Vinelott J. held that a solicitor has the implied authority of his partners to accept trust monies as agent of the trustees, but has no implied authority to accept office as trustee, nor to constitute himself a constructive trustee, and so make his partners liable for any misapplication of the trust property. The monies had not been received by the partnership as trustees, thus H's partner was not liable as constructive trustee. Nor was he liable under the provisions of the Partnership Act 1890.[1]

The decision in *Blyth* v. *Fladgate,*[2] where, in similar circumstances, the solicitor's partners were held jointly liable, was treated as a case on "very special facts," where the partners became trustees because there were no trustees at the time the money was paid into the firm's account, and, consequently, the partners could not be considered to be merely agents of the trustees.[3] There was no principle that the partners

---

[96] *Williams* v. *Williams* (1881) 17 Ch.D. 437; *Competitive Insurance Co. Ltd.* v. *Davies Investments Ltd.* [1975] 1 W.L.R. 1240.

[97] (1986) 102 L.Q.R. 114 (C. Harpum). See also Birks, *Introduction to the Law of Restitution*, p. 445, distinguishing agents who received beneficially and those who receive ministerially.

[98] [1980] 1 W.L.R. 1217; [1981] Conv. 310 (P. Luxton).

[99] *Quaere* if he had acted honestly but failed to make inquiries which a reasonable solicitor would have made.

[1] See s.13, providing that if a partner, being a trustee, improperly employs trust property in the business or on the account of the partnership, no other partner is liable for the trust property to the beneficiaries. It is otherwise if the partner has notice of the breach of trust, and nothing in this section prevents the recovery of trust money from the firm while still in its possession or under its control. Nor was the firm liable under ss.10 or 11 of the Act. On this aspect of the decision, see [1981] Conv. 310 (P. Luxton).

[2] [1891] 1 Ch. 337.

[3] Whose liability was discussed above.

became liable merely by reason of the fact that the monies received and paid in breach of trust had passed through the firm's client account. That this was the correct explanation was clear from *Mara* v. *Browne*,[4] where Lord Herschell said "it is not within the scope of the implied authority of a partner in such a business that he should so act as to make himself a constructive trustee, and thereby subject his partner to the same liability."[5]

C. Mutual Wills[6]

Two persons (usually husband and wife, but not always)[7] may agree that, on the death of the first to die, all their property shall be enjoyed by the survivor, and after his (her) death by nominated beneficiaries; and may make mutual wills to that effect. The survivor may be given a life interest[8] or an absolute interest.[9] The question is whether, and to what extent, such an agreement controls the devolution of their property.

(i) **Agreement Necessary.** Before any remedy can be obtained, an agreement to make wills and not to revoke them[10] between the parties must be proved. The standard of proof is the ordinary civil standard (*i.e.* on balance of probabilities); the evidence must be "clear and satisfactory" and may be extrinsic, as where the agreement is substantiated by family conversations.[11] The mere fact that the wills were made simultaneously and in the same form is not, of itself, proof of an agreement although it is a relevant circumstance to be taken into account.[12] But the court may infer an agreement from the conduct of the parties, the circumstances and the terms of the wills.[13] Preferably the agreement, if there was one, should be recited in the will.

In *Re Oldham*,[14] a husband and wife made mutual wills in similar form; each spouse left his (or her) property to the other absolutely with the same provisions in the event of the other predeceasing. There was no evidence of an agreement that they should be irrevocable. After the husband's death, the wife married again, and made a new will which was quite different from the earlier one. The second will was upheld; Astbury J. saying: "The fact that the two wills were

---

[4] [1896] 1 Ch. 199, *ante*, p. 296. But see [1981] Conv. 310 (P. Luxton).
[5] *Ibid.* at p. 208.
[6] (1951) 15 Conv.(N.S.) 28 (G. B. Graham); (1951) 14 M.L.R. 140 (J. D. B. Mitchell); (1970) 34 Conv.(N.S) 230 (R. Burgess).
[7] *Walpole* v. *Lord Orford* (1797) 3 Ves.Jr. 402.
[8] *Dufour* v. *Pereira* (1769) Dick. 419.
[9] *Re Green* [1951] Ch. 148.
[10] *In the Goods of Heys* [1914] P. 192.
[11] *Re Cleaver* [1981] 1 W.L.R. 939.
[12] *Ibid.*
[13] *Dufour* v. *Pereira* (1769) Dick. 419; *Stone* v. *Hoskins* [1905] P. 194; *Re Hagger* [1930] 2 Ch. 190; *Re Green* [1951] Ch. 148.
[14] [1925] Ch. 75.

made in identical terms does not necessarily connote any agreement beyond that of so making them . . . there is no evidence . . . that there was an agreement that the trust in the mutual will should in all circumstances be irrevocable by the survivor who took the benefit." The parties had left their estates to each other "absolutely." They "may have thought it quite safe to trust the other. . . . But that is a very different thing from saying that they bound themselves by a trust that should be operative in all circumstances and in all cases."[15]

In *Re Cleaver*,[16] on the other hand, the evidence of mutual wills was sufficient. An elderly couple married in 1967. The husband had three children. They made wills in each other's favour absolutely, and in default to the three children. In 1974, each of them reduced the share of one daughter, Martha, to a life interest. After the husband's death the wife made a new will consistent with the earlier one. Thereafter she made a further will enlarging Martha's share from a life interest to an absolute interest; and by her last will she left her residue to Martha and her husband, and nothing to the other two children. It was held that the wife's executors held the estate on the trusts of the 1974 will. Sufficient evidence of an agreement to make mutual wills was shown by the simultaneity and similarity of the original wills; the pattern of successive wills made together; the fact that both parties reduced Martha's interest; the faithful terms of the first will made after the husband's death; and the fact that, in family conversations, the wife had regarded herself as under an obligation to leave her estate to the children.

(ii) Remedies on the Contract. The agreement is binding between the parties. If it is broken by the first party to die, his estate will be liable in damages to the survivor.[17] If the breach is by the second party to die, as by revocation or alteration of his will, it has always been assumed that no remedy could be obtained against him or his estate under the contract. The law which has developed on the subject is based upon a trust which arises in appropriate cases in favour of the beneficiaries.

There seems, however, to be no reason why the principle of *Beswick* v. *Beswick*[18] should not be applied in this situation. The agreement between the parties is a contract for valuable consideration. The beneficiaries are not parties to the contract, and not within the consideration. The estate of the first to die, however, is in a similar position, analytically, to Mrs. Beswick, the administratrix of her husband. It seems that an action for specific performance of the contract would lie

---

[15] *Ibid.* at pp. 88–89; *Gray* v. *Perpetual Trustee Co.* [1928] A.C. 391.
[16] *Supra.*
[17] *Robinson* v. *Ommanney* (1883) 23 Ch.D. 285; but not where the revocation of the first will is by the subsequent marriage of the covenantor.
[18] [1968] A.C. 58.

by the estate against the survivor or his estate; and a decree of specific performance would effect the carrying out of the trusts. There has been no opportunity yet for this line of argument to be considered. An examination of the problems which have arisen in treating the interests of the beneficiaries as trusts, as will be seen, makes a contractual solution stand out as very attractive.[19]

(iii) Trusts Created by Mutual Wills. A will is always revocable; an agreement not to revoke it does not make it irrevocable.[20] Thus, if the survivor of an agreement to make mutual wills destroys his will, he will die intestate: and if he makes a new will, that later one will be admitted to probate. But the disposition of his property on his death will be affected by the agreement. For the principle is established that the agreement between the parties, followed by the death of the first party, relying on the undertaking of the other party to observe the agreement, creates trusts in favour of the intended beneficiaries, which are enforceable against the property of the survivor.[21] Of the leading case of *Dufour* v. *Pereira*,[22] Clauson J. said[23]: "*Dufour* v. *Pereira* decides that where there is a joint will . . . on the death of the first testator the position as regards that part of the property which belongs to the survivor is that the survivor will be treated . . . as holding the property on trust to apply it so as to carry out the effect of the joint will." A number of difficulties arise concerning the operation of such trusts.[24]

(a) *When Does the Trust Arise?* Mitchell says that there are three possibilities[25]: When the agreement was made; When the first testator dies; When the survivor dies. It is clear that no trust exists from the date of the agreement. For either party can revoke before either dies, on giving notice to the other[26]; and even notice is not necessary in the case of the first to die, for the survivor has notice on the first death and will not be prejudiced.[27] And the survivor in such circumstances is unable to establish any trust in his favour against the estate of the first to die.[28] Nor can the death of the survivor be the correct time. For where a beneficiary died between the date of the death of the first to

---

[19] See (1979) 29 U. of Toronto L.J. 390 (T. G. Youdan). The executor must be willing to sue. See [1982] Conv. 228 (K. Hodkinson), suggesting that the ultimate beneficiary should be the executor. The contractual solution is doubted in Pettit, p. 114, n. 8.

[20] *Vynior's Case* (1609) 8 Co.Rep. 81b.

[21] *In the Goods of Heys* [1914] P. 192; *Stone* v. *Hoskins* [1905] P. 194 (later will of first to die).

[22] (1769) Dick. 419; a case of a joint will, but the same principles apply to mutual wills.

[23] *Re Hagger* [1930] 2 Ch. 190 at p. 195.

[24] These difficulties are discussed in (1979) 29 U. of Toronto L.J. at pp. 411–419 (T. G. Youdan).

[25] (1951) 14 M.L.R. 137 (J. D. B. Mitchell).

[26] *Dufour* v. *Pereira* (1769) Dick. 419 at p. 420.

[27] *Ibid.*

[28] *Stone* v. *Hoskins* [1905] P. 194.

die and the survivor, the estate of that beneficiary was able to claim its share on the ground that the interest was vested and there was no lapse.[29] Of these three possibilities, it seems therefore that the trust arises on the death of the first to die.

There is, however, a fourth possibility. That is that the trust arises when the survivor receives the benefit under the first will.[30] This date is highly significant, if, as is submitted here, these trusts are constructive trusts, and they are imposed only where the survivor takes a benefit under the first will. Even if this is correct, however, the trust may relate back to the death. On this question there are dicta both ways, but no decision. Most of the dicta favour the view that the trust is imposed only where the survivor takes the benefit.[31] Clauson J., however, in *Re Hagger*[32] said *obiter* that the trust would arise "even though the survivor did not signify his election to give effect to the will by taking benefits under it."

Whether or not the receipt of benefits is material will depend upon the type of trust imposed. If the trust is express, it must be possible to show who declared it, and when. The survivor must be the person who declared it, if anyone, for it affects his property. He could not, however, at the date of the agreement, declare trusts of future property,[33] nor, apart from a suit for specific performance by the estate of the first to die under the *Beswick* principle,[34] could the agreement be enforced as a covenant to settle, for the beneficiaries are volunteers; and there is no question here of trustees suing; for the survivor, if anyone, is the trustee. As we have seen, equity insists upon a clear manifestation of an intention to declare one's self a trustee.

On the other hand, there is no reason why the survivor should not be free to elect whether to keep to the agreement or to disclaim the benefits—unless, of course, the agreement is specifically enforceable against him.[35] It would, however, be fraudulent of him to disregard the agreement *and* keep the benefits. This is a typical example[36] of the imposition of a constructive trust in order to prevent fraud or unjust enrichment.

---

[29] *Re Hagger* [1930] 2 Ch. 190; *cf. Re Gardner (No. 2)* [1923] 2 Ch. 230.
[30] But see (1970) 34 Conv.(N.S.) 230 (R. Burgess); [1982] Conv. 228 at p. 230 (K. Hodkinson).
[31] *Dufour* v. *Pereira* (1769) Dick. 419 at p. 421; *per* Barnes P. in *Stone* v. *Hoskins* [1905] P. 194 at p. 197; *per* Astbury J. in *Re Oldham* [1925] Ch. 75 at p. 87; *per* Sir John Collier in *Denyssen* v. *Mostert* (1872) L.R. 4 P.C. 236 at p. 255; Keeton and Sheridan, *Law of Trusts* (10th ed.), p. 181; (1951) 15 Conv.(N.S.) 28 at pp. 35, 36. See also *Re Cleaver* [1981] 1 W.L.R. 939.
[32] [1930] 2 Ch. 190 at p. 195.
[33] *Ante*, p. 131.
[34] *Ante*, p. 128.
[35] *Ibid.*
[36] Like cases of fully secret trusts; *ante*, p. 140; *post*, p. 306. See *Re Cleaver* [1981] 1 W.L.R. 939 at p. 947.

(b) *To what Property Does the Trust Attach?*[37] This may be clear from the express terms of the will.[38] Failing that, and subject always to a contrary intention, there are four possibilities; that the trust attaches to the property which the survivor receives from the estate of the first to die: or to all the property that the survivor owned at that time: or to all the property which the survivor owned at *his* death: or to all the property which the survivor owned at any time since the first death.

Clearly the trust must include property received from the first to die. If the will gave only a life interest, there is no scope for the trust. If the gift is absolute, the imposition of a trust in favour of ultimate beneficiaries will in effect reduce the survivor's interest to a life interest.

The position is more complex in relation to the property of the survivor. The decision in *Re Hagger,*[39] holding that the interests of the beneficiaries in the joint fund are vested suggests that the trust attaches at least to all the property which the survivor had at the time of the first death. This means that a disposition *inter vivos* by the survivor would be a breach of trust; indeed it would make nonsense of the trust if he could so dispose of the property.[40] This leaves the question of acquisitions by the survivor by his own efforts after the first death. After all, the property acquired after the date of the wills by the first to die was included in his estate; and the agreement, in the absence of a contrary provision, would apply to all property. The agreement thus acts like a covenant to settle after-acquired property, and the property becomes subject to the trust on its becoming vested in the trustee.[41] If this is correct, the effect of mutual wills is to reduce the survivor to the position of a life tenant in respect of all his property. He may use the income, but the capital is held on trust for the ultimate beneficiaries.

In *Re Cleaver*[42] Nourse J., relying on the Australian decision *Birmingham* v. *Renfrew,*[43] adopted the view there expressed that the survivor could enjoy the property as an absolute owner[44] in his lifetime "subject to a fiduciary duty which, so to speak, crystallised on his death and disabled him only from voluntary dispositions *inter vivos.* "[45] This meant dispositions calculated to defeat the agreement. There was no objection to ordinary gifts of small value. The difficulty however, is that any such duty not to dissipate the assets *inter vivos* will be unenfor-

---

[37] See (1977) 15 Alberta L. Rev. 211 (L. A. Sheridan).

[38] As in *Re Green* [1951] Ch. 148, where the wills provided that if the other spouse predeceased, the residue was to be divided into halves, one half being considered as the testator's personal property and the other as the benefit received from the other spouse. It was held that the trust attached only to the latter.

[39] [1930] 2 Ch. 190. A case of a joint will, but the principles are the same.

[40] See however Astbury J. in *Re Oldham* [1925] Ch. 75 at pp. 87, 88; suggesting that the trust attaches only to property held by the survivor at death.

[41] *Paul* v. *Paul* (1882) 20 Ch.D. 742; *Re Ralli's W.T.* [1964] Ch. 288.

[42] [1981] 1 W.L.R. 939.

[43] (1936) 57 C.L.R. 666.

[44] It would of course be otherwise if the will gave him a life interest only.

[45] (1936) 57 C.L.R. at p. 690. *cf. Palmer* v. *Bank of N.S.W.* (1975) 7 A.L.R. 671.

ceable if the beneficiary does not discover his rights until the survivor's death. Although Nourse J. affirmed the requirement of certainty of subject-matter, this is not fully consistent with his formulation of the rights and duties of the parties.[46] If, on the other hand, the survivor's obligation is merely not to dispose of the property *by will* inconsistently with the agreement,[47] then the difficulties are all the greater; for the trust property would be indefinite until his death.

(c) *The Survivor as Trustee.* If it is correct that the survivor becomes a trustee of all the property he owns, it is, to say the least, a very peculiar form of trusteeship. It is a sole trusteeship, with the trustee immediately interested, with the trusts declared by someone else's will, and with the beneficiaries unable to know until the trustee's (the survivor's) death whether mutual wills were made. There is very little opportunity in such circumstances to ensure that proper control over the trustees is maintained. Purchasers have no notice of the trusts, and the trust property may be lost on alienation to them.[48] And the survivor may have no idea that he is a trustee. If land is included in the trusts, it will presumably become settled land,[49] and because of the lack of knowledge of all parties concerned, may cause disputes and uncertainties as to title if it is alienated without observing the proper procedures laid down by the Settled Land Act 1925.[50] And, as noted above, further problems arise if the trust is treated as attaching only on the death of the survivor; and as "floating"[51] or as being "in suspense"[52] in the meantime. This is the problem, it should be noted, created in the field of secret trusts by *Ottaway* v. *Norman.*[53] The possibilities of trouble are unlimited; they have not yet been finally worked out.[54]

(iv) Conclusion. It is clear that the imposition by law of a trust in cases of mutual wills is a clumsy and inadequate way of dealing with a complicated problem. A contractual solution under the *Beswick* principle would be much more satisfactory; but could not, as yet, be relied on. A solution based on the idea of a floating charge has also been suggested.[55] For the present, persons who wish to leave property to each other by way of mutual wills should be advised to consider most carefully the trusts on which they wish the property to be held; what property is to be included; the position during the survivor's lifetime;

[46] See [1982] Conv. 228 (K. Hodkinson).
[47] See *Palmer* v. *Bank of N.S.W., supra.*
[48] *Pilcher* v. *Rawlins* (1872) L.R. 7 Ch.App. 259.
[49] Because the survivor's interest is limited to a life interest, S.L.A. 1925, s.1.
[50] ss.13, 18.
[51] *Ante*, p. 159; (1972) 36 Conv.(N.S.) 129 at p. 132 (D. J. Hayton).
[52] *Per* Brightman J. [1972] Ch. 698 at p. 713; *Re Cleaver, supra.*
[53] [1972] Ch. 698; *ante*, p. 159.
[54] (1951) 14 M.L.R. 140–142 (J. D. B. Mitchell).
[55] [1982] Conv. 228, at p. 231 (K. Hodkinson). This does not solve the problem that the "beneficiaries" are often unaware of the situation.

who they wish to be trustees; what administrative powers the trustees should have; and how best the scheme desired can be carried out from an inheritance tax point of view. Merely to draft mutual wills and then leave the law to sort out such a host of problems is no service to a client. The law in this context, as in most other areas of constructive trusts, imposes a trust in an attempt to prevent one party obtaining an unjust benefit. It is a kind of salvage operation; a salvage of a wreck which competent legal advice would have avoided in the first place.[56]

D. The Vendor under a Specifically Enforceable Contract for Sale

A contract for sale is specifically enforceable where the remedy of damages would be inadequate.[57] Contracts relating to personalty are rarely specifically enforceable, as the property may be purchased elsewhere. If this is not so, as in the case of shares in a private company, then the contract will be specifically enforceable.[58] In the present context, however, we are mainly concerned with contracts relating to land. The availability of specific performance means that, in equity, the purchaser is regarded as already the owner. Thus it has many times been said by high authority that a vendor of land, on the conclusion of the contract of sale, becomes a trustee of the land for the purchaser.[59] Opinions have differed as to the time at which the trustee-ship arises.[60] Any changes in the nature of the property after that time, for example by fire or flooding, if they occur without the fault of the vendor, are at the purchaser's risk.[61] If the vendor sells to another, he holds the purchase money on trust for the purchaser.[62] Beyond that, however, there is little agreement.[63] It is clear at least that this is not an ordinary trusteeship. Cotton L.J. said that the vendor was trustee only

---

[56] For a different view, see (1988) 138 N.L.J. 351 (F. H. G. Sunnucks).

[57] *Post*, p. 652.

[58] See *Oughtred* v. *I.R.C.* [1960] A.C. 206.

[59] Jessel M.R. in *Lysaght* v. *Edwards* (1876) 2 Ch.D. 499 at p. 507; (1959) 23 Conv. (N.S.) 173 (V. G. Wellings); Waters, *The Constructive Trust*, Chap. 2; Oakley, *Constructive Trusts*, Ch. 6.

[60] It may be the date of the contract; or the date the vendor makes title. If the latter, the trust relates back to the contract date. See *Lysaght* v. *Edwards* (1876) 2 Ch.D. 499; *Rayner* v. *Preston* (1881) 18 Ch.D. 1.

[61] *Paine* v. *Meller* (1801) 6 Ves.Jr. 349; *Harford* v. *Purrier* (1816) 1 Madd. 532; as to insurance, see L.P.A. 1925, s.47; *post* p. 529. For the view that the risk does not pass to the purchaser see [1984] Conv. 43 (M. P. Thompson). See further Law Com. Working Paper No. 109 (1988), *Transfer of Land; Passing of Risk from Vendor to Purchaser*. It is there suggested that the risk should pass only on completion.

[62] *Lake* v. *Bayliss* [1974] 1 W.L.R. 1073; relying on *Daniels* v. *Davidson* (1809) 16 Ves.Jr. 249 at p. 254; *Shaw* v. *Foster* (1872) 5 H. L. 321 at p. 327; (1974) 38 Conv.(N.S.) 357 (F. R. Crane).

[63] Cotton, Brett and James L.JJ. in *Rayner* v. *Preston* (1881) 18 Ch.D. 1 expressed different views on the situation. Farrand, *Contract and Conveyance* (4th ed.), Chap. VII.

in a qualified sense[64]; Lord Greene M.R. called him a quasi-trustee,[65] and Stamp L.J. a "constructive trustee or a trustee *sub modo*"[66]; and Lord Cairns[67] explained that the trustee was entitled to protect his own interest in the property. Similarly, the vendor is entitled to keep for himself the rents and profits of the land until the date of completion of the sale,[68] and to retain possession against the purchaser until the purchase price has been paid; and he retains a lien on the land for the price if the land is conveyed before the price is paid[69]; and time runs under the Limitation Act 1980 against the vendor in respect of possession of the land.[70] The relationship between the parties contains a number of aspects in which they are hostile and the vendor self-interested.

Once the date for completion has arrived and the price is paid in full, the vendor must immediately convey. This is an example of a trusteeship arising because the bare legal estate is in one person, and the entire beneficial ownership in another. Until that situation has arisen, it does not seem that any useful purpose is served by stating that the relationship between the parties is one of trustee and beneficiary. The position at law is that they are parties to a contract and no more. In equity additional rights arise by reason of the fact that specific performance is available as a remedy in favour of an innocent party. Equity then treats as done that which ought to be done, and considers the purchaser as being the owner in equity. Hence, where a receiver was appointed upon the vendor company's insolvency before completion, the contract remained specifically enforceable against the receiver as opposed to merely sounding in damages.[71] This is not attributable to any trust, but to the characteristics of a specifically enforceable contract for sale, whereby the equitable interest passes to the purchaser and is not destroyed by the subsequent insolvency of the vendor. In many other respects the contractual nature of the relationship is apparent; each party is continuing to guard his own interests against the other in a way which is quite inconsistent with the existence of the relationship of trustee and beneficiary.

A further question of difficulty, but of no great practical importance, is whether the vendor becomes trustee for a sub-purchaser, if

---

[64] *Rayner* v. *Preston, supra,* at p. 6; *Lysaght* v. *Edwards* (1876) 2 Ch.D. 499 at p. 506; see also Kekewich J. in *Royal Bristol Permanent Building Society* v. *Bomash* (1887) 35 Ch.D. 390 at p. 397 ("a modified sense"); *Re Hamilton-Snowball's Conveyance* [1959] Ch. 308.

[65] *Cumberland Consolidated Holdings Ltd.* v. *Ireland* [1946] K.B. 264 at p. 269.

[66] *Berkley* v. *Poulett* (1977) 242 E.G. 39 at p.43.

[67] *Shaw* v. *Foster* (1872) L.R. 5 H.L. 321 at p. 338.

[68] *Cuddon* v. *Tite* (1858) 1 Giff. 395.

[69] *Mackreth* v. *Symmons* (1808) 15 Ves.Jr. 329.

[70] *Bridges* v. *Mees* [1957] Ch. 475; *cf. Hyde* v. *Pearce* [1982] 1 All E.R. 1029.

[71] *Freevale Ltd.* v. *Metrostore (Holdings) Ltd.* [1984] 1 All E.R. 495 (a receiver, unlike a liquidator, has no statutory right to disclaim contracts); [1984] Conv. 446 (D. Milman and S. Coneys); *Re Coregrange Ltd.* [1984] B.C.L.C. 453.

the purchaser has entered into a contract to sell to the sub-purchaser. In such a case, the sub-purchaser, by virtue of his contract with the purchaser, is entitled to specific performance and is treated as the owner in equity. The question arose in *Berkley* v. *Earl Poulett*[72] because the vendor, with the knowledge and concurrence of the purchaser, had allowed certain items in a mansion, which were alleged to be fixtures, to be taken away. The sub-purchaser claimed that the vendor was in breach of the trustee's duty to take proper care of the property. The question was *obiter*, because a majority of the Court of Appeal held that the items were not fixtures. Goff L.J. dissented, and would have held the vendor liable. Stamp L.J., in a view which it is submitted is to be preferred, found no fiduciary duty owed to the sub-purchaser.[73] It was not that the vendor was a trustee and therefore had fiduciary duties; rather that the vendor owed duties to the purchaser and was labelled a trustee. There was no such duty owed to the sub-purchaser. The sub-purchaser's right is to have the purchaser enforce the contract against the vendor.

No doubt it is too late now to say that the relationship between vendor and purchaser is not that of trustee and beneficiary. The terminology must, however, be received with reserve. Unlike other cases of constructive trusts, the element of improper conduct is absent and the situation must, at best, be treated as anomalous.[74]

E. Secret Trusts

It is unsettled whether secret trusts, and more particularly half-secret trusts, are to be regarded as express or constructive. The practical significance of the distinction is that, in the case of land, section 53 of the Law of Property Act 1925 requires written evidence in the case of express trusts, but not in the case of constructive trusts. The matter is examined in detail in Chapter 5.

F. Conveyance by Fraud

Where property has been obtained by the fraud of the defendant, he may be compelled to hold it as a constructive trustee. The trust is not imposed in every case; while it is difficult to define the circumstances in which the trust will be imposed, some broad principles are in practice clear. In the case of a conveyance of land *inter vivos*, the transferee may be prevented, by the imposition of a constructive trust, from setting up the apparently absolute nature of the conveyance in order to

---

[72] (1977) 242 E.G. 39.
[73] *Ibid.* at p. 43.
[74] (1959) 23 Conv.(N.S.) 173 (V. G. Wellings). We have seen that it is not treated as a constructive trust for the purpose of L.P.A. 1925, s.53(2); *Oughtred* v. *I.R.C.* [1960] A.C. 206, *ante*, p. 87.

defeat a beneficial interest which, by oral agreement, was intended to remain in the transferor,[75] or in some third party.[76]

Similarly, situations in which a will is fraudulently revoked, or where the testator is fraudulently prevented from making a will, or fraudulently induced to leave property to a legatee or devisee, are all appropriate for the imposition of a constructive trust. These situations are discussed under the heading of secret trusts.[77]

G. Acquisition of Property by Killing[78]

Where a beneficiary kills the testator, or next of kin kills an intestate, there is good reason to prevent him from benefiting from his crime.[79] The English courts have established a rule to this effect, but they "have worked out no rational theory for their actions in depriving killers[80] . . . there has been little discussion of the theoretical basis for a deprivation . . . and generally they have considered that the killer does not gain legal title."[81] Such a result is contrary to the enactments relating to succession, testate or intestate, but clearly a rule of public policy can override statutory provisions.[82] If the killer does not acquire any title to the property in question, as in the pension and insurance cases, then there is no need for the imposition of a constructive trust. If, on the other hand, the killer acquires legal title, as is arguably the position in some of the succession cases, then he will be subjected to a constructive trust which is imposed to prevent unjust enrichment. A bona fide purchaser from the wrongdoer would then be protected.[83]

Whichever solution is reached, a number of problems remain, on which there is little authority.

(i) *Type of Killing.* Killing may be effected by any means from murder to accident. The deprivation principle only applies to criminal killing. There is much to be said for the view that "the killer should only be deprived when he does or causes to be done a dangerous act

---

[75] *Rochefoucauld* v. *Boustead* [1897] 1 Ch. 196; *Bannister* v. *Bannister* [1948] 2 All E.R. 133; *Hodgson* v. *Marks* [1972] Ch. 892; *ante*, p. 241. See also *Chief Constable of Surrey* v. *A.*, *The Times*, October 27, 1988, where it was held arguable that the profits of fraud were subject to a constructive trust.

[76] *Binions* v. *Evans* [1972] Ch. 359; *Peffer* v. *Rigg* [1977] 1 W.L.R. 285; *Lyus* v. *Prowsa Developments Ltd.* [1982] 1 W.L.R. 1044; *post*, p. 314. See also [1987] Conv. 246 (J. D. Feltham).

[77] *Supra.* For a fuller discussion, see Chap. 5.

[78] Goff and Jones, pp. 624–631; (1973) 89 L.Q.R. 235 (T. G. Youdan), which has been used as the basis of this account; Scott's *Trusts*, § 492; *Restatement of Restitution*, § 187; (1969) 68 Mich. L.R. 65 (W. M. McGovern).

[79] *Cleaver* v. *Mutual Reserve Fund Life Association Ltd.* [1892] 1 Q.B. 147; *In the Estate of Crippen* [1911] P. 108; *In the Estate of Hall* [1914] P. 1; *Re Sigsworth* [1935] 1 Ch. 89.

[80] (1973) 89 L.Q.R. 235.

[81] *Ibid.* at p. 251.

[82] See, for example, *R.* v. *Chief National Insurance Commissioner, ex p. Connor, infra.*

[83] *Re Cash* (1911) 30 N.Z.L.R. 571; *Beresford* v. *Royal Insurance Ltd.* [1938] A.C. 586 at p. 600.

intending[84] harm to the person whose death occasions his acquisition; and that person dies as a result of that act."[85]

(ii) *Means of Acquisition.* The principle applies when the killer benefits by testamentary gift,[86] or under his intestacy,[87] and also under a life insurance policy on the victim's life[88]; and, in the days when suicide was a crime,[89] the estate of a suicide was held to be unable to claim the benefits of an insurance policy.[90] Similarly, a woman who kills her husband cannot claim a widow's pension.[91] More complicated questions arise where one joint tenant kills another, or a remainder-man kills the life tenant. Following decisions in Canada,[92] Australia[93] and New Zealand[94] it has been held that the joint tenant cannot profit from his wrong. He becomes entitled under the common law rule of survivorship to the whole legal estate, but he holds it as to one half on trust for his victim's estate.[95] In the case of the remainderman killing the life tenant, the best course would be to postpone the killer's enjoyment until the time at which the victim's life expectation would terminate.[96]

(iii) *Destination of Property.* To deprive the wrongdoer does not solve all the problems. Persons claiming through the wrongdoer should not benefit from the crime, but the position is different with the wrongdoer's next of kin if they are also next of kin of the victim. They should not be deprived of an independent right of succession. It is suggested that they should be allowed to take "provided that they would have taken as next of kin of the murdered person if the murderer

---

[84] Including recklessness.
[85] (1973) 89 L.Q.R. 235 at p. 240, where the matter is examined in detail; Goff and Jones (3rd ed.), p. 625; *Re Giles* [1972] Ch. 544. (Manslaughter by reason of diminished responsibility); (1972) 35 M.L.R. 426 (J. G. Miller); *Re Hall* [1914] P. 1 (rule applied to manslaughter); *Re K. (deceased)* [1986] Ch. 180. (See also the discussion in the High Court at [1985] Ch. 85, at p. 97). See further *Evans* v. *Evans, The Times*, August 8, 1988 (periodical payments order discharged and arrears remitted where divorced wife convicted of inciting others to murder former husband, who survived).
[86] *Re Pollock* [1941] Ch. 219.
[87] *Re Sigsworth* [1935] Ch. 89.
[88] *Cleaver* v. *Mutual Reserve Fund Life Association Ltd.* [1892] 1 Q.B. 147.
[89] Until Suicide Act 1961, s.11.
[90] *Beresford* v. *Royal Insurance Ltd.* [1938] A.C. 586.
[91] *R.* v. *Chief National Insurance Commissioner, ex p. Connor* [1981] 1 Q.B. 758 (manslaughter); (1981) 44 M.L.R. 718 (St. J. Robilliard). See also (1972) 31 C.L.J. 144 (J. Shand). As submitted above, this is not a case of constructive trust, as the claimant acquires no title to any property.
[92] *Schobelt* v. *Barber* (1967) 59 D.L.R. (2d) 519 (Ont.).
[93] *Re Barrowcliff* [1927] S.A.S.R. 147; *Rasmanis* v. *Jurewitsch* (1970) 70 S.R. (N.S.W.) 407.
[94] *Re Pechar* [1969] N.Z.L.R. 574.
[95] *Re K. (deceased), supra,* in the High Court. The Court of Appeal affirmed the decision without discussing this point. See also [1987] Conv. 33 (M. P. Thompson). For variants, see *Re Barrowcliff, supra,* and *Kemp* v. *The Public Curator of Queensland* [1969] Qd.R. 145; and Scott: *Trusts,* § 493.2; *Restatement of Restitution,* § 188.
[96] Scott, *op. cit.* § 493.1; (1973) 89 L.Q.R. 235 at p. 250.

had predeceased his victim."[97] In other cases, the proper solution will be for the property to go to the victim's residuary legatee, or as on his intestacy, or to the other members of a class of which the wrongdoer was one[98]; or, where there are special circumstances to show what the victim's intention was, as where it was shown that the killing took place in order to prevent the victim from changing his will in favour of another, then the flexibility introduced by the concept of the constructive trust should allow the property to be claimed by "the person who, in the eyes of equity, has the best right to it."[99]

(iv) *Statutory Relief.* It is now provided by the Forfeiture Act 1982[1] that the court may grant relief from forfeiture of inheritance and other rights to persons guilty of unlawful killing[2] other than murder,[3] where the court is satisfied that the justice of the case so requires.[4] The convicted person must bring proceedings for this purpose within three months of his conviction.[5] The Act applies to killings before and after its coming into operation, unless the property has already been acquired by someone else before that date in consequence of the forfeiture principle.[6] The Act applies to benefits under a will or upon intestacy; nominations; a *donatio mortis causa*; and property held on trust before the death which would devolve on the offender as a result of the death.[7] The court may grant relief as to all or part of the property.[8] In the case of social security benefits, such as a widow's pension, the Act confers the discretion not on the court but on the Social Security Commissioner.[9] Finally, it is provided that the forfeiture principle does not preclude an application under the Family Provision legislation.[10]

H. Constructive Trusts of a New Model: Justice and Good Conscience

Some modern developments indicate a wide extension of the operation of constructive trusts by the introduction of what Lord Denning

---

[97] Goff and Jones (3rd ed.), p. 628; Scott, *op. cit.* § 492; *Restatement of Restitution*, § 187.

[98] *Re Peacock* [1957] Ch. 310.

[99] (1973) 89 L.Q.R. 235 at p. 257.

[1] (1983) 46 M.L.R. 66 (P. H. Kenny); (1983) 80 L.S.Gaz. 910 (A. Mithani and A. Wilton).

[2] Including aiding, abetting, counselling or procuring the death; s.1(2). The Act does not apply to suicide, nor to attempts to kill.

[3] s.5.

[4] s.2(2). Degree of moral blame is significant; *Re K. (deceased)* [1986] Ch. 180.

[5] s.2(3).

[6] s.2(7). See *Re K. (deceased), supra* (property not "acquired" within s.2(7) if held by personal representatives who have not completed the administration).

[7] s.2(4). It does not appear to apply to insurance policies.

[8] s.2(1) and (5); *Re K. (deceased), supra.*

[9] s.4. See (1984) 81 L.S.Gaz. 288; (1988) 85 L.S.Gaz. 37 (sequel to *Re K. (deceased), supra).*

[10] s.3. This section does not apply retrospectively to applications made before the Act was in operation; *Re Royse (decd.)* [1985] Ch. 22; (1985) 48 M.L.R. 723 (N. S. Price).

M.R. has called "a constructive trust of a new model."[11] The broad
principle is that a constructive trust may be imposed, regardless of
established legal rules, in order to reach the result required by equity,
justice and good conscience.[12] The principle was thus articulated in
Hussey v. *Palmer*[13]: "It is a trust imposed by law wherever justice and
good conscience require it. It is a liberal process, founded on large
principles of equity. ... It is an equitable remedy by which the court
can enable an aggrieved party to obtain restitution." Such a principle,
if it survives, would effect a complete swing of the pendulum so far as
the principles of English law concerning constructive trusts are concerned. The law in this field was once criticised as being too restricted[14]; in that the older cases would find a constructive trust only
where the facts brought the case within one of the limited and established categories of constructive trust, usually requiring a fiduciary
relationship. The new model opens up the possibility of finding a
constructive trust in any situation in which the established rules lead to
a result which would appear to be inconsistent with equity, justice and
good conscience. "It is possible to read into recent decisions a rule that
in cases in which the plaintiff ought to win, but has no legal doctrine or
authority to support him, a constructive trust in his favour will do the
trick."[15]

Not surprisingly, this doctrine has been applied in reaching solutions
in cases where satisfactory solutions under established doctrines have
proved particularly difficult to find. Illustrations come from the plight
of the deserted wife or mistress; the problem of the licensee of land
whose expectations have been disappointed; and the position of a bona
fide purchaser of registered land. The "new model," however, seems
to have declined since the retirement of Lord Denning M.R.

(i) *Family Arrangements*. In Chapter 11 we saw that, in the context
of claims to an interest in the family home, some decisions are difficult
to reconcile with the principles of *Pettitt* v. *Pettitt*[16] and *Gissing* v.
Gissing,[17] to the effect that the interests of the parties must be determined according to the principles of property law. In *Eves* v. *Eves*,[18]

---

[11] *Eves* v. *Eves* [1975] 1 W.L.R. 1338.
[12] However, it may not be imposed if to do so would contradict the terms of an express
trust; *Godwin* v. *Bedwell* (1982) 79 L.S.Gaz. 578.
[13] [1972] 1 W.L.R. 1286 at p. 1289; *cf. Spence* v. *Brown* (1988) 18 Fam. Law 291,
confirming that a loan does not give rise to a constructive trust. See also Cardozo J. in
Beatty v. *Guggenheim Exploration Co.* (1919) 255 N.Y. 360 at p. 385: "A constructive
trust is the formula through which the conscience of equity finds expression." (1973)
26 C.L.P. 17 at p. 35 (A. J. Oakley).
[14] Waters, *The Constructive Trust*.
[15] (1977) 28 N.I.L.Q. 123 (R. H. Maudsley).
[16] [1970] A.C. 777.
[17] [1971] A.C. 886.
[18] [1975] 1 W.L.R. 1338 *ante*, p. 258; *Cooke* v. *Head* [1972] 1 W.L.R. 518.

involving an unmarried couple, the man bought a house as a joint home. He had it conveyed into his sole name, giving as an excuse the fact the woman was under 21 years old. She did a great deal of heavy work in the house and garden, beyond ordinary housework. When they separated, she claimed a share of the house. "In strict law she has no claim upon him whatever. She is not his wife. He is not bound to provide a roof over her head. He can turn her into the street. . . . And a few years ago even equity would not have helped her. But things are altered now. . . . " It would be "most inequitable for him to deny her any share in the house. The law will impute or impose a constructive trust by which he was to hold it in trust for both of them."[19] Her share was one quarter. A similar principle was applied in *Heseltine* v. *Heseltine*[20] where a wife gave to her husband, *inter alia*, two capital sums, one being £40,000 for the purpose of saving estate duty if she predeceased him; and the other being £20,000 for the purpose of enabling him to provide the deposits necessary to become a member of Lloyd's. The Court of Appeal decided that the husband held the sums on constructive trust for his wife. The conclusion seems at variance with the principles of resulting trusts.[21] The presumption of a resulting trust should have been rebutted because the stated purposes could only be achieved if the husband became beneficial owner. A constructive trust appears to have been imposed in order to reach what the court regarded as a just solution.

More recent decisions, however, seem to have turned away from this use of the constructive trust. As we have seen, the Court of Appeal in *Grant* v. *Edwards*[22] has restated the principles governing the acquisition of an interest in the home. Insofar as the "common intention" is, in these cases, a somewhat artificial concept, the court retains a measure of discretion. It does not, however, have any discretion to impose a constructive trust simply to achieve a "fair" result. So in *Burns* v. *Burns*[23] a woman who looked after the home for many years but who made no financial contribution referable to its acquisition failed in her claim to a share. Where the woman has made no contribution but the parties assert a common intention to share, it was held in *Midland Bank Ltd.* v. *Dobson*[24] that an undocumented common intention cannot give rise to a constructive trust unless the woman has acted to her detriment in reliance upon it. Without such an act, section

---

[19] *Ibid.* at p. 1341. The reasoning of Browne L.J. and Brightman J. was more orthodox.

[20] [1971] 1 W.L.R. 342; *Re Densham* [1975] 1 W.L.R. 1519 (constructive trust imposed to meet the parties' undocumented intention to hold jointly). See also (1973) 26 C.L.P. at p. 27. (A. J. Oakley).

[21] *Ante*, p. 244.

[22] [1986] Ch. 638; *ante*, p. 256.

[23] [1984] Ch. 317; *ante*, p. 255. A strict view of the requirement that the contribution be "referable to the acquisition" was also taken by the House of Lords in *Winkworth* v. *Edward Baron Development Co. Ltd.* [1986] 1 W.L.R. 1512.

[24] [1986] 1 F.L.R. 171. The wife was attempting to defeat the husband's creditors. *cf. Re Densham*, *supra*, p. 253.

53(1)(*b*) of the Law of Property Act 1925 is not displaced by section 53(2).[25] In *Layton* v. *Martin*[26] a man invited his mistress to live with him, promising to provide for her by will. When he did not, she claimed a constructive trust to give effect to his intention. Her claim faifled because she had not contributed to the acquisition or preservation of any of his assets. In *Re Basham*,[27] on the other hand, the constructive trust was utilised as a means of filling what were perceived to be gaps in the proprietary estoppel doctrine. The plaintiff had acted to her detriment in reliance on her stepfather's assurances that she would inherit from him. There was little authority on the application of that doctrine where the belief related to a future right and to non-specific assets.[28] These problems were overcome by holding that if the belief related to a future right, a species of constructive trust arose. Hence reliance could be placed on other branches of constructive trusts such as mutual wills, where the doctrine was not confined to present rights in specific assets.[29]

(ii) *Licences.* The new model constructive trust has been most active in the context of licences. The matter will be treated in more detail in Chapter 27. Here let it merely be said that a licensee is a person who is physically present on land whether in occupation or not, but without any proprietary interest in the land. In the simplest case, such as that of a guest invited to dinner, the licensor may revoke the licence and require the guest to leave, allowing him a reasonable time to collect his belongings. But more complex cases arise: as where the licensee has given consideration for the licence; or where the licensee has been encouraged to act to his detriment in reliance on promises by the licensor, in such a way as to raise an estoppel against the licensor. Under the doctrine of proprietary estoppel,[30] the licensee can obtain a proprietary interest in the land. In the absence of such proprietary interest, a number of problems arise concerning the protection of the licensee. He is protected against the licensor; but how is he protected against third parties? The constructive trust has been called in aid as a means of enforcing a contractual licence against a third party, thus circumventing the rule that contractual rights are not binding on third parties even if they had notice.[31] Lord Denning M.R. pioneered this

[25] *Ante*, p. 80.
[26] [1986] 2 F.L.R. 277. Alternative claims based on contract and proprietary estoppel also failed. See further *Coombes* v. *Smith* [1986] 1 W.L.R. 808; *post*, p. 856.
[27] [1986] 1 W.L.R. 1498; [1987] Conv. 211 (J. Martin); (1987) 46 C.L.J. 215 (D. Hayton); All E.R. Rev. 1987, p. 156 (P. J. Clarke) and p. 263 (C. H. Sherrin); (1988) 8 L.S. 92 at pp. 101 *et seq.* (M. Davey); *post*, p. 856.
[28] *cf. Layton* v. *Martin, supra.*
[29] See *Re Cleaver* [1981] 1 W.L.R. 939; *ante*, p. 299.
[30] *Post*, p. 850.
[31] *King* v. *David Allen & Sons (Billposting) Ltd.* [1916] 2 A.C. 54; *Clore* v. *Theatrical Properties Ltd.* [1936] 3 All E.R. 483.

use of the constructive trust in *Binions* v. *Evans*,[32] where an employer agreed to allow an employee's widow to reside in a cottage rent free for life. The cottage was sold at a reduced price, expressly subject to her interest. Lord Denning M.R. regarded her interest as a licence, binding on the purchaser under a constructive trust. This principle was next applied in *D.H.N. Foods Ltd.* v. *Tower Hamlets London Borough Council*.[33] This case did not involve the question whether a licence could bind a third party, but the constructive trust theory enabled a contractual licensee to be treated as having a sufficient interest to qualify for compensation on compulsory purchase of the land. In *Re Sharpe (a Bankrupt)*[34] the aunt of the bankrupt had lent substantial sums of money to the bankrupt to purchase a shop and maisonette. She had been told that she could remain on the premises as long as she wished. She was held to have a right, as against the bankrupt, to remain in occupation while the loan was outstanding, and an interest by way of constructive trust against the trustee. The trustee had contracted to sell the premises to a bona fide purchaser. By a procedural oversight, the purchaser was not a party to the proceedings, and no decision was made on the question of her right, if any, against him.

Thus a principle was evolving that a constructive trust could be imposed on a purchaser with notice of a contractual licence, in order to achieve what was perceived as the just result. The Court of Appeal has now clarified and restricted the use of the constructive trust in this context, while leaving it with some scope for operation. In *Ashburn Anstalt* v. *Arnold*[35] the question arose whether an occupier's rights were binding on a purchaser. In fact the occupier was held to have a tenancy, but the Court of Appeal nevertheless considered *obiter* what the position would have been in the case of a licence. The basic principle that a contractual licence is only a personal right was confirmed, but the constructive trust solution was justified if the facts were appropriate to support it. A purchaser of the land would not automatically be bound by a constructive trust. The test was whether he had so conducted himself that it would be inequitable to allow him to deny the licensee's rights. The mere fact that the purchaser had notice or that property was conveyed "subject to" the licence was not enough. Such a term may be included merely to protect the vendor against claims by the purchaser should it turn out that he is bound by third party rights. The constructive trust solution was appropriate in *Binions* v. *Evans*[36]

---

[32] [1972] Ch. 359; (1972) 88 L.Q.R. 326 (P.V.B.); (1972) 37 Conv.(N.S.) 266 (J. Martin); (1977) 36 C.L.J. 123 (R. J. Smith). The majority view was that she had a life interest.

[33] [1976] 1 W.L.R. 852; (1977) 36 C.L.J. 12 (D. J. Hayton).

[34] [1980] 1 W.L.R. 219. [1980] Conv. 207 (J. Martin).

[35] [1988] 2 W.L.R. 706; (1988) 104 L.Q.R. 175 (P. Sparkes); (1988) 47 C.L.J. 353 (A.J. Oakley); *post*, p. 845. Decision criticised in (1988) 51 M.L.R. 226 (J. Hill) and in [1988] Conv. 201 (M. P. Thompson), the latter preferring a solution based on the economic torts.

[36] *Supra*. Also in *Lyus* v. *Prowsa Developments Ltd.* [1982] 1 W.L.R. 1044; *post*, p. 314.

because the purchaser paid a low price and was intended to give effect to the widow's rights. In *Re Sharpe (a Bankrupt)*,[37] on the other hand, the constructive trust was not appropriate, because the aunt did not reply to the trustee's enquiries as to her interest. In the instant case the imposition of a constructive trust would not have been justified. Although the vendor had disclosed the occupier's rights, this was done to protect the vendor, rather than with the intention that the purchaser should give effect to them, and the price was not reduced. The Court of Appeal emphasised that in matters relating to title to land, certainty was of prime importance, and that constructive trusts should not be imposed in reliance on slender materials. Thus the constructive trust survives as a means of achieving justice in appropriate cases, but the wide principle that a contractual licence automatically give rise to a constructive trust binding on a purchaser with notice has gone.

(iii) *Registered Land.* A constructive trust was also found in *Peffer* v. *Rigg*,[38] where a purchaser with notice of an interest under a trust for sale was held to take subject to it, applying general equitable principles, notwithstanding that the title to the property was registered and the interest was not protected on the register, as required by the Land Registration Act 1925. It has since been affirmed by the House of Lords in *Williams & Glyn's Bank Ltd.* v. *Boland*[39] that the concept of notice has no relevance to dealings with registered land: "The only kind of notice recognised is by entry on the register."[40] The land registration system has provided a code in which, it is submitted, the constructive trust doctrine has no part to play.[41]

Fraudulent or sham transactions would raise different considerations. There is a well known principle that a statute must not be used as an instrument of fraud. This principle was invoked in *Lyus* v. *Prowsa Developments Ltd.*,[42] where land was bought expressly subject to the plaintiff's contractual rights, but the defendants sought to defeat them by relying on the Land Registration Act 1925.[43] A constructive trust was imposed on the defendants on the ground that the statute was not to be used as an instrument of fraud. It has been said, on the highest authority, that it is not fraud to rely on legal rights conferred by an Act of Parliament.[44] Here, however, the defendants had gone further, by reneging on a positive stipulation in favour of the plaintiffs. Where the agreement expressly creates a right which a third party is to

---

[37] *Supra.*
[38] [1977] 1 W.L.R. 285; (1977) 93 L.Q.R. 341 (R. J. Smith); [1978] Conv. 52 (J. Martin); (1977) 36 C.L.J. 227 (D. J. Hayton); (1977) 40 M.L.R. 602 (S. Anderson).
[39] [1981] A.C. 487. *Peffer* v. *Rigg* was not cited on this point.
[40] *Ibid.* at p. 504 (*per* Lord Wilberforce).
[41] See especially s.59(6) and s.74 of Land Registration Act 1925.
[42] [1982] 1 W.L.R. 1044.
[43] ss.29, 34(4).
[44] *Midland Bank Trust Co. Ltd* v. *Green* [1981] A.C. 513 at p. 531.

have against the purchaser, a constructive trust arises if the purchaser seeks to defeat that right. The result would have been the same in unregistered land.[45] The application to these facts of the maxim that a statute cannot be used as an instrument of fraud has been much criticised.[46] The Court of Appeal, however, has recently approved the decision, emphasising that the parties intended the purchaser to give effect to the contract and that an assurance to that effect had been given.[47]

(iv) *Conclusion.* The courts, in some of these cases, are "invoking the constructive trust as an equitable remedy to do justice inter partes."[48] While a liberalisation of the application of equitable remedies is generally to be welcomed, it is important to appreciate that the "new model" constructive trust leaves a number of problems in its wake. The concept of justice alone is too vague to be used as the basis for determining property rights, and, inevitably, the imposition of the constructive trust on this basis is impossible to forecast. Further, a trust creates equitable proprietary rights, and these can operate more widely than the dispute between the parties. The question of the rights of third parties arises: whether, in particular, a bona fide purchaser or creditor is bound by a licensee's right of occupation, or by a woman's claim to a share in the home. The constructive trust is too powerful a solution for these cases. The knock-on effects are incalculable. It is submitted that a better solution to the question is to find a just solution between the parties on the basis of a personal decree not affecting the interests or rights of third parties.[49]

It is important also to appreciate that the "new model" constructive trust goes far beyond what was laid down by the American writers who have regarded a constructive trust as a remedy to prevent unjust enrichment. The provision of a remedy for unjust enrichment does not require an unlimited free-wheeling discretion as to the imposition of a constructive trust. There must at least be general guide-lines for the exercise of the discretion. Unjust enrichment has often been regarded in England as a principle too vague to be of any practical value.[50] This is no longer so.[51] The law of unjust enrichment lays down with reasonable clarity when an action will lie. The *Restatement of Restitution*

---

[45] Applying *Bannister* v. *Bannister* [1948] 2 All E.R. 133, and the judgment of Lord Denning M.R. in *Binions* v. *Evans* [1972] Ch. 359.

[46] All E.R. Rev. 1982, p. 165 (P. J. Clarke); (1983) 46 M.L.R. 96 (P. H. Kenny); [1983] Conv. 64 (P. Jackson); (1983) 42 C.L.J. 54 (C. Harpum); (1985) 44 C.L.J. 280 (M. P. Thompson); *cf.* (1984) 47 M.L.R. 476 (P. Bennett).

[47] *Ashburn Anstalt* v. *Arnold* [1988] 2 W.L.R. 706, *ante*, p. 313.

[48] (1973) 26 C.L.P. 17 at p. 35 (A. J. Oakley). The trend is further criticised in Oakley, *Constructive Trusts* (2nd ed.), p. 47.

[49] See *Muschinski* v. *Dodds* (1986) 62 A.L.R. 429 (constructive trust took effect only from date of court order); New South Wales De Facto Relationships Act 1984 (giving the woman a personal claim against the man).

[50] (1939) 55 L.Q.R. 37 at pp. 51–53 (Holdsworth).

[51] See Goff and Jones, *The Law of Restitution* (3rd ed.), *passim.*

describes a constructive trust as a remedy to prevent unjust enrichment[52]; it is not itself the basis of the claim. A proprietary remedy is
secondary to a personal remedy, and available where unjust enrichment is shown, and the personal remedy is inadequate. Some of the
modern English cases go further by giving a proprietary remedy where
there would be no personal action at all. They seem to treat a constructive trust as a magic formula to reach a just result between the parties,
regardless of existing proprietary rights in them, or of the interests of
persons who are not parties to the dispute. Present indications,
however, are that the "new model" constructive trust will not develop
further. The most recent decisions, as we have seen, favour a return to
more orthodox principles of property law. Similarly in the Commonwealth, where it has been said that "the legitimacy of the new model is
at least suspect; at best it is a mutant from which further breeding
should be discouraged."[53]

---

[52] § 160; *ante*, p. 285. See also *Chase Manhattan Bank N.A.* v. *Israel-British Bank
(London) Ltd.* [1981] Ch. 105, *post*, p. 628.   '
[53] *Allen* v. *Snyder* [1977] 2 N.S.W.L.R. 685 at p. 701. The "new model" was also
rejected in *Carly* v. *Farrelly* [1975] 1 N.Z.L.R. 356; (1978) 94 L.Q.R. 347 (G.
Samuels); *Avondale Printers & Stationers Ltd.* v. *Haggie* [1979] 2 N.Z.L.R. 124;
Muschinski v. *Dodds* (1986) 62 A.L.R. 429. The "new model" was accepted in a
modified form in *Pettkus* v. *Becker* (1980) 117 D.L.R. (3d) 257; (1982) 12 Fam. Law 21
(M. Bryan). See further (1978) 94 L.Q.R. 351 (W. M. Gummow); (1975) 53 C.B.R.
366 (D. Waters); [1982] Conv. 424 (F. Bates); [1983] Conv. 420 (K. Hodkinson)
(reviewing the position also in N. Ireland). The unjust enrichment approach was
favoured in *Baumgartner* v. *Baumgartner* (1988) 62 A.L.J. 29; [1988] Conv. 259 (D.
Hayton).

CHAPTER 13

TRUSTS WHICH CONTRAVENE THE LAW

A TRUST, though otherwise valid, may fail because it contains an element of unlawfulness or immorality, or is contrary to public policy. It is impossible to categorise all the possible grounds of unlawfulness, and only some of the more important ones can be mentioned here.

1. TRUSTS CONTRARY TO THE GENERAL POLICY OF THE LAW

A. Purposes Contrary to Law, Public Policy or Morality

It will be appreciated that such trusts are likely to fail in any event, apart from any question of unlawfulness, on the ground that they are non-charitable purpose trusts.[1] There are, perhaps for this reason, few examples of cases decided on the basis of illegality, but one such is *Thrupp* v. *Collett*,[2] where a testator attempted to provide for paying

---

[1] *Post,* Chap. 14. See, for example, *Brown* v. *Burdett* (1882) 21 Ch.D. 667, where a "useless" trust to seal up a house for 20 years failed.

[2] (1858) 26 Beav. 125. See also *Harrison* v. *Tew, The Times*, November 30, 1988 (protective trust of settlor's interest in litigation not illegal or contrary to public policy as savouring of champerty or maintenance).

the fines of convicted poachers. Sir John Romilly M.R. held the trust void on the ground that it was against public policy. It was held in *Bowman* v. *Secular Society*[3] that the denial of Christianity was not *per se* an illegal purpose, but it was suggested in *Thornton* v. *Howe*[4] that a trust whose purpose was adverse to all religion or subversive of morality would be void. It remains to be decided whether this would be the fate of any trust for the benefit of bodies such as the Church of Scientology.[5] It need hardly be added that trusts for the furtherance of illegal or immoral activities, such as, for example, terrorism or prostitution,[6] would fail. Likewise a trust for a fraudulent purpose, such as placing money with a company in order to give it the false appearance of a credit balance.[7]

It was at one time established that gifts by deed or will for future illegitimate children were void as being *contra bonos mores*, on the ground that they would tend to encourage immorality.[8] This is still the position as far as dispositions made before January 1, 1970 are concerned (although the more recent decisions have taken a less strict view of the matter[9]), but for dispositions made on or after that date,[10] the position was reversed by section 15(7) of the Family Law Reform Act 1969 (now replaced by the Family Law Reform Act 1987, section 19).[11]

B. Statutory Provisions Against Discrimination

(i) **Race Relations Act 1976.** Discrimination, as defined by the 1976 Act, on the ground of colour, race, nationality, or ethnic or national origins is unlawful.[12] The 1976 Act applies to certain specified situa-

---

[3] [1917] A.C. 406 (Lord Finlay L.C. dissenting).

[4] (1862) 31 Beav. 14.

[5] As to whose doctrines see *Hubbard* v. *Vosper* [1972] 2 Q.B. 84, *post*, p. 738. See also *R.* v. *Registrar General, ex p. Segerdal* [1970] 2 Q.B. 697; *Re Newsam*, March 14, 1973 (unreported); *The Church of the New Faith* v. *The Commissioner for Payroll Tax* (1983) 49 A.L.R. 65, noted [1984] Conv. 449 (St. J. Robilliard); (1984) 43 C.L.J. 218 (G. T. Pagone). But the sect known as the "Exclusive Brethren" has been held charitable; *Holmes* v. *Att.-Gen., The Times*, February 12, 1981. For the position as to the sect known as the "Moonies," see *post*, p. 393.

[6] See Harman L.J.'s example of a "school for prostitutes or pickpockets" in *Re Pinion* [1965] Ch. 85.

[7] *Re Great Berlin Steamboat Co.* (1884) 26 Ch.D. 616.

[8] *Occleston* v. *Fullalove* (1874) L.R. 9 Ch. App. 147. The claim of an illegitimate beneficiary might have failed in any event on the ground that gifts to children (or other relatives) were generally construed as confined to legitimate children. This is no longer the position: Family Law Reform Act 1987, s.19 (replacing F.L.R.A. 1969, s.15).

[9] *Re Hyde* [1932] 1 Ch. 95.

[10] A disposition made by will is made on the date of the execution of the will although, of course, it cannot come into operation until the death. See F.L.R.A. 1969, s.15(8) (now replaced by F.L.R.A. 1987, s.19(7)).

[11] This Act replaces the concept of the illegitimate child with that of the unmarried parent.

[12] s.1.

tions, including employment, the provision of goods and services, and the disposal of property. In these situations a person discriminates against another, for the purposes of the Act, if on any of the above-mentioned grounds he treats that other less favourably than he treats or would treat other persons.[13] It will be noted that religion as such is not covered by the Act.[14]

Subject to what is said below about charitable trusts, the Act does not extend to discrimination in the making of a gift or trust.[15] But trustees, just as any other individuals, are bound by the provisions relating to employment, disposal of property and so on. This is especially significant in the administration of charitable trusts.

Special provisions relating to charitable trusts are contained in section 34 of the 1976 Act. The general position is that the Act does not affect a provision in a charitable instrument which provides for conferring *benefits* on persons of a class defined by reference to race, nationality, or ethnic or national origins.[16] In other words, it is lawful to discriminate in favour of such groups, but not against them.[17] But it is not permissible to discriminate even in favour of a class defined by reference to colour.[18] Any such provision is to take effect as if it provided for conferring the benefits in question on persons of the class which results if the colour qualification is disregarded.

Finally, it should be noted that even where discrimination in a charitable trust is not made unlawful by the Act, the removal of discriminatory provisions is possible under the *cy-près* doctrine.[19]

(ii) Sex Discrimination Act 1975. Sex discrimination is not a ground for invalidating any provision in a private trust. As far as charitable trusts are concerned, section 43 provides that the Act does not apply to any provision in a charitable instrument for conferring benefits on persons of one sex only. Thus there is nothing unlawful in single sex charities, such as the YMCA or the Boy Scouts. Of course, the trustees

---

[13] The 1976 Act includes indirect discrimination: s.1.

[14] The position of the Jewish religion is unclear. See the Race Relations Board First Annual Report. A condition requiring Jewish parentage was considered racial in *Clayton* v. *Ramsden* [1943] A.C. 320. Jews were held to be an ethnic group in *King-Ansell* v. *Police* [1979] 2 N.Z.L.R. 531, approved by the House of Lords in *Mandla* v. *Dowell Lee* [1983] 2 A.C. 548, where Sikhs were held to be a racial group.

[15] For the American position on racially discriminatory trusts, see (1972) A.A.L.R. 101 (Sheridan).

[16] s.34(2) and (3).

[17] Thus the provisions contained in *Re Dominion Students' Hall Trust* [1947] Ch. 183 would now be unlawful. (This was also the case under the Race Relations Act 1968). See also *Re Gwyon* [1930] 1 Ch. 255.

[18] s.34(1).

[19] *Post*, p. 430. See *Re Lysaght* [1966] Ch. 191; *Re Dominion Students' Hall Trust, supra.* The promotion of racial harmony is now considered a charitable purpose; Annual Report of the Charity Commissioners for 1983, para. 19.

are bound by the Act in matters such as the employment of staff. Special provisions relating to educational charities enable restrictions based on sex to be removed or modified on application to the Secretary of State.[20]

C. Conditions Precedent and Subsequent; Determinable Interests

Questions involving illegality often arise in connection with the validity of conditions imposed upon otherwise valid gifts.[21] A condition precedent is one which must be satisfied before the gift can vest, whereas a condition subsequent operates to defeat an already vested gift by forfeiture. A determinable interest, on the other hand, is one which will automatically determine on the occurrence of the determining event, no question of forfeiture being involved.[22] It is not always easy, as a matter of construction, to decide whether a condition is intended to operate as a condition precedent or subsequent, or to distinguish conditional and determinable interests.[23] It seems that the latter are less susceptible to, although not immune from, attack on the ground of public policy.[24]

Apart from any question of illegality, conditions have frequently failed on the ground of uncertainty. A distinction has been drawn between conditions precedent and subsequent. A stricter test of certainty applies to a condition subsequent, which must be so framed that at the outset the beneficiary knows the exact event which will divest his interest.[25] Lord Denning M.R., has described this distinction as a "deplorable dichotomy," serving only to defeat the settlor's intention.[26] Even in the case of a condition subsequent, however, the court is reluctant to pronounce the condition void for uncertainty. So in *Re Tepper's Will Trusts*,[27] where a condition subsequent required the beneficiaries to remain within the Jewish faith and not to marry outside it, the court regarded as admissible extrinsic evidence of the Jewish-

---

[20] s.78

[21] Where several conditions are attached to one gift, the valid conditions may be severed from any which are invalid: *Re Hepplewhite Will Trusts, The Times*, January 21, 1977.

[22] *Ante*, p. 182. For a detailed account of the distinctions and their significance, see Cheshire and Burn's *Modern Law of Real Property* (14th ed.), pp. 326 *et seq.*

[23] See, for example, *Re Tuck's Settlement Trusts* [1978] Ch. 49; *Re Johnson's Will Trusts* [1967] Ch. 387; *Re Tepper's Will Trusts* [1987] Ch. 358.

[24] See *Re Johnson's Will Trusts, supra*, at p. 396; *Re Moore* (1888) 39 Ch.D. 116; Megarry and Wade, *The Law of Real Property* (5th ed.), pp. 71–72.

[25] *Re Tepper's Will Trusts, supra.* The test applying to conditions precedent is that laid down in *Re Allen* [1953] Ch. 810: conceptual uncertainty may not defeat such conditions. A recent example is *Re Barlow's Will Trusts* [1979] 1 W.L.R. 278, *ante*, p. 108. See generally Underhill's *Law of Trusts and Trustees* (14th ed.), pp. 59–64; [1980] Conv. 263 (L. McKay).

[26] *Re Tuck's Settlement Trusts* [1978] Ch. 49 at p. 60. But the distinction was acknowledged by the House of Lords in *Blathwayt* v. *Lord Cawley* [1976] A.C. 397 at p. 425.

[27] *Supra.*

faith as practised by the testator, to elucidate the meaning of his words.[28]

Assuming that the condition does not fail for uncertainty, the next question is whether it will be void as being illegal or otherwise contrary to public policy. The categories discussed below involve the types of condition which have been most frequently encountered.

(i) **Marriage, Separation and Divorce.** Where property is given by way of a determinable gift until marriage, and then to other beneficiaries, the limitation is unobjectionable.[29] Conditions, on the other hand, will be void if they are designed to prevent marriage or to encourage divorce or separation.

As far as conditions restraining marriage are concerned, a distinction is drawn between total and partial restraints. A condition subsequent, operating to divest the property on marriage, is void if its object is to restrain marriage altogether.[30] But conditions operating only in the event of a second or subsequent marriage, or merely requiring consent to marriage,[31] are not void.[32] Nor is there any objection to a condition in restraint of marriage with certain persons, or a certain class.[33] The rules relating to partial restraints on marriage differ according to whether the gift is of realty or personalty, the reason being that the personalty rules evolved in the ecclesiastical courts, whereas the realty rules were developed by the common law. The result of this historical distinction is as follows: in the case of personalty a condition imposing a partial restraint on marriage is invalid as being merely "*in terrorem*" if there is no express gift over on the occurrence of the marriage[34] whereas in the case of realty, a partial restraint is never invalid, whether or not there is a gift over.[35]

---

[28] Relying on *Re Tuck's Settlement Trusts, supra,* where, however, the will expressly provided that the Chief Rabbi could determine the meaning of "Jewish faith" and "approved wife." *cf.* A.J.A. 1982, s.21. See All E.R. Rev. 1987, p. 159 (P. J. Clarke) and p. 260 (C. H. Sherrin).

[29] *Re Lovell* [1920] 1 Ch. 122.

[30] *Lloyd* v. *Lloyd* (1852) 2 Sim.(N.S.) 255. This includes a condition which in practice amounts to a general restraint: *Re Lanyon* [1927] 2 Ch. 264. (Condition against marriage with any blood relation). It seems that similar rules would apply to a condition precedent. See *Re Wallace* [1920] Ch. 274.

[31] *Re Whiting's Settlement* [1905] 1 Ch. 96.

[32] *Allen* v. *Jackson* (1875) 1 Ch.D. 399.

[33] *Jenner* v. *Turner* (1880) 16 Ch.D. 188; *Perrin* v. *Lyon* (1807) 9 East. 170: condition against marrying a person born in Scotland or of Scottish parents upheld. See also the cases on religion, discussed below.

[34] *Leong* v. *Lim Beng Chye* [1955] A.C. 648 (A residuary gift is not a gift over).

[35] Another possible distinction is that in the case of realty, but not personalty, even a general restraint is valid if intended merely to provide for the beneficiary while unmarried, rather than to promote celibacy: *Jones* v. *Jones* (1876) 1 Q.B.D. 279.

Conditions designed to induce the separation or divorce of a husband and wife are void as being contrary to public policy.[36] But if the parties have already decided upon a separation, the trusts in any deed of separation are not invalid.[37] Nor is there any objection where the true object of a disposition is merely to make provision for a party during the separation.[38]

It will be seen that most of these cases were decided at a time when the sanctity of marriage was perhaps regarded more highly than it is today. A stricter view was taken of "immoral relations" than is now the case. Thus in the past trusts or covenants to create trusts have been held void if created in consideration of a future immoral association.[39] The modern tendency might be to discover some other form of consideration from the beneficiary.[40]

A question which might arise is the effect of a condition designed to restrain the modern practice of "living in sin."[41] Such a condition might fail for uncertainty,[42] but, in any event, it might be said that while such a practice is not unlawful, "it is not yet a virtue."[43]

(ii) Parental Duties. A condition calculated to bring about the separation of a parent from his child is void as being contrary to public policy,[44] even where the parents are divorced.[45] Similarly, a condition designed to interfere with the exercise of parental duties.[46] In *Blathwayt* v. *Lord Cawley*[47] a settlement provided for the forfeiture of the interest of any child who became a Roman Catholic. It was argued that the condition was void on the ground that it would hamper parental duties in religious instruction. The House of Lords rejected this argu-

---

[36] *Re Johnson's Will Trusts* [1967] Ch. 387; *Re Caborne* [1943] Ch. 224. See also *Re McBride* (1980) 107 D.L.R. (3d) 233; *Re Hepplewhite Will Trusts, The Times*, January 21, 1977.

[37] *Wilson* v. *Wilson* (1848) 1 H.L.C. 538. It is otherwise if the provision is designed to discourage reconciliation. See also *Egerton* v. *Egerton* [1949] 2 All E.R. 238 at p. 242: "a settlement which contains provisions as to what should happen in the case of divorce is not contrary to public policy" (*per* Denning L.J.).

[38] *Re Lovell* [1920] 1 Ch. 122. As to the admissibility of any evidence of the settlor's motive, see *Re Johnson's Will Trusts* [1967] Ch. 387.

[39] See *Re Vallance* (1884) 26 Ch.D. 353; *Ayerst* v. *Jenkins* (1873) L.R. 16 Eq. 275.

[40] See, for example, *Tanner* v. *Tanner* [1975] 1 W.L.R. 1346 where a contract was inferred between a man and his mistress in consideration of her looking after the house and family; *cf. Coombes* v. *Smith* [1986] 1 W.L.R. 808.

[41] Another example might be a condition restraining a homosexual relationship.

[42] See *Re Jones* [1953] Ch. 125, where a condition prohibiting a "social or other relationship" with X failed for uncertainty.

[43] Borrowing Lord Denning's description, in a different context (tax avoidance), in *Re Weston's Settlements* [1969] 1 Ch. 223.

[44] *Re Boulter* [1922] 1 Ch. 75.

[45] *Re Piper* [1946] 2 All E.R. 503.

[46] *Re Borwick* [1933] Ch. 657; *Re Sandbrook* [1912] 2 Ch. 471. These two decisions must now be read in the light of the comments made in *Blathwayt* v. *Lord Cawley* [1976] A.C. 397, discussed below.

[47] [1976] A.C. 397.

ment: "To say that any condition which in any way might affect or influence the way in which a child is brought up, or in which parental duties are exercised, seems to me to state far too wide a rule."[48]

(iii) Religion. It has already been noted that discrimination on religious grounds falls outside the Race Relations Act 1976. Conditions restricting freedom of religion have long been popular with settlors and testators. While such conditions have sometimes failed for uncertainty, especially in the case of conditions subsequent,[49] it has never been held that such provisions are contrary to public policy, even in the case of charitable trusts.[50] In *Blathwayt* v. *Lord Cawley*,[51] of which the facts have already been given, Lord Cross said that while it may be wrong for the government to discriminate on religion, it does not follow that it is against public policy for an adherent of one religion to distinguish in disposing of his property; any other view amounts to saying that "it is disreputable for him to be convinced of the importance of holding true religious beliefs and of the fact that his religious beliefs are the true ones."[52] It had been argued that the Race Relations Acts and the European Convention of Human Rights showed that the law was now against discrimination. Lord Wilberforce said "I do not doubt that conceptions of public policy should move with the times and that widely accepted treaties and statutes may point the direction in which such conceptions, as applied by the courts, ought to move. It may well be that conditions such as this are, or at least are becoming, inconsistent with standards now widely accepted."[53] But this did not justify the introduction of a new rule, for to do so would reduce another freedom, that of testamentary disposition. "Discrimination is not the same thing as choice: it operates over a larger and less personal area, and neither by express provision nor by implication has private selection yet become a matter of public policy."[54]

(iv) Race. We have already seen that discrimination on the grounds

---

[48] *Ibid.* at p. 426 (*per* Lord Wilberforce).
[49] *Clayton* v. *Ramsden* [1943] A.C. 320 (forfeiture on marriage to person not of Jewish parentage and faith); *Re Abraham's Will Trusts* [1969] 1 Ch. 463; *Re Tepper's Will Trusts* [1987] Ch. 358. A condition precedent is less likely to fail on this ground: see *Re Allen* [1953] Ch. 810; *Re Selby's Will Trusts* [1966] 1 W.L.R. 43; *Re Tuck's Settlement Trusts* [1978] Ch. 49 (marriage to "approved wife" of Jewish blood and faith not uncertain). See also *Re Evans* [1940] Ch. 629.
[50] See *Re Lysaght* [1966] Ch. 191. (Discrimination against Jews and Roman Catholics was merely "undesirable").
[51] [1976] A.C. 397. See also *Re Remnant's Settlement Trusts* [1970] 1 Ch. 560; *Clayton* v. *Ramsden, supra.* For a discussion of racial and religious discrimination in restrictive covenants, see [1978] Conv. 24 (J.D.A. Brooke-Taylor). The heir to the throne may not be, or marry, a Roman Catholic: Act of Settlement 1701.
[52] [1976] A.C. 397 at p. 429.
[53] *Ibid.* at p. 426.
[54] *Ibid.*

of race or colour is made unlawful by the Race Relations Act 1976. We have also seen that, apart from special provisions relating to charities, that Act has no application to private trusts. It seems that it is not contrary to public policy for a settlor to discriminate on these grounds, although the point is not unarguable.[55] There is little authority on the point, which has arisen mainly in connection with charitable trusts.[56] Many of the comments made by the House of Lords in *Blathwayt* v. *Lord Cawley*[57] in the context of religion would apply equally to racial discrimination, save that the dictum of Lord Cross[58] loses all conviction if race is substituted for religious beliefs.

(v) **Alienation.** Conditions operating as a complete restraint on the alienation of property are void as being contrary to public policy.

In *Re Brown*,[59] a testator devised realty among his four sons, subject to a condition which would have produced forfeiture of his interest by any son who mortgaged or sold his interest other than among his brothers. The condition was held to be equivalent to a general restraint on alienation, and therefore void, since the class of permitted alienees was small and bound to get smaller.

But a partial restraint on alienation is valid.[60] Restrictions upon alienation to groups identified by religion may be unobjectionable, but the Race Relations Act 1976 forbids racial discrimination in the disposal of property.[61]

Restraints even of a general nature may be valid if they take the form of a determinable interest.[62] Section 33 of the Trustee Act 1925 itself provides such an example.[63]

(vi) **Other Cases.** Much difficulty has been encountered in the past with "name and arms" clauses, whereby settlors seek to ensure that the beneficiary adopts a specified name and coat of arms, usually those of the settlor. Such clauses were at one time held to be contrary to public policy, on the ground that, if the beneficiary was a married woman, the taking of another name might lead to dissension between husband and

---

[55] See Underhill, *loc. cit.* at p. 167.

[56] See *Re Gwyon* [1930] 1 Ch. 255; *Re Dominion Students' Hall Trust* [1947] Ch. 183. In neither case was public policy discussed.

[57] [1976] A.C. 397.

[58] *Ibid.* at p. 429; *supra.*

[59] [1954] Ch. 39; S.L.A. 1925, s.106; *cf. Caldy Manor Estate Ltd.* v. *Farrell* [1974] 1 W.L.R. 1303 (covenant against alienation not unlawful).

[60] See *Re MacLeay* (1875) L.R. 20 Eq. 186. (Doubted in *Re Rosher* [1884] 25 Ch. 801). It is suggested in Cheshire and Burn's *Modern Law of Real Property* (14th ed.), at p. 330, that even partial restraints should be invalid as repugnant to ownership.

[61] s.21.

[62] *Re Dugdale* (1883) 38 Ch.D. 176 at pp. 178–181, *per* Kay J.; *Re Leach* [1912] 2 Ch. 422.

[63] *Ante,* p. 184 (the protective trust).

wife. It is now settled that such clauses are neither uncertain nor contrary to public policy.[64]

It was held in *Egerton* v. *Brownlow*[65] that a condition requiring the beneficiary to obtain a dukedom was contrary to public policy as tending to encourage corruption, but a similar provision involving a baronetcy was upheld in *Re Wallace*,[66] the distinction being that, unlike a dukedom, no legislative powers and duties would be involved, consequently the public interest could not be affected. Conditions forbidding entry into the naval or military services have also been held void.[67] The validity of conditions relating to bankruptcy has already been discussed.[68]

Finally, a condition whereby a beneficiary was to become entitled to property on becoming destitute has been held void as contrary to public policy in that it could encourage irresponsibility with money.[69]

D. The Consequence of Illegality

The general position is that if an express trust fails on the ground of unlawfulness, a resulting trust to the settlor or his estate ensues.[70] This is so even if the trust was designed to encourage an offence prohibited by statute.[71] Where the trust is only partly unlawful, the whole fails if the proportion to be devoted to the unlawful purpose is unascertainable,[72] whereas if that proportion is ascertainable, only that part fails.[73]

(i) **Fraudulent Settlements.** Where the purpose of the trust is not merely unlawful, but also fraudulent, then the court will not assist the settlor to recover the property, applying the principle *in pari delicto potior est conditio defendentis*.[74] But the settlor may recover if the trust is still executory and no fraud has in fact been perpetrated, whatever the motive; or if he repents before performance[75]; or if it is not necessary to plead his own illegality.[76]

There is some authority that even if the settlor cannot recover, an

---

[64] *Re Neeld* [1962] Ch. 643, where the Court of Appeal overruled many previous authorities.
[65] (1853) 4 H.L. 1.
[66] [1920] 2 Ch. 274.
[67] See *Re Beard* [1908] 1 Ch. 383.
[68] *Ante*, p. 182.
[69] *Re Hepplewhite Will Trusts, The Times* January 21, 1977.
[70] *Ante*, p. 228. *cf. Ayerst* v. *Jenkins* (1873) L.R. 16 Eq. 275.
[71] *Thrupp* v. *Collett* (1858) 26 Beav. 125.
[72] *Chapman* v. *Brown* (1801) 6 Ves. 404.
[73] *Mitford* v. *Reynolds* (1842) 1 Ph. 185. There is some authority that in such a case the whole can go to the lawful part: *Fisk* v. *Att.-Gen.* (1867) L.R. 4 Eq. 521.
[74] *Re Great Berlin Steamboat Co.* (1884) 26 Ch.D. 616; *cf.* where the parties are not *in pari delicto*: *Reynell* v. *Sprye* (1852) 1 De G.M. & G. 600 at p. 679.
[75] *Symes* v. *Hughes* (1870) L.R. 9 Eq. 475.
[76] *Chettiar* v. *Chettiar* [1962] A.C. 294.

innocent person claiming through him can do so,[77] but this seems contrary to principle.[78]

(ii) Conditional and Determinable Interests. Where a condition subsequent is unlawful, the gift takes effect as an absolute interest: the condition alone is void.[79] In the case of a condition precedent, a distinction is drawn between realty and personalty. As far as realty is concerned, the gift itself fails if the condition is bad.[80] Where the gift is of personalty, however, it takes effect free of the condition where the illegality is only a *malum prohibitum*.[81] But where the illegality is a *malum in se*, the gift fails. In the case of a determinable interest, the gift fails if the determining event is unlawful.[82]

2. PERPETUITY, DURATION AND INALIENABILITY

A. General

One of the most common causes over the years of invalidity of interests under a trust has been the failure to comply with the Rule Against Perpetuities. The hazard has been much reduced, and the law simplified by the Perpetuities and Accumulations Act 1964, which applies to dispositions coming into effect after July 15, 1964.[83] Questions may still arise in respect of earlier instruments, as a decision on a will, for example, may be delayed until the death of a life tenant.[84] But the Act has been in operation for over 25 years, and each year which passes will reduce the likelihood of a question arising which is not governed by the Act. There is not space to deal with the subject in detail here. It is covered by books on real property,[85] a practice which can have a historical justification only; the rule grew up in connection with settlements of land, but in modern times has its most common operation in trusts of personalty. The subject is one which has caused much confusion and misunderstanding, not least in connection with the Act; and a few general comments may be helpful.

---

[77] *Muckleston* v. *Brown* (1801) 6 Ves. 52 at p. 68 (Lord Eldon).
[78] *Ayerst* v. *Jenkins* (1873) L.R. 16 Eq. 275 at p. 281 (Lord Selborne).
[79] *Re Beard* [1908] 1 Ch. 383. This is so whether the gift is realty or personalty.
[80] *Re Elliott* [1952] Ch. 217.
[81] *i.e.* something made unlawful only by statute. See *Re Piper* [1946] 2 All E.R. 503. The distinction was apparently not discussed in *Re Hepplewhite Will Trusts, The Times*, January 21, 1977.
[82] *Re Moore* (1888) 39 Ch.D. 116. For the application of the perpetuity rule to conditional and determinable interests, see Perpetuities and Accumulations Act 1964, s.12: the interest becomes absolute if the determining event or breach of condition does not occur within the perpetuity period.
[83] s.15(5).
[84] See *Re Drummond* [1988] 1 W.L.R. 234, concerning a 1924 settlement.
[85] Cheshire and Burn, pp. 273 *et seq.*, M. & W., pp. 231 *et seq.*; Morris and Leach, *The Rule against Perpetuities*; Maudsley, *The Modern Law of Perpetuities*.

B. Tying Up Land

The perpetuity rule should be regarded as one of the ways in which the law has insisted on the observance of a basic policy against the tying up of lands for an undue length of time. The struggle began in the earliest years of the common law. Conditions against alienation were held void. Entails were by statute inalienable, but by 1472 it was recognised that an entail could be barred, turned into a fee simple and alienated.[86] The Old Rule Against Perpetuities prevented a series of contingent life estates. Alienability was successfully being maintained. But once it was decided that executory interests were valid and indestructible,[87] it was possible to project interests limited to vest at an indefinite time in the future. The Rule Against Perpetuities was designed to restrict the extent to which future vesting could be postponed.

C. Remote Vesting. Life in Being Plus 21 Years

The permitted period was a life in being plus 21 years; permitting, in effect, a grant to the first son of A to attain the age of 21 years. For A's son must attain the age of 21 years, if he ever does, within 21 years of A's death. A period of gestation was also allowed in the case of posthumous children.

One would have thought it obvious that the limitation which offended was one that failed to vest by the end of the period; and so rendered the ownership of the land uncertain for too long a period. But, no. The common law rule was that the interest was void if it *might* vest outside the period; even if in fact it vested the next day. The Rule is:

> "No interest is good unless it must vest, if at all, not later than twenty-one years after some life in being at the creation of the interest."[88]

Thus, a gift to the first son of A to attain the age of 22 years was void at common law if A was still alive; even if A had a son of 21½ at the time. For that son might die, another son be born, and A die; and A's first son to attain the age of 21 might do so more than 21 years after the death of any persons alive at the date of the gift. A long series of bizarre situations showing the ruthless operation of the rule has often been catalogued, and need not be repeated. The one simple example makes the point. The complexities of some of the cases are formidable.

---

[86] *Taltarum's Case* Y.B. 12 Edw. 4, 19; and "clauses of perpetuity" designed to prevent barring were also held void; *Corbet's Case* (1599) 1 Co. Rep. 83b; *Mildmey's Case* (1605) 6 Co. Rep. 40a; *Mary Portington's Case* (1613) 10 Co. Rep. 35b.
[87] *Pells* v. *Brown* (1620) Cro. Jac. 590.
[88] Gray, *The Rule Against Perpetuities* (4th ed.), § 201.

D. Wait and See

The Act deals with this situation in three ways; first, by permitting a settlor to specify as the perpetuity period for the purpose of the disposition a period of years not exceeding 80[89]; secondly, by a number of specific reforms on individual points which had caused difficulty, and thirdly, by introducing a system of wait and see.[90] If the law was difficult and unrealistic because it made void an interest which vested in fact within the period merely because it might have vested outside it, an obvious solution would be to make its validity depend on whether or not it does in fact vest within it. That is the theory of wait and see.

There is much disagreement as to the identity of the lives in being at common law.[91] The 1964 Act, however, lays down, in section 3, its own list of statutory lives in being, which must be used where the wait and see rule is invoked. Although certain common law lives in being, such as "royal lives," are not included, the statutory class is generally wider than the class of common law lives in being.

One would have thought it obvious that, on enacting wait and see, the common law rule should be abolished. It no longer has any part to play. If a disposition must vest, if at all, within the period, then it will vest, if at all, within the period. Thus, the common law test is contained within the wait and see test. There is no advantage in knowing that an interest complies with the common law test. Being "valid" within that test is of no advantage. The interest remains contingent, and its value is dependent, not on compliance with the common law rule, but upon its likelihood of vesting. Assume that A has a son X aged 21. A gift to A's first son to attain the age of 22 is void under the common law rule, but likely to vest within the period; and would be of greater value than a gift to the first son of A to go to the moon in A's lifetime, which would be valid at common law. Compliance with the common law rule is irrelevant in a system of wait and see.[92]

Nevertheless, the Act retained the common law rule. Wait and see only applies to "void" limitations.[93] So it is necessary to apply the common law rule to test validity, and to apply wait and see, if it fails to comply with the common law rule. It is tempting to ignore the common law rule. Every limitation which was valid at common law would also be valid under wait and see; unless, however, there could be some situation in which a gift was validated by a common law life who is not in the statutory list, and the interest does not in fact vest within 21 years

---

[89] s.1.

[90] s.3.

[91] (1964) 80 L.Q.R. 486 at pp. 495–508 (J.H.C. Morris and H.W.R. Wade); (1965) 81 L.Q.R. 106 at p. 108 (D.E. Allan); (1970) 86 L.Q.R. 357 (R.H. Maudsley), (1975) 60 Cornell L.R. 355 (R.H. Maudsley); Maudsley, *The Modern Law of Perpetuities*; (1981) 97 L.Q.R. 593 (R. Deech); (1986) 102 L.Q.R. 251 (J. Dukeminier).

[92] (1970) 86 L.Q.R. 357 at p. 372 (R.H. Maudsley); (1975) 60 Cornell L.R. 355 (R.H. Maudsley); Maudsley, *The Modern Law of Perpetuities*.

[93] s.3.

of the death of the survivor of the statutory lives. Because the class of statutory lives does not coincide exactly with the common law lives, that is theoretically possible.[94] But it is absurd to retain all the common law learning in order to save a rare gift which will probably never occur. The common law rule should have been abolished.[95]

If it had been, the application of the wait and see rule would have been simple. In the case of any gift, all that would be necessary would be the writing down of the measuring lives, the recording of their deaths, and the addition of 21 years.[96] The interests which had then vested would be valid; those which had not vested would be void. Just like the administration of a limitation governed by a royal lives clause. That is all that there need be to the operation of the perpetuity rule in the era of wait and see.

E. Duration and Inalienability

Separate from the perpetuity rule governing remoteness of vesting, but a further manifestation of the same policy, is the rule which declares void trusts which are required to continue for too long a period; longer, that is, than the perpetuity period.

The matter will be discussed in connection with non-charitable purpose trusts.[97] In so far as they are permitted, they must be limited to the perpetuity period. The restriction upon duration does not apply to charitable trusts.[98]

It should be added that this rule is not in any way inconsistent with the ownership of property in fee simple by a person or a corporation. Those owners may alienate at any time. They may of course keep the property for ever; but the property is not tied up in any way. Thus in *Bowman* v. *Secular Society*,[99] a gift to the "Secular Society" a society devoted to furthering anti-Christian beliefs, having survived an attack on the grounds of public policy, had nothing to fear on the score of perpetuity, as the Society was a limited company, and able to deal freely with its property.

In *Re Chardon*,[1] a testator gave the income of a fund to a cemetery

---

[94] For example: In "the first of my lineal descendants to shake hands with X." The gift is valid at common law because it must take effect, if at all, within X's lifetime. But X is not a statutory life. If the event took place more than 21 years after the dropping of the last of the statutory lives, the gift would take effect under the common law rule, but would fail under wait and see. Similarly dispositions governed by a royal lives clause.

[95] (1975) 60 Cornell L.R. 355 at p. 370 (R.H. Maudsley).

[96] Even simpler is the approach of the American Uniform Statutory Rule Against Perpetuities, discussed in (1987) 46 C.L.J. 234 (L. W. Waggoner), whereby the wait and see period is 90 years, without any lives in being.

[97] *Post*, p. 348; *cf. Re Dean* (1889) 41 Ch.D. 552. For difficulties arising with unincorporated associations, see *Re Grant's Will Trusts* [1980] 1 W.L.R. 360, *post*, p. 357.

[98] *Post*, p. 373.

[99] [1917] A.C. 406.

[1] [1928] Ch. 464.

company "during such period as they shall continue to maintain and keep in good repair" two specified graves; and there was a gift into residue on the company's failure to do so. The gift was upheld.

No property was rendered inalienable, for the cemetery company could alienate its interest; so could those entitled to the residue, and they could combine together to sell the fee.[2] Nor did the gift offend the rule against excessive duration. There was no requirement that the income should be applied in the maintenance of the graves[3]; and no requirement therefore that the capital fund should be maintained indefinitely for the purpose of producing the income.

The gift succeeded as a conveyancing device to effect the maintenance of the graves,[4] and would continue to do so as long as the cemetery company found the income paid was sufficient to make the operation profitable. The gift over might of course take effect at a time beyond the end of the perpetuity period; but the common law rule did not apply to possibilities of reverter. If the instrument were governed by the Perpetuities and Accumulations Act 1964, the wait and see provision would apply, and, if the determining event did not occur within the perpetuity period, the interest of the cemetery company would become absolute.[5]

3. ATTEMPTS TO KEEP PROPERTY FROM CREDITORS

A. General

A creditor can demand payment from his debtor out of the debtor's property. If the debtor's property is insufficient to pay his debts, he is insolvent, and it will not be possible to pay all the creditors in full. Generally speaking, before bankruptcy the debtor may choose which creditors he pays first[6]; but after bankruptcy the bankruptcy law provides for a fair sharing out of his property.

When a person foresees the danger of his own[7] future insolvency—as where he is entering upon a business venture—there is the temptation to put property out of the reach of creditors, by, for example, creating a settlement in favour of the family. If the business venture succeeds the profits will flow in; if it fails, the creditors will be

---

[2] *Per* Romer J. [1928] Ch. 464 at p. 470.
[3] As there was in *Re Dalziel* [1943] Ch. 277; *Re Wightwick's W. T.* [1950] Ch. 266.
[4] *Post*, p. 365. There is a substantial literature on this topic. See especially Gray, *Rule against Perpetuities* (3rd ed.), App. H; (1902) 15 Harv. L.R. 509 (J.C. Gray); (1917) 33 L.Q.R. 236, 357 (C. Sweet); (1957) 53 L.Q.R. 24 (W.O. Hart); (1938) 54 L.Q.R. 258 (M.J. Albery); (1961) 25 Conv.(N.S.) 56 (J.D. Davies). The distinction between determinable and conditional interests is explained *ante*, pp. 182, 320.
[5] s.12.
[6] *Middleton* v. *Pollock* (1876) 2 Ch.D. 104; *Glegg* v. *Bromley* [1912] 3 K.B. 474; *Re Lloyd's Furniture Palace Ltd.* [1925] Ch. 853.
[7] Where he foresees his beneficiary's insolvency, the protective trust may be employed; *ante*, p. 181.

unpaid; but the family will be cared for.[8] It may also be that a settlement is made for other reasons, such as the reduction of tax liability,[9] but insolvency subsequently occurs. The question for consideration here is the extent to which a creditor can upset dispositions made by debtors of property which would otherwise be available for the creditors, whether or not there is a bankruptcy.

The relevant provisions were formerly Law of Property Act 1925, section 172 (transactions to defraud creditors) and Bankruptcy Act 1914, section 42 (settlements prior to bankruptcy). These sections were repealed by the Insolvency Act 1985 (now the Act of 1986), and replaced by other provisions. It is proposed to give a brief outline of the old law, partly because it is relevant to the transitional provisions of the new legislation,[10] and partly because some of the decisions on the old law will continue to be relevant.

B. Position Prior to Insolvency Act

(i) Law of Property Act 1925, s.172. This section provided that a conveyance of property[11] made with intent to defraud creditors was voidable at the instance of any person thereby prejudiced. The transferee had a defence if he was in good faith and without notice at the conveyance of the intent to defraud creditors, and had given valuable or good consideration.[12]

In the event of the debtor's later bankruptcy, section 172 remained applicable, but the action to set aside the conveyance would be brought by the trustee in bankruptcy (or by an individual with leave of the court). Any property made available to creditors under the section would then be distributable under the bankruptcy laws, giving no priority to those creditors who were intended to be defrauded by the conveyance. The section also applied to insolvent estates.[13]

(a) *Proof of Intent to Defraud.* The onus of proof was upon the party seeking to set aside the conveyance.[14] Inferences drawn from surrounding circumstances could be relied on to establish a prima facie case of intent to defraud,[15] the burden then shifting to the debtor to disprove it. The fact that the conveyance was voluntary made the task

---

[8] "If I succeed in business, I make a fortune for myself. If I fail, I leave my creditors unpaid. They will pay the loss." *per* Jessel M.R.; in *Re Butterworth, ex p. Russell* (1882) 19 Ch.D. 588 at p. 598.

[9] *Ante*, p. 206.

[10] See Insolvency Act 1986, Sched. 11, paras. 9, 17 and 20, providing that transactions prior to the commencement date shall not be set aside save to the extent that they could have been set aside under the previous law.

[11] The section applied to every kind of property.

[12] Good consideration meant natural love and affection, but little effect seems to have been given to it; see *Re Eichholz* [1959] Ch. 708.

[13] *Re Eichholz, supra.* s.42 of the Bankruptcy Act 1914, *post*, did not.

[14] *Lloyds Bank Ltd.* v. *Marcan* [1973] 1 W.L.R. 1387.

[15] *Twyne's Case* (1602) 3 Co. Rep. 80b.

of upholding it all the more difficult. Although it was laid down in *Freeman* v. *Pope*[16] that an intent to defeat creditors must be inferred if a debtor made a settlement of property without which he could not pay his debts, such an extreme rule was described as "monstrous" by Lord Esher M.R. in *Re Wise, ex p. Mercer*,[17] where a master mariner, engaged to a girl in England, married a different one in Hong Kong. The English girl started an action for breach of promise; and the same post brought to Hong Kong the writ in the action, and also news that Wise had become entitled, on his mother's death, to a legacy of £500. Not being otherwise indebted, and thinking that nothing would come of the action for breach, he settled the £500 on his wife and any future children. The English girl obtained judgment for £500, and took steps to upset the settlement. She was unable to prove an intent to defraud and the settlement stood.

Under a more recent formulation of the rule, it was held sufficient to show an intent to deprive creditors of timely recourse to property which would otherwise be applicable for their benefit.

In *Lloyds Bank Ltd.* v. *Marcan*,[18] M and his wife carried on a horticultural business on land owned by M. M was indebted to the Bank, and he mortgaged the premises to them as security. After the Bank had started proceedings for possession, M assigned his share in the business to his wife, and, acting consistently with the counsel's opinion that it was legitimate to do so, purported to grant her a lease for 20 years in consideration of a rack rent. It was held the lease was voidable under section 172. M's intention was expressly to deprive the bank of its ability to obtain vacant possession and to diminish its position as a creditor. His conduct was "less than honest," and, notwithstanding the legal advice, amounted to sharp practice.

(b) *"Any person thereby prejudiced."* The settlement could be set aside by existing or subsequent creditors, even though all the debts existing at the date of the settlement had been paid.[19] The satisfaction of all debts existing at that time may have made the proof of fraudulent intent more difficult; but this was clear in *Re Butterworth, ex p. Russell*,[20] where a prosperous baker made the settlement immediately before purchasing a grocer's business, a trade in which he had no experience. Indeed in such circumstances it seems that there was no need for there to have been any creditors at all at the date of the

---

[16] (1870) L.R. 5 Ch. App. 538.
[17] (1886) 17 Q.B.D. 290 at p. 298.
[18] [1973] 1 W.L.R. 1387; (1975) 91 L.Q.R. 86 (B. J. F. Langstaff).
[19] *Mackay* v. *Douglas* (1872) L.R. 14 Eq. 106.
[20] (1882) 19 Ch.D. 588.

conveyance.[21] The settlor could not of course himself set aside the settlement unless it contained an express power of revocation.[22]

Although intent to defraud creditors had to be shown, the section possibly included as a person prejudiced someone who was technically not a creditor.[23] In *Cadogan* v. *Cadogan*,[24] a wife submitted a claim for financial relief in reply to her husband's petition for divorce. The husband then made a voluntary settlement in favour of their son, and then died; his death had the effect of abating the wife's claim for relief; and so she never became a creditor. She took steps to set aside the settlement; and the son attempted to strike out the claim under Ord. 18, r. 19 on the ground that it was clearly unsustainable, but the Court of Appeal refused to do so.

(ii) **Bankruptcy Act 1914, s.42.** Section 42(1) provided that a settlement[25] of property was void[26] as against the trustee in bankruptcy if the settlor became bankrupt within two years of the settlement. If he became bankrupt within 10 years of the settlement, the same result followed unless the beneficiaries could show that the settlor could pay his debts at the time of the settlement without the settled property, and that his interest in the property passed to the settlement trustee. There was no need to show any intention to defraud creditors. The settlement could not be set aside under the above rules if supported by marriage consideration[27] or if made in favour of a purchaser in good faith and for valuable consideration.[28]

"Purchaser" here meant a purchaser "in a commercial sense." Thus in *Re Densham*,[29] where the husband held the home on trust for himself and his wife jointly, the wife having contributed one-ninth of the purchase money, it could not be said that she was a purchaser for valuable consideration of her half-share. The trustee in bankruptcy was entitled save to the extent of her one-ninth share. Although the wife had given valuable consideration, which at law need not equal the

---

[21] See *Mackay* v. *Douglas* (1872) L.R. 14 Eq. 106; *Stileman* v. *Ashdown* (1742) 1 Atk. 477; *Cadogan* v. *Cadogan* [1977] 1 W.L.R. 1041.

[22] And where property was conveyed with such a fraudulent intention, then even though no creditors materialised, the presumption of advancement could not be rebutted by evidence of such an intention: *Tinker* v. *Tinker* [1970] P. 136, *ante*, p. 244.

[23] Although it may be established that there was no need for existing creditors at the date of the conveyance, as discussed above, in those cases creditors did come into existence subsequently.

[24] [1977] 1 W.L.R. 1041.

[25] Defined as "any conveyance or transfer of property," and interpreted as confined to a disposition in the nature of a settlement.

[26] Interpreted as voidable.

[27] See *Rennell* v. *I.R.C.* [1964] A.C. 173; *Re Densham* [1975] 1 W.L.R. 1519.

[28] Or if made on the wife or children in respect of property accruing to the settlor after marriage in right of his wife. This was designed to meet the case of property coming to the husband under the law as it applied to marriages prior to 1882.

[29] [1975] 1 W.L.R. 1519, criticised [1983] Conv. 240 (R. Griffith).

value of that which she received, she was not a purchaser for valuable consideration within section 42(1), as that expression had to be construed in a commercial sense rather than a legal sense. A similar result followed in *Re Windle*,[30] where a husband transferred the home to his estranged wife upon her undertaking to make future mortgage payments. She was not a purchaser within section 42(1), which postulated a person who, in a commercial sense, provided a *quid pro quo*. It would be otherwise if the equity of redemption was of no appreciable value.

But a more lenient view was taken in *Re Abbott (a bankrupt)*,[31] where, on divorce, the wife sought a tranfer of the jointly owned matrimonial home. A compromise was reached, embodied in a consent order, whereby the house was to be sold and she would be paid £18,000 and half of any excess. The house was sold for over £18,000. On the husband's subsequent bankruptcy his trustee claimed that the arrangement was a settlement of £9,000 on the wife which could be set aside under section 42. His claim failed. The wife was a purchaser for valuable consideration.[32] That expression was wide enough to cover a spouse whose bona fide claim to a property adjustment order on divorce had been compromised. "Good consideration" would not be enough, nor nominal consideration, even though sufficient to support a contract at law. It must have a real and substantial value, but need not take the form of a tangible asset, nor be measurable in monetary terms, nor be of equal value to the consideration given by the debtor. It was clear from section 39 of the Matrimonial Causes Act 1973 that property transfer orders could be avoided under section 42 of the 1914 Act, but this construction, as Peter Gibson J. admitted, made it harder for the trustee in bankruptcy to succeed. The problem remained that if the claim had not been compromised but the same order had been made by the court, the wife could not have been described as a purchaser for valuable consideration. It would be anomalous if she could improve her position by a compromise. This point was left open by the court.[33]

C. Insolvency Act 1986[34]

(i) **Transactions Defrauding Creditors.** Section 423 of the Insolvency Act 1986, replacing section 172 of the Law of Property Act 1925, provides that a transaction at an undervalue may be set aside if the court is satisfied that the person entering into the transaction (the debtor) did so for the purpose

[30] [1975] 1 W.L.R. 1628.
[31] [1983] Ch. 45.
[32] No doubt she would not be bona fide if she compromised her claim in order to defeat the trustee in bankruptcy.
[33] See [1983] Conv. 240 (R. Griffith); *cf.* [1983] Conv. 219 at p. 226 (C. Hand).
[34] See (1987) 17 Fam. Law 316 (N. Furey).

(a) of putting assets beyond the reach of a person who is making, or
   may at some time make, a claim against him, or

(b) of otherwise prejudicing the interests of such a person in relation to the claim which he is making or may make.

The court may make such order as it thinks fit for

(a) restoring the position to what it would have been if the transaction had not been entered into, and

(b) protecting the interests of persons who are victims of the transaction (defined as a person who is, or is capable of being,
   prejudiced by the transaction).

The section applies equally to transactions entered into by individuals and by corporate bodies.[35]

   (a) *Transaction at an undervalue.* By section 423(1), a person enters
into a transaction with another person at an undervalue if

(a) he makes a gift to the other person or he otherwise enters into a
   transaction with the other on terms that provide for him to
   receive no consideration; or

(b) he enters into a transaction with the other in consideration of
   marriage; or

(c) he enters into a transaction with the other for a consideration
   the value of which, in money or money's worth, is significantly
   less than the value, in money or money's worth, of the consideration provided by himself.

   It will be seen that these provisions are narrower than section 172 of
the 1925 Act, which allowed a transaction for full value to be set aside
where the transferee had notice of the intent to defraud, as in *Lloyds
Bank Ltd.* v. *Marcan.*[36] Under the new provisions that case would be
decided differently. As the transaction was not at an undervalue, the
court would have no jurisdiction to make any order. Another difference is that a purchaser for marriage consideration (or "good consideration") without notice of the intent to defraud had a defence under
section 172, but is not immune under the new provisions, which treat
such a transaction as at an undervalue.

   (b) *Intention.* As stated above, the court must be satisfied that the
person entering into the transaction did so for the purpose of putting
assets beyond the reach of, or of otherwise prejudicing, an existing or
potential claimant. This resembles the old "intent to defraud" requirement, as interpreted in *Lloyds Bank Ltd.* v. *Marcan.*[37] It seems also
that the new provisions resemble the previous law insofar as it is not

[35] See also I.A. 1986, s.207.
[36] [1973] 1 W.L.R. 1387, *ante*, p. 332.
[37] *Supra.*

necessary that there should be existing creditors at the time of the transaction,[38] nor that the person seeking to set aside the transaction should be technically a "creditor."[39]

(c) *Persons who may apply to court.* Where the debtor, being an individual, is now bankrupt, or, being a body corporate, is being wound up or is the subject of an administration order under Part II of the 1986 Act, the application may only be made by the official receiver, the trustee of the bankrupt's estate or the liquidator or administrator of the body corporate. The victim of the transaction, as defined above,[40] may apply with the leave of the court. Where a voluntary arrangement has been approved under Part I (corporate bodies) or Part VIII (individuals) of the 1986 Act, the application may be made by the supervisor of the voluntary arrangement or the victim of the transaction. In any other case, for example where there is no insolvency, the application may be made by the victim of the transaction. These provisions are found in section 424 of the 1986 Act, which further provides that any application made under the section is treated as made on behalf of every victim of the transaction.

(d) *Orders to be made.* Section 425 of the 1986 Act sets out the orders which may be made by the court. These include orders

(a) requiring any property transferred by the impugned transaction to be vested in any person, either absolutely or for the benefit of all the persons on whose behalf the application is treated as made, or
(b) requiring any property representing the application of the proceeds of sale of property transferred by the impugned transaction or of money transferred by it to be so vested, or
(c) requiring any person to pay to any other person in respect of benefits received from the debtor such sums as the court may direct.

(e) *Third parties.* Section 425(2) provides that any order made may affect the property of, or impose an obligation on, any person whether or not he was a party to the transaction, but the order shall not prejudice any interest in property acquired from a person other than the debtor which was acquired in good faith, for value and without notice of the circumstances making section 423 applicable, or prejudice any interest deriving from such an interest. Nor shall the order require a person who received a benefit from the transaction in good faith, for value and without notice of the circumstances to pay any sum

---

[38] See *Re Butterworth, ex p. Russell* (1882) 19 Ch.D. 588; *Mackay* v. *Douglas* (1872) L.R. 14 Eq. 106; *ante*, p. 332.
[39] See *Cadogan* v. *Cadogan* [1977] 1 W.L.R. 1041, *ante*, p. 333.
[40] *Ante*, p. 335.

unless he was a party to the transaction. "Value" here bears its ordinary meaning.

(ii) **Bankruptcy Provisions.** The Insolvency Act 1986 replaces section 42 of the Bankruptcy Act 1914 with new provisions dealing with transactions at an undervalue and preferences by individuals or corporate bodies within a certain time limit prior to insolvency.

(a) *Transaction at an undervalue.* In the case of the insolvency of an individual, section 339 permits the trustee of the bankrupt's estate to apply to court for an order where the individual entered into a transaction at an undervalue within certain time limits discussed below. The court may make such order as it thinks fit for restoring the position to what it would have been but for the transaction. "Undervalue" here bears the same meaning as under section 423.[41] Thus marriage consideration no longer affords any defence. Questions will arise, as under section 423, concerning the meaning of that part of the definition which treats a transaction "for a consideration the value of which, in money or money's worth, is significantly less than the value in money or money's worth, of the consideration provided by the individual" as a transaction at an undervalue. The definition reflects the interpretation of "purchaser for valuable consideration" in the 1914 Act as meaning a purchaser "in a commercial sense."[42] No doubt *Re Densham*[43] and *Re Windle*[44] would be similarly decided under the new law. *Re Abbott (a bankrupt)*,[45] however, is more problematical: the compromise of a claim to a property adjustment order on divorce may be difficult to assess in money or money's worth.

(b) *Preference of creditors.*[46] Where an individual is adjudged bankrupt and has given a preference to any person within time limits discussed below, the trustee of the bankrupt's estate may apply to court for an order under section 340. The court may make such order as it thinks fit for restoring the position to what it would have been if that individual had not given that preference. An individual gives a preference to a person if that person is a creditor, surety or guarantor,

[41] *Ante*, p. 335.
[42] *Re Densham* [1975] 1 W.L.R. 1519, *ante*, p. 333.
[43] *Supra.*
[44] [1975] 1 W.L.R. 1628, *ante*, p. 334.
[45] [1983] Ch. 45, *ante*, p. 334. Section 39 of the Matrimonial Causes Act 1973 is amended in order to preserve under the new regime the principle that a property transfer order may be set aside under the bankruptcy provisions; I.A. 1986, Sched. 14.
[46] Under the previous law the preference of one creditor over another could not be challenged under s.172 of the L.P.A. 1925, but if the debtor was adjudicated bankrupt on a petition presented within three months of the preference, it would be deemed fraudulent and void against the trustee in bankruptcy; Bankruptcy Act 1914, s.44(1). This result could be avoided if the apparent "creditor" was in reality a beneficiary under a trust who never became a creditor. See *Re Kayford* [1975] 1 W.L.R. 279, *ante*, p. 52.

and the effect is to put that person into a better position than he would otherwise have been in in the event of the individual's bankruptcy. An order may only be made if the effect mentioned above was intended by the individual, but this is presumed where the other person was an associate.[47]

(c) *Time limits.* Section 341 provides a five year time limit, ending with the day of the presentation of the bankruptcy petition, in the case of a transaction at an undervalue. This, therefore, reduces the previous time limit under the 1914 Act by half. In the case of a preference which is not an undervalue, the period is six months save in the case of associate, where the period is two years.

Except in the case of a transaction at an undervalue made within two years before the bankruptcy, no order may be made with respect to a transaction entered into within the above time limits unless the individual was insolvent at the time or became insolvent in consequence of the transaction or preference.[48] In the case of a transaction at an undervalue entered into with an associate, there is a rebuttable presumption that the individual was or became insolvent at the time of the transaction. A person is insolvent for this purpose if he cannot pay his debts as they fall due, or if the value of his assets is less than his liabilities.

(d) *Orders to be made.* Section 342 sets out the orders which the court may make for the benefit of the bankrupt's estate. These are similar to the orders which may be made under section 425.[49]

(e) *Third parties.* As in the case of section 425,[50] no order may prejudice any interest in property acquired from a person other than the bankrupt and acquired in good faith, for value and without notice of the "relevant circumstances." This means the circumstances making sections 339 or 340 applicable upon subsequent bankruptcy within the time limit (*i.e.* the undervalue or preference),[51] and the fact that the individual has been adjudged bankrupt within that limit if it has

---

[47] As defined by section 435. The definition includes relatives of the individual or of his spouse, partners, employers, employees and related companies. For the position in Scotland, see *Bank of Scotland* v. *Pacific Shelf (Sixty Two) Ltd*, *The Times*, June 24, 1988.

[48] See further s.341(4) and (5), dealing with criminal bankruptcy orders.

[49] *Ante*, p. 336.

[50] *Ante*, p. 336.

[51] See (1987) 84 L.S.G. 2257–2258 and (1988) 85 L.S.G. No. 7, p. 17 (I. Storey), discussing the position with respect to land. Where there is a deed of gift of land, the practical effect of s.342 seems to be that the property will be frozen in the hands of the donee at least until the two year time limit has expired, because any purchaser will have notice of the undervalue. Where two years (but not five) have passed without bankruptcy supervening, a purchaser from the donee would still be at risk if he had notice that the donor was insolvent at the time of or in consequence of the transaction. Only after five years would his title be safe from attack. S.339 is to be amended in order to resolve these problems; (1988) 85 L.S.G. No. 34, p. 3.

expired. Similarly, a person who has received a benefit from the transaction or preference in good faith, for value and without notice of the relevant circumstances shall not be required to pay any sum to the trustee unless he was a party to the transaction or was given a preference at a time when he was a creditor of the bankrupt.

(f) *Corporate insolvency*. Sections 238 to 241 of the 1986 Act lay down similar provisions in the case of transactions at an undervalue and preferences prior to liquidation or the making of an administration order. "Undervalue" is defined as in the case of an individual, but, of course, without any reference to marriage consideration. However, no order will be made concerning a transaction at an undervalue if the court is satisfied that the company entered into it in good faith and for the purpose of carrying on its business, and at that time there were reasonable grounds for believing that the transaction would benefit the company.

The time limits are shorter than in the case of an individual. In the case of a transaction at an undervalue or a preference given to a person connected[52] with the company, the period is two years ending with the onset of insolvency, as defined by section 240(3). In the case of a preference which is neither a transaction at an undervalue nor given to a connected person, the period is six months.[53] But no transaction within these time limits may be set aside unless the company was unable to pay its debts at the time, or became unable to do so in consequence of the transaction.[54]

Section 241, dealing with the orders which may be made and the protection of third parties, contains provisions similar to those already discussed in relation to individual insolvency.

D. Protection of the Spouse and Family

The previous sections dealt with attempts by a debtor to deprive his creditors of satisfaction by transferring property by way of voluntary settlement to other persons, usually members of his family, whom the debtor wishes to protect. We now deal with what is in effect the converse of that problem; cases where the defendant is trying to deprive his spouse or family of assets which should properly be available to them. This occurs in matrimonial proceedings, and also in relation to the rights of dependants upon a death.

(i) Matrimonial Causes Act 1973, s.37.[55] Section 37 protects a spouse

---

[52] Defined by s.249.

[53] A transaction at an undervalue or a preference may also be set aside if made between the presentation of a petition for an administration order and the making of the order.

[54] Such inability is presumed in the case of a transaction at an undervalue with a connected person unless the contrary is shown.

[55] Which in this respect reproduces provisions of M.P.P.A. 1970, s.16(4). As to overseas divorces, see Matrimonial and Family Proceeding Act 1984, ss.23, 24.

from activities of the other spouse which may injuriously affect the assets available for the purposes of financial relief under the Act. If the court is satisfied that one spouse is about to make a disposition[56] or transfer with the intention of depriving the applicant of financial relief, it may make such order as it thinks fit for the purpose of protecting the applicant's claim.[57] And where the defendant spouse has made a disposition of property, other than one made for valuable consideration to a bona fide purchaser without notice of any intention to defeat the applicant's claim,[58] the disposition may be set aside.

The intention to defeat the applicant's claim must be affirmatively proved, except in cases where the disposition was made within three years before the date of the application, in which case there is a statutory presumption[59] that the intention is to defeat the applicant's claim for financial relief.

(ii) Inheritance (Provision for Family and Dependants) Act 1975.[60] A similar problem arises in connection with statutory schemes which restrict the decedent's powers of free disposal of his property by will, in order to provide for the surviving spouse and children and other dependants. This is an old problem; originally answered by the surviving spouse's right to dower or curtesy, and now governed by a wide variety of provisions in various parts of the world. A common solution is to give to the surviving spouse, and sometimes to children, a fractional share of the estate. The system in England and Wales is to give to the court a discretionary power to make an award to a surviving spouse and other dependants on the ground that the disposition of the deceased's estate (whether by will or intestacy) is not such as to make reasonable financial provision for the applicant.[61] But these schemes could be thwarted if the decedent who wished to deprive a widow and dependants could give away all his property before death.[62] There would then be nothing left in the estate for the satisfaction of the claim.

Provisions to deal with this problem are contained in sections 10–13 of the Act and came into effect on April 1, 1976.[63] In short, the court is given power to require a donee from the decedent to provide sums of

---

[56] The wide definition in s.37(6) includes a trust, but not any provision made in a will.
[57] s.37(2)(a).
[58] Called a "reviewable disposition" and defined in s.37(4).
[59] s.37(5); rebuttable, of course. The provisions do not apply to dispositions made before January 1, 1968.
[60] The ways in which the dependants' claims could be defeated under the old law are discussed in Mellows, *The Law of Succession* (2nd ed.), Chap. 14.
[61] s.2.
[62] See *Schaefer* v. *Schuhmann* [1972] A.C. 572. It is possible that such transfers could be set aside independently of any statutory provisions in a case of fraud. See *Cadogan* v. *Cadogan* [1977] 1 W.L.R. 1041.
[63] s.27(3). s.10 could have assisted in *Cadogan* v. *Cadogan, supra*, had the testator died after April 1, 1976.

money,[64] up to, but not in excess of, the value of the gift,[65] if the gift was made within six years before the death of the decedent, and was made "with the intention of defeating an application for financial provision under this Act."[66] Protection is given to persons who gave full valuable consideration for a transfer. The intention is to be determined on a balance of probabilities,[67] and need not be the sole intention of the decedent in making the gift. Similar provisions in section 11 deal with contracts to leave property by will; and transfers to trustees in section 13.

[64] s.10(2); see also s.10(6), giving the factors which the court shall take into consideration.
[65] Valued, in the case of gifts other than cash, at the date of death of the decedent, or, if the property was disposed of by the donee, the value at the date of disposal.
[66] s.10(2).
[67] s.12.

CHAPTER 14

NON-CHARITABLE PURPOSE TRUSTS

1. THE GENERAL PROBLEM

A. Private Trusts, Purpose Trusts, Charitable Trusts

A private trust is essentially a trust in favour of ascertainable individuals. A charitable trust is a trust for purposes which are treated in law as charitable. The question for consideration in this chapter is whether or not it is possible to establish a trust for non-charitable purposes.

We have considered in earlier chapters questions relating to the setting up of trusts for individuals. Charitable trusts are dealt with in Chapter 15. For the present purpose, it will be sufficient to state that charitable purposes are grouped into four categories: Trusts for the Relief of Poverty, Trusts for the Advancement of Religion, Trusts for the Advancement of Education, and Trusts for other purposes Beneficial to the Community. The purpose trusts at present under consideration are those which do not come within these categories. A trust, for example, to provide a cup for a yacht race,[1] for an annual dinner for a society,[2] to feed the testator's horses and hounds,[3] to set up a monu-

[1] *Re Nottage* [1895] 2 Ch. 649.
[2] *Re Barnett* (1908) 24 T.L.R. 788.
[3] *Re Dean* (1889) 41 Ch.D. 554.

ment,[4] or to be applied for useful or benevolent purposes.[5] There is no question of any such trusts having any privilege in relation to taxation or to perpetuity, such as are allowed in the case of charitable trusts. The question is whether they are valid or void. This is a matter on which opinions have differed, both here and in the United States.[6]

B. Trusts for Persons and Purposes

With any particular trust, there may be a question of construction to determine whether the trust is for persons or for purposes. Most purposes affect persons; and there is no reason why a trust should not be treated as a trust for persons where the beneficiaries are to be benefited in some way other than by payment of money. Thus, a trust for the education of the children of X can be construed as a trust of which the children of X are the beneficiaries.[7] A trust for the promotion of fox-hunting would be treated as a trust for a purpose, although it might be said that the individual sportsman might benefit from it.[8]

There are various examples of trusts in which the beneficiaries enjoy only a limited proprietary interest. Where, for example, a debtor assigns an asset to trustees for the payment of his debts, his creditors do not, unless there has been an absolute assignment, take any surplus[9]; similarly, where money is given for the planting of trees and shrubs for the improvement of settled land.[10] Yet trusts have been upheld for both these purposes. In *Re the Trusts of Abbott Fund*[11] it was accepted that a trust for the maintenance of two old ladies was valid although it seems that they did not become owners of any proprietary interest; and in *Re Gillingham Bus Disaster Fund*,[12] a fund collected for the benefit of injured cadets and other "worthy purposes" was not invalid although there was no suggestion that the cadets could ever have claimed the assets of the fund. It may be possible to support these latter decisions as examples of discretionary trusts[13] for the benefit of individuals; but they were not so drafted, and it may be preferable to regard

---

[4] *Mussett* v. *Bingle* [1876] W.N. 170; *Re Endacott* [1960] Ch. 232.

[5] *Morice* v. *Bishop of Durham* (1804) 9 Ves.Jr. 399.

[6] (1953) 17 Conv.(N.S.) 46 (L. A. Sheridan); (1953) 6 C.L.P. 151 (O. R. Marshall); Morris and Leach, Chap. 12; Maudsley, *The Modern Law of Perpetuities*, pp. 166–178; (1970) 34 Conv.(N.S.) 77 (P. A. Lovell); (1973) 37 Conv.(N.S.) 420 (L. McKay); (1971) 87 L.Q.R. 31 (J. W. Harris); (1977) 40 M.L.R. 397 (N. P. Gravells); (1977) 41 Conv.(N.S.) 179 (K. Widdows). For American views, see Gray, *Rule Against Perpetuities*, Appendix H, §§ 894–909; Scott, *Trusts*, §§ 119, 123–124; (1892) 5 H.L.R. 389 (J. B. Ames).

[7] See [1968] A.S.C.L. at p. 439 (J. D. Davies). See also *Re Osoba* [1979] 1 W.L.R. 247, *ante*, p. 231.

[8] *Re Thompson* [1934] Ch. 342, *post*, p. 352.

[9] *Re Rissik* [1936] Ch. 68.

[10] *Re Bowes* [1894] 1 Ch. 507 (beneficiaries held absolutely entitled); *Re Aberconway's S.T.* [1953] Ch. 647.

[11] [1900] 2 Ch. 326, *ante*, p. 229; contrast *Re Andrew's Trust* [1905] 2 Ch. 48; *Re Foord* [1922] 2 Ch. 599; *ante*, pp. 54, 231.

[12] [1959] Ch. 62, *ante*, p. 229.

[13] Where there is a similar difficulty in locating the equitable interest; *ante*, p. 198.

them as examples of trusts for persons to be benefited in a particular
way. The proper analysis of trusts of this kind was little discussed until
the decision of Goff J. in *Re Denley's Trust Deed* in 1969.[14]

A plot of land was conveyed to trustees to hold, for a period
determined by lives, "for the purpose of a recreation or sports ground
primarily for the benefit of the employees of the company and secon-
darily for the benefit of such other person or persons (if any) as the
trustees may allow."

Goff J. upheld the trust as one for the benefit of the employees.
They were ascertainable, and the trust was one which the court could
control. If it had been construed as a trust for non-charitable purposes,
it would have been void. "The objection [to non-charitable purpose
trusts] is not that the trust is for a purpose or an object per se, but that
there is no beneficiary or cestui que trust."[15] Here, however, "the trust
deed expressly states that . . . the employees of the company shall be
entitled to the use and enjoyment of the land."[16] And he contrasted
this situation with a "purpose . . . trust, the carrying out of which would
benefit an individual or individuals, where that benefit is so indirect or
intangible or which is otherwise so framed as not to give those persons
any locus standi to apply to the court to enforce the trust"[17]; in which
case the trust would have been a non-charitable purpose trust, and
void.

The same line of reasoning was applied in *Re Lipinski's Will Trusts*,[18]
a case of a gift to an unincorporated association.

The testator bequeathed his residuary estate to trustees in trust as to
one-half for the Hull Judeans (Maccabi) Association "in memory of
my late wife to be used solely in the work of constructing the new
buildings for the association and/or improvements to the said
buildings."

At first sight, this would appear to be a gift to an unincorporated
association to be applied for its (non-charitable) purposes.[19] We will
see,[20] however, that recent cases on unincorporated associations show
a "retreat from *Leahy*"[21]; and that what at first sight looks like a trust
for purposes, may find a favourable construction which allows it to fit
into one of the categories listed by Cross J. in *Neville Estates Ltd.* v.

---

[14] [1969] 1 Ch. 373.
[15] [1969] 1 Ch. 373 at p. 383.
[16] *Ibid.* at p. 383.
[17] *Ibid.* at p. 382. For discussion of *locus standi* to enforce the *Re Denley* type of trust,
see [1982] Conv. 118, at p. 124 (A. R. Everton).
[18] [1976] Ch. 235; (1977) 93 L.Q.R. 167; (1977) 41 Conv.(n.s.) 139 (F.R. Crane); (1977)
41 Conv.(n.s.) 179 (K. Widdows); (1977) 40 M.L.R. 231 (N. P. Gravells); *Re
Turkington* [1937] 4 All E.R. 501.
[19] In favour of this construction, counsel relied on the reference to the testator's late
wife's memory, as indicating an intention to create an endowment; and on the
requirement that the money was to be used "solely" for the stated purposes.
[20] *Post*, p. 356.
[21] (1977) 41 Conv.(n.s.) 139 (F. R. Crane).

Madden[22] and discussed in *Re Recher's Will Trusts*.[23] Oliver J. found that the proper category was Cross J.'s second category: "As a gift to the members of the association at the date of the gift not as joint tenants, but subject to their contractual rights and liabilities towards one another as members of the association. . . . If this is the effect of the gift, it will not be open to objection on the score of perpetuity or uncertainty unless there is something in its terms or circumstances or in the rules of the association which preclude the members at any given time from dividing the subject of the gift between them on the footing that they are solely entitled to it in equity."[24] There were no such restrictions.

Thus, having decided that there was a trust for the members, *Re Denley's Trust Deed*[25] became "directly in point."[26] The beneficiaries, the members of the association, were ascertainable; there was no problem of perpetuity,[27] because they could, according to the rules of the association, terminate the trust for their own benefit.[28] The implication of these factors will be discussed later in the chapter.

These cases show a more liberal judicial tendency in connection with the construction of gifts of this type.[29] *Re Denley*, however, could not save the trust in *R. v. District Auditor, ex p. West Yorkshire Metropolitan County Council*,[30] where a local authority, purporting to act under statutory powers,[31] resolved to create a trust "for the benefit of any or all or some of the inhabitants of the County of West Yorkshire" in any of four ways: (i) to assist economic development in the county in order to relieve unemployment and poverty; (ii) to assist bodies concerned with youth and community problems in West Yorkshire; (iii) to assist and encourage ethnic and minority groups in West Yorkshire; (iv) to inform all interested and influential persons of the consequences of the abolition (proposed by the Government) of the Council and other metropolitan county councils and of other proposals affecting local government in the county. The capital and income were to be applied within a short period, obviating any perpetuity problems, but the trust was void as a non-charitable purpose trust. It was not within the purpose trust exceptions illustrated by *Re Denley* and *Re Lipinski*

---

[22] [1962] Ch. 832 at p. 849.

[23] [1972] Ch. 526.

[24] [1976] Ch. 235 at p. 244, quoting the summary of Cross J.'s categories in *Tudor on Charities* (6th ed., 1967), p. 150.

[25] [1969] 1 Ch. 373.

[26] [1976] Ch. 235 at p. 247.

[27] *Post*, p. 348. *cf. Re Grant's W.T.* [1980] 1 W.L.R. 360, *post*, p. 357.

[28] By altering the constitution of the association. The beneficiaries in *Re Denley*, on the other hand, would seem to have no right to divide up the assets under the *Saunders* v. *Vautier* principle (*post*, p. 579), but no perpetuity problem arose because the trust was expressly confined to the perpetuity period.

[29] (1970) 34 Conv.(N.S.) 77 (P. A. Lovell); (1972) 87 L.Q.R. 31 (J. W. Harris).

[30] [1986] R.V.R. 24; (1986) 45 C.L.J. 391 (C. Harpum). The certainty aspects are discussed in Chap. 3, *ante*, p. 104.

[31] Local Government Act 1972, s.137(1).

because there were no "ascertained or ascertainable beneficiaries."
Even if "inhabitant" was sufficiently certain, the class of 2,500,000
potential beneficiaries was so large that the trust was unworkable. It
has never been established what certainty test applies to a *Re Denley*
trust,[32] but this decision suggests that the class of beneficiaries, even if
conceptually certain and not capricious, must not be too wide. A
private trust which fails for "administrative unworkability"[33] cannot be
rescued by the *Re Denley* principle.

It is necessary now to consider the objections to non-charitable
purpose trusts.

2. Objections to Purpose Trusts

If a disposition is construed as a trust for non-charitable purposes,
there are various objections which may be made to it. The first of these
objections denies the possibility of existence of non-charitable purpose
trusts. It has not however been consistently applied; and purpose trusts
for the building of graves and monuments and the care of specific
animals, which succeeded in the nineteenth century[34] are now
regarded as anomalous exceptions to the rule.[35] The other objections
accept the possibility of the existence of non-charitable purpose trusts,
but impose restrictions upon them.

A. The Beneficiary Principle; Enforceability

The first objection stemmed from a celebrated dictum of Sir William
Grant M.R. in *Morice* v. *Bishop of Durham*.[36] "Every other [*i.e.*
non-charitable] trust must have a definite object. There must be
somebody in whose favour the court can decree performance."[37] A
trust, as we have seen, is an obligation. The objection is that there
cannot be an obligation upon the trustees unless there is a correlative
right in someone else to enforce it. With charitable trusts, the Attorney-General is charged with the duty of enforcement. With private
trusts, no public official is involved. The trust is void unless there are
human beneficiaries capable of enforcing the trust. Acceptance of this
principle renders non-charitable purpose trusts void *in limine*.

B. Uncertainty

If non-charitable purpose trusts are recognised at all by the law, they
are only valid if the purposes are expressed with sufficient certainty to
enable the court to control the performance of the trust. This point

[32] *Ante*, p. 100.
[33] *Ante*, p. 103.
[34] *Post*, p. 350.
[35] *Per* Roxburgh J. in *Re Astor's S.T.* [1952] Ch. 534 at p. 547.
[36] (1804) 9 Ves.Jr. 399.
[37] At p. 404.

commonly arises in the cases where incompetent draftsmanship has failed to create a charitable trust; where, for example, the property is to be applied for charitable or benevolent purposes,[38] or, as in *Morice* v. *Bishop of Durham*[39] for "such objects of benevolence and liberality as the Bishop of Durham in his own discretion shall most approve of." "Benevolence" and "liberality" are wider concepts than "charity," and the trust was not therefore applicable for charitable purposes only. The purposes were uncertain and the trust void.[40] Indeed, this reason was more clearly emphasised by Sir William Grant M.R. than was the earlier objection. Having established that the trust was not for charitable purposes, and that the Bishop did not claim any personal benefit for himself, he said[41]:

> "That it is a trust, unless it be of a charitable nature, too indefinite to be executed by this Court, has not been, and cannot be denied. There can be no trust, over the exercise of which this Court will not assume a control; for an uncontrollable power of disposition would be ownership and not trust. If there be a clear trust, but for uncertain objects, the property, that is the subject of the trust, is indisposed of; and the benefit of such trust must result to those, to whom the law gives the ownership in default of disposition by the former owner. But this doctrine does not hold good with regard to trusts for charity. Every other trust must have a definite object. There must be somebody, in whose favour the Court can decree performance."

This objection can be met by specifying in sufficient detail the purposes to which the property is to be applied. Trusts for specific purposes like feeding the testator's animals, or maintaining a tomb or monument, usually pass this test. But general projects, even carefully drafted, are likely to be held void; especially by a court, as in *Re Astor's Settlement Trusts*,[42] which looks unsympathetically upon non-charitable purpose trusts as a whole. The point only becomes significant, of course, if the problem of the beneficiary principle has been surmounted.

C. Excessive Delegation of Testamentary Power

There are judicial statements[43] to the effect that purpose trusts created by will are void because, in the absence of anyone to enforce the trust, the trustees are left to determine the application of the

---

[38] *Blair* v. *Duncan* [1902] A.C. 37; *Houston* v. *Burns* [1918] A.C. 337; *Chichester Diocesan Fund and Board of Finance* v. *Simpson* [1944] A.C. 341; *Re Atkinson's Will Trusts* [1978] 1 W.L.R. 586.

[39] (1804) 9 Ves.Jr. 399.

[40] *Re Wood* [1949] Ch. 498.

[41] (1804) 9 Ves.Jr. 399 at pp. 404–405.

[42] [1952] Ch. 534; *post*, p. 353; also *Re Endacott* [1960] Ch. 232.

[43] Quoted in (1953) 69 L.Q.R. 334 (D. M. Gordon); see also (1959) 4 U. of W.A.L.R. 251–353 (L. A. Sheridan); (1974) 9 M.U.L.R. 650 (I. J. Hardingham); (1974) 48 A.L.J. 527 (R. A. Sundberg).

property. In that situation, "the testator has imperfectly exercised his testamentary power; he has delegated it, for the disposal of his property lies with them, not with him."[44] The objection is not relevant to trusts created *inter vivos*. Of the trust in *Re Denley's Trust Deed,* Goff J. said[45]: "If this were a will, a question might arise whether this provision might be open to attack as a delegation of the testamentary power. I do not say that would be so, but in any case it cannot be said of a settlement inter vivos." The status of the objection is, however, not established, even with wills. Special and general powers are permitted in wills; and "an anti-delegation rule is really an anti-power rule. Hence, to claim that there is a rule against delegation, that is, a rule against the use of power, but that general and special powers can still both be used, is a direct contradiction which makes no sense."[46] In *Re Abraham's Will Trusts,*[47] Cross J. upheld a testamentary power to appoint to anyone except the trustee.[48] It seems, therefore, that this objection is of no significance in determining the validity of purpose trusts. What is significant, however, is the fact that there seems to be no objection to the creation of testamentary powers. For one way, as will be seen,[49] of effecting a non-charitable purpose where there are willing trustees, may be to give them *power* to perform, and not attempt to require them to do so.

D. Perpetuity

A charitable trust may last for ever; a non-charitable trust is void if it is to continue beyond the perpetuity period. The reason is that perpetual non-charitable purpose trusts would conflict with the *policy* of the perpetuity rule, which is the prevention of the tying up of property for too long a period.

In its more usual context, the rule against perpetuities deals with the limit of time to which the vesting of future interests may be postponed. An outline of this has already been given.[50] In the present context, however, we are not concerned with future vesting. We are concerned with a situation in which the property is vested in the trustees to be applied by them for certain non-charitable purposes for a period which may exceed that of perpetuity. This situation will arise if either the capital or the income of the fund is to be so applied. If the trust relates to income, then the capital must be maintained in order to produce the income. It is no answer to say that, since the trustees may sell the

---

[44] *Leahy* v. *Att.-Gen. for New South Wales* [1959] A.C. 457 at p. 484; *Re Wood* [1949] Ch. 498 at p. 501.

[45] [1969] 1 Ch. 373 at p. 387.

[46] (1953) 69 L.Q.R. 334 at p. 342.

[47] [1969] 1 Ch. 463.

[48] *Re Park* [1932] 1 Ch. 580; *Re Eyre* (1883) 49 L.T. 259; *Re Gulbenkian's Settlements* [1970] A.C. 508; *Re Manisty's Settlement* [1974] Ch. 17; *Re Hay's Settlement Trusts* [1982] 1 W.L.R. 202.

[49] *Post,* p. 366.

[50] *Ante,* p. 326.

present investments and purchase others, the capital is not inalienable. The objection relates, not only to alienability, but to duration. And, whatever happens to individual investments, an obligation to retain the capital as a fund for an excessive period violates the rule. Accordingly, a non-charitable purpose trust is valid only if it is confined to the perpetuity period. The matter is examined below.[51]

3. EXCEPTIONAL CASES UPHOLDING PURPOSE TRUSTS[52]

Until *Re Astor's Settlement Trusts*[53] in 1952, it was arguable that it was possible to establish a trust for a non-charitable purpose for the period of perpetuity. The authorities cover a narrow field, being nearly all concerned with trusts for building or maintaining monuments or tombs, or for caring for the testator's animals. But the language of the judgment is general, and there are occasional cases outside those fields. As will be seen, *Re Astor's Settlement Trusts*[54] underlined the beneficiary principle; and it is clear now that trusts for non-charitable purposes will fail unless they are kept strictly within the narrow confines of these limited and exceptional cases.

A. Tombs and Monuments

Reasonable provision for the building of a tomb or a gravestone for a testator may be regarded as a funeral expense, and valid independently of any doctrine relating to purpose trusts.[55] But bequests for family burial enclosures have been upheld as purpose trusts[56]; as have bequests for monuments to other people, such as the testator's wife's first husband.[57] Such a gift may be for the building of the monument which, it seems, may be assumed to be done within the period of perpetuity[58]; or for the care or the maintenance of the graves for a period limited to the period of perpetuity. A modern example is *Re Hooper*,[59] where

> A testator gave a sum of money to trustees for the care and upkeep of certain family graves and monuments, and a tablet in a window in a church so far as the trustees could legally do so. Maugham J. upheld the gift for a period of 21 years, admitting that

---

[51] *Post*, p. 360.
[52] Morris and Leach (*op. cit.*), pp. 310–319; Maudsley, *The Modern Law of Perpetuities*, pp. 168–176.
[53] [1952] Ch. 534; *post*, p. 353.
[54] *Supra*.
[55] *Mellick* v. *President and Guardians of the Asylum* (1821) Jac. 180; *Trimmer* v. *Danby* (1856) 25 L.J.Ch. 424; Gray thought that it was the only justification for upholding such trusts: *The Rule Against Perpetuities*, pp. 310–311.
[56] *Pirbright* v. *Salwey* [1896] W.N. 86; *Re Hooper* [1932] 1 Ch. 38.
[57] *Mussett* v. *Bingle* [1876] W.N. 170.
[58] *Post*, p. 360.
[59] [1932] 1 Ch. 38.

he would have had some difficulty in so doing if he had not had direct authority in *Pirbright* v. *Salwey*.[60]

Similarly, in *Mussett* v. *Bingle*,[61] Hall V.-C. held that since the executors were ready to carry out a bequest of £300 to erect a monument to the testator's wife's first husband, "it must be performed accordingly." But he held void for perpetuity a further gift for its upkeep.

Such trusts must of course comply with the requirement of certainty. In *Re Endacott*,[62] the Court of Appeal held void a residuary gift amounting to some £20,000 "to the North Tawton Devon Parish Council for the purpose of providing some useful memorial to myself." Such a trust, though specific in the sense that it indicated a purpose capable of expression, was "of far too wide and uncertain a nature to qualify within the class of cases cited."[63] No doubt was cast upon *Re Hooper*[64] and the early cases. Yet *Re Endacott*[65] may illustrate the stricter modern approach to purpose trusts; or perhaps it indicates the willingness of the court to allow reasonable sums to be spent upon these purposes, and a reluctance to uphold such grandiose schemes. This policy, as will be seen, is articulated in *Re Astor*.[66] The Law Reform Committee[67] recommended that it should be permissible to use the income of "a limited sum of money (say £1,000) for the maintenance of a grave, tomb or monument in perpetuity." The Parish Councils and Burial Authorities (Miscellaneous Provisions) Act 1970, s.1, now provides that a burial authority or a local authority may agree by contract to maintain a grave, or memorial or monument for a period not exceeding 99 years.

B. Animals

Gifts for the care of specific animals, though not charitable, have also been upheld. There was no argument on the point in *Pettingall* v. *Pettingall*[68] where an annuity of £50 to be applied in maintaining the testator's favourite black mare was held valid. In *Re Dean*,[69] the leading case, North J., relying on *Mitford* v. *Reynolds*[70] and the monument cases, upheld a gift of £750 per annum for the period of 50 years for the maintenance of the testator's horses and hounds if they should

---

[60] [1896] W.N. 86.
[61] [1876] W.N. 170. See also *Trimmer* v. *Danby* (1856) 25 L.J.Ch. 424.
[62] [1960] Ch. 232.
[63] At p. 247.
[64] [1932] 1 Ch. 38.
[65] [1960] Ch. 232.
[66] [1952] Ch. 534.
[67] Fourth Report (1955), § 53.
[68] (1842) 11 L.J.Ch. 176.
[69] (1889) 41 Ch.D. 552.
[70] (1848) 16 Sim. 105.

so long live. He met head-on the argument that the court will not recognise a trust unless it is capable of being enforced by someone, by pronouncing: "I do not assent to that view."[71] There was nothing obnoxious to the law in such a provision "provided, of course, that it is not to last for too long a period."[72] It is difficult to see how the gift could be upheld for a 50-year period; for the horses and hounds could not be the measuring lives for the period of perpetuity. This aspect of the matter is discussed below.[73] The case has been accepted as authority for the proposition that trusts for the upkeep of specific animals are valid for the perpetuity period; and it is believed that this exception to the general rule has been relied on in countless cases since *Re Dean*.[74]

A possible difficulty, it has been suggested,[75] is that the fund might be claimed by the person who now owns the animal (*e.g.* as specific or residuary legatee). A fund to maintain another's property can be claimed by that other without applying it to the purpose.[76] Another solution might be to give the fund to the person acquiring the animal on the testator's death, determinable on the death of the animal or on the trustee's decision that it is improperly maintained.[77]

C. Other Purposes

Trusts for other purposes have on occasion been upheld; and others which have failed have been refused on the ground of perpetuity, without any indication that they would not have been valid if confined to the permitted period.

It may be that trusts for the saying of masses for the benefit of private individuals will come into this category. Until the House of Lords decision in *Bourne* v. *Keane* in 1919,[78] such trusts were regarded as being trusts for superstitious uses and void.[79] *Bourne* v. *Keane* held them valid. *Re Caus*[80] held them charitable. Since then, however, greater emphasis has been placed upon the requirement of public benefit as a qualification for charitable status by religious trusts,[81] and doubt has been cast upon *Re Caus*.[82] If trusts for masses for the benefit of individuals are no longer held charitable, it would be necessary to decide whether they will be upheld as non-charitable purpose trusts. It

---

[71] (1889) 41 Ch.D. 552 at p. 556.
[72] At p. 557.
[73] *Post*, p. 361.
[74] (1889) 41 Ch.D. 552.
[75] (1983) 80 L.S.Gaz. 2451 (P. Matthews).
[76] *Re Bowes* [1896] 1 Ch. 507 (money directed to be laid out in planting trees on an estate belonged to the owners of the estate absolutely.) See also *Re Lipinski's Will Trusts* [1976] Ch. 235.
[77] See Matthews, *op. cit.*, discussing other possibilities.
[78] [1919] A.C. 815.
[79] *West* v. *Shuttleworth* (1835) 3 My. & K. 684, overruled in *Bourne* v. *Keane* [1919] A.C. 815.
[80] [1934] Ch. 162.
[81] *Gilmour* v. *Coats* [1947] A.C. 426, *post*, p. 415.
[82] By Lord du Parcq in *Gilmour* v. *Coats*, *supra*, at pp. 451–452, 454.

is thought unlikely, in view of modern emphasis on the beneficiary principle, that they will be upheld in England.

There is however Irish authority on a gift to the testator's executor to dispose of it "to my best spiritual advantage, as conscience and sense of duty may direct."[83] There was no problem of perpetuity, for the money was to be disposed of in the lifetime of the executors. The Irish court upheld the gift. There was no beneficiary who could enforce it; but there was no reason to prevent the executors from carrying it out if they wished to.

Another possible member of this category of miscellaneous purpose trusts is a trust for non-Christian private ceremonies. In *Re Khoo Cheng Teow*,[84] the Supreme Court of the Straits Settlements held valid a gift to be applied for the period of perpetuity in the performance of ceremonies called Sin Chew to perpetuate the testator's memory. The gift was not charitable; but the Court held that it was valid for a period measured by royal lives plus 21 years.

A decision which has perhaps been elevated to a position of importance which it does not merit is *Re Thompson*[85]:

An alumnus of Trinity Hall, Cambridge, bequeathed a legacy to one Lloyd, an old friend, to be applied in such manner as he should think fit towards the promotion and furtherance of fox-hunting, and gave the residuary estate to Trinity Hall. Lloyd made no claim to any beneficial interest, but desired to carry out the testator's wishes if he should be permitted to do so. Trinity Hall also was anxious that the trust should be performed; but felt it its duty, as a charity, to submit that the trust was void for lack of a beneficiary. There was no problem of perpetuity, and Clauson J. held that the purpose was sufficiently certain. He upheld the gift by ordering the money to be paid to Lloyd upon his giving an undertaking to apply for these stated objects, and gave to Trinity Hall liberty to apply if the money should be used for other purposes.

The case is one of very limited significance. It does not, as some have claimed,[86] provide a solution to the beneficiary problem, by holding that the party entitled in default can enforce a purpose trust. Enforcement is contrary to the interest of the party entitled in default; he is interested to restrain misapplication, which is a very different matter. In *Re Thompson*,[87] there was no contest, as all parties desired enforcement. The case was only litigated because Trinity Hall, as a charity, could not, without the court's approval, forgo its strict legal claim to the property.

---

[83] *Re Gibbons* [1917] 1 Ir.R. 448.
[84] [1932] Straits Settlements L.R. 226.
[85] [1934] Ch. 342.
[86] See Roxburgh J. in *Re Astor's S.T.* [1952] Ch. 534 at p. 543.
[87] *Supra.*

4. THE FAILURE OF THE ASTOR TRUST[88]

Modern decisions have made clear that this line of cases will not be extended.[89] They are regarded as "concessions to human weakness or sentiment,"[90] "troublesome, anomalous and aberrant,"[91] and as "occasions when Homer has nodded."[92] Purpose trusts generally have failed under the beneficiary principle, and on the ground of uncertainty. In these circumstances, compliance with the perpetuity rule is no escape.

In *Re Astor's Settlement Trusts*,[93] an *inter vivos* settlement was made in 1945, expressly limited to a period of lives in being plus 21 years, under which the trustees were to hold a fund upon various trusts for non-charitable purposes, including "the maintenance of good relations between nations . . . the preservation of the independence of the newspapers," and other similar purposes in favour of independent newspapers. Roxburgh J. held the trust void; both because there was no one who could enforce the trust, and also on the ground of uncertainty.

Re Shaw[94] concerned the will of George Bernard Shaw, which provided that the residue of the estate should be applied to research the utility of the development of a 40-letter British alphabet in the place of the present one, and for the translation of his play "Androcles and the Lion" into the new alphabet. Harman J. held that the trust was not charitable, and that it failed on the beneficiary principle. The trustees were willing to carry out the testator's wishes if they were permitted to do so. But "I am not at liberty to validate this trust by treating it as a power.[95] A valid power is not to be spelled out of an invalid trust."[96]

These cases show the current trend in situations where the gift is construed as a gift for purposes. The insistence upon an ascertained beneficiary reflects the analysis of the law of trusts before the days when discretionary trusts became common. We have seen that a beneficiary under a discretionary trust is not entitled to specific property; only to a limited right to be considered. It has been argued that *McPhail* v. *Doulton*[97] manifests a basic change in the conceptual development of the law of trusts. "It has broken the stranglehold imposed

---

[88] (1953) 6 C.L.P. 151 (O. R. Marshall); (1953) 17 Conv.(N.S.) 46 (L. A. Sheridan); (1955) 18 M.L.R. 120 (L. H. Leigh).
[89] *Re Endacott* [1960] Ch. 232 at p. 246.
[90] *Re Astor's S.T.* [1952] Ch. 534 at p. 547.
[91] *Re Endacott, supra,* at p. 251.
[92] *Ibid.* at p. 250.
[93] [1952] Ch. 534.
[94] [1957] 1 W.L.R. 729. The litigation started when the success of "My Fair Lady" "brought the interpretation of the will into the realm of practical politics." At p. 731.
[95] *Ibid.* at p. 731.
[96] *Per* Jenkins L.J. in *I.R.C.* v. *Broadway Cottages Trust* [1955] Ch. 20 at p. 36.
[97] [1971] A.C. 424; *ante,* p. 98.

·on the development of trusts . . . by a rigid conception of a framework of fixed equitable interests and correlatively narrow obligations . . . it does not take much crystal-ball gazing to see the impact this extension will have on all the old sterile purpose trust and unincorporated association debates."[98] Reliance on the beneficiary principle has over-ruled much discussion of the policy factor; but that is the real issue: whether, as a matter of policy, purpose trusts ought to be enforceable.

5. Unincorporated Associations

An unincorporated association exists where two or more persons are bound together for one or more common purposes by mutual under-takings, each having mutual duties and obligations, in an organisation which has rules identifying in whom control of the organisation and its funds is vested, and which can be joined or left at will.[99]

Special problems arise in connection with the holding of property by unincorporated associations.[1] An unincorporated association is not a legal person, and, with the exception of trade unions,[2] cannot be the owner of property or the subject of legal rights and duties.[3] The question we will consider here is the effect of gifts to such associations, and the various ways in which their property is held. The latter is determined by the terms of the instrument of creation or by the constitution or rules of the association. The question of entitlement to the funds on the dissolution of the association is dealt with elsewhere.[4]

A Charitable Purposes. The assets of an unincorporated association may be held by its officers or by a group of trustees upon charitable trusts. For example, a society for the relief of suffering among the poor. This is a charitable trust; it is valid as a purpose trust; the usual rules of certainty of objects do not apply; it may continue for ever; and it enjoys a number of tax privileges.[5]

B Non-Charitable Purposes. We have seen that, generally speak-

---

[98] (1974) 37 M.L.R. 643 at pp. 655–656 (Y. Grbich); (1972) 89 L.Q.R. 31 (J. W. Harris); [1970] A.S.C.L. 189 (J. D. Davies).

[99] *Conservative and Unionist Central Office* v. *Burrell (Inspector of Taxes)* [1982] 1 W.L.R. 522. See [1983] Conv. 150 (P. Creighton), doubting the last requirement.

[1] See Warburton, *Unincorporated Associations: Law and Practice*, Chap. 5.

[2] Trade Union and Labour Relations Act 1974, s.2. See also *Maclaine Watson & Co. Ltd.* v. *Dept. of Trade and Industry* [1988] 3 W.L.R. 1033 (International Tin Council).

[3] Halsbury (4th ed.), Vol. 7, p. 11. *The Restatement of the Law of Trusts* lays down a more liberal rule, § 119. It is otherwise in the context of tax; *Worthing Rugby Football Club Trustees* v. *I.R.C.* [1987] 1 W.L.R. 1057; *Blackpool Marton Rotary Club* v. *Martin (Inspector of Taxes)*, *The Times*, November 2, 1988. As to rates, see *Verrall* v. *Hackney London Borough Council* [1983] Q.B. 445; *Westminster City Council* v. *Tomlin* [1988] E.G.C.S. 122.

[4] *Ante*, pp. 231 *et seq.*

[5] *Post*, p. 375.

ing, trusts for the promotion of non-charitable purposes are void. Hence gifts to non-charitable unincorporated associations will fail if construed as purpose trusts. But, as will be seen, such a result may be avoided if it is possible to regard the gift as in favour of the members, as described below. Such a construction may be adopted even where the donor has expressly stated that his gift is for particular non-charitable purposes.[6]

C Property Held on Trust for the Members. The property of an unincorporated association may be held on trust for the members of the association, and not for its purposes. Such a trust must comply with the usual rules for the creation of a trust. There must be a manifestation of an intention to create a trust, and there must be ascertainable beneficiaries. This will often be made clear by the terms of the constitution of the society; or, in the case of societies governed by statute, such as friendly societies, by the terms of the statute governing them. The Friendly Societies Act 1974,[7] s.54(1), provides that the property of a friendly society shall vest in the trustees for the time being of the society, for the use and benefit of the society and the members thereof.[8] It was at one time thought that there was no need to identify the beneficiaries of property held by unincorporated associations; and that a gift to persons holding the property as trustees was good so long as the trustees had power to spend the capital. A society could then dispose of any of its assets at any time; there would be no more tendency to perpetuity than in the case of an individual holding a fee simple, and, it was argued, no reason for invalidating it. Thus, in *Re Drummond*[9], a gift was made to the Old Bradfordians Club, London, to be utilised as the committee should think best in the interests of the club or school. Eve J. upheld the gift. It was not, he said, a gift to the members, but the committee was free to spend the money as it thought fit on the specified objects. It did not tend to a perpetuity, and was valid.

If the trustees could spend only the income however—if, in other words, the trust was an endowment—the trusts on which the assets were held would be perpetual and void. This view, which appeared to have been approved by the House of Lords,[10] dealt, however, only

---

[6] *Re Lipinski's Will Trusts* [1976] Ch. 235, *ante*, p. 344.
[7] Replacing the Act of 1896.
[8] *Re Bucks Constabulary Fund (No. 2)* [1979] 1 W.L.R. 937; [1979] Conv. 302 (F. R. Crane).
[9] [1914] 2 Ch. 90, *Re Patten* [1929] 2 Ch. 276; *Re Prevost* [1930] 2 Ch. 383; *Re Price* [1943] Ch. 422 ("To the Anthroposophical Society of Great Britain to be used at the discretion of the Chairman and Executive Council of the Society for carrying out the teaching of the founder Dr. Rudolf Steiner."); (1937) 53 L.Q.R. 24 at p. 46 (W. O. Hart).
[10] *Macaulay* v. *O'Donnell*, July 10, 1933; reported at [1943] Ch. 435n.; *Carne* v. *Long* (1860) 2 De G.F. & J. 75.

with the perpetuity aspect of the problem. It ignored the necessity to analyse the property interests which were created.

In *Leahy* v. *Att.-Gen. for New South Wales*,[11] a testator provided that Elmslea, a sheep station of some 730 acres, should be held upon trust for "such order of nuns of the Catholic Church or the Christian Brothers as my executors and trustees shall select." The gift was not valid as a charitable trust because some of the orders were purely contemplative orders which are not charitable in law.[12]

Nor was it valid as a private trust. There was no intention to create a trust in favour of the individual members of selected orders.[13] The testator's intention clearly was to establish an endowment. The gift would have failed if it had not been rescued by a statute of New South Wales which permitted partly charitable trusts to be applied wholly in favour of those parts which were charitable.[14] The trustees' power of selection did not therefore extend to contemplative orders.

Other modern cases, however, have been able to find a different construction, enabling the gift to be held valid as being a trust for the benefit of members of the association.[15] This has even proved possible, applying the principle of *Re Denley's Trust Deed*,[16] where the donor has stated that his gift is to be applied for specific non-charitable purposes.[17] The position was analysed in *Neville Estates* v. *Madden*,[18] where Cross J. held that the property interests of the members of an association would fall into one of three categories. There might be a gift to the members at the relevant date as joint tenants, giving each a right of severance of his part; or a gift subject to the contractual rights and liabilities of the members towards each other, which prevent severance and cause a member's interest, on his death or resignation, to accrue to the remaining members; or a gift to present and future members, in which case the gift, unless confined to the perpetuity

---

[11] [1959] A.C. 457.

[12] *Gilmour* v. *Coats* [1949] A.C. 426; *post*, p. 415.

[13] "With the greatest respect to those judges who have taken a different view, their Lordships do not find it possible to regard all the individual members of an Order as intended to become the beneficial owners of such a property" at p. 486; *cf. Re Smith* [1914] 1 Ch. 937, where a bequest to the Society of Franciscan Friars of Clevedon County, Somerset was construed as a gift to the members of the community at the date of the testator's death; *Bacon* v. *Pianta* (1965) 40 A.L.J.R. 187 ("The Communist Party of Australia"); *Cocks* v. *Manners* (1871) L.R. 12 Eq. 574 (a share of residue to the "Dominican Convent of Carisbrooke payable to the Superior for the time being"); *Re Clarke* [1901] 2 Ch. 110 ("The Corps of Commissionaires" (veterans of the Crimean War)).

[14] New South Wales Conveyancing Act 1914–54, s.37(D).

[15] (1977) 41 Conv.(n.s.) 179 (K. Widdows); (1980) 39 C.L.J. 88 (C. E. F. Rickett); [1985] Conv. 318 (J. Warburton).

[16] [1969] 1 Ch. 373, *ante*, p. 344. This did not involve an unincorporated association, but the reasoning is applicable to gifts to such associations.

[17] *Re Lipinski's Will Trusts* [1976] Ch. 235, *ante*, p. 344.

[18] [1962] Ch. 832 at p. 849; *Re Recher's W.T.* [1972] Ch. 526 at p. 538, *post*, p. 358; *News Group Newspapers Ltd.* v. *SOGAT 82* [1986] I.C.R. 716.

period, would be void. A fourth possibility is that this situation creates a specialised form of co-ownership, whose rules should be worked out separately, and independently of the law of trusts.[19] All these possible solutions fail to explain how the equitable interest of a member passes on his resignation without compliance with Law of Property Act 1925, s.53(1)(c), or on his death without compliance with the Wills Act 1837, s.9.[20]

Gifts to unincorporated associations can involve perpetuity problems of two distinct kinds, relating to remoteness of vesting and perpetual duration. To avoid both problems, the trust must be for the benefit of members who are both ascertainable during the perpetuity period and also able to claim a division of the funds before that period expires. If the members are not so ascertainable, the trust will fail, subject to what is said below, for remoteness of vesting. If the capital is to be retained as an endowment, the trust will be void as a perpetual trust.[21]

Cross J. in *Neville Estates* v. *Madden*[22] referred to the problem of remoteness of vesting in his third category (gift to present and future members). This problem has been resolved by the Perpetuities and Accumulations Act 1964, which excludes from the gift any members not ascertainable within the perpetuity period.[23] The 1964 Act does not remove the problem of perpetual duration (inalienability). This aspect of the perpetuity rule caused the gift to fail in *Re Grant's Will Trusts*.[24] The trust was for the purposes of the Chertsey Labour Party Headquarters, which were not charitable. The members of this local association did not control the property, nor could they change the rules of the association and thereby gain control, because the rules were subject to the approval of, and capable of alteration by, an outside body (the National Executive Committee). Although it seems that a way around this problem could have been found,[25] the trust was held void for perpetuity, even though the restriction on disposing of the capital was not one imposed by the testator.

---

[19] Ford, *Unincorporated Non-Profit Associations*, Part 1, especially at pp. 5–8, 21–23.
[20] Morris and Leach, pp. 313–318; [1971] A.S.C.L. p. 379 (J. Hackney). The *Re Denley* approach (*ante*, p. 344), whereby the beneficiary has no proprietary interest, does not encounter these difficulties.
[21] *Carne* v. *Long* (1860) 2 De G.F. & J. 75.
[22] *Supra.*
[23] s.4(4). The Act applies to dispositions made after July 15, 1964.
[24] [1980] 1 W.L.R. 360; (1980) 43 M.L.R. 459 (B. Green); [1980] Conv. 80 (G. A. Shindler).
[25] See Heydon, Gummow and Austin, *Cases and Materials on Equity and Trusts* (2nd ed.), pp. 451–452, suggesting that control by the outside body was not as significant as the case suggests. The beneficiaries could be treated as including the members of that body also. Another possibility is that the members could disaffiliate from the national body. See also *News Group Newspapers Ltd.* v. *SOGAT 82* [1986] I.C.R. 716, where *Re Grant* was distinguished because the members of a local branch of a trade union had control over the branch assets and could in theory secede from the union and divide the assets.

D Ownership by Members on Contractual Basis. The contractual analysis provides a method by which unincorporated associations can validly hold property without the necessity of discovering an intention to create a trust, and by which gifts to the association, in order to escape invalidity as purpose trusts, need not be regarded as taking effect as immediate distributive shares in favour of the members, which is unlikely to have been the donor's intention. Members of an association can "band themselves together as an association or society, pay subscriptions and validly devote their funds in pursuit of some lawful non-charitable purpose. An obvious example is a members' social club[26]—where it would in most cases be difficult to find an intention to create a trust. Their assets, whether donations or members' subscriptions, are held by the trustees or by the committee[27] or officers of the club on the terms of the constitution or rules of the club, which are themselves a contract among the members *inter se*.

This solution avoids some of the difficulties which arise from an analysis which regards the members as beneficiaries under a private trust. The members' rights are contractual, and of course they depend upon the rules of the association. A member will not usually be able to claim his share at any time; but the members as a whole control the committee's activities in accordance with the rules, and can usually take the decision to wind up the association and share out the proceeds. A member's rights terminate on death or resignation, and a new member obtains his rights in relation to the assets owned by the association during his period of membership. Questions concerning the contractual rights of members usually arise on the termination of an association, as we have seen.[28] Theoretical difficulties of course can arise where the membership includes minors or other persons with less than full contractual capacity.

The fact that the assets are held by the members on a contractual basis of course does not prejudge the construction of a gift by a third party to the association. But the court will lean in favour of validity, and is likely to regard such a gift as one to the members beneficially but subject to their contract. In *Re Recher's Will Trust*[29] there was a gift in trust for "The London and Provincial Anti-Vivisection Society." Brightman J. held that the assets of the society were owned by the members in accordance with the rules. "There is no private trust or trust for charitable purposes or other trust to hinder the process."[30] If it was correct that a gift to such an association must be construed as a (void) purpose trust or as distributive shares in favour of the members,

---

[26] *Re Recher's W.T.* [1972] Ch. 526 at p. 538, *per* Brightman J.
[27] *Re Bucks Constabulary Fund (No. 2)* [1979] 1 W.L.R. 937.
[28] *Ante*, p. 231.
[29] [1972] Ch. 526; (1972) 35 Conv.(N.S.) 381; (1971) 8 M.U.L.R. 1 (P. W. Hogg); (1973) 47 A.L.J. 305. The "accretion to funds" solution is adopted by the Queensland Succession Act 1981, s.63.
[30] *Ibid.* at p. 539; *Re Bucks Constabulary Fund (No. 2), supra.*

then it would be difficult to make a donation in favour of the body, which would be contrary to common sense. The solution was that the gift could be construed as a beneficial gift in favour of the members, not so as to entitle them to an immediate distributive share, but as an accretion to the funds of the society subject to the contract of the members as set out in the rules. Such a construction was equally available whether the society existed to promote the interests of its members ("inward-looking") or, as in the present case, to promote some outside purpose ("outward-looking"). If the society had remained in existence, the gift would have been good. In fact, however, it had been dissolved before the date of the gift.

6. Mandate or Agency

The principles described above apply to unincorporated associations, which have already been defined.[31] It may be that an organisation (which is not incorporated) fails to satisfy the requirements of an unincorporated association. This was the case in *Conservative and Unionist Central Office* v. *Burrell (Inspector of Taxes)*,[32] where the Crown claimed that the Conservative Party was an unincorporated association. If this were so, Central Office would be assessable to corporation tax, as opposed to income tax, on certain income. The Court of Appeal rejected the Crown's claim. The Party was an amorphous combination of various elements, but not an unincorporated association, because the members had no mutual rights and obligations, there were no rules governing control (which lay in the party leader), and no event in history could be identified as marking the creation of the Party as an association.[33]

Of interest in the present context was the analysis of the legal effect of a contribution to such a body. Where the body was not an unincorporated association, the *Re Recher*[34] analysis could not apply. The legal basis was mandate or agency. The contributor gives the recipient (*e.g.* the treasurer) a mandate to use the gift in a particular way. He can demand its return unless the mandate becomes irrevocable, as when

---

[31] *Conservative and Unionist Central Office* v. *Burrell (Inspector of Taxes)* [1982] 1 W.L.R. 522; *ante*, p. 354. This case decides the meaning of "unincorporated association" for the purposes of I.C.T.A. 1970 (now I.C.T.A. 1988), but it would seem that the definition is of general application. Partnerships are excluded from the definition for the purposes of the Act.

[32] [1982] 1 W.L.R. 522. See generally [1987] Conv. 415 (P. St. J. Smart).

[33] Convincingly criticised in [1983] Conv. 150 (P. Creighton); "It may be as misleading to deny the organisation its status as an unincorporated association because its origins are obscure as it would be to deny the existence of a living human being on the ground that his birth certificate could not be found."

[34] *Ante*, p. 358.

the gift is added to a mixed fund with the authority of the contributor. There is no trust, only the fiduciary element inherent in the relationship of principal and agent. Once the mandate has become irrevocable, the contributor's rights are to an account of expenditure, and to restrain a misapplication.[35] Difficulties might arise where there was a change of the office-holder to whom the mandate was given. More seriously, the mandate theory could not explain the validity of bequests to such organisations, as agency cannot be set up at death. No solution to this problem was offered, the Court of Appeal being content to suggest that the answer was "not difficult to find."[36]

It remains to be seen whether the mandate theory will be applied in other situations.[37] In view of its limitations, especially with regard to testamentary gifts, this is perhaps doubtful.

7. PERPETUITY

A. Excessive Duration[38]

It has been said that a non-charitable purpose trust, even though otherwise valid, is void if it may last beyond the period of perpetuity; this being a rule designed to produce an effect analogous to the rule controlling remoteness of vesting, and applying the same general policy. If, therefore, a purpose trust survives an attack under the beneficiary principle, it must be restricted to the period of perpetuity.

In applying the rule against excessive duration, the courts have been more generous than in other aspects of perpetuity law. First, they have assumed that a monument will be erected within the period.

> In *Mussett* v. *Bingle*,[39] a testator gave £300 to be applied in the erection of a monument to his wife's first husband, and £200 the interest on which was to be applied in maintaining it. The latter gift was perpetual and void. The former was upheld. In the absence of any objection on the ground of perpetuity, the court must have assumed that the monument would be erected within the period.

Secondly, a trust will be upheld if the instrument provides that it is to continue "so long as the law allows" or some similar period. The gift is

---

[35] The contribution may be recoverable if made under duress; *Universe Tankships Inc. of Monrovia* v. *International Transport Workers' Federation* [1983] 1 A.C. 366.

[36] Perhaps referring to the principle of *Re Denley's Deed Trust* [1969] 1 Ch. 373, *ante*, p. 344. See also [1983] Conv. 150 (P. Creighton); [1987] Conv. 415 (P. St. J. Smart).

[37] It was referred to in connection with members' subscriptions in *Re Recher's Will Trusts* [1972] Ch. 526 at p. 539. The reasoning might apply to cases such as *Re Gillingham Bus Disaster Fund* [1959] Ch. 62, *ante*, p. 343, involving public donations to non-charitable purposes.

[38] Morris and Leach, pp. 321–327; Maudsley, *The Modern Law of Perpetuities*, pp. 166–178.

[39] [1876] W.N. 170.

good for 21 years.[40] If no such saving phrase is included, the trust is wholly void.[41] The court will not supply the necessary words to meet the testator's obvious intention. The wait and see principle does not apply to purpose trusts.[42] If it did, it would at least have solved this problem.

Thirdly, the courts have on various occasions taken judicial notice of the fact that an animal's life span is limited to 21 years. If the animal could not live that long, the trust could not endure beyond the period. Danckwerts J. in *Re Haines*[43] took judicial notice of the fact that a cat could not live for more than 21 years. Biologists have corrected him, showing that a cat may live for 25 years.[44] It seems that, if the courts are willing to accept judicial notice of longevity, it should be permissible to take evidence of the age of the cats in question; for if the youngest cat is over four, the particular trust would not last for more than 21 years.

B. Human Lives Only

Perhaps North J. in *Re Dean*[45] should be taken to have applied some such doctrine. He upheld a gift of annual sum for the period of 50 years if any of the testator's horses and hounds should so long live. The perpetuity point was not dealt with, and it seems almost as if the learned judge assumed that the life of an animal could be used as a measuring life for the purposes of the rule. The better doctrine however was provided by Meredith J. in *Re Kelly*[46]:

"If the lives of dogs or other animals could be taken into account in reckoning the maximum period of 'lives in being and twenty-one years afterwards' any contingent or executory interest might be properly limited, so as only to vest within the lives of specified carp, or tortoises, or other animals that might live for over a hundred years, and for twenty-one years afterwards, which, of course, is absurd. 'Lives' means human lives. It was suggested that the last of the dogs could in fact not outlive the testator by more than twenty-one years. I know nothing of that. The court does not enter into the question of a dog's expectation of life. In point of fact neighbours' dogs and cats are unpleasantly long-lived; but I have no knowledge of their precise expectation of life. Anyway the maximum period is exceeded by the lives of specified butterflies and twenty-one years

[40] *Pirbright* v. *Salwey* [1896] W.N. 86; *Re Hooper* [1932] 1 Ch. 38.
[41] *Contra, Re Budge* [1942] N.Z.L.R. 356, where a trust to apply the income in keeping a grave neat and tidy was held valid for 21 years. Morris and Leach, p. 322.
[42] s.15(4); *post,* p. 362; *cf.* New Zealand Perpetuities Act 1964; Maudsley, *The Modern Law of Perpetuities,* App. D.
[43] *The Times,* November 7, 1952.
[44] See Comfort: *The Biology of Senescence*; Morris and Leach, p. 323; Maudsley, *op.cit.* p. 170.
[45] (1889) 41 Ch.D. 552.
[46] [1932] I.R. 255 at pp. 260–261.

afterwards. And even, according to my decision—and, I confess, it displays this weakness on being pressed to a logical conclusion—the expiration of the life of a single butterfly, even without the twenty-one years, would be too remote, despite all the world of poetry that may be thereby destroyed ... there can be no doubt that 'lives' means lives of human beings, not of animals or trees in California."

Re Dean[47] is unsupportable on this point. All other purpose trusts which may last beyond the period of perpetuity have been held void.

C. A Fixed Number of Years

As we are dealing here with a question of duration and not one of remoteness of vesting of beneficial interests, it would be much more convenient to have a perpetuity period which was gauged by a number of years, rather than one measured by lives. It is possible to argue that a court should hold that purpose trusts can last for 21 years only; for no purpose trust, with the exception of *Re Howard*,[48] when a parrot was to be fed during the lives of the survivor of two servants, has been upheld for any other or longer period. Yet a royal lives clause was not challenged in *Re Astor's Trusts*.[49] In *Re Moore*,[50] the objection was to the excessive number of lives chosen and not to the fact that lives were chosen, and in *Re Khoo Cheng Teow*,[51] the Supreme Court of the Straits Settlements has upheld a non-charitable purpose trust for the period of royal lives plus 21 years.

It was reasonable therefore to hope that the Perpetuities and Accumulations Act 1964 would make such provision. Purpose trusts were not within the Law Reform Committee's terms of reference. They commented on the matter as we have seen by suggesting that it should be possible to provide for reasonable sums to be spent on the maintenance of a grave.[52] Some provision on these lines would have been welcome. So would a restriction to a period of 21 years. The 80-year period would have been an improvement. The worst alternative is to leave the period at lives plus 21 years.

Section 15(4) provides:

"Nothing in this Act shall affect the operation of the rule of law rendering void for remoteness certain dispositions under which property is limited to be applied for purposes other than the benefit of any person or class of persons in cases where the property may be so applied after the end of the perpetuity period."

---

[47] (1889) 41 Ch.D. 552.
[48] *The Times*, October 30, 1908.
[49] [1952] Ch. 534.
[50] [1901] 1 Ch. 936.
[51] [1932] Straits Settlements Reports 226; *ante*, p. 352.
[52] Fourth Report, § 53; *ante*, p. 350.

Although the contrary is not unarguable,[53] it appears that the effect of this provision is that the 80-year period permitted by section 1 of the 1964 Act does not apply to the duration of purpose trusts.[54]

8. USELESS OR CAPRICIOUS PURPOSES

One question which has to be faced when considering whether, as a matter of policy, purpose trusts should be enforced is that of excluding trusts which are useless, wasteful, capricious, or even harmful or illegal. This aspect of the matter was in the mind of Roxburgh J. in *Re Astor's Trusts* when he said[55]: " . . . it is not possible to contemplate with equanimity the creation of large funds directed to non-charitable purposes which no court and no department of state can control, or in the case of maladministration reform." The question ultimately is that of the extent to which one person, usually deceased, should be allowed to deprive the community or individuals within it, of the beneficial use of capital. The larger the amount, and the longer the period of application, the greater the problem. No attempt has been made to draw a precise line between those which are acceptable and those which are not. We will see that the greatest difficulty has been experienced in trying to draw a line between charitable and other trusts.[56] This does not augur well for the creation of a recognisable line between acceptable and non-acceptable non-charitable purpose trusts; but it is no reason for insisting on holding all non-charitable purpose trusts void. "The answer, of course, is that the courts will have to strike down the silly purposes and uphold the sensible ones."[57]

In *Brown* v. *Burdett*,[58] the testator devised a freehold house to trustees upon trust to block up almost all the rooms of the house for a period of 20 years, and, subject thereto, to a devisee. Bacon V.-C. decided that he must "unseal" this "useless, undisposed of property," and declared that there was an intestacy as to the period of 20 years.

Scottish judges have been forthright in their disapproval of the waste of money on useless projects. "I consider that, if it is not unlawful, it

---

[53] This was the view expressed in earlier editions of this work. See also Maudsley, *The Modern Law of Perpetuities*, p. 177; (1965) 29 Conv.(N.S.) 165 (J. A. Andrews).

[54] Morris and Leach Supp., p. 3; Hayton and Marshall, *Cases and Commentary on the Law of Trusts* (8th ed.), p. 175; Pettit, p. 49.

[55] [1952] Ch. at p. 542.

[56] *Post*, pp. 369 *et seq.*

[57] (1959) 4 U. of W.A.L.R. at p. 239 (L. A. Sheridan).

[58] (1882) 21 Ch.D. 667; see also *McCaig* v. *University of Glasgow*, 1907 S.C. 231; *McCaig's Trustees* v. *Kirk-Session of United Free Church of Lismore*, 1915 S.C. 426 (bronze statues at £1,000 each); *Aitken* v. *Aitken*, 1927 S.C. 374 (massive bronze equestrian statue); *Mackintosh's Judicial Factor* v. *Lord Advocate*, 1935 S.C. 406 (erection of vault); *Lindsay's Executor* v. *Forsyth*, 1940 S.C. 568 (£1,000 on trust to provide a weekly supply of fresh flowers on the graves of my mother and my own).

ought to be unlawful, to dedicate by testamentary disposition, for all time, or for a length of time, the whole income of a large estate . . . to objects of no utility, private or public, objects which benefit nobody, and which have no other purpose or use than that of perpetuating at great cost, and in an absurd manner, the idiosyncrasies of an eccentric testator."[59] "The prospect of Scotland being dotted with monuments to obscure persons cumbered with trusts for the purpose of maintaining these monuments in all time coming, appears to me to be little less than appalling. . . . "[60]

9. Alternative Solutions

It seems therefore that non-charitable purpose trusts are void under the beneficiary principle; that there are recognised exceptions in trusts for animals and monuments, which, to be valid, must be certain, not useless or capricious, and confined to the period of perpetuity; and that a trust may be upheld if, although expressed as a purpose trust, it is directly for the benefit of ascertainable individuals. Some take the view that this is too restricted a position. We now consider in what ways the effecting of a non-charitable purpose can be achieved.

A. By the Draftsman

(i) **Incorporation.** A society may be incorporated to advance such purposes. The matter then leaves the law of trusts, and the problem here discussed disappears. This is the simplest practical solution.[61]

(ii) **Mandate or Agency.** Consideration should also be given to the possibility of utilising the mandate or agency theory expounded in *Conservative and Unionist Central Office* v. *Burrell (Inspector of Taxes)*,[62] discussed in section 6, above. The principle could also be invoked in the case of gifts to unincorporated associations, although it is doubtful whether it has much to offer here, not least because it cannot be the basis of a testamentary gift.[63] Where this principle can be utilised, the matter then leaves the law of trusts, as in the case of incorporation. The problem of purpose trusts disappears, but other problems, as we have seen, take its place.

(iii) Gift to Members of an Association and Not for Purposes Only. In

---

[59] *McCaig* v. *University of Glasgow, supra,* at p. 242.
[60] *McCaig's Trustees* v. *Kirk-Session of United Free Church of Lismore, supra,* at p. 434.
[61] Report of the Goodman Committee on Charity Law and Voluntary Organisations, p. 24.
[62] [1982] 1 W.L.R. 522; [1983] Conv. 150 (P. Creighton); [1987] Conv. 415 (P. St. J. Smart).
[63] *Ante,* p. 360.

Re Lipinski's Will Trusts,[64] Oliver J. emphasised the distinction between "the case where a purpose is prescribed which is clearly intended for the benefit of ascertained or ascertainable beneficiaries . . . and the case where no beneficiary at all is intended . . . or where the beneficiaries are unascertainable." This distinction is crucial. A gift to provide recreational facilities may be a gift for beneficiaries if those persons are intended to be benefited[65]; and similarly a gift to an association where it is construed as a gift for the members subject to their contractual rights according to the rules of the association.[66] The problem of construction was substantial in the cases discussed; but there is no need for any difficulty to arise if the draftsman is aware of the possibilities and the difficulties and drafts the gift accordingly.

(iv) Conveyancing Devices. A gift over from one charity to another may validly take place at any time in the future; the rule against perpetuities does not apply.[67] Advantage was taken of this rule in *Re Tyler*,[68] to achieve a non-charitable purpose.

A gift was made to the London Missionary Society, committing to their care the family vault, and if they failed to comply with the request the money was to go to the Bluecoat School. The gift was upheld. It could last perpetually if the value of the gift was sufficient to encourage the London Missionary Society to perform the task. If the task became unprofitable, as no doubt it would do by the progress of inflation, the gift over would take effect. The Bluecoat School would be under no obligation to perform the task. Indeed, if an attempt was made to impose an obligation on either donee by requiring any part of the income to be applied for the non-charitable purpose, the trust would have been void.[69]

A similar result could have been produced before 1964, even without making the gift in favour of charity. In *Re Chardon*,[70] a gift of income was made to a cemetery company so long as it maintained a grave. This was held valid. There was no danger of a perpetuity because the cemetery company and the owner of the possibility of reverter could combine at any time to sell. Under the Perpetuities and Accumulations Act 1964, the possibility of reverter would be subject to the perpetuity rule.[71] It is still possible however to frame a limitation

[64] [1976] Ch. 235, at p. 246.
[65] *Re Denley's Trust Deed* [1969] 1 Ch. 373.
[66] *Re Recher's W.T.* [1972] Ch. 526; *Re Lipinski's W.T.* [1976] Ch. 235.
[67] *Christ's Hospital (Governors)* v. *Grainger* (1849) 1 Mac. & G. 460.
[68] [1891] 3 Ch. 252.
[69] *Re Dalziel* [1943] Ch. 277. See further [1987] Conv. 415 (P. St. J. Smart).
[70] [1928] Ch. 464.
[71] s.12.

on these lines which will secure the maintenance of a grave for the period of perpetuity.

(v) Draft as a Power; not as a Trust. The beneficiary principle applies to trusts. There must be someone who can enforce the trust. With a power, there is no question of enforcement; questions of certainty and perpetuity arise; and, with testamentary powers, questions of excessive delegation. Assuming however that these are overcome, could not the purpose be achieved by giving the property, not to a trustee upon trust, but to the ultimate beneficiary subject to a power in a third party to apply the property for the stated purpose for the perpetuity period?

There is little authority on the validity of such a power. Clearly, a power can be something other than a general or special power to appoint to persons. There was a power in *Re Douglas*[72] to appoint "among such charities, societies and institutions . . . as the said Earl of Shaftesbury shall by writing nominate." The context of the will showed that the gift was limited to charitable societies and institutions. But even if that was not so, the Court of Appeal decided that the gift was good. "All I decide," said Cotton L.J., "is, that the mere addition to the general charitable purposes of certain definite objects does not make the gift bad because one of these objects is itself not a charity."[73] Lord Shaftesbury could appoint to such institutions under the power given to him. It may be, then, that a power to apply the income for the improvement of land,[74] or for research into the advantages of the 40-letter alphabet,[75] or for the Oxford Group[76] could, if limited to the period of perpetuity, be valid. And it seems that the same rule should apply to repairing monuments, feeding animals, providing a cup for a yacht race, or contributing to a police or social club.

There seems to be nothing contrary to policy in allowing the purpose to be effected in this way. Policy questions will arise, of course, where an eccentric testator provides for large sums to be applied for useless, capricious or harmful purposes for a substantial period.[77] The problem here is the same as that discussed in section 8 above.

B. By the Courts

Arguments have been put forward to the effect that an instrument which purports to create a purpose trust should be construed as a

---

[72] (1887) 35 Ch.D. 472; (1902) 15 H.L.R. 67 (J. C. Gray); (1959) 4 U. of W.A.L.R. at p. 260 (L. A. Sheridan). See also *Re Clarke* [1923] 2 Ch. 407, where a power to appoint to *uncertain* non-charitable objects failed.

[73] *Ibid.* at p. 486.

[74] *Re Aberconway's S.T.* [1953] Ch. 647.

[75] *Re Shaw* [1957] 1 W.L.R. 729.

[76] *Oxford Group* v. *I.R.C.* [1949] 2 All E.R. 537.

[77] See Morris and Leach (2nd ed.), p. 320.

power so as to allow the purpose to be carried out.[78] Supporters of this view argued that this is a way of achieving the testator's or settlor's intention without conflicting with any rules of policy. A better draftsman would have drafted it as a power. A trust contains a power. As Scott says: "Should the failure of the duty drag down with it the power?"[79] In *Re Shaw,*[80] Harman J. appeared to find some attraction in the argument; but he rejected it, following what Jenkins L.J. had said in *Commissioners of Inland Revenue* v. *Broadway Cottages Trust*[81]: "We do not think that a valid power is to be spelt out of an invalid trust. This also was the view of the learned author of *Gray on Perpetuities* (4th ed.) the leading work on the subject (see Appendix H), and I feel bound to accept it." The point may be arguable in the House of Lords.

C. By the Legislature

If reform is to come, it will come best from the Legislature. The basic question is whether gifts for non-charitable purposes should be upheld. If so, it is necessary to find a means of overcoming the beneficiary principle, and this would most conveniently be done by enacting that trusts for non-charitable purposes should be construed as powers.[82] The purpose could then be carried out by the trustees if they elected to do so. If they did not, the purpose would fail and the property would go to those entitled in default. The power would be valid only if it was sufficiently certain. It may be thought best to limit such trusts to a period of 21 years[83]; or require them to be restricted to the common law perpetuity rule, or a longer specified period such as 80 years or for the period of Wait and See,[84] or either. The danger of maladministration would be no greater than that already encountered in the case of the permitted purpose trusts discussed in section 3 above.

To this solution, it may be objected that it does not answer the anxiety expressed by Roxburgh J. in *Re Astor's Settlement Trusts*[85] that it was not in the general interest that large sums of money should be applied for non-charitable purposes for long periods of time. The period of perpetuity can be about 100 years, and non-charitable purposes include all those which at one end are nearly charitable and those which are so useless or hostile that they are invalidated as capricious.

---

[78] (1949) 13 Conv.(N.S.) 418 at p. 424 (D. C. Potter); (1950) 14 Conv.(N.S.) 374 (A. K. R. Kiralfy); (1959) 4 U. of W.A.L.R. at pp. 240–244 (L. A. Sheridan); (1953) 17 Conv.(N.S.) 46 at p. 59; Scott, *Trusts,* § 124; *Restatement of Trusts,* § 124; (1892) 5 H.L.R. 389 (J. B. Ames); (1930) 30 Col.L.R. 60 (B. Smith); (1945) 58 H.L.R. 548 (A. W. Scott).

[79] Scott, *Trusts,* § 124.

[80] [1957] 1 W.L.R. 729 at p. 746; *Restatement of Trusts,* § 124.

[81] [1955] Ch. 20 at p. 36.

[82] See Ontario Perpetuities Act 1966.

[83] New Zealand Perpetuities Act 1964, s.20.

[84] Maudsley, *The Modern Law of Perpetuities,* App. D.

[85] [1952] Ch. 534; *ante,* p. 353.

In validating gifts for purposes, it is important to ensure that funds are made available for purposes which are useful to the public rather than for the satisfaction of the private interests of a settlor or testator. Resources are scarce, and need to be put to good use. The problem is one which exists also in the case of gifts which are drafted in the form of powers. The courts exercise a broad discretion in determining which trusts are to be labelled capricious and void. No doubt, the amount of money involved, and the duration of the trust will be factors which will be relevant to a decision. The line is difficult to draw. But capricious trusts are the rare ones. And the fact that they exist is no reason for failing to establish a rational method of validating the useful ones.

CHAPTER 15

CHARITABLE TRUSTS

I. INTRODUCTION[1]

CHARITABLE purposes are those which are considered to be of such value and importance to the community that they receive especially favourable treatment. These purposes, which will be examined in detail, are the relief of poverty, the advancement of education and religion, and other purposes beneficial to the community. Such a list is vague and old-fashioned. That is because the scope of charity originates in the Preamble to the Charitable Uses Acts of 1601, an Act which was passed for the purpose of remedying abuses which had grown up in the administration of charitable trusts. The Preamble contained a general catalogue of the purposes then regarded as charitable. Since that time, purposes which are regarded as being within the "spirit and intendment"[2] or "within the equity"[3] of the statute have been accepted as being charitable. And in 1891, Lord Macnaghten summarised these purposes into four categories given above.[4] In 1952, the Nathan Committee[5] recommended that a new statutory definition

---

[1] See generally *Tudor on Charities* (7th ed., 1984); Sheridan and Keeton, *The Modern Law of Charities* (3rd ed., 1983); Picarda, *The Law and Practice Relating to Charities* (1977); Nightingale, *Charities* (1973); Chesterman, *Charities, Trusts and Social Welfare* (1979); Maudsley and Burn, *Trusts and Trustees, Cases and Materials* (3rd ed.), Part II. See also the Annual Reports of the Charity Commissioners for England and Wales. For important reviews of the law and practice, see the Goodman Committee Report on Charity Law and Voluntary Organisations (1976); Annual Report of Charity Commissioners for 1976, paras. 7–14; (1976) 39 M.L.R. 77 (M. Partington); (1976) 5 *Anglo-American Law Review* 153 (L. A. Sheridan); The Wolfenden Committee Report on the Future of Voluntary Organisations; Annual Report 1977, paras. 6–13, 1978, paras. 4–7; The Woodfield Report, Efficiency Scrutiny of the Supervision of Charities (1987).

[2] "Those purposes are charitable which that statute enumerates or which by analogies are deemed within its spirit and intendment," *per* Sir William Grant M.R. in *Morice* v. *Bishop of Durham* (1805) 9 Ves. 399 at p. 405.

[3] See *Incorporated Council of Law Reporting* v. *Att.-Gen.* [1972] Ch. 73 at pp. 87–88.

[4] *Ante*, p. 342.

[5] The Committee on the Law and Practice relating to Charitable Trusts (1952) Cmd. 8710, para. 140.

of charity should be enacted, based on that classification. This recommendation was not implemented.[6] And, in spite of further recommendations from the Expenditure Committee of the House of Commons, the Government decided not to promote a legislative definition of charity.[7] The Preamble was, however, repealed by the Charities Act 1960.[8] No definition replaced it. The matter is now governed by the case law, and current developments by the decisions of the Charity Commissioners on the question of the registration of Charities under the Charities Act 1960, s.4.[9]

We will see that charitable trusts are accorded a number of concessions over other trusts in terms of enforcement, perpetuity, certainty and taxation.[10] To earn these concessions, especially in relation to the growing significance of relief from taxation, a trust must be of a public nature; of benefit to the public, and not merely to private individuals. This is obvious in the fourth category. It exists also in connection with trusts for the advancement of religion and education, but only minimally in trusts for the relief of poverty.[11] The policy in question behind most litigation concerning charitable trusts is an examination of whether the purposes are so useful to the public as to earn the concessions. This has to be carried out against a background of cases decided in earlier times when the condition of society was very different. In the days when the State made little or no provision for the poor and uneducated or for other general welfare purposes, and at a time when religious observance was unchallenged, trusts for these four categories were clearly for the public benefit. At the present time, however, many of the welfare and educational needs of society are provided from public sources, and religious observance, for better or worse, plays a smaller part in community life.[12] Are these purposes so vital to

---

[6] The task proved to be impossible. There is much to be said for retaining the flexibility which the present situation provides. See *Government Policy on Charitable Trusts in England and Wales* (1955) Cmd. 9538, paras. 2–3; Annual Report 1973, paras. 1–3.

[7] House of Commons Report, Vol. I, paras. 24–34 (a laconic guideline based on public benefit); Goodman Committee, para. 32, App. 1 (A lengthy guideline based on an updated version of the Preamble to the Act of 1601).

[8] s.38.

[9] The more significant decisions are discussed in the Annual Reports of the Charity Commissioners (referred to herein as *Annual Reports*). These reports give a better understanding of current practical problems than the older cases.

[10] *Per* Lord Cross in *Dingle* v. *Turner* [1972] A.C. 601 at p. 624.

[11] *Post*, p. 409.

[12] The main categories of recent charitable trusts are for: (i) social welfare, *e.g.* for drug addicts, the consequences of the break-up of family life, care for latchkey children, victim support schemes, care of AIDS sufferers, and the relief of youth unemployment; (ii) cultural purposes; (iii) conservation of the environment; (iv) religious cultural teachings of immigrant communities and the promotion of racial harmony. Goodman Committee, paras. 137–138; Annual Report 1978, para. 60; Annual Report 1980, paras. 74–77; Annual Report 1981, paras. 65–67; Annual Report 1982, paras. 28–30; Annual Report 1983, paras. 12–20; Annual Report 1986, para. 35; Annual Report 1987, para. 14.

present-day society that trusts for them should receive special encouragement by being permitted to exist as purpose trusts, for ever, supported by the court's *cy-près* power,[13] and tax free?[14] The pendulum has swung in the attitude of the courts to gifts for charitable purposes. In 1908, Lord Loreburn said "now there is no better rule than that a benignant construction will be placed upon charitable bequests."[15] But since the 1940s when taxation became penal the courts have been astute to restrict the scope of charity especially by emphasising the requirement of public benefit.[16] In a recent case in the House of Lords, however, Lord Hailsham of St. Marylebone referred to Lord Loreburn's dictum and said "In construing trust deeds the intention of which is to set up a charitable trust, and in others too, where it can be claimed that there is an ambiguity, a benignant construction should be given if possible."[17] In similar vein, the Government's intention is to encourage the liberality of the donor, and, within the present financial restraints, the development of the voluntary sector as a whole.[18] The policy changes which have been effected by changing social and economic conditions should be borne in mind when considering the cases relating to the definition of charity.

Before the definition is examined, the extent of the concessions granted to charitable trusts should first be explained.

2. Advantages Enjoyed by Charitable Trusts

A. Purpose Trusts

Charitable trusts are purpose trusts. But there is no need for human beneficiaries to enforce them, as there is in the case of non-charitable purpose trusts.[19] Individuals who may benefit from a charitable trust have no *locus standi* to enforce them.[20] Charitable trusts are public trusts, and are enforced by the Attorney-General in the name of the

---

[13] *Post*, p. 427.

[14] (1956) 72 L.Q.R. 187 at p. 204 (G. Cross); (1977) 40 M.L.R. 397 (N. P. Gravells); *Scottish Burial Reform and Cremation Society* v. *Glasgow Corporation* [1968] A.C. 138 at p. 153; *Dingle* v. *Turner* [1972] A.C. 601 at p. 624.

[15] *Weir* v. *Crum-Brown* [1908] A.C. 162 at p. 167.

[16] The Royal Commission on the Taxation of Profits and Income (1955) Cmd. 9474, recommended (paras. 168–175) that some charitable trusts should be subject to tax liability, and others, measured by a stricter definition, should be entitled to the present exemptions.

[17] *I.R.C.* v. *McMullen* [1981] A.C. 1 at p. 14; *Re Koeppler's W.T.* [1986] Ch. 423.

[18] House of Commons, January 24, 1980; 124 S.J. 102. The Goodman Committee recommended increasing the fiscal privileges of charities; Chap. 5. Some of these recommendations have been implemented; F.A. 1982, s.129; I.H.T.A. 1984, s.29(5); I.C.T.A. 1988, ss.86, 339, 577, 660, 671. See too *Incorporated Council of Law Reporting* v. *Att.-Gen.* [1972] Ch. 73 at p. 88, *per* Russell L.J., p. 395, *post*.

[19] *Ante*, p. 346.

[20] *Re Belling* [1967] Ch. 425; *Hauxwell* v. *Barton-on-Humber U.D.C.* [1974] Ch. 432, where the Att.-Gen. was substituted plaintiff in place of two individuals; Charities Act 1960, s.28.

Crown[21]; though, as will be seen,[22] the general administration of charitable trusts is carried out by the Charity Commissioners.[23] There must of course be an obligation upon the trustees; a mere power to apply to charitable purposes cannot be a trust.[24]

B. Objects Need Not be Certain

There is no requirement, as with other trusts, that the objects of the trust must be certain. Thus, a trust for "charitable purposes" will be valid. The court and the Charity Commissioners[25] have jurisdiction to establish a scheme for the application of the funds for specific charitable purposes. There must, of course, be no doubt that the objects of the trust are exclusively charitable.[26] And the purpose expressed must not be so vague and uncertain that the court could not control the application of the assets.[27] The relaxation of the certainty rule is only in respect of the particular form of charitable purpose intended.[28]

Where no trust has been created, but only a general intention expressed that the property should go to charity, the court has no jurisdiction. In such a case the Crown disposes of the gifts by sign manual.[29] But the Crown acts on principles very similar to those by which the court is governed.

C. May be Perpetual

Statements have often been made by judges to the effect that the Rule against Perpetuities does not apply to charities.[30] That is not so. With the exception of the rule in *Christ's Hospital* v. *Grainger*,[31] explained below, the rule governs the remoteness of vesting in the case of gifts to charities in the same way that it governs remoteness in the

---

[21] For recent examples, see *Att.-Gen.* v. *Wright* [1988] 1 W.L.R. 164; *Att.-Gen.* v. *Cocke* [1988] Ch. 414.

[22] *Post*, p. 443.

[23] Charities Act 1960, ss.1(4), 28.

[24] *Re Cohen* [1973] 1 W.L.R. 415, where a gift to trustees to apply "the whole or any part" of the fund "in such manner and at such time or times as my trustees shall in their absolute and uncontrolled discretion think fit," was held to create a trust. *Post*, p. 382.

[25] Charities Act 1960, s.18(1); *post*, p. 443.

[26] *Post*, p. 421.

[27] *Re Koeppler's Will Trusts* [1986] Ch. 423, where the formation of an informed international public opinion and the promotion of greater co-operation in Europe and the West were held too vague and uncertain to be charitable in themselves, but these aims did not destroy the charitable nature of the gift, which was to further the work of an educational project.

[28] See *Moggridge* v. *Thackwell* (1792) 1 Ves.Jr. 464; (1803) 7 Ves.Jr. 36; (1807) 13 Ves.Jr. 416; *Mills* v. *Farmer* (1815) 1 Mer. 55; *cf. Re Willis* [1912] 1 Ch. 44.

[29] *Moggridge* v. *Thackwell, supra*; *Paice* v. *Archbishop of Canterbury* (1807) 14 Ves. 364 at p. 371; *Re Pyne* [1903] 1 Ch. 83; *Re Smith* [1932] 1 Ch. 53; *Re Bennett* [1960] Ch. 18.

[30] *Goodman* v. *Mayor of Saltash* (1882) 7 App.Cas. 633 at p. 642, *per* Lord Selborne; *Commissioners for Special Purposes of Income Tax* v. *Pemsel* [1891] A.C. 531 at pp. 580–581, *per* Lord Macnaghten; *Att.-Gen.* v. *National Provincial and Union Bank Ltd.* [1924] A.C. 262 at p. 266.

[31] (1849) 1 Mac. & G. 460; *post*, p. 374; *Re Tyler* [1891] 3 Ch. 252; *Royal College of Surgeons* v. *National Provincial Bank Ltd.* [1952] A.C. 631.

case of other gifts.[32] In the case of gifts coming into effect after July 15, 1964, the wait and see provisions of the Perpetuities and Accumulations Act 1964 apply.[33]

Charitable trusts, however, may be perpetual. Indeed, the purpose of many charitable trusts could be said never to be capable of final achievement.[34] Many existing charitable trusts continue after centuries of existence, and many schools and churches and almshouses are dependent on them. Trustees of a charity require the permission of the court or the Charity Commissioners before dealing with property which forms part of the permanent endowment of the charity,[35] and with land which is used or occupied for the purposes of the charity.[36] If a perpetual gift of income only is made to a charity, the charity cannot claim the capital, as an individual could do in such circumstances.[37] But where property is given absolutely to a charity with a direction to accumulate the income for a period of time, a charity may terminate the accumulation, and claim the principal forthwith.[38]

The exception to the rule regulating remoteness of vesting is that a gift over from one charity to *another charity* is not subject to the rule.[39] The gift over to the second charity is valid even if it takes effect outside the perpetuity period.[40]

The reason for the exception is that "there is no more perpetuity created by giving to two charities rather than by giving to one."[41] "If the reason for upholding a gift to a charity for an indefinite period is that a charity in its nature is not obnoxious to the rule against perpetuities, I fail to see why the same reason should not apply to a gift over from any one charity to any other charity."[42] These reasons have been criticised on the ground that they confuse vesting with perpetual duration.[43] But this is not so. The explanation looks to the vesting for charitable purposes, rather than vesting in one specific charity, or group of trustees. Once vested in charity, then, subject to express

---

[32] *Chamberlayne* v. *Brockett* (1872) L.R. 8 Ch.App. 206; *Re Lord Stratheden and Campbell* [1894] 3 Ch. 265; *Re Wightwick's W.T.* [1950] Ch. 547; *Re Green's W.T.* [1985] 3 All E.R. 455.

[33] s.3.

[34] *Re Delius* [1957] Ch. 299.

[35] Charities Act 1960, s.29(2). "Permanent endowment" is defined in ss.46 and 45(3). There are exceptions, s.29(4); Cheshire and Burn, pp. 897–898.

[36] s.29(2).

[37] *Re Levy* [1960] Ch. 346.

[38] *Wharton* v. *Masterman* [1895] A.C. 186; *Re Knapp* [1929] 1 Ch. 341.

[39] A gift from non-charity to a charity is caught: *Re Bowen* [1893] 2 Ch. 291; *Re Mill's Declaration of Trust* [1950] 1 All E.R. 789; [1950] 2 All E.R. 292. So also a gift from a charity to a non-charity; *Re Bowen* (*supra*); *Re Peel's Release* [1921] 2 Ch. 218; *Re Engels* [1943] 1 All E.R. 506.

[40] *Christ's Hospital* v. *Grainger* (1849) 1 Mac. & G. 460.

[41] *Per* Shadwell V.-C. in the court below (1848) 16 Sim. 83 at p. 100.

[42] *Per* Lord Morton of Henryton in *Royal College of Surgeons* v. *National Provincial Bank Ltd.* [1952] A.C. 631 at p. 650.

[43] Morris and Leach: *The Rule Against Perpetuities* (2nd ed.), pp. 192–194; Maudsley, *The Modern Law of Perpetuities*, pp. 181–183; Picarda, *The Law of Charities*, p. 212.

provision to the contrary, a trust will continue, even if the purposes become impossible of fulfilment; the property will be applied *cy-près*.[44] All that is done by the provision for vesting in another charity is to make expressly the selection of the charity to be benefited when the first gift terminates.

This rule therefore seems logical; and also reasonable when the gift over is to take effect upon the happening of some event related to the carrying out of the purposes of the charity, as was the case in *Christ's Hospital* v. *Grainger*,[45] and *Royal College of Surgeons* v. *National Provincial Bank*.[46] In the hands of conveyancers, however as has been seen,[47] it can be used to produce, in effect, a perpetual non-charitable trust by making a gift to one charity conditional upon carrying out a non-charitable purpose, and terminable in favour of another charity upon its failure to do so. This is not a satisfactory use of charity privilege: but this conveyancer's technique was not questioned in the *Royal College of Surgeons* case, and remains possible after the Perpetuities and Accumulations Act 1964.

D. Fiscal Advantages[48]

Charities which are under the jursdiction of the English courts are exempt from income tax on rents, interests, dividends and annual payments, provided that the income is applied for charitable purposes only.[49] They may recover from the Revenue income tax paid or credited prior to the payment of interest or dividends, and also in respect of income received by charities under "four-year" covenants.[50] Alternatively, donors who are employees may utilise the new payroll deduction scheme.[51] Further, no income tax is chargeable in respect of profits of any trade carried on by the charity, if the profits are applied solely to the purposes of the charity and either the trade is exercised in the course of the actual carrying out of a primary purpose of the charity, or the work in connection with the trade is mainly carried out by beneficiaries of the charity.[52] Again the profits must be applied solely to the purposes of the charity. Similarly, charitable corporations are exempt from paying corporation tax.[53]

Gifts of any amount in favour of charity are exempt from inheritance

---

[44] *Post*, p. 427.

[45] *Supra*.

[46] [1952] A.C. 631.

[47] *Ante*, p. 365, *Re Tyler* [1891] 3 Ch. 252.

[48] [1972] B.T.R. 346 (G. N. Glover). See *Camille and Henry Dreyfus Foundation Inc.* v. *I.R.C.* [1956] A.C. 39.

[49] I.C.T.A. 1988, s.505; See *I.R.C.* v. *Educational Grants Association Ltd.* [1967] Ch. 993; *I.R.C.* v. *Helen Slater Charitable Trust Ltd.* [1982] Ch. 49.

[50] Reduced from seven years by F.A. 1980, s.55. See now I.C.T.A. 1988, s.660(3).

[51] I.C.T.A. 1988, s.202. See also s.339; F.A. 1988, s.70. The scheme raised £1,000,000 in its first year; *The Times*, July 21, 1988.

[52] *Ibid.*, s.505(1).

[53] *Ibid.*, ss.505(1), 506(1).

tax if made by way of payment from a discretionary trust,[54] or by way of gift by an individual during his lifetime or on death.[55] Similarly, transfers from a charitable trust are exempt from inheritance tax.[56]

No capital gains tax arises where a gain accrues to a charity and the gain is applicable and is applied for charitable purposes.[57] Nor will a donor be under any such liability in respect of a disposal to charity.[58] Charities are also exempt from stamp duty on conveyances,[59] and from National Insurance Surcharge.[60]

Charities, however, do have to bear Value Added Tax on goods and services which they purchase.[61] This liability will be particularly burdensome for many charities in respect of the maintenance and repair of buildings. Also, VAT may be chargeable in respect of goods and services provided, on payment, by some charities.[62]

All charities are entitled to exemption in respect of one-half of the rates of the properties which they occupy,[63] wholly or mainly used for charitable purposes. This includes administrative premises,[64] and premises used wholly or mainly for the sale of goods donated to a charity and applied for the purposes of a charity.[65] Relief can also be granted at the discretion of the rating authority up to the whole amount of the rates[66]; but "few rating authorities will grant relief beyond the one half which can be claimed as of right."[67] Churches, church halls and similar premises used for religious purposes are entitled to relief in respect of the whole of the rates.[68]

---

[54] Inheritance Tax Act 1984, s.76.
[55] *Ibid.* s.23. See also ss. 25, 26.
[56] *Ibid.* s.58(1)(*a*).
[57] C.G.T.A. 1979, s.145.
[58] *Ibid.* s.146.
[59] F.A. 1982, s.129.
[60] F.A. 1977, s.57.
[61] For specific exemptions, see Value Added Tax Act 1983, Scheds. 5 and 6.
[62] See [1972] B.T.R. 346 at p. 356; *Customs and Excise Commissioners* v. *Automobile Association* [1974] 1 W.L.R. 1447; Annual Report 1974, paras. 17–21. However, some goods supplied to or by charities are zero-rated. See, for example, V.A.T. (Charities) Order 1987 (S.I. 1987/437).
[63] General Rate Act 1967, s.40(1). See [1971] B.T.R. 86 (G. N. Glover); *Tudor Charities* (7th ed.), pp. 440–448. The 1967 Act ceases to have effect on March 31, 1990. Thereafter charities will enjoy discretionary relief from the community charge under Local Government Finance Act 1988, s.47.
[64] *Aldous* v. *Southwark Corporation* [1968] 1 W.L.R. 1671 (the management of Dulwich College Estates).
[65] Rating (Charity) Shops Act 1976; which reverses *Oxfam* v. *Birmingham District Council* [1976] A.C. 126.
[66] *Ibid.* s.40(2).
[67] [1971] B.T.R. 86 at p. 93.
[68] General Rate Act 1967, s.39(2). Similarly in respect of the community charge; Local Government Finance Act 1988, Sched. 5, para. 11. In *Henning* v. *Church of Jesus Christ of Latter-Day Saints* [1962] 1 W.L.R. 1091, the Mormon Church failed to obtain exemption in respect of premises to which only selected members of the faith were admitted. Similarly, the Exclusive Brethren in *Broxtowe Borough Council* v. *Birch* [1983] 1 W.L.R. 314.

In view of the extent of income and other assets thus exempted,[69] this is a formidable list of fiscal advantages. In 1975 the Inland Revenue "hazarded a guess that the total annual exemption must run into well over three figures (in terms of millions of pounds)."[70] This explains the prominence of Revenue cases in charity litigation.

Measures have recently been taken to prevent abuse of these tax advantages, for example by requiring charities to take reasonable steps to ensure that payments made to overseas bodies will be applied to genuine charitable purposes and requiring them to justify certain loans or investments as being for the benefit of charity and not for tax avoidance.[71] These provisions restrict tax relief where funds are applied for non-charitable purposes and prevent manipulation of charity tax advantages by individuals. So far they are working well.[72]

3. THE DEFINITION OF CHARITY[73]

A. The Four Categories

(i) **Lord Macnaghten's Classification.** A claim to charitable status is determined by considering whether the purpose in question comes within Lord Macnaghten's classification as exemplified by the cases decided in accordance with it. Lord Macnaughten said; "Charity in its legal sense comprises four principal divisions: trusts for the relief of poverty; trusts for the advancement of education; trusts for the advancement of religion; and trusts for other purposes beneficial to the community."[74] Each of these heads will be considered in turn. It is obvious that the heads provide no precise definition. Lord Wilberforce had this comment to make[75]: "first, that, since it is a classification of convenience, there may well be purposes which do not fit neatly into one or other of the headings." He might also have added that there are many purposes which overlap.[76] "Secondly that the words used must not be given the force of a statute to be construed; and thirdly, that the law of charity is a moving subject which may well have evolved even since 1891." Indeed, it is continually changing, and as has been

---

[69] In 1987 it was estimated that £12 billion a year flows through charities; Annual Report of the Charity Commissioners 1987, para. 27.

[70] Report of Expenditure Committee of H.C. (1975), Vol. 1, para. 16. For a review and criticism of fiscal advantages see Goodman Committee, Chap. 5.

[71] I.C.T.A. 1988, ss.339, 427, 505, 506, 683.

[72] Annual Report 1987, para. 28.

[73] (1945) 61 L.Q.R. 268 (J. W. Brunyate); (1949) 2 C.L.P. 102 (G. W. Keeton); Nathan Committee Report, paras. 120–140; Annual Report of the Charity Commissioners 1973, para. 2; for the text of the Preamble see Maudsley and Burn, p. 292.

[74] *Commissioners of Special Income Tax* v. *Pemsel* [1891] A.C. 531 at p. 583.

[75] *Scottish Burial Reform and Cremation Society Ltd.* v. *Glasgow Corporation* [1968] A.C. 138 at p. 154.

[76] Thus, a gift for the preparation of "poor students for the Ministry" might come under all four heads.

explained,[77] the impact of heavy taxation and the resulting significance of tax exemption, and also the development of State agencies to provide education, relief from poverty, and other purposes needed by society have transformed the concept of charity.[78] It should be appreciated that the Charity Commissioners have a major role in the development of this concept.[79]

(ii) **Public Benefit.** It should also be noted at this stage that each head involves two elements; an element of benefit, such as the advancement of education, and also an element of *public* benefit, that is to say, education being advanced in a way that will benefit the whole community, or a sufficiently substantial part of it. The requirement of public benefit varies from head to head, and will be discussed in detail.[80]

(iii) **Exclusively Charitable.** A trust will not fail to be charitable because it may in its operation incidentally benefit the rich, or other non-objects of charity.[81] But if a non-charitable purpose is an object, the trust cannot be charitable, for then it ceases to be wholly and exclusively "for charitable purposes."[82] And a statement of objects which includes non-charitable purposes is not saved by adding "in so far as they are of a charitable nature."[83]

(iv) **Charitable Purposes Overseas.** A number of special problems arise where the benefits arising from charitable trusts are to be enjoyed abroad. For at least 200 years there has been no rule requiring the benefits to be retained in this country.[84] But, how can the court or the (English) trustees control the application of the funds? What relationship is there between the Preamble of 1601 and the problem of an under-developed country suffering from drought, floods or earthquake? And, should tax privileges be given by the British Revenue for the benefit of communities abroad?[85]

---

[77] *Ante*, p. 372.
[78] See *Incorporated Council of Law Reporting* v. *Att.-Gen.* [1972] Ch. 73 at pp. 88–89, *per* Russell L.J. discussing the fourth head.
[79] *Post*, p. 443. The Commissioners take a generous view as to what is charitable, to reflect changes in society; Annual Report 1985, para. 5.
[80] *Post*, p. 408.
[81] *Verge* v. *Somerville* [1924] A.C. 496; *Re Resch's W.T.* [1969] 1 A.C. 514; *sub. nom. Le Cras* v. *Perpetual Trustee Co.* [1967] 1 All E.R. 915. But a trust for the relief of poverty will fail if it may benefit persons who are not poor; *Re Gwyon* [1903] 1 Ch. 255; *post*, p. 382.
[82] *Post*, p. 421, *Ellis* v. *I.R.C.* (1949) 31 T.C. 178; *Re Cole* [1958] Ch. 877; *Att.-Gen. of the Bahamas* v. *Royal Trust Co.* [1986] 1 W.L.R. 1001.
[83] See Annual Report 1964, Appendix C, para. B 1; *McGovern* v. *Att.-Gen.* [1982] Ch. 321.
[84] *Re Robinson* [1931] 2 Ch. 122 at p. 126, *per* Maugham J. (gift to German Government for the benefit of its soldiers disabled in the late war held charitable).
[85] Annual Report 1963, paras. 69–76. See (1965) 29 Conv.(N.S.) 123 (D. M. Emrys Evans).

There is insufficient case material to determine the way in which trusts for charitable purposes abroad compare with those producing benefits domestically. The Charity Commissioners have disclosed the principles on which they operate.[86] They consider that the relief of poverty and the advancement of education and religion are charitable in all parts of the world; but in connection with trusts coming under the fourth head, they take a defensive position, and say that there must be a benefit, albeit indirect, to the community of the United Kingdom,[87] and add that it is easier to establish this benefit in relation to Commonwealth than to foreign countries. The Commonwealth link is however weaker than it was when this statement was made in 1963. The position probably is that the Commissioners will be more likely to uphold trusts under the fourth head where they will benefit an under-developed country for which this country feels special responsibility.

Assuming that it is necessary to establish a benefit to the community in this country, it has been said that the court would still be bound to take account of the probable results of the execution of the trust on the inhabitants of the country concerned, which would doubtless have a history and social structure quite different from that of the United Kingdom. So in *McGovern* v. *Att.-Gen.*,[88] a trust to procure the abolition of torture or inhuman or degrading treatment or punishment[89] in all parts of the world was not charitable, one reason being that the court would have no satisfactory means of judging the probable effects of, say, legislation to abolish the death penalty on the local community. If the purpose of a trust was to secure abolition of the death penalty for adultery in Islamic countries, the court would not be competent to deal with it because it would either have to apply English standards as to public benefit, which might not be appropriate in the local conditions, or attempt to apply local standards of which it knew little or nothing.

The advancement of the Christian religion abroad has been upheld in the form of trusts for missionary work.[90] There is little recent authority on education abroad.[91] Such trusts are within the Commissioners' principle, and, again, they would probably lean more strongly in favour of education in under-developed countries. Similarly with

---

[86] *Ibid.* para. 70.
[87] See *Camille and Henry Dreyfus Foundation Inc.* v. *I.R.C.* [1954] Ch. 672 at p. 684. For the Australian position, see *Re Stone* (1970) 91 W.N. (N.S.W.) 704 at p. 717.
[88] [1982] Ch. 321, *post*, p. 405.
[89] Including punishment inflicted by process of law.
[90] *e.g.* The Universities Mission to Central Africa, and the Society for the Propagation of the Gospel in Foreign Parts, which combined in 1964 to become the United Society for the Propagation of the Gospel.
[91] In *Re Vaughan* [1905] W.N. 179, the trusts included educational objects on the Island of Cephalonia.

the relief of poverty and distress,[92] and the work overseas of organisations like Oxfam and War on Want is well known. But, even in these
cases, the Commissioners, concerned about the problem of controlling
the application of funds given for large projects of development, draw
a distinction between cases where the poverty is "observable" and the
results "reasonably direct,"[93] as opposed to cases where the object is of
more general improvement of the economy of an under-developed
country. It is difficult to see how the Commissioners, charged with the
duty of ensuring the proper application of charity money could do
otherwise; but in this field, it is those large assistance projects which
are most needed, and massive financial aid is provided in the form of
foreign aid for those purposes. If the taxpayer is going to pay for it in
any case, why not allow charitable trusts for such purposes?

In support of their position under the fourth head, the Commissioners can call in aid the case of *Keren Kayemeth Le Jisroel Ltd.* v.
I.R.C.,[94] where a trust for the purchase of land in Israel and for the
settlement there of Jewish people was held not charitable. But, as will
be seen,[95] the decision turned on the character of the purposes, and not
on the fact that the benefit would be enjoyed abroad. And in *Re Jacobs*
in 1970[96] a trust for the purpose "of planting a grove of trees in Israel to
perpetuate my name on the eternal soil of the Holy Land" was upheld.
Soil conservation is of crucial importance in the arid parts of Israel. It
was the benefit to the community abroad which was significant.

B. The Relief of Poverty

(i) **Meaning of Poverty.** There is no definition of poverty. Its meaning can only be understood by examining the cases on the subject. "It is
quite clearly established," said Sir Raymond Evershed M.R., "that
poverty does not mean destitution; . . . it may not unfairly be para-
phrased as meaning persons who have to 'go short' in the ordinary
acceptance of that term. . . . "[97] It is thus a matter of degree. Most of the
cases come from a time before public assistance and other welfare
payments were available from public funds. Such payments are
intended to relieve poverty and hardship, and it could be argued at the
present day that eligibility for such payments should be the test of
poverty. But, if that were so, charity in this area would duplicate the
work of a good welfare programme. If relief of poverty is the duty of

---

[92] See *Re Niyazi's Will Trusts* [1978] 1 W.L.R. 910 (trust for construction of working
men's hostel in Cyprus charitable).
[93] Annual Report 1963, paras. 69–76.
[94] [1932] A.C. 650.
[95] *Post*, p. 391.
[96] Annual Report 1970, para. 78; *Re Levy Estate* (1988) 28 E.T.R. 29.
[97] *Re Coulthurst* [1951] Ch. 661 at pp. 665–666.

the State, what scope is there for private charity? This is a problem which is met in many of the areas of charity today, especially in connection with trusts for the relief of poverty and for education and health. Private charity is useful to fill the gaps which the welfare state programme leaves uncovered.[98] But in doing so, it creates some controversies. If a trust's purpose is not appealing enough to justify the expenditure of public money, should it justify the tax exemptions to which charity is entitled?

(ii) **Illustrations.** Gifts for the benefit of the poor are clearly charitable.[99] Also "needy" persons,[1] or "indigent"[2] persons. Often a group of poor is confined to a particular location,[3] or religion,[4] or to a group which is assumed to be in need of help,[5] or victims of a disaster.[6] Persons of "limited means"[7] are included, and trusts for gentlewomen and distressed gentlefolk.[8] In *Re De Carteret*, in 1933,[9] a trust was upheld for the payment of annuities to women whose income was not less "than eighty or more than one hundred and twenty pounds per annum." On the other hand, a gift which includes persons who are not in need will be excluded. Thus gifts to employees of a company are not charitable[10] unless the qualification of poverty is clearly imposed.[11] In

---

[98] See Annual Report 1967, paras. 17–21; 1971, paras. 76–79; 1978, paras. 61–63, App. A, suggesting ways in which the income of charities for the relief of poverty may be effectively applied.

[99] *Att.-Gen.* v. *Peacock* (1676) Cas. *temp.* Finch 245: "for the good of the poor people for ever"; *Re Darling* [1896] 1 Ch. 56: "to the poor and the service of God."

[1] *Re Reed* (1893) 10 T.L.R. 87; "fifty needy and deserving men and fifty needy and deserving old women. ... " *Re Scarisbrick* [1951] Ch. 622: "shall be in needy circumstances"; *Re Cohen* [1973] 1 W.L.R. 415: "in special need."

[2] *Weir* v. *Crum-Brown* [1908] A.C. 162: "indigent bachelors and widowers who have shown sympathy with science."

[3] *Re Lousada* (1887) 22 L.T.Jo. 358 (London poor); *Re Lucas* [1922] 2 Ch. 52 (oldest respectable inhabitants in Gunville).

[4] *Re Wall* (1889) 52 Ch.D. 570.

[5] *Att.-Gen.* v. *Painter-Stainers Co.* (1788) 2 Cox. Eq.Cas. 51; *Att.-Gen.* v. *Ironmongers Co.* (1834) 2 My. & K. 526 (debtors); *Thompson* v. *Thompson* (1844) 1 Coll. 381 at p. 395 (unsuccessful literary men); *Reeve* v. *Att.-Gen.* (1843) 3 Hare 191; *Loscombe* v. *Wintringham* (1850) 13 Beav. 87 (servants); *Biscoe* v. *Jackson* (1887) 35 Ch.D. 460 (soup kitchen for the parish of Shoreditch); *Re Coulthurst* [1951] Ch. 661 (widows and orphaned children of employees).

[6] *Re North Devon and West Somerset Relief Fund Trust* [1953] 1 W.L.R. 1260 (flood disaster).

[7] *Re Gardom* [1914] 1 Ch. 664.

[8] *Att.-Gen.* v. *Power* (1809) 1 Ball & B. 145; *Mary Clark Home Trustees* v. *Anderson* [1904] 2 K.B. 745; *Re Gardom* (*supra*); *Shaw* v. *Halifax Corporation* [1915] 2 K.B. 170; *Re Young* [1951] Ch. 344.

[9] [1933] Ch. 103.

[10] *Re Drummond* [1914] 2 Ch. 90; *Re Hobourn Aero-Components Air Raid Distress Fund* [1946] Ch. 194.

[11] *Gibson* v. *South American Stores (Gath & Chaves) Ltd.* [1950] Ch. 177; *Dingle* v. *Turner* [1973] A.C. 601.

Re Sanders' Will Trusts,[12] a gift for the provision of housing for the working classes was not charitable. An in *Re Gwyon*,[13] a fund providing for a gift of clothing to boys in Farnham and district failed on the ground that the conditions for qualification, precise though they were in many ways, failed to exclude affluent children.[14] It is no objection, however, that the scheme operates by way of bargain rather than bounty, *i.e.* that the beneficiaries are required to contribute to the cost of the benefits they receive.[15]

There is no need for the trust to be an endowment. A trust may be charitable although the trustees may distribute the capital. A trust was upheld in *Re Scarisbrick*[16] "for such relations of my . . . son and daughters as in the opinion of the survivor of my . . . son and daughters shall be in needy circumstances . . . as the survivor . . . shall by deed or will appoint." This was a trust for "poor relations," and there is no requirement, in poverty cases, for public benefit.[17] But there can be no charitable trust, even in the poverty category, where the persons to be benefited are specified individuals; and such a construction is more likely where the capital of a trust may be immediately distributed. But it is not decisive.

Nor is it an objection that the persons to be benefited are to be selected at the discretion of the trustees.[18] It is necessary, of course, that there should be a duty and not a mere power to select,[19] and that the discretion is exercisable only in favour of those who are poor. Jenkins L.J. in *Re Scarisbrick* dismissed the words "in the opinion of the survivor" as having no potential bearing on the character of the trust.

C. The Advancement of Education

(i) **Meaning of Education.** The second head has its origin in the phrases in the Preamble which speak of "the maintenance of schools of

---

[12] [1954] Ch. 265. *Re Mead's Trust Deed* [1961] 1 W.L.R. 1244 (membership of a Trade Union). *cf. Re Niyazi's W.T.* [1978] 1 W.L.R. 910 (gift for "the construction of a working men's hostel" in Famagusta, Cyprus held charitable by Megarry V.-C., "although it was desperately near the border-line."). But some homes for working classes have been registered as charities where there were other factors which indicated a requirement of poverty. Annual Report 1965, App. C, para. I. A.9.

[13] [1930] 1 Ch. 255.

[14] They also excluded black boys. This caused no comment at the time; but would no doubt do so today, *ante*, p. 319. Annual Report 1978, para. 73–81 (Lionel and Hilda Barnet Trust). See further [1981] Conv. 131 (T. G. Watkin); Annual Report 1983, para. 19; Annual Report 1987, para. 14.

[15] *Re Cottam's W.T.* [1955] 1 W.L.R. 1299; *Le Cras* v. *Perpetual Trustee Co. Ltd.* [1969] 1 A.C. 514; *Joseph Rowntree Memorial Trust Housing Association Ltd.* v. *Att.-Gen.* [1983] Ch. 159 (dwellings for sale to elderly at 70 per cent. cost).

[16] [1951] Ch. 622; *Re Cohen* [1973] 1 W.L.R. 415.

[17] *Dingle* v. *Turner* [1972] A.C. 601; *post*, p. 409.

[18] *Gibson* v. *South American Stores (Gath & Chaves) Ltd.* [1950] Ch. 177; *Re Scarisbrick* (*supra*), *Re Cohen* (*supra*).

[19] *Re Cohen* (*supra*).

learning, free schools and scholars in universities" and "the education and preferment of orphans." The endowments, some of course very ancient, of many schools and colleges and universities are based on this provision. Education in school and university is now however accepted as being within the responsibility of the State; and it is not surprising that modern cases have substantially widened the concept of educational charity. It can now cover almost any form of worthwhile instruction or cultural advancement, except for purely professional or career courses. It is not possible to provide a formula to delineate the area of education. This can only be indicated by examples; and some matters needing specific mention will then be discussed.

The following trusts have been held charitable under this head: Education in business management,[20] and in the art of government,[21] the production of a dictionary[22]; the support of London Zoological Society,[23] the establishment and maintenance of museums,[24] the support of learned literary, scientific and cultural societies,[25] a search for the Shakespeare manuscript,[26] choral singing in London,[27] the promotion of the music of Delius,[28] classical drama and acting,[29] the publication of the Law Reports,[30] the founding of lectureships and professorships,[31] the study and dissemination of ethical principles and cultivation of a rational religious sentiment[32] and even a "sort of finishing school for the Irish people" where "self-control, oratory, deportment and the art of personal contact" were to be taught.[33] Educational purposes include matters ancillary to the main purposes, such as the payment of teachers and administrative staff.[34]

---

[20] *Re Koettgen's W.T.* [1954] Ch. 252.
[21] *Re McDougall* [1957] 1 W.L.R. 81. But not for the promotion of political causes; *post*, p. 388. The holding of conferences with a "political flavour" but not of a party political nature was upheld in *Re Koeppler's W.T.* [1986] Ch. 423.
[22] *Re Stanford* [1924] 1 Ch. 73.
[23] *Re Lopes* [1931] 2 Ch. 130.
[24] *British Museum Trustees* v. *White* (1826) 2 Sm. & St. 594; *Re Holburne* (1885) 53 L.T. 212; *Re Pinion* [1965] Ch. 85 at p. 105.
[25] *Royal College of Surgeons* v. *National Provincial Bank Ltd.* [1952] A.C. 631; *Re Shakespeare Memorial Trust* [1923] 2 Ch. 398; *Re British School of Egyptian Archaeology* [1954] 1 W.L.R. 546. The English Speaking Union was registered in 1977: Annual Report 1977, paras. 48–50.
[26] *Re Hopkins' W.T.* [1965] Ch. 669.
[27] *Royal Choral Society* v. *I.R.C.* [1943] 2 All E.R. 101.
[28] *Re Delius* [1957] Ch. 299.
[29] *Re Shakespeare Memorial Trust* (*supra*).
[30] *Incorporated Council of Law Reporting for England and Wales* v. *Att.-Gen.* [1972] Ch. 73; the first appeal under Charities Act 1960, s.5(3), against a decision of the Charity Commissioners on a question of entitlement to registration as a charity: (1972) 88 L.Q.R. 171. See also Annual Report 1980, para. 78 (The National Law Library Trust).
[31] *Att.-Gen.* v. *Margaret and Regius Professors in Cambridge* (1682) 1 Vern. 55.
[32] *Re South Place Ethical Society* [1980] 1 W.L.R. 1565.
[33] *Re Shaw's W.T.* [1952] Ch. 163.
[34] *Case of Christ's College, Cambridge* (1757) 1 Wm. Bl. 90.

(ii) Research. Education requires something more than the mere accumulation of knowledge. There must be some sharing, or teaching or dissemination, some way of showing that the public will benefit. There is no difficulty in the case of research which is likely to produce material benefit to the community, such as medical or scientific research.[35] Such purposes would in any case come under the fourth head. But, on literary, cultural and scholarly subjects, the matter is less obvious. "I think, therefore," said Wilberforce J. in *Re Hopkins*,[36] "that the word 'education' . . . must be used in a wide sense, certainly extending beyond teaching, and that the requirement is that, in order to be charitable, research must either be of educational value to the researcher or must be so directed as to lead to something which will pass into the store of educational material, or so as to improve the sum of communicable knowledge in an area which education may cover— education in this last context extending to the formation of literary taste and appreciation."

In *Re Hopkins*,[37] there was a testamentary gift to the Francis Bacon Society "to be earmarked and applied towards finding the Bacon-Shakespeare manuscripts." This was held to be a valid charitable trust. It was possible that the manuscript would be found. A "search, or research, for the original manuscripts of England's greatest dramatist (whoever he was) would be well within the law's conception of charitable purposes. The discovery would be of the highest value to history and to literature."[38] The gift was held to be a valid charitable trust under this head and the fourth head.

Re Shaw[39] was distinguished.

George Bernard Shaw, by his will, directed that his residuary estate should be devoted to researching the advantages to be gained by substituting the present 26-letter alphabet by a new proposed British alphabet of 40 letters, in which each letter would indicate a single sound; and to translate his play "Androcles and the Lion" into the new alphabet, for comparison with the original.

Harman J. held that the gift was not charitable "if the object be merely the increase of knowledge, that is not in itself a charitable object unless it be combined with teaching or education."[40]

---

[35] *Royal College of Surgeons* v. *National Provincial Bank Ltd.* (*supra*). See also Annual Report 1987, para. 12.

[36] [1965] Ch. 669 at p. 680.

[37] [1965] Ch. 669; A trust for completing research on Voltaire and Rousseau was held to be valid; *Re Besterman, The Times*, January 22, 1980. See also *McGovern* v. *Att.-Gen.* [1982] Ch. 321, where research into human rights and dissemination of the results would have been charitable. The trust failed for other reasons; *post*, p. 405. Trusts for research into human rights have been registered; Annual Report 1987, para. 12.

[38] *Ibid.* at p. 679.

[39] [1957] 1 W.L.R. 729.

[40] *Ibid.* at p. 737, referring to Rigby L.J. in *Re Macduff* [1896] 2 Ch. 451.

This is thought to be too narrow a view of education. Whether the trust in this case would be held charitable under Wilberforce J.'s test depends on the usefulness of the research, and that is a matter of individual judgment. Not every type of knowledge, whether researched, disseminated or taught is capable of being education. Not schools for prostitutes or pickpockets,[41] nor the training of spiritual-istic mediums.[42]

(iii) Artistic and Aesthetic Education. Education is not confined to the directly inculcative. In *Royal Choral Society* v. *I.R.C.*,[43] the Court of Appeal upheld as charitable a trust to promote the practice and performance of choral works. Lord Greene said in speaking of the view that education meant a master teaching a class[44]: "I protest against that narrow conception of education when one is dealing with aesthetic education. In my opinion, a body of persons established for the purpose of raising the artistic state of the country . . . is established for educational purposes.

In *Re British School of Egyptian Archaeology*[45] a trust to excavate and discover Egyptian antiquities, to hold exhibitions and to promote the training and assistance of students in the field of Egyptian history was held educational. In *Re Delius*,[46] there was a gift to increase the general appreciation of the musical work of the composer, Delius. Roxburgh J. had no doubt that the trust was for the advancement of education, even though it related to the work of a particular composer.

But it seems that a trust for "artistic" purposes is not charitable.[47] Upjohn J. dealing with a clause in the Associated Artists Ltd. Memorandum which empowered it to present "artistic . . . dramatic works' " found it difficult to attach any real charitable concept to an artistic dramatic work; it is too wide and too vague . . . "[48] Many artistic purposes, as we have seen, are educational; but a trust is not charitable unless its purposes are exclusively charitable.[49]

(iv) Subjective Evaluation. It is clear from what has so far been said that the question whether a purpose is educational or not will depend in many cases upon the evaluation of its quality and usefulness for that purpose. Music, drama, literature, archaeology, museums; these and

---

[41] *Per* Harman J. [1957] 1 W.L.R. 729 at p. 737; and in *Re Pinion* [1965] Ch. 85 at p. 105.

[42] *Re Hummeltenberg* [1923] 1 Ch. 237.

[43] [1943] 2 All E.R. 101.

[44] *Ibid.* at p. 104.

[45] [1954] 1 W.L.R. 540.

[46] [1957] Ch. 299.

[47] *Re Ogden* (1909) 25 T.L.R. 382; *Associated Artists* v. *I.R.C.* [1956] 1 W.L.R. 752.

[48] [1956] 1 W.L.R. 752 at p. 758; see also *Royal Choral Society* v. *I.R.C.* [1943] 2 All E.R. 101 at p. 107, *per* Lord Greene M.R.

[49] *Post*, p. 421.

many more are included. But not bad music, ham acting, pornography, useless digging or collections of rubbish. In *Re Delius*,[50] Roxburgh J. recognised that there would be difficulty if a manifestly inadequate composer had been chosen. A judge may be assisted by expert evidence.[51] But that may not be conclusive. And artistic evaluation changes with the fashion and the times. It is clear that the court will require to be satisfied of the merit of artistic work.[52] The opinion of the donor that the gift is for the public benefit does not make it so. The matter is to be decided by the court on the evidence before it.[53]

In *Re Pinion*,[54] a testator gave his studio, together with its contents, to trustees to enable it to be used as a museum for the display of his collection of furniture and objets d'art, and paintings, some of which were by the testator himself.

Expert opinion was unanimous that the collection had no artistic merit. One expert expressed his surprise that "so voracious a collector should not by hazard have picked up even one meritorious object."[55] The Court of Appeal held the trust void. "I can conceive," said Harman L.J., "of no useful object to be served in foisting upon the public this mass of junk. It has neither public utility nor educational value."[56]

(v) Youth. Sports at School and University. Education is specially concerned with the young. In many situations a provision for the young will be held charitable although the same provision for older people would fail.

In *Re Mariette*,[57] there was a gift to provide, *inter alia*, Eton fives courts and squash rackets courts at Aldenham School. Eve J. upheld this, on the principle that learning to play games at a boarding school was as important as learning from the books.[58]

The sporting facilities need not be limited to a particular school or

---

[50] [1957] Ch. 299.

[51] *Per* Russell L.J. in *Re Pinion* [1965] Ch. 85 at p. 108.

[52] The same problem arises with many situations under the fourth head. *Post*, p. 394.

[53] In *Re Shaw's W.T.* [1952] Ch. 163 at pp. 168, 172, Vaisey J. was reluctant to impose his personal evaluation.

[54] [1965] Ch. 85.

[55] *Ibid.* at p. 107.

[56] *Ibid.*

[57] [1915] 2 Ch. 284; *London Hospital Medical College* v. *I.R.C.* [1976] 1 W.L.R. 613. See also *Re Chesters* (1934) (unreported) cited in *I.R.C.* v. *McMullen* [1981] A.C. 1 at p. 17 (bequest for playgrounds for children charitable). For sport outside universities and schools, see *post*, p. 398.

[58] "No-one of sense could be found to suggest that between [the ages of 10 and 19] any boy can be properly educated unless at least as much attention is given to the development of his body as is given to the development of his mind. ... To leave 200 boys at large and to their own devices during their leisure hours ... would not be educating, but would probably result in their quickly relapsing into something approaching barbarism."

institution. In *I.R.C.* v. *McMullen*,[59] a trust to provide facilities for pupils at schools and universities in any part of the United Kingdom to play association football or other games or sports was held valid by the House of Lords. Lord Hailsham of St. Marylebone said[60]: "The picture of education when applied to the young . . . is complex and varied . . . It is the picture of a balanced and systematic process of instruction, training and practice containing both spiritual, moral, mental and physical elements[61] . . . I reject any idea which would cramp the education of the young within the school or university campus, limit it to formal instruction, or render it devoid of pleasure in the exercise of skill." But this wide definition of education is not without its limits. Lord Hailsham stated that the mere playing of games or enjoyment or amusement or competition was not *per se* charitable nor necessarily educational; and that a trust for physical education *per se* and not associated with persons of school age or just above was not necessarily a good charitable gift.[62]

Trusts for sport outside educational facilities and the services are not charitable[63] unless they come within the scope of the Recreational Charities Act 1958.[64] But intelligent games like chess are educational for young people; though Vaisey J. in *Re Dupree's Deed Trusts*[65] recognised that here, as with outdoor games, the problem of distinguishing between the influence of one activity and another was very difficult. He foresaw a slippery slope from chess to draughts, to bezique, to bridge and whist, and stamp collecting and acquiring birds' eggs.[66] All that can be said is that purposeful activities for the young receive favourable treatment. The Boy Scout Movement[67] and the National Association of Toy Libraries[68] are charities, and a gift for an annual treat or field day for school children at Turton has been upheld as encouraging a study of natural history.[69]

(vi) **Professional Bodies.** We have seen that learned societies may be

---

[59] [1981] A.C. 1; [1978] Conv. 355 (A. C. Hutchinson); [1980] Conv. 173, 225 (J. Warburton); (1986) 1 Trust Law & Practice 22 (D. Evans).

[60] *Ibid.* at p. 425.

[61] Borrowed from Education Act 1944, s.7. See also s.53(1), (2).

[62] In 1973, the Kent Youth Cricket Trust was registered, but attempts by other counties were refused: Annual Report 1973, paras. 80–82; Annual Report 1974 para. 64. The whole matter will no doubt be reconsidered in the light of *I.R.C.* v. *McMullen* (*supra*).

[63] *Re Nottage* [1895] 2 Ch. 649 (a prize for a yacht race).

[64] *Post*, p. 400.

[65] [1945] Ch. 16; (a chess contest in Portsmouth for males under 21). This is not contrary to Sex Discrimination Act 1975. Charities are excepted: s.43. Sex Discrimination Act 1975 (Amendment of Section 43) Order 1977 (S.I. 1977 No. 528). A similar trust was established for girls in Portsmouth under 18; see (1977) 41 Conv.(N.S.) 8.

[66] *Ibid.* at p. 20.

[67] *Re Webber* [1954] 1 W.L.R. 1500.

[68] Annual Report 1973, para. 41.

[69] *Re Mellody* [1918] 1 Ch. 228; *Re Ward's Estate* (1937) 81 S.J. 397.

charities. So also professional bodies, if their object is the advancement of education.[70] The object of the Royal College of Surgeons[71] was stated in the recitals of the royal charter of March 1800 to be: "the due promotion and encouragement of the study and practice of the . . . art and science of surgery."

The fact that the College gives assistance and protection to its members is ancillary only; and the College was held to be a charity for the purpose of taking a gift under the rule in *Christ's Hospital* v. *Grainger*.[72] Similarly, the Royal College of Nursing[73] was entitled to a reduction of rating liability on the ground that the advance of nursing as a profession in all or any of its branches was a charitable purpose.[74] The Construction Industry Training Board was held to be charitable,[75] and subsequently most of the Industrial Training Boards established under the Industrial Training Act 1964 have been registered as charities.[76]

But if the object or one of the objects of the society is to promote the status of the profession or the welfare of its members, it will not be charitable. In another nursing case,[77] the General Nursing Council for England and Wales, which is a statutory body, set up under the Nurses Registration Act 1919,[78] had as its main function the regulation of the nursing profession; and was not therefore entitled to the rating reduction.

(vii) **Political Propaganda Masquerading as Education.**[79] Political purposes are not charitable. They may be for the public benefit, but they are partisan. The court cannot determine whether any particular programme is for the public benefit.[80] Nor can such a trust be charitable even where the testator's project has subsequently been endorsed

---

[70] *Ante*, p. 383.

[71] *Royal College of Surgeons* v. *National Provincial Bank Ltd.* [1952] A.C. 631.

[72] (1849) 1 Mac. & G. 460; *ante*, p. 374.

[73] *Royal College of Nursing* v. *St. Marylebone Borough Council* [1959] 1 W.L.R. 1077; *I.R.C.* v. *Yorkshire Agricultural Society* [1928] 1 K.B. 611 (exhibitions and "the general promotion of agriculture"); *Brisbane C.C.* v. *Att.-Gen. for Queensland* [1979] A.C. 411 ("showground purposes" held to be for the protection of agriculture); *Institute of Civil Engineers* v. *I.R.C.* [1932] 1 K.B. 149 ("the general advancement of mechanical science and more particularly for providing the acquisition of the sources of knowledge which constitute the profession of a civil engineer").

[74] Similarly a gift to provide extra comforts for the nursing staff (as opposed to individual nurses) will be charitable; *Re Bernstein's W.T.* (1971) 115 S.J. 808.

[75] *Construction Industry Training Board* v. *Att.-Gen.* [1973] Ch. 173.

[76] Annual Report 1973, para. 39.

[77] *General Nursing Council for England and Wales* v. *St. Marylebone Borough Council* [1959] A.C. 540; *Chartered Insurance Institute* v. *London Corporation* [1957] 1 W.L.R. 867 (promoting the insurance profession).

[78] The objects are summarised at [1958] Ch. 429; [1959] A.C. 553–554.

[79] Annual Report 1966, para. 38 (warning the overworking of the word "education"); 1969, para. 11; 1971, paras. 7–10; 1981, para. 54.

[80] *Bowman* v. *Secular Society* [1917] A.C. 406 at p. 421, *per* Lord Parker of Waddington.

by Parliament.[81] A trust for political purposes will fail. Attempts have been made to foster the doctrines of a political party under the guise of a trust for education by providing for the advancement of adult education on the lines of the principles of that party.[82] In *Re Hopkinson*,[83] Vaisey J. explained the principle as follows: "Political propaganda masquerading ... I do not use the word in any sinister sense ... as education is not education within the statute of Elizabeth. . . . In other words it is not charitable."[84] But there is no doubt that the prospects of success are greater if purposes are presented in the form of education. In *Re Scowcroft*,[85] the gift was of income to be applied "for the furtherance of Conservative principles and religious and mental improvement," and this succeeded. And it is said that when the National Committee for the Commonwealth Immigrant was unable to obtain registration for its constituent branches on the ground that interracial harmony was not charitable, the Commissioners suggested that the purposes should be altered so as to be presented in the form of the promotion of education among the different races.[86] Similarly in *Re Koeppler's Will Trusts*[87] a gift to further the work of an educational project was held charitable even though the testator's express aspirations (the formation of informed international public opinion and the promotion of greater co-operation in Europe and the West) were not regarded as charitable. The project involved conferences with a "political flavour," but did not further the interests of a particular political party, nor seek to change the law or government policies.

While a students' union is a charitable body, as being ancillary to the educational purposes of the college or university,[88] the donation of union funds for political, or indeed for charitable purposes which are not educational, is not permitted. So in *Baldry* v. *Feintuck*[89] the use of union funds to campaign for the restoration of free school milk was

---

[81] *Re Bushnell* [1975] 1 W.L.R. 1596 (national health system introduced after testator's death but before the litigation); *post*, p. 404; (1975) 38 M.L.R. 471 (R. B. M. Cotterrell).
[82] *Bonar Law Memorial Trust* v. *I.R.C.* (1933) 49 T.L.R. 220 (Conservative); *Re Hopkinson* [1949] 1 All E.R. 346 (Socialist); *cf. McDougall* [1957] 1 W.L.R. 81. See also *Re Ogden* [1933] Ch. 678, where, however, a trust for Liberal institutions was upheld on other grounds; *ante*, p. 98.
[83] [1949] 1 All E.R. 346. See also *McGovern* v. *Att.-Gen.* [1982] Ch. 321, *post*, p. 405, where an essentially political trust was not saved by educational elements.
[84] *Ibid.* at p. 350.
[85] [1898] 2 Ch. 638; *cf.* in the field of religion, *Re Hood* [1931] 1 Ch. 240 (spreading Christian principles by extinguishing "the drink traffic").
[86] *Nightingale on Charities*, pp. 52–53. See now Annual Report 1983, paras. 15–20.
[87] [1986] Ch. 423; [1985] Conv. 412 (T. G. Watkin); (1986) 49 N.L.J. *Annual Charities Review* 12 (S. P. de Cruz).
[88] *London Hospital Medical College.* v. *I.R.C.* [1976] 1 W.L.R. 613, *post*, p. 399. The National Union of Students is not a charity; see *Att.-Gen.* v. *Ross, infra.*
[89] [1972] 1 W.L.R. 552. A donation to the charity War on Want was also restrained, as it was not an educational charity. See Annual Report 1983, paras. 95 and 96 and App. A; (1986) 1 *Trust Law & Practice* 47 (J. Warburton).

restrained as political, although the fact that a students' union has political clubs is not inconsistent with its charitable status.[90]

(viii) Private and Independent Schools. An educational institution cannot be charitable if it is operated for profit.[91] Most preparatory schools in England were for many years operated by the owners as commercial ventures, and for profit. In recent years, however, with increasing expenses and unavoidable fee rises, the practice has been to transform them into non-profit-making bodies which can then obtain the fiscal benefits available to educational charities.

A private school is a charity if it does not operate for profit.[92] There has been no challenge in law to the charitable status of the boys' and girls' public schools, which for many years have operated on that basis. There is, however, a political challenge at the present time. Labour Party policy is to deprive independent schools of the fiscal benefits of charitable status, on the ground that they exercise a divisive influence on our society, and are hostile to the public, and not beneficial.[93] Withdrawal of fiscal privileges would create a new form of charity, on the lines of that discussed by the Radcliffe Commission,[94] having the right to exist in perpetuity, but no fiscal privileges. Such a change could only come by legislation; and it is not profitable here to speculate upon the form which it might take.

D. The Advancement of Religion[95]

(i) What is Religion? In *Bowman* v. *Secular Society*,[96] Lord Parker of Waddington suggested that any form of monotheistic theism will be recognised as a religion. Religion requires a spiritual belief, a faith, a recognition of some higher unseen power which is entitled to worship. It may include, but is greater than, morality, or a recommended way of life. In *Re South Place Ethical Society*,[97] one question was whether the

---

[90] *Att.-Gen.* v. *Ross* [1986] 1 W.L.R. 252; All E.R. Rev. 1985, p. 320 (P. J. Clarke). (Preliminary issue as to whether Attorney General had *locus standi* to seek injunction to restrain donation of union funds to striking miners and famine aid in Ethiopia). By similar reasoning, a charity cannot guarantee the liabilities of a non-charity; *Rosemary Simmons Memorial Housing Association Ltd.* v. *United Dominions Trust Ltd.* [1986] 1 W.L.R. 1440. See further [1988] Conv. 275 (J. Warburton).

[91] *Re Girls' Public Day School Trust* [1951] Ch. 400.

[92] *Abbey, Malvern Wells Ltd.* v. *Minister of Local Government and Housing* [1951] Ch. 728.

[93] Recommended by the Public Schools Commission (1968); see Annual Report (1974), para. 16. See also Chesterman, *Charities, Trusts and Social Welfare*, pp. 336–339.

[94] *Ante*, p. 372, n. 16.

[95] The only reference to religion in the Preamble is to the repair of churches.

[96] [1917] A.C. 406. See *Tudor on Charities* (7th ed.), pp. 54–55, suggesting that the religion need not be monotheistic.

[97] [1980] 1 W.L.R. 1565; [1980] Conv. 150 (St. J. Robilliard).

Society's objects, which were the "study and dissemination of ethical principles and the cultivation of a rational religious sentiment," were charitable under this heading. Dillon J. held that they were not. "Religion as I see it, is concerned with man's relations with God, and ethics are concerned with man's relations with man. The two are not the same, and are not made the same by sincere enquiry into the question; what is God?"[98] Similarly, the objects of a body such as the Freemasons, whose rules demand the highest personal, social and domestic standards, do not constitute a religion, even though they insist upon a belief in a divine spirit.[99] Nor did *Keren Kayemeth Le Jisroel*, the organisation whose object was the settlement of Jews in Palestine and neighbouring lands.[1] In any event, to be charitable, a trust must be for the *advancement* of religion; and this means "the promotion of spiritual teaching in a wide sense and the maintenance of the doctrines on which this rests, and the observances that serve to promote and manifest it—not merely a foundation or cause to which it can be related."[2]

(ii) Religious Toleration Within Christianity. The advent of religious toleration in the seventeenth century permitted the recognition of Christian sects other than the Established Church, and it seems now that no distinction is drawn between them.[3] Thus, trusts for Roman Catholics,[4] Unitarians,[5] Quakers,[6] Baptists,[7] Methodists,[8] and the Exclusive Brethren,[9] have been upheld. So also small groups, promoting minority religions. In *Thornton* v. *Howe*,[10] Romilly M.R. went so far as to hold as charitable a trust for the publication of the sacred

---

[98] *Ibid.* at p. 1571. The Society was charitable under the second and fourth headings; *ante*, p. 382, *post*, p. 394.

[99] *United Grant Lodge of Ancient Free and Accepted Masons of England and Wales* v. *Holborn B.C.* [1957] 1 W.L.R. 1080; *Re Thackrah* [1939] 2 All E.R. 4 (The objects of the Oxford Group held not to be for the advancement of religion: but has since been registered in a different form). See also *Re Macaulay's Estate* [1943] Ch. 475n; *Berry* v. *St. Marylebone B.C.* [1958] Ch. 406. (Theosophy; Romer L.J. said "The teaching of the Fatherhood of God, and the recognition of the corresponding Brotherhood of Humanity, without distinction of creed, appears to us to be at best the teaching of a doctrine, which is of a philosophical or metaphysical conception, rather than the advancement of religion." At p. 418.) *Re Fyshe, The Times*, July 1, 1957. (Church of the Agapemonites not a religious institution; on the Agapemonites, see *Nottidge* v. *Prince* (1860) 2 Giff. 246);

[1] *Infra*, n. 2.

[2] *Keren Kayemeth Le Jisroel* v. *I.R.C.* [1931] 2 K.B. 465; *affd.* [1932] A.C. 650.

[3] *Dunne* v. *Byrne* [1912] A.C. 407; *Re Flynn* [1948] Ch. 24.

[4] *Dunn* v. *Byrne, supra.*

[5] Unitarian Relief Act 1813; *Re Nesbitt's W.T.* [1953] 1 All E.R. 934.

[6] *Re Manser* [1905] 1 Ch. 68.

[7] *Re Strickland's W.T.* [1936] 3 All E.R. 1027.

[8] "The Voice of Methodism" was registered in 1965; Annual Report App. C, para. 1.

[9] *Holmes* v. *Att.-Gen., The Times*, February 12, 1981. But their place of worship did not qualify for rating exemption in *Broxtowe Borough Council* v. *Birch* [1983] 1 W.L.R. 314; Annual Report 1982, App. B. See also App. C.

[10] (1862) 31 Beav. 14. As this gift was to take effect out of land, it was void as infringing the Statutes of Mortmain, now repealed.

writings of Joanna Southcott, who claimed that she was with child by the Holy Ghost and would give birth to a new Messiah. And more recently, in *Re Watson*,[11] Plowman J. upheld a trust for the continuation of the work of God . . . in propagating the truth as given in the Holy Bible" by financing the continued publication of the books and tracts of one Hobbs who, with the testator, was the leading member of a very small group of undenominational Christians. Expert evidence regarded the intrinsic value of the work as nil; but it confirmed the genuineness of the belief of the adherents of that small group.

Cases like these raise the question of the limits of such trusts. This is an area where crankish views can be held with the greatest fervour and good faith. Should any belief, however outlandish, shared perhaps by only a handful of friends, be entitled to the perpetuity and fiscal privileges given to charities? Or, should such a religion be required to show some relation to orthodox religious thought? This is not a question of public benefit; there is no problem here of the benefits being available only to a select few; and "where the purpose in question is of a religious nature . . . the court assumes a public benefit unless the contrary is shown."[12] It seems, therefore, that, if a movement can establish that its tenets are within the scope of the Christian religion, it is no objection that those tenets are theologically unsound, or that the number of followers is minimal. Minority groups are well looked after. But "doctrines adverse to the very foundation of all religion"[13] cannot found a charity. It is difficult to see how a gift to propagate arguments calculated to disprove, no matter in how sober a manner, all religious beliefs, could be upheld as a trust for the advancement of religion. Such a trust might, however, be brought within another head of charity; for instance rationalism as well as moral philosophy might, in certain circumstances, be educational.[14]

(iii) **Non-Christian Religions.** "As between different religions, the law stands neutral, but it assumes that any religion is at least likely to be better than none."[15] There is little authority upon the status of non-Christian religions. A provision for the performance of pious, religious ceremonies for the gratification of the spirits of the ancestors failed, mainly on the ground that it could be of benefit to the family only and not to the public.[16] But it seems that the court could also hold that it was not for the advancement of religion. That was a decision of the Privy Council on appeal from Penang. The matter is of domestic

[11] [1973] 1 W.L.R. 1472.
[12] *Per* Plowman J. at p. 1482. See also *Holmes* v. *Att.-Gen.*, *The Times*, February 12, 1981.
[13] *Per* Romilly M.R. (1862) 31 Beav. 14 at p. 20.
[14] See the approach of Cohen J. to a philosophic question in *Re Price* [1943] Ch. 422; and *cf. Re Stemson's W.T.* [1970] Ch. 16.
[15] *Per* Cross J. in *Neville Estates Ltd.* v. *Madden* [1962] Ch. 832. See also Lord Reid in *Gilmour* v. *Coats* [1949] A.C. 457–458.
[16] *Yeap Cheah Neo* v. *Ong Chen Neo* (1875) L.R. 6 P.C. 381.

importance now, because of the increase in the numbers of members of non-Christian religions among the immigrant population.

A gift for the promotion of the Jewish religion has been upheld.[17] The reference in Statutory Instruments to "the advancement of religion other than Christianity" clearly implies recognition.[18] It is believed that Sikh temples and other centres of non-Christian worship have been accorded the rating privileges applicable to charities,[19] and there seems little doubt that all non-Christian religions will be treated equally. This situation may give rise to a number of difficult questions if charitable status is claimed for some mystical oriental cults.[20]

(iv) Satellite Purposes. A large number of purposes have been accepted as charitable, although indirectly connected with the advancement of religion. Again, only a few illustrations can be selected. Many of these relate to the erection of churches or the maintenance of the fabric of religious buildings; which includes a window,[21] a tomb in the church,[22] bells,[23] and parts of the structure.[24] A trust for a graveyard, even though restricted to one denomination, is charitable,[25] but not a trust for individual tombs in the churchyard.[26]

Similarly, a trust for the benefit of the clergy,[27] or for sick, aged and retired clergy,[28] or for the church choir,[29] and also for retired missionaries.[30] It has been held, however, that a gift for missionary work is

---

[17] *Straus* v. *Goldsmid* (1837) 8 Sim. 614; *Re Michel's Trust* (1860) 28 Beav. 39; *Neville Estates Ltd.* v. *Madden* [1962] Ch. 832. The position of Buddhism was left open in *Re South Place Ethical Society* [1980] 1 W.L.R. 1565.

[18] S.I. 1962 No. 1421; 1963 No. 2074.

[19] Under General Rate Act 1967, s.39(2). See now Local Government Finance Act 1988, s.47 and Sched. 5, para. 11, providing a similar exemption from the community charge, which comes into effect in April 1990.

[20] On "fringe" religious organisations, see Annual Report 1976, paras. 103–108; and on exorcism, paras. 65–67. The Unification Church (the "Moonies") has also been registered; Annual Report 1982, paras. 36–38, App. C. The Attorney General announced on February 3, 1988, that a High Court action to deprive the "Moonies" of charitable status was being dropped. See also (1986/87) 36 *King's Counsel* 23 (S. R. Sutherland). As to Scientology, see *R.* v. *Registrar General, ex p. Segerdal* [1970] 2 Q.B. 697 (meeting place not registrable under Places of Worship Registration Act 1855); *cf. The Church of the New Faith* v. *The Commissioner for Payroll Tax* (1983) 49 A.L.R. 65; [1984] Conv. 449 (St. J. Robilliard); (1984) 43 C.L.J. 218 (G. T. Pagone) (Scientology a religion in tax context).

[21] *Re King* [1923] 1 Ch. 243; *Re Raine* [1936] Ch. 417.

[22] *Hoare* v. *Osborne* (1866) L.R. 1 Eq. 585.

[23] *Re Pardoe* [1906] 2 Ch. 184; an extreme case, as the purpose was to commemorate the restoration of the Monarchy.

[24] *Re Palatine Estate Charity* (1888) 39 Ch.D. 54; *Hoare* v. *Osborne* (*supra*); *Att.-Gen.* v. *Day* [1900] 1 Ch. 31.

[25] *Re Manser* [1905] 1 Ch. 68; *Re Eighmie* [1935] Ch. 524.

[26] *Lloyd* v. *Lloyd* (1852) 2 Sim.(N.S.) 225.

[27] *Middleton* v. *Clitheroe* (1798) 3 Ves. 734 (stipends); *Widmore* v. *Woodruffe* (1766) Amb. 636 (Queen Anne's Bounty); *Re Williams* [1927] 2 Ch. 283 (education of candidates for Ministry).

[28] *Re Forster* [1939] Ch. 22.

[29] *Re Royce* [1940] Ch. 514.

[30] *Re Mylne* [1941] Ch. 204; *Re Moon's W.T.* [1948] 1 All E.R. 300.

not charitable on the ground that the description was too wide.[31] In this situation, however, as with many other phrases like; "for God's work,"[32] "for the service of God,"[33] "for his work in the parish,"[34] the court will often find circumstances to indicate that the purposes are intended to be limited to charitable religious purposes.[35]

E. Other Purposes Beneficial to the Community[36]

This is the residual head of charity; the most difficult, as Sir Samuel Romilly called it as he presented the formulation.[37] The earlier three heads are in their nature charitable. There is no need in those cases to prove that the relief of poverty or the advancement of education or religion is beneficial. They are. The public element there, as we will see,[38] concerns the extent to which those benefits are made available to the public or a section of the public as opposed to a group of individuals. With the fourth head, however, it must be shown that the selected purposes are beneficial; beneficial, that is, in the way which the law regards as charitable.

(i) **The Spirit and Intendment of the Preamble.** The Preamble has always constituted the general statement of charitable purposes. Since its repeal, the cases themselves are the source of the principle. A purpose which is expressly included in the Preamble is charitable; and also one covered by case authority. But "not every object of public general utility must necessarily be a charity."[39] The purpose need not be *eiusdem generis* with those listed in the Preamble, but must be charitable in the same sense.[40] When new purposes arise, it is not sufficient to show that the purpose is beneficial. It must be shown to be beneficial within the spirit and intendment of the Preamble, or by analogy from the principles established by the cases.[41] In *Williams' Trustees* v. *I.R.C.*,[42] a trust for promoting the interests of the Welsh community in London failed, on the ground that the objects of the trust, though beneficial to the community, were not beneficial in the

---

[31] *Scott* v. *Brownrigg* (1881) 9 L.R.Ir. 246.
[32] *Re Barker's W.T.* (1948) 64 T.L.R. 273.
[33] *Re Darling* [1896] 1 Ch. 50.
[34] *Re Simson* [1946] Ch. 299; *post*, p. 421.
[35] *Re Moon's W.T.* [1948] 1 All E.R. 300.
[36] See generally (1983) 36 C.L.P. 241 (H. Cohen). Most new registrations are under this heading; Annual Report 1985, para. 8.
[37] *Morice* v. *The Bishop of Durham* (1805) 10 Ves. 522 at p. 531.
[38] *Post*, pp. 408 *et seq.*
[39] *Per* Lindley L.J. in *Re Macduff* [1896] 2 Ch. 451 at p. 456, quoted by Lord Simonds in *Williams' Trustees* v. *I.R.C.* [1947] A.C. 447 at p. 455; *Att.-Gen.* v. *National and Union Bank of England* [1924] A.C. 262 at p. 265; *per* Lord Cairns.
[40] *Re Strakosch* [1949] Ch. 529.
[41] See *Williams' Trustees* v. *I.R.C.* [1947] A.C. 447, at p. 455, *per* Lord Simonds. This approach was followed by Dillon J. in *Re South Place Ethical Society* [1980] 1 W.L.R. 1565. See also *Brisbane C.C.* v. *Att.-Gen. for Queensland* [1979] A.C. 411 at p. 422.
[42] [1947] A.C. 447. The trust was later validated under the Charitable Trusts (Validation) Act 1954, p. 425, *post*; Annual Report 1977, paras. 71–80.

way which the law regards as charitable. Similarly, trusts for international co-operation have usually failed, either on the ground that their purposes are not within the spirit and intendment of the statute,[43] or because they are political.[44] On the other hand, in *Scottish Burial Reform and Cremation Society*,[45] a non-profit-making cremation society was held charitable by analogy with cases holding burial grounds to be so, though neither facility receives specific mention in the Preamble. Over the years, of course, the law has been developed in a radical manner. There is no definitional boundary to the fourth class; any purpose can be argued as coming within it; and Russell L.J. went so far as to say that the courts are accepting that if a purpose is beneficial to the community, it is prima facie charitable in law, and that the analogy approach is too restrictive.[46] The treatment of the problem has been much improved by the obligation imposed by the Charities Act 1960 to register charities with the Charity Commissioners.[47] For, as part of their jurisdiction to register or to refuse registration, the Commissioners have built up a valuable range of precedents by which they can be guided, and though this has had to be based on the existing case law, nevertheless the Commissioners feel that they can develop from it "such a concept of the field of charity as may meet the needs of the community."[48] The process of developing the notion of the "benefit to the community" is thus far more in the hands of experts than hitherto, and the Commissioners have shown courage and enterprise in their efforts to keep the concept of "benefit to the community in line with modern needs." There is an appeal from the Commissioners' decision to the court.[49]

(ii) **The Test is What the Law Treats as Charitable.** A preliminary point however needs to be taken. The question whether a purpose is beneficial to the community is one that the court must decide in the light of all the evidence available. What the donor thought, or what other people think is not the issue. In a sense, the test is objective, yet

---

[43] *Re Strakosch* [1949] Ch. 529 (the furthering of understanding between the Union of South Africa and the Mother Country); *cf.* Annual Report 1983, para. 18; *Keren Kayemeth Le Jisroel* v. *I.R.C.* [1932] A.C. 650 (resettlement of Jews). See Picarda, pp. 118–119.

[44] *Re Buxton* (1962) 41 T.C. 235. Amnesty and the United Nations Association failed to obtain registration. See also *McGovern* v. *Att.-Gen.* [1982] Ch. 321, *post*, p. 405; *Re Koeppler's W.T.* [1986] Ch. 423 (formation of an informed international public opinion and promotion of greater co-operation in Europe and the West not regarded as charitable, although gift upheld as being for the furtherance of the work of a charitable educational project); *ante*, p. 389.

[45] [1968] A.C. 138, *ante*, p. 377.

[46] *Incorporated Council of Law Reporting* v. *Att.-Gen.* [1972] Ch. 73 at p. 88. *cf. Re South Place Ethical Society* [1980] 1 W.L.R. 1565, where Dillon J. preferred the analogy approach. See Annual Report 1985, paras. 24–27 (analogy required, but strict approach to it undesirable).

[47] *Post*, p. 445.

[48] Annual Report 1966, paras. 27–41.

[49] *Post*, p. 446.

the judges, as we saw in the case of artistic questions, cannot avoid making a subjective choice.

In *National Anti-Vivisection Society* v. *Inland Revenue Commissioners*,[50] the question was whether the Society was entitled to relief from income tax on the ground that its object, which was the total suppression of vivisection, was charitable. The protection of animals from cruelty is a charitable purpose.[51] Vivisection, on the other hand, is a necessary part of medical research and, as such, is itself beneficial to the community. The question, as Lord Simonds said "is whether the court, for the purposes of determining whether the object of the society is charitable may disregard the finding of fact that any assumed public benefit in the direction of the advancement of morals and education was far outweighed by the detriment to medical science and research and consequently to the public health which would result if the society succeeded in achieving its object, and that on balance, the object of the society, so far from being for the public benefit, was gravely injurious thereto. The society says that the court must disregard this fact, arguing that evidence of disadvantages or evils which would or might result from the stopping of vivisection is irrelevant and inadmissible."[52]

The court undertook to make the value judgment, "weighing conflicting moral and material utilities." On balance, on the evidence available to it, the suppression of vivisection was not beneficial to the public, and the claim failed.

The House overruled *Re Foveaux*,[53] where Chitty J. had held that the court stood neutral on the question whether the abolition of vivisection would benefit the community. Under that view, presumably a gift to benefit medical research by vivisection would also be charitable, public benefit being shown. The American Restatement follows this view.[54] It sees nothing improper in upholding trusts for both armament and disarmament and, by a parity of reasoning, vivisection and anti-vivisection being charitable. This view greatly simplifies the task of the court. The balancing of the merits of two different forms of public benefit is a matter on which opinions may vary, and one on which the court may not be the best judge.

(iii) Examples of Trusts under the Fourth Head. The number of cases decided under the fourth head is enormous, and there is no possibility

[50] [1948] A.C. 31.
[51] *Post*, p. 402.
[52] [1948] A.C. 31 at pp. 60–61.
[53] [1895] 2 Ch. 501.
[54] *Restatement of the Law of Trusts*, § 374, comment 1; "The courts do not take sides or attempt to decide which of two conflicting views of promoting the social interest of the community is the better adapted for the purpose, even though the views are opposed to each other. Thus, a trust to promote peace by disarmament, as well as a trust to promote peace by preparedness for war, is charitable."

of doing more than directing attention to the main groupings. The imprecision of the category is obvious, and the difficulty of making a decision in any new situation is very great.

(a) *Specific Mention in the Preamble. The Aged, Impotent and Sick.* The Preamble refers to the "relief of aged, impotent and poor people." The phrase is construed disjunctively, and there is no need to show that the purpose of a trust includes all three. Thus, in *Re Robinson*,[55] a gift for old people over 60 years of age was upheld; and also trusts for the provision of housing for the aged.[56] Impotent means physically handicapped; and in *Re Lewis*,[57] a gift of £100 each to 10 blind girls and 10 blind boys in Tottenham was valid, there being no requirement that they should also be poor. "It would be as absurd to require that the aged must be impotent or poor as it would be to require the impotent to be aged or poor, or the poor to be aged or impotent."[58]

But difficulties arise where the rich participate. What would be the effect, it is asked, of a gift for the relief of aged peers or impotent millionaires?[59] The answer surely is that, as with trusts for the relief of poverty, the purpose must be the *relief* of age or impotence; and money payments would not appear in these situations to provide any relief[60]; unless the aged were required also to be poor. "The word 'relief' implies that the persons in question have a need attributable to their condition as aged, impotent or poor persons which requires alleviating, and which those persons could not alleviate, or would find difficulty in alleviating, themselves from their own resources. The word 'relief' is not synonymous with 'benefit.' . . . Thus a gift of money to the aged millionaires of Mayfair would not relieve a need of theirs as aged persons."[61] We will see later that if the group to be benefited was bound together by a personal nexus, they may then fail to be a section of the public,[62] and, again the gift would be valid only if it included a qualification of poverty as well.

Some of the other instances given in the preamble occasionally

---

[55] [1951] Ch. 198; *Re Gosling* (1900) 48 W.R. 300 ("old and worn-out clerks" of the bank); the lowest age which has qualified under this heading is believed to be 50 years; *Re Wall* (1889) 42 Ch.D. 510.

[56] *Re Glyn's W.T.* [1950] 2 All E.R. 1005n.; *Re Cottam* [1955] 1 W.L.R. 1299; *Re Payling's W.T.* [1969] 1 W.L.R. 1595; *Joseph Rowntree Memorial Trust Housing Association Ltd.* v. *Att.-Gen.* [1983] Ch. 159, (1983) 46 M.L.R. 782 (R. Nobles), All E.R. Rev. 1983, p. 356 (P. J. Clarke); *Re Dunlop (deceased)* (1984) 19 *Northern Ireland Judgments Bulletin*. See Annual Report 1967, Paras. 22–29 (Homes for old people).

[57] [1955] Ch. 104; *Re Elliott* (1910) 102 L.T. 528.

[58] *Joseph Rowntree Memorial Trust Housing Association Ltd.* v. *Att.-Gen.* [1983] Ch. 159 at p. 171.

[59] (1951) 67 L.Q.R. 164; (1955) 71 L.Q.R. 16 (R.E.M.). For the view that the poor cannot be excluded, see *Re Macduff* [1896] 2 Ch. 451.

[60] *N.S.W. Nursing Service, etc.* v. *Willoughby Municipal Council* [1968] 2 N.S.W. 791.

[61] *Joseph Rowntree Memorial Trust Housing Association Ltd.* v. *Att.-Gen., supra,* at p. 171.

[62] *Post*, p. 411.

receive mention,[63] but there is reluctance to rely on them if the gift would not otherwise be charitable under Lord Macnaghten's classification. Their effect, now that the preamble is no longer on the Statute Book, is obscure, but those that have been acted on by the courts will presumably continue in effect, for the preamble was never a substantive provision and hence its repeal cannot affect the authority of cases based on it.

A trust for the relief of the sick is charitable, and so are trusts for the support of hospitals.[64] Indeed, prior to the introduction of the National Health Service in 1946, such hospitals were probably the greatest beneficiaries of charitable gifts, and the main hospital service of the nation was dependent on charity. It is no objection in this context that the benefits will be received by the rich as well as the poor; nor that the hospital was a private hospital for paying patients.[65] Satellite purposes consistent with the object of the hospital are included, such as benefits for the sick in hospital[66] or for nurses,[67] which improve the quality of the service, and the provision of accommodation for the relatives of the critically ill,[68] and for rest homes for those suffering from nervous strain.[69] A nursing home privately owned and run for profit is not however a charity.[70]

(b) *Social, Recreational and Sporting Trusts*. Great difficulty has been experienced in establishing a dividing line to determine the validity of trusts for social, recreational or sporting purposes. The uncertainty caused by a series of cases in the 1940s and 1950s created doubts as to the charitable status of a number of institutions of national importance which had always been assumed to be charitable, such as the National Playing Fields Association, the Women's Institute, boys' clubs, missions to seamen and a number of local activities such as village halls. The Recreational Charities Act 1958 rescued them, but made no attempt to deal with the many problems thrown up by these cases. They will provide a useful background to the Act.

A trust to provide sporting facilities was not charitable,[71] unless, as has been seen, the facilities were for pupils of schools or universities, in

---

[63] *e.g.* "The setting out of soldiers"; *Re Driffill* [1949] 2 All E.R. 933.
[64] *Re Smith's W.T.* [1962] 2 All E.R. 563. On charities engaged in fringe medicine, see Annual Report 1975, para. 70.
[65] *Re Resch's W.T.* [1969] 1 A.C. 514, [1978] Conv. 277 (T. G. Watkin).
[66] *Re Roadley* [1930] 1 Ch. 524.
[67] *Re White's W.T.* [1951] 1 All E.R. 520; *Re Bernstein's W.T.* (1971) 115 S.J. 808.
[68] *Re Dean's W.T.* [1950] 1 All E.R. 882.
[69] *Re Chaplin* [1933] Ch. 115; *Re Banfield* [1968] 2 All E.R. 276.
[70] *Re Resch's W.T., supra*, at p. 540.
[71] *Re Nottage* [1895] 2 Ch. 649 (prize for a yacht race); *Re Clifford* (1911) 106 L.T. 14 (angling); *Re Patten* [1929] 2 Ch. 276 (not even cricket); *cf. Re Laidlaw Foundation* (1985) 480.R.2d 549 (foundation to promote amateur athletic sports charitable). See (1956) C.L.P. 39 (O. R. Marshall); *I.R.C.* v. *McMullen* [1981] A.C. 1 at p. 15, where the point was expressly left open. See generally (1988) 52 N.L.J. *Annual Charities Review* iv (H. Picarda).

which case they would be regarded as being for the advancement of education[72], or within the armed forces, when they would contribute to the safety and protection of the country,[73] or where the game was itself of an educational nature.[74]

In *I.R.C.* v. *Glasgow Police Athletic Association*,[75] the respondent Association, whose object was "to encourage and promote all forms of athletic sport and general pastimes" was held not to be charitable. In so far as the objects were concerned with the "encouragement of recruiting, the improvement of the efficiency of the force and the public advantage"[76] they would have been charitable. But the provision of mere recreation was not charitable; nor could it, in the circumstances of the case, be held to be merely incidental to the main purpose. It was therefore fatal to the claim.

Gifts for the establishment of recreation grounds for the public generally or for the inhabitants of a particular area were upheld in *Re Hadden*[77] and in *Re Morgan*.[78] However, as has been seen, in *Williams' Trustees* v. *I.R.C.*,[79] a trust for the promotion of Welsh interests in London by various means, most of which were charitable, failed because they involved a "social" and recreational element.[80] Further problems arose with *I.R.C.* v. *Baddeley* in 1955.[81]

Land was conveyed to a Methodist Mission "for the promotion of the religious,[82] social and physical well-being of persons resident in . . . West Ham and Leyton . . . by the provision of facilities for religious services and instruction; and for the social and physical training and recreation of . . . persons who . . . are in the opinion of [local Church] leaders members or likely to become members of the

---

[72] *Re Mariette* [1915] 2 Ch. 284; *ante*, p. 386; *London Hospital Medical College* v. *I.R.C.* [1976] 1 W.L.R. 613; [1978] Conv. 92 (N. P. Gravells).

[73] *Re Gray* [1925] Ch. 362.

[74] *Re Dupree's Deed Trusts* [1945] Ch. 16, *ante*, p. 387.

[75] [1953] A.C. 380.

[76] *Per* Lord Normand, *ibid.* at p. 395.

[77] [1932] Ch. 133. See also *Re Chesters* (1934) (unreported), *ante*, p. 386.

[78] [1955] 1 W.L.R. 738, where there was no argument to the contrary. This view was accepted by Lord Simonds in *I.R.C.* v. *Baddeley* [1955] A.C. 572 at p. 589, and by Lord Somervell at p. 615. King George's Fields Foundation, whose object was "to promote and assist in the establishment throughout the United Kingdom of playing fields for the use and enjoyment of the people" was a charity. Annual Report 1965, para. 25. The Oxford Ice Skating Association Ltd. was registered in 1984 as being charitable under the 1958 Act and the general law; Annual Report 1984, paras. 18–25. Athletics has been upheld in Canada as promoting health; *Re Laidlaw Foundation* (1985) 48 O.R. (2d) 549; (1986) 1 *Trust Law & Practice* 22 (D. Evans).

[79] [1947] A.C. 447, *ante*, p. 394.

[80] This element was deleted in 1977, when the Charity Commissioners validated the Trust under Charitable Trusts (Validation) Act 1954, *post*, p. 425; Annual Report 1971, paras. 71–80.

[81] [1955] A.C. 572.

[82] In a second deed in similar form, "moral" appeared instead of "religious."

Methodist Church . . . and of insufficient means otherwise to enjoy the advantages provided. . . . "

The question was whether the conveyances could be stamped at the reduced rate on the ground that the purposes were charitable. By a majority of four to one (Lord Reid dissenting), the House of Lords held that the purposes were not exclusively charitable, because of the inclusion of purely "social" purposes; and three of their Lordships further held that the requirement of public benefit was not satisfied.[83]

The Recreational Charities Act 1958[84] attempted to remove the uncertainty caused by these decisions. The object[85] was to give statutory recognition to a number of trusts which had always been regarded as charitable, "without enlarging the definition of charity or encroaching on existing authorities (including *Baddeley's* Case[86] itself), or making any institution charitable which was not ordinarily regarded as charitable before that decision." It validates prospectively and retrospectively certain cases of the provision of recreational or other leisure-time occupations if the facilities are provided in the interests of social welfare.[87] Section 1 reads:

"—(1) Subject to the provisions of this Act, it shall be and be deemed always to have been charitable to provide, or assist in the provision of, facilities for recreation or other leisure-time occupation, if the facilities are provided in the interests of social welfare:

Provided that nothing in this section shall be taken to derogate from the principle that a trust or institution to be charitable must be for the public benefit.[88]

(2) The requirement of the foregoing subsection that the facilities are provided in the interests of social welfare shall not be treated as satisfied unless—

(a) the facilities are provided with the object of improving the conditions of life for the persons for whom the facilities are primarily intended; and

(b) either—

(i) those persons have need for such facilities as aforesaid by reason of their youth, age, infirmity or disablement, poverty or social and economic circumstances; or

(ii) the facilities are to be available to the members or female members of the public at large.

[83] *Post*, p. 418.
[84] (1959) 23 Conv.(N.S.) 15 (S. G. Maurice); (1958) 21 M.L.R. 534 (L. Price); [1980] Conv. 173 (J. Warburton).
[85] *Halsbury's Statutes*, Vol. 3, p. 585.
[86] [1955] A.C. 572.
[87] Selected as the criterion because the phrase appeared in other similar provisions, and had been judicially interpreted; *Halsbury's Statutes*, Vol. 3, p. 582; House of Commons Official Report, p. 322; February 11, 1958.
[88] *Post*, pp. 408 *et seq.*

(3) Subject to the said requirement, subsection (1) of this section applies in particular to the provision of facilities at village halls, community centres and women's institutes, and to the provision and maintenance of grounds and buildings to be used for purposes of recreation or leisure-time occupation and extends to the provision of facilities for those purposes by the organising of any activity."[89]

Two points of importance should be noted. First, it will be seen that the Act has no effect upon the cases previously discussed. The "Welsh people" do not come within section 1(2)(*b*)(i)[90]; nor would the "Methodists or persons likely to become Methodists" in *Baddeley*[91]; nor the Glasgow police, who would presumably not be covered by "youth" or by "social and economic circumstances."[92] If the village halls and Women's Institute and any other institutions intended to be covered by the Act were charitable before, the Act appears to be merely declaratory. But it would surely have been arguable that a Women's Institute, youth club, or the National Playing Fields Association, though beneficial to the public, was not within the spirit and intendment of the Preamble; if that is so, then they, and similar Institutions, included within the definition of "social welfare" in subsection (2), are rescued by the Act. Express provision is made also for Miners' Welfare Trusts in section 2.[93] Other trusts are left to the general law.

Secondly, it seems that, where the persons to be benefited are within subsection (2), the spirit and intendment of the Preamble no longer has any relevance. If subsection (2) is complied with, the test of charitable status is whether the facilities are for recreation or other leisure-time occupation, whether they are for public benefit, and whether they are provided in the interests of social welfare. To meet the latter qualification, they must be provided with the object of improving the conditions of life for the persons for whom the facilities are primarily intended. In *I.R.C.* v. *McMullen*[94] (the Football Association Youth Trust case), Walton J. at first instance[95] and the majority of the Court of Appeal[96] adopted a restrictive view of the qualification. Walton J. held that the words implied that only "the deprived" can benefit. Stamp L.J. said[97] that it "cannot with any show of reason be argued that facilities primarily intended for pupils of schools and universities in any part of the United Kingdom . . . are provided with the object of

---

[89] Such as the National Council for Social Service.
[90] *Williams* v. *I.R.C.* [1947] A.C. 447.
[91] *Supra.*
[92] *I.R.C.* v. *City of Glasgow Police Athletic Association* [1953] A.C. 380.
[93] *Wynn* v. *Skegness U.D.C.* [1966] 1 W.L.R. 52.
[94] *Ante*, p. 387.
[95] [1978] 1 W.L.R. 664 at p. 675.
[96] [1979] 1 W.L.R. 130.
[97] At p. 138. *Cf.* Annual Report 1984, paras. 18–25 (Oxford Ice Skating Association Ltd.), where the Commissioners expressed the view that any recreational charity which promotes health must improve conditions of life. The Association was charitable under the Act and the general law.

improving the conditions of life for such pupils. . . . The facilities are to be provided for those of them who are persuaded to, or do, play football, or some other game or sport quite irrespective of their conditions of life." On the other hand, Bridge L.J. adopted a more liberal approach. Social welfare is not limited to the deprived. "Hyde Park improves the conditions of life for residents in Mayfair as much as for those in Pimlico or the Portobello Road."[98] In the House of Lords,[99] the point was expressly left open.

Further guidance on the construction of social welfare can be obtained from other statutes in which the phrase has been used.[1] The question has been much litigated in connection with claims for rating relief available to organisations "whose main objects are charitable or are otherwise concerned with the advancement of religion, education or social welfare."[2] It is not possible to examine all the decisions,[3] but a few points may be extracted. The rating cases are not concerned with the problem of public benefit, though that requirement remains under the Recreational Charities Act.[4] "A person is commonly said to be engaged in 'social welfare' when he is engaged in doing good for others who are in need . . . in the sense that he does it, not for personal or private reasons . . . but because they are members of the community or a portion of it who need help."[5] It does not necessarily involve the presence of an eleemosynary[6] element.[7] The source of the benefits is relevant. Thus, while it is not necessary to find that there was an element of benevolence in the donor, there must be something more than a group of individuals combining together, as a club or society, to benefit themselves.[8] A women's social club would not, it seems, be charitable, nor a football club established by young people for their own enjoyment. It seems that there must be some element of providing help to others. But the details can only be worked out as questions arise for decision under the Act.

(c) *Animals.* Trusts for the welfare of animals generally are charitable, though gifts for specified animals are not.[9] The charitable status of gifts to animals was originally limited to the welfare of animals which were useful to man,[10] and this rule was justified on the basis of public

---

[98] At p. 143.
[99] [1981] A.C. 1. See also Annual Report 1978, para. 93.
[1] e.g. Miners Welfare Act 1952, ss.12, 16; Clean Air Act 1956, s.15(2)(c).
[2] General Rate Act 1967, s.40. See now Local Government Finance Act 1988, s.47.
[3] See (1959) 23 Conv.(N.S.) 365 (D. W. M. Waters).
[4] s.1(1) proviso.
[5] *National Deposit Friendly Society* v. *Skegness U.D.C.* [1959] A.C. 293 at p. 322, *per* Lord Denning.
[6] For the meaning of which, see p. 444, n. 32, *post.*
[7] [1959] A.C. 807 at p. 824.
[8] *National Deposit Friendly Society Trustees* v. *Skegness U.D.C.* [1957] 1 Q.B. 531. See also *Re Lipinski's W.T.* [1976] Ch. 235, *ante,* p. 344.
[9] *Ante,* p. 350.
[10] *London University* v. *Yarrow* (1857) 1 De G. & J. 72.

utility. More recently, the category has widened. It is difficult to find words in the Preamble to demonstrate that such gifts are within its spirit and intendment. The grounds of validity of such gifts have been differently stated in England and in Ireland. In Ireland, it is the simple and obvious good of the welfare of the animals, themselves.[11] In England, the cases are justified on the ground that they "tend to promote and encourage kindness towards [animals], and to ameliorate the condition of the brute creation, and thus to stimulate humane and generous sentiments in man towards the lower animals, and by this means to promote feelings of humanity and morality generally, repress brutality, and thus elevate the human race."[12] On this basis, trusts have been upheld for a home for lost dogs,[13] cats and kittens needing care and attention,[14] the Society for the Prevention of Cruelty to Animals,[15] and for hospitals,[16] and humane slaughtering[17]; and, it is thought, animal sanctuaries such as the Home of Rest for Horses[18] and The Wild Fowl Trusts.[19] But there are limits. We have seen that a trust for the abolition of vivisection was not charitable because its purposes would, on balance, cause more harm than good to the public. So also, a trust for the preservation of animals harmful to mankind could not be charitable.[20] The borderline in these cases is hard to draw. In *Re Grove-Grady*,[21] the Court of Appeal decided that it had been over-stepped, Russell L.J. expressing the view that the authorities had reached the furthest admissible point of benevolence in construing as charitable, gifts in favour of animals. There was a trust for the setting up of an animal refuge where the animals, birds and other creatures should be safe from molestation by man. A sanctuary which deprived mankind of all rights of involvement could not be for the public benefit,[22] either materially or morally. The decision does not cast doubt upon the charitable status of animal sanctuaries whose activities do benefit the public. And many purposes connected with animals

[11] *Armstrong* v. *Reeves* (1890) 25 L.R.Ir. 325.
[12] *Re Wedgwood* [1915] 1 Ch. 113, *per* Swinfen-Eady L.J. at p. 122. See also *Re Green's W.T.* [1985] 3 All E.R. 455.
[13] *Re Douglas* (1887) 35 Ch.D. 472; *Swifte* v. *Att.-Gen.* [1912] 1 Ir.R. 133.
[14] *Re Moss* [1949] 1 All E.R. 495.
[15] *Tatham* v. *Drummond* (1864) 4 De G.J. & Sm. 484; *Armstrong* v. *Reeve* (1890) 25 L.R.Ir. 325. See the evidence of R.S.P.C.A. in House of Commons Report, Vol. II, pp. 133–134, 140–144; Annual Report 1979, para. 20.
[16] *London University* v. *Yarrow* (1857) 1 De G. & J. 72.
[17] *Tatham* v. *Drummond* (*supra*).
[18] Annual Report 1971, para. 26; *Re Murawski's W.T.* [1971] 1 W.L.R. 707.
[19] *Re Wedgwood, supra*, at p. 121.
[20] Such as mad dogs; *Re Wedgwood* [1915] 1 Ch. 113 at p. 121, *per* Kennedy L.J.
[21] [1929] 1 Ch. 557 (compromised on appeal; *Att.-Gen.* v. *Plowden* [1931] W.N. 89). *Cf. Att.-Gen. (N.S.W.)* v. *Sawtell* [1978] 2 N.S.W.L.R. 200; Pettit, p. 224.
[22] And probably not for the animals, for they remained "liable to be molested and killed by other denizens of the area." *ibid.* at p. 586.

could be made charities by being expressed in terms of education[23] or of environmental preservation.[24]

(d) *Political Trusts*. Trusts whose object, direct or indirect, is the support of one political party are clearly not charitable.[25] The border-line between such trusts and trusts where political propaganda was "masquerading as education" has been discussed.[26]

A further question arises. Political trusts are not charitable. Most political activities involve a programme of reform which requires a change of the law. Conversely, programmes of reform involve legisla-tion, and therefore political activity. If political activity can never be charitable, should the same be said of programmes for law reform?

In *Re Bushnell*,[27] the testator left money for "the advancement and propagation of the teaching of socialised medicine." The trust was neither an educational charity nor charitable under the fourth heading. The testator had died in 1941, and at that time legislation would have been required to achieve the purpose. The desirability of such legisla-tion was a political matter. It made no difference that a national health service had subsequently been introduced, as the relevant time for judging the matter was the testator's death.

A second reason for the failure of the Anti-Vivisection trust[28] was that the objects of the Society required a change in the law. The majority treated this as necessarily being a "political purpose within the meaning of Lord Parker's pronouncement in *Bowman* v. *Secular Society Ltd.*[29]"[30] Lord Normand stressed that this should only be so where, as here, the change in the law was a *predominant object*,[31] while Lord Porter, who dissented, would have excluded only trusts which were *purely political*,[32] that is to say, where the object is to be attained *only* by a change in the law. There is clearly a distinction between a trust for the abolition of slavery or the protection of birds' eggs, and a

---

[23] *Re Lopes* [1931] 2 Ch. 130.
[24] The Advisory Committee on Oil Pollution of the Sea. See Annual Report 1973, para. 40; The Coral Conservation Trust; 1973, S.J. Supp. p. 3.
[25] *Bonar Law Memorial Trust* v. *I.R.C.* (1933) 49 T.L.R. 220 (Conservative); *Re Ogden* [1933] Ch. 678 (Liberal); *Re Hopkinson* [1949] 1 All E.R. 346 (Socialist: the whole tenor of the gift was to mask political propaganda as education). It is doubtful whether *Re Scowcroft* [1898] 2 Ch. 638 would now be followed; the case itself might have been differently decided had the gift been only for the furtherance of Conservative princi-ples. See also Annual Report 1982, paras. 45–51 (refusal to register Youth Training, whose purpose is to assist the Workers' Revolutionary Party). For the Canadian position, see *Re Public Trustee and Toronto Humane Society* (1987) 60 O.R. (2nd) 236.
[26] *Ante*, p. 388.
[27] [1975] 1 W.L.R. 1596; *ante*, p. 389.
[28] *National Anti-Vivisection Society* v. *I.R.C.* [1948] A.C. 31; *ante*, p. 396.
[29] [1917] A.C. 406 at p. 442.
[30] [1948] A.C. 31 at pp. 49–50.
[31] *Ibid.* at pp. 77–78.
[32] *Ibid.* at p. 56.

trust to nationalise the banking industry. But they all may require a change in the law. It may be possible to treat some trusts as political and others not. "It is a question of degree of a sort well known to the courts."[33]

The treatment as political of any trust requiring a change in the law has been criticised. It should however be appreciated that this view is not arrogantly asserting that the law is perfect, nor that the proposed change may not be for the public benefit. A reforming judge could believe this, and yet say "that is not for the court to judge, and the court has no means of judging."[34] The Legislature decides on changes in the law. The judges' duty is to apply it. The judges should not be put in a position of being asked to hold that a controversial object, often a minority object, is so obviously for the public good that it should be pursued perpetually and tax-free. It is difficult, however, to answer the criticism that organisations campaigning for modernisation of the law[35] cannot be registered as charities, while existing charities can and do campaign against change.[36]

The matter recently arose in *McGovern* v. *Att.Gen.*,[37] where a non-charitable body, Amnesty International, sought to obtain charitable status for part of its activities by setting up the Amnesty International Trust, to which were transferred those aspects of its work which were thought to be charitable. The objects were: (i) the relief of needy persons who were, or were likely to become, prisoners of conscience, and their relatives; (ii) attempting to secure the release of prisoners of conscience; (iii) the abolition of torture or inhuman or degrading treatment or punishment; (iv) research into human rights and disseminating the results of the research.[38] These objects were to be carried out in all parts of the world. Purposes (i) and (iv), if standing alone, would have been charitable, but the inclusion of the other objects caused the trust to fail on the ground that it was political.[39] A trust could not be charitable if its direct and main object was to secure a change in the law of the United Kingdom or of foreign countries, for example by repealing legislation authorising capital or corporal punishment. The court could not judge whether this would be for the

[33] *Ibid.* at p. 77.
[34] *Per* Lord Simonds [1948] A.C. 31 at p. 62.
[35] National Council for Civil Liberties; Amnesty; Campaign Against Racial Discrimination. See National Council for Voluntary Organisations, *Modernising Charity Law* (1984).
[36] Lord's Day Observance Society; Temperance Societies; see Nightingale; *Charities* pp. 46–52; Hayton and Marshall (8th ed.), pp. 278–279.
[37] [1982] Ch. 321; [1982] Conv. 387 (T. G. Watkin); (1982) 45 M.L.R. 704 (R. Nobles); (1983) 46 M.L.R. 385 (F. Weiss); [1984] Conv. 263 (C. J. Forder). See also *Re Koeppler's W.T.* [1986] Ch. 423; where the formation of an informed international public opinion and the promotion of greater co-operation in Europe and the West were not regarded as charitable, although the gift was upheld as being for the furtherance of the work of a charitable educational project; *ante*, p. 389.
[38] See Annual Report 1987, para. 12 (trusts for research into human rights upheld).
[39] It was not saved by a proviso restricting it to charitable purposes; *post*, p. 419.

public benefit, locally or internationally. Nor could a trust be charitable if a direct and principal purpose was to procure the reversal of government policy or of governmental decisions at home or abroad.[40] Object (ii) was not simply for the "relief or redemption of prisoners or captives,"[41] but involved putting pressure on foreign governments and authorities. To ascribe charitable status to such a trust could prejudice the relations of this country with the foreign country concerned. This public policy consideration could not be ignored.

A related problem arises where an existing charity is tempted to become involved in pursuing "causes" relating to the work with which it is concerned. It was suggested in *McGovern* v. *Att.Gen.*[42] that if the objects had been charitable, it would not have mattered that the trustees had incidental powers to employ political means to further these objects. The Charity Commissioners have offered some guidelines to charity trustees, including the following points[43]:

(i) Trustees engaging in political activity risk breach of trust; personal liability to repay the charity funds expended; and loss of tax relief.

(ii) Doubts could arise as to charitable status if the purposes of the institution are wide enough to cover such activities.

(iii) The governing instrument of a charity should not include power to exert political pressure except in a way which is merely ancillary.

(iv) It is permissible for a charity to help the Government on a particular issue by providing information and argument, with the emphasis on rational persuasion.

(v) Charitable funds may be spent on promoting public general legislation if ancillary to the charitable purposes.[44]

(vi) Charities must avoid seeking to remedy causes of poverty which lie in the social, economic and political structures of countries and communities; bringing pressure to bear on governments to procure a change in policy; and seeking to eliminate social, economic, political or other injustice.[45]

---

[40] The decision was distinguished in *Re Koeppler's W.T.*, *supra*, where an educational project involving conferences with a "political flavour" was held charitable. The project was not concerned with party politics, nor did it seek to change laws or government policies.

[41] Preamble to the Charitable Uses Act, 1601.

[42] *Supra.*

[43] Annual Report 1981, paras. 53–56; Annual Report 1986, App. A. In 1978 the activities of three international relief charities were reviewed (War on Want; Oxfam; and the Christian Aid Division), Annual Report 1978, paras. 21–29; and in 1979 three domestic charities (Abortion, the R.S.P.C.A., and the Howard League for Penal Reform); Annual Report 1979, paras. 18–22. See generally (1986) 49 N.L.J. *Annual Charities Review* 9 (P. Clarke).

[44] See Annual Report 1979, paras. 21–22 (Howard League for Penal Reform).

[45] See Annual Report 1981, paras. 57–60, criticising the "political" activities of War on Want. As to Oxfam's political campaigns in the third world, see *The Times*, April 8, 1986.

(vii) Educational charities should take care not to overstep the boundary between education and propaganda.

(viii) Charities may respond to Government Green or White Papers; supply information relevant to the debate on a Bill; support or oppose a Private Bill; or present a reasoned memorandum to a Government Department advocating changes in the law.

(ix) The Commissioners are always willing to advise the trustees on specific problems in this area.

(e) *Miscellaneous*. There is no way of explaining the full width of the fourth head. But some miscellaneous examples may be helpful. Gifts for the promotion of the efficiency of the fighting services are charitable. It has been seen that the promotion of sport in the Army is included[46]; so is the teaching of shooting,[47] an annuity to a volunteer company,[48] a gift to the officers' mess,[49] and for the poor of a regiment,[50] for the training of officers for the Navy or Merchant Marine,[51] for the protection of the Kingdom against attack by hostile aircraft.[52] On the other hand, a provision for ex-members of the services is not charitable, unless confined to the aged or poor.[53] The efficiency of the police is similarly a charitable purpose,[54] and also a gift to a voluntary fire brigade.[55] The National Trust is charitable,[56] and the Royal Naval Life Boat Institution; and the Council of Industrial Design[57]; so also are gifts for the promotion of agriculture[58] preservation of natural amenities,[59] and for environmental objects.[60] A gift for the founding of a children's home is charitable,[61] but, it seems a gift for the benefit of the children in such a home is too wide, unless expressly confined to the meeting of the children's needs at the home, otherwise it might be applied to the purchase of luxurious amenities.[62] The Incorporated Council of Law Reporting has been held to be charitable under the

[46] *Re Gray* [1925] Ch. 362.
[47] *Re Stephens* (1892) 8 T.L.R. 792.
[48] *Re Lord Stratheden and Campbell* [1894] 3 Ch. 265.
[49] *Re Good* [1905] 2 Ch. 60.
[50] *Re Donald* [1909] 2 Ch. 410.
[51] *Re Corbyn* [1941] Ch. 400.
[52] *Re Driffill* [1950] Ch. 92.
[53] *Re Meyers* [1951] Ch. 534.
[54] *I.R.C.* v. *City of Glasgow Police Athletic Association* [1953] A.C. 380. See also Annual Report 1984, para. 17 (Police Memorial Trust to commemorate officers killed on duty).
[55] *Re Wokingham Fire Brigade Trusts* [1951] Ch. 373; Annual Report 1979, paras. 74–81.
[56] *Re Verrall* [1916] 1 Ch. 100.
[57] Annual Report 1973, paras. 69–70.
[58] *I.R.C.* v. *Yorkshire Agricultural Society* [1928] 1 K.B. 611; *Brisbane C.C.* v. *Att.-Gen. for Queensland* [1979] A.C. 411.
[59] *Re Granstown* [1932] 1 Ch. 537; *Re Corelli* [1943] Ch. 332.
[60] Annual Report 1973, para. 40; Annual Report 1979, paras. 61–65 (Porthmadog embankment).
[61] *Re Sahal's W.T.* [1958] 1 W.L.R. 1243.
[62] *Re Cole* [1958] Ch. 877. But see *Tudor on Charities* (7th ed.), p. 107.

second and fourth heads[63]; and so has the study and dissemination of ethical principles and the cultivation of a rational religious sentiment.[64] A public memorial may be charitable, as in the case of the statue of Earl Mountbatten of Burma. The Charity Commissioners concluded that "the provision of a statue might be held to have a sufficient element of public benefit where the person being commemorated was nationally, and perhaps internationally, respected and could be said to be a figure of historical importance. In such a case the provision and maintenance of a statue can be held to be charitable as likely to foster patriotism and good citizenship, and to be an incentive to heroic and noble deeds." The Earl Mountbatten of Burma Statue Appeal Trust was accordingly registered as a charity.[65] Finally, in *Re Smith*, a gift "To my country, England,"[66] was upheld by the Court of Appeal, the court taking the view, based on some out-dated "locality" cases that,[67] in the context, the property could be applied only to charitable purposes.

4. PUBLIC BENEFIT[68]

A. Preliminary Points

It was said above,[69] that a gift could only be charitable if it was for the public benefit, and it is necessary to examine what this requirement involves. A few preliminary points must be made. First, it will be seen that the requirement differs in respect of each category,[70] and that it may differ within the fourth category, dependent upon the purpose concerned. Secondly, in categories two and three especially, the matter came to the fore in the post-war years, at a time when the great increases in personal taxation added significance to the privilege of tax exemption enjoyed by charities; we will see that there is disagreement among the Law Lords on the question whether this is a factor which

---

[63] *Incorporated Council of Law Reporting for England and Wales* v. *Att.-Gen.* [1972] Ch. 73; (1972) 88 L.Q.R. 171.

[64] *Re South Place Ethical Society* [1980] 1 W.L.R. 1565.

[65] Annual Report 1981, paras. 68–70.

[66] *Re Smith* [1932] 1 Ch. 153.

[67] The restriction of a benefit to a specified locality seemed at one time to enable the judge, by applying a benevolent construction, to find that a trust was charitable; *post*, p. 420.

[68] See generally (1956) 72 L.Q.R. 187 (G. Cross); (1958) 21 M.L.R. 138 (P. S. Atiyah); (1974) 33 C.L.J. 63 (G. H. Jones); (1975) 39 Conv.(N.S.) 183 (S. Plowright); (1976) 22 N.I.L.Q. 198 (J. C. Brady); (1977) 40 M.L.R. 397 (N. P. Gravells); [1978] Conv. 277 (T. G. Watkin); Goodman Committee Report Chap. 2 (Benefit to the "Community"); Chap. 3 ("Benefit" to the Community). For a discussion in the context of the Race Relations Act, see *Race Relations Board* v. *Charter* [1972] 1 Q.B. 545 at pp. 556 *et seq.*, *per* Lord Denning M.R.; *Race Relations Board* v. *Dockers' Labour Club and Institute Ltd.* [1976] A.C. 285.

[69] *Ante*, p. 378.

[70] *Per* Lord Simonds in *Gilmour* v. *Coats* [1949] A.C. 426 at p. 429; *per* Lord Somervell in *I.R.C.* v. *Baddeley* [1955] A.C. 572 at p. 615.

should be taken into consideration in deciding upon charitable status.[71] Thirdly, it may seem anomalous to speak in terms of a requirement of public benefit in the fourth category, for that category is defined in terms of trusts for the benefit of the community. To establish a trust as charitable within this category, it is necessary that the purposes are beneficial in the way which the law regards as charitable, and also that the benefits are available to a sufficient section of the public. With trusts coming under the first three heads, the matter is rather different. The beneficial aspect of trusts for the relief of poverty, or the advancement of education or religion is assumed.[72] The necessary public element needs to be shown.

B. Trusts for the Relief of Poverty

(i) A Class of Poor as Opposed to Selected Individuals. Poor Relations. The requirement of public benefit has been reduced, in the field of poverty, almost to vanishing point. A gift however to a group of persons chosen because they are poor is not charitable; as Harman J. said, a gift to amuse the poor would not be to relieve them.[73] But a gift to the poor members of a class is charitable, if the object of the gift is to relieve their poverty. Further, it is necessary to distinguish between a gift to a class or group of poor persons, and a gift to specified poor individuals. The former will be charitable, even if the group is small, and personally connected with the donor; gifts to poor relations have been upheld since the middle of the eighteenth century.[74] As Jenkins L.J. said: "I think that the true question in each case has really been whether the gift for the relief of poverty amongst a class of persons, or rather, as Sir William Grant, M.R. put it, a particular description of poor, or was merely a gift to individuals, albeit with relief of poverty amongst those individuals as the motive of the gift, or with a selective preference for the poor or poorest amongst those individuals. ... "[75] Thus, a gift to such of the testator's relatives as shall be poor or "in special need"[76] or "in needy circumstances"[77] is charitable. And it does not matter that recipients should be selected by one of the relatives,[78]

[71] *Dingle* v. *Turner* [1972] A.C. 601; *post*, p. 410.

[72] *Per* Lord Simonds in *National Anti-Vivisection Society* v. *I.R.C.* [1948] A.C. 31.

[73] [1953] 1 W.L.R. 84 at p. 88; [1969] A.S.C.L. 391; [1970] A.S.C.L. 187 at p. 199 (J. D. Davies).

[74] *Isaac* v. *Defriez* (1754) Amb. 595. They are discussed at length in *Re Compton* [1945] Ch. 123, and in *Re Scarisbrick* [1951] Ch. 622. See also *Dingle* v. *Turner* [1972] A.C. 601; *infra*.

[75] In *Re Scarisbrick* [1951] Ch. 622 at p. 655; see also at pp. 650–651; *per* Templeman J. in *Re Cohen* [1973] 1 W.L.R. 415 at p. 426; *Dingle* v. *Turner* [1972] A.C. 601 at p. 617.

[76] *Re Cohen* [1973] 1 W.L.R. 415.

[77] *Re Scarisbrick* [1951] Ch. 622.

[78] *Re Scarisbrick, supra.*

or by a trustee,[79] or the directors of a company,[80] nor that the distribution of capital can be made so as to exhaust the principal.[81]

(ii) Poor Employees. Poor relations trusts are said to constitute an anomalous exception to the requirement of public benefit,[82] and we will see that a personal nexus or relationship between the group of persons to be benefited is fatal to gifts under the other heads.[83] This relaxation in favour of poverty trusts applies also in connection with trusts for the relief of poverty among members of a friendly society,[84] or a professional association,[85] or employees of a company.[86]

> In *Dingle* v. *Turner*,[87] a testator provided a fund upon trust "to apply the income thereof in paying pensions to poor employees of E. Dingle and Co. Ltd. who are of the age of 60 years at least or who being of the age of 45 years at least are incapacitated from earning their living by reason of some physical or mental infirmity."
> At the date of the testator's death, the company employed over 600 persons, and there was a substantial number of ex-employees. The House of Lords, affirming Megarry J., from whom the case directly came, the first to do so under Administration of Justice Act 1969, s.12, upheld the gift as a charitable trust.

The poor relations cases had been recognised for 200 years, and, even if anomalous, should not now be overruled. It would be illogical to draw a distinction between poor relations, and poor employees or poor members. All forms of trusts for the relief of poverty should be treated the same, and there was no need to introduce into the poverty cases the stricter requirements of public benefit applicable to other forms of charitable trusts. Lord Cross suggested that one reason for the different treatment of poverty trusts—a practical justification but not the historical explanation—is that there is for a settlor a "temptation to

---

[79] *Re Cohen, supra.*

[80] The "London Board" in *Gibson* v. *South American Stores* (*Gath & Chaves*) *Ltd.* [1950] Ch. 177.

[81] *Re Scarisbrick, supra*; *Dingle* v. *Turner, supra.*

[82] *Re Compton* [1945] Ch. 123 at 139 *per* Lord Greene M.R.

[83] *Post*, p. 411.

[84] *Re Buck* [1896] 2 Ch. 727.

[85] *Spiller* v. *Maude* (1881), reported (1886) 32 Ch.D. 158n. (aged and decayed actors).

[86] *Dingle* v. *Turner* [1972] A.C. 601. The significance of this exemption is considerable. Counsel for Att.-Gen. stated that in 1972 nearly £100,000,000 capital was held on trust for poor employees, and poor members of associations, or professional groups, and a mere £68,000 on poor relations trusts. The figures for annual income were £4,690,000 and £3,400 respectively. See [1978] Conv. 277 (T. G. Watkin).

[87] *Supra. Re Gosling* (1900) 48 W.R. 300 (old and worn-out clerks in a banking firm); *Re Sir Robert Laidlaw* (unreported), where the Court of Appeal upheld a legacy of £2,000 for the relief of poor members of a family company; *Gibson* v. *South American Stores* (*Gath & Chaves*) *Ltd.* [1950] Ch. 177 ("necessitous and deserving employees, ex-employees and their dependants"); *Re Denison* (1974) 42 D.L.R. (3d) 652 ("impecunious or indigent members of the Law Society [of Upper Canada] and their wives, widows and children").

enlist the assistance of the law of charity in private endeavours"[88] in order to gain the tax benefits, though the danger is not so great in the field of relief of poverty. Three Law Lords[89] doubted whether the fiscal considerations should be given any relevance in deciding whether a gift was charitable. There seems little doubt, however, that they often have done so.[90]

C. Trusts for the Advancement of Education

(i) **Benefit to the Public or a Section thereof.** Much of what is said in this section also applies to the next two following sections. Poverty apart, a trust will only be charitable if it is "for the benefit of the community or an appreciably important class of the community."[91] It will be seen that this requirement has developed in recent years, and it was possible to argue some 25 years ago that an element of public benefit should be required only in the fourth category.[92] The principle appears to be that the privileges of charity, and the loss of public revenue, should only be accorded to trusts which provide a benefit to the public. There is no objection to a man educating his children expensively, nor to isolated religious communities, nor to friendly societies for the benefit of members; but there is no reason why these activities should be supported, indirectly, by the taxpayer. Poor relations trusts, as has been seen, are a long-established anomaly.

(ii) **Personal Nexus.** Not every member of the public can benefit from every charitable trust, and it becomes necessary to determine what is a section of the public for these purposes. Again, this will vary with the different categories. A trust for the advancement of education is charitable if it is for the education of the public or of a section of the public which is not selected on the basis of a personal nexus or connection, either with the donor or between themselves. Thus, a trust for the education of named persons or for descendants of named persons,[93] or the children of employees of a company,[94] or of members of a club is not charitable. But a trust for the education of the residents of a certain borough in 1880 and their descendants is charitable[95]; as are trusts for the education of children of members of a particular

---

[88] At p. 625.

[89] Lords Dilhorne, McDermott and Hodson.

[90] *Ante*, p. 372. The Goodman Committee recommended that the poverty exception for poor relations and poor employees cases should be abolished, paras. 37–39.

[91] *Per* Lord Westbury in *Verge* v. *Somerville* [1924] A.C. 496 at p. 499.

[92] (1946) 62 L.Q.R. 234 (F. H. Newark).

[93] *Re Compton* [1945] Ch. 123. "A trust established by a father for the education of his sons is not a charity"; *per* Lord Simonds in *Oppenheim* v. *Tobacco Securities Trust Ltd.* [1951] A.C. 297 at p. 306.

[94] *Oppenheim* v. *Tobacco Securities Trust Ltd.* [1951] A.C. 297.

[95] *Re Tree* [1945] Ch. 325.

profession,[96] and trusts for specified schools and colleges, and even "closed" scholarships from a specified school to a college at Oxford or Cambridge[97]; unless, of course, the number of possible beneficiaries was derisory.

In *Oppenheim* v. *Tobacco Securities Trust Co.*,[98] income was to be applied in "providing for . . . the education of children of employees or former employees of the British-American Tobacco Company Ltd. . . . or any of its subsidiary or allied companies in such manner . . . as the acting trustees shall in their absolute discretion . . . think fit" and there was power also to apply capital. The number of employees of the company and the subsidiary and allied companies exceeded 100,000. The House of Lords (Lord McDermott dissenting), following *Re Compton*,[99] held that there was a personal nexus between the members of the class of beneficiaries and they did not constitute a section of the public. The trust failed.

In the leading majority speech, Lord Simonds said that to constitute a section of the community for these purposes the "possible (I emphasize the word 'possible') beneficiaries must be not numerically negligible, and, secondly, that the quality which distinguishes them from members of the community . . . must be a quality which does not depend on their relationship to a particular individual. . . . A group of persons may be numerous but, if the nexus between them is their personal relationship to a single propositus or to several propositi,[1] they are neither the community nor a section of the community for charitable purposes."[2]

Lord McDermott, in his dissenting speech, pointed out the difficulties which arise in trying to lay down a positive rule in such a situation.[3] "But can any really fundamental distinction, as respects the personal or impersonal nature of the common link, be drawn between those employed, for example, by a particular university and those whom the same university has put in a certain category as the result of individual examination and assessment? Again, if the bond between those employed by a particular railway is purely personal, why should the

---

[96] *Hall* v. *Derby Sanitary Authority* (1885) 16 Q.B.D. 163, approved in *Oppenheim* v. *Tobacco Securities Trust Ltd.*, *supra*.

[97] Though it is difficult to see how some of these trusts are within the *Oppenheim* rule; see Lord McDermott in *Oppenheim*, *ante*, at p. 318. See also the anomalous "founder's kin" cases; Picarda, pp. 51–52; Tudor, p. 52.

[98] [1951] A.C. 297.

[99] [1945] Ch. 123.

[1] As in *Davies* v. *Perpetual Trustee Co. Ltd.* [1959] A.C. 439 (showing how the law has changed).

[2] [1951] A.C. 297 at p. 306.

[3] See also Cross J. in *Re Mead's Trust Deed* [1961] 1 W.L.R. 1244 at p. 1249; and Lord Denning M.R. in *I.R.C.* v. *Educational Grants Association Ltd.* [1967] Ch. 993 at p. 1009; "There is no logic in it."

bond between those who are employed as railwaymen be so essentially different? Is a distinction to be drawn in this respect between those who are employed in a particular industry before it is nationalised and those who are employed therein after that process has been completed and one employer has taken the place of many? Are miners in the service of the National Coal Board now in one category and miners in a particular pit or of a particular district in another? Is the relationship between those in the service of the Crown to be distinguished from that obtaining between those in the service of some other employer? Or, if not, are the children of, say, soldiers or civil servants to be regarded as not constituting a sufficient section of the public to make a trust for their education charitable?"[4] The question, he thought, should be one of degree, depending upon the facts of each particular case. All five Law Lords, sitting in *Dingle* v. *Turner*,[5] supported this view. This does not necessarily mean that *Oppenheim* would be decidedly differently. Taking all factors into account, these educational trusts for employees are attempts to use charity's fiscal privileges for the benefit of the company by providing a tax-free fringe benefit for the employees.[6] Such trusts should fail, not on the ground that the employees, however numerous, can never constitute a class of the public, but because the *purpose* of the trust, being a company purpose, is not charitable.[7] A trust for the advancement of religion among employees might be different[8]; as might an "entirely altruistic educational trust . . . if the size of the company is sufficiently large."[9] It is obvious that it is easier to criticise the "personal nexus" test than it is to improve upon it; and it may well be that Lord Cross's half-way house creates more problems than it solves."[10]

(iii) Benefiting Private Individuals. In this situation, the question arises as to the way in which a donor can effectively obtain benefits for a group of private individuals by means of a charitable trust. He cannot do so by setting up a charitable trust in favour of the public and relying on the trustees to make grants in favour of a narrow group.

In *I.R.C.* v. *Educational Grants Association Ltd.*[11] the defendant was an association established for the advancement of education in general terms and was a charitable corporation. It was financially

---

[4] At pp. 317–318.

[5] [1972] A.C. 601; see also Annual Report 1971, para. 21.

[6] "It is an admirable thing that the children of employees should have a higher education, but I do not see why that should be at the expense of the taxpayer" *per* Harman L.J. in *I.R.C.* v. *Educational Grants Association Ltd. supra*, at p. 1013; *cf.* Annual Report 1971, para. 21.

[7] *Dingle* v. *Turner, supra.*

[8] (1974) 33 C.L.J. 63 at p. 66 (G. H. Jones); *Dingle* v. *Turner, supra.*

[9] Annual Report 1971, para. 21.

[10] (1974) 33 C.L.J. 63 (G. H. Jones).

[11] [1967] Ch. 123, *affd.* 993; Annual Report 1976, paras. 45–49 (Cowen Charitable Trust).

supported by payments under a deed of covenant by the Metal Box Co. Ltd., and by senior executives of the company. The Association claimed the repayment of tax due in respect of payment under the covenant. Between 76 per cent. and 85 per cent. of the income of the relevant year had been paid towards the education of children of persons connected with the Metal Box Co. Ltd., and Pennycuick J. and the Court of Appeal held that the tax was not recoverable, because the money had not been applied for charitable purposes only.[12]

It is impossible to say what percentage of a trust for public charity could properly be spent in favour of a private group. In *Re Koettgen's Will Trusts*,[13] there was a trust for the promotion of commercial education among members of the public unable to acquire it at their own expense; and a direction that preference be given to the families of employees of a named company in respect of a maximum of 75 per cent. of the income. This was charitable. It would have been different if the trust had been for the employees' families with a provision in favour of the public in the absence of qualified applicants. Lord Radcliffe in *Cafoor* v. *Income Tax Commissioner, Colombo*,[14] thought that *Re Koettgen* "edged very near to being inconsistent with" *Oppenheim*,[15] and Pennycuick J.[16] had considerable difficulty with it. If a preference in favour of a private group is desired, it is essential to make it subsidiary to the trust in favour of the public; and the 75 per cent. which succeeded in *Koettgen* should be regarded as the outside maximum.[17] If, however, there is an absolute right in favour of a private group, and not merely a preference, then the trust cannot be charitable. It is a matter of construction into which category the gift falls.[18]

D. Trusts for the Advancement of Religion

The notion of public benefit in religious trusts is very similar to that in education. The advancement of religion among the public or a section of the public is charitable, and there is no room for the argument of the atheists that it is not beneficial. The section of the public may be a sect, whether of the Christian religion, such as the

---

[12] I.T.A. 1952, s.447(1)(*b*), now I.C.T.A. 1988, s.505(1), which permits exemption for a charitable body *so far as the income is applied to charitable purposes only*. In the *Educational Grants* case the non-charitable payments were *ultra vires*. If the objects permit such payments, the body is not charitable (subject to *Re Koettgen*) and there will be no tax exemption.

[13] [1954] Ch. 252.

[14] [1961] A.C. 584.

[15] *Ibid.* at p. 604.

[16] In *I.R.C.* v. *Educational Grants Association Ltd.* [1967] Ch. 123.

[17] See Annual Report 1978, paras. 86–89, where the Charity Commissioners followed *Re Koettgen* in three cases; 65 per cent. and 75 per cent.

[18] *Re Martin, The Times*, November 19, 1980.

Roman Catholic[19] or the Methodist Church,[20] or of a non-Christian religion, such as the Jewish.[21] And we have seen that the law is especially generous in favour of bona fide religions, even though they have minimal following[22]; similarly a gift to a Church will be charitable even though the congregation is small. A trust is charitable if it makes available a religious activity to the public if they should wish to take advantage of it. And it may be, as will be seen[23] that a sufficient benefit to the public is shown by having amongst it persons who have enjoyed the benefit of religious experience. But an enclosed, cloistered, monastic activity is excluded[24]; and a provision for services in a private chapel.[25]

In *Gilmour* v. *Coats*,[26] a gift of £500 was made to a Carmelite Priory "if the purposes of [the Priory] are charitable." The Priory consisted of a community of cloistered nuns, about 20 in number, who devoted their lives to prayer, contemplation and self-sanctification, and engaged in no external work.

The House of Lords held that the purposes were not charitable because they lacked the necessary public benefit. This could not be found in the benefits conferred upon the public by the prayers and intercessions of the nuns according to the doctrine of the Roman Catholic Church. Such benefit was "manifestly not susceptible of proof"[27] in a court of law, and the doctrinal belief of the Roman Catholic Church would be no substitute[28]; nor in the edification of a section of the public by the example of the spiritual life followed by the nuns, for that was too vague and intangible to constitute a proper test[29]; nor by the availability of the religious life being open to all women of the Roman Catholic faith.

Two important questions remain. The refusal to accept the doctrinal belief in the benefit provided for the public by intercessory prayer casts doubt upon the charitable status of gifts for the saying of masses. It has

---

[19] *Dunne* v. *Byrne* [1912] A.C. 407; *Re Schoales* [1930] 2 Ch. 75; *Re Flinn* [1948] Ch. 241.
[20] *I.R.C.* v. *Baddeley* [1955] A.C. 572.
[21] *Neville Estates Ltd.* v. *Madden* [1962] Ch. 832.
[22] *Re Watson* [1973] 1 W.L.R. 1472; (1974) 90 L.Q.R. 4.
[23] *Post*, p. 416.
[24] *Gilmour* v. *Coats* [1949] A.C. 426.
[25] *Hoare* v. *Hoare* (1886) 56 L.T. 147.
[26] [1949] A.C. 426; following *Cocks* v. *Manners* (1871) L.R. 12 Eq. 574. But sufficient public benefit was found in *Holmes* v. *Att.-Gen., The Times*, February 12, 1981 (Exclusive Brethren). See Annual Report 1982, App. C.
[27] *Ibid.* at p. 446. But extra-statutory tax concessions have been made; Halsbury (4th ed.), para. 1073.
[28] The Irish courts take a different view and accept the doctrine of the Church: *O'Hanlon* v. *Logue* [1906] 1 I.R. 247; *Re Sheridan* [1957] I.R. 257. See generally [1981] J.L.H. 207 (M. Blakeney), suggesting that the English law shows a Protestant bias.
[29] [1949] A.C. 426 at p. 446. *Cf. Re Wedgwood* [1915] 1 Ch. 113, *ante*, p. 403, where the uplifting example of kindness to animals constituted a benefit to the public. The views expressed in *Gilmour* v. *Coats* seem inconsistent with the acceptance of the advancement of religion as a charitable purpose.

been clear since *Bourne* v. *Keane*[30] that masses are no longer illegal as constituting a superstitious use. In *Re Caus*[31] Luxmoore J. accepted evidence in the form of Dr. Delaney's affidavit in *O'Hanlon* v. *Logue*[32] to the effect that a mass, even though offered for the benefit of one or more individuals, living or dead, was for the benefit also of the general objects of the Church, and that payments made for the celebration of masses are part of the ordinary income of priests, and in Ireland were usually distributed among those priests who were in need of assistance. He held that a gift for masses for 25 years "for my soul and the souls of my parents and relations" was charitable, on the ground that the gift enabled the ritual religious act to be performed and secondly because it assisted in the endowment of the priests. Doubts were expressed in *Gilmour* v. *Coats*[33] upon the validity of this decision. Clearly, the belief of the Church in the benefits conferred on the public by the saying of masses should now be disregarded. So also a mass, said in private, from which the public were excluded.[34] But, if the mass was said as part of a public act of worship, then it would seem to be entitled to be treated as a contribution to a religious service and so charitable; even if the attendance was small. The matter however is one of doubt.

Secondly, the argument that the gift in *Gilmour* v. *Coats*[35] was charitable on the ground that it was a provision for religious exercises among a group which was open to all women of the Roman Catholic faith, provides an interesting comparison with trusts for the advancement of education. Would there have been sufficient public benefit if the trust had been for the advancement of education? Lord Simonds accepted that there was a "speciously logical appearance" in the argument that "just as the endowment of a scholarship open to public competition is a charity, so also is a gift to enable any woman (or, presumably, any man) to enter into a fuller religious life a charity."[36] But he refused to be bound to apply to religious trusts the same test as that applied to educational trusts. Yet it may be that there is no conflict here. The explanation may be that a public benefit is supplied in educational trusts by the presence in society of educated people. A trust for the advancement of religion among the members of Catford Synagogue was held by Cross J. in *Neville Estates Ltd.* v. *Madden*[37] to be charitable because the court was "entitled to assume that some benefit accrues to the public from the attendance at places of worship of persons who live in this world and mix with their fellow-citizens."[38]

---

[30] [1919] A.C. 815.
[31] [1934] Ch. 162.
[32] [1906] 1 I.R. 247.
[33] [1949] A.C. 426.
[34] *Hoare* v. *Hoare, supra.*
[35] [1949] A.C. 426.
[36] *Ibid.* at p. 448.
[37] [1962] Ch. 832.
[38] *Ibid.* at p. 853.

And "if it can be imagined that it was made a condition of a gift for the advancement of education that its beneficiaries should lead a cloistered life and communicate to no one, and leave no record of the fruits of their study, I do not think that the charitable character of the gift will be sustained."[39]

This suggests that there must be some benefit to the public as a whole, however indirect, rather than the section which decides to participate. This point arises also under the fourth head. It is odd that a gift to enable pious women to spend their life in religious contemplation is not charitable; while a trust to propagate religious works of no value is.[40] The convent's problem can, however, easily be overcome by an extension of their activities to include external work.

E. The Fourth Head

In most of the situations which have been considered under this head, the trust is for the benefit of all the public. This is so with gifts which improve the efficiency of the fighting forces, or the police, or medical research, or public parks and sea walls, or law reporting, or the country generally. It does not matter that it is only a limited number of people who will take advantage of the benefit provided. "A bridge which is available for all the public may undoubtedly be a charity and it is indifferent how many people use it. But confine its use to a selected number of persons, however numerous and important: it is then clearly not a charity. It is not of general public utility: for it does not serve the public purpose which its nature qualifies it to serve."[41]

The problem arises where the purposes are restricted to a group of persons. We have seen that trusts for the relief of the aged, the impotent and the sick are charitable. Not everyone is aged or impotent or sick.[42] But if the benefits are generally available, there is some benefit, albeit indirect, to the public generally.[43] Clearly, a trust under the fourth head cannot be charitable if it is confined to persons bound together by a personal nexus.[44] The inhabitants of a geographical area are a section of the public in this context. But there are dicta in

---

[39] *Per* Lord Simonds in *Gilmour* v. *Coats* [1949] A.C. 426 at p. 450.

[40] *Re Watson* [1973] 1 W.L.R. 1472, *ante*, p. 392.

[41] *Per* Lord Simonds in *I.R.C.* v. *Baddeley* [1955] A.C. 572 at p. 592.

[42] For the imposition of further restrictions, such as aged peers and impotent millionaires, see *ante*, p. 397. See also *Re Dunlop (deceased)* (1984) 19 *Northern Ireland Judgments Bulletin*; [1987] Conv. 114 (N. Dawson), where a home for "Old Presbyterian Persons" was held charitable. It did not fail on the "bridge for Methodists" principle, as the public generally benefits from having some members housed.

[43] As suggested to be the test in (1958) 21 M.L.R. 138 at p. 140 (P. S. Atiyah).

[44] *Re Drummond* [1914] 2 Ch. 90; *Re Hobourn Aero Components Ltd. Air Raid Distress Fund* [1946] Ch. 86; *Re Mead's Trust Deed* [1961] 1 W.L.R. 1244; *Over-Seventies Housing Association* v. *Westminster London Borough Council* (1974) 230 E.G. 1593. This problem is not encountered with learned societies, where the benefit is not confined to the members; *Re South Place Ethical Society* [1980] 1 W.L.R. 1565. *Tudor on Charities* (7th ed.), p. 24, expresses the view that a personal nexus may not defeat trusts for the sick or aged, by analogy with poverty charities.

Williams v. *I.R.C.*[45] and in *I.R.C.* v. *Baddeley*[46] which suggest that trusts under the fourth head, even if otherwise charitable, are subject to a stricter rule than trusts under the other three heads in relation to the selection of persons who are to benefit.

In *Williams* v. *I.R.C.*[47] Lord Simonds suggested that, even if the trust would otherwise have been charitable, the "Welsh people," defined in the instrument to "mean and include persons of Welsh nationality by birth or descent or born or educated or at anytime domiciled in the principality of Wales or the county of Monmouth," would not have constituted a section of the public.[48] He returned to this in *Baddeley*.[49] It is necessary to distinguish between "relief extended to the whole community yet by its very nature advantageous only to the few and a form of relief accorded to a selected few out of a larger number equally willing to take advantage of it."[50] He doubted whether the test could be satisfied "if the beneficiaries are a class of persons not only confined to a particular area but selected from within it by reference to a particular creed."[51] "Who has ever heard of a bridge to be crossed only by impecunious Methodists?"[52] The persons to be benefited must be the whole community, or all the inhabitants of a particular area. Not a "class within a class." Lord Reid disagreed and found no justification in the suggestion that the test for determining what was a section of the community should be different under the fourth head.[53]

The matter must be considered to be one of uncertainty. The decision shows the difficulties which arise in this area from an attempt to lay down positive rules,[54] and Lord Simonds admitted that it "was often very difficult to draw the line."[55] The only solution appears to be to accept, in all heads of charity where public benefit is required, the more general and flexible test proposed by Lord McDermott,[56] and supported by the House in *Dingle* v. *Turner* through Lord Cross.[57] The question whether the beneficiaries constitute a section of the public "is

[45] [1947] A.C. 447.
[46] [1955] A.C. 572.
[47] [1947] A.C. 447. (The trust was confined to Welsh people in London.)
[48] Similarly with the Jews in *Keren Kayemeth Le Jisroel* v. *I.R.C.* [1942] A.C. 650. But see Annual Report 1977, para. 79, where the Charity Commissioners, when subsequently registering the *Williams* Trust as a charity under Charitable Trusts (Validation) Act 1954, held, citing *Idle* v. *Tree* [1945] Ch. 325, that the definition of the beneficiary class nevertheless did comprise a sufficient section of the public; *post*, p. 425.
[49] [1955] A.C. 572.
[50] *Ibid.* at p. 592.
[51] *Ibid.* See also *Re Lipinski's Will Trusts* [1976] Ch. 235, *ante*, p. 344.
[52] *Ibid.* This was a question posed by Stamp Q.C. in argument in the Court of Appeal.
[53] See also *Re Dunlop (deceased)*, *ante* p. 417, n. 42, which suggests that the test for each head is different, and that the test can differ even within the same head.
[54] (1974) 33 C.L.J. 63 (G. H. Jones).
[55] [1955] A.C. 572 at p. 592.
[56] *Oppenheim* v. *Tobacco Securities Trust Ltd.* [1951] A.C. 197; *ante*, p. 412.
[57] [1972] A.C. 601; *ante*, p. 413.

a question of degree and cannot be by itself decisive of the question whether the trust is a charity. Much must depend on the purpose of the trust. It may well be that, on the one hand, a trust to promote some purpose, prima facie charitable, will constitute a charity even though the class of potential beneficiaries might fairly be called a private class and that, on the other hand, a trust to promote another purpose, also prima facie charitable, will not constitute a charity even though the class of potential beneficiaries might seem to some people fairly describable as a section of the public."[58] One cannot go, with certainty, further than that.

5. THE INTERPRETATION OF CHARITABLE GIFTS AND PURPOSES

A number of special questions arise in connection with the construction of instruments which are claimed to create charitable trusts. The problems here discussed provide a further reminder of the importance of proper draftsmanship when setting up a charitable trust. The Charity Commissioners will help with advice,[59] and they will give reasons for the refusal to register, and make it possible for the trusts to be redrafted. The Commissioners warn draftsmen not to draft object clauses in unnecessarily wide terms, for this may allow non-charitable purposes to be included.[60] In *McGovern* v. *Att. Gen.*,[61] a trust included political objects, but the deed provided that the objects were "restricted to those which are charitable according to the law of the United Kingdom but subject thereto they may be carried out in all parts of the world." This proviso did not have the "blue-pencil" effect of cancelling out the non-charitable parts, and hence the trust was not charitable. The restriction was merely intended to make it clear that the trustees, when operating outside the United Kingdom, should be restricted to purposes charitable by United Kingdom law. In so far as the purposes of the trust included political and thus non-charitable objects, the proviso could not save it.

A. The Motive of the Donor

The charitable motive of the donor, even if expressed, is not of major significance. The rule cuts both ways. In *Re King*,[62] a will provided for the erection of a stained-glass window in a church in memory of her parents, her sister and the testatrix herself. This was held to be a valid charitable gift. The fact that the intention was "not to beautify the church or benefit the parishioners, but to perpetuate the

---

[58] *Ibid.* at p. 624.
[59] Charities Act 1960, s.24; Annual Report 1966, para. 19.
[60] Annual Report 1971, paras. 70–71; 1966, para. 39.
[61] [1982] Ch. 321, *ante*, p. 405.
[62] [1923] 1 Ch. 243, *post*, p. 435; following *Hoare* v. *Osborne* (1866) L.R. 1 Eq. 585.

memory of the testatrix and her relations"[63] was immaterial. Conversely, a non-charitable gift, such as a gift for the suppression of vivisection, cannot be made charitable by the donor's charitable motive.[64] But a clear charitable intent may help to turn an ambiguity in favour of charity; especially, as has been seen, where it is possible to find an intention to benefit the poor.[65] And if the intention is expressed too widely, it may again prove to be a double-edged weapon by letting in benevolent or other non-charitable objects.

B. The Locality Cases

Particular difficulty has been experienced with the "locality cases." The restriction of a benefit to a precise locality seemed at one time to colour the judges' views of the nature of the benefit. By a benevolent construction, the benefits conferred were construed as being charitable. These cases[66] were discussed by Lord Simonds in *Williams' Trustees* v. *I.R.C.*,[67] by Lord Greene M.R. in *Re Strakosch*,[68] and by the Court of Appeal in *I.R.C.* v. *Baddeley*.[69] They are to be treated as anomalous and not to be extended.[70] They will, however, be followed in cases directly similar.[71] At the other end of the locality scale, a gift "unto my country England" is a valid charitable gift.[72]

C. The Charitable Status of the Trustee[73]

The charitable nature of a trust is determined by the terms of the trust and not by the status of the trustee. Non-charitable trustees may hold property on charitable trusts, and charity trustees may, subject, in the case of a corporation, to the terms of their incorporation, hold property on non-charitable trusts. But the charitable status of the trustee can in some cases, where the terms of the trust are not spelled out, lead the court to construe the terms of the trust as charitable. A gift to a bishop or vicar, without the purposes being specified, may be charitable. In *Re Flinn*,[74] a gift to "His Eminence the Archbishop of

---

[63] *Ibid.* at p. 245.
[64] *National Anti-Vivisection Society* v. *I.R.C.* [1948] A.C. 31.
[65] *Biscoe* v. *Jackson* (1887) 35 Ch.D. 460; *Re Coulthurst's W.T.* [1951] Ch. 193; *Re Cottam* [1955] 1 W.L.R. 1299, *ante*, p. 381.
[66] *e.g. Goodman* v. *Saltash Corp.* (1882) 7 App.Cas. 633; *Att.-Gen.* v. *Lonsdale* (1827) 1 Sim. 105; *Re Christchurch Inclosure Act* (1888) 38 Ch.D. 520; *Jones* v. *Williams* (1767) Amb. 651.
[67] [1947] A.C. 447 at pp. 459–460.
[68] [1949] Ch. 529 at pp. 539–540.
[69] [1955] A.C. 572.
[70] *Houston* v. *Burns* [1918] A.C. 337; *Att.-Gen.* v. *National Provincial and Union Bank of England Ltd.* [1924] A.C. 262; *Re Gwyon* [1930] 1 Ch. 255.
[71] *Re Fishermen of Newbiggin by the Sea, The Times*, November 15, 1957.
[72] *Re Smith* [1932] 1 Ch. 153, following *Nightingale* v. *Goulburn* (1847) 5 Hare 484.
[73] (1960) 24 Conv.(N.S.) 306 (V. T. J. Delaney).
[74] [1948] Ch. 241.

Westminster Cathedral for the time being to be used by him for such purposes as he shall in his absolute discretion think fit" was upheld. So, also, gifts to such officers for their work, for this is treated as being wholly charitable. In *Re Rumball*[75] a gift "to the bishop for the time being of the diocese of the Windward Islands to be used by him as he thinks fit in his diocese" was upheld.

But there is a danger in saying too much; where the terms of the gift specify the purposes and allow any part of the fund to be used for non-charitable purposes, the gift is void. The cases turn on the finest points of construction. "Parish work," for example, includes some extra-charitable activities, and in *Farley* v. *Westminster Bank*[76] a gift to a vicar "for parish work" was held invalid, the House of Lords refusing to insert "his" before "parish." But in *Re Simson*,[77] a gift to a vicar "for his work in the parish" was held valid. The former phrase is held to be dispositive, thus enlarging the ambit of the gift and producing the result that a charitable trustee holds on non-charitable trusts, while the latter phrase is held to be merely descriptive of the vicar's responsibilities. The many pages in the reports dealing with these refinements and endeavouring to show at length that a dozen or so words mean nothing, bring no credit to our jurisprudence.

This principle does not apply to Local Authorities acting as trustees.[78] Indeed Local Authorities have no power to act as trustees of an eleemosynary charity.[79]

D. The Objects Must be Exclusively Charitable

To be charitable, the funds of a trust must be applicable for charitable purposes only.

(i) Main and Subsidiary Objects. A trust may be charitable, however, even if some expenditure is permitted on non-charitable purposes, but only if those non-charitable purposes are entirely subsidiary to the main charitable purposes. The question is whether "The main purpose of the body . . . is charitable and the only elements in its constitution and operation which are non-charitable are merely incidental to that purpose."[80]

Failure of a trust for this reason is fairly obvious in cases such as *Morice* v. *Bishop of Durham*,[81] and *I.R.C.* v. *Baddeley*[82] where the

---

[75] [1956] Ch. 105.
[76] [1939] A.C. 430; *Re Stratton* [1931] 1 Ch. 197.
[77] [1946] Ch. 299; *Re Bain* [1930] 1 Ch. 224; *Re Eastes* [1948] Ch. 257.
[78] *Re Endacott* [1960] Ch. 232; see especially pp. 242–243, *per* Lord Evershed.
[79] *Re Armitage* [1972] Ch. 438.
[80] *Per* Lord Cohen in *I.R.C.* v. *City of Glasgow Police Athletic Association* [1953] A.C. 380 at p. 405. See [1978] Conv. 92 (N. P. Gravells).
[81] (1804) 9 Ves.Jr. 399; (1805) 10 Ves.Jr. 522 ("objects of benevolence and liberality"); *ante*, p. 347.
[82] [1955] A.C. 572, *ante*, p. 399.

purposes are patently too widely expressed but it is less obvious in cases where the non-charitable element is latent.

In *Ellis* v. *I.R.C.*,[83] realty was conveyed to trustees upon trust for use "generally in such manner for the promotion and aiding of the work of the Roman Catholic Church in the district as the Trustees with the consent of the Bishop may prescribe." In *Oxford Group* v. *I.R.C.*,[84] a company had among its objects "the maintenance, support, development and assistance of the Oxford Group Movement in every way." In both cases the Court of Appeal held that assets could be spent on subsidiary objects which were not necessarily conducive to the main (and undoubtedly charitable) object; such subsidiary objects existed in their own right and prevented the gifts from being "for charitable purposes *only*."

An acute form of this problem occurs where the furtherance of a charitable purpose also benefits particular groups of persons. This may or may not be fatal according to the weight the courts place on it. For instance in *I.R.C.* v. *City of Glasgow Police Athletic Association*,[85] the House of Lords held that a police athletic association, intended to benefit policemen in Glasgow, was not wholly ancillary to increasing the efficiency of the Glasgow police force and therefore not charitable. Again, while the benefits to the nursing profession as such loomed too large in the constitution of the General Nursing Council in proportion to the advancement of healing,[86] this was not so of surgeons in relation to the advancement of surgery in the constitution of the Royal College of Surgeons.[87] In *Re Coxen*[88] a substantial gift to a charity included provision for an annual dinner for the trustees; and this was held charitable as being ancillary to the better administration of the charity. And in *London Hospital Medical College* v. *I.R.C.*,[89] a students' union was held to be a charitable trust where its predominant object was to further the purposes of the college, even though one of its objects was to confer private and personal benefits on union members.

(ii) And/Or Cases. Nowhere is the draftsman's error more nakedly displayed than in this group of cases. If a purpose is described as

---

[83] (1949) 31 T.C. 178, following *Dunne* v. *Byrne* [1912] A.C. 407. See also *I.R.C.* v. *Educational Grants Association Ltd.* [1967] Ch. 993 at pp. 1010 and 1015.

[84] [1949] 2 All E.R. 537. See particularly Tucker L.J.'s summary of the relevant rules at pp. 539–540; *Re Cole* [1958] Ch. 877.

[85] [1953] A.C. 380.

[86] *General Nursing Council* v. *St. Marylebone B.C.* [1959] A.C. 540; *ante,* p. 388.

[87] *Royal College of Surgeons* v. *National Provincial Bank Ltd.* [1952] A.C. 631; See also *Incorporated Council of Law Reporting* v. *Att.-Gen.* [1972] Ch. 73.

[88] [1948] Ch. 747.

[89] [1976] 1 W.L.R. 613. See also *Re South Place Ethical Society* [1980] 1 W.L.R. 1565 (social activities held to be ancillary to the objects of ethical humanist society).

"charitable and benevolent"—philanthropic, useful, or any other such adjective—the purposes are wholly charitable. For the purposes, to qualify, must be, *inter alia*, charitable; and that is enough. But if the draftsman says charitable *or* benevolent, there is prima facie an alternative; and the funds could be applied for purposes which are benevolent, but not charitable. But this is an oversimplification, and the question is one of construction in each case. Is the word conjunctive or disjunctive?

(a) *Cases of "or."* In *Blair* v. *Duncan*[90] the words were "such charitable or public purposes as my trustee thinks proper"; in *Houston* v. *Burns*,[91] "public, benevolent, or charitable purposes"; in *Chichester Diocesan Fund and Board of Finance* v. *Simpson*[92] "charitable or benevolent"; in each of these cases the gift was held not to be charitable, in that the words were wide enough to justify the trustees in disposing of the fund, or an unascertainable part of it, to non-charitable objects.

In *Re Macduff*,[93] a bequest of money "for some one or more purposes, charitable, philanthropic or—" was held to be bad, not by reason of the blank, but because there may be philanthropic purposes that are not charitable.

But in *Re Bennett*[94] the words were "charity, or *other* public objects in the parish of Faringdon," and Eve J. held that the addition of the word "other" entitled him to apply the *ejusdem generis* rule of interpretation, and dispensed him from the necessity of reading the two things disjunctively; the gift was, therefore, upheld as a charitable gift of the whole.

(b) *Cases of "and."* Lord Davey in *Blair* v. *Duncan*[95] said that if the words had been "charitable *and* public" effect might be given to them, because they could be construed to mean charitable purposes of a public character. Some cases support this view, the word "and" being regarded as having the power to draw the other word into the orbit of the charitable. This view is borne out by *Re Sutton*[96] and *Re Best*,[97] where gifts to "charitable and deserving objects" and "charitable and

---

[90] [1902] A.C. 37.
[91] [1918] A.C. 337. The purposes were also confined to a particular parish and its environs: on this point, see *ante*, p. 417.
[92] [1944] A.C. 341; the trustees of the will paid the sums over to various charities, not anticipating the litigation by the next-of-kin which, in the event, occurred and the sequel was *Ministry of Health* v. *Simpson* [1951] A.C. 251.
[93] [1896] 2 Ch. 451.
[94] [1920] 1 Ch. 305.
[95] [1902] A.C. 37 at p. 44.
[96] (1885) 28 Ch.D. 464.
[97] [1904] 2 Ch. 354; *cf. Att.-Gen.* v. *Herrick* (1772) Amb. 712 (charitable and pious uses—here, the objects being unspecified, and no trust being created, the gift fell to the Crown, to be disposed of by Sign Manual).

benevolent" objects respectively were upheld. In *Att.-Gen. of the Bahamas* v. *Royal Trust Co.*,[98] on the other hand, a gift for the "education and welfare" of Bahamian children and young people was held void on a disjunctive construction. To construe the words conjunctively would result in a single purpose of educational welfare, but the word "welfare" was regarded as too wide to permit such a construction. The addition of a third word, "without any conjunction, copulative or disjunctive,"[99] was in *Williams* v. *Kershaw*[1] held fatal to a gift to "benevolent, charitable and religious" purposes, and in *Re Eades*[2] Sargant J. refused to uphold a gift for "such religious, charitable and philanthropic objects" as three named persons should jointly appoint.

In *Att.-Gen.* v. *National Provincial and Union Bank of England*[3] there was a gift of part of the residuary estate "for such patriotic purposes or objects and such charitable institution or institutions or charitable object or objects in the British Empire" as the trustees should select. The House of Lords interpreted this as a gift for any or all of four categories, two of which might not be charitable, and so held the whole gift void.

So we cannot say more than that prima facie the word "or" causes the words to be read disjunctively; the word "and" causes them to be read conjunctively.

(iii) Severance. Where the language permits funds to be applied partly for charitable and partly for non-charitable purposes, the court will, in some cases, apply a doctrine of severance, separating the good from the bad, and allow the former to stand and the latter to fail.

In *Salusbury* v. *Denton*[4] a testator bequeathed a fund to his widow to be applied by her in her will, in part towards the foundation of a charity school, and as to the rest towards the benefit of the testator's relatives. The widow died without making any apportionment, but it was held, relying on the maxim "Equality is Equity," that the court would divide the fund into two equal halves.

The distinction between this and the "charitable or benevolent" cases is well brought out by Page-Wood V.-C.[5] "It is one thing to direct a trustee to give *a part* of a fund to one set of objects, and the *remainder*

---

[98] [1986] 1 W.L.R. 1001, criticised as too narrow in (1987) 50 N.L.J. *Annual Charities Review* 20 (S. P. de Cruz).
[99] *Per* Pearson J. in *Re Sutton* (1885) 28 Ch.D. 464 at p. 466.
[1] (1835) 5 Cl. & F. 111n.
[2] [1920] 2 Ch. 353.
[3] [1924] A.C. 262.
[4] (1857) 3 K. & J. 529.
[5] At p. 539; the italics are the Vice-Chancellor's.

to another, and it is a distinct thing to direct him to give 'either' to one set of objects 'or' to another. . . . This is a case of the former description. Here the trustee was bound to give a part to each." The crux of the matter is that the whole of a fund cannot be devoted to non-charity; once this is established, the court will endeavour to quantify what proportion of the capital assets is needed to support the non-charitable part,[6] and then hold the remaining part to be validly devoted to charity. In the absence of factors requiring a different division, the court will divide equally.[7] But there may be good reasons for making an unequal division.

In *Re Coxen*,[8] a testator gave the residue of his estate, amounting to more than £200,000 to the Court of Aldermen of the City of London for charitable purposes, providing however that one guinea should be paid to each of the six aldermen chosen to administer the trust on the occasion of his attending any meeting to administer the trust, and that £100 p.a. be used for an annual dinner for the Court of Aldermen when it should meet to discuss the business of the trust. On the assumption that these administrative provisions were not charitable,[9] quantification was desirable, for a division into equal parts would be absurd. Jenkins J. held that the court would find the necessary means to quantify the maximum slice of capital that would be needed to support them.

(iv) Charitable Trusts (Validation) Act 1954. If the terms of a trust coming into operation before December 16, 1952,[10] are such that the property could be applied exclusively for charitable purposes, but could also be applied for non-charitable purposes (called in the Act an "imperfect trust provision") then as from July 30, 1954, the terms shall be treated as if they permitted application for charitable purposes only.[11]

The simple case covered by this provision would be a gift, prior to December 16, 1952, for "charitable or benevolent purposes." It would have saved the trusts of the Diplock will,[12] or the terms of the Oxford Group Memorandum[13] and was applied in the case of a trust deed some of whose purposes were charitable and others not.[14] The difficulty

---

[6] In most cases this will produce *pro tanto* voidness.

[7] *Hoare* v. *Osborne* (1866) L.R. 1 Eq. 585; *Re Vaughan* (1866) 33 Ch.D. 187.

[8] [1948] Ch. 747.

[9] Jenkins J. later decided that they were charitable; *ante*, p. 422.

[10] The date of publication of the Nathan Report; see (1954) 18 Conv.(N.S.) 532; (1962) 26 Conv.(N.S.) 200 (S. G. Maurice).

[11] s.1(2); *Re Chitty's W.T.* [1970] Ch. 254.

[12] *Chichester Diocesan Fund and Board of Finance* v. *Simpson* [1944] A.C. 341; *ante*, p. 423, *post*, p. 625.

[13] [1949] 2 All E.R. 537.

[14] *Re Mead's Trust Deed* [1961] 1 W.L.R. 1244; *Re South Place Ethical Society* [1980] 1 W.L.R. 1565 ("purposes either religious or civil"). The trust in *Williams Trustees* v. *I.R.C.* [1947] A.C. 447, p. 394, *ante*, was eventually saved by the Act, and registered by the Charity Commissioners in 1977; Annual Report 1977, paras. 71–80.

arises where there is no express mention of any charitable purposes, but where the purposes are capable of including charitable purposes.[15] It was said in *Re Gillingham Bus Disaster Fund*[16] that a trust for "worthy causes" was covered, and in *Re Wykes' Will Trust*,[17] a trust for welfare purposes was upheld as those purposes are akin to the relief of poverty. On the other hand, a trust for division among institutions and associations, some of which were not charitable, was not validated[18]; nor was a trust providing various benefits for employees because it was essentially a private discretionary trust and contained no indication of an intention to benefit the public.[19] The principle seems to be that where there is a clear flavour of charity present, "a quasi-charitable trust" as Cross J. has put it,[20] the donor of such a gift would not feel that his intentions were being distorted by the whole of his gift being made available to charity. This accords with the view of the Privy Council on a comparable issue of New South Wales legislation.[21] It would thus cover "worthy causes," but not a case involving the mere possibility of charitable benefit.[22]

Commonwealth legislation[23] goes much further, and gives the courts a "blue pencil" power. Where non-charitable purposes are, or are deemed to be, within the ambit of a trust obviously intended to be charitable,[24] the trust is carried out as if the non-charitable elements were not present. The principle of such legislation seems acceptable and it is a pity that the Nathan Committee hesitated to recommend its adoption here.

E. Disaster Appeals

Problems can arise when public appeals for donations are made after some accident or disaster, if insufficient thought has been given to the question whether the fund is to be charitable or not. Such was the case with the loss of Penlee Lifeboat in Cornwall in 1982, when over £2 million was donated by the public to the dependants of the lost crew, numbering eight families. If charitable, the fund would attract tax

---

[15] *Re Gillingham Bus Disaster Fund* [1959] Ch. 62; *Re Wykes* [1961] Ch. 229; *Re Mead's Trust Deed* (*supra*).

[16] *Supra*, at p. 80.

[17] *Supra*. Apart from the 1954 Act, such a trust fails: *Re Atkinson's W.T.* [1978] 1 W.L.R. 586.

[18] *Re Harpur's W.T.* [1962] Ch. 78.

[19] *Re Saxone Shoe Co. Ltd.'s Trust Deed* [1962] 1 W.L.R. 943.

[20] *Ibid.* at pp. 957–958.

[21] *Leahy* v. *Att.-Gen. for New South Wales* [1959] A.C. 457 at pp. 474–476. It is strange that this analysis is not referred to in later English cases.

[22] *cf. Mead's Trust Deed* with *Re Saxone Shoe Co. Ltd.'s Trust Deed, supra. Re Mead* goes rather far in restricting a trust to "poor" members of a union.

[23] (New South Wales) Conveyancing Act 1919–1969; s.37D; (New Zealand) Trustee Act 1956, s.32; (Victoria) Property Law Act 1958, s.131; (Western Australia) Trustees Act 1962, s.102; (1940) 14 A.L.J. 58; (1946) 62 L.Q.R. 23; (1950) 24 A.L.J. 239; (E. H. Coghill); (1967) 16 I.C.L.Q. 464 (M. C. Cullity); (1973) 47 A.L.J. 68 (I. J. Hardingham). See also Charities Act (Northern Ireland) 1964, s.24.

[24] *Leahy* v. *Att.-Gen. for New South Wales* [1959] A.C. 457.

relief but, contrary to the expectations of some donors, it could not be simply divided amongst the families, as charitable funds, being essentially public in nature, cannot be used to give benefits to individuals exceeding those appropriate to their needs. Any surplus would, under the *cy-près* doctrine, be applied to related charities.[25] If, on the other hand, the fund was not charitable, it would not attract tax relief, but could be distributed entirely among the dependants if, upon construing the terms of the appeal, that was the intention of the donors. If that was not their intention, the surplus would not be applicable *cy-près*, but would result to the subscribers or perhaps devolve upon the Crown as *bona vacantia*.[26] Similar problems can arise if the appeal is on behalf of one specific person, such as a sick child. In the Penlee case[27] it was decided, after negotiations with the Attorney-General and the Charity Commissioners, to forgo tax relief and to treat the fund as private, so that the money could be divided among the families.[28]

The terms of the appeal are all-important in determining the status of the fund, and the consequences flowing from that status. In order to avoid uncertainty in the future, the Attorney-General has issued guidelines for consideration by persons planning to launch a public appeal of this sort.[29]

6. Cy-Près

A. The Cy-Près Doctrine Prior to 1960

Where property is given for charitable purposes and the purposes cannot be carried out in the precise manner intended by the donor, the question is whether the trust should fail, or whether the property should be applied for other charitable purposes. The *cy-près* doctrine, where it applies, enables the court (or now the Commissioners) to make a scheme for the application of the property for other charitable purposes as near as possible to those intended by the donor.[30] This is judicial *cy-près*. If a gift is to charity but not upon trust, it is disposed of

---

[25] *Infra.*

[26] *Re Gillingham Bus Disaster Fund* [1959] Ch. 62; *Re West Sussex Constabulary's Widows, Children and Benevolent* (1930) *Fund Trust* [1971] Ch. 1; *ante*, p. 234.

[27] Which was not litigated. See Annual Report 1981, paras. 4–8; (1982) 132 N.L.J. 223 (H. Picarda).

[28] The Charity Commissioners have stated that the fund was not charitable; Annual Report 1981, para. 6. If it had been charitable, as being for the relief of victims of a disaster (*Re North Devon and West Somerset Relief Fund Trusts* [1953] 1 W.L.R. 1260, *ante*, p. 381), presumably it would not be possible to forgo that status.

[29] See Annual Report, 1981, App. A. See also the South Atlantic Fund, for the needs of the Armed Forces and their dependants, arising from operations in the Falkland Islands; Annual Report 1982, paras. 31–35; Annual Report 1985, para. 19 (Bradford City Disaster Charitable Trust).

[30] See, generally, Sheridan and Delaney, *The Cy-Près Doctrine*; Sheridan and Keeton, *The Modern Law of Charities*; Nathan Committee Report (Cmd. 8710) Chap. 9; (1987) 50 N.L.J. Annual Charities Review 34 (P. Luxton), comparing the American position.

by the Crown under prerogative *cy-près*.[31] The distinction is not however always observed.

It is necessary to examine the circumstances in which the *cy-près* doctrine is applicable. It will be no surprise that the jurisdiction was very narrow; and, until the reforms of the Charities Act 1960, it was said to be available only where it was "impossible" or "impracticable" to carry out the purposes of the trust.[32] Thus, trusts for the distribution of loaves of bread to the poor or of stockings for poor maidservants continued until modern times. Their performance was cumbersome, uneconomical, inconvenient, but not impossible nor impracticable. But it had at least, by the turn of the nineteenth century, become impracticable to apply money for the advancement and propagation of the Christian religion among the infidels of Virginia,[33] or for "the redemption of British slaves in Turkey or Barbary."[34] *Re Dominion Students' Hall Trust*[35] showed the furthest development of the doctrine by the courts.

One of the objects of a company limited by guarantee was to promote community of citizenship, culture and tradition among all members of the British Community of Nations; and it maintained a hostel for students in Bloomsbury. But the benefits of the charity were restricted to students of European origin. The *cy-près* power was used to remove the "colour bar." It could not be said that it was "absolutely impracticable" to carry on the charity in its present state; but, by 1947, "to retain the condition, so far from furthering the charity's main object, might defeat it and would be liable to antagonize those students, both white and coloured, whose support and goodwill it is the purpose of the charity to sustain. The case, therefore, can be said to fall within the broad description of impossibility illustrated by *In re Campden Charities*[36] and *In re Robinson*.[37,38]

More recently, in *Re J. W. Laing Trust*,[39] concerning a settlement of

---

[31] *Paice* v. *Archbishop of Canterbury* (1807) 14 Ves. 364; *Moggridge* v. *Thackwell* (1802) 7 Ves. 36; *Re Bennett* [1960] Ch. 18. But even if there is no trust, the court has jurisdiction if there is an analogous legally binding restriction; *Liverpool and District Hospital for Diseases of the Heart* v. *Att.-Gen.* [1981] Ch. 193 (charitable corporation); [1984] Conv. 112 (J. Warburton).

[32] See *Re Weir Hospital* [1910] 2 Ch. 124.

[33] *Att.-Gen.* v. *City of London* (1790) 3 Bro.C.C. 121. Annual Report (1971), paras. 65–69; see also *Re Robinson* [1923] 2 Ch. 332. (The wearing of a black gown by the preacher was impracticable because it was likely to offend the congregation and defeat the main object.).

[34] *Ironmongers' Co.* v. *Att.-Gen.* (1844) 10 Cl. & F. 908.

[35] [1947] Ch. 183; see Race Relations Act 1976, s.34; *ante*, p. 319; Annual Report 1976, para. 20; Annual Report 1983, para. 19.

[36] (1881) 18 Ch.D. 310.

[37] [1923] 2 Ch. 332.

[38] [1947] Ch. 183 at p. 186, *per* Evershed J.

[39] [1984] Ch. 143, [1984] Conv. 319 (J. Warburton). Section 13 of the Charities Act 1960 did not apply; *post*, p. 439.

shares worth £15,000 in 1922, the question was whether the court could delete a term imposed by the settlor that the capital and income should be distributed no later than 10 years after his death. The investment was now worth £24 million. The trust was for Christian evangelical causes, and the individuals and bodies who would be the recipients were unsuited to receive large capital sums. The deletion of this term was approved under the court's inherent jurisdiction, as it had become inexpedient in the very altered circumstances of the charity.

It is convenient also at this stage to note that a distinction is made between the initial failure of a charitable trust, and a failure after the time when the trust has once been in operation. Application *cy-près* is much easier in the latter case; for, after application to charity, there is no resulting trust for the donor.[40] If the donor wants the property to pass to a third party, or to return to himself or his estate, he must expressly so provide by a gift over to take effect within the perpetuity period.[41] In the case of initial failure, the gift will lapse unless there is, on the proper construction of the instrument, a paramount intention to benefit charity. These situations will now be examined.

B. Initial Failure. Paramount Charitable Intent

(i) Width of Charitable Intent. Where a charitable trust fails as being ineffective at the date of the gift, the gift will either lapse and fall into residue, or the property will be applied *cy-près*. The decision depends on the width of charitable intent manifested by the donor. If the intention was that the property should be applied for a specified purpose, which cannot be carried out, or for one specific charitable institution which no longer exists, the gift will lapse. But if the court finds a wider intent, a paramount or general charitable intention, the property may be applied *cy-près*.

In *Re Rymer*,[42] there was a legacy of £5,000 "to the rector for the time being of St. Thomas's Seminary for the education of priests for the diocese of Westminster." At the time of the testator's death, the Seminary had ceased to exist, and the students had been transferred to another Seminary in Birmingham.

The Court of Appeal held that the gift failed. It was a gift "to a particular seminary for the purposes thereof." There was no wider intent.

This may be constrasted with *Re Lysaght*,[43] where the testatrix gave funds to the Royal College of Surgeons to found medical studentships.

---

[40] *Per* Romer L.J. in *Re Wright* [1954] Ch. 347 at pp. 362–363. But see [1983] Conv. 107 (P. Luxton).

[41] *Post*, p. 436.

[42] [1895] 1 Ch. 19; *Re Spence* [1979] Ch. 483. On the matter generally, see (1969) 32 M.L.R. 283 (J. B. E. Hutton).

[43] [1966] Ch. 191. See particularly at pp. 201–202.

The gift was subject to restrictions, in that the students were to be male, the sons of qualified British-born medical men, themselves British-born, and not of the Jewish or Roman Catholic faith. The Royal College of Surgeons declined to accept the gift on these terms. As it was held that the particular trustee was essential to the gift, the refusal of the College would cause the gift to fail. Buckley J. held that there was a paramount charitable intention. The particularity of the testatrix's directions was not fatal to such a construction, as the directions were not an essential part of her true intention. A scheme was ordered whereby the money was payable to the College on the trusts of the will, but omitting the religious disqualification.

This decision has been criticised as too lenient an application of the principles,[44] but criticisms of it were said to be ill-founded in *Re Woodhams (deceased)*,[45] where the testator left money to two music colleges to found annual scholarships for "the complete musical education of a promising boy who is an absolute orphan and only of British Nationality and Birth from any one of Dr. Barnado's Homes or the Church of England Children's Society Homes." The two colleges declined the gifts because it would be impractical to restrict the scholarships as required by the testator, but were prepared to accept them if available for boys of British nationality and birth generally. The gift failed for impracticability , but a paramount charitable intention to further musical education was found. The restriction to orphans from the named homes was not essential to the testator's purpose. Thus the gift was applicable *cy-près* under a scheme whereby the restriction was deleted.

(ii) Has the Gift Failed? Continuation in Another Form. A gift to a defunct charity may be regarded as not having failed at all, on the basis that it is continuing in another form. It may have been amalgamated with a similar charity by scheme, or have been reconstituted under more effective trusts. In such a case the gift may take effect in favour of the body now administering the assets of the old charity. Or the court may construe the gift as being for the purposes of the named charity, so that the nomination of a defunct charity does not cause the gift to fail. Provided the purposes still exist the gift takes effect in favour of a body furthering those purposes. It will be appreciated that the significance of holding that such a gift has not failed is that it is not necessary to find a general charitable intention. A scheme will be ordered to give effect to the gift, but it will not be a *cy-près* scheme.

---

[44] See *Tudor on Charities* (6th ed.), pp. 247–248, repeated in the 7th ed., p. 237, in spite of the comments in *Re Woodhams*.
[45] [1981] 1 W.L.R. 493.

(a) *Gift in Augmentation of Funds of Defunct Charity*

In *Re Faraker*,[46] there was a gift to "Mrs. Bayley's Charity, Roth-erhithe." A charity had been founded by a Mrs. Hannah Bayly in 1756 for the benefit of poor widows in Rotherhithe. This, with a number of other local charities had been consolidated under a scheme by the Charity Commissioners in 1905, and the funds were held in various trusts for the benefit of the poor in Rotherhithe. The Court of Appeal held that the Bayly trusts had not been destroyed by the scheme, and that the consolidated charities were entitled to the legacy. The gift had not failed, because a perpetual charity cannot die.[47]

(b) *Gifts for Purposes. Unincorporated Associations and Charitable Corporations.*

In considering whether a gift is effectively for the pur-poses of the named institution, a distinction is drawn between gifts to unincorporated societies and to corporations. "Every bequest to an unincorporated charity by name without more must take effect as a gift for a charitable purpose ... a bequest which is in terms made for a charitable purpose will not fail for lack of a trustee but will be carried into effect either under the Sign Manual or by means of a scheme"[48]; unless the testator's intention was to the contrary. On the other hand, "a bequest to a corporate body ... takes effect simply as a gift to that body beneficially, unless there are circumstances which show that the recipient is to take the gift as a trustee. There is no need in such a case to infer a trust for any particular purpose."[49] Thus a gift to a defunct charitable corporation lapses and fails,[50] and *cy-près* application is possible only if there was a general charitable intention. In *Re Finger's Will Trusts*,[51] there was a gift to the National Radium Commission (unincorporated) and to the National Council for Maternity and Child Welfare (incorporated). Both had ceased to exist by the date of the testatrix's death. The gift to the unincorporated charity was construed as a gift to charitable purposes. As those purposes still existed there was no failure, as a trust does not fail for lack of a trustee. A scheme

---

[46] [1912] 2 Ch. 488; *Re Lucas* [1948] Ch. 424; *cf. Re Slatter's W.T.* [1964] Ch. 512; (1964) 28 Conv.(n.s.) 313 (J. T. Farrand).

[47] Distinguished in *Re Stemson's W.T.* [1970] Ch. 16 (involving a terminable corporate charity), and *Re Roberts* [1963] 1 W.L.R. 406, *infra*.

[48] *Per* Buckley J. in *Re Vernon's W.T.* [1972] Ch. 300n; *Re Finger's W.T.* [1972] Ch. 286; (1972) 36 Conv.(n.s.) 198 (R. B. M. Cotterell); (1974) 38 Conv.(n.s.) 187 (J. Martin). See also *Liverpool and District Hospital for Diseases of the Heart* v. *Att.-Gen.* [1982] Ch. 193 (charitable corporation does not hold as trustee, but court has *cy-près* jurisdiction on winding-up; Companies Act 1985, s.558).

[49] *Ibid.* See [1984] Conv. 112 (J. Warburton).

[50] Unless the testator has indicated that the corporation was to take as trustee for its purposes.

[51] [1972] Ch. 286. The decision was applied by the Court of Appeal in *Re Koeppler's W.T.* [1986] Ch. 423. If the purposes had ceased to exist, the gift to the unincorporated charity would fail, but could be applied *cy-près* if there was a general charitable intention.

was ordered to settle the destination of the gift, but this was not a *cy-près* scheme and no general charitable intention was necessary.[52] In the case of the incorporated charity, on the other hand, it was a gift to a legal person which had ceased to exist, and was not a purpose trust. The gift therefore failed, but was saved from lapse by the finding of a general charitable intention, and was accordingly applied *cy-près*.

This is a technical distinction which might not be appreciated by the testator, but it has a certain logic. One difficulty which remains is that the same facts may allow either the *Re Faraker* construction or that adopted in *Re Finger's Will Trusts* in the case of the unincorporated charity, although the results are different. While both constructions avoid the finding of a failure and the need for a general charitable intention, the result of the *Re Faraker* construction is that the gift goes to the body now administering the funds of the defunct charity, even if its purposes are different. In *Re Faraker*[53] itself, the defunct charity was specifically for widows, while the new consolidated charity was for the poor generally, so that it "was not bound to give one penny to a widow,"[54] thus defeating the testator's intention to some extent. The result in *Re Finger's Will Trusts*[55] is that the gift is devoted, by means of a scheme, to the testator's purpose. It may be that the court would decline to apply *Re Faraker* where the purposes of the new body were widely different. Thus in *Re Roberts*,[56] a gift was made to the Sheffield Boys' Working Home, which had wound up and transferred most of its assets to the Sheffield Town Trust. The claim of the latter body was rejected as an undesirable extension of the *Re Faraker* principle, as its purposes were different. The money was applied, by means of an ordinary scheme, to the purposes to which the defunct Home had been dedicated.

Both constructions, however, were rejected in *Re Spence*,[57] where money was left to a specified Old Folks Home, "for the benefit of the patients." The home was no longer in use at the testatrix's death. Megarry V.-C. held that the gift failed and could not be applied *cy-près*. It was not a general gift to the old people of the district. Following *Re Harwood*,[58] it was said that if a particular institution is correctly identified, then it is that institution and no other which is intended: "It is difficult to envisage a testator as being suffused with a general glow of broad charity when he is labouring, and labouring successfully, to identify some particular specified institution or pur-

---

[52] It would be otherwise if the donor intended the particular institution and no other, as in *Re Rymer, supra*.
[53] [1912] 2 Ch. 488.
[54] *Ibid.* at p. 496.
[55] [1972] Ch. 286.
[56] [1963] 1 W.L.R. 406. See (1974) 38 Conv.(N.S.) 187 (J. Martin).
[57] [1979] Ch. 483.
[58] [1936] Ch. 285, *post* p. 433. *Re Rymer* [1895] 1 Ch. 19, *ante* p. 429, was also relied on.

pose as the object of his bounty."[59] This, with respect, is a very narrow view of the *cy-près* doctrine. A testator should always be careful to identify his beneficiary correctly. It is difficult to see why this should automatically negative a general charitable intention.

(iii) Projects. The cases so far discussed have dealt with gifts to institutions, corporate or unincorporated. The same rules apply in principle also to cases where there is a gift for a purpose or project such as, for example, the payment of a schoolmaster at a school to be built,[60] or a holiday home for clergymen of the Church of England and their wives,[61] or for the erection of rest homes,[62] or the establishment of a soup kitchen and cottage hospital.[63] In such cases, the question is whether the project is on the balance of probabilities capable or incapable or being implemented. If it is incapable, then, in the absence of wider intent, the gift will fail and will fall into residue. There is, it will be noted, no "wait and see" provision.[64]

(iv) Non-Existent Charity. In *Re Harwood*,[65] it was said that, where there was a gift for a non-existent charity, it was easier to find a general charitable intent in a case where the institution had never existed than it was in the case where an identifiable institution had ceased to exist.

In that case, a testatrix, who died in 1934, left £200 to the Wisbech Peace Society and £300 to the Peace Society in Belfast. The Wisbech Society had existed prior to 1934, but had ceased by that date to exist. There was no evidence that the Peace Society of Belfast had ever existed. The former failed, but Farwell J. was able to find an intention to "benefit societies whose object was the promotion of peace,"[66] and the £300 was applied *cy-près*. So also where there was an intention to benefit an ex-servicemen's charity, but it was not clear which one was intended.[67]

Similarly, in *Re Satterthwaite's Will Trusts*,[68] where a testatrix, who

---

[59] *Ibid.* at p. 493.
[60] *Re Wilson* [1913] 1 Ch. 314.
[61] *Re Packe* [1918] 1 Ch. 437.
[62] *Re Good's W.T.* [1950] 2 All E.R. 653.
[63] *Biscoe* v. *Jackson* (1887) 35 Ch.D. 460.
[64] *Re White's W.T.* [1955] Ch. 188; *Re Tacon* [1958] Ch. 447 at pp. 453–455, Lord Evershed M.R. admirably summarises these rules.
[65] [1936] Ch. 285; *Re Davis* [1902] 1 Ch. 876; *cf. Re Goldschmidt* [1957] 1 W.L.R. 524, where a gift to a non-existent charity was not applied *cy-près*, but fell into residue, which was also given to charity.
[66] *Ibid.* at p. 288. But the decision was doubted by the High Court in *Re Koeppler's Will Trusts* [1984] Ch. 243, on the basis that the purpose was political and not charitable. It was not cited in the Court of Appeal, [1986] Ch. 423.
[67] *Re Sargent* [1956] 1 W.L.R. 897. Ultimately a third organisation was held to be the one intended: [1956] 1 W.L.R. 1311.
[68] [1966] 1 W.L.R. 277.

hated the whole human race, left her residuary estate to a number of institutions concerned with animal welfare. Most of them were charitable, but a dispute arose over the share left to the London Animal Hospital. There was no charity of that name, but the plaintiff, a veterinary surgeon, carried on a practice under that trade name at a time prior to the date of the will and death. The Court of Appeal considered the gift as being to a non-existent charitable institution, and not to the plaintiff. A sufficiently wide charitable intent was found, and thus *cy-près* application was ordered.

(v) A Group of Donees; Mostly Charitable. A difficult question of construction arises where the testator has made a number of gifts to institutions, all of which are charitable except one. It can be argued that the intention clearly was to apply all the money for charitable purposes. On the other hand, "if you meet seven men with black hair and one with red hair, you are not entitled to say that here are eight men with black hair."[69] A gift to a non-charitable institution is not made charitable by being included in a list of other institutions which are charitable. So held Buckley J. in *Re Jenkins' Will Trusts*[70] where the offending gift was in favour of the British Union for the Abolition of Vivisection. This may be contrasted with *Re Satterthwaite's Will Trusts*,[71] where the gift in question was construed as charitable.

C. Subsequent Failure

Once assets are effectively dedicated to charity, there can be no question of a lapse or a resulting trust save where the gift effectively provides for it. Width of charitable intent is irrelevant. All that is necessary is that the property has been given "out and out" to charity, in the sense that the donor did not envisage its return in any circumstances.

In *Re Wright*,[72] a testatrix who died in 1933 provided for the foundation, on the death of a tenant for life, of a convalescent home for impecunious gentlewomen. The scheme was practicable in 1933, but the balance of probabilities was against it in 1942 when the tenant for life died. The Court of Appeal held that 1933 was the crucial date; at that date the scheme was practicable, dedication to charity occurred, and the possibility of a lapse or resulting trust was excluded. *Cy-près* was available in 1942 irrespective of width of charitable intent.

[69] *Per* Buckley J. in *Re Jenkins' W.T.* [1966] Ch. 249.
[70] *Supra.*
[71] *Supra.*
[72] [1954] Ch. 347; *Re Slevin* [1891] 2 Ch. 236, where the donee, the Orphanage of St. Dominic's, Newcastle-on-Tyne, was in existence at the testator's death, but came to an end before the money was paid over. *Cy-près* application was ordered; *Re Moon's W.T.* [1948] 1 All E.R. 300. See also *Harris* v. *Sharp* (unreported), noted [1988] Conv. 288 (D. Partington).

This rule is now firmly established,[73] but it was not always so, and it is not possible to reconcile some earlier cases on the subject, in particular the "surplus" cases.

In *Re King*,[74] residue worth £1,500 was bequeathed for one stained-glass window in a church. The cost of the window could not exceed £800. Romer J. held that the whole £1,500 had been dedicated to charity with the necessary consequences that any surplus would be applied *cy-près* (in fact for a second window) irrespective of width of intent.

But in *Re Stanford*,[75] where £5,000 was bequeathed for the purpose of completing and publishing an etymological dictionary and over £1,500 remained unspent when the task was complete, Eve J. held that the surplus fell into residue.

Such a result is only justifiable if the surplus can be regarded as a case of initial impossibility *pro tanto*.[76] Similar confusion can be seen in the cases where the surplus has arisen in the circumstances of a public appeal. In *Re Welsh Hospital (Netley) Fund*[77] and *Re North Devon and West Somerset Relief Fund Trusts*[78] money was collected for purposes which were fulfilled, leaving surplus. The surplus was held applicable *cy-près* on the basis that there was a general charitable intention. If these cases are to be regarded as involving subsequent failure, it is difficult to see why such an intention is necessary. All that is required is an "out and out" gift to charity. Thus in *Re Wokingham Fire Brigade Trusts*[79] a surplus was applicable *cy-près* without the need to discover a general charitable intention. It is submitted that this approach, which was approved *obiter* by the Court of Appeal in *Re Ulverston and District New Hospital Building Trusts*[80] (involving initial failure as insufficient funds were collected) is to be preferred.

D. Termination in Favour of Non-Charity

It was seen that a donor could, if he wished, make express provision for a gift over to a third party or to himself or to his estate upon the failure of a charitable gift within the period of perpetuity.[81] The cases

---

[73] *Re Tacon* [1958] Ch. 447, a case of a contingent gift; *cf. Re J. W. Laing Trust* [1984] Ch. 143, [1984] Conv. 319 (J. Warburton).

[74] [1923] 1 Ch. 243.

[75] [1924] 1 Ch. 73, criticised in *Tudor on Charities* (7th ed.), p. 278.

[76] See Picarda, p. 266; *Tudor on Charities* (7th ed.), pp. 268–273.

[77] [1921] 1 Ch. 655; *cf. Re British Red Cross Balkan Fund* [1914] 2 Ch. 419. The latter case is doubted in *Tudor on Charities* (7th ed.), p. 271, n. 86.

[78] [1953] 1 W.L.R. 1260.

[79] [1951] Ch. 373.

[80] [1956] Ch. 622. The case illustrates the difficulties now resolved by Charities Act 1960, s.14, *post.* p. 440. s.14 does not apply to the surplus cases unless it becomes established that a general charitable intention is necessary, contrary to the view expressed in the text.

[81] *Ante.* p. 429.

turn on the technicalities of conveyancing.[82] A possibility of reverter consequent upon the termination of what was known as a determinable interest was until 1964 immune from the perpetuity rule, while a gift over (in any form) was subject to it. The distinction was technical, being in effect only a matter of drafting,[83] but was well established.[84] In addition, the courts would occasionally imply a resulting trust by operation of law where the gift to charity was not absolute but the gift over to a third party was void for perpetuity, and such a resulting trust was also immune from the perpetuity rule.[85] Hence, it was possible by the use of appropriate language to bring about a devolution of charitable funds at a distant and uncertain point in time against the general policy of the perpetuity rule. Where the language of determinable interests was not used, however, but that of an absolute gift subject to an executory gift over which was void, the effect was to render the initial gift absolute. It could continue indefinitely,[86] if appropriate, or could be made the subject of a scheme *cy-près*.[87] There would never be a resulting trust.

Under Perpetuities and Accumulations Act 1964, s.12, which applies to instruments coming into effect after July 15, 1964, both possibilities of reverter and resulting trusts are subjected to the rule. But the rule is itself considerably altered by the Act, in that dispositions are no longer void on the ground that they might vest outside the perpetuity period. It is now necessary to "wait and see" whether or not a disposition vests within the period.[88] A few examples will show the considerations that now govern these cases.

In *Re Randell*,[89] a testatrix bequeathed £14,000 to trustees upon trust that they should pay the annual proceeds to the successive incumbents of a church "so long as the . . . incumbents shall permit all the sittings in the said church to be occupied free of all claims for pew rents." There was a void direction for the £14,000 to fall into residue should pew rents be claimed. North J. held that this was a determinable limitation, free from the application of the perpetuity rule, and that, on pew rent being claimed (at however remote a future date), a resulting trust would arise.

---

[82] See further Morris and Leach, Chap. 7; Maudsley, *The Modern Law of Perpetuities*, pp. 69–71, 190, and (1961) 25 Conv.(N.S.) 56 (J. D. Davies).

[83] "So long as," "until" and similar words denote a determinable interest; *ante*, p. 182.

[84] See (1937) 53 L.Q.R. 24 at p. 57 (W. O. Hart).

[85] *Re Cooper's Conveyance Trusts* [1956] 1 W.L.R. 1096; *post*, p. 437.

[86] *Re Engels* [1943] 1 All E.R. 506. For an unusual example with the effect of allowing the whole of a sum given by a settlor to be applicable to only a part of his scheme, see *George Drexler Ofrex Foundation Trustees* v. *I.R.C.* [1966] Ch. 675.

[87] *Re Peel's Release* [1921] 2 Ch. 218.

[88] s.3(1).

[89] (1888) 39 Ch.D. 213.

Under the present law such a resulting trust is subject to the rule, and a "wait and see" period will apply.[90] If, during the "wait and see" period, pew rents are claimed, the resulting trust will come into effect but, if the rents are not claimed within the period, the initial gift will become absolute.

In *Re Peel's Release*,[91] a donor conveyed land to trustees to be used for the education of 70 poor children, but he went on to provide that if certain conditions could not in the future be complied with, the land was to revert to the donor, his heirs or assigns. Sargant J. held that the provision for reverter, being conditional and not determinable, was caught by the rule against perpetuities and, as it could take effect at any time in the future, was void, and had been void from the very beginning. The land was accordingly devoted to charity in perpetuity. It was therefore, an "out and out" gift to charity, and applicable *cy-près*. Under the present law, the provision for reverter would not be void *ab initio*; section 3(5) of the Act would produce a "wait and see" period consisting of the life of the donor plus 21 years.

Limitations of the sort that arose in *Gibson* v. *South American Stores*[92] and *Re Cooper's Conveyance Trusts*[93] would also now raise different considerations. In the latter case there was a gift to charity "for ever" but subject to a gift over in more emphatic terms than those of *Re Peel's Release*,[94] in so far as the donor had specified that in certain events the property was to go to X and "for no other trust or purpose whatsoever." The gift over was void, but it was held to negative any intention to give "out and out" to charity, which was necessary to a *cy-près* application. Thus the property resulted to the donor. Under the present law, however, the prior gift becomes absolute where a possibility of reverter or a resulting trust is void for perpetuity.[95] This means that, whatever the donor's intention, the gift is by statute an "out and out" gift to charity. If neither the gift over nor the resulting trust can take effect, the *cy-près* doctrine is available. If, however, the gift over or resulting trust does not infringe the perpetuity rule, it will take effect, to the exclusion of that doctrine, because the gift to charity is not "out and out."

---

[90] Perpetuities and Accumulations Act 1964, ss.3 and 12; Maudsley, *The Modern Law of Perpetuities*, p. 190; *ante*, p. 365.
[91] [1921] 2 Ch. 218.
[92] [1950] Ch. 177 at. pp. 198–203.
[93] [1956] 1 W.L.R. 1096.
[94] *Supra*.
[95] Perpetuities and Accumulations Act 1964, s.12(1), *supra*.

E. The Widening of Cy-Près Jurisdiction. Charities Act 1960, s.13

(i) General. As part of the policy of modernising charitable trusts, the Charities Act 1960 introduced far-reaching reforms in the application of the *cy-près* doctrine.[96] Before examining these reforms it must be emphasised that it is the trustees' duty, where some or all of the property may be applied *cy-près*, to take steps to have the property so applied.[97] This situation will arise where there is an existing trust for outdated objects; for purposes which were once useful, but are now unnecessary, or overtaken by statutory services; or where the income of the trust has during the years become inadequate for the purpose, or, perhaps so large that there is a surplus. In short, the policy is to enable the trustees, with the help of the Charity Commissioners, to make the best use, in modern conditions, of funds dedicated to charity.

(ii) Section 13. Section 13 provides for application *cy-près* in five situations:

(1) Subject to subsection (2) below, the circumstances in which the original purposes of a charitable gift can be altered to allow the property given or part of it to be applied *cy-près* shall be as follows:
(*a*) where the original purposes, in whole or in part,—
  (i) have been as far as may be fulfilled; or
  (ii) cannot be carried out, or not according to the directions given and to the spirit of the gift; or
(*b*) where the original purposes provide a use for part only of the property available by virtue of the gift; or
(*c*) where the property available by virtue of the gift and other property applicable for similar purposes can be more effectively used in conjunction, and to that end can suitably, regard being had to the spirit of the gift, be made applicable to common purposes; or
(*d*) where the original purposes were laid down by reference to an area which then was but has since ceased to be a unit for some other purpose, or by reference to a class of persons or to an area which has for any reason since ceased to be suitable, regard being had to the spirit of the gift, or to be practical in administering the gift; or
(*e*) where the original purposes, in whole or in part, have, since they were laid down,—
  (i) been adequately provided by other means; or
  (ii) ceased, as being useless or harmful to the community or for other reasons, to be in law charitable; or

---

[96] It has recently been suggested that the doctrine might be redefined by statute; Annual Report 1987, para. 46.
[97] s.13(5).

(iii) ceased in any other way to provide a suitable and effective method of using the property available by virtue of
the gift, regard being had to the spirit of the gift.

(2) Subsection (1) above shall not affect the conditions which must
be satisfied in order that property given for charitable purposes may
be applied *cy-près*, except in so far as those conditions require a
failure of the original purposes.

In the case of subsequent failure, width of charitable intent is of no
significance, but the Commissioners endeavour to follow the spirit of
the original gift, so far as this is consistent with proper application of
the funds. "The paramount principle that the donor's intent must be
followed as closely as possibly has been preserved, but his intention is
now interpreted in the light of modern conditions and having regard to
the spirit of the gift."[98]

Many schemes have been made by the Commissioners under this
section. In their Annual Report for 1970, they say that they "have
made good use of the powers contained in section 13(1)(*e*)(i) [purpose
adequately provided for by other means]. . . . For example, we have
made schemes for a number of charities established for the repair of
roads and bridges, substituting for those purposes other general purposes for the benefit of local inhabitants which could include, for
instance, the promotion of the arts, the provision of seats and shelters,
the preservation of old buildings, or the improvement of local
amenities."[99]

The first occasion on which the section was litigated was *Re Lepton's
Charity*.[1]

A will dating from 1715, instructed trustees to pay £3 per annum
to the Minister, and the "overplus of the profits" to the poor. At that
time, the income was £5 per annum, and in 1970 the income from the
proceeds of sale of the land was nearly £800. Pennycuick V.-C.
raised the income payment to £100 per annum. This was consistent
with the spirit of the gift. Subsection (1)(*a*) applied because "the
original purposes" covered the purposes as a whole; it was not
necessary to consider separately the gift of the annuity and that of
the surplus. In any case (1)(*e*)(iii) would have applied.

More recently, in *Re J. W. Laing Trust*,[2] concerning a settlement of
shares worth £15,000 in 1922, the question which arose was whether
section 13 could be utilised in order to dispense with the donor's
requirement that the capital and income be distributed no later than 10
years after his death. The investment was now worth £24 million. The

---

[98] Annual Report 1970, para. 41; see also 1973, para. 11.
[99] *Ibid*. para. 43.
[1] [1972] Ch. 276.
[2] [1984] Ch. 143, [1984] Conv. 319 (J. Warburton); [1985] Conv. 313 (P. Luxton).

trust was for Christian evangelical causes, and the individuals and bodies who would be the recipients were unsuited to receive large capital sums. It was held that the provision could not be deleted under section 13(1), as "the original purposes" which the court could there review meant the objects of the trust, whereas the settlor's direction was merely administrative. The provision was, however, deleted under the court's inherent jurisdiction.[3]

Subsection (1)(*e*)(ii) may give rise to difficulty at some future time. Clearly, it will apply to the endowments of independent schools if the privileges of charitable status should be, as has been threatened, withdrawn.[4] Perhaps also the section would, if then available, have applied to anti-vivisection trusts, for these had been held charitable in *Re Foveaux*,[5] but non-charitable in *National Anti-Vivisection Society* v. *I.R.C.*[6] in 1948. The same may apply to charities which have been removed from the Register; for they were conclusively presumed to be charitable while registered, and have been removed on the ground that they are not. They would appear to have "ceased to be charitable." Similarly, it may be worth arguing that a trust for the education of persons in a private group comes within the section; for such trusts were accorded fiscal privileges by the Revenue prior to *Re Compton*.[7]

(iii) Section 14. Charity Collections. Finally, it is necessary to refer to section 14, which provides for application *cy-près*, regardless of width of intent, where property has been given for specific charitable purposes which fail,

    (a) by a donor who, after reasonable advertisements and inquiries, cannot be identified or cannot be found,[8] or

    (b) by a donor who has executed a written disclaimer of his rights.[9]

In the case of the proceeds of cash collections by means of collecting boxes or other means not adapted for distinguishing one gift from

---

[3] *Ante.* p. 428.

[4] *Labour Party Manifesto*, 1974, and subsequently.

[5] [1895] 2 Ch. 501.

[6] [1948] A.C. 31. Lord Simonds suggested at pp. 64–65 that application *cy-près* would have been possible before the Act.

[7] [1945] Ch. 123; counsel in *Dingle* v. *Turner* [1972] A.C. 601, suggested that the provision might apply to poor relations trusts if the House of Lords overruled the previous decisions and invalidated existing trusts. *Davies* v. *Perpetual Trustee Ltd.* [1959] A.C. 439. See also (1974) 38 Conv.(N.S.) 231 at p. 233.

[8] Such donors may claim within 12 months of the scheme, s.14(4). For an example of the operation of s.14 see *Re Henry Wood Memorial Trust* [1966] 1 W.L.R. 1601 (failure of Mile End Memorial Hall Fund through lack of financial support); Annual Report 1965, paras. 19–21.

[9] See Annual Report 1980, paras. 135–136 (South Scarborough Swimming Pool Association); Annual Report 1982, paras. 62–63 (South Petherton Swimming Pool Fund, Somerset).

another, or the proceeds of lotteries and similar money-raising activities, the property is conclusively presumed to belong to unidentifiable donors, without any advertisement or inquiry. In other cases the court may direct the property to be treated as belonging to unidentifiable donors, without any advertisement or inquiry, if it appears that it would not be reasonable, having regard to the amounts or the lapse of time since the gifts, to return it.

Section 14 applies only to cases of initial failure, subsection (5) providing that charitable purposes are deemed to fail, for the purposes of the section, where any difficulty in applying the property to those purposes makes it available for return to the donors.[10] In the case of subsequent failure, the property is not so available.

This solution is much more sensible than any attempt to solve the problem by applying the usual *cy-près* doctrine, involving either the imputation of an artificial general charitable intent, or, failing that, a search for the many donors of tiny gifts, with the possibility of a claim by the Crown to the property as *bona vacantia*.

F. Charities Act 1985[11]

The Charities Act 1985, "a modest and useful reform,"[12] introduces a new principle enabling certain charity trustees in effect to determine their own *cy-près* application with the concurrence of the Charity Commissioners. The procedure is simpler than under the 1960 Act and is designed to achieve a more effective use of the assets of small charities.

Section 2 of the Act allows the trustees to pass a unanimous resolution to alter the objects of the charity to other legally charitable objects which are not so dissimilar to the original objects as to constitute an unjustifiable departure from the founder's intentions or a violation of the spirit of the gift.

This may be done if the following conditions are satisfied:

(a) it is a local charity for the relief of poverty,
(b) it is not an exempt or incorporated charity,
(c) it was founded at least 50 years previously,
(d) the trustees consider that the objects are obsolete, lacking in usefulness or impossible of achievement, having regard to changed circumstances since it was founded,
(e) and that the objects should be altered in order to put the

[10] See [1983] Conv. 40 (D. Wilson), arguing that this is never the case where the donor is anonymous, because the property either goes *cy-près* by the imputation of a general charitable intent (see *Re Hillier* [1954] 1 W.L.R. 700) or to the Crown as *bona vacantia*.
[11] See [1986] Conv. 78 (M. Sladen); (1986) 1 *Trust Law & Practice* 76 (J. M. Fryer). The Act came into force on January 1, 1986.
[12] Annual Report 1984, para. 11.

resources to better use, consistently with the spirit of the original gift.

The trustees must take reasonable steps to secure the approval of the
founder, if still living, and must give reasonable public notice. Copies
of the resolution are to be sent to the Commissioners and the local
authority. If the Commissioners concur, the trusts of the charity are
deemed modified in accordance with the resolution.

Under section 3, trustees of a registered unincorporated charity (or
one not required to be registered) having an income of £200 or less in
the preceding accounting period may pass a unanimous resolution that
the property be transferred to another charity. The transferee charity
must be willing to accept it and must have objects not so far dissimilar
to those of the transferor as to make the transfer an unjustifiable
departure from the intentions of the founder of the transferor charity
or to violate the spirit of the gift. The section is subject to similar
safeguards as section 2 and likewise requires the concurrence of the
Commissioners. It is not confined to local poverty charities.

Section 4 applies to very small charities having a permanent endowment (*i.e.* capital) of £25 or less, no land, and a gross income of £5 or
less. Where the trustees consider that no useful purpose can be served
in spending the income, they can pass a resolution that the capital be
spent, after considering a transfer to another charity under section 3.
This is not confined to local poverty charities and is subject to the same
safeguards as sections 2 and 3.

In spite of publicity the response from trustees so far has been very
modest.[13] It has, accordingly, been suggested that the application of
the Act should be extended, for example by increasing the money
limits, and that the procedures should be simplified.[14]

7. The Administration of Charities[15]

A. The Need for Reform

Reform of the law of charities was long overdue when the Charities
Act, based upon the recommendations of the Nathan Committee[16] was
passed in 1960. The major problems were: the narrow limits of the
cy-près doctrine,[17] which prevented the bringing up to date of a number of old charities; the gap and the competition which existed between
the established charities and the statutory services of the welfare state;
the haphazard state of existing charities and the lack of information

---

[13] Annual Report 1986, para. 14; Annual Report 1987, para. 49.
[14] Annual Report 1987, para. 50.
[15] See generally Maudsley and Burn, *Trusts and Trustees, Cases and Materials* (3rd ed.),
  Chap. 11.
[16] The Committee on the Law and Practice relating to Charitable Trusts, Cmnd. 8710 of
  1952, para. 140.
[17] *Ante*, p. 427.

about them. The Charities Act 1960 contained reforms on these matters, and the opportunity was taken to consolidate all the statute law on charitable trusts since the days of Elizabeth I.

Reform at the present day is directed towards increasing the supervision of charities by the Charity Commissioners in order to minimise abuse and maladministration by charity trustees.[18] To this end the powers of the Commissioners are to be increased by legislation. The various recommendations are included in the relevant sections of the account which follows.

B. The Authorities

(i) **The Charity Commissioners.**[19] The Charity Commissioners, set up originally under the Charitable Trusts Act 1853, were modernised. There is a minimum of three, and two at least must be solicitors or barristers.[20] They are civil servants appointed by the Home Secretary,[21] but act independently of his Department. They are charged with "the general function of promoting the effective use of charitable resources by encouraging the development of better methods of administration, by giving charity trustees information and advice on any matter affecting the charity and by investigating and checking abuses."[22] Various aspects of the ways in which their general powers are exercised will be examined in the sections which follow.

The Commissioners are under a duty to submit an Annual Report to the Home Secretary,[23] and their reports since give an excellent picture of the administration of the law of charities, and of the problems of the day. The reports emphasise continually the duty and the desire of the Commissioners to be helpful to trustees.[24] At present they do not charge for their services, but this is likely to change in some areas.[25]

(ii) **The Official Custodian for Charities.** The Commissioners are required to appoint one of their officers to be the Official Custodian for Charities.[26] He is a corporation sole, and charity trustees may vest trust property in him as custodian trustee. They thereby avoid "the necessity for periodical transfers of land and securities upon the

---

[18] Efficiency Scrutiny of the Supervision of Charities (the Woodfield Report), 1987; National Audit Office Report, House of Commons Paper 380, 1986–87; Annual Report 1987; [1988] Conv. 163 (H. W. Wilkinson). A White Paper is to be published in 1989.

[19] See generally (1982) 79 L.S.Gaz. 984 (J. M. Fryer).

[20] Charities Act 1960, s.1; First Sched. para. 1(2), (3). More Commissioners are to be appointed; Annual Report 1987, para. 9.

[21] *Ibid.* para. 1(2).

[22] s.1(3).

[23] s.1(5).

[24] Leaflets for the guidance of charity trustees are regularly published by the Commissioners.

[25] Annual Report 1987, para. 69 (discussing the Woodfield Report).

[26] s.3. See Annual Report 1974, para. 107.

appointment of new trustees,"[27] and the necessity to reclaim income tax on investments, as dividends are remitted without deduction.[28] It has recently been recommended, however, that charity trustees should be discouraged from using the services of the Official Custodian. The purpose of this proposal is to increase the responsibility of the trustees. His function should be reduced to the holding of land and certain other investments, and he should charge for his services.[29]

(iii) **The Visitor.**[30] Ecclesiastical[31] and eleemosynary[32] corporations are subject to the jurisdiction of the visitor in relation to their internal affairs. Modern decisions illustrate that the visitor has an important role to play in the universities. Ecclesiastical corporations are visitable by the ordinary. In the case of eleemosynary corporations, the founder may appoint a visitor. If none is appointed, the founder (or his heirs) is the visitor by operation of law.[33] A similar principle applies where the Crown is the founder. Where visitatorial powers are exercisable by the Crown, they are in practice exercised by the Lord Chancellor.

The visitor's jurisdiction stems from the power recognised by the common law in the founder of an eleemosynary corporation to provide the laws under which it was to be governed and to be sole judge of the interpretation and application of those laws, either himself or via the person appointed as visitor. Thus the visitor has exclusive jurisdiction over matters of internal management, including the admission[34] and removal[35] of members, and the award of prizes and degrees,[36] but not

---

[27] Annual Report 1970, para. 75. See Law Reform Committee 23rd Report, *The Powers and Duties of Trustees* (1982, Cmnd. 8733), to the effect that failure to appoint charity trustees by deed has resulted in conveyancing difficulties where the land is not vested in the Official Custodian for Charities. It is therefore proposed that all such land should automatically be vested in the Official Custodian on a particular date. By s.17(2) of the Charities Act 1960, the trustees could then deal with the legal estate on behalf of the custodian. *Ibid.* para. 6.3.

[28] See also A.J.A. 1982, s.41.

[29] Annual Report 1987, paras. 57–63 (discussing recommendations of the Woodfield Report).

[30] Mitcheson, *Opinion on the Visitation of Charities* (1887). See generally (1970) 86 L.Q.R. 531 (J. W. Bridge); Picarda, Chap. 39; *Tudor on Charities* (7th ed.), pp. 312–328; (1981) 97 L.Q.R. 610 (P. M. Smith); (1986) 136 N.L.J. 484, 519, 567 and 665 (P. M. Smith), adopted in *Thomas* v. *University of Bradford, infra.*

[31] Corporations existing for the furtherance of religion and the perpetuation of the rites of the Church.

[32] The original meaning was corporations whose object was the distribution of free alms, or the relief of individual distress; *Re Armitage's W.T.* [1972] Ch. 438. But for the purpose of visitatorial powers, corporate schools and modern universities are included.

[33] *Phillips* v. *Bury* (1694) Skinn. 447. If the heirs die out or cannot act, the Crown is the visitor.

[34] *Patel* v. *University of Bradford Senate, supra; cf. Herring* v. *Templeman* [1973] 3 All E.R. 569, where a student of a teachers' training college was not a "member."

[35] *Thomas* v. *University of Bradford* [1987] A.C. 795; *Hines* v. *Birkbeck College* [1986] Ch. 524 (affirmed [1987] Ch. 457n.).

[36] *R.* v. *University of London, ex p. Vijaytunga* [1988] Q.B. 322; *Oakes* v. *Sidney Sussex College, Cambridge* [1988] 1 W.L.R. 431.

disputes between the foundation and outsiders.[37] The jurisdiction of the visitor in these matters is sole and exclusive, even though a member's contract of employment is affected.[38] The visitor has power to award damages or to order reinstatement.[39] No appeal lies from his decisions unless the statutes of the corporation so provide,[40] but he is subject to the prerogative remedies of prohibition,[41] mandamus[42] and certiorari[43]; and the rules of natural justice apply to the visitor's decisions.[44] While the court cannot invade the visitor's jurisdiction, Parliament can do so. So, for example, if a question arises concerning the internal laws of the corporation in proceedings under the Employment Protection (Consolidation) Act 1978, it must be resolved by the tribunal and not the visitor.[45]

C. The Register[46]

Section 4 requires the Commissioners to maintain a register[47] on which all charities are to be included except for (a) exempt charities,[48] (b) any charity excepted by order or regulation,[49] and (c) any charity having no permanent endowment, nor any income from property amounting to more than £15 per annum, nor the use and occupation of land, and (d) in respect of a place of worship. The purpose of the register is to obtain information about charities.[50] Those which are not required to register are those which are national institutions (exempt charities), very small ones not occupying land, and others such as ecclesiastical charities where provision for obtaining the necessary information already exists.

---

[37] *Casson* v. *University of Aston in Birmingham* [1983] 1 All E.R. 88 (dispute over contract entered into with student before he was a member). In *Thomas* v. *University of Bradford, supra*, this decision was upheld as correct on the facts but criticised as taking too narrow a view of the visitor's jurisdiction.

[38] *Thomas* v. *University of Bradford, supra*; (1987) 46 C.L.J. 384 (C. Lewis).

[39] *Ibid.*

[40] *Thorne* v. *University of London* [1966] 2 Q.B. 237; *Patel* v. *University of Bradford Senate, supra*; (1974) 37 M.L.R. 324 (D. Christie); (1974) 33 C.L.J. 23 (S. A. de Smith).

[41] *Bentley* v. *Bishop of Ely* (1729) 1 Barn. 192.

[42] *R.* v. *Dunsheath* [1951] 1 K.B. 127 at p. 134.

[43] *Thomas* v. *University of Bradford, supra*; *R.* v. *University of London, ex p. Vijaytunga, supra*.

[44] *R.* v. *Bishop of Ely* (1794) 5 Term Rep. 475.

[45] *Thomas* v. *University of Bradford, supra*.

[46] Computerisation has been recommended; Annual Report 1987, para. 10 (following the Woodfield Report).

[47] Annual Report 1970, para. 17.

[48] Charities Act 1960, Second Sched.

[49] S.I. 1963 No. 2074; S.I. 1964 No. 1825 (Religious Charities); S.I. 1961 No. 1044 (Boy Scouts and Girl Guides); S.I. 1965 No. 1056 (Armed Forces); S.I. 1966 No. 965 (Non-exempt Universities).

[50] See Annual Report 1961, para. 15; 1970, para. 17.

D. Decisions on Registration

It is the duty of trustees of charities to register, and the Commissioners have power to compel, though these powers have never been used.[51] Registration is much to the advantage of the trustees, for it raises a conclusive presumption of being a charity,[52] and of being entitled therefore to the privileges accorded to charity. Non-entry gives rise to no presumption either way.

The decision to register a claimant is that of the Charity Commissioners, and an account of recent decisions is given in the Annual Reports. In this way, the development of charity law is greatly influenced by the Commissioners. Any person who may be affected by registration, such as a residuary legatee in the case of a will charity, may object to registration, or apply for removal.[53] Nearly all these matters are finally disposed of by the Commissioners but there is provision for an appeal to the High Court from any decision of the Commissioners.[54] In making their decision, the Commissioners are aware of the need for flexibility, and for keeping the law of charities in tune with changing circumstances. They have not always been able to satisfy the critics, who assume that charitable purposes should include all useful projects of reform. The Commissioners sometimes have a narrow line to follow between the attacks of the critics and the decisions which bind them.[55] By the end of 1987, 161,376 charities had been registered, and during that year 198 charities were removed from the Register,[56] mainly because they had ceased to operate. On the matter of removal, the Commissioners are not bound by the view of the Attorney General.[57]

E. Advice

The Commissioners may also give to any charity trustees (without charge) an opinion or advice on any matter affecting the performance

---

[51] Charities Act, s.4(6): Annual Report 1970, para. 22.

[52] *Ibid.* s.5(1); *Re Murawski's W.T.* [1971] 1 W.L.R. 707.

[53] *Ibid.* s.5(2). Annual Report 1978, para. 84.

[54] *Ibid.* s.5(3); *Incorporated Council of Law Reporting for England and Wales* v. *Att.-Gen.* [1972] Ch. 73; *Re Murawski's W.T.* [1971] 1 W.L.R. 707; *Re Construction Industry Training Board* [1973] Ch. 173, following which decision, most industrial training Boards established under the provisions of the Industrial Training Act 1964 have been registered; Annual Report 1973, para. 39; *ante*, p. 388, *I.R.C.* v. *McMullen* [1981] A.C. 1, where H.L. upheld the decision of the Commissioners to register (reversing Walton J. and C.A.); p. 387, *ante*; *McGovern* v. *Att.-Gen.* [1982] Ch. 321, where Slade J. upheld the Commissioners' refusal to register; *Joseph Rowntree Memorial Trust Housing Association Ltd.* v. *Att.-Gen* [1983] Ch. 159, where refusal was reversed.

[55] Annual Report 1966, paras. 27–41.

[56] Annual Report 1987, para. 11. In 1987 3,672 were registered; *ibid.* It is estimated that there are 250,000 charities in the U.K.; *ibid.*, para. 27.

[57] See Annual Report 1982, paras. 36–38, App. C, for the Commissioners' refusal to accede to the request of the Attorney-General to remove the Church of Unification (The "Moonies") from the register. (The Attorney-General's action has since been dropped.)

of his duties, and a trustee acting upon it is deemed to have acted in accordance with the trust.[58] The Commissioners' advice is also available where an application is made to register a new charity. If the application is refused, the reason will be given so that the language may be amended. It is not of course possible to alter the terms of established trusts which fail to be registered. The *cy-près* doctrine only applies to charities.[59]

F. Powers of the Charity Commissioners

(i) **Schemes.** The Charity Commissioners have concurrent jurisdiction with the High Court in establishing schemes for the administration of a charity.[60] Much of their day-to-day work consists of making schemes and orders to help the trustees of charities to administer them more efficiently and to make better use of their funds and property. Schemes may cover the appointment of new bodies of trustees, the vesting of property in new trustees or in a custodian trustee, the provision of new *cy-près* objects in place of objects which have become impracticable, the extension of the trustees' investment powers, and the grouping or amalgamation of charities. Schemes which deal with only one or two of these subjects are usually short and comparatively simple, whereas others, including some which provide for the complete regulation of the charity, may be long and complicated and may necessitate detailed discussion with the trustees.[61] Schemes are usually made by the Commissioners on the application of a charity, or where the court, on directing a scheme, orders that the Commissioners shall settle the scheme.[62] We shall see that it is the duty of charity trustees to secure the effective use of charity property.[63] If they unreasonably refuse or neglect to apply for a scheme in circumstances in which they ought, in the interest of the charity, to do so, the Commissioners may apply to the Home Secretary for an order for a scheme to be made in the case of a charity at least 40 years old.[64] No such action has yet been taken by the Commissioners.

(ii) **Consent to Proceedings.** By section 28 of the Charities Act 1960, no court proceedings relating to a charity (other than an exempt

---

[58] Charities Act 1960, s.24.
[59] *Ante* p. 427.
[60] *Ibid.* s.18(1). See also Reverter of Sites Act 1987, s.2.
[61] Annual Report 1978, paras. 99–100. For illustrations see Annual Report 1982, paras. 52–54.
[62] *Ibid.* s.18(2). As to the right of appeal, see *Childs* v. *Att.-Gen.* [1973] 1 W.L.R. 497.
[63] *Ibid.* s.13(5).
[64] *Ibid.* s.18(6). The restriction to charities 40 years old was introduced in order to protect donors against official intervention to alter the terms of trusts within the donor's lifetime. It was thought that liability to earlier alteration would discourage charitable gifts.

charity) shall be entertained unless authorised by the Commissioners.[65] This is to prevent the dissipation of charitable funds in legal proceedings over matters which the Commissioners could resolve.

(iii) Dealings with Charity Property. Charity trustees are subject to various statutory restrictions on dealings in charity property.[66] The aim of these restrictions is "to preserve and husband the endowment so that it may continue to benefit the community."[67] Of particular importance is section 29 of the Charities Act 1960,[68] restricting the trustees' powers[69] to mortgage, sell, lease or otherwise dispose of charity land or to mortgage other property without an order of the court or of the Commissioners. Under section 23 of the Act of 1960 the Commissioners have a general power to authorise dealings with charity property which the trustees would otherwise have no power to do. Such authorisation usually applies to single transactions only, and the Commissioners prefer to "use the procedure of establishing a scheme, with its attendant publicity, in order to confer authority of a more general nature."[70] Some 4,000 orders are made annually under these provisions.[71] It has now been recommended, however, that section 29 should be repealed and replaced by a provision requiring charity trustees to follow certain statutory procedures before selling land. It is thought that the resources now devoted to the Commissioners' services in this area could be better utilised elsewhere.[72]

(iv) Accounts: Inquiries: Removal of Trustees. The Commissioners may also demand accounts,[73] and, if dissatisfied in any way, may institute inquiries.[74] Ultimately, they may remove trustees from

---

[65] See *Haslemere Estates Ltd.* v. *Baker* [1982] 1 W.L.R. 1109; *Brooks* v. *Richardson* [1986] 1 W.L.R. 385; *Bradshaw* v. *University College of Wales, Aberystwyth* [1988] 1 W.L.R. 190; *Re Hampton Fuel Allotment Charity* [1988] 3 W.L.R. 513; *Richmond upon Thames London Borough Council* v. *Rogers* [1988] 2 All E.R. 761; (1988) 2 *Trust Law & Practice* 128 (J.Thurston).

[66] See generally Picarda, *The Law and Practice Relating to Charities*, Chap. 36.

[67] *Ibid.* p. 383.

[68] As to which, see *Haslemere Estates Ltd.* v. *Baker* [1982] 1 W.L.R. 1109.

[69] Which derive from S.L.A. 1925, s.29(1), Charities Act 1960, s.23, or under the founding instrument or statute. The Law Reform Committee (23rd Report, *The Powers and Duties of Trustees*, 1982 Cmnd. 8733) has recommended that they should have power to raise money along the lines of S.L.A. 1925, s.71(1), to maintain or preserve trust property which is land; *ibid.* para. 6.5.

[70] Annual Report 1970, para. 63. See also Annual Report 1982, paras. 75–80 (sale of the Old Vic Theatre); Annual Report 1983, para. 76 (sale of Mermaid and Roundhouse Theatres).

[71] See Annual Report 1987, para. 55; (1987) 1 *Trust Law & Practice* 138 (J. Thurston).

[72] *Ibid.*, paras. 51–55.

[73] Charities Act 1960, ss.8, 32; Annual Report 1984, para. 7; Annual Report 1985, para. 10, App. C, (leaflet for the guidance of charity trustees); Annual Report 1987, App. B; Charities Act 1985, s.1.

[74] Charities Act 1960, s.6. For the wide scope of an enquiry under the section, see *Rule* v. *Charity Commissioners*, Annual Report 1979, paras. 24–36. Examples may be found in most of the Annual Reports.

office.[75] The Commissioners may be alerted by the Inland Revenue to the possible misapplication of charity funds.[76]

It is in the area of accounts and audit that much disquiet has been felt over the possibility of abuse and maladministration by charity trustees. Sanctions are now being considered for non-compliance by trustees with their obligations.[77]

G. Investment

(i) Investment Powers.[78] Until 1961, charity trustees could invest only in the old trustee securities, which in effect meant that they were restricted to government stocks and other fixed-income investments. A reference to Chapter 17 will show how serious the effect of inflation was upon the capital of such charities. The Trustee Investments Act 1961,[79] as will be seen, authorised the investment of one-half of a trust fund in shares of companies incorporated in the United Kingdom, quoted on a recognised Stock Exchange, and possessing certain qualifications as to size and record. This was not a solution to the charity trustees' problems, because Stock Exchange investment requires a considerable expertise; and sufficient capital funds to allow a reasonable spread of investments. The Official Custodian for Charities has issued a booklet, offering advice to trustees in selecting and managing their charity's investments.[80]

(ii) Pooling. C.O.I.F. Charities Deposit Fund. The court could authorise the pooling for investment purposes of the assets of different trusts held by the same trustees[81]; but, without statutory authority, different bodies of trustees could not pool their funds for investment purposes, for this would involve a delegation of the trustees' investment powers, and was inconsistent with the trustees' duty to act personally.[82] Section 22 gives power to the court or the Commissioners

---

[75] *Ibid.* ss.18, 20; *post*, p. 451. See also *Att.-Gen.* v. *Schonfeld* [1980] 1 W.L.R. 1182. (Educational charity in disarray, with uncertainty as to who could appoint new headmaster. Court, on application of Attorney-General, appointed receiver and manager to manage affairs until issues determined, so as to safeguard the assets and protect the welfare of the children).

[76] Charities Act 1960, s.9, as amended by F.A. 1986, s.33.

[77] Annual Report 1987, paras. 20–26 (following the Woodfield Report).

[78] As to whether the investment should be compatible with the purposes of the charity, see Annual Report 1987, paras. 41–45. For example, could a charity whose object is to relieve cancer invest in a cigarette company? See (1982) 45 M.L.R. 268 (H. Beynon); T.I.A. 1961, s.6(1)(b) (suitability to the trust); *Cowan* v. *Scargill* [1985] Ch. 270 (private trust); B.M.A. Report on Investment in the U.K. Tobacco Industry. See also (1987) 1 *Trust Law & Practice* 162 (J. Thurston).

[79] *Post*, p. 491. Wider powers may be approved by the court; *Trustees of the British Museum* v. *Att.-Gen.* [1984] 1 W.L.R. 418, *post*, p. 503; *Steel* v. *Wellcome Custodian Trustees Ltd.* [1988] 1 W.L.R. 167; Annual Report 1983, paras. 79 *et seq.*

[80] Annual Report 1978, para. 166, App. C; see also Annual Report 1970 paras. 69–72.

[81] *Re Royal Society's Charitable Trust* [1956] Ch. 87.

[82] *Post*, p. 532.

to create common investment schemes under which the investment of property transferred to the fund would be invested by trustees appointed to manage the fund, and the participating charities would be entitled to shares related to their contributions.[83] Under this power, the Commissioners established in 1963 the Charities Official Investment Fund, which is open to all charities. At the end of 1987 the value of the fund, including income shares and accumulation shares was over £257,000,000.[84]

In 1985 the Charities Deposit Fund was set up under section 22. The trustees of the Fund are the trustees of the C.O.I.F. The Fund is invested in banks, building societies, and local and central government. The interest rate compares favourably with money market funds and is paid without tax deduction. By the end of 1987 the Fund stood at £6.3 million.[85]

H. Trustees

(i) **Who May Be.** Any person who is capable of acting as a trustee may be trustee of a charity, except that a Local Authority may not be trustee of an eleemosynary charity.[86] We have seen that the appointment of a charity as trustee may colour the construction which a court will place upon the language of the trust, but does not ensure that a trust is charitable.[87]

(ii) **Number. Majority Vote.** There is no limit upon the number of persons who may be trustees of a charity.[88] Too great a number of trustees is an obvious inconvenience. But decisions of trustees of a charity may be taken by majority vote and need not be unanimous.[89]

(iii) **Retirement.** Charity trustees may retire in the same way as trustees of private trusts.[90] In 1982, however, the Law Reform Committee recommended that section 39 of the Trustee Act 1925[91] should be amended so as to permit a charity trustee to retire on giving formal written notice to his co-trustees, and also that some provision equivalent to section 35 of the Charities Act 1960 be introduced so that

---

[83] Annual Report 1970, paras. 68–74; 1971, para. 90; *Re London University's Charitable Trust* [1964] Ch. 284. See also A.J.A. 1982, s.42.
[84] Annual Report 1987, para. 65.
[85] *Ibid.*, para. 66.
[86] *Re Armitage* [1972] Ch. 438; *ante*, p. 421. Under new controls being drawn up by the Government, discharged bankrupts and persons with a criminal record are likely to be excluded; *The Times*, October 6, 1987.
[87] *Ante*, p. 420.
[88] T.A. 1925, s.34.
[89] *Re Whiteley* [1910] 1 Ch. 600 at p. 608.
[90] *Post*, p. 477.
[91] *Post*, p. 477.

charity trustees can produce a memorandum which will constitute evidence of the fact that one of their number has retired.[92]

(iv) Removal and Suspension. The Commissioners may remove or suspend a trustee on being satisfied as a result of inquiries[93] that there has been misconduct or mismanagement and that it is necessary or desirable in the interests of the charity,[94] and may on their own motion remove a charity trustee in case of bankruptcy, incapacity, absence, or refusal to act.[95] An inquiry was made in 1971, into the affairs of a charity called Sanctuary, whose purpose was the relief of suffering, hardship and distress among children, and in particular children born in this country of Indian or Pakistani descent. The Commissioner found mismanagement, and made an order removing the trustees; but subsequently a rehearing was obtained.[96]

(v) Supply of Goods and Services by Trustees. The question arose whether charity trustees should be prohibited from supplying goods or services to a charity. Under the ordinary rule, his fiduciary relationship would not allow him to be in a position where his duty as a trustee might conflict with his interests as an individual.[97] In many cases, however, trustees of a charity may be willing to supply goods and services on terms which are beneficial to the charity.

The Commissioners announced in their report for 1971[98] that they had altered the form of prohibitory clause commonly inserted in trusts in favour of one providing that a trustee should absent himself from any meeting of the trustees at which the provision of goods and services by him was being discussed, and that the other trustees must be satisfied that the transaction is advantageous to the charity.

(vi) Misapplication. An application by the trustee for purposes not covered by the terms of the trust is a misapplication of charity funds, which may give rise to personal liability on the trustee, and may be restrained by injunction,[99] or may be the subject of an inquiry by the Charity Commissioners.[1]

---

[92] 23rd Report, *The Powers and Duties of Trustees* (1982, Cmnd. 8733), para. 6.2.
[93] Under Charities Act 1960, s.6.
[94] s.20(1); Annual Report 1978, paras. 158–161 (Bedside Bingo).
[95] *Ibid.* subs. (3).
[96] Annual Report 1971, paras. 90–96; *Jones* v. *Att.-Gen.* [1974] Ch. 148; Annual Report 1978, paras. 31–32. (C.A. upheld decision of Brightman J. as "wholly unassailable"); Annual Report 1977, paras. 163–165 (Kidney Machine Fund).
[97] *Post*, p. 556.
[98] Para. 93. See also, on remuneration, Annual Report 1981, paras. 61–64.
[99] *Baldry* v. *Feintuck* [1972] 1 W.L.R. 552. (Resolution to apply Students' Union funds for political purposes). See Annual Report 1983, paras. 95 and 96 and App. A.
[1] *Ante*, p. 448.

I. Ex Gratia Payments

Difficulty and distress has been caused by the fact that a charity was thought to be unable to make *ex gratia* payments for non-charitable purposes, however compelling the moral obligation to do so. Thus, if a testator gave to his family his shares in certain companies, and left his residuary estate to charity, and at the time of the testator's death all the shares had been sold and the proceeds of sale fell into the residuary estate, the charity would be obtaining much more than the testator intended. Cross J. decided that, in appropriate circumstances, the court and the Attorney-General had power to give authority to make *ex gratia* payments from charitable funds; but only in case of strong moral obligation.[2] Trustees wishing to make such a payment should apply to the Charity Commissioners who will submit a report to the Attorney-General for his decision. A number of subsequent cases have been dealt with on these lines.

J. Co-operation Between Charities and Statutory Services[3]

If the best value is to be obtained from the resources available to charity trustees and local authorities, it is essential that they work in harmony. The social services of the Welfare State have taken over most of the ground of charity work, as it has been understood. This raises the question of the role of charity at the present time. Whatever view we take on this question, it has certainly changed in the last 100 years. If it is argued that all the important needs of the community are now the responsibility of the State, one conclusion is that the State should take over all funds held in charitable trusts. On the other hand, a giant bureaucratic system has its gaps and limitations; and, being users of public money, there is a danger of a lack of enterprise and experiment. Charitable trusts in this context look like a "private enterprise" social system; but it should never be forgotten that charitable trusts are users of public money too; for the fiscal privileges enjoyed by charities mean that the Revenue is losing income which it would otherwise receive. The role of charity is "to seek out the gaps in the statutory services and to pioneer new services."[4] Charities should remain independent, and "co-operation between them and the statutory services should be on the basis of partnership not subordination.[5] These are principles under which sections 10–12 of the Act are based.

[2] *Re Snowden* [1970] Ch. 700; *Re Henderson* [1960] Ch. 700; Annual Report 1969, paras. 26–31; Annual Report 1977, paras. 154–156.
[3] See Annual Report 1970, paras. 28–36; 1971, paras. 101 *et seq.*; 1972, para. 49. Social Services Act 1970. Local Authority Services Act 1970; Annual Report 1976, paras. 76–84; Annual Report 1977, paras. 51–56 (Motability: charity in partnership with State); paras. 58–62 (care of disabled). Annual Report 1978, paras. 61–63, App. A and B suggesting ways in which the income of charities for the relief of poverty and sickness may be spent without overlapping the statutory services; Annual Report 1987, para. 4.
[4] *Ibid.* para. 28.
[5] *Ibid.* para. 29, 1971, paras. 80, 84.

Section 10 authorises a county or county borough council to maintain a public index of local charities. Under section 11, the councils may initiate a review of local charities, and report to the Commissioners and make recommendations. Section 12 permits any local council to make arrangements for the co-ordination of the work of the council and of the charities in the interests of persons who may benefit from the service of either.

Although many schemes arising out of local reviews have been made,[6] few local authorities can now afford to initiate a review.[7] The ineffectiveness of many local authority reviews of charities to achieve modernisation and use of resources in co-operation with the welfare services led to the passing of the Charities Act 1985.[8] This Act, as we have seen,[9] was designed to promote greater accountability to the community by trustees of local poverty charities and to facilitate the modernisation of these and other small charities and the disposal of funds which can no longer be effectively used.

[6] H.C. Expenditure Committee Report, Vol. II, pp. 20–21; Goodman Committee Report, paras. 184–185; Annual Report 1979, para. 123.
[7] Annual Report 1980, para. 154.
[8] See Annual Report 1985, para. 1.
[9] *Ante*, p. 441.

PART III

TRUSTEES

CHAPTER 16

GENERAL PRINCIPLES: CAPACITY: APPOINTMENT: REMOVAL: RETIREMENT: CONTROL

1. ONEROUS NATURE OF OFFICE

THE office of trustee is an onerous one. We will discuss in some detail a trustee's duties, powers and liability; there is little to be said as to his rights. In the performance of his office a trustee must act exclusively in the interest of the trust. He stands to gain nothing from his work, unless special provision in the form of a clause authorising remuneration is made.[1] He is required to observe the highest standards of integrity,[2] and a reasonable standard of business efficiency in the management of the affairs of the trust; and he is subjected to onerous personal liability if he fails to reach the standards set. Nor may he compete in business with the trust; or be in a position in which his

---

[1] *Post,* p. 557. He is entitled to expenses; *post* p. 556.
[2] *Post,* p. 459.

personal interests conflict with those of the trust. He may thus be
forced to forgo opportunities which would be available to him if he
were not a trustee.[3]

It may well be asked why people consent to become trustees. To this
there are two answers. First, professional trustees undertake the work
only where express provision is made in the settlement or will providing for their remuneration. Solicitors, banks (Executor and Trustee
Departments) and insurance companies come into this category. The
Public Trustee is entitled to charge.[4] Most trusts of any size will have a
professional trustee. There may be non-professional trustees also; but
in any case the bulk of the work of administration—investment, distribution, accounting, tax payments, etc.—will in fact be done by
professionals, either the trustees or others employed by them.
Secondly, members of the family of the settlor or testator will often
consent to be trustees out of feelings of duty to the settlor or testator.
Where there is no professional trustee, the non-professionals will, as
will be seen,[5] usually employ professional agents such as a solicitor,
stockbroker and accountant to perform the technical duties of the
trust. It may well be better to have such experts appointed as trustees,
with a power to charge, in the first place, so that technical matters will
not be overlooked.[6]

It is usual and common to appoint a mixture of professional trustees
and non-professional. There is much to be said for appointing a
corporation such as a bank which has unrivalled facilities, dependability and permanence. There is, however, some disadvantage in allowing
trustees to be too "official"[7]; for such bodies can never take the
slightest risk in respect of a breach of trust however beneficial such a
course may be in the interest of the family.[8]

These general principles will be worked out in the sections which
follow. It will be convenient also to consider the extent to which the
very strict rules relating to the liability of trustees are also applicable to
other persons, such as agents, partners, etc., who, though not trustees,
are under special duties because of their fiduciary position.

---

[3] *Phipps* v. *Boardman* [1967] 2 A.C. 46; *post,* pp. 571 *et seq.*
[4] Public Trustee Act 1906, s.9; as amended by the Public Trustee (Fees) Act 1957.
[5] *Post,* p. 532.
[6] For the dangers inherent in appointing no professional trustees, see *Turner* v. *Turner*
[1984] Ch. 100, *ante,* p. 168. See generally (1988) 2 *Trust Law & Practice* 86 (C. Bell).
[7] In *Perrins* v. *Bellamy* [1899] 1 Ch. 797 at p. 798, Lindley M.R. during the argument
said, "My old master, the late Lord Justice Selwyn, used to say, 'the main duty of a
trustee is to commit judicious breaches of trust.' " But Lindley M.R. thought the
statement was an exaggeration and preferred "great use" to "main duty": *National
Trustees Co. of Australasia Ltd.* v. *General Finance Co. of Australasia* [1905] A.C. 373
at pp. 375–376.
[8] As, for example, by investing in equities before the Trustee Investment Act 1961 came
into force.

2. Standards Applicable to Trustees

A. Duties and Discretions

A distinction must be made between a trustee's duties and his powers or discretions. A duty is an obligation which *must* be carried out. The rules of equity (although, as we will see, they are often relaxed in practice) require strict performance of a trustee's duties; duties are imperative and a trustee must perform them with the utmost diligence.

On the other hand, a power as we have seen, is discretionary; it may be exercised, or it may not. This is so whether the power is one given to trustees by statute, or is a power or discretion contained in the instrument creating the trust, or relates to the general management of the affairs of the trust. Here the trustee must act honestly; and must take, in managing trust affairs, "all those precautions which an ordinary prudent man of business would take in managing similar affairs of his own."[9] This formula is varied in relation to the trustees' duties concerning investment. A trustee is under a duty to invest; he has a discretion in the selection of investments, but in the exercise of this discretion he is less free than a prudent man would be in investing his own money; for "business men of ordinary prudence may, and frequently do, select investments which are more or less of a speculative character; but it is the duty of a trustee to confine himself to the class of investments which are permitted by the trust [and now by the Trustee Investments Act 1961][10] and likewise to avoid all investments of that class which are attended with hazard."[11] If he properly performs his duties, powers and discretions, he is not liable for loss[12] to or depreciation[13] of the trust property arising from factors beyond his control.

We will see that many of the rules relating to trustees' duties are more strict in their terms than in their practical application. The past hundred years have brought a great alleviation in the lot of the honest trustee. We saw that much of the work of administration of a trust is necessarily done by professionals. This development has led to great relaxation, first by the courts[14] and then by statute,[15] of the requirement that the trustee should act personally. Further, the exculpatory clauses which were commonly inserted into trust instruments

---

[9] *Per* Lord Blackburn in *Speight* v. *Gaunt* (1883) 9 App.Cas. 1 at p. 19; in similar terms, Lord Watson in *Learoyd* v. *Whiteley* (1887) 12 App.Cas. 727 at p. 733.

[10] *Post,* p. 491.

[11] *Per* Lord Watson in *Learoyd* v. *Whiteley* (1887) 12 App.Cas. 727 at p. 733.

[12] *Morley* v. *Morley* (1678) 2 Ch.Cas. 2.

[13] *Re Chapman* [1896] 2 Ch. 763.

[14] *Speight* v. *Gaunt* (1883) 9 App.Cas. 1: *post,* p. 532; *Learoyd* v. *Whiteley, supra*; *Shaw* v. *Cates* [1909] 1 Ch. 389.

[15] T.A. 1925, ss.23, 30; *post,* pp. 533 *et seq.*

excluding the trustees' personal liability have become statutory[16]; and Trustee Act 1925, s.61, gives the court a discretion to excuse a trustee who has acted honestly and reasonably and ought fairly to be excused.[17]

B. Paid and Unpaid Trustees

As far as the standard of conduct required of trustees is concerned, it appears that a higher standard of care and diligence is expected of paid professional trustees than is required of unpaid voluntary trustees. The Law Reform Committee[18] described trustees as falling in practice into three groups:

   (i) unprofessional unpaid trustees of the "family friend" type;
  (ii) paid, often professionally qualified, trustees such as solicitors and accountants; and
 (iii) professional trustees, such as banks, who advertise themselves as such.

The standard of conduct required of an unpaid trustee is that laid down in *Speight* v. *Gaunt,*[19] namely that in the managing of trust affairs he must take the precautions which an ordinary prudent man of business would take in managing similar affairs of his own. But a higher standard is imposed on paid trustees in categories (ii) and (iii). In *Re Waterman's Will Trusts*[20] Harman J. said "I do not forget that a paid trustee is expected to exercise a higher standard of diligence and knowledge than an unpaid trustee and that a bank which advertises itself largely in the public press as taking charge of administrations is under a special duty." More recently, in *Bartlett* v. *Barclays Bank Trust Co. Ltd. (No. 1)*[21] Brightman J. said:

"I am of opinion that a higher duty of care is plainly due from someone like a trust corporation which carries on a specialised business of trust management. A trust corporation holds itself out in its advertising literature as being above ordinary mortals. With a specialist staff of trained trust officers and managers ... the trust corporation holds itself out, and rightly, as capable of providing an expertise which it would be unrealistic to expect and unjust to demand from the ordinary prudent man or woman who accepts, probably unpaid and sometimes reluctantly from a sense of family duty, the burdens of a trusteeship ... so I think that a professional

---

[16] *Ibid.*
[17] *Post,* p. 612.
[18] 23rd Report, *The Powers and Duties of Trustees* (Cmnd. 8733 (1982)), paras. 2.12–2.16.
[19] (1883) 9 App.Cas. 1.
[20] [1952] 2 All E.R. 1054 at p. 1055; *cf. Jobson* v. *Palmer* [1893] 1 Ch. 71; (1969) 33 Conv.(n.s.) 179 (M. Davies); (1973) 37 Conv.(n.s.) 48 (D. S. Paling).
[21] [1980] Ch. 515 at p. 534. See also *Re Rosenthal* [1972] 1 W.L.R. 1373.

corporate trustee is liable for breach of trust if loss is caused to the trust fund because it neglects to exercise the special care and skill which it professes to have."

The Law Reform Committee[22] saw no need to incorporate the existing distinction between unpaid and professional trustees into a statutory provision. The distinction is maintained through the application of section 61 of the Trustee Act 1925,[23] under which an unpaid family trustee is more likely to be relieved from liability than a professional trustee.[24] Further, a paid trustee will be expected to do more of the work himself and to delegate less; and a paid trustee will be given less opportunity to rely upon the fact that he acted upon legal advice.[25]

3. LIABILITY TO THIRD PARTIES

Persons entering into a contractual relationship with trustees, for example by supplying goods or by lending money, can enforce their rights against the trustees personally, but have no direct right to payment out of the trust assets. But the trustees are entitled to an indemnity out of the trust fund for liabilities properly incurred, to which the third party may be subrogated. The difficulty is that the creditor cannot make any claim against the trust fund which the trustees could not have made.[26] If the trustees have committed a breach of trust, then of course they are not entitled to an indemnity, and the creditor can be in no better position.

This absence of direct rights against the trust assets may cause difficulties with large commercial trusts, such as pension funds, wishing to borrow money on a large scale. The solution proposed by the Law Reform Committee[27] is that the trust deed should confer on the trustees a power to charge the trust fund in favour of the creditor. This power to charge should be confirmed by new legislation. The chargee's interest should be protected by endorsement on the trust instrument, along the lines of sections 137 and 138 of the Law of Property Act 1925.[28] The charge would be void if the creditor knew that the trustees were acting in breach of trust.[29]

---

[22] *Supra.*
[23] *Post,* p. 612.
[24] *National Trustee Co. of Australasia Ltd.* v. *General Finance Co. of Australasia* [1905] A.C. 373; *Re Pauling's S.T.* [1964] Ch. 303 at pp. 338, 339.
[25] *Re Windsor Steam Co. (1901) Ltd.* [1929] 1 Ch. 151. See also *Steel* v. *Wellcome Custodian Trustees Ltd.* [1988] 1 W.L.R. 167, at p.174.
[26] See *Re Johnson* (1880) 15 Ch.D. 548; *Re Oxley* [1914] 1 Ch. 604.
[27] 23rd Report, *The Powers and Duties of Trustees* (1982, Cmnd. 8733) paras. 2.17–2.24. See Hayton and Marshall (8th ed.), pp. 712 *et seq.*; (1987) 2 *Trust Law & Practice* 51 (D. Goddard).
[28] Relating to dealings with beneficial interests.
[29] If the creditor was unaware of the breach, the charge would be valid, but the beneficiaries could sue the trustees.

4. Unanimity[30]

Each trustee should be active in the administration of the trust. Equity does not recognise a "sleeping" trustee. A trustee who concurs with his co-trustees has, in so agreeing, as much "acted" as those others, and thus will be equally liable with them to beneficiaries who suffer loss if a breach results.[31] Nor will the concurring trustee necessarily escape liability when his co-trustee was a solicitor, though he may escape if, after considering the matter, he reasonably deferred to what could legitimately be regarded as superior knowledge.[32] But blind trust cannot safely be placed in a co-trustee. For although there is no rule that trustees are vicariously liable for the acts of co-trustees, a non-active trustee may himself be liable for neglecting to take the steps necessary to have prevented the breach.[33]

Trustees cannot act by a majority, unless expressly authorised in the trust instrument.[34] A majority binds neither a dissenting minority nor the trust estate.[35] The consequences of this rule need to be appreciated.

In *Re Mayo*,[36] for instance, one trustee of a trust for sale wished to sell, two to postpone. The trustees were by virtue of the trust to sell, under a *duty* to sell, but possessed *power* to postpone. Simonds J. held that their duty to sell prevailed unless they were unanimous in exercising their power to postpone. They were not unanimous on this point; the view of the single trustee who wished to sell prevailed, and the other two were directed to join in the sale.

5. Who may be a Trustee

In principle, any person who is able to hold property may be a trustee. But some categories need special consideration.

(i) Minors. A minor cannot hold a legal estate in land[37]; and Law of

---

[30] See Law Reform Committee, 23rd Report, *The Powers and Duties of Trustees* (1982, Cmnd. 8733), paras. 3.60–3.65, recommending no change in this rule.

[31] *Bahin* v. *Hughes* (1886) 31 Ch.D. 390; *Re Turner* [1897] 1 Ch. 536; *Wynne* v. *Tempest* (1897) 13 T.L.R. 360. But the co-trustee who concurs may be able to obtain an indemnity from the active trustee; *post*, p. 605.

[32] See *Head* v. *Gould* [1898] 2 Ch. 250; *Bahin* v. *Hughes, supra.*

[33] *Bahin* v. *Hughes, supra*; *post*, p. 605.

[34] *Re Butlins's W.T.* [1976] Ch. 251. The rule is different with trustees of charitable trusts; *Re Whiteley* [1910] 1 Ch. 600 at p. 608; *ante*, p. 450; see also T.A. 1925, s.63(3).

[35] *Luke* v. *South Kensington Hotel Ltd.* (1879) 11 Ch.D. 121.

[36] [1943] Ch. 302; *cf. Tempest* v. *Lord Camoys* (1882) 21 Ch.D. 571; but the unanimity rule did not affect the validity of a notice to quit served by only two of four joint landlords holding the reversion on trust for sale, because the characteristic of a periodic tenancy is that all parties must concur in its continuance; *Parsons* v. *Parsons* [1983] 1 W.L.R. 1390.

[37] L.P.A. 1925, s.1(6).

Property Act 1925, s.20, provides that a minor may not be a trustee in relation to any settlement or trust of land. A child of four years old was, however, held to be able to hold personalty on resulting trust.[38] As will be seen,[39] if a minor is a trustee of personalty, he may be replaced, whether or not he consents.

(ii) **The Crown.**[40] It is usually said that the Crown may be a trustee[41] "if it chooses deliberately to do so."[42] Older opinion was to the contrary. The Crown could not be a feoffee to uses[43]; and attempts to claim funds in the hands of the Crown on the ground that the Crown should be treated as a trustee have not been successful.[44] The circumstances in which the Crown will accept a trusteeship must be rare indeed, and there would be substantial difficulties in enforcing the trust if it did.[45]

(iii) **Judicial Trustees.** The High Court may, on the application of a person creating or intending to create a trust, or by or on behalf of a trustee or beneficiary, appoint a person to be a judicial trustee of that trust.[46] The court may appoint any fit or proper person,[47] and, in the absence of the nomination of such person, may appoint an official of the court.[48] Remuneration may be paid,[49] and the court may direct an inquiry into the administration of the trust by a judicial trustee.[50] The court may give a judicial trustee any general or special directions in regard to the trust or to the administration thereof[51]; not, however, so as to "reduce the administration of an estate by a judicial trustee to very much the same position as where an estate is being administered by the court and every step has to be taken in pursuance of the court's directions. . . . The object of the Judicial Trustees Act 1896 . . . was to provide a middle course in cases where the administration of the estate

---

[38] *Re Vinogradoff* [1935] W.N. 68; *ante,* p. 241.
[39] *Post,* p. 469.
[40] Hanbury, *Essays in Equity,* pp. 87–89.
[41] *Penn* v. *Lord Baltimore* (1750) 1 Ves.Sen. 444, *per* Lord Hardwicke at p. 453; *Burgess* v. *Wheate* (1757–59) 1 Eden 177.
[42] *Civilian War Claimants Association Ltd.* v. *R.* [1932] A.C. 14, *per* Lord Atkin at p. 27 (a claim by the Association for payment by the Crown of reparations money received from Germany: "There is nothing so far as I know, to prevent the Crown acting as agent or trustee if it chooses deliberately to do so.")
[43] See *Rustomjee* v. *R.* (1876) 1 Q.B.D. 487.
[44] *Re Mason* [1929] 1 Ch. 1; *Civilian War Claimants Association Ltd.* v. *R., supra*; *Tito* v. *Waddell (No. 2)* [1977] Ch. 106; *ante,* p. 72.
[45] Hanbury, *op. cit.*; Holdsworth H.E.L., Vol. IX, pp. 30–32.
[46] Judicial Trustees Act 1896, s.1(1); Judicial Trustee Rules 1983 (S.I. 1983 No. 370). The procedure has not been much used in practice.
[47] *Ibid.* subs. (3); Public Trustee Act 1906, s.2(i)(*d*).
[48] *Ibid.* subs. (3); usually the official solicitor of the court; Judicial Trustees Act 1896, s.5.
[49] Judicial Trustees Act 1896, s.1(5).
[50] *Ibid.* subs. (6), as amended by A.J.A. 1982, s.57(1). On the auditing of accounts, see Judicial Trustees Act 1896, s.4(1), as amended by A.J.A. 1982, s.57(2). See also Judicial Trustee Rules 1983, rr. 2, 13.
[51] *Ibid.* subs. (4); Judicial Trustee Rules 1983, r. 8.

by the ordinary trustees had broken down, and it was not desired to put the estate to the expense of a full administration ... a solution was found in the appointment of a judicial trustee, who acts in close concert with the court and under conditions enabling the court to supervise his transactions."[52]

A judicial trustee may also be appointed in respect of the administration of an estate.[53] At the time when there was no machinery whereby a personal representative could retire, this provided a method of replacing one who could no longer act. Now, however, the court may appoint a substitute executor or administrator under section 50 of the Administration of Justice Act 1985.[54] In an application under the 1896 Act for the appointment of a judicial trustee, the court may proceed as if it was an application under the 1985 Act, and vice versa.[55]

(iv) The Public Trustee. (a) *Functions.* The Public Trustee, established by the Public Trustee Act 1906,[56] may be appointed as trustee alone or jointly with another or others, and may act as a custodian trustee[57] or an ordinary trustee or as a judicial trustee. The Public Trustee is a corporation sole,[58] covered in respect of liability for breach of trust by the State,[59] and entitled to charge fees on a scale fixed by the Lord Chancellor.[60] His special function is the administration of small estates and, although he may decline to accept any trust, he may not do so on the ground "only of the small value of the trust property."[61] And he is required to undertake the administration of an estate less than £1,000 on the application of a person entitled to an order for administration by the court.[62] Once appointed, the Public Trustee has the same powers and duties and liabilities, and is entitled to the same rights and immunities as a private trustee.[63] Because the office of Public Trustee was not financially self-supporting, its abolition was recommended in 1972, but the Lord Chancellor announced in 1974 that it had been reprieved.[64] The functions of the Public Trustee have since been extended by the Public Trustee and Administration of Funds Act

---

[52] *Re Ridsdel* [1947] Ch. 597 at p. 605.
[53] Judicial Trustees Act 1896, s.1(2).
[54] The court may authorise the appointed person to charge; s.50(3).
[55] A.J.A. 1985, s.50(4); Judicial Trustees Act 1896, s.1(7), added by the 1985 Act.
[56] He is appointed by the Lord Chancellor, and may be the same person as the Accountant General of the Supreme Court; Public Trustee Act 1906, s.8(1); Public Trustee and Administration of Funds Act 1986, s.1 and Sched. He is paid such salary or fees as the Lord Chancellor determines; s.8(1A) of the 1906 Act, as amended.
[57] s.4, *post.*
[58] Public Trustee Act 1906, s.1.
[59] *Ibid.*, s.7.
[60] *Ibid.*, s.9; Public Trustee (Fees) Act 1957; Administration of Justice Act 1965, s.2; Public Trustee (Fees) (Amendment) Order 1988 (S.I. 1988 No. 571). See also Public Trustee and Administration of Funds Act 1986, s.3(6).
[61] *Ibid.*, s.2(3).
[62] *Ibid.*, s.3.
[63] *Ibid.*, s.2(2).
[64] *The Times*, August 1, 1974.

1986,[65] which confers on him all the functions conferred on the judge of the Court of Protection by Part VII of the Mental Health Act 1983 with respect to the property and affairs of mental patients. He may act as, or appoint a person to act as a receiver,[66] or carry on, as well as authorise a suitable person to carry on, a patient's profession, trade or business.

(b) *Restrictions.*[67] There are certain trusts that the Public Trustee may not accept; such as a trust exclusively for religious or charitable purposes,[68] or any trust under a deed of arrangement for the benefit of creditors, or the administration of an estate known by him to be insolvent,[69] and he may only accept a trust involving the management of a business under special restrictions limiting him to a short period of operation and requiring the Treasury's consent.[70]

(v) **Custodian Trustees.**[71] The Public Trustee[72] and a large number of other corporations[73] are authorised to act as custodian trustees, and they may all charge fees not exceeding those chargeable by the Public Trustee.[74] The custodian trustee holds property and the documents relating thereto while leaving to the managing trustee the day-to-day administration of the trust.[75] The Public Trustee cannot act in both capacities in relation to the same trust.

The advantage of the scheme of custodian trusteeship is that new managing trustees can be appointed without the necessity of undergoing the trouble and expense—which can be considerable in the case of a large trust—of vesting all the securities in the trust in new trustees whenever there is a death, retirement or new appointment. It should be noted that this advantage cannot be gained by appointing the holder of an office as trustee. If the chairman and secretary of a committee are

---

[65] s.3. The Act came into force on January 2, 1987.

[66] See Practice Direction [1987] 1 W.L.R. 63.

[67] These are subject to Public Trustee and Administrtion of Funds Act 1986, s.3(5), whereby functions conferred on the Public Trustee under Part VII of the Mental Health Act 1983 are exercisable notwithstanding any provision of the 1906 Act under which he would be obliged or empowered to decline to accept any trust or other duty.

[68] Public Trustee Act 1906, s.2(5).

[69] *Ibid.*, s.2(4).

[70] Public Trustee Rules 1912, r. 7.

[71] (1960) 24 Conv.(N.S.) 196 (S. G. Maurice).

[72] Public Trustee Act 1906, s.4(3).

[73] Public Trustee Rules 1912, r. 30, as substituted by the Public Trustee (Custodian Trustee) Rules 1975 (S.I. 1975 No. 1189), r. 2. See also Public Trustee (Custodian Trustee) Rules 1976 (S.I. 1976 No. 836) and 1981 (S.I. 1981 No. 358). Qualifying corporations include those of EEC States which comply with the requirements and have a place of business in the U.K. carrying on trust business.

[74] Public Trustee Act 1906, s.4(3).

[75] For the relationship between custodian trustees and managing trustees, see Public Trustee Act 1906, s.4(2); *Forster* v. *Williams Deacon's Bank Ltd.* [1935] Ch. 359; (a bank may not be appointed both custodian trustee and managing trustee in order to allow it to charge a fee as custodian trustee); *Re Brooke Bond and Co. Ltd.'s Trust Deed* [1963] Ch. 357; (custodian trustee may not take profit on insurance policy taken out with it by managing trustee).

trustees, the investments must be transferred to the names of the new holders of the office when a change is made. *Ex officio* trustees can only be effective in the case of a corporation sole.[76]

In determining a number of trustees for the purpose of the Trustee Act 1925, the custodian trustee shall not be reckoned as a trustee.[77]

(vi) Trust Corporations. Trust corporations are playing an increasing part in the administration of trusts. Their size, stability, dependability and expertise give them advantages over individual trustees; although, as was explained above,[78] there is a danger that they may become too professional and bureaucratic.

They enjoy, in some sense, a special status; in that they can often act alone in circumstances in which at least two individual trustees would be necessary. A trust corporation can give a valid receipt for capital money arising from the sale of land[79]; and a trust for sale has greater overreaching powers if a trust corporation is trustee[80]; as it would if there were as trustees two or more individuals approved by the court. Further, as will be seen, trustees may retire and leave a sole trustee only if that trustee is a trust corporation.[81]

In most cases of private trusts, a trust corporation means the Executor and Trustee Company of a bank. The legal definition is: "Trust corporation means the Public Trustee or a corporation either appointed by the court in a particular case to be a trustee, or entitled by rules made under subsection (3) of section four of the Public Trustee Act, 1906, to act as custodian trustee."[82] The qualifications are contained in the Public Trustee (Custodian Trustee) Rules 1975.[83] The Law of Property (Amendment) Act 1926, s.3 added, *inter alia,* a trustee in bankruptcy, the Treasury Solicitor, and the Official Solicitor. A trust corporation, unless acting as custodian trustee only, has no greater power to charge remuneration than any other trustee has. Fee earning is however their business, and express powers will always be given for a fee to be charged for the service.

---

[76] *Tufnell* v. *Constable* (1838) 7 Ad. & E. 798; *Bankes* v. *Salisbury Diocesan Council of Education* [1960] Ch. 631 at pp. 647–649.

[77] Public Trustee Act 1906, s.4(2)(*g*).

[78] *Ante,* p. 458.

[79] T.A. 1925, s.14; L.P.A. 1925, s.27(2); S.L.A. 1925, ss.18(1), 94, 95.

[80] L.P.A. 1925, s.2(2).

[81] T.A. 1925, s.39; *post,* p. 477.

[82] T.A. 1925, s.68(18); see also L.P.A. 1925, s.205(1)(xxviii); A.E.A. 1925, s.55(1) (xxvi); Settled Land Act 1925, s.117; Supreme Court Act 1981, s.128.

[83] S.I. No. 1189 of 1975. They include any corporation which (i) is constituted under the law of the United Kingdom or of any other Member State of the European Economic Community; and (ii) is empowered by its constitution to undertake trust business in England and Wales; (iii) has one or more places of business in the United Kingdom; and (iv) being a registered company has a capital (in stock or shares) for the time being issued of not less than £250,000 (or its equivalent in the currency of the state where the company is registered), of which not less than £100,000 (or its equivalent) has been paid up in cash. See also the Public Trustee (Custodian Trustee) Rules 1976 (S.I. 1976 No. 836) and 1981 (S.I. 1981 No. 358).

6. DISCLAIMER

Nobody can be compelled to accept the office of trustee against his will.[84] A person appointed as trustee who wishes to disclaim should do so by deed,[85] as this provides clear evidence of the disclaimer. However, a disclaimer may be implied; apathy will be evidence of an intention to disclaim, provided the apathy is consistent.[86] But if the trustee meddles with the estate, his conduct will be construed as an acceptance. Once he has disclaimed, he can no longer accept. Once he has accepted he can no longer disclaim[87] but as we will see, he may retire.[88]

7. NUMBER OF TRUSTEES

There is no restriction upon the number of trustees of personalty. It is inconvenient to have too many; and rare to have more than four. And where additional trustees are appointed under the statutory power, appointments may only be made up to a total of four.[89] A single or sole trustee is most unsatisfactory because of the opportunities for maladministration and fraud which then arise.

In trusts of land, the Trustee Act 1925, s.34, restricts the number of trustees of a settlement or of a trust for sale to four. There are exceptions, the most important of which is that of land vested in trustees for charitable, ecclesiastical or public purposes.[90]

While a sole trustee of land is not forbidden,[91] the Trustee Act 1925, s.14(2), makes it impossible for a sole trustee (not being a trust corporation)[92] to give a valid receipt for the proceeds of sale or other capital money arising under a disposition on trust for sale of land, or capital money arising under the Settled Land Act 1925.[93]

The Law Reform Committee[94] has recommended that the number of trustees should be limited to four, regardless of the nature of the trust property, on the ground that costs, administrative inconvenience and delays are increased if there are more than four; but the settlor should nevertheless be able to provide expressly for more than four trustees, subject to the present restrictions noted above, for example in the case of a trust for sale of land.

---

[84] A person can, of course, become a constructive or resulting trustee against his will.
[85] *Stacey* v. *Elph* (1833) 1 Myl. & K. 195 at p. 199; *Re Schär* [1951] Ch. 280; *Holder* v. *Holder* [1968] Ch. 353 (an executor).
[86] *Re Clout and Frewer's Contract* [1924] 2 Ch. 230.
[87] *Re Sharman's W.T.* [1942] Ch. 311; *Holder* v. *Holder, supra*.
[88] *Post*, p. 477.
[89] T.A. 1925, s.36(6), *post*, p. 471.
[90] T.A. 1925, s.34(3)(*a*).
[91] *Re Myhill* [1928] Ch. 100.
[92] *Ante*, p. 466.
[93] L.P.A. 1925, s.27(2); L.P.(A.)A. 1926, Sched.; S.L.A. 1925, ss.18(1), 94, 95.
[94] 23rd Report, *The Powers and Duties of Trustees* (1982, Cmnd. 8733), para. 2.2.

8. APPOINTMENT OF TRUSTEES

A. The First Trustees

The first trustees will ordinarily be appointed by the settlor or testator in the deed or will creating the trust. In the case of an *inter vivos* trust, the trustees will ordinarily be parties to the deed in their official capacity, and the trust is constituted upon the conveyance of the trust property to them. In a will, the same persons may be appointed executors and trustees. Where they are different persons, the trust is constituted upon the testator's death, for the title of the executors relates back to the death, and they hold as constructive trustees pending transfer to the persons appointed trustees in the will.

Trustees hold as joint tenants, and if one of several trustees dies, the survivors are the trustees, and they, and their successors, retain the same powers and duties as the original trustees.[95] On the death of a sole trustee, his personal representatives become trustees.[96] If he dies intestate, the trust estate will vest, pending the grant of administration, in the President of the Family Division.[97] A trust does not normally fail for lack of a trustee; hence if the trustees disclaim, the trust still subsists, save in the rare cases where the settlor or testator has himself made the validity of the trust dependent upon the acceptance of office by particular trustees.[98] If all the nominated trustees predecease the testator in the case of a testamentary trust, the personal representatives of the testator will hold until such time as trustees are appointed.[99]

B. Who May Appoint New Trustees

(i) **Express Power.** The trust instrument may include an express power to appoint new trustees. This is unusual,[1] as most settlors now think it sufficient to rely on the statutory power; where an express power is given, it is often reserved to the settlor. The extent of such power depends of course upon the construction of the particular instrument. The statutory power will be available in addition, unless a contrary intention appears in the instrument.[2]

---

[95] T.A. 1925, s.18; *contra,* a bare power given to two persons in their individual capacity: *Re Smith* [1904] 1 Ch. 139; *Re de Sommery* [1912] 2 Ch. 622; *Re Harding* [1923] 1 Ch. 182; *ante,* p. 164.

[96] A.E.A. 1925, ss.1–3; T.A. 1925, s.18(2).

[97] A.E.A. 1925, s.9; Administration of Justice Act 1970, s.1, Sched. 2, para. 5.

[98] *Re Lysaght* [1966] Ch. 191; *Re Woodhams (deceased)* [1981] 1 W.L.R. 493.

[99] *Re Smirthwaite's Trust* (1871) L.R. 11 Eq. 251.

[1] It is usual, however, to select a person to exercise the statutory power; *post,* p. 469.

[2] T.A. 1925, s.69(2). See *Cecil* v. *Langdon* (1884) 28 Ch.D. 1; *Re Wheeler and De Rochow* [1896] 1 Ch. 315; *Re Sichel's Settlements* [1916] 1 Ch. 358.

(ii) The Statutory Power: Trustee Act 1925, s.36(1) (2).[3]

"(1) Where a trustee, either original or substituted, and whether appointed by the court or otherwise, is dead,[4] or remains out of the United Kingdom for more than 12 months,[5] or desires to be discharged from all or any of the trusts or powers reposed in or conferred on him,[6] or refuses[7] or is unfit to act therein, or is incapable of acting therein,[8] or is an infant,[9] then, subject to the restrictions imposed by this Act on the number of trustees,—

(*a*) the person or persons nominated for the purpose of appointing new trustees by the instrument, if any, creating the trust; or

(*b*) if there is no such person, or no such person able and willing to act,[10] then the surviving or continuing trustees or trustee for the time being, or the personal representatives of the last surviving or continuing trustee;

may, by writing,[11] appoint one or more other persons (whether or not being the persons exercising the power) to be a trustee or trustees in the place of the trustee so deceased remaining out of the United Kingdom, desiring to be discharged, refusing, or being unfit or being incapable, or being an infant, as aforesaid.

(2) Where a trustee has been removed[12] under a power contained in the instrument creating the trust, a new trustee or new trustees may be appointed in the place of the trustee who is removed, as if he were dead, or, in the case of a corporation, as if the corporation desired to be discharged from the trust, and the provisions of this section shall apply accordingly, but subject to the restrictions imposed by this Act on the number of trustees."

---

[3] The statutory power does not apply to personal representatives (not being trustees); *Re Cockburn's W.T.* [1957] Ch. 438; *Re King's W.T.* [1964] Ch. 542; *ante,* p. 58. The court, however, may appoint a substitute personal representative under Administration of Justice Act 1985, s.50.

[4] Which includes the case of a person nominated trustee in a will but dying before the testator: T.A. 1925, s.36(8), and *ante,* p. 468.

[5] The period must be continuous: *Re Walker* [1901] 1 Ch. 259; see also *Re Stoneham S.T.* [1953] Ch. 59. T.A. 1925, s.25, permits a trustee in such a case to delegate his duties by power of attorney for a period not exceeding 12 months; *post,* p. 535.

[6] For retirement of a trustee, see *post,* p. 477.

[7] *Ante,* p. 467.

[8] "Unfit" has a wider meaning than "incapable." "Incapable" refers to personal incapacity, such as illness or mental disorder; see T.A. 1925, s.36(9). "Unfit" is more general and an absconding bankrupt has been held to be "unfit" but not "incapable": *Re Roche* (1842) 2 Dr. & War. 287. There is some doubt about an enemy alien: *Re Sichel's Settlements* [1916] 1 Ch. 358; *Re May's W.T.* [1941] Ch. 109. See subs. (3), providing that a corporation is "incapable" from the date of dissolution, and Mental Health Act 1983, s.148 and Sched. 4.

[9] L.P.A. 1925, ss.1(6), 20; *Re Parsons* [1940] Ch. 764.

[10] As where the donee cannot be traced; *Graddock* v. *Witham* [1895] W.N. 75.

[11] See *post,* p. 473, and T.A. 1925, s.40.

[12] *Post,* p. 478.

In favour of a purchaser of a legal estate, a statement in an instrument appointing a new trustee to the effect that a trustee is unfit, incapable or refuses to act, or has remained out of the United Kingdom for more than 12 months, is conclusive evidence of the matter. Similarly, any appointment of a new trustee depending on that statement, and the consequent vesting of the trust property in the new trustee, is valid in favour of such a purchaser.[13]

(iii) Exercise of the Statutory Power. It is usual to appoint someone to exercise the statutory power.

(a) *By Persons Appointed under section* 36(1)(*a*). If two or more persons are given power to exercise it jointly, the power is not, in the absence of a contrary intention, exercisable by the survivor. This is consistent with the usual rule relating to bare powers given to individuals.[14]

The power is usually given to individuals in simple terms. Complications can arise if the power is subjected to conditions and limitations.

In *Re Wheeler and De Rochow*,[15] the settlor gave power to donees to appoint a new trustee if one of the existing trustees should be (*inter alia*) "incapable." One of the trustees was bankrupt, and absconded. This made him "unfit" but not "incapable."[16] The question was whether a new trustee should be appointed by the donees under section 36(1)(*a*) or by the continuing trustees under section 36(1)(*b*). It was held that the situation was not within the terms of the power given to the donees and that section 36(1)(*b*) applied.

(b) *By the Surviving or Continuing Trustees under section* 36(1)(*b*). In the case of continuing trustees it is expressly provided by section 36(8) that the provisions of section 36 "relative to a continuing trustee include a refusing or retiring trustee, if willing to act in the execution of the provisions of this section." This provision enables a retiring sole trustee or a retiring group of trustees to appoint their successors. It raises the question, however, whether their participation is essential; whether an appointment in which they did not participate would be void. Such an objection failed in *Re Coates to Parsons*[17]; the retiring trustee is only included if it is shown that he is competent and willing to act. The concurrence of a trustee who is removed on the ground that he

---

[13] T.A. 1925, s.38.
[14] *Re Harding* [1923] 1 Ch. 182; *Bersel Manufacturing Co. Ltd.* v. *Berry* [1968] 2 All E.R. 552; *ante,* p. 164; *contra* where the power is given to persons as trustees: T.A. 1925, s.18(1), *ante,* p. 164.
[15] [1896] 1 Ch. 315; followed reluctantly in *Re Sichel's Settlements* [1916] 1 Ch. 358; *cf. Re Brockbank* [1948] Ch. 206.
[16] *Re Roche* (1842) 2 Dr. & War. 287, *ante,* p. 469.
[17] (1886) 34 Ch.D. 370.

remained outside the United Kingdom for more than 12 months[18] is not required.[19] It is advisable, in order to avoid these difficulties, that refusing or retiring trustees should participate in the appointment of new trustees if possible, and this is the usual practice.

The statutory power to appoint a new trustee can be exercised by the executor of a sole trustee appointed by will,[20] but not by the personal representative of the survivor of a body of trustees named in a will, who has died in the testator's lifetime, as the Act does not contemplate the case of all the trustees named in the will predeceasing the testator.[21] Nor can the sole surviving trustee exercise the power by his will, so as thereby to appoint new trustees in succession to himself.[22] The aim of the Act of 1925 is to ensure the making of an appointment in all events. The executors who have proved the will need not have the concurrence of those who have not proved or intend to renounce probate.[23] A sole or last surviving executor who intends to renounce probate can nevertheless fulfil this one function without thereby accepting the office of executor,[24] but the title of an executor to exercise the statutory power can only be proved by a proper grant of administration.[25]

(c) *Additional Trustees.* Before 1926 the statutory power of appointing new trustees only applied to the filling of vacancies. A broad power is given by section 36(6), restricted only by the limitation to a total number of four trustees, and by the fact that the power is to appoint "another person or other persons" and that consequently (and unlike appointments under subsection (1)) the appointor may not appoint himself.[26] Section 36(6) reads:

> "Where a sole trustee, other than a trust corporation,[27] is or has been originally appointed to act in a trust, or where, in the case of any trust, there are not more than three trustees (none of them being a trust corporation)[28] either original or substituted and whether appointed by the court or otherwise, then and in any such case—
>
> (*a*) the person or persons nominated for the purpose of appointing new trustees by the instrument, if any, creating the trust; or

---

[18] *Ante,* p. 469.

[19] *Re Stoneham S.T.* [1953] Ch. 59.

[20] *Re Shafto's Trusts* (1885) 29 Ch.D. 247.

[21] *Nicholson* v. *Field* (1893) 2 Ch. 511.

[22] *Re Parker's Trusts* [1894] 1 Ch. 707.

[23] T.A. 1925, s.36(4).

[24] T.A. 1925, s.36(5).

[25] *Re Crowhurst Park* [1974] 1 W.L.R. 583. (A grant of probate in Jersey insufficient in relation to leasehold land in England.)

[26] *Re Power's S.T.* [1951] Ch. 1074. The Law Reform Committee, 23rd Report, *The Powers and Duties of Trustees* (1982, Cmnd. 8733) recommends otherwise; para. 2.6.

[27] The Law Reform Committee, *supra,* recommends the removal of the restrictions on the power where a trust corporation is a trustee; para. 2.6.

[28] See n. 27.

(*b*) if there is no such person, or no such person able and willing to act, then the trustee or trustees for the time being;

may,[29] by writing, appoint another person or other persons to be an additional trustee or additional trustees, but it shall not be obligatory to appoint any additional trustee, unless the instrument, if any, creating the trust, or any statutory enactment provides to the contrary, nor shall the number of trustees be increased beyond four by virtue of any such appointment."

C. Appointment by the Court

(i) Trustee Act 1925, s.41.[30] Subsection (1) of section 41 provides:

"The court[31] may, whenever it is expedient to appoint a new trustee or new trustees, and it is found inexpedient difficult or impracticable so to do without the assistance of the court, make an order appointing a new trustee or new trustees either in substitution for or in addition to any existing trustee or trustees, or although there is no existing trustee.

In particular and without prejudice to the generality of the foregoing provision, the court may make an order appointing a new trustee in substitution for a trustee who is [incapable, by reason of mental disorder within the meaning of the Mental Health Act 1983, of exercising his functions as trustee] or is a bankrupt, or is a corporation which is in liquidation or has been dissolved."

(ii) Circumstances in which the Jurisdiction will be Exercised. The section gives the court a discretion. Cases arise in a variety of circumstances, *e.g.* where a sole surviving trustee has died intestate, or where all the trustees of a testamentary trust predeceased the testator,[32] and difficulty is experienced in obtaining administration of his estate,[33] or where the donee is incapable of making an effective appointment because of infancy.[34] The court has power to replace a trustee against his will[35]; and also where the trustees were the life tenant and remainderman and there was friction between them; or where a trustee has, through age or infirmity,[36] become incapable of acting, or who permanently resides abroad.[37]

---

[29] T.A. 1925, s.37(1)(*c*).

[30] As amended by the Mental Health Act 1983, s.148, Sched. 4, and the Criminal Law Act 1967, s.10, Sched. 3. The power does not apply to the appointment of personal representatives (s.41(4)).

[31] *i.e.* the High Court; or where the estate or trust fund does not exceed its financial jurisdiction, the county court.

[32] *Re Satterthwaite's Trust* (1871) L.R. 11 Eq. 251.

[33] *Re Matthews* (1859) 26 Beav. 463.

[34] *Re Parsons* [1940] Ch. 973; (1941) 57 L.Q.R. 25 (R.E.M.).

[35] *Re Henderson* [1940] Ch. 764.

[36] *Re Lemann's Trust* (1883) 22 Ch.D. 633.

[37] *Re Bignold's S.T.* (1872) L.R. 7 Ch.App. 223.

The court should not however be asked to exercise this jurisdiction where the power under section 36(1) can be exercised.[38] It has no jurisdiction to appoint a new trustee against the wishes of the persons who have the statutory power to appoint, even in a case where an application has been made to it by a majority of the beneficiaries.[39] The wishes of the beneficiaries in such a case can prevail if they are all *sui juris,* by terminating the trust and creating a new trust in which they will appoint the trustees.[40]

9. VESTING OF THE TRUST PROPERTY IN TRUSTEES

A. Requirement of Vesting

The trust property must be vested in the trustees to enable them to deal with outside parties. Even in the absence of a proper vesting, however, a trustee, whether appointed under section 36 or by the court under section 41, has "the same powers, authorities, and discretions, and may in all respects act as if he had been originally appointed a trustee by the instrument, if any, creating the trust."[41]

B. Vesting Declaration under Section 40

(i) Subsection (1). In order to obviate the necessity of a formal conveyance or other appropriate means of transfer of the trust property from the old trustees to the new, section 40 provides that the vesting may, with important exceptions, be effected by a vesting declaration, if the appointment of the trustees has been made by *deed.*[42] It does not apply, however, where the property is held by personal representatives and not by a trustee.[43]

Subsection (1) of section 40 provides:

"(1) Where by a deed a new trustee is appointed to perform any trust, then—

(*a*) if the deed contains a declaration by the appointor to the effect that any estate or interest in any land subject to the trust, or in any chattel so subject, or the right to recover or receive any debt or other thing in action so subject, shall vest in the persons who by virtue of the deed become or are the trustees for performing the trust, the deed shall operate, without any conveyance or assignment, to vest in those persons as joint

---

[38] *Re Gibbon's Trusts* (1882) 30 W.R. 287 (where, however, such an appointment was made); *cf. Re May's W.T.* [1941] Ch. 109.
[39] *Re Higginbottom* [1892] 3 Ch. 132.
[40] *Re Brockbank* [1948] Ch. 206; [1974] B.T.R. 68 (M. Jump). This would have tax disadvantages.
[41] T.A. 1925, ss.36(7), 43.
[42] *Ante,* p. 469.
[43] *Re Cockburn's W.T.* [1957] Ch. 438; *Re King's W.T.* [1964] Ch. 542; *ante,* p. 58.

tenants and for the purposes of the trust the estate interest or right to which the declaration relates; and

(b) if the deed is made after the commencement of this Act and does not contain such a declaration, the deed shall, subject to any express provision to the contrary therein contained, operate as if it had contained such a declaration by the appointor extending to all the estates interests and rights with respect to which a declaration could have been made."[44]

(ii) Exceptions under subsection (4). These in outline are:

(a) land mortgaged to secure money subject to the trust;
(b) land held under a lease which contains a covenant against assignment without consent, and the consent has not been obtained prior to the execution of the deed;
(c) stocks and shares.[45]

These exceptions are necessary. Where trust money is lent on mortgage, no mention is made in the mortgage deed of the existence of the trust, nor upon a transfer of the mortgage, such as would occur on the appointment of a new trustee. The second exception is included in order to avoid an unintended breach of trust, such as could occur in the appointment of a new trustee. The most serious exception in practice is the third; for this is the most important and valuable form of property in modern settlements. The provision, however, was necessary, because title to stocks and shares depends on the registration of the owners in the register of shareholders, and it is essential that the current trustees should be registered.

It will be seen that vesting orders relating to registered land are not excepted; however, the legal title cannot pass until registration. By the Land Registration Act 1925, s.47, the registrar is required to give effect on the register to any vesting order or vesting declaration made on the appointment or discharge of a trustee.[46] The provisions of the Trustee Act 1925 relating to the appointment and discharge of trustees and the vesting of trust property apply to registered land subject to proper entry being made on the register.

C. Vesting Orders under Sections 44 to 56[47]

Sections 44 to 56 contain the rules as to vesting orders by the court. These overlap section 40, for vesting orders as to all kinds of property can be made, not only where the appointment has been made by the court, but also where it has been made out of court under an express or

---

[44] See also L.R.A 1925, s.47, *infra*, for provisions relating to registered land.
[45] "Any share, stock, annuity or property which is only transferable in books kept by a company or other body, or in manner directed by or under an Act of Parliament." This includes money in a bank account, for example, but not bearer bonds.
[46] See (1971) 115 S.J. 512.
[47] s.54 was replaced by what is now M.H.A. 1983, s.148 and Sched. 4.

statutory power. The court is given wide powers to make such orders in a variety of eventualities, to which, *ex abundanti cautela,* is added the case "Where land or any interest therein is vested in a trustee whether by way of mortgage or otherwise, and it appears to the court to be expedient" to make the order.[48]

10. Selection of Trustees

A. On Appointment by the Court under Section 41

The factors which a court will take into account when exercising its jurisdiction to appoint a trustee were discussed by Turner L.J. in *Re Tempest.*[49] The court should always have regard to three prime requirements: the wishes of the person by whom the trust was created; the interests, which may be conflicting, of *all* the beneficiaries; the efficient administration of the trust. It is important that the trustees act harmoniously together; but Turner L.J. thought it would be going too far to say that the court should refuse to appoint a particular trustee on the ground that the continuing trustee refused to act with him. That would give the continuing trustee a veto; rather, the reasons for the refusal should be examined to see whether the objection is well founded.

The court is reluctant to appoint a person who, though not himself interested, is related to, or connected with, someone who is. Thus a relative of one of the beneficiaries is not a desirable appointment[50]; nor is one nominated by a relative of the testator with whom the testator was on bad terms.[51] Again, the solicitor to the trust,[52] or to one of the beneficiaries[53] or trustees, should not be appointed, as there might be a conflict of duties; unless, of course, no other person can be found to undertake the position. If the solicitor to the trust is a continuing trustee, his partner should not be appointed.[54] Persons out of the jurisdiction will not be appointed[55] except in a case where circumstances require it, or where the beneficiaries are resident outside the jurisdiction also.[56] Even where the trust can be more conveniently administered by trustees resident abroad, the court may exact an

---

[48] T.A. 1925, s.44(vii).

[49] (1866) L.R. 1 Ch.App. 485.

[50] *Wilding* v. *Bolder* (1855) 21 Beav. 222; *Re Parrott* (1881) 30 W.R. 97; *Re Coode* (1913) 108 L.T. 94; *Re Parsons* [1940] Ch. 973 (where an infant purported to appoint his mother).

[51] *Re Tempest* (1866) L.R. 1 Ch. 485.

[52] *Wheelwright* v. *Walker* (1883) 23 Ch.D. 752; *Re Orde* (1883) 24 Ch.D. 271.

[53] *Re Kemp's S.E.* (1883) 24 Ch.D. 485; *Re Earl of Stamford* [1896] 1 Ch. 288; *Re Spencer's S.E.* [1903] 1 Ch. 75; *Re Cotter* [1915] 1 Ch. 307.

[54] *Re Norris* (1884) 27 Ch.D. 333.

[55] *Re Guibert's Trust Estate* (1852) 16 Jur. 852; *Re Weston's Settlements* [1969] 1 Ch. 223.

[56] *Re Liddiard* (1880) 14 Ch.D. 310; *Re Simpson* [1897] 1 Ch. 256; *Re Seale's Marriage S.T.* [1961] Ch. 574; *Re Windeatt's W.T.* [1969] 1 W.L.R. 692; *Re Whitehead's W.T.* [1971] 1 W.L.R. 833. See also *Chellaram* v. *Chellaram* [1985] Ch. 409, *post,* p. 479.

undertaking from them that they will consult the court before proceeding to the appointment of new trustees out of the jurisdiction.[57] Trusts administered abroad have enjoyed a number of fiscal advantages, and this has encouraged the movement of many trusts overseas.

B. On Appointment under Express Power or under Section 36

(i) **Choice by Donee of Power.** It is said that the above principles should guide persons exercising their power to appoint under section 36. In practice, however, it is common for beneficiaries and other members of the beneficiaries' families, and for solicitors to the beneficiaries, to be appointed. A conflict of interest and duty or of two duties should of course be avoided. However, even if the trustee appointed is one whom the court itself would not have selected, it seems that the court will do little to rectify it.[58]

(ii) **Foreign Trusts.** Problems have arisen in relation to the appointment of foreign trustees with the intention of enjoying the tax advantages of foreign trusts over domestic trusts. We have seen[59] that the tax advantages are now minimal unless there are beneficiaries who are resident abroad, or the settlor was domiciled[60] abroad at the date of the creation of the settlement. We saw also that the court was unwilling to appoint trustees resident abroad unless the beneficiaries have made their homes in the country in question[61]; and that, although it was said that the donee of a power should only appoint foreign resident trustees in similar circumstances,[62] an appointment inconsistent with this rule would be a valid appointment.[63]

C. On Appointment by the Settlor
The settlor is under no restrictions in the selection of the original trustees whether English or foreign. It is of course in his interest to think long and hard before deciding on the persons to whom he will commit the administration of the trust. The question is not merely one of selecting efficient, businesslike and fair-minded trustees who will carry out their duties according to law. They are commonly given wide

---

[57] *Re Freeman's S.T.* (1888) 37 Ch.D. 148.
[58] In *Re Norris* (1884) 27 Ch.D. 333, the funds were being administered by the court; *Re Higginbottom* [1892] 3 Ch. 132; in *Re Coode* (1913) 108 L.T. 94, an appointment of an infant was held void; *Re Parsons* [1940] Ch. 973; (1941) 57 L.Q.R. 25 (R.E.M.).
[59] *Ante*, p. 222.
[60] Inheritance Tax Act 1984, s.267; *ante*, p. 225.
[61] *Re Weston's Settlements* [1969] 1 Ch. 223; *cf. Re Seale's Marriage S.T.* [1961] Ch. 574; *Re Windeatt's W.T.* [1969] 1 W.L.R. 692; *Re Whitehead's W.T.* [1971] 1 W.L.R. 833; (1976) 40 Conv.(N.S.) 295 (T. G. Watkin). See generally Parker and Mellows, *The Modern Law of Trusts* (5th ed.), pp. 437–441.
[62] *Re Whitehead's W.T., supra*, at p. 838.
[63] *Meinertzhagen* v. *Davis* (1844) 1 Coll. 353; *Re Smith's Trusts* (1872) 26 L.T. 820; cases of appointment under express powers not specifically authorising such an appointment; (1969) 85 L.Q.R. 15 (P.V.B.); *Re Whitehead's W.T., supra*, at p. 837.

discretions. They therefore must be people who will be relied on to respect the wishes of the settlor on matters on which they are in law virtually uncontrolled; and in circumstances which may have greatly changed since the trust was created.

11. RETIREMENT: SECTION 39

A trustee may retire from a subsisting trust in any one of the three ways explained below.[64] Retirement means a discharge from further responsibility and liability under the trust. A trustee should not retire when faced with disputes among beneficiaries and leave them to settle their differences among themselves. If he retires in order to facilitate a breach of trust by his successors, he will remain liable.[65]

A. Under an Express Power in the Trust Instrument
This is rare, since (the predecessors of) sections 36 and 39 made express powers unnecessary.

B. Statutory Power
We saw that a trustee desiring to be discharged could be replaced by a newly appointed trustee.[66] He may retire, without being replaced, if he complies with section 39.

"(1) Where a trustee is desirous of being discharged from the trust, and after his discharge there will be either a trust corporation or at least two individuals[67] to act as trustees to perform the trust, then, if such trustee as aforesaid by deed declares that he is desirous of being discharged from the trust, and if his co-trustees and such other person, if any, as is empowered to appoint trustees, by deed consent to the discharge of the trustee, and to the vesting in the co-trustees alone of the trust property, the trustee desirous of being discharged shall be deemed to have retired from the trust, and shall, by the deed, be discharged therefrom under this Act, without any new trustee being appointed in his place.[68]

---

[64] A personal representative may be discharged by the court; Administration of Justice Act 1985, s.50.

[65] *Head* v. *Gould* [1898] 2 Ch. 250.

[66] T.A. 1925, s.36(1); *ante*, p. 469.

[67] A sole trustee other than a trust corporation does not suffice even if he has power to give a valid receipt for capital money; see (1986) 1 *Trust Law & Practice* 16 (M. Jacobs), contrasting T.A. 1925, s.37(1)(c). This article also examines the position of a corporate trustee which is not a trust corporation under T.A. 1925, ss.37, 39, and L.P.A. 1925, s.27. *cf.* (1987) 2 *Trust Law & Practice* 43 (J. Hayes).

[68] It is unlikely that these conditions can be overriden by the terms of the settlement. See (1986) 1 *Trust Law & Practice* 95 (M. Jacobs).

(2) Any assurance or thing requisite for vesting the trust property in the continuing trustees alone shall be executed or done."

C. Under an Order of the Court

The court will only discharge a trustee under its statutory jurisdiction where it replaces him by a new appointment under section 41. There is however an inherent power in the court to discharge him without replacement in the case of an action to administer the trust. While it will not, in the exercise of this jurisdiction, encourage capricious retirement,[69] it will allow a trustee to retire where it is entirely proper for him to do so.[70]

12. REMOVAL

We have seen that the court may, on the appointment of a new trustee, remove an existing trustee and that some appointments by a donee of a power will have this effect.[71] The court has also an inherent jurisdiction in actions for the administration of trusts to remove a trustee compulsorily; but the principles on which this power is exercised are somewhat vague.[72]

Actual misconduct on the part of a trustee need not be shown, but the court must be satisfied that his continuance in office would be prejudicial to the due performance of the trust, and so to the interests of the beneficiaries. The court has a clear ground for removal in cases where a trustee is ignoring one of his recognised duties. Thus, though it will not necessarily constitute an actual breach of trust for a trustee of a will carrying on the business of his testator to set up a rival business, yet it will be a ground for his removal,[73] as he has put himself in a position wherein his duty and interest are bound to be in conflict. Similarly if trustees were to persist in an investment policy based on considerations other than the best interests of the beneficiaries.[74] And Harman J. has suggested that a member of a discretionary class would procure the removal of a trustee who "deliberately refused to consider any question" relating to the qualification of members to receive payments.[75]

In the case of a foreign settlement, the court has inherent juris-

---

[69] *Courtenay* v. *Courtenay* (1846) 3 Jo. & La.T. 519, 533.

[70] *Re Chetwynd's Settlement* [1902] 1 Ch. 692.

[71] T.A. 1925, ss.36, 41; *ante,* pp. 469–473; *Re Stoneham S.T.* [1953] Ch. 59; as to removal of a charitable trustee, see Charities Act 1960, s.20; *ante,* p. 451.

[72] *Letterstedt* v. *Broers* (1884) 9 App.Cas. 371; *Re Wrightson* [1908] 1 Ch. 789; *Re Pauling's S.T. (No. 2)* [1963] Ch. 576; *Jones* v. *Att.-Gen.* [1974] Ch. 148 (trustee of charitable trust); *ante,* p. 451; *Re Edwards' W.T.* [1982] Ch. 30.

[73] *Moore* v. *M'Glynn* [1894] 1 Ir.R. 74.

[74] *Cowan* v. *Scargill* [1985] Ch. 270, *post,* p. 496.

[75] *Re Gestetner Settlement* [1953] Ch. 672 at p. 688; see also *per* Lord Wilberforce in *McPhail* v. *Doulton* [1971] A.C. 424 at p. 456; *ante,* p. 203.

diction to make *in personam* orders removing and replacing foreign trustees, whether or not the assets are in England and whether or not the proper law of the trust is English law.[76] All that is necessary is that the individual trustee is subject to the jurisdiction of the English courts.[77]

In administration actions the powers of the court are very elastic.[78] The court can, at any time during such proceedings, remove the trustees, if it considers such removal necessary for the preservation of the trust estate or the welfare of the beneficiaries, notwithstanding that such removal has not been expressly asked for by the pleadings. But each case must be weighed carefully on its merits; and the court will sometimes find it necessary to place in one scale a minor breach of trust, and in the other the certain expense to the trust estate of a change of trustees.[79]

13. CONTROL OF TRUSTEES

The basic principle governing trustees is that, while duties must be discharged, the exercise of discretions needs only to be considered. The very fact of a discretion having been entrusted precludes the trustee from being obligated to exercise it in any particular matter, or indeed at all. Thus in *Tempest* v. *Lord Camoys*,[80] one trustee wished to take advantage of a power in a trust instrument to purchase land but his co-trustee would not agree. It could not be shown that he had failed to consider the matter, and the court refused to issue any directive to him.

Nor is there a general principle that trustees should consult beneficiaries, though they should inform them that they have certain rights.[81] Frequently consultation takes place as a matter of practice, but only occasionally does statute[82] impose an obligation on them to do so, and even then their wishes are not mandatory but must be related to the overall welfare of the trust.

But what is the position if trustees exercise a discretion in a manner that appears wholly unrealistic? Is it a satisfactory answer to state simply that the matter has been fully considered? The law on this subject is neither wholly clear nor wholly satisfactory.

[76] *Chellaram* v. *Chellaram* [1985] Ch. 409; (1986) 102 L.Q.R. 28 (D. Evans); All E.R.Rev. 1985, p. 62 (J. G. Collier); Hayton and Marshall (8th ed.), Chap. 11. See Recognition of Trusts Act 1987, Sched. 1, Art. 8.
[77] By reason of service of process in England, or because the trustee has submitted to the jurisdiction, or because the court has assumed jurisdiction under R.S.C. Ord. 11.
[78] *Re Harrison's Settlement Trusts* [1965] 1 W.L.R. 1492. On the removal of an executor, see *I.R.C.* v. *Stype Investments (Jersey) Ltd.* [1982] Ch. 456.
[79] *Re Wrightson* [1908] 1 Ch. 789.
[80] (1882) 21 Ch.D. 571; *cf. Gisborne* v. *Gisborne* (1877) 2 App.Cas. 300: *per* Lord Reid in *Re Gulbenkian's Settlements* [1970] A.C. 508 at p. 518.
[81] *Hawkesley* v. *May* [1956] 1 Q.B. 304; *post*, p. 524.
[82] *e.g.*, statutory trusts arising under L.P.A. 1925; see *ibid.* s.26(3) as amended by L.P.(A.)A. 1926, Sched., *ante*, p. 263.

A. Giving of Reasons

There is a basic rule that trustees cannot be compelled to explain their reasons for exercising or not exercising a discretionary power.

> In *Re Beloved Wilkes' Charity*,[83] trustees were directed to select a boy to be educated for Orders in the Church of England. Their freedom of choice was limited by a preference for certain parishes, if a fit and proper candidate therefrom could be found.
>
> The trustees selected Charles Joyce, a boy who did not come from one of these parishes. It appeared that Charles' brother was a Minister who had sought assistance on his behalf from one of the trustees. The trustees gave no reasons for their choice, but asserted that they had considered the candidates impartially.
>
> Lord Truro refused to set aside the trustees' selection, or to require the trustees to explain how they had arrived at their conclusion.[84]

No distinction exists in this context between oral and documentary evidence, which is a matter of some importance in view of the large amount of trust business which is now conducted by correspondence or at meetings with written agenda and minutes. In *Re Londonderry's Settlement*,[85] the court drew a sharp distinction between written material of this nature which related to management of the trust property (which should be disclosed to requesting beneficiaries) and material which related to the exercise of discretions (which need not be disclosed). But if trustees do give reasons, then the courts will look into their adequacy.[86]

B. Investigation

The cases are not clear, however, on whether the courts will look into the exercise of a discretion that *appears* to be wholly unreasonable. If there is an allegation of fraud or misconduct, the courts must investigate it; but the complainant is in a difficulty in that the evidence which he requires is the personal motivation of the trustees. If fraud is proved, or if the exercise of the discretion is shown to be "capricious,"[87] the court will declare the trustees' decision void. It is not clear what will happen if, on investigation, the discretion is shown to have been wrongly, but not fraudulently, exercised.[88] Some cases[89] in the

---

[83] (1851) 3 Mac. & G. 440.

[84] For a discussion on policy grounds, see (1965) 28 M.L.R. 220 (A. Samuels); (1965) S.J. 239 (A. J. Hawkins and F. W. Taylor).

[85] [1965] Ch. 918; *post*, p. 523; *Butt* v. *Kelson* [1952] Ch. 197.

[86] *Klug* v. *Klug* [1918] 2 Ch. 67.

[87] *Re Manisty's Settlement* [1974] Ch. 17; *ante*, p. 105.

[88] See (1965) 81 L.Q.R. 192 (R.E.M.), and *post*, p. 524, (1965) 28 M.L.R. 220 (A. Samuels).

[89] *Re Hodges* (1878) 7 Ch.D. 754; *Re Roper's Trust* (1879) 11 Ch.D. 272; *Re Brittlebank* (1881) 30 W.R. 99. But the jurisdiction may be confined to the protection of trust assets. *cf. Re D'Epinoix's Settlement* [1914] 1 Ch. 890.

nineteenth century reserve to the courts a jurisdiction to investigate the exercise of a discretion that has already been made and that, on external evidence only, appears to have been "mischievously and ruinously exercised." Lord Normand, in a Scottish appeal to the House of Lords, thought that "The principles on which the courts must proceed are the same whether the trustees' reasons for their decision are disclosed or not,"[90] but it is not clear whether all the propositions in this case are acceptable as part of the English law of trusts. A conclusion can only be drawn in the form that it will never be easy to persuade a court to review the exercise of a discretion by trustees in the absence of some clear facts from which it is not difficult to discern that the discretion has been irregularly exercised.

C. Power of Decision

A trust deed occasionally gives to trustees a power to decide a particular matter conclusively, so that the jurisdiction of the courts to decide it is ousted. For instance in *Re Coxen*,[91] a testator provided that his wife should cease to enjoy a right to live in a particular house if the trustees were of the opinion that she had ceased to reside there permanently. The condition was upheld, as the testator had sufficiently defined the state of affairs upon which the trustees were to form their opinion. And in *Re Tuck's Settlement Trust*,[92] the Court of Appeal would have accepted a decision by the Chief Rabbi of London on the question whether the beneficiary's wife should meet the qualifications of Jewish blood and Jewish faith.[93]

But the issue that they have to decide must be a reasonably clear one; unreasonably vague phrases are not to be given validity in this way.[94] And they cannot be given jurisdiction to determine conclusively the *identity* of beneficiaries as distinct from more limited issues such as where they lived, what is their ancestry or faith, or whether, being institutions, they are under "state" control.[95] The House of Lords in *Dundee General Hospitals* v. *Walker*[96] thought it possible that the

---

[90] *Dundee General Hospitals* v. *Walker* [1952] 1 All E.R. 896 at p. 900; *Re Hastings-Bass* [1975] Ch. 25, C.A.

[91] [1948] Ch. 747 at p. 761; *Re Tuck's S.T.* [1978] Ch. 49. A complete or wide ouster of the court's jurisdiction is not possible; *Re Wynn* [1952] Ch. 271.

[92] [1978] Ch. 49, *ante*, p. 102.

[93] Which was not necessary to the decision, because the condition was held to be sufficiently certain.

[94] *Re Jones* [1953] Ch. 125 ("if at any time X shall in the uncontrolled opinion of the trustee have social or other relationship with Y"); *Re Wright's W.T.* (1981) 78 L.S.G. 841 (to trustees to use at their discretion "for such people and institutions as they think have helped me or my late husband"); *ante*, p. 102.

[95] *Re Raven* [1915] 1 Ch. 673; *Dundee General Hospitals* v. *Walker* [1952] 1 All E.R. 896. In the latter case, the ouster was held not to be invalidated by the admixture of legal issues in the question of what constituted "state" control. But legal issues as such cannot be withdrawn from the court's jurisdiction.

[96] *Ibid.* See especially *per* Lord Reid at p. 905.

decisions of trustees in such cases could be attacked on the grounds of perversity or failure to appreciate the issue, as well as on grounds of bad faith; and Lord Denning in *Re Tuck's Settlement Trusts* would only have accepted the reference to the Chief Rabbi "so long as he does not misconduct himself or come to a decision which is wholly unreasonable."[97]

The general principle that beneficiaries cannot control trustees in the manner in which they exercise their powers applies even though all the beneficiaries are ascertained and *sui juris* and desirous of the power being exercised in a particular way.[98] But in such a case the trust can of course be brought to an end.

---

[97] *Supra*, at p. 62.
[98] *Re Brockbank* [1948] Ch. 206 (appointment of a new trustee); *ante*, p. 473; *cf. Re George Whichelow Ltd.* [1954] 1 W.L.R. 5 at p. 8.

CHAPTER 17

DUTIES OF TRUSTEES IN RELATION TO THE TRUST
PROPERTY

1. DUTY TO COLLECT IN THE ASSETS

A. Duty on Accepting Office

Trustees must, on their appointment, make themselves acquainted
with the terms of the trust and the state and the details of the trust
property, check that the trust fund is invested in accordance with the
provisions of the trust deed, and that the securities and any chattels are
in proper custody.[1] They should not wait until the trust property is
formally vested in them. The discharge of their duties will obviously
depend upon circumstances. Thus trustees of a trust newly constituted,
and with suitable assets, are in an easier situation than personal
representatives who find, as part of the estate, assets which are highly

[1] *Re Miller's Deed Trust* (1978) 75 L.S.Gaz. 454.

483

speculative or precarious. In the latter type of case the duty laid upon them is to consider the best method of protecting the value of the assets, and this may very well involve delaying a decision to dispose of them. Liability for loss will not be imposed on them if their decision to delay was reasonable, even though subsequent events show it to have been the less wise course.[2]

A trustee appointed in place of a former trustee must make all reasonable inquiries[3] to satisfy himself that nothing has been done by his predecessor and the continuing trustees which amounts to a breach of trust; and the continuing trustees must provide this information from trust documents.[4] Omission to inquire may render the new trustee liable, but he is not to be fixed with notice of matters that do not appear on any of the trust documents, though the matter may be known to the retiring trustee.[5] On a similar principle, if he is ignorant of the existence of some right forming part of the trust, he is not liable for loss of that right through non-enforcement unless he could have discovered its existence from materials at his disposal.[6]

B. Extent of Duty

The duty to safeguard trust assets is a stringent one; indeed, it has sometimes been almost too strictly applied.

> In *Re Brogden*,[7] the trustees of a marriage settlement took what they considered to be all reasonable steps to ensure that a covenant to pay £10,000 to them at the end of a stated period of five years was carried out. They did not sue because the covenantor's estate was the basis of the family partnership, the stability of which might have been imperilled by an action at a time of trade depression. The trustees were held liable. They should have taken every possible step to insist on payment, irrespective of the claims of sentiment within a family.

As with family sentiment, so with the commercial ethics that would govern the transactions of a private vendor.

---

[2] *Buxton* v. *Buxton* (1835) 1 My. & Cr. 80.

[3] *Harvey* v. *Olliver* (1887) 57 L.T. 239; *Re Lucking's W.T.* [1968] 1 W.L.R. 866. The Law Reform Committee, 23rd Report, *The Powers and Duties of Trustees* (1982, Cmnd. 8733), para. 4.15, takes the view that a new trustee must act as a prudent businessman in ascertaining the details of the trust. If these show nothing unusual, he is not liable for the defaults of his co-trustees. The same standard of care will apply in relation to the acts of his co-trustees during the trustee's office.

[4] *Tiger* v. *Barclays Bank* [1951] 2 K.B. 556.

[5] *Hallows* v. *Lloyd* (1888) 39 Ch.D. 686.

[6] *Youde* v. *Cloud* (1874) L.R. 18 Eq. 634. A similarly reasonable rule governs the inquiries trustees should make in relation to covenants to settle after-acquired property: *Re Strahan* (1856) 8 De. G.M. & G. 291.

[7] (1888) 38 Ch.D. 546. An extreme case, when litigation would have ruined a beneficiary, is *Ward* v. *Ward* (1843) 2 H.L.C. 777n. (Lord Lyndhurst L.C.). See also *Harris* v. *Black* (1983) 46 P. & C.R. 366 (duty to preserve assets did not require court to compel a trustee-beneficiary to seek the renewal of a business tenancy which he did not want, the partnership with the other trustee-beneficiary having been dissolved).

In *Buttle* v. *Saunders*,[8] trustees had orally agreed to sell the freehold reversion of premises in London to the leaseholder. Then a beneficiary made a higher offer. The trustees declined to consider it, feeling themselves bound by commercial morality to complete the agreement. Wynn-Parry J. held that, although there may be cases where a trustee should accept a lower offer—as where that offer may be lost if not honoured—and although the honourable course was to stand by the earlier offer, the trustees had an overriding duty to obtain the best price for their beneficiaries.

C. Litigation

In *Re Brogden*,[9] the Court of Appeal laid down that the only excuse for not taking action to enforce payment was a well-founded belief on the part of the trustees that such action would be fruitless; and the burden of proving their belief was on the trustees.[10] But the shoulders of trustees are lightened by the extensive powers of compounding liabilities, allowing time for the payment of debts, and compromising doubtful actions, etc., given by the Trustee Act 1925, s.15.[11] For trustees are not to be liable for loss caused by any acts done by them in good faith in exercise of these powers, provided they have directed their minds to the problem and not just let the matter slide.[12] A trustee will be allowed the costs of litigation by or against the trust from the trust assets, but not where the litigation results from an unreasonable withholding of property from those entitled to it,[13] nor where the litigation is speculative and turns out to be unsuccessful.[14]

D. A Continuing Duty

Trustees must of course regard their duty of safeguarding trust assets as a continuing one. In regard to investment in securities, the subject will fall to be treated at length. In regard to land, there is of course a duty to consider the maintenance and general welfare of the property, and in regard to deeds and chattels, a duty to see that they are kept securely.[15] These may be deposited with a bank or banking company whose business includes the safe custody of documents.[16] There is no duty to insure unless such a duty is imposed in the trust deed, but trustees have a power to insure.[17]

---

[8] [1950] 2 All E.R. 193; (1950) 14 Conv.(N.S.) 228 (E.H. Bodkin); (1975) 30 Conv. (N.S.) 177 (A. Samuels).
[9] (1888) 38 Ch.D. 546.
[10] *Re Brogden, supra*; *Clack* v. *Holland* (1854) 19 Beav. 262.
[11] *Post* p. 531.
[12] *Re Greenwood* (1911) 105 L.T. 509. *cf. Re Ezekiel's Settlements* [1942] Ch. 230.
[13] *Re Chapman* (1895) 72 L.T. 66.
[14] *Re Beddoe* [1893] 1 Ch. 547; *Re England's S.T.* [1918] 1 Ch. 24.
[15] *Jobson* v. *Palmer* [1893] 1 Ch. 71.
[16] T.A. 1925, s.21.
[17] *Post*, p. 529.

2. Duty to Invest[18]

A. Meaning of Investment

A trustee is under a duty to invest trust money in his hands. To invest means "to employ money in the purchase of anything from which interest or profit is expected."[19] From the point of view of an individual investing his own money, he does not mind whether the profit comes from income earned by the investment or from capital appreciation; probably he prefers the latter because the rates of tax are lower. But trustees usually have to consider the interests of a life tenant, who is entitled to the income, and also of the remaindermen who are interested in the capital. The trustees' duty is to act fairly between them. The investments must produce income, and maintain the capital. Thus premium bonds and chattels, such as antiques or silver, are not investments for this purpose. Similarly a purchase of a house for occupation by a beneficiary, and which therefore produces no income, has been held not to be an investment.[20] It is for this reason that power is usually given expressly to trustees to make such a purchase.[21] Similarly investments which yield a high rate of income because the capital is wasting away—as with short leaseholds,[22] or a loan which is dependent on the personal security of the borrower[23]—should be avoided. The law relating to authorised trustee investments is an attempt to give the trustees an area of choice within this principle. To what extent it succeeds can only be understood by an appreciation of some aspects of the economics of investment.

B. The Economics of Investment[24]

In most general terms, there are basically two types of investment. The first is a loan at a rate of interest; and there are, as will be seen, various forms of loan. The second is a participation in a profit-making activity; which in the present context means the purchase of ordinary shares in a company; "equities" as they are called. The great change

---

[18] As to the delegation of investment decisions, see Law Reform Committee, 23rd Report, *The Powers and Duties of Trustees* (1982, Cmnd. 8733), paras. 4.16 *et seq.* On the question how far the Financial Services Act 1986 applies to trustees and personal representatives, see (1988) 85 L.S. Gaz. No. 22, p.14 (R. Aldwinckle) and No. 45, p.30 (N. Reid). See further F.S.A. 1986, s.62.

[19] *Shorter Oxford English Dictionary*; *Re Wragg* [1919] 2 Ch. 58 at p. 64, *per* P.O. Lawrence J. who added: "and which property is purchased in order to be held for the sake of the income which it will yield."

[20] *Re Power* [1947] Ch. 572; *Re Peczenik's S.T.* [1964] 1 W.L.R. 720; it is otherwise if land is purchased for the sake of the income it will produce; *Re Wragg, supra*, at pp. 64, 65. The Law Reform Committee has recommended the reversal of *Re Power*; 23rd Report, *The Powers and Duties of Trustees* (1982, Cmnd. 8733), para. 3.5.

[21] See section D, *infra*.

[22] See *post*, p. 490.

[23] *Khoo Tek Keong* v. *Ch'ng Joo Tuan Neoh* [1934] A.C. 529.

[24] See Parker and Mellows, *The Modern Law of Trusts* (5th ed.), pp. 302–310.

made by the Trustee Investments Act 1961 was the inclusion of ordinary shares in the list of permitted investments for trustees in respect of part of the fund.

(i) **Fixed Interest Investments.** Fixed interest investments are also of two basic types.

(a) *Where the Value of the Capital does not Fluctuate.* National Development Bonds, deposit accounts at a bank, or in the Trustee Savings Bank or a Building Society earn interest for the depositor, and the loan is repayable according to the terms of withdrawal. The rate of interest earned may vary with the economic circumstances. The holders' or depositors' rights are governed by the terms offered by the borrowers.

(b) *Fixed Interest Securities with Fluctuating Capital Value.* Most fixed interest securities issued by the Government and local authorities are in the form of stock issued to the purchaser (lender), and pay a fixed rate of interest. The purchaser becomes the owner of the amount of stock purchased, and he may sell the stock, with all rights attached to it, to other purchasers. The value of the stock is whatever a purchaser will give for it. That depends on many factors; essentially the current rate of interest chargeable on borrowed money.

In times of prosperity, and where sterling is in demand as a reliable currency by foreign investors, interest rates on sterling are likely to be low. They were between 3 per cent. to 4 per cent. during most of the second half of the nineteenth century. And the Labour Government, in 1945, pursuing a policy of making money cheap to borrow, achieved the same rate. Thus 2½ per cent. Treasury Stock was issued in 1946 at par (100). Since then the value of the pound has fallen substantially, both against foreign currencies and in terms of purchasing power at home. Largely because of general inflation and the loss of international confidence in sterling, interest rates have increased. Of course, interest rates payable by a borrower are higher than those payable to an investor. The base lending rate is currently 13 per cent. So a 3 per cent. stock, paying £3 per annum on a nominal investment of £100, needs now, to be saleable, to pay 9 or 10 per cent. But the rate of interest is fixed. So the value of the stock declines. A 3 per cent. stock is now worth about £32. £3 per annum on an outlay of £32 is a 9.3 per cent. return.

(c) *Dated Stocks.* Some stocks however are "dated"; that is, they will be repaid at "par" (100) at a stated date in the future. A 3 per cent. stock, to be repaid next year, will be priced much higher than 33; for it will be 100 at a date during next year. Thus in December 1988, Treasury 3 per cent. 1989 is priced at 97. A purchaser will receive £3 per annum for each £100 nominal, which is a rate of return of 3.1 per cent. at a purchase price of 97. The holder will also receive a capital appreciation of £3 by the date of maturity of the stock. Capital gains on certain government stocks are free of capital gains tax.[25] This and other factors contribute to the price. The price of a selected number of government, local authority and commonwealth stocks are quoted daily in the financial pages of the press.

(d) *Debentures.* A debenture is an acknowledgement of indebtedness by a company, supported in practice by a charge upon the undertaking and assets of a company. This is a floating, as opposed to a fixed, charge. The company is free to deal with any of its specific assets unaffected by the charge. The charge crystallises when the debenture holders take the necessary steps in accordance with the terms of the debenture deed to enforce their security. The value of a debenture is dependent partly upon the ability of the assets and undertaking of the company to provide sufficient cover for the amount of the loan, and it is therefore to some extent dependent upon the commercial stability of the company.

(e) *Preference Shares.* Preference shares are shares in a company which have a preference in relation to the payment of a fixed rate of dividend, and may have other preferential rights as well. Being dependent upon the earning by the company of sufficient profits to pay the dividends, they are less secure than government securities or debentures, and consequently they normally carry a higher return. That does not mean of course that the rate of dividend rises. It is the price at which the shares can be purchased on the market which varies. If five per cent. preference shares, paying £5 per annum on their par value of £1 were priced at 50, the dividend of £5 per annum on an outlay of £50 would put the shares on a return of 10 per cent.

(ii) **Equities.** (a) *Ordinary Shares.* The capital of a company is laid down in its Memorandum[26] and its division into classes of shares usually contained in the Articles, and it normally includes ordinary shares. Ownership of an ordinary share entitles the purchaser to various rights, such as a vote at the general meeting, a right to participate in dividends when declared on the ordinary shares, and a right to participate in a winding up. The details of these rights are laid down in the general law as varied in the case of any particular company by the Articles.

The Annual General Meeting will declare the dividend payable for the year, if any. The amount will vary with the results of the year's trading. The value of ordinary shares thus varies with the fortunes of

[25] C.G.T.A. 1979, s.67 and Sched. 2; F.A. 1985, s.67; *ante*, p. 210.
[26] Companies Act 1985, s.2.

the company. Thus, they are an excellent investment in prosperous times, but disastrous if no profits are made, and no dividends paid. They necessarily contain an element of speculation, and it is for this reason that ordinary shares were not authorised investments for trustees until 1961.

(b) *Managed Fund.*[27] The selection of ordinary shares for investment is a highly specialised matter. Further, it is important that the investment of a trust should be spread over a wide range of companies operating in different fields.[28] This provides a "spread" of investments. But a small trust cannot provide a satisfactory spread. This can be achieved by participating in an investment fund which is managed by a team of investment experts. There are basically two types. First the unit trust, in which the managers receive money from investors, and form a single fund, divided up into units which are owned by the investors. The management is paid expenses and salary. The investors have the advantage of investment expertise, and of the spread of investments. Units in a trust can be bought and sold. Secondly, the investment trust. This is a limited company in which shares can be bought and sold through a stockbroker like other shares. The company buys shares in other companies, and the investors receive their return in the form of dividends from the investment trust.

C. Express Powers of Investment

A trustee may be given wide power by the express terms of the trust instrument to select investments; or his selection may be left to investments authorised by the general law. Express clauses at one time were strictly construed, and it used to be that the onus was on the trustees to prove that they were within the terms of the clause.[29] These cases reflect the court's fear of investment in ordinary shares in the nineteenth century. There was "a good deal of authority . . . to the effect that investment clauses should be strictly construed and should not be construed as authorising investments outside the trustee range unless they clearly and unambiguously indicate any intention to that effect."[30] Thus it seemed to be established that words such as a "power to invest in such securities as they might think fit"[31] gave power merely to select among trustee securities. In *Re Harari's Settlement Trusts*,[32] Jenkins J.

---

[27] (1973) 123 N.L.J. 354 (C. Woodhouse).
[28] *Contra*, Andrew Carnegie, who advised; "Put all your eggs in one basket, then watch the basket."
[29] *Stretton* v. *Ashmall* (1854) 3 Drew. 9.
[30] Jenkins J. in *Re Harari's S.T.* [1949] 1 All E.R. 430 at p. 432; *Re Peczenik's Settlement* [1964] 1 W.L.R. 720
[31] *Re Braithwaite* (1882) 21 Ch.D. 121; *Bethell* v. *Abraham* (1873) L.R. 17 Eq. 24; "as (to) the majority shall seem meet": *Re Maryon-Wilson's Estate* [1912] 1 Ch. 55; in *Re Smith* [1896] 1 Ch. 71, Kekewich J. held that such a clause entitled the trustees to invest in debentures of a limited company.
[32] [1949] 1 All E.R. 430.

accepted the fact that the older cases suggested a strict construction of investment clauses, but felt that he was "left free to construe this settlement according to what I consider to be the natural and proper meaning of the words used in their context, and, so construing the words 'in or upon such investments as to them may seem fit' I see no justification in implying any restriction."[33] The trustees could invest in equities.

It remains the usual practice since, as well as before, the Trustee Investment Act 1961 to include a clause giving trustees wide powers in investment in respect of the whole of the fund and thus to exclude the Act[34]; and the trustees, or other persons, may be given authority to amend the power.[35] The Act, however, will still apply where the express power does not cover all the property in the trust fund.[36]

D. The Purchase of Land

As a general rule, trustees may not purchase land unless the trust instrument so permits. Even where the instrument does authorise investment in land, we have seen that the purchase of a house for the occupation of a beneficiary is not an "investment."[37] However, trustees of settled land or land held upon trust for sale have statutory power to purchase land, either in fee simple or, if leasehold, where the lease has sixty years or more unexpired.[38] The Law Reform Committee[39] has proposed that all trustees should have the power to purchase land as an investment, with appropriate professional advice from surveyors and valuers. In the case of leasehold land, there should be no absolute prohibition on leases with less than sixty years to run, but where such an investment is made, a sinking fund should be set up, serviced out of income, or other steps should be taken to protect the capital.

E. Authorised Investments

(i) **Traditional Rule.** The rules governing investment by trustees have been governed by the principles, first that trustees must avoid all risk to the capital of the fund, and secondly, that the value of the £ will remain stable. Throughout the nineteenth century, the system worked well enough. At first, trustees were restricted to consols, and since

---

[33] *Re Jewish Endowments Trust* [1960] 1 All E.R. 764.
[34] See *Encyclopaedia of Forms and Precedents* (4th ed.) Vol. 20, p. 678.
[35] *Re Harari's S.T., supra,* at p. 434.
[36] *Post,* p. 494.
[37] *Re Power* [1947] Ch. 572, *ante,* p. 486.
[38] S.L.A. 1925, s.73(1)(xi) and L.P.A. 1925, s.28. See *Re Wakeman* [1945] Ch. 177; *Re Wellsted's W.T.* [1949] Ch. 296. The Trustee Investments Act 1961 permits investment in mortgages of such land.
[39] 23rd Report, *The Powers and Duties of Trustees* (1982, Cmnd. 8733), paras. 3.2–3.4. See also para. 3.8, proposing that land development is risky and should therefore have to be authorised by the instrument or by the court.

1859[40] they have been permitted to choose among a narrow range of fixed interest investments, known as trustee securities. Investment was not yet a technical or specialised matter. The income beneficiaries were assured of an income, and the capital was secure. But progressive inflation changed all that, as has been seen.

Much of the problem of the decline of the value of the currency should be solved by investment in equities. A purchaser of a share in a company owns a share of the operation. If the business prospers, its actual value may increase. Assume, however, that the actual value of the business remains the same; if the value of money is reduced to one-third, the value of the shares will treble. That may not sound to be great progress; but at least, as it is said, it is "a hedge against inflation."

But in times of economic depression, the prices of ordinary shares fall even faster than those of gilts. Prices on the Stock Exchange are established by buyers and sellers, and a number of emotional and irrational factors play their part in establishing and undermining confidence. The overall prices of industrial shares are gauged by an index called the *Financial Times* Index,[41] which started in 1937 at 100. In 1969 it was 500. In January 1975, it was 150, and is 1436 at the time of writing. The fluctuations underline the dangers involved in investment in ordinary shares, and emphasise the need for expertise in selecting investments; and the avoidance of speculation.

(ii) Trustee Investments Act 1961.[42] Authorised investments are now governed by the Trustee Investments Act 1961, which repeals and replaces the Trustee Act 1925, s.1.[43] The Act applies subject to a contrary intention in an instrument made after the passing of the Act,[44] but regardless of the provisions of such instruments coming into operation previously. The object of the Act is to permit trustees to invest a proportion of trust funds in equities. The present permitted proportion is one-half,[45] but the Treasury has power by order to direct that this will be increased to any proportion not greater than three-quarters.[46]

(iii) The Scheme of the Act. Trustees who wish to take advantage of the wider powers of investment given by the Act must divide the fund

---

[40] Law of Property Amendment Act 1859.

[41] This is now the FT30-share index. Since 1984 there is also the broader based FT-SE 100 Index.

[42] (1962) 26 Conv.(n.s.) 351 (A. Samuels). Most American states have given wider power of investment, controlling trustees' discretion only by the rule that they must act with the degree of care which a prudent investor would exercise. For a comparison between the English and American approaches, see (1954) 7 C.L.P. 139 (V. Latham); (1974) 23 I.C.L.Q. 748 (D. Grosh); and the Model Prudent Man Investment Act printed at p. 767; (1975) 39 Conv.(n.s.) 327 (D. Paling).

[43] T.I.A. 1961, s.16, Sched. 5.

[44] *Ibid.* s.1(3); and subject to Acts of Parliament or an instrument made under an enactment.

[45] *Ibid.* s.2.

[46] *Ibid.* s.13(1).

into two parts, equal at the time of the division,[47] and called the narrower-range part and the wider-range part. In making the division, a valuation in writing from a person believed by the trustees to be qualified to make it is conclusive.[48] The normal procedure is to have a valuation made by a stockbroker. The division sets the two parts of the fund for all time, and there is no need to ensure that each half remains of the same value. Indeed no further transfers from one half to the other may be made without a "compensating transfer."[49] Later the additions to the trust fund must similarly be equally divided between the two halves.[50]

(iv) Narrower and Wider Range. The First Schedule gives a list of authorised investments.[51] Part I consists of fixed interest investments whose capital value does not fluctuate, and which a trustee may select without taking expert advice.[52] Part II contains a long list of fixed interest investments, most of which may fluctuate in value, and trustees are required to take advice before making such investment. These two parts are a modern form of the Trustee Act 1925, s.1. Part III contains wider-range investments, and includes ordinary shares in United Kingdom companies, shares in building societies, and unit trusts. No investment in any part is permitted where the holder can be required to accept payment of principal and interest otherwise than in sterling.[53]

(v) Restrictions on Wider Range. As we have seen, trustees may, after division,[54] invest the wider-range part in wider-range investments. There is no need to do so. The wider-range half may be kept in narrower-range investments if the trustees so decide. If they decide, however, to purchase ordinary shares, their selection is restricted to shares with the following qualifications[55]: (i) they must be quoted on a recognised United Kingdom stock exchange; (ii) they must be fully paid up (or required by the terms of the issue to be fully paid up within nine months)[56]; (iii) the company must have an issued capital of £1,000,000 or more[57]; (iv) the company must have paid a dividend in each of the immediately preceding five years on all of its shares ranking for dividend.[57]

---

[47] T.I.A. 1961, s.2(1).
[48] *Ibid.* s.5.
[49] *Ibid.* s.2(1)(*b*).
[50] *Ibid.* s.2(3)(*b*). This includes interest and dividends.
[51] Reprinted in the Appendix.
[52] See *post*, p. 497.
[53] T.I.A. 1961, Sched. 1, Pt. IV, para. 1.
[54] *Ibid.*, s.2(1).
[55] *Ibid.* Sched. 1, Pt. IV, paras. 2 and 3.
[56] These requirements apply also to many of the fixed interest securities. The object is to prevent purchases of shares which are subject to a call.
[57] These requirements apply also to debentures under T.I.A. 1961, Sched. 1, Pt. II (narrower-range with advice), para. 6.

F. Alterations to the Fund

(i) **Accruals.** If property accrues to the trustee *as owner of property comprised in either part of the fund*, it shall be treated as belonging to that fund.[58] Thus a bonus issue of shares stays in wider-range; and a new issue of Government securities issued at the maturity[59] of a dated stock stays in narrower-range.

In every other case, however, the trustee must ensure, by apportionment of the accruing property or by the transfer of property from one part of the fund to another, that the value of each part of the fund is increased by the same amount.[60] This is so, as we have seen, with additions to the trust fund[61]; similarly with a "rights issue,"[62] because this comes to the trust fund, not by reason of the trustees' ownership of the original shares but by the purchase of the new shares. To the extent that the value of the new shares exceeds the purchase price, there must be a compensating transfer, as described above.

(ii) **Withdrawals.** Where trustees take property out of the trust fund in the exercise of any power or duty, the property may be taken at the trustees' discretion from either part[63]; no compensating transfer is necessary. It appears that this rule applies where the property is taken permanently out of the fund, as where an advancement is made to a beneficiary,[64] or to form a separate fund, as for example to establish an accumulating fund for an infant beneficiary,[65] or to purchase a "special range"[66] investment under a special power. In any of these cases, the balance between the narrower- and wider-range parts will be disturbed; indeed it seems that the narrower-range part might be completely used up.

(iii) **Separate Funds.** Where such a separate fund is set up out of a trust fund which has been divided into narrower-range and wider-range parts, then the separate fund must be divided either equally, or so that the parts bear to each other the same proportion as the two corresponding parts of the fund at the date of appropriation, or some intermediate proportion.[67]

For example, a £4,000 fund has been divided so that both parts were worth £2,000. The wider-range is increased to £3,000; the narrower

---

[58] T.I.A. 1961, s.2(3). This provision does not apply to interest and dividends.
[59] *i.e.* when the date arrives at which a dated stock is repaid at par.
[60] T.I.A. 1961, s.2(3)(*b*).
[61] *Ante*, p. 492.
[62] The right, given to shareholders by a company wishing to raise additional capital, to subscribe for newly issued shares, usually at a favourable price. See T.A. 1925, s.10(3); T.I.A. 1961, s.9.
[63] T.I.A. 1961, s.2(4).
[64] *Post*, p. 547.
[65] *Ante*, p. 220.
[66] *Post*, p. 494.
[67] T.I.A. 1961, s.4(3).

remained at £2,000. The trustees wish to establish a separate fund for a newly born beneficiary of £1,000. They may take this sum from the narrower-range. If they wish to use the investment powers of the Act in respect of the separate fund, they must divide it either £500 wider-range and £500 narrower-range, or £600/£400, or any intermediate proportion. The original fund will now of course be £3,000 and £1,000. If the trustees had decided to put £2,000 into the separate fund, and to take it all from the narrower-range part, the narrower-range part of the original fund would have disappeared.

G. Special Powers and Special Range

(i) **The Second Schedule.** The powers of investment conferred by the Act are in addition to express powers of investment or of postponing conversion. Such powers are referred to in the Act as "special powers."[68] A power to invest in any investment authorised by law for the investment of trust property conferred on a trustee before the passing of the Act has effect as a power to invest in accordance with the Act.[69]

Wider-range property which trustees are authorised to hold apart from the provisions of the Act or Part 1 of Trustee Act 1925 or a special power to invest in authorised investments[70] is called "special range" property, and is held subject to the provisions of the Second Schedule.[71] In effect, special range investments are those authorised under an express power of investment, or under a court order relating to the investment powers of a trust,[72] or under a special statute such as was obtained before 1961 in order to widen the investment power of various corporations and institutions. Common examples of special range investments include shares in private companies and the purchase of land. If the whole property of the trust is governed by any such power, the provisions of the Act have no relevance. Where, however, the trust contains other property, the Act applies to the remainder.[73] If the trustees then wish to exercise the investment powers under the Act, the trust funds must be divided into three parts; the special range, covering whatever part of the fund is so applicable, and the remainder divided equally between narrower- and wider-range.

(ii) **Purchases, Accruals and Disposals.** Property taken from the trust in pursuance of a power to invest in special range property may be taken either from the narrower- or the wider-range part.[74] Accruals of

---

[68] T.I.A. 1961, s.3(1).
[69] *Ibid.* s.3(2).
[70] See (1970) 120 N.L.J. 240 (R.T. Oerton).
[71] *Ibid.* s.3(3).
[72] Such as an order made under the Variation of Trusts Act 1958; *post*, p. 586.
[73] *Ibid.* Sched. 2, para. 2.
[74] *Ibid.* s.2(4).

special range property are added to the special range.[75] But any conversion *from* special range property must be apportioned equally between narrower- and wider-range,[76] or a compensating transfer made.

(iii) Exceptions. The provisions of the Second Schedule do not apply however where the special powers of the trustee have been conferred or varied within 10 years prior to the passing of the Act by an order of court or by an Act or statutory instrument relating specifically to the trust in question, or by a local Act of the same session as the 1961 Act.[77] The provisions of the Third Schedule then apply, which make no provision for special range property. The special powers may continue to be used; but the trustee may only use the powers of the 1961 Act to invest in wider-range investments if half of the fund is or becomes invested in narrower-range investments,[78] and trustees are no longer protected by Trustee Act 1925, s.4, in respect of non-narrower-range investments which have become unauthorised by virtue of the Third Schedule.[79]

H. General Duty in Choosing Investments

Trustees are under a duty not only to ensure that the chosen investments are authorised, but also that they are properly selected for the trust in accordance with the standard of a prudent man of business,[80] and "to avoid all investments of that class which are attended with hazard."[81] "The duty of a trustee is not to take such care only as a prudent man would take if he had only himself to consider; the duty rather is to take such care as an ordinary prudent man would take if he were minded to make an investment for the benefit of other people for whom he felt morally bound to provide."[82] In making an investment for the benefit of persons for whom he felt morally bound to provide he must show more caution than a private investor who may well benefit from making wisely chosen speculations.[83] This is so, however wide a discretion he may be given by the trust instrument.[84] The Act[85] requires that he shall have regard "to the need for diversification of investments

---

[75] *Ibid*. Sched. 2, para. 2(2)(*b*).
[76] *Ibid*. Sched. 2, para. 3.
[77] *Ibid*. s.3(4).
[78] *Ibid*. Sched. 3, para. 1.
[79] *Ibid*. Sched. 3, para. 2.
[80] *Speight* v. *Gaunt* (1883) 9 App. Cas. 1; *Learoyd* v. *Whiteley* (1887) 12 App. Cas. 727; *Bartlett* v. *Barclays Bank Trust Co.* [1980] Ch. 515. Trustees do not act as insurers or guarantee the results; *Nestlé* v. *National Westminster Bank plc* June 29, 1988 (unreported). See generally [1983] Conv. 127 (P. Pearce and A. Samuels).
[81] *Learoyd* v. *Whiteley* (1887) 12 App.Cas. 727 at p. 733, *ante*, p. 459.
[82] *Re Whiteley* (1886) Ch.D. 347 at p. 355, *per* Lindley M.R.
[83] *Learoyd* v. *Whiteley* (1887) 12 App.Cas. 727, *ante*, p. 459.
[84] *Chapman* v. *Browne* [1902] 1 Ch. 785.
[85] s.6(1). Diversification is especially important with large funds; *Cowan* v. *Scargill*, *infra*.

of the trust, in so far as is appropriate to the circumstances of the trust"
and "to the suitability to the trust of investments of the description of
investment proposed and of the investment proposed as an investment
of that description." He must also consider the competing interests of
the life tenant and the remainderman, investing so as to provide a
reasonable income, and to keep secure the capital.[86]

These matters recently arose in *Cowan* v. *Scargill*[87]

> A mineworkers' pension fund with large assets and very wide
> powers of investment was managed by ten trustees, of whom five,
> including the defendant, were appointed by the National Union of
> Mineworkers. They were assisted in investment decisions by an
> advisory panel of experts. An investment plan was submitted, which
> the union trustees, on the basis of union policy, refused to accept
> unless it was amended so that there should be no increase in overseas
> investments; those already made should be withdrawn; and there
> should be no investment in energies in competition with coal. It was
> held that the trustees would be in breach of duty if they refused to
> adopt the investment strategy. They must exercise their powers in
> the best interests of present and future beneficiaries. If the purpose
> of the trust was the provision of financial benefit, the best interests
> of the beneficiaries normally meant their best *financial* interests.
> This duty to the beneficiaries was paramount. The trustees must
> exercise their investment powers so as to yield the best return,
> putting aside personal interests and social and political views. If
> investments in, for example, armaments, tobacco or South African
> companies, were beneficial, they must not refrain because of their
> own views. Honesty and sincerity were not enough to satisfy the
> "prudent businessman" test, but financial benefit was not *inevitably*
> paramount. If all the beneficiaries were adults with strict views on,
> say, tobacco, it might not "benefit" them to make such investments.
> Here, however, there was no justification for reducing the benefit
> because the trustees had an investment policy intended to assist the
> union or the industry. The trustees were pursuing union policy, and
> the ultimate sanction was removal.

It is difficult to see, however, why the trustees would be failing in their
duties if they confined themselves to the investments proposed by the
union trustees. In the case of a pension fund, maintenance of the

---

[86] *Post*, pp. 508 *et seq*. Trustees are under no duty to preserve the real value of the capital
and have a wide discretion in the performance of their duty to hold the balance
between different classes of beneficiaries; *Nestlé* v. *National Westminster Bank plc*,
June 29, 1988 (unreported). The abolition of the investment income surcharge by
F.A. 1984, s.17(2) and Sched. 7, will generally increase the attraction of high income
yielding investments at the expense of capital growth investments.

[87] [1985] Ch. 270; (1984) 81 L.S.Gaz. 2291 (S. C. Butler); All E.R. Rev 1984, p. 306 (P.
J. Clarke). As to charity trustees, see p. 449, n. 78, *ante*.

prosperity of the industry must be in the financial interests of the beneficiaries, and to invest in a competing industry may be harmful.[88] Overseas investments may be risky, and there is an ample range of authorised investments at home: "no trust fund is so big as to exhaust the home market."[89] Perhaps the outcome would have been different if the union trustees had not argued their case on ideology rather than law.[90] It may further be suggested that the principles of private trust law are too narrow to meet the requirements of pension schemes.[91] In any event, it is unlikely that damages would have been recoverable if the union trustees' policy had been implemented, as it does not seem that any loss could have been established.[92]

I. Advice

Investment by trustees is now an expert's job; and it is inevitable that the Act should require them to take expert advice. Successful selection from the wider-range needs much more skill, knowledge and experience than do narrower-range investments, but the requirement of advice is not confined to the wider-range. Before investing under Part II (narrower-range requiring advice) or Part III (wider-range) of the First Schedule, whether in exercise of the statutory power, or under a special power[93] a trustee must obtain and consider advice either given, or subsequently confirmed, in writing[94] as to its suitability.[95] Such advice must be given by a person who is reasonably believed by the trustee to be qualified to advise, but he may give it in the course of his employment as an officer or servant.[96] The trustee must, as always, consider the advice, use his own judgment as a prudent man of business, and take his own decision.[97] He must not repose blind faith in his adviser.

These provisions do not apply where the advice is being given by one trustee to his co-trustees: nor where the trustees' decisions are taken by an officer or servant competent to advise, as in the case of a trust corporation acting as trustee.[98]

---

[88] This argument was rejected by Megarry V.-C. on the facts.
[89] [1985] Conv. 52 at p. 53 (P. Pearce and A. Samuels). See further Annual Report of the Charity Commissioners, 1987, paras. 41–45.
[90] (1986) 102 L.Q.R. 32 (J. H. Farrar and J. K. Maxton). See also (1980) 79 Mich. L.Rev. 72 (J. H. Langbein and R. A. Posner).
[91] *Ibid.*
[92] The suggested remedy in *Cowan* v. *Scargill* was removal of the trustees.
[93] See (1970) 120 N.L.J. 240 (R.T. Oerton).
[94] T.I.A. 1961, s.6(2).
[95] Except in the case of a mortgage, which is governed by T.A. 1925, s.8(1)(c); T.I.A. 1961, s.6(5).
[96] T.I.A. 1961, s.6(4).
[97] *Shaw* v. *Cates* [1909] 1 Ch. 389.
[98] T.I.A., 1961, s.6(6).

J. Retention of Investments: Section 6(3)

A trustee is required, in respect of investments for whose selection advice was required,[99] to determine at what intervals he should take advice on the question of retaining the investment.[1] The extent of this provision is not clear. It suggests that the trustee will be liable if loss occurs by reason of his failure to observe this requirement, or if he makes a determination in an unbusinesslike way. However, Trustee Act 1925, s.4, is still in force and protects a trustee from liability for breach of trust "by reason only of his continuing to hold an investment which has ceased to be an investment authorised by the trust instrument or by the general law." It is submitted that a trustee who retains an unauthorised investment will be liable if he fails to consider the matter at proper times under advice; the protection of Trustee Act 1925, s.4, only arises where the *only* reason for the breach was the fact that the investment became unauthorised.

K. Trustees Holding Controlling Interest in a Company

Difficult questions arise in relation to the trustees' duties where the trust contains a controlling interest in a company. The first question is whether the shareholding is a proper investment at all. If the company is a private company, as is the usual case in this situation, express authorisation would be needed to purchase such shares. Usually the question is one of retention, as where a wealthy person has his property held by a private company, and, as part of his estate planning, he puts some of the shares into a family trust. The trust deed in such circumstances ought to include a provision authorising retention. This will be needed whether the interest is a controlling or a minority interest. And, unless the authorisation covers the specific holding, the trustee may have to consider diversification.[2]

But that is not the end of the matter. It is not sufficient for the trustees to determine that the investment is suitable, and leave it at that. For the company or its directors may engage in practices which are wholly unsuitable for a trust investment, such as speculative activities. Can the trustees shelter behind the directors, whose acts they are in a position to control?

In *Bartlett* v. *Barclays Bank Trust Co. Ltd.*,[3] the bank was trustee of the Bartlett trust. The sole asset of the trust was a shareholding amounting to virtually all the shares in a family property company, which held some £500,000 worth of rent-producing properties. The beneficiaries were the settlor's children for their lives and, after their death, their children.

---

[99] *i.e.* those in Pts. II and III of Sched. I of the T.I.A. 1961.

[1] T.I.A. 1961, s.6(3); see *Rawsthorne* v. *Rowley* [1909] 1 Ch. 409n; *Re Chapman* [1896] 2 Ch. 763.

[2] Where the trust is testamentary, the rule in *Howe* v. *Lord Dartmouth* (*post*, p. 510) may apply.

[3] [1980] Ch. 515.

Tax would need to be paid on the death of the income beneficiaries, and a suggestion was made that cash would be more easily
raised if the company went public; and merchant bankers advised
that a public issue would be more successful if the company were not
only a manager of existing property, but a developer of new properties also. The bank agreed to a policy of active development, so long
as the income available to the income beneficiaries was not
prejudiced.

The board then embarked upon speculative developments, one of
which was a disaster, because planning permission for the intended
office development could not be obtained. This resulted in a large
loss to the trust.

The Bank was held liable. It was not sufficient that they believed the
directors to be competent and capable of running a profitable business.
Their duty was "to conduct the business of the trust with the same care
as an ordinary prudent man of business would extend to his own
affairs."[4] To do that it was necessary, especially as the bank was aware
that the company was moving into speculative development, to get the
fullest information on the conduct of the business; and not merely to be
content with the supply of information which they received as shareholders. Cross J. in *Re Lucking's Will Trusts*[5] held that a controlling
shareholder should insist on being represented on the board; but
Brightman J. treated this as one convenient way of ensuring that all the
necessary information was available.[6]

So the controlling shareholder must obtain the necessary information. The obtaining of the information is not an end in itself, but merely
a means of "enabling the trustee to safeguard the interests of the
beneficiaries."[7] How do the trustees do that? Ultimately, of course,
the majority shareholder will get its way; as by adopting "the draconian course of threatening to remove, or actually removing, the board
in favour of compliant directors,"[8] which is asking a lot of the trust
department of a bank. Brightman J. was able to avoid the practical
difficulties of such a course by finding that the members of the board
were "reasonable persons, and would (as I find) have followed any
reasonable policy desired by the bank had the bank's wishes been
indicated to the board."[9]

[4] *Ibid.* at p. 531, quoting *Speight* v. *Gaunt* (1883) 9 App.Cas. 1.
[5] [1968] 1 W.L.R. 866 at p. 874.
[6] [1980] Ch. 515 at p. 533. "Other methods may be equally satisfactory and convenient
depending upon the circumstances of the individual case. Alternatives which spring to
mind are the receipt of copies of the agenda and minutes of board meetings if regularly
held, the receipt of monthly management accounts in the case of a trading concern . . .
the possibilities are endless. . . . " See *Re Miller's Trust Deed* (1978) 75 L.S.Gaz. 454,
where one of the trustees was a member of a firm of accountants which acted as
auditors for the company.
[7] *Ibid.* at p. 534.
[8] *Ibid.* at p. 530.
[9] *Ibid.*

L. Mortgages of Land

(i) **The Security.** The Act includes in the list of narrower-range investments requiring advice, "mortgages of freehold property in England and Wales or Northern Ireland and of leasehold property in those countries of which the unexpired term at the time of investment is not less than sixty years. . . . "[10] This replaces the provisions of the Trustee Act 1925 which gave trustees power to invest in "real securities."[11] A number of restrictions had been established in relation to investments in real securities, and the question arises whether they still apply to mortgages under the 1961 Act. On a strict construction of the Act it appears that they do not. "Mortgage" unless the context otherwise requires, has the same meaning as in the Trustee Act 1925,[12] *i.e.* " . . . every estate or interest regarded in equity as merely a security for money . . . ."[13] Nothing in the 1961 Act appears to require a different construction, and it is arguable that the old restrictions no longer apply.

It would however be remarkable to sweep away these restrictions indirectly, and the safer view appears to be that the old rules still stand.[14] They established that trustees should lend money only on a first legal mortgage. Equitable mortgages[15] were unsatisfactory because of the danger of the appearance of a bona fide purchaser for value without notice. This is unlikely today, because an equitable mortgage is normally registrable.[16] Second mortgages were not authorised.[17] Nor was a contributory mortgage,[18] for, in spite of their many advantages in widening the spread of risk and choice of security, the trustees, needing to cooperate with strangers, lost effective control. A sub-mortgage, on the other hand, is a perfectly proper form of security.[19]

The Law Reform Committee[20] has recently proposed that second mortgages should be permissible, as their priority can be protected by registration. The two-thirds rule under section 8(1)(*b*) of the Trustee Act 1925, discussed below, would apply to the combined amount of the principal advanced on the first and second mortgages.

---

[10] T.I.A. 1961, Sched. I. Part II, para. 13.

[11] T.A. 1925, s.5(1).

[12] T.I.A. 1961, s.17(4).

[13] T.A. 1925, s.68(7).

[14] This is the view of the Law Reform Committee, *infra.*

[15] *Webb* v. *Ledsam* (1855) 1 K. & J. 385; *Swaffield* v. *Nelson* [1876] W.N. 255.

[16] Under L.C.A. 1972, or protected by notice or caution under L.R.A. 1925 in the case of registered land. An equitable mortgage protected by a deposit of title deeds is not registrable.

[17] *Chapman* v. *Browne* [1902] 1 Ch. 785 at p. 800.

[18] *i.e.* a mortgage where several mortgagees joined; *Webb* v. *Jonas* (1888) 39 Ch.D. 660; *Re Massingberd's Settlement* (1890) 63 L.T. 296; *Re Dive* [1909] 1 Ch. 328.

[19] *Smethurst* v. *Hastings* (1885) 30 Ch.D. 490.

[20] 23rd Report, *The Powers and Duties of Trustees* (1982, Cmnd. 8733), para. 3.13.

(ii) The Amount. Guidance to trustees as to the amount of money which should be advanced on mortgage is contained in Trustee Act 1925, s.8.

> 8.—(1) A trustee lending money on the security of any property on which he can properly lend[21] shall not be chargeable with breach of trust by reason only of the proportion borne by the amount of the loan to the value of the property at the time when the loan was made, if it appears to the court—
>
> (a) that in making the loan the trustee was acting upon a report as to the value of the property made by a person whom he reasonably believed to be an able practical surveyor or valuer instructed and employed independently of any owner of the property, whether such surveyor or valuer carried on business in the locality where the property is situate or elsewhere; and
> (b) that the amount of the loan does not exceed two third parts of the value of the property as stated in the report; and
> (c) that the loan was made under the advice of the surveyor or valuer expressed in the report.

The section is intended to give relief to trustees[22]; it does not deprive a trustee of the protection given by the pre-existing law.[23] It is important to take into consideration all relevant factors in determining a valuation for mortgage purposes. The current market value is not a sufficient guide, for example, in a situation in which there may be unusual fluctuations in value, connected perhaps with a business carried on there[24]; but a trustee "is justified in acting on expert advice not only as to the value of the property, but also as to the amount he may properly advance thereon ... it being, of course, assumed that in giving the advice the expert will consider all the circumstances of the case, including the nature of the property, and will not advise a larger advance than under all the circumstances can be prudently made."[25] But the trustee, to obtain protection, must comply strictly with the section. It is his responsibility to select the valuer,[26] who must be instructed and employed independently of the mortgagor[27]; and his

---

[21] See *Re Walker* (1890) 62 L.T. 449; *Shaw* v. *Cates* [1909] 1 Ch. 389.
[22] *Palmer* v. *Emerson* [1911] 1 Ch. 758 at p. 769.
[23] *Re Dive* [1909] 1 Ch. 328 at p. 342; *Shaw* v. *Cates, supra,* at p. 404.
[24] *Learoyd* v. *Whiteley* (1887) 12 App.Cas. 727. The security upon which the trustee may lend is the land and buildings, and not the additional value of a business conducted there. See *Palmer* v. *Emerson* [1911] 1 Ch. 758.
[25] *Shaw* v. *Cates, supra,* at p. 398.
[26] *Fry* v. *Tapson* (1884) 28 Ch.D. 268.
[27] *Shaw* v. *Cates, supra; Re Stuart* [1897] 2 Ch. 583; *Re Solomon* [1912] 1 Ch. 261. It is not sufficient that the trustee "reasonably believed" the valuer to be so instructed and employed. The words in quotes refer in s.8(1)(a) to the trustees' belief in the valuer's ability, and do not govern the provision that the valuer be instructed and employed independently; see Kekewich J. in *Re Somerset* [1894] 1 Ch. 231 at p. 253.

report must be followed. Even then, the mortgage may for other reasons be improper. If wholly unauthorised, and a loss results, the offending trustee is liable for the whole loss. If the fault is only in respect of the amount of money lent, the mortgage is treated as a proper investment for the smaller sum; and the trustee is only liable to make good the excess.[28]

It is possible that a trustee who fails to comply with the provisions of section 8 will obtain relief under section 61.[29] Section 8 does, however, in the case of investment of trust funds on mortgage, "constitute a standard by which reasonable conduct is to be judged."[30] The trustee will not be liable where the value of the land has decreased through economic circumstances outside the trustee's control, and where the trustee has taken reasonable steps to safeguard the trust property.[31] Finally, trustees may, on a sale, leave on legal mortgage not more than two-thirds of the purchase price without having first obtained a report.[32]

M. Extension of Investment Powers by the Court

Trustees may apply to court under section 57 of the Trustee Act 1925[33] for the authorisation of specific dealings, or under the Variation of Trusts Act 1958[34] to widen investment powers generally. Although section 15 of the Trustee Investments Act 1961 expressly preserves the power of the court to confer wider powers of investment, applications under the 1958 Act have been rare since the passing of the Act of 1961, the court generally taking the view (here described as the *Re Kolb* principle[35]), that special circumstances have to be shown to justify an extension beyond the powers conferred by a modern statute. The question recently arose in *Mason* v. *Farbrother*,[36] concerning a pension fund of the employees of the Co-operative Society. The fund had limited investment powers. By 1982, as a result of inflation, the fund had vastly increased, and the trustees wished to have wider powers. They applied to court under section 57 of the Trustee Act 1925.[37] It was

[28] T.A. 1925, s.9; *Shaw* v. *Cates* [1909] 1 Ch. 389; *Re Walker* (1890) 62 L.T. 449; See also s.10, permitting the postponement of repayment by contract for up to seven years.
[29] *Post*, p. 612.
[30] *Re Stuart* [1897] 2 Ch. 583 at p. 592; *post*, p. 613.
[31] *Re Chapman* [1896] 2 Ch. 763 (a case of retention while values were falling). Where the security, although proper, diminishes, the loss will be apportioned amongst the beneficiaries under the rule in *Re Atkinson* [1904] 2 Ch. 160, *post*, p. 519.
[32] T.A. 1925, s.10(2).
[33] *Post*, p. 583.
[34] *Post*, p. 586.
[35] *Re Kolb's Will Trusts* [1962] Ch. 531; *Re Cooper's Settlement* [1962] Ch. 826; *Re Clarke's Will Trusts* [1961] 1 W.L.R. 1471.
[36] [1983] 2 All E.R. 1078; [1984] Conv. 373 (H. E. Norman); All E.R. Rev. 1984, p. 308 (P. J. Clarke).
[37] The application under the 1958 Act did not proceed because of difficulties with the representative parties. The aspect concerning the court's inherent jurisdiction to approve a compromise is dealt with *post*, p. 582.

held that there was no absolute rule that the court should not widen investment powers after the 1961 Act. The court approved a wide modern clause, not restricted to investments permitted by the 1961 Act, which was out of date.[38] This could be done if there were special circumstances, which included the effect of inflation and the fact that it was in the nature of a public fund.

A different approach was subsequently taken by Megarry V.-C. in *Trustees of the British Museum* v. *Att.-Gen.*,[39] where the trustees sought a relaxation of their present scheme, made in 1960, as they needed a wider choice and a power to invest abroad. The trustees were eminent and responsible, and had highly skilled advice. The size of the fund (£5 million–£6 million) made it unlike a private trust and more like a pension fund or large institutional investor. Megarry V.-C. pointed out that there had been significant changes in investment practice in the last twenty years, especially with large funds. The factors involved in this change included increased inflation and a movement from fixed interest investment to equities and property; the disparity between various countries' inflation rates; the effect of oil on particular currencies; the fact that economic growth was greater in some countries than in the United Kingdom; the fact that smaller companies had grown faster than larger ones; the abolition of exchange control; and the fact that unit trusts and some unsecured loans (*e.g.* Eurobonds), offered valuable opportunities. Referring to *Mason* v. *Farbrother*,[40] where, as we have seen, the court treated the *Re Kolb*[41] principle as still binding in the absence of special circumstances, Megarry V.-C. disagreed that inflation could be called a special circumstance, and preferred to say that the *Re Kolb* principle had gone. That line of cases should not be followed, although if the statutory powers were increased, the principle could apply again. Factors to be considered included the standing of the particular trustees and the width and efficiency of their provisions for advice and control; the size of the fund (wider powers being permissible for larger funds as the spread of investments justifies greater risks); the objects of the fund (here the desirability of increasing the capital value, so that objects for the museum could be acquired despite soaring prices, justified greater risks); and the wider the powers sought, the more

---

[38] Referring to the Law Reform Committee, 23rd Report, *The Powers and Duties of Trustees* (1982, Cmnd. 8733). The Committee took the view that applications under the 1958 Act after the proposed reform of trustees' investment powers (*post*, p. 504) would continue to be possible, although rare; *ibid.* para. 3.25.

[39] [1984] 1 W.L.R. 418. See also *Steel* v. *Wellcome Custodian Trustees Ltd.* [1988] 1 W.L.R. 167; [1988] Conv. 380 (B. Dale). (Trustees of large charity with funds of £3,200 million including share capital in W. Ltd. which could not be sold sought wider powers of beneficial owner. Variation approved, having regard to size of fund, eminence of trustees and provisions requiring advice).

[40] *Supra.*

[41] [1962] Ch. 531, *supra.*

important it became that part should be in relatively safe investments.[42] Applying these principles, the trustees' application succeeded.

N. Reform

Nearly a quarter of a century has passed since the Trustee Investments Act 1961 and, as we have seen, investment practice has changed and the Act has become out of date.[43] In any event, the Act is usually modified or excluded by the trust instrument. The Law Reform Committee has accordingly recommended the repeal of the 1961 Act,[44] which has proved to be "tiresome, cumbrous and expensive in operation with the result that its provisions are now seen to be inadequate. Furthermore, careful investment in equities is perhaps more likely in the long run to protect and benefit both income and capital beneficiaries than is investment in fixed-interest securities."[45] But the principle of control over trustee investments should be retained.[46] Investments should be divided into those which may be made with or without advice. In the latter category will be those which are presently narrower-range investments, plus unit trusts and investment trusts.[47] Investments requiring advice comprise any others quoted on the English Stock Exchange.[48] The trustees should be able to invest in the two categories in such proportions as they choose. As advice is expensive, trustees of small funds will be more likely to invest in those not requiring advice. Failure to obtain advice where required will be a breach of trust. Trustees will continue to be obliged to maintain a fair balance between income and capital beneficiaries, and the provisions in section 6 of the 1961 Act concerning the taking of advice and the need for diversification will be reproduced in the new legislation.[49]

3. Duty to Distribute. Satisfaction of Claims

A. Liability for Wrongful Payments

A trustee is obliged to make payments of income and capital as they become due, and to make them to the persons properly entitled. Failure to do so is a breach of trust, which the trustee must normally make good, such as for example, a payment based on a forged docu-

---

[42] In *Steel* v. *Wellcome Custodian Trustees Ltd.*, *supra*, a variation which did not require any narrower-range investments was, however, sanctioned.
[43] See *Mason* v. *Farbrother, supra*; *Trustees of the British Museum* v. *Att.-Gen., supra*.
[44] 23rd Report, *The Powers and Duties of Trustees* (1982, Cmnd. 8733), para. 3.20; [1984] Conv. 373 (H. E. Norman).
[45] *Ibid.* para. 3.17.
[46] *Ibid.* para. 3.19.
[47] As defined by I.C.T.A. 1988, s.842.
[48] Foreign securities will not be permitted unless authorised by the instrument or the court; 23rd Report, *supra*, para. 3.24.
[49] 23rd Report, *supra*, paras. 3.22 and 3.23.

ment,[50] or upon an erroneous construction of a document,[51] even if legal advice was taken,[52] or without regard to the entitlement of illegitimate beneficiaries.[53]

Where a trustee makes an overpayment of income or of instalments of capital, the error may be adjusted in later payments.[54] If the payment is to a person who is not entitled, the trustee's right of recovery is a quasi-contractual one, and the money will be recoverable if the mistake is one of fact, but not if it is a mistake of law.[55] An unpaid or underpaid beneficiary may, in addition to his right to sue the trustee, proceed against the property in the hands of the wrongly paid recipient not being a bona fide purchaser for value without notice.[56] A trustee-beneficiary who fails to pay himself in full has been held to have no remedy,[57] but this rule is thought to be too extreme.[58]

B. Doubtful Claims

(i) **Application to Court for Directions.** Where the trustees are in any doubt in relation to the claims of the beneficiaries, they may make an application to the court for directions; and will be protected if they obey the directions of the court.[59] This course can now be taken with a minimum of complication by the procedure of originating summons,[60] which avoids the earlier inconvenience whereby a suit for administration of the trust had first to be commenced.[61] In this way problems of construction of the trust instrument and difficulties in administering the trust can be brought before the court, so that the trustees are not forced to take upon themselves the risk of making decisions upon a false premise.[62] The power of going to the court can also be helpful in

[50] *Eaves* v. *Hickson* (1861) 30 Beav. 136.
[51] *Hilliard* v. *Fulford* (1876) 4 Ch.D. 389.
[52] *National Trustees Company of Australasia Ltd.* v. *General Finance Company of Australasia Ltd.* [1905] A.C. 373.
[53] Family Law Reform Act 1987, s.20, reversing the previous position under F.L.R.A. 1969, s.17.
[54] *Dibbs* v. *Goren* (1849) 11 Beav. 483 (administration by the court); *Re Musgrave* [1916] 2 Ch. 417.
[55] *Re Diplock* [1947] Ch. 716; the rule is different in respect of unpaid or underpaid beneficiaries in the administration of a deceased's estate: *Ministry of Health* v. *Simpson* [1951] A.C. 251; *post*, p. 644.
[56] *Re Diplock* [1948] Ch. 465.
[57] *Re Horne* [1905] 1 Ch. 76.
[58] *Lewin on Trusts* (16th ed.), p. 262.
[59] *Re Londonderry's Settlement* [1965] Ch. 918. On the costs of such applications, see Law Reform Committee, 23rd Report, *The Powers and Duties of Trustees* (1982, Cmnd. 8733) paras. 5.2–5.4. See also para. 5.1, recommending that the trustees should be able to write to potential creditors, enclosing a copy of counsel's opinion that distribution should be made, and telling the creditor to claim within three months. If there is no claim, the trustee is not liable, but the assets can be traced.
[60] R.S.C., Ord. 85, r. 2, and Ord. 5, r. 4.
[61] See *Re Medland* (1889) 4 Ch.D. 476.
[62] See also A.J.A. 1985, s.48, giving the court power to authorise action to be taken in reliance on counsel's opinion respecting the construction of a will or trust.

cases where the trustees are in difficulty in connection with the exercise of a discretion, for instance a discretionary power to make advancements. Trustees must not go to court just for their own convenience, and they are not able to surrender discretions *in toto* to the court.[63] Trustees or beneficiaries may, in suitable cases, apply for the trust to be administered by the court,[64] but an unsuccessful applicant may be liable for costs.

(ii) Payment into Court. Where beneficiaries cannot be ascertained, or where for some exceptional reason trustees cannot obtain a good discharge from the trust, there is a residual power in trustees to pay the trust moneys into court.[65] The residue of the fund in *Re Gillingham Bus Disaster Fund,*[66] for instance, was eventually paid into court.

But this will not be tolerated by the court as a means of trustees evading their obligations when difficulties arise.[67] It is a last resort when all other methods of dealing with the problem have proved unsuccessful. Trustees who pay trust funds into court when a different course was preferable, may be liable for costs.[68]

(iii) "Benjamin" Order. The court has a power to authorise distribution of the whole of the assets of an estate, although not all the beneficiaries or creditors have made themselves known so as to be able to receive their share. A typical situation is where the whereabouts or continued existence of a certain beneficiary is not known. The procedure is sometimes known as a "Benjamin" order, and its purpose is to protect those distributing the assets[69]; if those entitled who have received nothing under the distribution eventually come forward to establish their claim, they may still be able to proceed, within the period of limitation, against the person wrongly paid,[70] or against the property itself. Such an order will of course only be made after all practicable inquiries have been instituted. A recent example is *Re Green's Will Trusts,*[71] where the testatrix left her property to her son, providing that it should go to charity if he did not claim it by the year 2020. The son had disappeared on a bombing raid in 1943, and all but his mother were satisified that he was dead. A "Benjamin" order was

---

[63] *Re Allen-Meyrick's W.T.* [1966] 1 W.L.R. 499; (1967) 31 Conv.(N.S.) 117 (A.J. Hawkins).
[64] R.S.C., Ord. 5, r. 1; (1968) 84 L.Q.R. 68 (A.J. Hawkins).
[65] Payment into court furnishes an exception to the rule that a majority of trustees cannot defeat a dissentient minority, for T.A. 1925, s.63, provides that the payment may in certain circumstances be made by a majority of the trustees.
[66] [1959] Ch. 62; *ante*, p. 229.
[67] See *Re Knight's Trust* (1859) 27 Beav. 45.
[68] *Re Cull's Trusts* (1875) L.R. 20 Eq. 561; (1968) 84 L.Q.R. 64 at pp. 65–67 (A.J. Hawkins).
[69] *Re Benjamin* [1902] 1 Ch. 723; *Re Gess* [1942] Ch. 37; *Re Taylor* [1969] 2 Ch. 245.
[70] *Ministry of Health* v. *Simpson* [1951] A.C. 251; *Re Lowe's W.T.* [1973] 1 W.L.R. 882 at p. 887.
[71] [1985] 3 All E.R. 455.

made, allowing distribution to the charity, it being no bar to such an order that it was contrary to the intention of the testatrix.[72]

(iv) Distribution after Advertisement. Under the Trustee Act 1925, s.27, trustees have themselves the power to advertise for claimants[73] and, after compliance with certain formalities, the power to distribute the whole of their trust assets to claimants who have made themselves known. But again, those who subsequently demonstrate an entitlement are enabled to proceed against the property distributed, save when it is in the hands of a purchaser.[74]

(v) Setting Aside a Fund. The Trustee Act 1925, s.26, provides a procedure whereby trustees can set aside out of trust assets a sum to meet any potential liabilities under a lease or rentcharge, and then to distribute the remainder of the trust assets to those entitled. Again, should the sum set aside prove insufficient, those entitled to the extra sums may still follow the distributed property. In the case of contingent liabilities outside section 26, the trustees can either retain a fund, distribute under a court order, or obtain an indemnity from the beneficiaries and then distribute.[75]

C. Relief under Section 61

A trustee who makes an erroneous distribution may be relieved from liability if he acted honestly and reasonably and ought fairly to be excused.[76]

D. Discharge

On the termination of the trust, the trustees should present their final accounts and obtain a discharge from the beneficiaries. The best protection is provided by a release under seal, for that places on a complaining beneficiary the burden of proving fraud, concealment, mistake or undue influence.[77] But a trustee is not entitled to a release under seal.[78] If the beneficiaries are unwilling to give one, the trustees may apply to the court for the accounts to be taken and approved.[79]

---

[72] Criticised on this point in [1986] Conv. 138 (P. Luxton).
[73] Normally creditors, but also beneficiaries, for example claimants under an intestacy.
[74] s.27(2)(a); and see *Re Aldhous* [1955] 1 W.L.R. 459.
[75] See Mellows, *The Law of Succession* (4th ed.), p. 332.
[76] *Post*, p. 612.
[77] *Fowler* v. *Wyatt* (1857) 24 Beav. 232.
[78] *King* v. *Mullins* (1852) 1 Drew. at p. 311, *per* Kindersley V.-C.; *Lewin on Trusts* (16th ed.), p. 189.
[79] Underhill, *Law of Trusts and Trustees* (14th ed.) p. 711.

CHAPTER 18

DUTIES OF TRUSTEES IN RELATION TO THE
BENEFICIARIES

1. DUTY TO MAINTAIN EQUALITY BETWEEN THE BENEFICIARIES

A trustee is under a general duty to maintain equality between the
beneficiaries. This duty forms the basis of the specific rules of conversion and apportionment, discussed below, which apply as between life
tenant and remainderman. It is not, however, confined to such cases.
A recent example of the wider general duty is *Lloyds Bank plc* v.
Duker,[1] where a testator's residuary estate included 999 company
shares. He left 46/80 to his wife, and the rest to other beneficiaries. In
spite of the general rule that a beneficiary is entitled *in specie* to his
share of divisible personalty held on trust for sale, it was held that the
wife could not claim 574 shares, as such a majority holding would be
worth more than 46/80. The only fair solution was for the trustees to
sell the shares and divide the proceeds in the specified proportions.

---

[1] [1987] 1 W.L.R. 1324. See also *Nestlé* v. *National Westminster Bank plc*, June 29, 1988
(unreported), where Hoffman J., applying the principle in the context of investments,
expressed it as a duty to act fairly in making investment decisions which may have
different consequences for different classes of beneficiaries.

A. Rule in Howe v. Earl of Dartmouth[2]

(i) Life Tenant and Remainderman. A trustee must act impartially between life tenant and remainderman. This duty applies to the selection of investments[3]; and the rules governing investment by trustees are an attempt to strike a balance between the provision of income for the life tenant and the preservation of the capital for the remainderman.[4] So long as those rules are observed, a trustee is usually under no duty to rearrange the investments so as to balance equally the interests of the life tenant and remainderman.[5] Nor, if there are unauthorised investments in the fund, are the trustees under any duty to convert them into authorised investments.[6] However the fund is invested, the normal rule is that the tenant for life takes all the income; the remainderman's interest is in the capital. The capital is not of course available until the life tenant's death; but he may, if he wishes, deal with or dispose of his reversionary interest in the fund.[7]

There are, as we will see, some situations in which there is a duty to convert into authorised investments; and this duty carries with it a duty to apportion the income earned before the conversion is effected.

(ii) The Duty to Convert. A duty to convert and re-invest in authorised investments may arise by reason of the existence of an express trust to sell or to convert, or by statute,[8] or, in the case of a bequest of residuary personalty, under the rule in *Howe* v. *Earl of Dartmouth*.[9]

(a) *Express Trust for Sale.* The trustees' duties under an express trust, of course, depend on the terms of the trust. It is important to note that an express trust to convert involves, as does a duty to convert under the rule in *Howe* v. *Earl of Dartmouth*,[10] an apportionment of

---

[2] (1943) 7 Conv.(n.s.) 128 and 191 (S. J. Bailey); (1952) 16 Conv.(n.s.) 349 (L. A. Sheridan).
[3] *Raby* v. *Ridehalgh* (1855) 7 De G. M. & G. 104 at p. 109; *Re Dick* [1891] 1 Ch. 423 at p. 431.
[4] *Ante*, p. 486. There is no duty to preserve the real value of the capital. "It would be an inhuman law which required trustees to adhere to some mechanical rule for preserving the real value of the capital when the tenant for life was the testator's widow who had fallen upon hard times and the remainderman was young and well off." *Per* Hoffmann J. in *Nestlé* v. *National Westminster Bank plc*, June 29, 1988 (unreported).
[5] "It is perhaps surprising that equity has not cast upon trustees, in every such case, a duty to convert the trust property as soon as practicable into something more likely to produce an equitable result" (1943) 7 Conv.(n.s.) 128 at p. 129 (S. J. Bailey); *Re Courtier* (1886) 34 Ch.D. 136; *Re Searle* [1900] 2 Ch. 829 at p. 834.
[6] T.A. 1925, s.4.
[7] This can be done through brokers who specialise in this field. A sale of a reversionary interest is usually unprofitable. The value, when it falls into possession, depends upon many unknown factors, including the progress of the investments in the meantime, and the tax payable on the life tenant's death. These uncertainties lower the price.
[8] A.E.A. 1925, s.33.
[9] (1802) 7 Ves.Jr. 137.
[10] *Supra.*

the income pending conversion.[11] A mere power to sell is not sufficient to create a trust to convert.[12]

(b) *Rule in Howe* v. *Earl of Dartmouth. Howe* v. *Earl of Dartmouth* establishes that, subject to a contrary provision in the will, there is a duty to convert where residuary personalty is settled by will in favour of persons who are to enjoy it in succession. The trustees should convert all such parts of it as are of a wasting[13] or future or reversionary[14] nature or consist of unauthorised securities,[15] into property of a permanent or income-bearing character.

Thus property such as speculative investments,[16] royalties, copyrights,[17] etc., and (before 1926) leaseholds[18] should be converted in the interest of the remainderman. For these are non-permanent investments, and may be of reduced or of no value at the life tenant's death. On the other hand, "future" property such as a remainder or reversionary interest, or other property which at present produces no income, is of no immediate benefit to the tenant for life. In his interest therefore it should be converted into income-bearing properties. And, as we shall see, provision is made for apportionment between the life tenant and remainderman of the value of such property when it falls into possession.[19]

It will be seen that, on its terms, the rule is of limited application. It does not apply to property settled *inter vivos*[20]; nor to specific as opposed to residuary bequests[21] (for the settlor's or testator's intention in such cases is for the specific property settled to be enjoyed successively). Nor does it apply to freehold[22] land, nor to leaseholds held for a term exceeding 60 years, for these are now authorised investments[23]; the question of its application to shorter leaseholds will be discussed later.[24]

(iii) **Apportionment.** Where there is a duty to convert, whether under an express trust or under the rule in *Howe* v. *Earl of Dartmouth*,[25] there is, in the absence of an intention that the life tenant shall

---

[11] *Gibson* v. *Bott* (1802) 7 Ves.Jr. 89.
[12] *Re Pitcairn* [1896] 2 Ch. 199.
[13] Such as leases, which terminate after a period of time; or mines or ships which will eventually become worthless; or patents or copyrights which expire.
[14] *i.e.* property which will only fall in after the death of the life tenant.
[15] *i.e.* not authorised by the terms of the will, nor by T.I.A. 1961; *ante*, p. 491.
[16] *Howe* v. *Earl of Dartmouth* (1802) 7 Ves.Jr. 137.
[17] *Re Evans' W.T.* [1921] 2 Ch. 309; *Re Sullivan* [1930] 1 Ch. 84.
[18] For the present position, see *post*, p. 514.
[19] *Re Earl of Chesterfield's Trust* (1883) 24 Ch.D. 643; *post*, pp. 512.
[20] *Re Van Straubenzee* [1901] 2 Ch. 779.
[21] *Ibid.* at p. 782.
[22] *Re Searle* [1900] 2 Ch. 829. A power to postpone sale is implied in the case of every trust for sale of land unless a contrary intention is expressed: L.P.A. 1925, s.25(1)(3).
[23] S.L.A. 1925, s.73(1)(xi).
[24] *Post*, p. 514.
[25] (1802) 7 Ves.Jr. 137.

enjoy the income until sale, a duty also to apportion fairly between the life tenant and the remainderman the original property pending conversion. The detailed rules appear complicated at first sight; but they are simple and obvious if their purpose is understood.

(a) *Wasting, Hazardous or Unauthorised Investments.* It is assumed that wasting, hazardous and unauthorised securities produce income in excess of that which the life tenant should reasonably receive[26]; and do so at the expense of the security of the capital. With such property therefore the object of the apportionment rule is to provide that the life tenant receives an income which represents the current yield on authorised investments,[27] and that the excess is added to capital.[28] If the interest received is less than 4 per cent., the balance should be made up out of subsequent income or from the proceeds of the unauthorised investments when sold.[29]

The question arises of the time at which the capital should be valued for the purpose of calculating the 4 per cent. income. A distinction must be made between cases where the trustees are given power to postpone conversion and those where they are not.

First: where there is no power to postpone. In this situation the trustees should convert within the "executor's year"[30]—the period during which the administration of the deceased's estate is expected to be completed. If the investments are sold within the year, the net proceeds of sale are taken as their value[31]; if not, these investments are valued *en bloc* as at the end of one year from the death.[32] In either case the life tenant is entitled, as from the date of the death of the testator, to 4 per cent. on that sum.

Secondly: where the trustees postpone sale in the exercise of a power to postpone.[33] The executor's year here has no relevance. There is a duty to convert, but no time within which the conversion should be effected. The date of the valuation is the date of the testator's death.[34]

---

[26] *Post*, p. 516.

[27] The life tenant's income was fixed at 4 per cent. in *Re Baker* [1924] 2 Ch. 271, and applied at that figure in 1961 in *Re Berry* [1962] Ch. 97 at p. 113. However, this is so far out of line with the current return from gilt-edged investments (*ante*, p. 487) that it is difficult to see how it could now be supported. Trustees who have to decide what income to pay may be well advised to take instructions from the court. Interest rates in other contexts have recently been increased, for example judgment debts; legacies and overdue taxes. See also *Wallersteiner* v. *Moir (No. 2)* [1975] Q.B. 373; *Bartlett* v. *Barclays Bank Trust Co. Ltd. (No. 2)* [1980] Ch. 515; *Tehno-Impex* v. *Gebr. Van Weelde Scheepvaarkantoor B.V.* [1981] Q.B. 648 at pp. 665–666.

[28] The life tenant will of course receive the income from the capital as thus increased.

[29] *Re Fawcett* [1940] Ch. 402.

[30] See *Williams on Wills* (6th ed., 1987), p. 398; A.E.A. 1925, s.44.

[31] *Re Fawcett, supra.*

[32] *Dimes* v. *Scott* (1828) 4 Russ. 195.

[33] We are here concerned with an administrative power to postpone which is not sufficient to exclude the rule; see *post*, p. 514.

[34] *Brown* v. *Gellatly* (1867) L.R. 2 Ch. App. 751 (the ships); *Re Owen* [1912] 1 Ch. 519; *Re Parry* [1947] Ch. 23; where Romer J. submitted the authorities to an exhaustive review; *Re Berry* [1962] Ch. 97.

In *Brown* v. *Gellatly*,[35] the estate consisted of (i) some ships (wasting assets) which the testator directed his executors to continue to use until they could be conveniently sold, and (ii) unauthorised securities. Both were retained for more than a year from the death. The question was whether, for the purpose of apportionment, the assets should be valued at the date of death or at a year from the death.

Lord Cairns held that the ships, being subject to a power to postpone sale, should be valued at the death; the unauthorised investments, on the other hand, a year from the death.

(b) *Future, Reversionary or other Non-Income Producing Property.* Where personalty which is subject to a duty to convert includes reversionary property, it is necessary, in the interest of the life tenant, to provide for apportionment[36]; otherwise the life tenant would obtain no benefit from the property until it fell into possession. The reversion should be sold and the proceeds re-invested; until that is done there is no way of producing income for the life tenant. When it has been sold, there is still the problem of determining how much of the proceeds of sale should be apportioned to capital and how much to the life tenant. This is done by[37] ascertaining the sum "which, put out at 4 per cent. per annum ... and accumulating at compound interest at that rate with yearly rests,[38] and deducting income tax at the standard rate, would, with the accumulation of interest, have produced, at the respective dates of receipt, the amounts actually received; and that the aggregate of the sums so ascertained ought to be treated as principal and be applied accordingly, and the residue should be treated as income." In other words, put a value on the reversion, on falling in, or on sale; that sum is part principal, part interest. The principal is the sum which, if invested at 4 per cent. at the date of the testator's death, would have produced the sum now received. The balance goes to the tenant for life.[39]

---

[35] (1867) L.R. 2 Ch.App. 751.

[36] The interest may be contingent: *Re Hobson* (1855) 55 L.J.Ch. 422. The rule also applies where the sum in question is itself a mixture of capital and income; *Re Chance's W.T.* [1962] Ch. 593 (compensation under the Town and Country Planning Act 1947); *Re Duke of Cleveland's Estate* [1895] 2 Ch. 542 (debt bearing no interest); *Re Hollebone* [1919] 2 Ch. 93 (instalments on sale of business); but a reversionary interest in land is not within the rule (*Re Woodhouse* [1941] Ch. 336).

[37] *Re Earl of Chesterfield's Trusts* (1883) 24 Ch.D. 643.

[38] *i.e.* the income is transferred to capital at the end of each year.

[39] The calculation can be made by taking the value of the reversion on sale or on falling in (£x), and working backwards year by year until the date of the testator's death. If the standard rate of income tax is 25 per cent., the next income earned at 4 per cent. on £100 of capital is £3.00. The sum needed to produce £x after *one* year of investment can be found by applying the formula:

$$\frac{£x \times 100}{103}$$

The application of this formula *to the sum* so calculated will produce the sums needed

(iv) Contrary Intention. All the rules above discussed are subject to a contrary intention by the testator or settlor.[40] A number of very fine points of construction arise; but the matter can only be discussed in outline here. The onus is on the person alleging that the equitable rules are excluded.[41]

(a) *Express Trust to Convert.* An express trust to convert normally carries with it the duty to apportion the income received pending conversion.[42] There is no question in this situation of a contrary intention with regard to conversion; but there may be a contrary intention with regard to apportionment. This will arise where there is an indication of intention that, although the property should be converted, the life tenant is to enjoy the whole income produced by it pending conversion.

Such an intention is commonly indicated by the inclusion of a provision to the effect that "the income of so much of the residue as for the time being shall remain unsold, shall be applied as if the same were income arising from investments of the proceeds of sale thereof."[43]

It may of course be indicated in other ways. The question depends upon the construction of the particular instrument. A power in the trustees to postpone a sale in their discretion is not a sufficient indication. Such a provision does not entitle the life tenant to the income produced by unauthorised investments.[44]

(b) *No Express Trust to Convert.* Here it is necessary to examine two constructional questions: whether the will indicates an intention to prevent conversion; or to permit the life tenant to retain the whole income. Either such intent will be sufficient to exclude apportionment.

In *Gray* v. *Siggers*[45] the trustees were given power to retain any portion of the testator's property in the same state in which it should be at his decease, or to sell and convert the same *as they should in their absolute discretion think fit.* Such a power excluded the duty to convert.

An indication that the life tenant is to enjoy the whole income of the

---

to produce £x after *two* years of investment. The calculation then needs to be continued back to the date of the testator's death. See Parker and Mellows, *Modern Law of Trusts* (5th ed.), pp. 333–334; Maudsley and Burn, *Trusts and Trustees: Cases and Materials* (3rd ed.), p. 643.

[40] *Hinves* v. *Hinves* (1844) 3 Hare 609; *Alcock* v. *Sloper* (1833) 2 Myl. & K. 699; *Re Pitcairn* [1896] 2 Ch. 199.

[41] *Per* James L.J. in *MacDonald* v. *Irvine* (1878) 8 Ch.D. 101 at p. 124; *per* Leach M.R. in *Alcock* v. *Sloper, supra; per* Cozens-Hardy M.R. in *Re Wareham* [1912] 2 Ch. 312 at p. 315.

[42] *Gibson* v. *Bott* (1802) 7 Ves.Jr. 89.

[43] Key & Elphinstone, *Precedents in Conveyancing* (15th ed.), Vol. 2, pp. 926–928; (1943) 7 Conv.(N.S.) 128 (S. J. Bailey).

[44] *Re Chaytor* [1905] 1 Ch. 233; *Re Slater* (1915) 85 L.J.Ch. 432; *Re Berry* [1962] Ch. 97.

[45] (1880) 15 Ch.D. 74; *Alcock* v. *Sloper* (1833) 2 Myl. & K. 699; *Re Pitcairn* [1896] 2 Ch. 199; *Pickering* v. *Pickering* (1839) 4 Myl. & Cr.289; *Re Nicholson* [1909] 2 Ch. 111.

property also prevents apportionment and has the effect of excluding the duty to convert.[46] It may also have the effect of authorising the investments; or of making into settled land what would otherwise be held on trust for sale.[47] A power to retain investments or to postpone conversion is thus more likely to exclude the duty to convert and to apportion in cases where there is no express trust to convert. But it may be so framed that it is intended to do no more than allow a suitable time to be selected for the sale.[48] Such a power, being merely administrative, will neither prevent conversion nor apportionment.

(c) *Reversionary Interests.* Similarly, the rule in *Re Earl of Chesterfield's Trusts*[49] may be excluded where such intention is manifested.[50] A clause expressly excluding the rule in *Howe* v. *Earl of Dartmouth*[51] usually operates to exclude the rule in *Re Earl of Chesterfield's Trusts* also[52]; but it is the general practice to add a special clause for this purpose.

It was laid down in *Rowlls* v. *Bebb*[53] that even if the rule is impliedly excluded by a clause in the will giving the trustees a discretionary power to postpone sale, it will nevertheless operate unless it can be shown that the trustees had, when they refrained from selling, a clear perception that they were exercising the discretionary power. It is not enough that they did not appreciate the necessity of selling a particular asset. There can be no such thing as an unconscious exercise of a discretion.[54]

(v) **Leaseholds.** The rule in *Howe* v. *Earl of Dartmouth*[55] applied before 1926 to leaseholds; it is generally thought that it no longer applies. Leases with 60 years or more to run are now authorised investments, so there can be no question of application to leases of that length.[56]

With shorter leases, the question depends on the Law of Property Act 1925, s.28,[57] and *Re Brooker.*[58] This was a case of an *express* trust

---

[46] *Alcock* v. *Sloper, supra; cf. Re Evans' W.T.* [1921] 2 Ch. 309; *Re Gough* [1957] Ch. 323.

[47] *Re Gough, supra.*

[48] As with the ships in *Brown* v. *Gellatly* (1867) L.R. 2 Ch.App. 751, *ante,* p. 512.

[49] (1883) 24 Ch.D. 643; *ante,* p. 512.

[50] *Re Pitcairn* [1896] 2 Ch. 199.

[51] (1802) 7 Ves.Jr. 137.

[52] See *Rowlls* v. *Bebb* [1900] 2 Ch. 107.

[53] [1900] 2 Ch. 107 (a case of a reversion).

[54] This principle was applied in *Re Fisher* [1943] Ch. 377 (a case of intestacy) and in *Re Hey's Settlement Trusts* [1945] Ch. 294; *Re Holliday* [1947] Ch. 402.

[55] (1802) 7 Ves.Jr. 137; *ante,* p. 509.

[56] S.L.A. 1925, s.73; L.P.A. 1925, s.28; *Re Gough* [1957] Ch. 323.

[57] See also s.25(1), conferring a power to postpone sale.

[58] [1926] W.N. 93.

for sale of leaseholds, and the question was whether the tenants for life were entitled to the income *in specie*. It was held that they were. Section 28(2) provides that "Subject to any direction to the contrary in the disposition on trust for sale or in the settlement of the proceeds of sale, the net rents and profits of the land until sale . . . shall be paid or applied . . . in like manner as the income of investments representing the purchase money would be payable or applicable if a sale had been made and the proceeds had been duly invested." And, by subsection (5), the section "applies to dispositions on trust for sale coming into operation either before or after the commencement or by virtue of this Act." "Land" in section 205 includes "land of any tenure," and the tenant for life was thus entitled to the whole income, as a tenant for life of freeholds would have been.

Does the rule in *Howe* v. *Earl of Dartmouth*[59] apply to residuary leaseholds where there is *no express* trust to convert? Certainly, *Re Brooker*[60] does not cover the precise point, for that was a case of an express trust, and the rule in *Howe* v. *Earl of Dartmouth* was therefore not relevant. The issue was apportionment, not conversion. If the rule applies so as to create an implied trust to convert, would the rule of apportionment apply also? If section 28 applies there will be no apportionment. It is arguable[61] that the section does not apply, because a residuary bequest which includes leaseholds is not strictly a "disposition on trust for sale." It is a "disposition" within that term as defined in section 205 as including "a bequest . . . of property contained in a will"; but it is not, so it is argued, a disposition on trust for sale, for the trust for sale is imposed, not by the disposition, but by the rule in *Howe* v. *Earl of Dartmouth*.[62] However, it would be most inconvenient to differentiate between express[63] or statutory trusts for sale,[64] where there is no apportionment, and implied trusts for sale. The better view is that the tenant for life is entitled to the whole income from leaseholds; and this is in accordance with the view of Tomlin J. who said in *Re Trollope*,[65] "so far as leaseholds held in trust for sale are concerned, the rule of *Howe* v. *Earl of Dartmouth* is gone."

If it is accepted that the duty to apportion no longer exists, then the only significance in the question whether, in cases where there is no express or statutory duty to convert, such a duty is implied under the rule in *Howe* v. *Earl of Dartmouth* is this: if there is a duty to convert, the leasehold will be held on trust for sale; whereas if there is no such duty, it will be settled land, governed by the Settled Land Act 1925.

[59] (1802) 7 Ves.Jr. 137.
[60] [1926] W.N. 93.
[61] See (1930–32) 4 C.L.J. 357 (S. J. Bailey); *cf.* Hayton and Marshall (8th ed.), p. 659, n. 19.
[62] *Supra.*
[63] *Re Brooker, supra.*
[64] *Re Berton* [1939] Ch. 200 (a gift of land to be held in undivided shares).
[65] [1927] 1 Ch. 596 at p. 601.

Such is the position while short leaseholds remain unauthorised investments. The Law Reform Committee,[66] however, has recommended that leases with less than 60 years to run should be authorised, subject to the requirement of professional advice. Where such an investment is made, a sinking fund should be set up, to be serviced out of trust income, or the trustees should take other steps to protect the capital value of the fund.

(vi) Howe v. Earl of Dartmouth Today.[67] The rules relating to conversion and apportionment demonstrate basic principles of equity. But they should be understood in their proper perspective.

(a) *Exclusion of Duty to Apportion.* The duty to apportion is in practice nearly always excluded, both in respect of income from unauthorised securities and in respect of reversionary interests. The duty to convert, where it exists, thus appears in the context of a duty to change the investments.

(b) *Trustee Investments Act* 1961. Authorised securities now mean those investments which are authorised by the Trustee Investments Act 1961. It should be noted that wider-range securities and narrower-range requiring advice are only authorised when advice to retain them has been received. Presumably, therefore, "If the trustees follow advice to sell and re-invest such property it would seem the rule [in *Howe* v. *Earl of Dartmouth*] applies until such sale."[68]

(c) *Paradoxical Effect of Current Investment Situation.* In the investment context of the present day, the rules of conversion and apportionment are in some way misplaced. The problem still exists of speculative and wasting securities. But the rule requires unauthorised investments, in the form of equities (other than those authorised by the Trustee Investments Act 1961) to be sold in order to protect the capital for the benefit of the remainderman; and it deprives the life tenant of the high income which is supposedly earned by them. "At a time when investment in equities may be the only way in which the capital value of the fund can in fact be maintained the traditional theory that re-investment is necessary to protect those interested in the capital no longer holds good. Conversely, the yield on fixed interest investments is now such as to provide the tenant for life with an income which is as high and may be higher than the average yield on authorised equities."[69] The positions are therefore reversed. The life tenant now wants fixed interest investments in order to provide a high income; the

---

[66] 23rd Report, *Powers and Duties of Trustees* (1982, Cmnd. 8733).
[67] (1952) 16 Conv.(n.s.) 349 (L. A. Sheridan).
[68] Hayton & Marshall (8th ed.), p. 651.
[69] Law Reform Committee, 23rd Report, *supra*, para. 3.31. See also Maudsley and Burn, *Trusts and Trustees: Cases and Materials* (3rd ed.), p. 637.

remainderman wants unauthorised securities for the preservation of the real value of the capital. And it is the life tenant who will be pressing the trustees to convert urgently into gilt-edged securities; for they can bring an income three or four times the mere 4 per cent. allowed to the life tenant by the rule of apportionment.

(d) *Reform.* The apportionment rules have recently been reviewed by the Law Reform Committee,[70] whose conclusion is that, rather than complete abolition, the rules in *Howe* v. *Earl of Dartmouth* and *Re Earl of Chesterfield's Trusts* should be subsumed into a statutory duty to hold a fair balance between the beneficiaries. The trustees should have express power to convert income to capital and vice versa. They should have regard to the whole investment policy of the trust, and should convert and apportion to the extent necessary to maintain an even hand. Any beneficiary who could show that he was substantially prejudiced by the trustees' exercise of their discretion should be able to apply to court for an order that the trustees make or adjust an apportionment.

B. Other Methods of Apportionment

Apportionment is necessary in other situations, and these will be mentioned in outline only.

(i) Apportionment Act 1870. When a testator or a life tenant dies, the question arises of the entitlement to periodical income, such as rents, interest and dividends, earned in whole or in part, but not paid, at the time of the death. That which is treated as being earned before the death will be added to the estate, and that earned afterwards is payable as income to the income beneficiary under the will or, in the case of the death of a life tenant, to the next life tenant, or to the capital.

The division is governed by the Apportionment Act, section 2, which provides that "all rents, annuities, dividends, and other periodical payments in the nature of income ... shall ... be considered as accruing from day to day, and shall be apportionable in respect of time accordingly." It is necessary therefore to ascertain the proportion of the earning period which expired prior to the death, and to divide the payment, when received, in the same proportion. When rent is due, or a dividend earned, but not paid prior to the death, the whole income is paid to the testator's estate or to the life tenant. A similar situation arises where there is a class of income beneficiaries whose composition changes by births or deaths. It was held in *Re Joel*[71] that each member is entitled to a share of the income for the days when he was a member. The Apportionment Act may be excluded by an expression of an intention to do so.[72] This is now common in order to avoid the addition

[70] *Supra.* See paras. 3.36 and 3.37.
[71] [1967] Ch. 14.
[72] *Williams on Wills* (6th ed.), p. 1219.

of complications which are introduced into the administration of an estate.

The view of the Law Reform Committee[73] was that the 1870 Act could be both inconvenient and unfair. There was a case for arguing that section 2 should only apply if expressly included. Their recommendation was that, subject to a contrary intention, the Act should not apply on any death upon which a trust or settlement arises. In the case of the death of a tenant for life of an existing settlement, the Act should be amended so that income could be treated as belonging to the person entitled to the income at the date it becomes due. As far as *Re Joel*[74] was concerned, it was of limited application and caused little real difficulty, but fairness could be achieved by abrogating the rule and providing that income from a trust fund should be apportioned between the class of beneficiaries as constituted on the date of its receipt by the trustees.[75]

(ii) The Rule in Allhusen v. Whittell. This rule attempts to strike a fair balance between life tenant and remainderman in respect of the payment of the debts of an estate. The life tenant under a will is entitled to income earned after the testator's death. The debts of the testator must also be paid; and it may take some time to do so. In the meantime the assets of the estate are earning income for the life tenant. He should, in fairness, only have the income from the net estate. The rule in *Allhusen* v. *Whittell*[76] provides that the life tenant shall make a contribution.

Romer L.J. in *Corbett* v. *Commissioners of Inland Revenue*[77] laid down the rule as follows:

"For the purposes of adjusting rights as between the tenant for life and the remainderman of a residuary estate, debts, legacies, estate duties, probate duties and so forth, are to be deemed to have been paid out of such capital of the testator's estate as will be sufficient for that purpose, when to that capital is added interest on that capital from the date of the testator's death to the date of the payment of the legacy or debt, or whatever it may have been, interest being calculated at the average rate of interest[78] earned by the testator's estate during the relevant period."[79]

---

[73] 23rd Report, *supra.* See para. 3.40.
[74] *Supra.*
[75] 23rd Report, *supra*, para. 3.41.
[76] (1867) L.R. 4 Eq. 295.
[77] [1938] 1 K.B. 567.
[78] *Re Wills* [1915] 1 Ch. 769; *Re Oldham* (1927) 71 S.J. 491.
[79] Assuming a debt of £50, an average rate of income of 6 per cent., income tax at 25 per cent., and payment of the debt one year from the death, the apportionment will be:

From Capital: 47.85 (being $\dfrac{100}{104.5} \times 50$)

From Income: 2.15 (being $\dfrac{4.5}{104.5} \times 50$)

The rule may be excluded by an expression of contrary intent, or where its application would in the circumstances be inappropriate.[80]

Witnesses to the Law Reform Committee described the rule as "complex, fiddlesome and resulting in a disproportionate amount of work and expense," adding that where the rule was not excluded it was often simply ignored.[81] The committee accordingly recommended that, as in the case of the rules in *Howe* v. *Earl of Dartmouth* and *Re Earl of Chesterfield's Trusts*,[82] it should be subsumed into a new statutory duty to hold a fair balance between the beneficiaries, as described above.[83]

(iii) The Rule in Re Atkinson. Where an authorised mortgage security is sold and the proceeds are insufficient to satisfy the principal and interest in full, it is necessary to determine the way in which the loss is to be shared between life tenant and remainderman. The sum realised must be apportioned between the life tenant and the remainderman in the proportion which the amount due for the arrears of interest bears to the amount due in respect of the principal.[84] The rule applies to debenture stock,[85] but not to dividends or arrears of dividends on preference shares.[86]

(iv) Purchase or Sale of Shares Cum Dividend. One of the factors which affects the price of shares is the date of payment of the next dividend. A share whose dividend will be paid tomorrow is worth more than it would be if the dividend has been paid yesterday. It would seem reasonable to require an apportionment when shares are bought or sold cum dividend, but the general rule is that there is none.[87] In this respect, the beneficiaries take "the rough with the smooth."[88] This is probably more convenient overall than an insistence on an apportionment in every case. But an apportionment will be required if there would otherwise be "a glaring injustice."[89]

(v) Company Distributions. Questions can also arise as to the entitlements of life tenant and remainderman to certain distributions by companies. The question of entitlement and that of the liability of the

---

[80] *Re McEuen* [1913] 2 Ch. 704; *Re Darby* [1939] Ch. 905.
[81] 23rd Report, *supra*. See para. 3.31.
[82] *Supra.*
[83] 23rd Report, *supra*, para. 3.36. See *ante*, p. 517.
[84] *Re Atkinson* [1904] 2 Ch. 160.
[85] *Re Walker* [1936] Ch. 280.
[86] *Re Wakley* [1920] 2 Ch. 205.
[87] *Bulkeley* v. *Stephens* [1896] 2 Ch. 241; *Re Ellerman's S.T.* (1984) 81 L.S.Gaz. 430, where the decision to the contrary in *Re Winterstoke's W.T.* [1938] Ch. 158 was regarded as wrong; (1986) 1 Trust Law & Practice 62 (I. Pittaway). See also Law Reform Committee, 23rd Report, *supra*.
[88] *Re Maclaren's S.T.* [1951] 2 All E.R. 414 at p. 420.
[89] *Ibid.*

distribution to income tax are related questions, but are not identical.[90] The tax aspect is the reason for the attraction to shareholders generally of distributions as capital.

(a) *Distribution as Capital.* A company may only make a distribution of its capital to the shareholders in certain circumstances, such as liquidation.[91] A company, however, has power to increase its capital[92]; this may be done by capitalising profits and applying the money in paying up new shares which are distributed, as capital, to the shareholder.[93] Other payments to shareholders will be income payments; and the fact that the company calls a payment one of capital does not make it one.[94] The question is whether the company has taken proper steps to capitalise profits; the company effectively determines the nature of the payment as capital. The leading case is *Bouch* v. *Sproule*,[95] where a bonus dividend, declared out of accumulated (and capitalised) profits, and applied in the purchase of new shares, was held to be a distribution of capital.

Treatment of such bonus issues of shares as capital is reasonable. The capitalised profits may or may not have arisen from undistributed trading profits; but the price of the shares when purchased will have reflected the existence of the sums in the reserve fund. The distribution of bonus shares looks like a "present" to shareholders. It is however merely a division of the company's assets among more shares. If a bonus issue is made of one new share for every one held, the assets of the company are divided among twice the number of shares, and the share price is immediately halved.

If a "rights" issue is made, the company offers to its shareholders the right to purchase newly issued shares at an advantageous price. The "rights" therefore have value. The purchase is purely a capital transaction, and trustees wishing to take up the shares should sell sufficient of the "rights" to produce enough money to purchase the shares available to the "rights" they retain.

(b) *"Windfalls" as Income.* Where, however, a company enjoys a sudden "windfall"[96] and distributes the benefit to shareholders, that is a distribution of income to which the life tenant is entitled.[97] So it was

---

[90] *Re Bates* [1928] Ch. 682; *Hill* v. *Permanent Trustee Co. of N.S.W.* [1930] A.C. 720; *Re Doughty* [1947] Ch. 263; *Re Sechiari* [1950] 1 All E.R. 417; I.C.T.A. 1988, ss. 209–211, 234, 254.

[91] *Re Armitage* [1893] 3 Ch. 337. For other examples, reference should be made to the Company Law textbooks.

[92] Under power in the articles: Companies Act 1985, s.121.

[93] *Bouch* v. *Sproule* (1887) 12 App.Cas. 385; *I.R.C.* v. *Blott* [1921] 2 A.C. 171; *Re Evans* [1913] 1 Ch. 23; *Re Outen's W.T.* [1963] Ch. 291 (issue of unsecured loan stock).

[94] *Hill* v. *Permanent Trustee Co. of N.S.W.* [1930] A.C. 720.

[95] *Supra.*

[96] *Re Kleinwort's Settlement* [1951] Ch. 860 at p. 863, *per* Vaisey J.

[97] *Re Bates* [1928] Ch. 682; *Re Tedlie* (1922) 126 L.T. 644.

held in the *Thomas Tilling* cases.[98] On the nationalisation of part of Thomas Tilling Ltd. a block of British Transport 3 per cent. Guaranteed Stock was issued to the company in payment. The company decided to distribute the stock among its shareholders. The income beneficiaries were entitled.[99]

There is much to be said for requiring an apportionment in such circumstances. If the Tilling shares were sold the day before the distribution, the whole price of the shares, including the part which was created by the promise of the bonus distribution, would have been capital. It was suggested in *Re Kleinwort's Settlement*[1] that an apportionment should be required in special circumstances; as where the trustees had acted in breach of trust. If, for example, trustees had applied capital in the purchase of shares which they knew were to be the subject of a bonus dividend, they would not be observing their duty to maintain equality between the beneficiaries, and an apportionment might be ordered. But none has been ordered on this ground.

(c) *Where the Shareholders may Elect.* It seems that the same principle applies where the shareholders are given the right to choose between a cash dividend and an allotment of shares. Where, following the principle of *Bouch* v. *Sproule*,[2] the company intends to make a distribution of profits as dividend, either in the form of cash or in shares paid up from accumulated profits, the trustees' duty is to accept whichever is the more advantageous, usually the shares.[3] The tenant for life is then entitled to so much of the value of the new shares as represented the dividend. The surplus is paid to capital,[4] as is necessary to maintain an even balance, because the value of the other shares will be reduced by the issue of the new ones. Where, however, the company has shown an intention to capitalise the surplus profits, there will be a capital distribution.[5] Then, if the new shares are more valuable than the cash, the trustees "must take the dividend in what I will call the capitalised form."[6]

The question then is whether they can take the shares and make some apportionment between life tenant and remaindermen. It is submitted that they should be able to do so; on the analogy of the

---

[98] *Re Sechiari* [1950] 1 All E.R. 417; *Re Kleinwort's Settlement* [1951] Ch. 860; *Re Rudd's W.T.* [1952] 1 All E.R. 254; (1953) 17 Conv.(N.S.) 22 (A. J. Bland).
[99] In *Re Maclaren's S.T.* [1951] 2 All E.R. 414, the opposite result was reached on the ground that the life tenant knew of the situation, and consented to the purchase of the Thomas Tilling Ltd. shares as a capital investment.
[1] [1951] Ch. 860.
[2] (1887) 12 App.Cas. 385; (1975) 39 Conv.(N.S.) 355 (W. H. Goodhart).
[3] *Re Evans* [1913] 1 Ch. 23.
[4] *Rowley* v. *Unwin* (1855) 2 K. & J. 138; *Re Northage* (1891) 64 L.T. 625; *Re Malam* [1894] 3 Ch. 578.
[5] *Re Evans* [1913] 1 Ch. 23; *Re Taylor* [1926] Ch. 923.
[6] *Ibid.* at p. 33, *per* North J.

situation where the life tenant has paid money to meet a call on shares obtained for the trust. In such a situation, the life tenant is entitled to a lien on the shares to the extent of his payment.[7] In the present situation, the life tenant can be regarded as surrendering the value of the dividend in order to obtain the transfer of the shares. He would then have a lien on the shares to the value of the net dividend. The shares would be added to capital. It is right that the difference in value should be added to capital for, as has been seen, the value of the other shares will be to that extent reduced by the issue of the new shares.[8]

2. Duty to Provide Accounts and Information

A. Accounts

(i) **Extent of Duty.** A trustee must keep accounts and be constantly ready to produce them for the beneficiaries.[9] It seems that a beneficiary is entitled only to see and inspect the accounts; if he wants a copy himself, he must pay for it; but it is common practice to provide a copy for each of the beneficiaries.[10] An income beneficiary is entitled to full accounts, but a remainderman is entitled only to such information as relates to capital transactions.[11] Accounts are often produced in simplified form in order to be comprehensible to the beneficiaries.

(ii) **Audit.** It is neither necessary nor, except in large and complicated trusts or where trouble with a beneficiary is foreseen, usual to have trust accounts audited. However, trustees may, in their absolute discretion, have the trust accounts examined and audited by an independent accountant, and may pay the costs out of income or capital. Audit should not be effected more than once in every three years, except in special cases.[12]

Any trustee or beneficiary may apply for the accounts of any trust to be investigated and audited by such solicitor or public accountant as may be agreed upon, or in default of agreement by the Public Trustee

---

[7] *Rowley* v. *Unwin* (1855) 2 K. & J. 138.

[8] The trust obtains no tax advantage by receiving dividends in the form of capital rather than in cash: I.C.T.A. 1988, ss. 249, 251.

[9] *Pearse* v. *Green* (1819) 1 Jac. & W. 135, *per* Plumer M.R. at p. 140.

[10] *Ottley* v. *Gilby* (1845) 8 Beav. 602; *Kemp* v. *Burn* (1863) 4 Giff. 348; *Re Watson* (1904) 49 S.J. 54.

[11] Mellows, *The Trustee's Handbook* (3rd ed.), p. 52.

[12] T.A. 1925, s.22(4). For the audit by the court of the accounts of a judicial trustee, see Administration of Justice Act 1982, s.57; Judicial Trustee Rules 1983 (S.I. 1983 No. 370). By r. 2 there is to be no automatic audit by the court of the accounts of a "corporate trust," meaning the Official Solicitor, Public Trustee or a corporation appointed by the court to be a trustee, or which is entitled to be a custodian trustee by the Public Trustee Act 1906, s.4(3).

[13] Public Trustee Act 1906, s.13. The Law Reform Committee has recommended the repeal of s.13, which is rarely used and is ineffective because there are no powers to enforce the findings of the Public Trustee. (23rd Report, 1982, Cmnd. 8733, para. 4.48).

or by some person appointed by him.[13] Such an investigation however may not, except with the leave of the court, take place within 12 months of a previous such investigation. The costs are usually borne by the trust, but the Public Trustee may order that the applicant or the trustees must pay them or share them.[14] An appeal against a decision of the Public Trustee lies to a Judge of the Chancery Division.[15]

B. Information. Trust Documents

(i) Information for Beneficiaries. The beneficiaries are entitled to be informed about matters currently affecting the trust.[16] In order to have a ready supply of up-to-date information, the trustees should keep a trust diary or Minute Book which will record decisions and events affecting the trust. And a large trust will keep many other documents, such as the minutes of trustees' meetings. Documents connected with the trust are trust documents, and prima facie the property of the beneficiaries, and as such open to their inspection.[17]

On the other hand, a trustee's powers and discretions are not open to challenge if he has exercised them bona fide.[18] Further "trustees exercising a discretionary power are not bound to disclose to their beneficiaries the reasons actuating them in coming to a decision."[19] These principles come into conflict where, in the trust records or correspondence relating to the exercise of discretions, confidential matters are discussed and reasons given for them. Are the beneficiaries entitled to see the documents?

In *Re Londonderry's Settlement*,[20] the donees of a power under a discretionary trust decided to distribute the capital. One member of the discretionary class was dissatisfied with the sum which they intended to give her. She asked for copies of the minutes of trustees' meetings, documents prepared for the meetings, and correspondence between various interested persons. The trustees were willing only to show her documents giving the intended distributions and

---

[14] See *Re Oddy* [1911] 1 Ch. 532.

[15] Public Trustee Act 1906, s.10.

[16] But this does not go so far as to put the trustees "under any duty to proffer information to their beneficiary, or to see that he has proper advice merely because they are trustees for him and know that he is entering into a transaction with his beneficial interest with some person or body connected in some way with the trustees, such as a company in which the trustees own some shares beneficially.": *Tito* v. *Waddell (No. 2)* [1977] Ch. 106 at p. 243, *per* Megarry V.-C.; questioned at (1977) 41 Conv. (N.S.) 438 (F. R. Crane).

[17] *O'Rourke* v. *Darbishire* [1920] A.C. 581 at pp. 619, 626.

[18] *Re Beloved Wilkes' Charity* (1851) 3 Mac. & G. 440; *Klug* v. *Klug* [1918] 2 Ch. 67; *Re Gresham Life Assurance Society, ex p. Penney* (1872) L.R. 8 Ch.App. 446; *ante*, pp. 479–482.

[19] *Per* Harman L.J. in *Re Londonderry's Settlement, infra*, at p. 928.

[20] [1965] Ch. 918; (1965) 81 L.Q.R. 192 (R.E.M.).

the annual trust accounts. They declined, in the general interest of the family, to disclose further documents, and brought a summons to determine the nature and extent of their duties in relation to disclosures.

The Court of Appeal found great difficulty in defining in general terms what were the "trust documents" which a beneficiary prima facie had a right to see. Salmon L.J. said that the category of trust documents could not be defined. They have however[21] "these characteristics in common: (1) they are documents in the possession of the trustees as trustees; (2) they contain information about the trust, which the beneficiaries are entitled to know; (3) the beneficiaries have a proprietary interest in the documents and, accordingly, are entitled to see them." Documents connected with the trust may contain confidential information, disclosure of which "might cause infinite trouble in the family, out of all proportion to the benefit which might be received from the inspection of the same ... Where trustees are given discretionary trusts which involve a decision upon matters between beneficiaries, viewing the merits and other rights to benefit under such a trust, the trustees are given a confidential role and they cannot properly exercise that confidential role if at any moment there is likely to be an investigation for the purpose of seeing whether they have exercised their discretion in the best possible manner. Of course, if a case is made of lack of bona fides, that is an entirely different matter."[22]

But it is one of extreme difficulty. If a beneficiary suspects the trustees' discretionary decisions have been made from wrong motives, it may only be possible to establish this by examining the documents. Such an allegation may be an effective way of obtaining information, otherwise denied. It is likely, however, that it would be dealt with by the exercise of a right to discovery after the action was started. Indeed the final order made in the *Londonderry* case was without prejudice to the right of the defendant to discovery in separate proceedings against the trustees.[23]

A trustee's duty is not merely one of answering questions; but also to provide beneficiaries with information concerning their interests under the trust; or, in the case of an infant beneficiary, to inform him of his entitlement on coming of age.[24] Executors are under no such positive duty, as a will is a public document.[25]

---

[21] *Ibid.* at p. 938.

[22] *Ibid. per* Danckwerts L.J. at pp. 935–936. Salmon L.J. said at p. 938: "If any parts of a document contain information which the beneficiaries are not entitled to know, I doubt whether such parts can truly be said to be integral parts of a trust document."

[23] *Ibid.* at p. 939.

[24] *Hawkesley* v. *May* [1956] 1 Q.B. 304; including, it seems, his rights under the rule in *Saunders* v. *Vautier* (1841) Cr. & Ph. 240; *post*, p. 579; (1970) 34 Conv.(N.S.) 29 (A. Samuels).

[25] *Re Lewis* [1904] 2 Ch. 656; *Re Mackay* [1906] 1 Ch. 25.

(ii) Successor Trustees and Third Parties. As has been seen, trustees must provide information concerning the trust to a new or successor trustee,[26] and, by Law of Property Act, s.137(8), they must produce to any person interested a written notice which they may have received of dealings[27] with equitable interests in the trust property.

[26] *Tiger* v. *Barclays Bank* [1951] 2 K.B. 556; *ante*, p. 484.
[27] *e.g.* mortgages, charges or sales.

CHAPTER 19

POWERS OF TRUSTEES

TRUSTEES may exercise such powers as are given to them by the trust instrument or by statute. A power, as has been seen,[1] is to be distinguished from a duty, in that its exercise is permissive and discretionary, and not compulsory. In the absence of *mala fides*, the court will not interfere with the exercise of discretions by the donee of the power. At most, the holder of a fiduciary power, such as a trustee donee, is under a duty to consider; he will not be compelled to exercise.[2]

Originally, it was necessary to spell out a trustee's powers in detail in

---

[1] *Ante*, p. 61.
[2] *Ante*, p. 167.

the trust instrument. Now, however, the Trustee Act 1925 provides the basic powers needed by trustees.[3] They may unless otherwise stated be excluded or amended as desired.[4]

1. POWER OF SALE

A. Land

Land is generally held either by a fee simple owner absolutely entitled, or under a settlement or under a trust for sale. In the first case, there is, of course, no trust. Settled land is vested in the tenant for life upon the trusts of the settlement, and he can sell.[5] Land held on trust for sale is vested in the trustees, and they hold upon trust to sell, with a power to postpone sale at their discretion[6] and have all the powers of a tenant for life under the Settled Land Act 1925.[7] The receipt of at least two trustees or of a trust corporation is required for all capital money arising under the Settled Land Act 1925 or under a trust for sale.[8] Rarely, land may be vested in trustees who hold on trust for a sole beneficiary of full age. In such circumstances, the land appears to be "property in his hands not in a state of investment"[9] which the trustees have power to sell. But the beneficiary can then call for a transfer of the legal title and at any time terminate the trust.[10]

B. Chattels

Where chattels or other personalty are held upon trust for sale, the position is the same as with land except that the receipt of a sole trustee is sufficient discharge to a purchaser.[11] The trust for sale may arise expressly, or by statute,[12] or be implied, as we have seen, under the rule in *Howe* v. *Earl of Dartmouth*.[13] When chattels are settled to devolve with settled land the tenant for life has power to sell them with the consent of the court and the purchase money must be paid to the trustees as capital money under the Settled Land Act 1925.[14] Where

---

[3] The Act does not provide any power of appropriation of assets to beneficiaries. The Law Reform Committee, 23rd Report, *The Powers and Duties of Trustees,* (1982 Cmnd. 8733), para. 4.42, recommends that trustees should have similar powers to those conferred on personal representatives by A.E.A. 1925, s.41.

[4] T.A. 1925, s.69(2).

[5] S.L.A. 1925, s.38(1).

[6] L.P.A. 1925, s.25.

[7] L.P.A. 1925, s.28(1). The Law Commission has suggested that the powers of trustees for sale should be extended beyond the reforms suggested by the Law Reform Committee (*supra*), paras. 8.1–8.10. They should have the powers of an absolute owner over the land; Working Paper No. 94 (1985), *Trusts of Land,* para. 7.5.

[8] S.L.A. 1925, s.94(1); L.P.A. 1925, s.27(2); T.A. 1925, s.14.

[9] T.L.A. 1961, s.1.

[10] *Saunders* v. *Vautier* (1841) Cr. & Ph. 240; *post,* p. 579; *cf. Re Brockbank* [1948] Ch. 206.

[11] T.A. 1925, s.14; *post,* p. 529.

[12] A.E.A. 1925, s.33.

[13] (1802) 7 Ves.Jr. 137; *ante,* p. 509.

[14] S.L.A. 1925, s.67; *Re Hope* [1899] 2 Ch. 679 (refusal of permission to sell the "Hope" diamond).

personal chattels are settled without reference to settled land on trusts creating entailed interests, the trustees may sell the chattels with the consent of the beneficiary in possession if of full age,[15] and the purchase money will be held on the same trusts as the chattels. In other cases, where chattels are settled for successive interests, but neither the Settled Land Act 1925, s.67, nor the Law of Property Act, s.130, applies, the court may in appropriate cases order a sale under the Trustee Act 1925, s.57.[16]

C. Other Property

In the case of many other forms of property, a power of sale, if not given expressly, will usually be implied. We have seen that a trustee has power to sell property in his hands not in a state of investment; this, and unauthorised investments, and any investments which the trustees think are not suitable for the trust, should be sold and invested in accordance with the express terms of the relevant investment power, or with the provisions of the Trustee Investments Act 1961.[17]

Whenever trustees are authorised to pay or apply capital money for any purpose or in any manner, they have power to raise such money by sale, mortgage, etc., of the trust property then in possession.[18] But this does not authorise trustees to raise money by charging existing investments in order to purchase others.[19]

D. Sales by Trustees

The detailed provisions relating to sales by trustees are contained in the Trustee Act 1925, s.12. Trustees may

> "sell or concur with any other person in selling all or any part of the property, either subject to prior charges or not, and either together or in lots, by public auction or by private contract, subject to any such conditions respecting title or evidence of title or other matter as the trustee thinks fit, with power to vary any contract for sale, and to buy in at any auction, or to rescind any contract for sale and to re-sell, without being answerable for any loss.
>
> (2) A trust or power to sell or dispose of land includes a trust or power to sell or dispose of part thereof, whether the division is horizontal, vertical, or made in any other way."

As we have seen, trustees are under an over-riding duty to obtain the best price for the beneficiaries.[20] If they fail to do so, the beneficiaries may ask the court for an injunction restraining the sale.[21] But if the sale

---

[15] L.P.A. 1925, s.130(5).
[16] *Re Hope's W.T.* [1929] 2 Ch. 136.
[17] *Ante*, pp. 491 *et seq.*
[18] T.A. 1925, s.16(1).
[19] *Re Suenson-Taylor* [1974] 1 W.L.R. 1280 (land).
[20] *Buttle* v. *Saunders* [1950] 2 All E.R. 193; *ante*, p. 485. As to whether trustees can sell at a valuation to be determined by a third party, see [1985] Conv. 44 (G. Lightman).
[21] *Wheelwright* v. *Walker* (1883) 23 Ch.D. 752.

has taken place, it may not be impeached by a beneficiary on the ground that any of the conditions of the sale were unduly depreciatory, unless it also appears that the consideration for the sale was thereby rendered inadequate.[22] A purchaser will not be affected unless he was acting in collusion with the trustees.[23]

2. Power to Give Receipts: Section 14

By the Trustee Act 1925, s.14, the written receipt by a trustee for money, securities, etc., is a sufficient discharge to the person paying, and effectually exonerates him from being answerable for any loss or misapplication of the money. The section applies notwithstanding anything to the contrary in the trust instrument,[24] and applies to sole trustees, except in the case of proceeds of sale or capital money arising under a trust for sale or capital money arising under the Settled Land Act where, unless the trustee is a trust corporation, the receipt of at least two trustees is necessary.[25] Where there is more than one trustee, all must sign, in accordance with the rule that they must act together.[26]

3. Power to Insure: Section 19

A. Insurance

There is no duty upon trustees to insure the trust property. The rule is that they are not liable if the property is destroyed; and if the trustees differ on the question whether the property should be insured, it seems that nothing can be done to compel them.[27] However, it is difficult to see how, in some circumstances, failure to insure would be consistent with their general duty of caring for the trust property. A power to insure is contained in section 19, but does not apply where the beneficiaries are absolutely entitled and *sui juris*, and so can end the trust at any time.[28]

> "(1) A trustee may insure against loss or damage by fire any building or other insurable property to any amount, including the amount of any insurance already on foot, not exceeding three fourth parts of the full value of the building or property, and pay the premiums for such insurance out of the income thereof or out of the income of any other property subject to the same trusts without

---

[22] T.A. 1925, s.13(1); *Dance* v. *Goldingham* (1873) L.R. 8 Ch.App. 902; *Dunn* v. *Flood* (1885) 28 Ch.D. 586. The trustee may, of course, be liable.
[23] T.A. 1925, s.13(2).
[24] T.A. 1925, s.14(3).
[25] *Ibid.* s.14(2).
[26] *Ante*, p. 462; charitable trustees may act by a majority.
[27] *Re McEacharn* (1911) 103 L.T. 900.
[28] T.A. 1925, s.19(2).

obtaining the consent of any person who may be entitled wholly or partly to such income."

The policy moneys must be treated as capital and applied as capital money under the Settled Land Act 1925 or to accord with the terms of the trust for sale or other trust as the case may be.[29]

B. Reinstatement

Trustees may apply the money in reinstatement,[30] but such action on their part is subject to the consent of any person whose consent is required by the trust instrument, and, in the case of money deemed to be capital money under the Settled Land Act 1925, to the provisions of that Act as to the application of capital money by the trustees of the settlement.[31] The section is to operate without prejudice to the statutory or other right of any person to require the money to be spent in reinstatement.[32] Persons interested under the settlement can, therefore, insist on having the premises rebuilt if they wish; or, if they do not wish it, can prevent the trustees from using the money for that purpose, but in any case the money is to take the form of capital money.

C. Reform

The question of insurance has recently been reviewed by the Law Reform Committee.[33] Concerning the power to insure conferred by section 19, discussed above, it is recommended that, instead of the three-fourths rule, the trustees should have power to insure to the full replacement value in cases where, applying the prudent businessman test, such a course would be sensible, and in other cases up to the market value.[34] The statutory power should be extended to trustees of bare trusts in certain circumstances.[35]

No absolute duty should be imposed on trustees to insure the trust property, but there should be a duty to insure against any risk in circumstances where a prudent businessman would insure, which must include fire. This new duty, however, should not be imposed on trustees of existing trusts.[36]

Finally, while the normal rule is that the premiums should be paid out of income, trustees should have power to pay out of capital where such a course is necessary in order to maintain a fair balance between the beneficiaries, for example in cases where the property, such as heirlooms, produces no income.[37]

[29] T.A. 1925, s.20.
[30] For the general law as to this subject, and as to s.83 of the Fires Prevention (Metropolis) Act 1774 in particular, see Colinvaux, *Law of Insurance* (5th ed.), Ch. 11.
[31] T.A. 1925, s.20(4).
[32] *Ibid.* s.20(5).
[33] 23rd Report, *Powers and Duties of Trustees* (1982 Cmnd. 8733). See also (1982) 79 L.S.Gaz. 755 (A. & P. Kenny).
[34] *Ibid.* para. 4.31.
[35] *Ibid.* para. 4.35, referring to T.A. 1925, s.19(2), *supra.*
[36] *Ibid.* para. 4.33.
[37] *Ibid.* para. 4.37.

4. POWER TO COMPOUND LIABILITIES: SECTION 15

Trustees are given a wide discretion in settling claims which may be made by third persons against the trust estate, or by the trust estate against third persons. The jurisdiction under section 15 does not extend to the changing of the beneficiaries' interest under a trust. Adult beneficiaries who are under no disability may, of course, make any arrangement that they wish among themselves. But until the Variation of Trusts Act 1958[38] was passed, the court had no general power to approve adjustments in the beneficial interests. But the dividing line is difficult to draw. The Court has inherent power to compromise a genuine dispute between beneficiaries[39] and section 15 has been held to authorise the settlement of a dispute with a person claiming to be a beneficiary,[40] and also litigation between the trustees and beneficiaries on the question whether certain property was subject to the trust or not.[41] And it was no objection to the jurisdiction under section 15 that the proposed compromise involved an adjustment of interests among the beneficiaries.

Personal representatives and trustees[42] may enter into compromises,[43] accept compositions for debts, allow time for payment of debts, submit doubtful points to arbitration, accept property before the time at which it is made transferable, sever and apportion any blended trust funds or property, and may enter into such agreements and execute such instruments as may be necessary for the efficient performance of these duties.[44] A wide power of this nature is of great practical importance in enabling the trustee to make a reasonable compromise instead of being obliged to litigate in respect of every possible claim, or risk liability for breach of trust if he fails to do so.[45] Trustees are not liable for loss caused by any act done by them in the exercise of the powers conferred by this section as long as it is done in good faith, and they have reached their decision by exercising their discretion and not by failing to consider the matter.[46] They may apply to the court to sanction a compromise. The court must consider what is the best from the point of view of everybody concerned, paying especial attention to the interests of minors.[47]

---

[38] *Post*, p. 586.

[39] *Brooke* v. *Mostyn* (1864) 2 De G.J. & S. 415; *Re Barbour's Settlement* [1974] 1 W.L.R. 1198; *Re Downshire S.E.* [1953] Ch. 218.

[40] *Re Warren* (1884) 51 L.T. 561; *Eaton* v. *Buchanan* [1911] A.C. 253; *cf. Abdallah* v. *Rickards* (1888) 4 T.L.R. 622.

[41] *Re Earl of Strafford* [1980] Ch. 28. The trustee had surrendered its discretion to the court; but the court's discretion was no wider than the trustee's.

[42] Including the Judicial Trustee; *Re Ridsdel* [1947] Ch. 597.

[43] There must be a genuine dispute: *Chapman* v. *Chapman* [1954] A.C. 429; but one claim must necessarily be wrong; *Re Ridsdel, supra.*

[44] See *Re Shenton* [1935] Ch. 651.

[45] *Re Brogden* [1948] Ch. 206; *ante*, p. 484.

[46] *Re Greenwood* (1911) 105 L.T. 509; *ante*, p. 485.

[47] *Re Ezekiel's S.T.* [1942] Ch. 230; *Re Earl of Strafford* (*supra*).

5. POWER IN REGARD TO REVERSIONARY INTERESTS: SECTION 22

Where part of the trust property consists of choses in action or reversionary interests the trustees may, on such interests falling into possession, "agree or ascertain the amount or value thereof in such manner as they think fit," without being responsible for any loss, if they act in good faith.[48] Further, they need not place a *distringas* notice,[49] or apply for a stop order,[50] on securities whereout such an interest is payable, and need not take any proceedings against persons in whom securities for the time being are vested, *unless* required in writing to do so by some person beneficially interested under the trust, and adequate provision is made for the payment of the cost of such proceedings. But nothing in the section is to be construed as relieving trustees from the duty of getting in such interests as soon as possible after their falling into possession, for this is one of their primary duties.[51]

6. POWER TO DELEGATE[52]

A. The Early Rule in Equity

The basic rule is that a person entrusted with a fiduciary duty does not fulfil it if he simply lays it on the shoulders of someone else; he remains liable for the other person's default.[53] But this rule was never, even in the times when the most rigorous views were being taken of the standard of conduct required from a trustee, inflexible. Indeed, there are certain things which a man of business would always delegate to a skilled agent. Thus, the employment of solicitors for legal, and brokers and bankers for financial, business is sanctioned by the ordinary business practice. This was recognised as early as 1754, by Lord Hardwicke in *Ex p. Belchier*,[54] and the trend of judicial decision, fortified by occasional statutory provisions, grew more and more tolerant of delegation in cases of commercial necessity. Following the two famous decisions of the House of Lords in *Speight* v. *Gaunt*[55] and *Learoyd* v. *Whiteley*,[56] it could be said that delegation was permissible if the trustees could show that it was reasonably necessary in the circumstances or was in accordance with ordinary business practice.' The trustees must exercise proper care in the selection of the agent, must employ him in his proper field,[57] and must exercise general

---

[48] *Ibid*. s.22(1).
[49] A notice forbidding the transfer of stock on a company's books or the payment of dividends, without notice to the person on whose behalf the notice was given. This is now usually called a "stop notice." See R.C.S., Ord. 50, rr. 10–15.
[50] See R.S.C., Ord. 50, r. 10.
[51] See *ante*, p. 483.
[52] (1959) 22 M.L.R. 381 (G. H. Jones).
[53] *Turner* v. *Corney* (1841) 5 Beav. 515 at p. 517, *per* Lord Langdale.
[54] (1754) Amb. 218.
[55] (1884) 9 App.Cas. 1.
[56] (1887) 12 App.Cas. 727.
[57] *Fry* v. *Tapson* (1884) 28 Ch.D. 268.

supervision.[58] The trustee would not then be liable for the defaults of the agent; but a trustee's discretions could not be delegated[59]; the exculpatory clause expressly limiting his liability to cases of "wilful default" did not relieve him from the responsibility of acting as a prudent man of business.[60] Nor did the statutes of 1859 and 1893, the predecessors of the Trustee Act 1925, s.30(1), which restricted the liability of trustees to cases of wilful default, do more than change the onus of proof; these statutes placed the onus on "those who seek to charge an executor or trustee with a loss arising from the default of an agent, when the propriety of employing the agent has been established."[61]

B. Trustee Act 1925: s.23(1)

But the position under the Trustee Act 1925 rests on a different principle, for trustees are no longer required to show a need to delegate. For this reason, the matter is here treated as a power to delegate, and not as a duty not to do so. Delegation as such is accepted as a normal method of performing the duties incidental to trusteeship; but the overall duties of trusteeship remain of course on the trustees. The effect of the statutory powers upon the overall responsibilities of a trustee is a matter of dispute. The question turns on the proper construction of section 23(1) which provides:

"Trustees or personal representatives may, instead of acting personally, employ and pay an agent, whether a solicitor, banker, stockbroker, or other person, to transact any business or do any act required to be transacted or done in the execution of the trust, or the administration of the testator's or intestate's estate, including the receipt and payment of money, and shall be entitled to be allowed and paid all charges and expenses so incurred, and shall not be responsible for the default of any such agent if employed in good faith."

This provision was considered by Maugham J. in *Re. Vickery*[62]:

An executor (the defendant) employed, to wind up a small estate, a solicitor named Jennens, who, unknown to him, had twice been suspended from practice. The beneficiaries (the plaintiffs) objected to his appointment, and also the defendant's permitting the money to be under the control of the solicitor. The defendant pressed the solicitor for payment and was promised that this would come shortly. Eventually the plaintiffs instructed a different solicitor, and

---

[58] *Matthews* v. *Brise* (1845) 10 Jur.(o.s.) 105; *Rowland* v. *Witherden* (1851) 3 Mac. & G. 568.
[59] *Speight* v. *Gaunt, supra.*
[60] *Rehden* v. *Wesley* (1861) 29 Beav. 213.
[61] *Per* Lord Selborne in *Re Brier* (1884) 2 Ch.D. 238 at p. 243; *Re Chapman* [1896] 2 Ch. 763 at p. 776, *per* Lindley L.J.
[62] [1931] 1 Ch. 572.

Jennens absconded and the money was lost. Maugham J. held that
the defendant was not liable. His decision was based upon two
separate sections of the Act: sections 23(1) and 30(1), which raise
quite separate issues, but which do not appear to have been kept
separate in the case or in some of the comment upon it.

Section 23(1) was new in 1925. It widens the powers of trustees to
delegate. Indeed, Maugham J. said[63] "it revolutionises the position of a
trustee or an executor so far as regards the employment of agents. He
is no longer required to do any actual work himself, but he may employ
a solicitor or other agent to do it, whether there is any real necessity for
the employment or not. No doubt he should use his discretion in
selecting an agent, and should employ him only to do acts within the
scope of the usual business of the agent."
    It is sometimes suggested that the only requirement of a trustee now
is one of subjective good faith in the original appointment of the
agent.[64] So long as he appoints an agent whom he thinks to be the right
appointment, he is absolved from any further responsibility; so that, as
in *Re Vickery*,[65] a trustee who negligently leaves money in the hands of
an agent, employed in good faith, is free of liability, however long the
money is left, and however inadequate the supervision of the agent. It
is submitted that there is no need to reach this conclusion, either on the
judgment of Maugham J. or on the words of the section.
    Although regarding the issue of "good faith" as a subjective matter,
Maugham J. saw no reason to suppose that the pre-1926 rules relating
to the requirement of discretion in selecting the agent and the limitation of the agent to the usual scope of his business should not still
apply. Section 23(1) clearly allows delegation in circumstances in
which it would not have been permitted before. It is submitted that the
section can be construed so as to apply the pre-1926 rules to the wider
area of post-1925 delegation, and thereby to reach a result which is
more consistent with the needs of the protection of the beneficiaries.[66]
The Act is a consolidating Act, and should be construed so as to effect
as little change in the law as possible.[67] Two further lines of argument
support this less extreme construction of section 23(1).

(i) **Pre-1926 Principles.** Section 23(1) assumes the continuation of
the pre-1926 principles. It should therefore be construed so as to be
consistent with them. A number of difficulties arise if section 23(1) is

[63] *Ibid.* at p. 581.
[64] (1931) 47 L.Q.R. 330 (H.P.) and 463 (W.S.H.). For varying views of the effect of *Re
    Vickery*, see Parker & Mellows, *Modern Law of Trusts* (5th ed.), pp. 286–287; (1959)
    22 M.L.R. 381 (G. H. Jones).
[65] [1931] 1 Ch. 572.
[66] (1959) 22 M.L.R. 381; see *Green* v. *Whitehead* [1930] 1 Ch. 38.
[67] *Re Turner's W.T.* [1937] Ch. 15.

construed so as to excuse trustees from all responsibility other than bona fide appointment.[68]

(a) *The Proviso to Section 23(3)*. The proviso becomes meaningless. Section 23(3) permits delegation by a trustee "without prejudice to such general power of appointing agents" as is contained in section 23(1) in specified matters, including the receipt of money by agents in certain circumstances; but a proviso to subsection (3) retains the trustee's previous liability if "he permits any such money, valuable consideration, or property to remain in the hands or under the control of the banker or solicitor for a period longer than is reasonably necessary[69] to enable the banker or solicitor, as the case may be, to pay or transfer the same to the trustee." If the trustee is given a wider protection by the general exemption under subsection (1), this restriction on his exemption in these specific cases is meaningless.

(b) *The Indemnity Clause in Section 30(1)*.[70] This clause would be unnecessary if "a trustee need never act personally and will never be liable for loss save through his wilful default."[71]

(c) *The Relationship between Sections 23(1), 23(2) and 25*. Section 23(2) empowers a trustee to appoint an agent for the purpose of administering any part of the trust estate situated outside the United Kingdom, "or executing or exercising any discretion or trust or power vested in them in relation to any such property," and authorises also the appointment of sub-agents. Section 25[72] enables a trustee to delegate to any person[73] by power of attorney for a period not exceeding 12 months "all or any of the trusts powers and discretions vested in him as trustee either alone or jointly with any other person or persons." The instrument must be attested by at least one witness,[74] and written notice must be given within seven days to each of the other trustees and to each person who has the power to appoint new trustees.[75]

As will be seen, each of these provisions allows a wider delegation than is allowed by section 23(1); for they allow the delegation of "discretions" and "trusts." If Maugham J. is right, they should only be used when such additional delegation is essential, for the protection given by these subsections is less than that stated in *Re Vickery*[76] to be

---

[68] (1959) 22 M.L.R. 381 (G. H. Jones); (1931) 47 L.Q.R. 330 (H.P.).
[69] *Re Sheppard* [1911] 1 Ch. 50 (no liability unless the trustee knew or ought to have known of the receipt).
[70] See *post*.
[71] (1931) 47 L.Q.R. 330 at p. 331 (H.P.).
[72] As amended by Powers of Attorney Act 1971, s.9. See (1971) 121 N.L.J. 764. On the question whether two trustees may appoint the same person as their attorney, see [1978] Conv. 85 (J.T.F.). For enduring powers of attorney, see *post*, p. 540.
[73] Including a trust corporation; but not to a sole co-trustee; subs. (2).
[74] Subs. (3).
[75] Subs. (4). But failure to give notice does not, in favour of a person dealing with the donee of the power, invalidate any act done by the donee.
[76] [1931] 1 Ch. 572.

provided by section 23(1). Under section 23(2), protection is given to the trustees in respect of losses arising "by reason only of their having made any such appointment"; pre-1926 liability remains. And section 25 provides that the donor of the power of attorney remains liable for the acts and defaults of the donee.[77] In respect of general delegation of ministerial matters, the protection they give is therefore less than that under section 23(1) as construed in *Re Vickery*.

(d) *The Power of Delegation in the Law of Property Act 1925, s.29.* The wide interpretation of section 23(1) is inconsistent with the limited power of delegation conferred upon trustees for sale by the Law of Property Act 1925, s.29.[78] The 1925 legislation should be construed consistently, where possible.

It is submitted that Maugham J. should have construed section 23(1) in the light of these other provisions which assume the continued operation of the pre-1926 principles of liability. Subsection (1) would then give the wider power of delegation; and the phrase "shall not be responsible for the default of any such agent if employed in good faith" would extend the exemption given by the pre-1926 law to such agents as the trustees were then authorised to employ. In other words "to construe the words 'in good faith . . . ' so that they limit only the *act* of employment."[79] It is submitted that such a construction does less violence to the words of the Trustee Act as a whole than does Maugham J.'s solution.

(ii) **Primary and Vicarious Liability.** It can further be argued that the exemption is in respect of the trustee's vicarious liability, and does not affect his primary duties and liabilities.

The rule has always been that a trustee is vicariously liable for the defaults of an agent to whom the affairs of the trust were improperly delegated; but not where a loss occurred by reason of the act of an agent to whom a proper delegation was made.[80] Section 23(1) is a section which widens the powers to delegate, and it is possible to construe the exemption given in the concluding phrase as being applicable to the vicarious liability of trustees; and to leave intact their primary duty of managing the affairs of the trust, taking decisions and of supervising the work of agents to whom proper delegation had been made.[81]

Thus, the delegation was proper in *Re Lucking's Will Trusts*.[82] The

---

[77] T.A. 1925, s.25(5). Arguably the delegation of investment decisions can only be done under s.25.

[78] Allowing, within limits, trustees for sale to delegate their powers of management to the tenant for life.

[79] (1959) 22 M.L.R. 381 at p. 389 (G. H. Jones); *cf.* the views of the Law Reform Committee, *post*, p. 540.

[80] *Speight* v. *Gaunt* (1884) 9 App.Cas. 1.

[81] (1959) 22 M.L.R. 381 at pp. 394–395 (G. H. Jones). See also the Report of the Law Reform Committee, *post*, p. 540.

[82] [1968] 1 W.L.R. 866; *ante*, p. 499; [1979] Conv. 345 at p. 358 (J. E. Stannard).

fault of Mr. Lucking was that he failed adequately to supervise the activities of Lt. Col. Dewar, the managing director.

The trusts assets consisted of a majority holding of shares in a private family company. Mr. Lucking and another were trustees. They could not run the business themselves, and Lt. Col. Dewar, an old and trusted friend of Mr. Lucking, was appointed managing director.[83] He appropriated substantial sums of company funds for his own purposes, and became bankrupt. Mr. Lucking had trusted him implicitly throughout. Cross J. held Mr. Lucking liable for "failing adequately to supervise Mr. Dewar's drawings" on the funds after the time at which there was reason to suspect Dewar's honesty. The standard applied was that in which "an ordinary prudent man would conduct a business of his own."[84] The other trustee, however, was not liable. He was not a director of the company, and was in no position personally to supervise the drawings. The supervision of the running of the business was not "a duty to the trust which it was incumbent on the trustees to perform personally, so that [the other trustee] became automatically responsible for any deficiencies in Mr. Lucking, as does a passive trustee who allows his co-trustee to exercise alone discretions which it is their duty to exercise jointly."[85] Indeed the trustees would have been satisfied in the circumstances with having a nominee on the board, or in finding some other means of obtaining the necessary information relating to the company's affairs.[86]

To distinguish between primary and vicarious liability is not inconsistent with *Re Vickery,*[87] for in that case there was no disapproval of the original delegation; the executor would be protected under the suggested narrower construction of the subsection. Nor is it clear that the executor was in breach of his general duty of supervision; it is difficult to see what else he could have done. Once a matter is in the hands of a solicitor, it is difficult to know what the executor could do beyond pressing the solicitor to account. This he did; and, in the circumstances with less than £300 at stake, it was unlikely that such a sum would be a temptation to a solicitor even of dubious reputation. It is quite possible, as Maugham J. thought,[88] that the defendant would have been held not liable under the pre-1926 law.

---

[83] He was appointed not by the trustees but by the company, hence s.23(1) would seem inapplicable.

[84] *Ibid.* at p. 874.

[85] *Ibid.* at p. 875.

[86] *Re Miller's Deed Trust* (1978) 75 L.S.Gaz. 454; *Bartlett* v. *Barclays Bank Executor and Trustee Co. Ltd.* [1980] Ch. 515; *ante*, p. 498.

[87] [1931] 1 Ch. 572. The distinction is criticised in [1979] Conv. 345 at p. 351.

[88] [1931] 1 Ch. 572 at pp. 584–585.

C. Trustee Act 1925, s.30(1)

"A trustee shall be chargeable only for money and securities actually received by him notwithstanding his signing any receipt for the sake of conformity, and shall be answerable and accountable only for his own acts, receipts, neglects, or defaults, and not for those of any other trustee, nor for any banker, broker, or other person with whom any trust money or securities may be deposited,[89] nor for the insufficiency or deficiency of any securities, nor for any other loss unless the same happens through his own wilful default."

(i) Scope of Section 30(1): "Wilful Default." It should first be noted that the protection given by this subsection is limited to the situations mentioned therein. The words "for any other loss" are construed *ejusdem generis.*[90]

The extent of the protection given by the subsection depends largely upon the construction of the phrase "wilful default." We have seen that this phrase, when inserted into express exculpatory clauses, did not excuse a trustee from the necessity of acting as a prudent man of business, and that the incorporation of the clause in the predecessors of Trustee Act 1925 had the effect only of changing the burden of proof.[91] It is submitted that Maugham J. should have so construed section 30(1). However, he introduced a subjective construction to the phrase "wilful default" which had been applied to the construction of these words in *Re City Equitable Fire Insurance Co.*,[92] where Romer J. said that a person is not guilty of wilful default "unless he knows that he is committing and intends to commit a breach of his duty, or is recklessly careless in the sense of not caring whether his act or omission is or is not a breach of duty."[93] Romer J. was there construing a set of articles of association dealing with directors' liability, and his definition has no bearing upon the construction of the Trustee Act. It has been pointed out that the common law cases dealing with the phrase "wilful default" in the context of the law of contract have established a meaning wholly different from that established in equity in cases involving a liability to account on the basis of wilful default and in the construction of exculpatory clauses. The former case requires some intentional or conscious fault. The more technical meaning in equity is that of "failure to do what is reasonable" and involves no intentional misconduct.[94] Maugham J.'s application of the meaning applied in the common law cases to a case dealing with the liability of a trustee is as

---

[89] s.30(1) was held inapplicable in *Re Lucking's Will Trusts* [1968] 1 W.L.R. 866, *ante*, p. 536, because Lt. Col. Dewar was not a person with whom trust money had been deposited.

[90] [1931] 1 Ch. 572 at p. 582, *per* Maugham J.

[91] *Re Brier* (1884) 26 Ch.D. 238; *ante*, p. 533.

[92] [1925] 1 Ch. 407, followed by Astbury J. in *Re Munton* [1927] 1 Ch. 262.

[93] *Ibid*, at p. 434; quoted in the Court of Appeal by Warrington L.J. [1925] Ch. 407, 523–524.

[94] [1979] Conv. 345 (J. E. Stannard).

little justified by authority as by principle; it is to be hoped that the courts will return to the earlier test of the prudent man of business.[95]

(ii) **Capital and Income.** Section 30(1) includes a reference to co-trustees,[96] and this raises an important distinction between receipt of capital and receipt of income. The basic rule is that capital should be received by all the trustees unless some of them have power under statute or under their trust deed to give good receipts and discharges. It is most important for purchasers of trust property to remember this rule.[97] Similarly, investments of trust moneys should be made in the joint names of the trustees. If two trustees divide investments, and invest separately, and one trustee commits a breach of trust, the other will be liable to make good the loss.[98]

The receipt of income is, however, treated differently from the receipt of capital. In *Townley* v. *Sherborne*[99] it was decided that the duty of receiving rents may be delegated to one of several trustees, on the ground that a requirement of receipt by all the trustees would involve inconveniences that would outweigh all the advantages of such a course. In the case of an investment by trustees in shares in a limited company it will be found that the articles provide that trusts shall not be recognised,[1] and that, in the case of joint ownership, the dividend shall be paid to the first named who can give a valid receipt.[2] The practice is to pay the dividend to the first named "and another."

Where income payments are properly paid to one only of multiple trustees, the co-trustee may nevertheless be liable if he permits the payee to retain the money for a longer period than the circumstances of the case necessitate.[3]

D. Other Delegating Sections

Other sections in the Trustee Act 1925 giving to the trustees a power of delegation are discussed in other chapters where they are most particularly relevant.[4] If they are all considered together as a group it will be seen that, if the wide interpretation discussed above of section 23(1) is correct, many of them overlap and not all of them required specific enactment. There is, in this area of the law, one of the least apt marryings of old and new in the whole of the 1925 legislation.

---

[95] *Cf.* the views of the Law Reform Committee, *post*, p. 540.
[96] See further the Law Reform Committee, 23rd Report, *infra*, para. 4.15, *ante*, p. 484.
[97] See *Lee* v. *Sankey* (1873) L.R. 15 Eq. 204 and Trustee Act 1925, s.14; see also *ante*, p. 529.
[98] *Lewis* v. *Nobbs* (1878) 8 Ch.D. 591.
[99] (1634) J. Bridg. 35. Such a power may be countermanded in a particular trust deed: *Brice* v. *Stokes* (1805) 11 Ves.Jr. 319.
[1] Companies Act 1985, s.360.
[2] Companies (Tables A–F) Regulations 1985, Table A, reg. 106 (S.I. 1985/805).
[3] *Carruthers* v. *Carruthers* [1896] A.C. 659.
[4] See pp. 497, 501, 552.

E. Reform

The power to delegate has recently been reviewed by the Law Reform Committee.[5] The Committee recommended that section 23(1) should be amended so that the trustees should only be able to charge the trust with the cost of delegating if the charges are reasonably incurred, taking into account the trustees' knowledge, qualifications, experience and level of remuneration.[6] It was felt that the relationship between sections 23(1), 30(1) and 61 was not as clear as it should be. Section 23(1) was concerned with the trustee's vicarious liability for the misfeasance of an agent who was not employed in good faith. Section 30(1) was concerned with the trustee's primary liability where loss was caused by the acts of other persons, which could have been prevented but for the trustee's wilful default. While the wilful default test, requiring connivance, was correct here,[7] the standard in section 23(1) was not stringent enough. A trustee should be expected to keep a check on his agent. The reference to "good faith" should be replaced by a provision that the trustee should not be liable if it was reasonable to employ an agent and if reasonable steps were taken to ensure that the agent was competent and that the work was done competently.[8]

F. Delegation under the Enduring Powers of Attorney Act 1985

We have seen that section 25 of the Trustee Act 1925 permits a trustee to delegate all of his functions by power of attorney for a maximum of 12 months, subject to various procedural requirements.[9] This could be done, for example, if he was going abroad.

Until recently there was no possibility of a power of attorney which would continue in force after the donor had become mentally incapable, as such incapacity automatically revoked the power. The position has been changed by the Enduring Powers of Attorney Act 1985 which, subject to various safeguards, permits the creation of a power of attorney which will survive the donor's subsequent incapacity.

This Act is relevant to trustees in two respects. First, it is provided that a power of attorney under section 25 of the Trustee Act 1925 cannot be an enduring power.[10] The reasoning here is that mental incapacity is a ground for replacing a trustee.[11] Secondly, and inconsistently with the latter point, section 3(3) of the 1985 Act provides that

---

[5] 23rd Report, *The Powers and Duties of Trustees* (1982 Cmnd. 8733).

[6] *Ibid.* para. 4.6.

[7] This view is out of line with the criticisms of the interpretation of s.30(1) in *Re Vickery* [1931] 1 Ch. 572, *ante*, p. 534.

[8] *Ibid.* paras. 4.9–4.11; (1983) 133 N.L.J. 1096 (C. T. Emery). For liability for the defaults of co-trustees, see *ante*, p. 484.

[9] *Ante*, p. 535.

[10] Enduring Powers of Attorney Act 1985, s.2(8).

[11] See Law Com. No. 122 (1983), *The Incapacitated Principal*, para. 4.2. The 12 month limit under s.25 would in any event have made the concept of an enduring power under s.25 of little use.

the donee of an enduring power of attorney may "execute or exercise all or any of the trusts, powers or discretions vested in the donor as trustee" and may give a valid receipt for capital money. Thus a trustee cannot create an enduring power under section 25 of the 1925 Act, but such a power may be created under the 1985 Act.

The purpose of section 3(3) was to enable a trustee of a house under a co-ownership trust for sale to delegate the power to execute a conveyance of the house to his co-trustee in such a way that the subsequent incapacity of the delegating trustee would not terminate the power.[12] The subsection, however, is not limited to this situation, and appears to permit a trustee to delegate all his functions indefinitely.[13] The execution of an enduring power of attorney will have this effect whether or not the trustee has considered the matter. Unlike section 25, delegation to the only other co-trustee is permitted, there is no time limit, and no requirement of notice to co-trustees. The rule requiring payment of capital money to two trustees is also ousted. If this is correct, section 3(3) is a "legislative blunder."[14] If a trustee wants to delegate for more than 12 months and may become incompetent, he should retire.

7. POWERS OF MAINTENANCE AND ADVANCEMENT[15]

Where any person has a contingent interest in property the question arises as to the use which should be made of the income until the gift vests. Otherwise the income would not be put to any use during the period. The policy is to allow the gift to "carry the intermediate income" unless there are good reasons to the contrary. Generally speaking, all testamentary gifts except contingent pecuniary legacies carry the intermediate income unless it is otherwise disposed of.[16]

One of the most common contingencies is that of attaining the age of 21 or more. It is important to make provision for the use of the income for the maintenance and education of the young. There is no comfort in the prospect of a fortune at 21 if you starve for lack of money in your teens.

A similar question arises in the opposite case of a minor who has a vested interest in property; for it may then be desirable that he should not be entitled to draw the whole of the income. It is better that he should receive what is reasonably necessary for his maintenance and

---

[12] This overcomes difficulties illustrated by *Walia* v. *Michael Naughton Ltd.* [1985] 1 W.L.R. 1125.

[13] See (1986) 130 S.J. 23 (R. T. Oerton); (1986) 1 *Trust Law and Practice* 54. The provision was added by the Lord Chancellor's Department after the *Walia* decision, and was not considered by the Law Commission.

[14] (1986) 130 S.J. 23 at p. 25; (1988) 85 L.S.G. No. 19, p.4.

[15] The Law Reform Committee, 23rd Report, *The Powers and Duties of Trustees* (1982 Cmnd. 8733) recommends no change in the statutory powers.

[16] *Post*, p. 545.

education, and that the balance should be put aside and invested for him. Again, it may be that capital sums may be needed to establish him in a profession or in business or on his marriage.

These matters may be expressly provided for in the trust instrument. If not, the court has an inherent power to approve the use of income, or even of capital for the maintenance of minors.[17] But the statutory powers of maintenance[18] and advancement[19] about to be discussed are sufficient to meet the needs of most situations, and they can be amended as required to meet the needs of a particular trust. Such powers have commonly been used, not only, or mainly, for their original purposes, but rather for the fiscal advantages which they have in the past been able to offer.[20]

A. Maintenance.[21] Trustee Act 1925, s.31

(i) **Subsection (1).** "Where any property is held by trustees in trust for any person for any interest whatsoever, whether vested or contingent, then, subject to any prior interests or charges affecting that property—

(i) during the infancy of any such person, if his interest so long continues, the trustees may, at their sole discretion, pay to his parent or guardian, if any, or otherwise apply for or towards his maintenance, education, or benefit,[22] the whole or such part, if any, of the income of that property as may, in all the circumstances, be reasonable, whether or not there is—

(*a*) any other fund applicable to the same purpose; or

(*b*) any person bound by law to provide for his maintenance or education; and

(ii) if such person attaining the age of [18][23] years has not a vested interest in such income, the trustees shall thenceforth pay the income of that property and of any accretion thereto under subsection (2) of this section to him, until he either attains a vested interest therein or dies, or until failure of his interest:
. . ."

(a) *Prior Interests.* The power of maintenance can only arise where a

---

[17] *Wellesley* v. *Wellesley* (1828) 2 Bli.(n.s.) 124; *Barlow* v. *Grant* (1684) 1 Vern. 255; Lewin, pp. 301–302; *post*, p. 554.

[18] T.A. 1925, s.31.

[19] T.A. 1925, s.32.

[20] *Pilkington* v. *I.R.C.* [1964] A.C. 612.

[21] See (1953) 17 Conv.(n.s.) 273 (B. S. Ker) for a most helpful discussion of s.31.

[22] See *Re Heyworth's Contingent Reversionary Interest* [1956] Ch. 364; *Pilkington* v. *I.R.C., supra*; *Re Pauling's S.T.* [1964] Ch. 303; (1959) 23 Conv.(n.s.) 27 (D. W. M. Waters).

[23] Reduced from 21 by Family Law Reform Act 1969 in respect of instruments made (not only those coming into effect) on or after January 1, 1970. A will made before that date is not to be treated as made on or after that date by reason only that the will is confirmed by a codicil executed on or after that date. s.1, and Sched. 3, para. 1.

person is entitled to the income, whether by virtue of a vested interest, or by virtue of a contingent interest which carries the intermediate income.[24] If the income is applicable in favour of a prior interest, no question of its use for maintenance can arise. Similarly, a member of a discretionary class is not entitled to any income and the section does not therefore apply to payments made by the trustees in the exercise of their discretion.[25]

(b) *Minority*. The question of application of income for the minor's maintenance, education or benefit, whether his interest is vested or contingent, is a matter for the trustees' discretion. The decision to apply income for such minor's maintenance must be taken as a result of a conscious exercise of their discretion, and not automatically.[26] The trustees should, so far as practicable, arrange for maintenance payments to be shared proportionately among various funds available for the purpose.[27] The payments are usually made to the parent or guardian whose receipt is a sufficient discharge for the trustees.

(c) *Adult Contingently Entitled*. An adult contingently entitled to the principal becomes entitled under paragraph (ii) of subsection (1) to the income.[28] His entitlement to the capital must, of course, await the happening of the contingency. The entitlement to income at majority is subject to a contrary intention; and this has been found to exist where there is a direction to accumulate.

In *Re Turner's Will Trusts*,[29] a testator provided interests in favour of his grandchildren contingently on their attaining the age of 28, and expressly gave the trustees power to apply the income for their maintenance, education and benefit until that time, and instructed the trustees to accumulate the surplus.

One grandchild, Geoffrey, was 21 when the testator died; and himself died three years later aged 24. No income had been paid to him, and some £3,000 had been accumulated since the testator's death. The question was whether section 31(1) applied. If it did, Geoffrey would have become entitled to the income; and this would affect the distribution of the accumulations, and also the liability to estate duty on his death. The Court of Appeal held that, in spite of the imperative terms of section 31, it gave way to an expression of a contrary intention in accordance with the Trustee Act 1925, s.69(2).

---

[24] T.A. 1925, s.31(3); *post*, pp. 545, 546.
[25] *Re Vestey's Settlement* [1951] Ch. 209.
[26] *Wilson* v. *Turner* (1883) 22 Ch.D. 521.
[27] T.A. 1925, s.31(1), proviso.
[28] *Re Jones' W.T.* [1947] Ch. 48.
[29] [1937] Ch. 15; *Re Ransome* [1957] Ch. 348; [1979] Conv. 243 (J. G. Riddall); *Brotherton* v. *I.R.C.* [1978] 1 W.L.R. 610; *I.R.C.* v. *Bernstein* [1961] Ch. 399; *Re McGeorge* [1963] Ch. 544, where the contrary intention was shown by deferring the gift to a daughter until after the death of a widow; *Re Erskine's S.T.* [1971] 1 W.L.R. 162.

(ii) Subsection (2). (a) *Surplus Income to be Accumulated for Minors.*
Subsection (2) provides that the residue of the income, not applied for
maintenance, shall be accumulated by investment during the minority
of the person contingently entitled. Income from such investments
becomes available for future maintenance; and the accumulations
themselves may be applied, during the minority, as if they were income
arising in the then current year.

(b) *Disposal of Surplus.* On the majority (or earlier marriage) of a
minor, the question arises whether or not the surplus should be given
to him. As would be expected, he is entitled to the accumulations, if he
had a vested life interest during his minority (for he was entitled all
along to the income)[30]; or if, on attaining his majority, he "becomes
entitled to the property from which the income arose in fee simple,
absolute or determinable, or absolutely or for an entailed interest." In
short, he is entitled to the accumulations on his majority (or earlier
marriage) if he is then entitled to the capital.[31]

The question arose in *Re Sharp's Settlement Trusts*[32] whether the
provision covered the case where the children of the settlor became
entitled, subject to an overriding power of appointment, to the capital
on attaining the age of 21. Were they then entitled absolutely? Pennycuick V.–C. held that they were not: the fact that their interests could
be defeated by the exercise of the power prevented their becoming
entitled absolutely. It is anomalous that "a person having a determinable interest in realty should qualify to take accumulations at 21,"[33] but
"a person having a like interest in personalty should not equally so
qualify."[34] "This is just another one of those curious instances where
the 1925 legislation just did not go far enough in its expressed intention
so far as possible to assimilate the rules relating to realty and
personalty."[35] In all other cases, as for example the case of a life tenant
whose interest in the capital was contingent until his majority, and
does not then become absolute, or where the beneficiary, although
having a vested interest, fails to reach majority, the accumulations are
added to capital for all purposes.[36]

The provisions relating to the destination of accumulations in sec-

---

[30] But not so as to impose liability to higher rates of income tax in respect of income not
paid to the minor during his minority: *Stanley* v. *I.R.C.* [1944] K.B. 255.

[31] T.A. 1925, s.31(2)(i).

[32] [1973] Ch. 331; (1972) 36 Conv.(n.s.) 436 (D. J. Hayton). See also *Re Delamere's
Settlement Trusts, infra.*

[33] The words "fee simple, absolute or determinable," applying only to realty.

[34] [1973] Ch. 331 at p. 346.

[35] (1972) 36 Conv.(n.s.) 436 at p. 438. The accumulations of income were added to the
share of each child, subject to the exercise of the power: *Re King* [1928] Ch. 330; *Re
Joel's W.T.* [1967] Ch. 14; *post,* p. 547.

[36] T.A. 1925, s.32(2)(ii). On the distinction between contingent interests and interests
subject to defeasance, see *Phipps* v. *Ackers* (1842) 9 Cl. & F. 583; *Re Heath* [1936] Ch.
259; *Re Kilpatrick's Policies* [1966] Ch. 730; *Brotherton* v. *I.R.C.* [1978] 1 W.L.R. 610;
Jarman on Wills, pp. 1360 *et seq.*

tion 31(2) are also subject to a contrary intention in the trust instrument.[37] In *Re Delamere's Settlement Trusts*,[38] the trustees appointed income to beneficiaries "absolutely" in 1971. All the beneficiaries were then minors. By 1981, £122,000 had been accumulated. The question arose whether section 31(2) applied, so that the share of any beneficiary dying before majority would devolve with the capital, or whether there was a contrary intention, so that the accumulations were held indefeasibly for the appointees. It was held that the word "absolutely" in the 1971 appointment indicated indefeasibility, thus excluding section 31(2). Clearly the mere fact that the interest is vested is not sufficient to achieve this result.[39]

(iii) Vested Annuities. The section applies to a vested annuity as if the annuity were the income of property held by the trustees in trust to pay the income thereof to the annuitant. Where accumulations have been made during a minority, they are in any case payable to the annuitant on his majority or to his personal representatives on his earlier death.[40]

(iv) Gifts Carrying Intermediate Income. Section 31 only applies to contingent interests which carry the intermediate income; that is to say, to gifts which entitle the donee to claim the income earned by, or interest upon, the subject matter of the gift between the date of the gift and the date of payment. Whether or not a gift should do so is not self-evident, and there are, as will be seen, some complex and technical rules which do not provide any conceptual unity. Some rules are based on case law, and some on statute. It is unfortunate that there is not a single comprehensive code.

Vested gifts carry the intermediate income unless a contrary intention appears, as where the income is given to someone other than the donee for a period. But a direction to accumulate the surplus income until majority, on the other hand, does not indicate that the gift does not carry the income, but merely that the power of maintenance is excluded.

With contingent gifts, the rules, subject always to an expression of contrary intention, are as follows[41]:

(a) *Contingent Residuary Bequest.* A contingent bequest of residuary personalty carries all income earned from the testator's death.[42] The undisposed of income "becomes part of the residue."[43] But it seems that, if a residuary bequest of personalty (whether vested or

---

[37] T.A. 1925, s.69(2).
[38] [1984] 1 W.L.R. 813; [1985] Conv. 153 (R. Griffith).
[39] See T.A. 1925, s.31(2)(1)(*a*).
[40] *Ibid*. s.31(4).
[41] (1953) 17 Conv.(N.S.) 273 (B. S. Ker); (1963) 79 L.Q.R. 184 (P.V.B.).
[42] *Re Adams* [1893] 1 Ch. 329.
[43] *Ibid*. at p. 334.

contingent) is postponed "to a future date which must come sooner or later,"[44] the intermediate income is undisposed of and therefore not carried by the gift.[45]

(b) *Contingent or Future Specific Gifts of Personalty or Realty and Contingent Residuary Devises of Freehold Land.* The Law of Property Act 1925, s.175 provides that, in wills coming into effect after 1925, a contingent specific bequest of personalty or devise of realty and a contingent residuary devise of freehold land, and a devise of freehold land to trustees on trust for persons whose interests are contingent or executory shall carry the intermediate income. It will be noticed that the section does not affect a residuary gift of a leasehold interest, which ranks as personalty.[46]

(c) *Contingent Pecuniary Legacy.* A contingent pecuniary legacy does not carry the intermediate income.[47] To this rule there are three exceptions, in which cases the contingent pecuniary legacy will carry interest, and it will be available for the maintenance of a minor.

First: Where the legacy was given by the father of the minor, or by some person *in loco parentis*, so long as no other fund is provided for his maintenance,[48] and the contingency is the attainment of majority.[49]

Secondly: Where the testator shows an intention to maintain.[50]

Thirdly: Where the testator has set aside the legacy as a separate fund for the benefit of the legatee.[51]

Section 31, having laid down that the section applies only to a limitation or trust if it carries the intermediate income, refers expressly to the first of these exceptions, and provides that "it applies to a future or contingent legacy by a parent of, or a person standing in loco parentis to, the legatee, if and for such period as, under the general law, the legacy carries interest for the maintenance of the legatee, and in any such case as last aforesaid the rate of interest shall (if the income available is sufficient, and subject to any rules of court to the contrary) be" 5 per cent. Thus, the subsection refers only to the first of the recognised exceptions, and the question arises whether that is an indication that the other two are not intended to apply. The better view is that they are unaffected by subsection (3), and that "the specific mention of the rule in [the first exception] is only for the purpose of establishing a suitable rate of interest."[52] It will be seen that the statute

---

[44] *Per* Cross J. in *Re McGeorge* [1963] Ch. 544 at p. 551; such as the death of an annuitant.

[45] *Re Oliver* [1947] 2 All E.R. 161; *Re Gillett's W.T.* [1950] Ch. 102; *Re Geering* [1964] Ch. 136.

[46] *Guthrie* v. *Walrond* (1883) 22 Ch.D. 573; *Re Woodin* [1895] 2 Ch. 349.

[47] *Re Raine* [1929] 1 Ch. 716; *Re George* (1877) 5 Ch.D. 837.

[48] *Re George* (1877) 5 Ch.D. 837 at p. 843, *per* James L.J.; *Re Moody* [1895] 1 Ch. 101.

[49] *Re Abrahams* [1911] 1 Ch. 108.

[50] *Re Churchill* [1909] 2 Ch. 431.

[51] *Re Medlock* (1886) 54 L.T. 828.

[52] See (1953) 17 Conv.(N.S.) 273 at p. 279.

widens the rule in the exception by making it applicable in the case of either parent, and not only in the case of a father.

(v) Aggregation of Income of Children with that of their Parents. It has been seen[53] that an accumulation and maintenance settlement[54] giving contingent gifts to minors with power to use the income for maintenance, and to accumulate that not so used, offers tax advantages, both in the context of income tax,[55] and of inheritance tax[56] but that income so accumulated carries the income tax disadvantage of liability to the additional rate.[57] Where income is paid to a minor who is the unmarried child of the settlor, the income is treated as that of his parent.[58] In other cases, the income is treated as part of the minor's total income.[59]

(vi) Gifts to Classes. Where there is a gift to a class contingently on attaining the age of 21, the trustees may treat separately, for these purposes, each person's presumptive share. That is to say, that when one member of the class attains 21 and becomes entitled to his share, the trustees may continue to exercise their powers of maintenance in respect of the other members.[60] Similarly, income may only be used for the maintenance of any member of the class if that income was earned during the lifetime of that member,[61] but if a member of a class dies without obtaining a vested interest, the accumulation of income representing his contingent share is added to the capital under section 31(2)(ii), although this means that future born members will thus benefit from it.[62]

B. Advancement

(i) The Meaning of Advancement. We saw that maintenance was concerned with the payment of income for the benefit of infants. Advancement is concerned with the payment or application of capital sums to the beneficiary's advantage before the time comes when he is entitled to demand the fund. The scope of the power depends upon the

[53] *Ante*, pp. 220 *et seq.*
[54] *Ante*, p. 220.
[55] *Ante*, p. 221.
[56] *Ante*, p. 221.
[57] I.C.T.A. 1988, s.686.
[58] I.C.T.A. 1988, ss.663, 664. See *Butler (Inspector of Taxes)* v. *Wildin, The Times,* November 16, 1988.
[59] See Maudsley and Burn's *Trusts and Trustees: Cases and Materials* (3rd ed.), pp. 682–683, also discussing the taxation of accumulated income.
[60] *Re Holford* [1894] 3 Ch. 30; *Re King* [1928] Ch. 330.
[61] *Re Joel's W.T.* [1967] Ch. 14.
[62] *Ibid.*; not following *Re King, supra*, on this point. The Law Reform Committee, 23rd Report, *The Powers and Duties of Trustees* (1982 Cmnd. 8733), para. 3.41, recommends the abrogation of the rule in *Re Joel*, and that income from a trust fund be apportioned between the class of beneficiaries as constituted on the date the income is received by the trustees.

terms of the instrument giving it,[63] and, since 1925, upon Trustee Act 1925, s.32.[64] The purposes for which payments under such power have been desired and made, have greatly changed with the passage of years. It will be no surprise to be told that advancements have been made in recent years, not only for the purpose of providing capital sums when needed, but also for the purpose of tax saving.

Thus, suppose a fund is held on trust for A, the capital being payable to him on attaining 25. If A marries, or sets up in business or in a profession before that time, a power of advancement makes possible the payment to him of some or all of the capital of the fund to help with such a project. There is a similar but more complicated question if A's interest is subject to a prior life interest in X; for X's income will be affected by any payments out of the capital fund which produces it. Or if A's interest is contingent on his attaining 25; for if payments are made to A and A never attains 25 (*i.e.* "never vests") the capital payments will have been made to the wrong person.

The tax-saving question arises where trustees hold a large sum on trust for A for life and then to A's children equally at 21. Independently of the fund A is rich enough to provide the children with all they need. It may be advantageous to make transfers of capital from the trust for the children. Inheritance tax will be avoided if the advancement was made more than seven years before A's death.[65] Such a payment is certainly not an "advancement" within the usual meaning of the word, but no one could deny that the saving of tax on the trust is a benefit to the children. A further question arises, whether such sums must be held in trust for the children absolutely, or whether they may themselves be settled by the creation of sub-trusts for the benefit of themselves and also for other persons such as future dependants. These questions are dealt with below.

(ii) **Original Meaning of Advancement.** "The word 'advancement' itself meant in this context the establishment in life of the beneficiary who was the object of the power or at any rate some step that would contribute to the furtherance of his establishment.[66] ... Typical instances of expenditure for such purposes under the social conditions of the nineteenth century were an apprenticeship or the purchase of a

---

[63] See *Re Collard's W.T.* [1901] Ch. 293.

[64] *Post*, p. 549.

[65] F.A. (No. 2) 1987, s.96.

[66] See *per* Jessel M.R. in *Taylor* v. *Taylor* (1875) L.R. 20 Eq. 155; *Lowther* v. *Bentinck* (1874) L.R. 19 Eq. 166 (payment of debts); *Roper-Curzon* v. *Roper-Curzon* (1871) L.R. 11 Eq. 452 (starting a career at the Bar); *Re Breed's Will* (1875) 1 Ch.D. 226; *Re Long's Settlement* (1868) 38 L.J.Ch. 125 (passage money to go to a colony); *Re Williams' W.T.* [1953] Ch. 138 (purchase of a house as a surgery); *Hardy* v. *Shaw* [1976] Ch. 82 (shares in family company), (1976) 126 N.L.J. 117 (F. G. Glover).

commission in the Army or of an interest in business. In the case of a girl there could be advancement on marriage.[67][68]

(iii) Express Powers. Until 1925 there was no statutory power of advancement. Express powers of advancement were given narrow scope consistent with the established meaning of the word.[69] So, "to prevent uncertainties about the permitted range of objects for which moneys could be raised and made available, such words as 'or otherwise for his or her benefit' were often added to the word 'advancement.' It was always recognised that these added words were 'large words'[70] and indeed in another case[71] the same judge spoke of preferment and advancement of being 'both large words' but of 'benefit' as being the 'largest of all.' "[72] The combined phrase "advancement or benefit" is read disjunctively[73]; it now means "any use of the money which will improve the material situation of the beneficiary."[74] The scope of an express power depends of course upon its own language. The standard form of express power has now been incorporated in the Trustee Act 1925, s.32; and express provisions on the question of advancement are now usually confined to extensions of the statutory power by making the power applicable to the whole of the beneficiary's presumptive share,[75] or by giving express powers to the trustees to create sub-trusts.[76]

(iv) The Statutory Power. Trustee Act 1925, s.32.

Section 32—"(1) Trustees may at any time or times pay or apply any capital money subject to a trust, for the advancement or benefit, in such manner as they may, in their absolute discretion, think fit, of any person entitled to the capital of the trust property or of any share thereof, whether absolutely or contingently on his attaining any specified age or on the occurrence of any other event, or subject to a gift over on his death under any specified age or on the occurrence of any other event, and whether in possession or in remainder or reversion, and such payment or application may be made notwithstanding that the interest of such person is liable to be defeated by

---

[67] *Lloyd* v. *Cocker* (1860) 27 Beav. 645.
[68] *Per* Lord Radcliffe in *Pilkington* v. *I.R.C.* [1964] A.C. 612 at p. 634.
[69] *Per* Kennedy L.J. in *Molyneux* v. *Fletcher* [1898] 1 Q.B. 648 at p. 653.
[70] See Jessel M.R. in *Re Breed's Will* (1875) 1 Ch.D. 226 at p. 228.
[71] *Lowther* v. *Bentinck* (1874) L.R. 19 Eq. 166 at p. 169.
[72] *Per* Lord Radcliffe in *Pilkington* v. *I.R.C.* [1964] A.C. 612 at p. 634; *Re Brittlebank* (1881) 30 W.R. 99 at p. 100; *Re Halsted's W.T.* [1937] 2 All E.R. 570 at p. 571; *Re Moxon's W.T.* [1958] 1 W.L.R. 165 at p. 168; *cf.* the meaning of the word "benefit" in T.A. 1925, s.31, and in Variation of Trusts Act of 1958, s.1; *post*, p. 593; (1959) 23 Conv.(N.S.) 27 (D. W. M. Waters).
[73] *Lowther* v. *Bentinck* (1874) L.R. 19 Eq. 166; *Re Halsted's W.T., supra*, at p. 571.
[74] *Per* Lord Radcliffe in *Pilkington* v. *I.R.C.* [1964] A.C. 612 at p. 635.
[75] By proviso (a) to T.A. 1925, s.32, the statutory power extends only to one-half of the beneficiary's presumptive share; *infra*.
[76] *Post*, p. 552; (1959) 23 Conv.(N.S.) 27 (D. W. M. Waters).

the exercise of a power of appointment or revocation, or to be diminished by the increase of the class to which he belongs:
Provided that—

(*a*) the money so paid or applied for the advancement or benefit of any person shall not exceed altogether in amount one-half of the presumptive or vested share or interest of that person in the trust property; and

(*b*) if that person is or becomes absolutely and indefeasibly entitled to a share in the trust property the money so paid or applied shall be brought into account as part of such share; and

(*c*) no such payment or application shall be made so as to prejudice any person entitled to any prior life or other interest, whether vested or contingent, in the money paid or applied unless such person is in existence and of full age and consents in writing to such payment or application."

The section applies only where the trust property consists of money or securities, or property held upon trust for sale, provided the proceeds are not by statute[77] or in equity considered as land, nor applicable as capital money under the Settled Land Act 1925.[78] Its application is always subject to the expression of a contrary intention[79] and it has been held to be excluded by provision for accumulation.[80]

(v) Problems in the Application of section 32. Pilkington v. I.R.C.[81]
The wide construction of the phrase "advancement" or "benefit" must have been carried into the statutory power created by section 32, since it adopts without qualification the accustomed wording "for the advancement or benefit in such manner as they may in their absolute discretion think fit."[82] But this leaves open a number of questions; can payments be made for the "benefit" of a person who is not in any way in need? To what extent can an advancement re-settle the money advanced, the re-settlement changing the original trust? Can trustees, exercising the statutory power of advancement, delegate their discretion by giving a dispositive discretion to the trustees of the re-settlement; *i.e.* can they make an advancement on protective or discretionary trusts? These questions were discussed and largely settled in the long litigation over the will of William Pilkington.

The testator left a share of his residuary estate on trust for his

---

[77] See S.L.A. 1925, s.75(5).
[78] T.A. 1925, s.32(2), described as "difficult to understand" by Luxmoore J. in *Re Stimpson's Trust* [1931] 2 Ch. 77 at p. 82, where s.32 was held applicable to land held upon trust for sale.
[79] *Re Evans' Settlement* [1967] 1 W.L.R. 1294.
[80] *I.R.C.* v. *Bernstein* [1961] Ch. 399. This is so even if the direction for accumulation contravenes L.P.A. 1925, ss.164–166; *Re Ransome* [1957] Ch. 348; *Brotherton* v. *I.R.C.* [1978] 1 W.L.R. 610.
[81] [1964] A.C. 612.
[82] *Per* Lord Radcliffe in *Pilkington* v. *I.R.C. supra*, at p. 635; *Re Pauling's S.T.* [1964] Ch. 303.

nephew Richard upon protective trusts during his life and after Richard's death upon trust for such of his children or remoter issue as he should by deed or will appoint and in default of appointment in trust for such of Richard's children as attained 21 (or, if female, married under that age) in equal shares. Richard had three children all born after the death of the testator of whom a two-year-old daughter Penelope was one. Richard's father (brother of the testator and grandfather of Penelope) proposed to make a settlement in favour of Penelope, providing that the trustees hold the property on trust to pay the income to Penelope at 21, and the capital for her absolutely at 30 and if Penelope died under 30 leaving children, on trust for such children at 21 with further family trusts in default. The trustees had power to apply the income for Penelope's maintenance until she reached the age of 21, and were to accumulate the surplus income.

The trustees proposed to advance, with the consent of Richard, one-half of Penelope's expectant share under the testator's will, and pay it to the trustees of Richard's father's settlement.

The House of Lords, reversing the Court of Appeal, which had reversed Danckwerts J., held that this proposal was within the trustees' power under section 32. they held also that the exercise of the power of advancement was analogous to the exercise of a special power of appointment and that in the circumstances the advancement would be void for perpetuity.

(a) *Benefit.* On the question of the benefit to Penelope, Lord Radcliffe held that it was immaterial that other persons, such as her future dependants, would benefit also. " . . . if the disposition itself, by which I mean the whole provision made, is for her benefit, it is no objection to the exercise of the power that other persons benefit incidentally as a result of the exercise."[83] The relief from anxiety about the future maintenance of a wife and a family has been held to be a sufficient benefit[84]; as has the performance of the obligation felt by a rich man to contribute to a charitable trust where it would be a great burden to do so out of taxed income[85]; and also the payment from a wife's fund to her husband to enable him to set up in business in England and prevent a separation of the family.[86] Similarly, there was no need, as the Court of Appeal had held, to show that the benefit was "related to his or her

---

[83] *Per* Lord Radcliffe in *Pilkington* v. *I.R.C.* [1964] A.C. 612 at p. 636; *Re Halsted's W.T.* [1937] 2 All E.R. 570; *Re Earl of Buckinghamshire's Settlements, The Times,* March 29, 1977.
[84] *Re Halsted's W.T., supra.*
[85] *Re Clore's Settlement Trust* [1966] 1 W.L.R. 955.
[86] *Re Kershaw's Trusts* (1868) L.R. 6 Eq. 322.

own real or personal needs."[87] The estate duty saving was a sufficient benefit.[88]

(b) *Settlement of Funds Advanced. Sub-Trusts*. Nor was it any objection that the funds were being subjected to a settlement, and not paid for the sole benefit of Penelope; nor that her enjoyment was deferred. The settlement of advanced funds had many times been approved[89] and this inevitably meant that the trusts on which the funds would be held under the advancement were different from those laid down by the original settlor.

(c) *Delegation*. Closely connected with the question of resettlement is that of the extent to which trustees, in making an advancement on new trusts, can give discretionary powers to the trustees of the new settlement. In general, *delegatus non potest delegare*.[90] However, "the law is not that trustees cannot delegate: it is that trustees cannot delegate unless they have authority to do so. If the power of advancement which they possess is so read as to allow them to raise money for the purpose of having it settled, then they do have the necessary authority to let the money pass out of the old settlement into the new trusts. No question of delegation of their powers or trusts arises. If, on the other hand, their power of advancement is read so as to exclude settled advances, cadit quaestio."[91]

This does not, however, solve all the problems. The statutory power allows trustees to advance money by paying it to other trustees to hold on new trusts. Such trusts may include a power of advancement[92]; and presumably section 32 applies to the new trustees. Further, acting on the analogy of cases on special powers of appointment, it seems that the new trusts may include a protective and forfeitable life interest[93]; but that the discretionary trusts which come into effect upon the determination of the life interest may be invalid, because the duties of trustees of a discretionary trust involve dispositive (as opposed to

---

[87] *Per* Lord Evershed in *Re Pilkington's W.T.* [1961] Ch. 466 at p. 481.

[88] " . . . if the advantage of preserving the funds of a beneficiary from the incidence of death duty is not an advantage personal to that beneficiary, I do not see what is"; *per* Lord Radcliffe in *Pilkington* v. *I.R.C., supra*, at p. 640; see also Upjohn J. in *Re Wills W.T.* [1959] Ch. 1, 11–12; *Re Clore's S.T.* [1966] 1 W.L.R. 955.

[89] *Re Halsted's W.T.* [1937] 2 All E.R. 570; *Re Moxon's W.T.* [1958] 1 W.L.R. 165; *Re Ropner's S.T.* [1956] 1 W.L.R. 902; *Re Wills' W.T.* [1959] Ch. 1; *Re Abrahams' W.T.* [1969] 1 Ch. 463; *Re Hastings-Bass* [1975] Ch. 25; (1974) 38 Conv.(N.S.) 293 (F. R. Crane).

[90] *Re May* [1926] 1 Ch. 136; *Re Mewburn* [1934] Ch. 112; *Re Wills' W.T., supra*. This principle applies also to powers of appointment; *Re Hay's S.T.* [1982] 1 W.L.R. 202.

[91] *Per* Lord Radcliffe in *Pilkington* v. *I.R.C.* [1964] A.C. 612 at p. 639.

[92] *Re Mewburn* [1934] Ch. 112; *Re Morris* [1951] 2 All E.R. 528; *Re Hunter's W.T.* [1963] Ch. 372.

[93] *Re Boulton's S.T.* [1928] Ch. 703; *Re Hunter, supra*; *Re Morris, supra*.

administrative) discretions,[94] and these cannot be delegated without express authority.[95]

If that is correct, section 32 appears to give trustees no power to make an advancement upon a new settlement which takes the form of discretionary trusts. Such a situation appears necessarily to raise questions of delegation; and not to be covered by Lord Radcliffe's dictum quoted above.[96] Whether a settlement on discretionary trusts would satisfy the test of "benefit" is another matter; for under such a trust no interest of course is technically given to the advanced beneficiary.[97] The delegation problem can be met by expressly empowering the trustees of the original settlement to delegate their powers in that manner.[98]

(d) *Perpetuity*. For the purposes of the perpetuity rule, the exercise of a power of advancement is treated, as has been seen,[99] on the analogy of a special power of appointment. Where a sub-trust is created by an advancement, the limitation in the sub-trust is tested for validity by being read back into the original instrument under which the power was exercised.[1] The advancements made in *Re Abrahams' Will Trusts*[2] and *Re Hastings-Bass*[3] failed, in part, to comply; as the intended advancement would have done in *Pilkington* v. *I.R.C.*[4] In *Re Abrahams' Will Trusts*, the failure of the void parts of the sub-trust wholly changed the character of the benefit being conferred on the beneficiary, and the advancement was held void. In *Re Hastings-Bass*, however, the trustees' prime consideration was to create a life interest in the life tenant of the sub-trust in order to save estate duty on the death of his father, the life tenant of the original settlement. The fact that the interests in remainder in the sub-trust were void for perpetuity did not make the advancement itself void.

This problem would not exist in the case of advancements made under powers coming into existence after July 15, 1964 because the interests under the sub-trust would be treated as valid until it became known that they would in fact vest outside the perpetuity period.[5]

(vi) The Provisos.[6] (*a*) Only half the presumptive share of each

---

[94] See (1953) 17 Conv.(N.S.) 285 at p. 289 (A. K. R. Kiralfy).
[95] *Per* Eve J. in *Re Boulton's S.T. ante*, at p. 709.
[96] *Supra*.
[97] *Gartside* v. *I.R.C.* [1968] A.C. 553. This is not *per se* an objection; *Re Clore's Settlement Trust, supra*.
[98] For the view that *Pilkington* v. *I.R.C.* ([1964] A.C. 612) does authorise the creation of discretionary trusts under the statutory power of advancement, see (1963) 27 Conv. (N.S.) 65; Parker and Mellows, *The Modern Law of Trusts* (5th ed.), p. 376.
[99] *Pilkington* v. *I.R.C.* [1964] A.C. 612; *ante*, p. 552.
[1] *Re Paul* [1921] 2 Ch. 1.
[2] [1969] 1 Ch. 463.
[3] [1975] Ch. 25.
[4] [1964] A.C. 612.
[5] Perpetuities and Accumulations Act 1964, s.3.
[6] Set out *ante*, p. 550.

beneficiary may be advanced under the statutory power.[7] No doubt this is a wise limitation as a general rule; for if the contingent interest of the advanced beneficiary never vests, the fund in the hands of the person next entitled is reduced by the amount advanced. However, where it is advantageous to be able to advance one-half, it may be more advantageous to be able to advance the whole; and it is common to extend the statutory power so as to give the trustees power to advance the whole if they see fit.

(*b*) This is an application of the doctrine of "hotchpot," which attempts to effect an equality between the members of a class of beneficiaries, by requiring those who have received benefits in advance of other members of a class of beneficiaries to count the advancement against their ultimate share.[8] Of course it is otherwise if the share never vests.[9] The doctrine applies also in an intestacy.[10]

(*c*) By advancing some or all of the capital, the fund which provides the income of the tenant for life is reduced. The consent of the tenant for life is therefore requisite to the exercise of the power. The court has no power to dispense with this consent.[11] A member of a discretionary class is not, however, a person whose consent is required.[12]

C. The Court's Inherent Power to Provide Maintenance and Advancement

The court has inherent power to order provision to be made for a minor out of his property. This power is usually applied in respect of income[13]; but occasionally capital is used.[14] Also, as will be seen,[15] the court has statutory power to make an order authorising a person to make use of a minor's property with a view to the application of the capital or income for the minor's maintenance, education or benefit.

---

[7] See *Re Marquess of Abergavenny's Estate Act Trusts* [1981] 1 W.L.R. 843; [1982] Conv. 158 (J. W. Price); (express power to pay life tenant any part or parts not exceeding one-half in value of the settled fund was exhausted by the advance of one-half, even though the remainder subsequently increased in value).

[8] The advance is brought into account at its value at the date of advancement. In times of inflation this can have capricious results. A form of indexation is therefore recommended by the Law Reform Committee, 23rd Report, *The Powers and Duties of Trustees* (1982 Cmnd. 8733), paras. 4.43–4.47.

[9] *Re Fox* [1904] 1 Ch. 480 (express power).

[10] A.E.A. 1925, s.47(1)(iii).

[11] *Re Forster's Settlement* [1942] Ch. 199. See also *Henley* v. *Wardell, The Times*, January 29, 1988. (Power in will giving trustees "absolute and uncontrolled discretion" to advance whole capital did not give them power to dispense with the consent of the prior income beneficiary. The purpose of the clause was merely to enlarge the power as to the amount advanced).

[12] *Re Harris' Settlement* (1940) 162 L.T. 358; *Re Beckett's Settlement* [1940] Ch. 279.

[13] *Wellesley* v. *Wellesley* (1828) 2 Bli.(N.S.) 124.

[14] *Barlow* v. *Grant* (1684) 1 Vern. 255.

[15] *Post*, p. 584; T.A. 1925, s.53.

D. Responsibility of the Trustees to See to the Application of the Money Advanced

We have seen that the trustees must be satisfied that the proposed advancement is for the benefit of the beneficiary. The next question is whether the trustees, in making an advancement, are under an obligation to see that the money is applied towards the purposes for which the payment was made. In *Re Pauling's Settlement Trusts*[16] the Court of Appeal, dealing with an express power to advance one-half of an expected or presumptive share for the "absolute use" of a beneficiary, held that the power was fiduciary; the trustees could hand over a sum of capital quite generally to a beneficiary if they thought that he was the type of person who could be trusted with the money. Or, if the trustees made the advance for a particular purpose, which they stated, they could quite properly pay it over if they reasonably thought that he could be trusted to carry it out. "What they cannot do is prescribe a particular purpose, and then raise and pay the money over to the advancee leaving him or her entirely free, legally and morally, to apply it for that purpose or to spend it in any way he or she chooses without any responsibility on the trustees even to inquire as to its application."[17]

[16] [1964] Ch. 303; *post*, p. 607.
[17] [1964] Ch. 303 at p. 334.

CHAPTER 20

THE FIDUCIARY NATURE OF TRUSTEESHIP

1. REMUNERATION AND REIMBURSEMENT

THE basic principle is that a trustee acts voluntarily and is not paid for his services.[1] It does not matter whether his services are of a professional nature, as where he is a solicitor, or whether they are personal. It follows, therefore, that a trustee can only claim remuneration if he can show a specific entitlement to it; and the discussion that follows is essentially an account of how that entitlement can arise. It will appear that the basic principle is much honoured in its breach.

But it is also a basic principle that a trustee may recover for his legitimate out-of-pocket expenses, which include the payment of agents' fees wherever their employment is justified,[2] calls on shares,[3]

---

[1] *Robinson* v. *Pett* (1734) 3 P.Wms.249; *Re Barber* (1886) 34 Ch.D. 77; *Dale* v. *I.R.C.* [1954] A.C. 11 at p. 27. The rule is to the contrary in many of the American States, where statutory rates are usually established. English executors were held to be entitled to retain a fee earned by taking out a grant of probate in New York in respect of Amercian assets; *Re Northcote's W.T.* [1949] 1 All E.R. 442. For the views of the Law Reform Committee, see 23rd Report, *The Powers and Duties of Trustees* (1982 Cmnd. 8733) paras. 3.45–3.58; [1984] Conv. 275 (N. D. M. Parry), suggesting that the reforms are too cautious. See generally (1983) 46 M.L.R. 289 (W. Bishop and D. D. Prentice).

[2] This must be borne in mind when considering the principle that the trustee's office is gratuitous. His burden is alleviated to the extent that he can properly delegate the work to agents; *ante*, p. 532.

[3] *Hardoon* v. *Belilios* [1901] A.C. 118.

and the proper costs of litigation.[4] This right is now statutory,[5] and prevails against trust property generally, both corpus and income, and in some cases against the beneficiaries personally.[6]

A. Remuneration Authorised by the Trust Instrument

While equity remains true to its basic principle in that it construes strictly clauses authorising remuneration,[7] it is equally true that such clauses are at the present time extremely common, and are frequently drafted in a very wide manner. Indeed, if it were not so, it would be difficult to persuade professional people to act as trustees in view of the many and complex matters that now fall to be considered. The remuneration may take the form of the income from a part of the estate,[8] or the trustee may be given power to make use of trust money in other ways.[9] A clause in a will authorising remuneration is for many purposes equivalent to a legacy.[10]

B. Remuneration Authorised by Statute

Statutory provisions enable fees to be charged by the Public Trustee,[11] by persons appointed to be Judicial Trustees,[12] and by corporations appointed as custodian trustees.[13] In this last case, the corporation concerned cannot also be a managing trustee.[14] But where a corporation is appointed to be a trustee by the court, the court has full discretion as to its fees, and is not restricted by this distinction.[15]

---

[4] *Ante,* p. 485. It can extend to the costs incurred by trustees in defending actions brought against them personally, save in cases of misconduct: *Re Spurling's Will Trusts* [1966] 1 W.L.R. 920.

[5] Trustee Act 1925, s.30(2).

[6] See generally *Stott* v. *Milne* (1884) 25 Ch.D. 710; and *Re Grimthorpe* [1958] Ch. 615; Snell, pp. 255–257. *Cf. Holding and Management Ltd.* v. *Property Holding and Investment Trust plc.* [1988] 1 W.L.R. 644.

[7] *Re Chalinder & Herington* [1907] 1 Ch. 58; *Re Gee* [1948] Ch. 284. see Snell, pp. 254–255.

[8] *Public Trustee* v. *I.R.C.* [1960] A.C. 398. See (1988) 2 *Trust Law & Practice* 93 (J. Thurston).

[9] See *Space Investments Ltd.* v. *Canadian Imperial Bank of Commerce Trust Co. (Bahamas) Ltd.* [1986] 1 W.L.R. 1072 (settlement provided that bank trustee could deposit trust money with itself and use for own purposes, subject to normal obligation to repay).

[10] *Re Pooley* (1888) 40 Ch.D. 1; *Re Thorley* [1891] 2 Ch. 613; *Re White* [1898] 2 Ch. 217. See also *Re Chapple* (1884) 27 Ch.D. 584.

[11] Public Trustee Act 1906, s.9; Public Trustee (Fees) Act 1957; Administration of Justice Act, 1965, s.2; Public Trustee (Fees) (Amendment) Order, 1988 (S.I. 1988/ 571). He is paid such salary as the Lord Chancellor determines; Public Trustee Act 1906, s.8(1A).

[12] Judicial Trustees Act 1896, s.1.

[13] Public Trustee Act 1906, s.4.

[14] *Forster* v. *Williams Deacon's Bank Ltd.* [1935] Ch. 359; *Arning* v. *James* [1936] Ch. 158.

[15] Trustee Act 1925, s.42.

C. Remuneration Authorised by the Court

The court has an inherent jurisdiction, which is exercisable retrospectively[16] and prospectively, but in exceptional cases only, to authorise remuneration.[17] The power has even been exercised in favour of a
fiduciary who was guilty of undue influence. In *O'Sullivan* v. *Management Agency and Music Ltd.*[18] a contract between a performer and his
agent was set aside for undue influence and breach of fiduciary duty,
but the agent was awarded remuneration (including a reasonable
profit element) as he had contributed significantly to the plaintiff's
success. The argument that the jurisdiction was exercisable only in
favour of the morally blameless was rejected.

The court's power extends to trustees *de son tort*,[19] and also covers
the case of a corporation appointed, other than by the court, to be a
managing trustee.[20] The jurisdiction was recently reviewed by the
Court of Appeal in *Re Duke of Norfolk's Settlement Trusts*.[21] A corporate trustee, which was authorised to charge fees according to its scale
of fees at the commencement of the trust, and an individual, for whom
no provision was made in the trust instrument, asked for payment in
respect of exceptionally burdensome work in connection with the
development of what is now Arundel Court in the Strand, and in
respect of the additional work generated by the introduction of capital
transfer tax by the Finance Act 1975. The corporate trustee also sought
an increase in its scale of fees as to future work. Walton J. had
authorised payment in respect of the Strand development only.[22] The
corporate trustee appealed against the refusal to authorise an increase
in its future fees. The Court of Appeal held that there was inherent
jurisdiction to authorise remuneration if beneficial to the administration of the trust. The jurisdiction extended to increasing the rate of
remuneration authorised by the settlor. It would be illogical if the
court could sanction remuneration where the trust provided for none
but could not raise the level of that laid down by the trust, which was a
lesser interference. The fact that the office was essentially gratuitous
and the need to protect the beneficiaries from spurious claims must be

---

[16] *Re Worthington* [1954] 1 W.L.R. 526; *Re Jarvis* [1958] 1 W.L.R. 815; *Phipps* v.
Boardman [1967] 2 A.C. 46, *post*, p. 571; *O'Sullivan* v. *Management Agency and
Music Ltd.* [1985] Q.B. 428, *infra; cf. Guinness plc.* v. *Saunders* [1988] 1 W.L.R. 863
(no claim where defendant had wrongly retained plaintiff's property). For the views of
the Charity Commissioners on remuneration of trustees of a charitable trust, see
Annual Report 1978, paras. 11–20; Annual Report 1981, paras. 61–64; *cf.* (1987) 50
N.L.J. Annual Charities Review 24 (H. Picarda).

[17] Most applications are dealt with in chambers and not reported.

[18] *Supra*; (1986) 49 M.L.R. 118 (W. Bishop and D. D. Prentice).

[19] *Brown* v. *Litton* (1711) 1 P.Wms. 140; it also extends to those who administer the trust
without technically becoming trustees in any sense: *Phipps* v. *Boardman* [1967] 2 A.C.
46; and to constructive trustees, *Re Jarvis* [1958] 1 W.L.R. 815.

[20] *Re Masters* [1953] 1 W.L.R. 81.

[21] [1982] Ch. 61; (1982) 45 M.L.R. 211 (B. Green); (1982) 98 L.Q.R. 181 (P.V.B);
[1982] Conv. 231 (K. Hodkinson).

[22] [1979] Ch. 37. The decision of Walton J. was applied in *Re Keeler's S.T.* [1981] Ch.
156, which should now be read in the light of the decision of the Court of Appeal.

balanced against the fact that it was important that the trust be properly administered. The court would have regard to the nature of the trust, the experience and skill of the trustee, and the sums claimed in comparison with the charges of other trustees. Here the level of fees of the corporate trustee, even if increased as claimed, was low; the trustee had incurred a substantial and continuing loss as a result of its office; and the work exceeded that contemplated at the creation of the trust. The case was remitted to the Chancery Division for a decision whether the jurisdiction to increase the fees should be exercised.

Where an increase is sought, it should be the subject of a direct application, and not included as a term of a compromise of a dispute between beneficiaries which is unconnected with the trustees' rate of remuneration.[23]

D. Remuneration for Litigious Work by Solicitor-Trustees

Under the rule in *Cradock* v. *Piper*,[24] a solicitor-trustee may charge costs if he has acted for a *co-trustee as well as himself*[25] in respect of business done in an action or matter *in court*, provided that his activities have not increased the expenses. It is not necessary that the court action should be hostile in character, but it must be some form of litigious matter.[26] The rule will not be extended by analogies.

It may also be noted here that a solicitor-trustee may employ his *partner* in cases where it would be proper to employ an outside solicitor, provided that he himself will derive no benefit, direct *or* indirect, from such an employment.[27] There must be complete separation of the trust work from the firm's general work, so as to make it clear that the solicitor-trustee is not involved in the former. This power is not restricted to matters in court, but it does not enable a solicitor-trustee to employ his own *firm*.[28]

E. Authorisation by Contract

Trustees may contract for remuneration with those beneficiaries who are *sui juris*.[29] But such agreements may somewhat easily be brought under the head of undue influence,[30] and are not encouraged. Nor, in fact, are they at all common.

---

[23] *Re Barbour's Settlement* [1974] 1 W.L.R. 1198; *cf. Re Codd's W.T.* [1975] 1 W.L.R. 1139.

[24] (1850) 1 Mac. & G. 664. See (1983) 46 M.L.R. 289 at p. 306 (W. Bishop and D. D. Prentice).

[25] *Lyon* v. *Baker* (1852) 5 De G. & Sm. 622.

[26] *Re Corsellis* (1887) 34 Ch.D. 675.

[27] *Clack* v. *Carlon* (1861) 30 L.J.Ch. 639.

[28] *Christophers* v. *White* (1847) 10 Beav. 523; *Re Gates* [1933] Ch. 913; *Re Hill* [1934] Ch. 623.

[29] No remuneration may be paid out of the trust property by agreement with the beneficiaries if they are not all *sui juris*. In such a case, application must be made to court, as in *Re Duke of Norfolk's S.T., supra,* (living beneficiaries did not object, but some unborn).

[30] *Ayliffe* v. *Murray* (1740) 2 Atk. 58; *post*, pp. 788 *et seq.*

2. TRUSTEES MUST NOT BE PURCHASERS

A. Purchase of the Trust Property

A trustee may not place himself in a position where trafficking in the trust property may prove to be an irresistible temptation. The general rule is that trustees are not to become the owners or lessees of trust property. This rule is independent of any question of inadequacy of price, or unfairness, or undue advantage; the sale may have been at auction and the trustee may have taken the bidding well above the reserve price, but he is still caught by the rule, which derives from his status and position and not from his conduct in the particular case.[31] Nor does it matter that he left the decision to sell and the manner of sale wholly to his co-trustee; nor that he retired from the trust before making an offer.[32] His responsibility as trustee is such that he must not contemplate the purchase at all.

The rule was somewhat relaxed in *Holder* v. *Holder*,[33] involving a purchase by an executor who had purported to renounce the executorship, but invalidly, as he had already done some minor acts in the administration of the estate. After his purported renunciation, the executor took no further part in the administration. He later purchased at auction for a fair price some farmland belonging to the estate, of which he had previously been tenant. The Court of Appeal declined to set aside the purchase. The circumstances were special, because the executor had not interfered in the administration of the estate; nor had he taken part in organising the auction; nor was there any conflict of interest and duty, as the beneficiaries were not looking to him to protect their interests; and finally, any special knowledge he had about the property was acquired as tenant and not as executor. In any event, the plaintiff beneficiary had acquiesced in the sale. As a general rule, however, a trustee or executor who has once involved himself in his office is affected by the rule for a considerable period after retirement.

The effect of the rule is that the purchase is voidable at the option of a beneficiary, who is allowed a generous time to discover the position.[34] The right to avoid the sale is effective against a purchaser with notice of the circumstances. The rule cannot be got around by sales to nominees,[35] for a repurchase by the trustee will be regarded as on behalf of the trust (unless the original sale was bona fide).[36] A sale to

---

[31] *Campbell* v. *Walker* (1800) 5 Ves.Jr. 678; *ex p. Lacey* (1802) 6 Ves.Jr. 625.

[32] *Wright* v. *Morgan* [1926] A.C. 788; *Re Boles and British Land Co.'s Contract* [1902] 1 Ch. 244.

[33] [1968] Ch. 353. *Cf. Re Mulholland's W.T.* [1949] 1 All E.R. 460 (option to purchase acquired before trusteeship).

[34] For an illustration see *Re Sherman* [1954] Ch. 653.

[35] *Silkstone & Haigh Moor Coal Co.* v. *Edey* [1900] 1 Ch. 167.

[36] *Re Postlethwaite* (1888) 60 L.T. 514.

the trustee's wife is looked upon with suspicion,[37] and likewise a sale to a company in which the trustee has a substantial interest.[38]

The court may in certain circumstances prefer to order a re-sale, and, if the price is higher than the previous sale price, the trustee must convey; otherwise he is held to his purchase. The trustee will not be allowed to bid at the new sale if this is objected to.[39]

The rule discussed above is subject to certain exceptions. The trust instrument may expressly permit the purchase by a trustee. Secondly, the court has a discretion to allow such a purchase in a proper case,[40] or to permit the trustee to bid at an auction.[41] Finally, a tenant for life of settled land, which he holds on trust, is permitted by statute to purchase the property.[42]

B. Purchase of the Beneficial Interest

Equity's view is less stringent when dealing with a purchase by a trustee of the beneficial interest of a beneficiary.[43] This is a type of transaction which is carefully watched; the onus is on the trustee to show "that he gave full value, and that all information was laid before the *cestui que trust* when it was sold."[44] The principles of undue influence apply; but it is open to a trustee in this type of case to show that the whole transaction was conducted at arm's length. This must however be very distinctly proved.[45]

3. INCIDENTAL PROFITS

A. Trustees

The rules discussed below apply in full force to trustees. Many of them apply also to other fiduciaries. Although we are mainly concerned here with trustees, it will be convenient to mention also, where relevant, the application of the rules to persons who are not strictly trustees.

---

[37] See *Burrell* v. *Burrell's Trustees* 1915 S.C. 33, where the sale was upheld; *Tito* v. *Waddell (No. 2)* [1977] Ch. 106.

[38] See *Re Thompson's Settlement* [1986] Ch. 99, (1986) 1 *Trust Law & Practice* 66 (C. H. Sherrin), where the contract for sale to a company of which the trustee was managing director and majority shareholder was held unenforceable. A mortgageee is also debarred from selling the property to himself, but it has been held that he can sell to a company in which he has an interest if he acts in good faith and gets the best price reasonably obtainable; *Tse Kwong Lam* v. *Wong Chit Sen* [1983] 1 W.L.R. 1349. See also *Farrar* v. *Farrar's Ltd.* (1889) 40 Ch.Div. 395.

[39] See Cross J. in *Holder* v. *Holder* [1968] Ch. 353 at p. 371.

[40] *Farmer* v. *Dean* (1863) 32 Beav. 327. Or the beneficiaries, all being *sui juris,* may agree to it.

[41] *Holder* v. *Holder, supra,* at pp. 398, 402.

[42] S.L.A. 1925, s.68; *Re Pennant's W.T.* [1970] Ch. 75.

[43] *Tito* v. *Waddell (No. 2) supra,* at p. 241; *Re Thompson's Settlement* [1986] Ch. 99.

[44] *Per* Lord Cairns in *Thomson* v. *Eastwood* (1877) 2 App.Cas. 215 at p. 236; *Hill* v. *Langley, The Times,* January 28, 1988.

[45] See generally *Coles* v. *Trecothick* (1804) 9 Ves.Jr. 234; *Morse* v. *Royal* (1806) 12 Ves.Jr. 355; *cf. Williams* v. *Scott* [1900] A.C. 499.

(i) **Rule in Keech v. Sandford.**[46] This rule prevents a trustee from keeping for his own benefit a renewal of a lease which he was able to obtain for himself by reason of his being the trustee of the original lease[47]; and even though the trustee had tried unsuccessfully to obtain a renewal for the benefit of his infant *cestui que trust*. In the leading case, from which the rule takes its name, the defendant held a lease of the profits of a market on trust for a minor. Before the expiration of the lease, the defendant asked the lessor to renew the lease in favour of the minor. The lessor refused to grant a lease to the minor on the ground that, as the lease was of the profits of the market, he would be unable to distrain, and would be unable to enforce the covenant against the minor. The trustee then took a lease for his own benefit.

Lord Chancellor King held that the trustee must hold the lease on trust for the minor. "This may seem hard," he said,[48] "that the trustee is the only person of all mankind who might not have the lease; but it is very proper that the rule should be strictly pursued, and not in the least relaxed; for it is very obvious what would be the consequences of letting trustees have the lease, on refusal to renew to *cestui que use*."

It is otherwise, however, where there is no fiduciary relationship.

In *Re Biss*,[49] a lessor had refused to renew a seven-year lease of premises, and the lessee remained in possession as tenant from year to year. He died, leaving a widow and three children, one of whom was a minor. The widow, who was his administratrix, and the two adult children continued the business under the existing lease. The lessor terminated the lease, and then granted a three-year lease to one of the adult children. The Court of Appeal allowed him to keep the lease for his own benefit. Romer L.J. said that[50] "where the person renewing the lease does not clearly occupy a fiduciary position" he "is only held to be a constructive trustee of the renewed lease if, in respect of the old lease, he occupied some special position and owed, by virtue of that position, a duty towards the other persons interested." If such a person, by virtue of his position "is enabled to obtain a renewal of the lease, equity clearly demands that the new right obtained in virtue of the old, should be regarded as a graft on the old. ... "

(ii) **Purchase of the Reversion.** Where the trustee acquires the free-

---

[46] (1726) Sel. Cas. t. King 61; *Re Knowles' W.T.* [1948] 1 All E.R. 866; (1969) 33 Conv.(N.S.) 161 (S. M. Cretney); *Re Edwards' W.T.* [1982] Ch. 30; *cf. Harris* v. *Black* (1983) 127 S.J. 224.

[47] In *Re Thompson's Settlement* [1986] Ch. 99 it was left open whether the rule applies where a trustee of the reversion purchases the lease.

[48] (1726) Sel. Cas. t. King 61 at p. 62.

[49] [1903] 2. Ch. 40; *Brenner* v. *Rose* [1973] 1 W.L.R. 443. See also *Savage* v. *Dunningham* [1974] Ch. 181.

[50] [1903] 2 Ch. 40 at p. 61.

hold reversion, the position is unclear.[51] The trustee is liable if he has in any way made use of his position to get a personal benefit: thus if the lessor makes an offer to all his lessees giving them the right to enfranchisement on favourable terms, or if the lessee had any statutory right of enfranchisement, there could be no doubt that the trustee who sought to take the reversion for his own benefit would be liable. The courts have, however, vacillated in deciding whether there is any *absolute* liability in the absence of such abuse.[52] In *Protheroe* v. *Protheroe*[53] the Court of Appeal, without referring to the relevant authorities, held that the rule was applicable, without qualification, to purchases of the freehold. A husband held the lease of the matrimonial home on trust for his wife and himself in equal shares. After the wife had petitioned for divorce, he purchased the freehold reversion. When he sold, the wife was held to be entitled to a share of the proceeds.[54] In earlier cases the courts had limited the rule to cases where the lease, the reversion on which was being purchased, was renewable by law or custom.[55] The rationale of that limitation was that if the lease were normally renewed in practice,[56] the lessee would suffer if the lease passed to a third party who might not follow the custom (particularly if the lease, as was commonly the case with church leases, was generally renewed at less than the market rent). Thus it was wrong to allow the trustee, who ought to be protecting his beneficiary's interests, to damage them. Today, by statute, many lessees are given valuable rights of renewal or enfranchisement. It is submitted that the proper question in each case is: has the trustee taken advantage of his position to get a personal benefit? If so, he is liable, otherwise he is not. "It seems to me," said Pennycuick V.-C. in *Thompson's Trustee in Bankruptcy* v. *Heaton*,[57] "that apart from the fact that it binds me, this decision [*Protheroe* v. *Protheroe*], like the rule in *Keech* v. *Sandford*, is really in modern terms an application of the broad principle that a trustee must not make a profit out of the trust estate." The onus would

---

[51] The converse situation where a trustee of the reversion purchases the lease was left open in *Re Thompson's Settlement* [1986] Ch. 99.

[52] *Norris* v. *Le Neve* (1743) 3 Atk. 26; *Randall* v. *Russell* (1817) 3 Mer. 190; *Hardman* v. *Johnson* (1815) 3 Mer. 347; *cf. Phillips* v. *Phillips* (1885) 29 Ch.D. 673.

[53] [1968] 1 W.L.R. 519; (1968) 31 M.L.R. 707 (P. Jackson); (1968) 32 Conv.(n.s.) 220 (F. R. Crane); *Thompson's Trustee* v. *Heaton* [1974] 1 W.L.R. 605; (1974) 38 Conv.(n.s.) 288; (1975) 38 M.L.R. 226 (P. Jackson).

[54] "It may be that there were facts in the case which indicated that the husband obtained the freehold by virtue of his position as leaseholder, but they are not apparent from the report"; (1968) 84 L.Q.R. 309 (L. Megarry).

[55] *Longton* v. *Wilsby* (1897) 76 L.T. 770; *Bevan* v. *Webb* [1905] 1 Ch. 620; *cf. Griffith* v. *Owen* [1907] 1 Ch. 195; *per* Wilberforce J. in *Phipps* v. *Boardman* [1964] 1 W.L.R. 993 at p. 1009.

[56] See generally (1969) 33 Conv.(n.s.) 161 (S. M. Cretney), where the history of the doctrine is traced.

[57] [1974] W.L.R. 605 at p.606, *per* Pennycuick V.-C. Textbook criticisms of *Protheroe* were rejected.

be on the trustee to satisfy the court, and it can be a very difficult one to discharge.

(iii) Trustees as Company Directors. The question has arisen several times in connection with the remuneration of directorships which trustees have obtained by virtue of their position as trustees.

In *Re Macadam*,[58] trustees had power under the articles by virtue of their office to appoint two directors of a company. They appointed themselves, and were held liable to account for the remuneration which they received because they had acquired it by the use of their powers as trustees.

On the other hand, the remuneration may be retained if the trustees were directors before they became trustees,[59] or if the trustees were appointed directors independently of the votes of the shares of the trust,[60] or if the trustee did not obtain the remuneration by the use of his position as a trustee, but by an independent bargain with the firm employing him.[61] Indeed, as Cohen J. said in *Re Macadam*[62]: " . . . the root of the matter really is: Did [the trustee] acquire the position in respect of which he drew the remuneration by virtue of his position as trustee?" Trustees will not be liable even within that test if the terms of the trust authorised them to appoint themselves and receive remuneration.[63]

(iv) Other Profits by Trustees. Incidental profits come to trustees in a variety of ways and must always be disgorged. "Whenever it can be shewn that the trustee has so arranged matters as to obtain an advantage, whether in money or money's worth, to himself personally through the execution of his trust, he will not be permitted to retain, but will be compelled to make it over to his constituent."[64]

A few examples must suffice. A trustee who introduced to a firm, of which he was a member, business of the trust, was compelled to account for the profit[65]; similarly, a trustee who received a sum of £75 to induce him to retire[66] and a trustee who used trust funds in his own business was required to account for the profits he received[67]; and a

---

[58] [1946] Ch. 73; *Re Francis* (1905) 92 L.T. 77; *Williams* v. *Barton* [1927] 2 Ch. 9.
[59] *Re Dover Coalfield Extension Ltd.* [1908] 1 Ch. 65. See also *Re Orwell's W.T.* [1982] 1 W.L.R. 1337.
[60] *Re Gee* [1948] Ch. 284.
[61] *Re Lewis* (1910) 103 L.T. 495, as explained in *Re Gee, supra.*
[62] [1946] Ch. 73 at p. 82. Harman J. accepted this test in *Re Gee, supra.*
[63] *Re Llewellin's W.T.* [1949] Ch. 225. The court may sanction the retention of the fees; *Re Keeler's S.T.* [1981] Ch. 156.
[64] *Huntingdon Copper Co.* v. *Henderson* (1872) 4 R. (Court of Session) 294 at p. 308. Cf. *Patel* v. *Patel* [1981] 1 W.L.R. 1342 (no breach where trustees sought to live in the trust property where the beneficiaries were young children adopted by the trustees on the death of their parents).
[65] *Williams* v. *Barton* [1927] 2 Ch. 9.
[66] *Sugden* v. *Crossland* (1856) 3 Sm. & G. 192; *Re Smith* [1896] 1 Ch. 171.
[67] *Brown* v. *I.R.C.* [1965] A.C. 244 (a Scottish solicitor compelled to account for interest earned by deposits of clients' moneys).

trustee may be liable for profits which he ought reasonably to have received.[68]

(v) A Trustee must not be in Competition with the Trust. Conflict of Interest. A "trustee must not place himself in a position where his duty and his interest may conflict."[69] One possible area of conflict is where the trustee operates in business in competition with the trust. Such competition was inevitable in *Re Thomson*[70] where executors of a will were directed to carry on the business of the testator who had been a yacht broker. One of the executors was intending to set up on his own account as a yacht broker in competition. It was held that he must not set up in a competing business.

This rule applies to other fiduciaries who are not trustees. A partner is required by statute to "account for and pay over to the firm all profits made" by carrying on a business "of the same nature as and competing with that of the firm"[71] unless he has the consent of the other partners. It is a question of fact in each case whether or not the activity is in conflict with the fiduciary duty.[72]

B. Other Fiduciaries[73]

(i) The Principle. A similar rule applies to profits made by other persons in breach of a fiduciary relation; indeed such persons are grouped with trustees in many formulations of the rule, although there is no rule that they must act gratuitously. "It is an inflexible rule, of a Court of Equity that a person in a fiduciary position, . . . is not, unless otherwise expressly provided, entitled to make a profit; he is not allowed to put himself in a position where his interest and duty conflict."[74] But it is not safe to make the attractive over-simplification of saying that a fiduciary must always account for all gains which come to him by reason of his fiduciary position. Indeed, Lord Herschell in the paragraph containing the above quoted statement of the rule, "plainly recognised its limitations."[75] "But I am satisfied that it might be departed from in many cases, without any breach of morality, without any wrong being inflicted, and without any consciousness of wrong-

---

[68] *Re Waterman's W.T.* [1952] 2 All E.R. 1054.
[69] *Per* Lord Upjohn in *Boardman* v. *Phipps* [1967] 2 A.C. 46 at p. 123.
[70] [1930] 1 Ch. 203; *Aberdeen Railway Co.* v. *Blaikie Bros.* (1854) 1 Macq. 461; *cf. Moore* v. *M'Glynn* [1894] 1 Ir.R. 74.
[71] Partnership Act 1890, s.30.
[72] *Moore* v. *M'Glynn* [1894] 1 Ir.R. 74.
[73] Goff and Jones, Chaps. 34, 35; (1968) 84 L.Q.R. 472 (G. H. Jones); (1976) 92 L.Q.R. 360 at p. 372 (R. M. Goode); Oakley, *Constructive Trusts* (2nd ed.), Chap. 3; (1981) 97 L.Q.R. 51 (J. C. Shepherd); Shepherd, *The Law of Fiduciaries* (1981); Snell, pp. 250–252.
[74] Lord Herschell in *Bray* v. *Ford* [1896] A.C. 44 at p. 51; see also Lord Cranworth in *Aberdeen Railway Co.* v. *Blaikie Bros.* (1854) 1 Macq. 461 at p. 471; *Regal (Hastings) Ltd.* v. *Gulliver* [1942] 1 All E.R. 378; [1967] 2 A.C. 134n.
[75] Lord Upjohn in *Boardman* v. *Phipps* [1967] 2 A.C. 46 at p. 123.

doing. Indeed, it is obvious that it might sometimes be to the advantage of the beneficiaries that their trustee should act for them professionally rather than a stranger, even though the trustee were paid for his services."[76]

It is not always easy, however, to determine whether a particular relationship should be classified as fiduciary. While some examples are well established, the boundaries of the category of fiduciary relationships are not clear, and the category is not closed.[77] The rule has been applied to certain agents,[78] (including "self-appointed" agents[79]), solicitors,[80] company directors,[81] tenants for life,[82] partners,[83] confidential employees,[84] and certain bailees.[85]

Indeed, it may sometimes appear that the defendant may be classified as a fiduciary, or not, in order to achieve the desired result.

In *Reading* v. *Attorney-General*,[86] a staff-sergeant in the British

---

[76] *Bray* v. *Ford* [1896] A.C. 44 at p. 52.

[77] *English* v. *Dedham Vale Properties Ltd.* [1978] 1 W.L.R. 93. A public authority may owe fiduciary duties in the exercise of its statutory powers; *Bromley L.B.C.* v. *Greater London Council* [1983] 1 A.C. 768 (fiduciary duty to ratepayers).

[78] *De Bussche* v. *Alt* (1878) 8 Ch.D. 286; *N.Z. Netherlands Society* v. *Kuys* [1973] 1 W.L.R. 1126 at p. 1129, *per* Lord Wilberforce; *Boardman* v. *Phipps* [1967] 2 A.C. 46. And see the cases on the taking of double commission by an agent; Hanbury, *Principles of Agency*, (2nd ed.), p. 67. Not all agents are fiduciaries, although there may be a presumption that they are; *Hendy Lennox (Industrial Engines) Ltd.* v. *Grahame Puttick Ltd.* [1984] 1 W.L.R. 485; *Aluminium Industrie Vaassen B.V.* v. *Romalpa Aluminium Ltd.* [1976] 1 W.L.R. 676; *cf. Re Andrabell Ltd. (in liq.)* [1984] 3 All E.R. 407. See Goff and Jones, p. 71, n. 68, suggesting that "much depends on whether the agent is under a duty to keep separate his own money from his principal's money."

[79] *English* v. *Dedham Vale Properties Ltd.*, *supra.* (where the intending purchaser obtained planning permission in the vendor's name); (1978) 41 M.L.R. 474 (A. Nicol); (1978) 94 L.Q.R. 347 (G. Samuel).

[80] *Brown* v. *I.R.C.* [1965] A.C. 244; (1964) 80 L.Q.R. 480; *Oswald Hickson Collier & Co. (a Firm)* v. *Carter-Ruck* [1984] 2 W.L.R. 847; *Islamic Republic of Iran Shipping Lines* v. *Denby* [1987] 1 F.T.L.R. 30 (accountable for bribe). See also *Hanson* v. *Lorenz* [1987] 1 F.T.L.R. 23 (no liability to account to client for his profits from a joint venture where client had understood the agreement). As to whether a head of chambers is in a fiduciary position to the members, see *Appleby* v. *Cowley, The Times* April 14, 1982.

[81] *Regal (Hastings) Ltd.* v. *Gulliver, supra*; *Selangor United Rubber Co.* v. *Cradock (No. 3)* [1968] W.L.R. 1555; *Karak Rubber Co. Ltd.* v. *Burden* [1972] 1 W.L.R. 602, *ante*, p. 290; *Industrial Development Consultants Ltd.* v. *Cooley* [1972] 1 W.L.R. 443; (1973) 89 L.Q.R. 187 (A. Yoran); (1972) 35 M.L.R. 655 (H.Rajak); [1980] Conv. 200 (W. J. Braithwaite), *post*, p. 569. See also *Horcal Ltd.* v. *Gatland, The Times*, April 16, 1984.

[82] *Taster* v. *Marriott* (1768) Amb. 668; *Rawe* v. *Chichester* (1773) Amb. 715; *Pickering* v. *Vowles* (1783) 1 Bro.C.C. 197. *cf. Re Pelly's Will Trusts* [1957] Ch. 1.

[83] *Featherstonhaugh* v. *Fenwick* (1810) 17 Ves.Jr. 298; *Clegg* v. *Fishwick* (1849) 1 Mac. & G. 294.

[84] *Triplex Safety Glass Co.* v. *Scorah* [1938] Ch. 211; *British Celanese Co.* v. *Moncrieff* [1948] Ch. 564; *British Syphon Co.* v. *Homewood* [1956] 1 W.L.R. 1190; *Att.-Gen.* v. *Guardian Newspapers Ltd. (No. 2)* [1988] 3 W.L.R. 776 (The "Spycatcher" case).

[85] *Aluminium Industrie Vaassen B.V.* v. *Romalpa Aluminium Ltd.*, *supra*; *Re Andrabell Ltd. (in liq.)* [1984] 3 All E.R. 407.

[86] [1951] A.C. 507; *Jersey City* v. *Hague* (1955) 18 N.J. 584; *Amalgamated Industrials Ltd.* v. *Johnson & Firth Brown Ltd., The Times*, April 15, 1981.

Army stationed in Cairo was paid large sums of money by Egyptians for riding in their civilian lorries carrying contraband goods and enabling the lorries to pass civilian check posts without difficulty. The British authorities seized some £20,000 of such funds in Reading's possession; later Reading petitioned to recover it. He had obtained the money wrongfully, but he argued that this fact did not mean that the British Government was entitled to claim it. Reading failed, however, and one of the grounds for the decision in the House of Lords was that he, as a non-commissioned officer, was in a fiduciary relation to the Crown, and was therefore under a duty to account for the profit wrongfully made.

Illegal or secret commissions or bribes obtained by a confidential servant or agent are recoverable by the principal or employer regardless of any loss by him.[87] If the fiduciary relationship in this case is accepted, the result merely follows the earlier cases on agents. The application of the rule to a policeman[88] and a staff-sergeant may be an extension; indeed it has been said that the speeches in the House of Lords in *Reading* v. *Attorney-General*[89] "confirm that the status of a fiduciary may ... be easily acquired."[90]

In the context of tracing, where the existence of a fiduciary relationship is equally significant, it was held in *Chase Manhattan Bank N.A.* v. *Israel-British Bank (London) Ltd.*,[91] that a fiduciary relationship arose where one bank mistakenly made a double payment to another.

In *Swain* v. *The Law Society*,[92] on the other hand, the House of Lords declined to find such a relationship.

The Society negotiated a compulsory insurance scheme on behalf of all solicitors. It kept the commission on the policy, which it applied for the purposes of the profession. The plaintiff, a solicitor, objected to the scheme and claimed that the Society must account for the commission as a profit made out of a fiduciary position. The alleged conflict of interest and duty lay in the fact that it was in the interest of the Society to negotiate a high premium (resulting in a higher commission) while its duty to the solicitors was to obtain a low one. The House of Lords, reversing the Court of Appeal, found

---

[87] (1968) 84 L.Q.R. 472 (G. H. Jones); *Brown* v. *I.R.C.* [1965] A.C. 244; *Mahesan* v. *Malaysia Government Officers Cooperative Housing Society Ltd.* [1979] A.C. 374; (1979) 95 L.Q.R. 68 (A. M. Tettenborn); *Lister & Co.* v. *Stubbs* (1890) 45 Ch.D. 1, *post*, p. 627; *Re Att.-Gen.'s Reference (No. 1 of 1985)* [1986] Q.B. 491; *Logicrose Ltd.* v. *Southend United Football Club Ltd.* [1988] 1 W.L.R. 1256 (principal can recover from agent whether he affirms or repudiates the transaction between the agent and the third party).

[88] *Att.-Gen* v. *Goddard* (1929) 98 L.J.K.B. 743 (bribes received when on duty).

[89] *Supra.*

[90] Goff and Jones, p. 655.

[91] [1981] Ch. 105, *post*, p. 628.

[92] [1983] A.C. 598; [1982] Conv. 447 (A. M. Kenny).

in favour of the Society. It had not acted unconscionably, and there was no fiduciary relationship. The scheme was entered into with statutory authority.[93] The Society was acting in its public capacity. Private law concepts such as accountability and breach of trust did not apply. If there was a breach of its public duty (which there was not), the remedy was judicial review.

(ii) Company Directors.[94] Company directors are treated as fiduciaries[95] in so far as they are prohibited from making a profit out of their office.[96] The leading case is the House of Lords decision in *Regal (Hastings) Ltd.* v. *Gulliver.*[97]

In that case R. Ltd. set up a subsidiary, A. Ltd., to acquire the leases of two cinemas. A. Ltd. had an authorised share capital of 5,000, £1 ordinary shares. The owner of the cinemas was only willing to lease them if the share capital of A. Ltd. was completely subscribed for. However, R. Ltd. had resources to subscribe for only 2,000 of the 5,000 shares and it was therefore agreed that the directors of R. Ltd. should subscribe for the remaining 3,000. This the directors did and when subsequently the business of R. Ltd. was transferred to new controllers the directors made a profit from their holdings in A. Ltd. The new controllers of R. Ltd. caused the company to bring an action against the ex-directors of R. Ltd. to account for this profit on the ground that the directors had made the profit from their office. In this action R. Ltd. was successful. The directors had made the profit out of their position as directors and, in the absence of shareholder approval,[98] they were obliged to account.

There are a number of features of *Regal* which need to be emphasised: First, the directors were found by the court to have acted bona fide, but the court was of the opinion that the liability of a fiduciary to account

[93] Solicitors Act 1974, s.37.
[94] See also Mitchell, *Directors' Duties and Insider Dealing* (1982); Company Securities (Insider Dealing) Act 1985; Financial Services Act 1986, Pt. VIII.
[95] The duty is traditionally regarded as owed to the company, not to the shareholders; *Percival* v. *Wright* [1902] 2 Ch. 421. But see (1975) 28 C.L.P. 83 (D. Prentice).
[96] The office of director should not, however, be equated with that of trustee. The assets of the company, unlike trust property, are not vested in the director but in the company which is a separate legal entity and, more importantly, directors "are . . . commercial men managing a trading concern for the benefit of themselves and of all other shareholders in it . . . ": *per* Jessel M.R. in *Re Forest of Dean Coal Mining Co. Ltd.* (1878) 10 Ch.D. 450, at pp. 451–452. See also *Re Faure Electric Accumulator Co.* (1889) 40 Ch.D. 141, at pp. 150–152.
[97] [1967] 2 A.C. 134n. This case was first reported in [1942] 2 All E.R. 378, but only found its way into the official reports after it had been cited extensively by the House of Lords in *Phipps* v. *Boardman* [1967] 2 A.C. 46.
[98] Lord Russell of Killowen considered that the shareholders could have ratified the director's breach of duty: [1967] 2 A.C. 134n. at p. 150. This is a very controversial aspect of the case, on which see (1958) 16 C.L.J. 93 at 102–106; (K. W. Wedderburn); *Prudential Assurance Co. Ltd.* v. *Newman Industries Ltd. (No. 2)* [1981] Ch. 257; (1981) 44 M.L.R. 202.

for a profit made from his office "in no way depends on fraud, or absence of bona fides."[99] Secondly, the new controllers obtained what was in effect a windfall. Having paid an agreed amount for the R. Ltd. shares they were able, for all intents and purposes, to recoup part of their expenditure by compelling the directors to account.[1] Thirdly, it was arguable that the directors by purchasing the shares in A. Ltd. had enabled R. Ltd. to enter into a transaction which it was otherwise commercially impossible for the company to enter into. While there is some truth in this, the decision that R. Ltd. did not have the necessary financial resources to enter into the transaction was made by the directors who were the very persons who benefited from this decision. Because of this a compelling argument can be made that a "reasonable man looking at the relevant facts and circumstances of the particular case would think that there was a real sensible possibility of conflict."[2]

The courts have imposed liability on directors to account where the directors have made the profit out of an economic opportunity, or information, even though they acquired it in a personal capacity, if it was information which could have been exploited by their company.[3]

In *Industrial Development Consultants Ltd.* v. *Cooley,*[4] the defendant was a director and general manager of the plaintiffs, who provided construction consultancy services for industrial enterprises. He attempted to interest a public Gas Board in a project, but was unsuccessful because the Gas Board's policy was not to employ development companies. The defendant was a distinguished architect who had worked in the gas industry for many years. For this reason the Gas Board decided to offer the contract to him personally, which he accepted, obtaining a release from the plaintiffs by falsely representing that he was ill. He was held to be liable to account to the plaintiffs for the profits from the contract.

The significance of the case is twofold. In the first place the court rejected Cooley's first line of defence, that the information concerning

[99] [1967] 2 A.C. 134n. at p. 144.

[1] See (1979) 42 M.L.R. 215. (D. Prentice).

[2] *Phipps* v. *Boardman* [1967] 2 A.C. 46 at p. 124, *per* Lord Upjohn. Although Lord Upjohn dissented, Lord Scarman in *Queensland Mines Ltd.* v. *Hudson* (1978) 18 A.L.R. 1 at p. 3 adopted his reasoning on the grounds that Lord Upjohn had "dissented on the facts, but not on the law."

[3] In most of the cases the company had developed an interest in the particular business opportunity, but the reasoning of the courts could also extend to situations where the opportunity falls within the general line of the company's business. See *Canadian Aero Service Ltd.* v. *O'Malley* (1973) 40 D.L.R. (3d) 371 (S.C.C.). For a recent example of a constructive trust imposed on a director in breach of his duty to disclose his interest in the company's contract, see *Guinness plc* v. *Saunders* [1988] 1 W.L.R. 863.

[4] [1972] 1 W.L.R. 443; [1972] 2 All E.R. 162 (the reports on the case are not identical); (1973) 89 L.Q.R. 187 (A. Yoran); (1972A) 30 C.L.J. 222 (J. G. Collier); (1972) 35 M.L.R. 655 (H. Rajak); (1972) 50 C.B.R. 623 (D. Prentice).

the Gas Board's contract came to him in his private capacity, and not as director of the plaintiffs; this "is the first case in which it was decided that the prohibition on exploiting a corporate opportunity applies also to an opportunity which was presented to the director personally and not in his capacity with the company."[5] Secondly, the decision whether or not the contract went to the company lay, not with the fiduciary, Cooley, but with a third party, the Gas Board.[6] In *Cooley's* case there were special circumstances; this was exactly the type of opportunity which the company relied on Cooley to obtain; furthermore, the absence of bona fides was clear. Also, the imposition of liability will provide directors with an incentive to channel relevant economic opportunities to their companies and not exploit them for their personal advantage.

But there are more recent decisions which suggest that the courts are evincing a more benign attitude towards directors.

In *Queensland Mines Ltd.* v. *Hudson*[7] the plaintiff company had been interested in developing a mining operation and the defendant (Hudson), the managing director of the company, was successful in obtaining for the company the licences necessary to enable it to do so. However, because of severe liquidity problems it could not proceed. Hudson resigned his position as managing director and, with the knowledge of the plaintiff company's board, successfully developed the mines. In an action to compel Hudson to account, the Privy Council held that Hudson was not liable, for either of two reasons: (a) the rejection of the opportunity by the plaintiff company because of cash difficulties took the venture outside the scope of Hudson's fiduciary duties or (b) because Hudson had acted with the full knowledge of the plaintiff company's board, they should be taken to have consented to his activities.[8]

This decision causes some difficulties.[9] First, to argue that a board's rejection of the opportunity for commercial reasons immunises a director against liability is difficult to reconcile with *Regal (Hastings) Ltd.* v. *Gulliver.* Although in the case Lord Reid deliberately left open

---

[5] (1973) 89 L.Q.R. 187 at p. 189.
[6] Roskill J. found that there was only a 10 per cent. chance that the Gas Board would have awarded the contract to the plaintiff company. Thus the case involved the paradoxical situation that the plaintiff company only benefited because Cooley had breached his duty.
[7] (1978) 18 A.L.R. 1 (P.C.). See also *Island Export Finance Ltd.* v. *Umunna* [1986] B.C.L.C. 460 (defendant not liable for developing a business opportunity after resigning as managing director because company was not actively pursuing the venture when he resigned, and his resignation was influenced not by any wish to acquire the business opportunity but by dissatisfaction with the company).
[8] (1978) 18 A.L.R. 1 at p. 10.
[9] (1979) 42 M.L.R. 711 (G. R. Sullivan).

the question of the effect of board rejection,[10] it is difficult to see how there would still not be a serious conflict of interest if directors were permitted to acquire for themselves opportunities which they had rejected on behalf of the company. To argue that the board could condone Hudson's breach is also difficult to accept unquestioningly as the appropriate organ of the company is the shareholders' meeting.[11] If the line of reasoning in *Queensland Mines Ltd.* v. *Hudson* were to be expanded, it would lead to the development of a line of defences, (such as bona fides,[12] illegality,[13] *ultra vires,*[14] inability, or lack of desire on the part of the company to exploit the opportunity[15]) available to directors charged with breach of duty, a development which the law hitherto has not countenanced. Such a development would also have significant implications for fiduciary duties in general.[16]

(iii) Boardman v. Phipps. Many of the difficulties relating to the application of the rule came to the fore in *Boardman* v. *Phipps.*[17]

The Phipps trust owned a substantial minority holding of shares in L.H. Company. John Phipps, the plaintiff and respondent, was one of the beneficiaries under the trust, and the defendants (appellants) were Boardman, a solicitor, and Tom Phipps, also a beneficiary. The trustees were Mrs. Phipps, an elderly widow who died in 1958, Mrs Noble, her daughter, and Fox, an accountant. Boardman acted as solicitor to the trust.

In 1956 the appellants were dissatisfied with the way in which the affairs of the company were managed. They made various inquiries on behalf of the trust, and in that capacity obtained confidential information about the company. They learned that the value of the company's assets was high although the profits were low; and realised that it would be advantageous to sell some of the non-profit-

---

[10] [1967] 2 A.C. 137n. at pp. 152–153. In *Peso Silver Mines Ltd.* v. *Cropper* (1966) 58 D.L.R. (2d.) 1 (S.C.C.), it was held that board rejection did immunise a director against any action to account. But this decision has not gone uncriticised; (1967) 30 M.L.R. 450 (D. Prentice); (1971) 49 C.B.R. 80 (S. M. Beck).

[11] (1979) 42 M.L.R. at pp. 712–713 (G. R. Sullivan).

[12] *i.e.* the directors acted bona fide. This was rejected in *Regal (Hastings) Ltd.* v. *Gulliver* [1967] 2 A.C. 137n.

[13] *i.e.* it would be illegal for the company to enter into the transaction. This is implicity rejected by *Parker* v. *McKenna* (1874) 10 Ch.App. 96; *Reading* v. *Att.-Gen.* [1951] A.C. 507.

[14] *i.e.* it would be beyond the company's capacity to enter into the transaction. This was rejected in a dictum in *Fire Industrial Commodities Ltd.* v. *Powling* (1954) 71 R.P.C. 253 at p. 258.

[15] The inability would arise because the third party would not deal with the company or it lacked the necessary resources. These, of course, were the issues dealt with in *Regal (Hastings) Ltd.* v. *Gulliver* [1967] 2 A.C. 137n. and *Industrial Development Consultants Ltd.* v. *Cooley* [1972] 1 W.L.R. 443. *Cf. Island Export Finances* v. *Umunna* [1986] B.C.L.C. 460, *ante*, p. 570, n. 7.

[16] See (1968) 84 L.Q.R. 472 (G. H. Jones).

[17] [1967] 2 A.C. 46; (1968) 84 L.Q.R. 472 (G. H. Jones); [1978] Conv. 114 (B. A. K. Rider).

making assets. They obtained control of the company by purchasing the remainder of the company's shares, and carried out the desired sales and reorganisation. The transaction was highly profitable. The trust gained in respect of its holding and the appellants gained in respect of the shares which they had purchased for the purpose of obtaining control.

Boardman had informed the beneficiaries and the two active trustees (Mrs. Phipps being senile and taking no part in the affairs of the trust) giving them an outline of the negotiations and asking them whether they had any objection to his taking a personal interest, bearing in mind that his initial inquiry had been on behalf of the trust. Boardman acted bona fide throughout and thought that he had made a full disclosure and had the beneficiaries' consent. Wilberforce J. however found that the respondent was justified in thinking that he had only been told half the truth. The trustees had been invited to consider whether the trust should find the money for the purchase of the shares; but the trustees were unable and unwilling to do so.

John Phipps then called upon the appellants to account for the profits which they had made from the operation. Wilberforce J., the Court of Appeal and the House of Lords (3–2) held that they must account for the profits made; but having acted bona fide, they were entitled to payment on a liberal scale for the work and skill they had displayed.[18]

A number of points of importance arise from the case. First, Boardman was not, of course, a trustee. The fiduciary relation arose from the fact of his employment as solicitor by the trustees. He was not, however, employed to act for the trust in the dealings in question and he claimed, as he stated at the time, to have been acting in a private capacity. The members of the House of Lords took different views on this issue. In the early negotiations with L. H. Company, the appellants, who were not shareholders in their own right, purported to represent the trust, although strictly they did not do so. So Lord Cohen, in the majority, said[19] "that information and that opportunity they owed to their representing themselves as agents for the holders of the 8,000 shares held by the trustees." Lord Upjohn, dissenting[20]: "though they portrayed themselves as representing the Phipps Trust, it is quite clear the offer was made by these two personally."

Secondly, the liability of the appellants was unaffected by the fact

---

[18] *Ante*, p. 558.
[19] *Boardman* v. *Phipps* [1967] 2 A.C. 46 at p. 103.
[20] *Ibid.* at p. 120; see also Viscount Dilhorne at p. 91; and *N.Z. Netherlands Society* v. *Kuys* [1973] 1 W.L.R. 1126, (1973) 37 Conv.(N.S.) 362, where the honorary secretary of the appellant society was held not to be acting in a fiduciary capacity, when he launched a newspaper for the Dutch community in New Zealand in place of a previous bulletin which the Society produced and which failed.

that the trust had lost nothing; nor that the trust had greatly benefited; nor did it matter that the Phipps Trust could not have found the money; nor that the trustees would not have wished to use the money for that purpose even if they had it; nor that such user would have been in breach of trust, unless they had applied to the court and obtained consent to the investment.[21]

Thirdly, it is extremely difficult to determine the limits, if any, of this inflexible rule. In *Aas* v. *Benham*,[22] Lindley L.J. laid down that information obtained in the course of a partnership business must not be used by the partners for their own benefit within the scope of the partnership business; but that they may make use of it for "purposes which are wholly without the scope of the firm's business. . . . It is not the source of the information, but the use to which it is applied, which is important in such matters."[23] This was not disapproved in *Boardman* v. *Phipps*,[24] but it seems that a stricter view there prevailed; the appellants were held accountable because they had obtained the information by purporting to represent the trust; and although they were acting independently when they made the purchase. It is submitted that it is difficult to answer Lord Upjohn's argument in dissent[25]: "I think, again, that some of the trouble that has arisen in this case, it being assumed rightly that throughout he was in such a [fiduciary] capacity, is that it has been assumed that it has necessarily followed that any profit made by him renders him accountable to the trustees. That is not so. . . . It is perfectly clear that a solicitor can if he so desires act against his clients in any matter in which he has not been retained by them provided, of course, that in acting for them generally he has not learnt information or placed himself in a position which would make it improper for him to act against them. This is an obvious application of the rule that he must not place himself in a position where his duty and his interest conflict. So, in general, a solicitor can deal in shares in a company in which the client is a shareholder, subject always to the general rule that the solicitor must never place himself in a position where his interest and his duty conflict; and in this connection it may be pointed out that the interest and duty may refer (and frequently do) to a conflict of interest and duty on behalf of different clients and have nothing to do with any conflict between the personal interest and duty of the solicitor, beyond his interest in earning his fees." His Lordship concluded "To extend the doctrines of equity to make the appellants accountable in such circumstances, is, in my

---

[21] Lord Denning M.R. in the Court of Appeal mentioned this as a source of a potential conflict of interest and duty; [1965] Ch. 992, at p. 1020. The suggestion, however, seems unrealistic. See [1967] 2 A.C. 46 at pp. 92, 124; *cf.* Lord Cohen at pp. 103–104.

[22] [1891] 2 Ch. 244.

[23] *Ibid.* at p. 256.

[24] [1967] 2 A.C. 46.

[25] *Ibid.* at p. 126.

judgment, to make unreasonable and inequitable applications of such doctrines."[26]

If this rule applies, the only escape of the fiduciary is that he made full disclosure, and obtained the consent of the other parties. It is not, however, clear whether the "other parties" are the trustees or the beneficiaries. In the straightforward case of a profit made by a trustee, the relevant consent must be that of the beneficiaries, to whom the duty is owed. Difficulties will arise if any of the beneficiaries are minors or unborn. Also, as we have seen, the trustee runs the risk that what he, bona fide, thought was disclosure may later be held inadequate. *Boardman* v. *Phipps,*[27] however, was not such a case. Boardman was a fiduciary agent, the principals being the trustees. To whom did he owe his fiduciary duties? Presumably consent must be obtained from those persons. If the trustees had not consented, they would, as principals, have a right of recovery against their agent, any money thus recovered being held by them on trust for the beneficiaries. If the trustees had consented, the agent would nevertheless be liable to the beneficiaries if he owed fiduciary duties to *them.*[28] The result of *Boardman* v. *Phipps*[29] was that the beneficiary successfully sued the agent, but the basis of this is not clear. Their Lordships spoke, rather ambiguously, of his being a fiduciary "to the trust".[30] Lord Guest spoke of the "knowledge and assent of the trustees."[31] Lord Hodson held that the relevant consent was that of the beneficiary; Boardman "was in a fiduciary position *vis-à-vis* the trustees, and through them *vis-à-vis* the beneficiaries."[32] Viscount Dilhorne regarded the consent of the principals as necessary, but also referred to the fact that the beneficiary was not fully informed.[33] Lord Upjohn said that Boardman was "in a fiduciary capacity at least to the trustees. Whether he was ever in a fiduciary capacity to the respondent was not debated before your lordships and I do not think that it matters."[34]

It is important that a person acting bona fide in these matters should know exactly what his duties are. Boardman thought that he had made full disclosure both to the trustees and to the respondent. Wilberforce J., however, held that the disclosure to the respondent was inadeq-

---

[26] *Ibid.* at pp. 133–134, quoting Lord Selborne L.C. in *Barnes* v. *Addy* (1874) 9 Ch. App. 244, at p. 251.

[27] *Supra.*

[28] Presumably the beneficiaries could sue the trustees in such circumstances even if they could not sue the agent.

[29] *Supra.*

[30] [1967] 2 A.C. 46 at pp. 100, 104, 110.

[31] *Ibid.* at p. 117.

[32] *Ibid.* at p. 112. Lord Cohen also regarded the consent of the beneficiary as necessary; *Ibid.* at p. 104.

[33] *Ibid.* at p. 93.

[34] *Ibid.* at pp. 125–126.

uate.[35] Boardman had obtained the consent of the two active trustees to his taking a personal interest in the purchase at an early stage. The third trustee, Mrs. Phipps, was not informed because she was then too old to take any interest in the matters of the trust.

If therefore the duty in the particular circumstances was to obtain the consent of the trustees, the failure to do so was due to a mere formality. Although trustees must act jointly, it does not seem to be sound to make the issue in such a case as this depend on the technicality of the addressing of a third envelope to a trustee who in fact took no part; and whose consent would have been meaningless.

Finally, it is important to determine what remedy was decreed in *Boardman* v. *Phipps*.[36] This is discussed below.

(iv) The Extent of the Fiduciary Principle. Essentially the problem is one of determining the limits of the rule. "Rules of equity have to be applied to such a great diversity of circumstances that they may be stated only in the most general terms and applied with particular attention to the exact circumstances of each case."[37] If a fiduciary obtains a benefit for himself at the expense of his beneficiary, there is no difficulty. The case is one of unjust enrichment, and generally speaking, an action in the nature of a quasi-contractual action will lie. The position is more difficult where the beneficiary loses nothing; where he did not wish to make the profitable purchase which the trustee makes; where the fiduciary acted honestly; or even where the fiduciary conferred by his activities every possible benefit on the beneficiary, but received an additional benefit for himself. A windfall has been received through the exertions of the fiduciary; the beneficiary has risked nothing, and lost nothing; should he be entitled to the profits?[38]

Lord Hodson in *Boardman* v. *Phipps*[39] answered this question in the affirmative, allowing only one exception. "The proposition of law involved in this case is that no person standing in a fiduciary position, where a demand is made upon him by the person to whom he stands in the fiduciary relationship to account for profits acquired by him by reason of his fiduciary position and by reason of the opportunity and the knowledge, or either, resulting from it, is entitled to defeat the

---

[35] [1964] 1 W.L.R. 993; *cf. N.Z. Netherlands Society* v. *Kuys* [1973] 1 W.L.R. 1126; *Queensland Mines Ltd.* v. *Hudson* (1978) 52 A.L.J.R. 399; (1979) 42 M.L.R. 711 (G. R. Sullivan).

[36] [1967] 2 A.C. 46.

[37] *Boardman* v. *Phipps* [1967] 2 A.C. 46 at p. 123.

[38] See generally (1968) 84 L.Q.R. 472 (G. H. Jones). Oakley, *Constructive Trusts* (2nd ed.), p. 84 advocates liability only in cases of actual abuse of the fiduciary position.

[39] [1967] 2 A.C. 46; *Boston Deep Sea Fishing and Ice Co.* v. *Ansell* (1888) 39 Ch.D. 339; *Lister & Co.* v. *Stubbs* (1890) 45 Ch.D. 1; *Metropolitan Bank* v. *Heiron* (1880) 5 Ex.D. 319; *Parker* v. *McKenna* (1874) L.R. 10 Ch.App. 96; *Industrial Development Consultants Ltd.* v. *Cooley* [1972] 1 W.L.R. 443.

claim upon any ground save that he made profits with the knowledge and assent of the other person."[40]

Such a principle might be criticised on the ground that it fails to draw any distinction between the honest and the dishonest fiduciary. Both are equally liable. This is so; however, it should be borne in mind that the honest fiduciary may be remunerated by order of the court, as in *Boardman* v. *Phipps*.[41] A dishonest fiduciary, on the other hand, may be made to pay a higher rate of interest in cases where the remedy is personal accountability.[42]

But this still leaves open the question, to be determined on the facts of each case, whether the opportunity for profit arose by reason of the fiduciary position.[43] For example, a merchant banker, stockbroker, insurance broker, solicitor or company director learns through the proper course of his business information from a confidential source which may be of advantage to other clients in companies with which he is associated. Having satisfied the requirements of a particular client, is he precluded from making use of this information in respect of other trusts with which he is concerned? Or for himself? Similarly with the directors of several (non-competing) companies? Or, does his fiduciary duty to the second client place him under a duty to provide that client with the confidential information, to avoid the risk of liability for misrepresentation through failure to disclose relevant information to a fiduciary.[44] There is the danger that the rule, if applied inflexibly, may impose an impossible burden: As Lord Cohen said in *Boardman* v. *Phipps*,[45] " . . . it does not necessarily follow that because an agent acquired information and opportunity while acting in a fiduciary capacity he is accountable to his principals for any profit that comes his way as the result of the use he makes of that information and opportunity. His liability to account must depend on the facts of the case." Viscount Dilhorne[46] quoted Lindley L.J. as saying "to hold that a partner can never derive any personal benefit from information which he obtains from a partner would be manifestly absurd."[47]

It is difficult to formulate any single test which may be applied to determine whether a fiduciary has incurred liability. It is submitted that liability will arise if any of the following factors is present:

---

[40] *Boardman* v. *Phipps, supra,* at p. 105. As to acquiescence, see *Swain* v. *Law Society* [1982] 1 W.L.R. 17 (C.A.).

[41] *Supra.* A fiduciary guilty of undue influence has, however, been remunerated by the court; *O'Sullivan* v. *Management Agency and Music Ltd.* [1985] Q.B. 428, *ante,* p. 558; *cf. Guinness plc* v. *Saunders* [1988] 1 W.L.R. 863.

[42] *Post,* p. 602.

[43] (1970) 86 L.Q.R. 463 (G. H. Jones).

[44] See a valuable discussion in [1978] Conv. 114 (B. A. K. Rider); *Anglo-African Merchants Ltd.* v. *Bayley* [1970] 1 Q.B. 311; *North and South Trust Co.* v. *Berkeley* [1971] 1 W.L.R. 470; (1972) 35 M.L.R. 78 (M. Kay and D. Yates).

[45] [1967] 2 A.C. 46 at pp. 102–103; see also Lord Upjohn at p. 126.

[46] *Ibid.* at p. 90.

[47] *Aas* v. *Benham* [1891] 2 Ch. 244 at pp. 255–256.

(a) The fiduciary has used trust property, even if there was no actual or potential conflict of interest and duty (*Boardman* v. *Phipps.*)[48];

(b) The opportunity to make a profit arose from the fiduciary relationship, even if no trust property was used (*Reading* v. *Att.-Gen.*)[49];

(c) There was a conflict of interest and duty, even if no trust property was used, and the opportunity did not arise from the fiduciary relationship (*Industrial Development Consultants Ltd.* v. *Cooley*).[50]

C. Remedies

We have seen that profits may come to a trustee or other fiduciary in many ways. It is often said that a fiduciary who is required to account for such profits becomes a constructive trustee. But a duty to account is a personal liability; a constructive trust is a proprietary remedy; the significance of the distinction appears where the fiduciary is bankrupt, and the question is whether the beneficiaries can claim ahead of the general creditors. A related question is whether the proprietary remedy of tracing is available. The question is discussed in Chapter 22. Its significance can be clearly seen in the bribes cases, such as *Lister & Co.* v. *Stubbs.*[51] Liability to account is not synonymous with constructive trusteeship, but the cases do not always maintain the distinction. Indeed, Lord Lane C.J. has said "We find it impossible to reconile much of the language used in these decisions."[52]

In *Boardman* v. *Phipps,*[53] Wilberforce J. had held that the shares were held on constructive trust for the beneficiaries; and that Boardman was accountable for profits he made, less a sum for his skill and effort. The House of Lords did not distinguish between accountability and constructive trust. Lord Guest concluded that "the appellants hold the Lester and Harris shares as constructive trustees, and are bound to account to the respondent."[54] The other members spoke of accountability only.

As submitted above, there is a difference between a duty to hold specific property on trust and a duty to account. Could Boardman have

---

[48] *Supra*; but see *Guinness plc* v. *Saunders* [1988] 1 W.L.R. 863 at 870, where Fox L.J. said that the defendants in *Boardman* v. *Phipps* "had misused for their own benefit an opportunity (which belonged to the trust) to make a profit. They had not received trust property." See also Stephenson L.J. in *Swain* v. *Law Society* [1982] 1 W.L.R. 17 at p. 31: there must be a possibility of a conflict of interest and duty, and a nexus between the fiduciary position and the profit made.

[49] [1951] A.C. 507.

[50] [1972] 1 W.L.R. 443.

[51] (1890) 45 Ch.D. 1, *post*, p. 627; (1959) 75 L.Q.R. 234 (R. H. Maudsley); *Re Att.-Gen.'s Reference (No. 1 of 1985)* [1986] Q.B. 491.

[52] *Re Att.-Gen.'s Reference (No. 1 of 1985)*, *supra*, at p. 503.

[53] [1967] 2 A.C. 46. The decision in *Guinness plc* v. *Saunders* [1988] 1 W.L.R. 863, *post*, n. 55, was clearly the imposition of a constructive trust.

[54] *Ibid.* at p. 117.

satisfied the judgment by payment of the value of the shares at that time? Would a purchaser (with notice) have taken the shares subject to the same obligation? What would have been the position if Boardman had been bankrupt? Or if he had sold the shares and placed the money in a mixed account with his own, and then gone bankrupt? None of these matters arose, and it was not necessary to discuss them. They do however raise questions of great importance, which are discussed in Chapter 22. The point here is that the duty to hold property as constructive trustee is very different from a duty to account; and that each of these situations is related to, but again different from, the equitable remedy of tracing.

If the fiduciary has used trust property, as in *Boardman* v. *Phipps*,[55] then any profits made, it is submitted, should be held on constructive trust for the beneficiaries.[56] Where, on the other hand, the profit is made without any use of trust property, as in *Industrial Developments Consultants Ltd.* v. *Cooley*[57] and *Reading* v. *Att.-Gen.*,[58] then the result should be accountability.[59]

---

[55] *Supra,* where confidential information was held to be trust property. This finding is criticised in (1968) 84 L.Q.R. 472 (G. H. Jones) and Oakley, *Constructive Trusts* (2nd ed.), p. 78. See *Guiness plc* v. *Saunders* [1988] 1 W.L.R. 863 at p. 870, where Fox L.J. imposed a constructive trust on the basis of the combination of three factors: the fiduciary relationship; breach of duty arising in respect of that fiduciary relationship; and the receipt, in breach of duty, of property belonging to the person to whom the duty was owed. See also *Att.-Gen.* v. *Guardian Newspapers Ltd. (No. 2)* [1988] 3 W.L.R. 776, suggesting that the *Spycatcher* copyright was held on constructive trust for the Crown.

[56] *In Re Att.-Gen.'s Reference (No. 1 of 1985)* [1986] Q.B. 491 it was suggested that a trustee who profits from trust property holds the profit as constructive trustee (as opposed to being merely accountable) only if the profit is identifiable as a separate piece of property. This unorthodox view is examined *post*, p. 629.

[57] [1972] 1 W.L.R. 443, *ante*, p. 569.

[58] [1951] A.C. 507, *ante*, p. 566.

[59] As to whether this should preclude the tracing remedy, see *Lister & Co.* v. *Stubbs* (1890) 45 Ch.D. 1, *post*, p. 627; Goff and Jones, p. 657.

CHAPTER 21

VARIATION OF TRUSTS

1. The Background

A TRUSTEE must administer the trust according to its terms. Any deviation is a breach of trust for which the trustee will be personally liable at the instance of an injured party.[1] However, any adult beneficiary *sui juris* may deal with his equitable interest under the trust in any way he wishes; and may consent to the trustee dealing with the trust funds in a way which affects his interest. Further, adult beneficiaries who together are absolutely entitled to the trust property may terminate the trust and demand that the fund be handed over to them[2]; but not if any interests are outstanding.[3]

They may wish to do this for various reasons. In *Saunders* v. *Vautier*,[4] the beneficiary wished to terminate an accumulation which was to continue until he reached 25; he was able to claim the fund at 21. If property is given to A for life and then to B, and both A and B are adult, they may each wish to have capital immediately available, and may agree to partition the fund. The most potent factor however in persuading them to do so is the possibility of reducing tax liability and

---

[1] *Ante*, p. 457; *post*, p. 597.
[2] *Saunders* v. *Vautier* (1841) Cr. & Ph. 240; *Re Chardon* [1928] Ch. 464; *Re Smith* [1928] Ch. 915; *Re Nelson* [1928] Ch. 920n; *Re Becket's Settlement* [1940] Ch. 279; *Re A.E.G. Unit Trust* [1957] Ch. 415.
[3] *Berry* v. *Green* [1938] A.C. 575; *Re Robb* [1953] Ch. 459; *Re Wragg* [1959] 1 W.L.R. 922.
[4] (1841) Cr. & Ph. 240.

especially liability for inheritance tax on the death of A. Inheritance tax, an outline of which was given in Chapter 9, is chargeable on transfers on or within seven years before death. It is also chargeable on certain *inter vivos* transfers even if the transferor survives for seven years, for example the creation of a discretionary trust, although in such a case the rate is lower.[5] In the case of a non-discretionary trust, the advantage of partitioning the fund between life tenant and remainderman is that, provided the life tenant survives for seven years (which may be covered by insurance), no tax will be payable on the partition, whereas the whole capital is taxable if the life interest terminates on death.[6]

It may be advantageous in terms of income tax liability to share out the entitlement to income. Whether or not a variation is a disposal for capital gains tax purposes has never been decided.[7] As far as inheritance tax is concerned, trustees of a discretionary trust may wish to improve the tax position of the settlement by converting it to a trust where there is an interest in possession or to an accumulation and maintenance settlement.[8] Such a conversion will itself be taxable.[9] The tax saving aspect of the matter is emphasised here because it has been the motive force in the passing of the Variation of Trusts Act 1958, and the variations which have been made under it. "Nearly every variation" said Lord Denning M.R. "that has come before the court has tax-avoidance for its principal object."[10] Variations have, of course, been made for other purposes, as will be seen.

One particular tax exemption should be noted. Where, not more than two years after a death of a person, testate or intestate, the disposition of his property taking effect upon his death is varied by an instrument in writing, such a variation is not a transfer of value for inheritance tax purposes,[11] nor a disposal for capital gains tax purposes,[12] and the variation takes effect as if made by the deceased. These provisions may be of great help where, for example, a wealthy testator has created a disadvantageous discretionary trust in a will coming into effect after March 26, 1974.[13] They clearly apply to an agreed variation by adult beneficiaries and to a variation under the Variation of Trusts Act 1958. A similar principle applies to an order under the Family Provision legislation.[14]

---

[5] Inheritance Tax Act 1984, s.7.
[6] F.A. (No. 2) 1987, s.96.
[7] Harris, *Variation of Trusts*, pp. 97 *et seq.*
[8] *Ante*, p. 220.
[9] *Ante*, p. 219.
[10] In *Re Weston's Settlements* [1969] 1 Ch. 234 at p. 245.
[11] Inheritance Tax Act 1984, ss.17, 142.
[12] C.G.T.A. 1979, s.49(6).
[13] Inheritance Tax Act 1984, Part III, Chap. III, *ante*, p. 218.
[14] *Ibid.*, s.146.

2. Variations which Need the Approval of the Court[15]

We have seen that minors and persons not *sui juris* are not able to deal irrevocably with their property. If a situation arose where variations needed to be made to a trust in the interests of such persons, nothing could be done which involved any negotiation with or compromise by the persons under disability, without the approval of the court. The person under disability could be benefited at the expense of the adult parties. The life tenant may be willing to agree to an advancement by the trustees,[16] or to surrender his life interest. But if the life tenant wanted something in return, there was no way in which he could negotiate it.

Yet, especially in the tax context, it was in the interest of the remaindermen that the variation should be made. Adult remaindermen could agree to a variation; it was hard for infants, persons under a disability and unborn persons to be denied advantages which competent adults could obtain for themselves. The court, however, has no inherent jurisdiction to vary a trust in favour of infants and unborn persons.[17] But there are cases where the court can intervene, and these have been substantially increased by several statutes.

A. Inherent Jurisdiction

(i) **Salvage and Emergency.** A court has inherent power in the case of absolute necessity to sanction the mortgage of an infant's property in order to protect the property which he retains. The jurisdiction is very narrow and is usual where expenditure is necessary to save buildings from collapse.[18] An extension of this jurisdiction allows the court in an emergency, not foreseen or anticipated by the settlor, to authorise the trustees to perform certain acts which are beyond the powers given to them in the trust instrument, where this is in the best interests of the trust estate and where the consent of all the beneficiaries cannot be obtained because they are not in existence or are under a disability.

In *Re New*,[19] the court approved a scheme of capital reconstruction of a company, splitting the shares into different and smaller denominations, and authorised the trustees to take the new shares, subject to an undertaking to apply for further authorisation to retain the shares after one year. This decision was said in *Re Tollemache*[20] to be the

[15] (1954) 17 M.L.R. 420 (O. R. Marshall); Harris, *Variation of Trusts*.
[16] *Pilkington* v. *I.R.C.* [1964] A.C. 612, *ante*, p. 550.
[17] *Chapman* v. *Chapman* [1954] A.C. 429.
[18] *Re Jackson* (1882) 21 Ch.D. 786; *Conway* v. *Fenton* (1888) 40 Ch.D. 512; *Re Montagu* [1897] 2 Ch. 8 at p. 11, *per* Lopes L.J.
[19] [1901] 2 Ch. 534.
[20] [1903] 1 Ch. 457, affirmed, *ibid.* at p. 955.

"high water-mark" of the emergency jurisdiction. Kekewich J. and the Court of Appeal refused to sanction a widening of the trustees' investment powers merely because this would be for the advantage of the beneficiaries. There was no emergency. It is clear that the jurisdiction applies to administrative matters only, and does not cover schemes for the variation of beneficial interests.

(ii) **Compromise.**[21] Until the decision of the House of Lords in *Chapman* v. *Chapman*[22] in 1954, the courts had accepted a wide definition of the word "compromise" as the basis of a useful jurisdiction to approve a variation from the terms of a trust although there was no dispute between the parties in any real sense of the term. The cases were more akin to bargains or exchanges approved by the court as being fair to infants or remaindermen, than to compromised litigation. There was a question whether the jurisdiction effected a variation of beneficial interests as distinct from varying the property subject to the trusts,[23] and the jurisdiction did not extend to the redrafting of a settlement as such—there had to be some element of composition of rights.[24] But this distinction was of course paper-thin. Denning L.J., the minority judge in the Court of Appeal in the *Chapman* case, would have got round the difficulty by accepting for the courts a general jurisdiction to vary trusts on behalf of those unascertained or not *sui juris*, but the House of Lords preferred the other solution—that of limiting the jurisdiction to sanction compromises to cases where there was a genuine dispute. Nor could matters that did not genuinely contain an element of dispute be made to look as if they did.[25] Where there is a genuine dispute, the court of course has power to sanction a compromise, even if the compromise solution contains tax-saving advantages for the beneficiaries.

In *Allen* v. *Distillers Co. (Biochemicals) Ltd.*[26] the question was whether the court, in approving a settlement of the action of the child victims of the thalidomide drug, had jurisdiction to postpone the vesting of the capital in the children to an age greater than 18. Eveleigh J. held that the court had no inherent jurisdiction to order a postponement; a beneficiary with a vested interest under a trust was entitled to demand possession on majority.[27] Nor was there a trust to which the Variation of Trusts Act 1958 applied; the payment out to

---

[21] (1954) 17 M.L.R. 427 (O. R. Marshall).
[22] [1954] A.C. 429.
[23] *Re Downshire Settled Estates* [1953] Ch. 218, discussing *Re Trenchard* [1902] 1 Ch. 378.
[24] *Re Chapman's S.T.* [1953] Ch. 218.
[25] *Re Powell-Cotton's Resettlement* [1956] 1 W.L.R. 23. Nor should the trustees, in their application to court for the exercise of the compromise jurisdiction, insert an unrelated claim for increased remuneration; *Re Barbour's Settlement Trusts* [1974] 1 W.L.R. 1198.
[26] [1974] Q.B. 384.
[27] *Saunders* v. *Vautier* (1841) 4 Beav. 115; *ante*, p. 579.

trustees of sums paid into court did not give rise to the kind of trust contemplated by that Act. However, it was found that the terms of the settlement of the action were wide enough to authorise a postponement of payment.

A recent attempt to invoke the court's compromise jurisdiction occurred in the case of *Mason* v. *Farbrother*,[28] where trustees of a pension fund set up in 1929 for Co-operative Society employees had power to invest principally in the society itself and otherwise in authorised trustee securities. By 1982, as a result of inflation, the fund had increased to £127 million, and the trustees, who were anxious to have the wide powers of investment appropriate for modern pension funds, applied to the court for approval of an investment clause giving wider powers than those of the Trustee Investments Act 1961. The trustees were uncertain as to the proper construction of the original investment clause, one view being that the whole fund should be invested in the society, and the other that the whole should be invested under the 1961 Act. This was sufficient to give the court jurisdiction, as genuine points of difference existed. It was not necessary that there should be a contested dispute. While a compromise need not be something between the two views, it was doubtful whether the court could substitute an entirely new investment clause. Thus the variation was not permitted as an exercise of the court's jurisdiction to approve a compromise. (It was, however, authorised by section 57 of the Trustee Act 1925).[29]

B. Statutory Provisions (other than Variation of Trusts Act 1958)

(i) **Trustee Act 1925, s.57(1).** "Where in the management or administration of any property vested in trustees, any sale, lease, mortgage, surrender, release, or other disposition, or any purchase, investment, acquisition, expenditure, or other transaction, is in the opinion of the court expedient, but the same cannot be effected by reason of the absence of any power for that purpose vested in the trustees by the trust instrument, if any, or by law, the court may by order confer upon the trustees . . . the necessary power . . . on such terms . . . as the court may think fit . . . "

This subsection overlaps the "emergency" jurisdiction discussed above,[30] and widens it by making the statutory jurisdiction available in cases of expediency rather than emergency. It operates as if its provisions were read into every settlement.[31] It is clear from the opening words of the section that it is only available in questions arising in the *management* or *administration* of property; it is not therefore available

[28] [1983] 2 All E.R. 1078; All E.R. Rev. 1984, p. 308 (P. J. Clarke).
[29] *Post*, p. 583.
[30] *Ante*, p. 581.
[31] *Re Mair* [1935] Ch. 562; see also *Re Salting* [1932] 2 Ch. 57, *ante*, p. 187.

for the purpose of remoulding beneficial interests or for tax saving generally.[32]

Applications are usually made in Chambers, and it is not possible to learn from reported cases the full scope of the operation of the sub-section. It has however been effectively used to authorise the sale of land where necessary consents had been refused[33]; to authorise parti-tion,[34] and to blend two charitable trusts into a single fund[35]; to autho-rise wider investment powers,[36] the purchase of a residence for the tenant for life,[37] and the sale of a reversionary interest which under the terms of the trust instrument was not to be sold until it fell into possession.[38]

(ii) Settled Land Act 1925, s.64(1). "Any transaction affecting or concerning the settled land, or any part thereof, or any other land ... which in the opinion of the court would be for the benefit of the settled land, or any part thereof, or the persons interested under the settlement, may, under an order of the court, be effected by a tenant for life, if it is one which could have been validly effected by an absolute owner."[39]

It will be seen that this subsection is wider than Trustee Act, s.57(1). The transactions in respect of which the court is empowered to make an order are those which will be for the benefit of the settled land or of any persons interested under the settlement. "Transaction" is widely defined[40]; and there is no limitation restricting the court's powers to cases of management and administration.[41] The subsection enables the court to effect the alteration of beneficial interests in such a way as to reduce tax liability[42] and was the most effective vehicle for this purpose before 1958. It applies however only to cases of settled land, and to land held on trust for sale,[43] and not to the ordinary case of a personalty settlement.

(iii) Trustee Act 1925, s.53.[44] Under section 53 the court is given power to make an order authorising certain dealings with an infant's

---

[32] *Re Downshire S.E.* [1953] Ch. 218; *cf. Re Forster's Settlement* [1954] 3 All E.R. 714.
[33] *Re Beale's S.T.* [1932] 2 Ch. 15.
[34] *Re Thomas* [1930] 1 Ch. 194.
[35] *Re Harvey* [1941] 3 All E.R. 284.
[36] *Re Shipwrecked Fishermen and Mariners' Royal Benevolent Society* [1959] Ch. 220; *cf. Re Powell-Cotton's Resettlement* [1956] 1 W.L.R. 23; *Mason* v. *Farbrother* [1983] 2 All E.R. 1078.
[37] *Re Power* [1947] Ch. 572; (1947) 91 S.J. 541; Snell, p. 222.
[38] *Re Cockerell's S.T.* [1956] Ch. 372.
[39] See also Settled Land and Trustee Acts (Court's General Powers) Act 1943.
[40] S.L.A. 1925, s.64(2). See *Raikes* v. *Lygon* [1988] 1 W.L.R. 281.
[41] It is used for such purposes. *Re White-Popham's S.E.* [1936] Ch. 725; *Re Scarisbrick's Re-Settlement Estates* [1944] Ch. 229; *Re Mount Edgcumbe* [1950] Ch. 615; *Re Rycroft's Settlement* [1962] Ch. 263.
[42] *Re Downshire S.E.* [1953] Ch. 218; *Raikes* v. *Lygon* [1988] 1 W.L.R. 281.
[43] *Re Simmons* [1956] Ch. 125; L.P.A. 1925, s.28.
[44] (1957) 21 Conv.(N.S.) 448 (O. R. Marshall).

property "with a view to the application of the capital or income thereof for the maintenance, education, or benefit of the infant." As with section 57, the section overlaps and extends the inherent power to make provision for the maintenance of minors. The word "benefit" has been widely construed, and the court has authorised transactions whose object was the reduction of estate duty for the minor's benefit.[45] Thus, entails have been barred in order to exclude the interests of large numbers of remote beneficiaries with a view to raising money for the minor's benefit[46] or to simplifying an application to the court under the Variation of Trusts Act 1958[47]; and reversionary interests have been sold to the tenant for life.[48] However, the proceeds of sale should be resettled; this will be an "application" for the minor's benefit[49]; while an outright payment to him of the proceeds of sale will not be.[50]

(iv) Matrimonial Causes Act 1973. The court has wide power to make orders affecting the property of parties to matrimonial proceedings. It may order capital provision to be made, by cash payment, or property transfer, or by the making of a settlement for the benefit of the other spouse and the children of the family.[51] It may also effect the variation of ante-nuptial or post-nuptial settlements,[52] and the variation of orders for settlements made under the Act.[53]

(v) Mental Health Act 1983. Mental Health Act 1983, s.96(1)(*d*) gives to the Court of Protection a power to make a settlement of the property of the patient; and also, if any material fact was not disclosed when the settlement was made, or where there has been any substantial change in circumstances, to vary the settlement in such manner as the judge thinks fit.[54]

---

[45] *Re Meux* [1958] Ch. 154.
[46] *Re Gower's Settlement* [1934] Ch. 365.
[47] *Re Bristol's S.E.* [1964] 3 All E.R. 939; *Re Lansdowne's W.T.* [1967] Ch. 603.
[48] *Re Meux, supra. cf. Re Heyworth's Contingent Reversionary Interest* [1956] Ch. 364.
[49] *Re Meux, supra.*
[50] *Re Heyworth's Contingent Reversionary Interest, supra*; criticised (1957) 21 Conv. (N.S.) 448 at pp. 450–454 (O. R. Marshall).
[51] Matrimonial Causes Act 1973, ss.23 and 24. See also s.25, laying down the principles to be observed by the court in exercising its jurisdiction under ss.23, 24.
[52] s.24(1)(*c*), (*d*).
[53] s.31(2)(*e*). Further details must be obtained from the Family Law books.
[54] M.H.A. 1983, s.96(3).

C. Variation of Trusts Act 1958[55]

The Variation of Trusts Act 1958 gives to the court a "very wide and, indeed, revolutionary discretion"[56] to approve on behalf of four groups of persons[57] "any arrangement . . . varying or revoking all or any of the trusts, or enlarging the powers of the trustees of managing or administering any of the property subject to the trusts."[58] On its terms, this provision covers not only administrative matters, but also variations in the beneficial interests; but the court may only approve such an arrangement if the carrying out thereof would be for the benefit of the person on whose behalf the approval is given.[59]

The courts have approved a wide variety of variations, and, in addition to approving changes in the beneficial interests, have inserted a power of advancement,[60] terminated an accumulation,[61] inserted an accumulation period[62] and have widened the investment powers of trustees.[63] Investment clauses are rarely the subject of an application, for it became established that only in exceptional circumstances should a court give its approval to wider investment powers than those given to trustees in the Trustee Investments Act 1961[64]; and trustees automatically have those powers unless expressly excluded in an instrument coming into operation after the date of the Act.[65] The Act of 1961, however, has become outdated, and it seems that the courts are now willing to sanction an extension of investment powers.[66] But it is of

---

[55] Harris: *Variation of Trusts*, Chaps. 3 *et seq.*; (1958) 22 Conv.(N.S.) 373 (M. J. Mowbray); (1963) 27 Conv.(N.S.) 6 (D. M. Evans); (1965) 43 Can.B.R. 181 (A. J. Maclean); (1969) 33 Conv.(N.S.) 113 (J. W. Harris). The jurisdiction given by the Act is independent of T.A. 1925, s.57, and S.L.A. 1925, s.64, *ante*, p. 583. The jurisdiction of the 1958 Act should be invoked in preference to that of T.A. 1925, s.57. (But there may be technical reasons, *e.g.* difficulties as to representative parties, why this is not possible. See *Mason* v. *Farbrother* [1983] 2 All E.R. 1078.)

[56] *Per* Evershed M.R. in *Re Steed's W.T.* [1960] Ch. 407 at pp. 420–421.

[57] *Post*, p. 587.

[58] V.T.A. 1958, s.1(1). But see *Allen* v. *Distillers Co.* (*Biochemicals*) *Ltd.* [1974] Q.B. 384, *ante*, p. 582.

[59] Except for persons in para. (*d*), *infra*.

[60] *Re Lister's W.T.* [1962] 1 W.L.R. 1441.

[61] *Re Tinker's Settlement* [1960] 1 W.L.R. 1011.

[62] *Re Lansdowne's W.T.* [1967] Ch. 603; *Re Holt's Settlement* [1969] Ch. 100.

[63] *Re Coates' Trusts* [1959] 1 W.L.R. 375; *Re Burney's S.T.* [1961] 1 W.L.R. 545.

[64] *Re Kolb's W.T.* [1962] Ch. 531; *Re Cooper's Settlement* [1962] Ch. 826; *Re Clarke's W.T.* [1961] 1 W.L.R. 1471. See also *Re Rank's S.T.* [1979] 1 W.L.R. 1242, where an arrangement included a power of appointment in terms wide enough to permit the donee to give wider powers of investment to the trustees for the benefit of the appointees.

[65] T.I.A. 1961, s.1(3); *ante*, p. 491.

[66] In *Mason* v. *Farbrother* [1983] 2 All E.R. 1078, *ante*, p. 502, concerning T.A. 1925, s.57, the effect of inflation and the fact that the trust was in the nature of a public fund were regarded as special circumstances; *cf. Trustees of the British Museum* v. *Att.-Gen.* [1984] 1 W.L.R. 418, [1984] Conv. 373 (H. E. Norman), where Megarry V.-C. preferred the view that the *Re Kolb* principle, *supra*, had gone. This was discussed in Chap. 17. See also *Steel* v. *Wellcome Custodian Trustees Ltd.* [1988] 1 W.L.R. 167; [1988] Conv. 380 (B. Dale); Law Reform Committee's 23rd Report, *Powers and Duties of Trustees* (1982) Cmnd. 8733.

course in connection with schemes which vary beneficial interests for tax saving purposes that the Act has been mainly applied.

(i) Persons on whose Behalf Approval may be Given. In selecting the classes of persons on whose behalf approval may be given, the principle is that the court is not asked to approve on behalf of ascertainable adults who can consent for themselves. The classes (as set out in Variation of Trusts Act 1958, s.1) are:

"(*a*) any person having, directly or indirectly, an interest, whether vested or contingent, under the trusts who by reason of infancy or other incapacity is incapable of assenting, or

(*b*) any person (whether ascertained or not) who may become entitled, directly or indirectly, to an interest under the trusts as being at a future date or on the happening of a future event a person of any specified description or a member of any specified class of persons, so however that this paragraph shall not include any person[67] who would be of that description, or a member of that class, as the case may be, if the said date had fallen or the said event had happened at the date of the application to the court, or

(*c*) any person unborn, or

(*d*) any person in respect of any discretionary interest of his under protective trusts where the interest of the principal beneficiary has not failed or determined."

Paragraph (*b*) may well of course include adults; but because the class is ascertainable only at a future time, its members cannot yet be known. Under the proviso, however, those who would qualify if the future event happened at the date of the application to the court must themselves consent. If however they are infants, they come within paragraph (*a*).

In *Re Suffert*,[68] income was given under protective trusts to a spinster for life, and, in the event of her having no issue, and subject to a general testamentary power, in trust for those who would become entitled under her intestacy. She had three adult cousins, who would be entitled in equal shares to her estate if she had died at the date of the application to the court. One cousin was made a party, and consented, but the others were not. In asking the court to approve the arrangement, it was argued that the court should approve on behalf of those who would be entitled on intestacy, as they came within paragraph (*b*). Buckley J. however held that the proviso applied and that he could not approve on behalf of the two cousins. Otherwise he approved the arrangement.

---

[67] This presumably means any ascertained person; Harris, *op. cit.* pp. 39–40.
[68] [1961] Ch. 1.

The meaning of the words "may become entitled" in paragraph (b) were recently examined in *Knocker* v. *Youle*.[69]

> Property was held on trust for the settlor's daughter for life under a settlement in which her cousins had very remote contingent interests. It was not practicable to get the approval of the cousins to the proposed variation because they were very numerous, and some were in Australia.[70] Approval was therefore sought on their behalf under section 1(1)(*b*). The question was whether paragraph (b) included persons with an existing contingent interest, however remote. Warner J. held that it did not. A person having a contingent interest was not a person who "may become entitled" to an interest. Paragraph (b) covered the case of a person who had a mere *spes* (an expectation), such as the prospective next of kin of a living person in *Re Suffert*,[71] or a potential future spouse.[72] The court had jurisdiction under paragraph (b) to approve on behalf of persons having an expectation, but not, as in the present case, on behalf of persons having a contingent interest. The adult cousins were in any event excluded by the proviso to paragraph (b).

(ii) Parties. In general, the settlor, if living,[73] and all beneficiaries under the trusts, both adult and minor, should be made parties. The minors, unless their interests coincide with those of adult beneficiaries who consent, should be separately represented,[74] and a guardian *ad litem* must give full consideration to the way in which the proposed variation will affect the minors' interests.[75] In the case of a class, those who are members of the class at the date of the application should be included[76]; but it is not necessary to join persons who may become members later[77]; nor persons who may become interested under discretionary trusts[78]; nor those who are possible objects of a power.[79] Persons unborn cannot of course be made parties, but their interests

---

[69] [1986] 1 W.L.R. 934; criticised [1987] Conv. 144 (J. G. Riddall), also discussing persons who are objects of mere powers and discretionary trusts.

[70] The Act does not deal with the problem of the beneficiary who must consent on his own behalf but who is untraceable. In such a case a *Benjamin* order (*ante*, p. 506) could be used. See (1986) 136 N.L.J. 1057 (P. Luxton).

[71] *Supra; Re Moncrieff's S.T.* [1962] 1 W.L.R. 1344. But see [1987] Conv. 144 at p. 146 (J. G. Riddall) for the view that such persons do have a contingent interest in the *settlement*, although not, of course, in the estate of their living relative.

[72] See *Re Clitheroe's S.T.* [1959] 1 W.L.R. 1159; *Re Robert's S.T. The Times*, April 8, 1959; *Re Lister's W.T.* [1962] 1 W.L.R. 1441.

[73] R.S.C., Ord. 93, r. 6(2).

[74] *Re Whigham's S.T.* [1971] 1 W.L.R. 831.

[75] *Re Whittall* [1973] 1 W.L.R. 1027.

[76] *Re Suffert's Settlement* [1961] Ch. 1.

[77] *Re Moncrieff's S.T.* [1962] 1 W.L.R. 1344.

[78] *Re Munro's S.T.* [1963] 1 W.L.R. 145.

[79] *Re Christie-Miller's Marriage Settlement* [1961] 1 W.L.R. 462; *Practice Direction* [1976] 1 W.L.R. 884.

must be represented. Where a mental patient is involved the Court of Protection should be informed as soon as the originating summons has been issued and proceedings then taken in the Court of Protection to look after the interests of the patient.[80]

(iii) Applicants. The application should be made by a beneficiary, usually the person currently receiving the income. But the settlor may do so.[81] It is not usually satisfactory for the trustees to make the application because there might be an undesirable conflict of interest between their interest as an applicant, and as guardian of some of the beneficial interest for which they are responsible.[82] But they may apply if no-one else will do so, and the variation is in the interests of the beneficiaries.[83]

(iv) Foreign Trusts. The jurisdiction is not confined to trusts which are governed by English law.[84] The court will not however approve an agreement which provides for a settlement under the law of a foreign jurisdiction if the beneficiaries remain resident and domiciled in England; nor, as in *Re Weston's Settlement*,[85] where the connection with Jersey, the foreign jurisdiction, was recent and tenuous, and where the court doubted whether the living beneficiaries really intended to make Jersey their permanent home. Trusts have, however, been "exported" in favour of a settlement with foreign trustees and governed by foreign law where the beneficiaries have emigrated permanently to the foreign country[86]; and approval has been given for the transfer of funds from a trust governed by English law to one governed by the law of Guernsey where the primary beneficiaries were resident and domiciled in France and the remainderman in Indonesia.[87] The advantages of trust exporting have been much reduced since the introduction of capital transfer and inheritance tax.[88]

It should be added that the appointment of a foreign trustee may be made in a proper case without the intervention of the court.[89]

---

[80] *Practice Direction* [1960] 1 W.L.R. 17; *Re Sanderson's W.T.* [1961] 1 W.L.R. 36.
[81] *Re Roberts' S.T., The Times*, April 8, 1959; *Re Clitheroe's S.T.* [1959] 1 W.L.R. 1159.
[82] *Re Druce's S.T.* [1962] 1 W.L.R. 363.
[83] *Re Druce's S.T.* (*supra*) at p. 370.
[84] *Re Ker's S.T.* [1963] Ch. 553; *Re Paget's Settlement* [1965] 1 W.L.R. 1046.
[85] [1969] 1 Ch. 223.
[86] *Re Seale's Marriage Settlement* [1961] Ch. 574 (Canada); *Re Windeatt's W.T.* [1969] 1 W.L.R. 692 (Jersey); see also *Re Whitehead's W.T.* [1971] 1 W.L.R. 833.
[87] *Re Chamberlain* (unreported) discussed in (1976) 126 N.L.J. 1034 (J. B. Morcom); (1976) 40 Conv.(N.S.) 295 (T. G. Watkin).
[88] *Ante*, p. 224.
[89] *Re Whitehead's W.T., supra*. But application will often be made to the court, and a variation will be necessary if the form of the trust needs to be altered in order to comply with the foreign law, if there is no power in the trust instrument to do this. See generally Parker and Mellows, *The Modern Law of Trusts* (5th ed.), Chap. 24.

(v) **Effect of Approval by the Court.** It appears that the arrangement is effective from the time of the approval by the court. The reasons why this is so are not clear; and the result may be due to the practice established by *Re Viscount Hambleden's Will Trusts*.[90] Several, and in some cases conflicting, accounts have been given of the effect of approval by the court.

In *Re Joseph's Will Trusts*[91] Vaisey J. included in his order approving the variation a direction that the variation should be carried into effect. In *Re Viscount Hambleden's Will Trusts*,[92] Wynn-Parry J. thought that he had no jurisdiction to make such a direction. Nor was it required. "I hold that the effect of my approval is effective for all purposes to vary the trusts."[93] In *Re Holt's Settlement*,[94] Megarry J. was unconvinced. Before him it was argued that the Act gives the court power to approve only on behalf of the persons mentioned in section $1(1)$[95]; and the consent of the adults to a change in their beneficial interests was a "disposition," and ineffective unless in writing.[96] Megarry J. was reluctant to disturb what had become a very convenient practice based on *Re Viscount Hambleden*,[97] and searched for a theory to justify it. The suggestion that there was no "disposition" of the interests of the consenting adults, but a "species of estoppel"[98] operating against them was "unattractive." He was satisfied however that it could be explained on the ground that a "not impossible"[99] construction of the Act was that the court's jurisdiction was that of approving arrangements which did in fact vary the trusts, section $53(1)(c)$[1] being by necessary implication excluded; or that, where the variation was made for consideration, the consenting adults could be compelled to perform their contract and they held their original interests on constructive trusts, these being unaffected by section $53(1)(c)$.[2] The view that the variation obtains its effect by reason of the consent of the beneficiaries is supported by dicta in *I.R.C.* v. *Holmden*,[3] where however the question of section $53(1)(c)$ did not arise.

The arrangement coupled with the court's order is an "instrument" for the purposes of the Perpetuities and Accumulations Act 1964,

---

[90] [1960] 1 W.L.R. 82; *Re Holt's Settlement* [1969] 1 Ch. 100 at p. 113.

[91] [1959] 1 W.L.R. 1019.

[92] [1960] 1 W.L.R. 82.

[93] *Ibid.* at p. 86.

[94] [1969] 1 Ch. 100; (1968) 84 L.Q.R. 162 (P.V.B.).

[95] There is a clear contrast between the wording of this section and that of S.L.A. 1925, s.64, and T.A. 1925, s.57.

[96] L.P.A. 1925, s.53(1)(c); *ante*, p. 81; *Grey* v. *I.R.C.* [1960] A.C. 1.

[97] [1960] 1 W.L.R. 82.

[98] [1969] 1 Ch. 100 at p. 114; *Spens* v. *I.R.C.* [1970] 1 W.L.R. 1173.

[99] *Ibid.* at p. 115.

[1] L.P.A. 1925, providing that the disposition of subsisting equitable interests should be in writing; *ante*, p. 81.

[2] L.P.A. 1925; *Oughtred* v. *I.R.C.* [1960] A.C. 206; *Re Holt's Settlement* [1969] 1 Ch. 100 at pp. 115–116.

[3] [1968] A.C. 685; *cf.* T.A. 1925, s.57; *Re Mair* [1935] Ch. 562.

s.15(5), and future interests or accumulations permitted by the Act, which only applies to instruments coming into operation after July 15, 1964,[4] may be provided for in an arrangement.[5] Because the variation does not owe its authority to the settlor, its provisions need not be such that the settlor could have created them.[6] In contrast with powers of appointment and advancement,[7] the perpetuity period does not relate back to the original settlement. A variation which is inconsistent with the continuous existence of a power operates as a release of a power.[8]

(vi) Variation or Resettlement. The jurisdiction, as we have seen, is very wide. It is however a jurisdiction to "vary" and not to "resettle."[9] This is a difficult dividing line to establish. In *Re Ball's Settlement*, Megarry J. laid down the general test as follows[10]:

> "If an arrangement changes the whole substratum of the trust, then it may well be that it cannot be regarded merely as varying the trust. But if an arrangement, while leaving the substratum, effec- tuates the purpose of the trust by other means, it may still be possible to regard that arrangement as merely varying the original trusts, even though the means employed are wholly different and even though the form is completely changed."

(vii) Fraud on a Power. Nor will the court approve a variation which involves a fraud on a power, as for example where property is held on trust for A for life and to such of A's children as he shall appoint, and A, in order to avoid tax liability on his death, appoints in favour of his living children, and does so with a view to partitioning the fund, with the court's approval, between his children and himself. Such an appointment has been held to be fraudulent and void on the ground that it was made so that the appointor may obtain a benefit for himself under the variation.[11]

(viii) The Settlor's Intention. In giving approval, the court must be satisfied about the arrangement as a whole.[12] One important factor is

---

[4] Perpetuities and Accumulations Act 1964, s.12; Maudsley, *The Modern Law of Perpetuities*, Chap. 8.
[5] *Re Lansdowne's W.T.* [1967] Ch. 603; *Re Lloyd's Settlement* [1967] 2 W.L.R. 1078; *Re Holt's Settlement, supra.*
[6] *Re Holt's Settlement, supra.*
[7] *Pilkington* v. *I.R.C.* [1964] A.C. 612, *ante*, p. 553.
[8] *Re Christie-Miller's Marriage Settlement* [1961] 1 W.L.R. 462; *Re Courtauld's Settle- ment* [1965] 1 W.L.R. 1385; *Re Ball's S.T.* [1968] 1 W.L.R. 899; *ante*, p. 177.
[9] *Re T.'s S.T.* [1964] Ch. 158; *Re Ball's S.T.* [1968] 1 W.L.R. 899; criticised (1968) 84 L.Q.R. 458 (P.V.B.); *Re Holt's Settlement* [1969] 1 Ch. 100 at p. 117; *ante*, p. 590; *Allen* v. *Distillers Co. (Biochemicals) Ltd.* [1974] Q.B. 384.
[10] [1968] 1 W.L.R. 899 at p. 905.
[11] *Re Robertson's W.T.* [1960] 1 W.L.R. 1050; *Re Brook's Settlement* [1968] 1 W.L.R. 1661; *cf. Re Wallace's Settlement* [1968] 1 W.L.R. 711.
[12] *Re Burney's S.T.* [1961] 1 All E.R. 856.

whether or not the arrangement is consistent with the general plan of
the settlor or testator.

In *Re Steed's Will Trusts*[13] a testator had left property to a faithful
housekeeper for her life on protective trusts and after her death as
she should appoint, the trustee having power to pay capital moneys
to her as they should think fit. The property included a farm which
was let to the housekeeper's brother; and the terms of the will were
designed so as to give the maximum benefit in the property to the
housekeeper, without giving her an absolute interest, because of the
danger which the testator "thought was real, of being, to use a
common phrase, sponged upon by one of her brothers."[14]

The trustees decided to sell the farm. The housekeeper started
proceedings to stop them, exercised the power of appointment in
favour of herself, and applied under the Variation of Trusts Act, s.1,
for the elimination of the protective element in her life interest; " . . .
the result would be that the plaintiff would become absolutely
entitled to the property, because she would then be the life tenant,
having appointed . . . to herself the reversion."[15] The only persons
who might be prejudiced by such a variation would be those who
might benefit under the discretionary trusts which would arise if the
protective life interest were forfeited[16]; and under paragraph (*d*),
the court is not concerned to see that they benefit from a variation.
Was there any reason why approval should not be given?

The Court of Appeal refused. "It is the *arrangement*[17] which has to
be approved not just the limited interest of the person on whose
behalf the court's duty is to consider it . . . the court must regard the
proposal as a whole, and so regarding it, then ask itself whether in
the exercise of its jurisdiction it should approve that proposal on
behalf of the person who cannot give a consent . . . it was part of the
testator's scheme, made as I think manifest by the language which I
have read from the clauses in the will, that it was the intention and
the desire of the testator that this trust should be available for the
plaintiff so that she should have proper provision made for her
throughout her life, and would not be exposed to the risk that she
might, if she had been handed the money, part with it in favour of
another individual about whom the testator felt apprehension,
which apprehension is plainly shared by the trustees."[18]

The question also arose in *Re Remnant's Settlement Trusts*,[19] where

---

[13] [1960] Ch. 407; *Re Michelham's W.T.* [1964] Ch. 550.
[14] [1960] Ch. 407 at p. 415.
[15] *Ibid.* at p. 419.
[16] *Ante*, p. 189; assuming that she would not now have children, this was only a
prospective husband, described in the case of the "spectral spouse."
[17] Italics supplied.
[18] [1960] Ch. 407 at pp. 421–422.
[19] [1970] Ch. 560, *post*, p. 595.

the proposed variation was the deletion of a forfeiture clause whereby beneficiaries who practised Roman Catholicism or married a Roman Catholic would lose their entitlement. The fact that the variation would defeat the settlor's intention was regarded as a serious matter, but not conclusive. As the forfeiture clause was undesirable in the circumstances of the family (unlike the disputed provision in *Re Steed's Will Trusts*,[20] which was not cited), it was fair and proper to delete it, notwithstanding the settlor's intention.

(ix) **Benefit.** It is necessary that the variation should be for the benefit of the persons in categories (a) to (c) on whose behalf approval is sought. There is no such requirement of benefit in respect of persons under category (d).[21]

(a) *Financial Benefit.* There is usually no difficulty in showing financial benefit. But evidence must be presented to show that there is an advantage to each person required to be benefited.[22] Variations have commonly been made to save estate duty (prior to its replacement by capital transfer and inheritance tax),[23] capital gains tax,[24] and income tax[25]; any saving provides a larger sum for distribution, and remainder-men may also be benefited by the termination of an interest in possession as their interests will be accelerated. As stated above,[26] a partition of the settled fund between tenant for life and remainderman has inheritance tax advantages. Provided the tenant for life survives for seven years, no tax will be payable, whereas the whole capital is taxable if a life interest terminates on death. It is usual for the life tenant to pay the costs of the application.

(b) *Moral and Social Benefit.* But benefit is not only financial. The court must also consider the general welfare of the persons on whose behalf approval is sought; this does not necessarily coincide with their financial interest.

In *Re Weston's Settlements*,[27] two settlements had been made in 1964, one in favour of each of the settlor's sons (both young men and one still a minor) and their children. The settlor moved to Jersey in 1967, and the sons followed him. The application was for the appointment of new trustees under Trustee Act 1925, s.41,[28] and for the insertion into the settlement of a power for the trustees to

---

[20] *Supra.*
[21] V.T.A. 1958, s.1, proviso. See *Re Van Gruisen's W.T.* [1964] 1 W.L.R. 449.
[22] *Re Clitheroe's S.T.* [1959] 1 W.L.R. 1159 at p. 1163.
[23] *Re Druce's S.T.* [1962] 1 W.L.R. 363.
[24] *Re Sainsbury's Settlement* [1967] 1 W.L.R. 476.
[25] *Re Clitheroe's S.T.* [1959] 1 W.L.R. 1159.
[26] *Ante*, p. 580.
[27] [1969] 1 Ch. 223.
[28] *Ante*, p. 472.

discharge the trusts of the settlements and to create almost identical Jersey settlements. The object was to take advantage of the favourable fiscal situation in Jersey, relating to capital gains tax and estate duty. The Court of Appeal, affirming Stamp J.,[29] refused. The variation would make the beneficiaries richer but would not be for their benefit. "The court should not consider merely the financial benefit to the infant and unborn children, but also their educational and social benefit. There are many things in life more worth while than money. One of these things is to be brought up in this our England, which is still 'the envy of less happier lands.' I do not believe that it is for the benefit of the children to be uprooted from England and transported to another country simply to avoid tax . . . many a child has been ruined by being given too much.[30] The avoidance of tax may be lawful, but it is not yet a virtue. The Court of Chancery should not encourage or support it—it should not give its approval to it—if by so doing it would imperil the true welfare of the children, already born or yet to be born."[31]

The best interests of the children were to their financial disadvantage. Similarly, as has been seen, with the spinster lady who wished to become the absolute owner of a farm which would then have been at the mercy of her brother.[32] And in *Re C.L.*[33] it was held to be for the benefit of a mental patient to consent to the surrender of a protected life interest and a contingent remainder interest in favour of her adopted daughter. It was what the patient would have done if she had been of sound mind. Mental patients should not, it seems, be denied the satisfaction, whether they are aware of it or not, of taking proper steps to preserve the family fortune.

(c) *Postponing Vesting*. It may be for the benefit of a minor that the date of vesting of an interest in the capital of a fund should be postponed.

In *Re T.'s Settlement Trusts*,[34] a female minor who was irresponsible and immature was entitled to a vested interest on attaining her majority, which she would do a few months after the application to the court. The proposal was that the minor's interest should be varied to become a protected life interest. Wilberforce J. could not regard such protection to the minor as a "benefit in its own right";

[29] [1969] 1 Ch. 223.
[30] Each settlement was worth some £400,000.
[31] [1969] 1 Ch. 223 at p. 245.
[32] *Re Steed's W.T.* [1960] Ch. 407; *ante*, p. 592.
[33] [1969] 1 Ch. 587.
[34] [1964] Ch. 158; *Re Holt's Settlement* [1969] 1 Ch. 100. See also *Allen* v. *Distillers Co. (Biochemicals) Ltd.* [1974] Q.B. 384; *ante*, p. 582.

but he made an order postponing the vesting of the capital until a specified age and providing that the property should be held on protective trusts in the meantime.

(d) *Trouble in the Family*. Where a trust treats members of the family unequally, it may be for everyone's benefit, even for those who surrender a claim to property as a result, to vary the trust so as to treat each of them equally. Russell J. thought not in *Re Tinker's Settlement*,[35] where, owing to the draftsman's oversight, the settlement provided that the share of the settlor's son should accrue to his sister's share if he died under the age of 30 years, even if he left children. It was not for the benefit of the sister's children to surrender their contingent interest.

A broader view was taken in *Re Remnant's Settlement Trusts*.[36]

A trust fund gave contingent interests to the children of two sisters Dawn and Merrial, and contained a forfeiture provision in respect of any of their children who practised Roman Catholicism or was married to a Roman Catholic at the time of vesting, with an accruer provision in favour of the children of the other. Dawn's children were Protestant, but Merrial's were Roman Catholic.

Pennycuick J. approved an arrangement which deleted the forfeiture provision. This was clearly not for the financial benefit of Dawn's children, for they surrendered a very good chance of gaining by it. But it was overall for their benefit. "Obviously, a forfeiture provision of this kind might well cause very serious dissension between the families of the two sisters."[37] The forfeiture clause could also operate as a deterrent in the selection of a spouse. Freedom from such problems would be more important to the lives of the children than some more money.

(e) *Taking a Chance*. A difficulty arises where it is possible to say that a benefit is almost certain to arise, but there may possibly be circumstances in which it will not. Thus, in *Re Cohen's Settlement Trusts*,[38] an application was made to vary a settlement so as to make the interest of the grandchildren vest on a specified date, and not upon the death of a life tenant; which at that time would have avoided estate duty. But, although very unlikely that the life tenant would live until the date chosen, the alteration might possibly affect the number of grandchildren who may take. Similarly where the arrangement depends upon a woman of a certain age not having another child.[39] The

---

[35] [1960] 1 W.L.R. 1011.
[36] [1970] Ch. 560; (1971) 34 M.L.R. 98 (R.H.M. Cotterrell).
[37] [1970] Ch. 560 at p. 566. Another benefit, although not of great weight, was to be freed from having to choose between one's religion and the entitlement under the will.
[38] [1965] 1 W.L.R. 1229.
[39] *Re Westminster Bank Limited's Declaration of Trust* [1963] 1 W.L.R. 820 (over 50); *Re Pettifor's S.T.* [1966] Ch. 257 (no need for variation in case of woman over 70).

arrangements were approved. The question is one of degree. The court will not give its approval where the benefit is a matter of chance, but it will not require absolute certainty of benefit,[40] if the risk is one which a "prudent and well advised adult would be prepared to take."[41] Most risks can be covered by insurance.

---

[40] *Re Cohen's S.T.* [1965] 1 W.L.R. 1229; *Re Holt's Settlement* [1969] 1 Ch. 100; *Re Robinson's S.T.* [1976] 1 W.L.R. 806.
[41] (1960) 76 L.Q.R. 22 (R.E.M.).

CHAPTER 22

BREACH OF TRUST

1. Personal Liability to Beneficiaries

A. General[1]

(i) **Liability is Compensatory.** A trustee who fails to comply with the duties imposed upon him by equity and by the trust instrument is liable to make good to the beneficiaries the loss to the trust estate.[2] This liability is independent of fraud, intent or personal incompetence; it exists where the breach is innocent or merely technical. The object of the rule is not to punish the trustee, but to compensate the beneficiaries. However, the court will, on suitable occasions, authorise acts which are technical breaches of trust; a trustee will not be liable for a technical breach which the court would have authorised[3]; but there is no need to take the risk; he should obtain the directions of the court before acting.[4]

(ii) **Liability is Personal, not Vicarious.** The rule has always been that a trustee is liable for his own breaches and not for those of his co-trustees.[5] The dividing line however is extremely difficult to draw; for if there is a breach by a co-trustee, the trustee may himself be at fault by leaving the matter in the hands of a co-trustee without inquiry, or for standing by while a breach of trust is being committed,[6] or for allowing trust funds to remain in the sole control of a co-trustee, or for failing to take steps to obtain redress on becoming aware of a breach of trust.[7]

It became common to insert indemnity clauses protecting trustees from innocent and passive breaches of trust, and such a clause became statutory in the Act of 1859, s.31, which is essentially the same as the Trustee Act 1925, s.30,[8] considered above.[9] The Act of 1859 was strictly construed, and Lord Selborne went so far as to say that "It does not substantially alter the law as it was administered by Courts of

---

[1] See the definitions of breach of trust discussed by Megarry J. in *Tito* v. *Waddell (No. 2)* [1977] Ch. 106 at p. 247.
[2] In some cases the liability of a constructive trustee is different; *ante*, p. 282.
[3] *Lee* v. *Brown* (1798) 4 Ves. 362 at p. 369; *Brown* v. *Smith* (1878) 10 Ch.D. 377.
[4] *Ante*, p. 505.
[5] *Townley* v. *Sherborne* (1634) J. Bridg. 35 at pp. 37, 38.
[6] *Bahin* v. *Hughes* (1886) 31 Ch.D. 390; *ante*, p. 462.
[7] For further details see Hayton and Marshall, pp. 725–726.
[8] "A trustee shall be chargeable only for money and securities actually received by him notwithstanding his signing any receipt for the sake of conformity, and shall be answerable and accountable only for his own acts, receipts, neglects, or defaults, and not for those of any other trustee, nor for any banker, broker or other person with whom any trust money or securities may be deposited, nor for the insufficiency or deficiency of any securities, nor for any other loss, unless the same happens through his own wilful default."
[9] *Ante*, p. 535.

Equity."[10] It is possible however that the definition of the phrase "wilful default" which was applied in *Re Vickery*[11] to a case of a trustee leaving the money in the hands of a solicitor will now also be applied to the question of the liability of a trustee for the acts of his co-trustee.

(iii) Breaches before Appointment. A trustee is not liable for breaches of trust committed before his appointment in the absence of evidence indicating a breach of trust.[12] On appointment, however, he should examine the books and documents relating to the trust, and should ensure that the trust property is vested in him. If in the course of his inquiries he discovers a breach of trust, he should take steps against the former trustees; unless for some reason he can show that such proceedings would have been useless.[13]

(iv) Breaches after Retirement. A trustee remains liable after retirement for breaches committed by him during his term of office; and similarly his estate remains liable after his death. He may on the other hand have been released by the other trustees, or by the beneficiaries being *sui juris* and in possession of all the facts. He will not usually be liable in respect of breaches committed after his retirement; but he may be if he retired in order to facilitate a breach of trust. "Did (the retiring trustees)" asked Kekewich J. "denude themselves of the trust funds under circumstances that warranted any reasonable belief of the insecurity of the trust funds in the hands of those to whom they committed them?"[14]

(v) Trustee-Beneficiary. Where the trustee in breach is also a beneficiary, his beneficial interest bears the loss against the other beneficiaries,[15] and, as we will see,[16] against the trustees[17]; and this liability applies although the beneficial interest was acquired by him derivatively, even by purchase.[18]

---

[10] *Re Brier* (1884) 26 Ch.D. 238 at p. 243; *ante*, p. 533; *Underwood* v. *Stevens* (1816) 1 Mer. 712; *Dix* v. *Burford* (1854) 19 Beav. 409; *Brumridge* v. *Brumridge* (1858) 27 Beav. 5. For the application of the Unfair Contract Terms Act 1977 to indemnity clauses, see [1980] Conv. 333 (W. Goodhart).

[11] [1931] 1 Ch. 572; *ante*, p. 533.

[12] *Re Strahan* (1856) 8 De G.M. & G. 291.

[13] *Re Forest of Dean Coal Co.* (1878) 10 Ch.D. 450 at p. 452.

[14] *Head* v. *Gould* [1898] 2 Ch. 250 at p. 272. This question came into prominence in the context of pressure upon English resident trustees to retire in favour of foreign resident trustees in order to allow a trust fund to escape liability for capital gains tax: *Re Whitehead's W.T.* [1971] 1 W.L.R. 833; *ante*, p. 476.

[15] *Re Dacre* [1915] 2 Ch. 480; [1916] 1 Ch. 344; *Re Towndrow* [1911] 1 Ch. 662. Assignees are also bound, unless they took for value and without notice.

[16] *Post*, p. 606.

[17] *Chillingworth* v. *Chambers* [1896] 1 Ch. 685.

[18] *Jacubs* v. *Rylance* (1874) 17 Eq. 341; *Doering* v. *Doering* (1899) 42 Ch.D. 203; *Re Dacre, supra.*

B. Measure of Liability

The measure of liability is the loss caused to the trust estate, directly or indirectly,[19] and the onus is on the complainant to prove a causal connection between the breach and the loss.[20] As liability is restitutionary, rules of remoteness, such as those applicable in actions in contract or tort, are not relevant.[21] But a number of subsidiary rules have been established as being applicable to the particular situations.

(i) **Purchase of Unauthorised Investments.** When trustees make an unauthorised investment, they will be liable for the loss incurred on the sale. This is so even if the sale is at a time chosen by the court, and if the investments would have shown a profit if they had been retained until the decision of the court holding them to be improper.[22] The beneficiaries may, if they are *sui juris* and so wish, adopt the unauthorised investment[23]; if they do so, there is dispute whether that is the limit of their remedy,[24] or whether they may claim the difference between the value of the investment and the purchase price.[25]

(ii) **Improper Retention of Investments.** It is necessary to distinguish between authorised and unauthorised investments.

(a) *Unauthorised Investments.* A trustee who improperly retains unauthorised investments is liable for the difference between the present value (or selling price) and the price which it would have raised if it had been sold at the proper time. How hard this can be on a trustee holding property in a falling market is shown by *Fry* v. *Fry*[26] where trustees were liable for the difference between the price offered for a hotel in 1837 which they refused as inadequate, and the much lower price prevailing in 1859, the fall being largely due to the diversion of road traffic by the building of a railway.

(b) *Authorised Investments.* Before 1961 a trustee was not liable for loss occasioned by the retention of an authorised investment, unless he

---

[19] *Knott* v. *Cottee* (1852) 16 Beav. 77; *Bartlett* v. *Barclays Bank Trust Co. Ltd. (No. 2)* [1980] Ch. 515. It is otherwise in the case of unlawful profits, *ante*, p. 561.

[20] *Re Miller's Trust Deed* (1978) 75 L.S.Gaz. 454.

[21] Similarly the principle established in *British Transport Commission* v. *Gourley* [1956] A.C. 185, whereby tax is deducted in assessing damages for loss of earnings in tort, has no application to liability for breach of trust. It was held in *Re Bell's Indenture* [1980] 1 W.L.R. 1217 that a trustee who deliberately misappropriates trust property for his own benefit or for that of a third party must restore its value without deducting any tax which might have been paid if the property had not been appropriated. See also *Bartlett* v. *Barclays Bank Trust Co. (No. 2)* [1980] Ch. 515; *Re Dawson* [1966] 2 N.S.W.R. 211.

[22] *Knott* v. *Cottee, supra.*

[23] *Re Patten* (1883) 52 L.J. Ch. 787; *Re Jenkins and Randall's Contract* [1903] 2 Ch. 362; *Wright* v. *Morgan* [1926] A.C. 788 at p. 799.

[24] *Thornton* v. *Stokill* (1855) 1 Jur.(N.S.) 751.

[25] *Re Lake* [1903] 1 K.B. 439.

[26] *Fry* v. *Fry* (1859) 27 Beav. 144.

was guilty of wilful default.[27] We have seen that the Trustee Investments Act 1961, s.6(2), requires advice to be taken on the question of retaining investments.[28] Trustee Act 1925, s.4[29] has no application to such cases, nor to those to which it is expressly made inapplicable by Trustee Investments Act 1961, s.3(4).[30]

(iii) Improper Sale of Authorised Investments. When an authorised investment is improperly sold, the beneficiaries may require the trustees either to account for the proceeds of sale or to replace the investment, valued as at the date of judgment.[31] Thus where trustees sold consols and invested in an unauthorised investment, the whole matter was treated as a single transaction and the trustees were held liable to replace the consols at the higher price then prevailing.[32] This is so even though the improper investment was realised without loss.[33]

(iv) Failure to Invest. Trustees should invest within a reasonable time. Pending investment, moneys may be paid into a bank to a deposit or other account.[34] Interest should be obtained if possible; a trustee who unreasonably fails to find an investment will be chargeable with interest.[35]

If a trustee is required to invest in a specific investment and fails to make any investment, and the price of the specific investment has risen, he will be liable to purchase as much of that investment as would have been purchased at the proper time.[36] Similarly if he chooses an investment other than that specified[37]; profit in the unauthorised investment being surrendered, of course, to the trust.[38] Where, as is nearly always the case in practice, the trustees may select investments at their discretion, it is not practicable to base recovery upon the price of a particular investment, and the beneficiary will usually be entitled only to recovery of the trust fund with interest.[39]

---

[27] *Re Chapman* [1896] 2 Ch. 763; *Rawsthorne* v. *Rowley* [1909] 1 Ch. 409n.

[28] *Ante*, p. 497. The Law Reform Committee, 23rd Report, *The Powers and Duties of Trustees*, (1982 Cmnd. 8733) recommended retaining the advice requirement; *ibid.* paras. 3.21 and 3.22.

[29] *Ante*, p. 498.

[30] *Ante*, p. 495.

[31] *Re Bell's Indenture* [1980] 1 W.L.R. 1217, where Vinelott J. regarded the decision in *Re Massingberd's Settlement, infra,* as having been made *per incuriam* in so far as it is suggested that the date of valuing the asset was the date of the issue of the writ. But where the asset sold in breach of trust would have been properly sold at a later date, the trustee is liable to replace it at its value on that date, and not as at the date of judgment.

[32] *Phillipson* v. *Gatty* (1848) 7 Hare 516.

[33] *Re Massingberd's Settlement* (1890) 63 L.T. 296.

[34] T.A. 1925, s.11(1).

[35] *Att.-Gen.* v. *Alford* (1855) 4 De G.M. & G. 843.

[36] *Byrchall* v. *Bradford* (1822) 6 Madd. 235.

[37] *Pride* v. *Fooks* (1840) 2 Beav. 430.

[38] *Post*, p. 603.

[39] *Shepherd* v. *Moulis* (1845) 4 Hare 500; *cf. Watts* v. *Girdlestone* (1843) 6 Beav. 188.

(v) Employment of Trust Fund in Trade. A trustee who employs trust funds in his trade or business is liable as a constructive trustee for the profits he makes,[40] or for the sums involved with interest, whichever is the greater. Difficult questions arise when he employs a mixed fund, being partly his own and partly trust money. Here the rule is that the beneficiaries may claim a share of the profits which relate to the proportion of the trust fund employed,[41] or demand the return of the trust money with interest.[42]

(vi) Mortgage of Realty. We have seen that where trustees lend an excessive sum on a mortgage of realty which would have been a proper investment for a smaller sum, the mortgage is treated as an authorised investment for the smaller sum and the trustees are liable only for the excess, with interest.[43]

(vii) Interest. "It is well established in equity that a trustee who in breach of trust misapplies trust funds will be liable not only to replace the misapplied principal fund but to do so with interest from the date of the misapplication. This is on the notional ground that the money so applied was in fact the trustee's own money and that he has retained the misapplied trust money in his own hands and used it for his own purposes. Where a trustee has retained trust money in his own hands, he will be accountable for the profit which he has made or which he is assumed to have made with the use of the money. . . . The defaulting trustee is normally charged with simple interest only,[44] but if it is established that he has used the money in trade he may be charged compound interest. . . . Precisely similar equitable principles apply to an agent who has retained monies of his principal in his hands and used them for his own purposes."[45]"[46] If the trustee or agent has received a sum in excess of what the court would impose, he is accountable for what he has actually received, or the beneficiaries may adopt the investment.[47]

The rate of interest, and the choice between simple and com-

---

[40] *Re Davis* [1902] 2 Ch. 314; *Re Jarvis* [1958] 1 W.L.R. 815.
[41] *Lord Provost, etc., of Edinburgh* v. *Lord Advocate* (1879) 4 App.Cas. 823; *Re Tilley's W.T.* [1967] Ch. 1179.
[42] *Heathcote* v. *Hulme* (1819) 1 Jac. & W. 122.
[43] T.A. 1925, s.9; *ante,* p. 502.
[44] *Belmont Finance Corporation Ltd.* v. *Williams Furniture Ltd. (No. 2)* [1980] 1 All E.R. 393.
[45] *Burdick* v. *Garrick* (1870) 5 Ch.App. 233.
[46] *Wallersteiner* v. *Moir (No. 2)* [1975] Q.B. 373 at p. 397, *per* Buckley L.J.; distinguished in *O'Sullivan* v. *Management Agency and Music Ltd.* [1985] Q.B. 428, (1986) 49 M.L.R. 118 (W. Bishop and D. D. Prentice), *ante,* p. 558 (simple interest where profits used in trade, but trade benefited plaintiff, being in the nature of a joint venture).
[47] *Re Jenkins' and Randalls' Contract* [1903] 2 Ch. 362; *Wright* v. *Morgan* [1926] A.C. 788 at p. 799; *ante,* p. 600.

pound,[48] is in the discretion of the court. The nineteenth century cases laid down 4 per cent.[49] as the general rule, with an increase to 5 per cent. where the trustees or other fiduciary was guilty of fraud[50] or active misconduct,[51] or where he ought to have received more than 4 per cent.[52] These rates are out of line with current commercial interest rates, and more recent decisions have charged 1 per cent. above the London clearing banks' base rate[53] in force at the time[54]; or that allowed from time to time on the court's short-term investment account (now called the court special account), established under section 6(1) of the Administration of Justice Act 1965.[55] Compound interest is charged where that fairly represents what the trustee may reasonably be treated as having received,[56] or where there is a duty to accumulate,[57] and sometimes in cases of fraud or misconduct.[58]

(viii) Profit in One Transaction: Loss in Another. Any gains made out of the trust property belong to the beneficiaries while a loss incurred by reason of a breach of trust must be made good by the trustee. A trustee cannot set off a gain in one transaction against a loss made in another unauthorised transaction.

In *Dimes* v. *Scott*[59] trustees retained an unauthorised Indian mortgage returning 10 per cent. all of which was paid to the tenant for life. When the mortgage was paid off, trustees were able, because of the low price of trustee investments at that time, to purchase more Consols than they would have done if the conversion had taken place at the end of a year from the testator's death. Lord Lyndhurst held the trustees liable for the excess interest paid to the tenant for life[60] over that which would have been payable if the capital of the

---

[48] With yearly rests (*Jones* v. *Foxall* (1852) 15 Beav. 388 at p. 393; *Williams* v. *Powell* (1852) 15 Beav. 461; *Re Barclay* [1899] 1 Ch. 674); and sometimes half-yearly rests (*Re Emmet's Estate* (1881) 17 Ch.D. 142).

[49] *Att.-Gen.* v. *Alford* (1855) 4 De G.M. & G. 843; *Fletcher* v. *Green* (1864) 33 Beav. 426 at p. 430.

[50] *Att.-Gen.* v. *Alford, supra,* at p. 852.

[51] *Jones* v. *Foxall* (1852) 15 Beav. 388 at p. 393; *Vyse* v. *Foster* (1872) L.R. 8 Ch.App. 309; *Gordon* v. *Gonda* [1955] 1 W.L.R. 885.

[52] *Jones* v. *Foxall, supra,* at p. 388 (calling in a mortgage which was returning 5 per cent.); see *Re Waterman's W.T.* [1952] 2 All E.R. 1054.

[53] Now that the Bank of England's minimum lending rate is no longer posted.

[54] *Wallersteiner* v. *Moir (No. 2)* [1975] Q.B. 373; [1982] Conv. 93 (J.T.F.); *Belmont Finance Corporation* v. *Williams Furniture Ltd. (No. 2)* [1980] 1 All E.R. 393; *O'Sullivan* v. *Management Agency and Music Ltd.* [1985] Q.B. 428. See generally the comments of Lord Denning M.R., in a different context, in *Tehno-Impex* v. *Gebr. Van Weelde Scheepvaar Kantoor B.V.* [1981] Q.B. 648 at pp. 665–666.

[55] *Bartlett* v. *Barclays Bank Trust Co. Ltd. (No. 2)* [1980] Ch. 515.

[56] *Wallersteiner* v. *Moir (No. 2), supra.*

[57] *Re Emmet's Estate* (1881) 17 Ch.D. 142.

[58] *Jones* v. *Foxall, supra; Gordon* v. *Gonda, supra; cf. O'Sullivan* v. *Management Agency and Music Ltd., supra.* As to costs, see Snell, p. 287.

[59] (1828) 4 Russ. 195.

[60] The tenant for life was entitled only to 4 per cent. under the rule in *Howe* v. *Earl of Dartmouth* (1802) 7 Ves.Jr. 137; *ante,* p. 509.

unauthorised investment had been invested in Consols at the end of a year from the testator's death, and the trustees were unable to set against this the gain arising from the fall in the price of Consols.[61]

The rule is harsh though logical. It has not been applied where the court finds that the gain and loss were part of the same transaction. If that were not so, the liability of trustees purchasing unauthorised securities would automatically be calculated by a reference to the highest price reached by the unauthorised investment while the trustees held it. There is often difficulty in determining whether the question should or should not be regarded as a single transaction.

In *Fletcher* v. *Green*[62] trust money was lent on mortgage to a firm of which one trustee was a partner. The trustees reclaimed the money; the security was sold at a loss and the proceeds paid into court and invested in Consols. The question was whether the trustees' accounts should credit them with the amount of the proceeds of sale or with the value of the Consols, which had risen in price. They were held entitled to take advantage of the rise. No reasons were given. The case is usually explained on the ground that the whole matter was treated as one transaction. If that is so, they should logically have been at risk in relation to a possible fall in the price of Consols; the trustees can hardly be allowed to take advantage of a rise but not the burden of a fall; but it would be hard on the trustees if they have to run the risk of loss on an investment made by the court.

The difficulty of laying down a clear rule was recognised in *Bartlett* v. *Barclays Bank Trust Co. Ltd. (No. 1)*[63] where, it will be remembered, the defendant bank was held liable as trustee for failing to exercise proper supervision of the board of directors of a private company whose shares were almost wholly owned by the trust. The board embarked on speculative ventures in property development: The Old Bailey project was a disaster; the Guildford project was a success. In finding the bank liable, Brightman J. allowed the gain on the Guildford project to be set off against the Old Bailey. Without considering the case in detail, he said,[64] after recognising the general rule: "The relevant cases are, however, not altogether easy to reconcile. All are centenarians and none is quite like the present. . . . I think it would be unjust to deprive the bank of the element of salvage in the course of assessing the cost of the shipwreck." Thus a gain can be set off against a loss if, even though not arising from the same transaction, they resulted from the same wrongful course of conduct; in the present case a policy of speculative investment.

---

[61] See also *Wiles* v. *Gresham* (1854) 2 Drew. 258.
[62] (1864) 33 Beav. 426.
[63] [1980] Ch. 515; [1980] Conv. 155 (G. A. Shindler); *ante*, p. 498.
[64] *Ibid.* at p. 538.

2. LIABILITY INTER SE: CONTRIBUTION AND INDEMNITY

A. Joint and Several Liability

Where two or more trustees are liable for a breach of trust, their liability is joint and several. Thus a beneficiary may claim the whole loss by suing all or some or any one of those who are liable; and may levy execution for the whole sum against any one.[65]

B. Liability Inter Se: Contribution

The rule used to be that the joint liability of trustees required an equal sharing of the liability, regardless of fault, and therefore that one trustee who had paid more than his share of the liability for a breach of trust was entitled to equal contribution from the other trustees who were also liable[66]; or from their estates after death.[67] The effect of this rule was shown dramatically in *Bahin* v. *Hughes*,[68] where the Court of Appeal held that a passive trustee was liable with the active trustee. Cotton L.J. said[69]: "Miss Hughes was the active trustee and Mr. Edwards did nothing, and in my opinion it would be laying down a wrong rule to hold that where one trustee acts honestly, though erroneously, the other trustee is to be held entitled to indemnity who by doing nothing neglects his duty more than the acting trustee."

The Civil Liability (Contribution) Act 1978, following the principle of the Law Reform (Married Women and Joint Tortfeasors) Act 1935,[70] gives the court a discretion in relation to the amount to be recovered against two or more defendants who are liable in respect of the damage. The amount recoverable against any defendant shall be "such as may be found by the court to be just and equitable having regard to the extent of that person's responsibility for the damage in question"[71]; and includes breach of trust as one of the forms of liability to which the Act applies.[72] It will be interesting to see how the passive trustee will fare under this provision. The Act does not apply to situations in which one trustee is entitled to an indemnity.[73]

C. Indemnity

There are a few cases where one trustee is not liable to contribute; where, that is, he is entitled to an indemnity from his co-trustee against his own liability. Such cases are rare; for such relief "would act as an

---

[65] *Fletcher* v. *Green* (1864) 33 Beav. 426 at p. 430.
[66] *Lingard* v. *Bromley* (1812) 1 Ves. & B. 114; *Fletcher* v. *Green, supra*; *Ramskill* v. *Edwards* (1885) 31 Ch.D. 100; *Bahin* v. *Hughes* (1886) 31 Ch.D. 390; *Bacon* v. *Camphausen* (1888) 58 L.T. 851; *Robinson* v. *Harkin* [1896] 2 Ch. 415.
[67] *Jackson* v. *Dickinson* [1903] 1 Ch. 947.
[68] (1886) 31 Ch.D. 390.
[69] *Ibid.* at p. 396.
[70] s.1(1).
[71] s.2(1). This may extend to a complete indemnity; s.2(2).
[72] s.6(1).
[73] s.7(3); Law Commission Report on Contribution, No. 79 (1977), para. 26; *cf.* Snell, p. 294; Parker and Mellows, *The Modern Law of Trusts* (5th ed.), p. 456.

opiate upon the consciences of the trustees; so that instead of the *cestui que trust* having the benefit of several acting trustees, each trustee would be looking to the other or others for a right of indemnity, and so neglect the performance of his duties."[74] The situations are:

(i) Fraud. Where one trustee is fraudulent he alone will be liable.[75] If all are fraudulent the rule used to be that the one who has paid the damages could not claim contribution from the others,[76] because a plaintiff should not base his claim upon his wrong. No specific exception, however, is made under the modern legislation authorising the court to determine how liability will be shared, and the Civil Liability (Contribution) Act 1978 will presumably apply.[77]

(ii) Solicitor and Trustee. Many of the cases of indemnity are cases where one trustee is a solicitor and has exercised such a controlling influence that the other trustee has been unable to exercise an independent judgment.[78] There is no rule, however, that "a man is bound to indemnify his co-trustee against loss merely because he was a solicitor, when that co-trustee was an active participator in the breach of trust complained of, and is not proved to have participated merely in consequence of the advice and control of the solicitor."[79]

(iii) Beneficiary-Trustee. When a person who is a trustee and beneficiary participates in a breach of trust, he may not claim any share of the trust estate until he has made good his liability as trustee.[80] He will be required to indemnify his co-trustee to the extent of his beneficial interest; but this does not take away his right to contribution from his co-trustee. The rule in *Chillingworth* v. *Chambers*[81] effects a compromise between these rules. A beneficiary trustee must indemnify his co-trustee to the extent of his beneficial interest. That property is taken first to meet the claims; after that, their liability is shared equally. The non-beneficiary trustee is thus given a partial indemnity; partial in that it extends only to the value of the beneficiary-trustee's interest.

[74] *Per* Fry L.J. in *Bahin* v. *Hughes, supra,* at p. 398.
[75] *Re Smith* [1896] 1 Ch. 171 was an exceptional case of two trustees who acted together, but only one of whom was liable to the beneficiaries for the consequences. One trustee had honestly thought that an investment was a good one, but the other had received a bribe in order to induce him to make it.
[76] *Att.-Gen.* v. *Wilson* (1840) Cr. & Ph. 1 at p. 28.
[77] See (1948) 64 L.Q.R. 46 at p. 47, where P. H. Winfield doubted whether the Law Reform (Married Women and Joint Tortfeasors) Act 1935 would apply to such a case.
[78] *Re Partington* (1887) 57 L.T. 654.
[79] *Head* v. *Gould* [1898] 2 Ch. 250 at p. 265, *per* Kekewich J.; *ante,* p. 462; *Lockhart* v. *Reilly* (1856) 25 L.J. Ch. 697; *Re Turner* [1897] 1 Ch. 536.
[80] *Re Rhodesia Goldfields Ltd.* [1910] 1 Ch. 239; *Selangor United Rubber Estates Ltd.* v. *Cradock (No. 4)* [1969] 3 All E.R. 965.
[81] [1896] 1 Ch. 685; similarly if he becomes a beneficiary after the date of the breach, (1887) 37 Ch.D. 329, at p. 344.

3. Criminal Liability[82]

Breach of trust was not, at common law, a crime at all. The trustee was regarded as the owner of the trust property by the common law, which disregarded the rights of the beneficiary. It was therefore no larceny if the trustee converted to his own use property held upon trust. The Court of Chancery had no jurisdiction to punish him. But in 1857 breach of trust was made a statutory crime, and the law on the subject was incorporated in the Larceny Acts 1861 and 1916.

But these Acts were repealed and replaced by the Theft Act 1968, which defines "theft" as the dishonest appropriation of property "belonging to another" with the intention of depriving the other of it permanently. By section 5(2) of the Act, "any person having a right to enforce the trust" is regarded as a person to whom the subject-matter of the trust "belongs," so that the criminal liability of trustees is in this way brought within the general law, and does not require detailed consideration here.[83] The objects of a discretionary trust can presumably be regarded as having a sufficient right of enforcement to bring section 5(2) into operation for such trusts. Section 4(2)(*a*) also brings within the definition of "theft" an appropriation by a trustee of "land or anything forming part of it," and section 2(1)(*c*) makes a trustee guilty of theft if he appropriates property though he believes that the equitable owners cannot be discovered. A trustee cannot be convicted of theft on any evidence which has first been elicited from him in the course of civil proceedings instituted against him by the person aggrieved, but trustees have no privilege of refusing to incriminate themselves in civil proceedings.[84]

Finally, a trustee who is ordered to pay by a court of equity any sum in his possession or under his control, may be imprisoned in default of payment for a period not exceeding one year.[85]

4. Protection of Trustees

A trustee who has committed a breach of trust may be able to escape personal liability by bringing the case within one of the categories discussed below. Many of the relevant points arose in *Re Pauling's Settlement Trusts*.[86]

The children of the Younghusband family sued to recover from

[82] (1975) 39 Conv.(N.S.) 29 (R. Brazier). For guidelines on sentencing in trustee cases, see *R. v. Barrick* (1985) 81 Cr.App.R. 78.
[83] See further *Re Att.-Gen.'s Reference (No. 1 of 1985)* [1986] Q.B. 491, holding that the making of a secret profit for which a fiduciary was personally accountable was not within s.5(1) or (3) of the 1968 Act. The position as to constructive trusteeship of a profit was left open.
[84] Theft Act 1968, s.31(1).
[85] Debtors Act 1869, s.4.
[86] [1964] Ch. 303.

the trustees of their mother's marriage settlement various payments which were alleged to have been made in breach of trust. The Younghusbands were on many occasions in financial difficulties. Their main source of money was Mrs. Younghusband's marriage settlement under which she was tenant for life, and the trustees had power, with her consent, to advance up to one-half of the presumptive share of each child in the trust fund. Several advances were made under this power to the children when they had attained ages varying from 27 (in the case of Francis) to 21 (Ann and Anthony). In most cases the advances, although nominally made to the children, were, to the knowledge of everyone concerned, applied for family purposes and usually towards the reduction of Mrs. Younghusband's overdraft. On several occasions, but not on all, independent legal advice was obtained. In actions to recover the money from the trustees the defendants relied on the consent and acquiescence of the advanced beneficiaries, and claimed an indemnity under Trustee Act 1925, s.62, and asked for the benefit of the exercise of the court's discretion under section 61. Several of the payments were held to be in breach of trust and the defences set up by the trustees are considered in the following sections.

A. Participation in, or Consent to, a Breach of Trust

A beneficiary who has participated in, or consented to, a breach of trust may not proceed against the trustees. "It is clear to us," said Willmer L.J. speaking for the Court of Appeal in *Re Pauling's Settlement Trusts*[87] "that if the [trustee] can establish a valid request or consent by the advanced beneficiary to the advance in question, that is a good defence on the part of the [trustee] to the beneficiary's claim, even though it be plain that the advance was made in breach of trust." A reversioner is not "less capable of giving . . . assent when his interest is in reversion than when it is in possession,"[88] but he will not be treated as having given consent wherever he fails to take steps to remedy a breach of trust of which he has knowledge.[89]

(i) **Knowledge.** "Consent is not a mere formality. It is a judgment of a person who is interested. . . . "[90] For, if mere knowledge and a passive assent constituted consent, then a trustee could always escape liability by informing a beneficiary of what he proposed to do. The consent must be given by an adult, *sui juris*, in circumstances in which he had a free choice. However, a minor beneficiary may exceptionally be taken to have assented to a breach, for instance where he fraudulently

[87] *Ibid.* at p. 335; *Re Bucks Constabulary Widow's and Orphans' Fund Friendly Society (No. 2)* [1979] 1 W.L.R. 936 at p. 955.
[88] *Life Association of Scotland v. Siddal* (1861) 3 De G.F. & J. 58 at p. 73, *per* Turner L.J.
[89] *Ibid.*
[90] *Re Massingberd's Settlement* (1890) 63 L.T. 296 at p. 299.

misstated his age.[91] "The court has to consider all the circumstances in which the concurrence of the *cestui que trust* was given with a view to seeing whether it is fair and equitable that, having given his concurrence, he should afterwards turn round and sue the trustees: that, subject to this, it is not necessary that he should know that what he is concurring in is a breach of trust, provided that he fully understands what he is concurring in, and that it is not necessary that he should himself have directly benefited by the breach of trust."[92] Thus a beneficiary, who otherwise had a right to set aside a sale, was unable to do so when he had affirmed the sale, accepted part of the purchase money, and caused the purchaser to embark upon further liabilities which he could not repay.[93]

(ii) Benefit. It is not necessary that the beneficiary should have been motivated to derive a personal benefit from the breach, nor that he actually received one.[94] Where a beneficiary may recover even though he has received a benefit he must give credit for any benefit which he has received from the breach.[95]

(iii) Freedom of Decision. The decision must be freely taken by a person not under disability. Even where the beneficiary is adult and technically under no disability, it may be possible to show that the consent was due to undue influence. Thus, in *Re Pauling*,[96] the advancements were in each case delayed until the child had become 21; but several of the payments which had been made to, or indirectly for, the benefit of the parents were presumed to have been the result of undue influence exercised by them over the children. Indeed it was clear that the advances were all made to meet the financial needs of the father of the family. The Court of Appeal refused to accept the trustees' argument that undue influence was only relevant as between the children and their parents, where the parents had acquired the benefit; they suggested that "a trustee carrying out a transaction in breach of trust may be liable if he knew, or ought to have known, that the beneficiary was acting under the undue influence of another, or may be presumed to have done so, but will not be liable if it cannot be established that he so knew, or ought to have known."[97] It is impossible to say how long

---

[91] See *Overton* v. *Bannister* (1884) 3 Hare 503.
[92] *Per* Wilberforce J. in *Re Pauling's S.T.* [1962] 1 W.L.R. 86 at p. 108, accepted by counsel in the Court of Appeal but not commented on by the Court [1964] Ch. 303, at p. 339; approved in *Holder* v. *Holder* [1968] Ch. 353 at pp. 394, 399, 406.
[93] *Holder* v. *Holder, supra.*
[94] *Fletcher* v. *Collis* [1905] 2 Ch. 24.
[95] *Re Pauling's S.T.* [1964] Ch. 303. (The £300 received by Ann; and the policies received by Francis and George). See, however, *ibid.* at p. 354 for the reasons why Anthony was not required to account for benefits received indirectly through his mother.
[96] [1964] Ch. 303.
[97] *Ibid.* at p. 338.

after the attainment of majority the presumption continues; this depends upon the circumstances of each case.[98]

B. Release and Acquiescence

These defences relate to the conduct of the beneficiary after the breach has taken place; where they apply, they become equivalent to consent *ex post facto*. A release may be, but need not be, formal; it may be inferred from conduct, as where a beneficiary accepted benefits under his mother's will which prohibited him from setting up any claim in respect of the administration of his father's estate.[99] Length of time in making a claim will not of itself be fatal, but will assist the trustee by requiring less evidence to establish a release.[1] Many of the points raised in connection with consent, apply also here. "I . . . agree that either concurrence in the act, or acquiescence without original concurrence, will release the trustees; but that is only a general rule, and the Court must inquire into the circumstances which induced concurrence or acquiescence."[2] There will be no release for the trustees where the beneficiary acquiesced without knowledge of the fact; but, as with consent, it is not necessary that the beneficiary should have been aware of his legal rights.[3]

C. Impounding the Beneficiary's Interest: Trustee Act 1925, s.62

(i) **Inherent Power.** Independently of the Trustee Act 1925, s.62, the court has power to impound the interest of a beneficiary who has instigated or requested a breach of trust. The impounding of the beneficiary's interest means that it will be applied so far as it will go towards providing an indemnity to the trustee in respect of the breach. To obtain this indemnity, the trustee must show that the beneficiary acted with knowledge of the facts, although he may not have known that these amounted to a breach of trust. If the beneficiary instigated or requested the breach, it is not necessary to show that the beneficiary received a benefit[4]; but where a beneficiary merely concurred in or consented to a breach of trust, it seems necessary that a benefit be

---

[98] *Huguenin* v. *Baseley* (1807) 14 Ves.Jr. 273; *Allcard* v. *Skinner* (1887) 36 Ch.D. 145 at p. 171; *Powell* v. *Powell* [1900] 1 Ch. 243 at p. 246.

[99] *Egg* v. *Devey* (1847) 10 Beav. 444.

[1] *Stackhouse* v. *Barnston* (1805) 10 Ves.Jr. 453; *Life Association of Scotland* v. *Siddall* (1861) 3 De G.F. & J. 58 at p. 77.

[2] *Walker* v. *Symonds* (1818) 3 Swans. 1 at p. 64, *per* Lord Eldon; *Stackhouse* v. *Barnston, supra.* See also *Swain* v. *Law Society* [1982] 1 W.L.R. 17 (C.A.).

[3] *Holder* v. *Holder* [1968] Ch. 353.

[4] *Trafford* v. *Boehm* (1746) 3 Atk. 440; *Fuller* v. *Knight* (1843) 6 Beav. 205; *Chillingworth* v. *Chambers* [1896] 1 Ch. 685 (a trustee beneficiary).

shown.[5] The trustee, as has been seen, is protected against an action from the consenting beneficiary in respect of the breach.

(ii) Trustee Act 1925, s.62. Section 62 extends this jurisdiction,[6] permitting the court to make an impounding order regardless of any question of benefit. As will be seen, consent, if it is to be effective, must be in writing.[7] Section 62(1), which applies to breaches of trust committed at any time, reads as follows:

> "Where a trustee commits a breach of trust at the instigation or request or with the consent in writing of a beneficiary, the court may, if it thinks fit, . . . make such order as to the court seems just, for impounding all or any part of the interest of the beneficiary in the trust estate by way of indemnity to the trustee or persons claiming through him."

The effect of an impounding order is not only that the beneficiary is unable to recoup his own losses from the trustee, but also that the liability to make up losses suffered by other beneficiaries will fall on him, rather than on the trustee. The liability cannot, however, be for a greater sum than the subsisting value of his own interest in the trust, and it is subject to the discretion of the court. The discretion is exercised in the light of the earlier cases on which section 62 is founded,[8] and generally speaking an indemnity will be given to a trustee against a beneficiary who has been at all active in inducing a breach. Again, however, the knowledge of the beneficiary must amount to a definite appreciation of what is being done. In *Re Somerset*,[9] an impounding order was refused to trustees who had invested trust funds on a mortgage of a particular property at the instigation of a beneficiary, since the beneficiary had no intention of being a party to a breach and had left it entirely to the trustees to determine how much money to lend on the security.

An impounding order will not be made in respect of a loss sustained by a trustee who, only subsequently to the breach, became entitled to a beneficial interest.[10] The right of indemnity by impounding is, however, available to former trustees after their resignation or replacement. The trustees in *Re Pauling's Settlement Trusts (No. 2)*[11]

---

[5] *Booth* v. *Booth* (1838) 1 Beav. 125 at p. 130; *Chillingworth* v. *Chambers, supra*. It has, however, been said that, even in the case of a beneficiary who requests a breach, the indemnity is limited to the benefit received by the beneficiary: *Raby* v. *Ridehalgh* (1855) 7 De G.M. & G. 104.

[6] See Romer J. in *Bolton* v. *Curre* [1895] 1 Ch. 544 at p. 549.

[7] The requirement of writing applies only to consent; *per* Lindley M.R. in *Re Somerset* [1894] 1 Ch. 231 at pp. 265–266.

[8] See Romer J. in *Bolton* v. *Curre* [1895] 1 Ch. 544 at p. 549.

[9] [1894] 1 Ch. 231; *Mara* v. *Browne* [1895] 2 Ch. 69; *cf. Raby* v. *Ridehalgh, supra*.

[10] *Evans* v. *Benyon* (1887) 37 Ch.D. 329.

[11] [1963] Ch. 576; *ante*, p. 607; *Re Bucks Constabulary Widows' and Orphans' Fund Friendly Society (No. 2)* [1979] 1 W.L.R. 936 at p. 955.

claimed an indemnity out of the life interest of the parents of the plaintiffs, and Wilberforce J. held that they were entitled to it, and would remain so entitled, although, as was intended, they would at a future time be replaced by new trustees appointed by the court under the Trustee Act 1925, s.41.

D. Statutory Relief: Trustee Act 1925, s.61

Under this section the court is empowered to excuse trustees from the consequences of a breach of trust. It reads[12]:

> "If it appears to the court that a trustee, . . . is or may be personally liable for any breach of trust, whether the transaction alleged to be a breach of trust occurred before or after the commencement of this Act, but has acted honestly and reasonably, and ought fairly to be excused for the breach of trust and for omitting to obtain the directions of the court in the matter in which he committed such breach, then the court may relieve him either wholly or partly from personal liability for the same."

The power was first given in 1896 and was considerably attacked[13] on the grounds that trustees ought to go to the court for directions in any case in which they felt doubt[14] and that it gave a power to excuse mistakes of law. But it is in the latter type of case that the section can prove indispensable,[15] and the courts have preferred not to lay down formal rules for the application of the section. "It would be impossible," said Byrne J., "to lay down any general rules or principles to be acted on in carrying out the provisions of the section, and I think that each case must depend upon its own circumstances."[16] The only way to show how the discretion has been exercised is to catalogue the cases; but there is inadequate space here.[17] A few general rules, however, can be extracted.

The jurisdiction is available where a trustee "is or may be personally liable" for a breach of trust. There is thus no need to establish the liability; indeed it would put a trustee in a strange position if he had to prove his own liability in order to obtain relief. Several cases allowing relief have done so without reaching a conclusion on the question of liability.[18] However, " 'may be' has . . . been interpreted as indicating

---

[12] (1955) 19 Conv.(N.S.) 420 (L. A. Sheridan); [1977] *Estates and Trusts Quarterly* 12 (D. W. M. Waters). The section also applies to executors; T.A. 1925, s.68(17).
[13] See Maitland, pp. 99–100 and (1898) 14 L.Q.R. 159 (F. H. Maugham).
[14] *Perrins* v. *Bellamy* [1899] 1 Ch. 797.
[15] *e.g. Re Wightwick's W.T.* [1950] Ch. 260.
[16] *Re Turner* [1897] 1 Ch. 536 at p. 542; *Re Kay* [1897] 2 Ch. 518 at p. 524.
[17] See (1955) 19 Conv.(N.S.) 420 at p. 426 (L. A. Sheridan).
[18] *e.g. Re Grindey* [1898] 2 Ch. 593.

doubt, not futurity"[19]; the court will not commit itself in advance to giving relief in the case of a future breach of trust.[20]

In exercising the discretion three factors must be considered[21]; the trustee's honesty, reasonableness, and the question whether he ought "fairly" to be excused. There is little authority on honesty; dishonest trustees do not apply. But Kekewich J. once characterised as dishonest "a trustee who does nothing, swallows wholesale what is said by his co-trustee, never asks for explanation, and accepts flimsy explanations."[22] If this is right, there must be large numbers of trustees of family trusts who find themselves in that category.

There is some uncertainty as to the standard to be applied in determining reasonableness, but the usual standard is that of a prudent man of business managing his own affairs.[23] The amount of money involved will be a relevant factor.[24] In *Re Stuart*[25] it was said that, in connection with lending trust money on mortgage, the statutory procedure for valuations and reports[26] "constitute a standard by which reasonable conduct will be judged"; but failure to follow this is "not necessarily a fatal objection to the application of the section."

The distinction between conduct that is reasonable and that for which a trustee ought fairly to be excused is not easy to see. In *Davis* v. *Hutchings*[27] trustees, on the distribution of the trust fund, paid the share of one beneficiary to the solicitor to the trust in response to the solicitor's statement that he was the assignee of the share. The share had in fact been mortgaged and assigned to him subject to the mortgage. Kekewich J. held that the trustees were liable. They had acted honestly and reasonably, but they should not be excused.[28] Fairness should be considered in relation to all the parties, the trustees, the beneficiaries and the creditors, and is "essentially a matter within the discretion of the judge."[29]

Little seems to be added to this section by the reference to omission to obtain the directions of the court. "I do not see how the trustee can

[19] (1955) 19 Conv.(N.S.) 425.
[20] *Re Tollemache* [1903] 1 Ch. 457 at pp. 465–466; affirmed at p. 953; *Re Rosenthal* [1972] 1 W.L.R. 1273. The court may, however, authorise an act so as to prevent it being a breach.
[21] *Marsden* v. *Regan* [1954] 1 W.L.R. 423 at p. 434.
[22] *Re Second East Dulwich, etc., Building Society* (1899) 79 L.T. 726 at p. 727.
[23] See Chitty L.J. in *Re Grindey, supra,* at p. 601; *Re Turner* [1897] 1 Ch. 536 at p. 542; *Re Lord de Clifford's Estate* [1900] 2 Ch. 707 at p. 716; *Re Stuart* [1897] 2 Ch. 583 at p. 590; *Re Rosenthal, supra.* The trustees in *Bartlett* v. *Barclays Bank Trust Co. Ltd. (No. 1)* [1980] Ch. 515, *ante,* p. 604, were unable to rely on the section because they had not acted reasonably.
[24] *Re Grindey* [1898] 2 Ch. 593; *Marsden* v. *Regan, supra.*
[25] [1897] 2 Ch. 583.
[26] *Re Stuart, supra,* at pp. 591–592; *Shaw* v. *Cates* [1909] 1 Ch. 389; *Palmer* v. *Emerson* [1911] 1 Ch. 758.
[27] [1907] 1 Ch. 356.
[28] Some of the dicta of Kekewich J. were disapproved in *Re Allsop* [1914] 1 Ch. 1 at pp. 11, 12; see also *Marsden* v. *Regan* [1954] 1 W.L.R. 423, at pp. 434–435.
[29] *Marsden* v. *Regan, supra,* at p. 435.

be excused for the breach of trust without being also excused for the omission referred to, or how he can be excused for the omission without also being excused for the breach of trust."[30]

The onus of showing that he acted honestly and reasonably is on the trustee.[31] Applications for relief have most commonly arisen in connection with unauthorised investments.[32] A trustee will not usually be excused if he has "relied on a co-trustee, or on the testator's solicitor, or on some other adviser of the testator's, or on the testator's own course of conduct. ... The honest taking of what is conceived to be reliable advice will be no ground for excuse if the court believe a prudent man of business would have acted differently in ordering his own affairs."[33] Another and common situation is that of payment of the funds to the wrong beneficiary,[34] or the payment of void claims by creditors,[35] and relief may be given where the trustee's mistake was one of law.[36] The taking of legal advice is a relevant factor, but does not automatically entitle a trustee to relief.[37]

The section extends to professional trustees who are being paid for their services, but the court is less ready to grant relief in such cases.[38]

E. Limitation and Laches[39]

(i) Six-Year Period under Limitation Act 1980, s.21(3). Subject to exceptions discussed below, the Limitation Act 1980, s.21(3), provides a six-year limitation for the protection of trustees. The subsection reads:

"Subject to the preceding provisions of this section, an action by a beneficiary[40] to recover trust property or in respect of any breach of

---

[30] *Perrins* v. *Bellamy* [1898] 2 Ch. 521 at p. 528.

[31] *Re Stuart* [1897] 2 Ch. 583.

[32] *Re Turner, supra; Re Stuart, supra; Re Barker* (1898) 77 L.T. 712; *Re Dive* [1909] 1 Ch. 328; *Bartlett* v. *Barclays Bank Trust Co. Ltd. (No. 1)* [1980] Ch. 515, *ante,* p. 604.

[33] (1955) 29 Conv.(N.S.) 420 at p. 427.

[34] *Re Allsop* [1914] 1 Ch.1; *Re Pawson's Settlement* [1917] 1 Ch. 541; *National Trustees Co. of Australasia* v. *General Finance Co. of Australasia* [1905] A.C. 373; *Re Wightwick's W.T.* [1950] Ch. 260.

[35] *Re Lord de Clifford's Estate* [1900] 2 Ch. 707; *Re Mackay* [1911] 1 Ch. 300; *cf. Re Windsor Steam Coal Co. Ltd.* [1929] 1 Ch. 151.

[36] *Holland* v. *German Property Administrator* [1937] 2 All E.R. 807.

[37] *National Trustees Co. of Australasia* v. *General Finance Co. of Australasia* [1905] A.C. 373; *Marsden* v. *Regan* [1954] 1 W.L.R. 423 at pp. 434–435.

[38] *National Trustees Co. of Australasia* v. *General Finance Co. of Australasia* [1905] A.C. 373; *Re Windsor Steam Coal Co.* [1929] 1 Ch. 151; *Re Waterman's W.T.* [1952] 2 All E.R. 1054; *Re Pauling's S.T.* [1964] Ch. 303. at pp. 356–359; *ante,* p. 611; Law Reform Committee, 23rd Report, *The Powers and Duties of Trustees,* (1982 Cmnd. 8733), para. 2.16.

[39] See Preston and Newsom, *Limitation of Actions,* Chap. 5; Franks, *Limitation of Actions,* pp. 62–80.

[40] The section does not apply to a claim by the Attorney General against the trustee of a charitable trust, which has no "beneficiary"; *Att.-Gen.* v. *Cocke* [1988] Ch. 414; [1988] Conv. 292 (J. Warburton) (also holding the subsection inapplicable to an action for an account not alleging any breach of trust or claiming recovery of trust property).

trust,[41] not being an action for which a period of limitation is prescribed by any other provision of this Act, shall not be brought after the expiration of six years from the date on which the right of action accrued.

For the purposes of this subsection, the right of action shall not be treated as having accrued to any beneficiary entitled to a future interest in the trust property, until the interest fell into possession."

In this subsection, "trustee" includes personal representatives[42] and also certain fiduciary agents,[43] company directors[44] and a mortgagee in respect of the proceeds of sale,[45] but not a trustee in bankruptcy,[46] nor the liquidator of a company in voluntàry liquidation.[47] It will also be noted that there is no distinction between the protection given to an express trustee and that given to an implied or constructive trustee; until Trustee Act 1888, s.8, no protection based upon passage of time had been available to an express trustee.[48] It will be seen that the subsection only applies to cases where an action is brought by a beneficiary in respect of the trust property.[49] Under the proviso, time only begins to run against remaindermen or reversioners when their interest falls into possession; and it has been held that this does not occur when improper advancements are made in favour of remaindermen.[50] And if a beneficiary is entitled to two interests in the property, one in possession and one in remainder, he does not lose a claim in respect of the latter where time has run against him in respect of the former.[51]

(ii) Exceptions to the Six-Year Rule. There are some exceptions to the six-year rule

(a) *Limitation Act 1980, s.21(1).*

"(1) No period of limitation prescribed by this Act shall apply to an action by a beneficiary under a trust, being an action—
(*a*) in respect of any fraud or fraudulent breach of trust to which the trustee was a party or privy; or

---

[41] In *Tito* v. *Waddell (No. 2)* [1977] Ch. 106 at p. 249, Megarry V.-C. concluded that this provision did not apply to situations governed by the self-dealing and fair dealing rules applicable to trustees. Those cases are covered by the doctrine of laches.

[42] Limitation Act 1980, s.38(1); T.A. 1925, s.68(17).

[43] *Burdick* v. *Garrick* (1870) L.R. 5 Ch.App. 233.

[44] *Re Lands Allotment Co.* [1894] 1 Ch. 616; *Belmont Finance Corporation* v. *Williams Furniture Ltd. (No. 2)* [1980] 1 All E.R. 393.

[45] *Thorne* v. *Heard* [1895] A.C. 495.

[46] *Re Cornish* [1896] 1 Q.B. 99.

[47] *Re Windsor Steam Coal Co.* [1928] Ch. 609; affirmed on other grounds [1929] 1 Ch. 151.

[48] Franks, *loc. cit.* p. 64.

[49] *Re Bowden* (1890) 45 Ch.D. 444, at p. 451.

[50] *Re Pauling's S.T.* [1964] Ch. 303.

[51] *Mara* v. *Browne* [1895] 2 Ch. 69, reversed on another point [1896] 1 Ch. 199.

(*b*) to recover from the trustee trust property or the proceeds of
trust property in the possession of the trustee, or previously
received by the trustee and converted to his use."[52]

This subsection reproduces in the situations to which it applies the
rule of permanent liability which was applicable in equity to the case of
express trustees.

In *North American Land Co.* v. *Watkins*,[53] an agent had been sent
to America to buy land for his company. He bought it, and it was
duly conveyed to the company, but the agent made and retained a
profit for himself. After the expiration of the period applicable for
the recovery of money had and received, the company successfully
recovered the money on two grounds, first that the agent was in the
position of a trustee and had retained trust money, and secondly that
his conduct had been fraudulent.

It seems that the fraud must be that of the trustee himself.

In *Thorne* v. *Heard*[54] a trustee was protected where he had negligently left funds in the hands of a solicitor who had embezzled them;
for the trustee to come within section 21(1) he must be "party or
privy" to the fraud.

No question of dishonesty arises where a trustee is in possession of the
trust property.

In *Re Sharp*[55] trustees had paid to themselves annuities to which
they were entitled, but had done so without deduction of tax and
they were held to lose their protection within the provisions of the
subsection in respect of the amount which should have been
deducted for income tax.

And in *Re Howlett*[56] a trustee, who was income beneficiary until
remarriage, continued in possession of a wharf until he died, and the
remainderman was held able to sue the life tenant's representatives
after his death for an occupation rent for the premises.

Conversion to the trustee's own use requires some wrongful application in his own favour. A trustee was held to escape from the subsection where he applied the trust funds for the maintenance of a minor

---

[52] But where a trustee is also a beneficiary and has received his share on a distribution of
the trust property, paragraph (*b*) shall only apply in respect of the excess over his
share, so long as the trustee acted honestly and reasonably in making the distribution;
s.21(2).
[53] [1904] 1 Ch. 242; [1904] 2 Ch. 233.
[54] [1894] 1 Ch. 599; [1895] A.C. 495; *Petre* v. *Petre* (1853) 1 Drew. 371; *Re Fountaine*
[1909] 2 Ch. 382.
[55] [1906] 1 Ch. 793.
[56] [1949] Ch. 767; *Wassell* v. *Leggatt* [1896] 1 Ch. 554; *Re Eyre-Williams* [1923] 2 Ch. 533;
Re Clerk (1920) 150 L.T. Jour. 94; see also *Re Landi* [1939] Ch. 828; *Re Milking Pail
Farm Trusts* [1940] Ch. 996.

beneficiary,[57] or where trust funds advanced on mortgage were, with the concurrence of the mortgagor, used to pay a debt previously charged on the mortgaged property in favour of a bank of which a trustee was a partner,[58] or where the funds were dissipated by a co-trustee.[59]

(b) *Claim to the Personal Estate of a Deceased Person.* Under section 22, which is subject to section 21(1), an action in respect of any claim to the personal estate of a deceased person must be brought within the period of 12 years. Difficult questions on the inter-relation of this section and section 21(3) can arise where the personal representatives administering an estate would normally be treated as having become trustees. In that case the question is whether the 12-year or six-year rule is applicable.[60] The better view, it is submitted, is that the 12-year rule applies even though the personal representatives would for other purposes be treated as having become trustees.[61]

(c) *Sections 28 and 32.* Section 28 allows an extension of the period of limitation in cases in which the plaintiff has been under disability. Section 32 provides that where any action is based upon fraud or where the right of action is concealed by fraud or where the action is for relief from the consequences of a mistake, "the period of limitation shall not begin to run until the plaintiff has discovered the fraud, concealment or mistake . . . or could with reasonable diligence have discovered it."[62] This section applies to actions against trustees.[63]

(iii) **Assignees.** A transferee from the trustee is in the same position as the trustee was[64]; unless he is bona fide purchaser for value without notice in which case he will presumably be treated as if he had purchased from someone who was not a trustee.

(iv) **Where No Period is Applicable.** It has been seen that the Limitation Act 1980 deals comprehensively with the running of time in actions against trustees. In situations not covered, it is necessary to

---

[57] *Re Page* [1893] 1 Ch. 304; *Re Timmis* [1902] 1 Ch. 176.

[58] *Re Gurney* [1893] 1 Ch. 590.

[59] *Re Tufnell* (1902) 18 T.L.R. 705; *Re Fountaine* [1909] 2 Ch. 382.

[60] *Re Timmis* [1902] 2 Ch. 176; *Re Richardson* [1920] 1 Ch. 423; *Re Oliver* [1927] 2 Ch. 323; *Re Diplock* [1948] Ch. 465; [1951] A.C. 251.

[61] See Pettit, *Equity and The Law of Trusts,* pp. 440–441, for a discussion of the point; Franks, *Limitation of Actions,* pp. 49–50; Preston and Newsom, p. 188; *Re Diplock* [1948] Ch. 465, *sub nom. Minister of Health* v. *Simpson* [1951] A.C. 251.

[62] Re-enacting the provisions of the Limitation Act 1939, as amended by the Limitation (Amendment) Act 1980.

[63] See *Beaman* v. *A.R.T.S.* [1949] 1 K.B. 550; *Kitchen* v. *R.A.F. Association* [1958] 1 W.L.R. 563; *Phillips-Higgins* v. *Harper* [1954] 1 Q.B. 411; *Bartlett* v. *Barclays Bank Trust Co. Ltd.* [1980] Ch. 515 at p. 537.

[64] See *Re Dixon* [1900] 2 Ch. 561; *Re Eyre-Williams* [1923] 2 Ch. 533; *Baker* v. *Medway Building and Supplies Ltd.* [1958] 1 W.L.R. 1216; *Eddis* v. *Chichester-Constable* [1969] 2 Ch. 345.

return to the law as it existed before the statutory protection was given. No provision is made, for example, either for claims for equitable relief by way of specific performance, rescission or rectification, or injunction[65]; or in cases of redemption of a mortgage of pure personalty,[66] or the setting aside of a purchase of trust property by a trustee.[67] The rule of equity is that either no period is applicable, or that the relevant common law period is applied by analogy. In any situation for which no period of limitation is expressly applicable to an equitable claim, the defendant may rely on the doctrine of laches.[68] Delay by a plaintiff in pursuing his rights "may furnish a defence in equity to an equitable claim."[69] Whether such a defence is available in a particular case is a matter for the discretion of the court, and will depend to a large extent upon the hardship caused to the plaintiff by the delay, and the effect upon third parties; and generally upon the balance of justice in granting or refusing relief.[70] There is no maximum period beyond which the equitable relief cannot be sought but a period of 20 years may be taken as a convenient guide.[71] The defendant will be more likely to succeed if he can show not merely delay, but acquiescence. Both defences appear to have been retained by the Limitation Act 1980 which provides in section 36(2): "Nothing in this Act shall affect any equitable jurisdiction to refuse relief on the ground of acquiescence or otherwise."

These defences are therefore relevant to cases to which no period is applicable, including those within section 21(1). Prior to the Limitation Act 1939 the doctrine of laches applied differently in regard to express and other trustees; but it seems that there should no longer be a distinction,[72] and that the position of express trustees alone need be considered. The rule "seems to be that while the doctrine of laches applies to claims by beneficiaries, relief will only be refused in plain cases."[73]

A question which has recently arisen is whether any limitation period applies to an action for an account. Section 23 of the 1980 Act provides that "an action for an account shall not be brought after the expiration of any time limit under this Act which is applicable to the claim which is the basis of the duty to account." In *Att.-Gen.* v. *Cocke*[74]

---

[65] See Limitation Act 1980, s.36(1).

[66] *Weld* v. *Petre* [1929] 1 Ch. 33.

[67] *Baker* v. *Read* (1854) 18 Beav. 398; *Morse* v. *Royal* (1806) 12 Ves.Jr. 355; Snell, p. 37.

[68] *Re Pauling's S.T.* [1964] Ch. 303. See also *Alec Lobb (Garages) Ltd.* v. *Total Oil G.B. Ltd.* [1985] 1 W.L.R. 173.

[69] *Re Sharpe* [1892] 1 Ch. 154 at p. 168; *Smith* v. *Clay* (1767) 3 Bro.C.C. 639n.; Franks, *loc. cit.*, pp. 233 *et seq.*; Brunyate, *Limitation of Actions in Equity.*

[70] *Lindsay Petroleum Co.* v. *Hurd* (1874) L.R. 5 P.C. 221 at pp. 239–241; *Weld* v. *Petre* [1929] 1 Ch. 33 at pp. 51, 52.

[71] *Weld* v. *Petre, supra,* at pp. 54, 55.

[72] Franks, *loc. cit.* p. 260; *cf. Re Jarvis* [1958] 1 W.L.R. 815.

[73] Franks, *loc. cit.* p. 261.

[74] [1988] Ch. 414; [1988] Conv. 292 (J. Warburton); *ante*, p. 373. See also *Tito* v. *Waddell (No. 2)* [1977] Ch. 106 at p. 251.

an action for an account was brought in respect of an estate held upon charitable trusts. As there was no allegation of a breach of trust nor any claim to recover trust property (and also because there was no "beneficiary"), section 21(3) did not apply. The duty to account is based not on breach of trust but on the fiduciary relationship between the trustee and the person entitled to enforce the obligation. Harman J. considered, therefore, that section 23 had very little application. In the case of an action for an account *simpliciter*, based on fiduciary relationship and nothing more, there would be no period of limitation under the Act and nothing for section 23 to operate upon.

5. PROPRIETARY REMEDIES

A. Personal and Proprietary Actions

Most action at law and in equity are personal. We now have to consider the occasions on which a plaintiff has the right to proceed against a particular asset in the defendant's hands. Such proprietary remedies exist to a very limited extent at law; and these, for convenience and for the sake of comparison, will be described here.[75] In equity the right to follow or trace property is more extensive. We will see that a proprietary remedy may be available where the plaintiff is making a claim at law or in equity to a specific piece of property, and also where he is making a claim in equity against a mixed fund to which property of his (in equity) has contributed.

There are several advantages of a proprietary over a personal remedy. First and foremost, satisfaction of the plaintiff's demand does not depend on the solvency of the defendant. If the property traced is the plaintiff's in equity, it escapes the defendant's bankruptcy.[76] Secondly, in some cases, the plaintiff will be able to take advantage of increases in the value of the property. This is obvious where specific property is treated as being the plaintiff's in equity, and was more recently established where a mixed fund is in question.[77] Further, there appear to be some cases in which the proprietary remedy is available although no personal action will lie.[78] And, finally, judgment in a proprietary action concerning an income-producing asset carries interest from the date on which the property came to the defendant's hands, while claims *in personam* carry interest only from the date of judgment.[79]

[75] *Post*, p. 621.
[76] Insolvency Act 1986, s.283.
[77] *Re Tilley's W.T.* [1967] Ch. 1179; *post*, p. 639.
[78] *Sinclair* v. *Brougham* [1914] A.C. 398. (*ultra vires* loan).
[79] *Re Diplock* [1948] Ch. 465.

Finally, it should be said that, although the English and American rules on these matters are not identical, anyone who is faced with a question on proprietary remedies should be acquainted with paragraphs 160–162 and 202–215 of the *Restatement of Restitution*, whose authors have foreseen and provided solutions for most if not all the problems which have arisen in the English cases.[80]

B. Unjust Enrichment; Restitution[81]

Proprietary remedies cannot be fully understood without some appreciation of the doctrine of unjust enrichment. This is a doctrine which appears in nearly every system of law. It lays down as a general principle that where the defendant is unjustly enriched at the plaintiff's expense, the defendant must make restitution to the plaintiff.[82] Such a principle has its greatest scope in the area of quasi-contract, but it overlaps also into contract, tort, and into many areas of equity.

The development of unjust enrichment in England was bogged down by the dispute on the question whether or not a quasi-contractual action is theoretically based upon an implied contract.[83] In 1951, Lord Porter said[84]: "My Lords, the exact status of the law of unjust enrichment is not yet assured. It holds a predominant place in the law of Scotland and, I think, of the United States, but I am content for the purposes of this case to accept the view that it forms no part of the law of England. ... " Even though there is no such right to restitution in every case of unjust enrichment, all restitutionary claims are unified by the principle.[85] Ultimately, the search is to do justice between the parties.

Assume that A has a right to sue B on the ground that A has paid money to B by mistake, or under compulsion, or under a sudden emergency, or under a contract that was void, or in any other situation in which B is enriched at the expense of A. If B is solvent, a personal action will satisfy A's claim. What should be the effect on this situation if, (a) B is bankrupt, or (b) B invests the money and it doubles in value? In case (a) it is arguable that since B should never have had the money, nor should his creditors. The creditors run the risk of B's insolvency and there is no reason why they should have the advantage of a

---

[80] Including that of the personal claim in *Re Diplock* [1948] Ch. 465; see *Restatement of Restitution*, para. 126, comment (c), and *Restatement of Trusts*, para. 199.

[81] Goff and Jones, *The Law of Restitution* (3rd ed.); Birks, *An Introduction to the Law of Restitution*; *Restatement of Restitution*.

[82] *Restatement of Restitution*, para. 1.

[83] (1924) 40 L.Q.R. 34–36 (H. G. Hanbury); (1938) 54 L.Q.R. 201 (C. K. Allen); (1938) 6 C.L.J. 305; *Legal Essays and Addresses*, Chap. 1 (Lord Wright); (1939) 55 L.Q.R. 37 (W. S. Holdsworth); R. M. Jackson, *History of Quasi-Contract*, pp. 117–124; Winfield, *The Law of Quasi-Contract*, pp. 14–21; Stoljar, *The Law of Quasi-Contract*, pp. 2–9; *Sinclair* v. *Brougham* [1914] A.C. 398; *United Australia Ltd.* v. *Barclays Bank* [1941] A.C. 1; Goff and Jones (3rd ed.), p. 5.

[84] *Reading* v. *Att.-Gen.* [1951] A.C. 507 at pp. 513–514; *Orakpo* v. *Manson Investments* [1977] 1 W.L.R. 347.

[85] Goff and Jones (3rd ed.), pp. 12, 61.

payment into B's estate out of money of A's which B should never have had. A did not rely on B's solvency, and should have a prior claim to the available money. In case (b) it can be argued that neither B nor his creditors should reap the full measure of the profit which B has made out of money which he should never have had. Should A have it? Would it make any difference if the invested funds were part A's and part B's? We might here pose a further case (c). If B uses the money (*i.e.* A's) to pay off a mortgage on his property and is insolvent, should A be placed in the position, by subrogation, of the mortgagee? These are all interesting and difficult questions, to some of which the English cases provide answers; to others not. The cases have proceeded pragmatically from one point to another without keeping the various problems and principles in mind; and a number of unnecessary difficulties arise for this reason.

C. Tracing at Common Law[86]

A proprietary remedy is one which entitles a claimant to treat specific property, or a portion thereof, as his own. If the common law had developed a real action for chattels which entitled a plaintiff to specific recovery, the claimant would be able to demand the return of the chattel. But although the court recognised the plaintiff as being the owner, there was no such action at common law. The defendant had the choice of paying damages or returning the chattel. A discretion to award specific recovery in an action in detinue was given to the court in 1854.[87]

The plaintiff's ownership was relevant however in that his entitlement was to the chattel or to its value—its full value that is, even if the defendant was insolvent, and not merely to a dividend in the insolvency. In the case of a loan, the plaintiff's claim for the money lent to an insolvent defendant would abate; it was something owed. The position is different with the chattel; that was something owned.

The question then arises whether this right of the plaintiff's is limited to the case of a specific chattel. Should his right not continue if the defendant had exchanged one chattel for another; or the chattel for a sum of money; or had spent that money on another chattel? The answer of the common law is that of Lord Ellenborough in *Taylor* v. *Plumer*[88]: "It makes no difference in reason or law into what other form, different from the original, the change may have been made,

---

[86] (1966) 7 W.A.L.R. 463 (M. Scott); (1976) 40 Conv.(N.s.) 277 (R. A. Pearce); (1979) 95 L.Q.R. 78 (S. Khurshid and P. Matthews); (1976) 92 L.Q.R. 360 at p. 367 (R. M. Goode). See Hayton and Marshall, *Cases and Commentary on the Law of Trusts* (8th ed.), p. 513; Birks, *An Introduction to the Law of Restitution*, pp. 358 *et seq.*

[87] Common Law Procedure Act 1854, s.78. Detinue has now been abolished: Torts (Interference with Goods) Act 1977, s.2; but the discretionary power of the court to order specific recovery is retained by s.3.

[88] (1815) 3 M. & S. 562 at p. 575.

whether it be into that of promissory notes for the security of the money which was produced by the sale of the goods of the principal, as in *Scott* v. *Surman*,[89] or into other merchandise, as in *Whitecomb* v. *Jacob*,[90] for the product of or substitute for the original thing still follows the nature of the thing itself, as long as it can be ascertained to be such, and the right only ceases when the means of ascertainment fail, which is the case when the subject is turned into money, and mixed and confounded in a general mass of the same description. The difficulty which arises in such a case is a difficulty of fact and not of law, and the dictum that money has no ear-mark must be understood in the same way; *i.e.* as predicated only of an undivided and undistinguishable mass of current money. But money in a bag or otherwise kept apart from other money, guineas, or other coin marked, if the fact were so, for the purpose of being distinguished, and so far ear-marked as to fall within the rule on this subject, which applies to every other description of personal property whilst it remains (as the property in question did) in the hands of the factor [the bankrupt] or his general legal representatives."

In *Taylor* v. *Plumer*,[91] the defendant handed money to a stock-broker, Walsh, to purchase exchequer bonds. Walsh instead purchased American investments and bullion and hurried off to Falmouth to board a packet for America. He was apprehended, and the investments and bullion were seized. On his bankruptcy, his assignees sought to recover them from the defendant. They failed. The investments were the ascertainable product of the defendant's money and owned by the defendant. If the parties had been reversed, and Sir Thomas Plumer had been suing for the recovery of the securities and bullion, his action would have succeeded, but the assignees would have had the choice of returning them or of paying their full value in damages; just as if Walsh had taken the defendant's coach and horses and had had them in his possession on his bankruptcy.

It is important to appreciate the limitations of the tracing remedy at law. The available common law actions of conversion or the action for money had and received are personal actions as was detinue, though, as has been seen[92] the court may exercise a discretionary power to order the specific recovery of a chattel. Earlier editions[93] of the book had taken the view that this factor was a serious disadvantage to the common law claims, for personal actions, according to the ordinary rule, will abate in a bankruptcy, which is the normal situation in which

---

[89] (1742) Willes 400.
[90] (1710) Salk. 160.
[91] (1815) 3 M. & S. 562; *Re J. Leslie Engineers Co. Ltd.* [1976] 1 W.L.R. 292 at p. 297.
[92] *Ante,* p. 621.
[93] Prior to the 11th edition.

a tracing remedy is claimed. This view was criticised[94] on the ground that the right "remains proprietary. The limitation has resulted merely in an inability to compel the return of the property *in specie.* "[95] "If A's property is in B's hands and B goes bankrupt, title does not pass to B's trustee in bankruptcy. If the trustee nevertheless gets hold of it, he can be sued personally in conversion, so that he must either return the chattel or pay full damages."[96] And if the trustee has sold the property and converted it into money after the bankruptcy, the action for money had and received, so it is said,[97] will allow full recovery without abatement in the bankruptcy.

The right of full recovery in a bankruptcy appears to be limited to cases where the defendant, such as the trustee in bankruptcy, has taken a chattel of the plaintiff's, whether or not converted into money, or has taken money and purchased a chattel. *Giles* v. *Perkins,*[98] a case not involving a chattel, was a successful claim against an insolvent bank where the bank, at the time of its insolvency, held the plaintiff's bills which were payable after the date of the bankruptcy. The crucial question at common law, as *Taylor* v. *Plumer* shows,[99] was whether there was identifiable property, the title to which did not pass to the plaintiff. And in *Banque Belge pour L'Etranger* v. *Hambrouck*[1] money in a substantially unmixed bank account was treated by the majority of the Court of Appeal as identifiable, even though the payment into a bank account is a clear illustration of the creation of a debtor-creditor relationship. What the common law remedies could not do was to provide full protection to the plaintiff in the most important type of case in which these questions arise: that is, the case where the defendant has received the plaintiff's money, mixed it with other money in a bank account, and has gone bankrupt.[2] This, as we will see,[3] is the area in which the equitable tracing remedy, with all its limitations, is particularly relevant.

It is these limitations upon the availability of the equitable remedy which leave scope for tracing at common law. In practical terms, however, most of the situations in which a claim to trace arises are cases of money in mixed bank accounts, in which the common law remedy is not available. It has therefore little practical importance at the present day. The proper emphasis is on the equitable right, and

---

[94] (1976) 40 Conv.(N.S.) 277 (R. A. Pearce); (1979) 95 L.Q.R. 78 (S. Khurshid and P. Matthews); Goff and Jones (3rd ed.), p. 65, n. 31.
[95] (1976) 40 Conv.(N.S.) at p. 284.
[96] (1979) 95 L.Q.R. 78.
[97] (1966) 7 W.A.L.R. 463 at p. 481 (M. Scott); Goff and Jones (3rd ed.), pp. 65, 69.
[98] (1807) 9 East. 12; *Scott* v. *Surman* (1742) Willes 400.
[99] See (1966) 7 W.A.L.R. 463 at pp. 481 *et seq.*
[1] [1921] 1 K.B. 321.
[2] For the position at common law in respect of mixed or improved goods, see (1981) 34 C.L.P. 159 (P. Matthews).
[3] *Infra.*

upon overcoming the unnecessary restrictions which have been placed upon it.

D. Tracing in Equity

Equity has developed more sophisticated methods of tracing. The rules have developed, and are usually applied, in the context of property in the hands of trustees or other fiduciaries, and often on the bankruptcy of the fiduciary. But the rules apply also in a commercial context; as where a vendor, in order to protect himself in a customer's bankruptcy, provides expressly that property shall not pass in goods supplied until payment. This is dealt with below.[4]

(i) Who is Entitled to Trace. The remedy in equity is not confined to claims between trustee and beneficiary. *Re Hallett*[5] decided that the remedy was not restricted to such a case but was available between fiduciaries. "Has it ever been suggested," said Jessel M.R.,[6] "until very recently, that there is any distinction between an express trustee or an agent, or a bailee, or a collector of rents, or anybody else in a fiduciary position?"[7]

(a) *Requirement of Fiduciary Relationship.* The courts have insisted that the existence of a fiduciary relationship is a prerequisite to tracing in equity, although this relationship need not exist between the parties to the action.

In *Sinclair* v. *Brougham*[8] the Birkbeck Building Society operated a banking business which was held to be *ultra vires*. In the winding up of the Society, competition arose between the claims of the share-holders and of the bank customers (called the depositors). One of the questions that fell to be decided was whether the depositors had the right to trace into the general assets of the Society. The House of Lords held (as explained in *Re Diplock*[9]) that there was a fiduciary relation between the depositors and the directors; the directors had mixed the funds and the depositors had the right to trace them into

---

[4] *Post*, p. 633.

[5] (1880) 13 Ch.D. 696.

[6] *Ibid.* at p. 709; *Chase Manhattan Bank N.A.* v. *Israel-British Bank (London) Ltd.* [1981] Ch. 105.

[7] See Goff and Jones (3rd ed.), p. 71, n. 68, where they point out how difficult it is to define precisely who is a fiduciary. They refer to the analogy of decisions on the applicability of the Statutes of Limitation, which suggest that "much depends on whether the agent is under a duty to keep separate his own money from his principal's money."

[8] [1914] A.C. 398.

[9] [1948] Ch. 465, at p. 532.

the hands of the Society, recognising an equal claim of the share-holders with whom they shared *pari passu*.[10]

The matter was taken a step further in *Re Diplock*[11]; for the mixing was there done, not by the fiduciary agent, but by the innocent volunteer (the charities) to whom the agent handed the money.

By his will Caleb Diplock gave the residue of his property on trust "for such charitable institutions or other charitable or benevolent ... objects in England as my ... executors ... may in their ... absolute discretion select." He and the executors thought that this was a valid charitable gift, but a reference to Chapter 15 will show that this is not so.[12] The executors distributed £203,000 among a considerable number of charitable institutions; and when the invalidity of the charitable gift was discovered, the next-of-kin claimed to recover the money from the charities. They succeeded in a personal claim[13] and were also entitled to the tracing remedy, the Court of Appeal laying down as the test that[14] "equity may operate on the conscience not merely of those who acquire a legal title in breach of some trust, express or constructive, or of some other fiduciary obligation, but of volunteers provided that as a result of what has gone before some equitable proprietary interest has been created and attaches to the property in the hands of the volunteer." Although a beneficiary is not normally regarded as the equitable owner of assets in an unadministered estate,[15] the "equitable proprietary interest" was established for present purposes by the equitable claim by the plaintiffs as next-of-kin against the executors; and this gave the plaintiffs the right to trace against the charities.[16]

It has been questioned whether *Sinclair* v. *Brougham*[17] is in fact authority for the proposition that a fiduciary relationship is necessary to tracing in equity, although so regarded by the Court of Appeal in *Re Diplock*.[18] The insistence upon such a relationship has been said to be regrettable and capable of producing unjust and anomalous results.[19] The requirement has, however, been accepted without discussion by

---

[10] The validity of the explanation is doubted by Goff and Jones (3rd ed.), pp. 70–71; " ... the money had not passed through the directors' hands; moreover it is not easy to see how directors, who are never in a fiduciary relationship to their shareholders, can be in a fiduciary relationship to *ultra vires* depositors." It was agreed that outside creditors should take priority (as otherwise the *ultra vires* creditors would have been better off than the *intra vires* creditors).

[11] [1948] Ch. 465.

[12] *Ante*, p. 421, *Chichester Diocesan Fund* v. *Simpson* [1944] A.C. 341.

[13] [1951] A.C. 251. The appeal to the House of Lords concerned only the claim *in personam*; *post*, p. 644.

[14] [1948] Ch. 465 at p. 530.

[15] *Commissioner of Stamp Duties* v. *Livingston* [1965] A.C. 694; *ante*, p. 22.

[16] Applied in *Re J. Leslie Engineers Co. Ltd.* [1976] 1 W.L.R. 292.

[17] *Supra*.

[18] *Supra*.

[19] Goff and Jones (3rd ed.), p. 72. See also (1987) 103 L.Q.R. 433 (R. M. Goode).

the Court of Appeal.[20] But the position may be relieved by the apparent ease with which a fiduciary relationship may be recognised.[21]

(b) *Requirement of an Equitable Proprietary Interest.* In the days before the fusion of the jurisdiction of law and equity, it was only possible to obtain equitable remedies if the litigation were "in equity." It is not therefore surprising that the test which has been laid down historically for the availability of the equitable tracing remedy is that the plaintiff should be entitled to an *equitable* proprietary interest; and this requirement of an equitable proprietary interest is distinct from absolute ownership at law. Which makes little sense, because an absolute owner, having legal and beneficial ownership, is just as much owner in equity as is a beneficiary under a trust, and equity never disputed this. It merely did not have jurisdiction to adjudicate on it.

There seems to be no reason at all on the merits why the equitable tracing remedy should not be available also to the beneficial legal owner. Indeed, it was arguable, before *Re Diplock*[22] was decided, that this situation had been reached by the combined effect of *Sinclair* v. *Brougham*[23] and *Banque Belge* v. *Hambrouck*.[24] Atkin L.J. treated the equitable tracing remedy as a means of overcoming the common law's difficulty in identifying the plaintiff's money in a mixed fund.[25] "The question always was, Had the means of ascertainment failed? But if in 1815 the common law halted outside the bankers' door, by 1879 equity had had the courage to lift the latch, walk in and examine the books: *Re Hallett's Estate*.[26] I see no reason why the means of ascertainment so provided should not now be available both for common law and equity proceedings." It has seemed doubtful, since *Re Diplock*, whether the equitable tracing remedy will be available in the absence of some situation creating equitable as opposed to legal ownership.[27] In *Aluminium Industrie Vaassen B.V.* v. *Romalpa Aluminium Ltd.*[28] however,

---

[20] *Aluminium Industrie Vaassen B.V.* v. *Romalpa Aluminium Ltd.* [1976] 1 W.L.R. 676.
[21] See *Chase Manhattan Bank N.A.* v. *Israel-British Bank (London) Ltd.* [1981] Ch. 105, *post*, p. 628; *cf. Re Andrabell Ltd.* [1984] 3 All E.R. 407.
[22] [1948] Ch. 465; (1971) 34 M.L.R. 12 (F. O. B. Babafemi).
[23] [1914] A.C. 398.
[24] [1921] 1 K.B. 321.
[25] *Ibid.* at p. 335. See also *Chief Constable of Kent* v. *V.* [1983] Q.B. 34 at p. 41, *per* Lord Denning M.R.: "It may be that 150 years ago the common law halted outside the banker's door, but for the last 100 years, since the fusion of law and equity, it has had the courage to lift the latch, walk in and examine the books: see *Banque Belge pour l'Etranger* v. *Hambrouck* [1912] 1 K.B. 321 at p. 335, *per* Atkin L.J. and *Re Diplock's Estate, Diplock* v. *Wintle* [1948] Ch. 465, *per* Lord Greene M.R."
[26] (1880) 13 Ch.D. 696.
[27] For arguments to the effect that legal, as opposed to equitable, ownership is a sufficient basis for a right to trace, see (1975) 28 C.L.P. 64 (A. J. Oakley); (1976) 40 Conv.(N.S.) 227 (R. A. Pearce); Goff and Jones (3rd ed.), pp. 72, 77 (relying on the "fusion" of law and equity).
[28] [1976] 1 W.L.R. 676, *post*, p. 634; *cf. Re Andrabell Ltd.* [1984] 3 All E.R. 407. See Heydon, Gummow and Austin, *Cases and Materials on Equity and Trusts* (2nd ed.), p. 763.

the Court of Appeal permitted tracing by a legal owner to whom a fiduciary duty was owed, although this particular point was not discussed.

Consider this case; B owes £1,000 to his creditors and has only £100. He steals £1,000 from A and mixes that money in his account which now has £1,100. He now "owes" £2,000. Should the available money be shared equally between A and the creditors, each getting 55p in the pound? Or should A get back first his £1,000, which B should never have had? There is no such remedy available to A on the authorities. Common law tracing is not available because the funds are mixed; nor equitable tracing because there is not a fiduciary relation between a thief and his victim.

It is submitted that if proprietary remedies are to be based on ownership of property they should protect beneficial ownership in the full sense, and not only ownership recognised in equity alone.

It might further be asked whether the tracing remedy should be limited to cases of proprietary interests. In *Lister & Co.* v. *Stubbs*,[29] the defendant as purchasing agent for the plaintiffs had taken secret commissions from a firm from whom the plaintiffs obtained supplies. Part of the money was still in cash, but a large part had been invested in the purchase of land. There was no difficulty in recovering the money, but the plaintiffs moved also for an injunction to restrain Stubbs from dealing with the land, and for an order directing him to bring the investments or cash into court. The Court of Appeal held that, while the plaintiffs had a right to recover the money, they had no right to follow the money into the investments; for the money had never been their money; it was merely money owed to them by the defendant.[30]

The decision has been criticised on the basis that there is no reason why the property, which Stubbs should never have had, needs to be kept for his creditors; nor any reason why Stubbs should be able to enjoy the profit from the investment. On this view the plaintiff should have a tracing remedy wherever the defendant is unjustly enriched at the plaintiff's expense and the personal remedy is, for some reason, inadequate.[31] In such a case the defendant is in possession of property in circumstances in which he ought not to keep it, and it seems unjust that he or his creditors should benefit from the windfall. The *Lister* principle has, however, recently been re-affirmed by the Court of

---

[29] (1890) 45 Ch.D. 1; (1979) 95 L.Q.R. 536 (C. A. Needham) See also *Metropolitan Bank* v. *Heiron* (1880) 5 Ex.D. 319.

[30] *cf. Eden* v. *Ridsdales Railway Lamp and Lighting Co.* (1889) 23 Q.B.D. 368. The bribe is recoverable whether the principal affirms or repudiates the transaction between the agent and the third party: *Logiscrose Ltd.* v. *Southend United Football Club Ltd.* [1988] 1 W.L.R. 1256.

[31] *Restatement of Restitution*, para. 160, *ante*, p. 316; Goff and Jones (3rd ed.), p. 657; Oakley, *Constructive Trusts* (2nd ed.), p. 56.

Appeal in *Re Att.-Gen.'s Reference (No. 1 of 1985)*,[32] concerning a secret profit made by an employee in breach of his contract of employment. That decision, however, was in the context of the Theft Act 1968. The finding of a proprietary interest in the employer could have led to the conviction of the employee of theft, which the court regarded as undesirable.

A compromise solution is that the plaintiff should have a *personal* action to recover not merely the bribe or commission but also any profits made from it,[33] while nevertheless denying any proprietary interest.[34]

An opportunity to develop the law by accepting unjust enrichment as the basis of tracing was offered, but refused, in *Chase Manhattan Bank NA* v. *Israel-British Bank (London) Ltd.*[35]; but the result in that case, reached by straining the concept of the fiduciary relation to the utmost, was wholly consistent with this principle.

> Chase Manhattan Bank, by mistake of fact,[36] made a double payment of $2,000,000 to another New York Bank for the account of the defendant's bank which carried on business in London. The defendant's bank became insolvent, and the question was whether Chase Manhattan should prove with the other creditors in the insolvency, or whether it had a right to trace the money into the defendant's assets in priority to the general creditors.

Goulding J. held for the plaintiff on the ground that it retained an equitable proprietary interest in the money, and the defendant was subject to a fiduciary duty to the plaintiff. It is submitted that, although the reasoning was tortuous, the result is correct. It is difficult indeed to see how the court could find a fiduciary relationship, or an equitable property in the money, in a case in which the plaintiff had made a payment, through another bank, in settlement of what was believed to be a commercial debt. But this was surely a case in which Chase Manhattan ought to recover in full the money paid by mistake; rather

---

[32] [1986] Q.B. 491; (1986) 102 L.Q.R. 486; (1986) 136 N.L.J. 913 (P. St. J. Smart); (1986) 45 C.L.J. 367 (C. Gearty); [1987] Conv. 209 (J. Martin). See also *Islamic Republic of Iran Shipping Lines* v. *Denby* [1987] 1 F.T.L.R. 30 (solicitor personally accountable to client for accepting bribe from opposing litigant to persuade client to compromise claim, but no proprietary remedy).

[33] Birks, *An Introduction to the Law of Restitution*, p. 389 (although this was doubted in *Lister* itself).

[34] See (1987) L.Q.R. 433 (R. M. Goode), supporting *Lister*.

[35] [1981] Ch. 105; (1980) 39 C.L.J. 272 (A. Tettenborn); *ibid.* at p. 275 (G. Jones). See also *A.* v. *C.* [1981] Q.B. 956; *Bankers Trust Co.* v. *Shapira* [1980] 1 W.L.R. 1274; *R.* v. *Hamid Shadrokh-Cigari, The Times,* February 23, 1988.

[36] Presumably the result would be otherwise in cases of mistake of law, where no action generally lies at common law. With mistake of fact, a personal action is available at common law; the equitable remedy can thus be seen as concurrent, and available where the common law remedy is inadequate, as in cases of insolvency. A payment by mistake of law in *Re Diplock* [1948] Ch. 465 gave rise to no fiduciary relationship, but the recipient would take as constructive trustee if aware that the transfer was in breach of trust. See also (1986) 102 L.Q.R. 114 at p. 137, n. 57 (C. Harpum).

than present the creditors of the defendant with a windfall, which neither the defendant nor its creditors should have had. The real competition, as shown above, is between the plaintiff and the defendant's creditors. How much simpler it would be to accept the principle of unjust enrichment as the basis of tracing.

(ii) Unmixed Funds. The easy case is that in which there has been no mixing of the trust funds with the trustee's own money. If the trustee has sold the trust property, rightly or wrongly, the beneficiary may take the proceeds if he can identify them. And if the proceeds of sale have been used to purchase other property the beneficiary may "follow" them and may "elect either to take the property purchased, or to hold it as a security for the amount of trust money laid out in the purchase; or, as we generally express it, he is entitled at his election either to take the property, or to have a charge on the property for the amount of the trust money."[37] Claims in equity will never, of course, be valid against a bona fide purchaser for value.[38] If, however, the property has come into the hands of an innocent volunteer, the tracing remedy lies against him while he retains it.[39]

(iii) Mixed Funds. The position is more complicated where the trustee has mixed the trust funds with other money, and possibly converted the mixed funds into other property. The position differs according to whether the claim is against the trustee, or whether the ownership of the mixed fund must be apportioned between two trusts or a trust and an innocent volunteer. Also, as we shall see, there are special rules applicable to cases of mixed funds in bank accounts.

(a) *Position as Against the Trustee.* The rule here is that the beneficiaries have a first charge over the mixed fund or any property purchased with it. The onus is on the trustee to prove that part of the mixed fund is his own. " . . . if a trustee amalgamated [trust property] with his own, his beneficiary will be entitled to every portion of the blended property which the trustee cannot prove to be his own."[40] An unorthodox and narrow view was taken in *Re Att.-Gen.'s Reference (No. 1 of 1985)*,[41] where the employee of a publican secretly sold his own beer on his employer's premises in breach of contract. The money he received from the customers was made up of the profit element, for which he

---

[37] *Per* Jessel M.R. in *Re Hallett's Estate* (1880) 13 Ch.D. 696 at p. 709.

[38] *Post,* p. 642.

[39] *Post,* p. 639. He does not, however, have the additional liabilities of a constructive trustee; *ante,* p. 284.

[40] *Lewin on Trusts* (16th ed.), p. 223, quoted by Ungoed-Thomas J. in *Re Tilley's W.T.* [1967] Ch. 1179 at p. 1182; *Lupton* v. *White* (1808) 15 Ves.Jr. 432; *Re Oatway* [1903] 2 Ch. 356, *post,* p. 632; *Indian Oil Corp. Ltd.* v. *Greenstone Shipping S.A.* [1987] 2 Lloyd's Rep. 286; (1987) 46 C.L.J. 369 (P. Stein).

[41] [1986] Q.B. 491; criticised (1986) 102 L.Q.R. 486; (1986) 45 C.L.J. 367 (C. Gearty); (1986) 136 N.L.J. 913 (P. St. J. Smart); [1987] Conv. 209 (J. Martin).

would be accountable, and the reimbursement of his own expenditure on the beer. Applying *Lister & Co.* v. *Stubbs*,[42] he was held not to be constructive trustee of the profit, nor to be guilty of theft under section 5 of the Theft Act 1968. The Court of Appeal, however, went on to suggest that where a trustee uses trust property and his own property to make a profit, no part of the mixed property can be regarded as trust property until the profit element (to which the trust is entitled) is identifiable as a separate piece of property. While the profit element remains part of a mixed fund, the beneficiary has no proprietary interest in it and the trustee's liability is to account only. This view seems contrary to established principles of tracing, but, as mentioned above,[43] was put forward as a step in the argument against criminal liability, which the court was reluctant to impose.

In contrast, an extremely wide view of tracing into mixed funds emerges from *dicta* of the Privy Council in *Space Investments Ltd.* v. *Canadian Imperial Bank of Commerce Trust Co. (Bahamas) Ltd.*[44] A bank trustee deposited trust money with itself under an express power to do so, and was then wound up. The issue was whether the beneficiaries could trace the money. It was held that if a bank trustee misappropriated trust money for its own benefit, tracing would be possible. But where the mixing was done lawfully, as here, the trust money became the bank's, subject only to a personal obligation to repay. Hence the beneficiaries had no interest in the bank's assets and could only rank with unsecured creditors. The settlor had accepted the risk of insolvency by allowing the deposit. Lord Templeman went on to discuss the position if tracing had been available, saying that if the beneficiaries could not trace their money into any particular asset belonging to the trustee bank, equity would allow them "to trace the trust money to all the assets of the bank and to recover the trust money by the exercise of an equitable charge over all the assets of the bank."[45] The difficulty with this is that it suggests that if a commingled fund has been lost, the beneficiaries still have a proprietary claim to the trustee's remaining assets, which are impressed with a charge. Such a view would be unfair to the general creditors, and is supported neither by principle nor by policy.[46]

(b) *Position as Between Two Trusts, or Trust and Third Party.* It may be, however, that the trustee has mixed the funds of two trusts, whether or not with his own,[47] or has transferred the funds to an innocent volunteer, who has mixed them with his own. The rule here is

---

[42] (1890) 45 Ch.D. 1; *ante*, p. 627.

[43] *Ante*, p. 628.

[44] [1986] 1 W.L.R. 1072. See also *Ross* v. *Lord Advocate* [1986] 1 W.L.R. 1077.

[45] [1986] 1 W.L.R. 1072 at p. 1074.

[46] See the cogent criticisms in (1987) 103 L.Q.R. 433 (R. M. Goode).

[47] Any claim to ownership by the trustee will be governed by the principle discussed in paragraph (a) above.

that the two trusts, or the trust and the volunteer, share *pari passu* (*i.e.* rateably) in the mixed funds or any property purchased out of them.[48] The position of the innocent volunteer is further dealt with below.

(c) *Bank Accounts*. The mixing is likely, however, to occur in the context of a banking account, to which special rules apply. Again, it is necessary to distinguish the position as between trustee and beneficiary and as between two trusts or trust and innocent volunteer. These rules govern the allocation of payments out of the mixed fund.[49] The principle as between trustee and beneficiary is that the trustee is presumed to spend his own money first.

In *Re Hallett's Estate*,[50] Hallett, a solicitor, died after having mixed with his own money certain funds from two trusts, one his own marriage settlement of which he was trustee, and the other a trust of which a client, Mrs. Cotterill, was beneficiary. At his death there were insufficient funds to pay his personal debts and to meet these claims.

Three questions arose; (i) whether Mrs. Cotterill, not being a beneficiary of a trust of which Hallett was a trustee, was entitled to the tracing remedy on the ground of the fiduciary relationship; (ii) (assuming that she was) how to allocate the payments from the fund as between Hallett and the claimants; and (iii) as between the claimants themselves.

The Court of Appeal held that Mrs. Cotterill was entitled to trace, and that the payments out must be treated as payments of Hallett's own money. This left sufficient to satisfy the claims of Mrs. Cotterill and of the beneficiaries under the marriage settlement, so the third question did not arise.[51]

We are at present concerned with (ii). The other matters are discussed elsewhere.[52] The reason given by Jessel M.R. for allocating payments to Hallett's money and not to the trust is that wherever an act "can be done rightfully, [a man] is not allowed to say, against the person entitled to the property or the right, that he has done it wrongfully."[53]

It should be appreciated, however, that this principle operates in the

---

[48] *Sinclair* v. *Brougham* [1914] A.C. 398; *Re Diplock* [1948] Ch. 465.

[49] In the case of insuperable accounting difficulties, these rules will not be applied. See *Cunningham* v. *Brown*, 265 U.S. 1, 44 Sup.Ct. 424; 68 L.Ed. 873 (1923), where a tracing remedy was refused in respect of a mass of claims arising out of a fraud. Taft C.J. said "It would be running the fiction of *Knatchbull* v. *Hallett* into the ground to apply it here." The claimants shared equally.

[50] (1880) 13 Ch.D. 696; see (1975) 28 C.L.P. 64 (A. J. Oakley).

[51] In the court below, where, on the view taken by Fry J., the third question did arise, it was solved by applying the rule in *Clayton's Case* (1817) 1 Mer. 572.

[52] *Ante*, p. 624; *post*, p. 633.

[53] (1880) 13 Ch.D. 696 at p. 727.

context of a claim against a balance in the account, and does not derogate from the general principle, described above, that the beneficiaries have a first charge on any property bought out of a mixed fund.

In *Re Oatway*,[54] the trustee withdrew money from the mixed fund and invested it. Later he withdrew the balance of the fund and dissipated it. Joyce J. rejected the argument that the money drawn out first must be treated as his own, holding that the beneficiaries' claim must be satisfied from any identifiable part of the mixed fund before the trustee could set up his own claim. Thus the beneficiaries were entitled to the investments in priority to the creditors of the trustee.

The tracing remedy of course becomes especially significant when the defendant is insolvent. Should the beneficiary be given a prior claim over the other creditors? This factor must always be borne in mind when considering whether, theoretically, the tracing remedy ought to be available. The question is essentially one of competition between the beneficiary and the creditors. It is arguable that the tracing remedy in *Re Hallett*[55] is unfair to the creditors. They suffer when the defendant trustee pays money out of a mixed fund, for this, as we have seen, is normally treated as the payment of the trustee's own money. On the other hand, the part of the fund which consists of trust money is money which the trustee should never have had in his own account. We could go to the other extreme and say that, as the trustee's duty is to perform the trust, the whole of his property should be available for that purpose; and that any money he earns or receives after the mixing should be applied towards the remedying of the breach.[56] This however would be very harsh on the creditors; a creditor lends money or otherwise gives credit to the defendant on the basis of his estimate of the defendant's financial stability. It would be harsh to apply all the trustee's money in the first place to the satisfaction of the beneficiaries' claims. The rule is that the tracing remedy can be applied against a mixed fund in the bank account to the extent that the trust funds can still be shown to be there. If the account falls below that sum, that part of the trust money must have been spent.[57] Later payments in are not treated as repayments of the trust fund unless the trustee shows an intention to do so.[58] It is essential therefore to ascertain from the

---

[54] [1903] 2 Ch. 356; Scott, *Law of Trusts* (3rd ed.), para. 517; *Re Tilley's W.T.* [1967] Ch. 1179 at p. 1185; *City of Lincoln* v. *Morrison,* 64 Neb. 882; 90 N.W. 905 (1902).

[55] (1880) 13 Ch.D. 696.

[56] *Hungerford* v. *Curtis,* 43 R.I. 124; 110 A. 650 (1902); *Meyers* v. *Matusek,* 98 Fla. 1126, 125 S. 360 (1929); 30 Mich.L.R. 441.

[57] In *Roscoe* v. *Winder* [1915] 1 Ch. 62, 69 Sargant J. said that the tracing remedy applied to "such an amount of the balance ultimately standing to the credit of the trustee as did not exceed the lowest balance of the account during the intervening period."

[58] *Roscoe* v. *Winder, supra.*

accounts the lowest balance in the fund; to that extent the tracing remedy is available against that balance. Of course the personal claim remains as to any shortfall, in cases where the trust money withdrawn cannot be followed into other property.

It remains to consider the position where the mixed funds in the bank account represent the funds of two trusts,[59] or of a trust and an innocent volunteer. Here the rule in *Clayton's* case[60] applies, which lays down that in the case of an active continuing bank account, the first payment in is appropriated to the earliest debt which is not statute-barred; in other words, first in, first out. This is a rule which has some relevance and convenience in commercial matters. We have seen that it does not apply to accounts between trustee and beneficiary. Nor, it is submitted, should it appear in any aspect of the present subject,[61] but it has unfortunately been applied as a means of determining entitlement in a mixed banking account between rival persons with a right to trace,[62] and also between a person with a right to trace and an innocent volunteer.[63] It never appears in any context other than that of a continuing or current bank account.[64]

As has been said, the presumptions discussed above only work if the withdrawals and deposits are modest in number and amount. "But if millions of pounds flow daily into and out of a volatile bank, they are transparently wanting."[65]

(iv) **Retention of Title Clauses.** In recent years the rules of equity have been utilised in the context of the supply of goods to manufacturers. By means of a retention of title clause, the supplier stipulates that the property in the goods shall not pass until payment.[66] He may also seek to reserve ownership where his goods have been mixed with

---

[59] If the trustee's own money is also mixed, the principle of *Re Hallett's Estate, supra,* will apply to determine withdrawals to be allocated to the trustee; *i.e.* he is presumed to spend his own money before that of either trust.

[60] (1817) 1 Mer. 572; (1963) 79 L.Q.R. 388 (D. A. McConville); (1965) 6 W.A.L.R. 428, at p. 437 (P. F. P. Higgins). *cf. Re British Red Cross Balkan Fund* [1914] 2 Ch. 419 (where later subscribers to a fund could not claim surplus to the exclusion of earlier subscribers).

[61] (1963) 79 L.Q.R. 401–402 (D. A. McConville). See the Report of the Review Committee on Insolvency Law and Practice (1982, Cmnd. 8558) paras. 1076–1080, preferring a rateable distribution.

[62] *Re Hallett's Estate* (1879) 13 Ch.D. 696 (Fry J.). *Hancock* v. *Smith* (1889) 41 Ch.D. 456; *Re Stenning* [1895] 2 Ch. 433; *Re Diplock* [1948] Ch. 465 (in the case of the National Institute for the Deaf). It was not applied in *Re Ontario Securities Commission* (1986) 30 D.L.R. (4th) 1.

[63] *Re Stenning* [1895] 2 Ch. 433; *Mutton* v. *Peat* [1899] 2 Ch. 556 at p. 560 *per* Byrne J.; *Re Diplock, supra.*

[64] *Sinclair* v. *Brougham* [1914] A.C. 398; *Re Diplock* [1948] Ch. 465 at p. 554 (The Royal Sailors Orphan Girls' School and Home (Action 111C)).

[65] Goff and Jones (3rd ed.), p. 80, discussing the *Chase Manhattan Bank* case, *ante,* p. 628.

[66] See Sale of Goods Act 1979, s.19.

others in a manufacturing process, or of the proceeds of sale by the manufacturer on a sub-sale. He may further, by means of an "all-monies" clause, stipulate that the property shall not pass until all the buyer's obligations to him have been satisfied, not merely as to the particular consignment.[67] Retention of title clauses are often called "*Romalpa* clauses," and take their name from the leading case, *Aluminium Industrie Vaassen B.V.* v. *Romalpa Aluminium Ltd.*[68]

The plaintiff vendor sold aluminium foil to the defendant, a manufacturing company. One clause in the contract provided that legal ownership in the foil was not to pass to the defendant until payment. Until that time, the defendant could be required to store the foil in such a way that it was clearly the property of the plaintiff. Other clauses dealt with the position where the foil was mixed with other materials. The defendant company got into financial difficulties and a receiver was appointed by the debenture holders, at a time when over £122,000 was owing to the plaintiff. The receiver certified that £35,152 in his hands represented the proceeds of sale of unmixed foil sold by the defendant to third parties. The plaintiff claimed priority in respect of that sum over the secured and unsecured creditors. The Court of Appeal, applying *Re Hallett's Estate*,[69] upheld the claim. Although the third parties acquired title to the foil sold to them,[70] the position as between the plaintiff and defendant was that the foil was the plaintiff's property, which the defendant was selling as agent. The defendant's position as agent and bailee gave rise to a fiduciary relationship,[71] which entitled the plaintiff to trace the proceeds of the unmixed foil and recover in priority to the secured and unsecured creditors.

It was conceded in *Romalpa* that the defendant held the goods as bailee.[72] Normally, however, the relationship of the parties under a title retention clause hardly fits the concept of bailment or agency. It has been held that if sub-sales are permitted, the normal implication is

---

[67] See (1985) 82 L.S.G. 1075 (C. Whitehouse); (1986) 49 M.L.R. 96 (W. Goodhart); [1987] Conv. 434 (J. R. Bradgate). The Review Committee on Insolvency Law and Practice (1982, Cmnd. 8558), para. 1645, proposed that such clauses should be regarded as creating a charge (and hence be registrable).

[68] [1976] 1 W.L.R. 676; (1976) 92 L.Q.R. 360, 528 (R. M. Goode); (1976) 39 M.L.R. 585 (R. Prior); (1977) 93 L.Q.R. 324 (D. T. Donaldson) and 487 (R. M. Goode); (1977) 36 C.L.J. 27 (J. H. Farrow and N. E. Furey); [1978] Conv. 37 (O. P. Wylie); (1980) 39 C.L.J. 48 (J. W. A. Thornley); (1980) 43 M.L.R. 489 (W. Goodhart and G. Jones); (1986) 83 L.S.G. 1128 (C. Whitehouse). See T.B. Smith, *Property Problems in Sale*; R. M. Goode, *Proprietary Rights and Insolvency in Sales Transactions*.

[69] (1880) 13 Ch.D. 696.

[70] See also *Four Point Garage Ltd.* v. *Carter* [1985] 3 All E.R. 12 (purchaser in good faith from buyer where resale in the ordinary course of business gets legal title even though, as between buyer and supplier, buyer did not get title).

[71] Such relationships are not always fiduciary; *Hendy Lennox (Industrial Engines) Ltd.* v. *Grahame Puttick Ltd.* [1984] 1 W.L.R. 485; *Re Andrabell Ltd.* [1984] 3 All E.R. 407, indicating factors which negative such a relationship.

[72] See *Re Bond Worth Ltd., infra.*

that the buyer will sell on his own account and not as fiduciary agent for the seller.[73]

(a) *Unmixed Goods*. Retention of title clauses have proved effective where, as in *Romalpa*, the property has retained its identity. In *Clough Mill Ltd.* v. *Martin*[74] the Court of Appeal held that a clause reserving legal title to yarn until payment entitled the seller, on the buyer's insolvency, to recover unused yarn which had not been paid for. As no title passed to the buyer, the buyer could not be regarded as having created a (registrable) charge over the yarn in favour of the seller. Similarly in *Hendy Lennox (Industrial Engines) Ltd.* v. *Grahame Puttick Ltd.*,[75] where the seller reserved title to a diesel engine which had been used by the buyer as a major component of a diesel generating set. The plaintiff's claim to ownership of the engine succeeded as the engine remained readily identifiable and could be disconnected quite easily from the generator. In *Re Peachdart Ltd.*,[76] on the other hand, where leather was supplied for the manufacture of handbags, it was not regarded as retaining its identity even though it remained recognisable in the product. Thus the claim fell to be considered under the following heading.

(b) *Incorporation into Manufacturing Process*. Vendors have been unsuccessful, however, where the property has been incorporated into a manufacturing process. In *Re Bond Worth Ltd.*[77] the vendor supplied fibre to the purchaser, which was spun into yarn with other fibre and used in the manufacture of carpets, becoming an inseparable component of the yarn and the carpets. The contract provided that "equitable and beneficial ownership" should remain with the vendor until payment. If resold, the vendor's rights should attach to the proceeds. If converted to other products, the vendor's rights should extend to those products. Upon the purchaser's insolvency £587,397 was owing to the vendor. The receiver held little raw fibre but much yarn and carpets. Slade J. rejected the vendor's claim to priority. The contract was primarily a contract of sale, whereby the legal title and the risk passed

[73] *E. Pfeiffer Weinkellerei-Weineinkauf GmbH & Co.* v. *Arbuthnot Factors Ltd.* [1988] 1 W.L.R. 150, where Phillips J. regarded the clause in *Romalpa* as having "special features"; [1987] Conv. 434 (J. R. Bradgate).

[74] [1985] 1 W.L.R. 111, distinguishing *Re Bond Worth Ltd., infra,* as to unused material. See All E.R. Rev. 1984, p. 31 (N. E. Palmer); (1985) 135 N.L.J. 224, 271 (S. A. Jones); (1985) 36 N.I.L.Q. 165 (McKee); (1985) 44 C.L.J. 33 (J. W. A. Thornely); [1987] Conv. 434 (J. R. Bradgate).

[75] [1984] 1 W.L.R. 485. The plaintiff's proprietary claim to the engine was transferred to the proceeds of sale as the property in the engine had not passed to the defendant's customers at the time of receivership. As to other engines where the property had passed, see *infra.*

[76] [1984] Ch. 131; All E.R. Rev. 1983, p. 48 (N. E. Palmer); (1984) 100 L.Q.R. 35 (S. Whittaker); (1984) 43 C.L.J. 35 (J. W. A. Thornely); [1984] Conv. 139 (D. Milman). The contract expressly provided for a fiduciary relationship.

[77] [1980] Ch. 228.

to the purchaser, who was at liberty to resell or use the fibre in the manufacturing process. The purchaser was neither an agent nor a bailee. The retention of title clause, upon its true construction, did not reserve full equitable ownership to the vendor, but gave the vendor an equitable charge over the fibre or its products. This charge, which was created by the purchaser company, was void for non-registration under the Companies Act.[78] *Romalpa*[79] was distinguishable, primarily because there the clause reserved *legal* ownership to the vendor.[80]

The result was similar in *Borden U.K. Ltd* v. *Scottish Timber Products Ltd.*,[81] where the vendor supplied resin to the purchaser, to be used in the manufacture of chipboard, of which it became an inseparable component. The contract reserved legal ownership in the resin to the vendor until payment, but did not purport to give the vendor rights over the chipboard. Upon the purchaser's insolvency, £318,321 was owing to the vendor. The Court of Appeal held that the clause merely reserved rights over the resin, which had disappeared, leaving nothing to trace. There was no fiduciary relationship, as the contract was a contract of sale, giving the purchaser liberty to use the resin in the manufacturing process, destroying its very existence. It was doubted whether the tracing remedy could ever apply when heterogeneous goods were mixed in a manufacturing process wherein the original goods lost their character.[82] If there was such a remedy, how could the value of the original goods be quantified? There had been no mixing in issue in *Romalpa*,[83] where it was conceded that the defendant was a bailee of the foil. In the present case, even if the vendor had acquired rights over the chipboard, the claim would have failed for non-registration under the Companies Act. The vendor was similarly unsuccessful in *Re Peachdart Ltd.*,[84] where leather was supplied for the manufacture of handbags. The retention of title clause was held to create a charge over the handbags or their proceeds, which was void for non-registration. The question of mixing was not in issue in *Clough Mill Ltd.* v. *Martin*,[85] but the Court of Appeal there expressed the view that if the material is incorporated into other goods, it is assumed that they are owned by the buyer subject to a charge in favour of the seller, unless they are still in a separate and identifiable state.

---

[78] Now Companies Act 1985, s.395.
[79] *Supra.* Registration was not there in issue.
[80] Might the plaintiff in *Romalpa* have succeeded at common law?
[81] [1981] Ch. 25.
[82] This view is not inconsistent with the retention of proprietary rights prior to such mixing; *Clough Mill Ltd.* v. *Martin, supra.*
[83] *Supra.*
[84] *Supra.*
[85] *Supra.* See also *Specialist Plant Services Ltd.* v. *Braithwaite Ltd.* [1987] BCLC 1 (retention of title clause concerning parts incorporated into machines, and expressed to be as surety for debt, created charge which was void for non-registration).

(c) *Proceeds of Sale.* Even where the seller's goods have not been amalgamated with others, claims to proprietary rights in the proceeds of sale have been unsuccessful.

First, the plaintiff may fail because he cannot establish a fiduciary relationship, which is necessary for tracing into a mixed fund.[86] Such was the case in *Re Andrabell Ltd.*,[87] where a claim to the proceeds of sale of travel bags supplied by the plaintiff failed. The rights and duties of the parties were inconsistent with a fiduciary relationship and were merely those of debtor and creditor. Similarly in *Hendy Lennox (Industrial Engines) Ltd.* v. *Grahame Puttick Ltd.*,[88] where the plaintiff supplied engines for incorporation into generators. Where the property in the engines had passed to the defendant's customers, the plaintiff's claim to the proceeds failed, because the terms of the contract (in particular the granting of credit) were inconsistent with a fiduciary relationship.

Secondly, even if a fiduciary relationship can be established, the true analysis of the position is that the plaintiff has a charge over the proceeds,[89] which will fail unless registered under the Companies Act.[90]

The reform of this area of the law, which has been called "a maze if not a minefield,"[91] was considered by the Review Committee on Insolvency Law and Practice.[92] Some of the Committee's proposals have been enacted by the Insolvency Act 1986, the relevant provisions being confined to corporate insolvency. The Act provides that an administrator may be appointed to manage the affairs of a company which is in financial difficulties.[93] After the presentation of a petiton for an administration order, no steps may be taken to enforce any security or to repossess goods under a retention of title agreement[94] without leave of the court.[95] Nor may any such steps be taken while an administration order is in force without the consent of the administrator or the leave of the court.[96] Where any property of the company is subject to a security or goods are subject to a retention of title agreement, the administrator may dispose of the property or goods as if they were not subject to the security or the agreement, if the court is satisfied that the disposal would be likely to promote the purposes

---

[86] *Ante*, p. 629.
[87] [1984] 3 All E.R. 407.
[88] [1984] 1 W.L.R. 485; *ante*, p. 635.
[89] *Re Peachdart Ltd.* [1984] Ch. 131.
[90] Now Companies Act 1985, s.395. Registration was not argued in *Romalpa.*
[91] *Hendy Lennox (Industrial Engines) Ltd.* v. *Grahame Puttick Ltd.* [1984] 1 W.L.R. 485 at p. 493.
[92] (1982 Cmnd. 8558), paras. 1587–1651.
[93] Insolvency Act 1986, s.8.
[94] Defined in s.251 as an agreement which does not constitute a charge but which gives the seller priority over other creditors.
[95] Insolvency Act 1986, s.10.
[96] *Ibid.*, s.11.

specified in the administration order.[97] The net proceeds of the disposal must be applied towards discharging the sums secured by the security or payable under the retention of title agreement.[98] The object of these provisions is to enable the business to be kept as a going concern, for the benefit of all creditors.

The real question, however, is whether retention of title clauses are desirable as a matter of policy. Save where construed as creating charges and hence registrable, they effectively create a hidden security, enabling the seller to "leapfrog" other creditors.[99] This objection could be overcome if *all* retention of title clauses were registrable, but this view has yet to be accepted by the legislature.[1]

(v) Increase in Value. We saw that Jessel M.R. said in *Re Hallett's Estate*[2] that where trust funds, unmixed, could be traced, the claimant could choose to take the property purchased with them, or to have a charge upon it for the amount; but that if property had been mixed with the trustee's own, and property purchased with the mixed fund, the claimant's remedy was that of a charge. Lord Parker seemed to affirm this by saying in *Sinclair* v. *Brougham*[3]: "In such a case the beneficiary can only claim a charge on the property for the amount of the trust money expended in the purchase."

Such a rule would mean, however, that the beneficiary would be able only to claim the original money taken (with interest, and in priority to the creditors) and that the trustee would keep all the profits. This would be a startling result; all the more so in view of the extreme strictness with which the courts deal with cases of profits made by trustees.[4]

It appears that the appropriate remedy in such a situation is to allow the beneficiary to claim, if he wishes, a share of the fund in the proportion which the original trust funds bore to the mixed fund at the time of the mixing. If the fund increased in value, it would be in his interest to do so. If the fund decreased in value, it would be to his interest to have a charge. This is the rule in the United States of America, and has been applied in Australia.[5] The principle of proportionate entitlement has been applied in England as between two persons entitled to trace into a fund[6] but never between beneficiary

[97] *Ibid.*, s.15. See also s.43.

[98] s.15(5).

[99] See [1987] Conv. 434 (J. R. Bradgate).

[1] See *Security Interests in Property Other Than Land*, Dept. of Trade and Industry, July 1986.

[2] (1880) 13 Ch.D. 696; *ante*, p. 631.

[3] [1914] A.C. 398 at p. 442; quoted and explained in *Re Tilley's W.T.* [1967] Ch. 1179 at pp. 1187, 1188.

[4] *Boardman* v. *Phipps* [1967] 2 A.C. 46; *ante*, pp. 571 *et seq.*

[5] *Scott* v. *Scott* (1963) 37 A.L.J.R. 345.

[6] *Lord Provost of Edinburgh* v. *Lord Advocate* (1879) 4 App.Cas. 823.

and trustee. Its applicability was, however, conceded in *Re Tilley's Will Trusts*[7]:

> The testator's widow and executrix had paid small amounts from the testator's estate into her own account which she then used so successfully in property purchases that the modest capital with which she started became worth £94,000 at her death. She made full use of overdraft facilities allowed her by the bank, and could have carried out every one of her operations without the use of the trust money. The question on her death was whether those entitled in remainder could claim a share of the £94,000 in the proportion to which the trust money paid into her account bore to the balance in the account at the time; or whether they could claim only the return of the trust money with interest. In spite of the concession relating to the beneficiary's right to a proportionate share, Ungoed-Thomas J. allowed only the return of the trust money with interest; concluding, rather surprisingly, that "the trust moneys were not invested in properties at all, but merely went in reduction of Mrs. Tilley's overdraft which was in reality the source of the purchase-moneys."[8]

This right to a share in the fund is called in the United States of America a constructive trust, the theory being that it is the duty of the trustee to make over to the beneficiary that proportion of the fund which is the beneficiary's in equity. This is the remedial constructive trust[9]: "Where a person holding title to property is subject to an equitable duty to convey it to another on the ground that he would be unjustly enriched if he were permitted to retain it, a constructive trust arises." The English concept of a constructive trust is, as we have seen, different.[10] This remedy needs a name to differentiate it from a charge. Perhaps it should be called a "proportionate share."[11] The fact that a beneficiary, proceeding against a trustee has this choice of remedy does not mean that the choice should be available in every tracing situation; a dishonest trustee is in a very different situation from an innocent volunteer.[12]

(vi) The Innocent Volunteer. We have seen that the tracing remedy is never available against a bona fide purchaser for value.[13] A volunteer of course is in a different position. The usual rule in the case of volunteers is that they take the property subject to any equitable

---

[7] [1967] Ch. 1179 at p. 1189; (1968) 26 C.L.J. 28 (G. H. Jones).

[8] *Ibid.* at p. 1193

[9] *Restatement of Restitution*, para. 160; *Scott on Trusts*, Chap. 13; (1920) 33 H.L.R. 420 at p. 421 (Roscoe Pound); (1955) 71 L.Q.R. 41 (A. W. Scott); (1959) 75 L.Q.R. 234, 237 (R. H. Maudsley); *ante*, p. 285.

[10] *Ante*, pp. 285 *et seq.*

[11] Sometimes called a quasi-trust. Lord Wright, *Legal Essays*, Chap. 7; (1938) 6 C.L.J. 309; (1959) 75 L.Q.R. 234, 235 (R. H. Maudsley).

[12] *Restatement of Restitution*, paras. 202–204.

[13] *Ante*, p. 629.

interest affecting it.[14] In the tracing situation, however, it appears from *Sinclair* v. *Brougham*[15] and *Re Diplock*[16] that a person who receives a mixed fund bona fide but without payment (the innocent volunteer) is raised to a position equal to that of the equitable owner who is entitled to trace. "But this burden on the conscience of the volunteer is not such as to compel him to treat the claim of the equitable owner as paramount. That would be to treat the volunteer as strictly as if he himself stood in a fiduciary relationship to the equitable owner which *ex hypothesi* he does not. The volunteer is under no greater duty of conscience to recognise the interest of the equitable owner than that which lies upon a person having an equitable interest in one of two trust funds of 'money' which have become mixed towards the equitable owner of the other. Such a person is not in conscience bound to give precedence to the equitable owner of the other of the two funds."[17] Thus the shareholders in *Sinclair* v. *Brougham* and the charities in *Re Diplock* were allowed to claim rateably with the plaintiffs; in other words, they were treated in the same way as they would have been if they had themselves been entitled to a tracing remedy.

It is submitted that this analysis of the position of the innocent volunteer can be faulted in two ways. First, the question of conscience is irrelevant. The conscience is by definition unaffected. An innocent donee is generally made to take subject to the prior equitable rights of others because the principles of property law so require. Secondly, the Court of Appeal was not, as is suggested in the quotation above, faced only with the alternatives of treating the innocent volunteer as if he was either in the position of a person entitled to trace or of one being traced against.

Another solution appears if the difference between the remedies of "the proportionate share" and lien are appreciated. We have seen that where a trustee or fiduciary agent is defendant the plaintiff has his choice of remedy[18]; the fiduciary surrenders the profits and stands the losses. That is a harsh rule for the innocent volunteer. If he has spent the money on property which has increased in value, or been applied profitably in trade, it is submitted that he should keep the increase for it has been obtained through his efforts by the use of property which he believed to be his own.[19] The plaintiff would then have a lien. If, however, it has decreased in value it would be harsh to make him stand the whole loss; he and the claimants should take proportionate shares. Where the money has been partly dissipated but some remains, it is

---

[14] (1948–1949) 62 H.L.R. 1002 (G. K. Scott).
[15] [1914] A.C. 398.
[16] [1948] Ch. 465.
[17] *Ibid.* at p. 524.
[18] *Ante*, p. 638.
[19] Another view is that both parties should share the increase rateably, with an extra allowance to the volunteer for his effort, enforceable as a personal claim; [1983] Conv. 135, at p. 137 (K. Hodkinson).

submitted that the innocent volunteer should be taken to be spending his own money first[20]; but should be able in appropriate circumstances to make use of the doctrine of change of position.[21] If the fund is completely lost, no proprietary remedy is of course available.

We will see that, as far as any claim *in personam* is concerned, the action against the volunteer may be brought only after the remedies against the personal representatives have been exhausted.[22] Any money recovered from them reduces the sum recoverable from the volunteer. It is not clear whether the action *in rem* against a third party is similarly limited. Without suggesting that there was any obligation to sue the executors before proceeding *in rem* against the volunteer, the Court of Appeal in *Re Diplock* took the preliminary view that "prima facie and subject to discussion"[23] the next-of-kin's proprietary claim should be reduced by any amounts recovered from them. It is difficult to see why this should be so. Of course, the beneficiary should not recover twice over, but "it should be no defence to the volunteer that the next-of-kin have recovered *in personam* against the executors. The executors should then be subrogated ... to that part of the next-of-kin's fund which represents the difference between the total of the sums recovered from the executors and the volunteer and the loss suffered by the next-of-kin."[24] A better solution might be to require the claimant to sue the volunteer before suing the executors, who should be liable only for that which cannot be recovered from the volunteer.[25]

(vii) Loss of Right to Trace. There are some situations in which the right to trace will be lost. Some of these have already been mentioned, but they will be included here for the sake of completeness.[26]

(a) *The Property Ceases to be Identifiable.* It is clear from the preceding discussion that the remedy of tracing is not available to a plaintiff who cannot identify his property, for example where the trust funds or the proceeds of sale of trust assets have been dissipated.[27] Of course, the personal action remains.

---

[20] For a different solution, see [1983] Conv. 135, at pp. 138–139, proposing that the loss should be borne rateably.

[21] *Post*, p. 643; (1957) 73 L.Q.R. 48 (G. H. Jones); Goff and Jones (3rd ed.), Chap. 39.

[22] *Post*, p. 645.

[23] [1948] Ch. 465 at p. 556. The dictum may be confined to claims arising out of the administration of estates.

[24] Goff and Jones (3rd ed.), p. 77.

[25] This is the rule adopted by the New Zealand Administration Act 1952, s.30B(5) and the Western Australia Trustee Act 1962, s.65(7); *cf.* Trusts Act (Queensland), s.109, whereby the trustee must be sued before the third party.

[26] See also Goff and Jones (3rd ed.), pp. 76–77, on the question how far the right to trace against an innocent volunteer is reduced by the amount recoverable from the trustee; *Re Diplock* [1948] Ch. 465 at p. 556.

[27] *cf. Space Investments Ltd.* v. *Canadian Imperial Bank of Commerce Trust Co. (Bahamas) Ltd.* [1986] 1 W.L.R. 1072, *ante*, p. 630.

(b) *Bona Fide Purchaser.* Where trust property has been transferred to a bona fide purchaser for value without notice, the latter must take free of the claims of the beneficiaries, which must be pursued against the proceeds of sale or against the trustee personally.[28]

(c) *Where Tracing would be Inequitable.* Where the mixed fund was applied in making improvements or alterations to land of the innocent volunteer, the remedy of a charge was held not available to the plaintiff.[29] There is no space here to deal in detail with the reasons which were given for this refusal, nor to suggest the answers to them.[30] The result, it was thought, would be inequitable because a charge is enforceable by sale; it would be hard on the volunteer to be compelled to sell his own land. The matter is related to the question, discussed above,[31] whether or not the innocent volunteer should in all ways be treated as having an equal claim to the plaintiff who is entitled to the tracing remedy. It must be sufficient here to submit that a charge on the land should have been allowed; but limited to the amount, if any, by which the value of the land had been increased by the improvements, or to the money spent on them, whichever is the smaller.[32] This solution would permit the recovery of the plaintiff's money without making the charities liable for more than the benefit they had received.

(d) *Payment of Debts.* Payments were made to two of the charities in *Re Diplock*[33] on the understanding that the money would be used to pay off debts, one of these being an unsecured, the other a secured, debt. It was held in each case that the debt was extinguished, and, along with the security in the second case, no longer existed. The plaintiffs had no right to be subrogated to the position of the creditors.

Subrogation is a doctrine under which one person is entitled to stand in the shoes of another in respect of certain legal or equitable rights.[34] The most common application is that of a contract of insurance, or a contract of suretyship. An insurer who pays the loss is entitled to stand in the shoes of the insured in respect of his action against the party responsible for the loss. Similarly, a person who pays another's debt may in some circumstances stand in the shoes of the creditor.[35] It is

---

[28] *Thorndike* v. *Hunt* (1859) 3 De G. & J. 563; *Taylor* v. *Blakelock* (1886) 32 Ch.D. 560; *Thomson* v. *Clydesdale Bank* [1893] A.C. 282; *Coleman* v. *Bucks and Oxon Union Bank* [1897] 2 Ch. 243; *Re J. Leslie Engineers Co. Ltd.* [1976] 1 W.L.R. 292.
[29] [1948] Ch. 465, at pp. 546–548.
[30] Treated in detail in (1959) 75 L.Q.R. 240 at pp. 248–249 (R. H. Maudsley).
[31] *Ante*, p. 640.
[32] Admittedly the enforcement of the charge by sale would be difficult in the case of, say, improvements to part of a hospital, as in *Re Diplock*.
[33] [1948] Ch. 465.
[34] See Goff and Jones (3rd ed.), Chap. 27.
[35] See *Re Cleadon Trust* [1939] Ch. 286; *Wenlock (Baroness)* v. *River Dee Company* (1887) 19 Q.B.D. 155.

submitted that an application of the doctrine would have been a proper solution here. Where the defendant pays off debts with money which he should never have had, it is no hardship to him to be put back into the position he was in before using the money to pay the debts.

(viii) Change of Position. The doctrine of change of position lays down that "the right of a person to restitution from another because of a benefit received is terminated or diminished if, after the receipt of the benefit, circumstances have so changed that it would be inequitable to require the other to make full restitution."[36] Such a doctrine, not fully accepted in English law,[37] is essential to any satisfactory system of restitutionary remedies.

The absence of such a defence to the claim *in personam* in *Re Diplock*,[38] caused great hardship to those charities which had disposed of the Diplock money. In the case of proprietary remedies the doctrine applies to some extent automatically; if the property can no longer be traced, the proprietary remedy is no longer available.

But questions of change of position do arise in the context of proprietary remedies[39]; where for instance the property which is subject to the proprietary remedy has been improved by the defendant's expenditure[40]; or has been exchanged for other property[41]; or where the fund has been spent in improving the defendant's own property[42]; or has been spent in paying off secured debts of the defendant.[43] In these cases there is still some property or fund against which a proprietary remedy could be exercised. We have seen that *Re Diplock*[44] held that no tracing remedy existed in the last two cases, and that this decision was influenced by the fact that the non-availability of this defence might have made a tracing remedy inequitable in the circumstances.[45] This has been described as "an emasculated application of the defence of change of position."[46] The defence is necessary to a satisfactory system of restitution, and in connection with proprietary claims it is especially relevant where the *res* or its product is still in the defendant's hands, but where it is inequitable either to compel him to

---

[36] *Restatement of Restitution*, para. 142.
[37] *Durrant* v. *The Ecclesiastical Commissioners for England and Wales* (1880) 6 Q.B.D. 234; *Baylis* v. *The Bishop of London* [1913] 1 Ch. 127; *R. E. Jones Ltd.* v. *Waring and Gillow Ltd.* [1926] A.C. 670; *Ministry of Health* v. *Simpson* [1951] A.C. 251 at p. 276; (1957) 74 L.Q.R. 48 (G. H. Jones); Goff and Jones (3rd ed.), Chap. 39. See p. 647, n. 77, *post*.
[38] [1948] Ch. 465 at pp. 502–503; [1951] A.C. 251 at p. 276.
[39] (1948–1949) 62 Harv.L.R. 1002 (G. K. Scott).
[40] *Scott on Trusts* (3rd ed.), para. 479; *Restatement of Restitution*, para. 178.
[41] *Restatement of Restitution*, para. 142, comment (*b*); para. 178.
[42] *Re Diplock, supra*, at pp. 546–548.
[43] *Ibid.* at pp. 548–550.
[44] [1948] Ch. 465.
[45] [1948] Ch. 465 at p. 548.
[46] Goff and Jones (3rd ed.), p. 76.

hand it back to the plaintiff, or to submit to a lien to the extent of the full value of the plaintiff's claim.[47]

6. THE CLAIM IN PERSONAM IN DIPLOCK

It will be recalled that in *Re Diplock*[48] executors distributed large sums of money to numerous charities under the terms of a residuary bequest which was subsequently held to be invalid. The misapplied money belonged, therefore, to the testator's next-of-kin, whose claim to have the money *in rem* has already been considered.[49] The next-of-kin claimed alternatively that a direct action *in personam* lay against the innocent recipients in equity. This claim succeeded in the Court of Appeal, whose judgment was unanimously affirmed by the House of Lords.[50] Such an action may be brought by an unpaid or underpaid creditor, legatee or next-of-kin against the recipient, whether the latter is an overpaid creditor or beneficiary or a "stranger" having no claim to any part of the estate.[51] While the common law action for money had and received is, as a general rule, confined to mistakes of fact,[52] it was held that the action in equity lay whether the mistake was of fact or, as in the present case, of law. The mistake in such a case is not that of the plaintiff, but that of the personal representative, who is not a party to the action. The plaintiff has no way of finding out whether the mistake was of fact or law, nor whether it was a mistaken or deliberate misapplication,[53] hence "it would be a strange thing if the Court of Chancery, having taken upon itself to see that the assets of a deceased person were duly administered, was deterred from doing justice to a creditor, legatee or next-of-kin because the executor had done him wrong under a mistake of law."[54]

The action will not lie against a bona fide purchaser without notice, but, as far as a volunteer is concerned, it is no defence that he was

---

[47] *cf.* Heydon, Gummow and Austin, *Cases and Materials on Equity and Trusts* (2nd ed.), p. 784, questioning whether the defence of change of position would introduce an element of "palm-tree justice."

[48] [1948] Ch. 465, [1951] A.C. 251. (Where the earlier authorities are extensively reviewed). For a historical survey, see (1983) 4 Journal of Legal History 3 (S. J. Whittaker).

[49] *Ante*, p. 625.

[50] [1951] A.C. 251 (*sub. nom. Ministry of Health* v. *Simpson*).

[51] [1948] Ch. 465 at p. 502; [1951] A.C. 251 at p. 269.

[52] It seems that the decision in *Chase Manhattan Bank N.A.* v. *Israel-British Bank (London) Ltd.* [1981] Ch. 105, *ante,* p. 628, that where money is paid by mistake the equitable title remains in the payer, is confined to mistakes of fact. The recipient of a payment made under a mistake of law would, however, be a constructive trustee if he knew that the property was transferred in breach of trust; *ante,* p. 292.

[53] It seems that the action will also lie where the wrongful payment was deliberate: [1951] A.C. 251 at p. 270.

[54] [1951] A.C. 251 at p. 270 (*per* Lord Simonds). But the personal representative cannot himself recover from the recipient unless the mistake was of fact (although he can deduct the mistakenly paid sum from any future payments to the recipient: *Livesey* v. *Livesey* (1827) 3 Russ. 287).

unaware of the mistake[55]; "it is prima facie at least a sufficient circumstance that the defendant, as events have proved, has received some share of the estate to which he was not entitled."[56] But the claim will fail if the plaintiff has acquiesced in the wrongful payment,[57] or has failed to bring his action within the time permitted by the Limitation Act 1980.[58] It is doubtful whether the action lies against the recipient's successor in title.[59]

The equitable claim *in personam* lies for the principal sum only, without interest,[60] and is subject to two further important qualifications. First, the direct claim against the recipient is limited to the amount which cannot be recovered from the personal representative, who is primarily liable.[61] Thus the recipient will only be liable in respect of the whole sum if nothing can be recovered from the personal representative, for example because he is insolvent, or acted under a court order,[62] or is protected by section 27 of the Trustee Act 1925.[63] This limitation has been criticised.[64] Why should the recipient's liability depend on the personal representative's solvency? The solution adopted in *Re Diplock*[65] benefits the recipient at the expense of the personal representative, who, on paying the plaintiff, should be subrogated to the plaintiff's right to sue the recipient. Another solution might be to require the plaintiff to exhaust his remedies against the recipient before suing the personal representative.[66]

The second qualification is that the action appears to be limited to claims arising out of the administration of estates.[67] The action originated at a time when the Court of Chancery was attempting to acquire the jurisdiction then exercised by the ecclesiastical courts over the administration of assets, and is not necessarily available to

---

[55] This was, however, a defence to an alternative claim based on constructive trusteeship; [1948] 1 Ch. 465 at p. 478.

[56] [1948] Ch. 465 at p. 503 (*per* Lord Greene M.R.). But the innocent volunteer, having taken without notice, does not have the liabilities of a constructive trustee: *ibid.* at pp. 478–479.

[57] [1951] A.C. 251 at p. 276; *Blake* v. *Gale* (1886) 32 Ch.D. 571.

[58] By s.22, the period is 12 years. (For creditors the period is six years). See [1948] Ch. 465 at p. 514.

[59] Goff and Jones (3rd ed.), p. 574; Hayton and Marshall, *Cases and Commentary on the Law of Trusts* (8th ed.), p. 509.

[60] *Re Diplock, supra.* This is described as "curious" by Goff and Jones, *loc. cit.* at p. 574.

[61] [1948] Ch. 465 at p. 503. Here the executors paid £15,000 under a compromise approved by the court. For the position concerning the action *in rem*, see *ante*, p. 625.

[62] For example, a Benjamin order (*Re Benjamin* [1902] 1 Ch. 723), giving him liberty to distribute on the footing that a particular person is dead.

[63] *Ante,* p. 507.

[64] See (1949) 65 L.Q.R. 37 at p. 44 (A. T. Denning); Goff and Jones, *loc. cit.* at p. 574; (1983) 4 Journal of Legal History 3 (S. J. Whittaker).

[65] [1948] Ch. 465, [1951] A.C. 251.

[66] See New Zealand Administration Act 1952; Western Australia Trustee Act 1962.

[67] See [1951] A.C. 251 at pp. 265–266 (*per* Lord Simonds). But the action is not confined to cases where the estate is administered by the court: *ibid.* at p. 268.

beneficiaries of *inter vivos* trusts.[68] But more recent cases indicate that the court is not unwilling to extend the action beyond the administration of estates. This approach is consistent with the doctrine of unjust enrichment. In *Butler* v. *Broadhead*[69] it was suggested that the liquidator of a company had a sufficiently analogous position to that of an executor to allow a creditor of the company to recover from overpaid contributories in a winding-up, at any rate where the liquidator had not advertised for claims. But the action was held to be barred by the Companies Act 1948.[70] In *Re J. Leslie Engineers Co. Ltd.*[71] Oliver J. was prepared to allow a personal action where a liquidator claimed recovery of money paid to X after the commencement of a winding-up (the transaction being void under the Companies Act). But the claim failed in the present case because the liquidator had not exhausted his remedies against the person primarily responsible, and, in any event, it appeared that X had given consideration for the payment. In *Re Montagu's Settlements*,[72] on the other hand, it was assumed that the action would not lie in respect of dispositions by a trustee of an *inter vivos* trust: a volunteer who no longer had the property would have no liability unless he took as constructive trustee.

Much criticism has centred around the apparent refusal of the House of Lords in *Re Diplock*[73] to recognise the defence of change of position. Where the volunteer has received the money in good faith, his liability to repay it could cause hardship if he has acted to his detriment by spending the money in an exceptional and irretrievable manner.[74] It will be recalled that in *Re Diplock* money had been paid to a hospital charity, and used in the erection of new buildings. This, it was considered, made it inequitable to allow the tracing remedy.[75] If tracing would be inequitable in such circumstances, why is the claim *in personam* not similarly regarded?[76] On the other hand, it should be borne in

---

[68] Although if a trustee pays trust money under a mistake of fact, he may recover it, and may be compelled by the beneficiaries to do so: *Re Robinson* [1911] 1 Ch. 502.

[69] [1975] Ch. 97. See also *G.L. Baker Ltd.* v. *Medway Building and Supplies Ltd.* [1958] 1 W.L.R. 1216; *Nelson* v. *Larholt* [1948] 1 K.B. 339; *Eddis* v. *Chichester Constable* [1969] 1 All E.R. 566 (affirmed, without discussing this point, [1969] 2 Ch. 345).

[70] Now Companies Act 1985, s.557.

[71] [1976] 1 W.L.R. 292.

[72] [1987] Ch. 264, at p. 271; (1987) 50 M.L.R. 218 (C. Harpum).

[73] [1951] A.C. 251.

[74] See (1949) 65 L.Q.R. 37 at p. 50 (A. T. Denning); (1957) 73 L.Q.R. 48 at p. 61 (G. H. Jones); Goff and Jones (3rd ed.), pp. 696–699. The mere fact of spending the money, for example on living expenses, cannot be regarded as a change of position.

[75] *Ante.*

[76] The Court of Appeal rejected the claim that the volunteers were personally liable *as constructive trustees*, holding that they were not under any duty to investigate the validity of the gift and were entitled to assume that the executors were acting properly; *Re Diplock* [1948] Ch. 465 at pp. 477–479. Having rejected this claim as one which would lead to "startling results," it is perhaps ironic that the court went on to find the volunteers personally liable under another heading.

mind that the defence of change of position has not yet been generally accepted in restitutionary actions,[77] and that we are here concerned with adjusting the loss as between two innocent parties. The plaintiff is the rightful owner, and has not made the payment himself. It might be thought that his claim is the stronger unless the plaintiff by his conduct induced the change of position.[78]

Finally, it seems that the action does not lie if there was a sufficiency of assets at the date of the payment to the defendant. Where the deficiency has arisen subsequently, the personal representative alone is liable.[79]

---

[77] See Goff and Jones, *loc. cit.* There are exceptions; see, for example, *Barclays Bank Ltd.* v. *W. J. Simms* [1980] Q.B. 677; *Avon County Council* v. *Howlett* [1983] 1 W.L.R. 605. The position is otherwise in the U.S.; see *Restatement of Restitution*, para. 142. As to Commonwealth jurisdictions, see Goff and Jones, *loc. cit.*

[78] See (1961) 24 M.L.R. 85 (R. Goff).

[79] See *Fenwicke* v. *Clarke* (1862) 4 De G.F. & J. 240; *Peterson* v. *Peterson* (1866) L.R. 3 Eq. 111.

PART IV

EQUITABLE REMEDIES

CHAPTER 23

SPECIFIC PERFORMANCE

1. GENERAL PRINCIPLES[1]

AN outline of the nature of equitable remedies has already been given.[2] Their characteristics, in relation to specific performance in particular, must now be examined.

A. Discretionary

Specific performance, like other equitable remedies, is only given as a matter of discretion, although the discretion is exercised in accordance with settled principles.[3] Thus there are some cases, notably

---

[1] See Fry, *Specific Performance*; Spry, *Equitable Remedies*; Jones and Goodhart, *Specific Performance*; Sharpe, *Injunctions and Specific Performance*.

[2] *Ante*, p. 31.

[3] *Lamare* v. *Dixon* (1873) L.R. 6 H.L. 414; *Haywood* v. *Cope* (1858) 25 Beav. 140 at p. 151 (Romilly M.R.).

651

contracts for the sale of land,[4] where the plaintiff may expect to obtain specific performance as a matter of course, and other cases, such as contracts for personal services,[5] where he may expect not to. The discretionary nature of the remedy is well illustrated by a consideration of the matters, such as the conduct of the plaintiff, which the court may regard as a bar to specific performance.[6]

B. Common Law Remedies Inadequate

Equitable remedies are only available where common law remedies are inadequate[7]; for example where only nominal damages could be recovered at law,[8] or where the obligation is a continuing one, necessitating a series of actions at law for damages.[9] Indeed specific performance may be available where there is no remedy at law at all, as in the case of an oral contract for the sale of land, supported only by acts of part performance.[10] But specific performance will not be available if, on the true construction of the contract, the parties have agreed that a specified sum of money is to be paid as an alternative to performing the contract.[11]

C. Specific Performance is a Remedy in Personam[12]

A decree of specific performance issues against the individual defendant. If the defendant is within the jurisdiction of the court and can be compelled personally to carry out his obligation, the court may order him to do so even though the subject-matter of the contract is outside the jurisdiction of the court.

In *Penn* v. *Lord Baltimore*[13] the plaintiffs and defendant had entered into a written agreement fixing the boundaries of Pennsylvania and Maryland, the former of which belonged to the plaintiffs and the latter to the defendant, under various grants which were recited in the agreements. The plaintiffs sued the defendant in the Court of Chancery in England to have the agreement specifically performed, and one of the objections taken by the defendant was to the jurisdiction of the court. This objection was overruled by Lord Hardwicke on the ground that "the conscience of the party was bound by this agreement; and being within the jurisdiction of this

---

[4] *Post*, p. 658.
[5] *Post*, p. 666.
[6] *Post*, p. 674.
[7] See *Beswick* v. *Beswick* [1968] A.C. 58, *post*, p. 689; *Tito* v. *Waddell (No. 2)* [1977] Ch. 106 at p. 327.
[8] *Beswick* v. *Beswick, supra.*
[9] *Ibid.* but see *post*, p. 691.
[10] This will no longer be the case after the repeal of L.P.A. 1925, s.40; *post*, p. 658.
[11] *Legh* v. *Lillie* (1860) 6 H. & N. 165; Pettit, pp. 520–521.
[12] *Ante*, pp. 7, 19.
[13] (1750) 1 Ves.Sen. 444 (following the decision, further surveying of the boundaries was carried out by Jeremiah Mason and Charles Dixon, and their work produced the Mason/Dixon line; see Chafee, *Cases and Materials on Equity* (5th ed.), p. 70); *Richard West and Partners (Inverness) Ltd.* v. *Dick* [1969] Ch. 424.

court, which acts *in personam*, the court may properly decree it as an agreement."[14] He reasoned that though the land was not within the jurisdiction, the defendant was, and the court would hold him in contempt unless he complied.

But this jurisdiction is not, perhaps, so wide as might at first appear. The land in question was subject at that time to the Crown. The court was invited in *Re Hawthorne*[15] to apply it to land in Saxony (not subject to the Crown) but refused to do so. It appears that the tendency of modern decisions is to restrict rather than to enlarge the limits within which this jurisdiction will be exercised.[16]

D. Ensuring Observance

Equitable remedies will never issue unless the court can ensure that they will be observed. As equity does not act in vain,[17] specific performance will be decreed only where the defendant is in a position to comply with the order.

In *Jones* v. *Lipman*[18] the defendant entered into a binding contract to sell some land to the plaintiff. After the date of the contract, the defendant changed his mind, and sought to avoid specific performance by selling the land to a company acquired by him solely for this purpose and controlled by him. While specific performance would not normally be ordered against a vendor who no longer owned the property, here the defendant was still in a position to complete the contract, because the company was "the creature of the vendor, a device and a sham, a mask which he holds before his face in an attempt to avoid recognition by the eye of Equity."[19] Thus specific performance was decreed against the vendor and the company.

E. The Enforcement of Positive Contractual Obligations

Unlike injunctions, the remedy of specific performance is confined to the enforcement of positive contractual obligations. These obligations must be binding on the defendant.[20] A prohibitory injunction is appropriate to restrain the breach of a negative contract, while a mandatory injunction is used to force the defendant to take positive steps to undo an act already done in breach of contract. But this

---

[14] *Ibid.* at p. 447.
[15] (1883) 23 Ch.D. 743.
[16] See, *per* Parker J. in *Deschamps* v. *Miller* [1908] 1 Ch. 856, at p. 863; Dicey and Morris, *The Conflict of Laws* (11th ed.), pp. 928 *et seq.* See also Civil Jurisdiction and Judgments Act 1982, s.30.
[17] *Tito* v. *Waddell (No. 2)*, [1977] Ch. 106 at p. 326.
[18] [1962] 1 W.L.R. 832. And see *Elliot* v. *Pierson* [1948] Ch. 452.
[19] *Ibid.* p. 836 (*per* Russell J.).
[20] For specific performance against a party estopped from denying the existence of a contract, see *Spiro* v. *Lintern* [1973] 1 W.L.R. 1002; *Worboys* v. *Carter* [1987] 2 E.G.L.R. 1.

classification is not inflexible. Even where the plaintiff wishes to enforce a positive contractual obligation, he may ask for an injunction instead of specific performance. The advantage of such a course is that an injunction can be obtained on an interlocutory basis, while specific performance cannot.[21] It should also be added that specific performance does not lie against the Crown.[22]

F. Time for Performance

While specific performance is a remedy for breach of contract, it may in some circumstances be obtained before the time for performance has arrived. In *Marks* v. *Lilley*[23] the plaintiff issued a writ for specific performance of a contract for the sale of land after the contractual completion date but without first having served a notice making time of the essence of the contract. It was held that this action was not premature, as the equitable right to specific performance, based on the defendant's equitable duty to perform his contract, had already accrued. But the court would not normally interfere before the time for performance had arrived, and a premature plaintiff may be penalised in costs. In *Hasham* v. *Zenab*[24] specific performance of a contract for the sale of land was granted even before the contractual completion date where the defendant had been guilty of anticipatory breach of contract.[25] The decree would not, of course, take effect before the fixed date.

A novel point arose in *Oakacre Ltd.* v. *Claire Cleaners (Holdings) Ltd.*[26]

A vendor and purchaser discussed completing the sale on February 29, 1980, but the vendor failed to complete on that date, so on the same day the purchaser issued a writ claiming specific performance and damages. Completion took place on June 20, 1980, but the purchaser maintained the claim for damages for delay arising from the vendor's failure to complete on February 29. The court ruled that the contractual completion date was March 4, 1980, so that the writ was issued prematurely at law. It was held that although no cause of action for damages had accrued before the issue of the

---

[21] See *Sky Petroleum Ltd.* v. *V.I.P. Petroleum Ltd.* [1974] 1 W.L.R. 576; *Astro Exito Navegacion S.A.* v. *Southland Enterprise Co. Ltd. (No. 2)* [1983] 2 A.C. 787; *Peninsular Maritime Ltd* v. *Padseal Ltd.* (1981) 259 E.G. 860; *Parker* v. *Camden London Borough Council* [1986] Ch. 162.

[22] Crown Proceedings Act 1947, s.21(1)(*a*). The proper remedy is a declaration.

[23] [1959] 1 W.L.R. 749. It has since been held that there is a breach of contract at law and in equity if completion does not occur on the contractual date, even though time has not become of the essence: *Raineri* v. *Miles* [1981] A.C. 1050, *post*, p. 677.

[24] [1960] A.C. 316; (1960) 76 L.Q.R. 200 (R.E.M.). This is similar to the position at law, where an immediate right to damages accrues upon an anticipatory breach of contract: *Hochster* v. *De la Tour* (1853) 2 E. & B. 678.

[25] Anticipatory breach is not essential, but there must be a sufficient likelihood of breach; Spry, *Equitable Remedies*, pp. 71–73.

[26] [1982] Ch. 197.

writ, the claim to specific performance was not premature.[27] The court was not obliged to consider the damages claim as an isolated claim at law, and since the action was originally properly constituted and brought in good faith as a specific performance action, the court could consider the purchaser's whole case, including the claim for damages, which could be awarded in equity under Lord Cairns' Act.[28]

G. Specific Performance and Damages or Compensation

Damages may be awarded either in addition to or in substitution for specific performance.[29] Similarly, there are some cases, involving misdescription in contracts for the sale of land, where the court may grant specific performance with compensation in the form of an abatement of the purchase price. Both these matters are discussed below.[30]

2. THE EFFECT OF A DECREE OF SPECIFIC PERFORMANCE ON OTHER REMEDIES

If a decree of specific performance is attained, but enforcement subsequently becomes impossible, what remedies are available to the plaintiff?

A. Common Law Remedy not Excluded

In *Johnson* v. *Agnew*[31] the plaintiff, having contracted to sell mortgaged properties to the defendant, obtained a decree of specific performance. Subsequently, owing to the defendant's delay, the properties were sold by the mortgagees so that it became impossible to comply with the decree. The price obtained by the mortgagees was lower than the contract price, so the plaintiff sought damages from the defendant at common law for breach of contract.[32] The defendant claimed that the plaintiff's election to pursue the remedy of specific performance was irrevocable, so that he could not revert to the position before his election and claim damages at common law. The House of Lords found in favour of the plaintiff. Lord Wilberforce explained the vendor's position as follows:

If a purchaser fails to complete, the vendor can treat this as a repudiation[33] and claim damages for breach of contract, or he may seek

---

[27] Following *Hasham* v. *Zenab.*, *supra*.
[28] *Post*, p. 684.
[29] Lord Cairns' Act 1858; Judicature Act 1873; *post*, p. 684.
[30] *Post*, p. 684 (damages), and p. 680 (compensation). See also *Seven Seas Properties Ltd.* v. *Al-Essa* [1988] 1 W.L.R. 1272 (specific performance and damages combined with *Mareva* injunction).
[31] [1980] A.C. 367; (1979) 95 L.Q.R. 321 (P. V. Baker); [1979] Conv. 293 (F. R. Crane); (1979) 42 M.L.R. 696 (G. Woodman); (1980) 96 L.Q.R. 403 (M. Hetherington); (1980) 39 C.L.J. 58 (A. J. Oakley); (1981) 97 L.Q.R. 26 (D. Jackson).
[32] Or, alternatively, damages under Lord Cairns' Act, *post*, p. 684.
[33] This is sometimes referred to as "rescinding," but it is not rescission *ab initio*. The position is simply that both parties are discharged from further performance.

specific performance. If he proceeds for these remedies in the alterna-tive, he must elect at trial.[33a] If an order for specific performance is made, the contract still exists and is not merged in the judgment. If the defendant then fails to comply with the decree, the plaintiff may apply either to enforce or to dissolve the contract. It follows from the fact that the contract still exists that the defendant has committed a repu-diatory breach of it, for which the plaintiff can recover damages at common law. The argument based on irrevocable election is unsound: "A vendor who seeks (and gets) specific performance is merely elect-ing for a course which may or may not lead to implementation of the contract; what he elects for is not eternal and unconditional affirma-tion, but a continuance of the contract under control of the court, which control involves the power, in certain events, to terminate it. If he makes an election at all, he does so when he decides not to proceed under the order for specific performance; but to ask the court to terminate the contract."[34] If the plaintiff accepts a repudiation, he cannot afterwards seek specific performance, because the defendant has been discharged from further performance by the plaintiff's accep-tance of the repudiation. But if the plaintiff attains a decree of specific performance, and enforcement becomes impossible, there is no reason why the plaintiff should be precluded from seeking a remedy at com-mon law.[35]

B. The Court's Discretion

But the control of the court is exercised according to equitable principles: the relief sought by the plaintiff will be refused if it would be unjust to the other party to grant it. In *Johnson* v. *Agnew*[36] it was the purchaser's fault that it had become impossible to enforce the decree, therefore the vendor was entitled not only to an order discharging the decree of specific performance and terminating the contract, but to damages at common law for breach of contract.

C. Subsequent Performance Regulated by Terms of Decree

Although the contract still exists after specific performance is granted and does not merge into the decree until the legal title has been conveyed, the rights under the contract may be affected by the decree.

[33a] See *Meng Leong Development Pte. Ltd.* v. *Jip Hong Trading Co. Pte. Ltd.* [1985] A.C. 511 (P.C.): P claimed in the alternative and was awarded damages. V appealed against the amount. P insisted that the damages be placed with a stakeholder, otherwise he would levy execution. It was held that P was estopped from later seeking specific performance. He was not bound to make an election at that stage, and could have retained the right to elect until after the appeal. Here, however, he had elected to take the benefit of the damages award, and thereby relinquished the right to seek specific performance. The reasoning is criticised at (1985) 101 L.Q.R. 309 on the ground that the damages had not come under P's control.

[34] [1980] A.C. 367 at p. 398 (*per* Lord Wilberforce).

[35] Damages are also available in lieu of specific performance under Lord Cairns' Act (*post*, p. 684); *Biggin* v. *Minton* [1977] 1 W.L.R. 701.

[36] *Supra*.

By applying for specific performance, the plaintiff puts into the hands of the court how the contract is to be carried out: the performance of the contract is regulated by the provisions of the order and not those of the contract. In *Singh* v. *Nazeer*[37] a purchaser was granted specific performance of a contract for the sale of land. The purchaser then became dilatory, so the vendor served a completion notice under the general conditions of sale applicable to the contract and claimed damages and forfeiture of the deposit. Megarry J. held that the completion notice was invalid. The machinery provisions of the contract, for example as to mode and date of completion, were intended to apply to performance out of court. Once specific performance was granted, they must yield to any directions in the order. Unless the parties agree, the working out, variation or cancellation of an order for specific performance is a matter for the court. Applying these principles, a vendor who obtains specific performance is not free to sell to a third party if the purchaser fails to comply with the decree. Unless the purchaser agrees to the resale, the vendor's remedy in such a case is to apply to court either for enforcement of the decree or for an order terminating the contract.[38]

3. SPECIFIC PERFORMANCE IN PARTICULAR SITUATIONS

It is a fundamental rule that specific performance will not be granted where the plaintiff would be adequately compensated by the common law remedy of damages.[39] We will see that there are some situations, few in number, in which it is settled that the plaintiff may expect to obtain specific performance.[40] There are also numerous situations in which it can firmly be said that the plaintiff will *not* be awarded specific performance. It is perhaps for this reason that most of the books list the conditions for the award of specific performance in the negative—and state the circumstances in which a decree will not be granted.[41] It may

[37] [1979] Ch. 474; criticised in (1980) 96 L.Q.R. 403 (M. Hetherington). *Cf.* (1981) 97 L.Q.R. 26 (D. Jackson).
[38] *GKN Distributors Ltd.* v. *Tyne Tees Fabrication Ltd.* [1985] 2 E.G.L.R. 181. (Vendor's claim against purchaser for declaration, forfeiture of deposit and damages dismissed).
[39] *Hutton* v. *Watling* [1948] Ch. 26 at p. 36, affirmed [1948] Ch. 398. The approach of equity differs, as Lee has pointed out (*Introduction to Roman-Dutch Law* (5th ed.) App. 1) from that of Roman-Dutch law, under which specific performance is usually granted subject only to the overriding discretion of the court to refuse the remedy in the interests of justice in the particular case; *Abdeen* v. *Thaheer* [1958] A.C. 116. On the effect of the defendant's insolvency, see Spry, *Equitable Remedies*, p. 65; *Freevale Ltd.* v. *Metrostore (Holdings) Ltd.* [1984] Ch. 199; [1984] Conv. 446 (D. Milman and S. Coneys): receivership of the vendor company before completion is no bar to specific performance.
[40] See *Goring* v. *Nash* (1744) 3 Atk. 186; *White* v. *Damon* (1802) 7 Ves.Jr. 30; *Haywood* v. *Cope* (1858) 25 Beav. 140, *per* Romilly M.R. at p. 151; *Lamare* v. *Dixon* (1873) L.R. 6 H.L. 414.
[41] Fry, *Specific Performance*, Part III; Snell, p. 575; Pettit, pp. 522, *et seq.* We are not concerned here with contracts which are not enforceable at all, such as illegal or immoral contracts.

be that many of the arguments for restricting specific performance are no longer wholly convincing, and that the trend is towards expansion of the remedy.[42]

A. Contracts for the Sale of Land

A plaintiff seeking specific performance of a contract for the sale (or other disposition) of land must first of all satisfy the requirements of section 40 of the Law of Property Act 1925.[43] These requirements, it should be added, apply also to a claim for damages. Section 40(1) provides that "no action may be brought upon any contract for the sale or other disposition of land or any interest in land, unless the agreement upon which such action is brought, or some memorandum or note thereof, is in writing, and signed by the party to be charged or by some other person thereunto by him lawfully authorised." Under the doctrine of part performance, however, the Court of Chancery would grant specific performance in the absence of written evidence where it would be unjust not to enforce the contract. Thus the plaintiff could succeed by showing a sufficient act of part performance. This exception is now found in section 40(2), providing that the section does not affect the law relating to part performance. The doctrine of part performance is fully explained in the real property books.[44]

Assuming section 40 is satisfied, a decree of specific performance is readily granted to enforce a contract to create or convey a legal estate in land (for example, to sell land[45] or to grant a lease) unless some special consideration arises to prevent it.[46] It cannot however be said that the plaintiff is *entitled* to a decree; because the issue of a decree is always subject to the discretion of the court.

Each piece of land is unique, and it is accepted as a general rule that an award of damages is not adequate compensation for the purchaser

---

[42] Treitel, *The Law of Contract* (7th ed.), p. 785. See generally (1984) 4 Legal Studies 102 (A. S. Burrows).

[43] Replacing s.4 of the Statute of Frauds 1677.

[44] See Megarry and Wade, *The Law of Real Property* (5th ed.), pp. 587 *et seq.*; Cheshire and Burn, *Modern Law of Real Property* (14th ed.) pp. 114 *et seq.* S.40 is to be repealed when the Law of Property (Miscellaneous Provisions) Bill is enacted. This provides that contracts relating to land must be *in* writing. This will leave no scope for part performance, which can only cure *evidential* defects. Estoppel and restitution could provide remedies in situations presently covered by part performance.

[45] On specific performance of options and rights of pre-emption, see *Pritchard* v. *Briggs* [1980] Ch. 338; *Sudbrook Trading Estate Ltd.* v. *Eggleton* [1983] 1 A.C. 444. See also *Berkley* v. *Poulett* (1976) 120 S.J. 836, *ante*, p. 306. (Sub-purchaser would be entitled to specific performance of head contract, subject to notice of the sub-contract having been given to the vendor).

[46] As in *Wroth* v. *Tyler* [1974] Ch. 30. For the position in Canada, see [1984] Conv. 130 (J. Berryman).

or lessee.[47] If the purchaser does not acquire the fee simple he will not have to pay the price, thus "the damages for loss of such a bargain would be negligible and, as in most cases of breach of contract for the sale of land at a market price by refusal to convey it, would constitute a wholly inadequate and unjust remedy for the breach. That is why the normal remedy is by a decree for specific performance by the vendor of his primary obligation to convey, on the purchaser's performing or being willing to perform his own primary obligations under the contract."[48] The court, treating each party equally, will also give specific performance to the vendor or lessor,[49] although a monetary payment might be adequate compensation.

If a vendor fails to comply with the decree, the purchaser may apply to the court for an order nominating some person to execute the conveyance in the vendor's name.[50]

B. Contractual Licences

It was at one time thought that specific performance would not be granted of a contractual licence to occupy land, on the ground that the licence created no estate in the land.[51] This view has now been seen to be inconsistent with the court's power to grant an injunction to restrain the wrongful revocation of a contractual licence.[52] Thus in *Verrall* v. *Great Yarmouth Borough Council*[53] the Court of Appeal affirmed the grant of specific performance to enforce a contractual licence whereby the National Front was to occupy the defendant's premises for the purpose of its annual conference. The remedy of damages would be inadequate as the plaintiff could not find any other premises. Roskill L.J. held it to be the duty of the court "to protect, where it is appropriate to do so, any interest, whether it be an estate in land or a licence, by injunction or specific performance as the case may be."[54]

---

[47] *Cf.* Heydon, Gummow and Austin, *Cases and Materials on Equity and Trusts* (2nd ed.), p. 805, preferring the explanation that "the process of looking for, negotiating for and completing the purchase of land is a lengthy and irritating one; . . . so that it is better to get specific performance . . . rather than get damages and use them to buy something similar."

[48] *Sudbrook Trading Estate Ltd.* v. *Eggleton, supra,* at p. 478.

[49] *Cogent* v. *Gibson* (1864) 33 Beav. 557.

[50] Supreme Court Act 1981, s.39; Trustee Act 1925, s.50; A.E.A. 1925, s.43(2). If a trustee has wilfully refused or neglected to convey the land for 28 days after being required to do so, the court may make a vesting order. T.A. 1925, s.44(vi); this, where available, is cheaper and more expeditious. See section 2, *ante,* p. 655.

[51] *Booker* v. *Palmer* [1942] 2 All E.R. 674 at p. 677, *per* Lord Greene M.R.

[52] *Winter Garden Theatre (London) Ltd.* v. *Millenium Productions Ltd.* [1948] A.C. 173, *post,* p. 835.

[53] [1981] Q.B. 202, *post,* p. 669, [1981] Conv. 212 (A. Briggs). See also *Tanner* v. *Tanner* [1975] 1 W.L.R. 1346 at p. 1350. The decision is further discussed, *post,* p. 838.

[54] [1981] Q.B. 202 at p. 220. But the remedy of damages was adequate in *Webster* v. *Newham London Borough Council, The Times,* November 22, 1980, where, on otherwise similar facts, another hall had been hired.

C. Contracts for the Sale of Personal Property

Chattels and stocks and shares do not usually possess such individual character as land. Most commercial contracts for the purchase of goods,[55] or for a loan of money,[56] or contracts for the purchase of government stock, will not be specifically performed.[57] But if stocks or shares cannot always be bought in the market, the court may order specific performance[58] or where a chattel has especial value by reason of its individuality, beauty or rarity[59] indeed, in such situations, there is an ancient jurisdiction to order the specific recovery of such a chattel if wrongly detained.[60]

Further, the Sale of Goods Act 1979, s.52 (re-enacting a similar provision in the 1893 Act) enables the court to decree specific perform-ance of a contract for the sale of specific[61] or ascertained[62] goods, either unconditionally, or upon such terms as to damages, payment of the price or otherwise as to the court may seem just. The power is of course a discretionary one, and it must still be shown that the remedy of damages is inadequate.[63] It was intended to broaden the scope of the remedy of specific performance in connection with the purchase of chattels, but less use has been made of it than might have been expected.[64]

In *Cohen* v. *Roche*,[65] the plaintiff agreed to purchase from the defendants a set of eight Hepplewhite chairs. This was a contract for the sale of specific goods; but McCardie J., finding that the chairs were "ordinary articles of commerce and of no special value or interest," refused to order specific performance and awarded damages.

---

[55] *Dominion Coal Co. Ltd.* v. *Dominion Iron and Steel Co. Ltd.* [1909] A.C. 293; *Cohen* v. *Roche* [1927] 1 K.B. 169; *Société Des Industries Metallurgiques S.A.* v. *The Bronx Engineering Co. Ltd.* [1975] 1 Lloyd's Rep. 465. See the examples given by Goff L.J. in *Price* v. *Strange* [1978] Ch. 337 at p. 359.

[56] *South African Territories Ltd.* v. *Wallington* [1898] A.C. 309.

[57] *Cud (or Cuddee)* v. *Rutter* (1720) 1 P.Wms. 570 (South Sea Bubble Stock); *Mason* v. *Armitage* (1806) 13 Ves.Jr. 25. For other reasons against the grant of specific perform-ance, see Treitel, *The Law of Contract* (7th ed.), pp. 786, 787–789.

[58] *Duncuft* v. *Albrecht* (1841) 12 Sim. 189; (1953) 51 Mich.L.R. 408 (A. Neef).

[59] *Falcke* v. *Gray* (1859) 4 Dr. 651; *Thorn* v. *Commissioners of Public Works* (1863) 32 Beav. 490; *Philips* v. *Lamdin* [1949] 2 K.B. 33.

[60] *Pusey* v. *Pusey* (1684) 1 Vern. 273 (an antique horn, supposedly given by King Canute); *Duke of Somerset* v. *Cookson* (1735) 3 P.Wms. 390 (an altar piece); *Fells* v. *Reed* (1796) 3 Ves.Jr. 70; (the tobacco box of a club).

[61] Defined in Sale of Goods Act 1979; s.61, to mean "identified and agreed on and at the time a contract of sale is made."

[62] See *Re Wait* [1927] 1 Ch. 606 at p. 630, where "ascertained," which is not defined in the Act, was said "probably" to mean "identified in accordance with the agreement after the time a contract of sale is made." *Fothergill* v. *Rowland* (1873) L.R. 17 Eq. 132, (the "get" of coal in a colliery for five years held not to be within the section).

[63] *C.N. Marine Inc.* v. *Stena Line A/B., The Times,* June 12, 1982.

[64] [1969] J.B.L. 211; *Société Des Industries Metallurgiques S.A.* v. *The Bronx Engineer-ing Co. Ltd., supra.*

[65] [1927] 1 K.B. 169.

In *Behnke* v. *Bede Shipping Co.*,[66] Wright J. made an order for specific performance of a contract for the sale of a ship, being satisfied that the ship was of "peculiar and practically unique value to the plaintiff."

The boldest exercise of jurisdiction was in *Sky Petroleum Ltd.* v. *V.I.P. Petroleum Ltd.*[67]

A contract had been entered into whereby the plaintiff company would buy all the petrol needed for its garages from the defendant company, and the defendant would supply the plaintiff with all its requirements. The defendant, alleging breach, purported to terminate the contract in November 1973, at a time when petrol supplies were limited, so that the plaintiff would have little prospect of finding an alternative source. An interlocutory injunction was granted to restrain the withholding of supplies.

Goulding J. acknowledged that it amounted to specific performance, the matter being one of substance, and not of form; but held that the court had jurisdiction to order specific performance of a contract to sell chattels, although they were not specific or ascertained,[68] where the remedy of damages was inadequate. The usual rule that specific performance was not available to enforce contracts for the sale of chattels was well established and salutary; but it was based on the adequacy of damages, and was therefore not applicable to the present case, where the plaintiff company might be forced out of business if the remedy was not granted.

D. Contracts to Pay Money

Contracts to pay money are normally not specifically enforceable, because damages will usually be an adequate remedy. So, for example, specific performance of a contract of loan will not be awarded against the borrower, because the remedy of damages is adequate.[69] Exceptionally, however, specific performance may be obtainable in the following situations:

---

[66] [1927] 1 K.B. 649 at p. 661; *cf. Hart* v. *Herwig* (1873) L.R. 8 Ch.App. 680.

[67] [1974] 1 W.L.R. 576. See also *Howard E. Perry & Co. Ltd.* v. *British Railways Board* [1980] 1 W.L.R. 1375; (1980) 39 C.L.J. 269 (J. W. A. Thornely).

[68] *Ante*, notes 61, 62.

[69] See *Locabail International Finance Ltd.* v. *Agroexport* [1986] 1 W.L.R. 657 (no mandatory injunction); *City Centre One Association* v. *Teachers Insurance and Annuity Association*, March 31, 1987 (U.S. District Court, Utah), (1987) 137 N.L.J. 758.

i. Where the contract is to pay money to a third party, so that any damages awarded would probably be nominal[70];

ii. Where the contract is for the payment of an annuity[71] or other periodical sums. This exception is based on two different grounds: first that specific performance avoids the inconvenience of a series of actions for damages every time payment is not made; and, secondly, even if substantial damages were available, which was not the case in *Beswick* v. *Beswick*,[72] it has been suggested that the common law remedy would still be inadequate as the amount in the case of an annuity would be conjectural.[73]

iii. A contract with a company to take up and pay for debentures.[74]

iv. A contract of indemnity, if, on its true construction, the obligation is to relieve a debtor by preventing him from having to pay his debt. Instead of compelling the party indemnified first to pay the debt and perhaps to ruin himself in doing so, equity will order the indemnifying party to pay the debt. It will be otherwise if the obligation is merely to repay the debtor a sum of money after he has paid it. Damages will then be an adequate remedy.[75]

v. As has been seen, in the case of a contract for the sale of land, the vendor will be granted specific performance of the purchaser's obligation to make a money payment.[76] Although the remedy of damages may be adequate, specific performance is allowed because of the mutuality principle.

vi. A contract to pay a debt out of specific property segregated by the debtor for that purpose is specifically enforceable, and creates an equitable interest in the specific property, unless there is evidence of a contrary intention.[77]

E. Volunteers[78]

Specific performance will not be awarded to a party who has given no consideration. Indeed, unless the contract is under seal, consider-

---

[70] *Beswick* v. *Beswick* [1968] A.C. 58; *post*, p. 689; *Gurtner* v. *Circuit* [1968] 2 Q.B. 587; *Woodar Investment Development Ltd.* v. *Wimpey Construction U.K. Ltd.* [1980] 1 W.L.R. 227. It was held in *Jackson* v. *Horizon Holidays Ltd.* [1975] 1 W.L.R. 1468 that where one party contracts for the benefit of himself and others, he may recover substantial damages for the loss suffered by the others. This must now be read in the light of the reservations expressed by the House of Lords in the *Woodar Investment* case, *supra*, where it was also suggested that the *ius quaesitum tertio* doctrine should be reviewed. See (1980) 43 M.L.R. 696 (A. Nicol and R. Rawlings).

[71] *Beswick* v. *Beswick, supra.*

[72] *Supra*, note 70.

[73] *Adderly* v. *Dixon* (1824) 1 Sim. & St. 607 at p. 611. But see *post*, p. 691.

[74] Companies Act 1985, s.195.

[75] *McIntosh* v. *Dalwood (No. 4)* (1930) 30 S.R.(N.S.W.) 415 at p. 418. See Spry, *Equitable Remedies*, p. 67.

[76] *Ante*, p. 659.

[77] *Swiss Bank Corporation* v. *Lloyds Bank Ltd.* [1982] A.C. 584 at p. 613 (*per* Lord Wilberforce).

[78] *Ante*, p. 110.

ation is necessary for the validity of the contract itself. Parties to a contract under seal may sue at law, even though there is no consideration, but they will not be able to obtain specific performance.[79] Problems commonly arise in this connection in relation to covenants to make family settlements.[80] Inadequacy of consideration is not a bar to specific performance, but may be relevant to the exercise of the court's discretion.[81]

But it is no objection, provided that the party seeking specific performance is not a volunteer, that the decree will have the direct consequence of benefiting a volunteer[82]; nor, in the case of the due exercise of an option to purchase land, that the option was granted for a token payment or for no payment at all.[83]

F. Contracts Requiring Supervision

(i) **The Principle.** It is settled law that a court will not order specific performance where the decree would require constant supervision by the court.[84] The reason for this rule is that supervision would be impracticable. Equity does nothing in vain; and will not issue decrees which it cannot be certain to enforce. Of course, the issue of a decree supported by a threat of imprisonment would be effective in many cases; but imprisonment of the defendant for contempt, if he proves recalcitrant, will not get the duty performed.

Decrees for the specific performance of contracts to create or convey a legal estate in land do not meet with this difficulty. All that the defendant needs to do to perform such a contract is to seal the document; and, as has been seen, if he refuses, he may be threatened with imprisonment for contempt; and if he still refuses, the court may nominate any person to effect the conveyance[85]; it can therefore be certain that the decree will be effective.

Modern decisions indicate a relaxation of the principle.[86] The real

---

[79] See *Cannon* v. *Hartley* [1949] Ch. 213; *cf. Gurtner* v. *Circuit* [1968] 2 Q.B. 587.

[80] *Ante*, p. 120.

[81] Spry, *Equitable Remedies*, p. 57. See *post*, p. 679.

[82] See *Beswick* v. *Beswick* [1968] A.C. 58, *post*, p. 689.

[83] *Mountford* v. *Scott* [1975] Ch. 258, affirming on different grounds the decision of Brightman J., *ibid.*; (1975) 39 Conv.(N.s.) 270 (F. R. Crane); *Midland Bank Trust Co. Ltd.* v. *Green* [1980] Ch. 590 (C.A.); [1979] Conv. 441 (F.R. Crane). As to rights of pre-emption, see *Manchester Ship Canal Co. Ltd.* v. *Manchester Racecourse Ltd.* [1901] 2 Ch. 37; *Murray* v. *Two Strokes Ltd.* [1973] 1 W.L.R. 823; *First National Securities* v. *Chiltern District Council* [1975] 1 W.L.R. 1075; *Pritchard* v. *Briggs* [1980] Ch. 338.

[84] *Ryan* v. *Mutual Tontine Westminster Chambers Association* [1893] 1 Ch. 116; *Heathcote* v. *North Staffordshire Ry.* (1850) 2 Mac. & G. 100; *Blackett* v. *Bates* (1865) L.R. 1 Ch. App. 117 (maintenance of railway); *Phipps* v. *Jackson* (1887) 3 T.L.R. 387; *Barnes* v. *City of London Real Property Co.* [1918] 2 Ch. 18; *Joseph* v. *National Magazine Co.* [1959] Ch. 14 (contract to publish an article not yet in final form).

[85] *Ante*, p. 659.

[86] See Treitel (7th ed.), p. 795. As to injunctions, see *Sanderson Motors (Sales) Pty. Ltd.* v. *Yorkstor Motors Ltd.* [1983] 1 N.S.W.L.R. 513.

question is whether there is a sufficient definition of what has to be done in order to comply with the order of the court.[87]

In *Posner* v. *Scott-Lewis*[88] a lease contained a landlord's covenant to employ a resident porter, whose duties were to clean the common parts, to look after the heating and to carry rubbish to the dustbins. Specific performance of this covenant was granted, to procure the appointment of a porter. The earlier decision in *Ryan* v. *Mutual Tontine Westminster Chambers Association*,[89] where a decree had been refused on the ground of constant superintendence, was difficult to distinguish, but the authority of that case had been weakened by later decisions.[90] The relevant questions were: (a) was there a sufficient definition of what had to be done? (b) would an unacceptable degree of superintendence be involved? (c) what would be the respective hardship to the parties if the order was made or refused? In the present case, the answer to these questions supported a grant of specific performance; the remedy of damages was clearly inadequate.

Thus the court now seems ready to grant the remedy more freely, circumventing the older cases, and accepting the principle that specific performance should be decreed where it is the appropriate remedy.[91] Other modern illustrations include *Beswick* v. *Beswick*[92] where specific performance was ordered of a contract to make a regular payment to the plaintiff for life. In *Sky Petroleum Ltd.* v. *V.I.P. Petroleum Ltd.*[93] an interlocutory injunction, which was regarded as tantamount to specific performance, was granted to enforce the defendant's obligation to supply petrol regularly to the plaintiff. And, in the analogous sphere of mandatory injunctions, the requirement of supervision has not been regarded as an insurmountable obstacle.[94] Specific performance is more likely to be granted, in spite of supervision difficulties, against a defendant who has had some or all of the benefit to which he was entitled under the contract.[95]

(ii) **The Construction Cases.** The court does not, as a rule, order

---

[87] *Tito* v. *Waddell (No. 2)* [1977] Ch. 106 at p. 322, *per* Megarry V-C; (1977) 41 Conv.(N.S.) 432 at p. 436 (F. R. Crane).

[88] [1987] Ch. 25.

[89] [1893] 1 Ch. 116.

[90] *Giles (C.H.) & Co. Ltd.* v. *Morris* [1972] 1 W.L.R. 307 at p. 318; *Shiloh Spinners Ltd.* v. *Harding* [1973] A.C. 691 at p. 724; *Tito* v. *Waddell (No. 2)* [1977] Ch. 106 at p. 321.

[91] (1987) 46 C.L.J. 21 (G. Jones). *Posner* v. *Scott-Lewis* was, however, reluctantly distinguished in *F.W. Woolworth plc* v. *Charlwood Alliance Properties Ltd.* [1987] 1 E.G.L.R. 53, where a covenant in a lease to keep open during trading hours as a retail shop was held not specifically enforceable.

[92] [1968] A.C. 58; *post.*

[93] [1974] 1 W.L.R. 576.

[94] *Morris* v. *Redland Bricks Ltd.* [1970] A.C. 652; *Gravesham Borough Council* v. *British Railways Board* [1978] Ch. 379, *post*, p. 709.

[95] *Tito* v. *Waddell (No. 2)*, *supra* at p. 322.

specific performance of a contract to build or repair[96]; but there are certain exceptional cases. "The first [requirement] is that the building work, of which he seeks to enforce the performance, is defined by the contract; that is to say, that the particulars of the work are so far definitely ascertained that the court can sufficiently see what is the exact nature of the work of which it is asked to order the performance. The second is that the plaintiff has a substantial interest in having the contract performed, which is of such a nature that he cannot adequately be compensated for breach of the contract by damages. The third is that the defendant has by the contract obtained possession of land on which the work is contracted to be done."[97]

In *Wolverhampton Corporation* v. *Emmons*[98] a plot of land had been sold by the plaintiffs, an urban sanitary authority, in pursuance of a scheme of street improvement, to the defendant, who agreed to erect buildings thereon, and went into possession. A later agreement provided for the erection of the buildings in accordance with detailed plans. The Court of Appeal made a decree of specific performance.

This exception is said to be based on a "balance of convenience." Historically it originates in a series of cases relating to the early days of railways.[99] Where a railway was built through a farmer's land and the railway company undertook to provide a bridge or tunnel to connect the separated parts of the farmer's land, it would have been most unjust to leave the farmer to a remedy in damages. These specialised cases have been given more general application, and the formulation in *Wolverhampton Corporation* v. *Emmons*[1] was further extended in *Carpenters Estates* v. *Davies*,[2] where Farwell J. held that it was sufficient that the defendant was in possession of the land, whether he came in by the contract or not. After all, the defendant's possession is the material factor; for the plaintiff cannot then enter to perform the construction or repair work himself.

---

[96] *Wheatley* v. *Westminster Brymbo Coal Co.* (1869) L.R. 9 Eq. 538; *Haywood* v. *Brunswick Building Society* (1881) 8 Q.B.D. 403. But see *Jeune* v. *Queens Cross Properties Ltd.* [1974] Ch. 97; *post*, p. 666.

[97] *Wolverhampton Corporation* v. *Emmons* [1901] 1 K.B. 515 at p. 525, *per* Romer L.J., *Hounslow L.B.C.* v. *Twickenham Developments Ltd.* [1971] Ch. 233; (1970) 34 Conv.(N.S.) 421 (defendant in possession as contractual licensee), *post*, p. 832.

[98] [1901] 1 K.B. 515. See also *Price* v. *Strange* [1978] Ch. 337 at p. 359, *per* Goff L.J.

[99] *Per* Kay L.J. in *Ryan* v. *Mutual Tontine Westminster Chambers Association* [1893] 1 Ch. 116 at p. 128.

[1] [1901] 1 K.B. 515.

[2] [1940] Ch. 160.

(iii) Enforcement of Landlord's Covenants. The "construction contracts" exception was extended to cover a landlord's repairing covenant in *Jeune* v. *Queens Cross Properties Ltd.*,[3] where a balcony which was not part of the demised premises fell into disrepair. The three conditions laid down in *Wolverhampton Corporation* v. *Emmons*[4] were satisfied, as the landlord was in possession of the balcony, and the work involved was specific. There was a clear breach, and no doubt as to what was required to be done to remedy it. A mandatory order was much more convenient than an award of damages, leaving it to the plaintiff to do the work. The decision was extended by statute, now Landlord and Tenant Act 1985, s.17,[5] which provides that the court may order specific performance of a landlord's repairing covenant relating to any part of the premises in which the tenant's dwelling is comprised, notwithstanding any equitable rule restricting this remedy.

It will be seen that neither this section nor the decision in *Jeune* v. *Queens Cross Properties Ltd.*[6] will assist a landlord to get specific performance of a tenant's repairing covenant.[7]

G. Contracts for Personal Services

It is well established that contracts which are personal in nature or which involve the performance of personal services will not be specifically enforced.[8] In this respect, it is necessary to distinguish contracts of employment with other contracts for personal services. The former are governed by a firm prohibition against specific enforcement by Trade Union and Labour Relations Act 1974, s.16, which provides that "no court shall . . . by way of an order for specific performance . . . compel an employee to do any work or to attend at any place for the doing of any work." A contract of employment is defined in section 30 (1).[9] Not every contract for personal services constitutes a contract of employment; for it may be a contract between an employer and an independent contractor; in other words, it may be a "contract for service" and not a "contract of service."[10]

In cases of contracts not covered by the Act, or where enforcement

---

[3] [1974] Ch. 97; *post*, p. 672; *Francis* v. *Cowcliff Ltd.* (1977) 33 P. & C.R. 368. If the matter is urgent, a mandatory interlocutory injunction may be granted; *Parker* v. *Camden London Borough Council* [1986] Ch. 162 (boiler strike threatened tenants' health).

[4] [1901] 1 K.B. 515.

[5] Replacing Housing Act 1974, s.125. See *Gordon* v. *Selico Ltd.* [1985] 2 E.G.L.R. 79.

[6] [1974] Ch. 97.

[7] Although a mandatory injunction was suggested as a possibility in *Sedac Investments Ltd.* v. *Tanner* [1982] 1 W.L.R. 1342.

[8] Fry, *Specific Performance*, pp. 50–51; *Lumley* v. *Wagner* (1852) 1 De G.M. & G. 604, *post*, p. 748; *Thomas Marshall (Exports) Ltd.* v. *Guinle* [1979] Ch. 227. See (1984) 4 Legal Studies 102 at pp. 112–114 (A. S. Burrows).

[9] "Contract of employment" means "a contract of service or of apprenticeship, whether it is express or implied and (if it is express) whether it is oral or in writing."

[10] See *Massey* v. *Crown Life Insurance Co.* [1978] 1 W.L.R. 676.

is sought against an employer,[11] the equitable principle applies. The reasons traditionally given for the rule are first, that such contracts would require constant supervision, and would in practice be impossible to enforce; and secondly, that it is contrary to public policy to compel one person to submit to the orders of another. "The courts," said Fry L.J., "are bound to be jealous, lest they should turn contracts of service into contracts of slavery."[12] Nor, as we will see, can the rule be avoided by seeking an injunction instead of a decree of specific performance, where the injunction would in effect compel performance.[13] Megarry J. (as he then was) has expressed the hope that the court might look again at this "so-called rule." It was not based on these difficulties alone; but was rather a question of human nature. "If a singer contracts to sing, there could no doubt be proceedings for committal if, ordered to sing, the singer remained obstinately dumb. But if instead the singer sang flat, or sharp, or too fast, or too slowly, or too loudly, or too quietly, or resorted to a dozen of the manifestations of temperament traditionally associated with some singers, the threat of committal would reveal itself as a most unsatisfactory weapon, for who could say whether the imperfections of performance were natural or self induced? To make an order with such possibilities of evasion would be vain, and so the order will not be made . . . the matter is one of balance of advantage and disadvantage in relation to the particular obligations in question, and the fact that the balance will usually lie on one side does not turn this probability into a rule."[14]

The rule, however, is not absolute. In *Giles (C.H.) & Co. Ltd.* v. *Morris*,[15] a distinction was drawn between the performance of a contract of service and the execution of such a contract which provided for the plaintiff to be appointed managing director of a company for a period of five years. As we have seen, this approach was also adopted in *Posner* v. *Scott-Lewis*,[16] where specific performance was granted of a covenant in a lease to appoint a resident porter. Nor should it be assumed that as soon as any element of personal service or continuous services can be discerned in a contract, the court will always refuse an

---

[11] If an employee is unfairly dismissed the Employment Protection (Consolidation) Act 1978, s.69, empowers an industrial tribunal to order reinstatement or re-engagement of the employee, if he so wishes. But if the order is not complied with the sanction is an award of compensation; s.71. See also s.78 of that Act.

[12] *De Francesco* v. *Barnum* (1890) 45 Ch.D. 430. See also *Johnson* v. *Shrewsbury and Birmingham Ry.* (1853) 3 De G.M. & G. 914; *Bainbridge* v. *Smith* (1889) 41 Ch.D. 462, and see *post*, p. 747.

[13] *Post*, p. 748.

[14] [1972] 1 W.L.R. 307 at p. 318. This passage was approved by Goff L.J. in *Price* v. *Strange* [1978] Ch. 337 at p. 359; *cf.* Buckley L.J., *ibid.*, at p. 369. But the House of Lords in *Scandinavian Trading Tanker Co. A/B.* v. *Flota Petrolera Ecuatoriana* [1983] 2 A.C. 694, concerning a time charter, took the view that there was no jurisdiction to grant specific performance of a service contract.

[15] [1972] 1 W.L.R. 307.

[16] [1987] Ch. 25; (1987) 46 C.L.J. 21 (G. Jones); *ante*, p. 664.

order. In *Beswick* v. *Beswick*,[17] Lord Upjohn said that a small element of personal services in a contract did not warrant the refusal of specific performance on the ground of want of mutuality. And in *Hill* v. *C.A. Parsons & Co. Ltd.*[18]

The plaintiff was a senior engineer in the employment of the defendant. In May 1970, a trade union successfully introduced a closed shop, under which it became a term of employment that all the defendant's employees were to be members of the union. The plaintiff refused, and received a month's notice of dismissal. He successfully obtained an interlocutory injunction restraining the termination. The circumstances were special, in that the notice was short; a reasonable notice would probably have given him protection under the Industrial Relations Act 1971; and the employee and employer retained their mutual confidence.

Lord Denning M.R. said[19]: "It may be said that, by granting an injunction in such a case, the court is indirectly enforcing specifically a contract for personal services. So be it. Lord St. Leonards L.C. did something like it in *Lumley* v. *Wagner*.[20] And I see no reason why we should not do it here." But Stamp L.J., dissenting, felt that the rule against specific performance of service contracts, while not without exceptions, was deeply embedded in the law. The rule, he said, was a salutary one, which benefited the employer and employee equally.[21]

H. Contracts for the Creation of Transient or Terminable Interests

As equity does not act in vain, specific performance will not be granted of an agreement for a lease which has already expired by the date of the hearing,[22] nor of an agreement for a tenancy at will or a partnership at will.[23]

An agreement for a tenancy from year to year is specifically enforce-

---

[17] [1968] A.C. 58 at p. 97. See also *Regent International Hotels (U.K.) Ltd.* v. *Pageguide Ltd.*, *The Times*, May 13, 1985 (enforcement of long-term hotel management agreement by negative injunction pending arbitration).

[18] [1972] Ch. 305; *cf. Chappell* v. *Times Newspapers Ltd.* [1975] 1 W.L.R. 482, where the employer "had every reason to suspect the plaintiff's loyalty." It seems that injunctions of the kind granted in *Hill* v. *Parsons* are no longer rare; see *Powell* v. *London Borough of Brent* [1987] I.R.L.R. 466, *post*, p. 751.

[19] *Ibid.* at p. 315.

[20] (1852) 1 De G.M. & G. 604; *post*, p. 748.

[21] [1972] Ch. 305 at p. 324.

[22] *Turner* v. *Clowes* (1869) 20 L.T. 214. But the doctrine of *Walsh* v. *Lonsdale* (1882) 21 Ch.D. 9, *ante*, p. 16, will govern the rights and obligations of the parties if specific performance of a contract for a lease would have been available during its currency, even though it has terminated by the date of the hearing: *Industrial Properties (Barton Hill) Ltd.* v. *Associated Electrical Industries Ltd.* [1977] Q.B. 580; *cf.* (1977) 40 M.L.R. 718 at p. 720 (P. Jackson). See also *Tottenham Hotspur Football and Athletic Co.* v. *Princegrove Publishers* [1974] 1 W.L.R. 113; (1974) 90 L.Q.R. 149 (M. J. Albery).

[23] *Hercy* v. *Birch* (1804) 9 Ves. 357. Even if not merely at will, a partnership agreement involves the difficulty of supervision; *ante*, p. 663.

able,[24] but in *Lavery* v. *Pursell*[25] specific performance of an agreement for a lease for one year was refused, one ground being that, although rights should not be prejudiced by delays in litigation, it was normally impossible to get the action heard and the decree made within the year. This meant that the plaintiff had no remedy at all. Common law damages were not available as the contract was supported only by an act of part performance,[26] nor were damages in lieu of specific performance available under Lord Cairns' Act, as there was held to be no jurisdiction to award specific performance.[27]

But the nineteenth century authorities on transient interests must now be treated with caution.

In *Verrall* v. *Great Yarmouth Borough Council*[28] the defendant council had granted a contractual licence to the National Front to occupy its premises for two days (on a date which had not yet occurred) for the purpose of holding an annual conference. Fearing a breach of the peace, the defendant wrongfully repudiated the contract, but sought to avoid specific performance on the ground, *inter alia*, that the licence was a transient interest. This argument was rejected by the Court of Appeal, and the grant of specific performance was affirmed. It was held that there was no reason why the court could not order specific performance of a contractual licence of short duration. Authorities to the contrary were inconsistent with the decision of the House of Lords in *Winter Garden Theatre (London) Ltd.* v. *Millenium Productions Ltd.*,[29] whereby an injunction could be granted to restrain the wrongful revocation of the licence. "In my judgment the old view, such as it was, that courts of equity would not protect a so-called transient interest can no longer be supported, at any rate to its full extent."[30]

Thus while specific performance remains inappropriate in respect of an interest which has already expired or which is revocable at the will of the defendant, the mere fact that the interest is of short duration is no longer a bar to specific performance, which may be granted at the discretion of the court in an appropriate case.

I. Contracts to Leave Property by Will[31]

The remedy for breach of such a contract is normally damages, for any other result would amount to interference with testamentary

---

[24] *Manchester Brewery Co. Ltd.* v. *Coombs* [1901] 2 Ch. 608.
[25] (1888) 39 Ch.D. 508 at p. 519. See also *Gilbey* v. *Cossey* [1911–13] All E.R. 644 at p. 645.
[26] *Ante*, p. 658.
[27] *Post*, p. 684.
[28] [1981] Q.B. 202 *ante*, p. 659.
[29] [1948] A.C. 173.
[30] [1981] Q.B. 202 at p. 220 (*per* Roskill L.J.). See also the comments of Lord Denning M.R. at p. 215.
[31] See (1971) 87 L.Q.R. 358 (W. A. Lee); A.R. Mellows, *The Law of Succession* (4th. ed.); Chap. 3.

freedom.[32] But specific performance might be decreed in certain cases, as was indicated *obiter* by the Court of Appeal in *Synge* v. *Synge*.[33]

In consideration of marriage, the defendant promised to leave by his will certain real property to his wife for life. The property was later conveyed in breach of contract to a third party. The wife sued for damages only, but the Court of Appeal expressed the view that where a written agreement is made to induce a marriage, and the marriage takes place on the faith of it, then the court has power to order a conveyance of a defined piece of real property after the death of the contracting party, against those who have acquired it as volunteers. While the court could not order the defendant to make a will in any particular terms, it could order the executor or devisee to convey to the plaintiff.

In *Schaefer* v. *Schuhmann*,[34] in the Privy Council, Lord Cross of Chelsea treated it as established that where there is a contract to leave specific property by will, the plaintiff "can obtain a declaration of his right to have it left to him by will and an injunction to restrain the testator from disposing of it in breach of contract: *Synge* v. *Synge*.[35] No doubt if the property is land he could also register the contract or a caution against the title."[36] If the testator retains the property until his death, but dies insolvent, the promisee can only rank as a creditor for value in competition with other such creditors.[37]

Finally, it seems that specific performance will not be granted of a contract by the donee of a testamentary power of appointment to exercise the power in favour of the plaintiff.[38]

J. Contracts to Transfer Goodwill

A contract to sell the goodwill of a business alone is not specifically enforceable, because the subject-matter of the contract is too uncertain.[39] But specific performance will be granted of a contract to transfer the goodwill together with the premises or other assets of a business.[40]

---

[32] *Ante*, p. 300.

[33] [1894] 1 Q.B. 466. See also *Goilmere* v. *Battison* (1682) 1 Vern. 48; *Coverdale* v. *Eastwood* (1872) L.R. 15 Eq. 121; *Wakeham* v. *Mackenzie* [1968] 1 W.L.R. 1175.

[34] [1972] A.C. 572: see also Inheritance (Provision for Family and Dependants) Act 1975, s.11; Law Com. No. 61 (1974), paras. 222–242.

[35] [1894] 1 Q.B. 466.

[36] [1972] A.C. 572 at p. 586. If the contract relates to land, there must be a written memorandum or part performance, in order to satisfy s.40 of the Law of Property Act 1925: *Wakeham* v. *Mackenzie* [1968] 1 W.L.R. 1175. See *ante*, p. 658, n. 44.

[37] [1972] A.C. 572. See also *Beyfus* v. *Lawley* [1903] A.C. 411. For the situation where the parties agree to leave property to each other under mutual wills, see *Dufour* v. *Pereira* (1769) 1 Dick. 419, *ante*, p. 300.

[38] *Re Parkin* [1892] 3 Ch. 510. The proper remedy is damages. See also *Robinson* v. *Ommanney* (1883) 23 Ch.D. 285.

[39] *Darbey* v. *Whitaker* (1857) 4 Drew. 134.

[40] *Ibid.* at p. 140. And see *Beswick* v. *Beswick* [1968] A.C. 58; *post*, p. 689.

K. Contracts to Refer to Arbitration

Such a contract is not specifically enforceable.[41] But if the plaintiff sues on a contract which includes an arbitration provision, the defendant may ask for a stay of proceedings under Arbitration Act 1950, s.4(1) so that the plaintiff must proceed with the arbitration or be left with no remedy.[42] The court will, however, enforce the arbitrator's award.[43]

L. No Specific Performance of Part of a Contract[44]

A court will not usually decree specific performance of any part of a contract unless it can decree performance of the whole.

In *Ogden* v. *Fossick*,[45] an agreement between the parties provided that the defendant would grant to the plaintiff a lease of a coal wharf, and that the defendant should be appointed manager of the wharf. In a suit for specific performance of the agreement to grant the lease, specific performance was denied on the ground that the part of the agreement which the court could enforce was inseparably connected with the contract of employment which it would not.

But the rule is not absolute.[46] And it may be possible to construe a contract which contains several parts as being in effect several separate and distinct contracts, so that the enforcement of one part is independent of the others.[47] This question often arises where several lots of land are sold and the question is whether there is one sale of several lots,[48] or several sales of individual lots.[49]

4. MUTUALITY

A. Refusal of Specific Performance for Lack of Mutuality[50]

It has been seen that where equity will decree specific performance in favour of a purchaser or lessee, the remedy will be available also in

---

[41] *Doleman & Sons* v. *Ossett Corporation* [1912] 3 K.B. 257 at p. 268.
[42] See also Arbitration Act 1975, s.1. As to the court's jurisdiction to intervene by way of injunction, see *post*, p. 766.
[43] *Wood* v. *Griffith* (1818) 1 Swans. 43; Halsbury (4th ed.), para. 632. See also *Sudbrook Trading Estate Ltd.* v. *Eggleton* [1983] 1 A.C. 444, as to the possibility of specific performance of a contract to appoint a valuer or arbitrator to fix the price in an option to renew a lease. *cf. Re Smith & Service and Nelson & Sons* (1890) 25 Q.B.D. 545.
[44] Fry, *op. cit.*, Chap. 16. Compare the doctrine of partial performance; *Thames Guaranty Ltd.* v. *Campbell* [1985] Q.B. 210.
[45] (1862) 4 De G.F. & J. 426; *South Wales Ry.* v. *Wythes* (1854) 5 De G.M. & G. 880; *Brett* v. *East India and London Shipping Co. Ltd.* (1864) 2 Hem. & M. 404.
[46] *Beswick* v. *Beswick* [1968] A.C. 58; *C.H. Giles & Co. Ltd.* v. *Morris* [1972] 1 W.L.R. at pp. 317–318; *Astro Exito Navegacion S.A.* v. *Southland Enterprise Co. Ltd. (No. 2)* [1983] 2 A.C. 787.
[47] *Wilkinson* v. *Clements* (1872) L.R. 8 Ch. App. 96, *post*, p. 673.
[48] *Roffey* v. *Shallcross* (1819) 4 Madd. 227.
[49] *Lewin* v. *Guest* (1826) 1 Russ. 325.
[50] See Spry, *Equitable Remedies*, pp. 7–12, 85–97.

favour of the vendor or lessor.[51] Such a person can compel the other party to take the property or to accept a lease even though in many cases an award of damages would be adequate compensation for his loss. He can obtain specific performance under a principle of mutuality.

A similar principle applies to deny specific performance, on grounds of lack of mutuality, where the situation is one in which that remedy could not be available to the other party.[52] "It is not disputed," said Leach M.R., "that it is a general principle of courts of equity to interpose only where the remedy is mutual."[53] Thus one party is not compelled specifically to perform his obligation if he would himself be left with only a remedy in damages. In *Flight* v. *Bolland*,[54] a minor failed to obtain a decree of specific performance because a suit for specific performance could not be maintained against him.[55] Nor can a person whose own obligation is to perform personal services obtain a decree, for no decree could be obtained against him.[56]

Where there is a written memorandum of a contract concerning an interest in land, and it has been signed by the defendant but not by the plaintiff, the plaintiff may enforce it although the defendant could not have enforced it against him. This, at first sight, seems to offend the mutuality principle, but it was explained by Leach M.R. in *Flight* v. *Bolland*[57] that the plaintiff "by the act of filing the bill, has made the remedy mutual."[58] There is, however, a statutory exception to the mutuality principle in the Landlord and Tenant Act 1985, s.17, which allows a court to order specific performance of a landlord's repairing covenant, notwithstanding any equitable rule restricting this remedy, "whether based on mutuality or otherwise."[59] It might be added that the plaintiff may be able to overcome the absence of mutuality by waiving the benefit of a term,[60] or submitting to perform an obligation, which could not be specifically enforced against him.[61]

Finally, the mutuality principle goes only to discretion, not to jurisdiction. Thus the absence of mutuality does not deprive the court of

---

[51] *Ante*, p. 659.

[52] This defence based on lack of mutuality may be waived by the conduct of the defendant: *Price* v. *Strange* [1978] Ch. 337.

[53] (1828) 4 Russ. 298 at p. 301.

[54] (1828) 4 Russ. 298.

[55] *Lumley* v. *Ravenscroft* [1895] 1 Q.B. 683.

[56] *Pickering* v. *Bishop of Ely* (1843) 2 Y. & C. Ch. 249; *Johnson* v. *Shrewsbury and Birmingham Ry.* (1853) 3 De G.M. & G. 914; *Ogden* v. *Fossick* (1862) 4 De G.F. & J. 426; *ante*, p. 666.

[57] (1828) 4 Russ. 298.

[58] *Ibid.* at p. 301; *Spry, op. cit.*, p. 89. The signature of the pleadings by himself or by his agent provides the necessary evidence. See now Law of Property (Miscellaneous Provisions) Bill, *ante*, p. 658.

[59] *Ante*, p. 666. *Jeune* v. *Queens Cross Properties* [1974] Ch. 97.

[60] *Heron Garage Properties Ltd.* v. *Moss* [1974] 1 W.L.R. 148; *Usanga* v. *Bishop* (1974) 232 E.G. 835; *cf. Federated Homes Ltd.* v. *Turner* (1974) 233 E.G. 845; (1975) 39 Conv.(N.S.) 251 (S. Robinson).

[61] *Scott* v. *Bradley* [1971] Ch. 850; (1951) 67 L.Q.R. 300 (R.E.M.)

jurisdiction to award damages in lieu of specific performance under Lord Cairns' Act 1858.[62]

B. The Time at which the Remedy must be Mutual

Must the requirement of mutuality be satisfied at the date of the contract, or will it suffice that the remedy has become mutually available by some later date, such as the date of the hearing? This question has been the source of much academic disagreement. Fry's proposition was that, subject to certain exceptions, the contract must be mutual "that is to say, such that it might, at the time it was entered into, have been enforced by either of the parties against the other of them."[63] Ames, on the other hand, considered that "Equity will not compel specific performance by a defendant if, after performance, the common law remedy of damages would be his sole security for the performance of the plaintiff's side of the contract."[64]

The courts, it must be said, had never applied a principle as rigid as that propounded by Fry.[65] It was laid down in *Hoggart* v. *Scott*[66] that a vendor may obtain specific performance if he can show a good title at the time of the hearing, even though he had none when the contract was made. We have seen that a minor cannot obtain specific performance because he would not himself be liable to a decree; but it had been held in *Clayton* v. *Ashdown*[67] that if he commences his action after attaining his majority he is entitled to succeed, even though he would himself continue to have a defence for a reasonable time after his majority. We saw also that there could be no specific performance of a contract where the obligation of one party was the performance of services. It was held, however, in *Wilkinson* v. *Clements*[68] that if the plaintiff has already performed the services, he may enforce the contract.

The formulation of Ames has now been adopted by the Court of Appeal in preference to Fry's rule.

---

[62] *Price* v. *Strange* [1978] Ch. 337. For the jurisdiction under Lord Cairns' Act, see *post*, p. 684.

[63] Fry, *Specific Performance*, p. 219.

[64] Ames, *Lectures in Legal History*, p. 370. This is the basis of the rule accepted by the Restatement of Contracts. See also Spry, *op. cit.* pp. 85–97; Ashburner, *Principles of Equity* (2nd ed.), p. 404; Anson, *Principles of the Law of Contract* (26th ed.), pp. 518–519; Treitel, *The Law of Contract* (7th ed.), pp. 797–799.

[65] See the example of the memorandum signed only by the defendant, *ante*, p. 672.

[66] (1830) 1 Russ. & M. 293; *Eastern Counties Ry.* v. *Hawkes* (1855) 5 H.L.Cas. 331; *Salisbury* v. *Hatcher* (1842) 2 Y. & C. Ch. 54; *Joseph* v. *National Magazine Co. Ltd.* [1959] Ch. 14 (a case of personal property); *Price* v. *Strange* [1978] Ch. 337 at pp. 355 and 364. See (1977) 41 Conv.(N.S.) 18 (C. T. Emery).

[67] (1714) 2 Eq.Ca.Abr. 516. See also Ames, *op. cit.* p. 374.

[68] (1872) L.R. 8 Ch.App. 96; *Price* v. *Strange* [1978] Ch. 337. In this case the plaintiff had not performed all the obligations, but justice could be done by granting specific performance on terms of a monetary readjustment. See also *Wakeham* v. *Mackenzie* [1968] 1 W.L.R. 1175.

In *Price* v. *Strange*[69] D contracted to grant an underlease of a flat to P, and the agreement contained an undertaking by P to execute certain repairs, some internal and some external. P did the internal repairs, and was ready and willing to complete the external; but D repudiated the contract, and did the external repairs herself. P sued for specific performance of the contract to grant the underlease. D claimed that P was not entitled to specific performance because, relying on Fry's rule, there was no mutuality at the date of the contract: P's repair obligations were not specifically enforceable. It was held that Fry's rule was wrong; the time for considering mutuality was the date of the trial. If by that time those obligations which were not specifically enforceable had been performed, P could obtain specific performance.

After reviewing the authorities and academic criticisms of Fry's rule, Buckley L.J. said "I can discover nothing in principle to recommend the Fry proposition, and authority seems to me to be strongly against it. Accordingly in my judgment it should be regarded as wrong. The time at which the mutual availability of specific performance and its importance must be considered is, in my opinion, the time of judgment, and the principle to be applied can I think be stated simply as follows: the court will not compel a defendant to perform his obligations specifically if it cannot at the same time ensure that any unperformed obligations of the plaintiff will be specifically performed, unless, perhaps, damages would be an adequate remedy to the defendant for any default on the plaintiff's part."[70] Goff L.J. put it thus: "the court will grant specific performance if it can be done without injustice or unfairness to the defendant."[71] Specific performance was, accordingly, granted on terms that P should pay compensation to D for the cost of the repairs done by D.

It is submitted that this formulation of the rule is to be welcomed.

5. DEFENCES TO SPECIFIC PERFORMANCE[72]

The situations discussed below are those in which the discretion of the court is unlikely to be exercised in favour of a decree of specific performance, although the contract is of a type to which the remedy is appropriate. Most of the illustrations relate to land, for, as we have

---

[69] [1978] Ch. 337; (1978) 128 N.L.J. 569 (F. G. Glover). *Price* v. *Strange* was applied in *Sutton* v. *Sutton* [1984] Ch. 184 (wife agreed to consent to divorce and not to seek maintenance in return for a transfer of the home. Husband could not have enforced her promises, but once she had performed an appreciable part by giving formal consent to the petition, he could not rely on absence of mutuality).

[70] [1978] Ch. 337 pp. 367–378.

[71] *Ibid.* at p. 357.

[72] See also *BICC* v. *Burndy Corp.* [1985] Ch. 232; (1985) 101 L.Q.R. 145; (1985) 44 C.L.J. 204 (C. Harpum); All E.R.Rev. 1985, p. 36 (N. E. Palmer); discussing set-off as a defence to specific performance.

seen, few contracts outside this area are specifically enforceable. It will be noted that, in some of the circumstances discussed below, such as hardship or delay, the contract is unaffected, and the defendant remains liable in damages; the plaintiff is merely denied the remedy of specific performance. In others, as in some cases of mistake and misrepresentation, the contract may be rescinded in equity, which is of course a defence to specific performance, and which may or may not affect the parties' rights at law.[73] In cases of substantial misdescription or lack of good title, the vendor may be in breach; not only is the vendor unable in such circumstances to obtain specific performance; he may be liable in damages to the purchaser.

A. Mistake and Misrepresentation

There are situations in which equity, although refusing to rescind a contract or cancel a deed for mistake or misrepresentation, will decline to allow the other party positive equitable help in enforcing it. The plaintiff will be left to his remedy in damages.[74] The court is not bound to decree specific performance in every case in which it will not set aside the contract, nor to set aside every contract that it will not specifically enforce.[75]

A defendant cannot usually resist specific performance by alleging merely his own fault and mistake,[76] nor on the ground that he was mistaken as to the legal effect of the agreement,[77] although "unilateral mistake may, in some circumstances, afford an answer to a claim for specific performance."[78] Generally, equity will hold the defendant to enforcement of his bargain unless it can be shown that this would involve real hardship amounting to injustice.[79]

In *Webster* v. *Cecil*[80] A, by letter, offered to sell some property to

---

[73] *Ante*, p. 32.

[74] See *per* Lord Eldon in *Mortlock* v. *Buller* (1804) 10 Ves.Jr. 292.

[75] *e.g. Wood* v. *Scarth* (1855) 2 K. & J. 33 (in equity); 1 F. & F. 293 (at law).

[76] *Duke of Beaufort* v. *Neeld* (1845) 12 Cl. & F. 248 at p. 286; *Monro* v. *Taylor* (1851) 3 Mac. & G. 713; *Swaisland* v. *Dearsley* (1861) 29 Beav. 430.

[77] *Powell* v. *Smith* (1872) L.R. 14 Eq. 85; *Hart* v. *Hart* (1881) 18 Ch.D. 670.

[78] *Per* Brightman J. in *Mountford* v. *Scott* [1975] Ch. 258 at p. 261; *Malins* v. *Freeman* (1837) 2 Keen 25; *Riverlate Properties Ltd.* v. *Paul* [1975] Ch. 133, *per* Russell L.J. at p. 140; *Watkin* v. *Watson-Smith, The Times*, July 3, 1986.

[79] *Tamplin* v. *James* (1880) 15 Ch.D. 215; *Van Praagh* v. *Everidge* [1902] 2 Ch. 266; reversed on another ground [1903] 1 Ch. 434. The type of mistake that renders a contract liable to be set aside in equity though not at law would also be a defence to specific performance. See *Solle* v. *Butcher* [1950] 1 K.B. 671; *Grist* v. *Bailey* [1967] Ch. 532; *post*, p. 780; *Laurence* v. *Lexcourt Holdings* [1978] 1 W.L.R. 1128; [1978] Conv. 380 (F. R. Crane); *post*, p. 784.

[80] (1861) 30 Beav. 62; *Joynes* v. *Statham* (1746) 3 Atk. 388; *Day* v. *Wells* (1861) 30 Beav. 220; *cf. Hartog* v. *Colin and Shields* [1939] 3 All E.R. 566. See also *Watkin* v. *Watson-Smith, The Times*, July 3, 1986, *post*, p. 000 (no specific performance where elderly vendor offered bungalow for sale at £2,950 by mistake, intending £29,500. There was no contract).

B. He intended to offer it at £2,250 but by mistake wrote £1,250. B agreed to buy at £1,250. A immediately gave notice of the error and was not compelled to carry out the sale.

In *Tamplin* v. *James*[81] an inn was offered for sale, and was correctly described with reference to plans. At the rear of the inn was a piece of land, not belonging to the vendors, and so not included in the sale, which had commonly been occupied with the inn. The defendant knew the premises, but did not consult the plans, and he agreed to purchase in the belief that he was buying both the inn and the land at the rear. Specific performance was ordered against him.

A case that goes further, and perhaps too far, is *Malins* v. *Freeman*,[82] where an estate was purchased at an auction and the defendant bid under a mistake as to the lot put up for sale. Specific performance was refused although the mistake was due entirely to the defendant's fault and not in any way caused by the vendor; and the defendant waited until the auction was over before declaring the mistake.

Where the mistake is in the written record of the contract, the plaintiff may obtain rectification and specific performance in the same action.[83]

B. Conduct of the Plaintiff

A plaintiff must come to equity with clean hands. Before specific performance can be decreed in his favour, he must show that he has performed all his own obligations under the contract,[84] or has tendered performance, or is ready and willing to perform them.[85] Thus a person holding under an agreement for a lease is not entitled to a decree of specific performance of the lease if he is himself in breach of one of its covenants.[86] Nor could a purchaser obtain specific performance if he had taken advantage of the illiteracy of a defendant who was not separately advised.[87] The conduct in question must be connected to the contract of which specific performance is sought.[88]

If both parties have "unclean hands," there is no question of balancing the misconduct of the one against that of the other. The "clean

---

[81] (1880) 15 Ch.D. 215; *cf. Denny* v. *Hancock* (1870) L.R. 6 Ch.App. 1, where specific performance was refused because the mistake was induced unintentionally by the plaintiff.

[82] (1837) 2 Keen 25.

[83] *Craddock Bros.* v. *Hunt* [1923] 2 Ch. 136; *post*, p. 795.

[84] Except the most trivial ones; *Dyster* v. *Randall* [1926] Ch. 932 at pp. 942–943. See also *Cross* v. *Cross* (1982) 12 Fam. Law 182; *Sport International Bussum B.V.* v. *Inter-Footwear Ltd.* [1984] 1 W.L.R. 776.

[85] *Lamare* v. *Dixon* (1873) L.R. 6 H.L. 414; *Australian Hardwoods Pty. Ltd.* v. *Railways Commissioner* [1961] 1 W.L.R. 425; *Cornish* v. *Brook Green Laundry* [1959] 1 Q.B. 391. See also *Ailion* v. *Spiekermann* [1976] Ch. 158.

[86] *Walsh* v. *Lonsdale* (1882) 21 Ch.D. 9; *Coatsworth* v. *Johnson* (1886) 55 L.J.Q.B. 220; *Swain* v. *Ayres* (1888) 21 Q.B.D. 289.

[87] *Mountford* v. *Scott* [1975] Ch. 258.

[88] *van Gestel* v. *Cann, The Times*, August 7, 1987 (no defence where alleged fraudulent expenses claims not connected to contract).

hands" defence is concerned with the conduct of the plaintiff alone, although all the circumstances, including the conduct of the defendant, are relevant to the exercise of the discretion.[89]

C. Laches or Delay

Generally, in equity, time is not held to be of the essence of a contract,[90] thus specific performance may be decreed although the contractual date for performance has passed. Failure to complete on the contractual date may, however, render the delaying party liable to damages for breach of contract. The fact that time is not of the essence in equity does not negative a breach of contract in such a case. It means that the breach does not amount to a repudiation of the contract. Thus the delaying party, although liable to damages, does not lose the right to seek specific performance, nor will he forfeit his deposit, provided he is ready to complete within a reasonable time.[91]

There is no statutory period of limitation barring claims to specific performance or to the refusal of relief on the ground of acquiescence,[92] but a plaintiff who delays unreasonably in bringing an action for specific performance may lose his claim.[93]

There is no rule to lay down what is meant by unreasonable delay. One relevant factor is the subject-matter of the contract. If it has a speculative or fluctuating value, the principle of laches will be especially applicable.[94] Until recently it was thought that the plaintiff must normally seek specific performance well within one year,[95] but it now seems that this approach may be too strict.

In *Lazard Bros. & Co. Ltd.* v. *Fairfield Properties Co. (Mayfair) Ltd.*[96] a contract was entered into on March 12, 1975. The plaintiffs issued a writ for specific performance on May 14, 1977. In ordering specific performance, Megarry V.-C. said that if specific performance was to be regarded as a prize, to be awarded by equity to the

---

[89] *Sang Lee Investment Co. Ltd.* v. *Wing Kwai Investment Co. Ltd., The Times*, April 14, 1983.

[90] This rule now applies also at law; L.P.A. 1925, s.41. (Time may be made of the essence in a contract for the sale of land by the service of a notice to complete.)

[91] *Raineri* v. *Miles* [1981] A.C. 1050 (where £20,000 in legal costs were involved); *Inns* v. *D. Miles Griffiths, Piercy & Co.* (1980) 255 E.G. 623; *Oakacre Ltd.* v. *Claire Cleaners (Holdings) Ltd.* [1982] Ch. 197; *Canning* v. *Temby* (1905) 3 C.L.R. 419; *cf. United Scientific Holdings Ltd.* v. *Burnley Borough Council* [1978] A.C. 904 (as to rent review clauses). See (1980) 96 L.Q.R. 481; (1981) 44 M.L.R. 100 (A. Samuels).

[92] Limitation Act 1980, s.(36)(1), (2).

[93] *Southcomb* v. *Bishop of Exeter* (1847) 6 H. 213; *Eads* v. *Williams* (1854) 4 De G.M. & G. 674; *Lord James Stuart* v. *L.N.W. Ry.* (1853) 1 De G.M. & G. 721; *M.E.P.C. Ltd.* v. *Christian-Edwards* [1981] A.C. 205. Even a delay for which neither party is to blame may be a reason for leaving the purchaser to damages; *Patel* v. *Ali* [1984] Ch. 283, *post*, p. 679.

[94] *Mills* v. *Haywood* (1877) 6 Ch.D. 196; *Glasbrook* v. *Richardson* (1874) 23 W.R. 51.

[95] *Huxham* v. *Llewellyn* (1873) 21 W.R. 570 (delay of five months in the case of commercial premises prevented specific performance); *cf. Wroth* v. *Tyler* [1974] Ch. 30, Farrand, *Contract and Conveyance* (4th ed.), p. 216.

[96] (1977) 121 S.J. 793; [1978] Conv. 184.

zealous and denied to the indolent, then the plaintiffs should fail. But whatever might have been the position over a century ago that was the wrong approach today. If between the plaintiff and defendant it was just that the plaintiff should obtain the remedy, the court ought not to withhold it merely because the plaintiff had been guilty of delay. There was no ground here on which delay could properly be said to be a bar to a decree of specific performance.

An exceptional case where delay will not be a bar is where the plaintiff has taken possession under the contract,[97] so that the purpose of specific performance is merely to vest the legal estate in him. In *Williams* v. *Greatrex*[98] a delay of 10 years in such circumstances did not bar specific performance. But a significant factor there was that the transaction creating the proprietary interest was not in issue. It is otherwise where the contract itself is disputed. In such a case the doctrine of laches does apply.[99]

Where the plaintiff has delayed, but specific performance is refused for another reason, the effect of his delay may be that the date for assessing damages in lieu of specific performance under Lord Cairns' Act is moved back from the date of judgment to the date upon which the matter might have been disposed of.[1]

The situation discussed above is where the delay has occurred before the plaintiff has sought specific performance. It may, however, occur at some later stage. Where the plaintiff issues the writ for specific performance promptly but then delays in bringing the matter to trial, he may, in a clear case, be disentitled to the remedy.[2] Where the plaintiff obtains a decree for specific performance but then delays in enforcing it for a long period, leave to enforce it[3] will be refused only if there is an insufficient explanation and detriment to the defendant. Thus, in *Easton* v. *Brown*,[4] a delay of eight years in seeking to enforce the decree was no bar where the defendant's former wife and children had remained in occupation and the plaintiff had been legally advised that it would be difficult to remove them. The plaintiff had an explanation for the delay and had acted reasonably; detriment to the defen-

---

[97] It is otherwise if possession has been taken other than pursuant to the contract: *Mills* v. *Haywood, supra.*

[98] [1957] 1 W.L.R. 31. The position is the same where a tenant has taken possession under a contract for a lease: *Sharp* v. *Milligan* (1856) 22 Beav. 606; *Shepheard* v. *Walker* (1875) L.R. 20 Eq. 659.

[99] *Joyce* v. *Joyce* [1979] 1 W.L.R. 1170.

[1] *Malhotra* v. *Choudhury* [1980] Ch. 52.

[2] *Du Sautoy* v. *Symes* [1967] Ch. 1146 at p. 1168. *Towli* v. *Fourth River Property Co. Ltd., The Times,* November 24, 1976 (delay of nine years between writ and hearing) was such a clear case. See also *Lamshed* v. *Lamshed* (1963) 109 C.L.R. 440 (specific performance refused where delay of over five years between commencement of action and setting down for trial).

[3] See R.S.C. Ord. 44 r. 2(1).

[4] [1981] 3 All E.R. 278. The plaintiff also obtained an order for inquiry as to damages arising from the defendant's failure to complete.

dant was not on its own a ground for refusing leave to enforce the order.

Finally, in cases where time is of the essence, specific performance is not normally available after the stipulated date. The court may, however, in the exercise of its equitable jurisdiction to relieve against forfeiture, grant specific performance to prevent the "forfeiture" of the purchaser's equitable interest under the contract.[5]

D. Hardship

In general, specific performance may be refused in the discretion of the court where a decree would cause unnecessary hardship to either of the parties,[6] or to a third party.[7] Inadequacy of price is not, standing by itself, a ground for refusing specific performance; but it may be evidence of other factors, such as fraud[8] or undue influence,[9] which would render enforcement inequitable.

These matters recently arose in *Patel* v. *Ali*,[10] where the vendor and her husband were co-owners of a house which they contracted to sell in 1979. The husband's bankruptcy caused a long delay in completion, for which neither the vendor nor the purchaser was to blame. After the contract the vendor got bone cancer and had a leg amputated. She later gave birth to her second and third children. The purchaser obtained an order for specific performance, against which the vendor appealed on the ground of hardship. She spoke little English, and relied on help from nearby friends and relatives, hence it would be a hardship to leave the house and move away.

Goulding J. held that although a person of full capacity took the risk of hardship, the court in a proper case could refuse specific performance on the ground of hardship subsequent to the contract, even if not

---

[5] See the Australian decision, *Legione* v. *Hateley* (1983) 57 A.J.L.R. 292, noted (1983) 99 L.Q.R. 490.

[6] *Denne* v. *Light* (1857) 8 De G.M. & G. 774; *Pegler* v. *White* (1864) 33 Beav. 403; *Tamplin* v. *James* (1880) 15 Ch.D. 215; *Warmington* v. *Miller* [1973] Q.B. 877 (no specific performance of contract to sublet if result would be to expose tenant to liability for breach of covenant against subletting); *Mountford* v. *Scott* [1975] Ch. 258; *Francis* v. *Cowcliff* (1977) 33 P. & C.R. 368; *Shell U.K. Ltd.* v. *Lostock Garage Ltd.* [1976] 1 W.L.R. 1187 at p. 1202; *Cross* v. *Cross* (1982) 12 Fam. Law 182. For further details, see Fry, *Specific Performance*, Chap. 16; Spry, *Equitable Remedies*, pp. 191–198.

[7] *Earl of Sefton* v. *Tophams Ltd.* [1966] Ch. 1140; *Sullivan* v. *Henderson* [1973] 1 W.L.R. 333, *Watts* v. *Spence* [1976] Ch. 165; *Cedar Holdings Ltd.* v. *Green* [1981] Ch. 129 at p. 147 (*per* Goff L.J.); [1979] Conv. 372 (F.R. Crane); (1979) 38 C.L.J. 215 (M. J. Prichard). This case was disapproved, although not on this point, by Lord Wilberforce in *Williams and Glyn's Bank Ltd.* v. *Boland* [1981] A.C. 487 at p. 507. See also *Thames Guaranty Ltd.* v. *Campbell* [1985] Q.B. 210; *cf. Patel* v. *Ali* [1984] Ch. 283, *infra*, (interests of vendor's children in their own right not material, but relevant to hardship of vendor).

[8] *Coles* v. *Trecothick* (1804) 9 Ves.Jr. 234 at p. 246; *Callaghan* v. *Callaghan* (1841) 8 Cl. & F. 374.

[9] *Fry* v. *Lane* (1888) 40 Ch.D. 312 (sale set aside).

[10] [1984] Ch. 283; (1984) 100 L.Q.R. 337. There was evidence that the Muslim community would pay the damages.

caused by the plaintiff and not related to the subject-matter. On the facts, there would be hardship amounting to injustice, therefore the appropriate remedy was damages.

E. Misdescription of Subject-Matter

(i) **Specific Performance Subject to Compensation.**[11] If the property agreed to be sold is incorrectly described in the contract, the vendor cannot fulfil his promise to transfer property which corresponds exactly with that which he contracted to convey. A frequent instance is an inaccurate measurement in the plan.[12] A misdescription is a term of the contract; the vendor is therefore in breach. It might be thought that there is no problem; surely the purchaser, being the party not in default, cannot be subjected to a decree of specific performance? But that theory would introduce a rigid rule capable of producing injustice. Is the purchaser, who for some reason does not wish to complete, to be allowed to repudiate on account of some trivial mistake in acreage, which in no way affects the value or utility of the property?

Equity adopts a more flexible approach; the circumstances may be such that justice will be done by compelling completion, notwithstanding the error, compensating the purchaser by allowing him a reduction in the price he had agreed to pay ("abatement").[13] This course will not be followed if it would prejudice the rights of a third party interested in the estate.[14] On the other hand the misdescription may be so serious that to decree specific performance would be in effect to force the purchaser to take something wholly different from what he intended.[15] If so, the only way of achieving justice may be to permit the purchaser to rescind; or to refuse to grant specific performance to the vendor.[16]

---

[11] See (1981) 40 C.L.J. 47 (C. Harpum), taking the view that this should not be distinguished from specific performance with damages under Lord Cairns' Act, *post*, p. 684.

[12] See, *e.g. Watson* v. *Burton* [1957] 1 W.L.R. 19; *Topfell Ltd.* v. *Galley Properties Ltd.* [1979] 1 W.L.R. 446 (inability to give vacant possession); [1979] Conv. 375 (F. R. Crane).

[13] If the misdescription goes against the vendor, he cannot increase the price: *Re Lindsay and Forder's Contract* (1895) 72 L.T. 832. (But specific performance might be refused on the ground of hardship, *ante*, p. 679.) See also *Seven Seas Properties Ltd.* v. *Al-Essa* [1988] 1 W.L.R. 1272.

[14] *Cedar Holdings Ltd.* v. *Green* [1981] Ch. 129.

[15] See *Cedar Holdings Ltd.* v. *Green, supra*. (Specific performance with abatement not appropriate where vendor's interest merely a share under a trust for sale.)

[16] Misdescription must be distinguished from non-disclosure. A vendor is under a duty to disclose latent defects in title; but not physical defects, where the doctrine of *caveat emptor* applies (subject to possible negligence liability where the vendor has created the physical defect). Thus, in the case of latent physical defects, the purchaser can only resist specific performance if there has been a misdescription or misrepresentation; see *Re Puckett and Smith's Contract* [1902] 2 Ch. 258; Farrand, *Contract and Conveyance* (4th ed.), p. 67. The defence of hardship might perhaps apply. The *caveat emptor* doctrine is presently under review; *Caveat Emptor in Sales of Land*, Conveyancing Standing Committee of the Law Commission (1988).

(ii) Refusal of Specific Performance. The rule which has been developed is thus that a purchaser will not be forced to take something which is *different in substance* from that which he agreed to buy.[17] Differences of quality or quantity will not *by themselves* suffice as a defence to an action for specific performance (although of course they will give rise to a claim for compensation) unless they can fairly be said to make the property, as it in fact is, different in substance from that contracted to be sold.[18] A misdescription is substantial for this purpose if it so far affects "the subject-matter of the contract that it may be reasonably supposed, that, but for such misdescription, the purchaser might never have entered into the contract at all."[19] This will always be a question of fact in each case: obviously A, who has contracted to sell Blackacre to B, cannot force him to take Whiteacre, even if Whiteacre is larger, more valuable, and better suited to B's purposes. It is often difficult to say whether a misdescription of the area of land agreed to be sold involves a difference of substance or of quantity; the rule is "easy to be understood, though often difficult of application."[20]

(iii) The Purchaser's Choice. So much is true where a vendor seeks to compel a purchaser to take something different from that contracted to be sold. It is only just to give the purchaser the option of insisting on completion, and being paid compensation[21] for what he has lost. If it were not so, a person in default could in effect take advantage of his own wrong. "For the purpose of this jurisdiction, the person contracting under those circumstances, is bound by the assertion in his contract; and if the vendee chooses to take as much as he can have, he has a right to that, and to an abatement and the Court will not hear the objection by the vendor, that the purchaser cannot have the whole."[22] In short, the purchaser has a choice: he may elect to take the property,[23] notwithstanding that it may be substantially different from the contract description.

---

[17] *Flight* v. *Booth* (1834) 1 Bing.N.C. 370; *Re Puckett and Smith's Contract* [1902] 2 Ch. 258; *Watson* v. *Burton* [1957] 1 W.L.R. 19.

[18] If a vendor contracts to sell a lease of Blackacre, a purchaser cannot be compelled to take an underlease; *Madeley* v. *Booth* (1845) 2 De G & Sm. 718; nor if he contracts to sell a "registered freehold property," can he compel the purchaser to take a possessory (as distinct from *absolute*) freehold title; *Re Brine and Davies' Contract* [1935] Ch. 388.

[19] *Per* Tindal C.J. in *Flight* v. *Booth* (1834) 1 Bing.N.C. 370 at p. 377.

[20] *Per* Lord Esher M.R. in *Re Fawcett and Holmes' Contract* (1889) 42 Ch.D. 150 at p. 156; *cf. Watson* v. *Burton* [1957] 1 W.L.R. 19; *Dyer* v. *Hargrave* (1805) 10 Ves.Jr. 505.

[21] Which, however, he must generally claim before completion. Otherwise, unless he could not have discovered the defect, he will be deemed to have waived his claim to compensation; *Joliffe* v. *Baker* (1883) 11 Q.B.D. 255.

[22] *Per* Lord Eldon L.C. in *Mortlock* v. *Buller* (1804) 10 Ves.Jr. 292 at p. 316.

[23] In the absence of special circumstances, *e.g.* if he was himself aware of the misdescription at the date of the contract; *Castle* v. *Wilkinson* (1870) L.R. 5. Ch. 534. See [1978] Conv. 338 at p. 340 (C. T. Emery).

(iv) Conditions of Sale. The above is true of "open" contracts, but the parties are perfectly free to make their own conditions to regulate what is to happen if there is a misdescription. In the case of contracts for the sale of land, virtually all contracts prepared by a solicitor will be made subject to the conditions contained in either the Law Society's General Conditions of Sale, or the National Conditions of Sale. In every case, therefore, the first question must be: what does the contract provide? But even then caution is necessary, since the courts have been reluctant to permit either party to contract out of the rights conferred on him by equity.[24] Reference should be made to the standard textbooks on conveyancing for details of these conditions, and the interpretation which has been placed upon them by the courts.[25]

(v) Want of Good Title. The court will not force a doubtful title on a purchaser. The phrase "defect in title" is loosely used in some of the cases to indicate that the vendor, through some material error in description, fails in effect to convey to the purchaser the property he intended to buy. In other cases the expression may be used in a more literal sense; where, for example, the vendor's land is burdened with restrictive covenants.[26] Yet there are other cases where there is not merely a defect in the vendor's title, but no title at all. Clearly the purchaser cannot be compelled to take a bad title, nor be allowed to refuse a good one. Between the good and the bad is an infinite variety of doubtful titles, and the question inevitably arises of drawing a line between those titles which a purchaser will, and those which he will not, be compelled to accept. The test is whether there is likely to be litigation.[27] If the doubt is one of law, the court will normally resolve it.[28] If the doubt is one of fact, it is the court's duty, unless there are exceptional circumstances, to decide the question of title as between the vendor and purchaser. If the facts and circumstances are so compelling that the court concludes beyond reasonable doubt that the purchaser will not be at risk of a successful assertion against him of an incumbrance, then the court should declare in favour of a good title, and should not be deterred by the mere possibility of future litigation by a claimant to an incumbrance who is not bound by the declaration.[29]

---

[24] See *Topfell Ltd.* v. *Galley Properties Ltd.* [1979] 1 W.L.R. 446; [1979] Conv. 375 (F. R. Crane); *Rignall Developments Ltd.* v. *Halil* [1988] Ch. 190. Conditions of sale are subject to the Unfair Contract Terms Act 1977; *Walker* v. *Boyle* [1982] 1 W.L.R. 495; *Southwestern General Property Co. Ltd.* v. *Marton, The Times*, May 11, 1982.

[25] *e.g.* Farrand, *Contract and Conveyance* (4th ed.), pp. 54 *et seq.*

[26] *Re Nisbet and Potts' Contract* [1906] 1 Ch. 386; *Faruqui* v. *English Real Estates Ltd.* [1979] 1 W.L.R. 963; [1979] Conv. 444 (F. R. Crane). See generally [1978] Conv. 338 (C. T. Emery).

[27] A vendor and purchaser summons to establish whether the title is good is not litigation for this purpose: *M.E.P.C. Ltd.* v. *Christian-Edwards* [1978] Ch. 281 (C.A.).

[28] *Wilson* v. *Thomas* [1958] 1 W.L.R. 422.

[29] *M.E.P.C. Ltd.* v. *Christian-Edwards* [1981] A.C. 205 (doubt as to abandonment of 1912 contract: good title established). See also *Re Handman and Wilcox's Contract* [1902] 1 Ch. 599; *Selkirk* v. *Romar Investments Ltd.* [1963] 1 W.L.R. 1415.

But if good title is not shown, the purchaser will be entitled to rescind, unless the vendor removes the doubt. The court will not compel a party to purchase a law suit.[30]

(vi) Amount of Damages. For breach by either party, the normal rule is that the plaintiff can recover his loss as damages. Where, however, a sale of land goes off because the vendor cannot produce a good title, the anomalous rule laid down in *Flureau* v. *Thornhill*,[31] and adopted by the House of Lords in *Bain* v. *Fothergill*,[32] lays down that the purchaser is limited to the recovery of his deposit and interest thereon, together with expenses to which he has been put in relation to the transaction. The reason for the rule is said to be the great difficulty in English law of proving a title to land.[33] However, now that registration of title is the general rule, this rationale is no longer valid, if it ever was.[34] The modern tendency of the courts has been to restrict the operation of the rule. So, for example, it has been held applicable only if the vendor has established that he has taken all reasonable steps to remove the defect in title.[35] The rule in *Bain* v. *Fothergill*[36] will be abolished when the Law of Property (Miscellaneous Provisions) Bill[37] is enacted, following the recommendations of the Law Commission.[38]

F. Public Policy

The court will not decree specific performance of a contract where the result would be contrary to public policy.

In *Wroth* v. *Tyler*,[39] a husband, the owner of the matrimonial home, entered into a contract to sell with vacant possession. Before completion, his wife registered a charge under the Matrimonial Homes Act 1967.[40] The purchaser sued for specific performance, and failed on two grounds:

[30] *Re Nichols and Von Joel's Contract* [1910] 1 Ch. 43 at p. 46. See also *Pips (Leisure Productions) Ltd.* v. *Walton* (1981) 260 E.G. 601 (purchaser entitled to rescind contract for sale of lease which was already forfeited).

[31] (1776) 2 W.Bl. 1078.

[32] L.R. 7 H.L. 158. See also *Wroth* v. *Tyler* [1974] Ch. 30; *post*, p. 686.

[33] *Bain* v. *Fothergill*, *supra*, at p. 210, *per* Lord Hatherley; *J. W. Cafés* v. *Brownlow Trust* [1950] 1 All E.R. 894 at p. 896, *per* Lord Goddard C.J; *Ray* v. *Druce* [1985] Ch. 437.

[34] See *Sharneyford Supplies Ltd.* v. *Edge* [1987] Ch. 305. (An appeal to the House of Lords was settled).

[35] *Malhotra* v. *Choudhury* [1980] Ch. 52; (1979) 38 C.L.J. 35 (D. J. Hayton); *Sharneyford Supplies Ltd.* v. *Edge*, *supra*; [1987] Conv. 60 (M. P. Thompson); (1987) 46 C.L.J. 212 (C. Harpum).

[36] *Supra.*

[37] 1988.

[38] Law Com. No. 166 (1987), *Transfer of Land, The Rule in Bain v. Fothergill.*

[39] [1974] Ch. 30. See also *Malhotra* v. *Choudhury* [1980] Ch. 52 at p. 71; *Verrall* v. *Great Yarmouth Borough Council* [1981] Q.B. 202, *ante*, p. 659 (specific performance of contract to hire conference hall to National Front), where this defence failed: the risk of public disorder was outweighed by the freedom of speech and assembly and the sanctity of contract.

[40] Now the Act of 1983.

    i. The husband could only carry out his obligation by applying successfully to the court for an order terminating the wife's right of occupation, and this was a matter to be determined in the discretion of the court. To grant a decree would compel the husband to embark on difficult and uncertain litigation. He had attempted to obtain the wife's consent by all reasonable means short of litigation, and it would be most undesirable to require a husband to take proceedings against his wife, especially where they were still living together.

    ii. Nor could the purchasers get specific performance subject to the wife's right of occupation. The husband and daughter would remain liable to eviction by the purchasers, and the family would be split up. The court would be slow to decree specific performance in such circumstances.

6. DAMAGES IN SUBSTITUTION FOR, OR IN ADDITION TO, SPECIFIC PERFORMANCE

A. Chancery Amendment Act 1858. Lord Cairns' Act[41]

    Section 2 of Lord Cairns' Act gave to the Court of Chancery discretionary power to award damages either in addition to or in substitution for specific performance, the damages to be assessed in such manner as the court shall direct.

    Before this Act, it was only in the common law courts that damages could be awarded.[42] The Act gave power to award damages where none would be available at law, for example where a contract was supported only by an act of part performance.[43] But it did not give the Court of Chancery power to award common law damages.[44] It applied only to cases where the court had jurisdiction to award specific performance. Thus Lord Cairns' Act does not apply where the contract is of a type which is not specifically enforceable[45]; but it does apply where the contract is of a type which is, even though specific performance is

---

[41] See generally (1975) 34 C.L.J. 224 (J. A. Jolowicz); [1981] Conv. 286 (T. Ingman and J. Wakefield).

[42] *Cf.* Spry, *Equitable Remedies*, p. 542, suggesting that the Court of Chancery had inherent power to award damages in equity. See also the statute of 1393 (17 Ric. 2, c.6), whereby the Chancellor had power to award damages for what is now malicious prosecution.

[43] See *Johnson* v. *Agnew* [1980] A.C. 367 (Lord Wilberforce); *Price* v. *Strange* [1978] Ch. 337; *Crabb* v. *Arun District Council (No. 2)* (1977) 121 S.J. 86; *Oakacre Ltd.* v. *Claire Cleaners (Holdings) Ltd.* [1982] Ch. 197 (action for damages at law not accrued at date of writ).

[44] But see *Price* v. *Strange* [1978] Ch. 337 at p. 358, where Goff L.J. said "One purpose and a very important purpose of that Act was, of course, to avoid circuity of action by enabling the old Court of Chancery to award damages at law. ... "

[45] *Lavery* v. *Pursell* (1888) 39 Ch.D. 508 (tenancy for one year); *ante* p. 669. As to whether contracts for personal services come into this category, see the different views expressed in *Price* v. *Strange* [1978] Ch. 337 at p. 359 (Goff L.J.) and at p. 369 (Buckley L.J.). The House of Lords in *Scandinavian Trading Tanker Co. A.B.* v. *Flota Petrolera Ecuatoriana* [1983] 2 A.C. 694 took the view that there was no jurisdiction to grant specific performance of a contract for services.

refused on some discretionary ground, such as the absence of mutuality.[46] The jurisdiction under Lord Cairns' Act exists if, when the proceedings were begun, the court had jurisdiction to grant specific performance, notwithstanding that thereafter, but before judgment, specific performance has become impossible.[47] Similarly, the jurisdiction to award damages in lieu of specific performance exists where a decree of specific performance has been obtained but has proved useless.[48] But it has been held that the court has no jurisdiction to award damages in lieu of specific performance under Lord Cairns' Act where specific performance is not claimed by the plaintiff.[49]

It was not until the Judicature Act 1873 that the common law remedy of damages was available in the Chancery Division. Today it is only necessary to rely on Lord Cairns' Act if no damages would be available at law.[50] It was at one time thought that it could be advantageous to the plaintiff to rely on Lord Cairns' Act even where common law damages were available, as the measure of damages might be different.[51] This is now discredited.[52]

Lord Cairns' Act was repealed in 1883 by the Statute Law Revision Act, but section 5 of that Act preserved its general effect,[53] and its provisions are now found in section 50 of the Supreme Court Act 1981.

B. Measure of Damages under Lord Cairns' Act

Where a purchaser claims damages for breach of a contract for the purchase of land, he is normally entitled to full damages for loss of his bargain. But if the breach is caused by a defect in title which the vendor cannot remove, then, under the rule in *Bain* v. *Fothergill*,[54] he may only claim his expenses.

In *Wroth* v. *Tyler*[55] the plaintiffs contracted to buy a bungalow for

---

[46] *Price* v. *Strange* [1978] Ch. 337. Even where the contract concerns building or repair works, the court has jurisdiction under the 1858 Act: *ibid.* at p. 359. See also *Wroth* v. *Tyler* [1974] Ch. 30; *Malhotra* v. *Choudhury* [1980] Ch. 52, (1979) 38 C.L.J. 35 (D. J. Hayton); and the cases on injunctions, *post*, pp. 738, *et seq.*

[47] *Johnson* v. *Agnew* [1978] Ch. 176 (C.A.).

[48] *Biggin* v. *Minton* [1977] 1 W.L.R. 701; *cf.* (1978) 37 C.L.J. 41 (A. J. Oakley). This is less important since the decision of the House of Lords in *Johnson* v. *Agnew* [1980] A.C. 367 that common law damages are available in such a case, *ante*, p. 655.

[49] *Horsler* v. *Zorro* [1975] Ch. 302. (The plaintiff withdrew his claim to specific performance and sought damages.) But see (1975) 91 L.Q.R. 337 (M. J. Albery) at pp. 352–353, and the injunction case there cited: *Dixson* v. *Tangle* (1891) 12 L.R.N.S.W. Eq. 204. See also *Malhotra* v. *Choudhury* [1980] Ch. 52. *Horsler* v. *Zorro* was overruled in part on a different point in *Johnson* v. *Agnew* [1980] A.C. 367. It seems that damages may be awarded under Lord Cairns' Act, although not expressly claimed; (1985) 34 I.C.L.Q. 317 (A. Burgess).

[50] See *Oakacre Ltd.* v. *Claire Cleaners (Holdings) Ltd.* [1982] Ch. 197 (writ for damages in addition to specific performance not invalid although premature at law because issued before breach).

[51] *Wroth* v. *Tyler* [1974] Ch. 30, *infra*.

[52] *Johnson* v. *Agnew, infra*.

[53] See *Leeds Industrial Co-operative Society Ltd.* v. *Slack* [1924] A.C. 851.

[54] (1873) L.R. 7 H.L. 158. But see p. 683, *ante*.

[55] [1974] Ch. 30.

£6,000. Contracts were exchanged on May 27, 1971, but on May 28 the vendor's wife registered a charge under the Matrimonial Homes Act 1967,[56] and refused to remove it. The vendor was thus unable to pass a clear title. At the date at which completion was due, the property was worth £7,500, but at the date of the judgment in January 1973, its value had risen to £11,500.

Megarry J. refused specific performance for reasons mentioned above.[57] The rule in *Bain* v. *Fothergill*[58] did not apply because the charge, unregistered at the date of the contract, was not a defect in title. Therefore the main issue was the measure of damages. It was "common ground" that the normal rule is that damages for breach of a contract for the sale of land are measured by the difference between the contract price and the market price at the date of the breach, which is normally the completion date (with interest from that date until judgment). Applying that rule, damages would be £1,500.

Although Fry had said that "the measure would be the same under Lord Cairns' Act"[59] Megarry J. held that damages under the Act may be assessed on a basis which is not identical with that of the common law[60]: they should be a true substitute for specific performance, and must put the plaintiffs in as good a position as if the contract had been performed. Damages could be measured as at the date of judgment, and the plaintiffs were awarded £5,500.

The principle formulated in *Wroth* v. *Tyler*[61] was subsequently applied by Goff J. in *Grant* v. *Dawkins*,[62] where damages were being sought, in addition to specific performance, against a defendant in breach of a contract to sell a house free from incumbrances. For the purpose of assessing the damages, the property was valued not at the date of the breach, but at the date of the grant of specific performance. The *Wroth* v. *Tyler*[63] principle applied whether the damages were awarded in lieu of, or in addition to, specific performance.

It has since been doubted by the House of Lords[64] whether Lord Cairns' Act permits a departure from the common law rule on the quantum of damages, and, indeed, whether the damages awarded in *Wroth* v. *Tyler*[65] could not have been equally available at common law. There is no inflexible rule at common law that damages must be

---

[56] Now the Act of 1983.

[57] *Ante*, p. 683.

[58] (1873) L.R. 7 H.L. 158; [1983] Conv. 435 (C. Harpum).

[59] *Op. cit.* p. 602.

[60] [1974] Ch. 30 at pp. 58–60.

[61] [1974] Ch. 30. See also *Tito* v. *Waddell (No. 2)* [1977] Ch. 106 at p. 335.

[62] [1974] Ch. 30; (1974) 90 L.Q.R. 297 (P. H. Pettit); (1981) 40 C.L.J. 47 (C. Harpum). See also *Oakacre Ltd.* v. *Claire Cleaners (Holdings) Ltd.* [1982] Ch. 197 (damages awarded in addition to specific performance not limited to those accrued at writ).

[63] [1974] Ch. 30.

[64] In *Johnson* v. *Agnew, infra.*

[65] *Supra.*

assessed as at the date of the breach of contract.[66] The principle is that the plaintiff should be put in the same position as if the contract had been duly performed. The rule that damages are to be assessed as at the date of the breach evolved in times of financial stability when the subject-matter was unlikely to have increased in value between the breach and the judgment. The position at common law will be more readily appreciated by considering the doctrine of mitigation of damages. The principle that the plaintiff is to be put in the same position as if the contract had been performed is subject to the principle of mitigation of damages.[67] Thus in the case of chattels, damages will usually be assessed at the breach, because at that date the plaintiff could have acquired an equivalent property elsewhere. But in the case of a specifically enforceable contract, such as a contract to buy land, the purchaser cannot reasonably be expected to mitigate the damages by seeking an equivalent property elsewhere as soon as the breach occurs, because he will normally wish to wait and see if specific performance is obtainable. In such a case, the common law principle of putting the plaintiff in the same position as if the contract had been performed is only adhered to in times of inflation by assessing the damages at a date subsequent to the breach.[68]

In *Johnson* v. *Agnew*[69] Lord Wilberforce rejected the view that damages under Lord Cairns' Act could be assessed on a different basis from that of the common law. Subject to the point that in some cases damages would be available under the Act where none at all would be available at common law, the quantum is the same.[70] The words in section 2 that damages "may be assessed in such manner as the court shall direct" relate only to procedure.[71] *Wroth* v. *Tyler*[72] could not be supported in so far as it suggested that damages under the Act may be assessed on a different basis than at common law. Where, after the breach, the innocent party has reasonably continued to try for completion, the damages, however awarded, should be assessed as at the date

---

[66] *Wroth* v. *Tyler* [1974] Ch. 30 at p. 57; *Horsler* v. *Zorro* [1975] Ch. 302; *Radford* v. *De Froberville* [1977] 1 W.L.R. 1262, (1978) 94 L.Q.R. 327 (A. A. S. Zuckerman), [1978] Conv. 163 (F. R. Crane); *Malhotra* v. *Choudhury* [1980] Ch. 52, (1979) 38 C.L.J. 35 (D.J. Hayton); *Johnson* v. *Agnew* [1980] A.C. 367; *Techno Land Improvements Ltd.* v. *British Leyland (U.K.) Ltd.* (1979) 252 E.G. 805; *Forster* v. *Silvermere Golf & Equestrian Centre Ltd.* (1981) 42 P. & C.R. 255; *Suleman* v. *Shahsavari* [1988] 1 W.L.R. 1181.

[67] *Wroth* v. *Tyler* [1974] Ch. 30 at p. 57; *Radford* v. *De Froberville* [1977] 1 W.L.R. 1262; *Malhotra* v. *Choudhury, supra; cf. Kaunas* v. *Smyth* (1977) 75 D.L.R. 368.

[68] See generally (1979) 95 L.Q.R. 270 (D. Feldman and D. F. Libling); (1981) 97 L.Q.R. 445 (S. M. Waddams); (1982) 98 L.Q.R. 406 (I. N. Duncan Wallace); (1985)'34 I.C.L.Q. 317 (A. Burgess).

[69] [1980] A.C. 367. The facts have been given, *ante*, p. 655.

[70] This precludes any argument that the rule in *Bain* v. *Fothergill, ante*, p. 683, may be avoided by seeking damages under Lord Cairns' Act: see (1977) 41 Conv.(N.S.) 341 (A. Sydenham); [1978] Conv. 338 at p. 340 (C. T. Emery).

[71] This phrase does not appear in Supreme Court Act 1981, s.50.

[72] [1974] Ch. 30.

the contract was lost.[73] This will normally be the date of the hearing, provided the proceedings have been conducted with due expedition: an earlier date will be substituted if the plaintiff has delayed.[74]

7. SPECIFIC PERFORMANCE AND THIRD PARTIES

Claims for specific performance are usually made between the parties to the contract.[75] In such a case, all the parties to the contract must be parties to the suit.[76] Other difficulties arise where the issue is between assignees, or where the person to be benefited was not a party to the contract.

A. Specific Performance between Assignees[77]

It must always be shown that the contract in question is binding on the defendant.[78] Cases on agreements for leases suggest that the right to specific performance of an agreement will pass with the assignment of the interest of the lessor or of the intended lessee,[79] "It is well settled that the assign of one of the parties to a contract can obtain specific performance of that contract against the other contracting party."[80] And, since it has been held that Law of Property Act 1925, ss.141 and 142 apply although the lease is not under seal,[81] it follows that the burden of the lessor's covenants in an agreement for a lease will also run on the assignment of the freehold.

It has been held however that where a person holding under an agreement for a lease assigns his interest, the assignee is not liable on the covenants.[82] For the lessor is not entitled to specific performance against the assignee. " . . . suppose, in the case of an agreement for a lease, the intended lessee has assigned the benefit of the contract, can this Court, at the instance of the intended lessor, enforce the payment of the rent or the performance of the covenants by the assignee of the

---

[73] This was the date on which the vendor's mortgagees contracted to sell the property; *ante*, p. 655. See also *Domb* v. *Isoz*. [1980] Ch. 548; *Suleman* v. *Shahsavari* [1988] 1 W.L.R. 1181 (£29,500 awarded where property worth £76,000 at hearing but contract price £46,500).

[74] *Radford* v. *De Froberville* [1977] 1 W.L.R. 1262; *Malhotra* v. *Choudhury* [1980] Ch. 52.

[75] See generally Snell, pp. 573–574. For the rights of a sub-purchaser to obtain specific performance of the head contract, see *Berkley* v. *Poulett* (1976) 120 S.J. 836, *ante* p. 306.

[76] See *Tito* v. *Waddell (No. 2)* [1977] Ch. 106 at p. 324 (Megarry V.-C.).

[77] See Spry, *Equitable Remedies*, p. 81, on the question how far defences to specific performance which could be raised against the assignor can be raised against the assignee.

[78] *Tito* v. *Waddell (No. 2)*, *supra*, at pp. 285 *et seq.*

[79] *Manchester Brewery Co.* v. *Coombs* [1901] 2 Ch. 608; *Rickett* v. *Green* [1910] 1 K.B. 253. This is subject to the requirements of registration, as discussed below.

[80] *Per* Farwell J. in *Manchester Brewery Co.* v. *Coombs, supra*, at p. 616.

[81] *Rickett* v. *Green, supra*; *Rye* v. *Purcell* [1926] 1 K.B. 446; *Breams Property Investment Co.* v. *Stroulger* [1948] 2 K.B. 1; *Boyer* v. *Warbey* [1953] 1 Q.B. 234.

[82] *Cox* v. *Bishop* (1857) 8 De G.M. & G. 815; *Purchase* v. *Lichfield Brewery* [1915] 1 K.B. 184.

contract. I take it most clearly not; for there is no privity of contract between the lessor and the assignee."[83] "It is impossible that specific performance of a contract can be decreed against a person with whom there is neither privity of contract nor privity of estate."[84]

Although consistent with principles of contract, this rule has not escaped criticism[85]: the lessor ought to be able to enforce covenants against an assignee to whom the intended lessee has assigned his rights. And if there is any meaning in the principle of mutuality, it is strange that the assignee can have specific performance against the lessor, but not the lessor against the assignee. It is perhaps relevant that the only case in which the issue appears to have arisen since 1873 is *Purchase* v. *Lichfield Brewery*,[86] where the defendant was a mortgagee by assignment who did not enter into possession; it would be harsh to compel him to pay the rent.[87]

As far as estate contracts generally are concerned, it will be appreciated that, provided the agreement is specifically enforceable as between the original parties, an equitable interest is created in the intended purchaser or lessee, which is enforceable against an assignee, to whom the liability to specific performance passes unless he can show that he is bona fide purchaser for value without notice.[88] Since 1925 this means that his liability depends upon registration.[89] Thus a contract for a lease may be enforceable against the lessor's assignee, but there is nothing in these provisions which assists in the problem discussed above, as to whether the lessor can seek specific performance of the contract against the tenant's assignee.

B. Specific Performance for the Benefit of Third Parties

A number of problems will arise if A has contracted with B to confer a benefit on C. Sometimes,[90] C can enforce the contract in his own right, and obtain either an award of damages or specific performance according to the usual principles. If, however, because of the usual "privity" rule,[91] C cannot enforce the contract himself, the question is whether B may obtain specific performance, compelling A to confer the benefit on C.

In *Beswick* v. *Beswick*,[92] one Peter Beswick, a coal merchant who

---

[83] Turner L.J. in *Cox* v. *Bishop, supra,* at p. 824.
[84] *Per* Lush J. in *Purchase* v. *Lichfield Brewery* [1915] 1 K.B. 184 at p. 189. See generally (1978) 37 C.L.J. 98 (R. J. Smith).
[85] See *Boyer* v. *Warbey* [1953] 1 Q.B. 234 at p. 246 (*per* Denning L.J.).
[86] [1915] 1 K.B. 184.
[87] *Williams* v. *Bosanquet* (1819) 1 Brod. & B. 238. Save in the case of mortgages of equitable interests, which are not in point here, the situation is one which cannot arise after 1925; L.P.A. 1925, s.86.
[88] *Ante,* p. 33.
[89] L.C.A. 1972, s.2(4); *ante,* p. 37.
[90] For instance, where there is a trust of a chose in action, *ante,* p. 122.
[91] *Scruttons Ltd.* v. *Midland Silicones Ltd.* [1962] A.C. 466.
[92] [1968] A.C. 58; see also *Chitty on Contracts* (25th ed.), paras. 1793 *et seq.*; Treitel, *The Law of Contract* (7th ed.), pp. 799–800; (1988) 8 L.S. 14 (N. H. Andrews).

wished to retire, made an arrangement with his nephew under which
the business was transferred to the nephew, and the nephew promised to employ Peter as consultant for a weekly wage, and after his
death to pay to Peter's widow £5 per week for her life. Payments
were made to Peter during his lifetime, but soon after his death
ceased to be paid to his widow. The widow took out letters of
administration of Peter's estate and sued both as administratrix and
in her own right under the contract.

The House of Lords held that she was entitled as administratrix to
specific performance of the promise to make the weekly payments to
her as Peter's widow. She was unable to sue in her own right because
of the rule of privity, which was not affected in this respect by Law of
Property Act 1925, s.56.[93]

In view of the principles previously discussed relating to specific
performance, the difficulties which faced the widow in her action as
administratrix were essentially threefold: (a) Peter's estate, which she
represented, had lost nothing by the breach; (b) the widow, in her own
capacity, had suffered the loss but had no right of action; (c) the
agreement was for the payment of money and was not the type of
agreement where breach is usually remedied by a decree of specific
performance.[94]

The widow, as administratrix, overcame them all. Lord Upjohn
thought that (a) was an argument in favour of specific performance;
" . . . the court ought to grant a specific performance order all the more
because damages *are* nominal."[95] She had no other effective remedy;
"justice demands that [the promisor] pay the price and this can only be
done in the circumstances by equitable relief."[96] This, however, is to
disregard the principle. The principle is that equitable remedies are
available where the legal remedy is inadequate to compensate for the
loss. It is not that equitable remedies are available where the plaintiff
has suffered no loss,[97] nor where an independent person has suffered a
loss for which there is no cause of action.

Their Lordships found no difficulty in treating the case as a suitable
one for specific performance. "Had [the promisor] repudiated the
contract in the lifetime of [the promisee] the latter would have had a

---

[93] Reversing the majority of the Court of Appeal on this point: [1966] Ch. 538.
[94] *Ante*, p. 661.
[95] *Beswick* v. *Beswick* [1968] A.C. 58 at p. 102; *cf. Re Cook's S.T.*[1965] Ch. 902; *ante*,
    p. 129. On damages for loss suffered by third parties, see also *Jackson* v. *Horizon
    Holidays Ltd.* [1975] 1 W.L.R. 1468; *ante*, p. 124, *Woodar Investment Development
    Ltd.* v. *Wimpey Construction U.K. Ltd.* [1980] 1 W.L.R. 277; (1980) 96 L.Q.R. 321.
[96] *Ibid.*
[97] *cf. Marco Productions Ltd.* v. *Pagola* [1945] 1 K.B. 111; injunction available to
    restrain breach of negative covenant even though the breach causes no loss to
    plaintiff; or if only nominal damages would be available at law; *Rochdale Canal Co.* v.
    King (1851) 2 Sim.(n.s.) 78; *Wrotham Park Estate* v. *Parkside Homes Ltd.* [1974] 1
    W.L.R. 798; *cf. Stoke-on-Trent City Council* v. *W. & J. Wass Ltd.* [1988] 1 W.L.R.
    1406.

cast-iron case for specific performance."[98] The orthodox view has been that specific performance will not be ordered in cases where the promise is to pay money—unless[99] the plaintiff is a vendor or lessor against whom the purchaser or lessee could have demanded specific performance. *Beswick* v. *Beswick*[1] may have been regarded as such a case, for the nephew "could on his part clearly have obtained specific performance of it if Beswick senior or his administratrix had defaulted."[2] That, it is submitted, is questionable; for the contract was essentially for the sale of the goodwill of the business; such a contract is not normally specifically enforceable, in contrast to a contract to sell premises along with the goodwill.[3]

It is said also that a contract to pay an annuity is specifically enforceable. In *Adderly* v. *Dixon*,[4] Leach M.R. said of annuities[5]: "Damages might be no complete remedy, being to be calculated merely by conjecture; and to compel the Plaintiff in such a case to take Damages would be to compel him to sell the annual Provision during his life for which he had contracted, at a conjectural price."

While such a proposition may have been sound in 1824, it is questionable whether it is sound today. The development of the law and practice of life assurance and of the actuarial technique of calculation of values of life interests has made an annuity and a capital sum in effect interchangeable. Annuities are freely purchased from insurance companies in exchange for capital payments—the transaction having in many cases substantial fiscal advantages for the purchaser. And an annuity can similarly be freely sold for a capital sum. Thus the conjectural element is less marked than it was over a century ago. The value of an annuity need not be regarded as depending on the life of the annuitant; but upon the capital sum for which it could be sold in his particular case. If it is so regarded it becomes more difficult to maintain that the award of a capital sum in damages would be an inadequate remedy. If the plaintiff was awarded damages, and desired the annuity, all he has to do is to buy one.

The cases on which their Lordships relied[6] to support the view that the contract to pay was specifically enforceable, at the instance of a personal representative, were all cases either of a contract to transfer land or contracts to pay an annuity. It is possible to treat *Beswick* v.

---

[98] [1968] A.C. 58 at p. 98; see also, as quoted at pp. 90 and 99, *Drimmie* v. *Davies* [1899] 1 Ir.R. 176 at p. 190, *per* Holmes J.

[99] *Ante,* p. 662.

[1] [1968] A.C. 58.

[2] *Ibid.* at p. 89, *per* Lord Pearce.

[3] *Baxter* v. *Connolly* (1820) 1 J. & W. 576; *Darbey* v. *Whitaker* (1857) 4 Drew. 134 at pp. 139, 140; *ante,* p. 670.

[4] (1824) 1 Sim. & St. 607; (1966) 29 M.L.R. 657 at p. 663 (G. H. Treitel).

[5] *Ibid.* at p. 611.

[6] *Keenan* v. *Handley* (1864) 2 De G.J. & A. 283; *Hohler* v. *Aston* [1920] 2 Ch. 420; *Drimmie* v. *Davies* [1899] 1 Ir.R. 176; *Coulls* v. *Bagot's Executor and Trustee Co.* (1967) 40 A.L.J.R. 471; *ante,* p. 129.

Beswick[7] as consistent with authority by saying that there was mutuality, that the contract (being to pay an annuity) was capable of specific performance, and that the common law remedy of damages (assuming them to be nominal) was inadequate. The plaintiff barely succeeds on the first two; and only on the third by relying on cases which uphold it without explaining the logical dilemma of holding an award of nominal damages inadequate where no loss was suffered by the party able to sue.

In spite of the opportunities which exist for criticism in relation to orthodox doctrine, the House of Lords should rather be applauded for taking a broad equitable view of the situation. There was "an unconscionable breach of faith [and] the equitable remedy sought is apt."[8] Lord Pearce and Lord Upjohn both approved the dictum of Windeyer J. in *Coulls* v. *Bagot's Executor and Trustee Co. Ltd.* in which he said[9]: "It seems to me that contracts to pay money or transfer property to a third person are always, or at all events very often, contracts for breach of which damages would be an inadequate remedy—all the more so if it be right (I do not think it is) that damages recoverable by the promisee are only nominal. . . . I see no reason why specific performance should not be had in such cases . . . but of course not where the promise was to render some personal services. There is no reason today for limiting by particular categories, rather than by general principle, the cases in which orders for specific performance will be made." There were no technical or practical difficulties preventing an award of specific performance and "justice demands that [the promisor] pay the price and this can only be done in the circumstances by equitable relief."[10] Perhaps the correct explanation is that damages must be considered from the point of view of both plaintiff and defendant. Thus the remedy of damages is inadequate if it would lead to the unjust enrichment of the wrongdoer. Substantial damages have been awarded under Lord Cairns' Act, for this reason, where no loss was suffered.[11]

The decision in *Beswick* v. *Beswick*[12] has since been applied by the Court of Appeal in *Gurtner* v. *Circuit,*[13] concerning the Motor Insurers' Bureau's contract with the Minister of Transport. Under this contract, if an injured person's judgment against a motorist is not satisfied within seven days, the Bureau will pay the injured person.[14] While the injured person cannot sue, the Minister can get specific performance in his favour.

---

[7] [1968] A.C. 58.
[8] *Ibid., per* Lord Hodson at p. 83.
[9] (1967) 40 A.L.J.R. at p. 487; (1978) 37 C.L.J. 301 (B. Coote).
[10] *Ibid.* at p. 102, *per* Lord Upjohn.
[11] *Wrotham Park Estate Co.* v. *Parkside Homes Ltd.* [1974] 1 W.L.R. 798; *cf. Stoke-on-Trent City Council* v. *W. & J. Wass Ltd.* [1988] 1 W.L.R. 1406.
[12] [1968] A.C. 58.
[13] [1968] 2 Q.B. 587.
[14] It is the policy of the M.I.B. not to rely on absence of privity: see *Persson* v. *London Country Buses* [1974] 1 W.L.R. 569.

This chapter began by indicating how narrow was the scope of the remedy of specific performance in practice. Other systems of law tend to be much more free in their use of this type of remedy. *Beswick* v. *Beswick*[15] indicates a willingness in the House of Lords to make freer use of the remedy in the interests of justice. The case is however concerned with its own particular problem of the covenant to pay to a third party.[16] Time alone will tell whether this more liberal approach will be applied to other, and more usual, aspects of the law of specific performance.

8. Jurisdiction

Both the High Court[17] and the county court have jurisdiction to grant specific performance, but the jurisdiction of the county court, in cases of specific performance of contracts to sell or to let land, is limited to cases where the purchase money, or the value of the property in the case of a lease, does not exceed the county court limit.[18]

The county court must give effect to every defence or counterclaim to which effect would be given in the High Court.[19] Thus, in *Kingswood Estate Co. Ltd.* v. *Anderson*,[20] where the landlord brought an action for possession based on the termination of a common law periodic tenancy, the county court gave effect to the tenant's defence that she held the property under a specifically enforceable agreement for a lease for life, even though it had no jurisdiction to grant specific performance of that agreement. Similarly, in *Rushton* v. *Smith*,[21] the county court had no jurisdiction to grant specific performance of an agreement for a business tenancy where the value of the property exceeded the county court limit, but it nevertheless had jurisdiction to decide whether or not the tenant would be entitled to such a decree.

---

[15] [1968] A.C. 58.
[16] *Ante*, pp. 128 *et seq*.
[17] Where an expeditious procedure is available under R.S.C., Ord. 86, where the facts are not in dispute.
[18] County Courts Act 1984, s.23. The current limit is £30,000.
[19] County Courts Act 1984, s.38.
[20] [1963] 2 Q.B. 169. See also *Cornish* v. *Brook Green Laundry Ltd.* [1959] 1 Q.B. 394.
[21] [1976] Q.B. 480.

INJUNCTIONS

1. JURISDICTION

AN injunction is an order by the court to a party to the effect that he shall do or refrain from doing a particular act. Originally the Court of

Chancery alone[1] had jurisdiction to grant an injunction. This inevitably led to much duplication of proceedings; as where the plaintiff required an injunction as a remedy for a legal right. The Common Law Procedure Act 1854 gave to common law courts a power to grant injunctions in certain cases. The present jurisdiction is governed by the Supreme Court Act 1981, replacing the Judicature Acts, which vested the jurisdiction of the Court of Chancery and of the common law courts in the High Court.

A. The High Court

Section 37(1) of the Supreme Court Act 1981 provides that "The High Court may by order (whether interlocutory or final) grant an injunction . . . in all cases in which it appears to the court to be just and convenient to do so."[2] The jurisdiction is however not so wide as would appear from a first reading of the section. It is exercised, not on the individual preference of the judge, but "according to sufficient legal reasons or on settled legal principles."[3] There have been differences of opinion as to whether section 25(8) of the Judicature Act 1873, which introduced the provision similar to that now contained in the Act of 1981, gave the court power to grant injunctions in cases where they had not previously been granted.[4] It has been said that the Act of 1873 "has not revolutionised" but "has to some extent enlarged" the jurisdiction.[5] The restrictive approach, namely that the court's jurisdiction has not been extended, was affirmed by the House of Lords in *Gouriet* v. *Union of Post Office Workers*.[6] Lord Edmund-Davies said that section 25(8) of the Act of 1873 "dealt only with procedure and had nothing to do with jurisdiction."[7] But former rules of practice no longer hamper the exercise of discretion; thus enabling the merits of new situations to be dealt with as they arise.[8] A similar question is whether the Act of

---

[1] Or the Court of Exchequer in its equity jurisdiction, *ante*, p. 4. See generally Sharpe, *Injunctions and Specific Performance*.

[2] This consolidates the previous legislation. Compare the wording of s.25(8) of the Supreme Court of Judicature Act 1873 and s.45 of the Act of 1925: "just *or* convenient"; *Day* v. *Brownrigg* (1878) 10 Ch.D.294; *L.* v. *L.* [1969] P. 25.

[3] *Per* Jessel M.R. in *Beddow* v. *Beddow* (1878) 9 Ch.D. 89 at p. 93. Thus a plaintiff with no "rights" cannot obtain an injunction, however "just and convenient" it may be: *Gouriet* v. *Union of Post Office Workers* [1978] A.C.435; *Paton* v. *Trustees of British Pregnancy Advisory Service* [1979] Q.B.76, *post*, p. 705.

[4] See the different views expressed by Lord Esher M.R. and Cotton L.J. in *North London Ry.* v. *Great Northern Ry.* (1883) 11 Q.B.D. 30. See also *The Siskina* [1979] A.C. 210; *Maclaine Watson & Co. Ltd.* v. *International Tin Council (No. 2)* [1988] 3 W.L.R. 1191.

[5] *Cummins* v. *Perkins* [1899] 1 Ch.16 at p. 20.

[6] [1978] A.C. 435. See also *Bremer Vulkan Schiffbau und Maschinenfabrik* v. *South India Shipping Corp.* [1981] A.C. 909.

[7] *Ibid.* at p. 516. *cf.* the wider views of Lord Denning M.R. in *Rasu Maritima S.A.* v. *Perusahaan* [1978] Q.B. 644 at pp. 659–660.

[8] *Argyll* v. *Argyll* [1967] Ch. 302 at p. 345; *Rasu Maritima S.A.* v. *Perusahaan, supra*. See generally the *Mareva* and *Anton Piller* injunctions, *post*, pp. 766, 770.

1981 enlarged the previous jurisdiction, but the better view is that it did not.[9] A plaintiff with no cause of action cannot invoke section 37(1).[10]

Jurisdiction where a foreign element is involved is dealt with below.[11]

B. The County Court

The general rule is that the county court has jurisdiction to grant an injunction only if it is ancillary to a claim for some other specific relief, such as damages, within the ordinary jurisdiction of the county court.[12] Provided the claim to other relief is genuine, it is no objection that, in the case of damages, the sum claimed is small, or even nominal. The court is not obliged to weigh or balance the importance of the claim to an injunction against the other claim in order to decide which is ancillary to the other.[13] This rule is subject to certain statutory exceptions enabling the county court to grant an injunction where no other relief is claimed.[14] More particularly, the rule does not apply to injunctions relating to land.[15]

2. Types of Injunctions

A. Prohibitory and Mandatory Injunctions

The most common and natural form of an injunction, as the name implies, is one which is prohibitory or restrictive. However, if the unlawful act has been committed and an order restraining its commission is therefore meaningless, justice can sometimes be done by issuing a mandatory injunction ordering the act to be undone. Thus if, while A has been absent, B has built a wall which obstructs his ancient lights, the order which A requires is one requiring B to pull down the wall.[16] At one time the negative character of an injunction used to be insisted upon; if the court intended to order a party to pull down a wall, the order would be that he should refrain from permitting the wall to remain on his land. And such an injunction may have a positive effect,

---

[9] Contrast the views of Lord Denning M.R. with those of Donaldson and Slade L.J.J. in *Chief Constable of Kent* v. *V.* [1983] Q.B. 34; (1983) 99 L.Q.R. 1; (1983) 42 C.L.J. 51 (A. Tettenborn); All E.R. Rev. 1982, p. 205 (G. Zellick); *Richards* v. *Richards* [1984] A.C. 174. The wording of the 1981 Act and its predecessors is not identical.

[10] *Ainsbury* v. *Millington* [1986] 1 All E.R. 73; *Wilde* v. *Wilde* [1988] 2 F.L.R. 83; *Associated Newspapers Group plc* v. *Insert Media Ltd.* [1988] 1 W.L.R. 509.

[11] *Post*, pp. 698, 772–775.

[12] County Courts Act 1984, s.38(1). As to interlocutory injunctions, see s.39.

[13] *Hatt & Co. (Bath) Ltd.* v. *Pearce* [1978] 1 W.L.R. 885 (jurisdiction to grant injunction where damages of £1 claimed for breach of contract).

[14] For example, the Domestic Violence and Matrimonial Proceedings Act 1976, s.1 (1); *Spindlow* v. *Spindlow* [1979] Fam. 52, *post*, p. 762.

[15] County Courts Act 1984, s.22. The value of the land must be within the county court limits (currently £30,000). See generally (1977) 36 C.L.J. 369 and (1978) 37 C.L.J. 51 (P. H. Pettit).

[16] For recent examples, see *Allen* v. *Greenwood* [1980] Ch. 119; *Pugh* v. *Howells* (1984) 48 P. & C.R. 298.

as in *Sky Petroleum Ltd.*v. *V.I.P. Petroleum Ltd.*,[17] where an injunction restraining the defendant from withholding supplies of petrol was equivalent to specific performance of the contract. But a mandatory injunction is now couched in positive form,[18] but just for this reason it may be harder to obtain. For example, it has been held that it ought not to issue to compel a ferry owner to run a ferry, when it could only be run at a loss.[19] But the fact that a local authority may have to borrow money, or get a building licence to comply with a mandatory injunction is a ground, not for refusing the remedy, but for granting it subject to a suspension.[20]

B. Perpetual and Interlocutory Injunctions

Prohibitory or mandatory injunctions may be perpetual or interlocutory. "Perpetual" does not mean necessarily that the effect of the order must endure for ever; it means that the order will finally settle the present dispute between the parties, being made as the result of an ordinary action, the court having heard in the ordinary way the arguments on both sides. But a plaintiff may not always be able to wait for the action to come on in the normal course; it may be that irreparable damage will be done to him if the defendant is not immediately restrained. If such is the case, the plaintiff will serve on him a notice that on the next motion day[21] his counsel will apply to the court for an injunction. The service of this notice will enable the defendant's counsel also to be heard, if he wishes, but the hearing will not be a final decision on the merits of the case. If the plaintiff's affidavit has made out a sufficient case, the judge will grant an interlocutory injunction, which is effective only until the trial of the action.[22]

C. Ex Parte Injunctions

But if the urgency of the case is such that the plaintiff cannot even wait until the next motion day,[23] he is still not without a remedy, for he can apply for an *ex parte* injunction, which will hold good until the next motion day, by which time notice can have been served on the defendant, who will then have a chance of opposing the plaintiff's application for an interlocutory injunction. The phrase "*ex parte*" signifies that the court has not had an opportunity of hearing the other side.

---

[17] [1974] 1 W.L.R. 576; *ante,* p. 661. See also *Sanderson Motors (Sales) Pty. Ltd.* v. *Yorkstor Motors Ltd.* [1983] 1 N.S.W.L.R. 513.

[18] *Jackson* v. *Normanby Brick Co.* [1899] 1 Ch. 438.

[19] *Att.-Gen.* v. *Colchester Corporation* [1955] 2 Q.B. 207; *Gravesham Borough Council* v. *British Railways Board* [1978] Ch. 379, *post,* p. 709; *Morris* v. *Redland Bricks Ltd.* [1970] A.C. 652.

[20] *Pride of Derby Angling Association* v. *British Celanese Co.* [1953] Ch. 149.

[21] Every weekday in term is a motion day in the Chancery Division: *Practice Direction* [1980] 1 W.L.R. 751.

[22] *Jones* v. *Pacaya Rubber and Produce Co.* [1911] 1 K.B. 455 at p. 457, *per* Buckley J.

[23] But see note 21, *supra.* For procedure, see *Practice Direction* [1983] 1 W.L.R. 433.

D. Interim Injunctions

An interim injunction restrains the defendant, not until trial, but until some specified date, if for some special reason it would be unjust to protect the plaintiff beyond that date. An interim injunction is usually, but not always, *ex parte*. For example, if notice has been served on the defendant, but he is not given sufficient time to prepare his case, then an interim injunction until the next motion day is more likely to be granted than a full interlocutory injunction until trial.[24]

E. Quia Timet Injunctions

A *quia timet* injunction is one which issues to prevent an infringement of the plaintiff's rights where the infringement is threatened, but has not yet occurred. The jurisdiction is one of long standing, and exists in relation to both perpetual and interlocutory injunctions, and to both prohibitory and mandatory injunctions. The plaintiff must show a very strong probability of a future infringement, and that the ensuing damage will be of a most serious nature.[25] A defendant is not to lose his rights on anything short of the virtual certainty of unjustifiable injury to the plaintiff.

3. PRINCIPLES APPLICABLE TO THE ISSUE OF INJUNCTIONS

A. General

(i) **Discretionary Remedy.** While the injunction is a much wider remedy than specific performance, the characteristics of the two remedies are similar. Thus, the injunction is a discretionary remedy, based on the inadequacy of common law remedies. As will be seen, similar principles apply to the exercise of the discretion of the court. As in the case of specific performance, the court may award damages under Lord Cairns' Act, either in lieu of, or in addition to, an injunction.[26]

(ii) **Remedy in personam.**[27] Like specific performance, the injunction is a remedy *in personam*. It is possible to enjoin a defendant who is not personally within the jurisdiction, provided service out of the jurisdiction can properly be done under rules of court.[28] But, as a general rule, no injunction will be granted in connection with the title to land outside the jurisdiction, even if the defendant is within the jurisdiction.[29] It is otherwise in the case of actions relating to chattels, and,

---

[24] *Fenwick* v. *East London Ry.* (1875) L.R. 20 Eq. 544. For appeals procedure, see *Hunter and Partners* v. *Welling and Partners, The Times,* October 16, 1986.

[25] *Fletcher* v. *Bealey* (1885) 28 Ch.D. 688; *Att.-Gen.* v. *Nottingham Corporation* [1904] 1 Ch. 673; *Morris* v. *Redland Bricks Ltd.* [1970] A.C. 652; *post,* p. 733.

[26] *Post,* p. 738; *ante,* p. 684; Spry, pp. 589 *et seq.*.

[27] *Ante,* p. 652. See the *"Mareva"* cases; *post,* pp. 770 *et seq.*

[28] R.S.C., Ord. 11. See *Re Liddell's S.T.* [1936] Ch. 365.

[29] *Deschamps* v. *Miller* [1908] 1 Ch. 856; *Re Hawthorne* (1883) 23 Ch.D. 743. See Dicey and Morris, *The Conflict of Laws* (11th ed.), pp. 923 *et seq.,* discussing also the effect of Civil Jurisdiction and Judgments Act 1982, s.30.

even in the case of land, the rule is subject to exceptions.[30] Finally, an injunction may be granted against all the members of a class or organisation to restrain the unlawful acts of unidentified members.[31]

(iii) The Public Interest. Divergent views have been expressed in the Court of Appeal on the question whether the court, in considering an application for an injunction to protect a private right, has a duty to take into account the interests of the general public. In *Miller* v. *Jackson*[32] a cricket club committed the torts of nuisance and negligence in allowing cricket balls to land on the plaintiffs' property. But an injunction was refused by the Court of Appeal. The public interest in enabling the inhabitants to enjoy the benefits of outdoor recreation prevailed over the plaintiffs' private right to quiet enjoyment of their house and garden. But in *Kennaway* v. *Thompson*,[33] where the plaintiff sought an injunction to restrain a motor boat racing club from committing nuisance by excessive noise, the Court of Appeal granted the injunction, holding that the rights of the plaintiff should not be overridden by the interests of the club or of the general public. In considering whether to grant an injunction or damages in lieu under Lord Cairns' Act,[34] the public interest does not prevail over private rights. The views expressed in *Miller* v. *Jackson* ran counter to the well-established principles laid down in *Shelfer* v. *City of London Electric Lighting Co..*,[35] which was binding on the Court of Appeal.

(iv) Contempt. Non-compliance with an injunction (or an undertaking given in lieu[36]) is a contempt of court,[37] punishable by imprisonment, sequestration of property (in the case of a corporation) or a fine.[38] Acts done in breach of an injunction are void for illegality.[39] As

---

[30] One such exception is where there is "an equity between the parties": *Cook Industries Inc.* v. *Galliher* [1979] Ch. 439, *post*, p. 769. See also *Penn* v. *Lord Baltimore* (1750) 1 Ves.Sen. 444, *ante*, p. 652; *Hamlin* v. *Hamlin* [1986] Fam. 11.

[31] *M. Michaels (Furriers) Ltd.* v. *Askew, The Times*, June 25, 1983 (nuisance by members of "Animal Aid"); *E.M.I. Records Ltd.* v. *Kudhail, The Times*, June 28, 1983; *cf. United Kingdom Nirex Ltd.* v. *Barton, The Times*, October 14, 1986.

[32] [1977] Q.B. 966. In *Express Newspapers Ltd.* v. *Keys* [1980] I.R.L.R. 247, *post*, p. 707, the public interest was a relevant consideration in the grant of the injunction. See also the cases on libel and breach of confidence, *post*, pp. 753, 754.

[33] [1981] Q.B. 88; (1981) 97 L.Q.R. 3; (1981) 44 M.L.R. 212 (R. A. Buckley). The Scottish Court has rejected *Miller* v. *Jackson*; see *Webster* v. *Lord Advocate* (1984) S.L.T. 13. See also *Sevenoaks District Council* v. *Pattullo & Vinson Ltd.* [1984] Ch. 211.

[34] *Ante*, p. 684.

[35] [1895] 1 Ch. 287, *post*, p. 739. See (1982) 41 C.L.J. 87 (S. Tromans).

[36] *Hussain* v. *Hussain* [1986] Fam. 134.

[37] Contempt of Court Act 1981; Pettit, pp. 474–477. See also *Parker* v. *Camden London Borough Council* [1986] Ch. 162.

[38] See *Goad* v. *A.U.E.W. (No. 3)* [1973] I.C.R. 108 (Trade Union fined £50,000 for contempt of Industrial Court's order). Another consequence is that non-compliance with an injunction may be an element in a subsequent award to the plaintiff of exemplary damages: *Drane* v. *Evangelou* [1978] 1 W.L.R. 455.

[39] *Clarke* v. *Chadburn* [1985] 1 W.L.R. 78 (union rules); All E.R. Rev. 1985, p. 76 (C. J. Miller).

disobedience may lead to imprisonment, the injunction must be expressed in exact terms, so that the defendant knows precisely what he must do, or refrain from doing.[40] As committal proceedings are equivalent to a criminal charge, the standard of proof is that of the criminal law, thus the breach of injunction must be established beyond reasonable doubt.[41]

In matrimonial cases, committal orders should be made very reluctantly. As Ormrod L.J. said in *Ansah* v. *Ansah*,[42] "Committal orders are remedies of last resort; in family cases they should be the very last resort."

Rules of court provide for the service and enforcement of injunctions.[43] It should be added that a power of arrest may be attached to injunctions granted under the Domestic Violence and Matrimonial Proceedings Act 1976, s.2.[44]

A question which has recently been prominent is whether third parties commit contempt if they knowingly act contrary to an injunction. A third party who aids and abets a breach of injunction is guilty of contempt.[45] An agent of the party enjoined is also bound by the injunction.[46] It has been held that the court has jurisdiction in wardship cases to make an injunction against the world at large, although a person who contravened the order in good faith and without notice of its terms would not commit contempt.[47] In *Att.-Gen.* v. *Newspaper Publishing plc*[48] the question was whether newspapers which published confidential material which other newspapers had been enjoined from publishing could be guilty of contempt. The Court of Appeal held that strangers who knowingly took action to damage or destroy confidentiality in this way could commit contempt. The question was not whether third parties were bound by the injunction, but whether they could commit contempt even though they were not bound. As they were not parties to the order, the basis of the contempt would not be a breach of the order (unless they had aided and abetted a breach) but interference with the administration of justice.

---

[40] *Morris* v. *Redland Bricks Ltd.* [1970] A.C. 652; *P.A. Thomas & Co.* v. *Mould* [1968] 2 Q.B. 913 at p. 923.

[41] *Re Bramblevale Ltd.* [1970] Ch. 128; *Kent County Council* v. *Batchelor* (1977) 33 P. & C.R. 185.

[42] [1977] Fam.138 at p. 144. See also (1977) 40 M.L.R. 220 (P. H. Pettit); (1987) 17 Fam.Law 34 (T. Prime).

[43] R.S.C., Ord. 45, r. 5 (enforcement) and r. 7 (service).

[44] *Post,* p. 762.

[45] *Acro (Automation) Ltd.* v. *Rex Chainbelt Inc.* [1971] 1 W.L.R. 1676; (1972) 88 L.Q.R. 177 (P. Raynor).

[46] *Cretanor Maritime Co. Ltd.* v. *Irish Marine Management Ltd.* [1978] 1 W.L.R. 966. See the *Mareva* cases, *post,* p. 770, particularly the "world-wide assets" cases.

[47] *In re X. (a minor)* [1984] 1 W.L.R. 1422; All E.R. Rev. 1985, p. 74 (C. J. Miller); *Re L (a ward)* [1988] 1 F.L.R. 255; *Re W. (Minors)* (1989) 19 Fam.Law 17.

[48] [1988] Ch. 333 (the *Spycatcher* case). The matter was remitted to the High Court. See also *Att.-Gen.* v. *Observer Ltd., Re an application by Derbyshire County Council* [1988] 1 All E.R. 385; *Bank Mellat* v. *Kazmi, The Times,* December 27, 1988.

(v) **Crown Proceedings**. One disadvantage is that an injunction will not normally lie against the Crown.[49] The proper remedy in such a case is the declaration, but this leaves the plaintiff without a remedy in situations where an interlocutory injunction would be desirable, as it seems that an interlocutory declaration cannot be made.[50] A final declaration may be made in interlocutory proceedings in rare cases, but not against the Crown.[51] The Law Commission recommended that this gap be filled,[52] but this has not been fully implemented.[53] In certain circumstances, however, an interlocutory injunction may be obtained against an officer of the Crown in judicial review proceedings.[54]

B. Protection of Rights

(i) **Locus Standi**. "It is a fundamental rule that the court will only grant an injunction at the suit of a private individual to support a legal right."[55] The type of right which may be protected by injunction in the field of private law is dealt with below,[56] but the question also arises as to who may seek an injunction to protect a public right. This requires a consideration of the extent to which the civil courts may restrain a breach of the criminal law by injunction. The general rule is that public rights are protected by the Attorney-General, acting either *ex officio* or on the relation of a member of the public. He may obtain an injunction to restrain breaches of the criminal law even if there is a statutory remedy, where that remedy is inadequate,[57] and the view of the court is that injunctions should be granted at his request to prevent clear breaches of the law irrespective of the weighing of benefits and detriments which characterises most other injunctions.[58]

[49] Crown Proceedings Act 1947, s.21. See *Trawnik* v. *Lennox* [1985] 1 W.L.R. 532.
[50] *International General Electric Co. Ltd.* v. *Commissioner of Customs and Excise* [1962] Ch. 784; *Gouriet* v. *Union of Post Office Workers* (C.A.) [1977] Q.B. 729 at p. 770 (*per* Lawton L.J.); *cf.* (1977) 30 C.L.P. 43 at pp. 51–52 (I. Zamir). See also *Meade* v. *London Borough of Haringey* [1979] 1 W.L.R. 637 at pp. 648 and 657; *De Falco* v. *Crawley Borough Council* [1980] Q.B. 460 at p. 480; *R.* v. *I.R.C. ex p. Rossminster Ltd.* [1980] A.C. 952 at pp. 1000, 1007, 1014; *R.* v. *Secretary of State for the Home Department, ex p. Herbage* [1987] Q.B. 872.
[51] R.S.C., Ord. 15, r. 16; *Clarke* v. *Chadburn* [1985] 1 W.L.R. 78.
[52] Report on Remedies in Administrative Law, para. 51 (Cmnd. 6407).
[53] See R.S.C., Ord. 53, r. 3(10)(b); Supreme Court Act 1981, s.31(1), (2); (1978) 41 M.L.R. 437 at p. 439 (J. Beatson and M. H. Matthews).
[54] *R.* v. *Licensing Authority, ex p. Smith Kline & French Laboratories Ltd. (No. 2), The Times,* August 16, 1988 (Dillon L.J. dissenting); *R.* v. *Secretary of State for the Home Department, ex p. Herbage, supra.*
[55] *per* Lord Denning M.R. in *Thorne* v. *British Broadcasting Corporation* [1957] 1 W.L.R. 1104 at p. 1109. But compare the different views expressed in *Chief Constable of Kent* v. *V.* [1983] Q.B. 34.
[56] *Post,* p. 704.
[57] *Att.-Gen* v. *Sharp* [1931] 1 Ch. 121; *Att.-Gen* v. *Chaudry* [1971] 1 W.L.R. 1623. See also *Att.-Gen* v. *British Broadcasting Corporation* [1981] A.C. 303, C.A.: the Attorney-General is the proper party to bring an action for an injunction to restrain a criminal contempt in respect of civil proceedings. (Not discussed in the House of Lords [1981] A.C. 303).
[58] *Att.-Gen* v. *Bastow* [1957] 1 Q.B. 514; *Att.-Gen* v. *Harris* [1961] 1 Q.B. 74; *post,* p. 758.

By way of exception to this general rule, an individual may seek an injunction if interference with a public right, created by statute or existing at common law, would also infringe some private right of his or would inflict special damage on him,[59] save where statute has, for instance by providing an exclusive remedy, excluded it.[60] But an individual who does not come within the established exceptions has no remedy, for it is no part of English law that a person who suffers damage by reason of another person's breach of statute has a civil action against that person.[61] Thus a record company could not get an injunction against a defendant who traded in "bootleg" records in breach of statute,[62] as there is no principle that a plaintiff can restrain a crime affecting his property rights by injunction where the statute was not designed for the protection of the class of which he is a member.[63]

Another important question is whether a private individual may obtain an injunction to restrain a threatened criminal offence which would interfere with a public right when the Attorney-General has refused his consent to a relator action, the case not being one where private rights or special damage to the plaintiff are involved.[64]

In *Gouriet* v. *Union of Post Office Workers*[65] the plaintiff, a member of the general public, sought an injunction to restrain a threatened boycott of postal communications between Britain and South Africa, in breach of the Post Office Act 1953. The Attorney-General had refused consent to a relator action, without giving reasons. It was unanimously held in the House of Lords, reversing the Court of Appeal,[66] that the court had no jurisdiction to grant

---

[59] *Gouriet* v. *Union of Post Office Workers* [1978] A.C. 435; *Lonrho Ltd.* v. *Shell Petroleum Co. Ltd.* [1982] A.C. 173; *R.C.A. Corpn.* v. *Pollard* [1983] Ch. 135. On the narrow scope of this exception, see (1979) 42 M.L.R. 324 (I. M. Kennedy). An action also lies if the plaintiff can show that he is a member of the class for whose benefit the statute, upon its construction, was passed. See also *Francome* v. *Mirror Group Newspapers* [1984] 1 W.L.R. 892; *Barrs* v. *Bethell* [1982] Ch. 294; *Holmes* v. *Checkland, The Times,* April 15, 1987.

[60] *Stevens* v. *Chown* [1901] 1 Ch. 894; *cf. Meade* v. *London Borough of Haringey* [1979] 1 W.L.R. 637; Spry, pp. 339 *et seq.*

[61] *Lonrho Ltd.* v. *Shell Petroleum Co. Ltd., supra,* rejecting the wider principle of *ex p. Island Records Ltd.* [1978] Ch. 122; *CBS Songs Ltd.* v. *Amstrad Consumer Electronics plc* [1988] 2 W.L.R. 1191.

[62] Performers' Protection Acts 1958–1972 (repealed by the Copyright, Designs and Patents Act 1988).

[63] *R.C.A. Corpn.* v. *Pollard* [1983] Ch. 135; All E.R. Rev 1982, p. 308 (B. A. Hepple); (1983) 46 M.L.R. 224 (Wedderburn) and 274 (A. Staines); (1983) 99 L.Q.R. 182 (G. Samuel); [1984] Conv. 451 (H. Carty); *Rickless* v. *United Artists Corp.* [1988] Q.B. 40.

[64] The right to bring a private prosecution, once the offence is committed, is a different matter, but the Attorney-General has power to veto such proceedings.

[65] [1978] A.C. 435; (1977) 36 C.L.J. 201 (D. G. T. Williams); (1978) 94 L.Q.R. 4 (H.W.R.W.); (1978) 41 M.L.R. 58 (T. C. Hartley); (1978) 41 M.L.R. 63 (R. C. Simpson); (1979) 42 M.L.R. 369 (D. Feldman). See also Lord Denning's observations in *The Discipline of Law,* pp. 137 *et seq.*

[66] [1977] Q.B. 729; (1977) 93 L.Q.R. 162 (P.V.B) Dicta in *Att.-Gen., ex rel. McWhirter* v. *Independent Broadcasting Authority* [1973] Q.B. 629, were disapproved. See the arguments of the Attorney-General [1977] Q.B. 729 at pp. 741–746.

such an injunction,[67] nor to control the exercise of the Attorney-General's discretion in any way.[68]

It was a fundamental principle that private rights could be asserted by the individual and public rights by the Attorney-General, and that "the criminal law is enforced in the criminal courts by the conviction and punishment of offenders not in the civil courts."[69] Any interference by the civil courts exposes the defendant to "double jeopardy"; the penalty of imprisonment for contempt of court, if the offence is committed, is added to the criminal penalties fixed by Parliament.[70] Not only are the punishments different, but the contempt proceedings will be decided by a judge alone while the defendant may be entitled to a jury in the criminal proceedings.[71] These considerations are, of course, also present in cases where injunctions may be granted to enforce the criminal law. No doubt for this reason the House of Lords expressed the view that the cases where the Attorney-General can seek an injunction to restrain the commission of an offence are narrow and not to be extended. The jurisdiction is "of great delicacy and is one to be used with caution." The Attorney-General's power is "not without its difficulties and these may call for consideration in the future."[72]

In denying the plaintiff's action, the House of Lords affirmed that the Attorney-General is responsible to Parliament, not to the court. Any error he might make would be of political judgment, not law, and would not be appropriate for decision in the courts. Others have doubted whether responsibility to Parliament is a sufficient control to compensate for the exclusion of the court's jurisdiction.[73]

But the effect of the decision may not be so great as first appears. The prerogative remedies, with their broader concept of standing,[74]

---

[67] Ormrod L.J. in the Court of Appeal regarded the matter as one of jurisdiction, not *locus standi*: [1977] Q.B. 729 at p. 777.

[68] For commonwealth views, see (1978) 12 U.B.C. Law Rev. 320 (D. Lunny); Australian Law Reform Commission, Discussion Paper No. 4, p. 20.

[69] [1978] A.C. 435 at p. 490 (*per* Viscount Dilhorne). Although the case concerned criminal law enforcement, many statements in the House of Lords were wide enough to cover all public law actions. See also *Ashby* v. *Ebdon* [1985] Ch. 394; (1985) 44 C.L.J. 6 (J. A. Jolowicz); *R.* v. *Westminster City Council, ex p. Sierbien, The Times,* March 30, 1987.

[70] *Ibid.* at p. 498 (*per* Lord Diplock). See *Kent County Council* v. *Batchelor* [1979] 1 W.L.R. 213. But in other areas the civil court adds to the criminal penalty; see p. 307, *ante,* (forfeiture of property acquired by killing).

[71] But the standard of proof will be the same; see (1979) 42 M.L.R. 369 (D. Feldman).

[72] See also *Stoke-on-Trent City Council* v. *B. & Q. (Retail) Ltd.* [1984] A.C. 754; *Waverley Borough Council* v. *Hilden* [1988] 1 W.L.R. 246. These cases are further considered *post*, p. 758.

[73] [1977] Q.B. 729 at pp. 758–759 (*per* Lord Denning M.R.); (1977) 36 C.L.J. 201 (D. G. T. Williams); (1978) 41 M.L.R. 58 (T. C. Hartley); (1979) 42 M.L.R. 369 (D. Feldman); *cf.* (1978) 41 M.L.R. 63 (R.C. Simpson).

[74] *Post*, pp. 759–761.

may be available where the defendant is a public authority.[75] Here the court feels able to judge on matters of public interest, even where there are political implications,[76] but the House of Lords has doubted the analogy.[77]

In the case of a crime which has already been committed, it has been held that the police have *locus standi* to seek an injunction to "freeze" money in a bank account which is reasonably believed to be the proceeds of a crime.[78] This principle is not without difficulty, and is confined to an asset which can be identified as the stolen item or as property representing it.[79] No such injunction is available in respect of moneys not themselves obtained by fraud but which were profits made by means of a loan obtained by fraud.[79a]

Finally, the rule that only the Attorney-General may enforce public rights is subject to certain limited statutory exceptions, notably section 222 of the Local Government Act 1972, enabling a local authority to seek an injunction in its own name to protect public rights in the locality.[80]

(ii) Legal and Equitable Rights. A right that is to be protected by an injunction must be one that is known to law or equity.[81] Thus it must not be one of which cognisance will be taken only in ecclesiastical law.[82] The point was firmly made in *Day* v. *Brownrigg*.[83]

> The plaintiff lived in a house that had been called "Ashford Lodge" for 60 years. The defendant lived in a smaller neighbouring house called "Ashford Villa." The defendant started to call his

---

[75] See *R.* v. *Commissioner of Police of the Metropolis* [1968] 2 Q.B. 118; *R.* v. *I.R.C., ex p. National Federation of Self-Employed and Small Businesses Ltd.* [1982] A.C. 617 at p. 640, *post*, p. 759; *R.* v. *Her Majesty's Treasury, ex p. Smedley* [1985] Q.B. 657.

[76] See, for example, *Secretary of State for Education and Science* v. *Tameside Metropolitan Borough Council* [1977] A.C. 1014.

[77] *Gouriet* v. *Union of Post Office Workers* [1978] A.C. 435 at p. 483.

[78] *Chief Constable of Kent* v. *V.* [1983] Q.B. 34; *West Mercia Constabulary* v. *Wagener* [1982] 1 W.L.R. 127; (1982) 98 L.Q.R. 190 (D. Feldman); All E.R. Rev 1982, p. 205 (G. Zellick); (1983) 99 L.Q.R. 1; (1983) 42 C.L.J. 51 (A. Tettenborn). A search warrant is not available in respect of a bank account.

[79] *Chief Constable of Hampshire* v. *A. Ltd.* [1985] Q.B. 132; (1984) 100 L.Q.R. 537 (G. Samuel). See also *Malone* v. *Metropolitan Police Commissioner* [1980] Q.B. 49.

[79a] *Chief Constable of Leicestershire* v. *M.* [1989] 1 W.L.R. 20; *Chief Constable of Surrey* v. *A., The Times*, October 27, 1988. Recent interventions by Parliament (e.g. Criminal Justice Act 1988) suggested that the courts should not indulge in parallel creativity.

[80] *Post*, p. 758. See also *National Dock Labour Board* v. *Sabah Timber Co. Ltd., The Times*, September 3, 1987.

[81] In *Chief Constable of Kent* v. *V.* [1983] Q.B. 34, Lord Denning M.R. considered that this was no longer the case after the Supreme Court Act 1981, but Donaldson and Slade L.J.J. disagreed; All E.R. Rev. 1982, p. 205 (G. Zellick); (1983) 99 L.Q.R. 1; (1983) 42 C.L.J. 51 (A. Tettenborn). Subsequent decisions support the majority view; *Ainsbury* v. *Millington* [1986] 1 All E.R. 73; *Wilde* v. *Wilde* [1988] 2 F.L.R. 83; *Associated Newspapers Group plc* v. *Insert Media Ltd.* [1988] 1 W.L.R. 509; *Chief Constable of Leicestershire* v. *M., supra*.

[82] *Att.-Gen.* v. *Dean and Chapter of Ripon Cathedral* [1945] Ch. 239.

[83] (1878) 10 Ch.D. 294; *Beddow* v. *Beddow* (1878) 9 Ch.D. 89 at p. 93.

house "Ashford Lodge" and the plaintiff sought an injunction to restrain him from doing so. Malins V.-C. would have been willing to grant an injunction on the ground that an injury would otherwise be suffered by the plaintiff, but the Court of Appeal took the view that there was no violation of a legal or equitable right in the plaintiff so that no injunction would be granted.[84]

Similarly in *Paton* v. *Trustees of British Pregnancy Advisory Service*[85] it was held that a husband could not obtain an injunction to prevent his wife from having, or a registered medical practitioner from performing, a legal abortion: the husband had "no legal right enforceable at law or in equity."

The legal or equitable right in question does not, however, have to be one based on property. So in the cases of injunctions to restrain unlawful expulsion from a club or association, the *jurisdiction* to intervene is said to depend on the mutual, and possibly implied, contractual rights of the parties; though the actual *exercise* of the jurisdiction may be limited where proprietary rights, or rights analogous to them, such as the right to earn one's livelihood, are not affected.[86]

The courts have gone even further than this in protecting confidential material.[87] Before 1875, it was accepted that equity would, in suitable cases, restrain a defendant from revealing or distributing information or other material obtained in confidence,[88] regarding the breach of confidence as an equitable wrong needing protection by injunction even though it was not easy to say that it was protected by any other remedy. And it has now been accepted[89] that the jurisdiction in this type of case does not depend on any notion of property or contract, but that an obligation of confidence can exist by virtue of the circumstances, and independently of any actual agreement to that effect.

We have clearly moved a long way from a narrow view of *Day* v. *Brownrigg*,[90] but, it is safer to add, only in relation to specific areas of

---

[84] See also *Montgomery* v. *Montgomery* [1965] P. 46; *Mechanical Services (Trailer Engineers) Ltd.* v. *Avon Rubber Co. Ltd.* [1977] R.P.C. 66; *Patel* v. *Patel* [1988] 2 F.L.R. 179 (no tort of harassment). See Spry, pp. 317–321.

[85] [1979] Q.B. 276; (1979) 95 L.Q.R. 332 (J. Phillips); (1979) 30 C.L.P. 217 (C. M. Lyon and G. J. Benett). For a discussion of the position if the proposed abortion would be illegal, see (1979) 42 M.L.R. 324 (I. M. Kennedy); *C.* v. *S.* [1988] Q.B. 135; (1987) 103 L.Q.R. 340 (A. Grubb and D. Pearl).

[86] *Lee* v. *The Showmen's Guild of Great Britain* [1952] 2 Q.B. 329, especially at pp. 341–342, *per* Denning L.J., *post*, p. 764.

[87] *Post*, p. 754. See also *British Steel Corporation* v. *Granada Television Ltd.* [1981] A.C. 1096 (discovery).

[88] *Prince Albert* v. *Strange* (1849) 1 H. & T. 1 (copies of etchings made by the Prince and Queen Victoria: distribution restrained).

[89] See particularly *Argyll* v. *Argyll* [1967] Ch. 302 at p. 322; *Fraser* v. *Evans* [1969] 1 Q.B. 349 at p. 361; (1972) J.S.P.T.L. 149 (P. M. North).

[90] (1878) 10 Ch.D. 294. *cf.* on unlawful trade competition, *J. Bollinger* v. *Costa Brava Wine Co.* [1960] Ch. 262 at p. 283.

the law. But, as for personal confidences, so for confidential commercial information, which will be restrained from publication along similar lines.[91] Here too, it would now seem preferable to base the jurisdiction on confidence as such and not on a fiction of contract or an interest in property.[92] Other rights which may be protected by injunction include the right (contractual or otherwise) not to be harassed by arbitration proceedings which could not lead to a fair trial[93]; the right (contractual or otherwise) not to be sued in a foreign court[94]; the right of the police to "freeze" money in a bank account which is reasonably believed to be the identifiable proceeds of crime[95]; the right to restrain a breach of the E.E.C. Treaty[96]; the right to restrain the export of works of art by means of forged documents[97]; and the right to ensure the effectiveness of a court order.[98] The latter right is the basis of the recent novel use of the injunction to prevent the defendant from leaving the country.[99] Such an injunction may be granted even if the applicant has no legal or equitable right.[1]

C. Perpetual Injunctions

It is axiomatic that the jurisdiction to grant injunctions is purely discretionary. But, as with specific performance, the court, in exercising its discretion, pays attention to certain factors established by the precedents as being of particular relevance.

(i) **Prohibitory Injunctions.** If a plaintiff has established the existence of a right, infringement of that right should be restrained, but injunc-

---

[91] *Post,* p. 754.
[92] See also Law Commission Working Paper 58, proposing a new tort of breach of confidence; (1982) 41 C.L.J. 40 (G. Jones).
[93] *Bremer Vulkan Schiffbau und Maschinenfabrik* v. *South India Shipping Corpn.* [1981] A.C. 909.
[94] *British Airways Board* v. *Laker Airways Ltd.* [1985] A.C. 58; *South Carolina Insurance Co.* v. *Assurantie Maatschappij "De Zeven Provincien" N.V.* [1987] A.C. 24.
[95] *Chief Constable of Kent* v. *V.* [1983] Q.B. 34; *cf. Chief Constable of Hampshire* v. *A. Ltd.* [1985] Q.B. 132; *West Mercia Constabulary* v. *Wagener* [1982] 1 W.L.R. 127; *Chief Constable of Leicestershire* v. *M.* [1989] 1 W.L.R. 20; *Chief Constable of Surrey* v. *A.*, *The Times*, October 27, 1988, *ante*, p. 704; (1982) 98 L.Q.R. 190 (D. Feldman); All E.R.Rev. 1982, p. 205 (G. Zellick); (1983) 99 L.Q.R. 1; (1983) 42 C.L.J. 51 (A. Tettenborn).
[96] *Cutsforth* v. *Mansfield Inns Ltd.* [1986] 1 W.L.R. 558.
[97] *Kingdom of Spain* v. *Christie, Manson & Woods Ltd.* [1986] 1 W.L.R. 1120.
[98] *Maclaine Watson & Co. Ltd.* v. *International Tin Council (No. 2)* [1988] 3 W.L.R. 1191 (unpaid judgment debt); *Normid Housing Association* v. *Ralphs, The Times*, July 18, 1988.
[99] *Bayer A.G.* v. *Winter* [1986] 1 W.L.R. 497 (*Anton Piller* and *Mareva* injunctions), *post*, p. 771; *cf. Al Nahkel for Contracting and Trading Ltd.* v. *Lowe* [1986] Q.B. 235 and *Allied Arab Bank Ltd.* v. *Hajjar* [1988] Q.B. 787; (1988) 47 C.L.J. 364 (N. Andrews) (writ *ne exeat regno*). See also *Re I. (a minor)*, *The Times*, May 22, 1987.
[1] *In Re Oriental Credit Ltd.* [1988] 2 W.L.R. 172 (injunction granted to liquidator to prevent director leaving the country prior to examination pursuant to an order under Companies Act 1985, s.561); criticised as leading to uncertainty in (1988) 47 C.L.J. 177 (C. F. Forsyth).

tions will not be granted where an award of damages[2] would be sufficient. Damages will not be an adequate remedy if they are not quantifiable, or if money could not properly compensate the plaintiff, as in the case of nuisance and other continuous or repeated injuries requiring a series of actions for damages, or even where the remedy would be ineffective because the defendant is a pauper.[3]

The extent of the damage is not the crucial point. An injunction may be granted even if only nominal damages would be recoverable at law.[4] The smallness of the damage suffered by a plaintiff and the fact that a monetary sum could easily be assessed to compensate for it, is no reason for withholding an injunction if the consequence is that the defendant is in effect compulsorily "buying" a right which is the plaintiff's to sell only if he wants to.[5] This principle was applied in *Express Newspapers Ltd.* v. *Keys.*[6]

> Certain trade unions had issued instructions to their members to support a "Day of Action," a political strike in protest against Government policies. The plaintiffs sought an injunction to restrain the unions from inducing a breach of contract between the members and their employers.[7] One issue was whether the common law remedy of damages was adequate. Griffiths J., in granting the injunction, held that it was not. The plaintiffs did not want the unions' money; they wanted their newspapers to be published. To refuse the injunction would be giving a licence to the unions to commit an unlawful act merely because they could afford to pay the damages. Where it was clear that the defendant was acting unlawfully, "it would require wholly exceptional circumstances to be a proper exercise of the discretion to allow such conduct to continue."[8] It would not be fair to leave the plaintiffs to their remedy in damages, as there would be real difficulty in attributing any particular breach of contract to incitement by the unions as opposed to the voluntary act of the employees. "It is one thing to suffer damage and it is another to prove it."[9]

Similarly in cases in which the defendant has trespassed on the

---

[2] The jurisdiction to award damages under Lord Cairns' Act is considered below, *post*, p. 738.
[3] *Hodgson* v. *Duce* (1856) 28 L.T.(o.s.) 155.
[4] *Rochdale Canal Co.* v. *King* (1851) 2 Sim.(n.s.) 78; *Woollerton and Wilson Ltd.* v. *Richard Costain Ltd.* [1970] 1 W.L.R. 411.
[5] *Wood* v. *Sutcliffe* (1851) 2 Sim.(n.s.) 163. In *Express Newspapers Ltd.* v. *Keys* [1980] I.R.L.R. 247, and *Patel* v. *W.H. Smith (Eziot) Ltd.* [1987] 1 W.L.R. 853, it was held that this principle applied equally to interlocutory injunctions, and was not affected by *American Cyanamid Co.* v. *Ethicon Ltd.* [1975] A.C. 396, *post*, p. 716.
[6] [1980] I.R.L.R. 247. The injunction in this case was interlocutory (and, in part, mandatory) but the judgment on this aspect is of general application.
[7] As there was no trade dispute, there was no immunity under s.13(1) of the Trade Union and Labour Relations Act 1974.
[8] [1980] I.R.L.R. 247 at p. 250.
[9] *Ibid.*

plaintiff's property, as by laying water pipes under it, and in other cases of interference with rights of ownership: actual loss does not need to be shown before an injunction is granted to remedy a trespass.[10] But there may be cases in which injunctions will be refused even on such facts, for example if the infringement is occasional or temporary, or if it is a trivial matter. One such case was *Armstrong* v. *Sheppard and Short*,[11] where the plaintiff had misled the court and had suffered no real damage. Lord Evershed M.R. said "A proprietor who establishes a proprietary right is ex debito justitiae entitled to an injunction unless it can be said against him that he has raised such an equity that it is no longer open to him to assert his legal or proprietary rights."[12] Similarly in *Behrens* v. *Richards*[13] an injunction was not granted to restrain the public from using tracks on the plaintiff's land on an unfrequented part of the coast, causing no damage to the plaintiff. Such cases are, however, to be regarded as exceptional.[14]

It is obvious that these various factors are not to be considered in isolation and no complete list can be given of instances where an injunction will be refused. The principle applied by the courts is the protection of existing rights which are recognised by the law. But an injunction will not issue in every such case; it may be refused where damages are an adequate remedy, or where the plaintiff has by his conduct disentitled himself from injunctive relief,[15] or where the defendant gives to the court an undertaking not to do the act complained of[16]; or where, even if there is no other suitable remedy, the court considers that the plaintiff has suffered no injustice.[17]

(ii) **Mandatory Injunctions.** These are governed by the same general principles as prohibitory injunctions, save that the problems of enforcement, supervision and hardship may be more acute. Mandatory injunctions are less frequently granted than prohibitory injunctions, and, as Lord Upjohn has stated in *Redland Bricks Ltd.* v. *Morris*,[18] are entirely discretionary and can never be "as of course."

There are two broad categories of mandatory injunctions: the "rest-

[10] *Goodson* v. *Richardson* (1874) L.R. 9 Ch.App. 221; *John Trenberth Ltd.* v. *National Westminster Bank Ltd.* (1979) 39 P. & C.R. 104. See also *Marco Productions Ltd.* v. *Pagola* [1945] K.B. 111 on breach of contract.

[11] [1959] 2 Q.B. 384.

[12] [1959] 2 Q.B. 384 at p. 394.

[13] [1905] 2 Ch. 614.

[14] *Patel* v. *W.H. Smith (Eziot) Ltd.* [1987] 1 W.L.R. 853; *Anchor Brewhouse Developments Ltd.* v. *Berkley House (Docklands Developments) Ltd.* [1987] 2 E.G.L.R. 173; (1988) 138 N.L.J. 23 (E. McKendrick) and 385 (H. W. Wilkinson).

[15] Discretionary bars are considered below, *post*, p. 734.

[16] *Halsey* v. *Esso Petroleum Co. Ltd.* [1961] 1 W.L.R. 683; *Att.-Gen.* v. *Times Newspapers Ltd., The Times*, June 27, 1975 (interlocutory injunction refused where defendant undertook not to publish Crossman diaries before trial); *British Broadcasting Corporation* v. *Hearn* [1977] 1 W.L.R. 1004.

[17] See *Glynn* v. *Keele University* [1971] 1 W.L.R. 487.

[18] [1970] A.C. 652 at p. 655. See also *Leakey* v. *National Trust for Places of Historic Interest or Natural Beauty* [1980] Q.B. 485.

orative" injunction, requiring the defendant to undo a wrongful act in situations where a prohibitory injunction might have been obtained to prevent the commission of the act[19]; and the mandatory injunction to compel the defendant to carry out some positive obligation.[20] If the matter is one of contract, specific performance is more usual in the latter situation, but an injunction may be granted.[21] We have already seen that the terms of an injunction must be certain. It follows from this that a duty which is itself uncertain cannot be enforced by injunction.[22]

Problems of supervision may arise with mandatory injunctions as with specific performance.[23] This will not normally prevent the grant of a "restorative" mandatory injunction, which merely requires an act of restoration, but a mandatory injunction is unlikely to be granted in cases involving the continuous performance of a positive obligation.

In *Gravesham Borough Council* v. *British Railways Board*,[24] the defendant planned to curtail the services of its ferry. As this would cause inconvenience to some local workers, a mandatory injunction was sought to compel the defendant to maintain existing timetables, even though this would cause the ferry to be run at a loss. It was held that in fact there was no breach of the defendant's common law duty to operate the ferry, but even if there had been, a mandatory injunction would not be appropriate, because of enforcement difficulties and financial hardship to the defendant. Slade J. said that there was no absolute and inflexible rule that the court will never grant an injunction requiring a series of acts involving the continuous employment of people over a number of years. But the jurisdiction to grant such an injunction would be exercised only in exceptional circumstances.

As in the case of prohibitory injunctions, it is not necessary for the plaintiff to show grave damage or inconvenience. In *Kelsen* v. *Imperial*

---

[19] *Charrington* v. *Simons & Co. Ltd.* [1971] 1 W.L.R. 598; *Pugh* v. *Howells* (1984) 48 P. & C.R. 29. Failure to obtain a prohibitory injunction does not preclude the issue subsequently of a mandatory injunction: see *Wrotham Park Estate* v. *Parkside Homes Ltd.* [1974] 1 W.L.R. 798, *post*, p. 710.

[20] See also *Anton Piller* injunctions, *post*, p. 766.

[21] See *Evans* v. *B.B.C. and I.B.A., The Times*, February 26, 1974 (interlocutory); *SEDAC Investments Ltd.* v. *Tanner* [1982] 1 W.L.R. 1342.

[22] *Bower* v. *Bantam Investments Ltd.* [1972] 1 W.L.R. 1120 (interlocutory); *cf. Acrow (Automation) Ltd.* v. *Rex Chainbelt Inc.* [1971] 1 W.L.R. 1676; *Peninsular Maritime Ltd.* v. *Padseal Ltd.* (1981) 259 E.G. 860.

[23] *Ante*, p. 663.

[24] [1978] Ch. 379. See also *Dowty Boulton Paul Ltd.* v. *Wolverhampton Corporation* [1971] 1 W.L.R. 204 (no injunction to enforce a covenant to maintain land as an airfield); *F.W. Woolworth plc* v. *Charlwood Alliance Properties Ltd.* [1987] 1 E.G.L.R. 53 (no injunction to enforce covenant in lease to keep open in trading hours as a retail shop). This problem does not arise if only one act is required: see the cases on mandatory interlocutory injunctions, especially *Sky Petroleum Ltd.* v. *V.I.P. Petroleum Ltd.* [1974] 1 W.L.R. 576; *Camden* v. *London Borough Council* [1986] Ch. 162.

Tobacco Co. Ltd.[25] a mandatory injunction was granted to enforce the removal of a sign which trespassed in the airspace above the plaintiff's premises, causing no real damage to the plaintiff, save in so far as he could have charged for the use of the space.

While the extent of the damage is not crucial, the question of hardship to the defendant is more significant.[26] In *Charrington* v. *Simons & Co. Ltd.*,[27] Buckley J. thought that the criterion for the grant of a mandatory injunction was a fair result, taking into consideration the benefit which the order would confer on the plaintiff and the detriment which it would cause the defendant. But Russell L.J. in the Court of Appeal doubted the usefulness of the "fair result" test.[28]

In *Wrotham Park Estate* v. *Parkside Homes Ltd.*,[29] the defendant had erected houses in breach of a restrictive covenant which he had thought was unenforceable. Although purchasers were now in occupation, the plaintiffs sought a mandatory injunction for the demolition of the houses. For various reasons, the plaintiffs had not sought interlocutory relief to prevent the erection of the houses. Brightman J. said that it was not fatal to the grant of a mandatory injunction that the plaintiffs had not sought interlocutory relief at an earlier stage.[30] The fact that the writ was issued before much building had been done was a relevant but not a conclusive factor. The injunction was refused, as it would result in the unpardonable waste of needed houses. Instead, damages were awarded under Lord Cairns' Act.

Finally, it has been held that the court should be reluctant to intervene in industrial disputes by the grant of a mandatory injunction.

In *Harold Stephen and Co. Ltd.* v. *Post Office*,[31] an industrial dispute had arisen whereby postal workers were unlawfully "blacking" the mail of a certain company (Grunwick). This resulted in the suspension of these workers, so that the plaintiff company's mail was held up and its business seriously disrupted. The plaintiff sought a mandatory injunction against the Post Office to release its mail. The Court of Appeal refused the injunction, which would require the Post Office to take back the suspended workers, who would be likely to continue the unlawful discrimination against Grunwick. The

---

[25] [1957] 2 Q.B. 334; *Straudley Investments Ltd.* v. *Barpress Ltd.* [1987] 1 E.G.L.R. 69. *cf. Bernstein (Lord) of Leigh* v. *Skyviews & General Ltd.* [1978] Q.B. 479.
[26] *Gravesham Borough Council* v. *British Railways Board, supra.* See also *Colls* v. *Home and Colonial Stores Ltd.* [1904] A.C. 179, and other cases on Lord Cairns' Act, *post*, p. 738.
[27] [1970] 1 W.L.R. 725 at p. 730. See also *Shepherd Homes Ltd.* v. *Sandham* [1971] Ch. 340.
[28] [1971] 1 W.L.R. 598, *post*, p. 745.
[29] [1974] 1 W.L.R. 798; (1974) 39 Conv.(N.S.) 289 (F. R. Crane); (1975) 34 C.L.J. 224 (J. A. Jolowicz); distinguished in *Wakeham* v. *Wood* (1982) 43 P.&C.R. 40, where the building was in flagrant disregard of the covenant.
[30] See also *Shaw* v. *Applegate* [1977] 1 W.L.R. 970 at p. 978.
[31] [1977] 1 W.L.R. 1172.

injunction would, therefore, have the effect of revoking the Post Office's disciplinary measures and making it appear that the court endorsed the continuance of the unlawful discrimination. Enforcement would also be impossible as there could be no sanction against the Post Office should it find itself unable to comply with such an injunction. Geoffrey Lane L.J. said that "It can only be in very rare circumstances and in the most extreme circumstances that this court should interfere by way of mandatory injunction in the delicate mechanism of industrial disputes and industrial negotiations."[32]

Such an extreme case was *Parker* v. *Camden London Borough Council.*[33]

A strike of boilermen employed by the landlord council meant that the tenants, many of whom were elderly or had young children, had no heating or hot water. In these exceptional circumstances, involving risk to life and health, the court was prepared to grant a mandatory injunction to turn on the boiler even though industrial action was involved.

The principles applicable to the grant of mandatory interlocutory injunctions and mandatory *quia timet* injunctions are discussed below.[34]

(iii) Suspension of Injunctions. If it would be very difficult for the defendant to comply immediately with the injunction, he will not be made to do the impossible. The injunction may be granted but suspended for a reasonable period, particularly if such a course will not result in financial damage to the plaintiff. The defendant may be required to undertake to pay damages to the plaintiff if any loss is suffered by him. Suspension is not unusual where the defendant is a local authority, which must make alternative arrangements for the performance of its duties. Thus in *Pride of Derby Angling Association* v. *British Celanese and Others*[35] an injunction was granted against a local authority to restrain the pollution of a river. It was no defence that the authority was performing a public service, namely, sewage disposal. But the injunction was suspended for a reasonable time, with the possibility of further suspension should the circumstances require it.

But the courts have sometimes suspended injunctions not in order to give the defendant time to comply, but rather to enable him to continue his wrongful activity in cases involving no substantial injury to the plaintiff.

---

[32] *Ibid.* at p. 1180. See also *Meade* v. *London Borough of Haringey* [1979] 1 W.L.R. 637.
[33] [1986] Ch. 162 (interlocutory).
[34] *Post,* pp. 728, 733.
[35] [1953] Ch. 149. See also *Halsey* v. *Esso Petroleum Co. Ltd.* [1961] 1 W.L.R. 683 (suspension for six weeks in nuisance case); *Miller* v. *Jackson* [1977] Q.B. 966; *Waverley Borough Council* v. *Hilden* [1988] 1 W.L.R. 246.

In *Woollerton and Wilson Ltd.* v. *Richard Costain Ltd.*[36] the defendant's crane sometimes swung over the plaintiff's premises, causing no actual danger or damage. This aerial trespass was unavoidable if the defendant was to finish the work, which was due to be completed in a year's time, *i.e.* in November, 1970. An injunction was granted to restrain the trespass, but was postponed until November 1970, when the crane would no longer be needed, on the ground that there was no threat of trespass continuing indefinitely, and the defendant had acted reasonably and had offered £250 to the plaintiff for the right to continue. The airspace only had any value because of the defendant's activities.[37]

In *Charrington* v. *Simons & Co. Ltd.*,[38] the plaintiff owned two orchards divided by a track, and sold one to the defendant company, reserving a right of way over the track. In breach of a covenant not to raise the level of the track above that of the orchards, the defendant resurfaced the track with concrete, raising it several inches. This interfered with the plaintiff's use of his land, and he sought a mandatory injunction to reinstate the track.

Buckley J. granted the injunction, but, as it would cause substantial inconvenience and expense to the defendant, it was suspended for three years, to allow the defendant the opportunity to do works which would remove the inconvenience to the plaintiff. It was intimated that if the plaintiff refused to agree to these works, he would not have a favourable hearing if he sought to have the suspension removed.

But the Court of Appeal held[39] that the three-year suspension was improper, as in effect the judge had sought to force on a reluctant plaintiff something very like a settlement involving operations which would harm his business, as a term of his obtaining a mandatory injunction to which he was plainly entitled. Furthermore reservations were expressed as to whether *Woollerton and Wilson Ltd.* v. *Richard Costain Ltd.*,[40] was correctly decided.

D. Interlocutory Injunctions

(i) **General.** Interlocutory injunctions raise somewhat different considerations. The jurisdiction is related not to the most just method of protecting established rights, but to the most convenient method of preserving the status quo while rights are established. The object of an

---

[36] [1970] 1 W.L.R. 411; (1970) 33 M.L.R. 552 (G. Dworkin). This was an interlocutory injunction, but it is doubtful whether it would now be granted, in the light of *American Cyanamid Co.* v. *Ethicon Ltd.* [1975] A.C. 396, *post*, p. 716.

[37] Unlike *Kelsen* v. *Imperial Tobacco Ltd.* [1957] 2 Q.B. 324, *ante*, p. 709.

[38] [1970] 1 W.L.R. 725.

[39] [1971] 1 W.L.R. 598.

[40] [1970] 1 W.L.R. 411; *supra*. See also *John Trenberth Ltd.* v. *National Westminster Bank Ltd.* (1979) 39 P. & C.R. 104; [1980] Conv. 308 (H. Street). A better solution might have been an award of damages under Lord Cairns' Act: see (1975) 34 C.L.J. 224 at p. 247 (J. A. Jolowicz).

interlocutory injunction is "to prevent a litigant, who must necessarily suffer the law's delay, from losing by that delay the fruit of his litigation."[41]

Interlocutory injunctions may be prohibitory, mandatory, or *quia timet*. Normally such an injunction remains in force until the trial of the action, but an interim injunction may be granted, which endures for some shorter specified period.[42] If the parties consent, the interlocutory hearing may be treated as a final trial if the dispute is of law.[43] But this will not be possible if the dispute is of fact, as affidavit evidence is unsuitable for such issues.

As we have seen, failure to seek an interlocutory injunction to restrain the commission of a wrongful act will not necessarily preclude the plaintiff from later obtaining a final mandatory injunction to compel the defendant to undo the act.[44]

(a) *Ex Parte Procedure.* The plaintiff should give at least two clear days' notice, so that, when the motion is heard, the defendant can oppose it. But exceptionally an injunction may be granted *ex parte*, without serving notice on the defendant, if the matter is one of such urgency that irreparable damage would be caused if the plaintiff had to go through the normal procedure.[45] The *ex parte* injunction is usually an interim injunction, valid only until the next motion day,[46] for which formal notice can be given. An *ex parte* injunction may be granted even before the writ or summons has been issued. In *Re N. (No. 2)*,[47] an *ex parte* injunction was granted by a High Court judge at his residence on a Sunday, to prevent the applicant's husband from taking their children to Australia. The common law rule that judicial acts could not be done on a Sunday did not apply to the court's equitable jurisdiction. In *Bates* v. *Lord Hailsham of St. Marylebone*,[48] the plaintiff, a solicitor, applied for an *ex parte* injunction at 2 p.m. to stop a committee which was to meet at 4.30 p.m. from making an order about the abolition of scale fees. The injunction was refused, as the plaintiff had known of

---

[41] *Hoffman-LaRoche (F.) & Co.* v. *Secretary of State for Trade and Industry.* [1975] A.C. 295 at p. 355 (Lord Wilberforce).

[42] See, for example, *Erinford Properties Ltd.* v. *Cheshire County Council* [1974] Ch. 261.

[43] Though this may be less likely since the decision in *American Cyanamid Co.* v. *Ethicon Ltd.* [1975] A.C. 396, *post*, p. 716, which has reduced the significance of the merits of the case at the interlocutory stage. See also the judgment of Lord Denning M.R. in *Fellowes and Son* v. *Fisher* [1976] Q.B. 122, *post*, p. 721; *Medway* v. *Doublelock Ltd.* [1978] 1 W.L.R. 710.

[44] *Wrotham Park Estate* v. *Parkside Homes Ltd.* [1974] 1 W.L.R. 798. But such an omission may be relevant to the defence of acquiescence: *Shaw* v. *Applegate* [1977] 1 W.L.R. 970, *post*, p. 736.

[45] Where a trade dispute is involved, see the Trade Union and Labour Relations Act 1974, s.17(1), *post*, p. 723.

[46] Every weekday in term is a motion day in the Chancery Division: see *Practice Direction* [1980] 1 W.L.R. 741. For procedure, see *Practice Direction* [1983] 1 W.L.R. 433.

[47] [1967] Ch. 512.

[48] [1972] 1 W.L.R. 1373; see also *Beese* v. *Woodhouse* [1970] 1 W.L.R. 586.

the meeting for some weeks and had therefore had the opportunity to give notice.

In family matters injunctions should not be granted *ex parte* unless there is "real immediate danger of serious injury or irreparable damage."[49] Only in the most exceptional circumstances will an injunction be granted *ex parte* requiring a spouse to leave the matrimonial home.[50]

In the commercial sphere, *ex parte* injunctions should not normally be granted which will prevent banks from honouring contractual obligations, such as payouts under letters of credit.[51]

The *ex parte* procedure has been found most useful in the *Anton Piller* and *Mareva* cases, where there is a danger that the defendant, if aware of the application, would destroy or remove vital evidence, or move assets out of the jurisdiction. These developments are discussed below.[52]

(b) *Discharge of Interlocutory Injunctions.* The court has inherent jurisdiction to discharge an interlocutory injunction, even when the defendant against whom it was granted has not applied for its discharge.[53] Furthermore, where an injunction has been granted which affects someone who was not a party to the action, he can apply to court for the variation or discharge of the injunction.[54]

If an interlocutory injunction is granted, the plaintiff has no right to its continuance if it becomes apparent that it was based on a wrong view of the law.[55]

(c) *Injunctions Pending Appeal.* In *Erinford Properties Ltd.* v. *Cheshire County Council,*[56] it was held that where a claim for an interlocutory injunction is dismissed, the judge does not become *functus officio* but has jurisdiction to grant a limited injunction pending an appeal, on the plaintiff's *ex parte* application. Megarry J. rejected the argument that such a course was inconsistent with his decision on the main motion. Dismissal indicated that the plaintiff had not made out a

---

[49] *Practice Note* [1978] 1 W.L.R. 925; *Ansah* v. *Ansah* [1977] Fam. 138.

[50] *Masich* v. *Masich* (1977) 121 S.J. 645; (1977) 7 Fam.Law 245.

[51] *Bolivinter Oil S.A.* v. *Chase Manhattan Bank* [1984] 1 W.L.R. 392n.

[52] *Post,* pp. 766, 770.

[53] *R.D. Harbottle (Mercantile) Ltd.* v. *National Westminster Bank Ltd.* [1978] Q.B. 146 (*ex parte* injunction). Similarly an undertaking in lieu of an injunction; *Butt* v. *Butt* [1987] 1 W.L.R. 1351.

[54] *Cretanor Maritime Co. Ltd.* v. *Irish Marine Management Ltd.* [1978] 1 W.L.R. 966; *Iraqi Ministry of Defence* v. *Arcepey Shipping Co. S.A.* [1981] Q.B. 65, *post,* p. 776 (*Mareva* injunctions).

[55] *Regent Oil Co. Ltd.* v. *J.T. Leavesley (Lichfield) Ltd.* [1966] 1 W.L.R. 1210 (solus agreement).

[56] [1974] Ch. 261; *Chartered Bank* v. *Daklouche* [1980] 1 W.L.R. 107. See also *Att.-Gen.* v. *Jonathan Cape Ltd.* [1976] Q.B. 752 (an interim injunction may be granted while the losing party considers whether or not to appeal from a decision to refuse a perpetual injunction); *Att.-Gen.* v. *Guardian Newspapers Ltd. (No. 2)* [1988] 2 W.L.R. 805 (C.A.).

sufficient case to restrain the defendant *until trial*. But where an injunction pending appeal was sought, the issue was whether the judgment was one on which the successful party should be free to act despite the pendency of the appeal. The possibility of the decision being reversed or varied must be considered, if damages would be an inadequate remedy. The limited injunction was therefore granted, in order that the appeal, if successful, was not nugatory.

(d) *Complete Relief*. It is no objection that the grant of an interlocutory injunction gives complete relief to the plaintiff without requiring him to prove his case, so that he need bring no final action.[57] In *Woodford* v. *Smith*,[58] Megarry J. granted an interlocutory injunction to restrain a residents' association from breaking its contract by holding a meeting without permitting the plaintiff members to attend and vote. There was nothing to prevent the court in a proper case from granting on motion all the relief claimed in the action. It may be a more serious objection in the case of mandatory interlocutory injunctions,[59] where positive action is required, but in *Evans* v. *B.B.C. and I.B.A.*[60] a mandatory interlocutory injunction was granted to enforce the Welsh Nationalist Party's alleged contractual right to a Party Political Broadcast on television just before an election. The interlocutory injunction was thus a complete remedy, making it unnecessary to continue to trial and prove the case.

(e) *Injunction Ineffective*. As equity does not act in vain, an interlocutory injunction will not be granted where it would be of no effect.[61] In *Bentley-Stevens* v. *Jones*[62] a director was removed by irregular proceedings in that no valid notice had been served on him. This was not a case for an interlocutory injunction, as the irregularities could be cured by going through the proper processes and serving a valid notice; the result therefore would be the same.

(ii) **Principles Applicable to the Issue of Interlocutory Injunctions.** As in the case of mandatory injunctions, the interlocutory injunction is discretionary and is never granted as of course. Prior to the decision of the House of Lords in *American Cyanamid Co.* v. *Ethicon Ltd.*,[63]

---

[57] As to whether the principle of *American Cyanamid Co.* v. *Ethicon Ltd.*, *infra*, applies in such cases, see *post*, p. 725.

[58] [1970] 1 W.L.R. 806; see also *Manchester Corporation* v. *Connolly* [1970] Ch. 420, where there was plainly no defence.

[59] *Locabail International Finance Ltd.* v. *Agroexport* [1986] 1 W.L.R. 657.

[60] *The Times*, February 26, 1974. See also *Shepherd Homes Ltd.* v. *Sandham* [1971] Ch. 340 at p. 347, and *Acrow (Automation) Ltd.* v. *Rex Chainbelt Inc.* [1971] 1 W.L.R. 1676 at p. 1683.

[61] Similarly with final injunctions; *Att.-Gen.* v. *Guardian Newspapers Ltd. (No. 2)* [1988] 3 W.L.R. 776.

[62] [1974] 1 W.L.R. 638.

[63] [1975] A.C. 396; (1975) 38 M.L.R. 672 (A. Gore); (1976) 35 C.L.J. 82 (P. Wallington); (1975) 91 L.Q.R. 168 (P. Prescott); (1975) 4 I.L.J. 239 (P. L. Davies); (1981) 40 C.L.J. 307 (C. Gray).

discussed below, it was well established, and indeed accepted by the House of Lords in *J.T. Stratford & Son Ltd.* v. *Lindley*,[64] that the plaintiff had to show a strong prima facie case that his rights had been infringed. He was then required to show that damages would not be an adequate remedy if he succeeded at the trial, and that the balance of convenience favoured the grant. In other words, an interlocutory injunction would not be granted unless the plaintiff could show that it was more likely than not that he would succeed in obtaining a final injunction at the trial.

(a) *The Decision in American Cyanamid Co.* v. *Ethicon Ltd.*[65] The principles mentioned above have been replaced by the rules laid down by Lord Diplock in *American Cyanamid*, which were "designed to circumvent the necessity of deciding disputed facts or determining points of law without hearing sufficient argument."[66] The case concerned an application for a *quia timet* interlocutory injunction to restrain the infringement of a patent. It was unanimously held that there was no rule requiring the plaintiff to establish a prima facie case.[67] The rule is that the court must be satisfied that the plaintiff's case is not frivolous or vexatious and that there is a serious question to be tried. Once that is established, the governing consideration is the balance of convenience. The court should not embark on anything resembling a trial of the action. At the interlocutory stage it is no part of the court's function to resolve conflicts of evidence on affidavit nor to resolve difficult questions of law.[68] These are matters for the trial. At the interlocutory stage the facts may be disputed and the evidence incomplete and there is no cross-examination; the court's discretion would be stultified if, on untested and incomplete evidence, it could only grant the injunction if the plaintiff had shown that he was more than 50 per cent. likely to succeed at trial.

While the balance of convenience is the governing consideration, a significant factor in assessing it is the inadequacy of damages to each party. If that does not provide an answer, then other aspects of the balance of convenience will arise. If the balance of convenience does not clearly favour either party, then the preservation of the status quo will be decisive.[69] Only as a last resort is it proper to consider the

---

[64] [1965] A.C. 269, especially at p. 338 (Lord Upjohn). The contrary was not there argued.

[65] [1975] A.C. 396.

[66] *Smith* v. *Inner London Education Authority* [1978] 1 All E.R. 411, at p. 426 (*per* Geoffrey Lane L.J.).

[67] But Lord Diplock himself had said that an applicant for an interlocutory injunction had to show a "strong prima facie case" that he would succeed at trial: *Hoffman-LaRoche (F.) & Co.* v. *Secretary of State for Trade and Industry* [1975] A.C. 295 at p. 360.

[68] *Derby & Co. Ltd.* v. *Weldon, The Times,* August 2, 1988. See also *Porter* v. *National Union of Journalists, The Times,* July 30, 1980 (H.L.).

[69] This was once held to be the governing consideration: *Harman Pictures N.V.* v. *Osborne* [1967] 1 W.L.R. 723.

relative strength of the cases of both parties, and only then if it appears
from the facts set out in the affidavit evidence, as to which there is no
credible dispute, that the strength of one party's case is disproportionate to that of the other.[70] Finally, other special factors may have to be
considered in individual cases.

Thus it will be seen that there is a series of rules, most of which will
apply only if the previous one has not afforded a solution. But, as
Browne L.J. stated in *Fellowes & Son* v. *Fisher*,[71] the remedy is
discretionary and the principles enunciated by Lord Diplock contain
some elements of flexibility. The House of Lords cannot have intended
to lay down rigid rules.[72] They are best described as guidelines.[73]

But the new principles have not satisfied everybody. We have seen
that the House of Lords in *J.T. Stratford & Son Ltd.* v. *Lindley*[74] had
required a plaintiff seeking an interlocutory injunction to establish a
prima facie case. The point was not argued, but the decision reflected a
practice which had been settled for many years. Lord Denning M.R. in
Fellowes & Son v. *Fisher*[75] expressed a preference for the "prima facie
case" approach, because most cases never went to trial,[76] as the parties
usually accepted the court's prima facie view, which was a sensible and
convenient practice. A prima facie case had been required for a
century, and *American Cyanamid*[77] was not reconcilable with the
decision of the House of Lords in *Stratford*. Other members of the
Court of Appeal in *Fellowes & Son* v. *Fisher* agreed that *American
Cyanamid* seemed to conflict with *Stratford*, and expressed the need
for further guidance, as the new rules were a complete departure from
previous practice. But the majority of the Court of Appeal in *Hubbard*
v. *Pitt*[78] considered that the *American Cyanamid* principles were convenient and had often been adopted, adding that, in any event, the

---

[70] See *Cambridge Nutrition Ltd.* v. *British Broadcasting Corporation, The Times,*
December 5, 1987.

[71] [1976] Q.B. 122 at p. 139.

[72] See also the earlier decision of *Hubbard* v. *Vosper* [1972] 2 Q.B. 84, advocating the
flexibility of the remedy, and referred to with apparent approval by Lord Diplock in
American Cyanamid [1975] A.C. 396 at p. 407.

[73] *Cayne* v. *Global Natural Resources plc* [1984] 1 All E.R. 225.

[74] [1965] A.C. 269. Megaw L.J. in *The Camellia* [1976] 2 Lloyd's Rep. 546 at p. 548, said
the decision in *American Cyanamid, supra,* was not intended to overrule *Stratford,*
nor to disapprove the reasoning or approach of the House of Lords in that case.
Stratford, however, was not cited in *American Cyanamid.*

[75] [1976] Q.B. 122.

[76] See *British Broadcasting Corporation* v. *Hearn* [1977] 1 W.L.R. 1004; *Dunford &
Elliott Ltd.* v. *Johnson & Firth Brown Ltd.* [1977] 1 Lloyd's Rep. 505 at p. 513. *Cayne*
v. *Global Natural Resources plc.* [1984] 1 All E.R. 225; *cf. Dimbleby & Sons Ltd.* v.
National Union of Journalists [1984] 1 W.L.R. 427, *post,* p. 725. The *Stratford* case
itself never came to trial; see *J.T. Stratford & Sons Ltd.* v. *Lindley (No. 2)* [1969] 1
W.L.R. 1547. Even if there is to be a trial, *American Cyanamid* applies even though
the interlocutory decision might influence the trial, without any prima facie case
having been established; see *Budget Rent A Car International Inc.* v. *Mamos Slough
Ltd.* (1977) 121 S.J. 374.

[77] [1975] A.C. 396.

[78] [1976] Q.B. 142. Lord Denning M.R. dissented.

House of Lords could depart from its own decisions. If *American Cyanamid* conflicted with the *Stratford* case, the Court of Appeal must follow *American Cyanamid*, as it was later.

The principles laid down by Lord Diplock in *American Cyanamid* were these:

(i) PLAINTIFF'S CASE NOT FRIVOLOUS OR VEXATIOUS. This requirement was designed to remove "any attempt by plaintiffs to harass defendants, any case which was futile and any case which was misconceived or an abuse of the process of the court."[79] Such claims fail *in limine*. The plaintiff must also show that there is a serious question to be tried, which means that he must have a good arguable case,[80] or, in other words, a real prospect of success at the trial.[81]

(ii) THE BALANCE OF CONVENIENCE. This concept was well known before the decision in *American Cyanamid*,[82] thus the earlier cases remain useful illustrations, but it must be borne in mind that this is now the governing consideration, assuming that the preliminary require-ment outlined above is satisfied.

We have seen that the inadequacy of damages is a significant factor in assessing the balance of convenience.[83] The court must first of all consider the adequacy of damages to each party, and will not grant an interlocutory injunction if damages would adequately compensate the plaintiff for any loss caused by the acts of the defendant prior to the trial.[84] This is not unlike the position prior to *American Cyanamid*,[85] when the plaintiff had to show that if the injunction was refused, he would suffer substantial and irreparable injury that could not be compensated if he succeeded at the trial. From the defendant's point of view, the court must consider whether, should the plaintiff fail at the trial, any loss caused to the defendant by the grant of the injunction could be adequately compensated by the plaintiff's undertaking in damages.[86]

An example of irreparable loss is the distribution of a dividend to

---

[79] *Honeywell Information Systems Ltd.* v. *Anglian Water Authority, The Times*, June 29, 1976 (Geoffrey Lane L.J.).

[80] *Morning Star Cooperative Society Ltd.* v. *Express Newspapers Ltd., The Times*, October 18, 1978; *The Camellia* [1976] 2 Lloyd's Rep. 546; *cf. Derby & Co. Ltd.* v. *Weldon, The Times*, August 2, 1988; *post*, p. 774.

[81] *Re Lord Cable* [1977] 1 W.L.R. 7 at p. 20; *Smith* v. *Inner London Education Authority* [1978] 1 All E.R. 411 (the same test applies where the defendant is a public body); *Mothercare Ltd.* v. *Robson Books Ltd.* [1979] F.S.R. 466; *Cayne* v. *Global Natural Resources plc, supra.* See also *Carlton Realty Co. Ltd.* v. *Maple Leaf Mills Ltd.* (1979) 93 D.L.R. (3d) 106 ("serious question to be tried" means prima facie case).

[82] [1975] A.C. 396.

[83] But not conclusive; *Potters-Ballotini Ltd.* v. *Weston-Baker* [1977] R.P.C. 202.

[84] See *Lion Laboratories Ltd.* v. *Evans* [1985] Q.B. 526.

[85] *Supra.*

[86] *Chancellor, Masters and Scholars of the University of Oxford* v. *Pergamon Press Ltd.* (1977) 121 S.J. 758. See also *Laws* v. *Florinpace Ltd.* [1981] 1 All E.R. 659 (injunction to restrain nuisance by running "sex shop" in residential area).

shareholders on the basis of supposedly erroneous calculations.[87] Another is the loss of trade when members of the public "picketed" the plaintiff's business premises,[88] or when a trade union proposed unlawfully to induce the plaintiff's employees to break their contracts by supporting a political strike[89]; the loss cannot be measured, but it may be great. Similarly, the publication of confidential material,[90] or the loss of a job with good prospects.[91] Damages will also be inadequate if the defendant is a foreign company whose government's exchange control may not permit the payment, or is a foreign company of unknown financial status so that the chances of any substantial damages being paid are questionable.[92] Likewise if an individual defendant does not have the means to pay any appreciable damages,[93] or if the damages would be unquantifiable,[94] as in the case of injury to goodwill[95] or reputation.[96]

While the adequacy of damages is a most significant factor, other considerations may be taken into account in assessing the balance of convenience. Where the dispute between the parties is a political one, the damage to both parties may not be calculable in monetary terms.[97] All the circumstances must be considered, including difficulties of compliance or enforcement, and the principle that the court should be reluctant to interfere in industrial disputes[98] or political decisions[99] by injunction. In *Smith* v. *Inner London Education Authority*,[1] where an interlocutory injunction was sought to restrain an alleged breach of

---

[87] *Bloxham* v. *Metropolitan Ry.* (1868) L.R. 3 Ch.App. 337.

[88] *Hubbard* v. *Pitt* [1976] Q.B. 142, *post*, p. 721. See also *Cutsforth* v. *Mansfield Inns Ltd.* [1986] 1 W.L.R. 558.

[89] *Express Newspapers Ltd.* v. *Keys* [1980] I.R.L.R. 247.

[90] *Att.-Gen.* v. *Times Newspapers Ltd.*, *The Times*, June 27, 1975 (The Crossman Diaries); *Att.-Gen.* v. *Guardian Newspapers Ltd.* [1987] 1 W.L.R. 1248 (*Spycatcher*). But the perpetual injunctions were refused: *Att.-Gen.* v. *Jonathan Cape Ltd.* [1976] Q.B. 752; *Att.-Gen.* v. *Guardian Newspapers (No. 2)* [1988] 3 W.L.R. 776.

[91] *Fellowes & Son* v. *Fisher* [1976] Q.B. 122, *post*, p. 721; *Powell* v. *London Borough of Brent* [1987] I.R.L.R. 466.

[92] *Evans Marshall & Co. Ltd.* v. *Bertola S.A.* [1973] 1 W.L.R. 349.

[93] *Morning Star Cooperative Society Ltd.* v. *Express Newspapers Ltd.*, *The Times*, October 18, 1978; *De Falco* v. *Crawley Borough Council* [1980] Q.B. 460 (no injunction where plaintiff could not give worthwhile undertaking in damages). See also *Thomas Marshall (Exports) Ltd.* v. *Guinle* [1979] Ch. 227.

[94] *Morning Star Cooperative Society Ltd.* v. *Express Newspapers Ltd.*, *supra*. See also *Express Newspapers Ltd.* v. *Keys*, *supra*.

[95] *Chancellor, Masters and Scholars of the University of Oxford* v. *Pergamon Press Ltd.* (1977) 121 S.J. 758; *Kerr* v. *Morris* [1987] Ch. 90.

[96] *British Broadcasting Corporation* v. *Hearn* [1977] 1 W.L.R. 1004. (Injunction to restrain interference with plaintiff's broadcast of the Cup Final to South Africa); *Savoy Hotel plc* v. *British Broadcasting Corporation*, *The Times*, December 17, 1982; *Schering Chemicals Ltd.* v. *Falkman Ltd.* [1982] Q.B. 1.

[97] See *Lewis* v. *Heffer* [1978] 1 W.L.R. 1061. Geoffrey Lane L.J., at p. 1078, found great difficulty in applying *American Cyanamid* in such a case.

[98] *Meade* v. *London Borough of Haringey* [1979] 1 W.L.R. 637, *ante*, p. 710.

[99] *Walsh* v. *McCluskie*, *The Times*, December 16, 1982.

[1] [1978] 1 All E.R. 411. (Injunction to restrain phasing out of grammar schools refused.)

statutory duty, it was said that where the defendant is a public body, the balance of convenience must be looked at more widely; the court must consider the interests of the general public to whom the duty is owed. The public interest was also a relevant consideration in *Express Newspapers Ltd.* v. *Keys*,[2] where an interlocutory injunction was granted to restrain a trade union from unlawfully inducing a breach of contract by the plaintiff's employees, by persuading them to support the "Day of Action," a political strike. Where it was clear that the defendant was acting unlawfully,[3] "it would require wholly exceptional circumstances to justify a proper exercise of the discretion to allow such conduct to continue." If the injunction was refused, the plaintiff would suffer unquantifiable damage, whereas if it was granted, the union would suffer no harm save political embarrassment. It was in the interest of the members of the union and of the public that the injunction be granted.

If the balance of convenience does not clearly favour either party, then, as we have seen, the deciding factor will be the preservation of the status quo,[4] which means the circumstances prevailing when the defendant began the activity which the plaintiff seeks to restrain.[5]

We have also seen that the relative strength of each party's case is a factor to be considered as a last resort, and only then if the strength of one party's case is disproportionate to that of the other.[6] Prior to the decision in *American Cyanamid*,[7] however, this was a vital consideration: the plaintiff had to show a strong prima facie case.[8] This departure from the previous practice was regarded as a source of difficulty by the Court of Appeal in *Fellowes & Son* v. *Fisher*,[9] where it was felt that the relative strength of the parties must be a factor in assessing the balance of convenience, and that sometimes the court could not do

---

[2] [1980] I.R.L.R. 247, *ante*, p. 707.

[3] See also *Thanet District Council* v. *Ninedrive Ltd.* [1978] 1 All E.R. 703; interlocutory injunction granted to restrain plain breach of statute where defendant making profits by flouting the statute (Sunday trading) which he could not be required to disgorge.

[4] See *Lewis* v. *Heffer* [1978] 1 W.L.R. 1061; *Chancellor, Masters and Scholars of the University of Oxford* v. *Pergamon Press Ltd.* (1977) 121 S.J. 758.

[5] *Fellowes & Son* v. *Fisher* [1976] Q.B. 122 at p. 141 (Sir John Pennycuick); *Budget Rent A Car International Inc.* v. *Mamos Slough Ltd.* (1977) 121 S.J. 374 (Geoffrey Lane L.J.); *Garden Cottage Foods Ltd.* v. *Milk Marketing Board* [1984] A.C. 130. But delay by the plaintiff will be taken into account in considering this principle: *Shepherd Homes Ltd.* v. *Sandham* [1971] Ch. 340, *post*, p. 734.

[6] Relative strength was held the governing factor in *Cambridge Nutrition Ltd.* v. *British Broadcasting Corporation, The Times,* December 5, 1987, where neither party could be adequately compensated by damages.

[7] [1975] A.C. 396.

[8] See, for example, *Hubbard* v. *Vosper* [1972] 2 Q.B. 84. Relative strength is still a governing consideration in Scotland, where *American Cyanamid* does not apply. See (1980) 43 M.L.R. 327 (R. C. Simpson); s.17(3) of the Trade Union and Labour Relations Act 1974.

[9] [1976] Q.B. 122, *infra*.

justice without considering the merits. The view was expressed that perhaps the House of Lords had not had all types of cases in mind.[10]

(iii) OTHER SPECIAL FACTORS. Lord Diplock in *American Cyanamid*[11] concluded his exposition of the guiding principles by saying, as we have seen, that "other special factors" may have to be considered in individual cases. A question which arises is whether these special factors are merely an aspect of the balance of convenience, or whether they justify a departure from the principles laid down in *American Cyanamid* and a return to the previous practice of requiring a prima facie case.

In *Fellowes & Son* v. *Fisher*,[12] the plaintiffs, a firm of solicitors, sought to restrain the breach of a restrictive covenant in the contract of a former employee. The covenant was of doubtful validity, but there was a serious question to be tried. As there was no evidence as to the adequacy of damages to either party, the decisive factor, according to the majority of the Court of Appeal, was the balance of convenience, which favoured refusal of the injunction.

Lord Denning M.R., refusing the injunction on different grounds, did not feel bound by *American Cyanamid*.[13] There were two escape routes from it. First, Lord Diplock had indicated that other special factors could be considered in individual cases. These "individual cases" were numerous and important, and included the present case. Secondly, the relative strength of the parties could be looked at where the court found that there was little difference in the uncompensatable disadvantages to both sides. The present case was therefore governed by *J.T. Stratford & Son Ltd.* v. *Lindley*[14] rather than *American Cyanamid*, and the injunction should be refused because there was no prima facie case.

The question next arose in *Hubbard* v. *Pitt*.[15]

Certain members of the public disapproved of the extensive development which had taken place in Islington, and they organised a protest regularly outside a leading firm of estate agents which had acted in connection with many land developments in the area. The pickets held placards and distributed leaflets to passers-by, thus impeding access to the premises, and deterring potential clients. The estate agents obtained an injunction to restrain them and this was upheld by the majority of the Court of Appeal.

[10] Possible special cases are dealt with below.
[11] *Supra.*
[12] [1976] Q.B. 122.
[13] [1975] A.C. 396.
[14] [1965] A.C. 269.
[15] [1976] Q.B. 142; (1976) 35 C.L.J. 82 (P. Wallington).

There was a serious question to be tried, and the balance of convenience favoured the grant. Damages could not compensate the plaintiffs for loss of business, even if the defendants could pay, whereas the injunction would not prevent a legitimate campaign. The majority held that there were no circumstances in which "special factors" would take a case out of the general rule that no prima facie case was required. "It appears to me clear beyond peradventure that Lord Diplock was there referring to special factors affecting the balance of convenience and not to special factors enabling the court to ignore the general principles laid down or, more particularly, to ignore ... the admonition not to require of a party seeking an interlocutory injunction that he should have made out a prima facie case."[16] But Lord Denning M.R., dissenting on the ground that such picketing was lawful, again held that "special factors" took the case out of the *American Cyanamid*[17] rules. In his view a prima facie case was required, and the relative strength of each party could be considered. The appeal should be allowed because the injunction would interfere with free speech and the right to demonstrate and protest.

The better view, it is submitted, is that "special factors" are merely an aspect of the balance of convenience. But there have been few illustrations of "special factors." In *Smith* v. *Inner London Education Authority*[18] it was held, as we have seen, that where the defendant is a public body, the balance of convenience must be looked at more widely, and the interests of the general public, to whom the defendant's duties are owed, must be considered. This was treated as a "special factor." Similarly, interlocutory injunctions against officers of the Crown may be governed by different considerations.[19]

It has long been established that interlocutory injunctions will rarely be granted in libel cases where the defendant intends to justify.[20] It has been held that *American Cyanamid*[21] has not affected this principle,[22] which might, therefore, be regarded as a "special factor." Special

---

[16] *Ibid.* at p. 185, *per* Stamp L.J.

[17] *Supra.*

[18] [1978] 1 All. E.R. 411; applied in *R.* v. *Westminster City Council, ex p. Sierbien, The Times*, March 30, 1987. See also *Lewis* v. *Heffer* [1978] 1 W.L.R. 1061, *supra*; *Bryanston Finance Ltd.* v. *de Vries (No. 2)* [1976] Ch. 63, *infra.*

[19] *R.* v. *Secretary of State for the Home Department, ex p. Herbage* [1987] Q.B. 872.

[20] *Bonnard* v. *Perryman* [1891] 2 Ch. 269, *post*, p. 753. See also *Hubbard* v. *Vosper* [1972] 2 Q.B. 84 (similarly in copyright actions where there is a reasonable defence of fair dealing).

[21] [1975] A.C. 396.

[22] *J. Trevor & Sons* v. *P. R. Solomon* (1978) 248 E.G. 779 (*per* Lord Denning M.R.); *Bestobell Paints Ltd.* v. *Bigg* (1975) 119 S.J. 678; *Herbage* v. *Pressdram Ltd.* [1984] 1 W.L.R. 1160; *Att.-Gen.* v. *British Broadcasting Corporation* [1981] A.C. 303 at p. 311 (C.A) (expressing a similar principle as to contempt in civil actions); [1981] A.C. 303 at p. 342 (H.L.); *Gulf Oil (Great Britain) Ltd.* v. *Page* [1987] Ch. 327.

considerations affecting the grant of *Mareva* and *Anton Piller* interlocutory injunctions are discussed elsewhere.[23]

(b) *Exceptional cases.* The following might be considered as cases where the *American Cyanamid*[24] principles do not apply, or apply in modified form.

(i) TRADE DISPUTES. The Trade Union and Labour Relations Act 1974, s.17(1), provides that an *ex parte* injunction shall not be granted in a case where it is likely that the defendant would plead that he acted in contemplation or furtherance of a trade dispute unless all reasonable steps have been taken to give notice and an opportunity to be heard to the defendant.[25]

After the decision in *American Cyanamid*,[26] subsection 2 was added to section 17,[27] which provides that where, in an application for an interlocutory injunction, the defendant claims that he acted in contemplation or furtherance of a trade dispute, the court in exercising its discretion is to have regard to the likelihood of the defendant's establishing at the trial any of the matters which, under the 1974 Act, confer immunity from tortious liability.[28] Thus *American Cyanamid* is modified in trade dispute cases by the opportunity for the defendant to prove a prima facie defence under the 1974 Act.

The reason for this amendment was that applications for injunctions in industrial disputes rarely went beyond the interlocutory stage, and if *American Cyanamid*[29] was applied without modification, the balance of convenience would invariably favour the plaintiff (*i.e.* the employer),[30] thus denying the trade unions their power to pressurise employers. Industrial action is unlikely to be effective if it has to be postponed, thus the unions' bargaining counter would disappear. In view of the immunity from liability in tort mentioned above, this might be thought to be unfair.[31] But trade dispute cases should not be

---

[23] *Post,* pp. 766, 770. See *The Niedersachsen* [1983] 1 W.L.R. 1412; *Derby & Co. Ltd.* v. *Weldon, The Times,* August 2, 1988.

[24] *Supra.*

[25] The application of this provision does not depend on whether there is in fact a trade dispute; see *Gouriet* v. *Union of Post Office Workers* [1978] A.C. 435 at p. 487; (1978) 41 M.L.R. 63 (R. C. Simpson).

[26] *Supra.*

[27] By the Employment Protection Act 1975, Sched. 16. See also Employment Act 1980, s.17(8). s.17(1) and (2) of the 1974 Act have been said to have made little impact; (1987) 50 M.L.R. 506 (B. Simpson), discussing *Barretts & Baird (Wholesalers) Ltd.* v. *I.P.C.S.* [1987] I.R.L.R. 3.

[28] See ss.13, 15.

[29] [1975] A.C. 396.

[30] Especially in public service disputes, where the interest of the public is relevant to the balance of convenience; see *Beaverbrook Newspapers Ltd.* v. *Keys* [1978] I.R.L.R. 34.

[31] See *N.W.L. Ltd.* v. *Woods* [1979] 1 W.L.R. 1294; (1980) 43 M.L.R. 327 (R. C. Simpson); (1980) 96 L.Q.R. 189 (A. Clarke and J. Bowers). *Woods* was regarded as of general application and not confined to s.17 in *Cayne* v. *Global Natural Resources plc.* [1984] 1 All E.R. 225; *post,* p. 725.

approached on the basis that they will not go to trial.[32] Since the Employment Act 1982 the injunction may be sought against the union itself, as opposed to an office-holder personally, which increases the likelihood of a trial.[33]

A question which arises is whether section 17(2) restores the previous law, requiring a prima facie case, to interlocutory injunctions concerning trade disputes,[34] or whether it merely adds an extra element to the *American Cyanamid*[35] principles. It is submitted that the latter is the correct approach.[36] Sometimes the likelihood of the defendant's establishing the defence of statutory immunity has been regarded simply as an aspect of the balance of convenience.[37] Perhaps the better view[38] is that it adds a third stage to the enquiry. Thus the court must consider first whether there is a serious question to be tried, secondly the balance of convenience, and thirdly the likelihood of the establishment of the defence of statutory immunity.[39]

Section 17(2) requires the court to "have regard" to the likelihood of the defence of statutory immunity succeeding at the trial. Thus the injunction will not normally be granted where the likelihood is that this defence would succeed.[40] But even in such a case the court retains a residual discretion which it may exercise in favour of granting the injunction, for example if the industrial action "endangers the nation or puts at risk such fundamental rights as the right of the public to be informed and the freedom of the Press,"[41] or "would probably have an immediate and devastating effect on the applicant's person or property" or would "cause immediate serious danger to public safety or health."[42] But such cases would be "altogether exceptional," because "When disaster threatens, it is ordinarily for the government, not the

---

[32] *Hadmor Productions Ltd* v. *Hamilton* [1983] 1 A.C. 191; *Dimbleby & Sons Ltd.* v. *National Union of Journalists* [1984] 1 W.L.R. 427; (1984) 100 L.Q.R. 342 (H. Carty).

[33] *Post*, p. 725.

[34] See *The Camilla M* [1979] 1 Lloyd's Rep. 26; (1979) 42 M.L.R. 458 (B. Doyle).

[35] *Supra.*

[36] See *N.W.L. Ltd.* v. *Woods* [1979] 1 W.L.R. 1294; *British Broadcasting Corporation* v. *Hearn* [1977] 1 W.L.R. 1004; (1978) 41 M.L.R. 80 (Lord Wedderburn); (1977) 127 N.L.J. 654 (R. Kidner); *Hadmor Productions Ltd.* v. *Hamilton, supra.*

[37] *N.W.L. Ltd.* v. *Woods, supra* (Lords Diplock and Fraser).

[38] So considered by Lord Wedderburn in (1978) 41 M.L.R. 80 and (1980) 43 M.L.R. 319. See also (1980) 43 M.L.R. 372 (R. C. Simpson).

[39] *British Broadcasting Corporation* v. *Hearn* [1977] 1 W.L.R. 1004 at p. 1016 (Scarman L.J.); *N.W.L. Ltd.* v. *Woods, supra,* at p. 1315 (Lord Scarman).

[40] As to the degree of likelihood necessary to produce this result, see *Duport Steels Ltd.* v. *Sirs* [1980] 1 W.L.R. 142; *Examite Ltd.* v. *Whittaker* [1977] I.R.L.R. 312; (1980) 43 M.L.R. 327 (R. C. Simpson); *Hadmor Productions Ltd.* v. *Hamilton* [1983] 1 A.C. 191; *Monsanto plc* v. *Transport and General Workers' Union* [1987] 1 W.L.R. 617.

[41] *Express Newspapers Ltd.* v. *MacShane* [1980] A.C. 672 at p. 695 (Lord Scarman). See also the views of Lords Diplock and Scarman in *N.W.L. Ltd.* v. *Woods* [1979] 1 W.L.R. 1294; *Health Computing Ltd.* v. *Meek* [1980] I.R.L.R. 437.

[42] *Duport Steel Ltd.* v. *Sirs* [1980] 1 W.L.R. 142 at p. 166 (Lord Fraser).

courts, to act to avert it."[43] Where it is unlikely that the defence of statutory immunity will be established, it does not always follow that an injunction is appropriate, for example if it would be of no practical use.[44]

(ii) WHERE TRIAL OF THE ACTION UNLIKELY. We have seen that Lord Denning M.R. in *Fellowes & Son* v. *Fisher*[45] preferred the "prima facie case" approach to the principles laid down in *American Cyanamid*[46] because most cases never went to trial; and also that amendment was required in the area of trade disputes for the same reason.[47] It has since been held by the Court of Appeal in *Cayne* v. *Global Natural Resources plc*[48] that the *American Cyanamid* principles do not apply to cases where no trial is likely to take place. If the grant or refusal would have the practical effect of ending the action, the court should approach the matter on the broad principle of what it can do to avoid injustice. Whatever the strengths of either side, the defendant should not be precluded by the grant of an interlocutory injunction from disputing the claim at trial. Otherwise it would mean effectively giving judgment without the right of trial. An exceptional case would be where the plaintiff's case was so overwhelming that it would be a waste of time and expense to go to trial.

In the area of trade disputes, however, it is now possible to obtain an injunction and damages against the union itself as opposed to an office-holder personally, and to obtain substantial damages, with no limit on costs, fines or sequestration of assets for breach of the injunction.[49] This means that there is no reason for a judge to exercise his discretion on the assumption that the case will not proceed to trial in cases where the union itself is the defendant.[50]

(iii) WHERE NO ARGUABLE DEFENCE. It has been held that the *American Cyanamid*[51] rules do not apply where the defendant has no arguable defence.[52] In such a case it is not necessary to consider the

---

[43] *Ibid.* at p. 171 (Lord Scarman). But the existence of this residual discretion may be open to challenge; see (1980) 43 M.L.R. 319 at p. 326 (Lord Wedderburn), and at p. 327 (R. C. Simpson).

[44] *Hadmor Productions Ltd.* v. *Hamilton, supra*; (1982) 45 M.L.R. 447 (R. C. Simpson).

[45] [1976] Q.B. 122; *ante*, p. 721.

[46] [1975] A.C. 396.

[47] *N.W.L. Ltd.* v. *Woods* [1979] 1 W.L.R. 1294; *ante*, p. 723.

[48] [1984] 1 All E.R. 225; *Thomas* v. *National Union of Mineworkers (South Wales Area)* [1986] Ch. 20; (1985) 44 C.L.J. 374 (K. D. Ewing); *Cambridge Nutrition Ltd.* v. *British Broadcasting Corporation, The Times,* December 5, 1987.

[49] Employment Act 1982, ss.15–17.

[50] *Dimbleby & Sons Ltd.* v. *National Union of Journalists* [1984] 1 W.L.R. 427; (1984) 100 L.Q.R. 342 (H. Carty); (1984) 47 M.L.R. 577 (B. Simpson); *Hadmor Productions Ltd.* v. *Hamilton* [1983] 1 A.C. 191. See also *Mercury Communications Ltd.* v. *Scott-Garner* [1984] Ch. 37.

[51] *Supra.*

[52] *Redler Grain Silos Ltd.* v. *B.I.C.C. Ltd.* [1982] 1 Lloyd's Rep. 435; *Official Custodian for Charities* v. *Mackey* [1985] Ch. 168.

balance of convenience. Thus the plaintiff may obtain an interlocutory injunction to restrain a clear trespass even where it causes no damage[53]; or to restrain a clear misapplication of union funds.[54] It is probable that the principle that the plaintiff is entitled almost as of right to an injunction to restrain a plain breach of a negative contract provides another example.[55]

(iv) INJUNCTIONS TO RESTRAIN THE PRESENTATION OF A WINDING-UP PETITION. It has been held that a prima face case (of abuse of process) is still required where a company seeks to restrain a creditor from presenting a winding-up petition.[56] If a prospective petitioner intends to petition on the basis of a debt alleged to be presently due, and there is a bona fide dispute as to whether it is presently due, it has been held by the Court of Appeal that the company is entitled as of right to an interlocutory injunction restraining the presentation of the petition, other than on the basis of a contingent or future debt.[57]

Difficulty was also experienced in applying the *American Cyanamid*[58] rules where a company sought an interlocutory injunction to restrain a takeover bid.[59]

(v) MANDATORY INTERLOCUTORY INJUNCTIONS. *American Cyanamid*[60] itself involved a prohibitory injunction, but the principles there expressed were not in terms confined to such applications. But it may still be said that mandatory interlocutory injunctions, which are discussed below,[61] will be granted less readily than the prohibitory, as was the case before *American Cyanamid*,[62] because the balance of convenience is likely to favour the refusal more often than the grant.[63] The *American Cyanamid*[64] principles have been applied to manda-

---

[53] *Patel* v. *W.H. Smith (Eziot) Ltd.* [1987] 1 W.L.R. 853; *Anchor Brewhouse Developments Ltd.* v. *Berkley House (Docklands Developments) Ltd.* [1987] 2 E.G.L.R. 173.
[54] *Taylor* v. *National Union of Mineworkers (Derbyshire Area), The Times,* December 29, 1984.
[55] *Doherty* v. *Allman* (1878) 3 App.Cas. 709; *post,* p. 743; applied to interlocutory injunctions in *Hampstead & Suburban Properties Ltd.* v. *Diomedous* [1969] 1 Ch. 248; cf. *Mike Trading and Transport Ltd.* v. *Pagnan* [1980] 2 Lloyd's Rep. 546.
[56] *Bryanston Finance Ltd.* v. *De Vries (No. 2)* [1976] Ch. 63. But Buckley L.J., at p. 78, regarded this as a "special factor." The other members of the Court of Appeal said that *American Cyanamid* did not apply. See (1976) 35 C.L.J. 82 at p. 86 (P. Wallington). *American Cyanamid* was applied, albeit with difficulty, in *Re Euro Hotel (Belgravia) Ltd.* [1975] 3 All E.R. 1075.
[57] *Stonegate Securities Ltd.* v. *Gregory* [1980] Ch. 576 (*American Cyanamid* was not cited).
[58] [1975] A.C. 396.
[59] *Dunford & Elliott Ltd.* v. *Johnson & Firth Brown Ltd.* [1977] 1 Lloyd's Rep. 505. Lord Denning M.R. held that the *American Cyanamid* principles did not apply, but Lawton and Roskill L.JJ. preferred to apply those principles, notwithstanding the difficulties.
[60] [1975] A.C. 396.
[61] *Post,* p. 728.
[62] *Supra.*
[63] See *Shotton* v. *Hammond* (1976) 120 S.J. 780.
[64] *Supra.*

tory injunctions,[65] but a strong prima facie case was required in *De Falco* v. *Crawley Borough Council*,[66] where the plaintiff sought a mandatory interlocutory injunction to secure the provision of accommodation by the defendant under the housing legislation. The Court of Appeal, refusing the injunction, held that the plaintiff had to show a strong prima facie case that the defendant's decision was invalid. Lord Denning M.R. held *American Cyanamid*[67] to be inapplicable because the plaintiff could not give a worthwhile undertaking in damages.[68] Bridge L.J. held that *American Cyanamid*, which governed the grant of prohibitory interlocutory injunctions, did not apply to the present case, which exhibited "sufficiently unusual features to make a comparison even with other types of litigation where a mandatory injunction may be granted on an interim application difficult and possibly misleading."[69] If the defendant was wrong, the plaintiff would suffer homelessness which was not compensatable in damages. But if the plaintiff was wrong, a heavy financial burden, with no prospect of recovery, would fall on the ratepayers, and there would also be a detriment to others on the housing list.[70] Therefore such an injunction should be granted only if the plaintiff had a strong prima facie case. It is submitted that *De Falco* is a special case because of the public law element. The Court of Appeal has recently stated, however, that the "high degree of assurance," required in *Shepherd Homes Ltd.* v. *Sandham*[71] for the grant of mandatory interlocutory injunctions, was not affected by the *American Cyanamid*[72] principles.[73]

Finally, the *Anton Piller* injunction,[74] which may be partly mandatory, has been held to require an extremely strong prima facie case.[75] This, it is submitted, is an exceptional case because such applications

---

[65] *Meade* v. *London Borough of Haringey* [1979] 1 W.L.R. 637. See also *Taylor Woodrow Construction (Midlands) Ltd.* v. *Charcon Structures Ltd.* (1983) 266 E.G. 40.

[66] [1980] Q.B. 460; overruled in *Cocks* v. *Thanet District Council* [1983] 2 A.C. 286, on the point that an application for judicial review was the appropriate remedy; *post*, p. 760. See also *Miller* v. *Wandsworth London Borough Council, The Times*, March 18, 1980. The requirement of a strong prima facie case was upheld in *R.* v. *Kensington and Chelsea Royal London Borough Council, ex p. Hammell, The Times*, August 25, 1988.

[67] *Supra.*

[68] [1980] Q.B. 460 at p. 478. This, it is submitted, might more properly be regarded as a factor in assessing the balance of convenience. See further Yates and Hawkins, *Landlord and Tenant Law* (2nd ed.), p. 631.

[69] *Ibid.* at p. 481.

[70] This, again, might be regarded simply as an aspect of the balance of convenience, without departing from *American Cyanamid*.

[71] [1971] Ch. 340; *post*, p. 729.

[72] *Supra.*

[73] *Locabail International Finance Ltd.* v. *Agroexport* [1986] 1 W.L.R. 657; *post*, p. 729.

[74] *Anton Piller K.G.* v. *Manufacturing Processes Ltd.* [1976] Ch. 55.

[75] *Post*, p. 768.

are usually *ex parte*, and because of the "draconian" nature of the injunction.[76]

(iii) **Mandatory Interlocutory Injunctions.** These are less readily granted than prohibitory interlocutory injunctions,[77] especially on an *ex parte* application, because the mandatory order is more drastic in effect. If the defendant has been required to do some positive act, it may not be easy to restore the parties to their previous position if the plaintiff turns out to be wrong at the trial.[78] It might be thought that mandatory interlocutory injunctions are necessarily inconsistent with the principle that interlocutory injunctions are for the preservation of the status quo, but this objection will be seen to be unfounded; it is the rights of the parties that must be preserved.

Mandatory interlocutory injunctions will be granted in a suitable case, for example, to compel the demolition of a building where the defendant has deliberately evaded service of the writ and has hurried on with the building,[79] to reinstate a wrongfully evicted contractual licensee to possession[80]; to enforce the return of passports wrongfully detained by the police[81]; to compel performance of a landlord's obligations[82]; or in the *Anton Piller* cases,[83] to compel the defendant to submit articles for inspection.

The court will be reluctant to grant such an injunction where the case involves an industrial dispute,[84] but will do so in exceptional circumstances if the balance of convenience so requires. Such a case was *Parker* v. *Camden London Borough Council*,[85] where a strike of boilermen was endangering the life and health of council tenants. The court was prepared to grant a mandatory interlocutory injunction to resume the supply of heating and hot water.

It has been held, in a case concerning trespass by building operations, that if the plaintiff could have got a prohibitory *quia timet* injunction to restrain the commission of the wrongful act, had he

---

[76] See *Yousif* v. *Salama* [1980] 1 W.L.R. 1540, at p. 1544 (*per* Donaldson L.J.) *post*, p. 767.

[77] *Daniel* v. *Ferguson* [1891] 2 Ch. 27; *Shotton* v. *Hammond* (1976) 120 S.J. 780.

[78] See *Shepherd Homes Ltd.* v. *Sandham* [1971] Ch. 340 at p. 349.

[79] *Von Joel* v. *Hornsey* [1895] 2 Ch. 774; *London & Manchester Assurance Co. Ltd.* v. *O. & H. Construction Ltd.* [1988] E.G.C.S. 41.

[80] *Luganda* v. *Service Hotels* [1969] 2 Ch. 209.

[81] *Ghani* v. *Jones* [1970] 1 Q.B. 693; *cf. Malone* v. *Metropolitan Police Commissioner* [1980] Q.B. 49.

[82] *Hart* v. *Emelkirk Ltd.* [1983] 1 W.L.R. 1289; *Peninsular Maritime Ltd.* v. *Padseal Ltd.* (1981) 259 E.G. 860.

[83] *Post*, p. 766.

[84] *Meade* v. *London Borough of Haringey* [1979] 1 W.L.R. 637; (1979) 38 C.L.J. 228 (J. Griffiths). (Schools were closed by a strike. There was, prima facie, a breach of the Education Act 1944, but only Lord Denning M.R. would have granted the injunction to compel the opening of the schools.) See also *Harold Stephen and Co. Ltd.* v. *Post Office* [1977] 1 W.L.R. 1172, *ante*, p. 710. *cf. Express Newspapers Ltd.* v. *Keys* [1980] I.R.L.R. 247, where the dispute was political.

[85] [1986] Ch. 162; *ante*, p. 711.

known about it in time, then the defendant should be in no better position if he in fact commits the act: a mandatory interlocutory injunction should be granted to enforce the removal of the building works.[86]

Modern decisions illustrate an increasing readiness to grant mandatory interlocutory injunctions. The principles were reviewed in *Shepherd Homes Ltd.* v. *Sandham*,[87] where the defendant erected a fence in breach of covenant, which the plaintiff sought to have removed. Megarry J. said that the case has to be unusually strong and clear before a mandatory interlocutory injunction will be granted. The court must feel "a high degree of assurance" that at the trial it will appear that the injunction was rightly granted, and this is a higher standard than is required for a prohibitory injunction. In view of the plaintiff's delay, the preservation of the status quo required that the injunction be refused. An injunction would disturb rather than preserve anything that could fairly be called the status quo.[88]

The "high degree of assurance" test has been approved by the Court of Appeal,[89] holding that although the test was formulated before *American Cyanamid Co.* v. *Ethicon Ltd.*,[90] it was unaffected by that case. It was added that the application should be approached with caution where the relief sought on the motion would amount to a major part of the relief claimed at the trial. Hoffman J. has since held that in exceptional cases, where the refusal of the injunction carried a greater risk of injustice than the grant, then the injunction should be granted even though the "high degree of assurance" test was not satisfied. That test is a guideline which applies in "normal" cases.[91]

The following are cases where a mandatory interlocutory injunction was clearly required:

In *Esso Petroleum Co. Ltd.* v. *Kingswood Motors*,[92] the defendant agreed with the plaintiff that he would not sell a garage without first procuring that the purchaser would enter a solus agreement with the plaintiff. The land was sold to a purchaser who conspired with the defendant to effect a breach. A mandatory interlocutory injunction was granted to compel a retransfer of the land to the defendant. There could be no clearer case of inducing breach of contract, and damages would be wholly inadequate. The injunction enforced the

[86] *John Trenberth Ltd.* v. *National Westminster Bank Ltd.* (1979) 39 P. & C.R. 104.
[87] [1971] Ch. 340. See also discussion in *Astro Exito Navegacion S.A.* v. *Southland Enterprise Co. (No. 2)* [1982] Q.B. 1248 (C.A.); (1983) 99 L.Q.R. 5.
[88] See also *Agbor* v. *Metropolitan Police Commissioner* [1969] 1 W.L.R. 703.
[89] *Locabail International Finance Ltd.* v. *Agroexport* [1986] 1 W.L.R. 657. See also *Ford Sellar Morris Developments Ltd.* v. *Grant Seward Ltd.* [1988] E.G.C.S. 112.
[90] [1975] A.C. 396; *ante*, p. 716.
[91] *Films Rover International Ltd.* v. *Cannon Film Sales Ltd.* [1987] 1 W.L.R. 670; (1988) 47 C.L.J. 34 (N. H. Andrews). A mandatory interlocutory injunction will be granted against a Crown officer only in very special circumstances; *R.* v. *Secretary of State for the Home Department, ex p. Herbage* [1987] Q.B. 872.
[92] [1974] Q.B. 142. But see (1977) 41 Conv.(N.S.) 318 (R. J. Smith).

personal liability of the tortfeasor to undo the consequences of his tort, which could have been restrained before it had been committed.

In *Sky Petroleum* v. *V.I.P. Petroleum Ltd.*,[93] such an injunction was granted to enforce a contract to supply petrol to the plaintiff. As there was no alternative supply, damages would be inadequate, and the plaintiff might be forced out of business unless the court intervened.

In *Evans* v. *B.B.C. and I.B.A.*[94] an order was made to compel the television authorities to show a party political broadcast. On the balance of probabilities[95] there was a contract with the Welsh Nationalist Party to broadcast it. Damages would be manifestly useless, as the election was about to take place, and no-one could say what the consequences of not showing the broadcast would be. It was crucially important for the Party to get its views across before the election. In such a case the court should take the risk of it turning out that there was no contract.

(iv) Conditions and Undertakings. On the grant of an interlocutory injunction, the plaintiff is normally required to give an undertaking in damages[96] in the event that the injunction is discharged at the trial as having been granted without good cause[97]; but a defendant may also be put on similar terms as a condition of an injunction not being granted.[98] One reason for the practice of undertakings is that it aids the court in achieving its object of abstaining from expressing any opinion on the merits until the hearing.[99] While an undertaking by the plaintiff is exacted for the benefit of the defendant, it is not a contract with the defendant. The undertaking is given to the court, so that non-performance is a contempt of court and not a breach of contract.[1] The damages will become payable if the plaintiff is unsuccessful at the trial, either because he cannot establish his case or because the judge who granted the interlocutory injunction took a wrong view of the law. The plaintiff may be required to give security or to pay the money into court. Any damages will be assessed on the same basis as damages for breach of contract; that is, as if there had been a contract between the plaintiff

---

[93] [1974] 1 W.L.R. 576. (The injunction was negative in form, but mandatory in substance.) See also *Worldwide Dryers Ltd.* v. *Warner Howard Ltd.*, *The Times*, December 9, 1982.

[94] *The Times*, February 26, 1974.

[95] This seems to be a relaxation of Megarry J.'s requirement of a "high degree of assurance," *ante*, p. 729.

[96] Or to do some other act; *P.S. Refson & Co. Ltd.* v. *Saggers* [1984] 1 W.L.R. 1025.

[97] *Anton Piller* and *Mareva* injunctions, *post*, pp. 766, 770, provide good examples of the need for undertakings. See *Digital Equipment Corporation* v. *Darkcrest Ltd.* [1984] Ch. 512.

[98] *Elwes* v. *Payne* (1879) 12 Ch.D. 468. For discharge, see *Butt* v. *Butt* [1987] 1 W.L.R. 1351.

[99] *American Cyanamid Co.* v. *Ethicon Ltd.* [1975] A.C. 396, at p. 407.

[1] See *Hussain* v. *Hussain* [1986] Fam. 134.

and the defendant that the plaintiff would not prevent the defendant from doing what the injunction restrains him from doing.[2]

Where interlocutory injunctions are sought in matrimonial and children's matters in the High Court or the county court, undertakings may be required if the claim concerns the protection of property rights, but will not be required in respect of matters concerning personal conduct.[3]

In *Hoffman-La Roche (F.) & Co.* v. *Secretary of State for Trade and Industry*[4] the question arose whether the Crown should be required to give an undertaking as a condition of the grant of an interlocutory injunction. The Secretary of State sought an interlocutory injunction to restrain the company from charging prices for drugs in excess of those specified in an order, but was not prepared to undertake in damages in the event that the company's claim that the order was *ultra vires* succeeded at trial. While the court cannot compel the Crown (or any other party) to give an undertaking, the injunction may be refused if the undertaking is not given. But the House of Lords held that the undertaking should not be required.

The Crown used not to give undertakings before 1947, but there was no justification after the Crown Proceedings Act for the view that the "Crown was immune from the requirement." A distinction had to be drawn between two cases: first, where the Crown was engaged in litigation for the purpose of asserting a proprietary or contractual right,[5] the ordinary rule applied and the Crown should give an undertaking; but, secondly, where an injunction was sought to enforce the law, the defendant must show special reason why justice required that it should not be granted, or should only be granted on terms. The present case was within the second category, and therefore no undertaking should be required unless the company could show a strong prima facie case that the order was *ultra vires*. The reason for this distinction is that where a person is prosecuted and acquitted, he may suffer loss but cannot normally recover from the prosecutor. There is therefore no reason why the Crown should incur liability when an injunction is sought to enforce the law. Lord Diplock thought that

---

[2] *Hoffman-La Roche (F.) & Co.* v. *Secretary of State for Trade and Industry* [1975] A.C. 295 at p. 361, *per* Lord Diplock. The party seeking to enforce the undertaking must have a prima facie case that the damage was caused by the injunction; *Financiera Avenida SA* v. *Shiblaq, The Times*, November 21, 1988.

[3] *Practice Direction* [1974] 1 W.L.R. 576.

[4] [1975] A.C. 295. This case was described as "very special" by Browne L.J. in *Smith* v. *Inner London Education Authority* [1978] 1 All E.R. 411 at p. 419, because the statute in question expressly provided for the grant to the Crown of an injunction as the only means of enforcing the statute. See also *Att.-Gen.* v. *British Broadcasting Corporation* [1981] A.C. 303 at p. 311 (C.A.). A local authority does not fall within this principle; *Rochdale Borough Council* v. *Anders* [1988] 3 All E.R. 490.

[5] Including the case where the Crown is asserting proprietary rights on behalf of a charity; *Att.-Gen.* v. *Wright* [1988] 1 W.L.R. 164; All E.R.Rev. 1987, p. 190 (A. A. S. Zuckerman).

there was no rigid rule; the court still has a discretion to ask for an undertaking even in law enforcement cases.

These considerations will apply where the Attorney-General acts *ex officio* to enforce the law by injunction. But where the Attorney-General brings the action under the relator procedure, the relator must give the usual undertaking.[6]

E. Quia Timet Injunctions

A *quia timet* injunction may be available where the injury to the plaintiff's rights has not yet occurred, but is feared or threatened.[7] The injunction may be perpetual or interlocutory, prohibitory or mandatory. It may further be subdivided into two broad categories: "first, where the defendant[8] has as yet done no hurt to the plaintiff but is threatening and intending (so the plaintiff alleges) to do works which will render irreparable harm to him or his property if carried to completion . . . those cases are normally, though not exclusively, concerned with negative injunctions. Secondly, the type of case where the plaintiff has been fully recompensed both at law and in equity for the damage he has suffered but where he alleges that the earlier actions of the defendant may lead to future causes of action. . . . It is in this field that the undoubted jurisdiction of equity to grant a mandatory injunction . . . finds its main expression."[9]

How serious must the fears of the plaintiff be, and how grave the suspected damage? As Lord Dunedin has said, it is not sufficient to say "timeo."[10] The requirements have been described in the following terms: a strong case of probability[11]; proof of imminent danger, and there must also be proof that the apprehended damage will, if it comes, be very substantial.[12] Thus in *Att.-Gen.* v. *Nottingham Corporation*[13] a *quia timet* injunction was not granted to restrain the corporation from

---

[6] *Hoffman-La Roche (F.) & Co.* v. *Secretary of State for Trade and Industry, supra,* at p. 363.

[7] For different views on the meaning of *quia timet*, see (1975) 34 C.L.J. 224 (J. A. Jolowicz); *cf.* (1977) 36 C.L.J. 369, (1978) 37 C.L.J. 51 (P. H. Pettit); Spry, p. 360.

[8] The defendant must himself have threatened the act in question. It does not suffice that some other party has done so. See *Celsteel Ltd.* v. *Alton House Holdings Ltd.* [1986] 1 W.L.R. 512 (no injunction against freeholder where act threatened by tenant).

[9] *Redland Bricks Ltd.* v. *Morris* [1970] A.C. 652 at p. 665, *per* Lord Upjohn. See also *Hooper* v. *Rogers* [1975] Ch. 43 (damages awarded under Lord Cairns' Act where subsidence was threatened by an excavation). But where the existence of the plaintiff's proprietary rights is in issue, such a claim to a mandatory injunction may be registrable as a "pending land action" under the Land Charges Act 1972 or Land Registration Act 1925: *Allen* v. *Greenhi Builders Ltd.* [1979] 1 W.L.R. 136.

[10] *Att.-Gen. for the Dominion of Canada* v. *Ritchie Contracting and Supply Co. Ltd.* [1919] A.C. 999 at p. 1005.

[11] *Att.-Gen.* v. *Manchester Corporation* [1893] 2 Ch. 87 at p. 92.

[12] *Fletcher* v. *Bealey* (1885) 27 Ch.D. 688 at p. 698. *cf. John Trenberth Ltd.* v. *National Westminster Bank Ltd.* (1979) 39 P. & C.R. 104.

[13] [1904] 1 Ch. 673; *Att.-Gen.* v. *Guardian Newspapers (No. 2)* [1988] 3 W.L.R. 776 (no general injunction against publication of any material the media might obtain from Crown servants in breach of confidence).

building a smallpox hospital, as there was no proof of genuine danger to nearby residents.

The principles applicable to the grant of a mandatory *quia timet* injunction have been enunciated by the House of Lords in *Redland Bricks Ltd.* v. *Morris.*[14]

The defendant company's digging activities caused landslips on the plaintiffs' adjoining property, which they used as a market garden. The plaintiffs' land, of which about one-tenth of an acre was affected, was worth about £12,000, but the cost of remedying the landslips would be about £30,000. The plaintiffs were awarded damages, a prohibitory injunction to restrain further withdrawal of support, and a mandatory injunction that the defendants "take all necessary steps to restore support within six months." But the House of Lords allowed the defendant's appeal against the grant of the mandatory injunction on the ground that it did not specify exactly what the defendant company had to do. While each case must depend on its own circumstances, Lord Upjohn set out the following four principles applicable to the grant of a mandatory *quia timet* injunction:

i. The plaintiff must show a very strong probability that grave damage will accrue to him in the future. It is a jurisdiction to be exercised sparingly and with caution, but, in the proper case, unhesitatingly.

ii. Damages will not be an adequate remedy if such damage does happen, applying the general principle of equity.

iii. Unlike the case where a negative injunction is granted to prevent the continuance or recurrence of a wrongful act, the cost to the defendant to do works to prevent or lessen the likelihood of a future apprehended wrong must be taken into account:

(*a*) where the defendant has acted wantonly and quite unreasonably in relation to his neighbour, he may be ordered to do positive work even if the expense to him is out of all proportion to the advantage thereby accruing to the plaintiff;

(*b*) but where the defendant has acted reasonably, although wrongly, the cost of remedying his earlier activities is most important. If it seems unreasonable to inflict such expenditure on one who is no more than a potential wrongdoer the court must exercise its jurisdiction accordingly. The court may order works which may not remedy the wrong but may lessen the likelihood of further injury. It must be borne in mind that the injury may never in fact occur, and that, if it does, the plaintiff may then seek the appropriate legal or equitable remedy.

iv. If a mandatory injunction is granted, the court must see that

---

[14] [1970] A.C. 652. See critical commentary in Heydon, Gummow and Austin, *Cases and Materials on Equity and Trusts* (2nd ed.), p. 898.

the defendant knows exactly in fact what he has to do.[15] A more recent statement is that, in the issue of mandatory *quia timet* injunctions, "what is aimed at is justice between the parties, having regard to all the relevant circumstances."[16]

4. DEFENCES TO PERPETUAL AND INTERLOCUTORY INJUNCTIONS

A. Delay

As in the case of specific performance, laches may be a defence even though the plaintiff's rights have not yet become statute-barred.[17] But a smaller degree of delay will defeat a claim for an interlocutory injunction than is necessary in the case of a perpetual injunction.[18] This is because, if an interlocutory claim is dismissed, the plaintiff is not unduly prejudiced, as he can still bring an action for a perpetual injunction. But the refusal of a perpetual injunction amounts to a final dismissal.

As we have seen, the plaintiff must come promptly in the case of an *ex parte* injunction, as any delay illustrates that his case is not urgent.[19] Where the plaintiff has voluntarily delayed his motion for an interlocutory injunction, he is unlikely to establish that his case is such that it would be unreasonable to make him wait until trial. An unexplained delay of five months prevented the grant of an interlocutory injunction in *Shepherd Homes Ltd.* v. *Sandham*,[20] where Megarry J. explained that if the injunction is also mandatory, any delay by the plaintiff will mean that the injunction, if granted, would disturb rather than preserve the status quo.[21] It may be otherwise, however, if there is no arguable defence.[22]

The authorities are not reconcilable on the question of delay in perpetual injunctions. It is sometimes said that laches is no defence,[23] or, to go to the other extreme, that mere lapse of time is a bar.[24] In *Kelsen* v. *Imperial Tobacco Co. Ltd.*[25] a mandatory injunction was granted to restrain a trespass even though it appeared that the state of affairs had existed for seven years. In *Fullwood* v. *Fullwood*,[26] Fry J.

[15] See also *Harold Stephen & Co. Ltd.* v. *Post Office* [1977] 1 W.L.R. 1172.
[16] *Hooper* v. *Rogers* [1975] Ch. 43 at p. 50 (*per* Russell L.J.)
[17] See Limitation Act 1980, s.36.
[18] *Johnson* v. *Wyatt* (1863) 2 De G.J. & S. 18.
[19] *Bates* v. *Lord Hailsham of St. Marylebone* [1972] 1 W.L.R. 1373.
[20] [1971] Ch. 340; *ante*, p. 729; *Church of Scientology of California* v. *Miller, The Times*, October 23, 1987; *cf. Texaco Ltd.* v. *Mulberry Filling Station Ltd.* [1972] 1 W.L.R. 814; *Express Newspapers plc* v. *Liverpool Daily Post and Echo plc* [1985] 1 W.L.R. 1089 (explanation for delay).
[21] See *Shotton* v. *Hammond* (1976) 120 S.J. 780: mandatory interlocutory injunction granted in spite of delay of six weeks by the plaintiff, who was not legally aided.
[22] See *Patel* v. *W.H. Smith (Eziot) Ltd.* [1987] 1 W.L.R. 853.
[23] *Archbold* v. *Scully* (1861) 9 H.L.C. 360 at p. 383.
[24] *Brooks* v. *Muckleston* [1909] 2 Ch. 519.
[25] [1957] 2 Q.B. 334.
[26] (1878) 9 Ch.D. 176.

held that a delay of two to three years was no defence, on the ground that mere lapse of time unaccompanied by acquiescence was no bar unless the legal right itself was barred.

In *H.P. Bulmer Ltd. & Showerings Ltd. v. J. Bollinger S.A.*[27] the appellants had described their products as "champagne perry" and "champagne cider" since 1950 and 1906 respectively. The latter usage had been known to the respondents since about 1930. Injunctions were granted in the High Court to restrain both descriptions. The defence of delay failed. This was a continuing wrong, and the right in question was legal. Whitford J. held that in such a case the delay must be "inordinate" if it is to prevent the grant of an injunction. Here it was not, because advice had to be sought, and interests consulted. The court must consider the period of delay, the period of knowledge, and all the circumstances. There was no appeal against the injunction restraining the usage of the description "champagne cider," but the other injunction was discharged by the Court of Appeal because passing-off was not established. But if it had been established, their Lordships considered that the injunction would not have been refused on account of delay. Goff L.J. thought that "inordinate" delay would be a ground for refusing an injunction, even in the case of a legal right, but that delay in the present case was not of that order.

Laches may be regarded more strictly if third parties would be affected. It is possible that a plaintiff who has delayed will be awarded damages in lieu of an injunction under Lord Cairns' Act.[28]

It has been suggested that a longer delay is required before a plaintiff will be refused an injunction where the right is legal than where it is equitable[29]; or alternatively that a less strict view of laches might be taken as to matters within equity's exclusive jurisdiction, such as a breach of trust, where there is no alternative remedy at law.[30] But the Court of Appeal has recently described the distinction between legal and equitable rights in this context as archaic and arcane.[31]

Finally, where an injunction is sought in an application for judicial review,[32] it is provided that, in the case of "undue delay," the injunction may be refused if the granting of relief "would be likely to cause

---

[27] [1977] 2 C.M.L.R. 625 (C.A). *cf. Vine Products Ltd. v. McKenzie & Co. Ltd.* (1969) R.P.C. 1 (no injunction to restrain description as "sherry," the usage having been common knowledge for 100 years). See also *Erlanger v. New Sombrero Phosphate Co.* (1873) 3 App.Cas. 1218 at pp. 1279–1280.

[28] *Shelfer v. City of London Electric Lighting Co.* [1895] 1 Ch. 287 at p. 322; see also *Bracewell v. Appleby* [1975] Ch. 408.

[29] *Cluett Peabody & Co. Inc. v. McIntyre Hogg Marsh and Co. Ltd.* [1958] R.P.C. 335 at p. 354, *per* Upjohn J.; *H.P. Bulmer and Showerings Ltd. v. J. Bollinger S.A., supra.*

[30] See Spry, *Equitable Remedies*, pp. 420–421; and *Knight v. Bowyer* (1858) 2 De G. & J. 421.

[31] *Habib Bank Ltd. v. Habib Bank A.G. Zurich* [1981] 1 W.L.R. 1265 at pp. 1285 and 1287; *cf.* Spry, p. 421.

[32] *Post*, pp. 759, 761.

substantial hardship to, or substantially prejudice the rights of, any person or would be detrimental to good administration."[33]

B. Acquiescence[34]

Lapse of time will be taken into account in that it may indicate acquiescence. It is, of course, possible to find acquiescence without delay and delay without acquiescence but there is normally some overlap. As in the case of laches, a greater degree of acquiescence is needed to defeat a claim for a final injunction than an interlocutory injunction. It has also been suggested that acquiescence is easier to establish where the right in question is equitable only.[35] In *Richards* v. *Revitt*[36] it was said that the fact that the plaintiff has previously over-looked trivial breaches of covenant does not debar him, on the ground of acquiescence, from acting on a serious breach. The test is whether the plaintiff had represented that he would no longer enforce his rights.[37] A leading authority is *Sayers* v. *Collyer*,[38] where a house was being used as a beershop in breach of covenant. The plaintiff could not get an injunction, as he had known of the breach for three years, and, furthermore, had bought beer there. This was sufficient to bar any remedy. But a lesser degree of acquiescence, while not sufficient to bar the action completely, might be a reason for giving damages in lieu of an injunction under Lord Cairns' Act.

In *Shaw* v. *Applegate*[39] the plaintiff was the legal assignee of the benefit of a covenant entered into by the defendant in 1967 not to use his land as an "amusement arcade." Breaches of covenant occurred from about 1971. The plaintiff was aware of the facts but was unsure whether they constituted a breach of covenant. The plaintiff began proceedings for an injunction in 1973, but did not seek interlocutory relief, so that the defendant continued to carry on his business, investing money and building up goodwill, until the trial in 1976. It was held that the plaintiff was not guilty of such a degree of acquiescence as to bar all remedies, the real test being whether, on the facts of the particular case, it would be dishonest or unconscionable for the plaintiff to seek to enforce his rights.[40] This was not the case, because of the plaintiff's doubts as to his legal

---

[33] Supreme Court Act 1981, s.31(6); R.S.C., Ord. 53, r. 4; Wade, *Administrative Law* (6th ed.), pp. 674–675 (drawing attention to the amended r.4, overlooked in s.31(6)); *R.* v. *Stratford-on-Avon District Council, ex p. Jackson* [1985] 1 W.L.R. 1319; *R.* v. *Dairy Produce Quotas Tribunal, ex p. Caswell, The Times*, December 7, 1988.

[34] See Limitation Act 1980, s.36(2). The Act does not affect this defence.

[35] *Shaw* v. *Applegate* [1977] 1 W.L.R. 970 at p. 979 (*per* Goff L.J.). (The right in this case was legal.) But see *Habib Bank Ltd.* v. *Habib Bank A.G. Zurich, supra.*

[36] (1877) 7 Ch.D. 224 at p. 226.

[37] *Allen* v. *Veranne Builders Ltd.* [1988] E.G.C.S. 2.

[38] (1885) 28 Ch.D. 103.

[39] [1977] 1 W.L.R. 970; (1977) 41 Conv.(N.S.) 355 (F. R. Crane). See also on this point *Sayers* v. *Collyer* (1885) 28 Ch.D. 103 at p. 110.

[40] *Ibid.* at p. 978, *per* Buckley L.J. See also *H.P. Bulmer & Showerings Ltd.* v. *J. Bollinger S.A.* [1977] 2 C.M.L.R. 625 at p. 682, *per* Goff L.J.

rights. But there was sufficient acquiescence to bar the remedy of an injunction because the defendant had been lulled into a false sense of security by the plaintiff's inactivity and failure to seek interlocutory relief. Thus the appropriate remedy was damages in lieu of an injunction under Lord Cairns' Act.

C. Hardship

Hardship to the defendant is a relevant consideration in injunctions as in specific performance.[41] It is perhaps of more weight in the case of an interlocutory injunction[42] than in the case of a final injunction, where the infringement of the plaintiff's rights has been established. Hardship may also carry more weight in the case of mandatory injunctions,[43] where it has been said that the benefit to the plaintiff in granting the injunction must be balanced against the detriment to the defendant.[44] As we shall see, damages may be awarded in lieu of an injunction under Lord Cairns' Act if the injunction would be oppressive to the defendant.[45]

The element of hardship to the defendant might be overcome, as we have seen, by granting an injunction but suspending its operation.[46] Even if there is no hardship to the defendant, an injunction may be refused if it would prejudice an innocent third party.[47]

It has previously been noted that the disproportionate cost of complying with a mandatory *quia timet* injunction may be a ground for refusing the grant if the defendant has acted reasonably.[48] Lord Upjohn, however, thought that such considerations would not be taken into account in the case of a negative injunction to prevent the continuance or recurrence of a wrongful act; any argument by the wrongdoer that the injunction would be very costly to him, perhaps by preventing him from carrying out a contract with a third party, would carry little weight.

---

[41] See *Shell U.K. Ltd.* v. *Lostock Garages Ltd.* [1976] 1 W.L.R. 1187. As to difficulty in compliance, see generally *Att.-Gen* v. *Colney Hatch Lunatic Asylum* (1868) L.R. 4 Ch.App. 146.

[42] See the "balance of convenience" requirement, *ante*, p. 718.

[43] *Att.-Gen.* v. *Colchester Corporation* [1955] 2 Q.B. 207. *Gravesham Borough Council* v. *British Railways Board* [1978] Ch. 379, *ante*, p. 709. (A mandatory injunction would not be granted to compel the running of a ferry at a heavy loss, which would benefit few passengers.)

[44] *Shepherd Homes Ltd.* v. *Sandham* [1971] Ch. 340; *Charrington* v. *Simons & Co. Ltd.* [1970] 1 W.L.R. 725.

[45] There are other conditions: see *Shelfer* v. *City of London Electric Lighting Co.* [1895] 1 Ch. 287. See also *Shaw* v. *Applegate, supra*, at pp. 978–979.

[46] *Ante*, p. 711.

[47] *Maythorn* v. *Palmer* (1864) 11 L.T. 261; *Miller* v. *Jackson* [1977] Q.B. 966, *ante*, p. 699.

[48] *Redland Bricks Ltd.* v. *Morris* [1970] A.C. 652 at p. 666.

D. Conduct of the Plaintiff

The plaintiff must come to equity with clean hands.[49] If, therefore, he is in breach of his own obligations, or otherwise guilty of unfair conduct,[50] he will not be granted an injunction, although trifling breaches by the plaintiff may not disentitle him.[51] Similarly, he who comes to equity must do equity, therefore the plaintiff will not succeed if he is unable or unwilling to carry out his own future obligations.[52]

But the defence of "clean hands" must be related to the subject-matter of the dispute, and does not embrace the plaintiff's general conduct. Thus in *Argyll* v. *Argyll*,[53] the fact that the wife's conduct had caused the divorce was no answer to her claim to an injunction to restrain a breach of confidence by her husband. In *Hubbard* v. *Vosper*,[54] one reason for refusing the interlocutory injunction was that the plaintiff had not come with clean hands, in that he had protected his secrets by deplorable means, namely by a private criminal code for dealing with the "enemies" of scientology.

Similarly, the injunction may be refused if the court is not impressed with the plaintiff on the merits.[55]

5. The Jurisdiction under Lord Cairns' Act

The Chancery Amendment Act 1858[56] allowed damages to be awarded in lieu of, or in addition to, an injunction or specific performance. The Chancery Division has, of course, been able, since the Judicature Act 1873, to award damages in any case where the common law courts could have done so, but these are common law damages. It will still be necessary to rely on Lord Cairns' Act where no damages would be available at law, for example in lieu of a *quia timet* injunction where no legal injury has yet occurred[57]; or if some damage has occurred but may continue in the future, and damages are awarded to cover future loss[58];

---

[49] See *Malone* v. *Metropolitan Police Commissioner* [1980] Q.B. 49 at p. 71.
[50] *Shell U.K. Ltd.* v. *Lostock Garages Ltd.* [1976] 1 W.L.R. 1187.
[51] *Besant* v. *Wood* (1879) 12 Ch.D. 605.
[52] *Measures* v. *Measures* [1910] 2 Ch. 248; *Chappell* v. *Times Newspapers Ltd.* [1975] 1 W.L.R. 482 (employees failed to obtain injunction to restrain their dismissal where they refused to give an undertaking not to become involved in industrial action); *Consolidated Agricultural Suppliers Ltd.* v. *Rushmere* (1976) 120 S.J. 523.
[53] [1967] Ch. 302.
[54] [1972] 2 Q.B. 84.
[55] See *Glynn* v. *Keele University* [1971] 1 W.L.R. 487; *Shelfer* v. *City of London Electric Lighting Co.* [1895] 1 Ch. 287 at p. 317.
[56] *Ante*, p. 684; repealed and replaced by Statute Law Revision Act 1883 and Judicature Act 1873. The jurisdiction now derives from Supreme Court Act 1981, s.50. In *Leeds Industrial Co-operative Society* v. *Slack* [1924] A.C. 851 Viscount Finlay suggested that the repeal may have been a mistake, made under the false impression that it dealt only with common law damages, and was therefore redundant after the Judicature Act 1873. See, generally (1975) 34 C.L.J. 224 (J. A. Jolowicz); (1977) 36 C.L.J. 369 (P. H. Pettit); [1981] Conv. 286 (T. Ingmam and J. Wakefield).
[57] *Leeds Industrial Co-operative Society* v. *Slack*, *supra*; establishing the point after some doubt; *Hooper* v. *Rogers* [1975] Ch. 43; *Johnson* v. *Agnew* [1980] A.C. 367 at p. 400.
[58] See *Kennaway* v. *Thompson* [1981] Q.B. 88.

or where the plaintiff's right is exclusively equitable, as in the case of a restrictive covenant.[59] In other cases, it will not be necessary to invoke Lord Cairns' Act, and damages may be awarded at common law; but there is no need to distinguish the ground of jurisdiction. The discretion exercisable under Lord Cairns' Act is similar to the discretion which the court has had since the Judicature Act to grant injunctions or damages at common law, in cases where they are available. The principle is the same; the court will not give damages instead of an injunction if damages will not be adequate to protect the plaintiff's rights. It seems that the court will consider the principles set out in *Shelfer* v. *City of London Electric Lighting Co.*[60] governing the award of damages under Lord Cairns' Act even where the plaintiff has a cause of action at law, and there is jurisidiction to award damages at law.[61]

Lord Cairns' Act enables the award of damages in lieu of an injunction only if there is *jurisdiction* to grant one,[62] in the sense that the plaintiff has established a prima facie case for equitable relief. It does not matter that the injunction is refused on some discretionary ground, such as, for example, delay or acquiescence.[63] If, on the other hand, the plaintiff has no case at all for an injunction, then damages cannot be awarded under Lord Cairns' Act, but, as we have seen, such a plaintiff can be awarded common law damages, provided he has a cause of action at law.

A. Award of Damages under Lord Cairns' Act

If the plaintiff can establish that his rights have been infringed, he is prima facie entitled to an injunction. Damages will only be awarded in lieu in special circumstances; otherwise the defendant would be allowed to "buy" the right to continue the wrongful act.[64]

The leading case is *Shelfer* v. *City of London Lighting Co.*,[65] a case of nuisance. A.L. Smith L.J. laid down a "good working rule," that

---

[59] *Baxter* v. *Four Oaks Properties Ltd.* [1965] Ch. 816; *Wrotham Park Estate Ltd.* v. *Parkside Homes Ltd.* [1974] 1 W.L.R. 798; *Crabb* v. *Arun District Council (No. 2)* (1977) 121 S.J. 86.

[60] [1895] 1 Ch. 287; *infra.*

[61] See *Kelsen* v. *Imperial Tobacco Co. Ltd.* [1957] 2 Q.B. 334; *Woollerton and Wilson Ltd.* v. *Richard Costain Ltd.* [1970] 1 W.L.R. 411.

[62] See *Hooper* v. *Rogers* [1975] Ch. 43; *Wrotham Park Estate Ltd.* v. *Parkside Homes Ltd., supra.*

[63] *Shaw* v. *Applegate* [1977] 1 W.L.R. 970. Distinguish a case of *jurisdiction* being lost through the passage of time. See generally *Lavery* v. *Pursell* (1883) 39 Ch.D. 508 at p. 519. The position is the same where damages are awarded in lieu of specific performance, *ante*, p. 684.

[64] See *Wakeham* v. *Wood* (1982) 43 P. & C.R. 40; *Sampson* v. *Hodson-Pressinger* [1981] 3 All E.R. 710.

[65] [1895] 1 Ch. 287. See also Viscount Finlay's valuable account of Lord Cairns' Act in *Leeds Industrial Co-operative Society* v. *Slack* [1924] A.C. 851 at pp. 856–863. The remedy of damages is not appropriate where the nuisance is actionable without proof of damage; *Sevenoaks District Council* v. *Pattullo & Vinson Ltd.* [1984] Ch. 211 (right to hold market).

damages should only be awarded in lieu if all the following requirements were satisfied:

(i) the injury to the plaintiff is small; and
(ii) the injury is capable of being estimated in monetary terms; and
(iii) the injury would be adequately compensated by a small payment[66]; and
(iv) it would be oppressive to grant an injunction.

Lindley L.J. said[67] that the injunction should not be refused merely
because it would not greatly benefit the plaintiff, as the court is not a
tribunal for legalising wrongful acts where the wrongdoer is able and
willing to pay. Damages will not normally be substituted in a case of
nuisance, as they cannot be easily estimated, but it was suggested that
damages would be appropriate if it was a trivial or occasional nuisance,
or if it is a vexatious case, or if the plaintiff has shown that he only
wants money. If damages are awarded in a case where the wrong is
continuing, they must include a sum for the future as well as the past.

Even if the above four principles are satisfied, an injunction may still
be awarded if the defendant has acted in reckless disregard of the
plaintiff's rights,[68] or has acted in a high-handed manner, or tried to
steal a march on the plaintiff, or to evade the jurisdiction of the court.[69]

The Court of Appeal in *Redland Bricks Ltd.* v. *Morris,*[70] while
accepting the principles of *Shelfer's* case, disagreed on the question
whether the injury could be regarded as small, or could be adequately
compensated in money. The defendant's excavations caused damage
by subsidence to the value of £1,500, but the correction of the situation, if an injunction was issued, would require expenditure of some
£30,000. An injunction was granted, but the House of Lords reversed
on a different ground, and Lord Upjohn rejected the applicability of
Lord Cairns' Act to the case. But the reasons for his Lordship's
rejection of the Act are unclear and, it is submitted, unconvincing.[71]

The four principles have not always met with approval, notably in

---

[66] The jurisdiction to grant injunctions is based on the inadequacy of damages. It might
be argued that compliance with A.L. Smith L.J.'s third requirement should alone be
sufficient to prevent the grant of an injunction. But common law damages may not be
available. Also, the case may be one of a class normally protected by injunction, such
as trespass or nuisance, but in the particular circumstances the injury could be
compensated by damages. See (1975) 34 C.L.J. 224 (J. A. Jolowicz).

[67] *Ibid.* at pp. 315–316.

[68] *Shelfer* v. *City of London Electric Lighting Co.* [1895] 1 Ch. 287; *Pugh* v. *Howells*
(1984) 48 P. & C.R. 298.

[69] *Colls* v. *Home and Colonial Stores Ltd.* [1904] A.C. 179 at p. 193, a case on an
easement of light, where it was suggested that the court should incline to damages if
there is any doubt, and the defendant has acted fairly and not in an unneighbourly
spirit. See also *Pugh* v. *Howells, supra* (injunction to remove extension interfering
with easement of light, where built quickly over a bank holiday, although warning
given).

[70] [1967] 1 W.L.R. 967; *ante*, p. 733.

[71] See (1975) 34 C.L.J. 224 (J. A. Jolowicz); (1977) 36 C.L.J. 369; (1978) 37 C.L.J. 51 (P.
H. Pettit). See also *Hooper* v. *Rogers* [1975] Ch. 43.

cases concerning rights to light and trespass, each of them situations in which the burden of remedying the situation will often be out of all proportion to the injury to the plaintiff. In *Fishenden* v. *Higgs and Hill Ltd.*[72] the defendant erected a building which obstructed the plaintiff's light in a manner that justified substantial damages, but not, by reason of the very high property values involved and the conduct of the defendant, an injunction. The Court of Appeal said that the principles of *Shelfer's* case were a useful guide, but not intended to be exhaustive or rigidly applied, and not a universal or even a sound rule in the case of rights to light.

Similarly in the case of trespass, the injury to the plaintiff may bear no relationship to that imposed on the defendant by the grant of an injunction. It was assumed in *Kelsen* v. *Imperial Tobacco Co. Ltd.*[73] that *Shelfer's* case applied to trespass. The question was whether the defendant should be required to remove an advertisement which trespassed upon the plaintiff's airspace. The injury was minimal, but an injunction was granted. In *Woollerton and Wilson Ltd.* v. *Richard Costain Ltd.*[74] Stamp L.J. doubted whether the four principles of *Shelfer's* case could be regarded as applicable to cases of trespass involving nominal damage, as the award of damages would amount to a licence to continue the trespass. An injunction was granted although the four principles were satisfied, but the injunction was suspended.[75] It seems, however, from the subsequent decision in *Wrotham Park Estate Ltd.* v. *Parkside Homes Ltd.*[76] that this problem could be solved by awarding substantial damages under Lord Cairns' Act even where the plaintiff has suffered no loss.

But the Court of Appeal, in a case concerning nuisance, has recently accepted the principles of *Shelfer's* case as good law.

In *Kennaway* v. *Thompson*[77] the plaintiff sought an injunction to restrain a nuisance by excessive noise against a motor boat racing club. Mais J. in the High Court had awarded damages in lieu of an injunction under Lord Cairns' Act. The Court of Appeal, in granting the injunction, held that the jurisdiction to award damages in lieu of an injunction should be exercised only in very exceptional circumstances in cases of continuing nuisance. *Shelfer's* case had been applied countless times over the last 85 years, and was binding on the Court of Appeal. In the present case the injury to the plaintiff was not small, nor was it capable of estimation in monetary terms, nor could the sum awarded in the High Court (£16,000) be called a

---

[72] (1935) 153 L.T. 128; *Colls* v. *Home and Colonial Stores Ltd., supra*; *Lyme Valley Squash Club Ltd.* v. *Newcastle under Lyme Borough Council* [1985] 2 All E.R. 405.

[73] [1957] 2 Q.B. 334.

[74] [1970] 1 W.L.R. 411.

[75] *Ante*, p. 712. The decision is criticised in (1975) 34 C.L.J. 224 (J. A. Jolowicz).

[76] [1974] 1 W.L.R. 798. Trespass is an exception to the rule that damages require proof of loss; *Stoke-on-Trent City Council* v. *W. & J. Wass Ltd.* [1988] 1 W.L.R. 1406.

[77] [1981] Q.B. 88; (1981) 97 L.Q.R. 3; (1981) 44 M.L.R. 212 (R. A. Buckley).

"small payment." In considering whether to award damages in lieu of an injunction, the public interest does not prevail over the private rights of the plaintiff. Any statements to the contrary in *Miller* v. *Jackson*[78] ran counter to the principles of *Shelfer's* case and were based on old authorities decided before *Shelfer's* case and now subject to it.

But there is much to be said for the view which regrets an attempt to reduce the court's function to "a series of inelastic rules."[79] "The general principle is . . . that . . . a substitution [of damages for specific relief] ordinarily occurs only when the hardship caused to the defendant through specific enforcement would so far outweigh the inconvenience caused to the plaintiff if specific enforcement is denied that it would be highly unreasonable in all the circumstances to do more than to award damages."[80]

B. The Measure of Damages under Lord Cairns' Act

In *Leeds Industrial Co-operative Society* v. *Slack*,[81] Lord Sumner said[82]: "No money awarded in substitution can be justly awarded, unless it is at any rate designed to be a preferable equivalent to an injunction and therefore an adequate substitution for it." This principle was re-echoed in *Wroth* v. *Tyler*[83] in respect of specific performance. This decision was once regarded as authority for the proposition that greater damages may be awarded under Lord Cairns' Act than would be available at law. But in *Johnson* v. *Agnew*[84] the House of Lords held, in a case concerning specific performance, that there is no difference in the measure of damages obtainable under Lord Cairns' Act and at common law. Of course, damages may be recoverable under Lord Cairns' Act where none at all would be obtainable at law,[85] but in general equity follows the law, and it may generally be expected that if only nominal damages would be available at law, then no more will be awarded in equity.[86] But a different view was taken in *Wrotham*

---

[78] [1977] Q.B. 966, *ante*, p. 699. The principle of *Miller* v. *Jackson* was also rejected in *Webster* v. *Lord Advocate* (1984) S.L.T. 13. See also *Sevenoaks District Council* v. *Pattullo & Vinson Ltd.* [1984] Ch. 211.
[79] Spry, *Equitable Remedies*, p. 603.
[80] *Ibid.* p. 604.
[81] [1924] A.C. 851.
[82] *Ibid.* at p. 870.
[83] [1974] Ch. 30.
[84] [1980] A.C. 367, *ante*, p. 687.
[85] As in *Hooper* v. *Rogers* [1975] Ch. 43, *ante*, p. 732, when £750 was awarded for the reinstatement of the track. This was the maximum sum recoverable at that time in the county court, where the action commenced.
[86] *Johnson* v. *Agnew* [1980] A.C. 367.

Park Estate Ltd. v. *Parkside Homes Ltd.*,[87] a case where no damages were available at law.

The defendant had erected houses in breach of covenant. There was jurisdiction to grant a mandatory injunction against the defendant and the purchasers, who had aided and abetted the breach; but the injunction was refused, in order to avoid the demolition of valuable houses. As a restrictive covenant was involved, damages were available only under Lord Cairns' Act. The value of the plaintiff's estate was not diminished by the breach, but it did not follow that only nominal damages were available.[88] It would not be right either to leave the defendants in possession of the fruits of their wrongdoing, nor to restrict the plaintiffs to nominal damages. Justice would be done by assessing the damages on a fair basis. Brightman J. held that a just substitute would be such sum as the plaintiff could reasonably have demanded to relax the covenant, assessed at £2,500.

6. Injunctions in Particular Situations

A. To Restrain a Breach of Contract

An injunction is the appropriate remedy to restrain the breach of a negative undertaking in a contract. In some measure it corresponds to specific performance in the area of positive undertakings.[89] But, as will be seen,[90] the jurisdiction to grant an injunction is wider.

(i) Contract Wholly Negative

(a) *Perpetual Injunctions*. Where the essence of the contractual undertaking is negative, the court will grant an injunction to restrain a breach almost as a matter of course. As Lord Cairns L.C. explained in *Doherty* v. *Allman and Dowden*[91]: " . . . in such case the injunction

---

[87] [1974] 1 W.L.R. 798, *ante*, p. 710. This resembles the "unjust enrichment" approach of *Beswick* v. *Beswick* [1968] A.C. 58, *ante*, p. 689. The decision was not cited in *Johnson* v. *Agnew*, *supra*. It was followed in *Bracewell* v. *Appleby* [1975] Ch. 408 (trespass) and *Carr-Saunders* v. *Dick McNeill Associates Ltd.* [1986] 1 W.L.R. 922 (right to light); but it was distinguished in *Tito* v. *Waddell (No. 2)* [1977] Ch. 106 at p. 335. See [1978] Conv. 366 at p. 369 (A. M. Tettenborn).

[88] See also *Anchor Brewhouse Developments Ltd.* v. *Berkley House (Docklands Developments) Ltd.* [1987] 2 E.G.L.R. 173 (trespass). But *Wrotham* was regarded as standing "very much on its own" in *Stoke-on-Trent City Council* v. *W. & J. Wass Ltd.* [1988] 1 W.L.R. 1406, where it was said that *Wrotham* and the trespass cases were exceptions to the rule that damages depended on proof of loss.

[89] *Ante*, pp. 653 *et seq*. Mandatory injunctions may also be available.

[90] *Post*, p. 745; *Donnell* v. *Bennett* (1883) 22 Ch.D. 835.

[91] (1878) 3 App.Cas. 709 at p. 720; *Sefton* v. *Tophams Ltd.* [1967] A.C. 50; *Avon County Council* v. *Millard* (1985) 50 P. & C.R. 275; *Sutton Housing Trust* v. *Lawrence* (1988) 55 P. & C.R. 320 (granted to prevent tenant keeping dog in breach of covenant in lease).

does nothing more than give the sanction of the process of the court to that which already is the contract between the parties." It is not necessary even to prove damage,[92] except where the action is by a reversioner.[93] Similarly breaches of covenants against particular types of user are restrained by injunction.

But the *Doherty* v. *Allman*[94] principle is not without qualification. It must be applied "in the light of the surrounding circumstances in each case,"[95] and it does not prevent the court from considering the effect of delay or other supervening circumstances.[96]

Thus an injunction was refused in *Baxter* v. *Four Oaks Properties Ltd.*,[97] where the defendants, innocently, but in breach of covenant, intended to use a new building as flats. "The effect of granting such an order would . . . be to put the plaintiffs in a very strong bargaining position, for unless the defendants were prepared to leave the building unused, they would be forced to buy a release of the injunction . . . what the plaintiffs would get in the end would be damages—though, no doubt, more damages than they would get if no injunction were granted."[98]

(b) *Interlocutory Injunctions*. Interlocutory injunctions are not granted as a matter of course,[99] but it was said in *Hampstead and Suburban Properties Ltd.* v. *Diomedous*[1] that the *Doherty* v. *Allman*[2] principle applied where there was a plain breach of a clear negative covenant. In such a case, there was no reason why the defendant "should have a holiday from the enforcement of his obligation until the trial."[3] But where the validity of the covenant is in dispute, *Doherty* v. *Allman* cannot apply to interlocutory injunctions.[4]

(c) *Mandatory Injunctions*. Mandatory injunctions are entirely discretionary, and can never be granted automatically, even if a negative covenant is involved.[5] It is not possible to give precise guidance as to

---

[92] *Grimston* v. *Cuningham* [1894] 1 Q.B. 125; *Marco Productions Ltd.* v. *Pagola* [1945] K.B. 111, where a troupe of dancers agreed not to perform for another producer; injunction granted although the plaintiffs could not show that they would suffer greater damage if the dancers performed elsewhere than if they remained idle.

[93] *Johnstone* v. *Hall* (1856) 2 K. & J. 414; *Martin* v. *Nutkin* (1724) 2 P.Wms. 266 (injunction to restrain ringing of church bells at 5 a.m.).

[94] (1878) 3 App.Cas. 709.

[95] *Shaw* v. *Applegate* [1977] 1 W.L.R. 970 at p. 975 (*per* Buckley L.J.).

[96] *Ibid.* at p. 980 (*per* Goff L.J.).

[97] [1965] Ch. 816.

[98] *Ibid.* at p. 829, *per* Cross J.

[99] See *American Cyanamid Co.* v. *Ethicon Ltd.* [1975] A.C. 396, *ante*, p. 716.

[1] [1969] 1 Ch. 248, restraining excessive noise made in breach of covenant by a licensed restaurant.

[2] (1878) 3 App.Cas. 709.

[3] [1969] 1 Ch. 248 at p. 259.

[4] *Texaco Ltd.* v. *Mulberry Filling Station Ltd.* [1972] 1 W.L.R. 814 at p. 831. See also *Mike Trading and Transport Ltd.* v. *Pagnan* [1980] 2 Lloyd's Rep. 546.

[5] See *Wrotham Park Estate Ltd.* v. *Parkside Homes Ltd.* [1974] 1 W.L.R. 798, where such an injunction was refused as it would result in a waste of housing; *ante*, p. 743.

the way in which the discretion will be exercised. In *Shepherd Homes Ltd.* v. *Sandham*,[6] Megarry J. said of *Doherty* v. *Allman*[7] that "a court of equity which says by way of injunction 'that which the parties have already said by way of covenant that the thing shall not be done,' is not thereby in the same breath adding 'and what is more, if it has been done, it shall be undone.' "[8] The application of the principle of *Doherty* v. *Allman* is tempered by a judicial discretion which withholds a mandatory injunction more readily than a prohibitory injunction, even where the plaintiff is blameless. Benefit to the plaintiff must be balanced against detriment to the defendant. But the search is not merely for "a fair result."[9]

(ii) Positive and Negative Terms. Where a contract contains both positive and negative stipulations, and the positive ones are not susceptible to the remedy of specific performance, the question arises whether the plaintiff can restrain the breach of the negative stipulation by injunction. In suitable cases, this can be done. The jurisdiction to grant an injunction is wider than that to order specific performance.[10]

The principle is that an injunction will not be granted if that would amount to indirect specific performance of the positive terms. Thus, it used to be said with confidence that if an employer agreed with his manager not to terminate the employment except for misconduct or breach of the agreement, and then gave notice to the manager, no injunction would lie, for this would indirectly enforce the contract.[11] It has been seen, however, that in the special circumstances of *Hill* v. *C.A. Parsons & Co. Ltd.*[12] where an employer was reluctantly obliged to terminate the employment of a senior engineer who refused to join a trade union operating a closed shop principle, an interim injunction was issued to restrain the termination.

(iii) No Express Negative Stipulation. Where a contract, drafted in positive form, contains no express negative stipulation, it is possible, in suitable circumstances, to discover in the contract, on its proper construction, an implied negative undertaking which can be remedied by injunction.[13] This is especially important where the positive obligation

---

[6] [1971] Ch. 340; *Sharp* v. *Harrison* [1922] 1 Ch. 502, at p. 512; *Charrington* v. *Simons & Co. Ltd.* [1970] 1 W.L.R. 725, *per* Buckley J.; the point was not discussed on appeal.

[7] (1878) 3 App.Cas. 709.

[8] [1971] Ch. 340 at p. 346.

[9] *Charrington* v. *Simons & Co. Ltd.* [1971] 1 W.L.R. 598 at p. 603, *per* Russell L.J.

[10] See *Thomas Marshall (Exports) Ltd.* v. *Guinle* [1979] Ch. 227 at p. 243.

[11] *Davis* v. *Foreman* [1894] 3 Ch. 654.

[12] [1972] 1 Ch. 305; *C.H. Giles & Co. Ltd.* v. *Morris* [1972] 1 W.L.R. 307; (1975) 34 C.L.J. 36 (B. Napier).

[13] *Tulk* v. *Moxhay* (1848) 2 Ph. 774; *De Mattos* v. *Gibson* (1859) 4 De. G. & J. 276; *Catt* v. *Tourle* (1869) L.R. 4 Ch.App. 654; *Clegg* v. *Hands* (1890) 44 Ch.D. 503; *Jones & Sons Ltd.* v. *Tankerville* [1909] 2 Ch. 440. Breach of an obligation imposed by law can be restrained by injunction even though the contract contains no express negative term: *Hivac* v. *Park Royal Scientific Instruments* [1946] Ch. 169 (confidential information). On the *De Mattos* v. *Gibson* principle, see Pettit, pp. 503–504.

is not specifically enforceable. It is not possible to lay down a rule to determine the circumstances in which an injunction may be obtained. The question in each case depends upon the construction which the court places upon the particular contract.

The principle was laid down by Lord Selborne in *Wolverhampton and Walsall Railway Co. Ltd.* v. *L.N.W. Ry. Ltd.*[14] as being that the court should "look in all such cases to the substance and not to the form. If the substance of the agreement is such that it would be violated by doing the thing sought to be prevented, then the question will arise, whether this is the court to come to for a remedy. If it is, I cannot think that ought to depend on the use of a negative rather than an affirmative form of expression."

A negative stipulation is rarely implied in contracts of personal service, for to do so might allow the indirect enforcement of a contract which is not specifically enforceable.[15] Thus, it will not be implied although the servant has contracted to devote the whole of his time to his employer,[16] nor where there was a contract to sell to a purchaser all the "get" of a colliery for five years[17]; nor where a boxer agreed that his manager should have the "sole arrangements" for his boxing and other engagements.[18] However, in *Metropolitan Electric Supply Co.* v. *Ginder*,[19] the defendant applied for a supply of electricity on terms which provided that the defendant agreed to take all the electricity required by his premises from the plaintiff for a stated period. The plaintiff was not bound to supply, nor the defendant to take, any electricity. The contract was construed as an undertaking not to take electricity from any other persons, and the defendant was restrained by injunction from doing so. In *Manchester Ship Canal* v. *Manchester Racecourse Co.*[20] the grant of a "first refusal" was construed as an undertaking enforceable by injunction, not to sell to anyone else in contravention of the undertaking.

It is established that a negative term may be implied in the following types of case:

(a) *Contracts Affecting the Use of Land.* A covenant which touches and concerns the land so as to be binding in equity upon successors in

---

[14] (1873) L.R. 16 Eq. 433 at p. 440; *Whitwood Chemical Co. Ltd.* v. *Hardman* [1891] 2 Ch. 416 at p. 441, *per* Lindley L.J.; *Bower* v. *Bantam Investments Ltd.* [1972] 1 W.L.R. 1120.

[15] *Ante*, p. 666.

[16] *Whitwood Chemical Co. Ltd.* v. *Hardman* [1891] 2 Ch. 416; *Bower* v. *Bantam Investments Ltd.* [1972] 1 W.L.R. 1120.

[17] *Fothergill* v. *Rowland* (1873) L.R. 17 Eq. 132.

[18] *Mortimer* v. *Beckett* [1920] 1 Ch. 571. See also *Fraser* v. *Thames Television Ltd.* [1984] Q.B. 44.

[19] [1901] 2 Ch. 799. See also *Sky Petroleum Ltd.* v. *V.I.P. Petroleum Ltd.* [1974] 1 W.L.R. 576.

[20] [1901] 2 Ch. 37. See also *Gardner* v. *Coutts & Co.* [1968] 1 W.L.R. 173 (implied term in right of pre-emption that property will not be given to another); *cf. Pritchard* v. *Briggs* [1980] Ch. 338.

title to the land under the doctrine of *Tulk* v. *Moxhay*[21] will be construed as negative and subjected to an injunction if it is negative in substance although positive in form. Indeed, in *Tulk* v. *Moxhay* itself, the covenant was to "keep and maintain the said piece of ground in its then form, and in sufficient and proper repair ... in an open state, uncovered with any buildings in neat and ornamental order."[22] The fact that a court was powerless to interfere against third parties except by the use of an injunction no doubt encouraged the courts to extend its use of the concept.

(b) *Contractual Licences*. After a long search for the proper solution to the problem of the revocation by a licensor of a contractual licence in breach of contract, the courts have found it in the issue of an injunction to restrain the breach of contract.[23] Where the wrongful revocation occurs before the licensee has entered, the court may, in an appropriate case, grant specific performance or a mandatory injunction to compel performance of the licensor's obligations.[24] A contractual licence is commonly in positive form—permitting the licensee to occupy premises. But where the licence on its proper construction gives no right to the licensor to revoke in the way in which he has purported to do, the court will treat the matter as one in which the licensor has contracted not to revoke inconsistently with the terms of the licence, and will restrain him from doing so.[25]

(iv) Contracts for Personal Services. It has been seen that contracts for personal services would not be specifically enforced either by specific performance or by an injunction.[26] In the case of contracts of employment, the Trade Union and Labour Relations Act 1974, s.16 provides that "no court shall ... by way of ... injunction ... restraining a breach or threatened breach of [a contract of employment] compel an employee to do any work or to attend at any place for the doing of any work." This provision, as with the corresponding provision relating to specific performance, applies only to contracts of employment[27] and only to enforcement against an employee. The equitable principle which denies specific enforcement of contracts of service has in appropriate circumstances permitted the issue of an injunction to restrain a negative undertaking in a contract for personal services, and this may have the effect indirectly of causing a contract to be performed. It remains to be determined whether and how far the

[21] (1848) 2 Ph. 774.
[22] *Ibid.* at p. 775.
[23] *Post*, p. 837.
[24] *Verrall* v. *Great Yarmouth Borough Council* [1981] Q.B. 202, *ante*, p. 659.
[25] See *Jones (James) and Sons Ltd.* v. *Earl of Tankerville* [1909] 2 Ch. 440.
[26] *Ante*, p. 666.
[27] *Ante*, p. 666.

Trade Union and Labour Relations Act 1974, s.16 affects the operation of this principle. Two aspects of the question of the issue of an
injunction in this circumstance need to be examined.[28]

(a) *Restraining Breach by Employee or Independent Contractor.*

In *Lumley* v. *Wagner*,[29] Miss Wagner, a well-known opera star,
had agreed with Lumley that she would sing at Her Majesty's
Theatre during a certain period, and would not sing anywhere else
without his written permission. She made another engagement with
Gye[30] to sing at Covent Garden and abandoned her previous com-
mitment to Lumley, who sought an injunction to restrain her from
singing for Gye. Lord St. Leonards held that an injunction should be
granted to restrain the breach of the negative stipulation; it would
not of course have been possible to obtain specific performance of
the promise to sing.

The principle of *Lumley* v. *Wagner* has been much criticised.[31] It is
said that the issue of an injunction in this situation is the equivalent of
negative specific performance; and that a number of principles are
thereby disregarded, especially the rule that the court will not supervise the performance of contracts; and the principle that the contracting parties must not become tied together in a relationship involving a
status of servitude. Justice Holmes[32] has spoken of the giving of an
injunction and refusal of specific performance as a distinction without
a difference; and the concept of personal servitude introduces constitutional objections in the United States.[33]

On the other hand, the carrying out of agreements must be encouraged by the courts, whatever remedy is used.[34] This view is commonly
followed in the case of purely negative contracts or covenants. And if a

---

[28] Of course no question of enforcement will arise if the term of the contract is void as
being unreasonably in restraint of trade.
[29] (1852) 1 De G.M. & G. 604; (1973) 117 S.J. 160; an injunction will not be granted
where the new employer was unaware of the restriction and is not a party to the action;
(*Maythorn* v. *Palmer* (1864) 11 L.T. 261). See also *Thomas Marshall (Exports) Ltd.* v.
Guinle [1979] Ch. 227 at pp. 240–242; *Scandinavian Trading Tanker Co. A.B.* v. *Flota
Petrolera Ecuatoriana* [1983] 2 A.C. 694.
[30] Lumley also sued Gye for inducing her to break her contract, *Lumley* v. *Gye* (1853) 2
E. & B. 216.
[31] Ames, *Lectures on Legal History*, p. 370; *per* Lindley L.J. in *Whitwood Chemical Co.*
v. *Hardman* [1891] 2 Ch. 416 at p. 428; "I think that the court ... will generally do
much more harm by attempting to decree specific performance in cases of personal
service than by leaving them alone; and whether it is attempted to enforce these
contracts directly by a decree of specific performance, or indirectly by an injunction,
appears to me to be immaterial."
[32] *Javierre* v. *Central Altagracia*, 217 U.S. 502 at p. 508 (1910).
[33] (1921) 6 Cornell L.R. 235 (R. S. Stevens); (1906) 6 Col. L.R. 82 (C. D. Ashley);
(1917) 17 Col. L.R. 687 (G. L. Clark); Spry, p. 514.
[34] *Lane* v. *Newdigate* (1804) 10 Ves.Jr. 192.

contract contains both positive and negative stipulations, it is a curious objection that the enforcement of the negative term has the effect of enforcing the positive. It is submitted that the correct approach in these situations, as in other cases of injunctions, is that the injunction should issue to restrain the breach of a negative undertaking, unless the defendant can show that the court should in its discretion refuse on the ground that undesirable consequences may follow. Each case, in other words, should be treated on its merits.

Thus an employee should not be put into a position in which he must either perform the contract or do nothing.

In *Rely-a-Bell Burglar and Fire Alarm Co.* v. *Eisler*[35] the employee had contracted to serve the employer and to take no other employment for the period of the contract of service. An injunction was refused, and damages awarded.

In *Warner Bros.* v. *Nelson,*[36] a well-known actress, Bette Davis, contracted to work for the plaintiffs and not to work as a film actress for any other film company for the period of her contract, "or to be engaged in any other occupation." The term was not void under the restraint of trade doctrine,[37] and the question was whether an injunction was an appropriate remedy. "[I]t would, of course, be impossible to grant an injunction covering all the negative covenants in the contract. That would, indeed, force the defendant to perform her contract or remain idle; but this objection is removed by the restricted form in which the injunction is sought. It is confined to forbidding the defendant, without the consent of the plaintiffs, to render any services for or in any motion picture or stage production for any one other than the plaintiffs."[38] An injunction was given on these terms.[39] Miss Davis was still free to earn a living in other ways, even if they were less lucrative.

In *Evening Standard Co. Ltd.* v. *Henderson*[40] an employee had failed to give the required notice. The Court of Appeal was prepared to grant an interlocutory injunction to prevent him from working for a rival paper during the notice period. As the employer had undertaken to pay his salary for that period even if he did not work, the injunction did not compel him to perform the contract or starve, but was rather a means of enforcing the notice requirement.

---

[35] [1926] Ch. 609; *Ehrman* v. *Bartholomew* [1898] 1 Ch. 671; *Chapman* v. *Westerby* [1913] W.N. 277.

[36] [1937] 1 K.B. 209.

[37] *Per* Russell L.J. in *Instone* v. *A. Schroeder Music Publishing Co. Ltd.* [1974] 1 All E.R. 171 at p. 178 (C.A.). He also criticised Branson J. who suggested in *Warner Bros.* v. *Nelson* [1937] 1 K.B. 209 at p. 214 that the doctrine of restraint of trade could not apply during the continuance of the contract; see also *Clifford Davis Management Ltd.* v. *W.E.A. Records Ltd.* [1975] 1 W.L.R. 61.

[38] [1937] 1 K.B. 209 at p. 219, *per* Branson J.

[39] *Robinson & Co. Ltd.* v. *Heuer* [1898] 2. Ch. 451.

[40] [1987] I.R.L.R. 64.

(b) *Compelling Employer to Employ.*

In *Page One Records* v. *Britton*,[41] a group of musicians appointed the plaintiff as their manager for five years, contracting not to engage anyone else as manager. They wished to change, and the plaintiff sought an injunction to prevent the employment of another manager, arguing, on the lines of *Warner Bros.* v. *Nelson*[42] that the defendants could retain him or continue without a manager. The argument was rejected, on the ground that the injunction would *persuade* them to retain the plaintiff, which would be undesirable in a personal and fiduciary relationship in which the defendants had lost confidence in the plaintiff.

This decision has been criticised on the ground that the distinguishing of *Warner Bros.* v. *Nelson*[43] was unconvincing: the group could have earned their living in another way.[44] That may be so, but the realistic approach of the court in *Page One Records* v. *Britton*[45] is to be preferred. It is *Warner Bros.* v. *Nelson* which should be criticised for putting economic pressure on the defendant to perform an obligation which was not specifically enforceable.[46]

In *Hill* v. *C.A. Parsons & Co. Ltd.*,[47] however, we have seen that the Court of Appeal granted an injunction restraining an employer from acting on a wrongful dismissal. This amounted to indirect specific performance of a service contract; but the circumstances were special. Personal confidence still existed between the parties; a proper length of notice would have safeguarded the plaintiff's right under the Industrial Relations Act 1971; and the plaintiff was due to retire in two years, and his pension depended on his average salary during the last three years of employment. Stamp L.J. dissented, and would have allowed the pension claim to be included in an award of damages. The question arose again in *Chappell* v. *Times Newspapers Ltd.*,[48] where employees sought an injunction to restrain their dismissal during an industrial dispute. As mutual confidence no longer existed between the parties, the case was not within the *Hill* v. *Parsons* exception. The fact that unfair dismissal was unlawful under the Trade Union and Labour Relations Act 1974 did not mean that a service contract was

---

[41] [1968] 1 W.L.R. 157.

[42] [1937] 1 K.B. 209.

[43] *Supra.*

[44] Pettit, *Equity and the Law of Trusts* (5th ed.), p. 502.

[45] [1968] 1 W.L.R. 157.

[46] Treitel, *The Law of Contract* (7th ed.) p. 802.

[47] [1972] Ch. 305; *ante*, p. 668. See also *Jones* v. *Lee* [1980] I.R.L.R. 67. For the position where the employment is protected beyond the common law by procedural requirements relating to dismissal, see *R.* v. *British Broadcasting Corporation, ex p. Lavelle* [1983] 1 W.L.R. 23; *Irani* v. *Southampton and South West Hampshire Health Authority* [1985] I.C.R. 590.

[48] [1975] 1 W.L.R. 482; see also *G.K.N. (Cwmbran) Ltd.* v. *Lloyd* [1972] I.C.R. 214 at p. 220; *Sanders* v. *Ernest A. Neale Ltd.* [1974] I.C.R. 565 at p. 571, *per* Sir John Donaldson; *Ali* v. *London Borough of Southwark* [1988] I.R.L.R. 100.

enforceable by injunction. That would be a "plain recipe for disaster."[49]

It appears that the grant of an injunction within the *Hill* v. *Parsons* exception is no longer a rarity. Although the plaintiff must show that mutual confidence still exists, this is not inevitably precluded by the fact that the employer opposes the claim. It suffices to establish that the employer has no rational ground to lack confidence, as where there have been no complaints or criticisms, nor any friction at the workplace.[50]

B. To Restrain a Breach of Trust

There are many examples of the issue of an injunction to restrain a breach of an equitable obligation, and a few must suffice here. Trustees have been restrained from distributing an estate inconsistently with the terms of the instrument[51]; or from selling under depreciatory conditions of sale[52]; or for a price below that offered firmly by a prospective purchaser[53]; or selling land held on trust for sale without appointing a second trustee and without consulting the beneficiary.[54] Where the plaintiff has a claim to trace property in equity,[55] an injunction may be granted to restrain the defendant from disposing of the property.[56]

C. To Restrain the Commission or Continuance of a Tort

In each of the many cases in which an injunction issues to restrain the commission of a tort, equity is exercising its "concurrent" jurisdiction. Equity plays no part in determining whether a wrong has been committed; that is a matter solely of law. It is the remedy alone that is equitable. Thus the plaintiff must first establish the commission or threat of something which constitutes a tort at law. It is not within the province of this book to consider what is thus included. The point here is that there can be no injunction under the jurisdiction at present under discussion unless the plaintiff can establish that the act is a tort. If it is, the court may, in its discretion, grant an injunction. The rules and practice vary with the tort in question.

(i) **Nuisance.**[57] The act complained of must constitute a nuisance at

---

[49] *Ibid.* at p. 506. See also the Employment Protection (Consolidation) Act 1978, s.69: an industrial tribunal may order the reinstatement of an employee who has been unfairly dismissed. But the sanction in the event of non-compliance with the order is an award of compensation.

[50] *Powell* v. *London Borough of Brent* [1987] I.R.L.R. 466; (1988) 85 L.S.G. No. 5, p. 28 (J. Hendy and J. McMullen).

[51] *Fox* v. *Fox* (1870) L.R. 11 Eq. 142.

[52] *Dance* v. *Goldingham* (1873) L.R. 8 Ch.App. 902.

[53] *Buttle* v. *Saunders* [1950] 2 All E.R. 193 (*ante*, p. 485) where the trustee had promised (but not in binding form) to sell land to another purchaser.

[54] *Waller* v. *Waller* [1967] 1 W.L.R. 451.

[55] *Ante*, p. 624.

[56] *A.* v. *C.* [1981] Q.B. 956n.

[57] See generally (1982) 41 C.L.J. 87 (S. Tromans).

law. "There is no such thing as an equitable nuisance."[58] The interference must cause or threaten damage.[59] No injunction will issue to deal with a trifling interference[60]; and even if damage is proved, equity will not grant an injunction in every case in which the common law would award damages. The remedy is discretionary, and is particularly appropriate in cases of nuisance.[61] Damages may be awarded in lieu under Lord Cairns' Act.[62]

It was held in *Miller* v. *Jackson*,[63] by a majority of the Court of Appeal, that the court should weigh the interests of the public against those of the individual, and should refuse the injunction if, on balance, it was felt that the interest of the public should prevail. This proposition has since been doubted in *Kennaway* v. *Thompson*[64] by a differently constituted Court of Appeal. It was there held that, when considering whether to award damages in lieu of an injunction under Lord Cairns' Act in a nuisance case, the public interest does not prevail over the private interest of the plaintiff.[65]

(ii) Trespass. An injunction will issue to restrain a threatened or existing trespass. In minor cases, the court will leave the plaintiff to such remedy as he has at law; as where a clergyman of the Church of England held services on the seashore between high and low water mark which was leased by the Crown to the Corporation[66]; or where collectors chased a butterfly on to the plaintiff's land.[67] Where, however, the defendant entered the plaintiff's wood, cut down trees and clearly intended to cut more, he was restrained.[68]

Where the defendant has no arguable defence, the plaintiff may be granted an interlocutory injunction even where the trespass has caused no damage.[69]

---

[58] *Per* Kindersley V.-C. in *Soltau* v. *de Held* (1851) 2 Sim.(n.s.) 133 at p. 151.

[59] It is otherwise where the nuisance is actionable without proof of damage; *Sevenoaks District Council* v. *Pattullo & Vinson Ltd.* [1984] Ch. 211; *Halton Borough Council* v. *Cawley* [1985] 1 W.L.R. 15 (right to hold market).

[60] *Ankerson* v. *Connelly* [1907] 1 Ch. 678.

[61] *Halsey* v. *Esso Petroleum Co. Ltd.* [1961] 1 W.L.R. 683; *Leakey* v. *National Trust for Places of Historic Interest or Natural Beauty* [1980] Q.B. 485; *Laws* v. *Florinpace* [1981] 1 All.E.R. 659; *Liburd* v. *Cork, The Times,* April 4, 1981; *Pugh* v. *Howells* (1984) 48 P. & C.R. 298.

[62] *Ante,* p. 738.

[63] [1977] Q.B. 966, *ante,* p. 699; *Tetley* v. *Chitty* [1986] 1 All E.R. 663.

[64] [1981] Q.B. 88. It was also rejected in *Webster* v. *Lord Advocate* (1984) S.L.T. 13. See also *Sevenoaks District Council* v. *Pattullo & Vinson Ltd., supra; Rosling* v. *Pinnegar* (1987) 54 P. & C.R. 124.

[65] Authorities supporting the contrary proposition were decided before *Shelfer* v. *City of London Electric Lighting Co.* [1895] 1 Ch. 287, *ante,* p. 739, and must be read subject to that decision.

[66] *Llandudno Urban Council* v. *Woods* [1899] 2 Ch. 705.

[67] *Fielden* v. *Cox.* (1906) 22 T.L.R. 411; *Behrens* v. *Richards* [1905] 2 Ch. 614.

[68] *Stanford* v. *Hurlstone* (1873) L.R. 9 Ch.App. 116. See also *League Against Cruel Sports Ltd.* v. *Scott* [1986] Q.B. 240 (persistent trespass by hunt).

[69] *Patel* v. *W.H. Smith (Eziot) Ltd.* [1987] 1 W.L.R. 853; *Anchor Brewhouse Developments Ltd.* v. *Berkley House (Docklands Developments) Ltd.* [1987] 2 E.G.L.R. 173.

A mandatory injunction will be granted where necessary; requiring the removal of an advertising sign which projected into the airspace above the plaintiff's single storey shop[70]; or ordering a discharged ship's crew to leave the ship.[71]

(iii) Libel. The granting of injunctions to restrain the publication of a libel has caused particular difficulty, partly because of the complexity of proof of the tort, but largely because of the importance of allowing to be said things that ought to be said. It was not until *Quartz Hill Consolidated Gold Mining Co.* v. *Beall* in 1882[72] that the courts positively asserted a jurisdiction to restrain publication. The matter is usually one of urgency, requiring an interlocutory injunction, and Jessel M.R. was careful to point out the need for great caution in its exercise.

The plaintiff must satisfy the court of the falsity of the statements and, where they are privileged, the presence of malice. "The court will not restrain the publication of an article, even though it is defamatory, when the defendant says that he intends to justify it or to make fair comment on a matter of public interest. . . . The reason sometimes given is that the defences of justification and fair comment are for the jury, which is the constitutional tribunal, and not for a judge; but a better reason is the importance in the public interest that the truth should out."[73] The interest of the public in knowing the truth outweighs the interest of a plaintiff in maintaining his reputation.[74] Thus, it was laid down in *Bonnard* v. *Perryman*[75] as a working rule that an interlocutory injunction ought never to be granted except in the clearest cases, in which, if a jury did not find the matter complained of to be libellous, the court would set aside the verdict as unreasonable. Lord Denning M.R. has stated that all requests for "gagging injunctions" which seek to prevent true and fair comment on matters of public interest should fail.[76] But in *Hubbard* v. *Pitt*[77] the Court of Appeal

---

[70] *Kelsen* v. *Imperial Tobacco Co. Ltd.* [1957] 2 Q.B. 334, *ante*, p. 709. *cf. Bernstein (Lord) of Leigh* v. *Skyviews & General Ltd.* [1978] Q.B. 479. See also *John Trenberth Ltd.* v. *National Westminster Bank Ltd.* (1979) 39 P. & C.R. 104; *Straudley Investments Ltd.* v. *Barpress Ltd.* [1987] 1 E.G.L.R. 69; *London & Manchester Assurance Company Ltd.* v. *O. & H. Construction Ltd.* [1988] E.G.C.S. 41 (interlocutory).

[71] *Canadian Pacific Railway* v. *Gaud* [1949] 2 K.B. 239.

[72] (1882) 20 Ch.D. 501. In *Prudential Assurance Co.* v. *Knott* (1875) L.R. 10 Ch.App. 142 the Court of Appeal in Chancery declared that it had met no such jurisdiction.

[73] *Fraser* v. *Evans* [1969] 1 Q.B. 349 at p. 360, *per* Lord Denning M.R.; *Bryanston Finance Ltd.* v. *de Vries* [1975] Q.B. 703 (privileged occasions); *Crest Homes Ltd.* v. *Ascott, The Times,* February 4, 1975; (no injunction when defendant chose "flamboyant and vulgar method of airing his complaints"); *Al-Fayed* v. *The Observer Ltd., The Times,* July 14, 1986; *Khashoggi* v. *L.P.C. Magazines Ltd.* [1986] 1 W.L.R. 1412; *Att.-Gen.* v. *News Group Newspapers Ltd.* [1987] Q.B. 1.

[74] *Woodward* v. *Hutchins* [1977] 1 W.L.R. 760, at p. 764 (*per* Lord Denning M.R.).

[75] [1891] 2 Ch. 269. See also *Hermann Loog* v. *Bean* (1884) 26 Ch.D. 306; *Harakas* v. *Baltic Mercantile & Shipping Exchange Ltd.* [1982] 1 W.L.R. 958.

[76] *Att.-Gen.* v. *British Broadcasting Corporation* [1981] A.C. 303 at p. 311 (C.A.).

[77] [1976] Q.B. 142; (Lord Denning M.R. dissenting). See (1976) 35 C.L.J. 82 (P. Wallington).

upheld the grant of an interlocutory injunction to restrain, *inter alia*, the display of allegedly libellous placards and leaflets outside the plaintiffs' business premises. The necessity of preserving the freedoms of speech, assembly and demonstration should "not constrain the court to refuse a plaintiff an injunction to prevent defendants exercising these liberties in his front garden."[78] The injunction will also be granted if there is an arguable case that publication is part of a concerted plan to inflict deliberate damage without just cause.[79] In *Monson* v. *Tussaud's*,[80] an injunction was refused because it appeared that there might be a question at the trial whether the plaintiff had agreed to the publication.[81] The court will only intervene where the issue is clear and certain. It "will not prejudice the issue by granting an injunction in advance of publication."[82] It has been held that the principles laid down in *American Cyanamid Co.* v. *Ethicon Ltd.*[83] governing the grant of an interlocutory injunction have no application to libel injunctions, thus preserving the rule in *Bonnard* v. *Perryman*.[84]

Once libel has been proved at the trial, the plaintiff may obtain an injunction to restrain its repetition.

D. Breach of Confidence

An injunction will be available to restrain a breach of confidence, whether arising out of a personal, commercial or other relationship.[85] The conceptual basis of this action has already been considered.[86] Many of the questions which arise are similar to those discussed in connection with the cases on libel, but the principle of freedom of speech plays a less dominant part here. Unlike libel, the truth of the statement is no defence to a breach of confidence. As will be seen, the *Anton Piller*[87] injunction has evolved to protect the victims of commercial malpractice and espionage.

An obligation of confidence exists in respect of communications between husband and wife. "It is the policy of the law (which is the basis of the court's jurisdiction) to preserve the close confidence and

---

[78] *Ibid.* at p. 187, *per* Stamp, L.J.
[79] *Gulf Oil (Great Britain) Ltd.* v. *Page* [1987] Ch. 327 (airborne sign over Cheltenham racecourse).
[80] [1894] 1 Q.B. 671.
[81] The plaintiff, who had been tried in Scotland for murder, where the jury had returned a verdict of "not proven," complained of the exhibition of a figure of himself in a room next to the "Chamber of Horrors."
[82] *Fraser* v. *Evans, supra*, at p. 361, *per* Lord Denning M.R.
[83] [1975] A.C. 396, *ante*, p. 716.
[84] *Bestobell Paints Ltd.* v. *Bigg* (1975) 119 S.J. 678; *J. Trevor & Sons* v. *P. R. Solomon* (1978) 248 E.G. 779 (*per* Lord Denning M.R.); *Herbage* v. *Pressdram Ltd.* [1984] 1 W.L.R. 1160; *Gulf Oil (Great Britain) Ltd.* v. *Page* [1987] Ch. 327.
[85] See generally (1977) 30 C.L.P. 191 and (1976) 92 L.Q.R. 180 (M. W. Bryan); Goff and Jones, *The Law of Restitution* (3rd ed.), Chap. 35.
[86] *Ante*, p. 705. See also Law Commission Working Paper 58, proposing a new tort of breach of confidence; (1982) 41 C.L.J. 40 (G. Jones).
[87] [1976] Ch. 55, *post*, p. 766.

mutual trust between husband and wife."[88] Other kinds of confidential information will be restrained from publication along similar lines,[89] and even, in some cases, where the information is available from other public sources,[90] but not if it has been disseminated worldwide, for in such a case the injunction would be futile.[91] It is necessary that the plaintiff should himself have an interest in preventing the disclosure,[92] although he need not show that the use of the information would cause him detriment.[93] Even where the injunction is granted, it may be that the defendant is enjoined from making use of the confidential information only for a limited period rather than for all time.[94]

As the right to the preservation of confidence is an equitable interest, third parties with notice may be bound by the duty of confidence.[95] Injunctions may, therefore, be granted against third parties, such as the press, who seek to publish confidential information knowing it to be such.[96] The third party, however, is not necessarily in the same position as the original confidant, as their respective duties may be different.[97] But worldwide publication releases third parties[98] (but probably not the original confidant[99]) from any duty of confidence. Similarly if the duty of confidence is outweighed by a countervailing public interest requiring disclosure, as discussed below.

The injunction will be refused if the public interest in the preservation of confidence is overridden by some other public interest. While

---

[88] *Argyll* v. *Argyll* [1967] Ch. 302 at p. 332.

[89] *Saltman Engineering Co. Ltd.* v. *Campbell Engineering Co. Ltd.* [1963] 3 All E.R. 413n; *Peter Pan Manufacturing Corporation* v. *Corsets Silhouette Ltd.* [1964] 1 W.L.R. 96; *Seager* v. *Copydex* [1967] 1 W.L.R. 923; *Thomas Marshall (Exports) Ltd.* v. *Guinle* [1979] Ch. 227; *Fraser* v. *Thames Television Ltd.* [1984] Q.B. 44; (1983) 42 C.L.J. 209 (A. Tettenborn). See generally (1977) 9 Patent L. Rev. 271 (J. W. Berryhill); (1979) 95 L.Q.R. 323 (W. J. Braithwaite).

[90] *Schering Chemicals Ltd.* v. *Falkman Ltd.* [1982] Q.B. 1; *Att.-Gen.* v. *Guardian Newspapers Ltd.* [1987] 1 W.L.R. 1248 (*Spycatcher* at the interlocutory stage); (1988) 47 C.L.J. 2 (D. G. T. Williams).

[91] *Att.-Gen.* v. *Guardian Newspapers Ltd. (No. 2)* [1988] 3 W.L.R. 776 (*Spycatcher* final injunction refused).

[92] *Fraser* v. *Evans* [1969] 1 Q.B. 349; *Hubbard* v. *Vosper* [1972] 2 Q.B. 84.

[93] *X.* v. *Y.* [1988] 2 All E.R. 648. See the varying views in *Att.-Gen.* v. *Guardian Newspapers Ltd. (No. 2)*, *supra*.

[94] This is the "springboard" doctrine. See (1979) 42 M.L.R. 94 (W. J. Braithwaite); (1976) 92 L.Q.R. 180 (M. W. Bryan); *Bullivant (Roger) Ltd.* v. *Ellis* [1987] I.C.R. 464.

[95] *Att.-Gen.* v. *Guardian Newspapers Ltd. (No. 2)*, *supra* (*Sunday Times* liable to account for profits of publication before defence of worldwide dissemination available). See also *Printers and Finishers Ltd.* v. *Holloway* [1965] 1 W.L.R. 1; *Goddard* v. *Nationwide Building Society* [1987] Q.B. 670; Law Com. No. 110, *Breach of Confidence* (1981), para. 4.11.

[96] *Att.-Gen.* v. *Guardian Newspapers Ltd.* [1987] 1 W.L.R. 1248, and *(No. 2)* [1988] 3 W.L.R. 776 (*Spycatcher*).

[97] *Att.-Gen.* v. *Guardian Newspapers Ltd. (No. 2)*, *supra*.

[98] *Ibid.* (*Spycatcher* final injunction refused).

[99] *Ibid.*; the reasoning being that he must not profit from his own wrong (assuming that he was responsible for the publication).

the precise scope of the "public interest" defence remains uncertain,[1] it is clear that matters such as confidentiality or national security[2] must be balanced against the public interest in freedom of speech and the press and the right to receive information. More particularly, there is no confidence as to the disclosure of "iniquity." This principle was recently discussed by the House of Lords in *Att.-Gen.* v. *Guardian Newspapers Ltd. (No. 2)*,[3] where the question was whether newspapers should be enjoined from publishing *Spycatcher* (the Peter Wright memoirs). It was said that the "iniquity" defence was subject to two limitations. First, the disclosure of confidential information revealing wrong-doing should in some cases be to interested parties such as the police rather than to the public at large.[4] Secondly, the duty of confidence was not overridden by mere allegations of wrong-doing. While the wrong-doing need not be proved, there must be at least a prima facie case that the allegations have substance. Further, it was not the case that *any* breach of the law was within the "iniquity" defence. In the present case, the publication of the entire book or substantial extracts could not be within this defence when the allegations of "iniquity" covered only a few pages. The final injunction was, however, refused because the information was by this time within the public domain.

Where there is no wrong-doing by the plaintiff the public interest defence will succeed only in exceptional cases. Such a case was *Lion Laboratories Ltd.* v. *Evans*,[5] where the plaintiff failed to restrain the publication of confidential documents concerning the accuracy of a "breathalyser" device manufactured by the plaintiff. The public interest in confidentiality had to be weighed against its interest in the accuracy of a device upon which depended the citizen's liability to criminal penalties. There might be circumstances where it was right to

---

[1] Goff and Jones, *op. cit* at p. 682. See also *Att.-Gen.* v. *Jonathan Cape Ltd.* [1976] Q.B. 752 (the Crossman diaries); *Schering Chemicals Ltd.* v. *Falkman Ltd.* [1982] Q.B. 1; (1982) 41 C.L.J. 40 (G. Jones); (1982) 98 L.Q.R. 5 (A. M. Tettenborn).

[2] *Att.-Gen.* v. *Guardian Newspapers Ltd.* [1987] 1 W.L.R. 1248, and *(No. 2)* [1988] 3 W.L.R. 776 (*Spycatcher*). The latter decision, however, is not based on the balancing of public interests but on the fact that no further damage could be caused by publication.

[3] *Supra.* The "iniquity" involved alleged plots to overthrow the Wilson government and to kill President Nasser.

[4] See also *Francome* v. *Mirror Group Newspapers* [1984] 1 W.L.R. 892 (injunction to restrain publication of illegally taped telephone conversations revealing possible criminal offences and breaches of Jockey Club regulations. Public interest could be served by making tapes available to police of Jockey Club); *cf. Cork* v. *McVicar, The Times,* October 31, 1984 (Exposure of corrupt practices in the administration of justice not to be restrained by injunction, although clear breach of contract and confidence. Argument that disclosure should only be to the appropriate authorities rejected). The suggestion in *Att.-Gen.* v. *Guardian Newspapers Ltd. (No. 2)* was that the editor should inform the Treasury Solicitor or report the allegations to the appropriate Minister and proceed to publish only if no effective action was taken.

[5] [1985] Q.B. 526 (interlocutory); (1984) 100 L.Q.R. 517; (1985) 44 C.L.J. 35 (Y. Cripps); (1985) 48 M.L.R. 592 (N. V. Lowe and C. J. Willmore).

publish confidential material even if unlawfully obtained in flagrant breach of confidence, and irrespective of the motive of the informer. But, it was added, what is interesting to the public should not be confused with the public interest.

Other cases where the public interest defence has succeeded include *Woodward* v. *Hutchins*,[6] where "publicity seeking" pop singers failed to restrain the publication of newspaper articles revealing "discreditable incidents" about them, and *Church of Scientology of California* v. *Miller*,[7] where the Church sought to enjoin the publication of confidential material relating to its founder. In *X.* v. *Y.*,[8] on the other hand, the defence failed when a health authority sought to restrain publication of the identity of two doctors suffering from AIDS, disclosed by its employee in breach of contract and confidence.

In the sphere of judicial proceedings, the public interest requiring the truth to be disclosed in the administration of justice does not override the confidentiality of matters disclosed in other proceedings, which may be protected by injunction.[9]

E. Public Wrongs

Although an injunction normally issues to prevent a breach of the plaintiff's own rights, it is available, at the suit of the Attorney-General, to restrain an act which is illegal or detrimental to the public. Thus the Attorney-General may obtain an injunction to restrain a public nuisance, either on his own initiative, or on the relation of some other person.[10] A private individual may only sue in respect of public wrongs where a private right of his own is interfered with,[11] or where he suffers special damage from the interference with the public right.[12] We have seen that, subject to this exception, the individual cannot sue in his own name to enforce a public right. He must bring a relator action, with the consent of the Attorney-General.[13]

---

[6] [1977] 1 W.L.R. 760 (interlocutory); criticised in Goff and Jones, *op. cit.*, p. 678. See also *Khashoggi* v. *Smith* (1980) 124 S.J. 149; *Stephens* v. *Avery* [1988] Ch. 449.

[7] *The Times*, October 23, 1987.

[8] [1988] 2 All E.R. 648.

[9] *Medway* v. *Doublelock Ltd.* [1978] 1 W.L.R. 710, (1978) 94 L.Q.R. 488 (P. Prescott). See also *Distillers Co. (Biochemicals) Ltd.* v. *Times Newspapers Ltd.* [1975] Q.B. 613; *British Steel Corporation* v. *Granada Television Ltd.* [1981] A.C. 1096 (discovery); *XAG* v. *A bank* [1983] 2 Lloyd's Rep. 535 (injunction to restrain bank from complying with foreign subpoena to produce confidential documents in court); *Goddard* v. *Nationwide Building Society* [1987] Q.B. 670.

[10] *Att.-Gen.* v. *P.Y.A. Quarries* [1975] 2 Q.B. 169.

[11] *Lyon* v. *Fishmongers Co.* (1876) 1 App.Cas. 662.

[12] *Winterbottom* v. *Lord Derby* (1867) L.R. 2 Ex. 316 at pp. 320, 322; *Benjamin* v. *Storr* (1874) L.R. 9 C.P. 400; *Meade* v. *London Borough of Haringey* [1979] 1 W.L.R. 637. (Parents suffer special damage if schools shut in breach of Education Act 1944); *Gravesham Borough Council* v. *British Railways Board* [1978] Ch. 379; *Barrs* v. *Bethell* [1982] Ch. 294; *Lonrho Ltd.* v. *Shell Petroleum Co. Ltd.* [1982] A.C. 173; *Ashby* v. *Ebdon* [1985] Ch. 394; *Holmes* v. *Checkland, The Times,* April 15, 1987; *Rickless* v. *United Artists Corp.* [1988] Q.B. 40; *CBS Songs Ltd.* v. *Amstrad Consumer Electronics plc* [1988] 2 W.L.R. 1191.

[13] *Gouriet* v. *Union of Post Office Workers* [1978] A.C. 435, *ante*, p. 702.

An injunction may issue in circumstances where it is the only effective way of protecting the interests of the public, or where the criminal penalty has proved inadequate to prevent continuous breaches of the law. It should be added that where the Attorney-General brings such an action, the injunction is almost always granted. Thus injunctions were issued where the defendant ran buses in Manchester without licence and in defiance of the corporation's objections, the profits being greater than the fines,[14] and where the defendant operated a hotel without a fire certificate, causing danger to the public.[15]

We have already seen that the view of the House of Lords is that the cases where the Attorney-General can invoke the aid of the civil courts to restrain the commission of a criminal offence are narrow and not to be extended, and may require reconsideration.[16]

Some statutory provisions enable local authorities to seek injunctions in their own name to enforce public rights, without the concurrence of the Attorney-General, upon giving the usual undertakings.[17] For example, the Local Government Act 1972, s.222[18] enables the local authority to act where it is "expedient for the promotion or protection of the interests of the inhabitants of their area." Applications under section 222 are almost invariably successful. Although the Attorney-General's power to seek injunctions to restrain criminal offences is limited to cases of emergency or inadequate criminal penalty, it has been held that the local authority's power under section 222 is not limited in this way: the only limitation is that the action must promote or protect the interests of the inhabitants.[19] But the court will be reluctant to grant an injunction if the sanctions for disobeying it would be more onerous than the criminal penalty.[20] Where the defendant is flouting a statute, an injunction may be sought before the statutory remedies have been exhausted.[21] In exceptional cases, involving a plain breach and a clear intention to continue with it, the

---

[14] *Att.-Gen.* v. *Sharp* [1931] 1 Ch. 121; *Att.-Gen.* v. *Harris* [1961] 1 Q.B. 74; (selling flowers illegally from stalls); *Att.-Gen.* v. *Bastow* [1957] 1 Q.B. 514; *Att.-Gen.* v. *Smith* [1958] 2 Q.B. 173. Such cases could now be dealt with by an action by the local authority under the Local Government Act 1972, s.222, *infra*.

[15] *Att.-Gen.* v. *Chaudry* [1971] 1 W.L.R. 1623.

[16] *Gouriet* v. *Union of Post Office Workers* [1978] A.C. 435, *ante*, p. 702.

[17] *Rochdale Borough Council* v. *Anders, The Times*, July 15, 1988.

[18] This exception was described as "limited" in *Gouriet* v. *Union of Post Office Workers, supra*. For the meaning of "local authority," see *London Docklands Development Corporation* v. *Rank Hovis Ltd.* (1985) 84 L.G.R. 101.

[19] *Kent County Council* v. *Batchelor* [1979] 1 W.L.R. 213 (breach of tree preservation order); (1979) 95 L.Q.R. 174 (D. Feldman). See also *Thanet District Council* v. *Ninedrive Ltd.* [1978] 1 All E.R. 703 (Sunday trading); *Solihull Metropolitan Borough Council* v. *Maxfern Ltd.* [1977] 1 W.L.R. 127 (Sunday trading); *Hammersmith Borough Council* v. *Magnum Automated Forecourts Ltd.* [1978] 1 W.L.R. 50 (nuisance); *Westminster City Council* v. *Jones* (1981) 80 L.G.R. 241.

[20] *Stoke-on-Trent City Council* v. *B. & Q. (Retail) Ltd.* [1984] A.C. 754; *Bradford City Metropoliton Council* v. *Brown* (1986) 84 L.G.R. 731.

[21] *Avon County Council* v. *Millard* (1985) 83 L.G.R. 597; *Runnymede Borough Council* v. *Ball* [1986] 1 W.L.R. 353.

injunction may be granted before proceedings for the statutory remedy have even been commenced.[22]

Although injunctions under section 222 are typically granted in cases of deliberate flouting or where the criminal penalty is inadequate, the jurisdiction is not confined to these circumstances.[23] Flagrant breaches of the criminal law need not be shown where there is clear evidence of persistent and serious conduct.[24] However, an injunction in aid of the criminal law is a remedy of last resort and should not be granted if a less draconian means of securing obedience is available.[25]

In the sphere of public law an injunction, declaration or prerogative order may be sought, with leave of the court, in an "application for judicial review."[26] The court may grant the injunction or declaration if, in all the circumstances, it is "just and convenient" to do so.[27] On the question of *locus standi*, it is provided that the applicant must have a "sufficient interest" in the matter.[28] In a case concerning a declaration and an order of mandamus, it has been held that one taxpayer has no sufficient interest to ask the court to investigate the tax affairs of another taxpayer or to complain that the latter has been under or over-assessed.[29] The new Order 53 has not removed the established requirements for *locus standi* by giving the court a discretion, although the test is not the same for all the remedies.[30]

The question soon arose whether, in the field of administrative law, the "application for judicial review" was an exclusive remedy, so that the plaintiff could not seek an injunction in the ordinary way. In *O'Reilly* v. *Mackman*[31] the House of Lords held that, as a general rule, it would be contrary to public policy and an abuse of process[32] for a plaintiff complaining of a public authority's infringement of his public law rights to seek redress by an ordinary action and thus avoid the

---

[22] *Stafford Borough Council* v. *Elkenford Ltd.* [1977] 1 W.L.R. 324 (Sunday trading); *Stoke-on-Trent City Council* v. *B. & Q. (Retail) Ltd., supra,* (Sunday trading).

[23] *Runnymede Borough Council* v. *Ball* [1986] 1 W.L.R. 353; (1986) 45 C.L.J. 374 (S. Tromans).

[24] *City of London Corporation* v. *Bovis Construction Ltd., The Times,* April 21, 1988; *Portsmouth City Council* v. *Richards, The Times,* November 21, 1988.

[25] *Waverley Borough Council* v. *Hilden* [1988] 1 W.L.R. 246.

[26] R.S.C., Ord. 53, codified by Supreme Court Act 1981, s.31. See (1978) 41 M.L.R. 437 (J. Beatson and M. H. Matthews); (1978) 94 L.Q.R. 179 (H.W.R.W.). See also Ord. 15, r. 16.

[27] S.C.A. 1981, s.31(2).

[28] Ord. 53, r. 3(5); S.C.A. 1981, s.31(3). See the comments of Lord Denning in *The Discipline of Law,* p. 133.

[29] *R.* v. *I.R.C., ex p. National Federation of Self-Employed and Small Businesses Ltd.* [1982] A.C. 617; (1982) 45 M.L.R. 92 (D. Feldman); (1982) 41 C.L.J. 6 (J. Griffiths). *cf. R.* v. *Her Majesty's Treasury, ex p. Smedley* [1985] Q.B. 657.

[30] *Ibid.* at p. 631, *per* Lord Wilberforce.

[31] [1983] 2 A.C. 237; (1983) 99 L.Q.R. 166 (H.W.R.W.); (1983) 42 C.L.J. 15 (J. A. Jolowicz); (1983) 46 M.L.R. 645 (M. Sunkin); (1987) 103 L.Q.R. 34 (J. Beatson).

[32] The onus is upon the defendant to establish this; *Davy* v. *Spelthorne Borough Council* [1984] A.C. 262.

protection afforded to statutory tribunals.[33] It is otherwise where the plaintiff's private law rights have been infringed.[34] Neither Order 53 nor section 31 of the Supreme Court Act 1981 provides that judicial review is an exclusive remedy. Where an action is begun as an application for judicial review but it transpires that it involves a private law right, it can be treated as if begun by writ,[35] but the converse is not the case.[36]

An ordinary injunction is appropriate where the defendant is a domestic body with no public role.[37] Where the defendant is a public body, the distinction between its public and private law functions may be illustrated as follows: a local authority's decision as to whether it has a duty to house a homeless person is a public law function, while its executive functions once it has decided that there is such a duty are matters of private law[38]; and a planning authority's decision as to an enforcement notice is a public law function, while its negligent advice as to the plaintiff's right of appeal against the notice involves private law.[39]

This approach has been described as a return to formalism; and the distinction between public and private law as a "singularly unfortunate step back to the technicalities of a bygone age."[40] Lord Denning M.R., discussing the distinction between a public authority's private and public law functions, has said, "But the division is very difficult to

[33] Which includes the requirement of leave of the court, and a three-month time limit. The new Ord. 53 has removed all the previous disadvantages of the prerogative remedies, particularly as to discovery.

[34] No private right was involved in a decision as to remission of a prison sentence. There may be other exceptions, such as where none of the parties objects.

[35] Ord. 53, r. 9(5). See *R.* v. *Secretary of State for the Home Office, ex p. Dew* [1987] 1 W.L.R. 881, holding that the discretion is only exercisable if the alleged breach of a public law obligation would result in an entitlement to damages in private law. It could not be exercised if the application for judicial review is struck out as disclosing no arguable complaint in public law, as in the present case, where allegedly negligent medical treatment of a prisoner involved only private law.

[36] Thus cases may be lost by the wrong choice of procedure, defeating the purpose of Ord. 53; see (1983) 99 L.Q.R. 166 (H.W.R.W.).

[37] *R.* v. *British Broadcasting Corporation, ex p. Lavelle* [1983] 1 W.L.R. 23; (1983) 42 C.L.J. 180 (Y. Cripps); All E.R.Rev. 1983, p. 174 (P. Elias); *Law* v. *National Greyhound Racing Club Ltd.* [1983] 1 W.L.R. 1302; *Tozer* v. *National Greyhound Racing Club Ltd., The Times,* May 16, 1983; *R.* v. *East Berkshire Health Authority, ex p. Walsh* [1985] Q.B. 152; *R.* v. *Derbyshire County Council, ex p. Noble, The Times,* November 21, 1988; *cf. R.* v. *Sec. of State for the Home Department, ex p. Benwell* [1985] Q.B. 554 (Crown servant); (1984) 43 C.L.J. (Y. Cripps).

[38] *Cocks* v. *Thanet District Council* [1983] 2 A.C. 286, overruling *De Falco* v. *Crawley Borough Council* [1980] Q.B. 460, *ante,* p. 727.

[39] *Davey* v. *Spelthorne Borough Council* [1984] A.C. 262, where the House of Lords said that the distinction between public and private law was imported from countries with separate systems, and the terms were to be used with caution here. See All E.R. Rev. 1983, p. 1 (K. Davies); (1984) 43 C.L.J. 16 (A. Grubb). See also *An Bord Bainne Co-operative Ltd. (Irish Dairy Board)* v. *Milk Marketing Board, The Times,* May 22, 1984; (1984) 43 C.L.J. 255 (J. Shaw); *Wandsworth London Borough Council* v. *Winder* [1985] A.C. 461; *Guevara* v. *Hounslow L.B.C., The Times,* April 17, 1987.

[40] (1983) 42 C.L.J. 15 at p. 18 (J. A. Jolowicz); (1985) 44 C.L.J. 415 (C. F. Forsyth); (1985) 101 L.Q.R. 486 (A. Grubb).

make. So difficult indeed that I can foresee an infinity of trouble arising from it. It makes me regret that the dichotomy was ever made. But still it has been done and you will all have to live with it in perpetuity."[41]

F. Family Matters

The court has a statutory jurisdiction to grant injunctions to restrain a husband from dealing with property so as to defeat his wife's claim to maintenance.[42] Injunctions are commonly granted in relation to occupation of the home under the provisions of the Matrimonial Homes Act 1983[43] or the Domestic Violence and Matrimonial Proceedings Act 1976.[44] Thus injunctions have been granted to restrain a husband from installing his mistress in the matrimonial home,[45] or to exclude the husband from the home,[46] or to restrain a man from living near his former wife,[47] or, in a grave case, to exclude an adult child from his parents' home.[48] But the jurisdiction is sparingly exercised; it must be necessary to protect the applicant's person or property and should never be regarded as routine.[49] It will however be freely used to prevent molestation[50] (particularly if children of the marriage are threatened) and oppression of the parties pending suit.[51] It should be added that injunctions of this kind should not be granted *ex parte* unless there is real danger of serious injury or irreparable damage.[52]

The Matrimonial Homes Act 1983 permits the grant of an injunction excluding a spouse from the matrimonial home even where that spouse is the sole owner (or tenant) of it. Similar powers are conferred on the county court by Domestic Violence and Matrimonial Proceedings Act

---

[41] *The Closing Chapter*, p. 125. See also (1984) 81 L.S.Gaz. 2207 (N. Saunders).

[42] Matrimonial Causes Act 1973, s.37; Matrimonial and Family Proceedings Act 1984, s.24. See also *Roche* v. *Roche* (1981) 11 Fam.Law 243.

[43] Replacing the Act of 1967. The extent of the court's inherent jurisdiction, after *Richards* v. *Richards* [1984] A.C. 174, *infra*, is doubtful.

[44] (1977) 41 Conv.(N.S.) 330 (J. G. Miller); (1978) 37 C.L.J. 252 (D. Pearl); (1986) 16 Fam.Law 70 (P. Parkinson). See also Domestic Proceedings and Magistrates' Courts Act 1978, ss.16 *et seq.*; *McCartney* v. *McCartney* [1981] Fam. 59.

[45] *Pinckney* v. *Pinckney* [1966] 1 All E.R. 121.

[46] *Hall* v. *Hall* [1971] 1 W.L.R. 404; *Phillips* v. *Phillips* [1973] 1 W.L.R. 615.

[47] *M* v. *M* (1983) 13 Fam.Law 110. *cf. Patel* v. *Patel* [1988] 2 F.L.R. 179 (no non-statutory jurisdiction to prevent a person approaching another's house by injunction).

[48] *Egan* v. *Egan* [1975] Ch. 218 (a clear history of assaults, and threats of more).

[49] *Des Salles d'Epinoix* v. *Des Salles d'Epinoix* [1967] 1 W.L.R. 553; *Burke* v. *Burke* (1987) 17 Fam.Law 201; *Summers* v. *Summers* (1987) 137 N.L.J. 611; *Wiseman* v. *Simpson* [1988] 1 W.L.R. 35.

[50] *Nanda* v. *Nanda* [1968] P. 351. See also *Re G.* (1983) 13 Fam.Law. 50 (no power of arrest may be attached in wardship cases).

[51] *Pinckney* v. *Pinckney*, *supra*.

[52] *Practice Note* [1978] 1 W.L.R. 925; *Ansah* v. *Ansah* [1977] Fam. 138; *Masich* v. *Masich* (1977) 7 Fam.Law. 245.

1976, s.1, which extends to unmarried couples living together as husband and wife.[53] Such injunctions do not confer any proprietary rights on the applicant, and should normally be of limited duration.[54] If granted, the order should be made to take effect within a week or two. It should not be left hanging over the defendant's head or used as a threat: there is no such thing as an ouster order nisi.[55]

It has recently been held by the House of Lords in *Richards* v. *Richards*[56] that the needs of any children, while an important consideration, are not paramount in ouster injunctions. The majority held that the court's power to order a spouse to vacate the home derived from the Matrimonial Homes Act, and must be exercised according to the criteria laid down in section 1(3), namely the conduct of the spouses, their needs and resources, the needs of any children, and all the circumstances of the case, none of these considerations being paramount. The needs of the children were only paramount in cases where section 1 of the Guardianship of Minors Act 1971 applied, where their custody or upbringing was directly in question.[57] Lord Scarman, however, considered that the court's inherent jurisdiction was not excluded by the Matrimonial Homes Act. It appears, however, that the inherent jurisdiction remains where the welfare of children is involved, although the matter requires clarification.[58]

Section 1 of the 1976 Act also enables the county court to grant injunctions to restrain one spouse from molesting the other spouse or a child living with the applicant spouse.[59] Section 2 permits a power of arrest to be attached to an injunction granted to restrain violence against the applicant or child or to exclude the other party from the

---

[53] *Adeoso* v. *Adeoso* [1980] 1 W.L.R. 1535. No other relief need be sought in proceedings under s.1. See *Crutcher* v. *Crutcher* (1978) 8 Fam.Law. 227; *Spindlow* v. *Spindlow* [1979] Fam. 52. There is no jurisdiction if the cohabitation has ceased; *Ainsbury* v. *Millington* [1986] 1 All E.R. 73.

[54] *Practice Notes* [1978] 1 W.L.R. 1123, [1981] 1 W.L.R. 27; *Davis* v. *Johnson* [1979] A.C. 264; *Hopper* v. *Hopper* [1978] 1 W.L.R. 1342; *Galan* v. *Galan* (1985) 15 Fam.Law 256; *cf. Spencer* v. *Camacho* (1983) 13 Fam.Law. 114; *Baggott* v. *Baggott* (1986) 16 Fam.Law 129 (order under M.H.A. 1983).

[55] *Burke* v. *Burke* (1987) 17 Fam.Law 201.

[56] [1984] A.C. 174; All E.R.Rev. 1983, p. 212 (R. Deech); (1984) 100 L.Q.R. 4 (J. Thomson); (1984) 43 C.L.J. 38 (J. C. Hall). See also *Eade* v. *Eade* (1983) 13 Fam.Law. 142. For procedure, see *Practice Direction* [1983] 1 W.L.R. 999. As to unmarried couples, see *Lee* v. *Lee* [1984] 5 F.L.R. 243 (same principle applies to applications under Domestic Violence and Matrimonial Proceedings Act 1976 by the unmarried).

[57] *T.* v. *T.* (1986) 16 Fam.Law 298.

[58] *Wilde* v. *Wilde* [1988] 2 F.L.R. 83; *Webb* v. *Webb* [1986] 1 F.L.R. 541; *cf. Ainsbury* v. *Millington* [1986] 1 All E.R. 73; *M.* v. *M.* [1988] 1.F.L.R. 225. See (1988) Journal of Social Welfare Law 110 (S. Edwards and A. Halpern); (1988) 18 Fam.Law 273 (P. Moor and N. Mostyn) and 395 (Judge Nigel Fricker Q.C.).

[59] This provision extends to parties living together as husband and wife.

home.[60] The judge must be satisfied that the defendant has caused actual bodily harm and is likely to do so again. The power of arrest is not to be regarded as a routine remedy, and should be used only in exceptional circumstances.[61]

The remedy of injunction is also employed in the protection of minors; for example, to restrain a wife from passing on to a child a letter which she had written[62]; to restrain persons who had enticed a girl of 16 away from her father, from continuing to harbour her[63]; in support of a custody order[64]; to protect a ward from publicity[65]; or to restrain the mother of a ward from leaving the jurisdiction before submitting to a test to establish its paternity.[66] It is in connection with equity's special care concerning minors that most risks are taken with regard to the issue of injunctions against persons outside the jurisdiction.[67]

As we have seen, a husband cannot obtain an injunction to prevent his wife from having an abortion.[68]

Applications for injunctions in matrimonial causes in the High Court or county court are heard in chambers, but the judge has a discretion to hear any particular application in open court.[69]

Finally, the use of *Mareva* and *Anton Piller* injunctions in family matters is dealt with below.[70]

G. Trade Unions, Clubs and Colleges

Some use of the injunction has been made as a remedy against trade unions.[71] Perhaps the most important use of the injunction in this field has been to restrain the expulsion of a member by his union where such

---

[60] This power is also conferred on the High Court when granting injunctions in these terms: *Crutcher* v. *Crutcher, supra*; *Lewis* v. *Lewis* [1978] Fam. 60. See also *Boylan* v. *Boylan* (1981) 11 Fam.Law. 76. There is no inherent jurisdiction to attach a power of arrest; *Harrison* v. *Lewis* [1988] 2 F.L.R. 339.

[61] *Lewis* v. *Lewis, supra*. See also *McLaren* v. *Mclaren* (1978) 9 Fam.Law 153; *Horner* v. *Horner* [1982] Fam. 90; *White* v. *White* [1983] Fam. 54.

[62] *R.* v. *R. & I.* [1961] 1 W.L.R. 1334.

[63] *Lough* v. *Ward* [1945] 2 All E.R. 338.

[64] *Re W. (a minor)* [1983] 3 All E.R. 401; doubted (1982) 45 M.L.R. 468 (G. Douglas).

[65] *Re X. (a minor)* [1984] 1 W.L.R. 1422; All E.R.Rev. 1985, p. 74 (C. J. Miller).

[66] *Re I. (a minor), The Times,* May 22, 1987.

[67] *Re Liddell's S.T.* [1936] Ch. 365; *Harben* v. *Harben* [1957] 1 W.L.R. 261; *Re O.* [1962] 1 W.L.R. 724. See also *Practice Direction* [1983] 1 W.L.R. 558 (injunctions to restrain removal of child from jurisdiction).

[68] *Paton* v. *Trustees of British Pregnancy Advisory Service* [1979] Q.B. 276; (1979) 42 M.L.R. 324 (I. M. Kennedy) *ante*, p. 705; *C.* v. *S.* [1988] Q.B. 135; (1987) 103 L.Q.R. 340 (A. Grubb and D. Pearl).

[69] *Practice Direction* [1974] 1 W.L.R. 936.

[70] *Emanuel* v. *Emanuel* [1982] 1 W.L.R. 669; *Roche* v. *Roche* (1981) 11 Fam.Law. 243; *K.* v. *K.* (1983) 13 Fam.Law. 46; *Law Society* v. *Shanks* [1988] 1 F.L.R. 504; *post*, p. 767.

[71] See also Employment Act 1980, s.4, providing additional remedies against unreasonable exclusion or expulsion from a trade union.

expulsion is contrary to the rules of the union,[72] or the rules of natural justice.[73]

The right of a member of an association to invoke the assistance of the courts in resisting expulsion is essentially a contractual right,[74] the subject-matter of the implied contract being the property of the association. It was once thought that where the association had no property, the right of membership would not be protected by injunction.[75] But modern decisions have established that the right to an injunction is not confined to cases where the plaintiff has some proprietary right. A member may seek an injunction, for example, to protect his "right to work,"[76] or where matters of public importance are concerned.[77] But the mere fact of membership is not, in the absence of these special considerations, sufficient to found a claim to an injunction.[78] Equity will not compel persons to remain in continual and personal relations with one another.[79]

Injunctions have also been granted to professional men who have been dismissed contrary to the rules of their profession, though usually only where improper motive or bad faith can be shown,[80] and to members expelled by social clubs, either in breach of the rules of the club, or where the club has acted in breach of natural justice. Thus, in *Labouchere* v. *Earl of Wharncliffe*,[81] the general meeting of a club, summoned without proper notice, expelled the plaintiff without full inquiry, without giving him notice of any definite charge, and by a resolution carried by an insufficient majority. The court granted an injunction against such purported expulsion.

Injunctions are sometimes sought by students or teachers dismissed

---

[72] See *Osborne* v. *Amalgamated Society of Railway Servants* [1911] 1 Ch. 540; *Lee* v. *Showmen's Guild* [1952] 2 Q.B. 329. The plaintiff should normally, however, exhaust other remedies available to him under the rules before the court will entertain his application: *White* v. *Kuzych* [1951] A.C. 585; but *cf. Lawlor* v. *Union of Post Office Workers* [1965] Ch. 712. As to interlocutory injunctions, see (1977) 127 N.L.J. 654 (R. Kidner).

[73] *Edwards* v. *SOGAT* [1971] Ch. 354; *Breen* v. *A.E.U.* [1971] 2 Q.B. 175; *Shotton* v. *Hammond* (1976) 120 S.J. 780. The rules cannot oust the court's jurisdiction: *Leigh* v. *N.U.R.* [1970] Ch. 326.

[74] *White* v. *Kuzych, supra*; *Bonsor* v. *Musicians' Union* [1956] A.C. 104.

[75] *Rigby* v. *Connol* (1880) 14 Ch.D. 482.

[76] *Edwards* v. *SOGAT, supra*; *cf. Gaiman* v. *National Association for Mental Health* [1971] Ch. 317 (no injunction as membership involved no question of property, livelihood or reputation).

[77] *Woodford* v. *Smith* [1970] 1 W.L.R. 806, concerning membership of a ratepayers' association, where an injunction was granted to restrain a breach of contract (the holding of a meeting without permitting the plaintiff members to attend and vote), even though the value of any property rights of a member was negligible and no question of livelihood was involved.

[78] *Baird* v. *Wells* (1890) 44 Ch.D. 661.

[79] *Lumley* v. *Wagner* (1852) 1 De G.M. & G. 604; *cf. Rigby* v. *Connol* (1880) 14 Ch.D. 482 at pp. 487, 488, *per* Jessel M.R.

[80] *Hayman* v. *Governors of Rugby School* (1874) L.R. 18 Eq. 28; *Cassel* v. *Inglis* [1916] 2 Ch. 211; *Weinberger* v. *Inglis* [1919] A.C. 606.

[81] (1879) 13 Ch.D. 346; and see *Harington* v. *Sendall* [1903] 1 Ch. 921; *cf. Dawkins* v. *Antrobus* (1881) 17 Ch.D. 615.

from a university without a fair hearing, in breach of the rules of natural justice, to restrain the university authorities from acting on the dismissal.[82] But the court has no jurisdiction if the university constitution provides for the appointment of a visitor.[83] Where the university is incorporated by royal charter the Crown is entitled to appoint the visitor. Pending the appointment, the Crown is the visitor, and the visitatorial powers are exercisable by the Lord Chancellor on behalf of the Crown. Thus it appears that, in the case of most modern universities, the Crown is the visitor.[84] The visitor has sole and exclusive jurisdiction over the internal affairs of the university and all membership disputes, including admission and expulsion, but not disputes between the foundation and outsiders.[85] If the visitor exceeds, or refuses to exercise, his powers, then he will be subject to an order of prohibition, certiorari or mandamus by the court.[86]

H. Judicial Proceedings

In proper cases, judicial proceedings in inferior courts,[87] administrative tribunals,[88] and private prosecutions[89] may be restrained. So also the initiation of proceedings in the High Court,[90] but once commenced, proceedings in the High Court are not subject to injunction; indeed interference with such proceedings may itself be restrained by

---

[82] *Glynn* v. *Keele University* [1971] 1 W.L.R. 487; *Herring* v. *Templeman* [1973] 3 All E.R. 569; *cf. R.* v. *Senate of the University of Aston, ex p. Roffey* [1969] 2 Q.B. 538 (where certiorari was thought appropriate). See (1969) 85 L.Q.R. 468 (H. W. R. Wade); (1970) 86 L.Q.R. 531 (J. W. Bridge); (1981) 97 L.Q.R. 610 (P. M. Smith).

[83] *Patel* v. *University of Bradford Senate* [1979] 1 W.L.R. 1066, affirming the decision of Megarry V.-C. [1978] 1 W.L.R. 1488, where a fuller discussion appears.

[84] The universities of Oxford and Cambridge, as distinct from the colleges, have no visitor.

[85] See *Thomas* v. *University of Bradford* [1987] A.C. 795, *ante*, p. 444, where the House of Lords reviewed the authorities.

[86] *Thomas* v. *University of Bradford, supra; R.* v. *University of London, ex p. Vijaytunga* [1988] Q.B. 322.

[87] *Re Connolly Bros. Ltd.* [1911] 1 Ch. 731 (Lancaster Palatine Court); *The Teresa* (1894) 71 L.T. 342 (Liverpool Court of Passage); *Thames Launches* v. *Trinity House Corporation (Deptford Strond)* [1966] Ch. 197 (magistrates' court); *Murcutt* v. *Murcutt* [1952] P. 266 (county court). See also *Johns* v. *Chatalos* [1973] 1 W.L.R. 1437.

[88] de Smith, *Judicial Review of Administrative Action* (4th ed.), pp. 470 *et seq.*

[89] *Thames Launches* v. *Trinity House (Deptford Strond)* [1966] Ch. 197; followed in *Conteh* v. *Onslow Fane, The Times*, June 25, 1975.

[90] *McHenry* v. *Lewis* (1882) 22 Ch.D. 397; *Ellerman Lines* v. *Read* [1928] 2 K.B. 144; *Orr-Lewis* v. *Orr-Lewis* [1949] P. 347; *Settlement Corporation* v. *Hochschild* [1966] Ch. 10. See also *Bryanston Finance Ltd.* v. *De Vries (No. 2)* [1976] Ch. 63 (winding-up petition).

injunction as a contempt of court.[91] It might be added that arbitration proceedings may, in certain cases, be restrained by injunction.[92]

Judicial proceedings in foreign courts may be restrained by injunction, where this is appropriate to avoid an injustice, but this is a jurisdiction to be exercised with great caution. Such an injunction will only be issued against a party who is amenable to the jurisdiction of the English court. It is directed not to the foreign court, but to the parties.[93]

I. Legislative Proceedings

It is very doubtful whether an injunction will lie to restrain the introduction or enactment of a Bill,[94] or to restrain the making of a subordinate legislative instrument.[95] It is, however, possible that an injunction may be granted to restrain the breach of contractual obligations not to promote or to petition against a private Bill,[96] or to restrain unauthorised expenditure of public funds in promoting or opposing a private Bill.[97] But no injunction will lie to restrain any procedure concerning a public Bill.[98]

J. To Prevent Removal or Destruction of Evidence: The "Anton Piller" Injunction

This type of injunction is designed to secure that pending trial[99] the defendant does not dispose of any articles in his possession which could be prejudicial at the trial.[1] It is "an illustration of the adaptability of

---

[91] *Att.-Gen.* v. *Times Newspapers Ltd.* [1974] A.C. 273. But this decision was held by the European Court (April 26, 1979) to infringe Art. 10 of the European Convention on Human Rights, which guarantees freedom of expression. See (1979) 95 L.Q.R. 348 (F. A. Mann); (1979) 38 C.L.J. 242 (C. Gray); Lord Denning, *The Due Process of Law,* pp. 45–49. See also *Att.-Gen.* v. *London Weekend Television Ltd.* [1973] 1 W.L.R. 202.

[92] The difficulties caused by *Bremer Vulkan Schiffbau und Maschinenfabrik* v. *South India Shipping Corporation* [1981] A.C. 909 are reviewed in *Food Corporation of India* v. *Antclizo Shipping Corporation* [1988] 1 W.L.R. 603, where legislative reform is suggested. See Mustill and Boyd, *The Law and Practice of Commercial Arbitration in England,* pp. 451 *et seq.* See also Arbitration Act 1979, s.5.

[93] See Dicey and Morris, *The Conflict of Laws* (11th ed.), pp. 396 *et seq.*; Keeton and Sheridan's *Equity* (3rd ed.), pp. 401–405; *Société Nationale Industrielle Aerospatiale* v. *Lee Kui Jak* [1987] A.C. 871. See also Civil Jurisdiction and Judgments Act 1982, s.49.

[94] Bill of Rights 1688, s.1, Art. 9; see de Smith, *op. cit.* pp. 465 *et seq.*

[95] *Harper* v. *Secretary of State for Home Affairs* [1955] Ch. 238; see also *Bates* v. *Lord Hailsham of St. Marylebone* [1972] 1 W.L.R. 1373.

[96] *Bilston Corporation* v. *Wolverhampton Corporation* [1942] Ch. 391.

[97] *Att.-Gen.* v. *London and Home Counties Joint Electricity Authority* [1929] 1 Ch. 513.

[98] *Att.-Gen. for New South Wales* v. *Trethowan* [1932] A.C. 526; doubted in *Hughes and Vale Pty. Ltd.* (1954) 90 C.L.R. 203 at p. 204.

[99] Or after judgment, in aid of execution; *Distributori Automatici Italia SpA* v. *Holford General Trading Co. Ltd.* [1985] 1 W.L.R. 1066.

[1] The injunction may be granted in respect of a document which is not itself the subject-matter of the action; *Yousif* v. *Salama* [1980] 1 W.L.R. 1540 (accounts and a diary); *Emanuel* v. *Emanuel* [1982] 1 W.L.R. 669 (documents relating to husband's earnings and assets). See also Practice Note [1982] 1 W.L.R. 1420, as to hearings in camera, and *W.E.A. Records Ltd.* v. *Visions Channel 4 Ltd.* [1983] 1 W.L.R. 721, as to the hearing of appeals.

equitable remedies to new situations."[2] It is particularly useful to plaintiffs who are the victims of commercial malpractice, such as breach of confidence, breach of copyright and passing off. It has also been used in the family context, as in *Emanuel* v. *Emanuel*,[3] where a husband had been ordered in matrimonial proceedings to transfer properties and to pay a lump sum to his wife. He failed to comply, and had sold a property in breach of an undertaking and spent the proceeds. An *Anton Piller* order was granted to allow the wife's solicitors to enter his home to inspect documents relating to his earnings and capital. It is essential that such an order be available *ex parte*, so that the defendant is not forewarned: "If the stable door cannot be bolted, the horse must be secured. . . . If the horse is liable to be spirited away, notice of an intention to secure the horse will defeat the intention."[4]

The *Anton Piller* order has been variously described as "a draconian power which should be used only in very exceptional cases,"[5] and as "an innovation which has proved its worth time and time again."[6] The first reported decision in modern times was *EMI Ltd.* v. *Pandit*,[7] where an *ex parte* order was made in a breach of copyright action to enable the plaintiff to enter the defendant's premises to inspect, photograph and remove infringing articles. The practice was confirmed by the Court of Appeal in *Anton Piller KG* v. *Manufacturing Processes Ltd.*[8]

> The defendants had received confidential information and plans concerning the plaintiff's electrical equipment in their capacity as the plaintiff's selling agents in England. The plaintiffs had reason to believe that the defendants were selling the information to the plaintiff's competitors, but were unable to prove this without access to documents situated on the defendants' premises.
>
> The Court of Appeal made an *ex parte* order,[9] requiring the defendants to permit the plaintiffs to enter their premises, and

---

[2] *Rank Film Distributors Ltd.* v. *Video Information Centre* [1982] A.C. 380 at p. 439 (*per* Lord Wilberforce).

[3] [1982] 1 W.L.R. 669; *K.* v. *K.* (1983) 13 Fam.Law 46. See also *Roche* v. *Roche* (1981) 11 Fam.Law 243 (*Mareva* injunction).

[4] *Rank Film Distributors Ltd.* v. *Video Information Centre* [1982] A.C. 380 at p. 418 (Templeman L.J.).

[5] *Yousif* v. *Salama* [1980] 1 W.L.R. 1540 at p. 1544 (*per* Donaldson L.J.). His Lordship, dissenting, regarded the order granted by the majority as a power to 'take' discovery.

[6] *Rank Film Distributors Ltd.* v. *Video Information Centre* [1982] A.C. 380 at p. 406 (Lord Denning M.R.).

[7] [1975] 1 W.L.R. 302. See also the 19th century cases and modern unreported cases there cited.

[8] [1976] Ch. 55; (1977) N.L.J. 753 (P. Russell); [1977] *Public Law* 369 (M. Dockray); All E.R.Rev. 1982, p. 218 (A. A. S. Zuckerman); (1983) 46 M.L.R. 274 (A. Staines); Lord Denning, *The Due Process of Law*, pp. 123 *et seq.* See also *Vapormatic Co. Ltd.* v. *Sparex* [1976] 1 W.L.R. 939; *Universal City Studios Inc.* v. *Mukhtar & Sons Ltd.* [1976] 1 W.L.R. 568 (order to hand over unlicensed "Jaws" T-shirts); *EMI Ltd.* v. *Sarwar* [1977] F.S.R. 146.

[9] The practice was affirmed by the Court of Appeal in a decision *inter partes*: *Rank Film Distributors Ltd.* v. *Video Information Centre, supra*, which was upheld on appeal [1982] A.C. 380. See also Supreme Court Act 1981, s.33(1).

inspect documents relating to the equipment, and an injunction restraining the defendants from breaching their copyright or making improper use of the confidential information. Such an order would only be made in exceptional circumstances, where it was essential that the plaintiff should inspect the documents to enable justice to be done between the parties, and there was a danger that vital evidence would otherwise be destroyed.

Unlike a search warrant, the order does not authorise the plaintiff to enter against the defendant's will. But it does order him to permit the plaintiff to enter, so that, if the defendant does not comply, not only does he commit a contempt of court, but adverse inferences will be drawn against him at the trial. Ormrod L.J. laid down three conditions for the grant of the order.[10]

(i) The plaintiff must have an extremely strong prima facie case;

(ii) The plaintiff must show actual or potential damage of a very serious nature;

(iii) There is clear evidence that the defendant has incriminating documents or things and a real possibility of their destruction before an *inter partes* application can be made.[11]

A further requirement was added by Lord Denning M.R.: the inspection will do no real harm to the defendant. It might be added that the order should not be sought as a "fishing expedition."[12]

In the enforcement of the order, the plaintiff must act with circumspection. He should be attended by his solicitor,[13] and must undertake in damages, so as to safeguard the defendant's rights. Because of the draconian nature of the order, the applicant is under a strict duty to make full and frank disclosure of all relevant matters to the court.[13a] Having obtained the order, he must neither act oppressively nor abuse his power in executing it.[14] Where the plaintiff or his solicitor has acted improperly the court may set aside the order. Even if it is not set aside,

[10] In *Anton Piller KG* v. *Manufacturing Processes Ltd., supra.* For further guidelines, particularly as to delivery of chattels, see *CBS United Kingdom Ltd.* v. *Lambert* [1983] Ch. 37. See also *Digital Equipment Corporation* v. *Darkcrest Ltd.* [1984] Ch. 512.

[11] See *Yousif* v. *Salama, supra*; *Jeffrey Rogers Knitwear Productions Ltd.* v. *Vinola (Knitwear) Manufacturing Co., The Times*, December 5, 1984.

[12] *i.e.* as a means of finding out what charges can be made; *Hytrac Conveyors Ltd.* v. *Conveyors International Ltd.* [1983] 1 W.L.R. 44. See also *Systematica Ltd.* v. *London Computer Centre Ltd., The Times*, November 16, 1982 (costs).

[13] The solicitor should avoid arriving simultaneously with police executing a search warrant; *I.T.C. Film Distributors Ltd.* v. *Video Exchange Ltd.* [1982] Ch. 431. The court might consider restricting the hours during which the solicitor could effect the search; *Randolph M. Fields* v. *Watts, The Times*, November 22, 1984 (where held *Anton Piller* order should not be made against practising barristers and their clerks).

[13a] *Dormeuil Frères SA* v. *Nicolian International (Textiles) Ltd.* [1988] 1 W.L.R. 1362 (proper time to hear application for discharge for non-disclosure is at the trial rather than at the interlocutory stage, as normally order has been executed and issue is one of damages).

[14] *Columbia Picture Industries Inc.* v. *Robinson* [1987] Ch. 38; (1987) 46 C.L.J. 50 (N. H. Andrews).

the defendant may be entitled to exemplary damages,[15] and the solicitor may be found to be in contempt.[16] Scott J. has recently expressed grave disquiet that the development of the *Anton Piller* practice has gone too far in favour of the plaintiff and that the safeguards to the defendant are inadequate.[17]

After execution of the order, the plaintiff is subject to an implied undertaking not to use the documents or other articles for any collateral purpose without the defendant's consent.[18] This implied undertaking may be modified by the court, for example by permitting the use of documents to support a contempt action against the defendant.[19]

The utility of the *Anton Piller* injunction suffered a set-back when the House of Lords held in *Rank Film Distributors Ltd.* v. *Video Information Centre*,[20] a copyright case, that the defendant could invoke the privilege against self-incrimination. But the privilege was subsequently withdrawn by section 72 of the Supreme Court Act 1981, in the case of proceedings to obtain disclosure of information relating to the infringement of rights pertaining to any intellectual property[21] or passing-off. Matters disclosed as a result of such proceedings are not admissible in evidence against the defendant in proceedings against him for a related offence.[22] But the defendant may still invoke the privilege against self-incrimination in a case where the possible offence is not included in section 72.[23]

The court has jurisdiction, in exceptional cases, to grant an *Anton Piller* injunction permitting the inspection of premises which are outside the United Kingdom.[24]

---

[15] *Ibid.*
[16] *VDU Installations Ltd.* v. *Integrated Computer Systems & Cybernetics Ltd., The Times*, August 13, 1988.
[17] *Columbia Picture Industries Inc.* v. *Robinson, supra*; All E.R.Rev. 1986, p. 225 (A. A. S. Zuckerman); (1987) 1 *Trust Law & Practice* 146 (C. Bell).
[18] *EMI Records Ltd.* v. *Spillane* [1986] 1 W.L.R. 967. See also R.S.C. Ord. 24, r. 14A.
[19] *Crest Homes plc* v. *Marks* [1987] A.C. 829; All E.R.Rev. 1987, p. 193 (A. A. S. Zuckerman); *Garvin* v. *Domus Publishing Ltd.* [1988] 3 W.L.R. 344.
[20] [1982] A.C. 380. Templeman L.J. in the Court of Appeal thought the court would not be slow to award high damages where the defendant sought to rely on the privilege; [1982] A.C. 380 at p. 423.
[21] Defined as patents, trade marks, copyrights, design rights, registered designs, technical or commercial information or other intellectual property; s.72(5).
[22] s.72(3), modelled on Theft Act 1968, s.31(1). It is otherwise in the case of proceedings for contempt or perjury, s.72(4). For the construction of s.72, see *Universal City Studies Inc.* v. *Hubbard* Ch. 225; All E.R.Rev. 1983, p. 266 (A. A. S. Zuckerman); *Crest Homes plc* v. *Marks* [1987] A.C. 829. See generally (1983) 46 M.L.R. 274 (A. Staines).
[23] See *Emanuel* v. *Emanuel* [1982] 1 W.L.R. 669 (Revenue offences).
[24] *Cook Industries Inc.* v. *Galliher* [1979] Ch. 439 (inspection of Paris flat). If the defendant is foreign, he must be served in England or be able to be served outside the jurisdiction; *Altertext Inc.* v. *Advanced Data Communications Ltd.* [1985] 1 W.L.R. 457; All E.R.Rev. 1985, p. 223 (A. A. S. Zuckerman).

K. To Prevent Removal of Assets: The "Mareva" Injunction

(i) **General Principles.** This injunction takes its name from the case of *Mareva Compania Naviera S.A.* v. *International Bulkcarriers S.A.*,[25] although the first reported exercise of this novel jurisdiction occurred in the case of *Nippon Yusen Kaisha* v. *Karageorgis.*[26] It has been described by Lord Denning M.R. as "the greatest piece of judicial law reform in my time."[27]

"A *Mareva* injunction is interlocutory, not final; it is ancillary to a substantive pecuniary claim for debt or damages; it is designed to prevent the judgment . . . for a sum of money being a mere 'brutum fulmen.' "[28] The usual purpose of a *Mareva* injunction is to prevent the dissipation or removal of assets before trial, so that if the plaintiff succeeds in the action, there will be property of the defendant available to satisfy the judgment. But it may also be granted after final judgment if the plaintiff can show grounds for believing that the defendant will dispose of his assets to avoid execution.[29]

The *Mareva* injunction is always interlocutory, and usually *ex parte*: speed is of the essence.[30] It is frequently sought in conjunction with an *Anton Piller* order. The basis of the jurisdiction is now the Supreme Court Act 1981, s.37: the injunction may be granted whenever it is "just and convenient" to do so.[31] It is unlimited as to its subject-matter and the nature of the proceedings.[32] As in the case of interlocutory injunctions generally, the plaintiff must satisfy the conditions laid down by the House of Lords in *American Cyanamid Co.* v. *Ethicon*

---

[25] [1975] 2 Lloyd's Rep. 509. See generally (1978) J.B.L. 11 (D. G. Powles); (1980) 2 W.I.L.J. 60 (A. J. Bland); [1982] Conv. 265 (R. Horsfall); (1982) 99 L.Q.R. 7 (C. C. Hodgekiss); All E.R.Rev. 1982, p. 209 (A. A. S. Zuckerman); (1987) 137 N.L.J. 413 (R. Ough).

[26] [1975] 1 W.L.R. 1093. See *The Siskina* [1979] A.C. 210 at p. 229, where Lord Denning M.R. described the evolution of this injunction not as an invention but as a "rediscovery" of the procedure known as foreign attachment; *Z Ltd.* v. *A–Z and AA–LL* [1982] Q.B. 558.

[27] *The Due Process of Law*, p. 134, reiterated in *The Closing Chapter*, p. 225. See also Donaldson L.J. in *Bank Mellat* v. *Nikpour* [1985] F.S.R. 87 at 91–92, describing the *Mareva* injunction, along with the *Anton Piller* order, as "one of the law's two 'nuclear' weapons."

[28] *The Siskina* [1979] A.C. 210 at p. 253 (Lord Diplock). Compare the French "saisie conservatoire."

[29] *Orwell Steel (Erection and Fabrication) Ltd.* v. *Asphalt and Tarmac (U.K.) Ltd.* [1984] 1 W.L.R. 1097; R.S.C. Ord. 29, r. 1; *Babanaft International Co. SA* v. *Bassatne, The Times,* May 5, 1988.

[30] *Third Chandris Shipping Corp.* v. *Unimarine S.A.* [1979] Q.B. 645.

[31] *Mareva Compania Naviera S.A.* v. *International Bulkcarriers S.A., supra; Nippon Yusen Kaisha* v. *Karageorgis, supra; Third Chandris Shipping Corp.* v. *Unimarine S.A., supra; Rasu Maritima S.A.* v. *Perusahaan Pertambangan Minyak Dan Gas Bumi Negara (Pertamina)* [1978] Q.B. 644. On procedure, see *Stewart Chartering Ltd.* v. *C. & O. Managements S.A. (The Venus Destiny)* [1980] 1 W.L.R. 460.

[32] *Z Ltd.* v. *A–Z and AA–LL* [1982] Q.B. 558. See *Roche* v. *Roche* (1981) 11 Fam.Law 243. It may be combined with specific performance; *Seven Seas Properties Ltd.* v. *Al-Essa* [1988] 1 W.L.R. 1272.

Ltd.[33]: he must have a good arguable case and the balance of convenience must favour the grant.[34] The safeguard to the defendant is that the plaintiff must give an undertaking in damages in case he should be unsuccessful at the trial, and that the defendant may apply at any time for the injunction to be discharged.[35]

It has recently been held that the old writ *ne exeat regno*[36] may be granted in support of a *Mareva* injunction,[37] or, if the requirements of that writ are not satisfied, an interlocutory injunction under section 37(1) of the Supreme Court Act 1981 to restrain the defendant from leaving the country.[38] While this development increases the efficacy of the *Mareva* injunction, it has been criticised as an unjustified restriction on individual liberty.[39]

(ii) Guidelines for the Grant of the Injunction. While the discretion of the court is not fettered by rigid rules, Lord Denning M.R. has suggested the following guidelines for the court to consider[40]:

(a) The plaintiff must have a good arguable case[41];
(b) The injunction is not limited to money, but in the case of goods, caution is required if the injunction would bring the defendant's business to a standstill[42];
(c) The court should favour the grant if it would be likely to compel the defendant to provide security;

---

[33] [1975] A.C. 396, *ante*, p. 716.
[34] *Rasu Maritima S.A.* v. *Perusahaan, etc. supra; Third Chandris Shipping Corp.* v. *Unimarine S.A., supra; Allen* v. *Jambo Holdings Ltd.* [1980] 1 W.L.R. 1252; *Felixstowe Dock & Railway Co.* v. *United States Lines Inc.* [1988] 2 All E.R. 77; *Derby & Co. Ltd.* v. *Weldon, The Times*, August 2, 1988. See (1978) 41 M.L.R. 1 (M. Kerr) and n. 41, *infra*.
[35] *Mareva Compania Naviera S.A.* v. *International Bulkcarriers S.A., supra*. But a broad view must be taken of the plaintiff's ability to undertake in damages; see *Allen* v. *Jambo Holdings Ltd., supra* (legally-aided plaintiff).
[36] *Ante*, p. 32.
[37] *Al Nahkel for Contracting and Trading Ltd.* v. *Lowe* [1986] Q.B. 235; *cf. Allied Arab Bank Ltd.* v. *Hajjar* [1988] Q.B. 787; (1987) 137 N.L.J. 584 (L. Anderson).
[38] *Bayer A.G.* v. *Winter* [1986] 1 W.L.R. 497; (1986) 83 L.S.G. 2897 (L. J. Anderson); *In Re Oriental Credit Ltd.* [1988] 2 W.L.R. 172.
[39] (1986) 45 C.L.J. 189 (C. Harpum); All E.R.Rev. 1986, p. 225 (A. A. S. Zuckerman); (1987) 104 L.Q.R. 246 (L. Anderson).
[40] *Rasu Maritima S.A.* v. *Perusahaan, etc.* [1978] Q.B. 644 (a decision *inter partes*); *Third Chandris Shipping Corp.* v. *Unimarine S.A.* [1979] Q.B. 645. See also *Barclay-Johnson* v. *Yuill* [1980] 1 W.L.R. 1259; (1981) 97 L.Q.R. 4; *Z Ltd.* v. *A–Z and AA–LL* [1982] Q.B. 558; *Derby & Co. Ltd.* v. *Weldon, supra*.
[41] See *Etablissement Esefka International Anstalt* v. *Central Bank of Nigeria* [1979] 1 Lloyd's Rep. 445; *The Niedersachsen* [1983] 1 W.L.R. 1412; *Barclay-Johnson* v. *Yuill, supra*.
[42] For further guidelines as to chattels, see *CBS United Kingdom Ltd.* v. *Lambert* [1983] Ch. 37.

(d) The plaintiff must make full and frank disclosure of all material matters[43];

(e) He should give particulars of his claim and its amount,[44] and (in an *ex parte* application) he should fairly state the points made against it by the defendant;

(f) He should give grounds for believing that the defendant has assets in the jurisdiction[45];

(g) He should give grounds for believing that there is a risk of their removal before the claim is satisfied, and a danger of default if the assets were removed.[46] The mere fact that the defendant is abroad is not sufficient;

(h) He must undertake in damages, giving security in suitable cases, in case he is unsuccessful in the action.

In relation to (f) and (g) above, it should be added that the plaintiff need no longer establish in all cases that there is a risk of removal of the assets from the jurisdiction, as section 37(3) of the Supreme Court Act 1981 provides that the injunction may be granted to prevent the defendant from removing from the jurisdiction "or otherwise dealing with" the assets. Thus a risk of dissipation within the jurisdiction is sufficient.[47] The recent developments as to foreign assets are discussed below.

Exceptionally, the injunction may be made comprehensively against all the defendant's assets; but usually a limit will be specified.[48] In rare cases it may be made in respect of a joint account,[49] but not in respect of assets of the defendant's wife or another third party.[50]

(iii) The Jurisdiction of the Court. In the first case to reach the House of Lords, *The Siskina*,[51] their Lordships emphasised the following

---

[43] *Negocios Del Mar S.A.* v. *Doric Shipping Corp. S.A.* [1979] 1 Lloyd's Rep. 331. Failure to make full disclosure may result in discharge. See *Bank Mellat* v. *Nikpour* [1985] F.S.R. 87; *Eastglen International Corp.* v. *Monpare S.A.* (1987) 137 N.L.J. 56; *Columbia Picture Industries Inc.* v. *Robinson* [1987] Ch. 38; *Lloyd's Bowmaker Ltd.* v. *Britannia Arrow Holdings plc* [1988] 1 W.L.R. 1337; *Brink's-MAT Ltd.* v. *Elcombe* [1988] 1 W.L.R. 1350.

[44] A good arguable case for substantial damages suffices; *Darashah* v. *U.F.A.C. (U.K.) Ltd., The Times*, March 30, 1982.

[45] Having established this, the court has power to order discovery or interrogatories in aid of the injunction: *A.J. Bekhor & Co. Ltd.* v. *Bilton* [1981] Q.B. 923; *Bankers Trust Co.* v. *Shapira* [1980] 1 W.L.R. 1274; *cf. R.H.M. Foods Ltd.* v. *Bovril Ltd.* [1982] 1 W.L.R. 661.

[46] See *Montecchi* v. *Shimco* [1979] 1 W.L.R. 1180; *Etablissement Esefka International Anstalt* v. *Central Bank of Nigeria, supra.*

[47] See *Z Ltd.* v. *A–Z and AA–LL* [1982] Q.B. 558.

[48] *Ibid.* See also *Oceanica Castelana Armadora S.A. of Panama* v. *Mineralimportexport* [1983] 1 W.L.R. 1294. After-acquired assets may be included; *TDK Tape Distributors (U.K.) Ltd.* v. *Videochoice Ltd.* [1986] 1 W.L.R. 141.

[49] *Ibid.*

[50] *S.C.F. Finance Co. Ltd.* v. *Masri* [1985] 1 W.L.R. 876; *Allied Arab Bank Ltd.* v. *Hajjar, The Times*, January 18, 1988.

[51] [1979] A.C. 210; (1978) C.L.J. 241 (K. Lipstein); (1978) 94 L.Q.R. 169 (P.V.B.); (1978) 41 M.L.R. 1 (M. Kerr).

limitation: the injunction had to be ancillary to substantive relief which the High Court had jurisdiction to grant; there was no power to grant the injunction save in protection or assertion of some legal or equitable right which the High Court had jurisdiction to enforce by final judgment. But *The Siskina* was reversed on this point when section 25 of the Civil Jurisdiction and Judgments Act 1982 came into operation.[52]

(iv) The English-based Defendant. The *Mareva* injunction evolved as a remedy against a foreign-based defendant having assets within the jurisdiction. The question which subsequently arose was whether such an injunction could be granted against an English-based defendant. It was assumed in the earlier decisions that there was no such power, although the merit of such a distinction was questioned.[53]

The difficulty in the way of extending the *Mareva* injunction to English-based defendants was the clear line of authority to the effect that there is "no statutory or other power in the Court to restrain a person from dealing with his property at a time when no order against him has been made."[54] It must be said, however, that this principle had already been eroded by the development of the *Mareva* injunction against foreign-based defendants.[55]

Attempts to extend the scope of the *Mareva* injunction were made in *Chartered Bank* v. *Daklouche*[56] and in *Barclay-Johnson* v. *Yuill*,[57] where Megarry V.-C. said that some weight must still be given to the *Lister* v. *Stubbs*[58] line of cases, to the effect that no injunction could be granted to restrain a defendant from parting with his assets. This remained the rule, to which the *Mareva* principle was a limited exception.

Thus the jurisdiction to enjoin an English-based defendant became established,[59] and is now confirmed by section 37(3) of the Supreme Court Act 1981, providing that the court's power to grant an interlocutory injunction restraining a party to any proceedings from removing from the jurisdiction, or otherwise dealing with,[60] assets located within

---

[52] See *Republic of Haiti* v. *Duvalier, The Times,* July 28, 1988, *post,* p. 774. s.25 seems inapplicable to matrimonial property claims.

[53] See *The Siskina* [1979] A.C. 210.

[54] *Jagger* v. *Jagger* [1926] P. 93 at p. 102 (*per* Scrutton L.J.). See also *Lister & Co.* v. *Stubbs* (1890) 45 Ch.D. 1; *Robinson* v. *Pickering* (1881) 16 Ch.D. 660.

[55] See *Malone* v. *Metropolitan Police Commissioner* [1980] Q.B. 49 at pp. 61 and 68.

[56] [1980] 1 W.L.R. 107. See also *Rasu Maritima S.A.* v. *Perusahaan, etc.* [1978] Q.B. 644 at p. 663.

[57] [1980] 1 W.L.R. 1259 (an *ex parte* application); approved by the Court of Appeal in *Rahman (Prince Abdul) Bin Turki Al Sudairy* v. *Abu-Taha* [1980] 1 W.L.R. 1268 (*inter partes*); *A.J. Bekhor & Co. Ltd.* v. *Bilton* [1981] Q.B. 923.

[58] (1890) 45 Ch.D. 1. See also *Faith Panton Property Plan Ltd.* v. *Hodgetts* [1981] 1 W.L.R. 927.

[59] See *A.J. Bekhor & Co. Ltd.* v. *Bilton, supra.* See also *The Due Process of Law*, pp. 147 *et seq.*; the Payne Committee Report on Enforcement of Judgment Debts (Cmnd. 3909) especially paras. 1252 and 1253.

[60] See *Z Ltd.* v. *A–Z and AA–LL* [1982] Q.B. 558.

the jurisdiction shall be exercisable whether or not that party is domiciled, resident or present within the jurisdiction.

(v) Assets outside the Jurisdiction. In its earlier phase of development the *Mareva* injunction was confined to assets within the jurisdiction. A recent and fast-developing principle is that the injunction may be granted in respect of assets outside the jurisdiction, even on a world-wide basis. The objections to extending the injunction to foreign assets were that the order would be oppressive and unenforceable, and that the territorial limitations were confirmed by section 37(3) of the Supreme Court Act 1981.[61] But the Court of Appeal held in *Babanaft International Co. S.A.* v. *Bassatne*[62] that section 37(3) did not restrict the scope, geographical or otherwise, of section 37(1). This case involved a post-judgment *Mareva* injunction. Such an order would more readily be made against assets abroad than in a pre-judgment case, but would nevertheless be rare. A personal order binding the defendant alone was made. A suggested alternative was to grant the injunction subject to a proviso that it should not affect third parties save to the extent that the order was enforced by the courts of the country where the assets were situated.

The issue next arose in another division of the Court of Appeal in *Republic of Haiti* v. *Duvalier*,[63] which concerned the alleged embezzlement of $120m. from the Republic during the presidency of Jean-Claude Duvalier. No substantive relief in England was sought. The court granted a pre-judgment *Mareva* injunction in respect of world-wide assets, although recognising that this was a most unusual measure which should very rarely be granted. While the court would be more willing in a post-judgment case, or where the plaintiff had a tracing or other proprietary claim, the injunction could be granted in respect of a pre-judgment money claim such as the present case, where international co-operation was demanded. Previous limitations arose from practice rather than from any restriction on the court's power. The injunction was granted subject to a "*Babanaft* proviso"[63a] in respect of the foreign assets, to protect third parties outside the jurisdiction save to the extent that the order might be enforced by the local court. Even stricter safeguards were required by the Court of Appeal in *Derby & Co. Ltd.* v. *Weldon*,[64] where a pre-judgment world-wide *Mareva* injunction was granted. It was emphasised that the plaintiff must do more than satisfy the requirements for an internal *Mareva*. In addition to a good arguable case, he must show that any English assets are

---

[61] *Supra.* See *Ashtiani* v. *Kashi* [1987] Q.B. 888 (C.A.), which involved a pre-judgment *Mareva*.
[62] *The Times*, May 5, 1988.
[63] *The Times*, July 28, 1988.
[63a] Modified in *Derby & Co. Ltd.* v. *Weldon (No. 3 and No. 4)*, *infra.*
[64] *The Times*, August 2, 1988.

insufficient, that there are foreign assets, and that there is a real risk of disposal of the latter. The injunction will not be granted if it would be oppressive. The court must be satisfied, by means of undertaking or proviso (or both), that (a) the defendant will not be oppressed by exposure to a multiplicity of proceedings; (b) the defendant will be protected against misuse of information gained from the order for disclosure of assets; and (c) third parties are protected. The present case was sufficiently exceptional because a very large sum was involved (£15m.), the English assets were totally inadequate, and there was a high risk of dissipation of the foreign assets through inaccessible overseas companies. In *Derby & Co. Ltd.* v. *Weldon (No. 3 and No. 4)*[64a] a similar injunction was sought against other defendants, being companies in Luxembourg and Panama which had no assets within the jurisdiction. The injunction was granted. The Luxembourg company was resident in a Brussels Convention country and was therefore subject to the jurisdiction of a court which would enforce the orders of the English court under the Civil Jurisdiction and Judgments Act 1982. Concerning the Panama company, the fact that the order could not be specifically enforced was no bar. The order would not be made if there was no effective sanction, but the sanction of being debarred from defending in the event of disobedience normally sufficed.

(vi) Operation in Personam. The usual subject-matter of a *Mareva* injunction is a sum of money, often in a bank account. But there is no reason why other assets, such as a ship,[65] an aeroplane,[66] or the goodwill of a company,[67] should not be "frozen" by this method. It is important to note, however, that the *Mareva* injunction, even if related to a specified asset, operates only *in personam.*[68] It is not a form of pre-trial attachment. It does not effect seizure of the asset, nor is it analogous to a lien. It merely prohibits the defendant personally from removing or transferring the asset. It gives no proprietary right in the asset, nor priority over other creditors.[69] The plaintiff's right is merely to have the asset preserved so that, if he succeeds in his action, judgment may be executed against it, but the rights of a third party with an interest in the asset will not be prejudiced.[70] The injunction

---

[64a] (1989) 139 N.L.J. 11. It was held that a receiver could be appointed of the companies against which the *Mareva* injunction had been granted, to prevent further dissipation. Difficulties over enforcement in Panama were not an absolute bar to the appointment.

[65] *The Rena K* [1979] Q.B. 377. There is no conflict here with the jurisdiction to arrest ships. See [1982] Conv. 265, at p. 270 (R. Horsfall).

[66] *Allen* v. *Jambo (Holdings) Ltd.* [1980 1 W.L.R. 1252 (A fatal accident case).

[67] *Darashah* v. *U.F.A.C. (U.K.) Ltd., The Times*, March 30, 1982.

[68] *Cf. Z Ltd.* v. *A–Z and AA–LL* [1982] Q.B. 558 at p. 573, "it operates *in rem* just as the arrest of a ship does." (*per* Lord Denning M.R.).

[69] Nor does it entitle him to intervene in an action between the defendant and a third party; *Sanders Lead Co. Inc.* v. *Entores Metal Brokers Ltd.* [1984] 1 W.L.R. 452.

[70] *Cretanor Maritime Co. Ltd.* v. *Irish Marine Management Ltd.* [1978] 1 W.L.R. 966.

may be varied subsequently to enable the assets to be used to make payments in good faith in the ordinary course of business.[71]

(vii) Position of Third Parties. As far as the liabilities of a third party are concerned, we have seen that a third party who aids and abets the breach of an injunction by the defendant is guilty of contempt.[72] So in the case of a *Mareva* injunction against a sum of money in a bank account, the bank, once it has notice, must not facilitate the disposal of the money without a court order.[73]

More commonly the question has arisen as to the rights of innocent third parties. It is clear that any expenses incurred by a bank or other third party in complying with the injunction must be met by the plaintiff.[74] Furthermore, a bank holding funds subject to a *Mareva* injunction can exercise any right of set-off it had before notification of the injunction, which extends to interest becoming due after that date.[75]

Similarly, the injunction must not interfere with the convenience of a third party. So in *Galaxia Maritime S.A.* v. *Mineralimportexport*,[76] where a *Mareva* injunction had been obtained as to a ship's cargo, the shipowner obtained its discharge, as it would interfere with the crew's arrangements for Christmas. The plaintiff's offer to indemnify was not sufficient in a case where the injunction would interfere substantially with a third party's freedom to trade or freedom of action generally.

The protection of third parties where a world-wide *Mareva* injunction is granted has already been considered.[77]

---

[71] *Iraqi Ministry of Defence* v. *Arcepey Shipping Co. S.A.* [1981] Q.B. 65 (repayment of a debt). Or it may initially or by variation permit payments of the defendant's own living expenses: *A.* v. *C.* [1981] Q.B. 956n.; *A.* v. *C. (No. 2)* [1981] Q.B. 961n.; *P.C.W. (Underwriting Agencies) Ltd.* v. *Dixon* [1983] 2 All E.R. 158; 697; *Campbell Mussells* v. *Thompson, The Times*, May 30, 1984; *Z Ltd.* v. *A–Z and AA–LL* [1982] Q.B. 558; *TDK Tape Distributors (U.K.) Ltd.* v. *Videochoice Ltd.* [1986] 1 W.L.R. 141; *Law Society* v. *Shanks* [1988] 1 F.L.R. 504; *National Bank of Greece* v. *Constantinos Dimitriou, The Times*, November 16, 1987.
[72] *Ante*, p. 700. See *Bank Mellat* v.*Kazmi, The Times*, December 27, 1988.
[73] *Z Ltd.* v. *A–Z and AA–LL* [1982] Q.B. 558; *cf. Law Society* v. *Shanks, supra.* The injunction does not prevent payment under a letter of credit or bank guarantee, nor does it apply to a credit card, which the bank must honour unless used fraudulently.
[74] *Rahman (Prince Abdul) Bin Turki Al Sudairy* v. *Abu-Taha* [1980] 1 W.L.R. 1268; *Searose Ltd.* v. *Seatrain (U.K.) Ltd.* [1981] 1 W.L.R. 894. Undertakings will normally be given in this respect; *Z Ltd.* v. *A–Z and AA–LL, supra.*
[75] *Oceanica Castelana Armadora S.A. of Panama* v. *Mineralimportexport* [1983] 1 W.L.R. 1294; All E.R. Rev. 1983, p. 262 (A. A. S. Zuckerman).
[76] [1982] 1 W.L.R. 539. See also *Clipper Maritime Co. Ltd. of Monrovia* v. *Mineralimportexport* [1981] 1 W.L.R. 262 (plaintiff should pay lost income and expenses of port authority, which should have discretion to move vessel within jurisdiction or, in certain circumstances, outside it).
[77] *Ante*, p. 774.

CHAPTER 25

RESCISSION AND RECTIFICATION

1. RESCISSION

A. General

The right to rescind is the right of a party to a contract to have it set aside and to be restored to his former position. The contract remains valid unless and until rescinded, so that, as we shall see, third parties may acquire interests under it in the meantime. This is rescission in the strict sense, and must be distinguished on the one hand from contracts void *ab initio*, for example on the ground of illegality, and on the other hand from contracts with no inherent invalidity which are subsequently discharged by breach.[1] Rescission is not a judicial remedy as such, for it may be achieved by act of the parties, nevertheless the assistance of the court is often invoked, for example to secure restitution of any property. The role of equity is, first, that equity might set aside a contract in circumstances where the common law would not; secondly, that equity is more flexible in its view of *restitutio in integrum*, and can effect what is necessary, for example by ordering accounts and inquiries[2]; and thirdly that equity can grant relief on terms, by applying the maxim "he who comes to equity must do equity."[3]

The party rescinding is entitled to be restored to the position he

---

[1] See *Johnson* v. *Agnew* [1980] A.C. 367. On the right to rescind for fraud, see *Logicrose Ltd.* v. *Southend United Football Club Ltd.* [1988] 1 W.L.R. 1256.

[2] *Erlanger* v. *New Sombrero Phosphate Co.* (1878) 3 App.Cas. 1218. If all that was required was a return of money or other property without any adjustments, this could be achieved by the common law action for money had and received.

[3] See *Solle* v. *Butcher* [1950] 1 K.B. 671, *post*, p. 780.

would have been in had the contract not been entered into. He cannot recover damages, as that would put him in the position he would have been in had the contract been performed.[4]

B. Grounds for Rescission

(i) **Mistake.** While mistake alone may justify refusal of a decree of specific performance,[5] mistake alone is not an automatic ground for rescission, although a mistake induced by fraud, or by misrepresentation, or deliberately not corrected in a situation that called for full disclosure[6] is a more compelling case than a mistake arising without the responsibility of the other party. If two parties enter into a contract and one makes a mistake concerning it, the general principle is that behind the maxim *caveat emptor*; a party who knows he is making a better bargain than the other is under no duty to divulge the fact. A party who wishes to secure a form of guarantee as to any aspect of the transaction must raise the matter at the time and have it dealt with on the basis of representation or a term of the contract. All this is inherent in freedom of contract; but it is subject to some limits even at common law. For instance, a party cannot remain silent when he knows the other party is mistaken as to what the actual terms of the contract are,[7] or in certain cases of mistake as to the identity of the person contracted with.[8]

Equity does not disturb these long-established principles. It is true that equity has limited their effect when it has granted rescission on a ground not recognised at law, but it does not grant rescission except on a recognised ground. Generally speaking, the mistake of a plaintiff is no ground as such for rescission, but only when coupled with, for example, a misrepresentation that induced it. Thus there is no separate set of rules in equity relating to rescission for mistakes as to the person or mistakes as to the extent of the terms of a contract.[9] Of course, if the contract is void at law, no question of mistake in equity arises.

In the absence of misrepresentation, the general principle is that, in order to justify rescission, the mistake must be common to both parties.[10] The law concerning a mistake made in common by both parties is difficult to state due to common law's own ambivalent

---

[4] *Redgrave* v. *Hurd* (1881) 20 Ch.D. 1.

[5] *e.g. Wood* v. *Scarth* (1855) 2 K & J 33, *ante*, p. 675.

[6] *e.g. Gordon* v. *Gordon* (1816) 3 Swan. 400, *post*, p. 786.

[7] *Smith* v. *Hughes* (1871) L.R. 6 Q.B. 597; *Hartog* v. *Colin & Shields* [1939] 3 All E.R. 566.

[8] *Cundy* v. *Lindsay* (1878) 3 App.Cas. 459; *Ingram* v. *Little* [1961] 1 Q.B. 31; *Lewis* v. *Averay* [1972] 1 Q.B. 198.

[9] The judgment of Denning L.J. in *Solle* v. *Butcher* [1950] 1 K.B. 671, at pp. 692–693 contains propositions asserting a wider equitable jurisdiction than is usually accepted. See (1961) 24 M.L.R. 421 (P. S. Atiyah and F. A. R. Bennion); Goff and Jones (3rd ed.), p. 186; *Grist* v. *Bailey* [1967] Ch. 532; *Magee* v. *Pennine Insurance Co. Ltd.* [1969] 2 Q.B. 507, *post*, p. 782.

[10] See *Riverlate Properties Ltd.* v. *Paul* [1975] Ch. 133; *post*, p. 798.

attitude to it.[11] It has been said at various times that such a mistake may be so fundamental as to render an apparent contract based on it necessarily void,[12] and at the other extreme that, if there is an apparent agreement on all points, then the contract can be avoided only by reference to the further intention of the parties or by equity.[13] This is a larger problem than can be solved here, but the cases in equity can be considered to a substantial degree apart from it.

In *Cooper* v. *Phibbs*,[14] Cooper agreed to rent a salmon fishery from Phibbs, who was a trustee of a settlement. But the fishery had in fact already descended under an entail to Cooper. It had been generally believed that the fishery was not subject to the entail and, in this belief, substantial sums had already been spent in improving it by members of the family now represented by Phibbs. Phibbs made no misrepresentation to Cooper that could be said to have induced Cooper's false belief that the fishery was outside the entail (though one may have been made by other members of the family now dead), and so the validity of the agreement to rent the fishery could be attacked only on the ground of common mistake. Cooper brought an action requesting cancellation of the agreement upon suitable terms; it was thought at first instance that mistake as such, even though common, afforded no ground of relief. The House of Lords disagreed; the rule was laid down in Lord Westbury's oft-quoted words: "If parties contract under a mutual mistake and misapprehension as to their relative and respective rights, the result is, that that agreement is liable to be set aside as having proceeded upon a common mistake."[15] Thus equity may rescind for common mistake alone; in such a case, rescission will be on such terms as appear to equity to be just; in this way Cooper obtained rescission of the agreement only on the terms of admitting a lien in favour of Phibbs' beneficiaries in respect of the sums spent on improving the fishery.

Equity's jurisdiction has been reaffirmed in subsequent cases, and in the widest language.[16] The jurisdiction has not been confined to mistakes of fact in any technical sense; it has been said that it should not be

---

[11] See Heydon, Gummow and Austin, *Cases and Materials on Equity and Trusts*, (2nd ed.), pp. 207–208, where the common law position is described as "the most arcane mystery." See also Pettit at p. 563.

[12] *Bell* v. *Lever Bros.* [1932] A.C. 161; *Scott* v. *Coulson* [1903] 2 Ch. 249; *Associated Japanese Bank International Ltd.* v. *Credit du Nord SA* [1988] 3 All E.R. 902 (sale of machines which did not exist).

[13] *McRae* v. *Commonwealth Disposals Commission* (1951) 84 C.L.R. 377; *Solle* v. *Butcher* [1950] 1 K.B. 671; (1954) 70 L.Q.R. 385 (C. J. Slade); (1957) 73 L.Q.R. 340 (P. S. Atiyah); *Magee* v. *Pennine Insurance Co.* [1969] Q.B. 507.

[14] (1867) L.R. 2 H.L. 149; (reversing (1865) 17 Ir.Ch.Rep. 73).

[15] (1867) L.R. 2 H.L. 149 at p. 170.

[16] *e.g.* Lord Chelmsford in *Earl Beauchamp* v. *Winn* (1873) L.R. 6 H.L. 223 at pp. 233–234. See Goff and Jones, pp. 187–191.

exercised in respect of mistakes as to public law such as the construction of a statute[17] and that it should not be exercised in cases where parties have finally settled their difference but on an assumption which has since turned out to be false in point of law.[18] Attempts to formulate the jurisdiction more precisely in terms of "mistakes as to private rights" have not proved successful.

In *Solle* v. *Butcher*,[19] a flat was leased for seven years on an erroneous assumption (made by both parties) that structural alterations had taken the premises out of the provisions of the Rent Restriction Acts imposing rent control. The lessee sued to recover rent paid in excess of the amount permitted by the Act. He failed. The landlord obtained rescission of the lease on "just and equitable" terms on the ground of mistake.

The judgments in the Court of Appeal reveal a variety of possible views on the nature of the mistake. It can be viewed as one of fact, of private rights, of misconstruction of a statute, of misapprehension of the legal consequences of an agreement; and this variety is not surprising, as it is not feasible to distinguish the causes, natures and effects of mistakes in this way. There are elements of each in the mistake as it is eventually made, so that the only question for the courts can be whether it is right in a general sense to remedy by rescission the particular mistake in question, and this jurisdiction cannot be limited by reference to the kind or type of mistake made.

(ii) Policy Considerations. The question of the availability of rescission should therefore be answered only after considering the issues involved. For instance, would remedying a common mistake by rescinding a contract lead to insecurity of a certain type of contract, as in *Rogers* v. *Ingham*?[20] Further, the effect of the common law view of the question should be considered as a matter of policy before deciding whether equity should intervene by rescission.[21] These wide aspects are in fact implicit in some cases in which rescission has been refused,

---

[17] Lord Westbury and Lord Chelmsford both appear mindful of the need to make this reservation.

[18] *Rogers* v. *Ingham* (1876) 3 Ch.D. 351; contrast the facts in *Gordon* v. *Gordon* (1816) 3 Swan. 400, *post*, p. 786.

[19] [1950] 1 K.B. 671 (C.A., Jenkins L.J. dissenting), followed in *Grist* v. *Bailey* [1967] Ch. 532, and *Magee* v. *Pennine Insurance Co. Ltd*: [1969] 2 Q.B. 507, *post*, p. 782. See Jackson, *Principles of Property Law*, pp. 334, 358–364; (1987) 103 L.Q.R. 594 (J. Cartwright).

[20] (1876) 3 Ch.D. 451; (estate divided among family in accordance with counsel's advice cannot be reopened even if division incorrect).

[21] Thus the considerations discussed in *McRae* v. *Commonwealth Disposals Commission* (1951) 84 C.L.R. 377, based on the intentions and responsibilities of the parties, would seem to be a matter for determination prior to consideration of the question of rescission in equity. Yet the common law aspects are not fully discussed in cases such as *Solle* v. *Butcher, supra*, or *Grist* v. *Bailey* [1967] Ch. 532, *post*, p. 782. But see Winn L.J. (dissenting) in *Magee* v. *Pennine Insurance Co.* [1969] 2 Q.B. 507 at pp. 515–517.

for instance *Bell* v. *Lever Bros.*[22] and the contemporaneous case of *Munro* v. *Meyer.*[23] In the latter case, parties varied the provisions of a contract for the purchase of meal without it being realised that the meal in question did not comply with the terms of the original contract; this erroneous assumption did not vitiate the agreement to vary, which was on several grounds not suitable for rescission in equity. But the reasons given for refusing relief in equity are not always clearly expressed, and it is submitted that the reason for this lack of clarity is that the availability of rescission is not always seen as a straight policy issue. Nor are the cases in which rescission has been granted more helpful, as they rely, in the main, on past statements of the general jurisdiction. If, however, the exercise of the remedy can be seen as one of general policy, it can be understood why the cases in which the remedy has in fact been exercised involve fairly restricted areas of fact, areas where equitable intervention is required to deal with the complicated situations that the parties have arrived at.[24]

It can be seen also that this wide doctrine of rescission has less scope in ordinary commercial transactions. The common law is more disposed to examine such cases on their merits, and in many cases it will be best to let the loss lie where it falls. In such circumstances there is no need for the application of a doctrine like rescission which will readjust the loss. This can be perceived particularly well on the facts of *Oscar Chess* v. *Williams.*[25]

A car was disposed of to a garage without there being, as it was held by a majority of the Court of Appeal, any warranty as to its age. Both parties had in fact relied on the car's log-book, on which the car's date of manufacture had been altered from 1939 to 1948, by some person unknown. Not only was there no term of the contract as to the car's age, but the garage had not been misled by anything said by the owner of the car. The result was that the loss due to mistake

---

[22] [1932] A.C. 161. A central fact in this case is that the contract did not fall to be treated as a contract *uberrimae fidei*. In fact, Bell's mind was not directed to his breaches of duty at the time of the compensation agreement, and therefore the concealment was innocent. "It is perhaps not fanciful to suggest that in *Bell* v. *Lever Bros. Ltd.* a narrow doctrine of mistake corrected an injustice that would have flowed from the rule of law under which a relatively trivial breach, which caused the innocent party no loss, nevertheless gave that party a ground for rescinding the contract." (1988) 104 L.Q.R. 501 at 505 (G. H. Treitel). The position may be otherwise in the case of fraudulent concealment; *Sybron Corp.* v. *Rochem Ltd.* [1984] Ch. 112; All E.R.Rev. 1983 p. 65 (D. D. Prentice), p. 115 (M. P. Furmston) and p. 176 (P. Elias); (1983) 42 C.L.J. 218 (S. E. Honeyball). See also *Horcal Ltd.* v. *Gatland, The Times*, April 16, 1984, (agreement by a company to pay a director a "golden handshake" would be void for mistake of fact if the director failed to disclose a breach of his contract of service or of his fiduciary duty to the company which would justify his dismissal without compensation. But not set aside on the facts, as no breach at the relevant time); (1985) 44 C.L.J. 215 (M. Owen); *van Gestel* v. *Cann, The Times*, August 7, 1987.

[23] [1930] 2 K.B. 312 (Wright J., who tried *Bell* v. *Lever Bros.* a few days later).

[24] *e.g.* in *Cooper* v. *Phibbs* and *Solle* v. *Butcher, ante,* pp. 779, 780.

[25] [1957] 1 W.L.R. 370.

fell on the garage; no ground of action was available against the former owner. But in a dictum,[26] Denning L.J. canvassed the possibility of rescission for common mistake. This seems an unsuitable case for rescission. The effect of rescission would be to make the former owner pay a sum of money to the garage which was in excess of the value of the car which he would get back in exchange; he could only dispose of the car for a smaller sum. This is not different in effect from an award of damages, for which the court held there was no justification.

Despite, therefore, the very wide statement of the remedy to be found in some cases and the impossibility of limiting its width by reference to types or kinds of mistake, its exercise is to be associated with a comparatively narrow range of cases. These cases concern land more than commerce in the wider sense, and tend to involve mistakes as to private rights more than mistakes as to facts or to qualities. To be more exact than that, however regrettable, is not possible.

(iii) Modern Formulations of the Remedy

In *Grist* v. *Bailey*[27] a freehold house was sold for £850 in a belief shared by both parties that it was subject to a protected tenancy; in fact no protected tenancy existed, in which event a fair price would have been £2,500. The vendor refused to complete the purchase and successfully claimed rescission of the contract for sale; but rescission was made subject to an undertaking that he would sell to the purchaser at a proper price. Goff J. treated *Solle* v. *Butcher*[28] as authority for the exercise on such facts of the remedy of rescission, subject to (1) the mistake being common and (2) sufficiently fundamental, and (3) the vendor not being at fault.

In *Magee* v. *Pennine Insurance Co. Ltd.*,[29] the plaintiff obtained insurance cover for a car, having signed an application form, the details of which had been filled in by a third party. The form incorrectly stated that he had a provisional licence, and that the car would be driven by himself, his eldest son who was an experienced driver, and a younger son aged 18. In truth, Magee had no licence, and the car was for the younger son, who alone drove it.

---

[26] [1957] 1 W.L.R. 370, at p. 374; he did not proceed with this possibility as in his view too long a period of time had elapsed.

[27] [1967] Ch. 532; Jackson, *Principles of Property Law*, p. 361. The formulation of Goff J. in this case was applied in *Laurence* v. *Lexcourt Holdings Ltd.* [1978] 1 W.L.R. 1128, *post*, p. 784 where a common mistake as to the availability of planning permission was sufficiently fundamental to allow rescission.

[28] [1950] 1 K.B. 671.

[29] [1969] 2 Q.B. 507; (1969) 85 L.Q.R. 454; (1969) 32 M.L.R. 688 (J. W. Harris). If, however, the company had paid out under the policy without entering into any contractual compromise, the money would have been recoverable in quasi-contract as having been paid under a mistake of fact; *Kelly* v. *Solari* (1841) 9 M. & W. 54 (where the insurance company made a payment under a policy, forgetting the policy had lapsed).

The car was destroyed in an accident. The plaintiff's claim was compromised by an agreement to pay £385, the plaintiff not being fraudulent in that he was not aware that the policy was voidable for non-disclosure. The insurer refused to pay, arguing that the compromise could not be enforced. The Court of Appeal, Winn L.J. dissenting, held that the action for the money failed.

The difficulty lies in reconciling this decision with that of the House of Lords in *Bell* v. *Lever Bros. Ltd.*[30] The compromise was an agreement whose basis was the validity of the insurance contract. The contract was voidable for misrepresentation, but not void. The compromise was therefore not void for mistake. But, said Lord Denning M.R.[31]: "A common mistake, even on a most fundamental matter, does not make a contract void at law[32]; but it makes it voidable in equity . . . it is clear that, when the insurance company and Mr. Magee made the agreement to pay £385, they were both under a common mistake which was fundamental to the whole agreement." This view, if correct, would greatly increase the scope of equitable jurisdiction, but it appears inconsistent with many decisions on the effect of mistake.[33] It is doubtful whether *Bell* v. *Lever Bros. Ltd.*[34] can be regarded as dealing only with the position at common law.[35] It is submitted, therefore, that there is much force in the dissenting judgment of Winn. L.J. In any event, the decision cannot be said to have clarified the equitable principles.[36]

It is clear that the mistake must be one common to both parties; and that both parties must have acted on the common incorrect assumption; the mistake must result in something being contracted for where, but for the mistake, no such contract would have been made. A similar emphasis on the causative nature of the mistake appears in quasi-

---

[30] [1932] A.C. 161. See Goff and Jones, p. 188.

[31] [1969] 2 Q.B. 507 at p. 514. Fenton Atkinson L.J. agreed with Lord Denning's decision, but it is not clear whether he did so on the basis that the contract was voidable in equity or void at law.

[32] Steyn J. in *Associated Japanese Bank International Ltd.* v. *Credit du Nord SA* [1988] 3 All E.R. 902 p. 911 considered that Lord Denning's interpretation of *Bell* v. *Lever Bros.* did not do justice to the speeches of the majority. For a valuable commentary on this case, see (1988) 104 L.Q.R. 501 (G. H. Treitel).

[33] Treitel (7th ed.), p. 242.

[34] [1932] A.C. 161.

[35] Steyn J. in *Associated Japanese Bank International Ltd* v. *Credit du Nord SA*, *supra*, at p. 911 considered that it should be so regarded.

[36] See Heydon, Gummow and Austin, *Cases and Materials on Equity and Trusts* (2nd ed.), p. 220, describing the decision as "indicative of the confusion which swathes the subject of common mistake in contract."

contractual actions for the recovery of money paid under mistake of fact.[37]

It was said in *Grist* v. *Bailey*[38] that the plaintiff should not be "at fault." This concept is more enigmatic; it appears to reflect the discretionary nature of the remedy, and permits of all the factors leading to the creation of the contract being taken into account. This was done in *Magee* v. *Pennine Insurance Co. Ltd.*[39] for Magee had no claim under the policy, and "it is not equitable that he should have a good claim on the agreement to pay the £385. . . . "[40] If the vendor in *Grist* v. *Bailey*[41] had been at fault in any material way in not appreciating the circumstances of the tenancy, the loss might have remained on him, as common law would have ordained.[42] In *Laurence* v. *Lexcourt Holdings Ltd.*,[43] where the parties had entered into a tenancy agreement under a common and fundamental mistake of fact as to the availability of planning permission, the tenants' claim to rescission succeeded even though they had made no enquiries or searches. They acted imprudently, but were not "at fault" within the formulation of Goff J. in *Grist* v. *Bailey*,[44] because they owed no duty of care to the landlord to make the searches, nor were they responsible for the landlord's mistake. The discretionary character of the remedy is also emphasised by the rescission being granted in appropriate cases on the terms which appear to the court to be just and equitable,[45] the term in *Grist* v. *Bailey*[46] being the sale of the house at a fair price. A more precise account of the scope of the equitable jurisdiction to rescind on the ground of common mistake cannot be given; "In the present confused state of the authorities one can only conclude that the courts recognise the existence of the equitable jurisdiction; but no clear answer can be given to the question just when a contract which is valid at common law

---

[37] *Barclay's Bank Ltd.* v. *W.J. Simms Son and Cooke (Southern) Ltd.* [1980] Q.B. 677; Robert Goff J. said, at p. 692, that money paid under mistake of fact was prima facie recoverable "provided the plaintiff's mistake is 'vital' or 'material,' which I understand to mean that the mistake caused the plaintiff to pay the money." See also *Chase Manhattan Bank N.A.* v. *Israel-British Bank (London) Ltd.* [1981] Ch. 105, *ante*, p. 628.

[38] [1967] Ch. 532.

[39] *Supra.*

[40] *Ibid.* at p. 515, *per* Lord Denning M.R.

[41] [1967] Ch. 532.

[42] In *Associated Japanese Bank International Ltd.* v. *Credit du Nord SA* [1988] 3 All E.R. 902 at p. 913 Steyn J. regarded the lack of fault requirement of equity as consistent with the principle that a party cannot rescind at law for common mistake if he had no reasonable grounds for his mistaken belief.

[43] [1978] 1 W.L.R. 1128.

[44] [1967] Ch. 532.

[45] *cf.* the much more complicated terms in the rescission decree in *Solle* v. *Butcher* [1950] 1 K.B. 671 at p. 697, *ante*, p. 780.

[46] [1967] Ch. 532. *cf. Magee* v. *Pennine Insurance Co. Ltd.*, *supra*, where no terms were imposed, for example as to repayment of the insurance premiums by the company.

will be rescinded in equity."[47] As Treitel has said, the differing results in the cases illustrate a conflict of policies, "respect for the sanctity of contract" and "the need to give effect to the reasonable expectations of honest men." "The fact that each policy has its own validity accounts for the interest of this branch of the law and for the impossibility of explaining the authorities by reference to any single set of sharp distinctions."[47a]

(iv) Other Grounds. In addition to mistake in the sense discussed above, the right to rescind may arise where the mistake results from a misrepresentation; similarly in a case of constructive fraud, which embraces the doctrines of undue influence and unconscionable bargains. These will be discussed below. The right to rescind may also be granted expressly by the terms of the contract, which will then govern its exercise.[48] The right to rescind where there has been a substantial misdescription in a contract for the sale of land has already been discussed.[49]

(a) *Misrepresentation.*[50] Where the misrepresentation was fraudulent, the contract could be set aside both at common law and in equity. "Fraudulent" here means that the misrepresentation was made knowingly or recklessly.[51] It must have been intended to be acted upon, and actually have had this result. Equity alone, however, gave relief where the misrepresentation was not fraudulent. Such an "innocent misrepresentation" was not recognised at common law unless it had become a term of the contract.[52]

It should be noted that mere silence does not constitute a misrepresentation unless it creates a false impression by distorting the meaning of any positive statement,[53] or unless there is a duty of

---

[47] Treitel (7th ed.), p. 244. See also Goff and Jones, pp. 187–191. Steyn J. in *Associated Japanese Bank International Ltd.* v. *Credit du Nord SA* [1988] 3 All E.R. 902 at p. 912 was more optimistic: "No one could fairly suggest that in this difficult area of the law there is only one correct approach or solution. But a narrow doctrine of common law mistake (as enunciated in *Bell* v. *Lever Bros. Ltd.*), supplemented by the more flexible doctrine of mistake in equity (as developed in *Solle* v. *Butcher* and later cases), seems to me to be an entirely sensible and satisfactory state of the law."

[47a] (1988) 104 L.Q.R. 501 at 507, comparing *Bell* v. *Lever Bros. Ltd.* [1932] A.C. 161 with *Associated Japanese Bank International Ltd.* v. *Credit du Nord SA, supra.*

[48] See Snell, pp. 603–604.

[49] *Ante*, p. 681.

[50] Only an outline can be given here, and reference should be made to the standard works on contract.

[51] *Derry* v. *Peek* (1889) 14 App.Cas. 337. Damages for deceit are also available: *Archer* v. *Brown* [1985] Q.B. 401; *Saunders* v. *Edwards* [1987] 1 W.L.R. 1116.

[52] See *Heilbut Symons & Co.* v. *Buckleton* [1913] A.C. 30.

[53] *Oakes* v. *Turquand* (1867) L.R. 2 H.L. 325.

disclosure because it is a contract *uberrimae fidei*,[54] such as contracts of insurance of all kinds,[55] and contracts for family settlements. Thus in *Gordon* v. *Gordon*[56] a deed of settlement of property within a family was entered into by an eldest son in the belief that he was illegitimate, though a younger son knew of a secret marriage of his parents by virtue of which the eldest son was legitimate. Lord Eldon held that a duty of candour recognised in equity had been breached so that the settlement should be set aside.

Similar duties may be owed to the court. In *Jenkins* v. *Livesey (formerly Jenkins)*,[57] a divorcing couple agreed that the husband would transfer his half-share of the home to the wife, who would give up all claims to financial provision. Shortly after this agreement, the wife became engaged to marry a man she had met before the agreement. This was not disclosed to the husband nor to her own solicitor. The agreement was then embodied in a consent order under section 25(1) of the Matrimonial Causes Act 1973. Two days after the husband conveyed his share of the home, the wife remarried. The House of Lords set aside the consent order. The remarriage ended the wife's right to financial provision, thus the husband would not have entered into the agreement had it been disclosed. Under section 25(1) the court must have regard to all the circumstances, and therefore a duty is owed to the court to make full and frank disclosure of material facts to the other party and to the court. But not every failure to disclose would result in the setting aside of the order. The test was whether the order was substantially different from that which would have been made upon full disclosure.

As far as innocent misrepresentation was concerned, equity's jurisdiction depended on the force of the misrepresentation on the plaintiff's mind rather than the mental state of the defendant when he made it, or on the relative importance of the fact misrepresented to the contract as a whole. Thus a plaintiff seeking rescission on this ground did not have to prove negligence or any other degree of fault in the defendant but only the fact of his own reliance on the statement, and its untruth.

---

[54] Or where a fiduciary or other similar special relationship exists between the contracting parties; *van Gestel* v. *Cann, The Times*, August 7, 1987; *Guinness plc* v. *Saunders* [1988] 1 W.L.R. 863. *Cf. La Banque Financière de la Cité SA (formerly Banque Keyser Ullman SA)* v. *Skandia (UK) Insurance Co. Ltd., The Times*, August 24, 1988 (holding also that breach of a duty of disclosure was not a tort giving rise to damages).

[55] Also company prospectuses. See *London Assurance Co.* v. *Mansel* (1879) 11 Ch.D. 363, and Kindersley V.-C.'s well-known judgment in *The New Brunswick and Canada Railway and Land Company* v. *Muggeridge* (1860) 1 Dr. & Sm. 363 at p. 381.

[56] (1816) 3 Swan 400.

[57] [1985] A.C. 424, overruling *Wales* v. *Wadham* [1977] 1 W.L.R. 199. See (1985) 44 C.L.J. 202 (R. Ingleby); All E.R.Rev. 1985, p. 175 (S. M. Cretney). The decision is based on the requirements of s.25, rather than the concept of *uberrima fides* in the agreement for a consent order. See also Practice Direction [1984] 1 W.L.R. 674, Matrimonial Causes Act 1973, s. 33A and Matrimonial Causes Rules 1977, r. 76A, which did not alter the need for full and frank disclosure.

Until the Misrepresentation Act 1967 the plaintiff could rescind,[58] or possibly resist specific performance, but he could not recover damages on the basis of an innocent misrepresentation. Since that Act, however, the plaintiff may recover damages for an innocent misrepresentation unless the defendant had reasonable grounds to believe and did believe that the statement was true.[59] The effect of this provision is that "if the representee proves a misrepresentation which, if fraudulent, would have sounded in damages, the onus passes immediately to the representor to prove that he had reasonable ground to believe the facts represented." It is not a question of negligence as such; "the liability does not depend on his being under a duty of care the extent of which may vary according to the circumstances in which the representation is made. In the case of negotiations leading to a contract the 1967 Act imposes an absolute obligation not to state facts which the representor cannot prove he had reasonable ground to believe."[60] Such damages do not cover loss of bargain.[61] By section 2(2),[62] damages may be awarded in lieu of rescission wherever the court thinks it would be equitable to do so, having regard to the nature of the misrepresentation and the loss that would be caused by it if the contract were upheld, as well as the loss that rescission would cause to the defendant. Damages may be awarded under section 2(2) although the misrepresentation was wholly innocent, (*i.e.* non-negligent). The result intended would seem to be that damages are the most suitable remedy in cases of misrepresentations inducing a contract, save where the facts reveal a real justification for there being rescission of the contract as well. A term in the contract purporting to restrict or exclude liability for misrepresentation is of no effect except insofar as it satisfies the requirement of reasonableness as stated in section 11(1) of the Unfair Contract Terms Act 1977.[63]

Equity's remedy of rescission now forms part of a hierarchy of remedies for misrepresentation that are available generally to a plaintiff, instead of being the only and not always very apposite remedy available in the absence of fraud. It is thus now more important as a supplementary than as a basic remedy. The history and rationale of the

[58] See generally *Redgrave* v. *Hurd* (1881) 20 Ch.D. 1.
[59] s.2(1).
[60] *Howard Marine Dredging Co. Ltd.* v. *A. Ogden & Sons (Excavators) Ltd.* [1978] Q.B. 574 at p. 596 (*per* Bridge L.J.). See also *Esso Petroleum Ltd.* v. *Mardon* [1976] Q.B. 801 (negligent forecast of petrol sales); *Laurence* v. *Lexcourt Holdings Ltd.* [1978] 1 W.L.R. 1128 (negligent misrepresentation as to permitted user); *Walker* v. *Boyle* [1982] 1 W.L.R. 495 (negligent statement by vendor that no boundary disputes). See also *Resolute Maritime Inc.* v. *Merchant Investors Assurance Co. Ltd.* [1983] 1 W.L.R. 857.
[61] *Sharneyford Supplies Ltd.* v. *Edge* [1987] Ch. 305, criticising the decision to the contrary in *Watts* v. *Spence* [1976] Ch. 165; [1987] Conv. 423 (J. Cartwright); Law Com. Working Paper No. 98 (1986), p. 30.
[62] (1967) 30 M.L.R. 369 (G. H. Treitel and P. S. Atiyah).
[63] s.3, as amended by the 1977 Act. See *Walker* v. *Boyle* [1982] 1 W.L.R. 495; *Southwestern General Property Co. Ltd.* v. *Marton, The Times*, May 11, 1982.

remedy are, however, of interest in considering rescission for mistakes not induced by misrepresentation, discussed in the earlier part of this section.

(b) *Undue Influence.*[64] Under the head of constructive fraud,[65] equity recognises a wide variety of situations in which intervention is justified by reason of a defendant's influence or dominance over a plaintiff in procuring his execution of a document (such as a settlement) or his entering into an obligation; equity's intervention here is independent of any question of the accuracy of information supplied to the plaintiff. Equity intervenes in such cases, not because, as is the case with misrepresentations, the defendant has positively (albeit innocently) misled the plaintiff on a particular and relevant point of fact, but because the defendant has caused the plaintiff's judgment to be clouded, with the result that the plaintiff has failed to consider the matter as he ought.

Actual threats, or physical duress, are remedied both at law and in equity, but equity's view is the wider. Where threats have made it impossible for a plaintiff either to consider the relevant matter normally or to feel a free agent, as when a son was threatened with disclosure to his sick father of the forging of the father's signature by his brother, equity will intervene.[66] But influence by means other than threats is the more usual type of case. It is possible for a defendant to have obtained almost complete domination over the mind of another,[67] but in most cases the undue influence is exerted only to secure a specific objective.[68] The varieties of methods are infinite also; they may range from developing a sense of complete confidence[69] over many years to quick seizure of an opportunity presented by a defendant's weakness. In *Tufton* v. *Sperni,*[70] a plaintiff was prevailed upon to buy a house from the defendant at an over-value and at the same time to make it available to the defendant on a lease of absurdly favourable terms. The Court of Appeal, in rescinding the transaction, emphasised that these cases cannot be categorised, but are all variations on the one theme of undue[71] use of a mental domination pos-

---

[64] See generally Keeton and Sheridan's *Equity* (3rd ed.), pp. 255 *et seq.*; [1985] Conv. 387 (C. J. Barton and P. M. Rank); (1988) 2 *Trust Law & Practice* 98 (S. Foster).

[65] See Snell, pp. 538 *et seq*; *O'Sullivan* v. *Management Agency and Music Ltd.* [1985] Q.B. 428, at p. 455.

[66] *Mutual Finance Co.* v. *Wetton* [1937] 2 K.B. 389, following *Williams* v. *Bayley* (1866) L.R. 1 H.L. 200; *Barton* v. *Armstrong* [1976] A.C. 104. See (1939) 3 M.L.R. 97 (W. H. D. Winder).

[67] *Smith* v. *Kay* (1875) 7 H.L.Cas. 750; *Morley* v. *Loughnan* [1893] 1 Ch. 736.

[68] *Lyon* v. *Home* (1868) L.R. 6 Eq. 655.

[69] *Tate* v. *Williamson* (1866) L.R. 2 Ch.App. 55.

[70] [1952] 2 T.L.R. 516. Distinguished in *Alec Lobb (Garages) Ltd.* v. *Total Oil G.B. Ltd.* [1983] 1 W.L.R. 87, affirmed on appeal [1985] 1 W.L.R. 173.

[71] It may be undue without being for personal gain, as where a parent's influence leads to an improvident settlement by a child that is only of marginal benefit to the parent: *Bullock* v. *Lloyds Bank* [1955] Ch. 317.

sessed or gained over another. Undue influence may be exercised by a corporation, although there may be no special personal relationship with any individual representative.[72] The novel point as to whether undue influence could be exercised by an unincorporated association arose in *Roche* v. *Sherrington*,[73] where the plaintiff had been a member of Opus Dei (an international Roman Catholic association) for some years. After leaving, he sought repayment of gifts to the association on the basis of undue influence. Slade J. held it to be arguable that a transaction between an individual and an unincorporated association might give rise to a presumption of undue influence on the part of the members. But the plaintiff's action was dismissed as he had brought it against the defendant as representative of all present members, including many persons who were not members at the time of the gifts. There was no common fund into which the gifts were traceable, so the present members could not be regarded as the recipients.

It is possible to divide the cases up into those, first, in which equity readily presumes undue influence. While the presumption does not apply to every relationship of trust and confidence,[74] it does arise in certain well defined cases such as parent and child, guardian and ward, doctor and patient,[75] religious adviser and pupil,[76] and other situations where it is shown that a similar relationship of confidence existed,[77] cases in which equity requires positive evidence that no undue influence was in fact exerted. In cases outside this category equity requires positive proof of influence having actually been exerted.[78] But in all cases the question is whether a defendant has taken advantage of his position, or, *per contra*, has been assiduous not to do so. The

---

[72] See *Lloyds Bank Ltd.* v. *Bundy* [1975] Q.B. 326.

[73] [1982] 1 W.L.R. 599.

[74] *National Westminster Bank plc* v. *Morgan* [1985] A.C. 686; *Goldsworthy* v. *Brickell* [1987] Ch. 378.

[75] Including a mental patient and the person in charge of the mental hospital: *Re C.M.G.* [1970] Ch. 574.

[76] *Allcard* v. *Skinner* (1887) 36 Ch.D. 145 (nun and mother superior); *Huguenin* v. *Baseley* (1807) 14 Ves. 273.

[77] *Re Craig* [1971] Ch. 95 (aged widower and secretary); *Lloyds Bank Ltd.* v. *Bundy* (*supra*), (banker and aged customer); *O'Sullivan* v. *Management Agency and Music Ltd.* [1985] Q.B. 428 (manager and entertainer); *Re Brocklehurst* [1978] Ch. 14 at p. 42, *per* Bridge L.J.; *Simpson* v. *Simpson* (1989) 19 Fam.Law 20 (incapacitated elderly husband and younger wife); *Goldsworthy* v. *Brickell* [1987] Ch. 378 (elderly farmer and manager). See also *Mathew* v. *Bobbins* (1980) 41 P. & C.R. 1, (1981) 131 N.L.J. 1022 (A. Waite) (there is no presumption of undue influence arising from the relationship of master and servant or landlord and tenant, or a combination of the two).

[78] As in the case of gifts by will, where no presumption of undue influence arises by reason of the relationship of the parties. See Mellows, *The Law of Succession*, pp. 46 *et seq.* There is no presumption of undue influence between husband and wife, although a transaction may be set aside if a relationship of confidence is shown to have existed, or, failing that, on proof of undue influence; *Bank of Montreal* v. *Stuart* [1911] A.C. 120; *Kingsnorth Trust Ltd.* v. *Bell* [1986] 1 W.L.R. 119; *Simpson* v. *Simpson*, *supra*; *Midland Bank plc* v. *Shephard* [1988] 3 All E.R. 17.

question can only be answered in each case by a meticulous consideration of the facts.[79] In some specialised situations, the facts speak for
themselves: Contracts between employers and employees which restrict the future freedom of operation of the employee may be unenforceable, even in the absence of proof of undue influence, on the ground
that the restriction is unreasonable.[80] Many cases turn, as is natural, on
whether a defendant discouraged independent legal advice or proceeded in such a way as to make it unlikely that the plaintiff would
think of taking it.[81] For, as with many of the flexible remedies of
equity,[82] a defendant is not placed under an absolute bar by virtue of
this equitable obligation, but has to adopt proper steps, in view of the
obligation, if he wishes to proceed in certain ways. So a genuine
insistence on independent legal advice is a natural means of repudiat-
ing a charge of having exerted undue influence, even in a case where
the possibility of influence was strong,[83] and especially where there is a
conflict of interest and duty.[84] But the presumption of undue influence
is not rebuttable only by establishing insistence on independent legal
advice; it may also be rebutted by showing that the gift was a "spontaneous and independent act."[85] In any event, the presumption will not
operate unless the gift is so large or the transaction so improvident that
it cannot reasonably be accounted for on grounds of friendship, relationship, charity or other motives.[86]

The question is whether it is possible to extract general propositions
from these illustrations of the flexible approach of the courts to cases
involving undue influence. Most of the illustrations relate to situations
of special relationship existing between particular people, and often
involve settlements of property. The principle is less often seen in
operation in commercial matters, where it has had little impact in
derogating from the more widely applicable principle that lies behind
the maxim *caveat emptor*.[87] Mere inequality of bargaining power,
which is a relative concept, does not justify interference with a commercial transaction. There is rarely absolute equality, and the court

---

[79] *Per* Sir Eric Sachs in *Lloyds Bank Ltd.* v. *Bundy, supra,* at p. 510.
[80] *A. Schroeder Music Publishing Co. Ltd.* v. *Macaulay* [1974] 1 W.L.R. 1308; *Clifford Davis Ltd.* v. *W.E.A. Records Ltd.* [1975] 1 W.L.R. 61; *ante,* p. 748.
[81] *Baker* v. *Monk* (1864) 4 De G.J. & S. 388; *Backhouse* v. *Backhouse* [1978] 1 W.L.R. 243; *Cresswell* v. *Potter* (1968); [1978] 1 W.L.R. 255n.
[82] *e.g. Holder* v. *Holder* [1968] Ch. 353, *ante,* p. 560; *Phipps* v. *Boardman* [1967] 2 A.C. 46, *ante,* p. 571.
[83] See *Zamet* v. *Hyman* [1961] 1 W.L.R. 1442 at pp. 1445–1446.
[84] *Lloyds Bank Ltd.* v. *Bundy* [1975] Q.B. 326.
[85] *Re Brocklehurst* [1978] Ch. 14. See also *Simpson* v. *Simpson, The Times,* June 11, 1988; *Goldsworthy* v. *Brickell* [1987] Ch. 378.
[86] *Goldsworthy* v. *Brickell* [1987] Ch. 378; (1987) 104 L.Q.R. 160; All E.R.Rev. 1987, p. 311 (M. P. F. Furmston).
[87] "Extravagant liberality and immoderate folly do not provide a passport to equitable relief," *per* Evershed M.R. in *Tufton* v. *Sperni* [1952] 2 T.L.R. 516 at p. 519.

only interferes in exceptional cases as a matter of common fairness.[88] The principles of undue influence have generally been discussed in the types of transaction which attracted equity's particular attention in the nineteenth century, such as the cases on bargains with expectant heirs; and the modern form of such cases, as where a beneficiary under a trust, who, although past the age of majority, is still subject to parental influence, and is persuaded to use his fortune to support the family finances,[89] or to make a settlement for fiscal reasons, although technically contrary to his personal interests; or where a secretary companion takes advantage of her dominance of a weak, dependent and vulnerable old man[90]; or where an elderly farmer grants a tenancy on terms disadvantageous to himself to the manager upon whom he relies.[91] Bridge L.J. summarised these cases as those in which there is a "duty on the donee to advise the donor, or a position of actual or potential dominance of the donee over the donor."[92] But there was no such position of dominance in *Re Brocklehurst*,[93] where an "autocratic and eccentric old gentleman" made a valuable gift of shooting rights to the defendant, a "subservient garage proprietor." The relationship was not one of confidence and trust such as to give rise to a presumption of undue influence.

A recent formulation of the doctrine by the House of Lords appears in *National Westminster Bank* v. *Morgan*,[94] where a husband and wife mortgaged their home to the bank to secure a loan to the husband, who was in difficulties with his business. The wife claimed that the bank manager had exercised undue influence in obtaining her signature during a visit to the home. Although the wife had not received independent legal advice before signing, her claim failed because the relationship never went beyond the normal business relationship of banker and customer, nor was the transaction disadvantageous to the wife. The principle which justifies setting a transaction aside for undue influence is the victimisation of one party by the other. The party alleging undue influence must show that the transaction was wrongful

---

[88] *Alec Lobb (Garages) Ltd.* v. *Total Oil G.B. Ltd.* [1985] 1 W.L.R. 173; (1985) 101 L.Q.R. 306. *Cf.* the wider views of Lord Denning M.R. in *Lloyds Bank Ltd.* v. *Bundy, supra,* which were disapproved in *National Westminster Bank plc* v. *Morgan* [1985] A.C. 686, *infra.*

[89] *Re Coomber* [1911] 1 Ch. 732 at pp. 726, 727; *Bullock* v. *Lloyds Bank Ltd.* [1955] Ch. 317; *Re Pauling's S.T.* [1964] Ch. 303.

[90] *Re Craig* [1971] Ch. 95.

[91] *Goldsworthy* v. *Brickell* [1987] Ch. 378.

[92] *Re Brocklehurst* [1978] Ch. 14 at p. 41.

[93] [1978] Ch. 14 (Lord Denning M.R. dissented).

[94] [1985] A.C. 686; (1985) 101 L.Q.R. 305 and (1985) 44 C.L.J. 192 (N. Andrews); (1985) 48 M.L.R. 579 (D. Tiplady); All E.R. Rev. 1985, p. 20 (N. E. Palmer) and p. 89 (M. P. F. Furmston).

in that it was manifestly disadvantageous[95] to him (which will, of course, be easier to establish in cases of gifts). It is not sufficient to establish that there was a relationship of influence without this further element of disadvantage. While there are no precisely defined limits to the equitable jurisdiction to relieve against undue influence, the doctrine is sufficiently developed not to need the support of a principle of inequality of bargaining power.[96] This decision, in rejecting the broad approach of inequality of bargaining power, has restricted the scope of the doctrine or undue influence. But a party who fails to prove undue influence may sometimes succeed in a negligence action, as where a bank gives an incorrect explanation of a transaction.[97]

A further question which has arisen in the context of mortgages and guarantees is whether the creditor should be prejudiced by any undue influence exercised by the debtor over a third party who executes the mortgage or guarantee in favour of the creditor. It was established in the cases of *Turnbull & Co. Ltd.* v. *Duval*[98] and *Chaplin & Co. Ltd.* v. *Brammall*[99] that where a creditor entrusts a husband with the task of procuring the execution of a mortgage or guarantee by his wife without ensuring that the wife takes independent legal advice, the creditor is tainted by any undue influence exercised by the husband and cannot enforce the mortgage or guarantee against the wife. These cases were decided before it became clear that there was no presumption of undue influence between husband and wife.[1] Nevertheless the relationship is such that influence might be expected by the creditor, and the principle has been applied in modern cases.[2] This principle was extended beyond the relationship of husband and wife in *Avon Finance Ltd.* v. *Bridger*,[3] where a dishonest son persuaded his elderly parents to execute a charge over their property to secure a loan from the plaintiff to the son. The plaintiff could not enforce the charge because it had appointed the son to procure its execution by the parents in circumstances where it should have known that he would have influence over them, and it had not insisted on the parents' obtaining independent

---

[95] *Lloyds Bank Ltd.* v. *Bundy* [1975] Q.B. 326 was wrong insofar as it took a different view. On "manifest disadvantage," see *Midland Bank plc* v. *Phillips, The Times,* March 28, 1986; *Woodstead Finance Ltd.* v. *Petrou, The Times,* January 23, 1986; *Midland Bank plc* v. *Shephard,* [1988] 3 All E.R. 17. It is also required where actual undue influence is proved; *Bank of Credit and Commerce International Société Anonyme* v. *Aboody* (unreported), criticised [1988] Conv. 441 (B. Dale).

[96] Disapproving the formulation of Lord Denning M.R. in *Lloyds Bank Ltd.* v. *Bundy, supra.*

[97] *Cornish* v. *Midland Bank plc* [1985] 3 All E.R. 513; *Midland Bank plc* v. *Perry* (1988) 50 P. & C.R. 202.

[98] [1902] A.C. 429.   [99] [1908] 1 K.B. 233.

[1] See *Bank of Montreal* v. *Stuart* [1911] A.C. 120.

[2] *Kingsnorth Trust Ltd.* v. *Bell* [1986] 1 W.L.R. 119; All E.R. Rev. 1985, p. 24 and 1986, p. 34 (N. E. Palmer); (1986) 45 C.L.J. 194 (N. H. Andrews); [1986] Conv. 212 (J.E.M.); (1986) 102 L.Q.R. 351; (1988) 85 L.S.G., No. 9, p. 11 (A. M. Kenny); *Barclays Bank plc* v. *Kennedy* (1988) N. L. J. Law Rep. 334.

[3] (1979) 123 S.J. 705.

advice. Whether the debtor has acted as the agent of the creditor in procuring the execution of the mortgage or guarantee may involve difficult questions of fact.[4] If the debtor's conduct is an unauthorised intervention, the creditor will not be tainted by the debtor's undue influence over the third party.[5] Where the creditor has not appointed the debtor his agent in the conduct of the transaction, his only duty to the third party is to point out the desirability of independent advice. It does not extend to ensuring that such advice is obtained.[6] To require more would place too great a burden on commercial lenders.

(c) *Unconscionable Bargains.*[7] Equity intervenes to set aside unfair transactions made with "poor and ignorant" persons. It is not enough to show that the transaction was hard and unreasonable.[8] Three elements must be established[9]: first, that one party was at a serious disadvantage to the other by reason of poverty, ignorance or otherwise,[10] so that circumstances existed of which unfair advantage could be taken[11]; secondly, that the transaction was at an undervalue; and thirdly, that there was a lack of independent legal advice.[12] A similar principle applies in the case of unconscionable bargains with reversioners or "expectant heirs."[13]

There are also at the present time other types of situation which call for relief. Oppressive hire purchase contracts and other credit arrangements are controlled by legislation,[14] and statutory protection is now given to unfair contractual terms, especially in the field of exemption clauses, by the Unfair Contract Terms Act 1977. Relief has long been given against oppressive provisions in mortgages,[15] and a similar general principle is evident in the protection of the weak against the strong in the context of relief against forfeiture, in the development of

---

[4] See *Coldunell Ltd.* v. *Gallon* [1986] Q.B. 1184 (son and elderly parents).

[5] *Ibid.*; *Midland Bank plc* v. *Shephard* [1988] 3 All E.R. 17; *Midland Bank plc* v. *Perry* (1988) 50 P. & C.R. 202 (but bank liable to wife in negligence for not having satisfied itself that she understood the position).

[6] *Ibid.*; *Bank of Baroda* v. *Shah* [1988] 3 All E.R. 24.

[7] See Keeton and Sheridan's *Equity* (3rd ed.), pp. 255 *et seq.* and 280–282.

[8] *Alec Lobb (Garages) Ltd.* v. *Total Oil G.B. Ltd.* [1985] 1 W.L.R. 173.

[9] *Fry* v. *Lane* (1888) 40 Ch.D. 312. The list is not exhaustive; *Cresswell* v. *Potter* [1978] 1 W.L.R. 255.

[10] See *Watkin* v. *Watson-Smith, The Times,* July 3, 1986 (old age with diminution of capacity and judgment, together with a desire for a quick sale, satisfied the requirement). See also *Mountford* v. *Scott* [1975] Ch. 259.

[11] This requirement is not satsified where, unknown to the purchaser, the vendor is of unsound mind; *Hart* v. *O'Connor* [1985] A.C. 1000; [1986] Conv. 178 (A. H. Hudson).

[12] See *Butlin-Sanders* v. *Butlin* (1985) 15 Fam. Law 126, where the claim was in any event barred by laches and acquiescence.

[13] Mere undervalue is not sufficient. See L.P.A. 1925, s.174(1).

[14] Consumer Credit Act 1974. See *Woodstead Finance Ltd.* v. *Petrou, The Times,* January 23, 1986.

[15] A modern example is *Cityland and Property (Holdings) Ltd.* v. *Dabrah* [1968] Ch. 166; *cf. Multiservice Bookbinding Ltd.* v. *Marden* [1979] Ch. 84.

the principles of restraint of trade, and in certain other contexts.[16] The view of the House of Lords is that there is no need to erect a general principle of relief against inequality of bargaining power. Parliament has undertaken this essentially legislative task, and the courts should not formulate further restrictions.[17]

C. Loss of the Right to Rescind

Formerly a contract entered into in reliance upon an innocent misrepresentation could not be rescinded after execution of the contract by the transfer of property under it.[18] This rule was abrogated by the Misrepresentation Act 1967, s.1. However, the court has a discretion under section 2(2) to award damages in lieu of rescission in any case of innocent misrepresentation if it would be equitable to do so.[19] This discretion is more likely to be exercised where the contract has been executed than where it remains executory.

More generally, the right to rescind may be lost in any of three ways:

(i) *Affirmation*. Where the party entitled to rescind affirms the contract, for example by taking a benefit under it, with knowledge of the facts giving rise to the right to rescind and of his legal rights,[20] he will be taken to have waived that right.[21] Affirmation may be shown by words or acts, or may be indicated by lapse of time, the remedy being subject to the doctrine of laches.[22]

(ii) *Restitutio in Integrum not Possible*. A contract will cease to be capable of rescission if the parties can no longer be restored to their original position.[23] Any money paid or other property transferred under the contract must be restored. But a precise restoration is not required, particularly in cases involving fraud. Equity is concerned to restore the parties, and especially the defendant, to their former positions so far as practically pos-

---

[16] *e.g.* salvage agreements; *The Port Caledonia and The Anna* [1903] P. 184.

[17] *National Westminster Bank plc* v. *Morgan* [1985] A.C. 686, disapproving wider statements in *Lloyds Bank Ltd.* v. *Bundy* [1975] Q.B. 326.

[18] *Angel* v. *Jay* [1911] 1 K.B. 666; *Seddon* v. *North Eastern Salt Co. Ltd.* [1905] 1 Ch. 326. It was otherwise if the misrepresentation was fraudulent.

[19] (1967) 30 M.L.R. 369 (G. H. Treitel and P. S. Atiyah).

[20] *Peyman* v. *Lanjani* [1985] Ch. 457; [1985] Conv. 408 (L. Anderson). (Mere knowledge of facts not enough. Plaintiff can rely on ignorance of law unless estopped from denying affirmation by unequivocal act showing intention to proceed with the contract coupled with detriment to defendant; or unless plaintiff's solicitor aware of right to rescind); *cf. Goldsworthy* v. *Brickell* [1987] Ch. 378.

[21] *Clough* v. *London and North Western Rail Co.* (1871) L.R. 7 Ex.Ch. 26.

[22] *Life Association of Scotland* v. *Siddal* (1861) 3 De G.F. & J. 58; *Alec Lobb (Garages) Ltd.* v. *Total Oil G.B. Ltd., supra.* In the case of company shares it seems that delay is viewed more strictly; *Re Scottish Petroleum Co.* (1883) 23 Ch.D. 434. See also *Leaf* v. *International Galleries* [1950] 2 K.B. 86. For the application of the Limitation Act 1980, s.32(1)(*c*), see *Peco Arts Inc.* v. *Hazlitt Gallery Ltd.* [1983] 1 W.L.R. 1315.

[23] *Thorpe* v. *Fasey* [1949] Ch. 649; *Erlanger* v. *New Sombrero Phosphate Co.* (1873) 3 App.Cas. 1218.

sible.[24] This might be achieved by, for example, ordering an account of profits and making allowances for deterioration of the property.[25]

(iii) *Third Party Acquiring Rights.* The right to rescind is lost if an innocent third party acquires an interest under the contract for value before the plaintiff seeks to set it aside.[26] There is no bar to rescission if the third party is a volunteer, such as the defendant's trustee in bankruptcy.[27]

2. RECTIFICATION

A. Nature of the Remedy[28]

Rectification is a discretionary equitable remedy whereby an instrument[29] which does not accord with the intentions of the parties to it may be corrected. It operates as an exception to the "parol evidence rule," whereby oral evidence is not admissible to alter a written instrument. It must be emphasised that the court does not rectify a mistake in the contract itself, but only a mistake in the instrument recording the contract. It must be very clearly shown that the parties had come to a genuine agreement and that the instrument had failed to record it. Thus where both a written agreement to sell land and the ensuing conveyance incorrectly described the land which it had been agreed to sell, it was possible to obtain rectification on proof of the real oral agreement.[30] Rectification may also occur where there are grounds for rescission and the court grants rescission on terms which include an option to the defendant to submit to rescission or rectification.[31]

It is no objection that the rectification may have the effect of saving

---

[24] *Spence* v. *Crawford* [1939] 3 All E.R. 271; *Newbigging* v. *Adam* (1886) 34 Ch.D. 582. Where a principal rescinds a contract with a third party, there is no obligation to return a bribe paid by the third party to the agent and recovered by the principal, as it is not money paid under the contract; *Logicrose Ltd.* v. *Southend United Football Club Ltd.* [1988] 1 W.L.R. 1256.

[25] *Erlanger* v. *New Sombrero Phosphate Co.*, *supra.* See also *O'Sullivan* v. *Management Agency and Music Ltd.* [1985] Q.B. 428 (contracts between manager and entertainer rescinded for undue influence; *restitutio* principle not applied with full rigour in cases of breach of fiduciary relationship; practical justice achieved by ordering account of profits, giving credit for defendant's labour and skill).

[26] *Oakes* v. *Turquand* (1867) L.R. 2 H.L. 325.

[27] *Re Eastgate* [1905] 1 K.B. 465; *Scholefield* v. *Templer* (1859) Johns. 155.

[28] See Goff and Jones, pp. 192–198.

[28] See Goff and Jones, pp. 192–198.

[29] Distinguish cancellation of an instrument that is void or voidable on some ground, *e.g.* forgery: *Peake* v. *Highfield* (1826) 1 Russ. 559.

[30] *Craddock Bros.* v. *Hunt* [1923] 2 Ch. 136.

[31] See the terms imposed in *Solle* v. *Butcher* [1950] 1 K.B. 671 and *Grist* v. *Bailey* [1967] Ch. 532. But where the mistake is unilateral, see *post*, p. 797.

tax[32]; nor that the mistake arose through the negligence of the plaintiff or his legal advisers[33] nor that one of the parties has since died.[34]

When rectification is ordered, a copy of the order may be indorsed on the instrument. There is no need to execute a new document.[35] Rectification is retrospective, and affects steps taken by the parties in the meantime.[36] But the instrument remains binding in its uncorrected form until rectification is actually ordered. The plaintiff may obtain rectification and specific performance in the same action.[37]

Rectification must be distinguished from the court's power to correct an obvious error as a matter of construction. If an instrument contains a manifest mistake in its drafting, neither common law nor equity is prevented from discerning the fact and substituting the words that were intended to be there. But this is a limited jurisdiction for it applies only when the mistake is obvious from the instrument itself and what should have been written is obvious too.[38] Extrinsic evidence is not admissible. This jurisdiction is one based on the duty of the court to construe documents correctly and is not a jurisdiction to rectify as such.

B. The Nature of the Mistake

(i) **Common Mistake.** The general rule is that rectification requires a mistake common to both parties, whereby the instrument records the agreement in a manner contrary to the intention of both.[39] It must be shown that there was some prior agreement, although not necessarily an enforceable contract, whereby the parties expressed a common intention regarding the provisions in question.[40] It must also be shown that the common intention continued until the execution of the instrument. Rectification is not possible where the instrument departs from the prior agreement because the parties had agreed to vary the terms.[41]

---

[32] *Re Colebrook's Conveyance* [1972] 1 W.L.R. 1397; *Re Slocock's W.T.* [1979] 1 All E.R. 358.

[33] *Weeds* v. *Blaney* (1977) 247 E.G. 211 (discussing also the position as to costs); *Central & Metropolitan Estates Ltd.* v. *Compusave* (1983) 266 E.G. 900 (rectification ordered on terms in such a case); *Boots The Chemist Ltd.* v. *Street* (1983) 268 E.G. 817.

[34] *Johnson* v. *Bragge* [1901] 1 Ch. 28.

[35] *White* v. *White* (1872) L.R. 15 Eq. 247.

[36] *Malmesbury* v. *Malmesbury* (1862) 31 Beav. 407. See also *Freer* v. *Unwins Ltd.* [1976] Ch. 288, contrasting rectification under the Land Registration Act 1925.

[37] *Craddock Bros.* v. *Hunt* [1923] 2 Ch. 136.

[38] *Re Bacharach's W.T.* [1959] Ch. 245; *Re Doland* [1970] Ch. 267.

[39] *Murray* v. *Parker* (1854) 19 Beav. 305. See also *Fowler* v. *Fowler* (1859) 4 De G. & J. 250.

[40] *Joscelyne* v. *Nissen* [1970] 2 Q.B. 86, (1970) 86 L.Q.R. 303 (P.V.B.), (1971) 87 L.Q.R. 532 (L. Bromley), arguing that an outward expression of accord is not *per se* a requirement. See also *Shipley U.D.C.* v. *Bradford Corpn.* [1936] Ch. 375; *Crane* v. *Hegeman-Harris Co. Inc.* [1939] 1 All E.R. 662, [1939] 3 All E.R. 68, [1971] 1 W.L.R. 1390n.; *C.H. Pearce & Sons Ltd.* v. *Stonechester Ltd., The Times*, November 17, 1983 (a plaintiff who pleads two claims for rectification in the alternative based on inconsistent assertions of the parties' common intentions demonstrates at the outset that there was no certain intention which would found such a claim).

[41] *Breadalbane* v. *Chandos* (1837) 2 My. & Cr. 711.

Next, it must be established that the instrument is not in accordance with the true agreement of the parties, and that, if rectified in the manner claimed, it will represent the agreement. But only the actual agreement of the parties is relevant, not what they would have agreed if they had not been under a misapprehension. Thus in *Frederick E. Rose (London) Ltd.* v. *William H. Pim Jnr. & Co. Ltd.*,[42] rectification was not possible where the parties agreed to buy and sell horsebeans, and the written contract referred to horsebeans, but the parties mistakenly believed that horsebeans were the same as feveroles. The mistake was made when entering into the contract in the first place. The crux of the remedy is proof of what the parties actually had decided at the time of reaching their agreement and not what they, or one of them, had thought at a later date, or what they might have thought if they had considered the matter in greater detail or in the light of more information than that available to them. In other words, the remedy exists to correct, but not to improve, an instrument.

The mistake is usually one of fact, but relief may be possible where the mistake is of law, although the position is not completely clear. In *Re Butlin's Settlement Trust*,[43] rectification was ordered where the settlor and his solicitor were mistaken as to the effect of a clause giving power to the trustees to decide by a majority. Rectification has been granted where the parties used the ineffective phrase "free of tax"[44] to carry out their agreement to pay such sum as after deduction of tax would leave the sum in question[45]; although rectification was refused in *Whiteside* v. *Whiteside*[46] where a similar phrase was used as the parties had already corrected the error by executing a supplemental deed, and there was therefore no issue between them.

(ii) Unilateral Mistake. Where one party incorrectly records a term of the agreement, but it is bona fide accepted as it is written by the other party, the mistake is unilateral and there is no ground for rectification. Thus, the rent may be incorrectly stated, or the lessor's obligations, or the land or buildings incorrectly described. The party making the mistake can only obtain rectification if he can show that the mistake is due to the fraud[47] of the other party, or that the other party was aware of the mistake.

---

[42] [1953] 2 Q.B. 450, described as a "hard case" in Goff and Jones, p. 194. See also *London Regional Transport* v. *Wimpey Group Services Ltd.* (1987) 53 P. & C.R. 356.

[43] [1976] Ch. 251.

[44] No longer ineffective: see *Ferguson* v. *I.R.C.* [1970] A.C. 442.

[45] *Burroughes* v. *Abbott* [1922] 1 Ch. 86; *Jervis* v. *Howle & Talke Colliery Co. Ltd.* [1937] Ch. 67.

[46] [1950] Ch. 65. (The plaintiff's purpose in seeking the order was to improve his tax position). *cf. Napier* v. *Williams* [1911] 1 Ch. 361.

[47] Constructive fraud suffices. See *Lovesy* v. *Smith* (1880) 15 Ch.D. 655.

In *Riverlate Properties Ltd.* v. *Paul,*[48] the plaintiffs, who were the landlords of property in London, intended to provide in the lease that the defendant should be liable to contribute one half of the landlord's expenditure on matters contained in clauses 6(*a*), (*b*), (*c*). By mistake, the lease referred to 6(*b*), (*c*), (*d*). The defendant and her solicitors were unaware of the mistake. The lease stood, as signed.

On the other hand, in *A. Roberts and Co. Ltd.* v. *Leicestershire County Council,*[49] the plaintiffs had undertaken to build a school for the defendants. The agreement provided that the school should be completed within 18 months, but the officers of the Council altered the period to 30 months in the draft contract, not drawing the company's attention to the alteration. The company signed the contract without noticing the change, and one of the defendant's officials was aware of the mistake. Rectification was ordered.

The Court of Appeal has recently held[50] that, in order for the *Roberts* doctrine to apply, it must be shown first that one party, A, erroneously believed that the document sought to be rectified contained a particular provision; secondly, that the other party, B, was aware of the mistake and that it was due to an error on the part of A; thirdly, that B had omitted to draw the mistake to the notice of A; fourthly, that the mistake must be one calculated to benefit B.[51] Although it need not amount to sharp practice, the conduct of B must be such as to make it inequitable that he should be allowed to object to rectification. The graver the character of the conduct involved, the heavier the burden of proof, but the conduct must be such as to affect the conscience of the party who had suppressed the fact that he had recognised the presence of a mistake. Thus, rectification was ordered where a rent review clause in a lease failed to provide machinery for determining the rent in default of agreement. The landlord realised the omission only when the time for review arrived, whereas the tenant had been aware of the mistake at all times. An arbitration clause was ordered to be inserted into the lease, according to the original mutual intention of the parties.

---

[48] [1975] Ch. 133; (1974) 90 L.Q.R. 439; (1975) 53 Can.Bar.Rev. 339 (S.M. Waddams); *London Borough of Redbridge* v. *Robinson Rentals Ltd.* (1969) 211 E.G. 1125; *Taylor* v. *Johnson* [1982–1983] 151 C.L.R. 422 (High Court of Australia); [1985] Conv. 81 (H. W. Wilkinson); *Agip S.p.A.* v. *Navigazione Alta Italia S.p.A.* [1984] 1 Lloyd's Rep. 353.

[49] [1961] Ch. 555. See Goff and Jones, pp. 195–196, expressing the view that the decision is based on estoppel.

[50] *Bates (Thomas) & Son Ltd.* v. *Wyndham's (Lingerie) Ltd.* [1981] 1 W.L.R. 505; *Kemp* v. *Neptune Concrete Ltd.* [1988] 48 E.G. 71. See also *Central & Metropolitan Estates Ltd.* v. *Compusave* (1983) 266 E.G. 900 (20 year lease rectified to include rent review clause. Negotiations contemplated such a provision, but mistakenly omitted from lease. Tenant aware of landlord's mistake. Rectification on terms that tenant should have opportunity to surrender lease after first review).

[51] Or, *per* Eveleigh L.J., be detrimental to A.

It was at one time thought that the court could give the defendant a choice of submitting to rescission or rectification, even though the mistake was unilateral and the court was unable to satisfy itself that the defendant was aware of the mistake. A practice developed of imposing such an option, but these cases[52] were firmly disapproved by the Court of Appeal in *Riverlate Properties Ltd.* v. *Paul*[53] and can no longer be relied upon. Unilateral mistake can only give rise to rectification in cases of fraud or upon the principle of *A. Roberts and Co. Ltd.* v. *Leicestershire County Council,*[54] where rectification was particularly appropriate, for the school had been built at the time of the action; and if the contract had been rescinded or held void at law, the plaintiff would have been forced to sue in quasi-contract.

Where the transaction is unilateral, a unilateral mistake is sufficient. This is discussed below.

C. Proof of the Mistake

The burden of proof on the party seeking rectification is a heavy one. According to the older cases, the plaintiff must establish the mistake by "strong irrefragable evidence,"[55] or with a "high degree of conviction."[56] A more recent description is "convincing proof."[57] Oral evidence is admissible to prove the agreement, and there is no need to show anything in the nature of error on the face of the instrument. It is no objection that the transaction is one required by statute to be evidenced in writing; it suffices that the rectified instrument will comply with the statute.[58]

In the case of a settlement, the settlor's evidence alone,[59] or even a mere perusal of the document[60] may suffice to establish the mistake, but the court is slow to act without the support of other evidence such as any written instructions given by the settlor prior to the execution of the settlement.

---

[52] *Garrard* v. *Frankel* (1862) 30 Beav. 445; *Harris* v. *Pepperell* (1867) L.R. 5 Eq. 1; *Paget* v. *Marshall* (1882) 28 Ch.D. 255.

[53] [1975] Ch. 133 at p. 145: in the absence of fraud or sharp practice, mere unilateral mistake was not a ground for rescission "either with or without the option to the [defendant] to accept rectification to cure the [plaintiff's] mistake." *Solle* v. *Butcher* [1950] 1 K.B. 671, *ante*, p. 780, was there distinguished as being a case of common mistake. Rectification may, however, be ordered on terms. See *Central & Metropolitan Estates Ltd.* v. *Compusave, supra*, n. 50.

[54] [1961] Ch. 555.

[55] *Countess of Shelburne* v. *Earl of Inchiquin* (1784) 1 Bro.C.C. 338 at 341.

[56] *Crane* v. *Hegeman-Harris Co. Inc.* [1939] 4 All E.R. 68 at 71.

[57] *Joscelyne* v. *Nissen* [1970] 2 Q.B. 86 at 98. See also *Thomas Bates and Son Ltd.* v. *Wyndham's (Lingerie) Ltd.* [1981] 1 W.L.R. 505 at 514.

[58] *Craddock Bros.* v. *Hunt* [1923] 2 Ch. 136.

[59] *Hanley* v. *Pearson* (1870) 13 Ch.D. 545.

[60] *Banks* v. *Ripley* [1940] Ch. 719.

D. Instruments which may be Rectified

The remedy is widely available, being applicable to leases and other conveyances of land,[61] insurance policies,[62] bills of exchange[63] and many other instruments; but not the articles of a company.[64]

Rectification can also be obtained of a voluntary deed, such as a settlement, if the court is satisfied on the evidence that the donor's real intent at the time of entering into it was not accurately reflected in the instrument.[65] It is not necessary to show that the intent of the trustees was inaccurately reflected.[66] Clearly the requirement of a common mistake has no application to unilateral transactions.[67] Rectification of a settlement may be ordered not only at the instance of the settlor but also at the instance of a volunteer beneficiary, although this will not be done during the settlor's lifetime without his agreement.[68]

Formerly it was not possible to rectify a will except in the case of fraud,[69] although the court could, as a matter of construction, correct a manifest error in drafting.[70] It is now provided by section 20 of the Administration of Justice Act 1982[71] that a will may be rectified if the court is satisfied that it fails to carry out the testator's intentions in consequence of a clerical error or a failure to understand his instructions. Applications for rectification of a will may not be made after six months from the date on which a grant of representation was taken out, save with leave of the court. If the personal representatives distribute the estate after the six months' period they will not be liable for failing to take into account the possibility that the court might allow an application for rectification out of time, but any part of the estate so distributed is recoverable. This statutory power does not permit rectification where the testator himself has misunderstood the legal effect of the wording used.[72]

E. Defences

The remedy of rectification, which, like other equitable remedies, is discretionary, will not be granted where a bona fide purchaser for

---

[61] *Thomas Bates and Son Ltd.* v. *Wyndhams (Lingerie) Ltd.* [1981] 1 W.L.R. 505.

[62] *Collett* v. *Morrison* (1851) 9 Hare 162.

[63] *Druiff* v. *Lord Parker* (1868) L.R. 5 Eq. 131.

[64] *Scott* v. *Frank F. Scott (London) Ltd.* [1940] Ch. 794.

[65] *Lackersteen* v. *Lackersteen* (1864) 30 L.J. Ch. 5; *Behrens* v. *Heilbut* (1956) 222 L.T.J. 290; *Bonhote* v. *Henderson* [1895] 1 Ch. 742; [1895] 2 Ch. 202 (where rectification was refused).

[66] *Re Butlin's Settlement* [1976] Ch. 251 at p. 262.

[67] *Wright* v. *Goff* (1856) 22 Beav. 207.

[68] *Thompson* v. *Whitmore* (1860) 1 J. & H. 268; *Lister* v. *Hodgson* (1867) L.R. 4 Eq. 30; Goff and Jones, Chap. 31.

[69] *Collins* v. *Elstone* [1893] P. 1.

[70] *Re Bacharach's W.T.* [1959] Ch. 245; *Re Doland* [1970] Ch. 267; *ante*, p. 796.

[71] Following the recommendations of the 19th Report of the Law Reform Committee (Cmnd. 5301). See (1983) 46 M.L.R. 191 at 201 (A. Borkowski and K. Stanton).

[72] See *Collins* v. *Elstone* [1893] P. 1.

value without notice has acquired an interest under the instrument.[73] Laches or acquiescence will bar the claim[74]; similarly if the contract is no longer capable of performance,[75] or has been fully performed under a judgment of the court.[76] In the case of a voluntary settlement, it has been held that the court may decline to rectify if a trustee, having taken office in ignorance of the mistake, has a reasonable objection to the rectification.[77]

---

[73] *Garrard* v. *Frankel* (1862) 30 Beav. 445. *Smith* v. *Jones* [1954] 1 W.L.R. 1089; *Lyme Valley Squash Club Ltd.* v. *Newcastle under Lyme Borough Council* [1985] 2 All E.R. 405. In the case of registered land, the right to rectify may be asserted against the purchaser as an overriding interest under s.70(1)(g) of the Land Registration Act 1925: *Blacklocks* v. *J.B. Developments (Godalming) Ltd.* [1982] Ch. 183. The benefit of the right to rectify in cases concerning land will pass with the land; *Boots The Chemist Ltd.* v. *Street* (1983) 268 E.G. 817; L.P.A. 1925, s.63.

[74] *Beale* v. *Kyte* [1907] 1 Ch. 564.

[75] *Borrowman* v. *Rossell* (1864) 16 C.B.(N.S.) 58.

[76] *Caird* v. *Moss* (1886) 33 Ch.D. 22.

[77] *Re Butlin's S.T.* [1976] Ch. 251 (where rectification was granted).

PART V

MISCELLANEOUS EQUITABLE DOCTRINES AND EQUITIES

CHAPTER 26

EQUITABLE DOCTRINES OF CONVERSION, ELECTION, SATISFACTION AND PERFORMANCE

1. THE DOCTRINE OF CONVERSION

A. Basis of the Doctrine

The basis of the doctrine is the maxim "Equity looks on that as done which ought to be done." This can be illustrated by examining the simple case of an express trust for sale. If there is a trust for sale of land, equity notionally regards that land as money from the moment when the instrument creating the trust takes effect,[1] that is, the date of death in the case of a trust created by a will, or the date of execution of a deed.[2] The land will devolve as personalty irrespective of the precise

---

[1] The doctrine is shown as clearly established in *Lingen* v. *Sowray* (1715) 1 P.Wms. 172. The leading case is *Fletcher* v. *Ashburner* (1779) 1 Bro.C.C. 497. See generally (1984) 100 L.Q.R. 86 (S. Anderson).

[2] Even though sale cannot take place at that date: *Clarke* v. *Franklin* (1858) 4 K. & J. 257.

time at which the sale takes place, thus preventing the devolution of beneficial interests from being altered by failure or delay on the part of the trustees in executing this duty to sell. Conversely, if there is a trust of money for the purchase of land, equity notionally regards that money as turned into land at the corresponding moment. This notional conversion will determine the devolution of an estate. Land held subject to a trust for sale passes as personalty; money held on trust to purchase land is treated as realty. This was of greater significance before 1926, when different rules applied to the devolution of realty and personalty on intestacy. It is now relevant in cases where a testator devises his realty to A, and bequeaths his personalty to B.

B. Trust for Sale and Power of Sale Distinguished

It is most important, however, to distinguish a trust for sale, which produces an immediate notional conversion,[3] from a mere power of sale, which does not. In the case of a power of sale, the nature of the property only changes when the sale is effected.[4] The distinction is the same as that made in the earlier discussion of the distinction between trusts and powers. A trust for sale is mandatory, imposing a duty to sell and convert. A power is a discretion, allowing the donee of the power to sell or not as he thinks best. But a trust for sale, although mandatory, may contain a power in the trustees to postpone sale. Indeed such a power was commonly found in express trusts for sale before 1926,[5] and is now by statute included, subject to an expression of contrary intention, in all trusts for sale.[6] Similarly it is no objection to a trust for sale that the sale may be effected only with the consent of a third party.[7] Considerable difficulty was experienced in determining the proper construction of a trust "to retain or sell." By the Law of Property Act 1925, s.25(4), such language is to be construed as a trust to sell the land with power to postpone the sale.

C. Contracts for Sale and Options

Conversion is a doctrine which applies not only to trusts for sale,[8] but also to specifically enforceable contracts for the sale of land.[9] Such

---

[3] The effect of the doctrine, in the context of a trust for sale of the family home, was considered in Chap. 11. See also [1986] Conv. 415 (J. Warburton); Law Commission Working paper No. 94 (1985), *Trusts of Land, post*, p. 810.

[4] *Re Dyson* [1910] 1 Ch. 750.

[5] *Re Johnson* [1915] 1 Ch. 435.

[6] L.P.A. 1925, s.25(1).

[7] *Re Ffennell's Settlement* [1918] 1 Ch. 91; L.P.A. 1925, s.26.

[8] Whether express or statutory. It also applies to partnership land and orders for sale by a court, for instance in the case of minority. Conversion applies as from the date of the order: *Pole* v. *Pole* [1924] 1 Ch. 156. See Snell, p. 483.

[9] Including contracts imposed by a statute: *e.g. Re Galway's W.T.* [1950] Ch. 1. A notice to treat does not produce a conversion until the terms are agreed to the point at which the agreement would be enforceable as a contract. Presumably a similar rule applies to purchases of freeholds under the Leasehold Reform Act 1967; (1969) 33 Conv.(N.S.) 43, 141 (J. Tiley). See generally (1960) 24 Conv.(N.S.) 47 (P. H. Pettit).

a contract is, as has been seen, an estate contract. The vendor is under an obligation to convey, which is specifically enforceable. Again, equity looks on that as done which ought to be done, and from the moment the contract is signed, regards the purchaser as the owner in equity.[10] He becomes owner at law when the conveyance is executed. If he should die between contract and completion, the property passes to those entitled to his realty, but subject to the obligation to pay the balance of the purchase price.[11] Equity also regards the land in the vendor's hands as personalty; and if he should die before completion, those entitled to his personalty will accordingly receive the proceeds of sale.

The doctrine has been extended beyond the case of a contract, and held to apply to the exercise of an option. Here we are in a backwater of equity known as the rule in *Lawes* v. *Bennett*.[12] The rule is not a satisfactory one, in that it represents an abuse of the doctrine of conversion, which it forces into a situation to which there was no necessity to apply it. If A grants to B a lease of Blackacre, which contains an option for B to purchase the freehold, and then dies, to whom do the rents of Blackacre go pending the exercise of the option to purchase? Clearly they must go to the person in whom is vested the freehold, namely, the residuary or specific devisee, as the case may be, and in this sense the law is laid down in *Townley* v. *Bedwell*.[13] One would expect that, on the exercise of the option by B, he would be entitled to receive the purchase money. But, by an unnecessary extension of the doctrine of conversion, he is required to hand the purchase-money over to the residuary legatee, on the footing that conversion into personalty is effected as from the exercise of the option, though he may retain the rents which he previously received. This principle has been applied where the giver of the option died intestate, as well as where he made a will, and even, as in *Re Isaacs*,[14] where the option did not become exercisable for some time after his death. Of course, if the option is never exercised, no notional conversion ever takes place.[15]

But the principle is not applied where a testator has shown, on the face of his will, a clear intention that his *entire* interest in his land is to pass to a specific devisee, for such an intention is strong enough to override the doctrine of *Lawes* v. *Bennett*,[16] and to carry the purchase-money which results from the exercise of the option to that devisee, its proper recipient. But again, the operation of these rules is technical. There will be a conversion where the specific devise comes first and the

---

[10] The vendor is said to be a constructive trustee for the purchasers; *ante*, p. 304.
[11] A.E.A. 1925, s.35 (subject to any contrary intention).
[12] (1785) 1 Cox 167.
[13] (1808) 14 Ves.Jr. 591.
[14] [1894] 3 Ch. 506.
[15] *Re Marlay* [1915] 2 Ch. 264. It is not the *grant* of the option which causes the conversion.
[16] (1785) 1 Cox 167.

option is given afterwards,[17] but there may not be a conversion if the option is given first and the specific devise comes later; and it is even immaterial in this latter case that the will makes no express reference to the option.[18] The same result follows if the will, or a codicil confirming the will, is contemporaneous with the grant of the option.[19]

The doctrine in *Lawes* v. *Bennett*[20] makes the devolution of property depend upon events that occur subsequently to a testator's death. Little can be said in its defence, yet in *Re Carrington*[21] the Court of Appeal extended it to a case of an option to purchase shares given subsequently to the making of a will, thus taking the proceeds of sale away from the specific legatees and adding it to residue. More recently, in *Re Sweeting (deceased)*,[21a] Nicholls J. held the doctrine applicable to a conditional contract, where the conditions were fulfilled after the testator's death. There the testator, having specifically devised a yard in his will of 1978, exchanged contracts for the sale of the yard three weeks before his death. The contract was conditional upon certain events, and was completed after his death. In fact the fulfilment of the conditions was considered to have been within the testator's control at his death, but even if that were not so, the doctrine of conversion would still have applied. Although the doctrine as it related to options had been criticised, to apply it to conditional contracts was not an extension of it. Rather, the present case was a stronger example because the contract existed at the death, unlike in the options cases. Thus the devise was adeemed, if not at the date of the contract then no later than completion, and the proceeds went to the residuary legatee.

D. Failure of Conversion

Conversion depends upon a valid and imperative trust *and* someone to enforce it. This latter question raises some difficult points. If, when the instrument creating the trust comes into effect, there is a total failure of beneficiaries, no conversion will take place.[22] But if at that date there is a possibility that there may be beneficiaries, there is a wait and see principle; if a beneficiary comes into existence, a notional conversion will be assumed from the date the instrument took effect, but otherwise there will be no conversion at all.[23] If there has been a partial failure of beneficiaries, a distinction appears to be made be-

---

[17] *Weeding* v. *Weeding* (1861) 1 J. & H. 424.

[18] *Drant* v. *Vause* (1842) 1 Y. &. C.Ch. 580; *Re Calow* [1928] Ch. 710.

[19] *Emuss* v. *Smith* (1848) 2 De G. & Sm. 722; *Re Pyle* [1895] 1 Ch. 724.

[20] (1785) 1 Cox 167.

[21] [1932] 1 Ch. 1; criticised (1933) 49 L.Q.R. 173 (H. G. Hanbury). The court seems to have confused the doctrine of conversion with that of ademption.

[21a] [1988] 1 All E.R. 1016. See also *Re Marlay*, *supra*.

[22] *Re Lord Grimthorpe* [1908] 2 Ch. 675. Similarly with a covenant to lay out money in the purchase of land, and, at the date the covenant takes effect, the only beneficiaries are volunteers.

[23] *Re Hopkinson* [1922] 1 Ch. 65.

tween trusts created by deed and those created by will. Notional conversion unquestionably occurs in a deed; and the failed share accordingly results to the settlor in its converted form; but, in a will, it is probable that the lapsed share will devolve under the will in its unconverted form, though, because the trustees remain under a duty to convert the property, its recipient will receive it in its converted form. Thus if one of the beneficiaries under a trust for sale of land set up in a will predeceases the testator, the proceeds of sale will devolve as realty to the residuary devisee but, in his hands, will be personalty. These ramifications depend upon the old law favouring heirs-at-law,[24] but they still govern trusts of land and of money.[25]

E. Reconversion

Just as conversion depends upon the existence of some person who can enforce it, so a decision by that person against conversion may prevent conversion or, to be more accurate, may yield a reconversion; and, as a result, property which had notionally been converted will notionally return to its actual physical condition.

(i) **Reconversion by Person of Full Age and Absolutely Entitled.** A notional conversion effected by a trust for sale may at any moment be ended by a demand from a sole beneficiary, of full age and absolutely entitled, or by a unanimous demand from the whole body of beneficiaries, all of full age and absolutely entitled, that the property should be handed over to them unconverted, and the trust for sale terminated.[26]

Such a decision to reconvert may be indicated by express declaration or by other signification of intention. The onus of showing an intent to reconvert is on the party desiring to effect a reconversion,[27] and an intention to reconvert is more easily established in the case of unsold land held on trust for sale than in the case of money held on trust to invest in land.[28]

(ii) **Reconversion by Operation of Law.** Reconversion may also be effected by operation of law where the trusts on which the property was held have ended or failed, and the property was in the possession of a person absolutely entitled who died without indicating any intention in the matter. Thus in *Re Cook*[29]:

A freehold house had been conveyed to husband and wife as joint tenants. On January 1, 1926, the house became subject to a statutory

[24] *Ackroyd* v. *Smithson* (1780) 1 Bro.C.C. 503.
[25] *Curteis* v. *Wormald* (1878) 10 Ch.D. 172; *Re Richerson* [1892] 1 Ch. 379.
[26] *Saunders* v. *Vautier* (1841) Cr. & Ph. 240; see also L.P.A. 1925, s.23 (protection of purchaser); for the position of minors and mental patients, see Snell, pp. 492–493.
[27] *Griesbach* v. *Fremantle* (1853) 17 Beav. 314 at p. 317.
[28] *Crabtree* v. *Bramble* (1747) 3 Atk. 680; *Re Pedder's Settlement* (1854) 5 De G.M. & G. 890; *Mutlow* v. *Bigg* (1875) 1 Ch.D. 385; *Re Gordon* (1877) 6 Ch.D. 531.
[29] [1948] Ch. 212.

trust for sale.[30] In January 1944, H died; and eight months later W died, leaving by her will "all my personal estate" to her nephews and nieces. She was in possession of the house at her death and the question was whether it passed under the gift. Harman J. held that the trust for sale had terminated. The house was reconverted into land and did not pass under the will as personal estate.

(iii) Concurrent Owners and Remaindermen. So far as concurrent owners are concerned, the position depends on the presence or absence of inconvenience to co-beneficiaries: in a trust to buy land, there is no reason why one beneficiary should not receive his share in money, but as land loses value if not sold in one piece, one co-owner of a trust to sell land cannot choose to retain his share as land.[31] A remainderman can do nothing to prevent a conversion except to indicate that, if the property is not converted when it becomes his, he would elect not to convert it. This, if events turn out as he hopes, will yield a notional reconversion automatically, provided his interest in remainder was an absolute one; but not if it was, at the time of his death, subject to any contingency.[32]

F. Reform

The doctrine of conversion has recently been considered by the Law Commission in the wider context of a review of trusts of land.[33] One proposal put forward is that trusts for sale of land should be replaced by trusts of land with a power of sale, which would mean that the doctrine of conversion would no longer apply in this area.[34] Even if the present trust for sale is retained, the doctrine is artificial, unsatisfactory and confusing and should be abolished. "It seems to us that little purpose is served today by the doctrine of conversion, and that nothing would be lost by its abolition."[35] This reform, if enacted, would mean that all interests under a trust for sale would be treated as interests in land instead of personalty.

2. ELECTION

A. Introduction

The principle from which the doctrine of election derives is old, basic and wide. A person may not take a benefit and reject an asso-

---

[30] L.P.A. 1925, s.36(1).

[31] *Seeley* v. *Jago* (1717) 1 P.Wms. 389; *Holloway* v. *Radcliffe* (1856) 23 Beav. 163. For the beneficiary's right to take his share *in specie* where personalty is held on trust for sale, see *Lloyds Bank plc* v. *Duker* [1987] 1 W.L.R. 1324, *ante*, p. 508.

[32] *Re Sturt* [1922] 1 Ch. 416, reviewing a rather tangled web of authority; see also (1922) 38 L.Q.R. 261.

[33] Working Paper No. 94 (1985), *Trusts of Land*.

[34] *Ibid.*, para. 6.4. See *ante*, p. 278.

[35] *Ibid.*, para. 16.4. See also para. 3.18.

ciated burden or, to put it in another way, a person may not choose between parts of a single transaction. "He may not approbate and reprobate."[36] *Qui sentit commodum, sentire debet et onus.*[37] At the beginning of the eighteenth century this principle appears in a distinct form; a volunteer taking under a will must give effect, so far as he is able, to everything contained in the will. But in this form the principle is extended from wills to deeds and, by the end of the century, it is at the root of a wide variety of cases. Cases of excessive execution of a power, ineffective disposition of realty, and dispositions in conflict with a spouse's right such as dower are among the most common. Such cases may lead to an election, in this sense: the disappointed beneficiaries may be to some extent compensated by making those who do take under the instrument elect between their rights. T attempts to give property over which A has rights to B absolutely, and as part of the same transaction gives other property to A. A cannot take the latter without giving effect to the former.

In the first half of the nineteenth century the cases change. The right of alienation is less restricted, and forms of alienation less complicated. The principle of election comes to be associated more with cases where a testator has made a mistake than where he has made an eccentric or ineffective disposition. Election becomes formulated, as a doctrine, in the light of these changes. It becomes established that election leads to compensation not to forfeiture, that an actual intent to cause an election need not be shown, and that parol evidence is not admissible to explain the disposition. The doctrine becomes technical and refined, and an uncertain instrument of equity in the broad sense. A supportable basis for the doctrine in its developed form is, as will be apparent, hard to find.

In considering the present-day doctrine of election, then, we must remember three things: first, that we have a basic idea enshrined in a technical doctrine, secondly, that the basic idea has continued to have applications that are analogous to the technical doctrine but not part of it,[38] and, thirdly, that some parts of the technical doctrine are anomalous in that they inherit reasoning from the doctrine's earlier days.

A good modern statement of the doctrine is given by Jenkins L.J.[39] "The essentials of election are that there should be an intention on the part of the testator or testatrix to dispose of certain property; secondly, that the property should not in fact be the testator's or testatrix's own

---

[36] *Re Lord Chesham* (1886) 31 Ch.D. 466 at p. 473, *per* Chitty J.

[37] For modern appearances of this principle, see *Halsall* v. *Brizell* [1957] Ch. 169; *Ives (E.R.) Investments Ltd.* v. *High* [1967] 2 Q.B. 379; *Tito* v. *Waddell (No. 2)* [1977] Ch. 106 at pp. 289–311; [1965] A.S.C.L. pp. 313 *et seq.* (A. W. B. Simpson).

[38] *e.g. Guthrie* v. *Walrond* (1883) 22 Ch.D. 573; *Codrington* v. *Codrington* (1875) L.R. 7 H.L. 854.

[39] *Re Edwards* [1958] Ch. 168 at p. 175. See also *Re Mengel* [1962] Ch. 791 at p. 797 (*per* Buckley J.); *Re Gordon's Will Trusts* [1978] Ch. 145 at p. 153 (*per* Buckley L.J.). The doctrine applies to deeds as well as to wills.

property; and, thirdly, that a benefit should be given by the will to the true owner of the property." This statement of the doctrine will need careful consideration, but first an example may be helpful. (The letters in the example will be used throughout the section.) A is owner of Blackacre. T in his will devises Blackacre to B and bequeaths £10,000 to A. A cannot, of course, be compelled to transfer Blackacre to B. A is put to his election. This means that he can choose to take with the will or against the will. If A takes with the will, he will release Blackacre to B and get his £10,000. If A takes against the will, he will retain Blackacre but the £10,000 will be subject to an equity in B to claim compensation out of it to the extent of the value of Blackacre. If Blackacre is worth £12,000 at T's death, B will take the £10,000, but A is not obliged to find the extra £2,000 from his own money. If Black-acre is worth £6,000, B will take that much and A £4,000.

It is essential in the above example that the legacy to A should not have been *expressed* to be conditional upon A releasing Blackacre to B. If a condition attached to a legacy is not complied with, the legatee loses the legacy altogether, which falls into residue.[40] It is not just a matter between A and B. Accordingly it is not a question of A electing between forms of benefit. If he does not comply with the condition, he gets nothing, B gets nothing, and the residuary beneficiary takes the legacy.[41]

B. Requirements for Election

(i) The Intent to Dispose of Property. In this section only intent will be discussed. Jenkins L.J., in the passage already quoted, talks of the intent as being to "dispose of certain property"; not to "dispose of another's property." This distinction goes to the heart of the matter. The courts do not examine the state of a testator's knowledge. The question is—does the will purport to dispose of property? Was that property the testator's to dispose of? That the testator did or did not realise that the property was or was not his to dispose of is irrelevant. The testator is presumed to know what his interest is in property that he is devising. External evidence is not (though evidence *in* the will of course is) admissible to raise or rebut an election.[42] The equity of election arises because of the very co-existence of two particular gifts in the same instrument, and not because of any "conjecture of a

---

[40] *Robinson* v. *Wheelwright* (1856) 6 De G.M. & G. 535.

[41] This principle was always true of conditional gifts. The early cases on election talk of an election arising on an implied condition: *Noys* v. *Mordaunt* (1706) 2 Vern. 581. But it was finally held by Lord Eldon that election did not give rise to forfeiture: *Tibbits* v. *Tibbits* (1821) Jac. 317; and see Swanston's note at (1818) 1 Swan. 409. Thereafter it became more and more difficult to base election on intent or to use the language of implied conditions with any accuracy: see Lord St. Leonards in *Sugden on Powers* (8th ed.), p. 576.

[42] This rule became firmly established in the first half of the nineteenth century: *Dummer* v. *Pitcher* (1833) 2 Myl. & K. 262; *Clementson* v. *Gandy* (1836) 1 Keen 309; *Parker* v. *Sowerby* (1854) 4 De G.M. & G. 321.

presumed intention"[43] that equity makes about them. This was clearly put by Lord O'Hagan[44]: "But what is the intention that the Court must apprehend upon clear evidence? Not an intention on the part of the testatrix that there shall be an election. . . . A . . . testatrix does not generally know or understand anything about the doctrine of election. . . . The intention that must be clearly demonstrated in evidence to the Court, is an intention to do the particular thing—to give the property which the party has not a right to give, and to give a benefit to a person who has an interest in the property. Those two intentions being ascertained upon clear evidence, the law draws the conclusion. It is a conclusion of equity, . . . and there is an end of the matter."

The first requirement of election is therefore that it should appear from the will itself that the testator was purporting to dispose of property which was not in fact his to dispose of. But if this does so appear, then the requirement is satisfied though the testator may very well not have understood the position—as, indeed, in many cases of election he will not have done. In a modern case, a testator was presumed to know that property he was purporting to dispose of absolutely in his will was subject to the rights of his wife under Danish matrimonial law, though it was reasonably evident that it was just this that he had forgotten.[45]

Two considerations limit this strictness of construction, however. First, a disposition will not, as a matter of the construction of the will, be construed as including another's property if it has a sensible effect when construed in some other way. A gift in general terms, of residue for instance, will only exceptionally raise an election,[46] and the will of a testator who has a limited interest in property will only be construed as disposing of a larger interest in that property if, for instance by the use of clear words of limitation, the latter construction is the only reasonable one.[47] Secondly, though election operates on the facts existing at a testator's death, a further look is permitted to ascertain whether a legacy which appears to dispose of another's property has ceased to be operative by reason of an ademption. Thus no election will arise if T, having devised Blackacre to B and another property to A, subsequently sells Blackacre to A and dies, without changing his will; for the sale adeemed the legacy, which thereupon became inoperative.[48]

(ii) The Property of Another that is Disposed of. It is sufficient if a

---

[43] *Per* Lord Cairns L.C. in *Cooper* v. *Cooper* (1874) L.R. 7 H.L. 53 at p. 67.

[44] *Cooper* v. *Cooper, supra,* at pp. 74–75.

[45] *Re Mengel's W.T.* [1962] Ch. 791. But see Pettit, p. 624, doubting whether the particular dispositions in this case gave rise to an election.

[46] *Dummer* v. *Pitcher* (1833) 2 Myl. & K. 262; *Re Harris* [1909] 2 Ch. 206. One such exceptional case, involving community of property under foreign law, is *Re Allen* [1945] 2 All E.R. 264.

[47] *Parker* v. *Sowerby* (1854) 4 De G.M. & G. 321; *Wintour* v. *Clifton* (1856) 8 De G.M. & G. 641; *Howells* v. *Jenkins* (1863) 2 J. & H. 706 at p. 713.

[48] *Re Edwards* [1958] Ch. 168; *post,* p. 821.

testator is purporting to dispose of any interest in property that is in
fact another's. In illustrating the requirement, however, the more
complicated case of testamentary powers of appointment is taken, as
many of the cases arise in that context.

T has power to appoint by will among the children of Z, the property
to go to such children in default of appointment. T appoints half of the
property to A, a child of Z, and the other half to B, a stranger. T also
devises Greenacre to A. A will be put to his election. But the reason is
not because T made an appointment of half of the property to A, but
because A was one of the class entitled in default of appointment. Only
A's share under the latter gift counts as A's prior property for the
purpose of the doctrine of election.

(a) *Property Must be Alienable*. The property of A that T purports to
dispose of must be alienable by A. If it is not alienable, A is not obliged
to elect. He has no choice in the matter and election presupposes a
choice. In such a case A takes his gift under the will without any
obligation attaching to it.

> Thus, in *Re Lord Chesham*,[49] chattels were held upon trust to
> permit them to be enjoyed with settled land, of which A was tenant
> for life. T bequeathed the chattels to B, and his residuary estate to
> A. A was not put to his election, because he had no power to alienate
> the chattels.

An election does arise, however, where A is not absolute owner but
has only a limited interest in the property which T has purported to
dispose of absolutely.

> In *Re Dicey*,[50] T devised property to A, and purported to dispose
> of the entire interest in other property to B, which property was in
> fact owned (on T's death) as to a half-share by A, and as to a
> quarter-share each by B and by C. The Court of Appeal held that A
> must elect and that, on an election to take with the will, the equity of
> election is satisfied by his release of his property to B so far as he is
> able; a release of his half-share to B thus making B owner as to a
> three-quarter share.

This may not be what T intended, but the doctrine depends neither on
this consideration nor on the existence of an outstanding interest in

---

[49] (1886) 31 Ch.D. 466. But it is no objection that A's interest in the property was
originally defeasible; see the cases on powers of appointment (where, of course, the
default beneficiary's interest is no longer defeasible when the testator's will comes into
operation, as, *ex hypothesi*, no valid appointment has been made). A similar rule as to
alienability applies to T's gift to A, *post*, p. 818.

[50] [1957] Ch. 145; *Ward* v. *Baugh* (1799) 4 Ves. 623. Where several persons are called
upon to elect (*e.g.* joint owners) each has an independent right to elect: *Fytche* v.
Fytche (1868) 7 Eq. 494. The position is similar where the limited interests are
successive rather than concurrent.

another party. The principle of *Re Lord Chesham*[51] accordingly applies only where A cannot by any "relevant means" bring about anything resembling the result envisaged by the will.[52]

(b) *Void Disposition.* A more difficult problem arises if T's purported disposition of A's property to B is bad for a reason quite independent of it being A's property, for instance through informality, or the rule against perpetuities. Is A in such a case put to his election between the property purported to be given to B and the benefits given him by T's will? It is tempting to argue that a disposition that is legally bad is non-existent for all purposes. Indeed Lord Hardwicke seems to have argued this way.[53] But a century later it is clear that the judges are unwilling to draw a distinction, for the purposes of the doctrine of election, between mistakes of fact and law, and between grounds of voidness.[54] Save where "illegality" is involved, A is put to his election; in particular, an infringement of the rule against perpetuities is held not to be a special ground of invalidity, demanding separate treatment.[55] Subsequently, however, the judges have varied in their views in this one instance of the rule against perpetuities. In *Re Oliver's Settlement*,[56] an infringement of the perpetuity rule was said to be "illegal," so that equity would not, through causing an election, help to effectuate it. And this view was upheld by the Court of Appeal in *Re Nash*,[57] which purported to overrule the decision of Kekewich J. in *Re Bradshaw*[58] that A was put to his election in this type of case. Nevertheless, Younger J. in *Re Ogilvie*[59] did not regard the matter as finally established and the weight of academic opinion is in favour of an election arising.[60] For A, in being put to his election, is not asked to do more than *he* legally can; no perpetuity will attach to the manner in which A releases his property to B.[61] This may not produce all that T

---

[51] Envisaged by the will, rather than the testator. This statement of the rule is based on a passage in *Re Dicey, supra,* at p. 158 which distinguishes two cases involving foreign systems of law: *Re Ogilvie* [1918] 1 Ch. 492; *Brown* v. *Gregson* [1920] A.C. 860. The flexibility of "relevant means" is necessary for such cases.

[52] (1886) 31 Ch.D. 466.

[53] *Hearle* v. *Greenbank* (1749) 3 Atk. 695 at p. 715. *cf.* Pearson J. in *Re Warren's Trusts* (1884) 26 Ch.D. 208 at p. 219. This is also the reasoning in *Woolridge* v. *Woolridge, post,* p. 816, but this decision is to be supported, if at all, on another ground.

[54] *e.g.* Page-Wood V.-C. in *Schroder* v. *Schroder* (1854) 23 L.J. Ch. 916 at p. 918.

[55] *e.g. Tomkyns* v. *Blane* (1860) 28 Beav. 422, especially at p. 428, *per* Romilly M.R.

[56] [1905] 1 Ch. 191; see especially, *per* Farwell J. at p. 197.

[57] [1910] 1 Ch. 1.

[58] [1902] 1 Ch. 436.

[59] [1918] 1 Ch. 492 at p. 501, in a reserved judgment.

[60] See particularly Gray, *Rule against Perpetuities* (4th ed.), §§ 556 *et seq.*; Morris and Leach, p. 158, *cf.* Pettit, p. 626; Williams on Wills (6th ed.), p. 273.

[61] It is true that T, not A, *causes* the release of the property by A, but it would seem preferable to look at the actual dispositions of property, not their source. Nevertheless, if this view is upheld, other anomalies follow; see *post,* p. 818.

intended but, as we saw from *Re Dicey*,[62] that is no reason for avoiding an election.

(c) *Appointment to Object with Proviso in Favour of Non-Object.* A rather special group of cases, involving powers of appointment, must now be mentioned. If T, in making a valid appointment in A's favour, superadds some proviso in favour of B, (a non-object), there is no election. The proviso is simply ignored, and A takes the property validly appointed to him free from any obligation, together with any property to which he is entitled in default of appointment and any other property given him by T in his will.[63] The proviso is not treated as a purported gift of A's property but as non-existent.[64] But in terms of the doctrine of election, it is anomalous that this particular attempt to provide a benefit for B at A's expense should not put A to his election.[65]

(d) *A's Title Independent of Instrument Raising Question of Election.* A far more important rule that arises under this section is the rule that the property of A must be A's property independently of the will that raises the question of putting A to his election. Assume, for example, that T's gift of his own property to B is void for informality or perpetuity; B cannot take, and the property goes to A as residuary beneficiary. A is not required to elect between the property which T failed to give to B and other property which he receives as part of residue. The point was firmly taken by James V.-C. in *Wollaston v. King*,[66] a decision that is a turning point in the evolution of the doctrine of election.

Under a marriage settlement, T had a special power of appointment in favour of the children of her marriage, who were also the persons to take in default of appointment. By her will T appointed part of the fund to her son for life and the remainder to her daughters, A. The appointment included a general power of appointment given to the son. The appointments which the son made under it were void for perpetuity and consequently the property appointed by him was caught by the residuary appointment to the daughters, A. The daughters were also given other property by T's will.

---

[62] [1957] Ch. 145.
[63] *Carver* v. *Bowles* (1831) 2 R. & M. 301; *Churchill* v. *Churchill* (1867) L.R. 5 Eq. 44. *cf. Re Neave* [1938] Ch. 793. Fry J. in *White* v. *White* (1882) 22 Ch.D. 555 attempted to limit this rule, but his ground of doing so is not clear.
[64] *Woolridge* v. *Woolridge* (1859) Johns. 63 at p. 69; a view to be explained in terms of the special rule as to appointments that are prima facie absolute but with an improper qualification appended.
[65] *Jarman on Wills* (8th ed.), pp. 845–846 and note (*z*).
[66] (1869) L.R. 8 Eq. 165.

James V.-C. held that the daughters were not put to their election between this other property and the windfall. They took the windfall not in *default* of appointment under the marriage settlement, but as the result of an appointment under T's will, and their rights accordingly arose *wholly* under this will. It could not be said that any property of theirs outside of and independent of this will had been disposed of. "The rule as to election is not to be applied as between one clause in a will and another clause in the same will."[67]

This principle is at the basis of most recent statements of the doctrine, and the early cases based on a wide view of electing between any two benefits in the same instrument must accordingly be treated with caution.[68] Nevertheless the wide view was followed by Neville J. in *Re Macartney*.[69]

> T purported to bequeath to B stock that T held as a trustee; the legacy of course failed. The beneficial interest in the stock was vested in a company, which was a subsidiary of a company the shares in which were held mainly by T. He bequeathed the shares in this latter company to his children, A, who in this way received the beneficial interest in the stock intended for B. No property previously vested in A was disposed of by T in his will. It was rather a case of T giving the same property to A and to B in the same instrument, but Neville J. nevertheless took the view that equity would intervene to subject the shares bequeathed to A to a charge under which B would be compensated for the loss of her legacy.

This result could be justified only if there existed in equity a wide principle of producing rough justice among beneficiaries, as indeed the judge realised when he placed reliance on the view that "A volunteer under a will cannot take the benefit and at the same time wilfully defeat the expressed intentions of the testator."[70] Logically this would mean that residuary beneficiaries would always have to compensate beneficiaries of specific gifts that failed. This is not a general proposition of present-day equity and certainly is not part of the technical doctrine of election. Further difficulties inherent in *Re Macartney*[71] include the fact that, contrary to the doctrine of election, A was given no choice in the matter: the decision was that A's shares were charged with compensation to B. This may have been because a transfer of the shares themselves to B would have been *ultra vires* the rules of the company, thus raising a further problem as to the alienability of the property.[72]

---

[67] (1869) L.R. 8 Eq. 165 at p. 174. The judge spelt this principle out of *Carver* v. *Bowles* but this case is to be supported, if at all, on other grounds, *supra*, notes 63 and 64.

[68] See Viscount Maugham in *Lissenden* v. *Bosch* [1940] A.C. 412 at p. 419.

[69] [1918] 1 Ch. 300. A further criticism of this decision might be that Neville J. seemed to identify the shareholders with the company, a different legal entity.

[70] [1918] 1 Ch. 300 at p. 303. This is a maxim of uncertain application, not a rule. *cf. Re Sturt* [1922] 1 Ch. 416.

[71] [1918] 1 Ch. 300.

[72] This requirement is discussed below.

It is right, then, to regard James V.-C.'s decision in *Wollaston* v. *King*[73] as authoritative.[74] It is true that this principle does not emerge clearly out of earlier cases, but this is possibly because most of them involved realty which, unless effectively disposed of, went to the heir-at-law *by virtue of superior title*. Around the heir-at-law there arose some very complicated learning. Sometimes his interest as heir-at-law was regarded as causing an election. Sometimes his being heir-at-law (of English freeholds) was given as a reason for not making him elect. This learning has no relevance today. Suppose that T validly disposes of half his estate, ineffectively disposes of a quarter to B and fails to dispose altogether of the last quarter. A takes the two quarters on intestacy. It is submitted that A is not required to elect between the quarter not disposed of at all and the quarter ineffectively disposed of to B. Those taking on intestacy under the 1925 legislation have no prior proprietary interest[75] and should not be in a different position from residuary beneficiaries.

(iii) The Gift of Property to the Person Electing. The third requirement for election is that the testator should, in the same instrument,[76] have given some property of his own to A. This can be neatly illustrated by a comparison of *Bristow* v. *Warde*[77] and *Whistler* v. *Webster*.[78]

In the former case T, who had a power to appoint among children, A, appointed some of the property to them and some to strangers, B. It was held by Lord Loughborough L.C. that A could set aside the appointment to B and take the whole property. Election did not arise even though A were entitled in default of appointment, as A received no other benefits under T's will. But in the latter case, on analogous facts, A were put to their election as they did receive other benefits under T's will.

It is essential that the property given to A is given to him beneficially and in such form as to be alienable; for the property has to be available

---

[73] (1869) L.R. 8 Eq. 165.

[74] Under *Wollaston* v. *King, supra*, a devise of *his own property* by T that fails for, *e.g.* perpetuity, and benefits the residuary devisee, A, does not put the devisee to an election between that and other benefits. But if T's devise was void for perpetuity *and* was of A's property, not his own, on the view expressed above at p. 815, A would be put to an election between the property devised and other benefits given to him in T's will. So that a void gift is given some effect by being of another's property, which is an unpalatable conclusion. On this indirect ground, there is an advantage in supporting the trend of authority leading to *Re Nash* [1910] 1 Ch. 1 and not the academic view following *Re Bradshaw* [1902] 1 Ch. 436.

[75] *cf. Lall* v. *Lall* [1965] 1 W.L.R. 1249; *ante*, p. 60; *Cooper* v. *Cooper* (1874) L.R. 7 H.L. 53 has not received any discussion in this context. For the view that election would arise in such circumstances, see Snell, *Principles of Equity* (28th ed.), p. 501.

[76] A will and codicil are regarded as the same.

[77] (1794) 2 Ves.Jr. 336. It would be otherwise if A was simply an object of a mere power of appointment, for such a person has no proprietary interest, *ante*, p. 66.

[78] (1794) 2 Ves.Jr. 367.

to compensate B if A elects to take against the will.[79] The property need not be an absolute interest, but if it is a defeasible gift for instance, or a gift on protective trusts, so that it is not effectively alienable, no election will arise. This point recently arose in *Re Gordon's Will Trusts*.[80]

T and A owned the Old Rectory jointly, therefore A became absolutely entitled to it on T's death. T by her will purported to leave the Old Rectory on trust for sale for the benefit of A and B in equal shares. T's will also gave A some furniture, a legacy of £1,000, and a life interest on protective trusts in half of the residuary estate. It was conceded that a case for election arose. A elected against the will by selling the Old Rectory and keeping the proceeds, but the furniture and the £1,000 legacy were insufficient to compensate B. The question arose as to whether A's interest under the protective trusts was subject to the doctrine of election, in which case his life interest would terminate, leaving no property from which to compensate B. The Court of Appeal held that the interest under the protective trusts was not subject to the doctrine of election, whose essential feature was compensation, not forfeiture. A's determinable life interest was inalienable, and "the doctrine does not require a beneficiary to surrender for the purpose of compensation an interest which would be destroyed by the very act of surrender, and thereby rendered unavailable to make compensation."[81]

In earlier cases this rule was based on supposed intent, the theory being that a gift of an inalienable interest could not have been intended to cause an election. This is an unreal way of looking at the matter, as was perceived by Astbury J. in *Re Hargrove*.[82] What matters is the nature of the interest created: is it, at the time of the testator's death,[83] effectively available for compensation? As has been seen, if A elects to take with the will, B only gets whatever A has in an alienable form. Equally, if A elects to take against the will, there is no question of B being able to get more than what T provided for A in his will and is in an alienable form.[84] But this includes all that T has in fact provided for A by his will, whether or not the will takes effect precisely as T intended.[85] The distinction is between all the property acquired by A

[79] *Re Vardon's Trusts* (1885) 31 Ch.D. 275; *ante*, p. 121. Presumably an interest under a discretionary trust created by T's will would not suffice. See (1977) 41 Conv.(N.S.) 188 at p. 196 (T. G. Watkin).

[80] [1978] Ch. 145, reversing Goulding J. [1977] Ch. 27, whose decision was convincingly criticised in (1977) 93 L.Q.R. 65 (P. H. Pettit) and (1977) 41 Conv.(N.S.) 188 (T. G. Watkin).

[81] [1978] Ch. 145 at p. 162 (*per* Sir John Pennycuick).

[82] [1915] 1 Ch. 398 at 406. *cf. Re Fletcher's S.T.* [1936] 2 All E.R. 236.

[83] This date is preferable to the date of election in that it puts less premium on chance events.

[84] *Re Lord Chesham* (1886) 31 Ch.D. 466.

[85] *Cooper* v. *Cooper* (1874) L.R. 7 H.L. 53.

under T's will and property after-acquired by A independently of T's will: the latter is immune from the election.[86]

C. Nature of an Election and Conclusion

Where A is under a duty to elect, the property which he is given under T's will is regarded as being subject to a form of equitable charge. This is most clearly shown by the situation that arises if A dies before he has elected. Where his own property and that given to him under T's will devolve on the same person, that person is in the same position as A with regard to election.[87] But if A's assets devolve so that no one person can elect in his place, the property given to him under T's will devolves subject to the charge, and can only be claimed by the person entitled if B is compensated, so far as is possible, out of it.[88]

Benefits passing as the result of an election are of a testamentary character; what B will receive will be a testamentary gift, and, where A elects to take with the will, A's prior property will become part of T's assets liable for the payment of his debts.[89]

An election may be express, or implied, as by receiving rents or selling the property,[90] but it must have been made with a full appreciation of the issues involved.[91] When made, it refers back to the date of the gift; for instance, the amount of compensation B will receive depends upon the valuation *at the date of T's death* of the property A elects to retain.[92]

An overall consideration of these technical rules reveals a doctrine far removed from the apparently simple principle from which it derives. In its present form, election is too uncertain an instrument of equity. It does not even achieve a fair distribution. T must intend both A and B to benefit, but in fact A may get nothing, while B always takes something. We have seen that if T's legacy to A is worth no more than A's own property, A derives in reality no benefit from the will; indeed A benefits as much as B only if A's legacy is worth at least double the value of his own property. In all other cases the net benefit to B is greater than that to A, yet it is A alone who has an effective gift in the will. Is there an adequate rationale for it? In practice, most election cases arise not from eccentricity of testation but from mistake. Ordinarily, mistakes in a will are not remedied by equity, but in this context they are. Why? Because there is to hand a wide and ancient principle,

[86] *Grissell* v. *Swinhoe* (1869) L.R. 7 Eq. 291.
[87] *Cooper* v. *Cooper* (1874) L.R. 7 H.L. 53.
[88] *Pickersgill* v. *Rodger* (1877) 5 Ch.D. 163; *cf. Rogers* v. *Jones* (1876) 3 Ch.D. 688. If A has elected before his death, the position is not affected by the devolution of the properties in question on his death.
[89] *Re Booth* [1906] 2 Ch. 321; *Re Williams* [1915] 1 Ch. 450.
[90] See *Re Gordon's W.T.*, *supra*.
[91] *Kidney* v. *Coussmaker* (1806) 12 Ves. 136; *Dillon* v. *Parker* (1822) Jac. 505; (1833) 1 Cl. & Fin. 303. As to election on behalf of infants and mental patients, see Pettit, p. 631; Snell, pp. 503–504.
[92] *Re Hancock* [1905] 1 Ch. 16.

not invented to cover mistakes, but which in this context has come to be more concerned with mistakes than with anything else. But the real question, and the only one in relation to which it is justifiable to consider the merits of election, is whether a more general jurisdiction to correct mistakes should exist.[93] There is limited merit in a doctrine that deals only in mistakes as to other people's property.

3. SATISFACTION

A. General

"Satisfaction," "ademption" and "performance" must be distinguished. Ademption in the present context means the cancellation of a legacy by a subsequent life-time advance, but in its strict sense ademption deals with the disappearance of the subject-matter of a specific legacy, through its disposal or destruction before the testator's death. This topic belongs to a treatise on wills rather than to a general textbook on equity. So also the question of construction which arises where two legacies are given in the same will to the same person (sometimes termed satisfaction of legacies by legacies but not strictly satisfaction, as there is no obligation to satisfy). But at the heart of all these issues rests the maxim "Equity imputes an intent to fulfil an obligation," and the principle of preserving equality amongst children. In performance, the act which the party obligated himself to do is considered actually to have been done, while in satisfaction, something that is accepted as different from the act agreed to be done is taken as equivalent to it. Both doctrines are said to rest upon intention, but the courts do not allow much scope for subjective intention; presumptions are much relied on.[94]

B. Satisfaction of Debts by Legacies

(i) **The Presumption.** Suppose a legacy is given to a person to whom the testator owed in the ordinary way a debt (including a covenant to pay money in a lump sum or by way of an annuity, but excluding questions of portion debts[95]). Can the legatee claim the legacy and the debt? Equity's attitude to this question is certainly based on intention, for if the legacy is expressly said to be given in reduction of the debt, the legacy must be given that effect; and intention goes further than this, for in *Hammond* v. *Smith*[96] a legacy was taken as *pro tanto*

---

[93] See the limited measures in A.J.A. 1982, s.20, permitting rectification of wills in the case of certain mistakes. This has no application here.
[94] (1964) 38 Austr.L.J. 147 (M. C. Cullity).
[95] *i.e.* an obligation by a parent to make a payment to a child by way of an advancement; *post*, p. 823.
[96] (1864) 33 Beav. 452. The normal rule is that there is no *pro tanto* satisfaction of a debt by a legacy. *cf. Re Hall* [1918] 1 Ch. 562.

satisfaction of a debt, in view of the peculiar circumstance that the testatrix had in her lifetime made a proposal to that effect to her creditor, who had not objected to it. But, generally, the question is decided on presumptions of intention founded on the terms of the will itself.

There is a presumption that if a debtor, without mentioning the debt in his will, gives a legacy to his creditor, then the legacy destroys or swallows up the debt in the sense, of course, that the legatee has an option; he can choose to receive the legacy but he thereby admits that he can no longer enforce the debt.[97]

But while this presumption is unquestioned where it operates, it must be noted that its field of operation is greatly circumscribed.[98]

(ii) Limited Operation of the Presumption.

First, the presumption only applies where the debt existed prior to the making of the will[99]; and the presumption does not apply to a running account, *e.g.* a trade account.[1] Secondly, the presumption does not apply if the will contains a direction to pay debts,[2] which of course any well-drafted will should contain. Thirdly, the presumption only applies if the legacy is in sum as great as, or greater than, the debt and is in every circumstance as beneficial as the debt: there is thus no possibility of *pro tanto* satisfaction, as there is with performance. On this third point a large amount of unattractive learning reflects the desire of the courts to limit the operation of the basic presumption. Thus there will be no satisfaction where the gift by will is of the whole or of a share of the residue, nor where it is a devise of land, or a gift of chattels, or a conditional gift, or an unsecured gift if the debt was secured.[3] There is doubt whether a legacy can be satisfaction of a debt due at a specific time prior to the probable date of distribution under the will,[4] or whether a legacy can be satisfaction of a debt of exactly similar amount at a rate of interest[5];

---

[97] *Thynne* v. *Glengall* (1848) 2 H.L.C. 131; *Chichester* v. *Coventry* (1867) L.R. 2 H.L. 71.

[98] In *Re Horlock* [1895] 1 Ch. 516 at p. 518 Stirling J. said: "No sooner was it established than learned judges of great eminence expressed their disapproval of it, and invented ways to get out of it."

[99] *Cranmer's Case* (1702) 2 Salk. 508; *Horlock* v. *Wiggins* (1888) 39 Ch.D. 142. If the debt is discharged between the date of the will and the date of death, the legacy is adeemed, at least where the sums are identical: *Re Fletcher* (1888) 38 Ch.D. 373.

[1] *Rawlins* v. *Powel* (1718) 1 P.Wms. 297 (Earl Cowper L.C.). The reason being that, in such a case, the necessary intention is missing, as the testator would not know at the date of his will the amount of the debt, if any, at his death.

[2] *Bradshaw* v. *Huish* (1889) 43 Ch.D. 260; *Re Manners* [1949] Ch. 613.

[3] *Barret* v. *Beckford* (1750) 1 Ves.Sen. 519; *Eastwood* v. *Vinke* (1731) 2 P.Wms. 613; *Crichton* v. *Crichton* [1895] 2 Ch. 853; *Re Stibbe* (1946) 175 L.T. 198; *Re Van den Bergh's W.T.* [1948] 1 All E.R. 935.

[4] In *Re Rattenberry* [1906] 1 Ch. 667 the problem was solved by holding that a legacy in satisfaction of a debt carried interest from the date of death rather than from the end of the executors' year, and was therefore as beneficial as the debt.

[5] *Re Horlock* [1895] 1 Ch. 516; *Re Rattenberry* [1906] 1 Ch. 667; *Fitzgerald* v. *National Bank* [1929] 1 K.B. 394; *Re Stibbe, supra.*

on these points it would seem sensible to deny satisfaction when there was a particular difference between the debt and the legacy, but not to deny it on grounds which are merely a restatement of the differences in the manner of payment between testamentary and *inter vivos* discharges of obligation.

In *Re Haves*,[6] there was a covenant by the testator, made on the dissolution of marriage, to pay his wife £3 a week, charged upon specific assets. By his will, he gave her an annuity of £3 a week, charged on the whole of his estate. The testamentary annuity was held to be in satisfaction of the covenant.

Applying a similar principle, a debt may be satisfied by a subsequent payment *inter vivos*, whether the debt is between parent and child or other parties.[7]

C. Satisfaction of Portion Debts by Legacies. The Rule Against Double Portions

In the absence of special circumstances, most parents would wish to share out the family capital in equal shares among the children. There is, of course, no obligation to do so; but it would be unsatisfactory if a grossly uneven division occurred unintentionally. There is the danger that this could happen if a parent made a will providing for equal division, but then incurred an obligation to pay a portion, or made a distribution, to some of the children during his lifetime. "Equity leans against double portions," and provides for the satisfaction of portion debts by the legacy, or, in the case of *inter vivos* distributions, for the ademption of the legacy by the portion. A similar result is achieved in cases of intestacy by the principle of "hotchpot."[8] Of course, if the portion has actually been paid, the doctrine cannot apply even though a legacy is subsequently given. But if the will was made before the portion was given, the question of ademption, discussed below, will arise.

(i) What is a Portion? To bring the rule into operation, there must be both an unsatisfied portion debt and a testamentary provision by way of portion. The two provisions must normally have been made by and for the same persons.[9] Ordinary debts, even between father and child, are governed by ordinary rules. What then transforms a debt or a gift into a portion? It must be a gift made, or an obligation undertaken, by a parent to a child, or by one *in loco parentis* to one in his charge, with

---

[6] [1951] 2 All E.R. 928.

[7] *Wood* v. *Briant* (1742) 2 Atk. 521.

[8] A.E.A. 1925, s.47(1)(iii). On the meaning of the word, see Co.Litt. 176a; (1962) 78 L.Q.R. at p. 262 (J. E. S. Simon); Pettit, pp. 601 *et seq. Inter vivos* distributions to children are accounted for against the net estate; *Re Turner's W.T.* [1968] 1 W.L.R. 227.

[9] In some cases a provision for the spouse of the testator's child has sufficed; see *McClure* v. *Evans* (1861) 29 Beav. 422; *Nevin* v. *Drysdale* (1867) L.R. 4 Eq. 517.

the intent of setting that child up in life. This is a question of intent but, generally speaking, a portion must be substantial, though this, too, is relative to the wealth of the parent and the age of the child.[10] Separate sums will not be added together to constitute a portion, nor will casual gifts or gifts to discharge debts ordinarily count. The intent must be to *establish* the child, and not just make a gift.[11] A gift of stocks and shares, or a business itself, can constitute a portion.[12]

(ii) **To Whom Does the Rule Apply?** The presumption of satisfaction applies without question to father and legitimate child[13]; but in all other cases, it only applies where a person systematically acts in relation to a child so as to demonstrate the intention of making full provision for the child. This is easier to show in the case of a mother, or the father of an illegitimate child, than in the case of an uncle or a grandfather, but in *Pym* v. *Lockyer*[14] a wealthy grandfather was held to have placed himself *in loco parentis* to his grandchildren though their father was living.

(iii) **Strength of the Presumption.** The greater ambit of the presumption in respect of portions can be illustrated in several ways. In the case of an ordinary debt, a smaller legacy is not held to be in satisfaction of part of a larger debt; but in the case of portion debts, a legacy may be satisfaction *pro tanto*.[15] The same holds true of residuary gifts, which may constitute satisfaction *pro tanto* of portion debts. Greater flexibility is also shown in evaluating differences between the portion debt and the legacy, for instance in the precise character of the limitations[16]; in the case of an ordinary debt, small differences negative satisfaction, but this is not so in portions cases, where the differences must be of some substance. A contingent legacy cannot satisfy an absolute portion debt of course, but differences between forms of personal wealth, *e.g.* between money and stock, can be ignored.[17] It is all, of course, a matter of degree; there may well be a material difference between a fixed sum and a share in a business,[18] and gifts of land and chattels

---

[10] *Re Hayward* [1957] Ch. 528.

[11] *Taylor* v. *Taylor* (1875) L.R. 20 Eq. 155; *Re Scott* [1903] 1 Ch. 1; *Watson* v. *Watson* (1864) 33 Beav. 574.

[12] *Re Lacon* [1891] 2 Ch. 482; *Re George's W.T.* [1949] Ch. 154.

[13] It does not seem that the Family Law Reform Act 1987, which generally abolishes the distinction between legitimate and illegitimate children in property matters, affects this proposition.

[14] (1841) 5 Myl. & Cr. 29; see also *Powys* v. *Mansfield* (1837) 3 Myl. & Cr. 359; *ex p. Pye* (1811) 18 Ves.Jr. 140; *Rogers* v. *Soutten* (1839) 2 Keen 598; *Re Ashton* [1897] 2 Ch. 574; *Fowkes* v. *Pascoe* (1875) L.R. 10 Ch.App. 343. The result, sometimes, is that a child receiving a substantial provision in the ordinary way from his or her father is less favourably treated than other recipients of gifts.

[15] *Warren* v. *Warren* (1783) 1 Bro.C.C. 305.

[16] *Thynne* v. *Earl of Glengall* (1848) 2 H.L.C. 131; *Lord Chichester* v. *Coventry* (1867) L.R. 2 H.L. 71. See (1977) 93 L.Q.R. 65 (P. H. Pettit) at p. 74, as to whether a covenant to settle by way of protective trust can be satisfied by a legacy.

[17] *Bellasis* v. *Uthwatt* (1737) 1 Atk. 426; *Re Jaques* [1903] 1 Ch. 267.

[18] *Holmes* v. *Holmes* (1783) 1 Bro. C.C. 555; *cf. Weall* v. *Rice* (1831) 2 R. & M. 251.

rarely constitute satisfaction unless given by reference to their pecuniary value.[19]

The presumption of satisfaction may be rebutted by extrinsic evidence as well as by evidence of intent in the will itself.[20] But extrinsic evidence may only be used to rebut the presumption, not to raise it, though, once the evidence is admitted, other extrinsic evidence may be admitted to refute it.[21] Extrinsic evidence appears to extend to words, whenever uttered, but the circumstances will obviously affect their weight. The presumption is intended to produce equality among children, but it sometimes has a further effect. For instance, the fact that the presumption only affects children means that a legacy may in some cases be satisfaction of that part of a covenant that constitutes a portion debt in favour of a child while other beneficiaries, for instance the spouse of a child, can claim under the covenant and the will.[22]

D. Satisfaction of Portion Debts by Portions

What has been said in the previous section applies to portion debts being satisfied by the payment by a covenantor of a portion during his life. It is the fact of both the obligation and the payment being in the nature of portions that attracts to them the learning of the presumption against double portions, and it is in this way that these cases are distinguishable from those considered under the doctrine of performance.[23] The matter often arose in relation to settlements upon marriage, but it is in no way restricted to such circumstances.[24]

E. Ademption of Legacies by Portions

The principle of ademption has been explained.[25] It is relevant here because the equitable presumption against double portions may adeem a legacy. Indeed, many of the cases cited in discussing the satisfaction of portion debts are ademption cases. This is distinguishable from satisfaction because there is no obligation to satisfy, but merely a legacy. The rule is that a legacy by way of portion is adeemed and so cannot take effect if, subsequent to the making of the will,[26] the legatee actually receives a portion, or obtains an enforceable right, *e.g.* by way of covenant, to receive one. The law relating to portions applies as discussed above. Thus the presumption of ademption applies only to portions between a parent (or someone *in loco parentis*) and a child; ademption can be *pro tanto*; and extrinsic evidence is admitted on the same principle. But there are some differences. First, ademption gives the legatee no choice; the *inter vivos* provision made for him prevails

---

[19] *Bengough* v. *Walker* (1808) 15 Ves.Jr. 507; *Re Tussaud's Estate* (1878) 9 Ch.D. 363.
[20] *Re Tussaud's Estate, supra.*
[21] *Re Shields* [1912] 1 Ch. 591; *Re Vaux* [1939] Ch. 465.
[22] *Re Blundell* [1906] 2 Ch. 222.
[23] *Post*, p. 826.
[24] For an example see *Lawes* v. *Lawes* (1881) 20 Ch.D. 81.
[25] *Ante*, p. 821.
[26] If the portion is actually paid before the will is made, the child will take both.

over his testamentary claim. Secondly, the presumption in favour of ademption is much stronger than the presumption in favour of satisfaction.[27] The presumption in favour of satisfaction of ordinary debts by legacies may be excluded by small differences between the two; the differences must be substantial in order to exclude the presumption of satisfaction of portion debts by legacies; but the presumption in favour of ademption will yield only to really considerable differences, for example, a devise of land will not be adeemed by a portion. Special considerations arise if the will indicates the intent with which a legacy is given. Even among strangers, a legacy for a purpose which is indicated in the will itself may be adeemed, either wholly or *pro tanto*, by *inter vivos* gifts made with the identical purpose.[28]

It is sometimes said that an ademption which appears to have occurred in this type of case must not be allowed to benefit a stranger, as its aim is only to produce equality among children. This principle emerges from the judgments in *Re Heather*[29] and *Re Vaux*,[30] where it was said that strangers could not benefit from an accretion to residue as a result of the presumption occurring. But these were cases where the residue was divisible amongst children and strangers, so that there was an obvious method to hand of dealing with the accretion without benefiting the strangers. It is not easy to see how this method can be applied where the only residuary beneficiary is a stranger.

4. Performance

The equitable doctrine of performance[31] is closely related to the doctrines of satisfaction and ademption. All three doctrines can be traced to the maxim "Equity imputes an intention to fulfil an obligation"; and the principle of performance is, that where A is bound in equity to do something for B but leaves that thing undone, equity may in appropriate circumstances feel able to regard something else that A has done as performance of the obligation. It is not a matter of equity regarding that not done as done; rather one of equity regarding what has been done as done in performance of an obligation.[32] There must, accordingly, be some positive acts on the basis of which equity can impute this intention,[33] and this fact serves to distinguish performance from the doctrine whereby property subject, on it vesting in a covenantor, to an obligation to settle, may be regarded from the moment that it does vest as subject to the settlement.[34] The doctrine of performance, normally

---

[27] *Lord Chichester* v. *Coventry* (1867) L.R. 2 H.L. 71 at p. 87, *per* Lord Cranworth.

[28] *Re Pollock* (1885) 28 Ch.D. 552; *Re Jupp* [1922] 2 Ch. 359.

[29] [1906] 2 Ch. 230; *Meinertzhagen* v. *Walters* (1872) L.R. 7 Ch.App. 670.

[30] [1938] Ch. 581 (reversed on other grounds [1939] Ch. 465 (C.A.)).

[31] Which is quite distinct from part performance; *ante*, p. 658.

[32] See *per* Kenyon M.R. in *Sowden* v. *Sowden* (1785) 1 Cox Eq. 165 at p. 166 and *per* Lord Brougham in *Tubbs* v. *Broadwood* (1831) 2 R. & M. 487 at p. 493.

[33] *cf.* the intestacy cases, *infra*.

[34] *Ante*, p. 121.

involving contests between the heir-at-law and the next-of-kin, has become less important since the property legislation of 1925.

A. Covenants to Purchase and Settle Land

The doctrine[35] is associated first with covenants in a marriage settlement to lay out money on the purchase of land to be held on the trusts of the settlement. The problem is illustrated by *Lord Lechmere* v. *Lady Lechmere*.[36]

> Upon the marriage of Lord and Lady Lechmere, articles were entered into whereby Lord Lechmere covenanted to lay out, within a year after his marriage and with the consent of the trustees, £30,000 in the purchase of freehold lands in fee simple in possession. The lands, when purchased, were to be settled for his use for life, with remainder, subject to the payment of a jointure to his widow, to the first and other sons in tail male, with an ultimate remainder to Lord Lechmere himself.
>
> Lord Lechmere died intestate without issue, and without having complied with his covenants. Lord Lechmere's heir-at-law, who was entitled to all the realty on the death, claimed that the £30,000, which was to be considered as realty under the doctrine of conversion[37] should be raised from the personalty and laid out in accordance with the covenant. The next-of-kin claimed that, under the doctrine of performance, the value of other realty devolving on the heir-at-law should be subtracted from that sum. At the time of marriage, Lord Lechmere owned estates in fee simple; after marriage he purchased, and contracted to purchase, more, some being in possession, some in reversion, and some for life only. But for none of these purchases did he seek the trustees' consent.

Lord Talbot held that the purchases of, and contracts to purchase, the estates *in possession* should be regarded as intended as a partial performance of the covenant to lay out £30,000, although they had not been entered into within a year of marriage, nor had the trustees' consent been obtained, nor had the estates been settled. Equity would, despite the difficulties, identify these estates as purchased in performance of the covenant, so that their value could be deducted from the sum of money devolving on the heir-at-law. He could not have these estates and their value in addition. But Lord Talbot refused to identify the purchases of the estates in reversion and those for life only as in performance of the covenant, as they were different in nature from the lands in fee simple in possession covenanted to be settled. Nor could

---

[35] The doctrine of performance is occasionally cited as one of general application—see *per* James V.-C. in *Thacker* v. *Key* (1869) L.R. 8 Eq. 408 at p. 416—but is more frequently associated with the specific instances now to be discussed.

[36] (1733) 3 P.Wms. 211; (1735) Cas.T.Talb. 80. For some further problems, see (1964) 38 Aust.L.J. 147 at pp. 155–156 (M. C. Cullity).

[37] *Ante*, pp. 805 *et seq.*

estates already owned by Lord Lechmere at the time of his marriage be taken as intended performance of a covenant to purchase after marriage.

In this case the money was to be laid out by the covenantor. But when the covenant is to pay money to trustees to be laid out by them in the purchase of land, the covenantor can still be regarded as performing, wholly or partially, this covenant by purchasing land himself; again, when the covenant is to settle property of a certain value, purchases made subsequently to the covenants can be taken in performance, at least where the covenantor had no property which could have been settled at the time of his entry into the covenant.[38] In one case the doctrine was also applied to cover an obligation to settle imposed by a statute.[39] But the doctrine is, in general, probably restricted to covenants which can be enforced by those entitled under the settlement to enforce it, and so does not assist volunteers.[40]

Equity will regard property, which it identifies as bought in performance of a covenant, as subject to the rights of the beneficiaries from the moment of purchase. But this is a somewhat *ex post facto* rationalisation. For if meanwhile the covenantor has sold or mortgaged the land, equity will say that he did not mean his purchase to be in performance of his obligation. Hence a purchaser or mortgagee is not affected even if he had notice, and there is nothing for a beneficiary to register so as to secure his position.[41] Covenants to settle property already owned by the covenantor, and covenants to settle after-acquired property, both stand on a different footing.[42]

B. Covenants to Leave Money on Death

The second type of case with which the doctrine of performance is associated is that of performance through an intestacy. Where A covenants that he will leave by his will part of his personal estate to B, or that his executors shall pay a sum of money to B, and A dies intestate, and under his intestacy B becomes entitled to a portion of A's personal estate,[43] B cannot claim both the agreed sum or share and the intestate portion, for the intestate portion is deemed to be a

---

[38] *Sowden v. Sowden* (1785) 1 Cox Eq. 165; *Deacon v. Smith* (1746) 3 Atk. 323.

[39] *Tubbs v. Broadwood* (1831) 2 R. & M. 487.

[40] *Re Plumptre's Marriage Settlement* [1907] 1 Ch. 609. *cf.* in relation to the maxim that equity looks on that as done which ought to be done, *Re Anstis* (1886) 31 Ch.D. 596 at p. 605, *per* Lindley L.J.

[41] But see *ex p. Poole* (1847) 11 Jur. 1005. It is otherwise if the covenant is for value and relates to specific land. The beneficiaries then acquire an equitable interest (*Pullan v. Koe* [1913] 1 Ch. 9) capable of binding a purchaser: *Snell's Principles of Equity* (28th ed.), p. 507.

[42] *Pullan v. Koe* [1913] 1 Ch. 9; *ante*, p. 121; see *Mornington v. Keane* (1858) 2 De G. & J. 292; L.C.A. 1972, ss.2(4), 4(6).

[43] Whether more or less than that covenanted; *Garthshore v. Chalie* (1804) 10 Ves.Jr. 1, in which case the doctrine is reviewed at length by Lord Eldon.

performance, or *pro tanto* performance, of the covenant. This, like other aspects of the doctrine of performance, rests on presumed intention.

In *Blandy* v. *Widmore*,[44] by the marriage articles of A and B, it was agreed that A should leave B £620 by will if B survived him. A died intestate and B became entitled thereon to more than £620. It was held that she had no separate claim for the £620 covenanted, as this covenant was deemed performed.

But the position is different if the covenant was one to be performed during the covenantor's life and not later.

In *Oliver* v. *Brickland*,[45] A covenanted that he would, within two years of marriage, pay to B a sum of money. The sum taken by B on A's intestacy some years later could not be deemed performance of A's obligation, which had simply been broken. Performance can, however, take place by intestacy of a covenant to leave by will *or* by deed.[46]

Performance, as so far considered in this section, does not extend to obligations being satisfied by provisions in wills, though it may be added that performance does extend to cases where a will fails, so producing an intestacy.[47] The doctrine of performance is sometimes said, however, to extend to cases where a covenant is followed by a legacy[48] that yields a similar effect. Unfortunately the cases are confused in that, in them, performance as a doctrine is not kept sufficiently distinct from satisfaction. But the rules of performance are less inflexible than those of satisfaction,[49] particularly in relation to performance *pro tanto*, so that the possibility of performance having a role to play in this situation should not be overlooked.[50]

---

[44] (1716) 1 P.Wms. 323.
[45] (1732) cited 3 Atk. 420; *Lang* v. *Lang* (1837) 8 Sim. 451. Contrast *Lechmere* v. *Carlisle* (1733) 3 P.Wms. 211.
[46] *Lee* v. *Cox and d'Aranda* (1747) 3 Atk. 419.
[47] *Goldsmid* v. *Goldsmid* (1818) 1 Swan. 211.
[48] Not a devise, or a bequest of other than money. Nor can a covenant to pay an annuity be performed by a bequest of a lump sum: *Salisbury* v. *Salisbury* (1848) 6 Hare 526.
[49] *Ante*, pp. 821 *et seq*.
[50] See Cullity in (1964) 38 Aust.L.J. 147, especially at p. 153, reviewing the tangled web of authority. For an illustration in more recent times, see *Re Hall* [1918] 1 Ch. 562.

LICENCES

1. GENERAL

A LICENCE is a permission. We are here concerned with licences or permissions to enter land.[1] The licence makes lawful what would otherwise be a trespass.[2] The licence may be express; or it may be implied; as in the case of a shopkeeper's invitation[3] to enter the premises to do business; or the householder's implied invitation to bona fide visitors to approach his doorstep.[4]

Express licences arise in a myriad of factual situations, as where the occupier invites guests to dinner or to a tennis game; or to stay in a room in his hotel, or to "rent" a room in a lodging house.[5] It will be seen that some of these situations will be expected to give minimal

---

[1] A licence, however, may be a permission to a neighbour for the neighbour to do on his own land something which would otherwise be a wrong to the licensor, and the same general principles apply; *Winter* v. *Brockwell* (1807) 8 East 308, *Liggins* v. *Inge* (1831) 7 Bing. 682; *Hopgood* v. *Brown* [1955] 1 W.L.R. 213; *Ward* v. *Kirkland* [1967] Ch. 194.

[2] *Thomas* v. *Sorrell* (1673) Vaug. 330 at p. 351. This remains true even though consideration is given. "A licence created by contract is not an interest. It creates a contractual right to do certain things which otherwise would be a trespass." *Per* Lord Greene M.R. in *Winter Garden Theatre (London) Ltd* v. *Millennium Productions Ltd.* [1946] 1 All E.R. 678 at p. 680.

[3] *Davis* v. *Lyle* [1936] 2 K.B. 434 at p. 440, *per* Goddard L.J.

[4] *Robson* v. *Hallett* [1967] Q.B. 939.

[5] *Luganda* v. *Service Hotels Ltd.* [1969] 2 Ch. 209.

rights to a licensee. He has no interest in the land. The licence prevents him from being a trespasser, and no more. In other situations there will be a contract which gives certain rights to the licensee; and some situations create difficulties in determining whether a person is a contractual licensee or a lessee.[6] Different types of situations create different types of licences; and different levels of protection to the licensee.

The main question for discussion in this chapter is the protection of the licensee; as where the licensor purports to revoke the licence. The common law cases prior to the Judicature Acts will demonstrate what difficulties the common law met in dealing with this question; largely through the inadequacy of the remedies available at common law. If a licensee obtained a proprietary interest, the licensor clearly could not revoke; but, as a licence was not a proprietary interest, it was difficult to see how the licensee could be protected, and the situation was complicated by the fact that it only gradually became clear that an easement could not exist in gross[7]; and the common law judges found themselves saying that if a licence were granted by deed, it would not be revocable; which still leaves open the question of finding a proper remedy available to the licensee.

Equity provided the remedies. If the licensor could not lawfully revoke the licence, equity could grant an injunction to restrain him. The licence may be irrevocable for various reasons; most commonly because the terms of the contractual licence make it irrevocable; or because an estoppel has worked in favour of the licensee. Thus, the licensee would enjoy the licence for the period covered by the injunction.

The protection of the licensee against the licensor soon raised the question of whether the licensee should be protected against a third party; not being a bona fide purchaser of the legal estate for value without notice. Where the licensee is protected against third parties, the question arises whether the licence has, by this roundabout route, become an interest in land.

There are also situations in which the estoppel which works in favour of the licensee can only properly be satisfied by a positive remedy, and not merely by an injunction. In recent years, the doctrine known as "proprietary estoppel" has grown apace; allowing the courts to exercise a wide range of remedies in favour of the licensee, including the award to him of a proprietary interest in the land, with or without monetary compensation; and intended to provide the solution which is the most just and proper in all the circumstances.

---

[6] *Street* v. *Mountford* [1985] A.C. 809.
[7] *Hill* v. *Tupper* (1863) 2 H. & C. 121. *cf.* (1980) 96 L.Q.R. 557 (M. Sturley).

2. The Situation at Common Law

The common law never reached a satisfactory solution to the problem of the protection of the licensee. Essentially, this was because the inquiry was to see what it was that the licensor had *granted* to the licensee; and a licence *grants* nothing. The true issue, as will be seen, is the extent of the protection which should be given to a licensee against the licensor or against a third party; and, without the remedy of an injunction to restrain intervention, the common law had no adequate means of dealing with this situation. A number of propositions, relating to particular types of licences, were, however, established prior to 1875.

A. Bare or Gratuitous Licence

A simple permission to enter the licensor's land gives no contractual or proprietary right to the licensee. The permission may be withdrawn at any time by the licensor. On revocation, the licensee becomes a trespasser, but is allowed a reasonable time to collect his goods and perhaps to finish his business and to leave the land.[8]

B. Licence Coupled with a Grant (or an Interest)

It has long been established that a licence coupled with a grant of a proprietary interest is irrevocable.[9] If anything less than a proprietary interest was required, "it is not easy to see any fair stopping place in what amounts to an interest, short of any legitimate reason for being on the land."[10] The concept of a licence coupled with a grant is clearly seen where the grant is of a chattel interest; where for example an occupier sells a stack of hay on his land to a purchaser,[11] or some cut timber,[12] and expressly or by implication gives the purchaser permission to enter the land to collect it. Such a licence is irrevocable. Similarly where there is a grant of a right to take away part of the realty, as with a *profit à prendre*. The grant carries with it an irrevocable licence to enter. We do not speak of a licence coupled with a grant where the proprietary interest is one which itself includes a presence

---

[8] *Minister of Health* v. *Bellotti* [1944] K.B. 298 (not a gratuitous licence); *Canadian Pacific Ry. Co.* v. *R.* [1931] A.C. 414; *Winter Garden Theatre (London) Ltd.* v. *Millennium Productions Ltd.* [1948] A.C. 173 at p. 199; *Australian Blue Metal Co.* v. *Hughes* [1963] A.C. 74; *Greater London Council* v. *Jenkins* [1975] 1 W.L.R. 155 at p. 158, *per* Lord Diplock.

[9] *Webb* v. *Paternoster* (1619) Palm 71; *Wood* v. *Manley* (1839) 11 A. & E. 34; *James Jones & Son Ltd.* v. *Tankerville* [1909] 2 Ch. 440.

[10] *Per* Megarry J. In *Hounslow L.B.C.* v. *Twickenham Garden Developments Ltd.* [1971] Ch. 233 at p. 244, discussing *Vaughan* v. *Hampson* (1875) 33 L.T. 15.

[11] *Wood* v. *Manley* (1839) 11 A. & E. 34.

[12] *James Jones & Son Ltd.* v. *Tankerville, supra.*

on the land; with a lease or an easement, the grantee enters by force of the grant and not under any licence.

C. Contractual Licences

Most of the difficulties which arose at common law were concerned with contractual licences. If the licensor (A) contracted for valuable consideration to allow the licensee (B) to enter his land for a particular purpose or for a particular period of time, and A, in breach of contract, ordered B to leave, and perhaps, forcibly ejected him, the common law held that B had become a trespasser and could be ejected.

In *Wood* v. *Leadbitter*,[13] the plaintiff purchased a ticket of admission to the grandstand at Doncaster Racecourse. The defendant, on the orders of the steward of the course, required him to leave. He refused to go, and was physically removed, no more force being used than was reasonably necessary. He sued for assault and false imprisonment, and failed. The Court of Exchequer distinguished between a mere licence, such as this, which was revocable; and a licence coupled with an interest, which was not.

In the circumstances, nothing was *granted* to the plaintiff. Any grant of an interest in land would have required a deed. A contract for valuable consideration to grant an interest would not, in a court of common law in 1845, have made any difference. Nor could a grant of an interest in land arise in the situation in question. As Latham C.J. said in *Cowell* v. *Rosehill Racecourse Co.*[14]: "50,000 people who pay to see a football match do not obtain 50,000 interests in the football ground." An action for breach of contract no doubt lay,[15] but that was not the issue. Whether or not the defendant had the *right*, under the terms of the contract, to eject the plaintiff, he had a *power* to do so.[16]

The conclusion must be that the common law provided no adequate doctrine to deal with the problem of protection of licensees; neither the doctrine nor the remedies were adequate.

3. CONTRACTUAL LICENCES AFTER THE JUDICATURE ACTS

The treatment of contractual licences at common law was clearly unsatisfactory. This situation, and that of licences generally, has been transformed by a number of factors, of which the most significant are discussed below. The application of equitable remedies, not available

---

[13] (1845) 13 M. & W. 838. See (1954) 12 C.L.J. 201 and (1955) 13 C.L.J. 47 (H. G. Hanbury).
[14] (1937) 56 C.L.R. 605 at p. 616.
[15] *Per* Viscount Simon L.C. in *Winter Garden Theatre (London) Ltd.* v. *Millennium Productions Ltd.* [1948] A.C. 173 at p. 190.
[16] *Per* Goddard L.J. in *Thompson* v. *Park* [1944] K.B. 408 at p. 410; later disapproved in *Verrall* v. *Great Yarmouth Borough Council* [1981] Q.B. 202.

to common law courts, has been crucial; as also has been the recognition of the part that estoppel has to play; and finally the willingness of modern courts to seek and select the most appropriate remedy for the particular situation. "It is for the court in each case to decide in what way the equity can be satisfied."[17]

A. Injunction to Restrain a Licensor from Breaking a Contractual Licence

We have seen that the reasoning of the common law, established in the leading case of *Wood* v. *Leadbitter*,[18] was that a licence was revocable unless it validly granted a proprietary interest. In the absence of such a grant, it was said, even as late as 1944,[19] that, though the licensor had no *right* to revoke, he had a *power* to revoke, and could then turn the licensee into a trespasser. The opposite conclusion had been reached in 1915 in *Hurst* v. *Picture Theatres Ltd.*,[20] but on grounds that show that the courts still thought that it was the grant of a proprietary interest which made the licence irrevocable. In that case the plaintiff paid to watch a cinema show in the defendants' theatre. The defendants mistakenly thought that he had entered without paying. On being requested to leave, he refused and was ejected. He sued for assault and false imprisonment and succeeded.

Buckley L.J. gave two grounds for distinguishing the case from *Wood* v. *Leadbitter*,[21] both based upon the availability of equitable doctrine, the first reason being, it is submitted, clearly wrong, and the second being the basis of the modern doctrine protecting contractual licensees. The first ground was that the plaintiff had a licence coupled with an interest—"the right to see"—and that the interest can now be granted in equity by a contract, whereas before 1875 a deed was required. The fallacy in this reasoning is that there was no identifiable proprietary interest to be granted.[22] A "right to see" is not a piece of

---

[17] Lord Denning M.R. in *E.R. Ives Investment Ltd.* v. *High* [1967] 2 Q.B. 379 at p. 395; *Inwards* v. *Baker* [1965] 2 Q.B. 29 at p. 37; *Plimmer* v. *Wellington Corporation* (1884) 9 App.Cas. 699 at p. 714; *Chalmers* v. *Pardoe* [1963] 1 W.L.R. 677 at p. 682; *Crabb* v. *Arun District Council* [1976] Ch. 179 at p. 189.

[18] (1845) 13 M. & W. 838; which was distinguished in *Butler* v. *Sheffield and Manchester Rly. Co.* (1888) 21 Q.B.D. 207, where the plaintiff sued for assault on being forcibly ejected from a railway carriage, having paid the fare, but lost his ticket. The plaintiff succeeded in the Court of Appeal, the matter being dealt with on the basis of his rights under the contract. "The present case . . . has nothing to do with . . . any licence to go upon land." (*Per* Lopes L.J. at p. 214).

[19] *Thompson* v. *Park* [1944] K.B. 408 at p. 412. The reasoning was disapproved by Megarry J. in *Hounslow L.B.C.* v. *Twickenham Garden Developments Ltd.* [1971] Ch. 233; and by Watkins J. and the Court of Appeal in *Verrall* v. *Great Yarmouth Borough Council* [1981] Q.B. 202.

[20] [1915] 1 K.B. 1.

[21] (1845) 13 M. & W. 838.

[22] These matters are demonstrated by Phillimore L.J. in his dissenting judgment; see *Hounslow L.B.C.* v. *Twickenham Garden Developments Ltd.* [1971] Ch. 233 at p. 244, *per* Megarry J.; *cf. Cowell* v. *Rosehill Racecourse* (1937) 56 C.L.R. 605.

property; deed or no deed, nothing in the circumstances would have been granted because there was no proprietary interest to grant.

As a second ground for the decision, Buckley L.J. treated the matter as one of construing the parties' rights under the contract. Here "there was included in that contract a contract not to revoke the licence until the play had run to its termination."[23] This is the germ of the later development; and the significance of the Judicature Act in this context is that it makes available the equitable remedy of an injunction to restrain the breach of contract by the licensor. This precludes the argument that he has no right to revoke, but has a power to do so; he has no power if an injunction is available to restrain him.

Winter Garden Theatre (London) Ltd. v. *Millennium Productions Ltd.*[24] finally established that the rights of the parties must be determined upon the proper construction of the contract.

> The respondents were given by contract the right to present plays at a theatre for a period of six months from July 6, 1942, with provision for an extension, which was agreed, for an unstated period, terminable by the respondents (the licensees) at a month's notice. No provision was made for termination by the licensors. In September 1945, the licensors, wishing to terminate, served notice accordingly. The House of Lords held that, on the proper construction of the contract, the licence was terminable on the giving of notice, the length of which must be reasonable in the circumstances.[25]

As the licence was held to have been revoked in accordance with its terms, the problem in *Hurst's* case[26] did not arise. In the Court of Appeal, however, the contract had been construed as irrevocable by the licensor. In that situation, they held, the licensee would be protected by the issue of an injunction to restrain a breach of contract by the licensor. Sir Wilfrid Greene M.R., in words referred to with approval in the House of Lords, explained that the revocation of the licence was a breach.[27] "It may well be that, in the old days, that would only have given rise to a right to sue for damages. The licence would have stood revoked, but after the expiration of what was the appropriate period of grace the licensees would have been trespassers and

---

[23] *Hurst* v. *Picture Theatres ltd.* [1915] 1 K.B. 1 at p. 10; see also Kennedy L.J. at p. 14.

[24] [1948] A.C. 173. A successor in title has been held to be able to revoke on giving reasonable notice; *Re Spenborough Urban District Council's Agreement* [1968] Ch. 139.

[25] There is no presumption relating to revocability, [1948] A.C. 173 at p. 203, *per* Lord MacDermott; *Re Spenborough U.D.C.'s Agreement* [1968] Ch. 139; *Beverley Corp.* v. *Richard Hodgson and Sons Ltd.* (1972) 225 E.G. 799. Lord Parker said at p. 195 that a licence was prima facie revocable. Presumably, it will be more difficult to establish the non-revocability of a licence unlimited in time, than it would be in the case of a licence for a specific period.

[26] [1915] 1 K.B. 1.

[27] [1946] 1 All E.R. 678 at pp. 648 *et seq.*

could have been expelled, and their right would have been to sue for damages for breach of contract, as was said in *Kerrison* v. *Smith*.[28] But the matter requires to be considered further, because the power of equity to grant an injunction to restrain a breach of contract is, of course, a power exercisable in any court. The general rule is that, before equity will grant such an injunction, there must be, on the construction of the contract, a negative clause express or implied. In the present case it seems to me that the grant of an option which, if I am right, is an irrevocable option, must imply a negative undertaking by the licensor not to revoke it. That being so, in my opinion, such a contract could be enforced in equity by an injunction."[29]

B. The Licensee's Remedy for the Breach

(i) **Damages.** The normal remedy for breach of contract is, of course, damages; and there is little doubt that this was recognised even in the old common law cases which held that the licensee could be evicted. The question did not arise in *Wood* v. *Leadbitter*,[30] because the form of action was for assault and not for breach of contract.[31] An action for damages was held to be maintainable in *Kerrison* v. *Smith*,[32] and assumed to be so in *Hurst's* case.[33] The amount of damages has been little considered. An award to Hurst of 6d, the price of admission to a cinema in those days, may well be the correct measure of damages for breach of contract,[34] but wholly inadequate as compensation to the plaintiff for the assault.

In *Tanner* v. *Tanner*,[35] the defendant was the mistress of the plaintiff, and bore him two daughters. She lived in a rent-controlled flat; which she left in 1970, when the plaintiff purchased a house for her and for the children. The relationship ended, and in 1973 the plaintiff offered her £4,000 to vacate. She refused, claiming that she could stay in the house until the children left school. The Court of Appeal would have permitted her to stay. But the county court had made an order for possession, and the defendant had been rehoused by the local authority before the case came to the Court of Appeal. The defen-

---

[28] [1897] 2 Q.B. 445.

[29] In *Hounslow London Borough Council* v. *Twickenham Garden Developments Ltd.* [1971] Ch. 233, a contract by the defendant to construct a building on the plaintiff's land was held to involve an implied negative obligation on the part of the plaintiff not to revoke during the currency of the construction contract; *Mayfield Holdings Ltd.* v. *Moane Reef Ltd.* [1973] 1 N.Z.L.R. 309.

[30] (1845) 13 M. & W. 838.

[31] *Winter Garden Theatre (London) Ltd.* v. *Millennium Productions Ltd.* [1948] A.C. 173 at pp. 189–190, *per* Viscount Simon.

[32] [1897] 2 Q.B. 445.

[33] [1915] 1 K.B. 1.

[34] *Ibid.* at pp. 15, 20, *per* Phillimore L.J.; *Cowell* v. *Rosehill Racecourse* (1937) 56 C.L.R. 605.

[35] [1975] 1 W.L.R. 1346. See also *Wallshire Ltd.* v. *Advertising Sites Ltd.* [1988] 33 E.G. 51 (damages awarded for termination of licence in breach of notice term).

dant's remedy was in the form of compensation for the loss of the licence; expressed by Lord Denning M.R. as requiring the plaintiff to make restitution for the unjust benefit which he had received; or, by Brightman J., as the amount which might reasonably be payable for a surrender of the licence; which was quantified at £2,000.

(ii) Injunction. The normal way of protecting a contractual licensee against improper revocation is by issuing an injunction to restrain the breach by the licensor. A number of questions arise:

(a) *The Judge at your Elbow.* It was said in 1915[36] in connection with *Hurst's* case, that an injunction would be a useless remedy unless a Chancery judge was sitting at your elbow, because the breach and ejection would take place before the injunction could issue. But the court will treat the licence as not revoked in circumstances in which an injunction would issue, and this will prevent the licensee from being a trespasser. As has been seen, monetary compensation was awarded in *Tanner* v. *Tanner*[37] where it was no longer practicable to issue an injunction. And, it may be added, a mandatory injunction may be obtained, in a suitable case, to enable the licensee to re-enter.[38]

(b) *Discretionary Nature of the Remedy.* An injunction, like all equitable remedies, is discretionary. An injunction will not therefore be available to a licensee who is himself in breach of the terms of the licence. A licensee who himself misbehaves will not be protected.[39] Further, an injunction will not be granted where it will have the effect of compelling persons to live together in circumstances which are intolerable. If this situation arises in the case of a licence, an injunction may be refused, and the parties may be left to their rights at common law to sue for breach of contract.

In *Thompson* v. *Park*,[40] an arrangement between two preparatory schoolmasters provided that some places should be reserved for the duration of the war for the defendant's pupils at the plaintiff's school. After various disagreements, the defendant (the licensee)

---

[36] See (1915) 31 L.Q.R. 217 at p. 221 (Sir John Miles); and Lord Greene M.R. in *Millennium Productions Ltd.* v. *Winter Garden Theatre (London) Ltd.* [1946] 1 All E.R. 678 at p. 685. The damages recoverable for assault in *Hurst's* case were more than would be recoverable for breach of contract.

[37] [1975] 1 W.L.R. 1346.

[38] As in *Luganda* v. *Services Hotels Ltd.* [1969] 2 Ch. 209.

[39] *Thompson* v. *Park* [1944] K.B. 408. See also *Ivory* v. *Palmer* [1975] I.C.R. 340. For a consideration of the question of the circumstances in which misbehaviour by a licensee by estoppel will allow his licence to be terminated, see *Williams* v. *Staite* [1979] Ch. 291; [1986] Conv. 406 (M. P. Thompson), suggesting that termination is only possible where the previous court order was not the grant of an estate in the land. A smaller degree of misconduct will prevent an estoppel licence arising, under the "clean hands" principle, than will cause it to terminate; *J. Willis & Son* v. *Willis* [1986] 1 E.G.L.R. 62.

[40] [1944] K.B. 408.

was ordered to leave. He refused; and eventually the plaintiff wrote to the parents of the defendant's boys stating that they would not be able to return in the following term. The defendant then assembled a number of friends and supporters, entered the school, forced several locks, disconnected a pump and left the school without water; in Goddard L.J.'s words, he was "on his own showing . . . guilty at least of riot, affray, wilful damage, forcible entry, and, perhaps, conspiracy."[41]

In the circumstances, it is not surprising that the plaintiff obtained an interim injunction to restrain a breach of the peace. The defendant was so obviously in breach of his own obligations under the contract that there could be no question of his obtaining an injunction against the plaintiff to restrain a breach of the contract.

An interesting situation would, however, have arisen on these facts if the defendant (the licensee) had behaved impeccably. The first question then would have been whether, on its proper construction, the licence was revocable by the licensor on giving reasonable notice. If it was held revocable, he could so revoke. But if the court had held that, as the licence was given for a specific period of time, it was irrevocable, the court would be faced with the question whether or not to issue an injunction. The court will not "enforce an agreement for two people to live peacably under the same roof,"[42] and in such circumstances the court would be likely to leave the parties to their remedy at law.

(c) *Scope of Injunction.* It has been seen that an injunction can exist in many forms, and can be "tailored" to meet a particular situation. This proposition is demonstrated in many of the licence cases; in contractual licence cases, as will be seen in the next section, and all the more dramatically in the cases on estoppel.[43]

(iii) Specific Performance. The Court of Appeal had no hesitation in holding in *Verrall* v. *Great Yarmouth Borough Council*[44] that a contractual licence was enforceable by specific performance.

The National Front entered into a contract in April 1979 with the Council to hire a hall for the Front's national two-day Conference. In May 1979, after local authority elections, the new socialist controlled Council purported to revoke the licence; essentially on the ground that the Front's extremist political stance would create unrest in the borough. Specific performance of the contract was granted.

The old argument that a licence can be revoked by the licensor on

[41] *Ibid.* at p. 409.
[42] *Per* Goddard L.J. [1944] K.B. 409.
[43] *Post*, p. 847.
[44] [1981] Q.B. 202; [1981] Conv. 212 (A. Briggs).

payment of damages was firmly and finally disposed of, and the reasoning of *Thompson* v. *Park*[45] was disapproved. The Front was entitled to the benefits of the contractual licence.

The issue of a decree of specific performance raised a number of questions of principle relating to the availability of the decree. It used to be said that a decree of specific performance would not issue in relation to a transient matter; because the issue may not come to the court in time.[46] That view was held to be out of date. Presumably, however, it would have been a defence if the date of the conference had passed before the issue was tried. Another possible difficulty might be the question of the continued supervision by the court, although, as we have seen,[47] inroads have already been made into the supervision principle. A further question is whether specific performance is available to enforce a contract which does not create a proprietary interest. The older view was that the decree would not issue in such a case.[48] But more recent authorities indicate that specific performance is a remedy based on the inadequacy of damages rather than on the vindication of some proprietary interest.[49] This, it is submitted, is the correct approach today; "it is the duty of the court to protect, where it is appropriate to do so, any interest, whether it be an estate in land or a licence, by injunction or specific performance as the case may be."[50] Such an approach is consistent with the court's power to grant a prohibitory injunction to restrain the wrongful revocation of a contractual licence, or to grant a mandatory injunction to re-instate a licensee whose licence has been revoked in breach of contract.[51]

C. Express or Implied Contracts

The contract may be express or implied. In the older cases, which dealt mainly with commercial transactions of one sort or another, it was not difficult to recognise the existence of a contract, though its terms may have been difficult to construe. Many of the recent cases concern arrangements within the family, using that term widely enough to include mistresses and their children. These are situations in which the terms of an agreement are usually not spelled out; and a contract may in any case fail because of a lack of intention to create

---

[45] [1944] K.B. 408; *ante*, p. 837.

[46] *Ante*, p. 668.

[47] *Ante*, p. 663.

[48] *Booker* v. *Palmer* [1942] 2 All E.R. 674 at p. 677 (*per* Lord Greene M.R.); Spry, *Equitable Remedies* (3rd ed., 1984), pp. 52 and 534. This was the view that prevailed at the time of *Hurst's* case.

[49] *Beswick* v. *Beswick* [1968] A.C. 58; *Tanner* v. *Tanner* [1975] 1 W.L.R. 1346 at p. 1350; *Hutton* v. *Watling* [1948] Ch. 26 at p. 36 (affirmed, *ibid.* p. 398); (1980) 96 L.Q.R. 483. See also *Tailby* v. *Official Receiver* (1888) 13 App.Cas. 523 at p. 548.

[50] [1981] Q.B. 202 at p. 220 (*per* Roskill L.J.).

[51] *Winter Garden Theatre (London) Ltd.* v. *Millennium Productions Ltd.* [1948] A.C. 173 (prohibitory); *Luganda* v. *Service Hotels Ltd.* [1969] 2 Ch. 209 (mandatory).

legal obligations; or, in the case of a contract for co-habitation, on the ground of the unlawfulness of the consideration.

In these circumstances, it is not to be expected that it will be possible to distinguish clearly between cases in which a contract has been found and those where it has not. As has been seen, a contractual licence was implied in *Tanner* v. *Tanner*.[52] That indeed was the only way to find an adequate remedy; and Lord Denning M.R., conscious of the difficulty of finding a contract in the circumstances, went so far as to say that the court should "imply a contract by him—or if need be impose the equivalent of a contract by him."[53] In *Coombes* v. *Smith*,[54] the court failed to find a contract in circumstances which were basically similar. There the defendant bought a house into which the plaintiff, his lover, moved. As she was pregnant, she gave up her job, the defendant assuring her that he would always provide for her. The defendant paid the outgoings, but the plaintiff did some decorating and gardening. When the couple separated 10 years later, the defendant offered the plaintiff £10,000 to move out, but she claimed a contractual licence for life. Her claim failed, as she had provided no consideration, and it was impossible to infer a contract. *Tanner* v. *Tanner*[55] was distinguished as the claimant there had provided consideration in giving up her rent-controlled flat and was not claiming a licence for life. The defendant, however, conceded that the plaintiff could remain until the child was 17. It is indeed easier to see why there was not a contract in *Coombes* v. *Smith*,[56] than it is to see how one could be implied in *Tanner* v. *Tanner*.[57] In making that decision, the court seemed to be influenced by the desired result.

In other cases the occupier has received protection by the court's finding that there was a contractual licence which was irrevocable for a period of time.

In *Hardwick* v. *Johnson*,[58] a mother purchased a house, on her son's marriage, for occupation by him and his bride. The young couple were to pay £7 a week as rent to the mother. But this soon ceased to be paid, and the mother did not demand it because the couple had little money.

The marriage collapsed. The son left his bride, now pregnant, for another woman. The mother sued for possession. The baby was born. The wife claimed to be entitled to remain in possession on payment of £7 per week.

---

[52] [1975] 1 W.L.R. 1346; (1976) 92 L.Q.R. 168 (J. L. Barton).

[53] *Ibid.* at p. 1350.

[54] [1986] 1 W.L.R. 808; (1986) 45 C.L.J. (D. Hayton); *post*, p. 851. See also *Horrocks* v. *Forray* [1970] 1 W.L.R. 230; (1970) 40 Conv.(N.S.) 362 (M. Richards).

[55] *Supra.*

[56] *Supra.*

[57] [1975] 1 W.L.R. 1340.

[58] [1978] 1 W.L.R. 683. See also *Chandler* v. *Kerley* [1978] 1 W.L.R. 693 ("mistress" entitled to remain for a period determinable upon 12 months' notice).

The Court of Appeal found a contractual licence; though Lord Denning M.R. thought that no enforceable contract could arise in a family situation of this kind,[59] preferring to find a licence by estoppel. On the face of it, it would seem to be unlikely that the parties would intend to bind themselves contractually in a situation of this type. The mother was trying to help her son, who had had a prior unsuccessful marriage. It is unlikely that she would have answered affirmatively if she had been asked whether she had agreed to the arrangement being continued in favour of the daughter-in-law after the collapse of the marriage. Such cases provide situations in which some steps for the protection of the licensee seem eminently just. A solution might have been reached by the application of the principle of proprietary estoppel, discussed later.[60] But the application of that doctrine will usually provide a final solution, affecting the proprietary rights of the parties. Something less was needed here. The daughter-in-law in *Hardwick* v. *Johnson*[61] was entitled, subject to resuming the weekly payments, to protection by injunction for an indefinite period of time.

D. Contractual Licences and Third Parties

Protection of the licensee against the licensor inevitably gives rise to the question whether a licensee will be protected also against an assignee of the licensor. On the one hand, protection given to a licensee is in many cases of little use if the licensor can transfer the land and leave the licensee helpless. On the other hand, if a licensee is protected against third parties, his licence begins to look like some sort of proprietary interest.[62]

The extent to which a licence is binding on a third party will vary with the type of licence. Bare licences are obviously not binding. Licences which create proprietary interests in land, whether by way of constructive trusts,[63] or by way of proprietary estoppel,[64] are binding on third parties in the sense that the licensee is the owner of an equitable proprietary interest which is so binding. The question whether a licence has given rise to a constructive trust or an estoppel is considered later. First the position as to contractual licences outside these situations will be examined.

It is important to appreciate that there is no principle which requires that the availability of an injunction against one contracting party will make it available against third parties coming to the land. The jurisdiction to apply an injunction against a third party was demonstrated

---

[59] *Ibid.* at p. 688.
[60] *Post*, p. 850.
[61] [1978] 1 W.L.R. 683.
[62] See, however, (1986) 49 M.L.R. 741 (J. Dewar), suggesting that it is wrong to attempt to fit licences into traditional academic land law.
[63] *Post*, p. 844.
[64] *Post*, p. 850. For further discussion see [1981] Conv. 212 (A. Briggs) and 347 (P. N. Todd); [1983] Conv. 50 (M. P. Thompson) and 285 (A. Briggs).

by the development of the law of restrictive covenants from *Tulk* v. *Moxhay*.[65] The policy decision to refuse an injunction against third parties was shown by the unsuccessful attempts to make covenants run with chattels.[66]

As far as contractual obligations are concerned, the estate of a deceased party to the contract is not properly a third party. The devisee of the licensor is a third party, but one in a special situation, taking as a volunteer. One of the landmark cases on the enforcement of licences against third parties, *Errington* v. *Errington and Woods*[67] is such a case; the report fails to say whether the licensor's widow, who was the devisee, was also his executrix; but both Lord Denning M.R. and Hodson L.J. refer to her as successor in title. Such a person is in a different position from a purchaser.

Authority leads to the conclusion that contractual licences are not ordinarily binding on third parties.

In *King* v. *David Allen & Sons, Billposting Ltd.*,[68] the licensor agreed that the licensees should have the exclusive right of affixing advertisements upon a building. Later the licensor leased the building to a cinema company, no provision being made to protect the rights of the licensees. The licensees sued the licensor for breach of contract. The licensor was liable if the lease to the company deprived the licensees of their contractual right. The House of Lords held that it did. The action succeeded.

In *Clore* v. *Theatrical Properties Ltd.*,[69] an indenture which was drafted in the form of a lease purported to grant the lessee the "front of the house" rights in a theatre; that is, the right to use refreshment rooms etc. to provide for the needs of patrons. The instrument provided that the terms "lessor" and "lessee" should include their executors, administrators and assigns.

It was held to be a licence and not a lease. The "lessor" and "lessee" both assigned; and the question was whether the "lessee's" assignee could enforce the right under the agreement. He failed; because the licence was a personal contract and enforceable only between the parties to it.

As has been recently reaffirmed,[70] these cases lay down a correct doctrine relating to contractual licences. Licences were indeed treated as binding on third parties in a number of cases decided in the days when a deserted wife was treated as a licensee protected by injunc-

[65] (1848) 2 Ph. 774.
[66] *Taddy & Co.* v. *Sterious* [1904] 1 Ch. 354; *McGruther* v. *Pitcher* [1904] 2 Ch. 306; *Port Line* v. *Ben Line Steamers* [1958] 2 Q.B. 146; *post*, p. 869; *Lord Strathcona S.S. Co.* v. *Dominion Coal Co.* [1926] A.C. 108.
[67] [1952] 1 K.B. 290.
[68] [1916] 2 A.C. 54; *Edwardes* v. *Barrington* (1901) 85 L.T. 650; *Warr (Frank) & Co. Ltd.* v. *L.C.C.* [1904] 1 K.B. 713; *Re Solomon* [1967] Ch. 573 at p. 585.
[69] [1936] 3 All E.R. 483.
[70] *Ashburn Anstalt* v. *Arnold* [1988] 2 W.L.R. 706, *post*, p. 845.

tion[71]; and these provided a very compelling case for applying the injunction also against the party to whom the deserting husband sold the house. But these cases were incorrect; because the House of Lords decided that a deserted wife was not a licensee of her husband, and had no interest capable of binding the land.[72] Legislation followed.[73] There are some cases in which a contractual arrangement, outside the context of a deserted wife, was held to bind a third party, but they are best explained as being decided on other grounds.

In *Errington* v. *Errington and Woods*[74] the father (A) of a young man who was about to be married purchased a house through a building society, made a down-payment and told the young couple that the house would be theirs when they had paid all the instalments due under the mortgage. They went into possession and paid all the instalments which fell due. Nothing was stated concerning the rights of the young couple during the currency of the mortgage payments. A died, leaving all his property to Mrs. A. The son returned to his mother, who took steps to evict the daughter-in-law. She failed. The daughter-in-law was held to be a licensee who was entitled to protection not only against A in his lifetime, but also against Mrs. A, taking as a volunteer.

There was clearly a flavour of contract in the licence, and the case is usually treated as one of contractual licence. But the wide views expressed in the case as to the enforceability of such licences were disapproved, *obiter,* by the House of Lords in *National Provincial Bank Ltd.* v. *Ainsworth*,[75] and have recently been said by the Court of Appeal in *Ashburn Anstalt* v. *Arnold*[76] to be neither practically necessary nor theoretically convincing. They could not be reconciled with *King*[77] and *Clore*,[78] but the decision was, however, correct on the facts. It could be justified on one of three grounds: (i) there was a contract to convey on completion of the payments, giving rise to an equitable interest in the form of an estate contract which would bind the widow as a volunteer; (ii) the daughter-in-law had changed her position in reliance upon a representation by the deceased, the estoppel binding the widow; (iii) the payment of instalments gave rise to a direct proprietary interest by way of a constructive trust under the principle later formulated in *Gissing* v. *Gissing*.[79] Thus the result could have been achieved without accepting Lord Denning's broad principles,

[71] *Bendall* v. *McWhirter* [1952] 2 Q.B. 466; *Lee* v. *Lee* [1952] 2 Q.B. 489n; *Street* v. *Denham* [1954] 1 W.L.R. 624; *Ferris* v. *Weaven* [1952] 2 All E.R. 233.
[72] *National Provincial Bank Ltd.* v. *Ainsworth* [1965] A.C. 1175.
[73] Matrimonial Homes Act 1967 (now the Act of 1983).
[74] [1952] 1 K.B. 290; *Duke of Beaufort* v. *Patrick* (1853) 17 Beav. 60.
[75] [1965] A.C. 1175.
[76] [1988] 2 W.L.R. 706, *infra*.
[77] *Supra*.
[78] *Supra*.
[79] [1971] A.C. 886, *ante*, p. 254.

which were unnecessary and *per incuriam*. The principle now affirmed by the Court of Appeal is that a contractual licence cannot bind a third party unless the circumstances are such that a constructive trust has arisen. Further examination of this principle will be deferred until the development of the constructive trust solution has been outlined.

4. Constructive Trusts

A few cases in this field have been decided on the basis of a constructive trust. We have seen that, in modern times, the constructive trust solution has been widely defined.[80] Lord Denning has described a constructive trust as one "imposed by law whenever justice and good conscience require it. It is a liberal process, founded upon large principles of equity, to be applied in cases where the legal owner cannot conscientiously keep the property for himself alone, but ought to allow another to have the property or the benefit of it or a share of it. ... It is an equitable remedy by which the court can enable an aggrieved party to obtain restitution."[81] Similarly in *Binions* v. *Evans*,[82] he quoted Cardozo J. in *Beatty* v. *Guggenheim Exploration Co.*[83] "A constructive trust is the formula through which the conscience of equity finds expression."

In those terms, the constructive trust solution is at once too vague and too far-reaching. Too vague in that such broad statements provide no way of determining when such a trust will be held to exist.[84] It is almost as if we look to see where the merits of the case are, and then impose a constructive trust in favour of the victor. This used to be called "palm-tree" justice, and it may well be a satisfactory method of reaching a solution in some cases, as in *D.H.N. Food Distributors Ltd.* v. *Tower Hamlets London Borough Council*,[85] where the issue was whether a contractual licensee could claim compensation for disturbance upon compulsory purchase. But it is not appropriate where title to land is at stake.

Authority for the constructive trust solution is hard to find in the cases involving title to land and enforceability against third parties.

Lord Denning M.R. pioneered this solution in *Binions* v. *Evans*.[86]

Mrs. Evans was the widow of an employee of the Tredegar Estate.

---

[80] *Ante*, p. 309.
[81] *Hussey* v. *Palmer* [1972] 1 W.L.R. 1286, at p. 1290.
[82] [1972] Ch. 359 at p. 368.
[83] (1919) 225 N.Y. 380 at p. 386.
[84] (1973) 32 C.L.J. 123 at p. 142 (R. J. Smith).
[85] [1976] 1 W.L.R. 852. See also *Pennine Raceway Ltd.* v. *Kirklees Metropolitan Council* [1983] Q.B. 382 (Licensee entitled to compensation for withdrawal of planning permission as "person interested in the land" within Town and Country Planning Act 1971, s.164).
[86] [1972] Ch. 359; (1972) 88 L.Q.R. 336 (P.V.B.); (1972) 3 Conv.(N.S.) 266 (J. Martin); (1973) 32 C.L.J. 123 (R. J. Smith); Oakley, *Constructive Trusts* (2nd ed.), p. 45.

The Estate made an agreement with her, under which she would be allowed to reside in a cottage, free of rent and rates, for the rest of her life. She undertook to keep the cottage in repair.

Two years later, the Tredegar Estate sold the cottage to Mr. and Mrs. Binions, expressly subject to the agreement, the purchase price being reduced accordingly. The purchasers claimed possession of the cottage.

It is hardly surprising that Mrs. Evans was protected. Lord Denning M.R. held that the purchasers were bound by Mrs. Evans' contractual licence and also by a constructive trust in her favour, whereas Megaw and Stephenson L.JJ. relied upon the agreement as creating a life interest.[87]

The difficulties of the majority solution, giving a life interest to Mrs. Evans, and thus making her a tenant for life under the Settled Land Act 1925, will be considered below. Clearly, the case provides no support for the view that contractual licences generally are binding on third parties. Nevertheless, it was cited subsequently as authority for the proposition that a contractual licence is capable of binding a third party. Such statements have been *obiter*, being made in cases not involving a transfer of the land.[88] One case, however, which did involve a third party was *Re Sharpe*.[89]

An elderly aunt lent money to her nephew towards the purchase of a house on the understanding that she would live there with the nephew and his wife for the rest of her life. The nephew subsequently went bankrupt, and his trustee in bankruptcy contracted to sell the house to a purchaser. The trustee failed in his claim to recover possession of the house from the aunt. Her rights were held to be more than merely contractual, and gave rise to a constructive trust binding upon the trustee in bankruptcy. The purchaser was not a party to the action, and it was left open whether he would also be bound.[90] However, as the aunt had sold her home and paid for improvements to the nephew's house, a preferable basis for the decision might have been proprietary estoppel.

The position has now been clarified by the Court of Appeal in *Ashburn Anstalt* v. *Arnold*,[91] where the plaintiff purchaser sought possession against the defendant, who was in occupation under an agreement with the plaintiff's predecessor in title. The plaintiff had

---

[87] Feeling themselves bound by *Bannister* v. *Bannister* [1948] 2 All E.R. 133.
[88] *Tanner* v. *Tanner* [1975] 1 W.L.R. 1346; *D.H.N. Food Distributors Ltd.* v. *Tower Hamlets London Borough Council* [1976] 1 W.L.R. 852.
[89] [1980] 1 W.L.R. 219; [1980] Conv. 207 (J. Martin). The correctness of this decision was left open in *Bristol and West Building Society* v. *Henning* [1985] 1 W.L.R. 778. See also *Midland Bank Ltd.* v. *Farmpride Hatcheries Ltd.* (1981) 260 E.G. 493; [1982] Conv. 67 (R. Annand).
[90] See further Murphy and Clark, *The Family Home*, pp. 199–204.
[91] [1988] 2 W.L.R. 706; (1988) 51 M.L.R. 226 (J. Hill); (1988) 104 L.Q.R. 175 (P. Sparkes); [1988] Conv. 201 (M. P. Thompson); (1988) 47 C.L.J. 353 (A. Oakley).

been aware of the agreement and had purchased expressly subject to its provisions "so far as the same are enforceable against the Vendor." In fact it was held that the defendant had a tenancy which was binding on the plaintiff under the Land Registration Act 1925.[92] However, the Court of Appeal proceeded to consider the position if the defendant had been a contractual licensee. On the clear authority of *King* v. *David Allen & Sons, Billposting Ltd.*,[93] the correct principle was that a contractual licence could not normally bind a third party. However, the law must be free to develop, and the finding of a constructive trust was considered a beneficial adaptation of old rules to new situations in appropriate circumstances. But there could be no bare assertion that a licence gives rise to a constructive trust. It would arise only if the conscience of the third party was affected. Mere notice would not be sufficient, nor the fact that the property was conveyed "subject to" the interest. Such a term does not mean that the grantee is necessarily intended to be under an obligation to give effect to the interest, but may be merely to protect the grantor against claims by the grantee (for example as in the case of an old restrictive covenant which may or may not be enforceable). The question is whether the grantee has acted in such a way that, as a matter of justice, a trust must be imposed on him. In the present case there would be no constructive trust because the transfer "subject to" the defendant's rights was done to protect the vendor, and the purchaser had not paid a reduced price. As far as the previous cases were concerned, *Binions* v. *Evans*[94] was a legitimate application of the constructive trust doctrine because the parties intended the purchaser to give effect to the interest and the price was reduced accordingly. Also approved was the decision in *Lyus* v. *Prowsa Ltd.*,[95] where the intention had been similar and the purchaser had given assurances. The doctrine was not, however, appropriate in *Re Sharpe*,[96] where the aunt had not replied to the trustee in bankruptcy's enquiries as to her interest.

The Court of Appeal added that certainty was of prime importance as far as title to land was concerned, and it was not desirable to impose a constructive trust on slender materials. As we will see, the difficulty is that the imposition of a constructive trust, in the case of a fee simple, creates an equitable interest which is neither registrable (in unregistered land) nor overreachable.[97] If the interest protected by a constructive trust is for life only, it may bring the Settled Land Act into operation.[98] A similar problem arises with the doctrine of proprietary

[92] As an overriding interest under s.70(1)(g).
[93] [1916] 2 A.C. 54, *ante*, p. 842.
[94] [1972] Ch. 359, *supra*.
[95] [1982] 1 W.L.R. 1044, *ante*, p. 314.
[96] [1980] 1 W.L.R. 219, *supra*.
[97] *Hodgson* v. *Marks* [1971] Ch. 894.
[98] See *Dodsworth* v. *Dodsworth* (1973) 228 E.G. 1115, *per* Russell L.J.; *Bannister* v. *Bannister* [1948] 2 All E.R. 133.

estoppel, as discussed below.[99] In that context also the constructive trust has been invoked in order to achieve a just result.[1]

The new formulation, it is submitted, provides welcome guidelines as to the circumstances in which a constructive trust will be imposed, and thereby achieves a compromise between the sometimes divergent goals of certainty and justice.

5. Licences by Estoppel

The doctrine of estoppel has played a significant part in the modern development of the law of licences.[2] A situation in which a licensee has acted to his detriment in reliance upon a representation or promise by the licensor presents a compelling case for the intervention of equity in order to protect the licensee; more compelling, in a sense, than the case of a contractual licence, because the licensee by estoppel has no alternative remedy in damages.[3] It will be seen that the doctrine of estoppel by encouragement or acquiescence has found a fruitful area of operation in the field of licences, under a newly acquired name of proprietary estoppel; its success in this area has been largely due to the fact that, unlike estoppel by representation or promissory estoppel, it can found a cause of action and, in the licence context, enables the court to award a proprietary interest to the licensee. It will also be seen that, in the enthusiasm for the application of this doctrine, the doctrine has become confused with other estoppels, its separate origin, and even the historical requirements for its operation, being often overlooked; and also that it has been credited with the solution to many cases in which it is quite clear that the judges reached their decision on other grounds. The utility of the doctrine stems from the fact, in the estoppel cases, that the court will "look at all the circumstances in each case to decide in what way the equity can be satisfied"[4]; and the most suitable solution is often an award to the licensee of a proprietary interest, rather than merely giving negative protection. A sword and not a shield is sometimes required.

---

[99] *Post*, p. 860. See also [1982] Conv. 118 (A. R. Everton).

[1] *Re Basham* [1986] 1 W.L.R. 1498, *post*, p. 856.

[2] It seems that a licence by estoppel was first so referred to judicially in *Inwards* v. *Baker* [1965] 2 Q.B. 29 *per* Danckwerts L.J. at p. 38, *post*, p. 861.

[3] As to how far a contractual licence may also be a licence by estoppel, see [1983] Conv. 50 (M. P. Thompson) and 285 (A. Briggs); *post*, p. 857.

[4] *Plimmer* v. *Wellington Corporation* (1884) 9 App.Cas. 699 at p. 714; *Greasley* v. *Cooke* [1980] 1 W.L.R. 1306 at p. 1312. It may be held that the claimant has already had sufficient satisfaction for his expenditure; *Appleby* v. *Cowley, The Times*, April 14, 1982. See (1984) 100 L.Q.R. 376 (S. Moriarty).

A. Types of Estoppel

There are many different types of estoppel at law and in equity. We are concerned with three of these, each having a separate origin and history.[5]

(i) Estoppel by Representation. Estoppel by representation operates over a wide field of common law and equity. The basic principle is that a person who makes an unambiguous[6] representation, by words,[7] or conduct,[8] or by silence,[9] of an existing fact, and causes another party to act to his detriment in reliance on the representation will not be permitted subsequently to act inconsistently with that representation. The doctrine was originally applied only where there was a representation of existing fact,[10] and not where the representation was one of law or of intention. The representor could not subsequently allege, in dealing with the representee, that the facts were different from those represented. And, apart from a few long-established exceptions,[11] such an estoppel works negatively. It is not capable of creating a cause of action. It works like a rule of evidence, a rule which excludes a particular defence or line of argument. Thus, an owner of goods would be estopped from claiming them if he stood by at the sale, thereby indicating that he was not the owner, and encouraging the sale.[12]

This is not to say that estoppel is available only to a defendant. A plaintiff may take advantage of the doctrine if he has an independent cause of action, and can show that the defence is inconsistent with a representation of the defendant on which hé relies.[13]

A well-known example is *Robertson* v. *Minister of Pensions*,[14] where an officer claimed a pension, relying upon a statement by the War Office that his disability had been accepted as due to military service,

---

[5] For estoppel by convention, *i.e.* by a course of dealing, see *Amalgamated Investment and Property Co. (in liquidation)* v. *Texas Commerce International Bank Ltd.* [1982] Q.B. 84; *Pacol Ltd.* v. *Trade Lines Ltd.* [1982] 1 Lloyd's Rep. 456; *Keen* v. *Holland* [1984] 1 W.L.R. 251; *Troop* v. *Gibson* [1986] 1 E.G.L.R. 1; (1982) 79 L.S. Gaz. 662 (P. Matthews).

[6] *Low* v. *Bouverie* [1891] 3 Ch. 82.

[7] *Hunt* v. *Carew* (1649) Nels. 46; or through an agent: *Moorgate Mercantile Ltd.* v. *Twitchings* [1977] A.C. 890.

[8] *Waldron* v. *Sloper* (1852) 1 Drew. 193.

[9] *Hunsden* v. *Cheyney* (1690) 2 Vern. 150; *Fung Kai Sun* v. *Chan Fui Hing* [1951] A.C. 489; *Pacol Ltd.* v. *Trade Lines Ltd.* [1982] 1 Lloyd's Rep. 456.

[10] *Jorden* v. *Money* (1845) 5 H.L.C. 185.

[11] *e.g.* a tenancy by estoppel, M. & W., pp. 660 *et seq.*; see also *Stiles* v. *Cowper* (1748) 3 Atk. 692; *Ramsden* v. *Dyson* (1866) L.R. 1 H.L. 129; *post*, p. 853.

[12] *Pickard* v. *Sears* (1837) 6 A. & E. 469; *Gregg* v. *Wells* (1839) 10 A. & E. 90.

[13] Similarly with promissory estoppel; *Amalgamated Investment and Property Co. (in liquidation)* v. *Texas Commerce International Bank Ltd.* [1982] Q.B. 84; *Pacol Ltd.* v. *Trade Lines Ltd.* [1982] 1 Lloyd's Rep. 456.

[14] [1949] 1 K.B. 227; *Combe* v. *Combe* [1951] 2 K.B. 215 at p. 219, *per* Denning L.J.; *Evenden* v. *Guildford City A.F.C. Ltd.* [1975] Q.B. 917. On the operation of estoppel in Public Law, and especially in the context of erroneous statements that planning permission is not required, see (1975) 125 N.L.J. 279 (C. Joseph) and 279 (D. J. Bentley). See also *Western Fish Products Ltd.* v. *Penwith District Council* [1981] 2 All E.R. 204; *Rootkin* v. *Kent County Council* [1981] 1 W.L.R. 1186.

and forbore to obtain an independent medical opinion. It was held that the Crown, through the Minister of Pensions, could not go back on the statement previously made. The officer was no longer in a position to supply the necessary evidence; but the Minister was estopped from denying that he qualified.

(ii) Promissory Estoppel. The doctrine is expanded in equity, so as to include, not only representations of fact, but also representations of intention; or promises. The doctrine came into prominence with the decision of Denning J. in *Central London Property Trust Ltd.* v. *High Trees House Ltd.* in 1947,[15] and became firmly established in later cases.[16]

Where, by words or conduct, a person makes an unambiguous representation as to his future conduct, intending the representation to be relied on, and to affect the legal relations between the parties,[17] and the representee alters his position in reliance on it, the representor will be unable to act inconsistently with the representation if by so doing the representee would be prejudiced.[18]

The doctrine emerged in *Hughes* v. *Metropolitan Railway Co.*,[19] and developed through a line of cases which was little known until 1947. Denning J. then applied it to the problem of waiver of rights under a contract in *Central London Property Trust Ltd.* v. *High Trees House Ltd.*[20]

The plaintiff company in 1937 leased to the defendant (a subsidiary of the plaintiffs) a block of flats for 99 years at a rent of £2,500 a year. Early in 1940, and because of the war, the defendants were unable to find sub-tenants for the flats, and unable in consequence to pay the rent. The plaintiffs agreed to reduce the rent to £1,250 from the beginning of the term. By the beginning of 1945 all the flats were let, and the plaintiffs claimed the full rent as from the middle of that year. They succeeded. Denning J., however, stated that they would have been estopped from claiming the full rent for the period from 1940 to 1945, on the ground that though not technically bound

---

[15] [1947] K.B. 130.
[16] *Combe* v. *Combe* [1951] 2 K.B. 215; *Ajayi* v. *R.T. Briscoe (Nigeria) Ltd.* [1964] 1 W.L.R. 1326; *W.J. Alan & Co. Ltd.* v. *El Nasr Export and Import Co.* [1972] 2 Q.B. 189; *cf. D. & C. Builders Ltd.* v. *Rees* [1966] 2 Q.B. 617 (promise obtained by undue pressure).
[17] *Foot Clincs (1943) Ltd.* v. *Cooper's Gowns Ltd.* [1947] K.B. 506.
[18] See *Combe* v. *Combe* [1951] 2 K.B. 215 at p. 220.
[19] (1877) 2 App.Cas. 439.
[20] [1947] K.B. 130; *Birmingham and District Land Co.* v. *L. and N.W. Ry.* (1888) 40 Ch.D. 268; *Panoutsos* v. *Raymond Hadley Corp. of New York* [1917] 2 K.B. 473; *Salisbury (Marquess)* v. *Gilmore* [1942] 2 K.B. 38; *Ledingham* v. *Bermejo Estancia Co.* [1947] 1 All E.R. 749; *W.J. Alan and Co. Ltd.* v. *El Nasr Export and Import Co.* [1972] 2 Q.B. 189; *Ogilvy* v. *Hope-Davies* [1976] 1 All E.R. 683; *Pacol Ltd.* v. *Trade Lines Ltd.* [1982] 1 Lloyd's Rep. 456.

because of the lack of consideration, the plaintiffs had intended the defendants to rely on the promise and the defendants had acted on the faith of it.

Promissory estoppel contains a number of features which distinguish it from estoppel by representation of fact.[21] First, in that the representation may be one of intention and not one of fact; which raises the question whether it is inconsistent with the House of Lords decision in *Jorden* v. *Money*.[22] But the doctrine is now well established.[23] Secondly, the requirement of detriment to the representee is less stringent in the case of promissory estoppel. Financial loss or other detriment is of course sufficient; but it seems that it is not necessary to show more than that the representee committed himself to a particular course of action as a result of the representation.[24] Thirdly, the effect of the estoppel may not be permanent. The representor may escape from the burden of the equity if he can ensure that the representee will not be prejudiced.[25] But, consistently with estoppel by representation, promissory estoppel does not create a cause of action; it operates to give a negative protection. It is a shield and not a sword.[26]

(iii) Proprietary Estoppel. Distinct from the types of estoppel by representation previously explained is estoppel by encouragement or by acquiescence. This doctrine is applicable where one party knowingly encourages another to act, or acquiesces in the other's actions, to his detriment and in infringement of the first party's rights. He will be unable to complain later about the infringement, and may indeed be required to make good the expectation which he encouraged the other party to rely on. Unlike other estoppels, therefore, this doctrine may, in some circumstances, create a claim, and an entitlement to positive proprietary rights; in others, it can operate negatively, or can produce a compromise situation appropriate to the particular circumstances.

Detrimental reliance need not involve the expenditure of money on the land. In *Greasley* v. *Cooke*,[27] the plaintiff served notice to quit on

---

[21] See generally (1947) 63 L.Q.R. 283 (G. C. Cheshire and C. H. S. Fifoot); (1951) 67 L.Q.R. 330 (J. F. Wilson); (1952) 15 M.L.R. 1 (Denning L.J.); (1952) 15 M.L.R. 325 (L. A. Sheridan).

[22] (1854) 5 H.L.Cas. 185.

[23] But it "may need to be reviewed and reduced to a coherent body of doctrine by the Courts": *Woodhouse A.C. Israel Cocoa Ltd.* v. *Nigerian Produce Marketing Co. Ltd.* [1972] A.C. 741 at p. 758 (*per* Lord Hailsham).

[24] *Central London Property Ltd.* v. *High Trees House Ltd.* [1947] K.B. 130; *W.J. Alan & Co. Ltd.* v. *El Nasr Export and Import Co.* [1972] 2 Q.B. 189; *Ajayi* v. *R.T. Briscoe (Nigeria) Ltd.* [1964] 1 W.L.R. 1326.

[25] *Tool Metal Manufacturing Co. Ltd.* v. *Tungsten Electric Co. Ltd.* [1955] 1 W.L.R. 766.

[26] *Combe* v. *Combe* [1951] 2 K.B. 215 at p. 224; *Syros Shipping Co. S.A.* v. *Elaghill Trading Co.* [1980] 2 Lloyd's Rep. 390. See generally (1983) 42 C.L.J. 257 (M. P. Thompson). A wider approach has been taken in Australia; *Waltons Stores (Interstate)* v. *Maher* (1988) C.L.R. 387; (1988) 104 L.Q.R. 362 (A. Duthie).

[27] [1980] 1 W.L.R. 1306; (1981) 44 M.L.R. 461 (G. Woodman); *cf. Maddison* v. *Alderson* (1883) 8 App.Cas. 467.

the defendant, who had moved into the property as a maid, but had cohabited with the owner's son, K, and had stayed on after the owner's death, continuing to care for the family, which included a mentally-ill daughter. She had remained without payment since 1948, encouraged by K, now deceased, and his brother (the plaintiff) to believe that it was her home for life. The Court of Appeal held that she was entitled to remain as long as she wished. Once it was shown that she had relied on these assurances, the onus of proving that she had acted to her detriment was not upon her. Lord Denning M.R. appeared to suggest that it was not necessary that the claimant should have acted to her detriment[28]: "it is sufficient if the party, to whom the assurance is given, acts on the faith of it—in such circumstances that it would be unjust and inequitable for the party making the assurance to go back on it. ... There is no need for her to prove that she acted to her detriment or to her prejudice."[29] Subsequent cases, however, have made it clear that these comments related only to the burden of proof. In *Coombes* v. *Smith*[30] Lord Dennings' statement was interpreted as meaning merely that where the plaintiff has adopted a detrimental course of conduct after the defendant's assurances, there is a rebuttable presumption that this was done in reliance upon the assurances. Here the plaintiff, who was the defendant's lover, moved into a house provided and maintained by the defendant. Being pregnant, she gave up her job, and was assured by the defendant that he would provide for her. Subsequently she did some decorating and gardening. After 10 years the couple separated, but she refused to leave the house. Her claim based on proprietary estoppel failed. She had no mistaken belief that she had a right to remain indefinitely, and in any event there was no detrimental act. Her acts in leaving her husband, becoming pregnant and looking after the house were not on in reliance on any expectation of an interest and were not detrimental.[31]

Early illustrations of the doctrine dealt with the protection of a lessee; as where a life tenant granted a 30 year lease, to the knowledge of remainderman who "stood by and encouraged" the tenant to take the lease and incur expenditures. Lord Hardwick confirmed the tenant in the balance of his lease after the life tenant's death.[32]

Other cases deal with activities on a party's own land which require facilities from a neighbour; allowing that party to acquire a right in the nature of an easement; as where a millowner erects a mill on the

---

[28] Here in any event the claimant had foregone wages and perhaps lost job opportunities.

[29] *Ibid.* at pp. 1311–1312. This resembles the requirements of promissory estoppel (*supra*, note 24).

[30] [1986] 1 W.L.R. 808, *ante*, p. 840 (the contract claim); (1986) 45 C.L.J. 394 (D. Hayton); *Watts* v. *Story* (1984) 134 N.L.J. 631; *Grant* v. *Edwards* [1986] Ch. 638.

[31] *cf. Grant* v. *Edwards, supra, ante*, p. 256.

[32] *Huning* v. *Ferrers* (1711) Gilb.Eq. 85; *East India Co.* v. *Vincent* (1740) 2 Atk. 83; *Stiles* v. *Cowper* (1748) 3 Atk. 692; *Jackson* v. *Cator* (1800) 5 Ves. 688 (tenant making alterations to landlord's knowledge).

understanding, to the knowledge of a canal owner, that he could use canal water to generate steam[33]; or where the defendants constructed a sewer over a strip of the plaintiff's land, and the plaintiff failed to complain until the construction of the sewer was complete[34]; or where a landowner subdivides his land in reliance on a right of way being granted by a neighbour (the local authority) through a specified outlet[35]; or where one party with the knowledge and consent of his neighbour, builds so as to encroach on the neighbour's land.[36] The doctrine does not, however, apply where the claimant does acts on his own land which are not done in the expectation of acquiring rights over the land of another.[37]

The most extreme cases are those where a non-owner, in reliance upon a gratuitous promise of a gift of the land, has built on the land. Clearly, it would be wrong to allow him to be turned out. The court has on occasion ordered a conveyance of the land.[38] On other occasions, the non-owner has been given a lien on the land for his expenditure[39]; or compensation for the value of the improvements[40]; or awarded the improved land on payment of a reasonable price for the site[41]; or has been given protection from eviction without obtaining a proprietary interest in the land.[42]

The leading case is *Dillwyn* v. *Llewelyn*[43] where a father encouraged his son to build a house on the father's land, and signed a memorandum purporting to convey the land to the son; but it was not sealed. And the father's will left all his real estate upon certain trusts in favour of others.

The son spent some £14,000 in building a house on the land, with

---

[33] *Rochdale Canal Co.* v. *King* (1853) 16 Beav. 630; *Cotching* v. *Bassett* (1862) 32 Beav. 101.

[34] *Armstrong* v. *Sheppard & Short Ltd.* [1959] 2 Q.B. 384; *Ward* v. *Kirkland* [1967] Ch. 194.

[35] *Crabb* v. *Arun D.C.* [1976] Ch. 179. See also *Salvation Army Trustee Co. Ltd* v. *West Yorkshire Metropolitan County Council* (1981) 41 P. & C.R. 179.

[36] *Hopgood* v. *Brown* [1955] 1 W.L.R. 213; *Ives (E.R.) Investment Co.* v. *High* [1967] 2 Q.B. 379.

[37] *Western Fish Products Ltd.* v. *Penwith District Council* [1981] 2 All E.R. 204 (no estoppel where plaintiff spent money on own land relying on planning officer's assurance that planning permission would be granted; doctrine in any event not available against statutory body exercising statutory discretion or performing statutory duty; *Rootkin* v. *Kent County Council* [1981] 1 W.L.R. 1186).

[38] *Dillwyn* v. *Llewelyn* (1862) 4 De D.G. & J. 517; *Pascoe* v. *Turner* [1979] 1 W.L.R. 431, *post*, p. 862; *Thomas* v. *Thomas* [1956] N.Z.L.R. 785; *Chalmers* v. *Pardoe* [1963] 1 W.L.R. 677; *Raffaele* v. *Raffaele* [1962] W.A.R. 29; (1963) 79 L.Q.R. 238 (D. E. Allan).

[39] *Unity Joint Stock Mutual Banking Association* v. *King* (1858) 25 Beav. 72.

[40] *Raffaele* v. *Raffaele (supra)*.

[41] *Duke of Beaufort* v. *Patrick* (1853) 17 Beav. 60.

[42] *Jackson* v. *Cator* (1800) 5 Ves. 688; *Cotching* v. *Bassett* (1862) 32 Beav. 101; *Hopgood* v. *Brown* [1955] 1 W.L.R. 213; *Inwards* v. *Baker* [1965] 2 Q.B. 29.

[43] (1862) 4 De G.F. & J. 517; *Plimmer* v. *Wellington Corporation* (1884) 9 App.Cas. 699; *Ahmed Yar Khan* v. *Secretary of State for India* (1901) L.R. 28 I.R. 21.

his father's knowledge and approval. On the father's death, the House of Lords held that the son was entitled to a conveyance of the fee.

On its face, the decision is inconsistent with two basic rules, namely that a gratuitous promise is not enforceable, and that an incomplete gift will not be completed in favour of a volunteer.[44] Lord Westbury seemed to find consideration in the detrimental reliance of the son upon his father's promise. But detrimental reliance does not provide a consideration under English law. A solution based on estoppel may well have been appropriate, but estoppel was not mentioned by the House of Lords at any stage; the case was decided as one of law, not equity. Further, the solution is not just and equitable. There was no reason why the son should have a transfer of the land at the expense of the father's estate. Too much has been read into this case. It is even claimed now to be an illustration of the new doctrine of proprietary estoppel; though that phrase would have meant nothing to their Lordships.[45]

What is clear, however, is that there is a doctrine, based on encouragement and acquiescence, under which a court of equity will adjust the rights of the parties so as to do substantial justice between them. The doctrine is obviously not confined to cases of licences as currently understood.[46] Two early judicial formulations of the doctrine come from statements of Lord Kingsdown and Fry J. Lord Kingsdown, with the old cases of disappointed lessees in mind, explained the doctrine as follows[47]:

"If a man, under a verbal agreement with a landlord for a certain interest in land, or, what amounts to the same thing, under an expectation, created or encouraged by the landlord, that he shall have a certain interest, takes possession· of such land, with the consent of the landlord, and upon the face of such promise or expectation, with the knowledge of the landlord, and without objection by him, laid out money on the land, a Court of Equity will compel the landlord to give effect to such promise or expectation."

Fry J. in *Willmott* v. *Barber*[48] laid down the principle in more specific detail, in what have been called the "five probanda." He said:

"What, then, are the elements or requisites necessary to constitute fraud of that description? In the first place the plaintiff must

---

[44] See (1980) 96 L.Q.R. 534 at pp. 539–542 (S. Naresh).
[45] Dawson & Pearce, p. 34.
[46] As to whether it applies to property other than land, see *Western Fish Products Ltd.* v. *Penwith District Council* [1981] 2 All E.R. 204, at p. 218; *Moorgate Mercantile Co. Ltd.* v. *Twitchings* [1976] Q.B. 225, p. 242. *cf. Greenwood* v. *Bennett* [1973] 1 Q.B. 195; (1981) 40 C.L.J. 340 (P. Matthews); Torts (Interference with Goods) Act 1977, s.6(1).
[47] *Ramsden* v. *Dyson* (1866) L.R. 1 H.L. 129 at p. 170.
[48] (1880) 15 Ch.D. 96 at pp. 105–106. See *post*, p. 854.

have made a mistake as to his legal rights.[49] Secondly, the plaintiff must have expended some money or must have done some act (not necessarily upon the defendant's land) on the faith of his mistaken belief. Thirdly, the defendant, the possessor of the legal right, must know of the existence of his own right which is inconsistent with the right claimed by the plaintiff. If he does not know of it he is in the same position as the plaintiff, and the doctrine of acquiescence is founded upon conduct with a knowledge of your legal rights. Fourthly, the defendant, the possessor of the legal right, must know of the plaintiff's mistaken belief to his rights. If he does not, there is nothing which calls upon him to assert his own rights. Lastly, the defendant, the possessor of the legal right, must have encouraged the plaintiff in his expenditure of money or in the other acts which he has done, either directly or by abstaining from asserting his legal right.[50] Where all these elements exist, there is fraud of such a nature as will entitle the Court to restrain the possessor of the legal right from exercising it, but, in my judgment, nothing short of this will do."

Spencer Bower[51] emphasises that the doctrine is distinct from estoppel by representation and promissory estoppel, and warns against the danger of allowing this doctrine to merge with estoppel proper; and, for that reason, his editor declines to use the modern term "proprietary estoppel," which causes this confusion. Scarman L.J., however, in *Crabb* v. *Arun District Council*,[52] did not find helpful "the distinction between promissory and proprietary estoppel." Similarly, Robert Goff J. has doubted whether proprietary estoppel was a separate category,[53] and Purchas L.J. has said that not much importance is to be attached to different types of estoppel.[54]

Modern judicial formulations of the doctrine have moved away from the inflexibility of the "five probanda." In *Taylors Fashions Ltd.* v. *Liverpool Victoria Trustees Co. Ltd.*,[55] Oliver J. held that, contrary to Fry J.'s requirements, estoppel by acquiescence was not restricted to cases where the defendant knew his rights. There were many circumstances of estoppel, and it was not possible to lay down strict and

---

[49] The claim failed on this ground in *Att.-Gen. of Hong Kong* v. *Humphreys Estate (Queen's Gardens) Ltd.* [1987] A.C. 114 (expenditure in reliance upon "subject to contract" agreement which was never finalised).

[50] See *Brinnand* v. *Ewens* (1987) 19 H.L.R. 415 (tenant had no claim for voluntary improvements where no reliance on any interest and no encouragement or acquiescence by landlord).

[51] *The Law Relating to Estoppel by Representation* (3rd ed.), p. 289.

[52] [1976] Ch. 179 at p. 193.

[53] *Amalgamated Investment and Property Co. Ltd. (in liquidation)* v. *Texas Commerce International Bank Ltd.* [1982] Q.B. 84 at p. 103; *cf.* (1981) 97 L.Q.R. 513.

[54] *Troop* v. *Gibson* [1986] 1 E.G.L.R. 1 at p. 5 (distinguishing, however, estoppel by representation and by convention). *Cf.* [1988] Conv. 346 (P. T. Evans).

[55] [1981] 2 W.L.R. 576; [1982] Q.B. 133n.; [1982] Conv. 450 (P. Jackson).

inflexible rules. The application of the *Ramsden* v. *Dyson*[56] principle "requires a very much broader approach which is directed to ascertaining whether, in particular individual circumstances, it would be unconscionable for a party to be permitted to deny that which, knowingly or unknowingly, he has allowed or encouraged another to assume to his detriment rather than to inquiring whether the circumstances can be fitted within the confines of some preconceived formula serving as a universal yardstick for every form of unconscionable behaviour."[57] "The inquiry which I have to make therefore . . . is simply whether, in all the circumstances of the case, it was unconscionable for the defendants to seek to take advantage of the mistake, which, at the material time, everybody shared. . . . "[58]

This broad approach was adopted in *Amalgamated Investment and Property Co. Ltd. (in liquidation)* v. *Texas Commerce International Bank Ltd.*,[59] where Robert Goff J. said that "Of all doctrines, equitable estoppel is surely one of the most flexible . . . it cannot be right to restrict [it] to certain defined categories."[60] Similarly, Lord Denning M.R., in the Court of Appeal, considered that:

> "The doctrine of estoppel is one of the most flexible and useful in the armoury of the law. But it has become overloaded with cases. . . . It has evolved during the last 150 years in a sequence of separate developments: proprietary estoppel, estoppel by representation of fact, estoppel by acquiescence, and promissory estoppel. At the same time it has been sought to be limited by a series of maxims: estoppel is only a rule of evidence; estoppel cannot give rise to a cause of action; estoppel cannot do away with the need for consideration; and so forth. All these can now be seen to merge into one general principle shorn of limitations. When the parties to a transaction proceed on the basis of an underlying assumption—either of fact or of law—whether due to misrepresentation or mistake makes no difference—on which they have conducted the dealings between them—neither of them will be allowed to go back on that assumption when it would be unfair or unjust to allow him to do so. If one of them does seek to go back on it, the courts will give the other such remedy as the equity of the case demands."[61]

It seems that we have moved away, in the context of licences at least,

---

[56] *Supra.*

[57] [1981] 2 W.L.R. 576 at p. 593. See also *Ives (E.R.) Investment Co.* v. *High* [1967] 2 Q.B. 379; *Shaw* v. *Applegate* [1977] 1 W.L.R. 970 at pp. 977–978, 980.

[58] *Ibid.* at p. 596. It was suggested that the "five probanda" might be necessary in a case of "standing by," where the defendant has done no positive act. The "five probanda" were, however, applied without comment in *Coombes* v. *Smith* [1986] 1 W.L.R. 808, *ante*, p. 851.

[59] [1982] Q.B. 84; *Pacol Ltd.* v. *Trade Lines Ltd.* [1982] 1 Lloyd's Rep. 456.

[60] *Ibid.* at p. 103.

[61] *Ibid.* at p. 122. See also *Att.-Gen. of Hong Kong* v. *Humphreys Estate (Queen's Gardens) Ltd.* [1987] A.C. 114; *Re Basham* [1986] 1 W.L.R. 1498.

from the basic rule that an estoppel is a shield and not a sword. The modern practice appears to be to find circumstances sufficient to create an estoppel. If an injunction suffices as the remedy, the estoppel operates in the traditional way as a shield and not a sword. But if something more is needed, like the grant to the licensee of a proprietary interest, then we call it a case of proprietary estoppel, and make use of the additional remedies. The constructive trust has even been called upon to fill in possible gaps in the estoppel doctrine.

In *Re Basham*[62] the plaintiff's mother married her stepfather in 1936 when the plaintiff was aged 15. The plaintiff lived with them until her marriage in 1941, helping to run the business without pay on the understanding that she would inherit from her stepfather. He dissuaded the plaintiff's husband from taking a job with a tied cottage, saying he would help them to get a house. After the mother's death in 1976, the plaintiff and her husband helped her stepfather in his house and garden, prepared his meals, bought carpets for the house, and paid solicitors for advice over a boundary dispute. The stepfather constantly assured the plaintiff that the house would be hers, but he died intestate. The plaintiff, who did not benefit under the intestacy, succeeded in her claim to the whole estate under the doctrine of proprietary estoppel. It was held that the doctrine was not confined to a case where the plaintiff's belief related to an existing right and to specific assets.[63] Where the belief related to a future right, a species of constructive trust arose. The doctrines of estoppel, mutual wills[64] and secret trusts[65] had a common theme, and thus reliance could be placed on cases such as *Re Cleaver*,[66] where an expectation of inheritance of non-specific assets gave rise to a constructive trust under the mutual wills doctrine. The proper remedy was an award of the entire estate, to satisfy the expectations encouraged by the deceased.

Clearly the plaintiff should have some remedy, however it is doubtful whether the introduction of the constructive trust is either necessary or desirable.[67] Under the new flexible approach to proprietary estoppel,[68] the plaintiff may succeed without a constructive trust. If

[62] [1986] 1 W.L.R. 1498.

[63] *cf. Layton* v. *Martin* (1986) 16 Fam. Law 212, where the deceased's assurances that he would provide for the plaintiff by will could not found a claim to proprietary estoppel, which arose only in connection with specific assets.

[64] *Ante*, p. 298.

[65] *Ante*, p. 140.

[66] [1981] 1 W.L.R. 939, *ante*, p. 299. If the analogy with the surviving testator in *Re Cleaver* is taken too far, a finding that the estopped party holds his estate on constructive trust seems to restrict the choice of discretionary remedies open to the court.

[67] See [1987] Conv. 211 (J. Martin); (1987) 46 C.L.J. 215 (D. Hayton); All E.R.Rev. 1987, p. 156 (P. J. Clarke) and p. 263 (C. H. Sherrin); (1988) 8 L.S. 92 at pp. 101 *et seq.* (M. Davey).

[68] *Supra.*

that is not so, the plaintiff should not succeed under estoppel but should look to other remedies.[69]

B. Conveyancing Problems Caused by Licences by Estoppel[70]

It seems to be clearly established that protection given to a licensee by estoppel will affect third parties. This is obvious enough in grants of proprietary interests in land under the doctrine of proprietary estoppel. And a licensee by estoppel, protected by an injunction only, is protected also against third parties, not being bona fide purchasers for value without notice.[71] This is to be contrasted with the case of contractual licensees and third parties, discussed above.[72] And it is wholly reasonable that a licensee by estoppel should be so protected. He has no other remedy.

It may be noted in passing that situations will occur in which an estoppel arises between the parties to a contractual licence.[73] We saw that this was so in *Errington* v. *Errington*[74] and in *Hardwick* v. *Johnson*.[75] In such circumstances, the licensee may rely either on the contract or on the estoppel. Where the issue is a claim for damages between the parties, he will rely on the former.[76] If the licensor has transferred the land to a third party, he may rely on the estoppel; as a right to protection based on estoppel is binding on third parties, whereas a contractual licence is not unless a constructive trust has arisen.[77]

Any decision to give to a licensee protection against third parties creates a conveyancing problem. Ideally, a conveyancing system should provide a purchaser with a documentary statement of the title and of all restrictions and limitations upon it. This is basically what the 1925 legislation attempted to do; requiring documentary proof of the location of the legal estate, and providing that most other interests were over-reachable or registrable. Similarly, the Land Registration Act 1925 attempted to provide a complete record within the Land Registry of matters by which the purchasers would be bound. But it is never possible to reach finality. The registered land system listed, as overriding interests, those interests which were to be binding on purchasers in spite of the absence of documentary evidence in the

---

[69] For example, under the Inheritance (Provision for Family and Dependants) Act 1975.
[70] See generally (1984) 100 L.Q.R. 376 (S. Moriarty).
[71] *Hopgood* v. *Brown* [1955] 1 W.L.R. 213. See also [1981] Conv. 212 (A. Briggs) and 347 (P. N. Todd); [1983] Conv. 50 (M. P. Thompson) and 285 (A. Briggs).
[72] A contractual licence does not bind third parties unless a constructive trust has arisen; *ante*, p. 841.
[73] See [1983] Conv. 50 (M. P. Thompson) and 285 (A. Briggs).
[74] [1952] 1 K.B. 290, *Foster* v. *Robinson* [1951] 1 K.B. 149.
[75] [1978] 1 W.L.R. p. 683.
[76] *Tanner* v. *Tanner* [1975] 1 W.L.R. 1346.
[77] *Ashburn Anstalt* v. *Arnold* [1988] 2 W.L.R. 706; *ante*, p. 845. See (1988) 51 M.L.R. 226 (J. Hill), suggesting that the position is unsatisfactory without clearer guidelines for distinguishing contractual and estoppel licences.

Registry.[78] Decisions, not satisfactory to all, have increased the number of such situations, both with registered[79] and unregistered[80] land. Some such situations are inevitable. The point here is that any new such situation increases the complications of conveyancing.

The discussion which follows is primarily concerned with estoppel licences, but also applies to contractual licences so far as they create proprietary interest, as where a constructive trust arises.[81]

(i) Unregistered Land. Non-Registrability of Licences. There is no provision in the Land Charges Act 1972 for the registration of licences. It was argued in *E.R. Ives Investment Ltd.* v. *High*[82] that a permanent licence of access over a driveway was void against a purchaser (with notice) of the land because it was not registered as an equitable easement. This is defined in the Land Charges Act 1972, section 2 as:

> "An easement, right or privilege over or affecting land created or arising on or after 1st January 1926, and being merely an equitable interest."

On their face, these words were capable of covering the situation. The Court of Appeal, however, applied a restrictive construction, limiting equitable easements to "a proprietary interest in land such as would before 1926 have been recognised as capable of being conveyed or created *at law*, but which since 1926 only takes effect as an equitable interest."[83] Thus, the interest was not registrable.

An important policy factor in favour of this decision is the fact that licences, arising as they do as a result of informal arrangements unsupervised by lawyers, will not, as a practical matter, be registered. To hold them registrable would thus result in their being void against purchasers.[84] This point has been made in the context of the provision for registration of a spouse's right of occupation as a Land Charge Class F.[85]

In unregistered land, therefore, estoppel licences and contractual licences giving rise to constructive trusts depend on the doctrine of notice.

[78] L.R.A. 1925, s.70.
[79] *Hodgson* v. *Marks* [1971] Ch. 892, (1973) 36 M.L.R. 25 (R. H. Maudsley); *Williams & Glyn's Bank Ltd.* v. *Boland* [1981] A.C. 487; [1980] Conv. 361 (J. Martin).
[80] *Ives (E.R.) Investment Ltd.* v. *High* [1967] 2 Q.B. 379 (equitable easement); *Poster* v. *Slough Estates* [1968] 1 W.L.R. 1515 (right of entry to remove a fixture on termination of lease); *Kingsnorth Finance Co.* v. *Tizard* [1986] 1 W.L.R. 783 (beneficial interest of wife who had contributed towards purchase price); *Shiloh Spinners Ltd.* v. *Harding* [1973] A.C. 691 (equitable right of entry on breach of covenant).
[81] *Ashburn Anstalt* v. *Arnold, supra.*
[82] [1967] 2 Q.B. 379 (on the Land Charges Act 1925). The right in question may have been an easement rather than a licence.
[83] *Ibid.* at p. 395; (1937) 53 L.Q.R. 259 (C. V. Davidge); (1948) 12 Conv.(N.S.) 202 (J. F. Garner).
[84] *Shiloh Spinners Ltd.* v. *Harding* [1973] A.C. 691 at p. 721; *per* Lord Wilberforce.
[85] *Ante*, p. 269.

(ii) Licences in Registered Land.[86] With registered land the doctrine of notice does not apply. Protection is given to interests which are within the definition of minor interests,[87] or overriding interests. In the case of a minor interest, the correct procedure[88] should be followed in order to obtain protection.

The definition of minor interests effectively covers all interests in land, other than those which are registered, or which are overriding interests. It includes, therefore, licences capable of binding third parties in unregistered land, such as estoppel licences or contractual licences giving rise to constructive trusts. One form of protection which might be appropriate is the caution.[89] A caution may be entered by "any person interested under any unregistered instrument, . . . or otherwise howsoever, in any land or charge registered in the name of any other person."[90] But, as explained above, the context in which these licences arise is rarely one in which steps are likely to be taken to obtain protection by any formal act.

More promising is the argument that a licence is an overriding interest within section 70(1)(*g*), which includes "The rights of every person in actual occupation of the land or in receipt of the rents and profits thereof, save where enquiry is made of such person and the rights are not disclosed." The rights of course must be property rights of some kind: that is to say "rights in reference to land which have the quality of being capable of enduring through different ownerships of the land according to normal conceptions of title to real property."[91]

The difficulties which arise where there is multiple occupation have already been examined in the context of the trust for sale.[92] No doubt the solutions adopted by the courts in those cases would be equally applicable in the present context. Thus a licensee who can establish an estoppel or a constructive trust can presumably claim an overriding interest within section 70(1)(*g*), even where the licensor is also in occupation.

If an estoppel licensee is not in occupation,[93] it seems that his right will fail against a third party unless protected by a caution. Similarly where a contractual licence gives rise to a constructive trust, although

---

[86] See generally [1983] Conv. 99 (T. Bailey).
[87] Defined L.R.A. 1925, s.3(xv).
[88] By Notice, Caution, or Restriction or Inhibition.
[89] See Ruoff and Roper, *Registered Conveyancing* (4th ed.), pp. 723–724; (1985) 44 C.L.J. 280 (M. P. Thompson).
[90] L.R.A. 1925, s.54(1).
[91] *National Provincial Bank Ltd.* v. *Hastings Car Mart* [1964] Ch. 665 at p. 690, *per* Russell L.J. See also (sub nom.). *National Provincial Bank Ltd.* v. *Ainsworth* [1965] A.C. 1175, at pp. 1226, 1228–1229, 1240, 1262.
[92] *Williams and Glyn's Bank Ltd.* v. *Boland* [1981] A.C. 487, [1980] Conv. 361 (J. Martin), (1980) 43 M.L.R. 692 (S. Freeman); *Hodgson* v. *Marks* [1971] Ch. 892 (bare trust); *ante*, p. 267.
[93] *e.g. Ives (E.R.) Investment Ltd.* v. *High* [1967] 2 Q.B. 379.

the party upon whom the constructive trust is initially imposed presumably could not rely on the absence of protection.[94]

(iii) Other Problems Arising Under the Doctrine of Proprietary Estoppel. (a) *Necessity for Litigation*. The problems here are the same as those met in the context of licences giving rise to a constructive trust. No one knows, before the court's decision, whether or not the licensee is entitled to have an interest in the land transferred to him, nor what the interest will be.[95] If the court orders the transfer of any interest, the documentation will be completed. Until then, a third party's position is as discussed above.

(b) *Application of Settled Land Act 1925*. A special problem arises where, as is quite usual in the case of licences within the family, the licensor has permitted the licensee to remain in the premises for the rest of his or her life. A positive proprietary solution in such a case may give a life interest to the licensee. This problem was first realized in *Bannister* v. *Bannister*,[96] a "constructive trust" case, but one which would probably have been analysed as an estoppel licence case if it had arisen a few years later.[97] In *Dodsworth* v. *Dodsworth*,[98] Russell L.J. noticed that the award of a life interest "will lead, by virtue of the provision of the Settled Land Act, to a greater and more extreme interest than was ever contemplated by the plaintiff and the defendants," giving the licensee the tenant for life's powers of sale and leasing. Lord Denning[99] had earlier suggested that the Settled Land Act would not be applicable, because there was no "instrument" which was capable of being the settlement. But, even if this is correct, it will still leave a most complex situation in which the beneficial interest is divided between life tenant and remainderman, and the legal estate in the remainderman, which is the type of situation which the Settled Land Acts were designed to avoid. It is noticeable that the recent cases have striven to avoid a solution which will attract the application of the Settled Land Act.[1]

C. Illustrations of the Application of Estoppel Doctrines

It remains now only to see how the doctrines have been applied in the cases. The solutions are varied; but the principle on which these are

---

[94] See *Lyus* v. *Prowsa Ltd.* [1982] 1 W.L.R. 1044, approved in *Ashburn Anstalt* v. *Arnold* [1988] 2 W.L.R. 706, *ante*, p. 845.

[95] As to the possibility of registering a pending land action, see *Haslemere Estates Ltd.* v. *Baker* [1982] 1 W.L.R. 1109.

[96] [1948] 2 All E.R. 133.

[97] (1977) 93 L.Q.R. 561 (J. A. Hornby).

[98] (1973) 228 E.G. 1115; *post*, p. 862.

[99] *Binions* v. *Evans* [1972] Ch. 359 at p. 366; see also Goff L.J.'s comments at (1977) 248 E.G. 947 at p. 949.

[1] *Griffiths* v. *Williams* (1977) 248 E.G. 947; *Pascoe* v. *Turner* [1979] 1 W.L.R. 431. See also Murphy and Clark, *The Family Home*, pp. 187–188; Law Commission Working Paper no. 94 (1985), *Trusts of Land*, pp. 73–75.

reached is not in doubt; "The court must look at all the circumstances in each case to decide in what way the equity can be satisfied."[2]

(i) Negative Protection

In *Inwards* v. *Baker*,[3] Mr. Baker's son, Jack, decided to build a bungalow upon land which he hoped to purchase, but the project proved to be too expensive. Mr. Baker suggested that Jack should put the bungalow on land already owned by him; that would save some expense, and Jack could build a bigger bungalow. This was done. Jack lived there some 40 years before the proceedings began in 1963. The father died in 1951, leaving a will dated 1922, under which the realty was left to trustees on trust for sale in favour of others.

The Court of Appeal held that the son should not be disturbed as long as he wished to stay. He did not, it will be noticed, obtain a conveyance, as did the son in *Dillwyn* v. *Llewelyn*.[4] This is the first case, as far as is known, in which a licence is expressly referred to as one "created by estoppel."[5] Negative protection only was considered, because "proprietary estoppel" had not yet been introduced into the licence cases. Thus, the son was protected; and was not awarded a windfall of a conveyance of the land without payment. It may be thought that a better solution would have been to order a conveyance of the land on payment of the site value; a remedy which, as we have seen, is available to the court.[6]

(ii) Proprietary Remedies. We have seen that a coveyance of the land was ordered, without compensation, in *Dillwyn* v. *Llewelyn*.[7]

In *Plimmer* v. *Wellington Corporation*[8]; the question was whether Plimmer, a licensee, had "any estate or interest in" a jetty in Wellington, New Zealand, so as to entitle him to compensation under the Public Works Loan Act 1882. Plimmer had obtained permission of the Crown to moor an old hulk on the foreshore of Wellington Bay, and to use it as a wharf and store. The level of the ground rose after an earthquake, and Plimmer added a jetty; and, later, at the request of the Provincial Government, he extended it. When the Government took over the jetty under statutory powers, Plimmer claimed compensation under the statute. The Privy Council applied Lord Kingsdown's principle, and awarded the compensation.

[2] *Plimmer* v. *Wellington Corporation* (1884) 9 App.Cas. 699 at p. 714; *Chalmers* v. *Pardoe* [1973] 1 W.L.R. 677 at p. 682; *Ives (E.R.) Investment Ltd.* v. *High* [1967] 2 Q.B. 379 at p. 395; *Pascoe* v. *Turner* [1979] 1 W.L.R. 431 at p. 437.
[3] [1965] 2 Q.B. 29; *Hopgood* v. *Brown* [1955] 1 W.L.R. 213; *Jones* v. *Jones* [1977] 1 W.L.R. 438.
[4] (1862) 4 De G.F. & J. 517.
[5] By Danckwerts L.J. at p. 38.
[6] *Duke of Beaufort* v. *Patrick* (1853) 17 Beav. 60.
[7] (1862) 4 De G.F. & J. 517.
[8] (1884) 9 App.Cas. 699.

Similarly, incorporeal interests have been awarded, as in *Crabb* v. *Arun District Council*,[9] where the defendant was estopped by its conduct from denying the plaintiff a right of way.

Perhaps the most extreme of the cases on proprietary estoppel is *Pascoe* v. *Turner*.[10]

> The plaintiff and defendant lived together in the plaintiff's home. Later the plaintiff purchased another house and the couple moved in. He told the defendant that the house was hers and everything in it. In reliance on this gratuitous promise, she expended, to the plaintiff's knowledge, her own money on repairs, improvements and redecoration, and also on furniture. Later, when the relationship ended, the plaintiff gave the defendant two month's notice to determine the licence. The Court of Appeal held that the defendant occupied the house as a licensee. There was no valid declaration of trust of the house, but an estoppel operated in her favour. Cumming-Bruce L.J. sought to find the way in which "the equity can here be satisfied." "Should the equity be satisfied by a licence to the defendant to occupy the house for her lifetime, or should there be a transfer to her of the fee simple?"[11] And, even though the licensee never sought to establish that she had spent more money on the house than she would have done had she believed that she only had a licence to live there for her lifetime, the court felt that protection for her lifetime was insecure, and awarded a conveyance of the house.

This resulted in an extraordinary windfall for the licensee. Other cases have gone more deeply into the detailed circumstances in order to find a solution which avoids injustice to either party, and is specially adjusted to meet the circumstances.

> In *Dodsworth* v. *Dodsworth*,[12] the plaintiff's brother and his wife, the defendants, returned to England from Australia and were looking for a home. The plaintiff persuaded them to join her and live in her bungalow. The defendants spent over £700 on improvements in the expectation, induced by the plaintiff, that the defendants would be able to live in the bungalow as their home for as long as they wished to do so. The judge in the court below held that the defendants should be allowed to stay in occupation unless and until they were compensated for their outlay on improvements to the bungalow. By the time of the appeal hearing the plaintiff had died. The defendants argued that they should be allowed to remain for the rest of their lives; but this, the court thought, would put them in the

---

[9] [1976] Ch. 179.
[10] [1979] 1 W.L.R. 431. But see (1984) 100 L.Q.R. 376 (S. Moriarty), suggesting that the result gave effect to the intentions of the parties; *cf.* [1986] Conv. 406 (M. P. Thompson). See also *Re Basham* [1986] 1 W.L.R. 1498, *ante*, p. 856, where an award of the entire estate made good the expectations encouraged by the deceased.
[11] *Ibid.* at p. 438.
[12] (1973) 228 E.G. 1115.

position of being joint tenants for life under the Settled Land Act, and sought a solution which would avoid that situation. They decided that the equity should be satisfied by securing the defendants' occupation until the expenditure had been reimbursed which, as is pointed out, was the effect of the judge's order or declaration. An alternative solution could have been that the defendants should become entitled to the bungalow on payment of a reasonable purchase price after deducting the amount expended on the improvements.

In *Griffiths* v. *Williams*[13] a daughter had looked after her mother in her latter years and expended her own money on repairs and improvements to the house. She did so primarily for the care of her mother, but also in the belief that she would be entitled to live in the house for the rest of her life. However, the mother left the house by will to another relative. The Court of Appeal held that the daughter should be protected under the doctrine of estoppel. The award of a life interest would not be appropriate, because that might create a settlement under the Settled Land Act 1925. The most appropriate solution was for the daughter to receive a lease determinable upon her death, with no power to assign, and at a nominal rent which did not give her protection under the Rent Act. The case is a good example of the wide jurisdiction which the court exercises and also of a solution reached without introducing the complications which follow from the award of a life interest in the land.[14]

6. SUMMARY

The history of licences is a remarkable story of false trails and confused thoughts. In the early days, the common law would accord no protection to a licensee, unless some interest in property had been conveyed to him. Relics of this view are manifested in the majority opinion in *Hurst's* case[15]—saying that the passage of the Judicature Act allowed an (equitable) property interest to be granted by virtue of the contract. And relics of the old doctrine continued up to 1944.[16] The turning point in the case of contractual licences came with the decision in the *Winter Garden*[17] case to the effect that the rights of the parties were dependent on the proper construction of the contract; and the court's willingness to grant an injunction to protect it.

But litigation on the subject of licences moved from the commercial

---

[13] (1977) 248 E.G. 947. *Cf. Cadman* v. *Bell* [1988] E.G.C.S. 139, where an irrevocable licence for life was the solution.
[14] For another solution, see Murphy and Clark, *The Family Home*, p. 119.
[15] [1915] 1 K.B. 1.
[16] *Thompson* v. *Park* [1944] K.B. 408.
[17] *Winter Garden Theatre (London) Ltd.* v. *Millennium Productions Ltd.* [1948] A.C. 173.

sphere to that of the family. There were clear injustices in cases in which husbands who owned the family home could desert their wives and treat them as unprotected licensees. The "deserted wife's licence" sprang up quickly in the 1950s to deal with this situation; and expired even more quickly in 1965,[18] to be replaced by the unsatisfactory provisions for registration in the Matrimonial Homes Act 1967.[19]

The doctrine of estoppel was also called into play to protect a licensee. Protection at first was negative; until the doctrine of encouragement and acquiescence established itself as a doctrine which enabled the court to provide positive proprietary remedies in estoppel licence cases. The courts adopted the new jurisdiction rapidly; and there is no point now in enquiring whether this was justified on authority.

So the court now has the powers it needs to reach the just solution in these cases; with a constructive trust as a back-up.[20] The conveyancing problems which are thereby created are considerable, as has been discussed. The truth is that proprietary estoppel and constructive trusts will create proprietary interests which were not included in the scheme of the 1925 legislation; and which neither comply with the usual rules for creation, nor fit in with the registration system of the Land Charges Act 1972 or the Land Registration Act 1925; and which are dependent for their very existence on the exercise of a discretion by the court which deals with the case. This is all in the course of the advancement of justice. It is to be hoped that it is not so complex and uncertain as to make the system unworkable.

---

[18] *National Provincial Bank Ltd.* v. *Ainsworth* [1965] A.C. 1175.
[19] Now the Act of 1983.
[20] See *Ashburn Anstalt* v. *Arnold* [1988] 2 W.L.R. 706, *ante*, p. 845.

CHAPTER 28

EQUITABLE INTERESTS AND EQUITIES: A PROBLEM OF PRIORITIES

1. INTRODUCTION

THIS difficult question has been left until the end of the book, partly because it enables us to tie together certain aspects of equity which have hitherto been considered separately, and partly because the nature of the question can best be understood after the width of manner of equitable intervention has been appreciated.

It is necessary to appreciate the various uses of the phrase "equitable interests."

A. Equitable Interests in Land and Personalty

The property legislation of 1925 uses the phrase in the context of interests *in* land; thus the tenant for life of land has an equitable interest, namely, an equitable tenancy for life, *in* the land. All successive interests in land, other than leasehold estates, can now, as has been seen,[1] exist only in equity. But the terminology of "equitable interests" is also appropriate to personalty, and it is common usage to speak of such interests in relation, for example, to life interests in trust funds.[2] The phrase is not appropriate, however, to rights under a will in the course of being administered; here equity recognises in the beneficiaries only a right that the estate be properly administered.[3]

B. Equitable Interests over Land

The phrase also occurs in the context of rights *over* land. Some rights over the land of another have the characteristic that they can be made

[1] *Ante*, p. 38.
[2] *e.g.* L.P.A. 1925, s.53(1)(*c*), *ante*, p. 81; *Cave* v. *Cave* (1880) 15 Ch.D. 639. Contrast the position taken in Ireland; *Re ffrench's Estate* (1887) 21 L.R. Ir. 283; (1957) 21 Conv. (N.S.) 198–199 (V. T. H. Delaney).
[3] *Ante*, p. 59.

865

to benefit and burden land in the hands of successors in title to the creators of the rights. This is true of certain legal interests, such as easements and profits. It is also true of certain "equitable interests," such as restrictive covenants, equitable mortgages, vendors' liens, equitable easements and estate contracts, and some of these can be bought and sold in the market place.[4] The manner in which they can be made to bind land will of course vary with the equitable or legal interests in question. But, where the interest is an equitable interest only, it will be defeated if the land gets into the hands of a bona fide purchaser of a legal estate for value without notice, actual or constructive, of the equitable interest.[5] The ascertainment of the question whether or not the purchaser had constructive notice caused a lot of difficulties prior to 1925. The Land Charges Act 1925[6] produced a system for the registration of certain interests over unregistered land (mostly, but not exclusively, equitable interests) and provided that registration should constitute notice to all the world. There is therefore no question, in the cases of registered equitable interests, of the appearance of a bona fide purchaser of a legal estate for value without notice. Conversely, a registrable, but unregistered equitable interest is void against a purchaser of the land, even if he has actual notice of it.[7]

Notice is not the *cause* of equitable interests being able to bind the land. A right does not become binding on third parties *because* the third party has notice or even because the right may have been registered. Notice or registration may be one essential factor in enabling the rights to be binding on third parties. The reason why they are so binding is that equity has decided to give this status to them. The characteristics which are influential in leading to this status are definability, identifiability and stability.[8] These characteristics must be possessed by an "equitable interest" respecting the land of another if it is to bind the land in the hands of successors. The rights which so qualify are well known; and, though the courts have not closed the door to the possibility of new ones emerging,[9] a new right of this type is reluctantly admitted, especially if its admission would conflict with the principle that equitable interests in land should either be over-reachable or registrable; otherwise the binding effect of such interests in unregistered land will be dependent on the doctrine of notice, and all

---

[4] See (1955) 19 Conv. (N.S.) 343 (F. R. Crane) for a full discussion.
[5] *Ante*, p. 33.
[6] Now the Act of 1972.
[7] *Hollington Bros.* v. *Rhodes* [1925] 2 All E.R. 578n; *Midland Bank Trust Co. Ltd.* v. *Green* [1981] A.C. 513.
[8] See particularly *National Provincial Bank Ltd.* v. *Ainsworth* [1965] A.C. 1175, at pp. 1247–1248, *per* Lord Wilberforce, and at p. 1237, *per* Lord Upjohn.
[9] See Lord Upjohn in *National Provincial Bank Ltd.* v. *Ainsworth, supra,* at p. 1239; *Pennine Raceway Ltd.* v. *Kirklees Metropolitan Council* [1983] Q.B. 382 at p. 392. The contractual licence may be such a case; *ante*, pp. 841 *et seq. Cf.* L.P.A. 1925, s.4(1).

the problems return of deciding whether or not a purchaser has notice of the interest.

(i) **Unregistered Land.** It might be thought that the introduction in 1925 of a system of registration of land charges would make the courts more willing to accept new rights as being interests which will be binding as equitable proprietary interests on third parties. Insofar as registration is notice to all the world,[10] and failure to register a registrable interest makes it void against a purchaser,[11] there is no problem of the bona fide purchaser of the legal estate for value without notice. But many of the rights under consideration are informal arrangements arising without the assistance of professional advice, and in ignorance, therefore, of the statutory provisions concerning registration. To make such rights registrable may therefore play into the hands of the unscrupulous well-informed at the expense of the innocent ignorant.

We have seen that the general pattern of the 1925 legislation envisaged that all equitable interests should be registrable or over-reachable. That would dispose once and for all of the problem of notice relating to equitable interests. But the system was not foolproof, and equitable interests and equities have been held to exist, and to be binding on third parties, including purchasers with actual or constructive notice; for example, an equitable co-owner's right upon a sale by a sole trustee[12]; a right to enter land to remove fixtures;[13] an equitable right of re-entry[14]; and some of the licence cases could be said to fit into this category[15]; but, whether or not a licence is correctly described as an equitable *interest*, is a matter discussed below. Some of these rights might have been held to be within the definition of an equitable easement (Class D(iii)). That is defined as[16] an easement, right or privilege over or affecting land created or arising on or after January 1, 1926, and being merely an equitable interest. But a narrow construction has been put on this definition,[17] restricting it to "a proprietary interest in land such as would before 1926 have been recognized as

[10] L.P.A. 1925, s.198(1).
[11] L.C.A. 1972, s.4(6). As respects a land charge Class D or an estate contract the land charge is void only in favour of a purchaser of a legal estate for money or money's worth. This includes an equitable easement (Class D(iii)).
[12] *Kingsnorth Finance Co. Ltd.* v. *Tizard* [1986] 1 W.L.R. 783; *ante*, p. 266.
[13] *Poster* v. *Slough Estates Ltd.* [1969] 1 Ch. 495. A right of pre-emption, on the other hand, although expressly included in the statutory definition of "estate contract," has been held not to be an interest in land until the owner of the land decides to sell; *Pritchard* v. *Briggs* [1980] Ch. 338, [1980] Conv. 433 (J. Martin); *Kling* v. *Keston Properties Ltd.* (1985) 49 P. & C.R. 212.
[14] *Shiloh Spinners Ltd.* v. *Harding* [1973] A.C. 691.
[15] *Ante*, p. 841.
[16] L.C.A. 1972, s.2(5).
[17] *Ives (E.R.) Investment Ltd.* v. *High* [1967] 2 Q.B. 379; *Shiloh Spinners Ltd.* v. *Harding, supra*; *Poster* v. *Slough Estates Ltd.* [1969] 1 Ch. 495. See (1937) 53 L.Q.R. 259 (C. V. Davidge); (1956) 14 C.L.J. 255–256 (H. W. R. Wade).

capable of being conveyed or created *at law* but which since 1926 only takes effect as an equitable interest," thus excluding equities arising out of estoppel and acquiescence, and out of the principle that "he who takes the benefit must accept the burden," and possibly even equitable easements which fail to qualify as legal interests by reason of their informal creation. Such interests may thus be binding on third parties regardless of registration; their effect depends on notice, and the old problem of the bona fide purchaser revives.

(ii) Registered Land. The situation is entirely different with registered land. The distinction between legal and equitable interests is no longer significant; nor is notice relevant.[18] Interests in land, apart from those freehold and long leasehold estates[19] which entitle the owner to be registered as proprietor, are binding on purchasers only if they are minor interests and protected in the proper manner,[20] or are overriding interests.[21]

As with unregistered land, there are many situations where undocumented interests can bind purchasers. This has arisen, as has been seen, because of a wide construction of section 70(1)(g), which includes, among the list of overriding interests, "the rights of every person in actual occupation of the land or in receipt of the rents and profits thereof, save where enquiry is made of such person and the rights are not disclosed." In *Hodgson* v. *Marks*,[22] a fraudulent lodger of Mrs. Hodgson became the registered proprietor of a house upon transfer by Mrs. Hodgson. He was held to hold the house on resulting trust for Mrs. Hodgson. The interest of Mrs. Hodgson, an equitable fee simple, was not over-reachable on a sale.[22a] It was held to be an overriding interest under section 70(1)(g), and binding on a bona fide purchaser. Mrs. Hodgson could presumably have avoided all the trouble by registering a caution. Similarly, a wife who had contributed to the purchase of a house which was registered in her husband's name alone was held to have an overriding interest under this provision.[23] Again, as has been seen, many types of licences to occupy land have

---

[18] *Williams & Glyn's Bank Ltd.* v. *Boland* [1981] A.C. 487 at p. 504 (*per* Lord Wilberforce); *cf. Peffer* v. *Rigg* [1977] 1 W.L.R. 285, [1978] Conv. 52 (J. Martin); *Lyus* v. *Prowsa* [1982] 1 W.L.R. 1044.

[19] Even a substantively registered leasehold estate should be protected by a notice on the freehold register if it is to bind a purchaser of the freehold estate. Usually, however, it will be overriding under s.70(1)(g), discussed below.

[20] L.R.A. 1925, Part IV. It seems that interests which in unregistered land depend on the doctrine of notice can only be protected by a caution in registered land; *Poster* v. *Slough Estates Ltd.* [1969] 1 Ch. 495.

[21] L.R.A. s.70(1). These interests must be "subsisting in reference" to the land.

[22] [1971] Ch. 892.

[22a] The Law Commission recommends that a bare trust should be overreachable; Working Paper 106 (1988), *Trusts of Land, Overreaching*, pp. 16–17. It is further recommended, however, that overreaching should not operate without the consent of an occupying beneficiary.

[23] *Williams & Glyn's Bank Ltd.* v. *Boland* [1981] A.C. 487, [1980] Conv. 361 (J. Martin).

been held to be binding on third parties[24]; perhaps on the principle of estoppel; or by finding a constructive trust in favour of the licensee[25]; or as it may be held in the future, because the licensee has an overriding interest. Again, the licensee could presumably protect himself by registering a caution.

These are all cases where the courts have felt that the victim of some misfortune has required protection. Protection is given at the expense of the smooth and efficient working of the system of registered conveyancing. That point was, of course, put to the court in *Hodgson* v. *Marks*[26] and in *Boland*,[27] but was not in either situation thought to be decisive.[28]

C. Personalty

Covenants affecting the use of personalty do not constitute "equitable interests" in the sense of binding the personalty in the hands of third parties; the fact that a purchaser of a chattel has notice of an undertaking in respect of the user of the chattel is not relevant so far as property law is concerned.[29]

On the other hand, a contract to sell a specific chattel, or to pay a debt out of specific property segregated by the debtor for that purpose, is capable of creating an equitable interest in personalty in favour of the purchaser or the creditor. It will do so if the court will grant specific performance of the contract.[30] This situation is similar to, but less common than, the parallel cases of contracts for the sale of land or agreements to lease or to mortgage. It should not be thought, however, that the availability of specific performance necessarily connotes the creation of an equitable interest. This will be so only if the contract is for the creation or transfer of a proprietary interest and not, for example, if it is merely for the grant of a licence.[31]

D. Equities

There are, however, a number of situations in which equity will interfere to protect a party without according to that party any interest which can be described as an equitable interest. To all these various

---

[24] *Ante*, p. 841.
[25] See *Ashburn Anstalt* v. *Arnold* [1988] 2 W.L.R. 706; *ante*, p. 845.
[26] [1971] Ch. 892; (1973) 36 M.L.R. 25 (R. H. Maudsley).
[27] [1981] A.C. 487.
[28] See further *Third Report on Land Registration*, Law Com. No. 158 (1987), paras. 2.54–2.70.
[29] *Port Line Ltd.* v. *Ben Line Steamers Ltd.* [1958] 2 Q.B. 146; see (1966) 29 M.L.R. 657 (G. H. Treitel); (1982) 98 L.Q.R. 279 (S. Gardner); (1982) 41 C.L.J. 58 (A. Tettenborn).
[30] See *Swiss Bank Corporation* v. *Lloyds Bank Ltd.* [1979] Ch. 548; [1982] A.C. 584; where Browne-Wilkinson J. held that an undertaking to repay the loan out of an identifiable fund created an equitable charge in favour of the lender. The Court of Appeal and House of Lords reversed, holding that the undertaking did not have that effect in the particular case, but accepting the principle; [1982] A.C. at p. 595 (C.A.) and p. 613 (H.L.).
[31] *Verrall* v. *Great Yarmouth Borough Council* [1981] Q.B. 202, *ante*, p. 659.

situations, the phrase "an equity" has been applied.[32] Many such situations are long-established, and past precedent will show generally what relief the court is likely to give. Thus, it is common to speak of the equities of estoppel, of rescission, of rectification,[33] of undue influence, of consolidation of mortgages; to which may now be added the equity arising from the principle that "he who takes the benefit must accept the burden"[34]; and the list is not exclusive. But there are other situations, exemplified particularly in the cases of licences and of confidential information, in which the court finds an "equity" and exercises the broadest discretion in deciding what the remedy should be. An interesting article in the University of Tasmania Law Review[35] recognises this distinction, and calls the former "defined equities," to which certain consequences attach, and the latter "undefined equities," for which no obvious proprietary protection is available. The authors point to the flexibility and natural evolution of the law as among the advantages of allowing new developments of the law on these lines. And they point out that this is not a static situation; what may be an undefined equity today may become a defined equity tomorrow, and then develop into an equitable interest. But whether any labelling of emerging rights can help in guiding their development or in predicting its course is doubtful when they include such differing areas as estoppel (or acquiescence) and confidential information.[35a]

2. THE DISTINCTION BETWEEN EQUITABLE INTERESTS AND EQUITIES

A. The Effect of the Distinction

It sometimes happens, however, that "equities" are treated as a group in order to solve certain questions of priorities. These questions of priorities occur in relation not only to land but also to personalty,

[32] See generally Heydon, Gummow and Austin, *Cases and Materials on Equity and Trusts* (2nd ed.), pp. 55 *et seq.*; Meagher, Gummow and Lehane, *Equity, Doctrines and Remedies* (2nd ed.), pp. 111 *et seq.*; (1976) 40 Conv.(N.S.) 209 (A.R. Everton).

[33] Although there is some authority that a defendant against whom a right to rectify may be asserted holds the land on trust for the plaintiff. See *Leuty* v. *Hillas* (1858) 2 De G. & J. 110; *Craddock Brothers* v. *Hunt* [1923] 2 Ch. 136; *Blacklocks* v. *J.B. Developments (Godalming) Ltd.* [1982] Ch. 183; [1983] Conv. 361 at pp. 366 *et seq.* (D. G. Barnsley).

[34] *Tito* v. *Waddell (No. 2)* [1977] Ch. 106; *Halsall* v. *Brizell* [1957] Ch. 169; *Ives (E.R.) Investments Ltd.* v. *High* [1967] 2 Q.B. 379; *Poster* v. *Slough Estates Ltd.* [1969] 1 Ch. 495. It may be that a right of pre-emption should be added to the list. It was held not to be a proprietary interest in *Pritchard* v. *Briggs* [1980] Ch. 338, [1980] Conv. 433 (J. Martin), but the majority of the Court of Appeal held that it could become such an interest when the owner decided to sell. But its status in the meantime was described as a "mere spes." The majority view was applied in *Kling* v. *Keston Properties Ltd.* (1985) 49 P. & C.R. 212.

[35] (1979) U. of Tasmania L.R. 24, 115 (M. Neave and M. Weinberg).

[35a] See *Att.-Gen.* v. *Guardian Newspapers Ltd. (No. 2)* [1988] 3 W.L.R. 776, *ante*, p. 755, particularly on the question how far third parties are bound by the duty of confidence.

though the policy issues in respect of land and personalty may well be very different. For, as has been shown,[36] a general distinction exists between the bona fide purchaser of a legal, and of an equitable, interest in property. The purchaser of a legal estate, if he has no notice of equitable interests, takes free of them. The purchaser of an equitable interest does not; it appears that he does, however, take free of equities,[37] if he has no notice of them. The theory behind this distinction is that dispositions of equitable interests in property are always "innocent"[38]; this curious description, which proceeds by way of contrast with "tortious" conveyances at law,[39] implies that only what can be disposed of is disposed of. "If, therefore, a person seised[40] of an equitable estate (the legal estate being outstanding) makes an assurance by way of mortgage, or grants an annuity, and afterwards conveys the whole estate to a purchaser, he can grant to the purchaser that which he has, *viz.*, the estate subject to the mortgage or annuity, and no more."[41]

This view presupposes that the mortgage or annuity constitutes an "equitable interest." If the prior right were only, for instance, a right to rescission of a contract of sale, which is an "equity," a different result ensues. Such a right does not constitute a subtraction from the equitable interest then subsisting in the owner in equity, so that the equitable interest can still be disposed of *in toto*, despite the existence of the right of rescission.[42] The prima facie result is that, as between equitable interests, the prior in time prevails, but as between equitable interests and equities, equitable interests prevail.[43] Thus it appears to follow that priorities between prior equities and later equitable interests are generally determined by reference to their status as such; and an equity is a lesser right, at least to the extent that the principle of bona fide purchaser without notice prevails in such cases.[44] So for this purpose, it is necessary to draw a line between "equities" and "equitable interests," a task which has proved no easy one. The problem of priority is

---

[36] *Ante*, p. 33.
[37] Some "equities," however, may not bind even with notice, *post*, p. 875.
[38] *Phillips* v. *Phillips* (1862) 4 De G.F. & J. 208, at p. 215; (1955) 71 L.Q.R. 480 (R.E.M.); *post*, p. 874.
[39] M. & W., p. 1182.
[40] *i.e.* entitled to.
[41] *Phillips* v. *Phillips, supra*, at p. 215 *per* Lord Westbury L.C.
[42] See (1957) 21 Conv.(N.S.) 195 (V. T. H. Delaney), especially at p. 197.
[43] The conduct of the parties may also be relevant, however. In *Rice* v. *Rice* (1853) 2 Drew. 73, a contest between a prior vendor's lien and an equitable mortgage was resolved in favour of the latter due to the conduct of the former in indorsing the deeds with a note of receipt of the purchase money. Kindersley V.-C.'s judgment is classic, and shows that time is not the only factor; but the contest in the case seems to be between two equitable interests and not between an equity and an equitable interest. To what extent conduct other than notice is relevant in the latter situation has not been authoritatively determined.
[44] The position in registered land is dealt with below.

further complicated by the fact that there are several rules governing the matter, and that the relationship between these rules is not clear.[45]

B. The Determination of the Category

It is impossible to lay down a test to determine what is an equitable interest and what is an equity. An "equitable interest" suggests something of a proprietary nature, and most of the long-established equitable interests are capable of being bought and sold and devised by will.[45a] But that cannot be a precise test, because the benefit of a restrictive covenant cannot be bought and sold in the market place: at best, it can, unless annexed to the benefited land,[46] be transferred or not, according to the wish of the person entitled to the benefit of it, by an express assignment no later than the transfer of the land.

It is often assumed, especially in the context of licences, that a right acquires the characteristics of an equitable proprietary interest if it is held to be binding on third parties. But that cannot be right, for, as the illustrations below will show, most equities are "binding" on third parties other than a purchaser for value without notice. Apart from those situations the normal rule of priority in equity applies—and they take priority according to their order of creation.

Academic explanations of the characteristics that help to distinguish equities and equitable interests have from time to time been attempted, but have all run into difficulties. It has been said that it is "indeed difficult to find two writers who share the same view."[47] Professor Wade,[48] for instance, cautiously suggests that "The dividing line between equitable interests and mere equities is perhaps the discretionary character of the latter," but has to admit that "a purchaser's rights under an estate contract are surely more than a 'mere equity,' yet they rest on the court's willingness to award specific performance." Professor Crane puts it somewhat differently.[49] "The common feature of equitable interests appears to be that they are immediately enforceable against the land through the estate owner for the time being whereas until rectification even the court must act on the deed as it stands." But it is far from clear that the language of "immediately enforceable" interests is the most apt guide to its solution.

---

[45] See, for example, the rule in *Dearle* v. *Hall* (1828) 3 Russ. 1 (assignments or other successive dealings with equitable interests).

[45a] See also *Midland Bank plc.* v. *Pike* [1988] 2 All E.R. 434 at 436, classifying an equitable charge as a proprietary interest because it endures through changes of ownership of the property charged, binds the trustee in bankruptcy or successor in title of the chargor, and the benefit of the charge is transmissible.

[46] It seems that most restrictive covenants, entered into after 1925, will be held to be annexed to the benefited land; *Federated Homes Ltd.* v. *Mill Lodge Properties Ltd.* [1980] 1 W.L.R. 594.

[47] Pettit, p. 17.

[48] (1955) 13 C.L.J. 160–161; *cf.* (1955) 71 L.Q.R. 482 (R. E. Megarry).

[49] (1955) 19 Conv.(N.S.) 346.

It is submitted that, accepting the reservation about a restrictive covenant, the better test is whether the "interest" is capable of being bought and sold in the market place. There is no doubt that an interest under a trust is so capable, and also the interest of an equitable mortgagee, and that of a person holding under an agreement for a lease or a contract of sale. On the other hand, a right to rectification, or a right to consolidate mortgages, cannot be the subject of an independent sale.[50] This, it is submitted, is the basis of the distinction between an equitable interest and an equity. But it is not foolproof, and, in any case, it only helps in classification once it is established that the particular interest is or is not capable of independent sale.

Recent developments in the law of estoppel, especially in the context of licences, have added to the confusion. Estoppel is essentially an equity, entitling the victim to certain rights for his protection against the person on whose statements or promises he relied. And it is long established that estoppel by representation and promissory estoppel are capable of giving negative protection only.[51] But these limitations upon the effect of estoppel have been wholly changed by the development of the doctrine of proprietary estoppel.[52] We have seen that the courts, in cases where a licensee is protected under the doctrine of estoppel, now exercise a wide discretion in tailoring the remedy to meet the circumstances; sometimes giving negative protection only, and applying a wide variety of intermediate remedies up to the extreme of awarding a fee simple or life interest, or a form of incorporeal hereditament to the licensee. This does not mean, of course, that estoppel has become an "equitable interest"; it means rather that the remedy in a particular situation might be the creation of an equitable interest. The results of the court's intervention are in many cases impossible to foresee; thus these cases come within the category of the undefined equity. Further, the recent practice of deciding these cases by the discovery of a constructive trust in favour of the licensee has the effect also of creating equitable interests.[53]

C. Illustrations of Cases Testing the Distinction

The determination of the distinction between an equity and an equitable interest is commonly required in the cases where questions of priority are raised; and it is most often encountered in the context of

---

[50] Although they are transmissible along with the interest in question. See *Boots The Chemist Ltd.* v. *Street* (1983) 268 E.G. 817, relying on L.P.A. 1925, s.63(1). (Right to rectify lease passed to landlord's successor in title). See also *Stump* v. *Gaby* (1852) 2 De G.M. & G. 623; *Dickinson* v. *Burrell* (1866) L.R. 1 Eq. 337; *cf.* Snell (28th ed.), p. 26; *Gross* v. *Lewis Hillman Ltd.* [1970] Ch. 445 (right to rescind for fraudulent misrepresentation did not run with the land, distinguishing *Dickinson* v. *Burrell, supra*).

[51] See (1983) 42 C.L.J. 257 (M. P. Thompson).

[52] *Ante*, p. 850.

[53] *Ante*, p. 844.

mortgages, charges, and the various grounds for rescission and cancellation of transactions and deeds. For it is in this area that a competition for priority can easily arise. Other subjects that have been discussed obviously have relevance, though questions of priority may of course arise in other contexts also.

In *Rice* v. *Rice*,[54] a question of priorities arose between a vendor's lien for unpaid purchase money and a subsequent equitable mortgage without notice of the lien. Kindersley V.-C. held that, "as relates to the nature and quality of the two equitable interests abstractedly considered, they seem to me to stand on an equal footing"[55]; so that, prima facie, the prior in time prevailed.

In *Phillips* v. *Phillips*,[56] the question of priorities arose between an annuity of £20 p.a., charged upon land by the fee simple owner in equity, and a later settlement of the owner's equitable interest. The annuity was to take effect only at a future date; the settlement was made before the date when the annuity was to come into operation, and it contained no notice of the annuity. Lord Westbury held that the settlement was "diminished by the estate which had been previously granted to the annuitant."[57] Again, the prior in time prevailed.

In *Cave* v. *Cave*,[58] a sole trustee of trust funds used part of them to buy land in the name of his brother, who obtained loans on the security of the land from legal and equitable mortgagees who had no notice of the fraud. Fry J. held that the right of the beneficiaries under the trust to follow the money representing the trust assets into the land was an equitable interest of equal quality with the rights of the equitable mortgagees, so that, as between these two rights, the first in time, namely, the rights of the beneficiaries, prevailed; but the rights of the beneficiaries did not of course prevail against the legal mortgagee.

Not all the rights of beneficiaries under trusts are necessarily equitable "interests," however. Thus the right[59] of beneficiaries to have a sale by trustees to one of themselves set aside is probably only an "equity."

Certain other rights, such as a right to rescind a transaction for fraud or undue influence, a right to rectify or cancel documents, and a right of consolidation of mortgages,[60] have been established for some time as mere "equities." Modern discussion of these problems comes from a decision of the High Court of Australia.

---

[54] (1853) 2 Drew. 73, *ante*, p. 871, n. 43.
[55] *Ibid.* at p. 79.
[56] (1862) 4 De G.F. & J. 208.
[57] *Ibid.* at pp. 218–219.
[58] (1880) 15 Ch.D. 639. *Re Morgan* (1881) 18 Ch.D. 93.
[59] This right is discussed at length in *Holder* v. *Holder* [1968] Ch. 353, where, however, no subsequent equitable interest had arisen.
[60] *Garrard* v. *Frankel* (1862) 30 Beav. 445; *Bainbrigge* v. *Browne* (1881) 18 Ch.D. 188; *Harter* v. *Colman* (1882) 19 Ch.D. 630; *Smith* v. *Jones* [1954] 1 W.L.R. 1089. The last case is further mentioned, *post*, p. 876.

In *Latec Investments Ltd.* v. *Hotel Terrigal Pty. Ltd.*,[61] a mortgagee exercised a power of sale over mortgaged land by contriving a sale at a favourable price to one of its subsidiary companies. The mortgagor was held to have a right to have the sale set aside as against the mortgagee and the purchaser. But before the mortgagor had acted on this right, the purchaser had charged the land in favour of a third party who had no notice of the fraudulent character of the sale. The mortgagor's delay may in itself have been a sufficient reason for giving priority to the third party,[62] but the court went on to consider, independently of any issue of estoppel, the nature of the rights of the mortgagor and the third party. Both parties had rights only in equity. The third party had a right which was unquestionably an "equitable interest"; but what was the mortgagor's right? After exercise, it would yield to the mortgagor an equitable interest, namely, the equity of redemption in the land. But was the mortgagor's right an equitable interest before its exercise? Kitto and Menzies JJ. answered this question with a clear negative. In their view, the right was a mere equity, like the equity of rectification, and the matter was not affected either by the fact that an equitable interest would result from its exercise, or that the equity (before its exercise) was a devisable interest.[63] For some purposes, such as devisability, the mortgagor's right might have a proprietary flavour, but not for all purposes, and they held that it was not an equitable interest such as to attract the principle that the first in time prevailed. Accordingly, priority between the mortgagor's right and the third party's right lay, independently of estoppel, in the third party, since his right was an equitable interest and the mortgagor's right was, for this purpose, a mere equity.

D. The Distinction in Different Contexts

It is not possible to draw clear distinctions in the use of terminology in this area of equity. Rather, it is preferable to bear in mind on all occasions why a classification has to be made. We have seen that the High Court of Australia felt able to accept that an equitable right might constitute an equitable interest for one purpose, *e.g.* devisability, but not for another, *e.g.* priority. This approach points to the only way to a breakdown of the general problem into manageable components. There is no reason why equitable rights should have to be classified in

---

[61] (1965) 113 C.L.R. 265. For a critical view, see Jackson, *Principles of Property Law*, pp. 75–77; (1979) U. of Tasmania L.R. 24, 115 (M. Neave and M. Weinberg).

[62] *Ibid.* at p. 276 *per* Kitto J.; *cf. Rice* v. *Rice*, *ante*, p. 874. See also *Re King's Settlement* [1931] 2 Ch. 294.

[63] *Stump* v. *Gaby* (1852) 2 De G.M. & G. 623; *cf. Dickinson* v. *Burrell* (1866) L.R. 1 Eq. 337. Taylor J. took the view that these cases established the mortgagor's right as an equitable interest, apparently for all purposes, but agreed with Kitto and Menzies JJ. in the result since the interest was, in the case before him, subject to an "impediment to title" which the court would not remove: see at p. 286. There is more of linguistics than of substance in this difference of opinion.

the same way for all purposes.[64] Policy considerations are bound to vary in different areas of law, and it would seem less productive of anomalies to contemplate different solutions of the problem—"equity or equitable interest"—in different areas of the law than to insist, despite the obvious objections, that there must be one classification for all purposes. This general approach is clearly shown in the recent developments of estoppel. It seems that, in the licensee cases, an estoppel may create an equity or an equitable interest; the choice being dependent upon the policy considerations applicable to ascertaining the most suitable solution on the facts of the particular case.

By accepting this explanation, it is easier to deal with the difficulties of rectification referred to by Lord Upjohn in *Smith* v. *Jones*[65] and again in *National Provincial Bank Ltd.* v. *Ainsworth*.[66] In the latter case he said, "I myself cannot see how it is possible for a 'mere equity' to bind a purchaser unless such an equity is ancillary to or dependent upon an equitable estate or interest in the land."[67] This remark, in its context, is closely related to the question of which, if any, non-registrable interests are at all capable of binding land in the hands of successors in title with notice of them. This is a question of the utmost importance, because outstanding equities and equitable interests, if not capable of protection by registration, can play havoc with conveyancing practice. But this factor has been treated in some recent cases as subsidiary to that of protecting innocent people in the occupation of their home.[68] The issue appears differently when no question of registrability arises, as for example, in relation to chattels.[69] Here it may not be necessary to draw lines between kinds of competing equitable rights so strictly. For instance, a problem in priorities could arise between a party entitled under a non-registrable charge and a party entitled to rescission. In dealing with this sort of problem, it may be preferable to weigh the conduct of each of the parties in a more detailed manner than would be possible if the inquiry were restricted according to lines predetermined by a technical status attaching to the rights in question.

The position of mere equities in registered land has received little attention. Depending upon the context, such rights are presumably capable of being minor interests.[70] A question which recently arose was whether the right to rectification could be an overriding interest under section 70(1)(g) of the Land Registration Act 1925 when the

---

[64] As with the *in rem/in personam* classification discussed in Chap. 1.

[65] [1954] 1 W.L.R. 1089. *Cf. Westminster Bank* v. *Lee* [1956] Ch. 7.

[66] *Ante*, p. 269.

[67] [1965] A.C. 1175 at p. 1238.

[68] *Hodgson* v. *Marks* [1971] Ch. 892; *Williams & Glyn's Bank Ltd.* v. *Boland* [1981] A.C. 487.

[69] Difficult problems arise where chattels are affixed to land, see (1963) 27 Conv.(N.S.) 30 *et seq.* (A. G. Guest and J. F. Lever); and *cf. Poster* v. *Slough Estates Ltd.* [1968] 1 W.L.R. 1515 at pp. 1520–1521, *per* Cross J.

[70] L.R.A. 1925, s.3(xv).

claimant was in actual occupation. In *Blacklocks* v. *J.B. Developments (Godalming) Ltd.*[71] V contracted to sell part of some land to P in 1968. By common mistake, the plans included land not intended to be sold, as to which P was registered as proprietor. Neither party realised the mistake, and V continued in occupation of the disputed land. In 1972 P sold to the defendant, against whom V successfully claimed rectification. Applying Lord Upjohn's principle in *National Provincial Bank Ltd.* v. *Ainsworth*,[72] the right to rectify,[73] although often described as a mere equity, was ancillary to or dependent upon an equitable estate or interest in the land. It was capable of enduring through different ownerships of the land, and was accordingly of such a nature as to qualify as an overriding interest under section 70(1)(*g*) when accompanied by actual occupation. This decision deals with the position as against a subsequent registered proprietor, and not with the question of priorities as between competing equities and equitable interests. As the legislation is silent upon the latter, presumably the equitable principles applicable in unregistered land apply here also.[74]

3. Conclusion

It is suggested, then, that the classification of the various equitable rights discussed in this and in earlier parts of this book is not of itself a matter of crucial or primary importance. It is certainly necessary to know that certain equitable rights constitute equitable interests; for certain definite consequences[75] flow from that status. But the status is rather one of attribution for a purpose than of conceptual analysis. The same result could be obtained jurisprudentially by proceeding straight from the equitable right in question to the consequence, without using the intermediate terminology. Similarly with "mere equities"; consequences may also flow from a decision to treat a right as a "mere equity."[76] But, again, the statement of the consequences would be no more difficult and might be easier without reference to jurisprudential categories. Indeed the width and variety of the contributions of equity to English law are such that it might be surprising if they could be parcelled up and labelled in neat and precise categories.

---

[71] [1982] Ch. 183; criticised [1983] Conv. 361 (D. G. Barnsley).

[72] [1965] A.C. 1175, *ante*, p. 876.

[73] The judgment might be regarded as ambiguous on the point whether the right in question was the right to rectify the documents or the right to rectify the registered title. It is difficult to see why rectification in the latter sense needs to be an overriding interest (see L.R.A. 1925, s.82). See the editorial notes in [1983] Conv. pp. 169–171 and 257–260; [1983] Conv. 361 (D.G. Barnsley).

[74] See *Barclays Bank Ltd.* v. *Taylor* [1974] Ch. 137. See *Third Report on Land Registration*, Law Com. No. 158 (1987), paras. 4.94–4.104.

[75] Concerning matters such as priority and transmissibility.

[76] For example, if the owner of the "equity" is in actual occupation of the land, he may have an overriding interest under L.R.A., s.70(1)(*g*); *Blacklocks* v. *J.B. Developments (Godalming) Ltd.* [1982] Ch. 183, *supra*.

AUTHORISED INVESTMENTS

TRUSTEE INVESTMENTS ACT 1961: SCHEDULE 1.

PART I

NARROWER-RANGE INVESTMENTS NOT REQUIRING ADVICE

1. In Defence Bonds, National Savings Certificates and Ulster Savings Certificates, Ulster Development Bonds,[1] National Development Bonds,[2] British Savings Bonds,[3] National Savings Income Bonds[4] National Savings Deposit Bonds,[5] National Savings Indexed-Income Bonds[6] and National Savings Capital Bonds.[6a]

2. In deposits in the National Savings Bank,[7] and deposits in a bank or department thereof certified under subsection (3) of section 9 of the Finance Act 1956.

PART II

NARROWER-RANGE INVESTMENTS REQUIRING ADVICE

1. In securities issued by Her Majesty's Government in the United Kingdom, the Government of Northern Ireland or the Government of the Isle of Man, not being securities falling within Part I of this Schedule and being fixed-interest securities registered in the United Kingdom or the Isle of Man, Treasury Bills or Tax Reserve Certificates or any variable interest securities issued by Her Majesty's Government in the United Kingdom and registered in the United Kingdom.[8]

---

[1] Trustee Investments (Additional Powers) (No. 2) Order 1962 (S.I 1962 No. 2611).
[2] Trustee Investments (Additional Powers) Order 1964 (S.I. 1964 No. 703).
[3] Trustee Investments (Additional Powers) Order 1968 (S.I. 1968 No. 470).
[4] Trustee Investments (Additional Powers) Order 1982 (S.I. 1982 No. 1086).
[5] Trustee Investments (Additional Powers) (No. 2) Order 1983 (S.I. 1983 No. 1525).
[6] S.I. 1985 No. 1780.
[6a] Trustee Investments (Additional Powers) Order 1988 (S.I. 1988 No. 2254).
[7] Post Office Act 1969, ss.94, 114, Sched. 6, Part III.
[8] Trustee Investments (Additional Powers) Order 1977 (S.I. 1977 No. 831).

2. In any securities the payment of interest on which is guaranteed by Her Majesty's Government in the United Kingdom or the Government of Northern Ireland.

3. In fixed-interest securities issued in the United Kingdom by any public authority or nationalised industry or undertaking in the United Kingdom.

4. In fixed-interest securities issued in the United Kingdom by the government of any overseas territory within the Commonwealth or by any public or local authority within such a territory, being securities registered in the United Kingdom.

References in this paragraph to an overseas territory or to the government of such a territory shall be construed as if they occurred in the Overseas Service Act 1958.

4A. In securities issued in the United Kingdom by the government of an overseas territory within the Commonwealth or by any public or local authority within such a territory, being securities registered in the United Kingdom and in respect of which the rate of interest is variable by reference to one or more of the following:

(a) The Bank of England's minimum lending rate[9];
(b) the average rate of discount on allotment on 91-day Treasury bills;
(c) a yield on 91-day Treasury bills;
(d) a London Sterling inter-bank offered rate;
(e) a London sterling certificate of deposit rate.

References in this paragraph to an overseas territory or to the government of such a territory shall be construed as if they occurred in the Overseas Service Act 1958.[10]

5. In fixed-interest securities issued in the United Kingdom by the African Development Bank, the Asian Development Bank, the Caribbean Development Bank, the International Finance Corporation, the International Monetary Fund or by[11] the International Bank for Reconstruction and Development, being securities registered in the United Kingdom, and in fixed interest securities issued in the United Kingdom by the Inter-American Development Bank,[12] and in fixed interest securities issued in the United Kingdom by the European Atomic Energy Community, the European Economic Community,[13] the European Investment Bank, or by the European Coal and Steel community,[14] being securities registered in the United Kingdom.

5A. In securities issued in the United Kingdom by

(i) the International Bank for Reconstruction and Development or

[9] This is no longer posted.
[10] Trustee Investments (Additional Powers) (No. 2) Order 1977 (S.I. 1977 No. 1878).
[11] Trustee Investments (Additional Powers) Order 1983 (S.I. 1983 No. 772).
[12] Trustee Investments (Additional Powers) (No. 2) Order 1964 (S.I. 1964 No. 1404).
[13] Trustee Investments (Additional Powers) (No. 2) Order 1977 (S.I. 1977 No. 1878).
[14] Trustee Investments (Additional Powers) Order 1972 (S.I. 1972 No. 1818).

by the European Investment Bank or by the European Coal and Steel Community, being securities registered in the United Kingdom; or

(ii) the Inter-American Development Bank

being securities in respect of which the rate of interest is variable by reference to one or more of the following:
  (a) the Bank of England's minimum lending rate;
  (b) the average rate of discount on allotment on 91-day Treasury bills;
  (c) a yield on 91-day Treasury bills;
  (d) a London sterling inter-bank offered rate;
  (e) a London sterling certificate of deposit rate.[15]

5B. In securities issued in the United Kingdom by the African Development Bank, the Asian Development Bank, the Caribbean Development Bank, the European Atomic Energy Community, the European Economic Community, the International Finance Corporation or by the International Monetary Fund, being securities registered in the United Kingdom and in respect of which the rate of interest is variable by reference to one or more of the following—

  (a) the average rate of discount on allotment on 91-day Treasury Bills;
  (b) a yield on 91-day Treasury Bills;
  (c) a London sterling inter-bank offered rate;
  (d) a London sterling certificate of deposit rate.[16]

6. In debentures issued in the United Kingdom by a company incorporated in the United Kingdom, being debentures registered in the United Kingdom.

7. In stock of the Bank of Ireland and in Bank of Ireland 7 per cent. Loan Stock 1986/91.[17]

8. In debentures issued by the Agricultural Mortgage Corporation Limited or the Scottish Agricultural Securities Corporation Limited.

9. In loans to any authority to which this paragraph applies charged on all or any of the revenues of the authority or on a fund into which all or any of those revenues are payable, in any fixed-interest securities issued in the United Kingdom by any such authority for the purpose of borrowing money so charged, and in deposits with any such authority by way of temporary loan made on the giving of a receipt for the loan by the treasurer or other similar officer of the authority and on the giving of an undertaking by the authority that, if requested to charge

[15] Trustee Investments (Additional Powers) (No. 2) Order 1977 (S.I. 1977 No. 1878).
[16] *Ibid.*
[17] Trustee Investments (Additional Powers) Order 1966 (S.I. 1966 No. 401).

the loan as aforesaid, it will either comply with the request or repay the loan.

This paragraph applies to the following authorities, that is to say—

(a) any local authority in the United Kingdom;

(b) any authority all the members of which are appointed or elected by one or more local authorities in the United Kingdom;

(c) any authority the majority of the members of which are appointed or elected by one or more local authorities in the United Kingdom, being an authority which by virtue of any enactment has power to issue a precept to a local authority in England and Wales, or a requisition to a local authority in Scotland, or to the expenses of which, by virtue of any enactment, a local authority in the United Kingdom is or can be required to contribute;

(d) the Receiver for the Metropolitan Police District or a combined police authority (within the meaning of the Police Act 1946)[18];

(e) the Belfast City and District Water Commissioners;

(f) the Great Ouse Water Authority[19];

(g) any district council in Northern Ireland.[20]

(h) the Inner London Education Authority;

(i) any residuary body established by section 57 of the Local Government Act 1985.[20a]

9A. In any securities issued in the United Kingdom by any authority to which paragraph 9 applies for the purpose of borrowing money charged on all or any of the revenues of the authority or on a fund into which all or any of those revenues are payable and being securities in respect of which the rate of interest is variable by reference to one or more of the following:

(a) the Bank of England's minimum lending rate;

(b) the average rate of discount on allotment on 91-day Treasury bills;

(c) a yield on 91-day Treasury bills;

(d) a London sterling inter-bank offered rate;

(e) a London sterling certificate of deposit rate.[21]

10. In debentures or in the guaranteed or preference stock of any incorporated company, being statutory water undertakers within the meaning of the Water Act 1945[22] or any corresponding enactment in force in Northern Ireland, and having during each of the 10 years

---

[18] See now the Police Act 1964.

[19] Trustee Investments (Additional Powers) Order 1962 (S.I. 1962 No. 658). See the Water Resources Act 1963, s.6(6) and Sched. 4, para. 33.

[20] Trustee Investments (Additional Powers) Order 1973 (S.I. 1973 No. 1332).

[20a] (h) and (i) added by S.I. 1986 No. 601.

[21] Trustee Investments (Additional Powers) (No. 2) Order 1977 (S.I. 1977 No. 1878).

[22] As amended by the Water Act 1948, s.1.

immediately preceding the calendar year in which the investment was made paid a dividend of not less than 3½ per cent.[23] on its ordinary shares.

10A. In any units, or other shares of the investments subject to the trusts, of a unit trust scheme which, at the time of investment, is an authorised unit trust, within the meaning of subsection (1) of section 468 of the Income and Corporation Taxes Act 1988, in relation to which that subsection does not, by virtue of subsection (5) of that section, apply.[24]

11. [Repealed by the Trustee Savings Bank Act 1976 and S.I. 1976 No. 1829].

12. In deposits with a building society within the meaning of the Building Societies Act 1986.[25]

13. In mortgages of freehold property in England and Wales or Northern Ireland and of leasehold property in those countries of which the unexpired term at the time of investment is not less than 60 years, and in loans on heritable security in Scotland.

14. In perpetual rent-charges charged on land in England and Wales or Northern Ireland and fee-farm rents (not being rent-charges) issuing out of such land, and in feu-duties or ground annuals in Scotland.

15. In Certificates of Tax Deposit.[26]

PART III

WIDER-RANGE INVESTMENTS

1. In any securities issued in the United Kingdom by a company incorporated in the United Kingdom, being securities registered in the United Kingdom and not being securities falling within Part II of this Schedule.

2. In shares in a building society within the meaning of the Building Societies Act 1986.[27]

3. In any units of an authorised unit trust scheme within the meaning of the Financial Services Act 1986.[28]

---

[23] Replacing 5 per cent. from 1973: Trustee Investments (Water Companies) Order 1973 (S.I. 1973 No. 1393).
[24] I.C.T.A. 1988, Sched. 29.
[25] Building Societies Act 1986, s.120(1), Sched. 18, Pt. I, para. 4.
[26] Trustee Investments (Additional Powers) Order 1975 (S.I. 1975 No. 1710).
[27] Building Societies Act 1986, s.120(1), Sched. 18, Pt. I, para. 4.
[28] Financial Services Act 1986, s.212(2), Sched. 16, para. 2.

INDEX